端居せる宇宙に近きところ得て

i found a place close to space sitting out on the veranda　　gotô masaharu　　*zarabanda lejana*

後藤昌治著

遠く聴こゆるザラバンド

The cover picture was going to be Edward Morse's man wearing a crab carapace, but he was pushed within the book in favor of this print by Hokusai (1760-1849), the most prolific artist of all history. Whether or not one recalls the name of the device pictured, the contrast of geometrical science and legendary geography, Mt. Fuji exaggerated in a fashion surveyed by Morse, evokes the surreal, or hyperlogical style of the best of the mad-cap verse called *kyôka*.

"the literature of reversal"

Haruo Shirane in *Traces of Dreams*, a book about Bashô, quoted by Peipei Qiu in *Celebrating Kyô: The Eccentricity of Bashô and Nampo*, found in Early Modern Japan: An Interdisciplinary Journal Vol XVI (2008), kindly on-line.

日本人の皆さまよわないで
じっとして読書こそ省エネ

狂歌の原文と敬愚の狂訳を
もろ共にご笑納ください

"Kyô, literally meaning madness or insanity, implies behavior or thought that so radically transcends worldly concerns that it appears eccentric."

Peipei Qiu (above)
writing about how Bashô
successfully used eccentricity
based on Daoist ideals to elevate
popular linked verse from the status
of *zoku* 俗 to profound poetry *ga* 雅
and how the Bashô of *kyôka*, Ôta
Nampo (Nanpo), likewise, was
inspired by both the great
haiku master and the
original Chinese
ideal of 狂

Benediction

空一杯なる我駄作それでも名
お役に立てばプーの脳味噌だ

If you find this book, so full of naught, of service, nonetheless,
Rename it "The Brain of Pooh" and you, too, will be blessed!

~~~~~~

狂歌とて天明ばかりとしたがる　手前の目から鱗こそ散れ
開け胡麻かしよりもかりこそ多き　駄作ながらさくら待望

狂歌集を開けば、お目出度、読み終われば
桜鯛、一匹ならぬ一首が飾るところを折々
拝見しながら、何故、大俵もの海鼠どんに
そういふ名誉を与へなかったのか。外人な
がら不思議におもったがやっと解かったぞ

狂 歌 師 に 鯛 ほ ど に あ ふ 魚 な き
食 ふ も 食 わ れ も 同 じ 目 出 た ひ

~~~~~~

The Brain of Pooh. In case you forgot. This was the name Christopher Robin gave to the empty bottle of honey upon which the little stuffed bear called *Winnie the Pooh* floated to safety in the big flood.　蛇足　熊のプーさんが大洪水を乗り越えた蜂蜜の空瓶の舟号、「プーさんの脳」。名づけ親は、むろん、親友のクリストファー・ロビンくん。ただし、英文詩の祝福の言葉「と君も幸運に恵まれる」が三十一音には、入れ切れなかったという訳。しかも blessed（神のおかげで恵まれた）という語は昔「痴呆」の婉曲である。

鯛こそ大メデタイと云われても、狂歌の世が広々して、異見は必ずあり、竜宮で忌むべき魚のなきがらを取りかはす世ぞめでたかりける　恋川春町

Acknowledgements
are in the back of the book
as readers feel more appreciative
of help rendered to the author *after* reading it.

~~~~~~

This Book is Dedicated to the Poor Scholars of the World,
Who labor/ed without the time, space, health, respect,
and, if isolated, the companionship and civilities
All humans should enjoy, in order to serve
the greater good, despite lack of access
to many of the means to best do so,
lack of remuneration (money)
honors and appreciation
in their lifetimes or
the better part
of them,

&

*To All Poets
of Good Wit.*

~~~~~~

火の車をひきながらの痩せ我慢ぞ
美と智の宝を世にわかち合うが為
一生懸命に物創る文化浪人諸君へ

*All
translations*
are by the author
unless otherwise specified.

いざ子ども狂業なせそ天地の固めし国そ大倭島根は
iza kodomo tawawaza na se so ametsuchi no
Well, kids, crazy doings not-do-not+emph heaven-earth's
katameshi kuni zo yamato shimane wa
solidified country! yamato isle-root-as-for
藤原朝臣奏之 万葉集 #4487

From a Minister to his men
speaking for the Empress
who expected big things

Get with it, Kiddos,
Stop thy craziness, start work!
Is this not Yamato,
the Isle where land and sky
out of murk solidified?

Yeah, right!

I do not know if Minister Fujiwara Sônosuke sang out this *waka* to his cabinet who were out in the garden playing *kemari* (keep-the-ball-in-the-air-as-long-as-you-can-kick-it-up), *go* (the world's top intellectual board-game, a Chinese invention), chugalugging *sake*, singing dirty songs or other activities all of which any sane and healthy man enjoys, or, instead, was written down and a copy sent to each *kodomo* to call them back from their vacations on Day-18 of Month-11 of the Founding Year of the Tenbyôhôji 天平宝字 or Heaven's Fair Treasure Letter era, *i.e.,* 757 anno Domini; but, I do know that the big dreams of the Empress Kôken 孝謙天皇 (718-770) did not come to fruition, or at least created so much discord she became the excuse for ending the practice of female heads of state in Japan! Maybe, the men – kids/children is a paternalistic term of endearment Bashô would later use to address his disciples, calling on them to run about in the hail – should have been left to their *tawawaza* or horse-play, which I translated as "craziness" because of the 狂 character we will see a lot of in this book. The *katameshi,* "solidified" or "made stable" seems a good antithesis for the same, and the "murk" was added less for the rhyme with "work" (also added in lieu of a preface), then because readers unfamiliar with the Japanese myth referred to may have a concept of the Beginning different from one where heaven and earth are not *created,* or set into motion, but fertilized and/or congealed. That dripping and stirring (a jeweled halberd in the sea) is halfway to the nature of translation, which, mad or not, is neither creation nor procreation, but *recreation.*

Fig. 109

~~~~~~

★ The man walking about "wearing the carapace of the gigantic crab on his head" in lieu of the hat (that Japanese did not wear as commonly as "we" did at the time) was sketched by Edward Morse in the 19c (*Japan Day by Day*) who observed that "many looked at the man as he passed and some smiled." He also generalized: *"An illustration of the tolerance of the people and the good manners of the children is shown in the fact that no matter how grotesque or odd some of the people appear in dress, no one shouted at them, laughs at them, or disturbs them in any way."* It goes without saying that a similar eccentric in the United States would not only have been jeered at, but risked bodily harm. Even as late as the early 1960's, one could be assaulted in the United States simply for wearing odd clothing or long hair. Japanese in the USA in the late-19c wrote of the danger of being physically attacked merely for being different unlike the case in England, where people where kind to the curious. Usanians were more tolerant of oddity in print, but not if it touched upon things that mattered to them. Tom Paine was all but tarred and feathered for his free-thinking; Mark Twain did not publish his *Letters From the Earth* for fear of the same or worse. ♪In parts of Japan, the carapace of a crab was sometimes hung on a gate to repel disease (「蟹の甲は悪病除けになる」), so maybe . . .

robin d. gill

Mad in Translation

*A thousand years of kyôka,
comic japanese poetry in the classic waka mode.*

para*verse* press

Alternative titles for this book include, *In Search of the Wild Waka, The Unbearable Lightness of Kyôka, Fun Poems from the Land of the Surprising Sun, Welcome to the Crazy Verse, Wacky Waka, Mad-cap Poems for the Man Who Wore a Carapace on His Head, Kyôka & other Kooky Japanese Poems, The Paraverse of Japanese Mad Poetry,* and (my favorite) *Please, No Songs to Move Heaven and Earth!* – rdg

With this book, Paraverse Press, home to *root* (not *rote*) writing, puts on perfection!
A sensitive Lafcadio Hearn once wrote, *"Words will eventually have their rights
recognized by the people."* — Our radically creative nonfiction sets them free
to play and grow in a garden of fanciful thought far from the well-crafted,
beautiful, but utterly boring journalism & plodding personal 'reality'
narratives taught to a generation of Usanian writers, but close
to the playful Aubrey, Borges, Chesterton, Darwin (Erasmus),
Lucretius, Montaigne, Newcastle (Duchess of ~), Ôta,
Plutarch, Rabelais, Sterne, Twain, Wilde, . . . *etc.*
Whatever the subject happens to be, our books
hold something of broad interest – *ideas.*

©
2009
paraverse press
all rights reserved

But, please quote freely, so long as you cite
this book and take care to check the *Errata*
at **http://paraverse.org**

Again, we invite the LC to help us catalog, meanwhile
please enjoy our Publisher's Cataloging-in-Publication:

Mad in Translation
*A thousand years of kyôka, comic japanese poetry
in the classic waka mode.* **Compiled, translated,
explained and essayed by robin d. gill.
Includes the Japanese originals,
romanization, a bibliography,
poet and poem indexes.**

ISBN # 0-9742618-7-4 (pbk)
13-digit: 978-0-9742618-7-4

1. Japanese poetry – comic – translations into English 2. English poetry – comic – translations from Japanese. 3. Kyôka (mad poems) – 8c ~ 19c. 4. Waka – 8c ~ 19c. 5. Kyôku (kyôka-like haiku. 6. Japanese poets – Bokuyô, Lady Daibu, Getsudôken, Henjô, Ikkyû, Lady Ise, Issa, Jakuren, Jihinari, Jinkyû, Kisshû, Kôfû, Kotomichi, Magao, Meshimori, Mitoku, (A.) Motokata, Munenaga, Ryôkan, Saigyô, Jihinari, Ryôkan, Sakuden, Sanekata, Sanetaka, Sengai, (I.) Shikibu, Shokusanjin (aka Ôta Nanpo), Shunzei, Sôchô, Sosei, Tabito, Takuan, Teiryû, Teitoku, Tameie, Tsurayuki, Yakamochi, Yayû, Yomo no Akara (Ôta Nanpo), Yûchôrô. 7. Squibs – Asahi Bunzaemon

I. gill, robin d.

1st edition: florida hurricane season 2009

Printed by Lightning Source
in the United States and United Kingdom.
Distributed by Ingram, Baker & Taylor, etc..
Available from Amazon, Barnes & Noble & elsewhere.

For more information, please visit our web site, www.paraverse.org.
For further questions, contact the author, at a social networking site, or
write to uncoolwabin *at* hotmail *dot* com, or whatever e-mail address
is given at the site (and good luck!). *Forget snail-mail. As it stands,*
your poor author-publisher *is* a snail . . or, maybe, a hermit crab?

Attitude

The only serious reason which I can imagine inducing any one person to listen to any other is, that the first person looks to the second person with an ardent faith and a fixed attention, expecting him to say what he does not expect him to say. – G.K. Chesterton

~~There are two types of people, those who want to be surprised and those who want what they want. We of the first type wish to hear something new or old but not of our choice on the radio. We desire surprise at the table and eating out may even ask the chef to "Cook me something for under ten dollars, but don't tell me what!" People of the second type want to hear only the songs they choose and eat only the food they choose. Whether they give up the joy of novelty because of fear of the unknown, with its occasional disaster, do not trust other people, or simply live for more of the same, I cannot say. They are probably more numerous than surprise seekers and include as many, if not more, seemingly artsy liberals as dyed-in-wool conservatives. After all, the instinct to be continually cool, or recognizably "creative," makes someone want to have or do whatever is faddish: hence, the cool crowd is always a crowd, though each member of it may fancy himself or herself to be more his or her own person than someone brave enough not to be cool. Though *hot,* an antonym for cool, is more appropriate to describe the way the cool adopt fashions and read books hot off the production line or press (unlike the truly discriminating who are open to books and clothing of all ages) provided they are puffed cool by the hottest reviews, I call them *cool* because the expression associated with coolness fits the state of mind so perfectly. People who fancy themselves to be cool (though most may not admit it) are all *know-it-alls* who have trained their all-too-neo cortex to suppress any surprise they might feel the instant the news jumps from one of their senses to the tip of a ganglia threatening to bring it to their attention. Such a person is not likely to find a book that no one reads. All of which is to say, if you are reading this, you may be a fool, but at least you're probably not cool.~~

敬愚 ~~aka,~~
~~Uncool Wabin~~

和歌より出てわかよりをかしく
Out of waka but wackier than waka.

蜀山人 Shokusanjin 大田南畝 1749-1823 蜀山家集

~~~~~~

*"There is an absolute freedom
both in respect of language and choice of subject.
The kiôka must be funny, that is all."*

William J Aston   *History of Japanese Literature*   1899

~~~~~~

真面目の趣を解して滑稽の趣を解せ
ざる者は共に文学を語るに足らず

*He who appreciates serious literature
but not the comic should discuss neither.*

Matsuyama Shiki 「万葉集巻十六」 講談社『子規全集』第七巻 明治三十二 1899

~~~~~~

♪ **The wacky words** are part of the flatulent rhetoric of the *kyôbun* – the *kyôka* master's equivalent of *haibun,* prose by *haikai* masters – of Ôta Nanpo, aka Yomo no Akara, later, Shokusanjin, the mad poem genius. They play upon the commonplace of a fabric dyed of indigo being *more indigo* (blue) *than indigo itself* (*ai yori idete ai yori ao*). The original does not, however, claim *kyôka* are more *waka* than *waka*, just that they are more *okashi* (funnier/stranger/wackier). Still, the implication is that *waka* had *something* wacky in them from the start. As Alice put it, one cannot have *more* tea unless . . . ♪♪ **Aston**, probably the first to introduce *kyôka* to English, had it right, though his *attitude* toward comic poetry was far more complex than this snippet suggests (pg.655). The succinct definition of *kyôka* by Kaneko Jitsuei (1927) 狂歌とは用語及び取材に絶対的自由を与へられたる卑俗なる短歌であり、滑稽を旨とするものである("A *kyôka* is a low or vulgar *tanka* with comic intent enjoying absolute freedom of language and theme") is amazingly close to Aston's. Re. that "absolute freedom," 18c *waka* poet Ozawa Roan 小沢 蘆庵 charged that the vocabulary of songs (31-syllabet poetry in Japan) was too exclusionary, so most of what we see and hear was excluded (今の世の歌は言(こと)えりのみして、常に見、聞くものも多くは詠まずなりにたり). He exampled it w/ a poem full of vegetables (いにしへは大根はじかみ韮なすび蒜干し瓜も歌にこそよめ *inishie wa ône hajikami nira nasubi hiru* . . .). Ozawa may be regarded as an early *tankaist*, who, like generations of tanka poets to come, may not have known *kyôka* already did what he espoused. ♪♪
♪ **Shiki, best known for establishing haiku as *haiku*, did the same for *tanka*.** As Yoshioka Ikuo 歌の未来図〜あるいは歌の円寂するとき has observed, he did this by re-incorporating the comic and colloquial into the seriously dead *waka*. In the process, he pretty much destroyed mad poetry *per se*, as it was no longer needed as a haven!

*A particular and extraordinary variety
of comic poetry . . . . . about which little
or nothing has yet been written in English.*

Lafcadio Hearn. *Goblin Poetry* in *Romance of the Milky Way* 1905

泪の種ではなくて、笑の種を秘めて居る三十一字詩である.

31-syllabet poems that contain not seeds of tears, but of laughter.

金子実英 from a 'History of *Kyôka* by Kaneko Jitsue in *Shokusankashû,* 1927.

---

*mad (light) waka . . . not so much making a fool
of the original writer as in European verse;
rather "lightening" it, in the sense of
omitting all the seriousness that
so easily falls into
sentimentality.*

R. H. Blyth. *Oriental Humor* 1959

---

*Kyôka uses allusion and poetic devices
to create an exquisite subterfuge . . . the mixing
of high and low language expresses freedom and
radically redefines the traditional waka form.*

Rokuo Tanaka *"Forgotten Women: Two Kyôka Poets of the Tenmei Era"*
in Jessica Milner Davis ed. *Understanding Humor in Japan,* Wayne St.U.P., 2006

♪ **Hearn's** is the earliest mention of *kyôka* in English I saw until reading Aston in Rokuo Tanaka's *Forgotten Women*. Because Hearn writes "little or *nothing* has yet been written in English" about *kyôka,* I suspect his passage was written before Aston was published. More of the passage from which I pulled and combined the above:

"The word 'kyoka' is written with a Chinese character signifying 'insane' or 'crazy'; and it means a particular and extraordinary variety of comic poetry. The form is that of the classic tanka of thirty-one syllables (arranged 57577); — but the subjects are always the extreme reverse of classical; and the artistic effects depend upon methods of verbal jugglery which cannot be explained without the help of numerous examples . . . a class of Japanese poetry about which little or nothing has yet been written in English . . . Lafcadio Hearn *Ibid*

Please do not worry about what the Japanese words mean; you will pick up the vocabulary as you read. Here, let me just say that a "classic tanka" is a short *waka*.

The *kyôka* scholar Hamada Giichirô defines *kyôka* as traditional waka in a thirty-one-syllable verse form that expresses nontraditional, incongruous content and which eschews elegant diction and sophisticated prosody designed to move heaven and earth. In other words, he says a satirically humorous perspective is invoked by, as it were, the heart of a poet who wears a "robe made of silk brocade" but who ties it with a "sash made of straw." In my view, this captures the genre exactly. . . . *kyôka* extracts wit and humor from materials found in ordinary daily life, invariably transforming elegance into plebianism and seriousness into mockery by its improvisations.

Rokuo Tanaka *"Forgotten Women: Two Kyôka Poets of the Tenmei Era"* in J. M. Davis ed. *Understanding Humor in Japan,* Wayne St. U. P., 2006

I added a page to this book to fit this beautiful summary of Hamada Giichirô and Tanaka's own view of *kyôka*. While it is almost perfect as is, I think one correction *might* be made: the mad poet of Japan *also* liked to wear a hempen robe and tie it with a sash made of silk. For example, gift of some agricultural product might be accompanied with an equally earthen message bound up in elegant grammar, which is to say classic *waka* trimming. I suppose that *could* be seen as "transforming elegance into plebianism," but, in my opinion, it makes more sense to see such as *making the plebian outrageously elegant*. *Mad in Translation* has examples enough to allow critics to make up their own minds on this and other defining matters.

一方、洋狂とは

Mad in the West – or what *kyôka* poets are **not**.

Yet, fellow poets, us it behoves to stand
Bare headed beneath God's thunderstorms,
To grasp the Father's rays, no less, with our own two hands
And, wrapping in song the heavenly gift,
To offer it to people.

Seeing the above translation of the literally mad poet Holderlin (in Jacques Derrida, trans. Alan Bass - 1990 - Language Arts & Disciplines) reminded me of how far apart *kyôka* 'mad' is from the Romantic tradition of poets/artists as mad. Some 17c *kyôka* poets do boast of the greatness of their art, but their spirit is comic, i.e., *sane*, not serious.

Apology for the arrangement of the Contents

The tiny two-page *chapters*, if they can be so called, were invented because your author began to write before he knew diddlywink about the subject. With all too few examples of this or that, and no grasp of the larger picture, real chapters were out of the question. (So, why start in the first place? Because translating wit helped him forget his tinnitus and country exile.) Later, knowing more, he might have made a stab at it, were he not writing in a house ruled by the needs of others. The rail-track running by us was no problem. I love most R & R sounds; but a poor short-term memory cannot cope with sounds demanding attention (Help the old dog out to poop! Find out why the cows are mooing! etc..) without the train of thought derailing. Complex synthesis was out of the question. But later he – *let's switch to the first-person* – I came to wonder whether those two-pagers might not have something *good* to be said for them. *Are they not just the right length for the reader to enjoy yet still get off the john before his or her legs fall asleep?* And, is it not convenient for the studious soul? *By starting chapters on the left page rather than the right, we can always see the explanation for the poem, without turning the page and may, if we wish, glance back at it!* At last minute, I rearranged some of the two-page units to fit larger themes – chaptering on the cheap – but want to wait until I hear from you before doing more, for the pleasure of seeing themes neatly clustered and ordered must be balanced against the monotony of reading something that does not include enough hop, skip and jump. About the overall order, I did not put all the interesting stuff in front (as is the common practice in publishing), but held much, perhaps most, for later, because I thought it would become even *more* interesting if you read what came before. I also tend to put what I read first before what I read last, for interpreting poetry bears some resemblance to detective work and rightly or wrongly, I imagine my readers want to enjoy the process as well as solution. For the same reason, when I add things, I do not always smooth the seams. Patchwork holds more information. But, all said, I must confess that the arrangement *is* pretty haphazard, even sloppy. A friend and critic who is *always* dismayed by my lack of editing, may find it absolutely appalling, yet another example, and *the worst*, of a book published before it was, properly speaking, a *book*. He would be right. But here & now, L.C. et al, I can do no more.
..

& the Table *of ~ . . . . for what it's worth!*

FORE-MATTER
A nominal stab at the poems called "mad" 18.   By any other name – or a one-page history   21
On the Nature of *Kyôka* & Nurture of Mad Translation   23
ONE OUTRAGEOUS, UNHERALDED POEM
People as spiteful as silverfish. – What haiku-master Issa's furiously mad Tom-swifty means   29
THE ODDLY ENCHANTED WORLD OF JAPANESE MAD POETRY
Why good poems are dangerous   –   If Meshimori's much-Englished *kyôka* were read by Belloc.   32
Loony-solar calendar conundrum   –   Defending this much-maligned *waka* is defending wit itself.   34
New years for better or worse   –   Monk Ikkyû turns the celebration of new life into a death march.   36
A round bow for time's arrow   –   Taoist beginnings in a round bow, or Teitoku's puzzling *kyôka*.   38
Can a pebble grow into rock-of-ages?   –   The supernatural turns surreal in *kyôka* by Yûchôrô, et al.   40
Flying ships of stone – An idea which should have launched 10,000 kyôka but apparently has not.   42
Cow slobber and milked icicles – A mad-cap look at an infamous, supposedly worthless *haiku*.   44
Why Dreams of Fuji beat the real thing – A well-known *kyôka* & unknown treasure-ship *kyôku*.   46
Princess Sao's country matters – Teitoku's unsung erotic masterpiece, or a *kyôka* landscape.   48
Mountains dressed & undressed – *Haikai*-style elegant vulgarity by *kyôka* star Kisshû.   50
Old Issa cuts farts into plum scent – A peek into a subject dear to mad poems and perhaps. . .   52
WITH SOME RUDENESS FOR GOOD MEASURE?
Manyôshû's mean little poems – Cruel if not mad: picking on long underarm hair & red noses.   54

Two More, picking on bean poles – Kidding is mad: these are cited as examples of *bullying*. 56

LOVE POEMS – WHERE MAD METAPHOR IS TOO COMMON TO BE MAD
The burning passion of *waka* – hearts burning robes, a *kyôka*-class metaphor by Tsurayuki. 58
Yam lovers become eel and split – The sleight of tongue of *kyôka's* first man. 60
Mad love *Manyô* style: shot deer – allegory that astounds and has an odd pedigree. 62
The king of Siam & hairy *zôri?* – An old and yet unsolved *kyôka* and sex-as-sandals! 64
The furious loves of cats & man – Yayû's question. Mad poets take on a *haikai* subject. 66
Cats too lazy to make love – More *kyôka* from Issa the *haikai* master with a cat. 68
Leveling Hills for quality time – The desire for more hours of light at night. 70
Will one-wing lovers fly in translation? – and other sexual *kyôka,* including a fake Ikkyû 72
Love approached by fire, rain, roads – mediocre *kyôka* but representative. 74
& by ashtrays, lightning, etc. – ditto. 76
Love w/ all twelve animals – vs. the Braddock+Braddock song *I lobster but never flounder.* 78
Pursued by the love-sick blues – Fighting that miscreant from ancient times. 80
My love is an otter & other dreams – Love and dreaming in old *waka*. 82
To pluck a sleeping zither – And march back into the bog of love again. Shokusanjin. 84

SOME FAVORITE KYÔKA THAT ARE SWEET, EDO/EGOISTIC, AWFUL, ...
Thank goodness tôfu lacks wings! – & how a bean pole gets to heaven according to Ryôkan. 86
The bare-faced moon. Or, anthropomorphism & mixed feelings about a cloudless moon. 88
Why the moon was envious of Japan – Cultural nationalism, even among mad poets. 90
Shy Bald Mountains & Nostril Hairs by Moonlight – And the moon feeding world peace. 92
Should on-the-rag enter the temple? – A god's *kyôka* reply to Shikibu & Yûchôrô's vile parody! 94
Trading blood for a drink beats being a monkey – 8c *kyôka* in praise of wine. 96
More drink, wine as dew & octopus – Yûchôrô's sweet Ise parody & Shokusanjin's fleas. 98
In Praise of Getting Plastered and Puking – or, the heavy-drinking first men of *kyôka*. 100
Poop as omen and in a dream – The good luck of getting beshitted, not a *kyôka* invention, but. 102
More good shit, snowy outhouses – Half Ozarks and half the Dean. 104
Why bad poems are good, too – A lesson for editors from the worst poem in the *Manyôshû*. 106

LAMPOONS, OR *RAKUSHU,* THAT ARE KYÔKA, EDO TO MEIJI.
The pen the sword & the mosquito – The anonymous *rakushu,* or, *kyôka* as dead-head lampoon. 108
Steam-boat tea & stone dumplings – Famous *rakushu* that are *kyôka*, or the best comic squibs. 110

12C WAKA MASTER SAIGYÔ AS A METAPHYSICAL, OR MAD, POET
The good ole days of bamboo ponies – Reminiscence, or infantile old age as somewhat mad. 112
The monk who cried rivers – Did you know Saigyô the esteemed poet had a maudlin wit? 114
The man with a baby in his heart – Or, Saigyô, master of spanking new mad metaphor? 116
Kyôka-masters on Saigyô's maudlinity – Should moonshine make a strong man cry? 118
Silly as Saigyô: more waka weepers for perspective – from the 1205 *Shinkokinshû* 120
Silly as Saigyô: more waka weepers for perspective – from the 1310 *Fuboku wakashô* 上 122
Silly as Saigyô: more waka weepers for perspective – from the 1310 *Fuboku wakashô* 中 124
Silly as Saigyô: more waka weepers for perspective – from the 1310 *Fuboku wakashô* 下 126
Silly as Saigyô: wild waka with dust & smoke – a break from tears also from the 1310 . . . 128
Silly as Saigyô: more waka weepers for perspective – from the 1313 *Gyokuyôshû* 130
The man who troped transience – And wrote poems as hyperlogical as any? 132

A SUNDRY SAMPLE OF WILD OLD WAKA & NEW KYÔKA, MOSTLY
Testing snipe and riding clouds – Meshimori takes melancholy & sticks it up a clam. 134
It may not get used up, but . . . – The great wife-lending debate from *waka* to *kyôka.* 136
Sooty wives & sleeping w/ virgins – Mad as a matter of interpretation & Akara on first-sex. 138
An empress w/ a mountain of laundry – & scabies: real matins moon misery by Takuan. 140
Things that cannot be – A list of impossibilities made up over 1000 years ago 142
Segregated beaches, b&w stones – Saigyô's go-playing islands, Hakushû's lactating mother island 144
Perverse nursery verses: snails – Beware of cows, ponies and children as revised by Jakuren. 146
Country vs city vs country – Shokusanjin's crude pelts of time (wearing sun-mice?) 148

CHINESE-STYLE MAD VERSE, SOME BETTER SOME WORSE
Loving women & chinese poems – (double-length chapter) Ikkyû's rhyming *kyôshi* in lively   150
Rectangular translation, including three more readings of the already translated female part   152
All-character blue camels & buoyant boobs – or 18-19c Chinese-style poems as broadsides   154
Almost mad 10c Chinese-style, *kanshi* – drunken moon rats & a cuckoo-hating woman   156

THE POETRY OF FREE THINKING & ONE UNIT OF MORALITY
Playing with myths of beginning & end – When logic looks at detail and chuckles   158
One world at a time – *Heaven or hell, one thing is true / You cannot take them with you!*   160
Life after death, death after death – Mark Twain would have loved Ikkyû's best *kyôka*   162
Nothing Sacred: Buddha, Gods, Heaven & Hell – Religion in *kyôka* 1679 vs 1785.   164
Dew passed off as gems by a lotus? – Escalating Bishop Henjô play w/ the symbol of purity   166
If dewdrops were delicious – Issa's *kyôka* and *kyôku* celebrating literal tastelessness   168
Witty wisdom, or weighing the 'way songs' – *Dôka:* Can paradox make morality palatable?   170
Less Witty Wisdom, or Weighing Way Poems II – some truly mediocre *dôka* and *kyôkunka*.   172

CAPPING, DUELING & GREETING POEMS
40-year-old chickadee & other caps – From *100 Frogs* to recognizing wit in haikai link-verse.   174
Mad debates: *kyôka* vs *kyôka* – Chamber maid vs. captious man, grandpa vs. grandma . . .   176
The Piss-proud Drunk vs. The Sharp-tongued Teetotaler – a 10-point 17c dissing contest 上   178
The Piss-proud Drunk vs. The Sharp-tongued Teetotaler – a 10-point 17c dissing contest 下   180
A witness of salutations & warnings – Complimenting entertainers, giving watermelons, etc.   182
Ancient mad exchanges found by Cranston – A palace maid and traveling governor's wit.   184

SPRING PASSION
The naughty nightingale – Or, bird watching us, a *kyôka* from an illustrated 18c book   186
A violent nightingale – Pure *kyôka* in wordplay from the 10c Kokinshû   188
If Only There Were No ~~Cherry Blossoms~~ Women? – a *waka* only I think mad is *made* so.   190
How can blossoms be stopped from falling? – More Saigyô *kyôka* and a Sôgi *kyôku*.   192
In defense of the blossom wind – More craziness from Saigyô, Sôgi and other haikai poets.   194

SUMMER IS ICUMEN . . .
Cuckoo, headaches & tabby cats – A kyôka obvious after knowing the *waka* and Katô Ikuya's *kyôku*.   196
A touché of mosquito makes all men kin – The amorous stab and shellfish in the 'squito net.   198
The dirty tails of fireflies – How haikai link-verse made the light of scholarship obscene, etc.   200
Unnatural love and buried souls – Burning from the wrong end and sparking up rivers.   202
Mostly Wacky Waka Fireflies – from the 1313 Gyôkuyôshû Collection.   204
Burning moths & burning people – Why are we drawn to fire, and sequence in the *Kokinshû*.   206
Third-rate poet, first rate *kyôka?* – Lady Daibu, or more than one measure of good poetry.   208

FALL ROMANCE
Loving Stars, Lady Daibu & Maiden Flowers – Kooky cosmic voyeurism in waka and haikai.   210
Magpie bridges, Teitoku & more Lady – Rationalism brought to bear on heavenly bodies.   212
From ox slobber to the Amazon – Shokusanjin rises above contradiction to the surreal.   214
The maiden flower and the monk – from Henjô's famous fall to my imagined one.   216
Maiden flowers & young blades – Two totally off-the-wall *Kokinshû* name-game poems.   218
Deer write & larvae dance sutra – Pop buddhism, ancient 'now-style' to 19c *kyôka & kyôku*.   220
Hairy crickets & old chestnuts – Natural monsters from *haikai* and *kyokâ*.   222
Bug-songs, Morning Glory, Mum-wine & Star-babies – a fair sample of Fall senryû.   224
Maple & homo-wisteria rumps – Making an ass of the maudlin Manyô's monkey-guy.   226
Blushing or drunk fall leaves – Shokusanjin gives the oddest reason ever for blushing leaves.   228

WINTER MADNESS
The honest rain that came in with the cold – playing with proverbs in the absence of the gods.   230
Three takes on the snow: dick, swell-fish & fools – Polymath Gennai's bio of limp ones.   232
Kicking the year in the rear – Mixed feelings about sending off the old one.   234

AROUND THE CALENDAR, TWO PAGES AT A TIME
Five seasons mad, or almost mad – Mostly Shokusanjin.   236

Another round of five seasons, mixed Tenmei ⊕ 238
Another round of five seasons, mixed Tenmei ⊤ 240
A final round of five mad seasons – Mostly Yûchôrô. 242
Just geese coming in – Tenmei and post-Tenmei run-of-the-mill *kyôka*. 244
One for the Birds, or Saigyô Kyôka Master – geese and some other birds in season. 246

WHERE CELEBRATORY WILD WAKA & KYÔKA RESEMBLES LETTER-PICTURES
Composite characters and a charm – Combining lucky symbols, where mad & magic meet. 248
Playing w/ 'Spring' radicals & mom's age – Deconstructing & reconstructing 春. 250

DO THE ELDERLY LIKE MAD POEMS OR VICE-VERSA?
Roly-poly old age – A sea slug mistaken for eighty-eight tries a tart, & Shokusanjin stays put. 252
Making light of your old age – Shikibu shows how to lose your looks but still bloom! 254
Old age minutely described *is* mad – Yokoi Yayû's 7 poems of which 6 are tanka & 1 mad. 256
The third leg before viagra (canes) – & one *kyôka* where Yûchôrô sells his soul to the devil. 258
Rewinding the Spool – Akera Kankô on "always looking young" & Sôchô on stopping old age. 260

A FEW ODDITIES
Displeasure in the Pleasure Q *de arinsu* – Akera Kankô's bolting beauty & foreign accents. 262
Women of Pleasure in a Mad Poem Portrait Gallery – & his Unkempt Wife's masterpiece. 264
Lice rosaries that could have been soroban – How a mistranslation can make mad madder. 266
Pleasing fleas, loving lice – A *haikai* about symbiosis with bugs & my 'flea hell' *kyôku*. 268

THINGS AS LISTS, THINGS AS RIDDLES
Nothing but *things* – Things to show off & other lists of things, or *monowazukushi* poems. 270
Things as riddles – Lessons learned while revisiting Sôkan's fart by father's death-bed. 272

GOBLIN POETRY OR NIGHT-MADNESS
Spooky creatures 1 – Long tongues/necks: 100-demon night-madness + Hearn's goblin poetry. 274
Spooky creatures 2 – Bad trees, charm-peelers: more of the best Tenmei spooks & Hearn, too. 276
Spooky creatures 3 – House-shakers, mermen, flesh-suckers: more Tenmei vs. revival *kyôka*. 278
Spooky creatures 4 – Changeling clams and toads: two unidentified *kyôka* and Hearn's cutest. 280

SWEET LAND OF POVERTY
What the have-nots have plenty of – The live-wires, Teitoku, Yûchôrô & Ikkyû on poverty. 282
On the prosperity of poverty – The paradoxes and pushiness of poor wit. 284
The more poverty the merrier? – Boasting hyperbole, the god Poverty as me, pity for the god. 286
Bor-row, row your boat! – *Kyôka* along the lines of John Heywood's "Be Merry Friends." 288

BEYOND PARODY, OR MAD TAKE-OFFS ON 100 POEMS 1 POET
Shokusanjin's Hundred Poet take-off 1 – Linking content and card-game reality. From #1~8. 290
Shokusanjin's Hundred Poet take-off 2 – Kidding the poet as parody that is no take-off. #9~19. 292
Shokusanjin's Hundred Poet take-off 3 – A roach for a carp & scenery as an offering. From #9~19. 294
Shokusanjin's Hundred Poet take-off 4 – It's lonely with no one but us, mountain cherries. #20~65. 296
Shokusanjin's Hundred Poet take-off 5 – Bleeding heart meets bleating hart. #66~82. 298
Shokusanjin's Hundred Poet take-off 6 – Kindness for Go Toba & 100 hidden in #100. #83~100. 300
In Praise of Kyôka, or Why Blyth Beats Keene – On seeking the best, regardless. 302

AND TIME FOR A SMOKE
Puffing pictures: white heron & Saigyô smoking – With three of ten reflections of a smoker. 304
Play Pictures and Play Words, or Illuminated Kyôka – mad poems and asobi-e. 306
Wacky Waka Twisting Tongues & Crossing Sashes – with good stereo Manyôshû, too. 308
Wishing for Nothing? Or, Nothing to Wish for? – (S)OV Monk Sôchô vs. SVO Krishnamurti. 310
One Almost Flew Over the Cuckoo's Nest: Sanekata! ⊕ – 10c, but definitely mad. 312
One Almost Flew Over the Cuckoo's Nest: Sanekata! ⊤ – And a Casanova, to boot. 314

SAVAGE SONGS, THE GREAT 1666 KYÔKA COMPILATION, & 1672 KYÔKA TOURISM.
Ye Olde & Now Savage Songs, or Mad in 1666 I – A tobacco, parrot & cloudy-cake New Year. 316.

II – Time like musket shot & dandy lion teeth 318. Dandelion break: Shokusanjin, Issa, Nenten – milk problems & mimesis 320. III – Lice don't fawn, poets do boast, milky morals. 322. IV – Clicking tongues, washing hearts, soul sushi. 324. V – Lice dawn & dying dancer. 326. Supplement: Gay & corny 328

THE BIG FAN: VARIOUS KYÔKA FROM 2000+ BY ONE MAN, ca.1700
Getsudôken 1 – a *kyôka* master in the era of Bashô– Tears like poles and lunatic hyperbole.   330
Getsudôken 2 – Some *tanka*, or soft-boiled *kyôka* – The moon as a hare and wagging ducks. 332
Getsudôken 3 – Talk about hard-boiled *kyôka!* – Jacking-off birds and killing cicada.   334
Getsudôken 4 – The spirit of casual *kyôka!* – Suitable words for gifts and correspondence. 336
Getsudôken 5 – Fuji, mountain of mad metaphor – a fan big as a moor and a volcanic airhead. 338
Getsudôken W-extra – Buttering up the salt-butts – so many *wakashu* I marked the poems "W." 340
Getsudôken W(omen)-extra II – Love & Libido – and back to women. 342

A 17-SYLLABET POET'S PROGRESS W/ 31-SYLLABET POEMS
Issa's *kyôka* start to finish 1 – Dirty bird, raspy heart & cactus, or so-and-so early attempts. 344
Issa's *kyôka* start to finish 2 – Conch spells, leeches for cuckoo & discovering Shokusanjin. 346
Issa's *kyôka* start to finish 3 – Excellence at last: springs from rain-stones, hills w/ stylish coiffure. 348
Issa's *kyôka* start to finish 4 – Dew becomes doo, hands & legs, pestles, & old age wastes fireflies. 350

ADDITIONS, LEFT-OVERS, UNTRANSLATEABLES, & LEAD-INS TO NEXT SECTION
Real & Fake: Why I Must Wait to Translate N/Ise ⊕ Subtle 10c wit vs. Easy 17c wit. 352
Real & Fake: Why I Must Wait to Translate N/Ise ⊤ Sexy 10c wit vs. Stinky 17c wit. 354
The Untranslatable Lightness of Nakarai Bokuyô – A 17c match for Shokusanjin? ⊕   356
The Untranslatable Lightness of Nakarai Bokuyô – A 17c match for Shokusanjin? ⊤ 358
After Issa & Ryôkan, Wordway's Wacky Waka – or the re-integration of *kyôka* by Kotomichi 360
Buddhist grapes & persecuted X'tians – The difficulty of translating religion. 362   62   9b
Marine trope meets land-culture I – Komachi's shore, dirty reeds and algal trails in teary seas. 364
Marine trope meets land-culture II – Duckweed turns to jellyfish & *T of Ise's* translator gives up. 366
Literal/figuratively lousy translations – Imayo & kyôka on lice & a two favorites that failed. 368
Spiteful *kyôka* sans silverfish – Garden stolen, Monk Kyôgetsu insults an Empress's privates! 370
Near-kyôka by Sosei, a late-10c chestnut who didn't fall far from the 木 (Arch-bishop Henjô)   372
Near-kyôka by Lady Ise, or early-10c lovelorn *waka* in mad translation 374
Kyôka that is as bad as its detractors think it is, yet still valuable and *why*. 1740, Ôsaka. 376
Sorry woman & sorry man – Turning a now-world song (*imayo*) & 9c *waka* into *kyôka*? 378
The straight ones die – Kyôka where men as trees play on Zhuang-ze & tears become silverfish. 380

DEATH POEMS WITH LIFE TO SPARE
Poems for bowing out of life – Sôkan's business, Kyôriku's manure & more from Hoffman 382
Death takes an encore! – Strange, heroic and *haikai* argot puns. 384 Dying for more *haikai* – a second encore. 386. Death haiku as *kyôku* – or a third encore 388. And where is thy sting? – Kyôka's first man's takes on death for a fourth 390. The world's most macho death poem: *Wanzakure!* for a fifth 392. Sick of living and ready to go for a sixth! 394. & Death as a jellyfish with bones, or a celebration of death for the seventh and final encore! 396

FART! FART! & (in the notes, *ARF! ARF!*)
Hey, hey, hey for *he-no-he* – By Fool-Buddha, the most worthless poem of all time, or? 398

追加艸 *OVERLOOKED 16 -17C SOURCES & SURIMONO KYÔKA FROM ART PUBLISHERS*
Laughs to Banish Sleep, 402. More 16c wacky *waka*, 408. Sanetaka: a *waka* master's journal, 412. Kôfû horsing around w/ *'my rain'* & the *yu-girls* in Arima 414. Our Star the Shrimp, Our Sun the Crab – netted *surimono* 424. McKee's *surimono* 426. M&C's *surimono* 436. Carpenter's *surimono* 440.

AFTER-MATTER
The Silent Fart, or a meaningless postscript – On expecting the unexpected, after Chesterton. 454
On Mad Translation – three more takes (there is one up front!). 457
♪'s *Snake-legs, or Grass by the Road* – Over a hundred pages of elaboration and diversion. 464

By Any Other Name – Short & Inadequate yet Extraordinarily Broad History of 'Mad Poems.' 595
Biblios 648. Glossarios 664. Bios 674. Acknows 707. Gen. Index 715. Poet Ind. 718. Poem Ind. 726

A Nominal Stab at the Poems Called *"Mad"*

Japanese *kyôka* (*kyouka, kyoka*), usually Englished as "mad poems" are rarely translated. As we shall see, there are good reasons for this. But let us first try to define the genre starting with its name and ending with a subjective history including some value judgments.

Kyô comes from the Chinese 狂 which, like all interesting characters, defies explanation in a word. Modifying a human, 狂 generally means *crazy*, not merely eccentric but mad. Madness is nothing to laugh about. In Japan, as elsewhere, possession by bad spirits was greatly feared. But, it has also long been recognized as a blessing. To be "out of one's mind" is to be free of worry and liberated from the straight-jacket of convention. Late-20c squeamishness has made the word *kyôjin* 狂人, or *mad man*, taboo, so that even Japanese, if they do not know what 狂歌 *mad poems* are, tend to feel the same revulsion a naive English reader might. That is too bad; the character and concept of 狂 has something in it we need. As the 犭, or *beast* radical on the left, implies, madness has a touch of the *wild* – the natural world without – in it. A *wolf*, for example, is 狼, a *fox* 狐, a *monkey* 猿, a *boar* 猪, a *cat* 猫, an *otter* 獺. And, it is associated with *cats in heat* – need I say more? *As a verb*, applied to a missile, thrown or shot, a pen-stroke, schedule etc., 狂 more tamely means it went *off-course*. In this sense, 狂 resembles another fine character 遊 or, *play*, for some-thing with *play* in it may *wander or stray from the prescribed path*. On the other hand, combined with other characters, it describes the absurdly rigid mind of the monomaniac or idealist. This attribute is ambivalent. Such *maniacs* entertain tolerant people, but are rarely respected. This gives 狂, or *madness*, the proper character to deprecate one's own unconventional language or ideas in the Sinosphere, where rhetorical humility was, and to a lesser degree, is still *de rigor*. Today, 狂 is not used that way. Japanese prefer to call their own work "駄 crude" or "拙 wretched" or present it to someone to "store away with a laugh ご笑納下さい."

Ka comes from the Chinese character 歌. Usually Englished as *song*, in Japanese poetry it means 17+14=31-syllabet poems, unless prefaced with *long,* 長, in which case, it means longer poems likewise combining 5 and 7-syllabet phrases, but going on and on, though never so long as poems often do in the long-winded Occident. Most old 31-syllabet Japanese poems are called 和歌, *i.e., waka,* or *"harmonious-song/s."* The "song" character 歌 literally suggests they were *sung* – from what I have heard, I think *"sing-song"* would be more like it – but, actually serves primarily to differentiate Japanese poetry from Chinese (and, later, Occidental) poetry, which are called 詩, "poem/poetry," but sometimes also "song" (eg. *The Book of Songs* for Waley's translation of the 経詩). The *wa* 和 in the *waka* can also stand for Japanese, or *Yamato-style* – literally 大和 = *big-harmony/peace* – so the *waka* is doubly Japanese; indeed it is *the* national form of high literary art. This puts the alter-*waka*, our *kyôka* 狂歌, likewise 31-syllabets, closer to the heart of Japanese literature than generally recognized, especially when you realize that the difference between the two is not so clear as definitions might lead one to believe, but we are getting ahead of ourselves.

Putting together the parts, we have our word, 狂歌, or mad-poem. If after seeing the many examples in this book, you would define it for me, be my guest. I will only say the poems may be as vitriolic yet pleasant and learned as Samuel Butler's epic of heroic couplets, *Hudibras*, amateur yet up-to-date as the all-too-neglected scientific whimsy of Margaret Cavendish, the Duchess of New Castle, as naively nonsensical as Edward Lear (but, with more variety in the fun-for-fun's sake nonsense, paralleling that found visually expressed in the under-rated but highly developed genre of "play-paintings" called *asobie*), as punfully crafted as Lewis Carroll's hyperlogical fantasies, as down-to-earth yet off-the-wall inventive as Samuel Clemens's with his exuberantly flatulent *1601* or essayist+ novelist Li Yu李漁 (1611-80) with his hole-less female and dog-penis-grafting male, as charmingly inconsequential (stinking of the peculiarities of time and place) as Ogden Nash's enjambed and butchered-English, as convolutedly arcane as John Donne, as clearly clever as the pleasantly paradoxical and always wise grooks of Piet Hein . . . . . While rarely serious, they may be seemingly so. The facetious double entendre or teasingly allusive pun, not uncommon even in formal *waka,* is a stable for *kyôka*. Parody, usually the first thing associated with *kyôka*, is indeed common, *if take-offs of all types are equated with that genre*, but rare in the strict sense of it, as borrowing was normal for most Japanese poetry – smart, too, for a known phrase brings a poemful of allusion – and there is nothing particularly perverse about it. Pure play dominated *kyôka.* The take-offs are usually ridiculous, but they rarely make the original seem so, or intend to do that. They are meant to entertain, rather than to educate us with the difference. In other words, they are by and large as good-natured as the take-offs found on Garrison Keillor's *Lake Wobegon,* a place, incidentally, where most of the people are as supremely self-effacing – or, *modest,* if you prefer – as most Japanese.

To convey this with less explanation, I considered alternatives to "mad poem" such as "crazy verse," or "mad-cap verse," after Steven Carter (*Anthology of Traditional Japanese Poetry*). The former, while less angry or obviously insane, would fail to convey the intellectuality of the *kyôka*, while the latter, as felicitous as it is, would only be appropriate had I confined my book to the most narrowly defined urbane *kyôka* of the late 18-c, as does Carter. I wanted something broader to do justice to this literature often belittled as mere parody. Another possibility was dropping *mad/crazy* for one of three connotations of 狂 that seem good to us. 1) *Free*. Unfortunately, "free verse" implies a lack of formal restraint while the 狂歌 keeps the traditional 31-syllabets. If "free-thinking" were only as salient as it was in the 19c, *"Japanese Poems for Free-thinkers"* might have worked as a title, but it is *not*. 2) *Play*. I was tempted by *"Poems With Some Play in Them"* or, *"Playing Poetry."* That title would still, however, leave us without a simple name for the genre. True, *the united states of (north) America*, lacking a proper name – in consideration of other national states in the hemisphere, I call it *Usania* – has survived for over two centuries, but that required the monopolization of a distinct Proper noun. The phrase "31-syllabet Japanese comic poems" has no such *America* to steal. 3) *Wild.* If only the word *"waka,"* like *haiku*, was well-known in English and I had the guts to put an argument about the identity of *kyôka* right in the title, I might have followed the gourmet naturalist Eul Gibbons and given this book a title with the proper wit and gravitas for one addressing the literate reader: *"In Search of the Wild Waka."* So, why, you might ask, not just keep *kyôka,* as is? Because, I am afraid, the word just does not *sound* good enough. I will, however use it often within this book.

There is something positive to be said for "mad" in the classic sense of the word. It would be wrong to completely divorce the poetic license that is *kyôka* from insanity. The masses can appreciate simple paradox and pun, both of which abound in Japanese folk song, but *kyôka* often include more labored thought, the sort of hyper-logical, convoluted stuff that people not used to oddly linked chains of logic might find demented. It was no accident the only syndicated popular music show in late-20c Usania specializing in thematic humor was called *The Doctor Demento Show* (its absence in my home state, Florida, proves that too much fun in the sun does indeed addle the brain). Intelligence, to those who lack it or fail to exercise it, is a strange animal. And, even when complexity is not involved, and we have only a novel idea or an off-the-wall manner of expressing an old idea, there is a tendency for the common man to roll his eyes before he opens them wide enough to take it in. Hence, I think it truly extraordinary that the "mad poem," the *kyôka,* was able to achieve in its heyday greater popularity than that achieved by any similar genre of poem, if there is a similar genre, anywhere in the world. It speaks well for the broadmindedness of the Japanese, does it not?

As my approach toward mad poems is far, far from nominal, I will move away from the character 狂 now but, if you would continue, on pages 713-714, there are several thousand more words you may pour over with a magnifying glass.

♪**Butler, Cavendish, Donne, etc.** I gave no information for they are historical figures known to all who read broadly in English. But a few words are in order. I regret not having samples of Cavendish's playful scientific verses and other "fancies" to share; the bias for novels on the part of our cultural gate-keepers has kept them confined to the British Library, where I once glimpsed them. Li Yu (李漁 1611-80) is Chinese and his non-fiction essays not yet translated, but from tantalizing excerpts found in his novels, he brought to bear logic, the mother of humor, to many things to a ludicrous degree. His comic pornographic novel 肉布団(meat/flesh cushion) includes a marvelous list of ways a big heavy woman beats a thin one (the Chinese aesthetic ideal) in bed. Piet Hein, the great Dane, whose grooks should be immortalized, needs a major publisher to keep his name and work in circulation in English. We will see more of him in this book. Were copyright not a possible problem, I would introduce a score of his grooks in their tiny entirety right here, for they are perfect examples of the hyperlogical humor that marks the best *kyôka*. Mark my word, Piet Hein will still be here in a hundred or a thousand years. On the other hand, who can say if Garrison Keillor, the top radio presence in Usania for three decades, will survive as long as, say, this book, for his best work is written not on paper or water, but in the *air*! (But see M&J Pankake: *A Prairie Home Companion Folk Song Book* for take-off lyrics, some comparable to parody-style *kyôka*). Ah, people of the 22c – if it is called that – look for the recordings, you know not what you miss!

♪ **Mad Boast**. Cosmopolitan sophisticates, please do not attack me for what may be hyperbole rather than fact when I make the unsubstantiated claim the mad poem craze is a uniquely Japanese phenomenon! Instead, please *prove* me wrong by sending information about *your* pet outbreaks of mad poetry in other cultures – include general background, at least two example poems in translation (or multiple translations), and, if possible the original and its romanization, names, dates, etc. – and I will be happy to add a comparative section to a second volume of *Mad In Translation* and give you full credit.

♪ a wild & wooly history of *kyôka* in one page ♪
By Any Other Name

There are half a dozen schools of thought on what should be called a *kyôka*. That means there are, or could be, as many histories. For generalizing, three will do.

The narrow school admits comic poems written earlier were sometimes called *kyôka*, but holds that the only genuine ones come from the Tenmei era (1780s) *kyôka* explosion set-off by the genius Ôta Nanpo (1749-1823), *aka* Yomo no Akara, Shokusanjin, etc., when the form became a very popular literary genre. While I have never seen it expressed *quite* that baldly – except with respect to the fraternal form, *kyôshi* a mad sub-genre of all-character (Chinese) *kanshi*, likewise canonized by Ôta – the way *kyôka* tends to be equated with those by Ôta *et al* and earlier work largely ignored, leads me to think this may be the largest school.

The middle school admits as *kyôka* most of what was so called. It tends to exclude 13c *waka* called *kyôka* by the author merely to be humble, but include those born of the first flowerings of *kyôka* in the 14-17c when noble *monks, renga* and *haikai* link-verse masters (Sôchô, Ikkyû, Yûchôrô, Teitoku, etc.) played with *kyôka* and the 17-18c when *Naniwa kyôka-shi*, or Ôsakan mad-poem masters, were in some ways as successful as Ôta Nanpo was to be. Ôta himself does not completely deny this school, for he included more than a handful of old poems in his first anthology (万歳集 1783), even if a prefatory subtitle to a broadside 万歳集著微来歴 (1784), celebrating its success with respect to another *kyôka* anthology just published by his rival, seems to suggest the contrary when he boasts *"That book is trad; this one is mad!"*「夫は本歌是は狂歌」(岩波の大系 57『川柳狂歌集』の解説より)

The wide school holds that what is or is not a mad poem is a matter of form and content. *Kyôka*, by whatever name, go back at least as far as the *Manyôshû* (8c) and may be found in subsequent collections, mixed (incognito) among other *waka* (especially in minor, allegedly substandard collections) or in separate books/chapters going under other names, of which *haikai* (comic *waka* not identical with, but sharing something with the later link-verse *haikai* that gave birth to haiku) is best known. Didactic religious or secular 31-syllabet poems, or even anonymous broadsides, *if playful in language and/or thought*, were prima facie, *kyôka*. The champion of the wide school today, Yoshioka Ikuo, a *tanka* poet who respectfully rebels against the tendency for the canons of literature to be established by the exclusion of humor and would like to restore the *warai* (laughter) to the history of *waka*, notes with astonishment that Hamada Giichirô, the annotator of a collection of *kyôka* in the classic literature series of Japan's top literary publisher, Iwanami, chose the narrow nominal definition/history because "to call *kyôka* simply "comic song (31-syllabet poetry)" would be to lose its origin in that of *waka*." (狂歌を単に滑稽歌と定義づけるならば、その起源は和歌の起源に埋没してしまう) To translate and condense Yoshioka's feelings, which I share: *Huh!?*

I love Akara/Shokusanjin/Ôta and translate scores of his poems. Still, my school is the wide one. I hope I will not discredit it by ranging further yet to include not only 17-14 *haikai* link-verse but some 14-17, somewhat longer *Imayo* songs, squibs (*rakushu*) the conventionally further removed *wild waka* and even look at *haiku* (*kyôku*). To fully survey a field, one must step outside of its boundaries.

♪ *For the Scholarly*. A longer *Short & Broad History* may be found in the Appendix. Below, find 1) part of a letter from Yoshioka Ikuo 吉岡生夫, responding to my questions about approaches toward studying the history of *kyôka*, and 2), an exclusionary definition of the 18c Chinese-style mad poem, 狂詩*kyôshi* you may want to see again after reading examples of Ikkyû's and other Zen poems (pgs. 150-3, 506-9).

～～～～～～～～～～～～～～～～～～～～～～～～～～～～～～～～～

浜田義一郎という偉い学者がいました。『日本古典文学大辞典』の「狂歌」の項目を書いています。抜粋すると「『古事記』の夷振（ひなぶり）、『万葉集』の戯笑歌、『古今和歌集』の俳諧歌、あるいは軍記物の中の落首などに起こるとする古人の説には賛しがたい。狂歌という語は平安時代すでに用いられ、現に『明月記』建久二年（1191）の条に「当座狂歌アリ」と記されているし、狂歌の上手と評される歌人もいた。しかし歌道の権威を憚って、狂歌は「言捨て」るのが不文律となっていたから、記録されることはなかった」。これは大変なことを言っています。「古人の説には賛しがたい」この「古人」には遠く藤原定家の父俊成の「俳諧といふは狂歌なり」（『和歌肝要』、但し仮託書と言われています）に及ぶと思われるからです。『江戸狂歌本撰集』は表紙を捲ると「故浜田義一郎先師に捧ぐ」となっています、その弟子なのでしょう。江戸狂歌本撰集刊行委員会の一員である塩村耕は岩波書店の『新日本古典文学大系』第六十一巻に収録されている『狂歌略史 源流から二つの選集まで』を次のように書いています（執筆は高橋喜一ですが浜田門下に繋がるのでしょう）。

　　「狂歌を単に滑稽歌と定義づけるならば、その起源は和歌の起源に埋没してしまう。なぜならば、滑稽は和歌が本来持っていた機能の一分野であるからである。『万葉集』には「戯に嗤へる歌」があり、勅撰集に「俳諧歌」の部立が見られるが、これを狂歌の古例とすることはできない。狂歌の始原は「狂歌」の語が文芸のジャンルの名として文献に現われ始める鎌倉初期を待たねばならないのである」。

はたしてそうか。狂歌の起源が和歌の起源に埋没して何か不都合なことがあるのか。『和歌肝要』が「歌にあまたのしなあり」としてそこに狂歌を数えて何が不都合なのか。それから文献に現れないということは存在しなかったということなのか。ともあれ浜田義一郎の門下が圧倒している気配です。唯一見つけたのが「狂」の文字から万葉時代まで遡る金子実英の説です（「狂歌逍遥」。しかし「狂」の字に頼らずとも説明できることに気がついた、それが「私の五句三十一音詩史」です。　★ 皆様、Kaneko の文は藤井乙男編『蜀山人歌集』昭和二年。オンラインですから、関心あればじっくりとご覧になってください！

～～～～～～～～～～～～～～～～～～～～～～～～～～～～～～～～～

"一休、単に滑稽な詩を作ったというだけでは、まだ文学と称するには足りない。作者が、狂詩という様式の特性——形式と内容のアンバランスという構造が本来的に内包している批評性——を認識し、胸中の思いを託するのにもっともふさわしい様式として、それを自覚的に選択した時、換言すれば、狂詩という様式が作者にとって必然のものとなった時、戯れは戯れなりに質の高い表現が達成され、初めて狂詩は文学でありうる。"（日野龍夫+高橋圭一　編者『太平楽府他』平凡社 1991 の解説：日野龍夫より）　★ 皆様、大田南畝は偉い– has anyone else canonized two genres of literature? – と小生もおもいますが、上記は、一休などにとって不公平。I.m.h.o., a gross overstatement!

On *the* Nature *of* Kyôka & Nurture *of* Mad Translation

Finally, we come to the third and last of our preambles. After it, we are ready for the fun, the poems themselves. Let us start with an old quote –

> It is not possible that the rest of the world will ever realize the importance of Japanese poetry, because of all poetries it is the most completely untranslatable. *The originality of Japanese civilization* Arthur Waley, 1929

Of course, this would not hold for translating Japanese into Korean which shares the same syntax, but, for English, Japanese is indeed difficult, as English is for Japanese. With prose, where one can work with entire paragraphs, a gifted translator can break, combine and shuffle sentences to restore the good sense of the original unless it is a witty aphorism or humorous definition where the word order matters in which case, nine times out of ten the snapper at the tail shakes its hook (Hence, Ambrose Bierce's *Devil's Dictionary* is for the most part flat in Japanese). For literary translation, the translator must have an ear and a tongue for language above and beyond the usual. Waley did. He beautifully Englished classic Japanese prose that even most Japanese translators (putting it into modern Japanese) found challenging. So why did he find Japanese poetry a problem?

> Its beauty consists in the perfection with which a thought and a body of sound are fitted into a small rigid frame. An *uta* runs into its mold like quicksilver into a groove. In translation, only the thought survives; the poem no longer 'goes', any more than a watch goes if you take its works out of their casing and empty them upon a sheet of paper. (同)

Uta generally means a *waka*. Most *waka* include a long serial thread of modification with one slight knot in the middle usually called a *pivot word*, though often a phrase, that allows what came before to morph into something else, thus squeezing in a surprise and additional information into the small poem. That single thread of modification can run all the way to the last word of the poem, the subject leaving no room whatsoever for a plot. Even if the order of our syntax were the same, doing that in English would require hyphen after hyphen for Japanese is agglutinative, while English is not. That largely explains this:

> In the few examples I am about to give, the reader must for himself discover the possibility of poetry. If he is a poet, this will present no difficulty; just as a watch-maker would see in the scattered springs and wheels the possibility of a watch. (Waley 同)

We will not embarrass Waley with examples. Let me just say that Ivan Morris, in his foreword to his translation of *As I Crossed a Bridge of Dreams* (*Sarashina Nikki*), claims that Waley *demonstrated* "the peculiar resistance of Japanese classical poetry to translation" because his best Japanese poem translations were not up to his worst Chinese ones, and wonders whether the best solution might not be to simply avoid translating *uta*. I am not sure if even a poet can discover poetry in a language he cannot read which the translator could not re-create as a poem, but I can say that if Waley thought classical *waka* were categorically hard, he should have tried the most convoluted of them all, the *kyôka!*

Kyôka not only share the quicksilver-in-the-groove form of all *waka*, but have characteristics that make it hard for even the thought to survive translation. Let us see what three traits commonly ascribed to the genre mean for translation.

The first, *exceptionally imaginative content*, is, *in itself,* no problem, for paradox, hyperbole and most other comic rhetorical devices tend to translate well and the background or context for novel ideas can always be explained outside of the poem. The difficulty lies in the way long chains of logic are used to create the ideas in a manner which makes them witty rather than simply philosophical. What was said earlier about losing snappers in humorous prose is equally true for poems in translation. The more restrictive form makes it harder to get around, but the greater license given to poetry to use otherwise awkward grammar, and ellipsis makes it easier for the exceptionally creative translator.

The second, *word play*, is, in itself, a problem. Some is found in most *kyôka,* and much is found in many. It generally requires re-creation rather than translation, for, with mutually exotic languages, there is slim chance of a shared pun deriving from common homophones or shared ambiguity coming from the connotative spread of a key word. With nonsense verses or lullabies, the reason may be determined by the *rhyme* – which, in my opinion, makes rhyme a variety of pun – so a "translator" can simply change unimportant elements in the plot to fit whatever word-play he or she invents, but *kyôka* are usually have a message, so there is a limit on our license. Moreover, the phonemic poverty of Japan makes it a punning superpower where even mediocre writers can out-pun master wordsmiths in English. There are *kyôka* (and *haikai*) that squeeze all the integers, ten fish, or more vegetables than most Usanians or English can even name into a single 31-syllabet poem. And they can do it so *gracefully*; you do not feel like groaning. Indeed, you might miss them all! In the words of the only native English speaker I know as well-published *in his own Japanese* as I am, Roger Pulvers, *"Whoever said that the pun is the lowest form of humor obviously didn't speak Japanese."* (*Corny corkers add life to lingo, you elephant!* Japan Times: 2008/2/xx)

The third is *parody* in the broadest sense of the word, including playing with an older *waka,* either because it asks for it, or simply because it is well known, *satire* addressing the characteristics, nominal or factual, of a historical figure, and less pointed allusions to sayings, etc.. To appreciate parody, you must know the parodied. It, too must be translated. That would only be inconvenient – more explanation – were not *the linguistic gap between our languages so large the parody and the parodied may lose much if not most of their similarity in translation*. Moreover, some parodies are presented within stories because the original *waka* themselves were part, sometimes the main part, of a tale. I will introduce some such, but the only way to do them proper justice would be to do the entire tales. Again, note that "parody" is used for lack of a broader term, in most cases, the play upon the original, which may change as little as one letter, might better be called a *mutation*, and if that sounds too random, too natural, the only suitable word I can think of would be a term I invented to describe poems that changed so much in translation that I was forced to admit I was creating something new, alternative to or taking off on the original: *paraverses*. (*Variation,* even *allusive,* will not do for it implies a sort of identification not necessarily there).

In this book, for better or worse, I have had to grant myself a broader poetic license and do more of this *paraversing* than in any of my previous books (with a total of 8,000 translated poems) for it was the only way to translate the delightful soul of *kyôka*. In so far that this makes my poems differ more from the original than is usual with translation, one could say that I tend to create a *kyôka* of a *kyôka*. Thinking of this gave me my title, *Mad In Translation*, which, in *kyôka* style plays upon the title of a movie which I am sorry to say, I have yet to see: *Lost in Translation* (and, is this not a good example of the type of allusion often mistaken for parody?). Readers who fancy themselves to be traditionalists and are unfamiliar with my work, may be wary of a translator who confesses from the start that he will be literally unfaithful to the originals in order to be spiritually true. If you know my work, however, you know there is nothing to fear, for I always provide the original Japanese, a romanization, a word-by-word gloss and ample explanation (of which the numerous composite translations play a role) of what cannot be translated. This permits me to play without compunction and you, the reader, to see what is what and make your own judgment.

Needless to say, *kyôka* is not alone in being hard to translate. If another witty genre of poetry, classical *senryû,* has done better than *kyôka* – i.e., enjoyed considerable success in English translation – it is only because 17-syllabet humor requires a shorter sequence of improbable coincidences to be miraculously reborn in the target language than 31, and because it plays with a more limited number of stereotypes which facilitate a more economical theme-by-theme explanation. With *kyôka*, the best examples tend to be totally off the wall. Few who are not Japanese can guess what they mean, much less reincarnate them in translation. And, to be frank, I have seen, even bought, entire books of translated Japanese poetry of types far less difficult to do that make me want to surreptitiously paste in a card with the following disclaimer before selling them to a second-hand book store, or returning them to the library:

> This is a book of poems that, like the Wicked Witch of the West in the Wizard of Oz, are not merely dead but really most sincerely dead. These are poems in which even bookworms have lost interest. (Adapted from Roger M Knutson: *Flattened Fauna, A Field Guide to Common Animals of Roads, Streets, and Highways* (Ten Speed Press, 1987) which mentioned *animals* and *flies*.)

This is not to say that mad poems are the most difficult poetry to translate. Some are, indeed, *impossible* to translate – we shall see examples, too, for your author believes in sharing failure as well as triumph – but most *kyôka can* be done in one way or another. I think of them as the *second* most difficult genre to translate. Being singular, they are easier to recreate than the wit weaving through *haikai* link-verses, where poets cap verses with puns, allusions, parodies and other associations (sometimes leap-frogging one another's lines) so odd as to be on the far side of surreal. Look at the samples of gross *haikai* sequences in *The Moon Duty* chapter of my book of dirty senryu (*The Woman Without a Hole*, 2007) to see what I mean. I have seen some game efforts, but know of none, including my own, that do it full justice. *Kyôka* in translation may become popular in English, but *haikai* in translation will probably ever remain an academic exercise.

♪ *Sun*dry & *moon*wet *notes to be read or skipped, as you like.*

狂 **Pronouncing Japanese.** The vowels are like those of Latin tongues. Learn to say *Buenos Aires* correctly and you have mastered them. Well, almost, the vowels with " ^ " over them (the long-vowel line used for a century is not on our keyboards) will take you years or decades to learn unless you have mastered them already. Just know that they sound a syllabet longer than the vowels without the " ^ " and count that way in the poetry! The consonants are a snap, except *tsu* (say *datsun* minus the *da* and *n*) and *ky* before *a, o* or *u* (do *not* make it a "key" but go straight from k to y and unite that with the vowel). Then, put some *h* in *f, l* in *r,* slightly palatalize *g* and swallow *n* at the end, and pause briefly before gently exploding with any consonant written double.

狂 **A *Syllabet?*** – what I call the uniformly short syllables represented by one phonetic letter in Japanese, for which the highly variable and often very long English *syllable* is a poor substitute, while the Latin *mora* is completely opaque to all but the specialist. If you want the ease, or the snap, of the Japanese 17-syllabet poem, try 7-9 beats, for the 31-syllabet poem, try 13-15. If you do not know what such a *beat* is, "Mary had" has two, and so does "a little lamb." In other words, beats are accented syllables.

狂 **Why Is Japanese So Punny?** Besides boasting few phonemes to start with, the Chinese characters that allow Japanese to tell apart a large vocabulary are mixed with phonetic letters and optional. They can always be dropped to permit *polysemy* – *ambiguity* implies choice of one meaning or another, while *polysemy* implies more than one meaning is intended, as is commonly the case with *kyôka,* so I prefer it. Moreover, until the mid-20-c, *Japanese chose to use their phonetic letters in a way that increased the potential for puns.* Despite the fact that the letters, like those of Romance languages are generally pronounced as written, *as written* was not always *fully* written, even in print. Writers were not obliged to make explicit the distinctions between the sharp and dull sounds, or as Japanese put it, *clear* and *muddy* sounds of "k, h, s, t, ch" *vs.* "g, b, z, d and j," respectively. Since all these consonants come with various vowels, *we are talking about close to half of the* 50-sound *Japanese syllabary*. Take the first letter with a consonant sound (there are five vowels first) in the syllabary, か, pronounced *"ka,"* for example. With two muddy marks on it, が is pronounced *"ga."* Now *"ka"* could signify a question (a sound, not a mark in Japanese) and/or a *mosquito*, and in combination with the preceding or following syllabet, hundreds or even thousands of things, including *flower* or *fire* or *river.* The *"ga"* with which it could be conflated for lack of usage of those muddy marks, by itself, is a demonstrative article, the *self* or a *moth,* and, in combination with another syllabet a *picture* and . . . . This lack of distinction is usually no matter to the fluent reader who, with no conscious thought, chooses the intended pronunciation and does not even think of punning possibilities; but in the context, or lack of context of a short poem, the phonetic play resulting from rare use of diacritical marks made punning easier than it is nowadays, when Japanese are expected to be more explicit, though the addition of tens of thousands of occidental words to what is surely the world's largest vocabulary, has made up for this loss of ambiguity or polysemy.

狂 **Puns as Visual.** Homophonic puns may be aimed at the ear but, as explained above, they often must be taken in *by the eyes* to be appreciated as reading them aloud forces a choice and kills the ambiguity/ polysemy. Because of this, up to a double digit number of *kyôka* in old collections may only be appreciated visually. In the Occident, the acceptance by the literary critics of puns that required a visual read pretty much began and ended with Joyce, whose spelling reveals more than pronunciation possibly can. Today, despite the ability of the eyes to take in more than the ears, all poets – and Joyce is a poet to my mind – and their audiences might as well be blindfolded. We have come full circle from blind old Homer to boom-box homey. The joy of more informative, faster and long-lived visual language has been traded in for the sensually satisfying but more limited – to humans, who lack radar, at any rate – world of sound. The change came from both above – the ivory-tower elite feeling guilt for our sins against unlettered cultures chose to glorify the ears – and from below, because the most creative musical culture (remember, music is part of poetry whether poetry knows it or not) is black, and Afro-american culture is, for better or worse, oral/aural, at the far end of the spectrum from the Sinosphere, where visual language has been highly appreciated for millennia.

狂 **On Proper Form in Translation.** While Japanese books tend to print 31-syllabet poems *in one line,* as 17-syllabet poems (haiku and senryû) are almost always printed, we sometimes find a slight space between the first and second part or, if the page dimension calls for it, two lines. In English translation, five lines are as uniform for 31-syllabet poems as three are for 17-syllabet poems. There are very rare one or two or four-line translations. In this book, I am inconsistent. I rarely use one-line, often use two, rarely three, rarely four and often five, some of which have a space of varying width between the third and fourth lines, reflecting the tendency for 31-syllabet kyôka to split like *waka* 17-14, and others between the second and third lines reflecting the most common old *haikai* style as that is where the original, *kyôka* or not, happens to split, or simply that it works best that way in translation. Such variation may upset the formalist, but the fact is that the natural joints or breaks in *waka, haikai* and *kyôka* are not as consistent as our lines. While 5-7-5+7-7 is the ideal way a *waka* (including *kyôka*) parses – with the hyphen a joint and the plus a break – some small internal breaks go missing in many if not most of the poems – call them enjambed, if you wish – and even the large break is not de rigor. It is not uncommon to have *no* break from start to finish. Sometimes in both *waka* and *kyôka*, we find 5-7+5-7-7, something closer to the ideal haikai-linkverse form, 7-7+5-7-5. In cases where the middle 5-syllabets serve as a pivot phrase for what comes before and after, we might describe it as 5-7+5+7-7 and separate the third-line ever so slightly from the second and fourth. And, if that were not enough, it is not uncommon to find some breaks occurring that disregard the 5 or 7-syllabet ideal, occurring, say 10-syllabets into the poem, or 27. If a translator wishes to demonstrate formal consistency in parsing throughout a book, fine, but it does not bring us closer to the original. (Check the first three poems in this book, Issa's un-known *kyôka* has *no* break, Meshimori's famous *kyôka* and Motokata's infamous *waka* are both 14-17.) Yes, there *is* satisfaction in formal constraint. But, in translation, we need to carefully consider what the original constraints are before setting our own. I try to match the breaks of each poem, but luck of language often does not allow it. Two-lines are suitable for translations that refuse to divide well into five lines. Am I the only one to have noticed that excessively long or short lines look horrible and done something about it? I also feel my two-line translations are often closer to the originals as I have read them in Japanese. Sometimes, I confess, the choice is made for the sake of the page design. That, too, is poetic license. Finally, you might note there is one way I limit myself *more* than any translator I know of, with the exception of the playful Hofstadter, who sets constraints for constraint's sake, another game altogether). Until very recently, you might note the poems in almost all Japanese anthologies of *haiku, waka, kyôka,* or *senryû* are exactly the same length despite the different number of letters and characters used to write them varying by a factor of two or three. This is done by varying the distance between, and less commonly, the size of, the font, and altering the orthography. I try to maintain the figure (size & proportion) of my poems by these three means and by choosing words that will expand or shrink lines. While I do not often line up one poem after another in the Japanese style, I embody that uniformity by creating far more physical/visual alignment than would occur naturally.

狂 **Is It a Crhyme?** I do *not* apologize for using more explicit rhymes than found in the originals as I am obliged to make up for the loss of puns and uniform syllabets. Though wit is often divided between nominal, or wordplay-dependent, and conceptual varieties, with the former declared to be inferior, or, in the case of puns, even a sort of demerit, the truth of the matter is far more complex. Just as a piece of prose may contain the same information as a poem yet not be poetic, a plain unryhming poem may expound the same concept as a witty rhymed one, yet not seem humorous. To be witty, the concept must be elaborated in such a way as to lead the reader on until suddenly coming together at the end, or, if it comes together prematurely, graced with something extra to tickle the fancy. With syntax requiring a different order of the major parts of speech in Japanese and English, the concept must often be adjusted to keep the surprise in just the right part of the poem. Rhyme helps save the wit by making that change seem natural, justifying it.

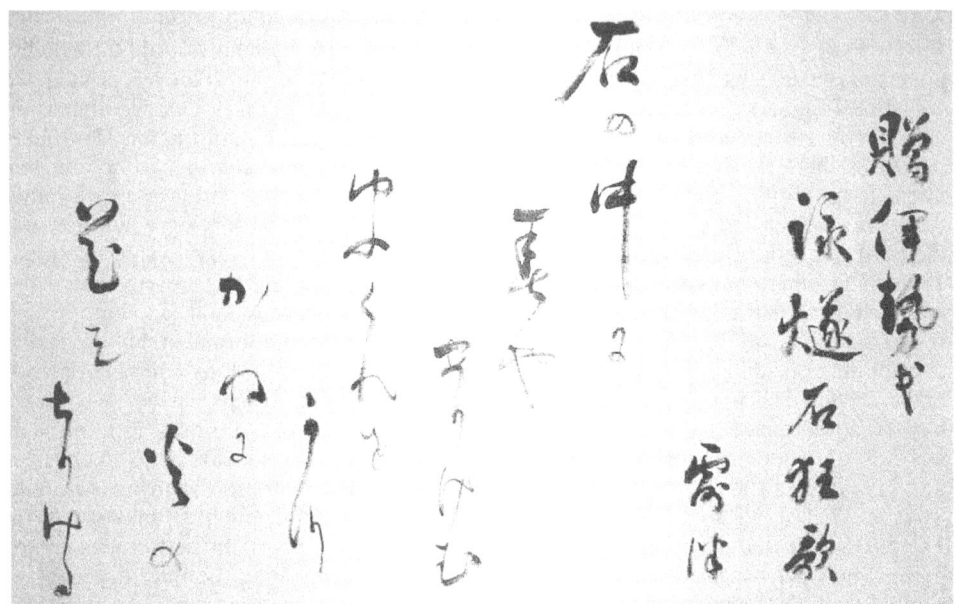

The above is an a *kyôka* for a store selling fire-making equipment (see pg.647). Note it is broken into nine lines and it really does not matter. Below is 80% of a third of a page from *Broadview* with standardized modern parsing of Bokuyô's *kyôka*. The first poem is better not broken into two for it flows smoothly from start to finish. In the old books one finds poems in single lines, in two lines split where space runs out or at the standard 17-14 juncture, but spaces are rarely made artificially where lines do not really need to break.

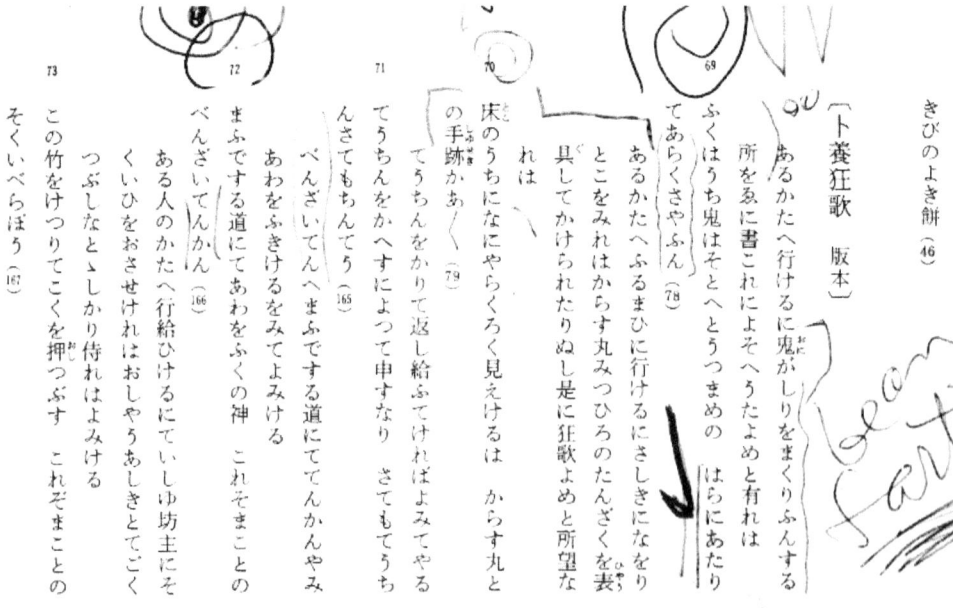

番外曲
A Poet Betrayed

書物も残らず棒にふる郷の人の紙魚／＼憎き面哉　一茶
shômotsu mo nokorazu bô ni furu^sato no hito no shimijimi nikuki tsura kana   issa
print-matter even remain-not pole-on-swing/hometown folks' keenly:paperfish spiteful faces!

The Poet Betrayed

Like silverfish, they don't give a shit for written stuff,
My countrymen, my ass! They live to eat it up!

Written shortly after *haikai*-master Issa (1763-1827) finally returned to his hometown after decades in the big city, this *kyôka* fuses *bô-ni-furu* (an idiom for *letting go to waste* – literally, *swing as or on a pole*) to *furusato* (home-town) and turns "intensely" (*shimijimi*) into "silverfish-zilverfish" by repeating the bug's Chinese characters 紙魚+ditto. The philologist might call it a visual Tom Swifty (But, note: *kyôka* adverbial puns are not limited to describing quotations)! Your translator first imagined Issa's manuscripts were used to heat baths or wipe arses, as the greater part of a carefully collected superb collection of bawdy English ballads once was.

Fuck my town of illiterate assholes w/ bad behavior
To them, a book means but one thing: toilet-paper!

Eventually, I read an annotation to the effect that Issa entrusted something, more likely to be documents concerning his father's will rather than what I imagined, to someone and returned to find them damaged and/or missing (害失).

My father's deeds mean squat to my countrymen – in anguish
I look at their faces and all I see are silverfish!

I have seen this vicious mad poem in Issa's journal (文化十年) and nowhere else. He kept it under wraps, not copying it into anything he published. This is understandable as it puts down the people of his hometown while he still wanted to live there; but why has it languished unread in the modern reprint by Mainichi (newspaper) of Shinano prefecture now *for decades?* I have not found a single mention of it anywhere. Even one of Japan's most prolific novelists, Tanabe Seiko, despite her obvious attraction for Issa's earthy side, failed to find it, for it would certainly have graced her 800-page "faction" novel *Warped Issa* (*hinekureta issa*) if she had. As a *kyôka*, it was not in any selection of Issa's collected haiku a busy novelist might have had time to read. It caught my eye before I knew anything about *kyôka,* by chance, because I happened to like Issa enough – or value my time little enough – to read his journals from start to finish.

. Living with Silverfish!

If they had their way, all books would wipe asses or burn:
The spiteful faces in my hometown, make my stomach churn!

Pardon the large number of *paraverses*. Your translator cannot help but identify with Issa and that affects his reading. Considered one of the top three or four classic haiku poets today, in his time Issa was but one of a score of top haikai masters, and lacking independent wealth, he was poor his entire life. The acerbic wit that flows from a deftly welded poison pen, or brush in the Sinosphere, is cheap medicine for the soul of all whose well-being largely depends upon the consideration of those who enjoy the security we are denied. And, as writers, we know that, in the long run, the fruit of our resentment may entertain and bring food for thought to others. I had hoped the annotation would prove wrong and we were talking about notes, poem journals and books; but not only did the date match the time when Issa was fighting what we might call illegal disinheritance, as the town including the relatively well-off man who was entrusted with his fathers will/s and whatnot, favored those who had been there all along to this poet who spent all of his adult life away, but a variation of the same poem minus the saving grace of the silverfish pun, specified the *shômotsu* or written things were his deceased father's (*waga mida no*). Still, the fact is that by making those *shômotsu* "books," the silverfish come to life and the poem gains broader currency which I would cash in translation.

What Spiteful Faces!

All books must go: that is their wish –
In my hometown, capital to silverfish!

Waka punning on the *furu* in *furusato* (hometown) as *falling* rain, snow and flowers, *passing* years or *aging* were common, but Issa's is the only insulting usage I know. There is an equally furious *waka* in the *Manyôshû* where a lover describes the location where his lover loved another using a word close to the English *damn*, namely *shiko*, literally "piss" three times! But Issa's *kyôka* is a uniquely mad mad poem. I have kept it separate from the merely mad majority.

Papa's papers, saved for me, the fruit of his hard labor –

Gone! My hometown's motto? "Silverfish thy neighbor!"

Finally – days after the *reading copy* version of the first-edition was published – this, my best translation, came to me like the proverbial true-love who suddenly reappears when, tired of the single life, you've just married another.

狂 **How Amazing this Odious Bug** that turns manuscript into coralline mazes! Squashed as easily as warm butter, they feel like the dust on a butterfly's wing and make me feel guilty. Look for a book of silverfish haiku. ♪ *Notes will be at book's end* and *chapters will start on even-numbered pages* and *end on odd-numbered pages* from now on.

This is page 43, vol.2 of Issa's Haiku Journals 句帖 (*All Works: Zenshû* 全集 v.3, as v.1 compiles his poems by seasonal themes) 文化七年三月, April/May, 1810. Issa, 48, was in Edo. Visiting 'National Mound 国塚, he found *haikai* poet Kûsui's poem 極楽も地獄も活て居るうちぞ 死ての後は何か有べし 空翠 (*gokuraku mo jigoku mo* . . see pg. 160 for the full gloss) on a grave marker. I suppose it means something like *Heaven & Hell, who can deny they exist when we're alive; / but all that talk of where we go once dead is so much jive!* but such a translation (done now, as I cannot help retranslating poems each time I read them) is painfully heavy next to one I jotted into the book in the mid-nineties: *Heaven or Hell one thing is true / You cannot take them with you!* and promptly forgot. Coming across it again in early 2008 reminded me that, sometimes, wit might not just be kept but *improved* in translation and helped to give me the courage to do this book. Issa's furious *kyôka* is likewise mixed among his haiku a few years later, on page 257. Who knows how many other extraordinary mad poems hide like those silverfish or this Heaven and Hell within books or papers not ostensibly harboring the same!

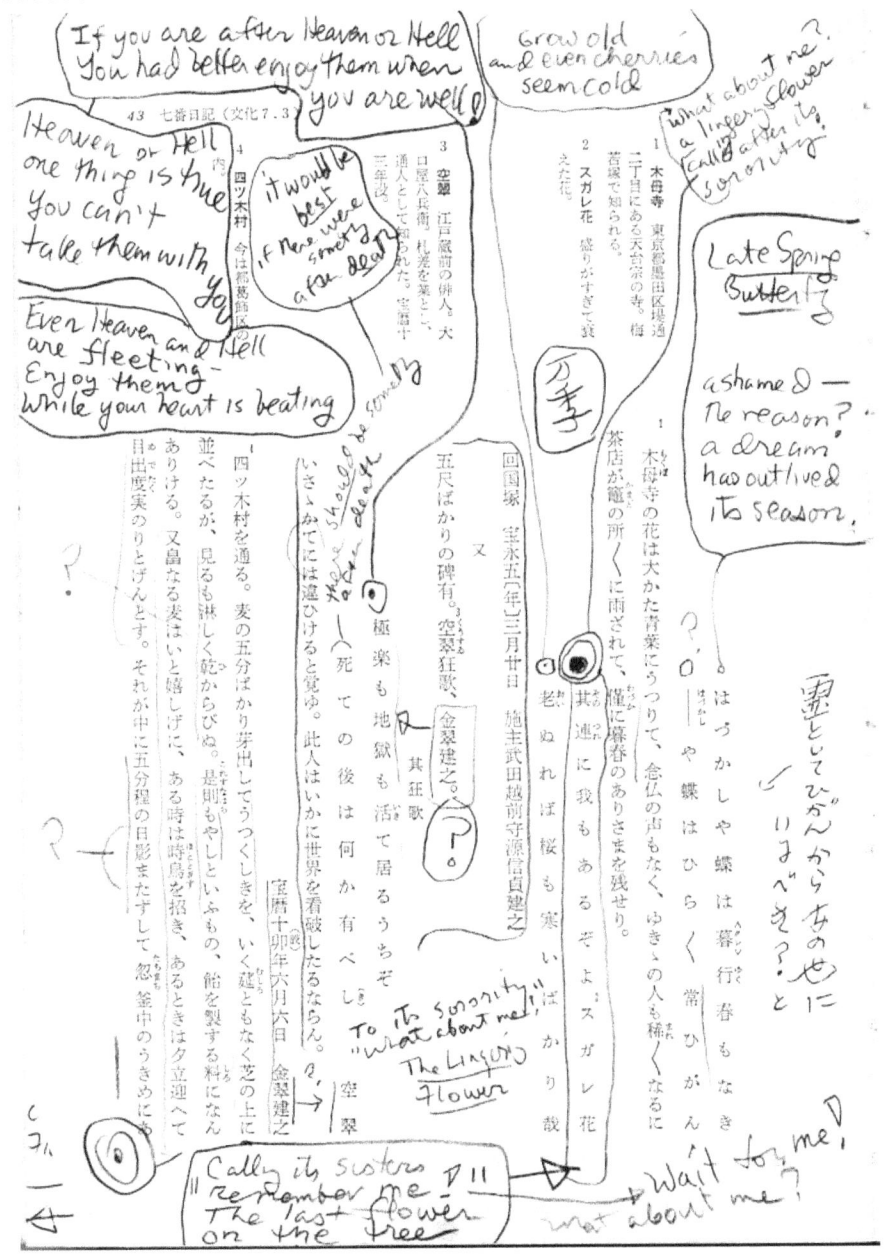

So, *What* Do We Want of Our Poets, Anyway?

歌よみは下手こそよけれ あめつちの動き出してたまるものかは 飯盛
uta-yomi wa heta koso yokere ametsuchi no ugoki-idashite tamaru mono ka wa meshimori
poem-composing-as-for lousy+emph., good heaven-earth(world) move-start put up w/!/? 1752-1830

To my mind, bad poets are the ones to be preferred:
Who wants to see Heaven and the Earth disturbed?

This poem by 18-19c *kyôka* master Yadoya no Meshimori should be in *every* anthology of traditional Japanese poetry. Conceptually speaking, the quintessential mad poem, the *kyôka* of all *kyôka,* it is less unlikely than Issa's adverbial silverfish, but, nonetheless, brilliant in the way of Charlie Chaplin as described in a four-line grook by Danish Poet-scientist Piet Hein which ends *"You think of what all of us think of / but nobody else could have thought of."* When Hein visited Japan in the mid-1970's, an *Asahi Shinbun* reporter noted his grooks resembled classic Japanese comic poems. But one thing splits Chaplin's skits from Meshimori's wit. For the *kyôka,* "all of us" includes only those familiar with the preface to China's oldest anthology of song/poem, the *Shi-ching* 詩経 (also *Shijing,* 2-3,000 yrs. b.p.), which claimed poetry could move heaven and earth and influence gods or demons, or the same in Japan's second major anthology of poetry, the *Kokinshû* (905). *Ametsuchi,* or Heaven-Earth, was standard high-language for the whole shebang. By "move," I doubt the ancient editors meant cause earthquakes, mud-slides or typhoons. I like to think Meshimori pulled that idea straight from his playful child-mind – mad poems not uncommonly exhibit the mistaken concreteness of children – but, truth be said, it was already in the air. The foreword of a 1769 book of *kyôshi* (太平楽府) lamented that the only one moving heaven and earth in *that* day was Mr. Money. A poet in one of a thousand anecdotes published in 1628 (*Laughs to Banish Sleep* by Anrakuan Sakuden) warns someone not to praise him too much for, according to the translator H. Mack Horton's note, *shrines and temples were believed to be liable to shake as a sign of the deities' favor.* And, I recall a Chinese creation myth, where heaven and earth separate to create the world, with the corollary being that when they started moving back together it would mean the end was nigh!

~ A Silly Notion About Grading Poems ~

In a wacky waka world, bad is better than good;
– for who the hell would want to see in motion
our earth, the firmament & even the ocean?

Doubtless, most literate Japanese had their doubts about poem-power. They were free-thinkers. Growing up in the clear-headed rationalism of the Sinosphere, they thought religion little more than superstition useful for governing the masses. That is no big thing. People *playing* with, rather than denying belief, i.e., pretending to take a belief at face value, i.e., as a *fact,* then showing the ridiculous place anyone would see it led to if they only looked – *that* is much more rare, but, in *kyôka,* quite common. Now, my version, after Belloc:

The Kokinshû Revisited
by a cowardly conservative

They say a good song
can move heaven and earth;
I hope they're wrong!
But, just to be safe, my Lad,
Let us learn to love the bad.

When I wrote that this poem should be in *every* anthology of traditional Japanese verse, I assumed it was *not*. I was *almost* wrong. It is indeed not among the seven *kyôka* in Steven D. Carter's *Traditional Japanese Poetry*, but *is* one of four in Geoffrey Brownas and Anthony Thwaite's older *Penguin Book of Japanese Verse* and one of nine in Shirane's larger, later anthology, which borrows a translation by Burton Watson, itself an evident improvement of B & T's ("mess" is no coincidence). Carter may have left out the poem to ensure his limited space for "madcap uta" – no one gives them much room, which is why I wrote this book – added to the tiny body of commonly available translation, or to avoid comparison, for he tends to be long and this happens to be one of B&T's best short & sweet efforts. Were I not mad enough to *enjoy* being outclassed, I, too, would bow out before them (Brownas+Thwaite, left; Watson's later 'mess,' right):

Our poets had best	when it comes to poets
Be rather weak:	the clumsier the better
If heaven and earth	what a mess
Began to move –	if heaven and earth
What a terrible mess!	really started to move

Now, let us see a less celebrated yet similar sort of naive take-off by a slightly older contemporary of Akera Kankô, Tegara no Okamochi. The target for his *tegara,* or skill, is a poem from the third most famous anthology of Japanese poetry, the *Shinkokin-shû* (1205): *"May Heaven's Door not be barred to your world for a thousand reigns, / so long as the sun shines and the moon waxes and wanes"* (君が世は千代ともささじ天の戸やいづる月日のかぎりなければ 俊成 skks 1205, *kimigayo wa chiyo to mo sasaji amanoto ya izuru tsuki-bi no kagiri nakereba* Shunzei). This is probably a New Year's toast. So, too, the *kyôka*:

久かたの空錠なれや天の戸をあけたつ春のかぎりなければ　手柄岡持 1785/6
hisakata no sorajô nare ya amanoto o ake tatsu haru no kagiri nakereba tegara-no-okamochi
far-off/long-ago's sky=keyless-lock is:/! opening-appears spring while=key not-if

May the door to heaven away in the sky locked without a key
Open up for Spring so long as 'so long' continues to be!

Three puns in the *kyôka* are lost in translation (蛇足：空錠は鍵のかけぬ錠、明立＝開閉、かぎりにも鍵), but if you can find it, perhaps I did save the core of the conceptual wit. Heaven's Door will be described in detail elsewhere in this book.

Calendar Conundrums and the Right to be Silly

としのうちに春はきにけりひととせをこぞとやいはむことしといあいはむ
toshi no uchi ni haru wa kinikeri hitotose o kozo to ya iwamu kotoshi to ya iwamu
year-within-in spring-as-for came: one-year+acc lastyear-as say-not, thisyear-as say-not

*Spring is in the air today,
so tell me if we may,*

*Call this year last year
before New Year's day!*

The original, which *I* consider mad, is neither the oldest *kyôka* nor, for that matter, ever called a *kyôka*. Nor was it an AABA verse; but I submit that my reading of Ariwara no Motokata's *waka* is, nonetheless, closer to the *spirit* of the original than the usual boring translation. I have seen several; and promise that none were interesting enough to add to the plain, parenthetical translation by Brower included in the following quote of Shiki's opinion about the *waka*:

> Tsuruyuki is a bad poet, and the *Kokinshu* a worthless collection . . . . Take down the *Kokinshu* and open it to the first page. The first thing you will come across is this really disgustingly insipid poem:
>
> *Toshi no uchi ni / Haru wa kinikeri / Hitotose o / Kozo to ya iwamu / Kotoshi to ya iwamu* (Spring has come within the old year: shall we call the year "this year," or shall we call it "last year"?)
>
> The poem is so silly that it fails to rise even to the level of vulgar wit, as if one were to say, "This child of mixed blood, born between a Japanese and a foreigner – are we to call it 'Japanese,' or should we call it a 'foreigner'?" . . . (from Brower transl., cited by McCullough & further abbreviated & unparsed by me.)

Shiki, considered, with Kyoshi, co-father of modern haiku, could not have been harder on the poem and the editor, Ki no Tsurayuki for featuring it in his *Kokinshû* (905), the second most famous anthology of *waka*. It is refreshing to hear someone attack a man and a book revered for a thousand years; but, is it fair? "Silly" or not, the poem embodies one of the best traditions of Japanese poetry: it plays with high culture. Tsurayuki chose and placed the poem first because it reminds us that calendars and editing have no pat solution. For example, poems in the last pages of the most famous anthology, the *Manyôshû* (9c), alternate between Spring signs seen in the winter (#4492 月数めば) and New Year poems, ending with snow on the first day of the year (#4516). And don't such contradictions between lunar, solar and local (or climatic) years make life more interesting? If the natural calendar jumped the gun, not just Spring, but the New Year itself was called into question. The poet, Ariwara no Motokata, was playing. The original has a witty snap. My rhyme would compensate for that and the boringly descriptive terms "last year," "this year" and "New Year's Day." Their Japanese counterparts have the pleasant ring of proper names. Shiki, of course, read it in Japanese and *still* was not impressed. Having grown up with the Gregorian calendar, could he have lacked sufficient *feeling* for the pleasure people once derived from the complex ancient system? In the 17c, Teimon school *haikai* poets, including young Bashô, so enjoyed the contradictions, which may seem artificial but actually come from the nature of nature (Does the earth not keep growing colder after the sun turns around?). Scores of examples of their calendrical play may be found in my book of New Year haiku, *The Fifth Season* (2007). Here is something not in my book, a *kyôka* published in 1649, composed by Mitoku 未得, a Teimon school *haikai* and *kyôka* master, for someone whose child was born when the solar Spring fell within the old year:

年の内の春にむまるゝみどり子をひとつとや言はん二つとや言はん　吾吟我集
toshinouchi no haru ni mumaruru midoriko o hitotsu to ya iwan futatsu to ya iwan　mitoku
year-within's spring-in born infant+acc one+emph say=celebrate-should, two+emph say=celeb.

Born on the day Spring calls on the Old Year
Do we celebrate this baby's 1ˢᵗ birthday, or is his 2ⁿᵈ here?

~~~~~~

A child born in the spring within the year – what can we do?
We want to call him "one" and we want to call him "two!"
~~~~~~~~~~~~~~~~~ or ~~~~~~~~~~~~~~~~~~~
We cannot call her "one" and we cannot call her "two!"

In the Sinosphere, one is one at birth, not just because of the gestation time but because of an idea of time similar to that in the Classic West which we continue when we call the 1900's the 20ᵗʰ century. But parody seldom moves us; no poem I know of succeeded in tying the premature Spring to real emotion, until this:

年の内に春は来にけりいらぬ世話　一茶 文化十三
toshi-no-uchi ni haru wa kinikeri iranu sewa　issa 1816
(year-inside=house, spring's done come: unneeded help)

Thanks but no thanks	*There is a season*	*Early Spring*
Spring, go home!	*Do-goody Spring,*	*Hold your horses!*
Old man Winter doesn't	*must you barge right into*	*the Winter and I do not*
need your help.	*Winter's house!*	*need your help.*

Issa took the first 13 syllabets of his virtually unknown *ku,* that I consider a prime example of a *kyôku,* or mad haiku, directly from Motokata's in/famous *waka.* His last 5, *iranu sewa,* a rude colloquialism for "unneeded help," bring to life the puns on the "inside" (*uchi*) of the year as a *house* and the "year" (*toshi*) as an *elder.* Issa was not the first to use those puns, but his *ku* trumps his predecessors' *because it has feeling.* We do not always *want* the winter to be over any more than we always want to jump out of bed at dawn. Hibernating can be good when you are deeply troubled; spring thaws out things better left frozen. As a *waka* by Gyôson (1055-1135) put it *"When spring comes / my iced-up sleeves / melt down / and serve only / to lodge the moon."* (*haru kureba sode no kôri mo tokenikeri morikuru tsuki no yadori bakari ni* skks #1439). 蛇足 = Wet sleeves mean *tears.*

New Years – More Laurels or Nails in your Casket?

門松は冥土の旅の一里塚　めでたくもありめでたくもなし　一休

kadomatsu ⊼ *gantan wa meido no tabi no ichirizuka medetaku mo ari medetaku mo nashi* ikkyû
gatepine/s (newyear's-morn)-as-for hades/purgatory's travel's 1-mile-mound: lucky r & lucky r-not

What are gate-pines
But milestones on the Way
to the Netherworld?

Lucky and Unlucky, they
bring us cheer & tears.

What's the first Day,
but a milestone on the way
to the world below?

A new year is propitious
And very much not so!

The sad contrast between the ever-young natural world and our aging, or metaphysical regret for another year to bear is felt at New Year's, when Japanese aged collectively. These feelings generally crested with the Year-forget parties for the old year. If you drink and think, it does seem odd the old years always "leave" while *ours* sticks fast. Still, expressing this anxiety through the evergreen New Year decoration – generally a pair of black (male) and red (female) trident pine branches standing in bamboo vases outside the gate – is unusual, though not for Ikkyû (1394-1481), the Zen monk exemplar of shocking thought and behavior, one of which was walking around with a skull on New Year's Day. In Ernest Tubb's old country song, each drink drives another "nail in my coffin." Change them to the *wreaths* placed on the same and we get an English mad thought where the Christmas wreaths each year add up to a quantity sufficient to fill a funeral parlor. Still, with the Occidental New Year just another holiday – competing with Christmas, Easter, etc. – no translation can satisfy. The version of the Ikkyû poem on the right is found within a Tale of Ikkyû and only differs in the first four syllabets, given within parentheses. The concrete *gate pines* are funnier, but *first Day* (lit. original-morn) evokes an imaginary *core sample of time* made of vertically stacked New Year's Days. The mad quality of the poem is enhanced by the poet belonging to a faith that made a point of death being nothing much (and shocking everyone before his own death by admitting *he* did not want to die). It also borrows from a poem by Ariwara no Narihira (825-80):

おほかたは月をもめでじこれぞこのつもれば人のおいとなるもの　伊勢八八
ôkata wa tsuki o mo medeji kore zo kono tsumoreba hito no oi to naru mono
mostly moon+acc even delight-not this+emp these pile-when person's/s' age(=burden) becomes+

For the most part, even full moons do not delight me –
They pile up on us, they do, and, soon, we are buried!

There is a pun on *age* 老=*oi* as a *burden* =負. I change *old* to *buried* to keep it in translation. To me, the pun make this a near-*kyôka*. Neither book I have on hand mention it. R&H (KKS #880) handle the metaphor thus: *"for every wax and wane / numbers the months of our lives,"* and Harris's odd moon sinks *"every night . . . / and these losses all amount / to making each of us old."*

春立やにほんめでたきかどの松　徳元
haru tatsu ya nihon medetaki kado no matsu　tokugen 1559-1647
spring arrives=stands!/: two=Nihon(Japan) ⇒legs? joyous gate-pines

Spring stands on
its own two legs, gate-pines:
Nippon is fine!

The puns in this, the most famous gate-pine *ku,* do not English. The *"nihon,"* or, *two,* with the counter *hon/bon/pon,* signifying long things such as these decorations, sounds like the name of the nation, and this, together with the fact that the verb used for *the coming* of the season, also means *to stand,* subtly turns the long upright decorations into legs: *the Spring = infant Year stands up, hurrah!*

門口に立や阿吽の二本松　隋言 桜川
kadoguchi ni tatsu ya aun no nihon-matsu　zuigen 1674
gate-mouth/entrance-at/in stand: aum's two pines

Ahum

Standing by the mouth
of the gate two pines
breath in and out

Aum is an Indian/sanskrit term that accompanied Buddhism to Japan. It Englishes as *Alpha & Omega, Inspiration & Expiration, open & closed mouth* (dog statues, etc.), *heavy breathing*. The in-and-outness suggests *fe/male;* if you recall, these pine are sexed. If they were wet or water was just poured into the bamboo vases, we might see vapor. Unfortunately, in English, unlike Japanese, entrances are not called *mouths* unless they lead into a tunnel, cave or body of water.

年波の今やこえんと門々にたてし師走の末のまつやま　蜀山百集
toshi-nami no ima ya koen to kadokado ni tateshi shiwasu no sue no matsuyama　shokusanjin
year-waves' anytime passover when gate-gate-by placed shiwasu's end's pine-mount

This most clever and untranslatable gate-pine *kyôka* of all, by Shokusanjin (1749-1823) puts the pine into the sea by alluding to a *waka* from the *Hundred Poets One Poem Anthology* where the sea flows over a pine-topped mountain (末の松山 こさじとは) and pegging that on the common conceit of the New Year as a wave passing over or bounding back. There may also be a hint of feeling swamped with debt-related anxieties at the year's end, as the term *shiwasu* (師走: "teacher-runs") is used and the pine mountain is deliberately not written in Chinese characters so the "pine: *matsu*" may also be read as "wait." Another, less clever but more interesting sour-grapes *kyôka* about these decorations records that a gate-pine seller to whom Shokusanjin offered 64 *mon* – one for each year of his life – to no avail, ended up with an unsold inventory. (六十四歳になりければ　わがとしも 六十四文 ねがならで うれのこりたる 河岸の門松　*waga toshi mo . .* 家集).

New Year Zen+Zaniness, or, Dao and How!

天下皆 はるにわなりの下手の弓 いられぬ道をゝしへ給はれ 貞徳
tenka mina haru ni wa nari no heta na yumi irarenu michi o oshie-tamaware Teitoku 〜狂歌抄 tk1
heaven-below-all/everyone spring=stretching-in/as-for/harmony-becoming(=humming?)'s poor/unskillful bow fretful-not=shoot-cannot=un-needed way+acc teach+hon. (a polite way to request something of a superior)

All of us below
the heavens string and bend
our bows in spring

Aimless arcs, meant for show,
Show us the way to harmony!

Oh, useless Bows
we string for pure harmony
our arc of spring

Teach us not what's hit or miss
But this: The way to stay calm.

Teitoku's *kyôka* are usually mentioned in asides as being as hopelessly nominal as his *haikai*. That is to say, all wordplay and no substance. It is easy to prove, for he left many poems to serve as examples of just that. But he also left many poems that prove he deserves better from literary critics and historians. This mad poem, with far more puns than could be re-created, may be one of them. I say "may be" because, to tell the truth, I am not sure I get it. What if it's this?

> *In spring, our minds bend round, like useless toy bows –*
> *Help we need to hit that road where no arrow ever goes.*

Regardless, the final 14-syllabets unite the mellow mindset of the New Year with the original WOW! or Way of Ways that is not *a* way but always flowing here and there. The New Year spirit of *wa* 和, meaning *peace*, *harmony* and *pliancy* is homophonous with a *ring/circle/hoop* 輪. When a strung bow describes a semi-circle, however, you can bet it will not shoot well, and that, Teitoku hopes will teach us to do all things with aimlessness. I read of ceremonial bows made from bamboo on shrine/temple premises strung with (weak) hempen string. I imagine it is really cane-bamboo (*yadake*), weak enough for a child to draw. Believe it or not, this hard-to-read bow poem had an envoi by the poet, himself, and it is this.

弓の句にひずみのあらばなをせとは　やさしき人の心たてかな 貞徳
yumi no ku ni hizumi no araba naose to wa yasashiki hito no kokorodate kana
bow poem-in dent/fault is-if/when fix as-for gentle person's mind/heart-set

> *If this bow ku turns out to be a bit bent, can I trust*
> *Ye gentle men to guess my intent and fair adjust it?*

Foolishness, or rather, the return to it (愚に帰る), was *proper* to the Japanese New Year for many reasons. The critical moment in the Japanese myth of the beginning, the return of the sun, which becomes one with the New Year sunrise, was itself proof of the saving grace of humor, for the Sun Goddess only opened the boulder door of the primal cave when another goddess did a clown-like strip-tease which caused such an uproar by the other gods that she just had to peek out.

To the educated class, such foolishness echoes Taoist myths of the beginning with all those silly sack and egg and gourd stories Taoists themselves are sane enough not to take too seriously. Yet New Year humor wells up from a place deeper than myth. The idea of a metaphysical return to infancy of the mindlessness of the beginning, whether it be ontogenic or phylogenic comes naturally to all who have observed seasonal and biological renewal. This is not in itself, funny, but the conflation of the old and the young the New Year embodies *is*. It comes from the very nature of history – of ancient times being both older and younger than us – and the nature of our individual lives, where maturity ends up in diapers, drooling like Teitoku's cow. As a corollary to this concept, the largest body of crazy poems by poets who do not belong to the mad school were written to celebrate their 50/1 or 60/1 birthdays (like centuries, there was some disagreement when things started, so some poets wrote such poems two years in a row!). The former marks the end of one standard fifty-year lifetime, while the latter marks the end of another more optimistic one comprising five cycles of the twelve year-animals. I do not think they have ever been gathered, as death poems have, into anthologies, because, on the whole, they are not masterpieces, but I can provide a few. Here is Issa (1763-1827) turning sixty-one:

Born Again

spring is here
an old fool turns into
a new one

春立や愚の上に又愚にかへる 文政六
haru tatsu ya gu no ue ni mata gu ni kaeru Issa
spring=new-year's comes! folly-upon again folly-to return

Blyth finishes *"upon folly / folly returns;"* Lanoue, *"nonsense / piled on nonsense."* Japanese rarely uses personal pronouns, so one cannot tell for certain if something is an aphorism or personal. Knowing Issa's self-deprecatory bent – not to mention age – I think it benefits from a personal take which also makes it seem more delightfully mad because, for haikai poets turning fifty or sixty, both ages formally appropriate for going *Back to Start* (*fifty* an old convention, *sixty* 5 year-animal cycles), or really aging – living into the late 70's or 80's was common among the *haikai* poets of a comic bent – foolishness was a sort of seasonal theme, though it was not actually made into a *kigo* (season-word) as far as I know. If you read the 2000-odd New Year haiku translated in *The Fifth Season*, you will find a good tenth that can only be called *kyôku,* though I should caveat, they are rarely called that, perhaps because *kyôku* is used as a broad generic term for mad 31-syllabet poems of both the Chinese style (*kyôshi*) and the Japanese *waka*-style (*kyôka*) because Japanese has no term as general as "poem." Since the general word is seldom used, I am trying to push *kyôku* for 17-syllabet mad poems. I am not alone. The Saint of haiku, Bashô, himself, used the term once and I am delighted to see it is the meaning the enormous *Morohashi* dictionary provides: 「狂句」おどけの意を含めた俳句。句に遊び楽しむこともいふ。〔芭蕉、冬の日〕狂句、木枯らしの身は竹斎に似たる哉。

Growing the Rock of Ages from a Pebble

君かかほ千代に一たひあらふらし　よこれ／＼て苔のむすまて 雄長老百
kimi ga kao chiyo ni hito-tabi arau rashi yogore yogorete koke no musu made yûchôrô
your/lord/darling's face thousand-reigns-in once wash-seems, soiling-soiling moss grows-till

My girl, your face would seem washed but once in a 1000 reigns
Dirty, dirty, I'll be blunt: Is growing moss your aim?

At a glance, this might seem a parody of one of the most well known of all Japanese poems, *Kokinshû* poem #343, the one that with one change (my lord => lord's reign) eventually became the lyrics of the national anthem:

わが君は千代に八千代に さざれいしの いはほとなりてこけのむすまで 無名
waga kimi wa chiyo ni yachiyo ni sazareishi no iwa hodo tonarite koke no musu made
my lord/you-as-4, 1000-ages 8000 ages, pebble/s' boulder/s-into becoming, moss grows until

Long live my Lord,
1000 reigns, 8000 reigns,

Until our pebbles
into giant boulders grown,
boast each a mossy crown!

This *Kokinshû* poem of celebration, in turn, borrows heavily from one of two poems lamenting the drowning death of a pretty maiden in the 8c *Manyôshû*: "*Let my girl's name flow down a thousand reigns until the buds of the young pines of Princess Island are solid moss.*" (妹が名は千代に流れむ姫島の子松が末に苔むすまでに *imo ga na wa chiyo ni nagaremu himejima no komatsu ga ure ni koke musu made ni* mys #228). Young pines evoke root-pulling festivities and roots, sleeping together, while *musu*, the verb for growing moss (or mold, etc) sounds a bit like *musubu* or unite, so we feel a particularly male chagrin for this death. The girl would not really be his girl friend, for the preface mentions an *otome*, or maiden, but the phrase seems to imagine what was never to be. The fact *washing* is close to *flowing* and only a *thousand* (no *eight: eight* has an infinite feeling in old Japanese) is mentioned in the *kyôka* suggests Yûchôrô also borrowed from the older *Manyôshû* poem, but the repeated soiling, soiling (*yogorete yogorete*) evokes pebbles rolling, and a late variant of the *Kokinshû* poem (拾玉集) starts with *kimi ga yo wa*, close to *kimi ga kao*, so who knows!

You Rock, Girl!   Roll Not, Stone!

Your face it's plain   *Majesty's face*
has only been washed once   *washed once in a 1000 reigns*
in a 1000 reigns   *is no disgrace*

Dirt upon dirt, without loss   *Dirt upon dirt is age's gain,*
Until we celebrate its moss!   *Behold the verdant moss in place!*

I recall my amazement at learning that "the rolling stone gathers no moss" originally meaning that one must stay still to prosper was taken as reason to move when transplanted to the hyperactive Yankee and could not help playing with the concept a bit. One thing is certain, in time, the pebble/s got far more attention than the young pine. The parodies could fill a book. Few translate well enough to merit parsing and presentation, but I cannot help mentioning a couple:

Eg., by *haikai* poet Ichû (1638-1711) *"May my lord's reign of men drunk as plovers, coral & turban shells; / Rolling free on pointed butt, until moss grows, age well!"* (君が代は 千代にやちよにさゞいにし ころ／＼／＼と苔のむすまで 惟中 狂歌五十人 TK2 *kimi ga yo wa chiyo ni yachiyo ni sazai ni shi koro-koro-koro to koke no musu made*). The original has one obvious pun. The pebble becomes a *turban shell* 栄螺, suitable for the first character means *prosperity*. I may be wrong to find pun readings of the *chiyo* and *yachiyo* but my OJD can back me up. Because I followed the pun readings alone, the poem seems unrelated, but it really is close to the original and the "thousand reigns, eight thousand reigns" still there.

Eg., 16c *waka*-master Yûsai 幽斎公 changes the *Kokinshû* poem, in a later version starting *kimi ga yo,* by just one syllabet, the last in the poem. The *made* まで, or "until," becomes *mame*, "bean/s" (君が代は..こけのむすまめ in 醒睡笑TK2). That had me confused. Having just finished a book on bawdy Japanese poetry, I imagined a woman's bean, the clitoris. As it turns out, there was a confection made of a parched bean wrapped in a sheet of green sea-laver and the poem was an impromptu composed when such was offered to the Imperial prince by the noble warrior-poet 太閤の御前 (『醒睡笑』in 山田孝雄『君が代の歴史』).

While none of this is parody slapping the face of the original, the mad poems do play with sacred cows. Speaking of which, another by Yûchôrô 雄長老:

神子たちのかぐらにけはう唐の土 更におもてはしろ／＼として 狂歌五十 tk2
kamiko-tachi no kagura ni kewau kara no tsuchi sara ni omote wa shirojiro to shite

> Shrine maidens do a sacred dance wearing Chinese earth,
> Making whiteness whiter still, faces beyond death or birth.

Shinto, "the way of the gods," was considered to be the font of the quintessential Japanese spirit and purely native ritual. For the pure maidens in pure white dress on sacred soil dancing a sacred dance to be wearing something imported from the contrary rationalistic world of Chinese civilization would have been a sacrilege if Japanese had such a concept. Sixteenth century Jesuits were amazed at the amount of white powder Japanese imported from China for make-up (See *Topsy-turvy 1585,* Items 2-15 and 2-66 in Frois's *Tratado*), so Yûchôrô is probably not kidding. Imagine the Chinese making not only the Stars & Stripes but Bibles for Usania. I first translated *"~ whiter still, the very face of mirth,"* for the myth where the Japanese Goddess invented white make-up to be more visible in the starlight, excite the Gods and draw the Sun Goddess from her cave is said to be the birth/etymology of *omoshiroi*, "white-visage," which is to say, the *interesting*. I changed because *kewai* has a powerful somewhat spooky presence, and lacking a good way to express that, invented the phrase "faces beyond death or birth."

If Stone Ships Can Fly, then Coconuts Can Sail?
あま雲に いはふねうけし そのかみを 思へはつきし やまとしま人
amagumo ni iwafune ukeshi sonokami o omoeba tsukiji yamatoshimabito minister tokiwai-nyûdô
heaven-clouds-in boulder-ships floated that upriver/before think-if end-not yamato islanders

常盤井入道太政大臣　百首御歌 賀
1 of 100 celebratory poems

*Boats of boulders
floating in on heaven's clouds
and who can go*

*Beyond that I do not know
the island folk of Yamato!*

*Boulder ships
that floated on the clouds;
it's all we know.*

*Who can trace where from
The island race of Yamato!*

I expected to find as many poems about these boulders – *ama no iwafune* (lit. heaven's/sky's boulder-boat) sailing in to earth as I did flying maidens (pg.293), but all I have found so far are a couple *waka* where the Herder Star uses a stone boat to cross the Milky Way. In one, Shinkei (1405-75) has it operate like a barge, pulled from the shore! (草根集). On the web, most of the interest is Christian; boulders and clouds up mountains are linked to said flood. The *best* news, however, is the presence of the ship-shaped boulder the god Nigihaya no Mikoto flew down from heaven. It still rests at the Iwafune shrine in Osaka which includes the shrine to aviation made by the man claimed (not necessarily correctly for the comparisons are made only with the Wright brothers in mind) to have practically invented heavier-than-air aviation, albeit rubber-band powered, with wheels for take-off, practical moveable wings, pull-tensioned struts and a screw-type propeller for use in the air, Ninomiya Chûhachi (1866-1936) who intended it for the repose of the souls of experimental aviators (For more, see *Practically Religious* by Ian Reader, et al. 1998). While boulder boats are the stuff of myth; a poem with them is not ipso-facto mad. Still, I did have to dig the lead poem out of the *Fuboku Wakashô* 夫木和歌抄(c1330), a collection of *waka* considered too odd or poor for the major collections. Since the poem is a beauty, either the poet or subject must have been thought beyond the pale. The poem, 雑部十八 歌 #18, is followed or grounded by the following *waka* by the beloved 12c poet Saigyô:

苔うつむゆるかぬ岩のふかきねは君かちとせをかためたるべし 西行上人
koke uzumu yuruganu iwa no fukaki ne wa kimi ga chitose o katametarubeshi
moss buried budge-not boulder's deep root-as-for lord your 1000-years solidify-ought

*How long of root
this boulder fixed in place
buried in moss!*

*May you grow ever solid
a thousand years without loss!*

*Like a boulder
green with moss and rooted
deeply in the earth*

*May my Lord remain in place
A thousand years from birth*

Where English speaks of *deep-seated* boulders, Japanese has its *roots*. Still, the idea of solidifying (*katametaru*) years in the original – similarity in the mineral and vegetable world that also caught the fancy of "our" metaphysicians (Kircher et alia) – may have struck some Japanese as far-fetched, and the root *and* hardening, together, dovetail beautifully with the most famous of all the mossy boulder metaphors, the one that grew from a pebble in the last chapter.

R I D D L E

What is this boat, that after floating in to shore,
Raises a sail, drops anchor and goes to sea no more?

When I read about boulder boats up mountains, *this* is what I think of – *coconuts!* That is because I grew up on a coconut plantation in a time before palm blight, when coconut trees were so abundant on the coast of Florida and the Caribbean that their progeny were constantly floating up on the beach and raising their first green sail. For readers unfamiliar with palms, the frond comes up solid, like a banana leaf, but somewhat curved like a sail running with the wind and only splits into tassels later. Hurricanes would always decapitate a number of trees – and we would dig out and enjoy their delicious raw hearts. Adults mourned the loss, but there was no shortage of trees back then, and if you were, like me, a dreamer, you would imagine the grown tree's sacrifice was not in vain. For, you see, only hurricanes that flooded the island gave the trees not growing right on the beach the opportunity to send their progeny out to colonialize new worlds. Back in the USA after decades in Japan, a few years ago, I joined my mom and fled from the island for a hurricane that gave us little wind and less water. Most people were relieved, but I did not forget the opportunity my nutty friends lost:

Down on the beach
after the storm missed I throw
coconuts out to sea!

Did Icicle Tears Begat *that* Cow Slobber?

丑年　今朝たるゝ氷柱やたれの涎かな　貞愚

ushidoshi: kesa taruru tsurara ya dare no yodare ka na   teigu (teitoku+keigu)
(ox/cow-year: this morning dripping icicle/s:/! whose slobber[+exclam. interrogative])

\\ Year of the Ox //

The icicles drip:
Whose slobber is it,
This Morning?

This is the only 17-syllabet lead in the book. Not only is not *kyôka*, but not even genuine. It is my improvement of Teitoku's in/famous haiku called "Teitoku's slobber," *i.e. dribble*, by Bashô. The *ku* that occasioned that criticism is this:

けさたるゝつらゝやよたれ牛の年　貞　徳

kesa taruru tsurara ya yodare ushinotoshi   teitoku 1570-1653
(this morning drips/hangs icicle/s!/?/: slobber/drool ox year)

synchronicity

this morning	dripping icicles
the icicles slobber	today, call them *slobber*
year of the cow	year of the ox

"This morning" in the absence of other clear seasonal signs means the morning of mornings, New Year's Day. Every year in the Sinosphere comes with, or *as* an animal. Far Easterners identified with these twelve creatures, as Occidentals do with their more eclectic (human, animal and chimera) monthly birth-signs. Pre-Bashô poets *reveled* in these animals and, even today, every child and adult with a child in his heart *should* enjoy reading or writing haiku about them. Yet, most *saijiki* (haiku almanacs) slight this practice by failing to give *jûnishi,* as the twelve animals are called, enough space. *Why?* I believe it is because Bashô held up this *ku* as an example of what was wrong with the *haikai* of his day. Called worthless for being contrived and nominal, the *ku* came to stand for what I'd call *Teitoku's slobberel*. This is unfair. Teitoku may well have seen a melting icicle and found the coincidence worth noting, but, even if he just imagined it, *what is wrong with that?* Icicles melt in early Spring. Moreover, *who says Teitoku was not himself taking an irreverent poke at the precious, artificial icicle tears of classical poetry* associated with teardrops on sleeves? There are at least three in the *Shin-Kokinshû* (1205) alone. Song #31 by Prince Koreaki where we learn that *"From the melting / icicle tears that drop / into his old nest // Even nightingale knows / another spring has come"* (*uguisu no namida no tsurara uchitokete furu su nagara* ~ 惟明親王 r.1179-1221), song # 633 with its virtual bed of icicles by a top advisor 攝政太政大臣: *"On my pillow and sleeves, icicle tears ~"* (*makura ni mo sode ni mo namida tsurara* ~ 後京極摂政前太政大臣 d.1206?), and, finally,

年暮れし涙のつらら解けにけり苔の袖にも春やたつらむ 俊成
toshi kureshi namida no tsurara tokenikeri koke no sode ni mo haru ya tatsuramu skks 1435
(year ends/ended, tear-icicle/s melt[+finality], moss-sleeve-to-even spring arrives[apparently])

A year ends;
Lachrymal icicles
melt down.

Has spring come
to mossy sleeve?

Icicles made
of last year's tears
have melted.

Could spring come to
even a monk's sleeve?

Fujiwara no Shunzei (1114-1204), provincial governor become monk, hence moss-colored sleeves. He would become *waka's* leading scholar. I was tempted to use this as the lead but, with icicle tears common trope already, it seemed trite not mad, while Teitoku's slobber was fresh. I thought Teitoku's *ku* should be a question and redid it, but on my final edit note that *if* we break *yodare* "drool" into an "emphatic + who?" (*yo dare*), the first 12 syllabets of Teitoku's *ku* already *pun* as a question and the last 5 provide the answer. Granted, the Year Animal is an artificial construct, but *isn't all culture that?* To me, finding something bovine in dripping icicles is not just a delightful image for the Year of the Ox, but a fine creative leap, easy – or trite – only in retrospect.

I cannot help wondering if Bashô was so intent upon his high mission that he never explored the tangled tropical jungle of the *Shinkokinshû* and therefore failed to understand the icicle slobber was partly meant to be a chuckle at icicle tears. Teitoku's *ku* is a fine *kyôku* because it parodies the old, and a fine *haiku* for capturing the present moment. Moreover, I just happen to *prefer* his *haikai* wit to pretty, description such as: *"The first sun: / the icicles on the eaves / melt away"* (日の始軒の氷柱の解にけり　不得　大三物 *hi no hajime noki no tsurara no tokenikeri* futoku 1697) or, *"Spring rises / from the drops of icicles / on the eaves* (春立つや氷柱の軒の雫より　希因　古選 *haru tatsu ya tsurara no noki no shizuku yori*　kiin -1748). These are all very lyrical, but if you ask me, too damn easy. I want that hard-found coincidence of year-animal and melting icicle.

To be mad, in the best sense, is to be happy. Issa was blessed to have a mad teacher, Sogan (1712-95) who celebrated Teitoku's death-day as follows:

この翁の書たまひし「天水抄」を開きて
貞徳翁忌：天水の氷柱しぼらん硯にも 素丸
ame mizu no tsurara shiboran suzuri ni mo sogan
heaven-water's icicles squeeze-would inkstone-in even

On Teitoku's Anniversary
(on reading his *Heaven's Water*)

heavenly water
i would milk his icicle
for my ink-stone

Spring Dreams: the Mountain & the Treasure Ship

不尽の山夢に見るこそ果報なれ 路銀もいらずくたびれもせず 鯛屋貞柳
fuji no yama yume ni miru koso kahô nare rogin mo irazu kutabire mo sezu teiryû
fuji-mount dream in see especially reward becomes road-tolls need-not tired get-not

Seeing Mt Fuji
in a dream your good luck
is already here.

No tolls to pay, no tired legs –
That I would call a good year!

貞柳翁狂歌全集類題 18c

What a marvelous disconnect! There was a night, once the New Year's Eve, but after people began to stay up to watch the sunrise, on the following night or the one after that, when Japanese tried to have lucky dreams and recall them. Mount Fuji was deemed luckiest of all, presumably because it is both lofty and one of a kind and that portended great success. And, it was sometimes written with the Chinese characters used in this *kyôka* meaning *inexhaustible*, as well. Still, the reward of a dream is so abstract it begs for a concrete putdown from a wise ass. Teiryû (1654-1735), student of a student of Teitoku, Naniwa (Osaka area) *kyôka* master with 3,000 門人 students/ members/ disciples, demonstrates just the kind of simple cock-eyed logic, or hyperlogical argument, I love above all other literary wit. It is what we saw in Meshimori's poem favoring bad poets (p.32). The *koso* I glossed as "especially" is especially hard to translate. It is an emphatic that targets what precedes it to the exclusion of all else and sometimes requires something Japanese lacks to match: *italics*. Still, I failed to pin the italics on the correct target, the dream *itself*. Here is one more try, that likewise fails a direct pin, but, again with italics, comes somewhat closer:

'Tis said Mt Fuji
is a lucky dream: I'd say
it *is* good luck,

If you can see it and keep
your money and your feet!

At the time the mad poem was composed, miniature model Fuji's were sprouting up in towns throughout Japan and pilgrimages to the real one 富士詣 had become popular; and, just as some Usanians (yours truly included) today think it insane to run about in circles sweating, or even worse, on treadmills like hamsters even though they do not live in cages, we may assume that some Japanese thought such travel and mountain climbing was a masochistic exercise better left for fools. Now, for comparison, let us see how *haijin* treated Mount Fuji of the New Year.

first dream:
the cat, too, sleeps like
he sees fuji!

初夢に猫も不二見る寝様哉　一茶
hatsuyume ni neko mo fujî miru neyô kana　issa -1827
(first-dream-in cat too fuji sees sleep-manner/appearance!/?/'tis)

a mount fuji	*that's kyôto!*
for your first dream sold	*selling edo's mount fuji*
in the capital	*for first dreams*

初夢の不二の山売都哉　一茶
hatsuyume no fuji no yama uru miyako kana　issa
first-dream's fuji mountain sell capital!/?/'tis -1827

The endearing cat *ku* is found in many *saijiki* and doubtless has many translations. Cats sleep on their back with their front legs over the head when they are feeling secure. People who have not lived with them might prefer a translation that makes the *First Dream* the title and defines the posture: *Our cat sleeps / on his back: is he looking / at Mount Fuji?* I added the bold second reading, not in *The Fifth Season* which I pillaged for New Year-related material, after giving more thought to what Issa might have meant to say. While Fuji was the most desirable dream, the most commonly sold charm for good dreams was generic:

宝船訳の聞こへぬ寝言かな　太祇　　　　　鼻息に飛んでは軽し宝船　子規　再現
takarabune wake no kikoenu negoto kana taigi　　*hanaiki ni tonde wa karushi takarabune* shiki
treasure-ship meaning hear-not sleep-words!/'tis -1772　　nose-breath-by flying-as-for light/easy tr.-ship -1902

Cargo Cult	*Dream-power*
a treasure ship	*the treasure ship*
impossible to make out	*how swiftly it sails in*
this sleep talk	*a nose wind*

The treasure ship was that charm and, if I am not mistaken, half the haiku about it seem like *kyôku*. Taigi alludes to the seven Chinese Gods aboard the ship and "Chinese-sleep-words" *i.e.,* "Greek to me" in English. As far as I know, Chinese did not sleep on pictures of treasure ships like Japanese did; but, long before the Occident began to explore, they sailed real ones the length of two football fields (with watertight compartments and many other modern features) around the Pacific and may have started something like the airplane-inspired cargo cults in 20c Oceania. While this was not *known* to the Japanese, there may have been a vague cultural memory. As far as Shiki's nose goes, the mad idea of nose-wind-power makes *some* sense when you know that Japanese depicted the *zzzzz* of sleep and the content of dreams in a balloon protruding from the nostrils!

A Soft Celebration of Princess Sao's Country Matters

棹姫の裳裾吹き返し やわらかな 景色をそそと見する春風 貞徳 貞徳百首狂歌
sao-hime no suso fukikaeshi yawarakana keshiki o soso to misuru harukaze teitoku 17c
sao princess's skirt blowing-back soft scenery+acc. gently:quim show/s spring-wind/s

♪ *mons vernâlis* ♪

how soft a scene
above her foothills pleasing
the eyes as softly

so softly the spring breeze
lifts sao hime's misty skirts

Sao Hime, the Princess of Spring, was identified with the mist, newly verdant hills and vales, and, of course, the flowers. A more appropriate title for Teitoku's original might have been *Ventus Adventis* or *The Coming of the Wind*, for the entire poem modifies the protagonist, found last: *"Blowing back the hem of Princess Sao's robe to gently reveal a soft scene, the Spring Wind."* I must confess it is hard to stay focused on the wind, rather than what *he* shows us in this verbal *shunga*, or spring-print (erotica). Shakespeare had a word for it: *country matters*. This beauty, one of all too few fine poems in Teitoku's *Hundred Kyôka* anthology, conceals *its* word where Issa would later put his *shimijimi* silverfishx2/very, in an *adverb – soso*, or *gently*, is also a fine old word for *cunt*, and with the accusative marker for the scenery (*keshiki*) that happens to precede it, gives us the more polite *o-soso*, preferred in Teitoku's Kyôto!

Mt. Tenderest

So so lovingly
the warm winds of spring
lift up the skirt

of princess sao and show
the tender heart of earth!

Even if I gave up on the puns, I probably could not capture the lyrical fluency of Teitoku's original. When I first read it in Issa's wordbook in 1995, I translated –

What a soft country, the scen'ry above her knees:
Sao-hime's skirts lifted gently by the April breeze!

At that time, I was correcting the translation of an 800 page biography of Darwin. The word "soft" (*yawaraka-na* in Japanese) was on my mind. As the boney butt of young Charles ground painfully into the hard wooden seats of the H.M.S.

Beagle, he listed the *pros* and *cons* of getting married on his return. I recall thinking *the* item in his list that decided it for marriage had to be the one about how comfortable he would be sitting with his *soft* wife on their *soft* sofa. He did not seek hard abs or buns of steel for himself or others, but *softness*. Me, too.

さほ姫のばりやこぼしてさく菫　一茶
sao-hime-no bari ya koboshite saku sumire   issa
sao-princess's piss!/?/: spilled/ing, bloom/s violet/s

        sweet pee   call of nature

where princess sao   *princess sao*
made water, who can miss   *took a leak & up peeked*
the violet scent?   *these violets*

just-so

princess sao's
piss: where it falls
violets bloom

There is no absence of Princess Sao *kyôka* – at least two in the *Tokuwa-kago-manzai-shû* alone – but I find more of interest in *haikai* or, at any rate, *kyôku*, such as Issa's. But why *violets?* Because they grow in the wettest places? Because they like the phosphate found in urine? (Issa notes, "The bone collector / is very familiar / with violets" (*hone hirou hito ni shitashiki sumire kana*). Or because of a certain affinity? Ben Franklin, in his letter to the French Academy of Science about the importance of finding a way to make farts smell good, described urine that pine nuts made aromatic as "like violets." Or, could the delicate beauty of the flower alone suffice to bait the poets? Regardless, it is easy to see Issa was developing the *haikai* tradition of a pissing goddess that started with Sôkan's famous *haikai* (variations in both 14-17 & 17-14 form) explaining the mist as the result of Sao accidentally wetting her hem as she/spring started=stood (a posture found in Kyôto – Sao's mountain was near – where women were known to piss into the public troughs for recycling). I will not translate *that* here, for it must already have a dozen published translations, including two or three of my own.

～～～～～～～

狂 **April?** I wrote *April* in one translation as it sounded good and another Teitoku *ku* about Sao included an April bloomer: "Princess Sao: / cherry blossom-colored / willow-hipped" (*sao-hime ya sakura-iro nite yanagigoshi*); but said *mist* belongs to early Spring.

狂 **My Mad Poem.** In the 1995 manuscript where I first pair Teitoku and Issa's mad poems, a note quotes Josephine Johnson: *"Winter is supposed to die this month. 'The back of winter is broken,' we say – a terrible expression, implying the old king lives, moves, but is helpless and in pain. But the old king still rises and scours the land with ice, typhoons, blizzards . . ." The Inland Island* (Story Press). This is followed by a couplet of mine titled *"Sadist Sao?"*

Winter's back breaks with the ice –
Spring smiles sweetly, "Oh, how nice!"

What would Herr Teufelsdröckh think of *this* Garb?

きのふまて丸裸なる山ひめも 霞のきぬをきそ初せり　方碩　銀葉夷歌集
kinô made maruhadaka naru yamahime mo kasumi no kinu o kisosome seri　hôseki　1679
yesterday-until round-naked is mountain-princess also mist's silk/dress+acc wear-starts

Even the princess of the mountain, buck-naked yesterday,
Has put on her misty robes, the year's first dress – Hooray!

The description of the princess as naked is funny in itself. While many poets make a big deal of Fuji's snow, nothing is said about mountains closer to hills in actual size near Kyôto that are identified with Princess Sao, so one might indeed wonder what *she* wore before the mist of spring, in the relatively dry and clear Japanese winter. The *"hooray!"* was added not just for the rhyme but to convey the joy of the ceremony or rite of first-dress, one of the most significant first-time this's and that's of the New Year. Here is something less interesting dated 1667:

雲の衣をたれかはぐらむ いつよりも 今宵の月は赤裸　新撰犬筑波集
kumo no koromo o dare ga haguramu itsu yori mo kesa no tsuki wa akahadaka　anon.
cloud-robes+acc who strips usual/when-more-than evening-moon-as-for red/buck-naked

Who stripped her
of her last cloudy gown?
What weather!
Tonight, Luna seems, well,
more naked than ever!

The moon in Japan is not thought of as feminine, but nudity usually was, so I called the moon by her Latin name and chose her over the "he" or "it" that English demands (and Japanese does not need). There are many emphatic adjectives for utter nudity in Japanese. If the princess above was 丸 *roundly*, or *wholly* so, the moon was 赤 or *redly* so, as would be a "complete" stranger or a "bald" lie. The moon can be red, but here, could she just be embarrassed?

今更に雲の下帯ひき締めて月の障の空ごとぞうき　唐衣橘洲　kisshû
ima sara ni kumo no shita-obi hikishimete tsuki no sawari no soragoto zo uki d.1802
now more-yet clouds under-belt pulls tight moon's obstacle/menses' empty/sky-act! sad

臨機変約恋と云ふ事を
Bloody or Just Blue?

Now, more than ever, cinching up her cloudy loin-cloth tight,
the moon's indisposed, or is it a pose, regardless, a sad night.

Kisshû was Yomo no Akara's main rival at the dawn of the Tenmei mad poem boom. From youth, he excelled at playing with *waka* trope in a dramatic *haikai*-style 戯歌 and supposedly popped up with this poem immediately when *asked for a poem on 'extemporaneous love'* by his *waka* teacher. His original combines the old trope of an obstacle to (seeing) the moon as the menses and the erotic word for a woman's loin-cloth "lower-belt," rarely applied to clouds around mountains (usually, just belts) puns sky-thing and fiction (*soragoto*) and sadness +float. I have seen this poem cited in a number of books, perhaps because it shows why Kisshû, unlike Yomo no Akara, did not become popular. For all its cleverness, it is not off-the-wall, and while it has been praised, the two simple older *kyôka* about utter nudity of Princess Sao and the moon are more appealing. However, I have not seen enough of Kisshû's work to judge it as a whole.

すゝはきの内より春はきにけらし ほこりたつ也霞立也 太女 銀葉夷歌集
susuhaki no uchi yori haru wa kinikerashi hokori tatsu nari kasumi tatsu nari futome
soot-cleaning-within-from spring-as-for come-has dust rising-is mist rising is

> *Spring has sprung and before our dusting is even done,*
> *!Up rise the clouds of soot!! Up rise the clouds of mist!*

The annual soot-cleaning day when everyone wraps a rag around their head and collectively carry on a war against the soot accumulated over the year (I mean, everyone – in modern times, even the officers of the company) is close enough to the end of the year that, occasionally, the astronomically calculated solar Spring may fall upon it. This *kyôka* by 太女 futome (or Kôfû 行風 pseudonym?) replaces the "(old) year-within," or *toshi-no-uchi* we saw in the *Calendar Conundrum* chapter, with "dusting-within." *Haikai* is full of clouds of soot rising to high heaven and many of those seventeen syllabet poems are as crazy or crazier than this. Indeed, I am tempted to call it a fine, even classy *waka*. A lesser poet would have had *". . . the soot into the mist become"*; and, to tell the truth, I had a hell of a time refraining from translating it so! But it is more elegant as is. I include the poem in this book less because mixing dirty old Soot Day with the pure mist associated with the new spring and coining "dusting-within" makes it a near-*kyôka,* than because it heads a 1679 anthology of 1186 "savage songs" or "wild waka" found in the 銀葉夷曲集 *Silver Leaf Ebisu Song Anthology* (*Ginyô-ikyokushû*) reprinted in the Broadview anthology, *Kyôka Taikan* 狂歌大観 *tk*) 夷 has a *barbarous*, or savage nuance – which includes a mixture of poems by recognized *kyôka-shi* (mad-poem masters) *haikai-shi* and *waka* poets. One more poem from the same old anthology caught my eye for being ahead of its time. It seems to be pr for a book (*of* which only the preface makes it to *Broadview*) of mad poems about the *young-crowd*, fashionable gay youth who sometimes sold their favors called 若衆 or *wakashu*. I was delighted to find 古今集 *Kokinshû* (the famous) anthology and 古今若衆 *Kokinwakashu* punned! Today, we are told, *shu* and *shû* utterly differ. Modern Japanese cannot imagine punning long and short vowels. As a foreigner, who sometimes cannot hear the difference, I say *Hah!*

きけはほんの名をは古今と申なり それは和歌集是は若衆　貞林
kikeba hon no na o ba kokin to môsu-nari sore wa wakashû kore wa wakashu teirin

> "From what I hear, the title of the book is *Kokin, Old-New:*
> That one is the *Wakashû* — *This* one is your *wakashu!*

Cutting Farts into Plum Scent

GrAsS hut airs

what wind i break
into sweet plum's bouquet
spring has finally come
to this old fart

梅が香に御ならの匂ひこき交ぜて 草の庵も春辺なりけり 一茶
ume ga ka ni onara no nioi kokimazete   kusa no iori mo harube narikeri issa
(plum scent in hon.fart's smell mixing grass=stinky hut too spring=swollen is!)

When Spring came, commoners eating gas-inducing *daikon* pickles and other salted greens that outlasted the winter were, shall we say, full of pep (or, as a Méxican might put it, full of *frijoles*) and ready to go. Issa (d.1827), using the double-verb *koki-mazete* in a number of *haiku*, confesses or boasts to mixing his stink with the scent of the plum. Married for the first time at age 52, his young wife was pregnant, so it is likely the plum blossom stands for her, with her breasts full of milk. *Plum* is written 梅. Can you see the 母 *mother* in it? And can you see the *tits* in the mother? While those tits also look like the little plums that resemble the full nipples of a nursing woman, in Japanese, the plum by itself, like the cherry, implies the bloom, not the fruit. The above reading, a paraverse rather than translation because of the blatant addition of "old fart," uses the "bouquet" to get that across. Issa's spring was in his fall. A usage of *koki-mazete* in *waka* he would have known mixes cherry blossoms and green willow to bring a trope associated with colored leaves, a Chinese robe, or *brocade*, into the spring. Reading Joyce on the toilet (who can take him more than a poop at a time?), I pulled Professor *Bloom* into another mad *harube* (*spring=harube=swell*) translation:

The scent of plum
in bloom and smelly farts
artlessly mixing
How my old grass hut
swells with the spring!

Issa's original, like most *kyôka*, including traditional poetic language, lies between the two readings. He is feeling both his age and his oats. Of all the haiku poets, Issa is the most full of farts. Find eight of his farty *ku* in *The Woman Without a Hole* also *Octopussy, Dry Kidney & Blue Spots* (2007) and composite translations of more of his fart-bug 放屁虫：屁ひり虫 *ku* in *A Dolphin in the Woods* (2008) if you are interested. He contributed to a *haikai* book 有なし草 with a flatulent preface and carefully wrote down one of the most famous fart *kyôka* of all time in his haiku journal (七番 9-11) as well as a miscellaneous notebook. Issa's *kyôka* is a prime example of punning that cannot be re-created with equivalent puns or even different ones of a similar class in translation because a proper name and particular variety of flower are involved. Likewise, the whiff of parody (the mixing of other scents with plum is done with the same compound verb, *kokimazete,* in an old *waka* we shall skip), and word for spring, *harube,* literally *spring-whereabouts,* but suggestive of flatulent swelling that may be a fartful allusion to the above-mentioned best-known fart poem, which has a 14-17 syllabic split common in *haikai,* but relatively rare in *waka* & *kyôka*.:

> *When it's breezy, our sleeves reek of spring:*
> *Ancient Nara=Fart, the capital's eight-fold=fart cherry!*

そよと春辺に匂ひぬる袖　古への御ならの京の八重桜 一滴 itteki
soyo to harube ni nioi-nuru sode　inishie no onara no miyako-no yae[he]zakura 18c?
blowing-w/ spring-about-in glow/scent wet sleeve ancient hon. nara-captal's 8-fold cher.

The most common words for *fart* in Japanese are *nara* and *he*. An honorific *o* before the ancient capital city of *Nara* makes it break wind politely, while the silent *"h"* in the *"e"* in *"yae,"* written in the old-style *"he,"* tempts one to mispronounce it as eight, *i.e., myriad* farts. And note how the optional *he*〜letter in the "inish*e*/ancient," written to visually accent the farts. *Haikai* or *kyôka,* this poem belongs to what may be the largest class of mad poems, parody. Its victim is a well-known 11c waka by Ise no Ôsuke (d.1060), *That eight-fold cherry of our ancient capital Nara – // Behold, it blooms anew, today, in nine-fold splendor!* いにしへの奈良の都のやへざくらけふここのへににほひぬるかな　伊勢 大輔 *inishie no nara no miyako no yaezakura　kyô kokonoe ni nioinuru kana*). The two poems are closer in the original, once you notice the first and last halves have been exchanged. Nine-fold, not normally a blossom term, means the Ninth Cloud, *i.e.,* Imperial Palace, whose denizens lived out of sight of us mortals. Blossoms and clouds in Japanese literature tend to be conflated. *Clouds of bloom* and *blossoming clouds* sound natural enough, but when the manifold is numbered, petals and clouds part ways in English. For the background of the poem and relationship to the ancient capital of this cherry, usually called double-petaled in English, see my *Cherry Blossom Epiphany* (2007). Among other things, I offer what may be a new hypothesis. Namely, this parody derives as much from the budding reaction against fancy breeds of flowering cherry as from a boyish poet's uncontrollable urge to cut farts into the flowery poems of lyrical elders.

M. Kei has described *kyôka* today as "about as popular among tankateers and haikuists as body odor at a beauty pageant." That is doubtless true (though I would make it *hair*). Most poets compete to be more poetic than others and those who take Japanese poetry seriously tend to take theirs religiously. I think the fact that Issa, who himself went through a more-Bashô-than-thou stage which slowed his progress as a poet (see the tell-tale quote, where he puts down Chiyojo's playful *ku,* in the foreword to *The Fifth Season*), still could not resist composing mad poems – and *hundreds* of his haiku are as "mad" as most *kyôka* – should tell us something about the mentality of not only Issa but, I would bet, *all* first-rate poets: they are wise enough to eventually indulge their foolish side, not simply to entertain others but to keep themselves in stitches.

Manyôshû's Mean Little Poems of Little Meaning

小児等 草者勿苅 八穂蓼乎 穂積乃阿曾 脇草乎可礼 万 葉 集
warawa domo kusa na kari so yahotade o okina no aso ga wakigusa? o kare mys #3842
children grass/weed don't crop yahotade oldman's aso's underarm grass=stink?+acc. crop!

The Alar Alarum
(a poem of priorities)

Hey, kiddos, skip that grass!
It's not half so thick
as the leek in old lord Aso's
armpit – Cut *it*!

Rank Garden   *Axillary Alarm*

Hey, boys,   Hey, kids,
   Let the green grass be!   the meadow can wait!
Rather cut the blooming cane
   below the arms of the old grandee   Mow Sir Aso's underarms
Aso, by name.   before it's too late!

The most memorable comic poems in the 8c *Manyôshû* remind one of the cruel kidding of children. Most, like this, are anonymous. Such is not the case with the 18c *kyôka*, but the hyperbolic wit and inane theme is mad enough.

Now you may talk about your horn of plenty
Compared to his armpit, it is empty.

Poems that are clearly minor ask us to relax and play with them; making it easier for translation as re-creation. Let's have the next poem picking on Minister Aso:

何所曾 真朱穿岳 薦畳 平群乃何曾我 鼻上乎穿礼 万葉集 #3843
izuku ni so masô horu okakomo tatami heguri no aso ga hana no ue o hore manyô
whenever+emph. vermillion dig okakomo tatami heguri aso's nose-upon+acc dig!

You want to mine vermilion from a vein that's big?
Go to the flat-top hills, find Aso's nose, then dig!

Looking for vermilion?
There's an inexhaustible vein
In the nose of Aso of Heguri plain
~~~~~~~~~~~~~~~~~~~~~~~~~~~~~~
You say you're short of cinnabar?
I've the answer for your woes:
Go find old Aso and
dig up his nose.

Aso's last name is a clan and its locality, a range of flat-topped hills near Nara. A paraverse two poems back, #3841, makes Aso's family name *pond-field* – a snot-allusion (Nakanishi) – specified – the implied use for the "true-vermilion" *i.e.,* copper for a giant Buddha statue. The obsolete word *masô* (真朱 "true-vermilion"), not in Japanese-English dictionaries, is the red or vermeil clay or tuff loam, source for vermilion and copper. Cinnabar, used for mercury, is different, but it is also described as vermilion, so poetic license excuses it, too.

> *Looking for red clay to mine?*
> *I know where there's a hill*
> *Try the flat-as-a-mat Heguri range*
> *Old Aso's nose should be there still.*

Aso is not only a rank in the bureaucracy but a term of endearment; hence "old." A heavy drinker? Not necessarily. Bulbous red noses pretty much grow themselves; I knew a sober Japanese man with a large, flat-topped red nose. Y's image, somewhat like the lion in *The Wizard of Oz*, came to mind many times while paraversing this poem. Then, after two poems roasting men for being too black or too white (skin color), my favorite hyperbolic insult in the *Manyôshû*,

法師等之 髭乃剃杭 馬繫痛勿引曾 僧半甘 # 3846
hôshira no hige no sorikui uma tsunagi itaku na hiki so hôshi wa nakamu
(bonzes' beards' shaving/en post/s horse/s tie/hitch painful/emph. not-pull!)

A Laugh at the Bonzes' Expense   The Bonzes' Choice Reply

Stubble that could,   *Go ahead & laugh, you asses!*
for hitching posts vie –   *When the reeve takes your taxes,*
Don't tug so hard, ponies,   *by and by, it will instead*
the bonzes will cry!   *be your turn to cry!*

Monks Who Could Shave More

Stubble that for hitching posts could double!
Try, ponies, not to pull, lest the bonzes cry.

◆

The Bonzes' Hair-raising Retort

Dear Parishioners, hush, lest your reeve should hear
Your words, & raising taxes, make you cry more!

檀越也 然勿言 五十戸長我 課イ役徴者 汝毛半甘 万葉集
dan-ochi ya shikamo na ii so sato-osa ga etsuki hataraba imashi mo nakamu
parishioners! say not reeve the tax/tithe impose-if you too cry will manyôshû #3847
♪ The response implies forced tithing, and suggests the monks were either too busy making a living to devote time to grooming, or could not afford the proper tools ♪

Two More Picking on the Involuntarily Thin

石麿にわれ物申す夏痩に良しといふ物そ鰻取り食せ　大伴家持　萬葉
iwamaro ni ware mono môsu natsuyase ni yoshi to iu mono zo munagi tori-mese　yakamochi
iwamaro[name]-to i thing say: summer-thinning-to end say thing! eel take eat!　manyô 8c

   Making fun of a thin man   Envoi

   IWAMARO, look!   Ever thinner
   Shall I tell you what?   Though you be,
   For summer sickness, catch   Better stay alive.
   An eel, and let it cook,   When you're after eels for dinner,
   Then – down the hatch!   Watch your step. Don't dive.

痩す痩すも生けらばあらむをはたやはた鰻を取ると川に流るな　同
yasuyasu mo ikeraba aramu o hata ya hata munagi o toru to kawa ni nagaru na
thin[vb]thin[vb] even live-if is-not[+exclam] conversely eel take and river in flow-not

   trans. Geoffrey Brownas & Anthony Thwaite: *The Penguin Book of Japanese Verse*

There are many tasteful translations in Brownas and Thwaite's Penguin Book of Japanese Verse, but this is the only clearly end-rhyming, albeit, enjambed – and, shall we say, delightfully irresponsible? – translation in it, though other light-verse, most notably, thirteen of Ôtomo Tabito's poems in praise of *sake* are included – unlike most Usanians, few English are prejudiced about drinking– and though they seem to ask for rhyme (see page 96-7, 488 for mine). Is it possible that the *cruelty* of the Thin Man poems caused the translators to either hand them over to a classics scholar well-versed in Martial's *Epigrams* (See Lesbia's *Wedgies* in *A Dolphin In the Woods* for an example) to do it right, or to reach deep down into their own gullets and pull it up themselves? (If my memory is correct, one of the translators is a classics scholar). Contentwise, I will not mention what was added in translation (you can ascertain that from the gloss) other than to point out that the alive ryme, "dive," was not free. The original idea of a man so slight the river current would *sweep him away*, was lost in translation. My first translation kept it:

   Kidding a Thin Man   *On Second Thought*

   I tell you, Bones, for summer-wasting,   *But e'er so thin a man may get, living*
     You must go catch and taste of eel.   *Still is his best bet! Sniggle with care,*

   Swallow it; then, see how you feel!   *Lest the river flush you into the mere!*

But, who cares! What is correctness in poetry? My translation is lame next to theirs. That is why I demoted it from the chapter lead translation in favor of their reading. Yet, as delighted with Brownas and Thwaite as I am, who likes to lose? Here is the first of two new tries:

♪ Kidding a Thin Man (two poems) 痩せたる人を嗤咲へる歌二首 ♪

Hey, Bones, I'll tell you what they say beats the summer blues:
Catch a big fat eel, then eat it, for weight you will not lose!

~~~~~~~~~~~~~~~~~~~~~~~~~~~~~~~~~~

No, no matter how thin, life is life, you'd best keep your seat,
& sniggle not, for any stream will sweep you off your feet!

By "new tries" I mean done after the reading copy first edition was published for a 300-page *Mad Reader* and *A Dolphin In the Woods,* and retrofitted so to speak. Are these any better? *Manyôshû* poems # 3853 # 3854 are sometimes cited in articles about 'the roots of bullying in Japan' for a note in the *Manyô-shû* tells us the thin man was a real man whose nickname was Iwamaro, Crag-guy (though the Chinese character is "stone"). In English, "Bones." Since youth, no matter how much he ate, he was bone-thin. This is no laughing concern. The fat were not kidded in the *Manyôshû*, as corpulence embodied wealth, happiness and good fortune. "Thin" 痩 is written with the sickness radical 疒 and most people feared thinning in the summer. I was surprised to find the word "summer-thinning" (*natsu-yase*), still used today, well over a thousand years ago, and *astounded* at the longevity of eel, eaten for the same reason, today. Of course, it does the involuntarily thin no good because the fat, unabsorbed, literally backfires or floats away (the supposed science of nutrician based almost completely upon what goes in the mouth, alone, is practically useless for the Bones of the world). The poet, Ôtomo Yakamochi, a fit man who could roam at night from wife to wife like a tom-cat and still have energy enough to do his work and write many passionate and clever poems on the side, could not feel the deep sorrow of those who can not get food to stick to their bones. Only the involuntarily thin know what it's like to be foresaken by the world of matter. The second half of my second new try is more a paraverse than translation:

Hey, Bones, I'll tell you the secret if you would stay fat
in the summer – you must catch and eat an eel for that.

~~~~~~~~~~~~~~~~~~~~~~~~~~~~~~~~~~

Though thin is not happy but sad, at least you are alive:
Let the fat sniggle, they float – Dive and you will sink!

~~~~~~~~~~~~~~~~~~~~~~~~~~~~~~~~~~

♪Originally, I thought to simply mention *Manyô-shû's* kidding poems in the short history of *kyôka* in the appendix and bail out, as I also have a handful in a different book sampling the poetic possibilities of *paraversing, composite translation* & *prose distillation* called *A Dolphin In the Woods* (after Horace's warning about where doing variations of poetry can eventually lead). I hate repeating myself, and fear it unfair to just the readers I most wish to delight, those who read more than one pf my books. At the same time, however, I realize that forcing readers interested in comic Japanese poetry to look at a more general book to encounter this material would be even more unkind than the average scholarly press book that forces us to read with a finger stuck in the back of the book for the segregated notes. So you got some here.

Volcanic Hearts, or Burning Passion as the Fashion

君こふる涙しなくば唐衣 むねのあたりは色もえなまし 紀つらゆき 古今集#572
kimi kouru namida shi nakuba karagoromo mune no atari wa iro moenamashi ki no tsurayuki
you longing tears +emph. not-if chinese robe breast's area-as-for color/desire burn-would   c 905

In Vain, My Love?

But for these tears
I shed for you, the silk
above my breast

Would burst into flame
as red as a Chinese dress!

In Japan, the metaphor of burning passion was fortified by a literal coincidence: "love," *kohi*, or thoughts of it, *omohi* (now, respectively, *koi* & *omoi*) both include "fire," *hi*. Chinese dress, *karagoromo*, was known for its bright reds, hence the simile. *Kara* meaning "Chinese," may homophonically evoke an "empty=*kara*" shell of oneself, *i.e.,* loving in "vain;" hence my title, also intended to bring out the humor – *wasted tears doing some good by keeping passion from burning out of control* (by removing trace elements, tears *do* have calming properties, according to research in a blue paperback in a cardboard box in a warehouse in Japan, waiting a decade for its owner, a pauper, to sell enough books of his own to be able to afford to settle down and be reunited with his library). The *waka* by *Kokinshû's* editor Tsurayuki could be a *kyôka* (or *haikai*) were it not a love poem.

中々二 如何知兼 吾山尓 焼流火氣能 外見申尾 万葉集 # 3033
nakanaka ni nani ka? shirikemu waga yama ni moyuru kemuri no soto ni mimashi o
rashly why? know[+done & bad] my mountain-at burning smoke's outside-by see-would+rather!

Volcano

fire & ash: i was rash
just once with you was once too much
i'd rather sit back and watch
another's heart erupt

This *Manyôshû* (8c) *waka* (left in its *Manyô* script of Chinese characters, just for the hell of it) lacks the nominal *hi*, or "fire" found in Tsurayuki's later poem. Rather than *kohi* (longing/desiring) or *omohi* (longing/worrying), this *waka* expresses love with that Biblical term, or at least the one found in English translation, *knowing* (知 *shiri*). It is not with the comic odds & ends in *Manyôshû* bk.16, but in a section of an earlier book "expressing thoughts by reference to things 寄物陳思." Needless to say, hyperbolic metaphor is comical for the reader even if the poet was serious. I added more than I should have in this early paraverse (you can always pare it down), but something like the "sit back" is needed to capture the strong emotion of the "rather" implied in that trailing "o." Another of my c. 1990 paraverses of the same in the style of Dorothy Parker:

> *See the volcano blow its top!*
>   *I wish it were not me.*
>
> *And had we never met, my dear,*
>   *It wouldn't be.*

More such may be found in *A Dolphin In the Woods* (2009), but to return to the subject, nominally burning passion, Cranston includes *Shûishû* (c.1005) song #597 – which he translates *"The furious gods / Also know the flames of love: / Must it not be so, / That across the endless years / The mountain Fuji burns?"* – among poems attributed to legendary poet Kakimoto no Hitomaro (fl.680-700), noting that its usage of the *fire* pun on the letter *hi* in *omohi* (*kami mo omoi no areba koso*) proves it to be post-9c. He also translates an allegory song, *Manyôshû* #1336 (*fuyu-gomori haru no . . .*), where a woman content with hibernating so to speak asks of a spring field-burner – *that's* a fireman for you! – *"Can he never burn enough, / That now he sets fire to my heart?"* It, too, has no pun, indeed no *koi* or *omoi* at all, just "my heart (he) burns" (*waga kokoro yaku*). So, my question is *why*, with fires in fields and mountains associated with passion, was that found within *words* not taken advantage of in the *Manyôshû?* My guesses: 1) *parts* of words were rarely punned at this time 2) and even if they were, "hi" was more likely to be punned as "sad" than "fire" for *Manyô* script often wrote *koi* as 孤悲, literally, "solitude+sadness; 3) the natural element of love tended to be *water*, rather than *fire*, with lots of ocean, stream, wave, shore and seaweed metaphors (Aren't your guts more likely to swim than to burn from uncertain love?), some achieving considerable allegorical complexity – Cranston translates one where the "heart" is a water plant that bobs in the current by the shore neither coming in nor going out. He notes that it *"captures the meaningless though not unpleasant motion of a love affair that is going nowhere,"* which may or may not capture the poet's feelings. Who says he isn't sea-sick and wishing with Willie (Nelson), *"♪ If you can't say you love me, say you hate me . . . . ♪"* ?

If the lead poem, while clearly crazy, is not generally considered a *kyôka*, it is because such metaphor was too common in love to be "mad." The first 100% *mad* fire in the breast may belong to old Monk Sôchô (1448-1532), whose paper robe actually caught fire when he slept below the *kotatsu*: *"Morning dawned / with nothing to show for the fire / that coursed through my breast / and my robe as well – / what an awful night!"* (*toru tokoro . . .* trans. Horton: 2002). Sôchô took advantage of Ono no Komachi's poem (*hito ni awan.. kks* #1030), where she wakes up with flames of passion barbecuing her heart (両方に「胸走り火」あり).

~~~~~~

狂 My KKS #572 first line was taken from Rodd+Henkeníus who translate *"but for the tears of / unrequited love that / gently stream for you / my Chinese robe would burn red / over my feverish breast."* The "unrequited," "gently stream for you" and "feverish" are explanation and/or padding to fill out the requisite number of syllables. Because, I provide glosses, readers can see what I do, but academics generally do not share that information =>I am not the only one adding and subtracting words; I am just open about it.

Yam Lovers Turn to Eel, then Get Split and Roasted

あなうなぎいづくの山のいもとせをさかれてのちに身をこがすとは 四方赤良
ana unagi izuku no yama no imo to se o sakarete nochi ni mi o kogasu to wa yomo no akara
pitiful=hole(waterhole)-eel, eventually's mountain-potato(a long thin variety)=girlfriend & boyfriend=back(of a body)+acc. // split/separating after body/self+acc. roast/burn-as-for

♪ *The Spitchcock Blues* ♪

Poor boy & girl,	*My poor Unagi,*
split up after the fashion	*born of wild potato, split*
of an oily eel,	*down your back,*
For roasting on the coals	*How sweet parting hurts*
of their very own passion!	*when you're burnt black!*

This is one of the three most cited *kyôka* (万載 1783) by the most famous *kyôka* poet – Akara = Shokusanjin = Ôta Nanpo – but I have yet to find one translation. Why? Because the reading must be split up. *One* will not do; it would have to be double, a composite translation showing both facets that in the original are a singularity. The *unagi*, a sea eel, is split open from the belly for roasting in most of Japan. Only in Kantô, which is to say greater Edo (now, Tokyo) was it split from the back as required for the pun – a boyfriend is a "back," *se,* short for "my baby," *waga seko,* or rather *papoose,* for that is how they are carried – and to turn the roast into a (possible) boast that "this is how we make mad poems in the capital city!" I am suffering as I write for the loss of a *senryû*, also from Edo, about this *yama(no)imo* – literally, "mountain (i.e., wild) potato:" an extremely starchy long (up to a meter) yam, *Discorea Japonica* – turning into an eel, where the latter stands for what more *senryû* call *zô no hana* or "an elephant's nose (trunk)" and stands (or rather does not) for the problem Mark Twain lamented as all too common for the proud possessors of a "mammoth cod." Now, all I can say is that of all the animals supposedly born of, or rather morphed of plants, none can boast circumstantial evidence for such magical ways as strong as that of the eel. One can read of small eels that dig and maintain finger-width tunnels between ponds that are not infrequently dug up on dry land (See John Fritchey: *Everglades Journal*, ed. Beth R. Read Florida Heritage Press 1992). I forgot to explain that "potato," *imo,* is homophonous with "little-sister," which meant *girlfriend.*

山のいもふちせにかわるなみだかわ うきみとなりてなをなかすらん
yama no i mo fuchise ni kawaru namida-kawa ukimi to narite na o nagasu ran
mountain-well (= taro = girlfriend/lover) pool-rapids-into changes tear-river floating/woeful-body/self becoming, name+acc. swept-off+huh! 四生の歌合

なまうなぎぬかりのぼう
~ by Live Eel Slimy Guy ~

A mountain well may turn into deep pools and rapids, a river of tears,
Flushed downstream, yam-girl's good name and her boy are gone.

This untranslatable 1643 *kyôka* shows that Shokusanjin's eel lovers were not born *ex nihilo*. It is too complex to split to present a readable composite. Take the first five syllabets. The *mountain well, even* (*yama no i mo*) doubles for a mountain or country girlfriend (*yama no imo*), then triples as a mountain yam, alluding to the eel the yam was said to become never mentioned in the poem itself – fitting, as the subject is the suffering maiden and her love's repressed love like a hidden eel that wells up and is lost, evoking a certain bean-pole in the *Manyôshû* a thousand years who was warned not to be swept away by the current sniggling for eels after he was advised to catch and eat them to cure his wasting away – akin to what happens when people pine for love. The *rapids* puns with *se* (back/boyfriend) but not in any significant way; it is simply to put him into the poem. And, so forth. There is no question that this, especially when paired, as it is in the original, with a more gutsy but equally complex pun-filled allusive allegory of catfish-catching and the disasters of love – including the "roasting" found in Shokusanjin's poem – is far more sophisticated than any of the Tenmei canonical mad-poem poets' work. If it was less widely read, the reason is probably the same as my reason for not translating it properly or John Donne's not being everybody's favorite poet. Most of us need to keep things reasonably simple. Perhaps, if I ever have the leisure to spend a day on translating each pair of poems, I will nonetheless try to English them, if necessary using triple- or quadruple-composite translation, each providing a different facet of the original and a page of explanation for the same. If that sounds boring, please note that the Japanese original's judgment as to which poem "wins," serves to indirectly, nay, gracefully, explain most of the puns and allusions to readers who might fail to catch them. Done right, explanations can, in themselves, entertain. Meanwhile, I do not want to ruin this 17c masterpiece, possibly by Kishita Chôshôshi 木下長嘯子, with four chapters comprising insects, birds, water-life and mammals (in tk1), most of which are depicted in relationship to humans *and* allegorically for human relationships. One exception will be made. The following poem supplies fine new adornment for the burning love metaphor we have seen and will see elsewhere in this book. I could not resist translating it. Or trying.

いかにして心の水にすみながら おもひはきへぬわか身なるらん
ika ni shite kokoro no mizu ni suminagara omoi wa kienu waga mi naruran
how (=squid) doing heart's water-in lives (=ink)-while おめてたいゐもん
longing(fire)-as-for extinguish-not my self/body is+emph. 四生の歌合 tk1

♪ Poem of the Happy-go-lucky Red Snapper ♪

How can it be that one who in a water-heart lives in fashion
may, catching fire, not go out, but rather burn with passion?

There were heart-shaped ponds, some were connected to the sea by underground conduits. At the same time, puns imply: *How, my squid, is it that our passion can burn so in ink / Within such tearful hearts yet blot not out I cannot think!* This is paired with a carping carp, the fish whose name puns with romance and there is an allusion to an old poem that would eat up another half-page to explain, so here we are, like the squid who can no longer hide himself . . . out of ink.

From Shot Deer to the King of Siam: More Mad Love

射ゆ鹿をつなぐ川辺の若草の身の若がへにさ寝し児らはも 万葉集 #3874
iyu shishi o tsunagu kawabe no nikokusa no mi wakagae ni sa-neshi korawa mo anon?
shot deer connected? river-area's young grass-body's young-in-add(?) slept child +emph.

> *Where is that girl with whom I slept, her body soft as young grass*
> *by the river where I trailed the deer I shot?*

In the original from the 8c *Manyôshû*, * "I slept," like the rest of the poem, is a mere modification of the *girl*, who comes last and is the subject of the plotless poem comic in the tastelessness of the modification of the metaphor "young grass," though, I suppose the loss of a trail, *i.e.,* losing touch with someone whom the poet might have left psychologically wounded years early can justify it. So this may not have been intended as black humor and was not just the natural language of a man who loved hunting to much to realize the implications of what he wrote. What I did not know when I translated the above was that the first 17 syllabets (except that "young grass" was pronounced differently) was lifted from a poem (*iyu shishi o tsu*, an odd lament for a prince who died at eight in 658 by his grandmother the Empress included in the historical account called the *Nihon-shoki* (c.720). In Cranston's translation, *"Not that he was young, / I do not say he was so young / As the young grass /* Along the river where they track / The arrow-wounded deer." I found it interesting that Cranston reversed the first and last half of the older poem (my italics), as I did the *Manyôshû* poem, which he began *"A wounded deer / Leaves a trail by the river / Into the soft grass: / But . . .."* Still, I find it hard to believe a poet could *seriously* recycle part of a lament in this way. Note: it is in chapter 16 of the *Manyôshû*, the one with poems one *waka* poet and literary critic (Kaneko) has called "substantially *kyôka*." Could the poet or *Manyôshû* editor have found the original lament so curious he could not resist recycling it as a different type of lament – though when you think about it, when you lose track of someone, it matters little whether they are in this world or that? Such recontextualized borrowing is common in *kyôka*. Sipping Cranston's *Gem-Glistening Cup* (*Waka* I), I also discovered something similar but thought-provoking in a different way with respect to *Manyôshû* poem #3806:

事之有者 小泊瀬山乃 石城尓母 隠者共尓 莫思吾背
事しあらば小泊瀬山の石城にも隠らばともにな思ひ我が背
koto shi araba obatsuse-yama no iwaki ni mo komoraba tomo ni na omoi waga se
(thing is-if obatsuse mt.'s stone-fort[crypt]s in even hide-out-if together don't-long/fret my boy)

..

A Grave Proposal

Honey, don't fret
if worst comes to worst
I know a pleasant place:
High on Mount Obatsuse
We can always embrace

This poem grabbed me the instant I saw it about twenty years ago, for I knew the "stone-fort" was a mountain-side cave used for noble graves in pre-Buddhist Japan. *What a thing for a maiden to say!* As one of *our* poets put it, *"The grave's a fine and private place, but none I think do there embrace."* A preface explains that the boyfriend of the girl who wrote the poem put off proposing because he was afraid to meet her parents. Fed up with his dilly-dallying, she called his bluff: *Was he not ready to die for or with her?* For half a dozen more readings, closer and farther from the original, see *A Dolphin In the Woods*. I was not sure I wanted the poem in *this* book; it may not be obvious in my mad translation but while it is in the comic poem chapter 16 of the *Manyôshû*, it seems more serious than the others. Then, last minute, I learned a variant of the poem first appeared as a folk song in the *Fudoki* (c.715) after mention of a female "mountain brigand" called Yukime or " 'Abura Okime,' 'Old Woman Oil' " (Cranston: 1993). Oddly, the name of the mountain did not match that of the locale. In other words, it, too, was handed down. To me, this sounds like what we might call *a ballad*, though the *Fudoki* variant is already in perfect 31-syllabet *waka/ kyôka* form, rather than the slightly different forms more common with folk song.

この頃のわが恋力記し集め功に申さば五位の冠 mys #3858
kono koro no waga koi-jikara shirushi . . .,
these days' my love-power

If I were to make a list of all the thankless things I've done for love
    And submit it, I would win the Fifth Rank, or above!

   Vs.

And if my efforts for the same bring no loving reward from you
    I am off for the capital, and see if I don't sue!

この頃のわが恋力給らず京兆に出でて訴へむ mys #3859
kono koro no waga koi-jikara tabarazu . . .
these days' my love-power

This competing pair of poems – in the original, beginning identically and using the same expression *"love-energy/power/effort"* (恋力 *koijikara*) – are in the *Manyôshû's* comic chapter. While less witty or novel than many *Manyôshû* love poems, they are closer in spirit to folksong and to the canonical *kyôka* by virtue of their lightness. I am reminded of a country novelty song where singer opines that a statue of himself with a gilded tear-drop rolling from one eye deserves to be erected at the Country Music Hall of *Pain*, which reminds me of another: *I Wish I Could Hurt That Way Again* and kkrj #3143 (*uki koto o oriori goto ni shinobureba tsuraki mo hito no katami narikeri* 古今和歌六帖 985 in Cran.v2a):

  If every heart-
 break were in silence born,
   Not a fracture
 but could be, at last, a mourn-
 ful yet dear keepsake of thee!

Love So Mad It Is ~~Almost~~ Impossible to Translate.

恋をしてのちはほとけといはませは 我そ浄土の あるしならまし ある好色の人 遠近草 TK2
koi o shite nochi wa hotoke to iwamaseba ware zo jôdo no aruji naramashi   aru kôshoku no hito
love/sex+acc doing after-as-for dead/buddha it's said-if I+emph. pure-land's boss am[not]!拾遺和歌集#1188

> ~~*'Tis said love is something made come hell or high water.*~~
> ~~*So take your pick: If I'm not Noah, I must be Old Nick!*~~

> *Make love and the world can go to hell! Unless all heaven*
> *Were to be under my thumb, why should I wait to get some?*

> ~~♪ *If making love brings us enlightenment, my dove* ♪~~
> ~~*Then crown me today, for I am the King of Siam!*~~

~ by one who loves sex ~

The uncrossed-out poem is my best guess, or *was* before more information gave me two more readings, not including Edwin Cranston's. We will get to them, but, first, let me say why I was so attracted to a poem I could only guess at. It is the phrase "Pure Land's Owner/boss" (*Jôdô no aruji*) in the original. I find it delightfully outrageous, whether or not it was intended to be. That made me equally so in translation – another version of the second reading ended something like ". . . *Unless you're head / of paradise, who would bet on being dead!*" Because, as far as I know, Japan had no tradition of sex in paradise ala Mohammedism (unless all those virgins are just meant to be gloated or drooled over), this *now-vs-then* approach to sex does not, however make much sense. Buddhists sitting on lotus pads looks as boring to me as Christians floating in the air playing harps. So, even my best guess must be wrong. Here is what I eventually came to think the most likely intent of the poet:

..
> *Do you really mean our having sex will forever set you free?*
> *Then, the God in charge of paradise would have to be me!*

I base it upon the example sentence for the third meaning of "becoming a buddha" 「仏に成る」 in Shogakukan's dictionary of proverbs 『ことわざ大辞典』, which is the ecstatic bliss brought by sex. A woman exclaims to her lord that his honorable usage (御用) of her would make her a Buddha (「仮・竹斎上」). I think it also could example the second meaning, namely achieving enlightenment. Then, it dawned on me. The poem was probably *a response* to such a woman. The only problem is that the usage example far postdates the poem, for though I found it in an Edo era *kyôka* collection, I later found it in Cranston (v2a), where I learned it was *Shûishû* (c1005) poem #1188. The poem was in the "referentially auspicious" section and was attributed to anonymous rather than a sex-lover. Judging from other exchanges in the boudoir regarding dreams, I imagine Anonymous may even have been an Emperor. My final reading follows that of a Japanese *Shûi Wakashû* editor (小町谷照彦), who wonders whether the tortures of love may not have been thought to create the reverse in the next world.

65

If love's tortures can really bring us Buddhahood, that is nice:
It makes me the future Lord of Pureland, the Paradise!

I.e., a macho-masochistic one-upping poem! (Want more? See the appendix!)

うつものもうたるゝものも奥女中 かはらけならぬ 毛沢山なり　蜀山家集
utsumono mo utaruru mono mo okujochû kawarake naranu ketakusan nari shokusanjin
striking one/thing struck one/thing even palace maid bare-pot is-not hair much is   18-19c

草履うちの画に
On a Picture of Straw Sandal Beating

The thumper and the thumped, both are palace maids;
Far from bare pies, these are hairy as the Everglades!

Senryû, following *haikai*, made a big deal of the quasi-harem existence of palace maids who strapped on dildos to assuage their loneliness and unlike women in the pleasure quarters did not shave their pubes – forgive my *Everglades* (that river of grass) and did not shy away from pre-pube(scent) girls; but Tenmei mad poems generally played with these things second-hand. By which I mean, not only did Shokusanjin only *use* sex to describe sandal-making, giving us a close-up of the tiny "hairs" sticking from the pounded straw twine used to make macramé sandals, but he amused his readers by playing with an early 16c poem:

うつものもうたるるものも土器の われての後はもとの塊　道寸　銀葉夷歌集
utsu mono mo utaruru mono mo kawarake no warete no ato wa moto no katamari
striking ones/things & struck ones/things earthen-ware broken-after original lump

Those striking and those struck, both unglazed pots today;
Once broken, all rejoin the original lump of clay.

Were this just a description of a pile for malformed work at a pottery, it would add little to Shokusanjin's sexy sandal-making. As it turns out, however, it is *a genuine death-poem* written by Michitake in 1516, before a battle that resulted in the extinction of the Miura clan (相模の守護、三浦道寸は1516年に北条早雲の攻撃を受けて家臣百余名とともに討ち死に). Composed for, or when the hundred-plus Miura vassals, knowing they were headed for virtually certain death, drank *sake* together from the unglazed earthenware cups Japanese used on ceremonial occasions (contrary to Europeans who used vessels made of precious metals and adorned with jewels for the same – see *Topsy-turvy 1585* for the reasons). In case you miss the connection between the poems, please note the verb I first translated "thump," and now "strike," is the same *utsu,* and I substituted "bare pies" (a semi-Japanese modernism from *pai-man,* or hairless vulva) for "unglazed pots" in Shokusanjin's poem, when both are the same *kawarake.* The "far from bare pies" (*kawarake naranu*) means, "~ *contrary to the mention of unglazed/bare vessels/ pies with respect to beating/throwing (utsu/utare) in the previous poem.* That is to say, the mad poem master facetiously contradicts the death poem.

Seasoning the Furious Loves of Cats & Yayû's Q.

野　風よりもそつとすこきはふうふうと 吹てかかれるのへののらねこ　如竹 堀川狂歌集
no *kaze yori mo sotto sugoki wa fû-fû to fuite kakareru nobe no noraneko* nyochiku
'field/s' wind-more than very dreadful-as-for huff-huff-with　blowing engage field's feral cats

< Winter Fields >

*Far more furious
than the wind, how curious
the caterwauling
of cats; To hear their hisses:
Love is not all hugs & kisses!*

Even cats have long had a proper time to make love in Japan; the early Spring, which the lunisolar calendar of old (pre-1870) put into what we would consider the cold tail of winter. *Fûfû*, the onomatopoeia of blowing suggests *fûfu*, or "mates," but the more significant pun is in *kakareru*, or "engage," *i.e.*, "doing it." We find *kareru*, which extending to the *nobe*, or "fields all about" means *withered* and *makes it sound like the cats may have some responsibility for the barren* January or February *landscape*. I believe that seeming causality supplies the craziness to the otherwise marginally mad poem. My aphoristic ending is nowhere in the original which, titled "field" (*no*), simply describes the dreadful sound and scary energy of cats in heat evoking the desolate fields. It is closer to the following, without my wolves and explicit just-so:

*Far more dreadful
than the wind, or wolves,
The huffing & puffing
of those cats: No wonder
all the fields are withered!*

Were I to start from scratch, you would get nine lives + fine wives and contrasting "heat" and *cold*, *i.e.*, basic English rhyme and idiom.

　　　年の内に春は来にけり猫の恋　一茶
toshinouchi ni haru wa kinikeri neko no koi issa
year-within-in spring-as-for comes+definite cats' love

*spring arrives
in the winter of the year
cats in heat!*

We have examined *toshi-no-haru*, or solar spring within the old lunar year, in Ariwara no Motokata's *waka* (pg.34), from which Issa lifts his first 12 syllabets, as he later does in a better *ku* which ends up chastising the Spring for intruding on his winter melancholy (or, so I read it, see my *The Fifth Season* ~いらぬ世話 (*iranu sewa*)). The ~ *nikeri* ending here suggests what happened was irrevocable and not necessarily good. *Indeed.* I have observed that when you find

snow-covered ground,
sure enough the cats
are in heat.

They mess up the snow's surface and the silence that snowflakes, like the feathers of an owl, bring us. It is also odd how often they come into heat at a particularly cold time. In the Tokyo area, I recall that the most miserable time in the winter was in February, after the flowering apricot (ume/plum) and before the flowering cherry bloom, when the cold from the desolate fields steals into your unheated room. At such a time, I recall thinking *Perversity, thy name is Cat!* That time would have been, formally speaking, Spring in Issa's time. And, today, while cats have been observed violating their season, the haiku almanac (*saijiki*) keeps them, as of old, in the Spring.

人の恋季はいつなりと猫とはゞ面目もなし何とこたへん 也有万代狂歌集
hito no koi ki wa itsu nari to neko towaba menmoku mo nashi nan to kotaen   yokoi yayû
people's loves season-as-for when becomes =quote asks-if/when face-not+emph what reply-should?

Asked by my cat
"What, then, is the season
for the loves of men?"

Blush: it stands to reason:
What should we reply?

"What season
for the loves of men?" ask
the cats in heat.

Talk about embarrassment
My reply is we are beat!

Asked by pussy
"What season, then, do men
come into heat?"

The cat's got my tongue:
We must admit defeat!

Ah, the shame!
How can one reply when
the cat has reason

To ask if the loves of men,
like felines, has a season?

The long-lived *haikai* poet Yayû (1657-1743) is one of the most pleasant poets of all time. His *Quail Robe* (*Uzuragoromo*) is *the* representative book of comic prose interlaced with haiku called *haibun*. He (or Buson) may also be the only pre-modern poet to have experimented with end-rhyme in Japanese. I had not known he wrote *kyôka* until finding this in Nada Inada's *Edo Kyôka* (1986), but it stands to reason that he did. I hope to find more and expect them to be sweet.

Tom at Home and Pussy Turned into a Banjo

朝夕に竈はなれぬ老猫の恋にはあらぬ身を焦すらん 一茶 文化 11
asa-yû ni kamado-hanarenu rô-neko no koi ni wa aranu mi o kogasuran issa
morning-night-in stove leave/s-not old cat's love-for is-not body+acc. burn+emph.

♪ day in, day out ♪
ne'er leaving the stove
old tom, you leave no doubt
even one who does not rove
for love can still get burnt

Cats in heat sound so *natural,* that when people are not angry at cats for keeping them up, they tend to be jealous (unless they are themselves doing it at the time) of them. We forget that not all cats are eager to join the fray. Some old Toms are too tired; some young Toms are afraid. Also, cats, despite their willingness to play in the snow, do, indeed, love heat. In Japan, where central heating is uncommon, once a cat finds a source of heat, it may hang on to it like a man to a life-raft. I had a felt-covered hot-water bottle-sized electric heater bought to keep my computer from fogging over that one cat literally sank her claws into. My added rhetoric, "you leave no doubt," compensates for the unEnglishable ending on the last verb, *"~ran,"* an audible exclamation with a grin or a laugh in it.

大空に妻祈るらん のら猫の月を見つめて夜たゞ鳴也 一茶 同
ôzora ni tsuma inoruran nora-neko no tsuki o mitsumete yoru tada nakunari issa
big sky-to wife pray!? feral-cat's moon-at staring night only cry

Praying to heaven
for a wife?
Gazing at the moon,
just singing all night?
Hey, Tom, get a life!

Do you, Tom, think
to find her up in the sky?
Mewing all night,
and staring at the moon,
you won't find her soon!

Issa left no doubt that the 31-syllabet poems mixed with the haiku in his journals were not pieces of link-verse *haikai* but stand-alone. Both of the above, like his mad silverfish, have no break whatsoever in the poem, as it would were they by two poets or composed as if they were. This makes them, in form, clearly *waka,* or what came to be called *tanka*. There is only one slight pun (the *hi,* or *fire* in the *omohi=omoi*) in the first, yet both feel like the unorthodox *waka* called *kyôka*. Why? I think it is because Issa kids his cat. That kidding quality is not as expressed in words as specific as my *"Hey, Tom, get a life!"* or *"you won't find her soon;"* but, as was the case with Issa's heater-loving cat, it is made with the chuckling and digging tail *"~ ran"* on the most important verb, which is "pray." Here is one of a surprisingly small number of feline mad poems:

猫の妻もし恋ひ死なば三味線の可愛やそれも色にひかれて　後西上皇 1638-85
neko no tsuma moshi koi-shinaba shamisen no kawaii ya sore mo iro ni hikarete emp. gosai
cat/'s mate/s if love-die-when shamisen's charming!/?/: that too color/sex-for scratch/played/ing

A cat that dies
from love gone wrong;

Reborn a Shami,
yet more charming, still
plucking for sex in song!

Piquant the song
of shamisen born of cats
that died for love

No fur flies, but sure enuf,
they're about getting some.

♪ Poetic Karma ♪

A shamisen made from a cat that died in season? Plaintive:
Clawed then, plucked now, and for the same damn reason!

In Japanese, *playing* a picked (plucked or strummed) string instrument is homophonic with being scratched: both are *hikarete,* a verb that also plays upon the *iro,* or color=sex, as "drawn to" or "attracted to" falls within its plethora of connotations, three of which are intended in this masterpiece by the 111th Emperor, Gosai. A *shamisen* is played with a plectrum the size of a small spatula, which might seem odd, but serves well to reduce sound-wave leakage. The sound of the *shami* (Japanese also abbreviate) resembles the banjo in that it can be alternately sharp and abrasive – more clawing than cloying – and the courtesans who played them and sang were called cats in some parts. Cat skin really was one of the skins used for the shamisen sound-box. A cat that died scratched up on the battlefield of love, or pined away at home would not be sought. The ideal was a kidnapped tortoise-shell house (better skin) cat, and the best shamisens, the *yatsuchichi,* are said to have been stretched so all eight tits of the belly are visible. I have not yet found out if the navel, found between the second row of tits from the bottom, is the sweet spot for strumming or good for the bridge, etc. One could take the love-making metaphor further, too, with *love-burning (koi-kogarete),* for the hair was burnt off (a *senryû* mentioning the dark inside of the home of a shamisen-maker tests the our knowledge of this).   Lacking such coincidences and a good "color" word to serve as a synonym for love of a sexual nature (plain *sex* would be too blatant and belittling), any translation is weak. Still, there is a way my above readings could be improved.

♪ Life After Death in the Pleasure Quarters ♪

Ah, mating cats, though you should die of love, as shamisen,
You would be more charming yet still scratching for a screw!

The original does not make it clear that a direct address was intended, but I think such was the intended reading, for, as we saw with Issa and his old tom, there is something I cannot put into words gained by having an audience, human or not.

Leveling Mountains for Love of the Moon & Sex?

をしなべてみねもたひらになりな〲む山のはなくは月もいらじを 伊勢 #82
oshinabete mine mo taira ni narinanamu yama no ha nakuba tsuki mo iraji o   tales of ise
all peaks+emph. level/flat-as become-would! mountain ridges not-if, moon too enter-won't+rhet.

> Why cannot we
> just flatten every peak?
> Think of the boon:
>
> Not one mountain left
> to hide the setting moon!

> ~~If only all peaks,~~
> ~~could leveled be, these blues~~
> ~~we could forget!~~
>
> ~~Behind the ridgeless mountains~~
> ~~a lover's moon would never set!~~

Why so dead set against the moon setting? First, people really viewed the moon with their friends and when it set, *party over*. Second, all lovers, even married, depended on the moon light for *him* to sneak in and out of the *her* house at night. Day visits were unmanly. A gentleman did his work by day and "crept" by night. Of course, there were torches, but the idea was a *discreet* visit. So, the moon pretty much set the social calendar. Having that limited time shaved off on both sides by mountain ridges naturally was resented. The above comes from the *Tales of Ise* (c.915), largely based on the life and borrowing the poems of a tireless lover, Ariwara no Narihira (d.880). Attributed to one Ki no Aritsune (a name punning into "always wants to"), it may be a takeoff on the definite Narihira poem (kks #884), in Carter's translation, *"Must the moon vanish / in such great haste, leaving us / still unsatisfied? / Retreat, O rim of the hills, / and refuse to let it set."* (*akanaku ni madaki ...*). I *assumed* it concerned *love*, but rereading *The Tales,* saw, *Oops!* the poems were side-by-side and the context, a party with a Prince. The desire for endless drink & entertainment (*miko*=shrine-maidens danced & sang) was expressed as the wish to contemplate the beautiful moon more.

あしひきの山は無くもが月見れば同じき里を心隔てつ 大伴家持 mys #4076
ashiki no yama wa naku mogana tsuki mireba onajiki sato o kokoro hedatetsu   ôtomo
leg-drag mt.-as4 not wish! moon see when same country yet heart separ. yakamochi d.785

> *I wish them gone, those leg-tiring mountains!*
> *The moon above our world is one village*
> *but they split our hearts.*

Even without the moon, mountains ate up travel time. In *Manyô* #2421, a woman wishes there were *none* as they trip her man's pony. In the preceding poem, the poet *views the moon, feeling it one land, but damn if the mountains keeping him from his* girl *don't ruin that thought!* (月見國同山隔愛妹隔有鴨 *tsuki mireba kuni wa onaji* . .) Yakamochi, main editor-compiler of the *Manyôshû*, openly borrowed the idea, calling it *a reply to the old poem* 答古人伝 to reassure a *male comrade in poetry* who, was sounding in *his* poems like "a neglected lover" (Cranston). Another version of the same, *Manyô* #4073, is prefaced "as said by people of old." This is marginally mad, but the spirit of borrowing is completely so.

おそくいづる月にもあるか葦引の山のあなたもおしむべらなり古今集877
osoku izuru tsuki ni mo aru kana ashibiki no yama no anata mo oshimu beranari anon
lately appears moon-to even have?! leg-drag mount/s farside too begrudge seems 905

So the late-rising moon has his lovers, too
Beyond that ridge, someone must be trying to hold him back!

This was a mountain given the "pillow word" *ashibiki*, literally *leg/foot-pulling/dragging*. Cranston translates it as *footsore, leg-cramping, foot-dragging, foot-wearying* and, here, *"weary with the feet of men."* R&H, from whom I took "hold him back," use "rugged mountain crests." ♪ I chucked that pillow, but as such mountains were often blamed for keeping lovers from visiting more *or asked to slow a lover's leaving*, made the "lovers" metaphor explicit. With the latter *slowing* effect wished for by women was alluded to, I made the moon male. To me, this as a mad poem, and a very good one, at that, though it is not apparent reading more timid translations. When you think about it, the wresting away of nature as a mere backdrop for human love to a subject for poetry in itself required such boldness. Those who criticize *Kokinshû* (905) editor Ki no Tsurayuki for artificiality fail to realize that we might not have gotten to haiku without such a contrived yet appealing transition. Here is Tsurayuki himself several poems later, right after Narihira's poem about the moon and aging (p.36),

かつ見れどうとくもあるかな 月影のいたらぬさともあらじと思へば kks #880
katsu miredo utoku mo aru kana tsukikage no itaranu sato mo araji to omoeba tsurayuki
before viewed but blue even am!/: moon-visage reaches-not locale+emph is-not think-when

I was a viewer   *I once gazed*
but it brings me down   *upon the moon but found*
to think of how   *it depressing*
the moon shows his face   *to think she was known*
to girls in every town   *by all in every town*

I used to see him
but it makes me sad to think
there is no place
that moon does not grace
w/ his fat & glowing face

Gender the moon as you wish; but with *envy* in this indirect paean to the moon's beauty, *"it"* will just not do. Kyûsojin claims this poem is just a repeat of the idea in KKS #147, where the cuckoo is told that his singing here, there and everywhere made his lover sad. I beg to differ. It is *much* wittier with the moon, which is *not* an old conceit for a lover. Tsurayuki wrote *kyôka*. He was a mad poet. This is a laugh as pure as moonlight. And, in case readers might miss his comic intent, he follows it with another: *"A beauty unique / or so I thought until / I saw its face: / a moon not over the ridge / but under the water!"* (*futatsu naki mono to omoishi o minasoko ni yama no ha nara de izuru tsukikage.*)

Love Sundry & Typed, but will it Fly in Translation?

はつかしさこはさ二ツを一ツ夜着袖を比翼にかはしてそぬる　撫彦 一萬集
hazukashisa kowasa futatsu o hitotsu yogi sode o hiyoku ni kawashitesomeru nadehiko? 18-19c
embarrassment fear two as/into one nightdress sleeve+acc pair-wing-into changing-start

Love's Consumption
初逢恋

Shyness and fear,　　　　　　　　　　　*Shyness and fear,*
when two souls become one　　　*when separate souls first don*
pair of pajamas.　　　　　　　　　　*one robe at night,*

Each sleeve a wing they take off.　　*Each sleeve a wing they flap*
Will their first flight stay aloft?　　　*And if lucky, stay in flight!*

Japanese had something very useful in the winter, bed quilts with built-in sleeves. Combining that with an allusion to the mythic Chinese bird that can only fly with its mate, for each has but one of the wings (see p.214), was a stroke of genius.

夏やせと人にはかくす苦しさよ我胸の火のあつさまけをも　蝸光 同 雑恋
natsuyase to hito ni wa kakusu kurushisa yo waga mune no hi no atsusa-make o mo
"summer-wasting" people-to-as4 hiding painfulness! my breast's fire's heat-losing though

How I suffer when I cover up – "It's only the summer thins."
I really cannot take the heat of passion burning from within!

The translation of Snail-shine's poem suffers for lack of words for thinness-as-a-summer-complaint and feeling the heat, but "cover up" makes up for it.

祈りても神無月は甲斐そなきあきはてられて忘らるゝ身は　連成 同 被忘恋
inorite mo kaminazuki wa kai zo naki aki haterarete wasuraruru mi wa tsurenari???
praying even gods-gone month-as-for worth+emph. not! fall exhausted body/myself-as4

Even praying is utterly worthless: It's Gods-gone Month!
Fall, an empty promise was, and winter, . . I'm forgotten.

うき人に忘らるゝ身はちり塚の骨となりゆく秋の扇か　琴弾 同 被忘恋
ukihito ni wasuraruru mi wa chirizuka no hone to nariyuku aki no uchiwa ka kotohiki???
fickle lover-by forgotten body/self-as4 trash-heap's bones becoming autumn fan-as4

Those forgotten by false-hearted lovers may still be found –
Fans of autumn, their peeling ribs fill the garbage mounds.

Because the subject is so well covered by old *waka*, most mad poems about love seem lacking. I had first planned to present only the best known *kyôka* about love by Shokusanjin – that split and roasted eel (pg.60). But, reading through page after page of poems about love in this single collection 狂歌一萬集 of what is probably mostly late-18c *kyôka*, I thought to gather enough of the more translatable poems to give the reader an idea of how run of the mill *kyôka* handled the subject. Call it *literary anthropology* if you will. Note that the last two translated represent a sub-theme, 被忘恋, "suffering/victimized(by)forgotten-love." *I.e.*, as opposed to love one wishes to forget which is altogether different. The Japanese (and Chinese) ability to type things, that is neatly categorize them with a few letters/characters makes English seem terribly crude by comparison.

人目をも忍ひ時計の音もなく只とき／＼と胸を打ちけり 皮人 同 雑恋
hitome o mo shinobi tokei no oto mo naku tada dokidoki to mune o uchikeri kawabito?
people's eyes +emph avoid/sneaking clock-sound even not just thumpthump breast beats

Avoiding all eyes, not even a clock ticks as I sneak in;
But oh, the loud knocking, the thumpity thump within!

からくりのからりと変る心根は外に糸引人やあるらん よみ人しらす 同 変恋
karakuri no karari to kawaru kokorone wa hoka ni itohiku hito ya aruran anon.
puppet quickly change heart-root/intent-as4 elsewhere string-puller+emph is+emph

The way puppets can flip about just like that, I smell a rat:
Someone must be pulling on the heartstrings of my baby!

..
The noise-making clock (first of the above batch) reminds us that the Japanese had mechanical clocks. The best ones could even adjust their hours for the seasonal variance of the day and night. The second, respecting 変恋 or changing love, mentions *karakuri*, which is usually translated "automata," but, with "strings" mentioned clearly means a puppet, though one where the operator is unseen.

問 奥行も間口も広き玉の門は、本来空を突く心地なり一休禅師諸色問答
okuyuki mo kadoguchi mo hiroki tamanomon wa honrai kû o tsuku kokochi nari anon
length and entrance both wide gem-gate-as4, original emptiness/space poking feeling

A jade gate w/ a wide entrance and a deep recess,
Feels like taking a poke at the original Emptiness!

~~~ ↑Q ~~~~~~ A↓ ~~~~

A down-bend covered by a pucker-point foreskin,
Perfect similitude for the original Not-one-thing!

答 下反りの上に、すぼけの皮かむり、これ一物のなきも同然
shitazori no ue ni suboke no kawakamuri kore ichimotsu no naki mo dôzen anon
down-arc (penis-type) moreover puckered skin-cover (phimosis), this one-thing-not even same

This is part of a *kyôka* take-off on Ikkyû's real & apocryphal 一休ばなし *koan*-like *mondô* (Q&A) fusing *bona fide* Buddhist terms for our reality as *emptiness* and *nothing* and Edo era sexual argot (See *Octopussy:* 2007). The relationship of the 問 *Question* and 答 *Answer* varies and recalls surreal associative technique.

蛇足：何をがなまいらせたくは思へども達磨宗には一物もなし 一休 *nani o ga..*
vs. 一物もなきをたまはる心こそ本来空の妙味なりけり 親当 *ichimotsu mo...*

Approaching Love by Fire, Rain, Roads, Stars, etc.

わすられし男日てりの我宿に 泪の雨のさりとては又　酒月米人 一萬集 寄雨恋
wasurareshi otoko-hideri no waga yado ni namida no ame no saritote wa mata sakazuki no
forgotten, men-drought's my lodge-in tears-of rain anyway once-again　komendo c. 1780

Love & Rain

Long forgotten, I suffer at home from a drought of men;
Not that I lack for water, with my endless rain of tears!

One Chinese character, 寄, suffices to show that a large subject, *Love*, is "approached" or "drawn together" with various things. I settled for "&." I first came across "a drought of men," referring to locales where the men are all away for seasonal employment, in Issa's haiku. If it is about an inn wench, *home* is *off*.

石ならでわりても見せん我心火の出る程に君をこそ思へ 引方 同 寄火恋
ishi nara de warite mo misen waga kokoro hi no deru hodo ni kimi o koso omoe hikikata?
stone-not-so splitting even show-not my heart fire exits enough/amount you+acc+emph love

Love & Fire

I'm not flint, but if I could I would split myself in two,
Just to show how brightly my heart burns for you!

猫の目のかわる心としるならは君を夜毎にたいて寝はせし 近喜 同寄猫恋
neko no me no kawaru kokoro to shiru naraba kimi o yoru goto ni daite ne wa seji kinki?
cat's eye's changing heart as know-if you+acc night-each-on embracing-slept-not c1800

Love & Cats

Had I known your heart could change as fast as a cat's eye,
I would not have let you near my pussy night after night!

我心あけてみせたき折/\は腹にあなある島もなつかし 金埒 同寄島恋
waga kokoro akete misetaki ori-ori wa hara ni ana aru shima mo natsukashi baba kinrachi
my heart opening show-want sometimes-as-for belly-in hole/s is/are isle even miss d.1807

Love & Islands

I would open my heart and show it to you now & then;
And, that is when I long for the Isle of Bored Bosoms!

Flint was "stone," probably not flint but *petrol*, as "rock-oil" was known to burn, or oolite, for in Edo era Japan, like Reformation Europe, busting open stones for crystal treasures was part of a vogue for oddities. I used flint for the sure fire-connection. I traded "pussy" for "sleep" to make up the loss of night's homophone "approach." The people of the Isle of Bored Bosoms 穿胸国 described as "belly-in hole is/has island" in the *kyôka* were one of many such imported fictions. I am unsure which details in Baba Kinrachi's poem are Chinese and which invented by the man who discovered young Ôta Nanpo, the polymath Hiranaga Gennai, whose five-volume novel 風流志道軒伝 included said isle where men of parts had a hole bored clean through the breast – the larger it was, the more it went to show that the *holey* one was a person of parts. They were useful, too. Well-bred, or rather bored, men and women who wished to go somewhere went to the road-side and paid to be shishkabobbed along by the sedan carriers, or rather sedan-less carriers, who made do with carrying poles alone. But, as Gennai pointed out (or made up), the most amazing thing was that these bored people lacked the very symbol of a human, the heart 心. So, unless there was another version of the legendary place where hearts *were* shown, the poem means either *"~ if I cannot show the heart to her, I would rather not have one,"* or the Isle is just pegged onto the hole in the belly (also seat of the heart, hence *hara*-kiri) as stylistic adornment. I favor the second, less significant reading, stylistically reversing the usual *waka* practice of starting with a meaningless or only vaguely allusive *jô* that puns into the real message in mid-poem. My translation, however, follows neither. It is a stop-gap reading, reflecting my first, probably, but not yet definitely mistaken reading (See the ♪s, for a different one by my respondent!) based upon a memory of Bulwer's words – which I found – in *Anthropometamorphosis* (*Man Transformed, or, The Artificial Changeling* 1643/1654). After introducing the men who pierced their paps with bamboo two-spans long and two-fingers thick in Mabada (?) – from side-to-side in front of the shoulders – he digressed,

> *Before the scene goes off, I ought to take notice of a prophane Cavill of Momus against the Fabrique of the Breast of man, who found fault that Nature had not made a Window in the breast of man that one might have seen the motions of his heart, and discovered the affections of his mind . . .*
> (It continues and is followed by an explanation as to why said window would have been of little use, as we already have the eyes that are . . .)

士になるより嬉しやる文を取上られし恋の奴は 真金 同寄武士恋
bushi ni naru yori ureshiyaru fumi o toriagerareshi koi no yakko wa magane?
warrior become more-than delighted/sent letter+acc purloined love's slave

~ Love & Warriors ~

A warrior knows the joy of winning, but a feeling still better
Comes to the slave of love freed by a purloined letter.

箱入の娘の年はいくつぞと隣の寶かそへてや見ん 蜀山人 同 寄寶恋
hako-ire no musume no toshi wa ikutsu zo to tonari no takara kazoete ya min shokusanjin
box-entered daughter's years-as-for how-many! neighbor's treasure counting+emph. try

~ Love & Treasure ~

How old is she, the pretty daughter kept inside a box next door?
If it brings pleasure, why not count your neighbor's treasure?

Were I willing to write an expansive translation of *Love & Warriors*, it would start: *"There is joy in being a warrior, cream of the human race"* for the original plays upon that old saw. The stolen letter might bring more relief than grief by getting the affair out in the open, or I have misread and love-as-the-blues delights in the tragedy of a purloined letter. A *box-put-in-daughter* 箱入れ娘 is a girl guarded at home by zealous parents. The word is still in common use today.

& by Ashtrays, Lightning, Chopping Boards, etc.

引よする煙草ぼんのう犬なれや君があたりを立もはなれぬ　東作　寄煙草盆恋
hiki yosuru tabako-bon nô inu nare ya　kimi ga atari o tachi mo hanarenu　tôsaku 1726-89
pull-close smoke-grass/tobacco tray's=desires' dogs become!/?/: your surroundings+acc rising leave-not

~ Love & Ash-trays ~

*Smoke hangs 'round
the Old Ash Tray, ever
faithful ever true*

The darkling dogs of desire　　　　　　　*I'm one of the dogs of desire*
have become attached to you!　　　　　*And cannot stay away from you!*

Old Dog Tray is mine. The *tabako-bon* (ash-tray) morphs into *desires=bonnô* which modifies *dogs=inu* to create the Buddhist *dogs/hounds of passions*, around, perhaps, a man waiting a long time for a courtesan, seated at a bordello. But, the first half of the poem is also nothing but a lead for the second half, *i.e.,* reading 2.

稲妻のちらと見初めし君故に心もうわの空になる神　呉竹世艶　同寄雷恋
inazuma no chira to mi-someshi kimi yue ni kokoro mo uwa no sora ni narugami
lightning/ricewife's blinking see-first you because-of heart too up empty/sky-in thunder

~ Love & Thunder ~

*One glimpse of you no longer than a lightning flash and I
Heard thunder clap in my heart's empty blue sky.*

◆

*Struck by a bolt from the blue I am, since one glimpse of you
No longer than a lightning flash left my heart up in the air!*

Electrical elements abound in mad poems; but the fact lightning is a "rice-wife" and puns "not" (蛇足「いないなっぱ！」と連想するのが小生斗り？) while thunder evokes a "groaning" or "sounding god," makes both as hard to catch as greased lightning so we have few in this book. The above starts with a commonplace in waka, then adds the thunder for good measure. Like *Love & Islands* (#___), above, the last part of the original, in this case the last half of the thunder (kami=god) is pegged on for the first half, usually sound (naru), in the context of what comes before it really means "is," as in "is empty-sky," i.e., painfully ungrounded from being swept off one's feet by love. My first reading, which, taken as is, is not that bad, nevertheless, fails to pick up on that playful disconnect. The second copies the jump from one idiom to another, but fails to do so as gracefully as the original, which also deserves points for doing so right at the very end. Perhaps, the biggest leap of lightning that I know in Japanese poetry is not, however, in an Edo era *kyôka*. It is in an old *waka*, as far as I know, unrecognized for its achievement: *"Even the flickers of lightning that glow upon the rice heads in autumn fields are spanned by my longing for you."* The 9c poem, which, in the original ends "(I) long for / miss you," is revolutionary for juxtaposing a positive emotion and something of short duration (*aki no ta no ho no ue ni mo terasu inazuma no hikari no ma ni mo kimi zo koishiki* (kkrj 813). All previous examples I know of, including the song (kks #548) that this one paraverses, couple such moments with "(*not*) forgetting" or "(never) not loving."

俎板の面やせしたる恋の身を切り刻みても逢んとぞ思ふ 中道 同寄俎板恋
manaita no tsura yaseshitaru koi no mi o kiri kizumitemo awan to zo omou nakamichi
chopping-board-face thinned love/longing's body+acc. chopping-even meet-would+emph think

~ Love & Chopping Boards ~

On my face as flat as a chopping board, I'd make mince
of my own love-sick body if it would only help us meet!

言よれと答へもうはの空豆のはしき出される身社つらけれ 頂 同寄青物恋
ii-yoredo kotae mo uwa no soramame no hajikidasareru mi koso tsurakere itadaki?
speaking-approach & reply+emph empty-sky=lima-bean's pop-out content/body espec. trying

~ Love & Vegetables ~

Words, like tendrils, seeking reply reach out but only find the sky;
While human beans popped from shells fall straight away to hell!

打あけて噺すはなしも実の入らぬ妹か心はうはの空豆 琴高 同 寄青物恋
uchi-akete hanasu hanashi mo mi no iranu imo ga kokoro wa uwa no soramame kotodaka?
emph+opening-up speak talk even content/truth put-in-not girlfriend's heart-as-4 empty-sky/lima

Love & Vegetables

Lies, lies, even when you open up you are not what you seem:
Your empty pod, my girl . . . . is just another lima bean.

Empty-sky=*uwa-no-sora*, an unfaithful (heart), puns into lima beans, called *sora-mame*, lit. "sky/empty-beans." Since a little girl's privates were called lima beans, the poet might be putting down the other as young slut. (See my dirty senryû book)

ぬかるまいと思なからも踏込で足のぬけぬが恋の路なり 袋町 同寄路恋
nukarumai to omoinagara mo fumikonde ashi no nukenu ga koi no michi nari fukurochô?
bog-down-not-should think-while+emph. treading-in legs extricate-cannot-the love's-road is

Love & Road

The road you take you think will surely never bog you down,
though it always does? A name is found: The Way of Love.

The poem I hoped to use as the lead-off, for I like it in Japanese, was: *In the dark night of a lover's soul, when the sight of shooting stars / makes him think of visiting . . . though his girl, too, is far!* (恋の闇心も空に飛星のよはひに物を思ふ ころかな 道頼 同 寄星恋 *koi no yami kokoro mo sora ni tobu hoshi no yobai ni mono o omou koro kana* michiyori?). But, without the term for nocturnal visits, "night-crawling=*yobai*," the poem fails (思えば、現在、よはいは 夜這 のみならず、齢にもなり得。星の齢にもの思えば、よほど深い詩になるでしょう！).

Love w/ All of Noah's Animals in Just One Poem

短夜も独はねうし寅の時うき たつ恋のみをしせかめは 次木 後撰夷曲集
mijika yo mo hitori wa ne-ushi tora no toki uki tatsu koi no mi o shi-segameba namiki? 1672
short-night even alone-as-for, sleeping=rat blue=cow tiger hour lone=hare=ly
arising=dragon longing body/self=snake[acc] badgered-when/if

a short dog-day night
still the blue *rats* gnaw and bite
this *cow*ardly *tiger*

heir to fears – how hours *drag on,*
snake-bit and badgered by love!

Japanese followed the Chinese in using the names of the zodiac animals for their twelve-hour days. You might think that would leave less than six animals for a summer night, but diurnal time units were split evenly between day and night with six for the former and six for the latter. The lengths of the hours waxed and waned with the seasons, but one could count on watching the sunrise or sunset with the same animal hours. The phonetic poverty of Japanese made it possible for a creative poet to hide all but one of the six animals (*rat, cow, tiger, hare, dragon, snake*) in the other nouns and verbs, *while maintaining the correct order*. Moreover, there might even be a *turtle* (*kame*) with a trail of water (*mio*) alluding to the seeming eternity of the night. My first try, with *love* and a *turtle dove* sounded better, but two of the requisite animals would not fit. I take no comfort in adding a dog and a badger: this poem defeated me. If anyone can do better, be my guest! (You may ruin a great example of what cannot be translated, but I am not holding my breath.) If, however, you *can* do it, why not raise the bar higher and try something harder yet. In the *Tokuwa Kago Manzaishû* we find poems with *ten* edible plant names, *ten* tree names, *ten* bird names and *ten* fish names! The only thing I know in English that even comes close is Braddock and Braddock's novelty song *I Lobster but Never Flounder*. Here are some of the best lines:

Oh I lobster but never flounder
He wrapped his line around her and they drove off in his carp!
. . . . .
I octopus his face in, he'll only break her heart
. . . . .
Now my life has no porpoise
. . . . .
If I get out of here alive — it'll be a mackerel.

(Select lines from *Braddock & Braddock Tree Publishing CO. Inc. BMI Warner Bros.* You really must see all of it!)

Not to carp, but even with allowance for imperfect homonyms, such as *"lobster/lost-her"* and *"flounder/found-her,"* Braddock and Braddock's lyrics do not pack in the fish like the Japanese *kyôka*, with 1 per every 3 syllabets, the equivalent of 1 per every 2 English syllables. Still, it is definitely funnier than the Japanese mad poems. Braddock, who, if you wonder, does work in a *haddock*, is humorous in a grotesque way not because that is *his* nature but because English puns are preordained by our obscenely large phonemic wealth to be groaners. The *kyôka*, by comparison, can pun up a storm and still be an art poem with wording as natural, even elegant as any *waka*. One must mull it over for a while to find the fish.

こいしさはいかにますかとふくかぜのなさけきゝたいいなのさゝはら
koishisa-w/ba ika ni masu ka to fuku kaze no nasake kikitai ina no sasa hara
longing-as-for how grows? blowing wind's sympathy ask-would rice-leave field
The fish: *koi, saba, ika, kani, masu, fuk(g)gu, sake, tai, ina, sawara*
carp,young-mackerel,squid,crab,trout,puffers,salmon,snapper,mullet, spanish-mackerel

*I would ask
the wind to be so kind
as to tell me*

*How to increase her longing, Oh,
Whisp'ring rice leaves on th' moor!*

山手白人　徳和歌後萬載集
by Yamanote no Shirohito 1726-87

The wind in Japan was the prototypical lady's man, who can persuade any plant bend to his will and carry off their flowers. A 12c *waka* by *Saigyô*, a noble monk who loved both cherry blossoms and women, put it like this:

寄花恋・つれもなき人に見せばや桜花 風にしたがふ心よわさを
tsure mo naki hito ni misebaya sakura bana kaze ni shitagau kokoro yowasa o

*I wish I could show this person who won't love me
the gentle heart of a blossom giving in to the wind!*

..

The subtle way the question in the *kyôka* leads to the rice leaves of a type associated with rustling, hence "whispering," and the field, *hara,* a homophone with belly. This may be doggerel but it has class and is a far better poem than the lead example. The only problem is that even if I changed the content, I could not possibly squeeze in *those* fish, or *any* "ten fish names" (魚十名=title). To think how primitives traded fish for favors, I chuckle at the choice of fish for this message, or the vice versa; but the main reason for the marriage is that a *carp* is a *koi,* and that is a homophonous with *romantic love, longing* and the very person of the *lovesick blues.* Whenever you come across an old print with carp, keep your eyes open, for there is a good chance you may be looking at a rebus of love.

How to Escape from the Love-sick Blues at Home

枕よりあとよりこひのせめくれば　せむ方なみぞとこなかにをる　古今集
makura yori ato yori koi no semekureba   senkata na mi zo toko naka ni oru   anon. kks c.905
pillow-from foot-frm longng attcks/forces-coms-when coping not! self+emph. bed-mddle-in am=fold

The lovesick blues
won't let me sleep, attacking
from my head & feet:

You will find me at mid-bed,
all curled up if i'm not dead!

I did that translation *without looking at the Japanese*, which I assumed was in the 8c *Manyôshû* but failed to find after a long search (my pb has no index), and only later, happened to come across it in the 10c *Kokinshû*. I recognized it from R & H's translation: *"when from my pillow / and from the foot of the bed / thoughts of love rise to / inflict their pain   I simply / cower here in the middle."* But, it took some doing to make a translation melodramatic *and* boring. Then, again, the original, excepting the humble *oru, "[I] am,"* a homophone for *double* or *fold*, that lets the poem with a novel idea end on a witty note, is only half so clever as mine. Japanese in hand, I checked Carter (*Traditional Japanese Poetry*) and found the proper balance: *"Beyond enduring / this passion that attacks me / from pillow and foot / I get up and seat myself / in the middle of the bed."* Carter's bold penultimate line, which makes us see the poet writing the poem right then and there, is great! Recalling the following *Manyôshû* poems was probably what made me think the better middle-of-the-bed poem was also in *that* anthology.

..

Hoping at least
to forget her face, i made
a fist to waste

The Lovesick Blues, but he
did not flinch an inch, not he!

面忘れだにもえ為やと手握りて打てども懲りず恋ふといふ奴　万葉
omo wasure dani moesu ya to tanigirite uttedomo korizu kou to iu yakko   anon mys
face forgetting even try for hand-clenching hit-but flinch-not love as-called guy 2574

～～～～～～～～～～～～～～～～～～～～～～

house-in was trunk-in lock barring keep/pt but love-slave's grabbing came 3816
*ie ni arishi hitsu ni kagi sashi osamete shi koi no yatsuko no tsukami kakarite*万葉
家にありし櫃に鍵さし蔵めてし恋の奴のつかみかかりて　穂積親王

I locked him up
for good in a trunk at home
but was I alone?

Suddenly that miscreant Love
had his hands around my throat

With respect to the first, please pardon the Usanian slang "waste," *i.e.,* to *utterly destroy*, or *kill*. The fist is a powerful threat, for fisticuffs has never been as much a part of popular Japanese culture as in the West. What is most remarkable about the second poem is the fact that it comes with a short explanation: the poet, Emperor Hôzumi (8c), was fond of reciting it at banquets when the drinking was in full swing. I follow Cranston (1996) with the "throat," not specified in the original, as it was also specified that *it was generally well received*, which leads me to envision a mime routine, with the Emperor turning about and pretending to choke himself, perhaps. What I called "the lovesick blues" and "miscreant love" is in the original *love=longing=blues* + *yatsuko* (later pronounced *yakko*), meaning "menial" or "slave," a most curious inversion, for it is the poet who is clearly that! Another *Manyôshû* proto-*kyôka*, song #2693, has the poet wish to be the sand his lover steps on rather than to be absent from her presence: love is no slave, *we* are. I prefer the equally love-crazed but less degrading song #3400, where the poet vows to collect pebbles on a river bank his or her love has, by stepping on, turned into precious gems! While the *Kokinshû* blues coming from both ends of the bed poem clearly beats the *Manyôshû* ones, there is one exceedingly abstract *koi* in the *Manyôshû* possibly absent from latter collections.

大地も採り尽さめど世の中尽し得ぬものは恋にしありけり 万葉集2442
ôtsuchi mo tori-tsukusamedo yononaka tsukushi-enu mono wa koi ni shi arikeri anon
big-earth too take-exhaust would-but world-among-exhaust-can't thing-as4 love/blues-as is+emph

Though you could
plunder the whole earth,
the world has one

inexhaustible resource:
Love will never run out.

Though we can
exhaust the bounty of earth,
there is one thing

With no end in this world:
It's called the Lovesick Blues

The verb is usually used for collecting plants or extracting mushrooms or metals from the earth. *Koi*, here, probably means "love," but it could also be the blues. Regardless, it is clearly not so clever, or should I say *mad*, as the following:

たよりにもあらぬおもひのあやしきは 心を人につくるなりけり もとかた
tayori ni mo aranu omoi no ayashiki wa kokoro o hito ni tsukuru narikeri   kks #480
message/messenger+emph. is-not longing's odd-as-for heart+acc person-to pack/send be+emph.

Love is nothing
like a carrier – How odd
It could take my heart

package, and deliver it
to her, my distant dove!

This is by Ariwara no Motokata, the man who wrote the oft-reviled first poem of the *Kokinshû* wondering what to call the old year whose spring had come. My reason for introducing so many *koi* poems is not only to show where old love poems meet the mad poem but to challenge Descartes' patent on *mind* vs *body*.

My Love is an Otter and Other Odd Dream Poems

夢 わか恋は海驢のねなかれさめやらぬ 夢なりなから絶やはてなん　表笠内大臣 夫木
waga koi wa michi no ne-nagare same yaranu yume narinagara taeya hatenan omokasa uchidaijin
my love/longing-as-for, otter's sleeping-drift-awaken-not dream-is-while breaks ends

My love? An otter
adrift, unable to snap
out of his dream,
That nonetheless must
break, and breaking, end.

What's my love?
An otter floating along
while fast asleep,
Never awakening though
his dream must surely end.

I have a particular affection for poems starting *waga koi wa,* "with respect to my love," because they are a type of *mono wa tsukushi,* or, *listing, i.e.,* an exercise in aesthetic sensibility. That is how the poem got my eye, but on closer reading, it does not describe the *object* of one's love, as is common for such poems, but the *nature* of it. As it turns out, *love* is one of the all-to-few examples of listing in English, and *"Love is ~"* treats the nature of it, too. The only problem is that the poem is (for me) hard to read. I thought it was a *never-ending dream* but my respondent assures me there is no way I can twist the grammar to say so. But I could not deep-six the otter. Most dream *waka* treat *love.* I read and marked scores in the *Manyôshû* not only because of the charming confusion as to whether one is awake or asleep, or ambiguity as to whether dreaming beats not meeting at all or is worse for the frustration of waking alone, and what dreams mean, not just in the details, but in a broader sense. Japanese were one of a minority of people in the world who held that dream visits arose from the desire of the party who appears, or visits the dream, yet *also,* were observant enough to note the influence of the dreamer's mind. These two concepts wove a particularly tangled web of dream poetry for our reading pleasure. But, here, we will return to *wild waka* (*waka* in un-canonical collections) and *kyôka*. First, two more *waka* from the "Dream" Section of the rogue *Fuboku* 夫木和歌抄 anthology (1310) :

夢 みぬもみえ きかぬもきゝつよのなかに 夢こそ恋のさとり也けれ 信実朝臣
minu mo mie kikanu mo kikitsu yononaka ni yume koso koi no satori narikere nobuzane
see-not even seen hear-not hearing world-among-in dream+emph. love's wake-up is!

Seeing the unseeable, hearing the unhearable, in this world,
Dreams are what awaken us to the reality of love.
~~~~~~~~~~~~~~~
In this world where we see the invisible and hear the inaudible
Love is what tells us that life is but a dream!
~~~~~~~~~~~~~~~
If I see what can't be seen and hear what can't be heard,
Only dreams of love strike me as real in this, my world.

Does *world-among* pun with "at night?" It does not matter. The end of the poem is puzzling. Does love enlighten *us?* Or, are we enlightened *about* love?

Regardless, it seems like a fine aphorism – something more common w/ *kyôka* than *waka* – if only I could settle on a meaning . . . (学者諸君、御異見下さい！).

とにかくに現にもあらぬこの世には 夢こそ夢の夢にはありけれ 民部爵為家
tonikaku ni gen ni mo aranu kono yo ni wa yume koso yume no yume ni wa arikere tameie
anyway actually even is/am-not this world-as-4 dream espec. dream's dream is/becomes!

Be as it may,
in a world a world apart
from all it seems,

What are dreams if not
dreams of what we dream?

In this world,
which, in reality, is
held not to be,

Dreaming is when we see
dreams within our dream.

In this world,
which, in reality, holds
no place for me,

My dreams are but dreams
of dreams that were to be.

With dreaming donne like this by *waka*, who would blame Edo era *kyôka* poets had they avoided dreams altogether! No wonder the mad dreams we see tend to be spectacular. I save the most outrageous dream (about *pooping:* p.102) for a more suitable chapter. Here is one *kyôka* completely novel that may or may not be gently influenced by the *wild waka* otter:

おもひ川寝て流れ行く水鳥は所のかはる夢やみるらん 竹壽園 狂歌一萬
omoi-kawa nete-nagareyuku mizutori wa tokoro no kawaru yume ya miruran chikushôen?
think/longing-river sleeping-flowing-go waterbirds-as4 place-the changing dreams! see+

Floating down the stream of thought, ducks, fast asleep.
I'll bet the dreams we/they see reflect the changing scenes!
~~~~~~
Stream of Thought: Like a river bird floating while asleep
Do not the dreams I see reflect a changing scenery?

The restless dreams of unsettled love? I am unsure what exactly is going on here, but is this not a precocious version of the modern *"stream of consciousness"* ? A slightly earlier mid-18c *zappai* from the *Mutamagawa* that I am even less sure of presents something else, perhaps, an organic theory of dreams:

念て見る夢は五臓がからくり師　武玉川五
nen de miru yume wa gozô ga karakuri-shi mutamagawa c1760
wishing/thought/concern-from see dream-as4 five-organs automata-master

Dreams that come
from thought: the 5 humors
pull the strings.

Ideas in dreams?
The automata master,
our five organs.

W/ deep dreams,
our five organs: fingers of
the puppet master.

our five humors
are what's behind the dreams
we wish to see

To Pluck the Sleeping Form of a Soundless Zither

やみぬれば緒のなき琴のねすがたをたゞかきなでゝみるばかりなる 蜀山人 才蔵集
yaminureba o no naki koto no nesugata o tada kaki-nadete miru bakari naru anon (shokusanjin)
stop-become-when strings-not-zither's sleeping form+acc just pluck-stroking try only am/become 1787

With silence, the sound of that zither without any strings –
Her body prone – just to take a lick I would give anything.

~~~~~~

When the music stopped, the sight of her recumbent form,
A stringless zither, that's what this poet was born to play!

My inability to do justice to this poem *hurts*. There is a phrase in the original so good that, if it is fresh, deserves everlasting fame. Describing *a recumbent woman's body as a stringless zither* evokes a natural beauty beyond the reach of the mechanical muse. It is not cheapened but enhanced by the enabling pun: *sound* (音) = *ne* = *sleeping* (寝) . It is no mere pun – as if any pun can be – but helps us for a moment to imagine the innocent beauty of sleep as comparable to the tree whose limbs played music with the wind more subtle than the simple tones men create in the old Taoist parable. And, Shokusanjin borrows from, *i.e.,* alludes to, a scene in the *Tale of Genji* where the already handsome teenage Kaori is drawn to the palace women's sleeping quarters by the sound of the moon lute and the 13-string zither (the string number a sign for girls coming of age?), to which he sings in harmony, knowing his attraction toward the zither-playing women was sinful, as desiring what a parent thought improper was wrong. That passage includes the phrase starting the *kyôka*. "When the zither music stopped 琴の声もやみぬれば." When it did, Kaori crept into the women's quarters. Shokusanjin is fusing the magical attraction of youth with his own feelings. While the poem expresses the desire to touch but not necessarily possess, that in no way makes the poem less erotic than a more knowing(?) poem. If anything, it brings out the natural beauty of the woman like no other poem I can recall. To others, it may look plain enough, but I *feel* it, as I do one of the best of Issa's haiku not to be included in the standard Maruyama (Iwanami) anthology:

寝むしろや尻を枕に夏の月　一茶　文政二
nemushiro ya shiri o makura ni natsu no tsuki issa
sleeping-mat!/: buttocks+acc. pillow-as/on, summer-moon

<table>
<tr><td>

An old straw mat.
Her ass for my pillow,
the summer moon.

</td><td>

The summer moon:
A straw mat, my head
upon a behind.

</td></tr>
</table>

This *ku*, unlike the others in this book, is no *kyôku,* unless the mere fact of resting one's head upon a buttocks seems improper, or improper for haiku. The *ku* is a natural, and what's more, the feeling of said pillow on the head, the texture of the mat and sight of the far-off moon create one of the richest pictures ever framed in 17-syllabets. I believe it got no attention (or none I know of) in Japan because when Issa was discovered in the early 20c (He was not *that* famous in his own time), such a *ku* might have been shunted aside as vulgar, better subject matter for a *senryû*. Because *senryû*, at least in Issa's time, were largely third-person and stereotype (not, necessarily a bad thing, but different from haiku in a manner more fundamental than nature vs. town-life), such comparison would be wrong. Unconventional *waka, kyôka* not intended for publication and the modern *tanka* would be a better comparison, for such did not serve stereotype and did not shy away from the unconventional and personal. *Back to mad love,*

おやまんとすれども雨の足しげく又もふみこむ恋のぬかるみ 蜀山人 遊戯三昧
oyaman to suredomo ame no ashi shigeku mata mo fumikomu koi no nukurumi shokusanjin
cease-try did but rain-legs frequent, again+emph. tread-into love's bog/morass

I tried to quit – but coming here as often as spring rain,
Marched right into the heart of the Bog o' Love, again!

The idiom "rain-legs," or rain seen falling from a cloud in mass as depicted by Turner with large brush-strokes, takes us to the expense of extra-marital love, as "legs" implies *support=>money*, and follows up on the initial, now rare verb, *oyamu,* which I took for a Yoshiwara Pleasure District slang phrase until, looking it up in the OJD, I learned it meant *a small-pause* or *break in the rainfall.* The *legs* then take us to the frequent rains/visits that create said bog-like conditions. Unlike the last poem I pretty much had to figure out (or, cook up?) for myself, this was reprinted in the hundred poem selection 蜀山百首 and has ample notes by the Iwanami editors. They note it appeared in a book crediting it to another but is really by our hero Shokusanjin in his Yomo no Akara days. So far so good. But I am puzzled they only mention his falling for a Yoshiwara Pleasure District Pine-needle shop's new girl 松葉屋の新造三穂崎 and fail to mention what a (net?) source mentions, namely, that his mistress Oshizu had died six years before (妾のお賤が死んで六年後に). Without that information, we cannot figure out where the "again" comes from. If it was indeed by "Yomo-no-Akara," rather than Shokusanjin, it suggests *kyôka's* first man had mistresses from a very young age (If that be so, poor samurai or not, he is to be envied!). Hamada notes a preface declares this poem was written on a rainy eve at a particular place, which suggests it was impromptu. His trepidation makes sense, as mistresses were not cheap; on the first full moon of Fall, sure enough, Yomo no Akara paid-off her debt to Yoshiwara – *There went the first profits of Tenmei mad poems!?* – and took her as his mistress. Judging from Shokusanjin's other work, there is *more*. Perhaps the girl had a nickname worked into the first word (eg. Oman in *oyaman*). Be that as it may, from what I have seen of *waka* and *kyôka*, wit alone creates few decent poems about love. Yomo no Akara's famous *yam-to-split-eel* poem (pg. 60) is a masterpiece of punning surreality and demonstrates the sort of genius usually found in a puzzle master. It *amazes* us. Yet, it definitcly does not *move* us. For that, there is no substitute for personal interest, or poems successfully pretending to it. For that reason, I have included as many *kyôka* as possible that were not written just to be writing *kyôka* in this book. And I hope to find more such for another edition. Meanwhile, please take note that the *kyôka* by Shokusanjin in this chapter were not as pun-filled, convoluted or hyperbolic as many a *waka* of love we will see in this book.

Thank Goodness for our *Wingless* Tôfu!

雁鴨はわれを見捨てて去りにけり 豆腐に羽根のなきぞうれしき 良寛 歌集
karigamo wa ware o misutete sarinikeri tôfu ni hane no naki zo ureshiki ryôkan 1758-1831
geese ducks-as-for me+acc abandoning leave+fin. tofu-on wings-not+emph. joyful

The geese & duck
abandoning me, leave.
Thank goodness
that our tôfu, at least
does not boast wings!

Geese & duck
fly & I am out of luck
happily, I see
My tôfu, lacking wings
cannot abandon me!

A creative individual reading in the heyday of *kyôka* and practicing Zen, with its surreal leaps of (al)logic, Monk Ryôkan came naturally to his wingless tôfu. His *kyôka,* not composed for *kyôka* publications but as part of his various poetic reparatory (including long stanzas between Chinese style and what came to be called modern poetry), are, like Issa's, one-of-a-kind. The kernel of the above poem is the *haikai* seasonal motif, the return of the geese to China and other places West. It was noted with bemusement how they left with the cherries in full bloom (pp. 246, 532) and Teitoku in one of his many amusing *ku*, attributed it to the birds choosing "dumplings over flowers," *i.e.*, food over decoration, the practical over the ideal. Issa, who expresses amazement over the thick-skin *shibutosa* of these birds capable of turning their backs on such beauty, himself professed to prefer the dumplings in his old age. Since the fowl was eaten – and mad-cap Zen monks did sometimes indulge – the *tôfu*, or protein, connection is *not* utterly off the wall. The expression of joy for what is not only taken for granted but so obvious that no one had ever bothered to record it, namely, the winglessness of tôfu, *is*, as is the delightfully *personal* nature of the poem. (A less dramatic *ku* in *Haiku for Jews* (Bader: 1999) observes the finless gefilte fish swims with difficulty – but even it is more aerodynamic than a block of *tôfu*.)

うちはとてあまり丸きは見よからず扇のかどを少し加へて
uchiwa tote amari maruki wa miyokarazu uchiwa no kado o sukoshi kuwaete
uchiwa=fan/home re. too round-as-for sight-fits-not uchi.=fan/home's corners+acc somewhat add

A fan called an uchiwa=house is good to have around, in fact,
They're even better squared off to show the corners they lack.

An *uchiwa* is a fixed (not folding) fan, usually round, sometimes oval, or trapezoid. Roundness evokes the full moon and Buddhist enlightenment or mercy, but Monk Ryôkan, catching the "*uchi*=home/house" in the name, gave voice to rectangularity, the *mark* of a house and the hopefully solid earth upon which we dwell . Perhaps, he recalled Bashô's cottage turning round moon's light into rectangular shadows. Maybe I overdo it. *Uchiwa* are *stiff* fans; roundness is psychologically *soft*. Ryôkan may just be playing with that paradox and he may removed a bit of the burden from an overly pliant old fan. Regardless, what a splendid image of squaring the circle, if ever so slightly! Some paraverses:

< on fans, when pursued by more than one fan to sign theirs >

Why not sign?
Begging is hot but this will
keep you cool:

Without them
no man is cool; but those
we call toadies

A big fool, I am
blessed with so many fans
but just 1 brush,

Fans, real and fake, seek
the autograph of a fool!

Best serve the fool – For wine,
The quiet paperkind, I'll sign!

Yes, doubly cool! I laugh,
giving out this autograph!

I wrote the above out of frustration at failing to translate the wit in Ryôkan's original. Call it an act of contrition. Here is another Ryôkan mad poem that is not quite so good, but exceedingly creative and more or less translatable.

一度さへやせたる殿を山蜘が絲引きかけて天へまひあがる
ichido sae yasetaru tono o yama-kumo ga ito hiki kakete ten e mai agaru
once+emph. skinny lord+acc. mountain-spider thread pull-catching heaven-to dancing-raise

Just once I'd see
our dear Lord Bean Pole
hoisted dancing

up to heaven by a thread
spun by an alpine spider!

Evidently, thin-man roasting did not stop with the 9c *Manyôshû* (p.56). But what ellipsis! The original lacks not just pronoun, but intent: *the first line is entirely mine*. The requisition of gossamer is brilliant. The usual way to ascend from a peak is on a cloud (*kumo*, a spider homophone!), high-flying bird, dragon or a carp. What a fine example of mad *ideas* 心の狂 as opposed to word-play! If Ryôkan lived a century later, what nursery verses he might have written! He also parodied in the conventional *kyôka* manner. The following plays with Sôsei's corny *Kokinshû waka* (p.195) telling off the big bad wind while contradicting a concept: *'Easy old age' – / Who the hell invented it? / Teach me / So I can go give him / a piece of my mind!* 老いらくを誰がはじめけん教へてよいざなひ行きてうらみましものを *oiraku o da ga hajimeken oshiete yo izanai ikite uramimashi mono o*. And he wrote poems that were only *kyôka* because baldly stating an absolute, yet unrecognized truth is not what most, supposedly sane people do; *eg.,*

大方の世をむつまじくわたりなば十に一つも不足なからん
ôkata no yo o mutsumajiku watarinaba jû ni hitotsu mo fuzoku nakaran
most part's world+acc dearly/closely cross/live-if ten-in-one even shortage is-not

If most of us felt close to the world, as a matter of fact,
not a tenth part would remain of what we claim to lack.

Unless most people become close to the world (nature and people), addiction to luxury, rationalized as normal needs, is bound to create hell on earth, even as we fly about it like flies on carrion bemoaning global warming and preaching an ecological lifestyle! 1970 - ? will surely be known as *The Age of Hypocrisy*.

What! No Pockmarks on the Bare-faced Moon?
こよひこの月は世界の美人にて素顔か雲の化粧だにせず　蓬莱帰橋
koyoi kono tsuki wa sekai no bijin nite sugao ka kumo no keshô dani sezu hôrai kikyô
tonight this moon-as-for world's beauty so bare-face? cloud's make-up even does-not 1785

This full moon is a world-class beauty queen, alright!
Bare-faced, I see her pass without one cloud of white.

Always mid-month, the full moon was usually called the *jûgoya*, or *fifteen-night*. But here, we have just *tsuki,* the moon, presumed full if not called otherwise. What shines is the novel double *kango* (2+2-character) phrase *"sekai no bijin,"* or *"(the) World's Beauty."* My translation fails to relate the moon's beauty and her bare-face. Neither does the original, but one feels there is something more.

♪Queen of the Firmament♪

Could tonight's moon
bare-faced as only
beauty dares

have sent
the cosmetic
clouds packing?

I also lose the wit in the word "beautiful person" (*bijin*), for in the late 18c, good readers would have known the Chinese used it to describe the moon as the Lord, or Ruler on high. But that cannot be helped. Back to relating *bare* and *beauty*:

Does her bare face prove the cosmic beauty of the Moon tonight
scorns cosmetics, hence, no powder-puff cloud remains in sight?

Annotator Hamada Giichirô points out this poem is just the sort of thing a well-known author of *kibyôshi* and *sharebon* – the intellectually stimulating comic and cool books of late-Edo – might write. Does he mean Hôrai Sanjin 山人 Kikyô's poem does not allude to other poems and, instead, laughs at the entire body of poetry, where men always swoon over this luminous heavenly body?

なか／＼にときどき雲のかかるこそ月をもてなす限なりけれ　西行
nakanaka ni tokidoki kumo no kakaru koso tsuki o motenasu kagiri narikere saigyô 12c
verymuchly sometimes clouds come/touch esp. moon+acc entertain enough be+emph

Sometimes we need	*Sometimes we need*
clouds and none too soon	*clouds and none too soon*
to cover the moon;	*to visit the moon;*
Enough to keep her	*Enough to keep her well*
entertaining, anyway.	*entertained at any rate!*

Or, was Hôrai Sanjin Kikyô's poem also meant to evoke and play with ideas dating back at least to Saigyô, who found the clouds a *complement* for the moon, rather than something to sully her face, or, worse, block out the pure light of

Buddhist Law/Mercy? That is not to say Saigyô went to the later extremes of another monk, Yoshida Kenkô, father of *shibui* (aesthetic minimalism/understatement), who found viewing the moon with clouds *more sophisticated* than without them and thought imagining the moon inside *without seeing it at all* even more laudable, if not desirable! Saigyô just found clouds a plus for moon-viewing (See ♪ for another transl.). As anyone who has spent time gazing at the moon knows, that is right. A moon without clouds is not worth viewing. Indeed, *that* is the train of thought that brings the *kyôka's* rhetoric home: any cloudless moon that *is,* would indeed need to be the beauty of all beauties! Since praising the moon is a proper thing for a moon-viewer to do – at least, in the *haikai* tradition – one might call Hôrai Sanjin Kikyô's *kyôka* simultaneously proper and playfully contradicting Saigyô, who wrote hundreds of moon poems including one that is hyperlogical in a *kyôka*-like way for treating the contradiction of one equal door to/from heaven and the different nature of the harvest moon:

天の原おなじ岩戸を出づれども 光ことなる秋の夜の月 西行 山家集 12c
amanohara onaji iwato o izuredomo hikari kotonaru aki no yo no tsuki saigyô

It comes out the same cavern door from high heaven,
but how the light of this Moon differs in the autumn!

～～～～～～～～～～～～～～～～～～～～～～～～～～～～～
よやせぬと賤かくたまきくりかへり まはらぬ舌もみしか夜の月 契因
yo ya senu to shizu kaku tamaki kurikaeri mawaranu shita mo mijika yoru no tsuki keiin
drunk+emph do-not: pauper/s wear bracelet turnng-over rotate-not tonge evn shrt night's moon

酔中夏の月, 狂歌活玉集 1740
The Summer Moon, Drunk

Losing my drunk,
I turn my pauper bracelet
inside-out, but soon

My tongue is tied and I'm as
short-changed as this moon!

I can't stay drunk,
when moonshine runs out
the cat takes my tongue:

Just one more damn line
& the short night is done.

This moon, subject of the poem modified by all that comes before it in the original, is rare. Even *kyôka* obeys the seasonal niceties so the moon, as a rule only shows her face in the Autumn. The poet's cheap bracelet parodies the ancient nobles' sleeping robes turned inside-out as a charm to entice a lover to visit. Please pardon my jump from Saigyô's poem, relevant to the lead, to this. Here are two Tenmei *kyôka* a bit closer to the theme for dwelling on the fame of the moon:

Though in the sky we know the famous moon of fall rides high,
Here below the rain clouds let not one blessed star come nigh!

大空に名高き月はありながらひとつ星さへみせぬ雨雲 銀杏満門
ôzora ni na-dakaki.. ichô mitsukado ↑ 1785 ↓ *sen kin no*.. yomo no akara
千金の名だかき月の雲間よりせめて一二分もれ出よかし 四方赤良

The million crown Moon they say and you'd think those Cloud
Banks with their silver linings would at least spit out a bit!

Is the Moon Jealous of Us for Parody's Sake Alone?

かくばかりめでたくみゆる世の中を うらやましくやのぞく月影 萬載集・蜀山百集
kaku bakari medetaku miyuru yo no naka o urayamashiku ya nozoku tsukikage shokusanjin 1783
this much lucky/happy appears world/society+<u>acc</u> enviously+emph. peek?! moon-form/light

i dunno

*our world seems
so damn happy – why
the moon in the sky*

*must be peeking in
out of sheer envy!*

かくばかり経がたく見ゆる世の中を 羨ましくもすめる月かな 拾遺 藤原高光
kaku bakari hegataku miyuru yo no naka o   urayamashiku mo sumeru tsuki kana
(this much cross-hard seems/ world+contra+lament. enviously-even clears/lives-can moon!)

Shokusanjin's poem plays upon a 10-11c *waka*: *"Given this world that seems so hard to live in or pass through, / How envious a thing to see the moon clear and serene!"* From the original, above, you may see how close they are. Readers of Japanese might note how the *kyôka* transforms the contradictory deplorative "o" (を) of the *waka* into an accusative post-position, or how the lack of homophonic verbs for *"live"* and *"[be] clear,"* and the more tenuous link between *clarity* and *serenity* in English hurts the *waka's* translation, as it kills otherwise translatable poems about hermit sages drinking cloudy *sake* because they have no interest in *clarity=living* in the world (eg. 隠居してのむへきものはにこりさけ とても此よにすむ身てはなし 夢窓 古今夷曲集 *inkyô shite nomu beki . . .* musô? p.1666). If I am not mistaken, the old *waka* is, *itself*, pretty wacky. Envy may be a compliment, but suffering poets usually found Buddha's grace and solace in the serenely clear face of the full moon. Perhaps, the main difference between this *waka* and *kyôka* is stylistic. What if I were to translate that *waka* as follows?

*How can ye moon
sit so high and pretty
in a world where
We all must get down
and dirty to survive?*

*Just look at Luna
not a wrinkle in her brow;
While we suffer
indignities here below
that diva does not know!*

*How envious to see
the full moon sailing through
this world of gloom;
While we, dog-paddling try
not to sink within our tombs!*

There are *kyôka* that amount to no more than this, or even less. That is, they do not reverse or even twist the logic. They simply dress it with slang &/or stretch it with hyperbole or ludicrous metaphors. My wild paraversing demonstrates how it that can be done. But the lead poem did reverse the original and make the moon jealous of *us*, or, of *Japan*, at any rate. I specify *Japan* for a reason. This was an era when expressions of boastful nationalism were widespread. There is a whole chapter on nationalism in *Cherry Blossom Epiphany* (2007), for mountains of *sakura* were one thing Japan had that its neighbors lacked. Even haiku master Issa, with his famous concern for little creatures and outbursts about the bad state of the world, nevertheless, has dozens of *ku* that might be called chauvinistic. But he was also a religious man and adopted the concept of the moon as the light of Buddhist law and mercy. Indeed, one of my favorite of Issa's moon *ku* goes even further and seems to turn it into what English used to call a sinne eater: *All of our sins / should vanish tonight:/ the fall moon* 許々多久の罪も消へ(ゆ)べし秋の月 一茶 *kokodaku no tsumi mo kiyubeshi akinotsuki issa* 文政一). So, as wild as he was, Issa would never have reversed that *waka* as Akara did. From the Buddhist point of view, it would have seemed not only *outrageous* but *perverse* to have the holy moon that helped raise men above their worldly attachments and even pacify wild animals look on with envy. Even the rudest genre of all, *senryû*, tended to celebrate the state of the nation, not with cherry blossoms but *balls,* for in at least two historical incidents they, the balls, *testified* to their owner being relaxed, and that came to be stretched into a barometer of peace, though unlike the air pressure, the *lower* they hang, the more peaceful the times and the more credit to the rulers presiding over them (Find half a dozen examples in the chapter on balls in *Octopussy, Dry Kidney & Blue Spots:* 2007). Also, Shokusanjin:

祝 戸をあけて ぬれどもさらにいさゝかの かぜさへひかぬ御代ぞめでたき
iwai: to o akete nuredomo sara ni isasaka no kaze sae hikanu mi yo zo medetaki
celebration: door+acc. opened sleep moreover wind/cold even catch-not hon.era+exclam joy/lucky

We open our doors to sleep and, what is more, never catch
The slightest cold in this, the most blessed, times e'er told!

Hamada's annotation of the Shokusanjin's lead *kyôka* calls it "reality-positive" or "reality-affirmative" (現実肯定的狂歌). Tanaka Yûko, an expert on the social networks of the Edo era called *ren*, citing the same, wrote

"In waka, the composer envies the moon, but in kyoka, the moon envies us. In waka, this world is difficult and blue, but in kyoka, this world is wonderful. In his kyoka, Nanpo always admires this real world, changes unhappy events into happy ones, and laughs at everything. This is connected with the traditional function of blessing. There were until the Second World War professional entertainers who blessed everything in each house on new year's day. The ren of kyoka produced laughter in all the meetings." 1993 Tanaka Yuko at Nissan Institute, Oxford University (Netted, already Englished, no translator named.)

That is a beautiful tribute to the genre, but the "always" is wrong and I still think a facetious or ironic reading, possibly a reaction to chauvinistic *waka*, many so *bad* they *seem* mad (see ch. 11 of *The Fifth Season:* 2007), as likely as a positive one. To my mind, this second *kyôka*, converting the common boast of *unlocked doors* = *safe times* into an *ad absurdum* claim, supports my risky minority reading.

Shy Bald Mountains & Nostril Hairs by Moonlight

うかうかと長き夜すがらあくがれて　月に鼻毛の数やよまれん　節松嫁嫁

ukauka to nagaki yosugara akugarete tsuki ni hanage no kazu ya yomaren   fushimatsu no kaka
carelessly long night-through longing, moon-by/(light)in nose-hairs' number+emph read-would

~~~~~~~~~~~~~~~~~~~(1)~~~~~~~~~~~~~~~~~~~

Lolling about the whole night long smitten by the moon;
handsome will count the hair in my nose and leave me in a ruin.

~~~~~~~~~~~~~~~~~~~(2)~~~~~~~~~~~~~~~~~~~

Forgetting yourself the whole night long, besotted by the moon;
soon she'll read your nostril hair and you will play her tune!

~~~~~~~~~~~~~~~~~~~(3)~~~~~~~~~~~~~~~~~~~

Lolling about from dusk to dawn in love that's how it goes;
in the moonlight, one can count every hair within a nose!

~~~~~~~~~~~~~~~~~~~(4)~~~~~~~~~~~~~~~~~~~

Putsing away a whole night in adoration? Take care,
in moon-light, the girls can read your nostril hair!

~~~~~~~~~~~~~~~~~~~(5)~~~~~~~~~~~~~~~~~~~

Absentmindedly, all through the night, admiring
the harvest moon can count your nostril hairs.

~~~~~~~~~~~~~~~~~~~~~~~~~~~~~~~~~~~~

The last, by Rokuo Tanaka, I deparsed.

Nostril-hair-counting means paying rapt attention to one's superior or a sugar-daddy. Why so many readings? The identity of the counter is ambiguous. A moon-viewer looks up at the beloved heavenly body from a lowly perspective while the moon shines down or rather up the nostrils, as looking up we lean back. *Reading* 1) assumes the poet Fushimatsu no Kaka, or The Unkempt Wife, one of the top two female Tenmei era *kyôka*-masters, is the protagonist and the moon *Katsurao* 桂男 the dangerously good-looking lady's man of the moon. The *ruin?* Pure rhyme – but staying up all night can that to you. *Reading* 2) assumes the poem is addressed to the poet's husband, Akera Kankô, who stayed up all night moon-viewing. The language (*yo-sugura*) may allude to Bashô's well-known *ku* of all-night (*yo-mo-sugura*) moon-viewing while circling a pond, implying the nature of *his* moon-viewing was less pure than that of the famous aesthete. *Reading* 3) "in love" is left personless. Moon-viewing memories? *Reading* 4) is the preferred reading. The moon, like Autumn leaves, was an excuse for men to paint the town. Kaka, a sophisticate in the good and not bad sense of the word, was cleverly warning her man not to paint himself into a corner. *Reading* 5), by Rokuo Tanaka (2006) does not quite match his preface: *"she is bantering with a flirting man,"* but he has done something fascinating here. Tanaka's "harvest moon" – unspecified, a moon is, by convention, mid-fall – serves as the object of admiration *and* a seeing subject, in turn. That is, he reproduces a Japanese-style pivot-word, though, to be fair to the poet, the original is grammatical both ways.

Forgetting myself the whole night long I'm stuck on one so fair,
The moon, my Laurel Man, must have read my nostril hair!

Forgetting yourself the whole night long stuck on one so fair;
My man, beware, your Luna reads your every nostril hair!

That covers the moon's sexes, but none of the readings captured Kaka's play with "moon and *blossoms*" (*tsuki ni hana*), suggesting the lifelong aesthetic pursuit of the poet (favoring readings addressed to her husband), before the would-be *blossoms* become a *nose* for the *hair* reading. Be that as it may, I favor reading 4), unless Akera Kankô liked men, for the moon was seldom a Luna ♀ in Japan. My Japanese respondent favors the lady-killer Laurel man (more in ♪'s).

兀山月 てら／＼と月のかつら男さす影もはづかしげなる老のはげ山 智恵内子
teratera to tsuki no katsurao sasu kage mo hazukashigenaru rô no hageyama chie no naishi
gleaming, moon's laurel-man beaming/pointing-out form embarrassed-becomes old bald mtn

Light beams from the Man in the Moon need no bush but, say,
Is that the crown Of Old Mount Baldy blushing bright as day?

The Man in the moon wears the laurels and makes the world swoon,
Poor old Mount Baldy, his blush is so bright you'd think it noon!

His features lit up by moon-beams from the Laurel Man so fair,
Old Mt. Baldy blushes bright to show the hair that is not there!

This poem by the most popular female *kyôka*-master Chie no Naishi, or Little Ignoramus, is not nearly as good as her *tears-turned-silverfish* (p.381), but it is better than the gloss shows. The moon man associates with a laurel tree, so we have a verdant moon and bare mountain; the word for *embarrassment* includes *shige*, as in *dense* with vegetation, which the mountain is not; the *kage* usually suggests the face of the *moon,* not mountain; the psychological mimesis *tera tera,* for gleaming/glowing, recalls temples, *tera,* up mountains, where we have old men viewing the moon, who, in a well-known *haikai* on the tip of my tongue but not my fingers are embarrassed not to have one good-looker among them.

くひたらぬうはさもきかずから大和 たつたひとつのもちの月影 濱邊黒人
kuitaranu uwasa mo kikazu kara yamato tatta hitotsu no mochi no tsukikage hamabe no kurohito
eat-suffice-not rumor+emph hear-not sino-japanese just one rice-cake-moon-form 1785

Let's pour our wine, then, lay back: when the cat's out, a man will play:
There's cheese enough in this fat moon to feed Japan and all Cathay!

In countless *waka* written long before the moon envied Japan, when the yet-to-be-united nation was at war within and without, the moon, as something many could enjoy simultaneously from many places without competition, embodied world peace. The first *kyôka*-master (of the Tenmei poets) said to charge a 入花料, or large sign-up fee, to join his group, added a new element, if only in good pun: the new (14-day) full-moon is called the *mochi-zuki,* which sounds like *rice-cake* moon (actually *mochizuki* 望月 *mochi* is written "hope"). And just one such miraculously suffices for all. The original is not only not cheese but alcohol-free. Rice cake, as something sweet, was thought repulse drinkers.

What's Wrong with Being on the Rag in the Shrine?

もとよりも塵にまじはる神なれば月の障も何かくるしき 熊野権現 風雅集
moto yori mo chiri ni majiwaru kami nareba tsuki no sawari mo nani ga kurushiki
origin-from+emph. scraps-in mix gods are-if moon-blockage+emph what's painful? c1350

Haven't the Gods,
one with paper, always mixed
with other litter?

What is wrong with riding horses
that they should mind our courses?

Izumi Shikibu (fl. 970-1030) was passionate in poetry and, unlike the "holeless" Ono no Komachi, in life. An hour away from the main shrine in Kumano, she noticed her menses coming on, and stopping, holed up in a hut in the woods to pray where she composed a poem about her sadness at clouding the moon (晴れやらぬ身のうき雲のたなびきて月のさわりとなるぞかなしき 風雅 *hare yaranu*). That night, the shrine's tutelary deity responded in a dream w/ the above, after which she visited the shrine. I added *"one with paper"* to cover the punning equation of *god/s* and *paper*, both *kami*, and the *"horses"* for rhyme, retroactively justifiable for protective devices resembled equestrian gear and the possibility of falling off the horse if one did not "ride" carefully resulted in just such a metaphor centuries later, when it gave rise to countless *senryû* (*The Woman Without a Hole* ch.3). Shikibu's *waka*, if it is hers – the source is 14c – is both elegant and gutsy merely for what is mentioned, while the apocryphal response – I'd guess is *hers,* too – challenging a taboo with a homophonic pun for proof is clearly *kyôka* mad.

If the Gods
have always mixed w/ dust,
and horses
How odd to think we must
sequester monthly courses.

If Gods and Paper
are both Kami and that
includes the Rag
Why should our Monthlies
make Shrine Guards gag?

Make the first-person plurals second-person if you wish. I first thought the poem was Shikibu's as the only thing in the Japanese suggesting a divine author is wording less polite than usual if addressing the gods. As no record has Shikibu visiting said Shrine; the legend (伏拝王子にまつわる伝説) is considered 1) an example of a *waka* getting gods to respond 歌徳説話, and 2) a teaching tool to overcome superstition so women would visit shrines more often. *Absurd argument fits absurd circumstances.* Men dressed as women in Turkey once rode backwards on asses (and just in the news, maidens plowed naked in West India) to draw rain by showing God how absurd it was that He would parch His earth. In *Ryôjinhishô,* a 12c collection of popular songs, a woman, objecting to the teaching that women had to be reborn as men before becoming enlightened, reasons that *if,* as per a tale, even a dragon girl could become a Buddha, why should *our* (a woman's) five obstructing clouds (Buddhist catechism) block the moon, i.e., the perfect Buddha whose halo light should, after all be able to pass through them? (龍女は仏に成りにけり などかわれらも成らざらん 五障の雲こそ厚くとも 如来月輪隠されじ *ryûnyo wa ...* 梁塵秘抄 巻第二 208). The women of early- Reformation England objected to their supposed perversity, pointing out in poetry that, far from being crooked ribs, *they* were *twice-refined* (Great examples in Angeline Gourneau: *The Whole Duty of Women*). Men could, however, be pretty mean to women who dared speak up. Take, for example, the following *kyôka* reaction to the possibly apocryphal Shikibu by the 42 year-old head of a Buddhist temple whose name 雄長老 means Male-chief-old. It is captioned "spring."

Night after night, Shikibu her soso washes – my, how stinky,
the Spring water she cups between her thumb and pinky!

泉 よるごとに式部がそそや洗ふらしむすぶいづみの水のくささは
yoru goto ni shikibu ga soso ya araurashi musubu izumi no mizu no kusasa wa
night-each-on shikibu's pussy+emph. washes-(it's said) cupping spring water's stink-as-for
by Yûchôrô 建仁寺の長老 1547-1602 『雄長老狂歌百首』 in 『狂歌大観1』

The insinuation that she was sniff-outable is outrageous. The most hard-boiled of all the mad-poem poets, Yûchôrô made even wine and woman-loving Shokusanjin seem a prude. Izumi Shikibu's family name, *izumi* means "spring;" *spring water* was, by convention, palm-cupped to drink. *Soso* is too folksy for *quim* and too pleasant for *cunt*. Like fellow translator, J.S., I favor "pussy," but chickened out. Beloved by two Emperors, Shikibu had fine marital relations. Her self-confidence might have allowed her to do a *waka* about her menses. So, this is an absolutely loony idea by a poet who simply could not resist being a wide-guy (eg., pp.,40,102,243,259,267,324)! The commentary in a book published in 1589 says *"I have not read anything at all about Izumi Shikibu having a bad odor, but one can hardly criticize such an okusetsu (deep/obscure-theory: a pun, for oku, while evoking her residence, the inner-palace, is slang for a woman's privates).* Or such *were* my thoughts, until I found an explanation by Suzuki Tôzô (鈴木棠三『狂歌鑑賞辞典』) to the effect that Yûchôrô referenced a well at the temple 誠心院 (俗：和泉式部寺) where Shikibu retired. Did the mad poet find the taste of the water drawn there offputting? Now, let us end with a far more reasonable – considering how the dream reply and Shikibu's question are willfully conflated – objection from the *Tokuwa Kago Manzaishû* 徳和哥後萬載集, the representative book of the late-18c *kyôka* craze:

Lady, how brash,
to say gods have always
mixed with trash!

Don't you go turning us
into litter bugs or bums!

Lady, must you
claim that we have always
mixed with crap?

Please clean your mouth:
gods don't need a bum rap!

もとよりも塵に交はる神じやとてあくたれ者となさせ給ふな　くれ竹世艶
moto yori mo chiri ni majiwaru kami ja tote akutare mono to nasase tamau na kuretake no yotsuya 1785
華紅葉 1729 ↓ basically trash/dust-w/ mix gods are says trashy/bad-ones as makeout-as do+hon.-not ↓ *danjiri ya*
オマケ みな月の御祓に　だんじりやチヤンチキ地祇の神〴〵も塵にましりてやれ〴〵といふ 桴雪

Trading Blood for a Drink Beats Being a Monkey?

さりとては けふまたしちにやれ 蚊帳 酒にそ我はくらはれにける　暁月房作
saritote wa kyô mata shichi ni yare kachô sake ni zo ware wa kurawarenikeri kyôgetsu-bô
regardless today again pawnshop-to give=emph. mosq.net sake-by i-as-for eaten+emph.

Once again, today
I'm off to the pawnshop!
My mosquito net

Will get some wine; and
I'll be eaten up this time!

A man will drink.
Today, the pawnshop gets
my mosquito net

and I will be, literally,
swallowed by my wine!

I love this *kyôka*, playing upon an old proverb warning that a one begins by imbibing wine and ends up imbibed *by* it. The father of a Japanese friend taught it to me in 1978 in a bar in Waikiki by. Pretending not to know the counters for glasses of drink (*ippai, nihai, sanbai*), with their damn *p*'s and *h*'s and *b*'s, I let the father refresh me, and as soon as he gave the third, piped up: *"So, one more would have to be "yopparai!"* (すると、も一杯は酔っ払い！) – the *yo* suggests *fourth* and there is the sound of a vessel (*hai*) in the word, which means "drunk." I beg the pardon of readers who do not know Japanese; but I want this in my obit, someday – could I forgo the perfect opportunity to publicize it? But, to return to the *kyôka*, attributed to the monk sometimes called the founder of *kyôka*, Kyôgetsu-bô 暁月坊 (1265-1328), it is not in the large 17c *kyôka* compilations, but only found in the 18c *Kyôka Hundred Poems on Sake* 狂歌酒百首 attributed to him 伝暁月坊 with a note *claiming* it is pre-1497. Now let us go back to the beginning, or at least the most famous early Japanese drinking *waka*.

験無 物乎不念者 一杯乃 濁酒乎 可飲有良師　大伴旅人万葉歌＃338
shirushi-naki mono o omowazu wa hitotsuki no nigoreru sake o nomu beku arurashi
results-not things think-not-as-for one cup/fill-up of cloudy sake drink should+emph.

When in doubt,
don't think, drink: cloudy wine
will clear you up.

Think not to rout
the blues but drink raw wine
& they will cloud.

If *love* is one source of mad poetry, *wine*, in this case made from fermented rice, is another. Since *every* translator of the *Manyôshû* (8c) includes a sip of Ôtomo no Tabito's 13 poems in praise of wine, I thought to pass, but failing to find any pursuit of the ideas in them, changed my mind. This one plays with the symbolism of *clear* and *muddy*. With clear springs and streams, memories run deep; specifying *cloudy sake*, cheaper than the clear stuff, as ideal for obscuring thought is a stroke of conceptual genius. My haiku-length paraverses, indirectly show my appreciation for it. The original is longer and simply says *you'd be better drinking a full saucer of muddy white wine than thinking about things thinking does not help*. The next poem of the series is even more in the mode of what came to be called a *kyôka*, as it plays upon an old Chinese saw.

酒名乎 聖跡負師 古昔 大聖之 言乃宜左 万葉 #339
sake no na o hijiri to ouseshi inishie no ôki hijiri no koto no yoroshisa tabito
sake's name+acc saint/sage as named ancient big s/s/s words suitability/goodness

♪A True Conservative to a Prohibitionist♪

The ancient sages called wine Sage,
So what gives with our Age?

The original says only that *the great sages of ancient times sure did a fine thing to call wine* 聖 *saint*. Proverbs call clear wine that, and cloudy wine 賢人 *sage*, a cut below saint. As moralists were probably down on drinking, I pulled up the last half of my short & mad reading+title by its ears from between the lines.

nakanaka ni hito to arazu wa sakatsubo ni nari nite shikamo sake ni nijimina #343
completely person-as be-not-as-for sake-jug into becoming, moreover wine-by stain-would

♪ Moderation, you say? ♪

Rather than play the half-hearted lug,
Let me soak myself in wine: I'd be a jug.

~~~~~~

♪A Red-Faced Riposte to Wrinkle-browed Teetotalers♪

How unsightly those men too damn smart to drink;
They look far more like monkeys than they think!

↑ *ana miniku sakashiru o su to sake nomanu hito o yoku miba saru ni ka mo mimu* mys #344↑
あなみにく酒には思ひます鏡 底なるかけはさるにかも似る 暁月房作 酒百↓
*ana miniku sake ni wa omoi*masu *kagami soko naru kage wa saru ni ka mo niru* kyôgetsu-bô

How ugly my face in a square cup, drinking blue
I look red as a monkey, thinking as I do of you!

Like all primates, red-faced Japanese macaque have a way of wrinkling their brows as if thinking, and that is used to turn the table on teetotalers who called drinkers "monkeys" for being red-faced. Monk Kyôgetsu plays with the *Manyôshû* poem, punning part of a conjugation, into a *masu*zake cup which immediately becomes a mirror. Another of his drinking poems – *When it's full, the Man in the Moon he drinks like one: / With potatoes for his tarts, I guess he always gets some!* 十五夜の月のかつらのおとこ酒 さかなのいもやちきりなるらん 百酒 *jûgoya no tsuki no katsura no otoko-zake sakana no imo ya chigiri naru ran* – is full of puns: the man in the moon pivots into a male drinking alone with nibbly/ies that become his girlfriend. I tired of typing in the old Chinese character *Manyô* inscription – modern renditions are transcriptions – & cut to the chase w/ romanization. The last, and most *kyôka* of the *Manyô* series (*kono yo ni shi tanoshiku araba komu yo ni wa mushi tori ni mo ware wa narinamu* #349):

♪*This is my life – so if I can have my fun,*
I'll gladly be a bug or bird in the next one♪

More Drink: *Heartburn, Sake as Mead & Octopus*

上巳 我むねは 今日はな焼きそ 若草の餅もこもれり酒もこもれり 孝雄 17c?
waga mune wa kyô wa na yakiso wakakusa no mochi mo komoreri sake mo komoreri yoshio 信海狂歌集
my breast-as-4 today-as-4 burn-not! young-grass-mochi (sweet-rice-cake) hidden, sake, too, hidden

Girl's Day

My heart burn not, not today, when we have a rendezvous
w/ soft sweet cakes of rice, grass-green, & wine for dew!

~~~~~~~~~~~~~~~~~~~~~~~~~~~~~~~

Heart burn not today, we need this space to lay away
Mochi fragrant as spring grass & cool rivers of *sake*!

Girl's Day, or the Doll Festival, takes place on the third day of the third month. Usually, wine and the glutinous, pounded cooked rice called *mochi* – translated as "cake" for lack of a word: the texture is far from cake – do not mix. Drinkers drink and teetotalers eat *mochi*. But girly day was an exception. It would seem the combination of sweet food and drink caused heartburn for some! The poem is also an exception. It is one of those few *kyôka* that *by itself is utterly boring, but with knowledge of the original is hilarious*, a masterpiece. Here is that original:

むさし(かすが)のはけふはなやきそわかくさのつまもこもれり我もこもれり 伊勢12
musashi/kasuga-no wa kyô wa na yakiso wakakusa no tsuma mo komoreri ware mo komoreri
musashi/kasuga moor-as-4 today-as-4 burn-not young-grass-spouse hidden I too hidden +古今#17

Not, today! Burn not Musashi moor! Soft spring grass
Lies hidden there, no less, my sweet young blade & I.

~~~~~~~~~~~~~~~~~~~~~~~~~~~~~~~

Not, today! Burn not the moor of Kasuga, for here we lie
My sweetheart as tender as the new spring grass, and I!

Yes, there were two versions of "the" original. The *Tales of Ise* (c905), puts the story in the mouth of a girl begging them not to burn a field to flush her kidnapper (a 'thief of peoples' daughters,' I assume he seduced her without her parents' permission). The *Kokinshû* (905) version is not prefaced. *Young-grass* eventually came modify maidens alone, but at this time, either sex could be so called.

酒のめばいつも慈童の心にて七百歳もいきんとぞおもふ 蜀山家集
sake nomeba itsumo jidô no kokoro nite nanahyaku-sai mo ikin to zo omou
wine drink-when always minion's heart-as 700-years-old even live-would so think

菊 の 絵 か き た る 盃 に
◆ *For a Sake Cup with a Picture of a Chrysanthemum* ◆

Drinking, call me the Chrysanthemum Kid, immortal I play,
Thinking I will live seven hundred years if not a day!

Shokusanjin did not so much drink like a fish as swim like one in a sea of *sake*: *Wealth keeps the wine shops numerous, wine, the body humorous. Heavy drinking is good if your mind stays free and your body tipsy, so you know enough not take a firm stance.* (富は酒屋を潤し、徳利は身を潤す。心広く体よろよろと、足元の定まらぬこそ上戸はよけれ). He stayed pleasantly drunk around the clock "360 days a year" and, adoring *sake,* rarely if ever abused it. On Day Nine Month Nine, people drank Chrysanthemum wine after a Chinese ritual coming from a legend of a stream of Chrysanthemum dew found high-up a mountain of youth, discovered by an exiled minion of the Emperor called the Chrysanthemum kid. In the *kyôka*, Shokusanjin marries his everyday with the annual ceremony and its enchanting mood.　And here is one by his *waka* teacher Gatei (1723-88):

盃へ飛びこむ蚤も呑み仲間つぶされもせず押さへられもせず　内山椿軒
sakazuki e tobikomu nomi mo nomi nakama tsubusare mo sezu osaerare mo sezu chinken
sake-cup-into dive –in flea too drinking=flea buddy squash do-not & repress do-not

Fleas hop into my sake cup: I drink up – but how can I flee,
Or pinching, pop, my drinking buddies who just won't stop?

Issa had a flea jump into his sake cup and swim with the moon, but here, with 14 extra syllabets, the *flea*, who could be swallowed easily enough, becomes *fellow drinkers* not so easily coped with – the original says they cannot be *squashed* or forcibly controlled. The verb *nomi* threatening to drink the flea, *nomi,* with *nakama,* becomes *nominakama, drinking-buddies.* Among the 611 ways Europeans and Japanese are contrary according to Portuguese Jesuit Luis Frois in 1585, we find Item #6-31 where a tendency to force others to drink is associated with the latter (*Topsy-turvy 1585:* 2004). While Islam-influenced South Europeans were particularly down on drinking and Frois, having left Europe at age 16, hardly knew how pushy his own compatriots could be, he may have had a point. Even Japanese noted the problem:

章魚をさかなに酒たうべて　蜀山狂歌家集
誰にても　酒をしひてや　足あれど　手のなきものぞ　たこの入道
dare nite mo sake o shiite ya ashi aredo te no naki mono zo tako no nyûdô shokusanjin
anyone-to-even sake+acc forced!/: legs have but hands not thing+emph. octopus-novice

◆ *Drinking with a Cephalopod for Nibblies* ◆

To push wine on all you have good legs to stand up drunk,
But your arms now go begging, my little Octopus Monk!

Monks were called *tako,* or *octopus,* for their round hats. Item #175 in Kenkô's, *Essays in Idleness* (*Tsurezuregusa,* c.1330), holds that for clergy to push drinks on someone was so horrendous a sin one would be reborn armless for 500 generations (some versions say *limbless*: a monk becomes a sea cucumber in one *ku* in *Rise, Ye Sea Slugs!* 2003). Why a *novice?* Because they lack wherewithal which puns as "hands" in Japanese and become nibblies for older monks.

In Praise of Getting Plastered and Puking

げに酒は愁をはらふはゝきとて　たはこともはく青反吐もはく　飯盛
ge ni sake wa urei o harau hahaki(hôki) tote tabako tomo haku aohedo mo haku meshimori
really sake-as4 trouble sweeps/exorczes broom/puking say, tobcco 2 spews, blue-puke spews

*You really can
call wine a broom to sweep
away thy trouble;*

*& tobacco, when thou spew it
blue – Thy exorcism's double!*

*With wine, by god,
a man can puke, or rather,
disengorge his blues,*

*So why not smoke tobacco, too:
'Tain't a puff that doesn't spew!*

I found the above once but did not think I could English it. Today, my last day to cram things into the book, I found it again and could not help trying. Even a composite translation falls short, for we do not have one basic verb that works for *exorcizing*, *sweeping*, *puking* and *smoking* (when smoke is *"puffed"*). If only a priests *puffed* out demons, brooms *puffed* dirt into dust-trays, drunks *puffed* vomit upon sidewalks, translation would have been a cinch! The closest we can come is with vile Latin words, such as *expectorate, regurgitate* and disengorge, and even they cover but two of the four. From the above, we can see that Shokusanjin whose love for being drunk was famous, was not alone, for his colleague and equal in poetry, Meshimori joined him. And the reason I found that poem again was that I was searching for the b&d dates of Kisshû, their contemporary and competitor, in Nada Inada's *Edo Kyôka* and there it was right after another *kyôka* I had read, lost and sought for the corvine onomatopoeia. That poem turned out to be by Kisshû:

とかく世はよろこび烏のんで　夜が明たかあ日がくれたかあ　橘州
tokaku yo wa yorokobi-garasu sake nonde yo ga aketakaa hi ga kuretakaa   kisshû
bewhatmay wrld-as4 happycrow sake-drnkng night brightns/dawnscaw? day duskscaw?

*A happy crow, just drinking wine, whatever will be will be.
Has dawn caw caw come? Is the sun in his caw-caw-fin?*

One reason I waited on and lost Kisshû's poem was to check two things. One was the *crow*. I only knew it could be old men wearing formal black robes, but, no, a *happy crow* is one that unlike most, whose call portends ill, sounds so happy (I think I have heard such, but, wow, that is a hard one to call!) it is a good omen! The other was the crow, *karasu,* itself, coupled with *yorokobi* to yield the pronunciation ~*garasu*. Not recalling which *glass* was which in Japanese, I had to check. Unfortunately, the glass one looks *through* is the one that came to be called *garasu* and the type one drinks *with* a *gurasu!* What a pun that poem lost! If this is not serendipity that never was, what is! Let me add that Nada Inada is a psychiatrist. He credited *kyôka* with curing him of his reflexive habit – he knew it did not work – of lecturing drunks about behavior amounting to suicide. The *kyôka* show a positive attitude approaching that of the lover who knows it is hopeless but has determined that *if I die, I would be killed by what I love.* (Nada

Inada writes about many things with a sure and kindly hand. I met him because his daughter discovered my books. My anti-stereotype agenda was easy for a psychiatrist to grasp and he was kind enough to review one.). Nada Inada also reprinted a *counting-song* of *sake*, a series of ten 31-syllabet *kyôka* about drinking he found with the others in a book of poems and passages about drinking called 酒仙伝 (a title, Japanese readers will note, gracefully punning the mountain sage element of drinking into the propaganda of it) by a science writer for the *Yomiuri Shinbun* (one of the newspaper big-three) published in 1971. Had I the time and money, I would let this book slip until next year, and translate *all* of them. Let me just do four easy ones lickety-split before returning to the torture of searching for names and dates to finish this book.

四かるべきその人柄も杯に　向かえば変わる人の面影　酒仙伝
shikaru-beki sono hitogara mo sakazuki ni mukaeba kawaru hito no omokage
firm/as-should-be that charctr/persnality evn winecup-to face-if changd persn's face

What is a man but character? And yet, within a sake cup
Another person altogether is all too often looking up!

五無理とは口に言えどもうれしさを　つつみかねたる意地の悪さ
gomuri to wa kuchi ni iedomo ureshisa o tsutsumi-kanetaru ijinowarusa
u're-forcng-it-as4 mouth-frm say but happinss+acc cram/drum-cannt maliciousnss

Don't over do it, please take care! I hear and do not mind,
But still, I cannot help but smack my lips to see my wine.

八景の中に入りたる酒ばやし　食らい倒れは絵にもかかれず
hakkei no naka ni iritaru sake-bayashi kurai-daore wa e ni mo kakarezu
8-sights w/in put wine-woods/kiddng, eatng-fall-as4 pictre-as evn draw-not

In scenic places, they always draw the same pictures of drunks
Heaven forbid the sight of those who ate until they fell, plunk.

九りかえし酔いのまわりて後先の　下らぬことをしずのおだまき
kurikaeshi yoi no mawarite atosaki no kudaranu koto o shizu no odamaki
repeatedly drunk/eness circlesround afterbefore's nonsense-talk is flax-bobbin

Drunken, we repeat ourselves when we pass our drinks around,
Like a spool of flaxen thread, our tongues are in a circle bound.

Please note several things. First that every part of Japan had its number – eight was only the most common, as it stood for many – of famous places to see and these were commonly depicted in prints. Second, the *spool* or *bobbin* in the last line is ancient trope for turning back time, Sôchô teased it into senile dementia (p.261). And, third, the second and fourth poems above may be misread. ♪ *Please see my alternate translations in the notes.* ♪ The poet, we assume is an anon. alcoholic. Nada Inada read the book to see if it had anything useful for his clinical practice and discovered the abandoned world of *kyôka*.

Poop as Omen & What It Means in a Dream

「夢」金ひろふ夢は ゆめにて 夢のうちにはこするとみし夢は まさ夢
kane hirou yume wa yume nite yume no uchi ni hako suru to mishi yume wa masayume Yûchôrô
money/gold find dream-as4 dream-in dream-within defecate and seeing dream-as4 true-dream

A dream about
finding money that will
come out true

is a dream in a dream
where you take a poo.

Finding money
is a dream, a dream
within a dream

where taking a poo
means it will come true.

雄長老 1547-1602 雄長老狂歌百首 tk1

This must be one of the most inane *kyôka* ever written, though the original is so convoluted who knows if I got it right, or *anyone* can! The 1589 評詞 gloss by 中院通勝? escapes me. I catch the *ben*s, or *bm*s, punned in, but not the content of his comment. About all I can say is that he found the dream within the dream of the man who was a butterfly inexplicable & this was *more* out of the question. 「化蝶翁の夢未夢を弁ず。此趣向まさ夢を弁ぜられたる尤も殊勝々々」 If I seem unsure of myself, well, so is my respondent (但し「化蝶翁」云々は不明である).

Right before the rice
w/ red beans is passed out,
Bird poop! How nice,

The mother's silk sleeves
will sure get a soaking now!

Shokusan-sensei 蜀山先生 狂歌百人一首

赤飯をいざやくばらん鳥のふんかけしや袖のぬれもこそすれ
akahan o iza yakubaran tori no fun kake ji ya sode no nure mo koso sure
red rice+acc. ever cook-distribute-would bird-shit puts!/&/: sleeves' wetness+emph. does

Poop was the only dirty subject *not* in my book about *senryû*, both because I do not enjoy writing about it very much and because there is less of it in *senryû* than one might think. While Japanese could use "shit" in the hard "k" pronunciation (*kuso*) as an explicative, ordure was, on the whole, less dirty, less bad in Japanese than the Occident, or what I know of it. This was partly because efficient recycling made it a valuable product (*Topsy-turvy 1585*, ch.14) and partly because other pronunciations, the common *fun* (*bafun*=horse shit, *gyûfun*=cowshit, etc.) and the childish *unko,* include *un*, the sound of "luck," or "fortune." Even today, students are said to visit the zoo and bait primates to act like Yahoos and throw shit at them in the hope that it sticks and good luck on exams with it! At the moment, I am helping care for an old dog that drops shit all over the house, so if I get lucky and this book sells like hot-cakes, I will know why.

Before I forget them, the poems. First, *the dream*. Some macro information: the *money* is written with the same character as *gold*, and shit in Japan was typically golden rather than brown. Not surprisingly, the house burglar's shit-for-money exchange found in many cultures is particularly well-developed (?) in Japan, as is, or was, the Freudian anal retentive idea, especially as associated with money. In Edo era art, the golden goose was not the only one to *doo* it. Cartoonists showed rich people literally pooping out gold coins when the Giant Catfish, i.e. earthquake, shook them up and leveled society. An Issa *ku* describes a lapdog belonging to wealthy people at a cherry blossom viewing as looking spoiled enough to shit the same. Second, the red rice *kyôka*. It celebrates marriage, childbirth or a girl's first period. If I *knew* it was the last, I would title the poem *Omense*. As poop is a good omen, the mother cries from joy. Shokusanjin plays on a *Hundred Poets One Poem waka* where the fake waves in a play, that is the emotional scene, wet Lady Kii's sleeves, that is, draw tears (音にきく高師の浜の あだ波はかけじや袖のぬれもこそすれ　祐子内親王家紀伊 *Oto ni kiku takashi no hama no ada nami wa kakeji ya sode no nure mo koso sure* kks # 486). One haiku:

鶯や餅に糞する縁のさき(の上)　芭蕉
uguisu ya mochi ni funsuru en no saki/ue bashô d. 1694
warbler/nightingale!/: rice-cake-on poop-does veranda-edge/on

the warbler he
poops on the mochi
out on the stoop

Rice cake is standard, but *mochi* is su generis. Hence I leave it as is. I translate for this book. Makoto Ueda's more subdued *"bush warbler – a dropping on the rice cake / at the veranda's edge"* may be closer to the original, style-wise, but Harold Stewart's bold *icing on the cake* couplet captures the magic. I include Bashô here for *a lot* is going on. *Mochi* was identified with smooth skin except when it dries out and cracks and molds, as the good-luck New Year decoration *mochi* tends to – icing on the cake = *double luck* = which is why it is put out and sunned, *and* said bird's poop is even today used in expensive facial creams . . .

鳥の糞　顔のはたけのこやし也
tori no fun kao no hatake no koyashi nari
bird shit face's garden/plot's fertilizer becomes
という句もある：西沢来　雑学艶学

Even birdshit has its place:
Use it to fertilize your face!

The above *senryû* is contemporaneous with the *kyôka*. To balance the chapter, here is an older *kyôka*, or rather, mad *dôka* by Ikkyû (d.1481): his didactic *baba* (baby-word: *poo-poo*) is *not* good: *Earthly desire, does the mind's eye fail to see it treads on poop? / Ordure becomes gold & blind greed won't stoop to wipe it off.* (煩悩の眼にばばをふんずけて　福はおしいと欲しいとのよく一休 *bonnô no manako ni baba o funzukete fuku wa oshii to hoshii to no yoku*). *Tread=fun* puns with "shit." *Wipe* and *wealth* are both *fuku*. Ikkyû has desire neglect the former for the latter.

More Shit: Snowy Outhouses & Counter-clockwise

雪降りて 雪隠遠く下駄は無し 心にかかる 尻の穴かな　木下勝俊 ＝ 長嘯子
yuki furite secchin tôku geta wa nashi kokoro ni kakaru shiri no ana kana　kinoshita katsutoshi b.1569
snow falling w.c. far geta-as-for none heart/mind-on sets/weighs butt's hole!　*i.e.* chôshôshi d.1649

The snow falls, the outhouse is far out & you got no geta:
Now it starts to prey upon the mind: your ass hole, fella!

~~~~~~

The more snow falls　　　　　　*Snow keeps falling,*
the further your outhouse　　　*The crapper's out in the yard*
if you're shoeless　　　　　　　*and you've no shoes*

What to d-do? You're clueless　*What comes to fill your mind?*
Butt in touch w/ your ass hole!　*A little thing: your ass hole!*

Snow falls & falls
You without shoes, exiled
from the outhouse

Now is when you find it
on your mind: your ass hole

Long-tooth *geta* were good for ferrying people across slushy snow, provided it was not too deep. *Geta* do not easily rhyme and *choppine* (the somewhat similar stilted medieval shoe of many spellings) are not well-known, so I favored shoes.

Shoeless and far from the outhouse, snow takes a heavy toll
Hell is being fixated upon your own asshole!

This is a sort of riddle. You wonder where it is heading long before you get there; the fundamental rule for translating it is *the ass hole must stay at the end.* I know that yet none of my translations has the natural grace of the original.

うづ高く左ねぢれの左大べん けつしてこれは公家の糞なり　蜀山人 寝物語
uzu takaku hidari-nejire no sa-daiben kesshite kore wa kuge no kuso nari　shokusanjin
whirl high left-turn's left/honorable big-business definitely this-as-4 noble's shit is

A high swirl to the left, a b.m. of honour, if it stank
would surely be proof of some nobleman's rank!

In the Occident, as far as I know, we have no accepted shit archetype, but if we did, I suppose it would be something like a fat cigar. In Japan, there is an image of shit everyone knows. Commonly appearing in cartoons, it resembles a swirl of soft ice-cream (as found on a cone). Hence, it is either clockwise or counter-clockwise. Japanese, like most languages, has sinister, i.e., anti-left metaphors, to have your "left-first/front" is to do something wrong and "left-wrap" is screwball.

But, when it comes to ranking, left is generally ahead of, or above right. Sadaiben 左大弁 is a high position held in the Imperial bureaucracy by a noble, the class called *kuge*, who tended to make marriage matches with merchant families because they had title without money and were despised by working samurai and commoners alike. It puns with *daiben* 大便 meaning "excrement" and the proudly high but screwy "left" prefix *sa* puns as "honorable/beautiful/precious." Suzuki notes that Ôta, visiting Kansai on business, composed it impromptu when pushed for a poem with words about his fame including an idiom meaning "nowadays" with "under-foot" in it 足下は蜀山とやらいふて名高い狂歌師だそうだが、何か承りたい. Looking about and spying shit nearby, he used it to prove *kyôka* can find a scoop anywhere. While Japanese found *Gulliver's Travels* and did a Japanese version, as far as I know, Swift's *Examination Of Certain Abuses Corruptions, And Enormities In The City Of Dublin* (1732), with its facetious identification of nationalities by the flatness or conical shape of their "excrements," had not yet made it to Japan.

はこはしりにぞみゆる石山・観音もこよひは慈悲や垂れぬらむ
hako wa shiri ni zo miyuru ishiyama kannon mo koyoi wa jihi ya tarenuramu
poop/ing?(=hakone)-as-for rear-on+emph. seeable stone-mountain
kannon too tonight-as-4 mercy+emph. drip/ooze-would

When you poop up on Rocky Top, your rear is patent to the town:
Will the Goddess of Mercy give us squat or send a present down?

Style and content-wise, this could be a classic *kyôka* though it is, in fact, an old *Shinsen-Inutsukuba* (1667 新撰犬筑波集 # 182) 7-7-5-7-5 *haikai*. While *kyôka* sometimes broke after 14 syllabets, this is *haikai* in the extreme laxity of the linkage between the first and last parts of the link-verse product. So saying, it is not quite the same in Japanese and English. Rocky Top is Ishiyama, literally Mt. Stone. Hakone, a place with the sound of *hako* (a now archaic word for *shit*) buried in it, can be seen in the background. There must be a temple on or near said mountain dedicated to the Goddess of Mercy, perhaps – I am going out on a limb here – boasting overhanging toilets where one's business soars through the air with the birds, splatting down on the fields below as described in loving detail by the novel- and essayist Tanizaki Junichirô (1886-1965). The Goddess in the original *drips* or *oozes* (*tarenuru*) mercy, a polite way to say *confers it*. *Tareru* is also the most common verb for evacuating one's bowels. The Usanian slang "squat" (for the information of foreign or future readers, means "nothing") translation of my second line was the only way I could think of maintaining any continuity with the previous line. Since it is content-wise contrary, I had to add the "present." I introduce the poem partly to show the surrealogical jumps that marked late 18-c *kyôka* were long found in *haikai* link-verse.

♪ A sample limerick   *A stingy old man of St Giles*   G. Legman #1683 ♪
Saved his shillings with miserly wiles.
Just to save a few bob
He would wipe with a cob,
And that way he got piles and piles!

The Good of Bad Poems and the Not So Bad

われはもや安見児得たり 皆人の得難にすといふ安見得たり 万葉集
ware wa mo ya yasumiko etari minahito no egata ni su to iu yasumi etari mys #95
i-as-for already+emph yasumiko got/earned all-people get-difficult say yasumi got

♪ Yasumiko Is Mine! ♪

Easy-on-the-eyes
Sweet Miss Easy-on-the-eyes!
Surprise, surprise, I

I'm the one, the one
who won Miss Easy-on-the-eyes!

This fulsome boast is the first & perhaps last poem in the 4,516-poem *Manyôshû* (8c) composed by a youth who is either a dunce or a six year-old at heart. *Kudos to the editor for not selecting only good poems.* Variety is what makes an anthology more interesting than a soap opera full of 100% pretty people. Still, I did the above translation *from memory*. Now, looking at the original, I will try to be more exact and not improve it with rhyme. Only her name, which I had recalled correctly as "*yasumi-ko*: easy-see/sight-child," will be naturalized.

I am the one
who won the cutie pie
the cutie pie

The one that every man
would win, I won!

This boast is a thank you for the gift of the beauty from Emperor #38, Ninji. The more famous Emperor #16, Nintoku, when still a young Prince called Wren (Big Sparrow), composed what Nakanishi considers a similar poem (同状況同想), after his father, Emperor Ôjin, gave him the Long Hair Princess 髪長比売.

道の後木幡嬢子を雷のごと聞こえしかども合枕まく 古事記 c710
michinoshiri kohada otome o kami no goto kikoe shikadomo aimakura maku
road-after kobada (name) maiden+acc. thunder/god-like hearing yet mutual-pillow wrap

From distant land	*This girl from afar*
beyond our ken, my maiden	*whose name recalls my fear*
whose fame resounds	*of thunder claps*
Like thunder, it is said – Just	*Must goddess be, but here*
clap, & we'll jump into bed!	*we are pillow to pillow*

I was tempted to trade "fear" for "dread," and finish with "together in bed," but further research put the poem/song into a banquet – resting in each other's arms perhaps, but nothing literally going on – immediately following poems by his father lauding the beauty of the girl and regretting he did not marry her himself! So the Prince was doubly blessed with a beautiful wife and a generous father, and I think that, unlike the case with the fulsome *Manyôshû* poem, this one meant for both parties is modest and even self-deprecating, though not without joy when he reaches the "mutual pillow" at poem's end. Unless I am mistaken, the poem has the wit of a *kyôka* and shows upcoming greatness. But, to tell the truth, I have yet to find support for my pun on the girl's name – *kohada/kowai da*, "is loud" – nor a single comment on the homophony of *thunder* and *god/dess* (I have seen the character for *thunder* in two Japanese texts and *god/dess* in one. I should add that the Chinese character transcription of the pillow-word for the distant land, *michino,* starts with 美知能, i.e., *beautiful, intelligent, capable*. Was the scribe also smitten by the Princess? Here is a less happy poem from the *Manyôshû*.

うつくしとわが思ふ妹は早も死なむか 生けりともわれに寄るべしと人の言はなくに
uruwashi to waga omou imo ga haya mo shinanu ka ikeri to mo ware ni yorubeshi to hito no iwanaku ni anon.
beautiful I think darling-the quickly die-not? living even me-to approach people say-not+emph 万葉2355

Sour Grapes?
(No, Blast Them!)

Why can't that girl
I find so beautiful
die, and fast!

Alive, what good is she,
Whom none say likes me?

This is far less obnoxious than the boastful *I-got-Yasumiko!* We can excuse the desire to be free from suffering. I confess to feeling some relief when someone on whom I had a long unrequited crush put on weight beyond the embonpoint and sprouted white hairs. Better to wish for a loss of beauty than of life!

――――――――――――

♪ Prince Nintoku's poem is called a 歌謡 or song in the sense of one that is actually sung, while the two *Manyôshû* songs in this chapter are poems. But, no matter: *any* traditional Japanese poem can be sung. Even the simple boast of the happy moron may have been sung, perhaps so well that it sounded as good as better poems merely recited. Maybe that is how the words got recorded to catch the eye of the editor who found it so bad he had to include it. Moreover, when a beauty is involved, poetic standards go out the window. I once read somewhere of a party of English or Irish poets (including someone famous) reacting poorly to one of their comrade's wretchedly boring ditties about his beloved sung as they strolled along. The defense by the poet was "If you, too, had seen her, the lyrics would not seem so bad." For all the fancy philosophical claims made in Occidental circles about *human beauty inspiring civilization* – a common idea up to the mid-20c, when it quietly slipped away, leaving us with something even worse, pure muscle worship – it is probably more common for beauty to turn men into barbarians: the only true ones, that is, *boys*.

Mosquitoes, Martial Preparedness & Fallen Heads

世の中に 蚊ほどうるさきものはなし ぶんぶというて 夜も寝られず 南畝？
yononaka ni ka hodo urasaki mono wa nashi   bunbu to iute yoru mo nerarezu shokusanjin?
world-in mosquito-amount bothersome thing-as-for (is)not. 'bunbu' saying, night even sleep-cannot

Pen, Sword, Mosquito

There is nothing
half so irksome, or small
as the mosquito

And when they go 'bunbu'
we cannot sleep at all!

What is as big
a bother, yet so minute
as the mosquito!

When they their boonboo toot
Woe to any man who'd sleep!

Much wit is lost with "trifling," *ka-hodo,* literally "mosquito-amount!" The main point lies in the slightly out-of-tune mosquitoes. Usually, they hum *bun* or *bun-bun,* but the second nasalized *"n"* syllabet is cut short to sound a word written in Chinese characters as 文武, i.e., *writing* (and other cultural activities)+*martial* (arts), referring to the new policy of the Kansei Reform (1787-1793), an attempt to re-instill a martial spirit in the warrior class that did not need to be told to practice the literary and fine arts because they already did. The poem was published anonymously as a *rakushu* 落首, or drop-head, falling within the broader category of *rakusho* 落書 or "drop-writing," lampoons which will be treated to the next chapter. It is said to be why Ôta Nanpô *aka* Yomo no Akara, retired after a decade of active *kyôka* composition and organizing. The authorities' suspicion was well-founded. Ôta was a famously heavy-drinker and all-night carouser – did his teenage *nom de plume* Dr. Sleepy-head 寝惚先生 mean he preferred to sleep by day? – and his late-night *kyôka* parties required the participation of others of the warrior class as well. Not only his lifestyle but livelihood would have been affected by policies pushing early morning exercise (*all* militarism – I experienced it in Korea – starts with that wake-up call!). Moreover, the exquisite combination of two puns, one so natural and different in type that it only adds to the other is indeed signature Ôta, as is this, though punless:

人はみな おきいづるその あかつきに小便をしてぬるぞたのしき
hito wa mina oki-izuru sono akatsuki ni shôben o shite nuru zo tanoshiki shokusanjin
people-as-for all waking-go-out that dawn-in/at piss+acc doing sleep+emph delightful

As day dawns, the whole world rises and out they head,
What a delight to take a piss, then, and go to bed!

That was written decades later (蜀山家集). Let me add Ôta's vice was time-honored. From what the Portuguese Jesuits wrote, even in the busy times when Japan was in the process of unification, *i.e., war,* the noble scholar-warriors were night owls beyond anything seen in Europe. They kept them up all night talking religion and left the early-rising Jesuits exhausted. (*Topsy-turvy 1585,* item #13-25). But, to get back on track, my point was that *kyôka* can be *rakushu* or vice-versa.

曲りても杓子は物をすくふなり すぐな様でも つぶすすりこ木
magarite mo shakushi wa mono o sukuu nari sugu na yô demo tsubusu surikogi
bent even/though ladle-as4 things scoop-up is; straight appear even crushing pestle

> *It can scoop as much as it is able, because it's bent, the ladle;*
> *Straightened out, you get a tool to grind and crush – a pestle.*

The government's reform is accused of harming rather than helping the body politic. *Sukuu*, or "scoop" is a homophone for "help." Weak rhyme cannot make up the loss of that pun in this protest recalling Burke on the insanity of logic taken to extremes (*The Rights of Man*). Like the other poem, it is attributed to Ôta, who denied it. Here are three more *rakushu*. The first probably never left Issa's journal (文政句帖・文政 6.8); the second is encountered often enough to be called famous; the third came to me only once on the world-wide web.

石はこびなげきこりツゝしめし野ゝ人の油にひかるしろ哉 一茶
ishi hakobi nageki koritsutsu shimejino no hito no abura ni hikaru shiro kana issa
stone-carrying lamenting-while marked-off fields' peoples' oil by shines castle!

> *Carrying stones and chopping trees, lamenting keep-out signs*
> *But elbow oil, grease of man – that's why this castle shines!*

〜〜〜〜〜

白河の清きに魚も住みかねて元の濁りの田沼恋しき 大田か
shirakawa no kiyoki ni uo mo sumi-kanete moto no nigori no tanuma koishiki
white-river clean/refreshing-in fish even live-cannot origl. murky paddy-marsh miss

> *It's hard to live in clean fast-waters, even for fish:*
> *They miss their paddy-marsh comfortably brackish.*

〜〜〜〜〜

御祭は目出たいあらのお吸物 だしばかりにてみどころはなし
omatsuri wa medetai ara no osuimono dashi bakari nite mi dokoro wa nashi anon
hon+festival-as-for joyous fishbone soup stock alone-with condiments place-as4 not

> *The festival, once such a joy, is New Year's soup: all stock.*
> *No goodies but float to greet the eye. The rest is under lock.*

Issa uses the old *waka* pun on tree-cutting=lament (*nageki*). A preface notes the castle (w/ a good overlook) was Minister Tanuma's doing. The second poem looks back on that corrupt but thriving time. Shirakawa=white-water is the clean new minister, and Tanuma=paddy-marsh the corrupt but popular previous one, whose laxity allowed Tenmei *kyôka* to bloom. The well-known poem may hold water but, like Issa's, as poetry, it is just so-and-so. The last, however, is a rare *rakushu* masterpiece. The basic *float* shouldered by the men of a shrine written with the Chinese characters as 山車 "mountain-car" is pronounced *dashi*, as is *soup stock*. The missing *condiments* and *seeing* are both *mi*. Those missing goodies refer to the dance floats/stages 踊り屋台, million lantern floats 万灯台, bottomless floats 底抜屋 entertainment tents & other such extras dastardly new 寛政三年 1791 sumptuary laws forbade the Kanda (a ward of Edo) Myôjin Festival.

Steam-boat Tea, Stone Dumplings & Other Concerns

太平の眠りを覚ます上喜撰＝蒸気船＝たった四杯＝隻＝で夜も眠れず　無名
taihei no nemuri o samasu jôkisen tatta yon hai de yoru mo nemurezu anon. 1853
indolence/pacific sleep-from wake jôkisen(tea)/steam-ship just 4cups/ships-from night=world sleep-can't

> *Stolid folk may be roused from their slumber –*
> *Just four packets of Joy Tea to stay up all night.*
> ~~~~~~~~~~~~~~~~~~~~~~~~~~~~~~~~~~~~
> *The Pacific ocean has awoken from its slumber,*
> *Just 4 steam ships & the world can get no sleep.*

All anonymous songs, poems or short treatises criticizing or parodying current events, policies or people, published, handed out, sung, or pasted on walls are *rakusho* 落書 in Japanese. In English, *lampoons* cover roughly the same ground. We also have the narrower term, *broadsides,* for the poems or ballads, sometimes posted and sometimes sold in the Colonies of America, for sure, but mostly in old London. The Japanese *rakushu* 落首 "drop-head" is a sub-category that includes only 31-syllabet poems (*head* is a counter and collective pronoun for such). Few *kyôka* are *rakushu,* but many *drop-heads* are mad. The lead poem is the only *rakushu* I have come across many times. It must be introduced in history textbooks with the Opening of Japan, a time when fearless Japanese fishermen tossed books with pornographic pictures up for the Yankee sailors to the disgust of their prissy officers and chaplains and traded fish for whatever they might get, while the rest of the country was thrown into a tizzy as terrified land and tradition-bound authorities and those who served them worked round the clock to throw up ramparts of fake forts on the hills overlooking the river Perry ascended. It would seem only two of the four "black ships" were steam-powered and even those were only partly steam-powered to supplement the sails, but no matter, the fact Japanese already had a word for such ships, *jôkisen*, that could be punned into the name-brand tea Jôkisen (up-joy-select), is in itself proof of how ready Japan was for the greater world. The second best known of these drop-head poems was the bothersome martial mosquitoes attributed to Ôta we saw in the last chapter. Now we will see more. The first two concern happenings in the reign of Nobunaga, the first shôgun to more or less unify Japan.

金銀をつかい捨てたる馬ぞろえ　将棋に似たる王の見物　安楽庵策伝　醒睡笑より
kingin o tsukai-sutetaru uma-zoroe shôgi ni nitaru ô no mimono pseudonym? c 1581
gold silver+acc using-throw-away horse-parade shôgi/chess-to resembles king's spectacle

> *Gold and silver thrown away for what! Horse play?*
> *Royal spectacle indeed! A chessboard walks today.*

In spring of 1581, Japan's first unifier Nobunaga put on the most spectacular parade anyone had seen. Recently obtained gifts from the West were in it. The generalissimo rode his favorite, a magnificent Arabian the Visitador Valignano S.J. had wisely, though at great expense, obtained for him in the horse parade, & showed-off his borrowed Africans (men). The *chess* is *shôgi,* like our "chess," a variant of China's second best board game (*go* being the best), including knights & elephants (our castle). In the original, throwing away precious metals for the gorgeously adorned array of horses shifts into chess, suggesting facetiously the sacrifices entailed in the game. The anonymous Idle Hut 安楽庵 poet evidently had mixed feelings about the wasteful pomp most people seem to have liked.

花よりも団子の京となりにけり けふもいしいしあすもいしいし
hana yori mo dango no kyô to narinikeri kyô mo ishi ishi asu mo ishi ishi anon 『寒川入道筆記』
blossom-more-than-dumpling-capital has become! today ishix2 tomorrow ishix2

> *In Kyôto has it come to pass that dumplings beat blossoms, at last?*
> *Today, it's "ishi!" "ishi!" and tomorrow will be no ishier!*

Nobunaga, not knowing he would be assassinated before long, set about making the mother of all castles for his selected heir in 1569. That required an enormous quantity of huge stones. It was like building a pyramid, though this king, unlike a pharaoh, tied a tiger hide to his waist (or wore it as a cloak, I forget) he could sit upon, and played foreman, barking orders himself. Stone is *ishi*. So, too, *dumplings* (usually *dango*) in wifely argot (女房詞), as is the pronunciation of *oishi* or "yummy" in this capital city famed for its flowers more than wealth or food (which mercantile Osaka boasted). As a laid-back place, it was the antithesis of the saying "dumplings beat blossoms" or *food over bloom*. All this activity, evoked by the triple pun *ishi* used as a mimetic adverb, evidently bothered the anonymous poet, as did the hardening of what had been the soft capital (except for the mountains of warrior monks who Nobunaga slaughtered).

上からは明治だなどといふけれど 治明と下からは読む 無名
ue kara wa meiji da nado to iu keredo osarumei to shita kara wa yomu
above-from-as-for meiji is etc. said, but control-not as below-from read

> *Though from above, Meiji reads* meiji, *i.e., "brilliant rule" —*
> *From below, it's* osamarumei: *"Control? Who do they think they fool!"*

After hundreds of years of the Tokugawa shogunate, the reformation of the government into an Imperial state with democratic features and a mandate to modernize before colonialization by the power-hungry Occident was not easy. The new state's first era was called Meiji. As always, everywhere, the bottom had it hardest. One way to show resentment was to mess with names. Meiji 明治 was reversed 治明 (with vectors of vertical writing, *up/down*). The name of an embassy sent abroad to renegotiate unequal treaties that found it tough going and compromised to buy time was even more brilliantly pun-criticized by a patriotic *rakushu*: 条約は結び損ない金奪られ世間に対して何といわくら *jôyaku wa musubi-sokonai kin ubaware sekken ni taishite nan to iwakura*. Translation is impossible. A gloss = *the treaty itself was left unmade, our gold was stolen, how do you explain that to the public?!* As far as I know, the Iwakura Embassy did need the money for expenses and the criticism was unfair, but public anger at having to bear continued discrimination is understandable. (♪For more squibs and poems between *rakushu* & *kyôka*, see the *Parrot Cage* added to the *History*).

An Older World: Bamboo Ponies from Childhood

懐旧　またがりし乳母が脊中を正真の馬と見し世ぞ　今は恋しき　蜀山人
kaikyû *matagarishi uba ga senaka o seishin no uma to mishi yo zo ima wa koishiki* shokusanjin d.1823
reminiscence // straddled wet-nurse's back+acc true horse-as saw+exclam now-as-for dear

♪Longing for Bygone Days♪

<table>
<tr><td>

How dear it was
those golden years I sat
upon her back
and Nanna was for me
My genuine war pony!

</td><td>

What a memory,
Those days when the ponies
we straddled
that felt so real, were only
The fannies of our nannies!

</td></tr></table>

蜀山人家集　附　網雑魚巻七　雑の部

The word "war" is not in the poem, but to any boy, ponies were largely about imagined military campaigns. While Japan was still isolated and at peace, the Kansei Reform's martial arts education and more recent altercations with rogue Russian traders helped create a vigilant mood. I write this because, thanks to the person/numberless language, we cannot rule out a collective statement. But, it is unlikely. There was a long tradition of poets recalling childhood. Those by the most famous *waka* poet of them all, Saigyô (1118-90), may be the best:

竹馬を杖にも今日はたのむかな わらわ遊びをおもひいでつつ　西行
takeuma o tsue ni mo kyô wa tanomu kana warawa asobi o omoiide tsutsu saigyô
stilt+acc cane-as-even today-as-for depend/pray!/?/: children's play+acc remembering-as

I put my faith in a bamboo pony as my cane, today,
Living together with memories of child-play.

Stilts in the Sinosphere are *"bamboo horses."* A later *kyôka* counsels a man celebrating his ordination as a monk at the hour of the first-horse to walk about on a bamboo pony so that happiness will ride into his new life 初午に元服するを賀して　竹馬を初午にせし元服は　さあ仕合ものつてきませふ　柳因　狂歌戒の鯛 *takeuma o hatsu-uma ni . . .* Ryûin (c1737). I have always liked the idea of taking a coincidence literally to make a figurative appeal, that is, *sympathetic magic*.

我もさぞ庭のいさごの土遊び さて生ひたてる身にこそありけれ　西行
ware mo sazo niwa no isago no tsuchi-asobi sate ôitateru mi ni koso arikere saigyô
me even! garden children's dirt/mud/clay play, yes age=living self/body-w/ esp. am 12c

I, too, am ever the little child in the garden at play;
The older I get, the more I feel at home with clay.

~~~~~~~~~~~~~~~~~~~~~~~~~~~~~~~~~~~~~~

I guess I am a thing of mud the kids make in play,
for I must animate myself each and every day!

The verb describing Saigyô's *aging* body is written with the character for *live* or *grow* or *energize*, 生 while the pronunciation *oi* allows it to be *aging* 老, which is the reading suggested by the context (coming before the *body-self* 身 *mi*), despite the different character. If my second reading, *by any chance*, hits the mark, it may be worth something, as more than sheer nostalgia animates the poem!

われら事たしかにかりの命ながら 千年ふるとも返済はいや 蜀山人
warera koto tashika ni kari no inochi nagara chitose furu to mo henzai wa iya shokusanjin
our thing surely borrowed life while thousand-years pass even return-as-4 yuck!

述 懐

That we and ours are only borrowed lives, we know for a fact,
But though a 1000 years may pass, we hate to give them back.

◆ ◆ ◆ ◆ ◆

Yes, of course, life is only mine on loan, but though
A 1000 years might pass, hell if I'd just let it go!

The caption for the poem is the same as that for the chapter lead 述懐 *jukkai*. I always thought of it as *nostalgia*, because poems it follows are usually sweet if not maudlin reminiscence. But, this *kyôka* sent me to the dictionaries where I found out, *oops!* that one meaning of the term was simply expressing those deep feelings that bubble up. Maybe it should be translated *con sentimento*. Still, for what reasons I cannot say, that caption pulls me out into a larger space and time. So, rather than reading old Shokusanjin's poem as the selfishness of one who is being stingy about *ever* giving back his life, I step back and feel a greater *nostalgia for life, itself*. So, for now, I will not try to English the caption. Were there an empty space in one of the chapters on aging or attitudes toward death, this poem and the next would probably have gone there not here, but the similarity of Shokusanjin to Saigyô attracted me. The former at age sixty-six:

更に文化十一年、六十六歳の「吉書初」に曰く。蜀山歌集
詩を作り歌を詠みしも昔にて芋ばかり喰ふ秋の夜の月 蜀山人
shi o tsukuri uta o yomishi mo mukashi nite imo bakari kuu aki no yoru no tsuki
chinese-rhymes making, poems composing, too oldtimes-in yam alone eat fall night moon

年をとつては、詩や歌もうるさくなる
As I age, even making poems becomes a pain in the ass.

Writing poems and rhyming tunes,
when, once upon a time, I was happy
just eating my potatoes with the moon.

I made the Chinese style poems 詩 "rhyming tunes," as they almost always *do*. We can see what makes *kyôka's* first man so likeable and we will soon see much more of him. But first, Saigyô. We need to see more of his work, because his *waka* show the mad wit associated with *kyôka* was in the mainstream all along.

The Monk Who Cried Rivers
& Turned into a Pond of Tears

よしさらば涙の池に身をなしてこころのままに月をやどさむ 西行
yoshi saraba namida no ike ni mi o nashite kokoro no mama ni tsuki o yadosamu
fine, then tear-pond-into body/self+acc making, heart's freely moon+acc+emph lodge 12c

*If such is to be
I might as well become
a pond of tears,*

*So I may see the moon
always has room in me!*

*If that's the case
I might as well become
a pond of tears,*

*The better to see Luna
whenever it pleases me.*

The moon in Japanese poetry has *always* taken up lodging (*yadoru*) here there and everywhere. What is fresh here is how Saigyô actively puts it up (*yadosu*), and what makes it a mad poem to my mind is the way the usual watery residence of the moon (for lovers, anyways), *i.e.,* the unmentioned wet sleeves, are expanded beyond anything anyone had ever done. And the very next poem in his *Sankashû* anthology (a 22-9 split) seems to show us why he left sleeves out of it:

うちたえてなげく涙に我が袖の朽ちなば なに月をやどさむ
uchitaete nageku namida ni waga sode no kuchinaba nani tsuki o yadosamu
active-enduring grieving tears-by my sleeves rot/ted-when/if what moon+acc lodge?

*If all the tears
I shed trying to endure
the unendurable
should rot away my sleeves –
How, then, to keep the Moon?*

Saigyô started playing with his tears (*namida*) a score of poems earlier in the love song section of his *Sanka-shû* (assuming it is chronological, but I do not know). The first example to catch my eye, was this:

寄水鳥恋 我が袖の涙かかるとぬれであれなうらやましきは池のをし鳥
waga sode no namida kakaru to nure de are na urayamashiki wa ike no oshidori 同
my sleeves' tears get-on and damp/wet are! envious-as-for pond's mallard/s

*When my tears run
down my sleeves, they get wet
And I think Ducks
have all the luck, floating high
and dry as the day they met!*

This one did not seem as mad as the first two poems introduced. My first two translations, despite or because of the added words (*When salty tears / stain the sleeves of my robe/ then how I envy // The brace of mallards afloat / in a pond of cool water* and *How lucky to be / love ducks afloat in a pond / backs dry as bone // Instead of wearing sleeves / steeped in teardrops, alone.*) killed it and I am unsure why my last try was not a third strike but a hit, maybe even a home-run! *Mallards* are exemplars of conjugal fidelity in the Sinosphere predating literacy in Japan. I *duck*ed them for the rhyme with *luck*, which together with *"have all the ~"* gives the English equivalent of Japanese *envy*, which, expressed openly and often by Japanese, is not unpleasant in the least. Providing detail on two characteristics of these loving birds left no space for the unnecessary "pond."
..

寄紅葉恋　わが涙しぐれの雨にたぐへばや紅葉の色の袖にまがへる
waga namida shigure no ame ni taguebaya momiji no iro no sode ni magaeru 同
my tears shigure rain-to equate-if crimson/maple-leaf colored sleeve-to morph

Were my tears of the pluvial ilk called shigure,
My silken sleeves would be crimson as the leaves today!

These clever tears preceded the *mallards* by three poems. Saigyô is taking one old Japanese conceit, that the cold showers called *shigure* dye the fall foliage and alluding to another Chinese conceit that heart-felt tears sometimes come out blood-red. Unlike the Chinese conceit, which is gruesome when you think about it, this whimsical hypothesis is charming. I feel such facetious metaphor is mad.

もの思ふ涙や　やがてみつせ河　人をしづむる淵となるらむ　西行 同
mono-omou namida ya yagate mitsusegawa hito o shizumuru fuchi to naruramu saigyô
thing-thinking tears!/: eventually mitsuse river person+acc sink/drown depth/pool-into become

Tears shed of longing pool and by and by leave one in a fix
Deep enough a man can drown and cross the River Styx.

In the reading-copy edition, Saigyô's poem was translated: *"Shed long enough / desire's tears crest higher / than the River Styx // That is they fill a deep pool / to drown your love-sick fool."* and *"Longing for love / tears rise and, by and by / The River Styx! // Water so deep you can / kiss your ass goodbye!"* Out of frustration at not being able to re-create the pun on the name of the river crossed on the journey to the underworld, Mitsusegawa, where Mitsu is a homophone for "to deepen," I used too much slang. The above is better.

松山の涙は海に深くなりてはちすの池にいれよとぞ思ふ　西行 同
matsuyama no namida wa umi ni fukaku narite hachisu no ike ni ireyo to zo omou
pine=wait-mount's tears-as4 ocean-into deep becoming lotus-pond-into put-will!

When tears shed on Pine Hill become as deep as the sea
Using them to fill a pond of lotus appeals to me!

This is followed by a yet madder poem with Saigyô still *waiting* (*matsu*, a homophone of "pine") *for lotus to grow in his pond to still the waves in his heart!*

The Man with a Wailing Baby in His Heart
君したふ心のうちは ちごめきて涙もろに/く?もなる我が身かな 西行
kimi shitau kokoro no uchi wa chigomekite namida moro ni/ku? mo naru waga mi kana saigyô
you/lord/lover(4) yearning heart-within-as-4 infantile tears maudlin+emph. becomes myself! 12c

*Within my heart
that yearns for thee, what's this,
a little baby?*

*Love has turned me into tears,
a study in maudlinity!*

Namida moroku means "tear-fragile," *i.e.* teary. The original is not so mad as my reading, for *chigomekite*, is baby*ish*, or infantile – not *a* baby. But the term is odd enough to pardon such liberty. Because this *waka* is oft-praised for demonstrating Saigyô's straight creativity, as opposed to the puns and play with old conceits we have seen that tend to be ignored as unbecoming a major poet, you may find a better translation of this poem elsewhere; but you will not find most of Saigyô's heart poems unless you read Japanese or my books. A score or so may be found in *Cherry Blossom Epiphany* (2007), half in chapter 46, *Soul/heart/mind Blossoms* 花の心, the last of Book II, *Drinking in the Bloom-shade*. Why so many slashes? Because the connotation of *kokoro* 心 is broader than that of *heart*, and includes *mind* and *spirit*. Yet, note also that Saigyô's *waka* are full of the mind-body separation so often described by scholars of both the pop and academic variety as an Occidental peculiarity, perhaps dreamed up by Descartes. Saigyô's heart *leaves his body* for the blooming trees, *waits for him* after they fall, laments their falling and *stays behind* at Yoshino *to seed the next Spring* – if anyone knows a more elaborate separated heart metaphor not about love between humans, please let me know! – and he *even needs to remind it to come back to him* after the wild cherry blossoms fall. This man was *a metaphysician of the heart*, yet, unlike metaphysical poets in English, never applauded, much less recognized for his extensive body of heart trope. Some of his cherry blossom-viewing hearts are mad enough to merit inclusion here but you would enjoy them more in a more blossomy context, so I defer. Not all of Saigyô's metaphor are mad,

涙川さかまくみをの底ふかみみなぎりあへぬ我がこころかな 西行
namidagawa sakamaku mio no soko fukami minagiri aenu waga kokoro kana
tear-river turbulent current bottom deep overflowing pitiful my heart!

*River of Tears, the turbulence runs so deep it cannot stay
Beat by the undertow, my heart is swept away!*

In my translation, this *seems* novel enough to be mad, but having read scores of older *tear-rivers* and *drifting hearts*, I would say he has only refined some details, such as adding the undertow. His *ponds* impress me more. The only Tear River poem I really like may be in *Tales of Ise*, where a Casanova who claims to be *awash in tears* is told, *"If so, why haven't they carried you away?"* I say *may be* for I could not re-find it and suspect I may have paraversed it myself from another telling a cry-baby would-be lover to go ahead and die. *When your imagination exceeds your memory . . .* The following heart poem is another story.

末の世の人の心をみがくべき玉をも塵にまぜてけるかな 西行
sue no yo no hito no kokoro o migakubeki tama o mo chiri ni mazetekeru kana saigyô
end of world's people's heart+acc polish-ought gem+acc+emph. rubbish-w/ mix-tumble!

*These are end times;
We need to polish our minds
as we would gems,*

*By mixing in some rubbish
to properly tumble them*

心 is still a *kokoro*, but *polish,* in English, wants a "mind" rather than a "heart." Usually, a *tama* (gem) puns on *soul* but, here, it is a concrete metaphor as well. Were the idea of mixing with bad elements to purify oneself an excuse for drinking in a bad bar, this could be a Tenmei era *kyôka.* As is, Saigyô seems to have composed an *apologia* for Wide Way Buddhist doctrine, maybe Pure Land. The poem is mad in the sense most clever moral poems (*dôka*) are.

心をば見る人ごとにくるしめて 何かは月のとりどころなる
kokoro o ba miru hito goto ni kurushimete nanika wa tsuki no toridokoro naru
heart+emph / viewing person-each-by torturing / what-as-for moon's draw-point is

*Torture is her art
Blues so personal she crafts,
They fit your heart!*

*Luna, author of this harm
What's the secret of your charm?*

I like this *wild waka* so much, I want to make a hundred translations. Some would have "attracts," at least one would rhyme "folly" and "melancholy," and all would play with this paradox only bold Saigyô, who courted and cultured melancholy – "masochism," too? – could have made explicit.

*In heart's room,
We are tormented each
a different way.*

*So, what is it that draws
us, crying, to the moon?*

*Reading hearts,
to each of us, she brings
a separate gloom;*

*So, what is it that draws
all men to view the moon?*

Saigyô, like metaphysical poets in the West, covered all angles, and one was that he did not seek loneliness: *In a world where the moon doesn't cloud & flowers don't die, / My melancholy blues & I will kiss and say goodbye!* (花ちらで月はくもらぬ世なりせば 物を思はぬわが身ならまし 西行 *hana chira de tsuki wa kumoranu yo nariseba mono o omowanu waga mi naramashi.* ♪The *kissing+goodbye* are *mine.*)

An Aside on Maudlinity and the Treatment of Tears

歎けとて月やは物を思はする かこち顔なる我が涙かな　西行　百人一首
nageke tote tsuki ya wa mono o omowasuru kakochigao naru waga namida kana saigyô
lament! as-if/says moon!/?-as-for thing-thinking-make sad/long-faced becomes my tears!

'Suffer!' Is *that* what Luna wants by making me blue?
The bitter tears on my long face say it is true!
~~~~~~

*How could it be that a man as tough as Saigyô
should melt into tears at the sight of the moon?*

what reason/cause? saigyô extent strong-braveman-a, moon/moonlight by/in crestfallen cries
nani yue ka saigyô hodo no kyôyû ga tsuki no kage nite shioshio to naku shokusanjin c.1790
何ゆへか西行ほどの強勇が月の影にてしほしほとなく　蜀山人　狂歌百人#86

Like one losing oneself in troubled thoughts, usually romantic, or, to use the Japanese, "thinking-things," I do not know where to start. *First*, I must confess that this poem from Shokusanjin's *Kyôka Hundred Poets One Poem* contradicts my earlier assertion that Saigyô, unlike Tsurayuki, has been pardoned his imagined sins of the sort Japanese considered Chinese and the Occident equally distastefully, belittled as Byzantine. Here Saigyô, who was, before becoming a monk, not only a noble but one with a fierce warrior pedigree (北面の武士), is accused, albeit in play, of having become effeminized. *Second*, the accusation was not invented by Shokusanjin. He has a forerunner in the Naniwa (greater Ôsaka area) *kyôka* master Teiryû, who also did a parody of *Hundred Poets*:

なけゝとて土やは物を思はする　あゝ西行は こんな坊ンさまか　貞柳
nageke tote tsuchi-yawamono o omowasuru aa saigyô wa konna bon-sama ka
lament/suffr?/! says earth/damn weaklng+acc think-make, aah, saigyô-as4 this boy?

*'Suffer!'? – That makes us imagine a weakling, not a tough!
Was Saigyô a spoiled monk not made of sterner stuff?*

This *kyôka* includes vernacular disparagement, disappointment and irony, not to mention fine parody, i.e., warped mimicry in the first part, such as turning the moon, *tsuki* into *tsuchi*, or "dirt," a term of disparagement (i.e. 土凡夫) and parts of speech (~ ya wa) into "weak" (*yawa*), . . . If I could English the style, Teiryû's *kyôka* would have headed the chapter. *Third,* there is a *senryû* temporally between these poets which says it all very well indeed in only 17-syllabets.

かこち顔見かねて定家集に入れ (don't have coll. name or date)
kakochigao mikanete teika-shû ni ire [teika ↓ = the 100 poet editor]
wretched/accusatory-face see-cannoting teika-collection-in included

Unable to bear his wretched face, Teika included his poem

When you read the chapters on/of Shokusanjin's *Kyôka Hundred Poet* parody later, recall this *senryû*, for it pioneers the meta-parody style of his freshest work. *Fourth,* the need to explain away Saigyô's maudlinity was felt earlier. The *kyôka* for this poem #86 in the 1669 *Dog Hundred Poets* (犬百人一首) has the *wine* rather than moon encouraging him to abandon himself and end up with a face full of drunken tears (あがけとて酒やは物に狂はする　酔泣がおの我なみたかな　酔狂法師 (佐心子賀近) *agake tote sake ya wa mono ni kuruwasuru ei-nakigao no waga namida kana*　Gakin.　Bashô, who loved Saigyô, would have been 25 when this was published. *Fifth*, Saigyô's poem is itself pretty mad. I actually toned it down a bit. See Carter's translation: *"As if to tell me, / 'Grieve on!' the moonlight shines down – / but that cannot be. / Yet still that is where my tears / seem to want to look for blame."* Of course, the original *means* that tears are what gives the poet the appearance of being someone teary with anger and love; but the construction does literally *seem* to give tears something a sea cucumber lacks, a brain.　Carter is, on the whole, a conservative translator; you can rest assured that the original is quite outlandish, even if he more boldly yet qualifies the same with *"but that cannot be."* Yet, on the page next to Saigyô's live tears, he timidly translates Monk Dôin (Fujiwara no Atsuyori, b.1090): *"Though deep in despair, / I have not yet felt my life / drained away by love; / but less resistant to pain / are my ever-flowing tears."* (*omoiwabi sate mo inochi wa aru mono o uki ni taenu namida narikeri*). Your mad translator will take it elsewhere – a) In the original *uki*, the suffering, puns as *floating*, so the dog-paddling poet is in danger of drowning despite himself, thanks to those weakling tears; or b) *taenu* means *cannot bear*, which for tears means "flowing" to be sure, but where Carter creates the lachrymal equivalent of a phlebotomy (the wealthy were often bled to death), I imagine the tears as rats fleeing a sinking ship.

> *Love has me down, but though I'm not yet finished off, I fear*
> *I must keep swimming to stay afloat: I cannot stop my tears!*

~ a ↑ ~~~~~~ ↓ b ~

> *Though deep in despair, love or not, I know I can make it,*
> *but my tears are another thing – They cannot take it!*

Where are we? Ah, *sixth* – are Saigyô's tears *that* exceptional? I have not read 3000 waka by any other man of his time. As we have seen, the *Kokinshû* (905) abounds in clever tear metaphor.　I have barely looked at many large anthologies that may contain floods of weepers.　Take these two by Anon. from the *Kokin waka-rokujô* (古今和歌六帖 c.985) found recently, thanks to Cranston:

hitorine no toko ni tamareru namida ni wa ishi no makura mo ukinubera nari
single-sleep-to bed-in gather tears-by-as-for stone-pillow/s even float-up/away be

> When I sleep alone, / In my bed the tears collect, / And on such a tide /
> Even a pillow of stone / Will surely rise and float.　tr. Cranston 2a

> *The teary flood that fills the bed of one who sleeps alone*
> *Can levitate a pillow, though it be of stone!*

~~~~~~

Nakitsumeshi fuyu no namida wa kôri ni ki token haruhi wa mi mo ya nagaren
cried packed-in winter tears-as4 froze-to-came+emph melt-will spring-sun/day-as4

> Cranston tr.: The winter tears / That I wept a riverful / Have frozen solid; /
> When the thaws of spring begin, / Will my whole body flow away?

> *The tears I cried all winter-long have frozen en masse;*
> *On a sunny spring day, will I just melt and run away?*

Humorous Slobber in a Sober 1205 Collection?

君がせぬわが手まくらは草なれや涙の露の夜な夜なぞ置く 光孝院 skks #1349
kimi ga senu waga tamakura wa kusa nare ya namida no tsuyu no yo na yo na zo oku mitsutaka?
you/lord/dear do-not my arm-pillow-as4, grass became tear-dew's night after night+emph sets c1205

The pillow your arm did not make made mine turn into grass
Night after night, tears run like dew, settling en masse.

Shinkokinshû is known for discontinuing the classic tradition of comic poem sections, but I note that in book 15, near the end of the fifth and last book (or chapter) on love=*koi*, we have a score of weepers many of which are witty if not risible. Some of them may even merit comparison with *kyôka* on the same subject.

露ばかり置くらむ袖はたのまれず涙の川の瀧つせなれば　無名#1350 読人不知
tsuyu bakari okuramu sode wa tanomarezu namida no kawa no takitsu senareba anon
dew only/amount setting sleeve-as-for depend-cannot, tear-river-waterfalls do-not-if

Who can trust a lonely sleeve that is only damp with dew?
I would be swept away by a cataract of tears from you.

1351 has seemingly sympathetic rain fall on colored leaves and 1351 has the poet get close to someone only to find the leaves changed their color/heart. Estrangement, I guess, but, *no, it's no typo:* there are *two* 1351's in some editions. As a. and b. are イ and ロ and read *iro* or *color/emotion/charm* in Japanese it seems an almost Tristam Shandy arrangement. 1352 (1353 in some eds. and so forth down the line) follows that fading or unfaithful love line with Lady Sagami's *Seeing the color of the lower leaves change on the clover, / We see one who fell in love, fall out: our harvest is over.* 色かはる萩の下葉を見てもまづ人のこころの秋ぞ知らるる　相模 *iro kawaru hagi no . . .*), setting up her next, 1353, as assurance to an anxious lover, *Not a night passes when the faint light of heat-lightning / like a visible phantom does not glow softly somewhere.* 稲妻は照らさぬ宵もなかりけりいづらほのかに見えしかげろふ *inazuma wa terasanu yoi mo nakari . . .*). Thinking of the way *lightning* is written *rice-wife* and *rice* is homophonous with *country*, I think I'd title it *Your Rice-wife in the Country*. Then, I'd title the next *Your Poet in the Palace.* It takes us back to *tears*, though I must admit they are pure *waka;* but that is followed by an ex-Emperor's masterpiece, which may be called a *kyôka*.

人知れぬ寝覚の涙ふり満ちてさもしぐれつる夜半の空かな 伊尹 koretada
hito shirenu nesame no namida furi-michite sa mo shiguretsuru yowa no sora kana
people know-not sleep-waking tears falling like+emph showering late-night sky!/? #1354

My tears at dawn well up and fall: who ever knows of them?
Think of me as the night-sky, raining when no one listens.

涙のみうき出づる蜑の釣竿の長き夜すがら恋ひつつぞぬる 光孝院 #1355
namida no mi uki-izuru ama no tsurizao no nagaki yosugara koitsutsu zo nuru kôkô-in
waves/teary body floatng-up shellfishr's gig/harvestng-pole's lengthy nght-long lnging-while sleep

Teary me, a diver pops up from the sea, her shellfish pole
Long but not so long as this night of longing for my soul.

まくらのみ うくとおもひしなみたかは いまはわかみのしつむなりけり 是則
makura nomi uku to omoishi namidagawa   ima wa waga mi no shizumunarikeri korenori
pillow only floats so i thought, tear-river now-as-for my body/self's sinking-am+enph! # 1356

> *I thought only pillows floated down a stream of tears;*
> *So what is happening to me! Am I not sinking, bodily?*

The *mi* in the middle poem, the masterpiece, with the *no* can mean "only" (I'm all tears) but, then becomes *myself* when the corporal connotation is brought out by floating up – *uki*, homophonous with being *depressed* – as a diver, no, a diver's long pole brings to mind the mountain-bird's long tail on Hitomaro's famous poem (pg.290). This, by retired Emperor #58 is not parody but improvement as this pole is used for hard work in the cold and wet sea which evokes the "sleep," *nuru,* homophonous with *wet* and takes us back to the teary start.

おもほえす そてにみなとの さわくかな もろこしふねのよりしはかりに
omoboezu sode ni minato no sawagu kana morokoshibune no yorishi bakari ni anon♪
aware-not sleeve-in port's clamor!/?/: chinese ships' approaching amount-with #1357

> *Before I knew, my sleeves had become ports, busy ones!*
> *Big enough for deep-draft Chinese junks on trading runs.*
> ~~~~~~~~~~
> *Before I knew, my sleeve became a very busy Watergate;*
> *It harbored even Chinese junks, with their monster wake.*

This *is* a poem about tears. Chinese boats were once by far the largest in the world. Next to them, our galleons would have looked like pints. The wake would swamp other boats and wet the sleeves/clothing of people on shore. *Watergate* is a transliteration on the philological meaning of *minato,* or harbor/port. #1358 picked up on that sleeve but lets us down, for it is boring. Better to have gone straight to #1359, a new twist on marine trope: *Meeting makes waves, below which the sea-grass, where we hide / Tears loose from the bed and floats, giving our hearts no respite.* 逢ふことのなみの下草みがくれてしづ心なくねこそなかるれ *au koto no nami no shitakusa mi-gakurete . . .*anon). And that led to the beach and a new tooth on another old saw, salt-making-smoke-as-bitter-memories: *That acrid smoke from burning seaweed for salt will not sink down;/ It rises up to black the sky though winds may blow from all around!* 浦にたく藻塩のけぶり靡かめや 四方のかたより 風は吹くとも #1361 *ura ni taku mo-shio no keburi nabikame ya . . .*anon). Lost in translation: the location, a bay=*ura* evokes *melancholy* from the homophonic *ura* as *back-side* (wrong side of the tracks, hidden aspects, etc.)♪ The next took the smoke, by pun (remember, this was the age haikai link-verse started) and we leave tears for other expressions of sad love for a while. Then, . . Jakuren!

涙川身も浮きぬべき寝覚かなはかなき夢のなごりばかりに　寂蓮 skks
namidagawa mi mo ukinu beki nesame kana hakanaki yume no nagori bakari ni jakuren
tear-rvr body/self float-seems awakenng!/: transient/empty drm's/s' detritus only-to #1385

> *River of Tears, it carries you out to sea, but then you wake*
> *alone with nothing but the flotsam and jetsam of dreams.*
> ~~~~~~~~~~
> *Down a river of tears I float and waking find I lie ashore*
> *Alone with the detritus of my dreams and nothing more.*

Silly as Saigyô: pre-1310 *waka* weepers *4* perspective 上

いまはとて なみたのうみに 梶をたえ 沖にわつらふ けさの舟ひと　後京極攝政夫木
ima wa tote namida no umi ni kaji o tae oki ni wazurau kesa no funabito go-kyôgoku 1169-1206
now-as-for and/say, tear-ocean-in rudder+acc end/broken/lost, offshore distressed morning's boatman

Sailor on a sea of tears at dawn and what's more, rudder broken off, now I cannot come ashore!

Writing in my short and broad history (at the book's end) of *kyôka* about how most old poems ridiculous enough to be considered mad are *waka* about love, the madness of which is taken for granted, and therefore not thought of as *kyôka*, it occurred to me that my claim was weakened by introducing many poems by Shikibu, Saigyô, and Lady Daibu, that might be excused(?) as the product of exceptionally creative minds, and few by others. So, I thought to interject a chapter of *waka* culled from the 1310 *Fuboku* collection. I opened the book where a piece of toilet paper happened to be marking poems with the *ocean* (*umi*) in them because I have a half-finished book on marine poems, and the first to catch my eye because I had 泪(tears) scribbled by it, was the above. Sitting on the john (freedom before heading out to feed the cows), I slowed down to read the source – all the poems in this anthology are sourced, though I rarely give that in this book – and discovered the above by Go-kyôgoku (d.1206) was but one of a hundred poems in *The Sea of Tears of Parting* 後朝恋涙の海, by a novice monk. It is possible, though not likely, that all the poems feature oceanic metaphor! The above is an example of the Japanese style where the entire poem modifies the subject that comes last: here, the boatman. I like the slightly odd personal twist at the start that a conservative editor would hate. The rudder is common enough in love poem metaphor but usually reserved for either the Seventh Night (*Tanabata*) when the Herder Star boats to his Weaver, or for the sounds of love-making. The next, three poems later, is better – paradoxically clever:

わか身こす涙の海にうくふねのゆたのたゆたにぬるゝそてかな　民部爵為家
waga mi kosu namida no umi ni uku fune no yutanotayuta ni nururu sode kana tameie
my body cover/exceeding tear-ocean-in floating boat's rocking by wetting sleeves!　同

How wet they are, my sleeves splashed by waves from the Sea of Tears breaking over me, a boat adrift, rocking endlessly!

Considering the source of the Sea of Tears, what could be sillier? Imagine a flipbook where *the crying poet* Minobe Tameie ends up tossed from the ark he built to save him from his self-induced flood to be eaten by a fish that grew in the same! The poem combines *tear* hyperbole with *Manyô* poem #122 metaphor, where a would-be lover pines away, heart rocking like one spending the night moored at a harbor for large boats. Tameie also wrote the most convoluted poem about dreaming in this book (p.83). His personal collection may be full of *kyôka*. The very next poem in the *Fuboku* collection is also made-for-flipbook : *As I sink below this sea of tears made of longing for you, / Like scum floating on water, puff goes my bubble of blues* (ひとこふるなみたの海にしつみつゝ水の沫とそおもひきえぬる 好忠 家集 *hito kouru namida no umi ni shizumitsutsu mizu no awa to zo omoi-kienuru*). The poet, Yoshitada is better known for this:

秋の野のくさむらごとにおくつゆはよるなくむしのなみだなるべし 好忠 詞花集
aki no no no kusamura goto ni oku tsuyu wa yoru naku mushi no namida narubeshi
autumn field's/s' grass-clumps-each-on place/d dew-as-for night crying bugs' tears are!/?

> *From dusk to dawn, all the grass and flowers caught 'em:*
> *The dew you see are the tears of bugs that cry in autumn!*
> ~~~~~~~~~~~~~~~~~~~~~~~~~~~~~~
> *On the leaves of plants that sprawl across the fields of fall,*
> *The dew. Could it be the tears of bugs that cried all night?*
> ~~~~~~~~~~~~~~~~~~~~~~~~~~~~~~
> *Heavy lies the dew in all unmown patches of the fields of fall,*
> *proof the bugs that cried last night waxed lachrymal.*

(又、よもすがらなくむしの涙か の七七)　This is not only *kyôka*, but a groaner. But let's get back to our ocean, the sea of human tears.

しくなみた ひとりやねなむ 袖のうら さわくみなとは よる舟もなし 家隆
shiku namida hitori ya nenamu sodenoura sawagu minato wa yoru fune mo nashi ietaka?

> *I'll just make tears my bed, and sleep in Sleeve Cove;*
> *As harbours go, it's busy, but no ship brings my Love.*
> ~~~~~~~~~~~~~~~~~~~~~~~~~~~~~~
> *Rivers of tears, flowing, descend into my bed – the Sea.*
> *My sleeve ports are busy, yes: melancholy's always wet.*

toko no umi ni nagarete-otsuru namida kawa sode no minato no sawagu na mo ushi tameie
とこのうみになかれておつるなみたかは そてのみなとのさわくなもうし 為家

In the *Shinkokinshû* poem, Chinese boats call, wetting the poet's – or singer's (it seems a song ♪) – sleeves. Here, many boats – splashing wakes implied – call, yet the Love-boat . . . Next, we are near the sea, with a brackish-water bird.

しるへなき 涙のかはの 河かせに おもひかねても ちとりをそきく 慈円
shirubenaki namida no kawa no kawakaze ni omoikanete mo chidori o zo kiku jien
guideless tears'river's riverbreeze-in thinking-cannot+emph. plovers+acc+emph hear

> *In the salt breeze blowing off Tear River, river with no guide,*
> *I never would have thought it, but I heard the plovers' cries!*
> ~~~~~~~~~~~~~~~~~~~~~~~~~~~~~~
> *Later tonight, I'll hear plovers on the banks of Tear River,*
> *Crying as they & I return; but this you won't know, dear.*

こよひこそ なみたのかはに ゐるちとり なきてかへると きみはしらすや 読人不知
koyoi koso namida no kawa ni iru chidori nakite kaeru to kimi wa shirazu ya anon
this evening esp. tear-river-in is plover crying return you-as-for know-not!

Jien's immediately previous poem #6781, *Waking from a sleep of longing late at night, the wind blew / and on the River of Tears – the plaintive plovers cried.* (おもひかぬる よはのねさめに かせふけて なみたのかはに ちとりなくなり *omoikanuru yowa no nesame ni kaze fukete . . .*) is probably the better *waka*, but "River with no Guide" is the more *kyôka*. The next *waka* by anon, #6783, strikes me as a probable folk song. It is also one of the best poems, period, in this book!

Silly as Saigyô: pre-1310 *waka* weepers *4* perspective 中

君なくて ひとりぬる夜の 床島は 寄するなみたそ いやしきりなる　よみびとしらず
kimi nakute hitori nuru yo no tokoshima wa yosuru namida zo iya shigerinaru　anon. 夫木
you/lord/dear not, alone sleepng night's bed-island-as4 approach tears+emph yuck/emph. freqent be

♪ *The Castaway's Lament* ♪

Without my love
marooned at night, my bed
becomes an isle;

Tears in waves erode the shore,
I'll be swimming in a while.

Desperately kicking to keep this masterpiece afloat, I came up with : *Without you, dear, marooned each night upon my Island Bed, / buffeted by tears, I shake: You'll find me swimming soon . . . or dead.* Ridiculous! *That* was the final straw. Oppressed by the weight of the loss in translation and fearing one tear poem after another largely limited to large bodies of water might drown the reader, I exiled the above and half a dozen more poems to the notes. Then, coming up with the *isle/while* rhyme, I reprieved it but not the others. By *swimming*, I hoped to make up for what could not be ferried across the linguistic divide. There are two losses in translation: *sleep=nuru=wet(yourself)* and *tears=nami ⇒ namida=waves*.

みなれかは わたすをふねに ことつてむ 涙にうくと 君にしらせよ　藤原章網
minaregawa watasu o fune ni kotozuten   namida ni uku to kimi ni shirase yo　akitsuna
wetness-used-to-river (p.n.?) crossing boat-to words-transmit! tears-upon floating you-to tell

I'm stuck in a river, the river is me – won't someone call a boat!
And tell my love/lord her/his sweetheart upon his/her tears doth float.

My first translation of this folksy Tear River attempted to English *minare*, meaning "used to being waterlogged" with *"I may be soaked already but . . . Someone, won't you call a boat! / . . .* It failed. Still. the *existence* of the one marvelous word eclipses all 200 varieties of Inuit snow. And, attached to river, Minare-gawa, it beats Dr. Lakoff's entire book of metaphor creating something that is simultaneously a river of tears *and* the *body=mi* of the lovesick poet. And now, a rarity: a poem English idiom *improves*, making up for loss of information. Akitsuna is male, but men could write as women; and "love" is not certain.

かくはかりせきわつらはは なみたかは　みやこのかたへ なかれいらなむ 長方
kakubakari sekiwazurawaba namida kawa miyako no kata e nagare-iranamu　nagakata?
thatmuch checkpoint bothered(by) tear-river   capital's person-to flowing enter not?

With checkpoints *causing us so much grief,* *River of Tears:*	*If the checkpoints* *are causing so much grief,* *I think you'd best*
Why not just keep running *to Kyôto – grab their ears!*	*Get thy Tear Rivers to run* *to the Capital for redress!*

The gain is in the *running*. Japanese rivers and watches do not "run." Here, as is often the case, cultural loss is no problem, so long as it is explained. It is enough to know that curfews and checkpoints around cities and within them made life hard for the roving lovers. The poem also teaches us that the capital had clout. It is uncertain whether the tears are being addressed directly or not. With Japanese poets writing from the point of view of either sex, the second reading assumes a woman in the Capital is kidding a lover stuck in the boondocks whom she does not necessarily want calling on her. Again, I think of the *Tale of Ise* exchange – possibly magnified in my mind – where a woman taunts a would-be Don Juan that were he really *that* pitiful a case, would his tears not have swept him out to sea rather than just wetting his pillow? Be that as it may, to me, the idea of putting Tear River to work is about as mad as mad can be. The *Miyako* (capital) in the original became Kyôto, as it *was* Kyôto and saved me a beat.

したとほるなみたにそてもくちはてて きるかひもなきあまころもかな 顕昭
shita tôru namida ni sode kuchihatete kiru kai mo naki amagoromo kana kenshô
below-passing tears-by sleeves rot-away, wearing worth nolonger raincoat is!/?

> *My clothing rots from within by the tears I would ignore;*
> *It makes no sense to wear my old rain-gear any more.*

Tears passing below, or within, do not start rumors but, like dew precipitating below a poorly ventilated floor, they can rot one from within. A more specialized variant plays on the sleeve-guard worn by traveling monks. *What have I done that under the protective guard of my sleeve / A rain of tears still falls, and even a monk must grieve?* (なにせんに我れかさすらし袖かさの下にそなみた雨とふりぬる 光俊 *nani sen ni ware kazasurashi sode . . .* mitsutoshi) A few centuries later, an out-and-out *kyôka* poet, Getsudôken, will make the above idea easier for us moderns to understand with his leaking eyes and a rain-hat (pg. 331). Ietaka:

とこはうみ まくらは山と なりぬへし 涙もちりも つもるうらみに 家隆 ietaka
toko wa umi makura wa yama to narinubeshi namida mo chiri mo tsumoru urami ni
bed-as4 oceans pillows-as4 mtn-into becme-should tears&dust build grudge/backbay-by d.1237

> *My Bed shall be the Sea, my Pillow a Peak – day after day,*
> *Bitter tears and lust-turned-dust compound by* Regret Bay.

This, like the lead poem, almost ended up in the notes. The way dust, *chiri*, for a second becomes *"falling"* tears is nice, but not important, but the lack of an *ura*, or *bay* with melancholic connotations, much less its expansion into an *urami* or overlook of said bay that is homophonic with *resentment/bitterness/grudge* is a killer. I had to "bitter" the tears, modify the dust – yes, I was thinking of "and into ashes all my lust" – and make the bay proper a proper name. I felt that all that panoramic and chronological development in one 31-syllabet poem was worthy of attention, so I kept it, but the losses in translation were so great, your translator is working on his own sad topography! The next needs no explanation:

うきひとに なみたのころも ひきかへし やとすとかたれ そてのつきかけ 為家
ukihito ni namida no koromo hikikaeshi yadosu to katare sode no tsukikage tameie 1310
woe(causing)person-to tear-robe remove-exchangng lodge & speak+imper. sleeve's moon

> *I would exchange my robe of tears with the one I love in vain;*
> *That done, Moon, lodge on her sleeve and tell her of my pain!*

Silly as Saigyô: pre-1310 *waka* weepers *4* perspective 下

なきかへる かりのなみたの つもるをや 苗代みつに 人はせくらむ 好忠 夫木
naki kaeru kari no namida no tsumoru o ya nawashiro mizu ni hito wa sekuramu yoshitada
cry/calling geese'tears' building-up+emph. (rice)paddies water-in people-as-for dam-up

> *And off they fly, crying as they go – could it be our paddies*
> *are made by damming streams of tears left by those geese?*

> *The showers pass with the fall wind and, from the treetops,*
> *Is that teardrops tinkling down? Bell-tone semi all around!*

fall wind-in shower-rain passes treetops-from tears dripping higurashi cicada's voice
aki kaze ni murasame suguru kozue yori namida shigururu higurashi no koe tameie
あきかせに むらさめすくる こすゑより なみたしくるるひくらしのこゑ 為家

The first *waka*, like most just-so stories, is wacky as a *kyôka*. After scores of love poems, natural(?) tears must be a relief. *Naki kaeru* might *also* mean "frogs cry" (they do croak grievously) but that's a long-shot. The second may *seem* mad if you have not heard this cicada, but as one who has been moved to tears by them, I would call it facetiously mad. My "tinkling down" rather than the original's "higurashi's voice" is meant to convey the crystalline clarity that people who think birds or humans the last word in mellifluous sound have yet to experience.

さゆるよに おつれはこほる なみたこそ まくらのもとの あられなりけれ 俊成
sayuru yo ni otsureba kôru namida koso makuranomoto no arare narikere shunzei
chilled night-on falling freeze tears esp. pillow/bed's base's hailstones become

> *On a cold night when any Tears that drop, freeze in the air,*
> *Look around my Pillow and you will see Hailstones there.*

> *I do not know exactly when my iced-up tears thawed out;*
> *But I, for one, can tell – Spring came early, beyond doubt.*

when tear-ice breaks/broke-apart year-within-in+emph. spring-as-4 arrives-ought
itsushika to namida no kôri uchitokete toshinouchi ni zo haru wa tatsubeki jien
いつしかとなみたのこほりうちとけて としのうちにそ はるはたつへき 慈円

Shunzei, if you recall, had spectacular *icicle* tears as well (pg.45). Add *slush* (*mizore*) and he will have covered all the salient tears of winter. Jien's spring "within the year=*toshi-no-uchi*" poem, madder than apparent at one read, reverses the usual causality having his thawing tears gauge the calendar. And, the *Fuboku* anthology did not forget Saigyô's lachrymal masterpiece (*yoshi saraba . . .*) which, once again – but in new translation – I'll give:

> *In that case, I'll turn myself into a pond of tears,*
> *And put up the Moon when and where I please!*

Moreover, it puts it right after a poem written about a hundred years earlier: *I wring my sleeves, and my eyes become ponds full of tears / Wanting to see him, I cried and cried aloud* そてはひち涙の池に目はなりてかけ見まほしき ねをのみそなく 成尋法師母 *sode wa hiji namida no ike ni me wa narite kage mi ma hoshiki ne o nomi zo naku.* "Him" here is "his *kage* meaning face but a word also used for a reflection, so it takes the double pond metaphor (wringing tears into it & eyes as ~) into the last half of the poem making it a hat trick. I was tempted to have her cries fill her ears or have them *swallow* her cries, but the original does not even have the wit of my *"cried and cried aloud."* It just says she cried aloud. The poet is in her eighties, her son, at age 62 had just departed for China and further religious study (入唐の時の歌). He died there at age 71, so chances are Jôjin's Mother did, indeed, never see him again.

おもへとも ひとめをつつむ なみたこそ おさへのいけとなりぬへらなれ
omoedomo hitome o tsutsumu namida koso osae no ike to narinuberanare anon
thinkng/lovng but people-eyes+acc avoidng tears most-of-all repress-pond as become!

When loving thoughts that I would hide from other people's eyes
Fill mine with tears, a place comes to mind: Chokeback Spring.
~~~~~~
Did someone hide from others eyes such thoughts that were too fond
Filling theirs with tears that after years made this Chokeback Pond?

Tsutsumu, or *conceal from discretion*, sounds like "wrap." We *also* have an eye wrapped in tears. That, the fact there doubtless was a real "Pond of Repression" (宮城県の「抑ノ池」か) and the im/personal polysemy were lost in translation. Now, let us return to the River and the *Hundred Poets* editor Fujiwara Teika.

なみた川 春の月なみ たつことに 身はしつみ木の したにくちつつ 定家 夫木
namidagawa haru no tsuki nami tatsu goto ni mi wa shizumi ki no shita ni kuchitsutsu teika
teariver sprng-moon/s sequence/wave arrive/rise each-w/ self/bdy-as4 sunkn tree-undr rottng-as

River of Tears,	*River of Tears,*
rising with each new moon	*waxing with the vernal moon,*
of spring, I know;	*waves spring up,*
For I, or rather my sleeves,	*I sink below: My sleeves,*
like sunken trees, rot below.	*trees on the riverbed, rot.*

The *nami* in the sequence of moons and their cycles, all in the word *tsukinami*, not only alliterates with *namida=tears,* but puns into *"nami:waves,"* which rise with the same verb, *tatsu,* the moons/months and Tear River do. The body/self *sinks*, presumably because of the chop on said river. No, not quite: *sinks* becomes a modifier for the tree that follows. That leads to rotting below (on the river-bed or bottom of the tree; little difference), alluding to the underwear or inner-sleeves of discreet maudlinity. With the unmentioned sleeve wet from repressed tears flowing from within, I think of a natural phenomenon which Erasmus Darwin was first to describe, namely the workings of an artesian spring.

こひわひて落るなみたのたまならは手箱の数もつきやしなまし 藤原雅親
koiwabite otsuru namida no tama naraba tebako no kazu mo tsuki ya shinamashi masachika
love-suffering fall-tears gems were-if treasureboxes number+emph exhaust would not?

If tear-drops born of hopeless love were counted as gems,
I would not have enough treasure chests to contain them!

I, who once penned a ditty with the words *"I'm bankrupt, I spent my last tear on you,"* cannot roll my eyes. There were far better 'tear' poems contending for this place, but this one is better proof that high and low poetry rubbed shoulders.

Silly as Saigyô: pre-1310 Wild *Waka* w/ Dust & Smoke

この世をも 後をもいかにいかにせん もえん 煙も むすほゝれつゝ　能宣朝臣　夫木
kono yo o mo ato o mo ika ni ika ni sen moen kemuri mo musubohoretsutsu　minister yoshinobu
this world+emph. after/behind+acc+emph. how-by do-should?/! burning smoke too choking-while p.1310

How can I leave this world behind, when burning makes smoke,
And smoke, well, . . . I hate the thought of having to choke!

~~~~~~~~~~~~~~~~~~~~~~~~~

I would be glad to leave this world, but how? All that smoke
would choke me long before I got out . . . and that's no joke!

~~~~~~~~~~~~~~~~~~~~~~~~~

How can I leave this world behind? I'll burn while I choke
of grief for my lord and, then, on both of our smoke!

~~~~~~~~~~~~~~~~~~~~~~~~~

What's to be done with our world and that to come
When we must choke on smoke in either one!

There is a caption: *"Telling some one of my secret aspiration"* (人しれぬ志あるひとにつかはしける). A desire to die? Or to accompany a dead Emperor? Or, does the "world after too" mean the next generation or reign in Japan? Does smoke imply incense offerings and not cremation? My last reading is all we *know*.

消かたき香のけふりのいつまてか立めくるへきこの世なるらん　寂蓮法師
kiegataki kô no keburi no itsu made ka tachimegurubeki kono yo naruran　jakuren d.1202
vanish-difficult incense's smoke's when-until stand/floating-circling-ought this world is!

~~Like the smoke of incense hard to put out that just hangs in the air,~~
~~How long can we count on this old world to be there!~~

~~~~~~~~~~~~~~~~~~~~~~~~~

Like the smoke of incense hard to put out that stays in the air,
How long will I hang around this world though my heart's not there?

Monk Jakuren composed the marvelous snail poem (pg.146), but *this* one re. impermanence (無常) is more like a *dôka,* or religious poem. The crossed-out reading may be grammatically possible, but is far too novel to be probable.

春ふかきまたきつけたる蚊遣火とみゆるはふしのけふり也けり　能宣
haru fukaki mata ki-tsuketaru kayari to miyuru wa fuji no keburi narireri　yoshinobu
spring deep again reviving mosquito-smudge-as looks/seems fuji's smoke is!　同

Spring grows late, and it comes once again – mosquito smudge, or
so seems this smoke from Fuji, the mountain that won't budge.

This by the same cabinet minister who wrote the chapter lead was composed for a smoking Fuji painted on a folding screen. *Fuboku* includes a *smudge* poem by Izumi Shikibu (かやり火の煙けふたきあふくまによるは暑さもおほえさりけり *kayaribi no kemuri kebutaki abuku . . .*) who felt it made the night hot when the smoke "boiled" up via a pun in the name of a cool summering place, 阿武隈(川), followed by her warning to rural travelers 田舎行人に about what I took for pollution until my respondent pointed out it referred to her cremation: *Look on it as me! On the mountains around our capital / It might be stifling when my smoke climbs up!"*(それとみよ都のかたの山のはにむすほゝれたるけふりのほらは　泉式部 *sore to miyo* . . .). Or, as Dorothy Parker would put it – or *did* put it, *Pardon my ashes!* For whatever reason, poems about *chiri=dust/trash*, though fewer in number (thirteen total), were far better. Here are three gems:

いくちりの山をいくへに重ねてもけにわか 國はうこきなき世に　後一条入道関白
iku chiri no yama o ikue ni kasanete mo ge ni waga kuni wa ugoki naki yo ni atoichijô?
howmany dust-mts+acc hwmnylayers-in double really our cuntry-as4 move-not world-in 夫木

> *How much trash and how many mounds must pile up before*
> *Our country becomes a world that stays for ever more?*

The above (原典：千五百番名所百首) suggests to me an awareness of the mounds left by the ancients and the warm spirit of identifying with them.

君か代はひかりつきせぬ日の本に朝たつちりのかすもえしらず 花園左大臣小大進
kimigayo wa hikari tsukisenu hinomoto ni asa tatsu chiri no kazu mo e-shirazu palace woman
lord's reign-as4 light exhausts-not sun's-source-in rising dust's # even gainsay-not p.1348

> *Your majesty's reign: who can begin to count the grains of dust*
> *illuminated by the rays of the also rising sun!*
> ~~~~~~~~~~~~~~~~~~~~~~~~~~~~~~~~~~~~~~
> *In this land of the rising sun, even the number*
> *of dust grains aglow bespeaks the wonder of your reign.*

A light play on the famous Manyô *kokumi* (Imperial *country-viewing* ritual) poem-as-benediction, where smoke from hearths and birds rise into the sky. On a fine day, dust in sun-beams looks beautiful. It really does, yet is rarely so credited. The poet is a palace woman (only her rank is given) for poet Emperor Hanazono.

玉箒ほしをみるにもきみか代はちりをさまりていやさかへなん 權僧正公朝 家集
tama-hôki hoshi o miru ni mo kimigayo wa chiri osamarite iyasakaenan kenzô? 1264
gem/pretty-broom star+acc see-to/for-even lord's reign-as4 dust controlling, no, prospering!

> ~~*A fancy broom — in this age even when we view the stars:*~~
> ~~*Does it mean we've conquered dust? No, just multiplied it!*~~

I could only guess the meaning of what nonetheless seemed the most exciting of the thirteen dust poems. ~~Were the paper strips with wishes blown from the branches after the Seventh Eve, or is this preparation for the same? The poet is a monk and monks at temples did seem to sweep around alot. Does the poet dare complain too much sweeping causes dust to rise and blur the view of the stars? Or is this, rather, a poem about a comet?~~ Comets were, after all, called Star-brooms and tiny stars, dust . . . .

~~~~~~~~~~~~~~~~~~~~~~~~~~~~~~~~~~~~~~

My respondent just dusted *my* guesses. A *tama-hôki* or "precious broom" was *alcohol* to sweep away melancholy 愁へを掃う玉帚! The poem concerns *drinking; chiri=dust* must pun on *scattering/leaving*. The lord may be the host of the party. And, I just recalled that *stars* of various number signified formal drinking trays. Yet, it still is an odd (and unsolved) poem! Could good wine mean less men leaving drinking parties and more leaving work, or, staying longer to party do they leave more litter? *Now, samples from a better-known anthology.*

Gem Leaf: Tears from the 1313 Imperial Anthology

よしさらは なみたのしたに くちもせよ みさへなかるる とこのさむしろ 玉葉集
yoshi saraba namida no shita ni kuchi mo seyo mi sae nagaruru toko no samushiro ng 番号外
ok be-it-so-if tears-below rot even do! self/body+emph drift/be-swept-away bed's mat

So be it if these sleeves, soaking in m tears, should rot!
I trust my sleeping mat will flood and I'll be carried off.

~~~~~~

Floating, you will drift somewhere – a River of Tears.
I may yet end up happy on a sandbar with my Dear.

sad/floating esp float-off whenever tear-river dear shallows(rendezvous)-to join even is!
ukite koso nagare izure to namidagawa koishiki sese ni awasu mo aru kana ng
うきてこそ なかれいつれと なみたかは こひしきせせにあはすもあるかな

The 1313 *Gyokuyôshû* (Gem-leaf anth.) is considered one of two last swan songs of the great court poets before the kill-sports completely took over. Times were bad, so there are plentiful tears, which means wit, for without it, they are just not palatable. The above are within what I think of as the mad love-poem tradition.

ゆくあきをしたひしそてのなみたより　しくれそめてや ふゆのきぬらむ 番号外
yuku aki o shitaishi sode no namida yori shiguresomete ya fuyu no kinuramu ng
going autumn+acc care-for sleeve's/s' tears-ratherthan coldshower-starting!/: winter comes!

The Tears that wet my sleeves are not for the departing Fall
Think of them as dyeing Rain, a Shigure, for Winter comes.

~~~~~~

My tears fall, and how now from this endless winter shower,
Will I find even an hour to dry out these charcoal robes?

tears only profusely fall-accompanyng wntershowrs-as4 drying time evn not charcl-dyed-sleeves
namida nomi itodo furisou shigure ni wa hosu hima mo naki sumisome no sode ng
なみたのみーいととふりそふーしくれにはーほすひまもなきーすみそめのそて

~~~~~~

ころもうし はつかりかねの たまつさに かきあへぬものは なみたなりけり 慈円
koro mo ushi hatsukarigane no tamatsusa ni kaki-aenu mono wa namida narikeri jien d.1225
time +emph depressing, first-geese's precious-epistle-with clean-up-can't thing-as-for tears are+emph.

The first geese flew in with their letters; the season is blue.
Something came with the text – these tears I look through!

These three, on the other hand, are all laments. The first and last presage the nature-centered yet comic *haikai*, while the second indirectly brings out the similarity of mourning poems and lovesickness, as there are similar no-time-to-dry poems for the latter. Translations by good scholars published by good presses often mistranslate *sumi* robes (or *sumi sakura*) as *black* (*No!* Jet-black robes were a luxury– for the b & w on clothing, see my long discussion for item #1-30+ in *Topsy-turvy 1585*). The last is a guess. The *kakiaenu* stumped me so I winged it.

たましひも わかみにそはぬ なけきして なみたひさしき よにそふりにし 定家
tamashii mo waga mi mi sowanu nageki shite namida hisashiki yo ni zo furi ni shi   teika
soul/s evn my body-w/ accompnies-not lamentng tears long-time-not wrld-in+emph fall do

Such is my grief, even my soul is not with me, so for a while,
I might as well let them, my tears, come out . . . in single file.

~~~~~~

As my tears, like dew-drops, beyond all telling cling,
I may have to wear my pearls for camouflaging!

numbers are-not (beyond count) tears' dew+acc wearing+emph. gem-adornment add+emph think
kazu naranu namida no tsuyu o kakete dani tama no kazari o soemu to zo omou   shikibu
かすならぬ なみたのつゆをかけてたに たまのかさりをそへむとそおもふ 式部

No, there is no "single file." but I hear Teika (1162-1241) got quite fastidious in his old age, so why not? And I really do not know if the "camouflage" idea is mine or Shikibu's intention. I do know that I had to be a bit mad in translation to properly bring the poems into *this* book. Because a Microsoft update destroyed a day's work right after I worked on this anthology, I suspect there may have been more obviously witty tears that were lost *before* translation. I cannot say. If that were the case, straighter translation might have worked. Finally, for comparison, here are some *waka* tears too pure to permit mad translation.

うきをうしと いはぬより <u>まつ</u> さきたちて こころのそこを しるなみたかな 番号外
uki o ushi to iwanu yori mazu sakidachite kokoro no soko o shiru namida kana ng
floating/excitment/love+acc depressng say before appearng heart-bottm+acc knws tears!

When did love's sweet melancholy turn into the lovesick blues?
Before it reached the tip of my tongue, tears said it was done.

~~~~~~

Before I thought my doubts strong enough to call me 'blue,'
From the bottom of my heart, up welled tears – they knew!

~~~~~~

So what is the cause of all my tears, why such a rout?
I, myself, would like to know what this is all about!

that amount-as-for what reason falling tears+emph., i too suspicious thing+emph think
ka bakari wa nani yue otsuru namida zo to ware mo ayashiki mono o koso omoe ng
かはかりは なにゆゑおつる なみたそと われもあやしき ものをこそおもへ

~~~~~~

おいらくは わかみのほかの はるなれは はなみてたにも なみたおちけり 雅有
oiraku wa waga mi no hoka no haru nareba hanami deta ni mo namida ochikeri masaari
oldage-as-for my self/body's other-than spring is-if blossom-viewing appeared even tears fall

Old age is this – when you know spring is outside of you
and just seeing a blossom makes tears fall from the blue.

I see I could not entirely refrain from the style of translation that *kyôka* have called from me; even relatively sleepy styles are becoming livelier on their own!

The Man who Troped Transience

さゝがにの糸に貫く露の玉をかけてかざれる世にこそありけれ
sasagani no ito ni tsuranuku tsuyu no tama o kakete kazareru yo ni koso arikere saigyô
spider's/s' threads/string/s-by perforate/s dew-drops=souls+acc placing adorned world-in+emph. be/are!

This world
is our world, it wears
a necklace
of dew drops strung
on threads a spider spun.

西行　山家集　哀傷歌

This is the world wherein we live, lovely with dewdrops
Atremble on silken threads, strung by a gossamer race.

Wearing strings	*Adorned with*
of dew-drops strung by	*dew-drop jewels strung*
the Gossamer kind,	*by little Arachne,*
Such Beauty is our World	*All pearls & rouge at dawn,*
fragile as the Human mind.	*My, the world looks tacky!*

Pendant with dew-drops strung on trembling silken thread
By spiders, the world where we live until we're dead!

Saigyô starts with the poetic word for spider, literally, "tiny crab." *Crab* by sound and image is far from poetic in English, so I left *spider* as is or used inventions and an English literary term. The allusive *tama*=drop/gem=soul-(tenuous)thread conceit is largely lost in translation. The side-by-side readings are *paraverses*, or mad translations, with some of my ideas added for good measure. (B sure 2C ♪s!)

天の川流れてくだる雨をうけて玉のあみはるささがにのいと　西行
amanokawa nagarete kudaru ame o ukete tama no ami haru sasagani no ito saigyô
heaven's rivr flowng falls rain+acc catchng drop/gem=soul-net stretchng spider's' thread

The thin thread of the spider that pitches the pearl-eyed net
that caught the rain spilt from the flow of the river of heaven.

The galaxy flowing fell as rain and now the drops are spread
Once again a net of pearls but made from spider thread.

Saigyô's *waka* examples what I call *the* Japanese style: *"The House that Jack Built"* with no *"This is,"* and in reverse order because of our topsy-turvy syntax. My first reading follows the Japanese content and *flow* more or less exactly –

only "thin" and two "thats" were added. The second tried to follow the original *order* beginning with the Milky Way and ending with the thread, but as you can see, I felt "then we see" had to be added. The "once again" only *seems* added. Japanese believed their souls, *tama* like rain *drops* commute from Heaven's River; *heaven* is a homophone of *rain*; *ukete=catch* also means receive, as one might grace; and the 糸 *thread*, I wistfully hope puns into 意図, the spider's *intent*.

Rain drops overflowing from the Milky Way, Spider catches,
Until her web is so bejeweled, Gaien beauty heaven matches.

~~~~~~~~~~~~~~~~~~~~~~~~~~~~

Rain-drops from heaven caught by webs twinkle with beauty;
Mimicking the Milky Way on earth – is that a spider's duty?

~~~~~~~~~~~~~~~~~~~~~~~~~~~~

The thread of spiders pitching their webs whose interstices
are pearls of rain descended from & modeling the Galaxy.

~~~~~~~~~~~~~~~~~~~~~~~~~~~~

From the Sky-river rain-drops fall: See Arachne spread
a web of stars to prove even heaven hangs by a thread.

石なごのたまの落ちくるほどなさに過ぐる月日はかはりやはする　西行
ishinago no tama no ochikuru hodonasa ni suguru tsukibi wa kawari ya wa suru
jackstones' falling-come amount-short-in pass months-days-as-for exchange do

Faster by far	*Faster than stones*
the months & days flip by	*tossed by children in play*
than jackstones	*drop to the ground,*
chucked at holes by kids	*old months & days leave,*
take time to fly	*new come around!*

あればとてたのまれぬかな明日は又きのふと今日はいはるべければ
areba tote tanomarenu kana asu wa mata kino to kyô o iwaru bekereba saigyô
is-if say, reliable? tomorrow-as-for again yesterday-as today+acc called will-if

Who can count	*Who can trust*
on things the same to stay!	*whatever Is to be –*
When tomorrow,	*When Tomorrow,*
what's today will change	*what we call Today we see*
its name to yesterday?	*is only Yesterday?*

~~~~~~~~~~~~~~~~~~~~~~~~~~~~

On the morrow, who knows what will stay, when what was
Only yesterday, 'today', today is only 'yesterday'?

The "only" in the second reading comes from Piet Hein's grook *Transmutation*. Wishing to try his double "only" – interesting for its change of nuance (the last four lines: *"How can what only yesterday / was now / be now already / only yesterday?"*) – we get the last reading, a paraverse. *"On the morrow"* comes from Carter, who uses it in the correct place (*"One cannot rely / on things to stay as they are – / for on the morrow / this day we call today / will be called yesterday."*).

The Testing of Snipe & Playing With Cherry Clouds

蛤に はしをしつかと はさまれて 鴫たちかねる 秋の夕ぐれ　宿屋飯盛
hamaguri ni hashi oshi-tsuka to hasamarete shigi tachikaneru aki no yugure 狂歌才蔵集 1787
clam in beak pushing-penetrate-would and stuck snipe takes-off-cannot fall evening

Caught by his bill
when he tried to force
a cherry stone

The snipe cannot fly off
at dusk this fall

yado no meshimori 18c

Even a monk
no longer of the world
can be moved

When snipe start at dusk
from the autumn marsh

archbishop saigyô 12c

心なき身にもあはれは知られけり 鴫たつ澤の秋の夕ぐれ　西 行
kokoronaki mi ni mo aware wa shirarekeri shigi tatsu sawa no aki no yugure saigyô
heart-not body/self-to even sadness/beauty-as-for known-is+emph snipe/s leave marsh's fall's dusk

Of all the mad poem masters, Yado no Meshimori had the easiest way with old poems. This translator, however, had it hard. "A clam" would have been too short for the third line, "short-neck clam" too scientific, "marsh clam" too informative, "big clam" too short, "a fat clam" too obviously licentious, etc.. Thank goodness, my Japanese-English dictionary supplied that *cherry-stone*, which I had never heard of and was just the sort of word a mad poem wants. Yet, part of me wanted to go full hog with this:

Thanks to his bill,
that snipe can not bolt
this autumn night.

The quahog he'd jimmy
is holding him still.

Phallic implications? *Of course*. Japanese legend has an adulterous couple locked like dogs for their sin. Meshimori obviously plays with the moral tale (漁夫の利『戦国策』) wihich features a hungry snipe and (hungry?) clam taken by a fisherman, locked in battle. There is a hint of eros there, too. And readers who carefully *read* Kitagawa Utamaro's erotic prints know the metaphor has been substantiated by the poem appearing on the fan held by one of two lovers in congress on the second floor of a tea-house. But this reading is faulty for detracting from the main target, Saigyô's famous *waka*.

For comparison, see long Carter (*Even one who claims / to no longer have a heart / feels this sad beauty: / snipes flying up from a marsh / on an evening in autumn.*) and short Brownas+Thwaite (*A man without feelings, / Even, would know sadness / When snipe start from the marshes / On an autumn evening*). Carter explains that the monk is not supposed to be attached to the things of the world, but Brownas + Thwaite either did not know what "heart-not meant," forgot to add a note, or thought it better to include all men dead to this world.

Regardless, the point is that this is a *waka* about sensitivities, about a delicate melancholy and that is why it *asks for* the slapstick, or rather snatch-pecker parody. Even so, I include this mad poem more because it is well known – probably among the top 20 – than because I like it. Here is a *ku* (in 西国紀行書込) by young Issa alluding to Saigyô's *waka* that I consider a superb *kyôku*.

つく／＼と鴫我を見る夕べ哉　一茶
tsukuzuku to shigi ware o miru yûbe kana issa d.1827
keenly snipes me-at look/ing evening 'tis!/?

*How keenly
the snipe looks at me;
and it is dusk.*

*this evening
when the snipes intently
stare at me*

*It's evening.
Is the snipe drawing
a bead on me?*

We cannot imagine many snipe all caught by clams, so I made the mad poem's single. With Saigyô and Issa's poems, it does not matter so we cannot tell. But let me try to explain what draws me to Issa's *ku*, which, aside from making it into Issa's top 2000 *ku* anthology (丸山選 岩波文庫), where it is unannotated, has received no attention to my knowledge. Issa may have played with sparrows as a lonely stepchild, but he had a country boy's feeling about the natural world, and expressed doubts about urban lyricism, especially as it related to snow, which he called "bad stuff" (*warui mono*). I think, he feels the snipe is/are gazing deep into his soul – or at least at his none-to-aesthete appearance – and, wondering if *he* had what it takes, the appreciation of *aware,* or what we might best call *melancholy*. Or, my interpretation could be bunk and we have here a mad *reading* rather than a mad *poem*. Now, a different but still fantastic Meshimori:

仙人も天狗も雲と見ちかへて梢をふむな三吉野の花　飯盛
sennin mo tengu mo kumo to michigaete kozue o fumu na miyoshino no hana
sages & tengu too cloud mistaking tree-top+acc step-on-not! +hon+yoshino-blossoms

*Adepts and tengu wizards all, step not to thy doom!
A cloud may be a treetop when Yoshino is in bloom!*

If more beats were possible, the "adept" might have been a mountain sage, an old Chinese Taoist master who retires up a mountain and walks on clouds rather than riding a dragon or a stork. One such encouraged dozens of *senryû* as he was said to have fallen off said cloud on seeing the white thigh of a laundress in a river. Belief in tengu, the long-nosed goblin, may have originated from sightings of the proboscis monkey in ancient times. Meshimori had the most natural style of all the mad-poets. He gently picks up on simple old conceits, such as the conflation of cherry blossoms on mountainsides with clouds, found in thousands of *waka* and *haiku* (Chapter 17 of *The Cherry Blossom Epiphany* (2007) is called *"How to tell the clouds from the blossoms"* in the Table of Contents, and *"Blossom Clouds, Cloud Blossoms"* at the head of the chapter).

Wife-borrowing – It May Not Get Used Up, but . . .

わか妻を人のとるとて 人ことに へらぬものをは なにおしむらん 教月法師
waga tsuma o hito no toru tote hitogoto ni heranu mono oba nani oshimuran kyôgetsu-bô 新旧狂歌
my/own mate+acc person takes-re. person-each-w/ diminish-not thing+emph what regret-should? 俳諧聞書

My wife, they say,
some one else had her.

Bad news? Hey,
If others do not use it up
what have I to lose!

What matter if
another does your wife?

Why regret what
diminishes not a whit
night after night

Kyôgetsu (1265-1328) is sometimes called the first *kyôka* master; but a monk writing *this* kyôka (also in 遠近草 tk2)? You never know. He could have been married himself. There was a Buddhist sect that allowed monks that privilege. Then, again, monks in Japan, as in Europe, were allegedly well-hung and on the prowl. A husband could be addressed, as per the second reading. That reading, like the original, can also be read as an aphorism. The idea of free sex as fine because sex with a third-party does not reduce the availability of the mate is proverbial –

女房は貸すとも擂木は貸すな

"Though you lend your wife, keep your pestle home"

– and international. Within a century, Chaucer's saucy Wife of Bath would echo the *kyôka*, but more convincingly, as she was the one with the goods under debate (What would she have thought about a man putting forward the argument?). Reading the *kyôka*, however, did not make me think of Chaucer first, but of a much older (9c) Japanese poem I first read in translation thirty years ago:

人妻と何かそいはむ然らばか隣の衣を借りて着なはも 万葉 3472
hitotsuma to aze ka so o iwamu shikaraba ka tonari no kinu o karite kinawa mo
person's-mate, what/why+emph. say-would? if-so-then neighbor's/s' dress+acc borrow wear not-even?

'She is married?'
Why say so? Why care?
Would you say

We should never borrow
another's dress to wear?

So, why does it
matter if I am a wife?
Have you, then

borrowed your neighbor's
robe even once in your life?

I recall this poem was used by Aoki Yayoi to document the sexual freedom of ancient women in Japan in one of her early (70's? 80's?) books. The first reading, which Cranston clearly Englishes *"Why do people say, / "She's somebody else's wife . . . ? / . . . "* is the usual interpretation, i.e., the poem rationalizes adultery. I added a second reading, an interpretation I have not read in Japanese or English, because Japanese, unlike Usanians (& other Occidentals?), have their own, individual eating utensils and, living in Japan, I witnessed so little borrow-ing between neighbors I can not help wondering if they were *ever* in the habit of lending one another clothing. It is fun to imagine a time before life-threatening sexually-transmitted disease when people were as free with their sex as Bonobo. Japanese, or at least those who wrote poems found in the *Manyôshû,* visited or were visited (i.e. male and female alike) by multiple lovers and seem to have been sexually liberated by some standards. But the fact they slunk around at night proves that sex was generally kept under wraps (not because it was sinful, but because of the jealousies and embarrassment it was bound to cause), and married couples – or, at least the women, once living with the man (or the man with the woman) – *generally* were *not* free to sleep around. So I made that second reading. *Manyô* poem #3548 calls sleeping with a married woman as dangerous as hitching your horse on the edge of a crumbling ravine, but the best proof of this is, conversely, the long poem #1759, describing a promiscuous sleep-in for people of all ages, where the male poet accepts that others will seduce his wife as he will theirs and says it is a time-honored rite, the one day when such behavior is alright and none should glare (目串 eye-skewer), *i.e.*, look askance at it. While the poem is sometimes cited as proof the *song-wall* tradition of seducing the other sex with poems/song survived to historical times, reading between the lines, we can easily imagine from its defensive tone that officials or visitors from the Capital put down the locals for their loose morals. The short envoi (反歌), rises above that and has the enthusiast proclaiming: *I don't know about you, even if it rains out here and I am drenched, no way I'm going home (tonight)!*

減りはせまいけれど広くはなろう 末四
heri wa semai keredo hiroku wa narô
diminish-as-for won't but wide-as-for become

盗まれてあとの減らぬは豆泥棒 三七
musumarete ato no heranu wa mamedorobô
stolen after's diminish-not-as-for bean-robber

*Well, it may not
diminish but who doubts
it can stretch out?*

*What was stolen
didn't diminish: how, then?
A bean-burglar!*

The debate about whether sexual goods did or did not diminish in the lending continued past Kyôgetsu until the Tenmei *kyôka* boom and overlapping heyday of *senryû*. For *kyôka,* sex was just one of many subjects. For *senryû*, it was by far the largest subject and there was book after book of nothing but dirty *senryû*. There are probably scores treating the debate. And speaking of borrowing, the two 18c *senryû* translated above are taken from my book of dirty *senryû Octopussy, Dry-kidney & Blue Spots,* also titled *The Woman Without a Hole* (2007). The "who doubts" added for the rhyme in the first, rhythmically odd *senryû* cannot adequately compensate for the lost pun of an exceptionally clever, allusive sort more common in *kyôka*. *Semai,* a form of "to be" that means *probably won't,* happens to be a homophone of "narrow," something ordinarily not noticed, but here, separated by just one "but" (*keredo*), from "wide/r" (*hiroku*), it *is*. The second *senryû* uses common slang for the *clitoris* or the *cunt,* namely a *bean* (for more sexy beans in *senryû*, see the above-mentioned book). If you don't mind semantic ambiguity, you may replace that *bean* with a *pussy*.

Sooty Wives and Sleeping with Virgins

難波人 葦火焚く屋のすしてあれど 己が妻こそ 常めづらしき 万葉集
naniwa hito ashihi taku ya no sushite aredo onoga tsuma koso tsune mezurashiki mys # 2651
naniwa people rush-fires burn room's sooty-make but own mate esp. regular rare/attractive/sexy

Nakanishi Pro Reading +

Naniwa people
are sooty as old houses
from burning cane

But all love most the sight
of their own sweet wife at night

The Naniwa folk
are sooty as old houses
from burning cane

But my love is amazing,
beauty that rare remains!

My Amateur Reading

Folk in Naniwa
Are sooty as old houses
from burning cane

How nice for your wife
to always seem strange!

Naniwa folk may
burn rush and turn so black
they cannot blush

But imagine your own mate
always strange, a new date!

I have never found this ancient *waka* called a mad poem, as it is understood to mean just what my first reading, minus the added "sight/ night" rhyme, does. If the first part of the poem is taken as a trope intended as a foil for the second part, which can be personal (possible for person is not indicated in Japanese), then the second reading is possible: the folk in Naniwa are sooty and look ugly all the time, while *my* mate is always fair. Both of these readings are *possible* from the somewhat modernized rendition of the poem by Nakanishi, for he avoided guessing one way or another on what the poems *meant*. From the little reading I have done, this seems common practice for *Manyô* scholars, who constantly advise us to "Just read it plainly, as it is," because *Manyôshû* is synonymous with good old-fashioned or legendary Japanese simple thinking and sincerity (*sunao + makoto*). Although the language, as far as I can see, often can *not* be read plainly, at least not by us today, the scholars pretend it *can*, as such, were it true, would support their strong belief in the direct, male style of the *Manyôshû*. The biggest problem here is the last word, *mezurashiki*. We will continue the discussion on the next page. First a 17-18c haiku, the knowledge of which, together with the memory of a married college friend, who constantly craved what he called "strange," *i.e.,* women other than his wife, influenced my reading.

煤掃てねた夜は女房めづらしや 其角？五元集
susu hakite neta yo wa nyôbô mezurashi ya kikaku? d.1707
soot brushing/sweeping slept night-as-for wife rare/attractive!

In bed the night
after we swept soot my wife
A rare delight!

In bed the night
after cleaning soot I cheated
With my wife!

Soot cleaning day is part of the calendar and no major *haikai* poet misses it. Do not confuse the poem for a *senryû* where the attitude and usually the word used for wife would be appropriate for the third-person. But to return to the subject, today, *mezurashi* generally means *rare* but, in ancient times most commonly meant *attractive*. Still, another *Manyô* poem, #4285, uses it to mean *rare* as well as *beautiful;* and when you consider there were other words for attractiveness also used at the time, I cannot help wondering *why* it is used in *Manyôshû* #2651, and my third and fourth readings, which go further than anyone would reading Nakanishi's diachronic translation, express my hope against hope that my rare reading is possible. Such a reading would bring the poem close to being a *kyôka!* Since one kind scholar checked a half dozen interpretations/explanations by Japanese scholars over the past four centuries, and none of them found what I found in the *Manyôshû* poem, I am sanguine about the chances of my reading ever becoming accepted. Still, I have not yet thrown in the towel, and catch myself wondering if it was too obvious for some to state and impossible for others to imagine. But, when it comes to reading the *Manyôshû*, I am a rank amateur, so if you bet on me, be warned, our odds are long, a hundred to one, if that. And, now, for a Yomo no Akara 四方赤良(Shokusanjin) *kyôka* playing with an altogether different sort of rare attraction:

初物は七十五日とは云えど　逢う夜はしぬる心地こそすれ　赤良
hatsumono wa shichijûgo hi to iedo au yo wa shinuru kokochi kososure akara
'first-thing-as4, 75 days' said-but meeting night-as4 dying feeling+emph. is 1784

四方赤良　巴人集　天明四

The first taste
they say gets you seventy
five days grace

But that night I felt like
I died & went to heaven

The first pickings
give a man seventy five
more days of life

they say, but on that night
you keep on dying & dying!

The old Chinese idea of sleeping with a living fountain of youth, a virgin, is found coupled with the Japanese idea that eating the first fruit, vegetable, fish of a given sort, or whatever comes into season, gains one 75 extra days of life in both *senryû* – pardon, I am afraid I have lost my examples – and *kyôka*. This proverb (初物七十五日) probably came in handy to excuse paying a high price for such products originally put aside for the gods. These first-things or *hatsumono* (sometimes just *hatsu*) are slang for *first sex*, particularly with reference to the penetrated party. "Dying" as an idiom for experiencing intense joy commonly associated with sex in much of the world. In the decades before this kyôka, zappai and senryû milked the association for all it was worth, giving us monks of a marrying sect delighted with their wives calling out *"I die! I die!"* as it was good luck for their profession (Buddhist monks took care of funerals), and children terribly worried about what they overheard at night, calling out "Momma, don't die!" and so forth (See my *senryû* book). Yomo no Akara mated the *dying=orgasm* association to the *first-thing* concept to bear a simple paradox.

An Empress w/ Laundry & a Monk w/ Scabies

いかほどの洗濯なればかぐ山で衣ほすてふ持統天皇　蜀山先生　狂歌百人一首
ika hodo no sentaku nareba kagu yama de koromo hosu chô jitô tenno   shôkusanjin c.1790
how much laundry become-would/if kagu-mountain-with/at clothing dries is-said jitô emperor ↓

With spring done,
summer seems to have come.
Behold the white
Robes of mulberry drying
on heavenly Mount Kagu.

How much laundry
did Empress Jitô have?
Enough, i guess,
That to dry it she had to
resort to Mount Kagu

↑ spring passng summr came-seems white/mulbrrybark robes dry say? heaven's kagu-mt.
haru sugite natsu kinikerashi shirotae no koromo hosu chô ama no kaguyama   emp. jitô
春過ぎて夏来にけらし　白妙の衣ほすてふあまの香久山　持統天皇　小倉百人一首集

This facetiously naive response to a variant of *Manyô* poem #28 (*hosu chô* is *hoshi-tari*) by Empress Jitô (645-702) in the Ogura *Hundred Poets One Poem* collection by Shokusanjin is not playing with the *words* of the poem – he parodies the content. The pure white robes, used for sacred ceremonies, are woven of pounded and bleached mulberry bark fiber. The name of the small mountain, near the Imperial palace, *Kagu*, sounds *fragrant* (to scent) and is also a homophone for household items (including laundry poles) which may or may not have helped evoke the *kyôka* that, in the original, includes the name of the Empress in the body of the poem. Having seen the myriad falls on Kawaii, I cannot help thinking the Empress may describe waterfalls, as the rains come in early summer, though I have read no such gloss. Nor, have I read anything like this:

With Spring done, summer is a sea of green: There, drying,
White robes like abalone girls, hence, Ama Mount Kagu!

I like to think the Empress might have been thinking of the women who dived for abalone and pearls, as they were called *ama* (海女 homophonic with *heaven* 天) and had Imperial ties. Shokusan's *kyôka* is badly beaten by the following *senryû:*

山で干すさすが女帝は衣裳持ち<u>Date!</u>
yama de hosu sasuga jotei wa <u>koromo</u> mochi
mountain-with dry surenuf empress-as-for clothes-owner

Needing a mountain
to dry them, man, that empress
had a wardrobe!

Why beaten? Because, all things equal, brevity is not only the soul of wit but its measure. The *senryû*, says it all. In Shokusanjin's defense, he *did* all 100 *waka*.
(*Senryû* were popular before & after Shokusanjin's *kyôka*. I hope to have a date by the next edit.)

有明のつれなく見えし別れより暁ばかり憂きものはなし　壬生忠岑
ariake no tsurenaku mo mieshi wakare yori akatsuki bakari ukimono wa nashi   mibu no
matin-moon wretched+emph looked parting-from dawn-as blue thing-as4 not   tadamine

> *Since that parting when in misery we saw the matin moon,*
> *Dawn, of all things in the world, always brings me gloom!*

Souring on dawn itself because of one sad parting is rather odd. Here, for once, Rodd and Henkenius reading of this *Kokinshû* (c905) poem #625– *"since that parting when / I saw the cold indifferent / countenance of the / fading moon   I have known / nothing so cruel as dawn"* (1984/96) – seems far more *kyôka* than mine and closer to the original intent, as Kyûsojin notes this poem (among those in *Hundred Poets One Poem*) is credited to "a woman ある女" in Tadamine's collection and probably concerns a meeting with waiting but no consummation.

有明のつれなくいへぬ皮癬瘡かくばかり身に憂きものはなし　沢庵和尚
ariake no tsurenaku ienu hizengasa   kakubakari mi ni ukimono wa nashi   monk takuan
matinmoon's wretched heal=say-not scabies(mites) scratch=such body/self-to blues-as4 not

> *Up with scabies at dawn too miserable to leave the room*
> *Scratching, tell me, itching, tell me of your matin moon!*

I tried translations closer to the original (eg., *Up with scabies, like that matin moon, they stay around / Of all things in this world, scratching brings me down!*) but went with what was interesting. Monk Takuan (1573-1645) was offered major religious and civil positions in his thirties but preferred a humble rural life. When Shôgun Iemitsu (r.1623-51) himself requested he return from exile (after he was banished, unnecessarily, for he wanted to go, for disobedience), to the new capital of Edo, he replied in a *kyôka*, far more famous than the above but untranslatable for including his name in a pun (~*taku* means "like to") saying he would go if the Shôgun *insisted*, but that he found crowded, filthy Edo repulsive (御意なれば 参りたく庵おもへども むさしきたなし江戸はいやいや *Goi nareba mairitakuan omoe-domo musashi kitanashi edo wa iya iya*).   The cleverest of Takuan's *kyôka* that I have seen was an allegorical report to a friend about the political situation:

大こうのもとはきけど糠みそに打ちつけられてしおしおとなる
taikô no moto wa kikedo   nukamiso ni uchi-tsukerarete shio-shio to naru   takuan
daikon(hideyoshi)'s basis-as4 asked-if, nuka-miso-in throw-soak/pickld limp becmes

> *You ask about making daikon pickles? Thrown into nuka miso, they become soft.*
> ◆　◆　◆　◆　◆　◆　◆　◆　◆
> *You ask about Hideyoshi's situation? Ieyasu pickled him, and he's turned softy.*

Taikô 太閤, "imperial advisor." The title the late-16c unifying shôgun Hideyoshi gave himself. *Daiko*. Colloquial for *daikon*, huge radish. The character for *nuka* (*nuka-miso* salted rice bran paste) is 糠; the second for Ieyasu, founder of the succeeding Tokugawa dynasty, was 康. The first name pun requires the mind's ear; the second its eye. ★ *Takuan* is a yellowish daikon pickle; one etymology credits the crotch-scratching monk w/ its invention (*Topsy-turvy 1585* re. its stink).

A Lantern in Daylight, or Things That Cannot Be

かるかやをほたるのひにはともすとも人のこころをいかがたのまん　古今和歌六帖
karu kaya o hotaru no hi ni wa tomosu to mo hito no kokoro o ikaga tanoman　kkrj #2226
sickled thatch-grass firefly's fire-by-as4 lit even human/other's heart+acc how trust-would!? c985

Say sickled thatch grass
Could be set alight with a spark
From a firefly,

Yet how on the human heart
Could you place your reliance?

Cranston trans. (v2a)

The improbability of such illumination, or conflagration if you prefer, was double for ancient Japanese readers, aware of the temporal contradiction. But, if we were to make the seasons explicit, the wit is diluted: *When the thatch-grass stacks* of fall *are torched by* summer *fireflies, / That will be the day when I, on human hearts rely!* Far better to add that *spark* , which, for whatever reason, improves the picture of *what could never happen*. So I used Cranston's translation (my centering, sorry!) for the first sample of forty *waka*, written by four top poets of the age (10-11c)♪, describing a variety of improbabilities in 17-syllabets as a foil for the single most improbable thing in the final 14-syllabet part. The preface for the series' lead mentions parting from an unfaithful woman, but all four poets were underpaid low-ranking aristocrats, with reason to begrudge the shifting sands of socio-politics, so the apparent sexism may cover broader discontent. Still, we can bet their main inspiration was natural: logic asked to play within limits, explodes in joy.

かたなもとながるるみづはきりつとも人のこころをいかがたのまん
katana mote nagaruru mizu wa kiritsu to mo   hito no kokoro o ikaga tanoman
sword take running water-as4 cut even/though man's heart+acc how trust-would?! kkr 2198

Though my sword a flowing stream might, cutting, part,
Could I ever put my trust in another person's heart?

wa ga sode no namida ni io wa suminu to mo ...
my sleeve's' tears-in fish-as4 living even/though kkr 2223

Though fish might swim within my tears, a sleeve of carp,
Could I ever put my trust in another person's heart?

haru kaeru kari o ba mina mo todomu to mo ...
spring returning geese+acc+emph all stop even/though kkr 2228

Though I might the geese home-bound stop before they start
Could I ever put my trust in another person's heart?

ami no me ni fukikuru kaze wa tomaru to mo . . .
net's' eyes/holes-by blown-comes wind-as4 stop even/though

Though wind might by the meshes of a net be caught,
Could I ever put my trust in another person's heart?

◆

tsuyujimo o tokete no nochi wa wakitsu to mo . . .
dew frost+acc melted after-as4 separate even/though   kkr 2232

Though once melted frost & dew I might tease apart,
Could I ever put my trust in another person's heart?

◆

he o hirite fujin raijin makasu to mo . . .
fart+acc fartng wind-god/s thundr-gd/s beat evn/thgh kkr 2233

Though I might ye gods of wind and thunder outfart,
Could I ever put my trust in another person's heart?

Were I to present all forty poems, *which do not include the last one above*, a ringer composed by my respondent (after reading my try: *eating a hill of green chestnuts yet not cutting a fart* (in the actual kkr #2233, a hand damns Japan's relatively small Niagara), I doubt I could have kept them rhyming, or nearly rhyming, with "heart." I probably would make it "then" so the first line could *always* end in "when," and save me from needing a new rhyme each time.

furu yuki o sora ni tomete wa arinu to mo . . .
falling snow+acc sky-in stop-as-for is even/though   kkr 2201

Say you suspend in the sky the falling snow, that's when
You'll find a human heart to trust, but not before then.

◆

kô no ishi o ari ni ôsete hakobu to mo . . .
kalpa-stone+acc ant/s-by back-carried even/though   kkr 2211

Say you have an ant haul off a kalpa stone, that's when
You'll find a human heart to trust, but not before then.

Unfortunately, *"Say + that's when"* up front slows the flow and adds beats better used for content, such as we find in Cranston's *"Load a kalpa stone / Onto the back of an ant – / Say it could haul it, / Yet how on the human heart / Could you place your reliance?"* English has a verb for *shouldering* but not *backing* objects in the meaning of *carrying* them there. How nice to have that *"Onto the back of an ant"* to evoke the image I only was able to imply by *haul*! Now, about that *kalpa stone*. Neither singular nor plural, it is a fiction in space representing a unit of time invented by Buddhist theology: *one kalpa* is defined as *the years required for such a stone with a radius of 40 leagues brushed by the feather robe of a heaven dweller once every 100 years to wear down to nothing!* (On line, in English, I am informed that is only 4320000000 years.)

Segregated Beaches with Heron and Crow

すが島やたふしの小石わけかへて 黒白まぜよ浦の濱風　西行
sugajima ya tôshi no koishi wake-kaete kuroshiro mazeyo ura no hama-kaze
suga island & tôshi's pebbles divide-exchanging black-white mix+imper.! bay's beach-wind

Suga island & Tôshi, day & night, segregate pebbles:
Mix the blacks and whites, Bay Breeze, put up a fight!

Traveling near Ise, Saigyô (1118-90) found neighboring islands, one with a black pebble beach, the other white. The Chinese characters for Suga and Tôshi are "管島 Tube Island" and "答志 Answer-will/aim-for." I had not intended to transliterate them because we usually do not think *literally* of names, while the sound of the same always matters to some degree. However, the next poem (さぎじまのごいしの白をたか浪のたふしの濱に打寄せてける *sagijima no goishi no shiro o takanami* . . .) in the four *waka* series includes one that is significant. Not wishing to have the names half-Englished, I also translated Tôshi.

Heron Island's white go *stones are brought within reach,*
Then slapped down by the breakers upon Answer Beach.

Lentil-shaped black and white "stones" the size of large pebbles are used to play *Go*, the best board game ever invented (minimum rules + maximum intelligence, AI still cannot beat good players). Held between the index finger-nail and middle finger-tip, the stones are plunked down with aplomb on thick wooden boards. The verb used, *utsu*, is that used for *hitting*, *shooting*, *typing*, or *slapping*. Saigyô borrowed the Chinese conceit of *crow+heron* standing for the stones and, by extension, the game (烏鷺の戦い). The poem falls flat, as it makes little sense for black stones to be played one by one when the white ones are all there. The next poem drops the *go* and reverts to the most popular theme in ancient poetry: "*How they must long for the pebbles on Cape Crow beach / The blacks on Tube Island unmixed with white seed.*" (からすざきの濱のこいしと思ふかな白もまじらぬすが島の黒 *karasu-zaki no hama no koishi to* . . .). Nothing could be more *kyôka*, but my treatment cursory, for even with *seed* substituted for *pebble*, English misses the charming pivot pun on *koishi*, that means *pebble* following "*hama*=beach" but, after what follows, retroactively changes into "long for," or "are so dear."

あはせばやさぎを烏と碁をうたば たふしすがしま黒白の濱　西行
awaseba ya sagi o karasu to go o utaba tôshi suga-shima kuroshiro no hama
match-let's! heron & crow-w/ go+acc strike/play-if tôshi suga island b+w's beach

Let's match up	*What a match,*
the Heron and the Crow	*heron & crow, the beaches*
for a go at go;	*black and white*
Black and white the beaches	*Tôshi Isle and Suga can*
wait on Tôshi Isle and Suga.	*fight it out in a game of go*

Because Heron and Crow are conceits rather than places here, I let the original island names stand. I imagine coves like the bowls from which stones are removed one by one while playing. This poem, unlike the others, works by being as vague as the surreality it sketches. Here's a pleasant old translation by Honda:

> *O that I could see*
> *Tohshi Island play*
> *the game of crow and egret*
> *with the Isle of Suga.*

I thought of putting this poem, obviously the maddest of the four, at the head of the chapter and working back to the first one, but when I found "segregate" to dress up the first just enough to make it *seem* a *kyôka*, I decided to keep the original order – a good start, a whimsical brainchild of the beach, followed by two mediocre follow-ups, one of which helped lead us to the final exuberant triumph of metaphor – which is, after all, the best one. But let us leave-off shop talk. Here is another island *kyôka*, one of but <u>two modern tanka</u> in this book.

ちちのみの父の嶋より見わたせば母の嶋見ゆ乳房山見ゆ『雀の卵』
chichi-nomi no chichi-no-shima yori miwataseba haha-no-shima miyu chibusa yama miyu
breast-drinking father-island from see-cross-when mother-island see titty-mountain see

From Pappa Island	*From Pappa Island*
w/ only milk on tap, I think	*with only pop on tap, I see*
on the far horizon	*on the far horizon*
I see the fount of all drinks:	*The fount of all drinks & free*
Momma Island's Mount Pap!	*Momma Island's Mount Pap!*

Other smaller islands on the Ogasawaras (once the Bonins) are called *brother* and *sister*, etc.. *Mother* Island (Hahajima) must be an Amazon, for she has but one large conical mountain, named as mentioned. Hakushû 白秋, whose poems always have a lyrical ease my labored English cannot match, might not like his poem to be called a *kyôka*, for his attitude, if I understand correctly, was that tanka (the modern, unbound *waka*) could itself encompass all humour: *"What I really hate is for tanka to trap itself in conventions that are not literary."* (つくづくいやなのは、短歌が文学以外の礼儀にもたやすく正装されることだ。) Of course, that refers first of all to courtly tradition, but Hakushû makes a broader point, that as far as content goes, *tanka* is, or ought to be free (Only haiku is different, for it is defined by content as well as form). Today, this concept has been taken up with a vengeance by soft-spoken Yoshioka Ikuo, a man with *tanka* roots who is examining the entire history of *waka* to understand how humor came to be segregated from the canon, or, given other names, became loose canons, so to speak. Like the wind on the beach that Saigyô called to come mix up those pebbles, he would re-unite *warai* (laughs) and *waka* – in history and thereby reappraise *tanka* from an ancient – pre-segregation – perspective.

♪An academic friend gave this chapter thumbs down for being too arcane. If so, I apologize, and hope the less pedagogical chapters make it up for you. *It stays.*)

Perverse Nursery Verse, or *Snails Beware!*

牛の子にふまるな庭のかたつむり 角のあるとて身をなたのみそ 寂蓮法師集
ushi no ko ni fumaru na niwa no katatsumuri   tsuno no aru tote mi o na tanomi so
cow/ox-child/ren-by tread-not garden-snail horns have because body/self+acc count-on not

Please, take care
Garden Snail not to be
tread by a cow

Trust not in your horns
to protect you somehow

1139?- Monk Jakuren -1202

I was unsure of *what* was *"na tanomi so"* or, *not to be counted on*. Probably you, yourself, the snail; but the original was ambiguous, to me, at least. All I consulted favored the above, so I went with it. Here are the less likely alternatives=rejects:

Don't you let / those oxen squash you, / garden snail!
And ask not my help; / You're the one with horns!
~~~~~~
Let not a cow / be the one to squash you, / garden snail!
Count not on mercy, just / because they too have horns!
~~~~~~
Do not get tread / by an ox my garden snail / Let him know
You, too, have horns & heaven / is not where you would go!

The Monk Jakuren had a daughter who became a poet herself and is known only as the daughter of Jakuren because he became that famous. I do not know if he was a monk when he had his daughter but it does not matter. What *does* is that he was probably reintroduced to nursery rhymes as an adult and reacted with this poem. Children around the world enjoyed playing with the "horns" of these timid creatures. The English Mother Goose has bread and barley *corns* offered to draw out those *horns*, and the Chinese Mother Goose has roasted mutton offered for the same. Oddly, the oldest recorded snail nursery verse, from the 12c *Ryôjin Hishô* collection of *Now-styles* (今様 *imayô*), or "contemporary ditties" which supplies the violence Jakuren must have been reacting to does not mention any horns! Its 66 syllabets are both sensitively and, for a translation from Japanese, precisely, translated by Brownas and Thwaite: *Dance, dance, little snail! / If you do not dance, / I shall have you kicked and crushed / By a pony, by a calf. / If you dance your dance / Well and prettily, / I shall let you go and play / In a garden full of flowers* (*The Penguin Book of Japanese Verse*). If I could have translated said poem half as well as they did, believe me, I would have. Only the "little" is added, which is fine, for making a horse or cow a 子 or *child* is more a term of endearment than a fact. It is all the more reason to make them *ponies* and *calves*, so it is no complaint. But, please note lest I mislead you, that while the *now-style* ditty is pretty and silly to be sure, without those horns and the logic that makes you scratch your head, the style here is far from mad. Though it, like Jakuren's, had 31 syllabets, it would be no *kyôka*. For *that,* one needs more than just a carrot and a stick. One needs something a bit screwy.

落書を此所にかきねの蝸牛習ひはしめの牛の角文字　苅穂 Kariho 一万
rakugaki o kono tokoro ni kakine no katatsumuri narai-hajime no ushi no tsunomoji c1780?
graffitti+acc this place on write-not=fence/hedge's snail practice-start's cow-horn letters

Snail, who said you could write on my wall this time?
Whatever it says must be dirty for slime is slime!

This *is* a mad poem about a snail, and a fine one, too. Unfortunately, it cannot be translated. The idea and pun are too tightly twined together around an idiom with no English equivalent. A snail has been caught writing graffiti on a fence, or *kakine*, the *kaki* of which is a homophone for "writing," and the writing is seen as pretty basic stuff represented by "the horn letter," i.e. the simple vowel い (*i*), because it looks like a pair of horns. That brings in the 牛 or cow which is a character in *snail* 蝸牛 as well as mentioned in nursery rhymes (maybe even the old Chinese expression of kingdoms' fighting on the horns of a snail), and adds a touch of bogus romance, for the horn letter which originally stood for innocent affection (see pp. 448-9) also came to stand for the "Dear" いとしい starting *love letters* and, by extension, all or *love/longing* こひ・こい *koi*. So we have the snail writing love letters for all to see in a juvenile style. Perhaps, I should add that *I* have seen snail tracks on the leaves that seemed dead-ringers for the purely *hiragana* cursive style of the female poets. So if you would make out exactly what those snails are writing, I would suggest studying medieval Japanese. Then, once you think you have found a particularly good passage, take a good photo of the leaf and send it to a scholar to see if your reading can be confirmed. I would do just that if *I* had time . . . Now, here is a *kyôka* that is not about snails, yet closer to Jakuren's poem than any other I know of.

草村にむさとな鳴きそ轡虫野飼の馬のはむ事もあり　浄治 古今夷曲集 1666
kusamura ni musato na naki so kutsuwa mushi nokai no uma no hamu koto mo ari jôji
grass clump/town-in overdoing don't call, katydid meadow-raise/feed horse/s munch thing+emph. is

I wouldn't call too much out on the heath, my Katybit bonny,
Lest ye find yourself between the teeth of a grazing pony!

Unlike Jakuren's snail, this song depends on a pun. I can demonstrate it in English by renaming the *kutsuwa mushi,* or *giant katydid* as "katy*bit*." *Kutsuwa* is a ring-like bit, and the poet assumes the ponies in the field would like to be back in action. But I am afraid English lacks a good verb for holding things between the teeth and one cannot really pun on a brand new word. If you would see an *English* mad poem, utilizing the bug's name as we know it, check out one of Oliver Wendell Holmes' few decent poems, or maybe his *only* decent poem, (his essays are another matter), the delightful *Katydid* who says she didn't.

Country Wants City Wants Country Life

山里は 冬ぞさびしさまさりける 矢張市中がにぎやかで よい　蜀山家集
yamazato wa fuyu zo sabishisa masarikeru yahari shijû ga nigiyaka de yoi　shokusanjin
mountain-as-for winter+exclam. loneliness grows+emph. sure city-inside-the busy-so good ↓

Back in the hills
Winter gets lonelier still,
and I think it's this:

The trickle of men runs dry
when all the grasses die.

Minamoto no Muneyuki 9-10c

Back in the hills
Winter gets lonelier still;
I shudda known:

The city big and busy
was just the place for me!

kyôka : Shokusanjin 18-9c

↑ mount-as-for winter+excl. loneliness grows+emph. people-eyes-& grass whither-not think-if
yamazato wa fuyu zo sabishisa masarikeru hitome mo kusa mo karenu to omoeba　kks #315
山里は冬ぞさびしさ増りける　人めも草もかれぬとおもへば　源宗于 古今集

An artless pun on "*me*=buds" in "*hitome*=people-eyes" in Muneyuki's *waka*, one of the select *Hundred*, aligns a drying stream of visitors with the withered fields. Forsaking puns, Shokusanjin translates that classical lyricism into blustery big-city-speak with the single colloquialism, "*yahari,*" meaning "*as I knew all along.*" Call it *Edo*fication without mentioning the name of the world's largest metropolis at the time. Were he Usanian and lived in the mid-20c, it would have been "*New York City is the place for me . . .*" Still, I find the following *senryû* parody – note the inclusion of the identical phrase (though pronounced slightly differently) – madder than the *kyôka* for the more tenuous association:

人目も草もいとはずに野糞たれ
jinmoku mo kusa mo itowazu ni noguso tare
human eyes and grass/weeds hating-not-w/ fieldshit hangs

fearing neither
human eyes or blades of grass
an al fresco shit

i not minding
the eyes of men or weeds
shit outdoors

There is no better weapon against pastoralism than the *noguso,* or field-shit. This makes it ideal for *haikai*, as it was anti-convention. Buson before and Issa later both have Buddhist high clerics doing it, but only Issa also described *himself:*

shitting outside
to gain some peace of mind
a damn long day

spring ennui
i walk out to the field
to relieve myself

relief-for field-shit+acc. drop/poop day-long!/how
nagusami ni noguso o tareru hinaga kana　issa
なぐさみに野糞をたれる日永哉　一茶

むだな身に勿体なさの日永哉　一茶
muda na mi ni mottainasa no hinaga kana
useless body-for wasteful day-long!/how

thrown away
on a good for nothing
these long days

老の身は日の永いにも涙かな　一茶
rô no mi wa hi no nagai ni mo namida kana
aged body-as-for day's/days' long-as-even tears!

old bodies sing　　　　　　　　　　　　*another spring*
a different song, for us a day　　　　*longer days that bring more*
can be too long　　　　　　　　　　　　*tears for the old*

wasted spring
when the day stretches
and you yawn

wasted weeds!/: you too stretch sun/day too stretch
muda-kusa ya nanji mo nobiru hi mo nobiru
むだ草や汝も伸る日も伸る　一茶

These *ku*, all within half a page of the *al fresco* relief in Issa's Journal are what I would call *kyôku*, or *guku,* "foolish *ku*," a word used by old Sôgi (1420-1502), whom I consider haiku's first father. One reason both terms are not common (aside from the former being used generically for *kyôka* and *kyôshi*) may be the difficulty of telling when a *ku* is or isn't *mad* or *foolish*. Indeed, one reason, I was not interested in *kyôka* earlier is because I found so much humor in *haikai*, even post-Bashô, that I did not feel I had to look elsewhere for it. Humor in solid *haikai* is seriously undervalued in Japan. Issa's self-deprecatory humor is well-known but one seldom comes across other epigrammatic fun he and other *haijin* came up with, by comparison to which most of the mad poems I read seem what those growing spring days became to old Issa: *wastefully long*. So saying, Issa's *al fresco* poop is not *kyôku* nor *senryû*, but as pure a haiku as a haiku can be, far more so than the famous poop of Bashô's bird, which, as I explain on page 103, cannot help but drop two significant meanings upon that rice cake.

日の鼠月の兎のかはごろもきて帰るべき山里もがな　蜀山百集
hi no nezumi tsuki no usagi no kawagoromo kite kaeru-beki yamasato mogana shokusan.
day-mice' moon-rabbits' pelt-robe/s wearing return-ought/could mountain-village wish-for!

Had I only a mountain village, a place to return with nothing
But day-mice and moon-hare pelts to show for my vestment!

..
Wearing sun-mice, an idea from the 9c *Taketori Tales*, evokes a rural mood, and moon-mice a leisurely months-flow-by one. They allude to the proverbial return home wearing a brocade robe (i.e. wealthy). Shokusanjin has aged. Poor and saddled with a disabled son, our elderly urbanite was stuck in the city, his old love, w/out the wherewithal to move and could only close the circle w/ a *kyôka*.

He Loved Both Women and Chinese Rhyme

女をは法のみくら といふそ実 しやかもたるまも出る玉門 一休諸国物語
onna o ba hô no mikura to iuzo geni shaka mo daruma mo deru tama mon ikkyû
woman/en+emph. law/buddhism's hon.+storage as say+emph. shaka & daruma exit gem-gate

The truth is this
Women alone are precious
Stores of the Law

Buddha and all the Saints
Exit her beautiful Maw

"Law" means Buddhist teachings. If you would chose accuracy over rhyme, it is "gem-gate," not "beautiful maw." I found what seems the light, or folk version of this *kyôka* attributed to Ikkyû in a notebook the poor 49 year-old Issa transcribed from various sources for his teacher and patron (boss?) Seibi. He attributes it to a *Kijin-den*, or "biography of eccentrics," written twenty-one years earlier:

女程めで度ものは又もなし 釈迦や達磨をひょいひょいとうむ
onna hodo medetai mono mo nashi shaka ya daruma o hyoi hyoi to umu
woman amount celebratory thing+emph not, shaka and daruma+acc nimbly bear

There is nothing
half so happily blessed
as a Woman. Why?

Popping out Buddha and
dharuma, as easy as pie!

The *kyôka* clash with *senryû* about Shaka (Buddha), for the latter claim he avoided being born from *that* place by choosing ? a Cesarean. *Medetai*, meaning happy, blessed, or propitious, includes the nuance of being a natural fool, so the folk version may be less than 100% feminist. Though the most important defender of women in Buddhism was probably not the crazy, likeable Ikkyû, but the rabid nationalist and vituperative enemy of all but his own faith, Nichiren (1222-82), Ikkyû is well known for both the above and the gratitude he expressed in purely Chinese character poems for one woman, his blind masseur cum lover. Here's one of these poems, not the best known, but known well enough to boast at least two English translations. It is novel enough to be called a *kyôshi*, or *mad Chinese-style* – which usually, but not always, means *rhyming* – verse.

Trying my hand at Describing Mori's

Mori's touch beats mine, hands down
The lady is an expert – I am a clown!
She can raise my spirits (and my rod)
So high my monks must think it odd!

The original for this poem, titled 換我手作森手 (replace my hand make mori's hand), which I think means "I wish I had Mori's hands for mine!" is four 6-character lines 我手何似森手・自信公風流主・発病治玉茎明・且喜我会裏衆 which follow the most common end-rhyme scheme used by the Chinese, AABA, albeit poorly, for they just repeat the syllabet "shu." The third line in the original is more direct: she *fixes his sick gem-stalk* (note the Chinese term), but I wanted to include the joy found in the problematic last line – which we shall skip – after it. To return to rhyme, Ikkyû did a far better job with the following *kyôshi*, where the *sound* of the poem is worth providing, *though I have yet to find a single book in Japan that tries to do so!* Odd, indeed, for Ikkyû belonged to the Five Mountain Temples 五山の寺院, one of the few scholarly enclaves in Japan noted for reading in the *ondoku* 音読 quasi-Chinese style, which would vocalize the rhyme 参考：『漢詩の事典』大修館書店). The title of the original is "Woman's Yin" 女陰 and a rough gloss would be *"originally has mouth still no words / billion hair heads(individuals) guard round pock(scar) / all group alive stray way place / million various buddhas leave body gate (alma mater)."*

        gan rai yû kô ko mu gon
        o yoku mo tô yô gan kon
        i' sai shu jô mei to sho
        jû man sho fu shu'shin mon

十	一	百	元
万	切	億	来
諸	衆	毛	有
仏	生	頭	口
出	迷	雍	更
身	途	丸	無
門	所	痕	言

    MOUTHED FROM THE START SPEECHLESS STILL
    MAN AND BEAST LOSE THEIR WAY ON THIS HILL
    SCARIFIED HOLE GUARDED BY A HAIRY HOST
    THAT BORE ALL BUDDHAS AND ALWAYS WILL!
    ~~~~~~~~~~~~~~~~~~~~~~
    BOASTING YE FIRST MOUTH – DUMB NONE-THE-LESS
    A HOST OF HAIRY HONOR-GUARDS, FOR BUT A HOLE!
    MAN AND BEAST LOSE THEIR WAY AT THIS ADDRESS
    BIRTHPLACE TO ALL BUDDHAS — CAN YOU GUESS?
    ~~~~~~~~~~~~~~~~~~~~~~
    THE VERY FIRST MOUTH, IT'S TOOTHLESS & DUMB.
    AN ARMY OF HAIR GUARDS A PIT BY THE BUM!
    IT GUIDES US HERE, THEN HELPS MEN GET LOST;
    YET OUT OF THIS GATE OUR BUDDHAS ALL COME.

..
The only translation I have, by John Stevens, and found in a book review by Donald Richie, is titled *A Woman's Sex* and Englished *"It has the original mouth but remains wordless / It is surrounded by a magnificent mound of hair / Sentient*

beings get completely lost in it / But it is also the birthplace of all the Buddhas of the ten thousand worlds." Excluding the second line and what may be a valid creative change in the fourth, it is correct, but lining up fine phrases hardly makes a poem. Translator's license may permit the substitution of "a magnificent mound" for the idea of guarding or protection, but so long as you go that far, why not go one step further and make that mound a *"forest?"* to connect with the idea of *getting lost* in line 3 to compensate for the weakening of the contrast by changing the crude 丸痕 *"round scar"* or *"pock"* to *"it?"* The ugly expression itself is worth noting as it seems 1) out of character from a monk unashamed of literally loving women, and 2) *the best proof we have that end-rhyme was important to at least one Japanese poet*. Ikkyû *needed* that awful *kon,* or "scar" for the rhyme, and brought in "round," a word full of good meaning, to make amends. Or, maybe 丸 *round* is a cover for 九 *nine* (the ninth-hole was slang for *it*). The rhyme *kyukon* would beat *gankon!* Here is a harder nut to crack:

示南坊偵

勇巴興尽対妻淫
狭路慈明逆行心
容易説禅能忌口
任他雲雨楚台吟

A NOTE FOR THE SOUTH MONK

BURNT OUT WITH MEN? THEN FUCK YOUR WIFE
THE NARROW OPENS BRINGING GRACE TO LIFE
ZEN IS EASY TO PREACH   I'LL SHUT MY MOUTH
AND LET OTHERS BLESS CLOUD-RAIN TONIGHT

Ikkyû also had a mad verse for the male part. It was less interesting than the female part, so I thought, instead, I would try a poem about which the Iwanami editors write: *"Content unclear. We dare not try to interpret it."* 内容不明。敢えて解釈をしない (失典,多分古典体系). The editors do note that 勇巴 (*brave fat*) is code for 男色, *male color* = homosexual sex, and that, according to a diary (菅原和長日記), Ikkyû was the South Monk's father, the South Monk was his disciple, and his hermitage was called Gathering Clouds Hut 集雲庵. The narrow road 狭路 alluding to the "narrow way" of esoteric Buddhism, would be the homosexual (anal) relations allowed to monks; and I would guess Ikkyû refers to his indulgences with women which brought him a fine son and to what his son, at this stage of his life, should consider doing. *Clouds+rain,* referring to the name of the new hermitage, means *sexual relations* in Chinese poetic trope. Maybe it was raining and someone went in Ikkyû's stead, or the rain was added because the last line mentions a "foundation song" and yin-yang sex is a fitting start for anything. Though unsure I got the above right, I am also tempted to try song #488, which the sex-shy editors also claimed to be *extremely hard*; but I will spare you a tedious exercise and end instead with something easier and more appropriate for a book of mad poetry:

若衆天然好富貴・摺切争可入御意・無酒無茶無餅・山僧風流只文字
(寄少人三首の其三 一休ばなし 第四 "We" in the original is *mountain monks*.
I follow one explanation of the second line which may well be wrong.)

        YOUNG MEN LIVE FOR RICHES' SAKE
        POVERTY'S RAGS ARE HARD TO TAKE
        WE HAVE NO TEA NO WINE NO CAKE
        WE ARE COOL 4 THE WORDS WE MAKE

One reason I have made this the only long chapter is because I feel pre-Tenmei Chinese-style mad-poems are unfairly denigrated by the only book my limited time and money allowed me on the subject of Edo era *kyôshi*. Here is what Hino Tatsuo and Takahashi Keiichi write about Ikkyû and kyôshi:

> To say Ikkyû wrote only ludicrous *kyôshi* is to say that *kyôshi* was not yet worth calling literature (一休、単に滑稽の狂詩 を作ったというだけでは、まだ文学と称するには足りない。) *Kyôshi* become literature when those who write them consciously choose this style or genre characterized by a critical attitude naturally born of a mismatch of form and content [the original uses the English "unbalanced"], and this play, as play, attains the heights of fine expression. (日野＋高橋『太平楽府、江戸狂詩の世界』1991)

Granting *kyôshi* became popular entertainment in the 18c largely due to young Ôta Nanpo's genius – Is that reason to discredit Ikkyû, deny other old *kyôshi* and credit Ôta alone with taking hitherto *stiff* (堅苦しい) *regulation* (正規) Chinese poems (漢詩), boldly introducing slang (日本語の俗語) and applying the form to vulgar matters (卑俗の素材)? Not, in my opinion, without a thorough study of three things: 1) Old *kyôshi* in Japan by whatever name, for I find it hard to believe Yûchôrô, Teitoku, Buson and others did not play with all-character poems; 2) Chinese poetry, to see just how 'mad' the Chinese *themselves* could be, for even in Chinese Nursery rhymes, no one out-vulgars the Chinese, and if parody is mad poetry, they own the field! And 3), how much Ôta may have read of 1) and 2). Yet, Nanpo's creative abandon and editorial sophistication does seem to lack precedent. H & T find *Professor Sleep-in's Anthology* (寝惚先生文集 1767), published when he was just nineteen, in a different class from others (eg. 桂井在高/古文鉄砲前後集/1761) and example the sort of novelty that inspired *kyôshi* as a real genre with the following poem. What it does, in short, is *play proverbs differently in each line*. The first points out that if "indigence dulls a man," it increases the poor man's handicap; the second splices a food proverb to an oral idiom for work; the long third rhetorically asks if you've heard that one's passage through Hades (purgatory) depends on money; the fourth reverses the proverb that work cures poverty. I cannot reproduce the allegedly revolutionary orthography and slang (eg.喰うや), and changed the order and some other details:

為貧為頓奈世何・食也不食吾口過ぎ・君不聞地獄沙汰金次第・拮追付貧乏多

    TO EAT OR NOT TO EAT, DEPENDS ON WHAT WE EARN,
    BUT IF INDIGENCE DULLS US, CAN A MAN EVER LEARN?
    MOST OF THE TIME POVERTY OVERTAKES HARD WORK,
    OR, HAVEN'T U HEARD? EVEN GOING TO HELL TAKES MONEY TO BURN!

Blue Camels & White Swimmers: News in Character

駱　駝　怨

一落山師手
日々見物多
却思野飼時
不食貧駱駝

THE BITTER BACTRIAN　　*RAKUDA-EN*

BOUGHT BY A MONTEBLANK UNFAIR
DAY AFTER DAY, I SPIT, THEY STARE;
STILL I DREAM OF THE SANDY MOOR
WHILE MY MASTER FEEDS ME LESS &
LESS, I REGRET MY SORRY CAMELOT!

The original is four lines & says "one-fall-mountain-master's-hand / day-day-audience-many / yet-think-field-raise-time / not-eat-poor-camel=poverty-ease

This is 19c *kyôshi*, a mad-poem in the Chinese style, though the *abcb* rhyme-scheme is actually a couplet and bactrian: it extends two characters (~ *butsuta* / ~ *rakuda*). The title mimics standard trope of a "bitter courtesan." The last line takes the saying *"if you don't eat, poverty's fun"* (*kuwazu binraku binraku*) – *binraku*, lit. *poverty-ease,* a slothful state of irresponsibility the wise prefer to the burdens of wealth – punned into the underfed *rakuda*, or camel. Thanks to *"Camelot = camel lot,"* miracle, miracle, *something* of the *style* of the original wit, for once, survived translation (!), though the exact meaning was sacrificed for it. My first glimpse of those camels came when I came across two camel *ku* of the sort I would call a *kyôku*, or mad haiku, in Issa's journal. Both *ku* play on the homophonic meaning of the name *rakuda*. One is sweetly boastful and the other, which comes half a dozen *ku* later, exchanges that banal chauvinism for something mates a possible aphorism with a report on the camels.

日本にとしをとるのがらくだかな 文政七 1824
nippon ni toshi o toru no ga rakuda (raku da) kana Issa
Japan-in year/age+acc take is/are easy/camel+exclam.

..

Growing old (passing the N.Y.) in Japan, why it's camels/easy!

どこでとしとつてもそちはらくだ哉 文政七 1824
doko de toshi totte mo sochi wa rakuda (raku da) kana
where-at year taking+emph there-as-for camel/easy+exclam

Wherever they/we age, that is where they/we're camels/at ease!

The pair of camels who were paraded from one major Japanese city to another in 1822 became famous not because of the punning name as one might imagine from the *kanshi* and Issa's *kyôku*, but as exemplars of what was at the time rare behavior. *To go camel*, so to speak, was for a husband and wife to walk together in public. So Issa's ku might *also* mean that they were *together*.

洋婦浴水海瀬邑
真裸飛込形浮々
胸張腹細尻又大
恰似瓢箪之川流

WESTERN WOMEN BATHE BY THE SEA
DIVING IN NUDE, FLOAT BUOYANTLY
FULL BREASTS, THIN WAISTS, BIG BUTTS
LIKE GOURDS BOBBING DOWN A STREAM

看西洋婦人水浴　安閑坊主　狂詩大全 明治廿二

This 19c *kyôshi* has only one metaphor and poor end-rhyme – but the subject is rare and the first metaphorical description of the exaggerated secondary sexual characteristics of the Occidental woman (compared to the Far Eastern) that I know. In 19c Europe at this time, scientists were boasting that curvaceous figures demonstrated that the sexes were more specialized in Caucasians than in the more unisex Amerindians or Mongolians, proving that "we" were the more advanced race. Obviously, aesthetics were behind that rationalization. In Tokugawa Japan, large breasts were the mark of stereotypically bestial wet-nurses and large buttocks seen as a flaw on a woman's beauty, probably because their clothing minimized rather than exaggerated *le difference*. Of course, not all Japanese failed to appreciate ample posteriors.   Male-loving men liked boys with big white butts and the greatest graphic designer the world has ever seen, Hokusai, favored big-butt women for his beautiful pornography. But the general attitude was clearly anti-ass. Viz., a *Tokuwa* 徳和歌後萬載集 (1785) *kyôka*:

さげ帯をみるにつけてもをたふくの衣がへ　うき尻にぞ有ける　橘鈴也
sage-obi o miru ni tsukete mo otafuku no koromo-gae uki-jiri ni zo arikeru tachibana suzunari
lowered belt+acc see adding even Otafuku's dress-changing woeful/floating-ass/hips-by is+emph

♪ Otafuku, or Ugly A-Bun-Dance ♪

Though her belt down low she wears on every dress-change day,
Miss Plump-cheeks' sorry rump insists on floating up to play!

Otafuku, though her name means *much luck* or *happiness*, has enormous cheeks which swallow up her clitoral nose and pinch her vulvic mouth. She is usually a mask, but also synonymic for an ugly woman. I could hardly *not* bring up the *kyôka* with its play on *float!* But, to return to the swimming Occidentals. The date corresponds with reports of the popularization of swimming for health on the part of one noble. Bifurcated swim-wear was probably considered *nude*.

Old Chinese-style Poems Not Quite Mad, *But*

夜月凝来夏見霜　　*Luna's light, so thick at night, in summer does frost fall?*
姮娥触処翫清光　　*Or, is this moonshine just Heng O, still stealing about?*
荒涼院裏終宵譠　　*At ev'ry ruined mansion, dusk to dawn, a drunken ball;*
白兎千群入幾堂　　*Squads of white hare a thousand-strong fill every hall!*

This 9c Chinese-style Japanese poem is risible for different moonshine metaphor in each of the three AABA rhyming lines. Heng O is said to play, here, but she was made the lady of the moon, so to speak (for there is a man of the moon, too), after she *stole* the fruit of immortality from the Mountain Queen, hence, *stealing about*. There may be a hidden metaphor in the B line, too, for drinking at that time generally meant milky colored sake. "Ball" isn't quite right, for Japanese had no social dances in the Occidental use of the word. The 譠, with radicals suggesting *conversation+meeting*, but meaning a boisterous drunken revel (*sakamori*), we could even English it as a drunken *brawl*. White hares, like white mice, are usually used to describe white-caps in the moonlight, but "thousands of squads" of them is new. Here is Cranston's reading *"Night moon congeals until we see frost in summer, / Wherever Heng O touches, she plays with clear shining. / In the desolate mansion carousing goes on all night; / White rabbits in troops of a thousand – how many the halls they enter?"* Or, perhaps, I should say, Cranston's translation of the Japanese editor's reading: よのつきこりきたりてなつしもをみる　こうがふるるところせいくわうをもてあそぶ　くわうりやうたるゐんりよもすがらさかもりす　はくとせんぐんいくばくかだうにいる. As Cranston (Waka v2a, <u>ssmys</u> c.893) explains, these "readings" of lines of Chinese verse

> "represent the way Chinese poetry has traditionally been vocalized in Japan, a kind of halfway translation technique that is the main excuse for the type of English translation presented (Chinese verse has rhymes and other structural features that call for more attention to pattern than is commonly provided by translators of that literature in its un-Japanized state)."

..
I do not bother to Romanize, for it is, with the exception of some of the fancy words not even a prose poem, and I do not give the Chinese-style pronunciation because I am unsure of some of it. Here is another, apparently ABAB:

One "cuckoo!" spoils the mood of the boudoir;　　郭公一叫誤閨情
flitting here & there, it stays ne'er near, nor far.　　怨女偸聞悪聞声
How our lady hates to hear the call of monsieur　　飛去飛来無定処
to whom no gate, north or south, is e'er barred!　　或南或北歳門庭

These are almost a thousand years older than *The Camel's Lot* we saw in the last chapter. While they are comical, they are further from *kyôshi* than the wildest of the *waka* are to *kyôka*. No small number of *waka* are crazier than the tamer poems in *kyôka* anthologies. If truly mad Chinese style verse was written in

Japanese prior to 18c *kyôshi,* Ikkyû excepted, I do not know it. I suspect I will find more, but for now, these exercises in Chinese poem-making must do. Once the choice to squeeze them into rectangles was made, such poems proved to be an extraordinary challenge and pleasure to translate. I had hoped to introduce a dozen or even a score more, but the only book I have at hand treating them at length – my source for *The Camel's Lot* – favors longer lyrical examples over the short stuff obviously a better match for *kyôka*. The length of the Chinese-style mad poems was not limited as the Japanese ones are. When I can afford to move to Japan or buy more books, that will be remedied. Ôta wrote more short ones and I cannot wait to see all of them, but must: they are not gathered in one book and the cost in time and money to read, select, figure-out and translate them is beyond me. But, here is one more Tenmei era *kyôshi* which provides a good example of how complex they could be. It is by Gubutsu 愚仏, whose name Englishes as Foolish-Buddha.

籠 細 工 釈 迦

釈 迦 沈 苦 界
乍 寝 設 金 銀
極 楽 未 身 抜
三 途 川 竹 身

Wickerwork Shakya

SHAKYA SINKS INTO THE WORLD
EARNING MONEY ON HIS BACK
NO HIGH WAY OUT OF PARADISE
CANE ON THE STYX OFF-TRACK

The Buddha, or "savior" had a name, Shakyamuni. Thanks to this *kyôshi* (or accompanying annotation) I finally get a *ku* by Issa chuckling at Buddhas raking it in incumbent. I figured he described an idol at the temple near his home, *but I should have known better. Haikai* was nothing if *au courant*. When Issa praised a peony for being a good Fukunosuke staying plunk-down on the ground, it turned out people were troubled by men masked as the boy-god of wealth, *traditionally seated*, who danced to beg money door to door. Here, sure enough, the poem refers to another passing concern. In 1819, a hundred yard-long covered stall to the North of the West exit of the Ôsaka temple Yontenôji boasted a thirty-meter cane/bamboo-framed recumbent Buddha to celebrate the Regent, Prince Shotoku's 1,200 year anniversary. This was, apparently, *very* popular. Please note that the "painful=world" the statue/s sinks into is the secular one, where money, which he makes so easily, talks. That image, in turn, takes us to Yoshiwara, where the women make it, lying on *their* backs. Yoshiwara was called "paradise" and a woman's debts had to be bought to escape from it. Ah, but the Buddha, himself, happens to be an avatar (who stays on earth to help) and has not yet crossed the River Styx. Then, again, he is not a hurricane, so why rush?

Playing With Myths of Beginnings & Ends

千早振神も御存ない道を いつのまにかはよく教え鳥　蜀山人　蜀山百集
chihayaburi kami mo gozonjinai michi o itsu no ma ni ka wa yoku oshie tori shokusanjin
powerful deities even know-not way/road+acc some-time-as-for emph. teaching bird　1749-1823

In the Beginning Was the *What!*

God and Goddess,
how odd that, until then, this
was beyond your ken:

The way of Women and Men
had to be learned from a bird!

Yuck! Was It, then, *Cloacal?*

Almighty Deities,
to think we must thank a bird
for wagging its tail

Up and down teaching you how
the world goes round! – absurd.

There may be small puns in the original – the "powerful" gods includes a "wag" (*f=buri*) and "bird" puns into a polite form of *being taught* (*oshiet(e)ori*) – but otherwise the poem is pretty much a straight comment about something many must have thought odd. To think the good-looking deities (always shown as a handsome youth and maiden) learned what to do from a magpie (that is usually depicted alone, no less) that flies in to perch and flicks its tail up and down, does test our credulity. Moreover, the bird model poses another problem and that I put in the second reading's title. ♪When the stories of religion are taken concretely, the fun begins. The first poem below is a mild *kyôka* touching upon the robes printed with sutra sold to the dying or their relatives. You might think *cool* would want warmth, but, no. It is associated with the time it is sweetest: the summer.

極楽は涼しき道ときくからに 経かたひらをきてや行らん　未得　吾吟我集
gokuraku wa suzushiki michi to kiku kara ni kyô-katabira o kite ya yukuran mitoku 1649
paradise-as-for cool road (i) hear-from sutra gown/slip+acc. wearing go-shall!

Since I hear that Paradise is the cool place to go;
I'll wear my sutras painted on a light linen robe!

念仏を強ひて申すもいらぬもの もし極楽を通り過ぎては　桃水和尚
nenbutsu o shiite môsu mo iranu mono moshi gokuraku o tôri-sugitte wa monk tôsui
prayers+acc forcing-say+emph unneeded thing, if paradise+dat pass-by-as-for d.1683

念仏 に 明け 暮れる うつけ を 嘲笑 して
Making light of blockheads who pray day and night.

If I were you,
my friend, I would take care
not to overdo

My prayers, & dying wake
on the far side of Paradise!

It's a bad idea
to overdo prayers: hark
lest when you die

It comes to pass that you
pass Paradise right by!

Taken literally, religion is a blast, a magazine – in the old meaning of the word – full of ammunition for humor. Popular Buddhism, like Catholicism, stereotypically prospered by providing people with concrete ideas of Paradise and the itinerary taken to get there, then charging them and their surviving family hefty fees for safe-passage. The *kyôka* is not about indulgences per se, but the frame of mind in which they thrive. Though not by Ikkyû, this is the sort of witty free-thinking rationalism usually identified with Zen monks.

お釈迦さま生れ落るとみそをあげ　俳風柳多留拾遺　四
oshaka-sama umare-ochiru to miso o age　(a *senryû* pre.1801)
shakamuni(buddha's name)+hon.　born-drop and boast-raises/says

Buddha's birth
He was already boasting
as he came out!

Shaka's the most:
As soon as he was born, out
pops a big boast!

As Shakamuni
fell from his mother he was
talking up himself

This is a *senryû* and not a *kyôka*, but I could not resist including it here, for no poem I know of addresses the central contradiction of most organized religions so well. Most cultures in the Far East admire modesty so much they even expect it from their leaders. For a newly born babe to pop out with the legendary words, *Above and below Heaven I alone am precious* (or *command respect*) 天上天下唯我独尊 is truly outrageous. That is the type of boastful me-ism one might expect of a boastful Occidental (*i.e.,* Judeo-Christian-Islamic) God, not a Far Eastern one. Then again, India is somewhere between East and West. . . I am turning a mouse colored reality into a dalmation, but there *is* a difference, and it is why such a *senryû* would be immediately understood as criticism.

ねてまてどくらせどさらに何事もなきこそ人の果報なりけれ　蜀山百首
nete matedo kurasedo sara ni nanigoto mo naki koso hito no kahô narikere shokusanjin
sleep waited but lived but, further nothing+emph. person's reward became　1749-1823

"Sleep on it and your time will come" they say. I did
And found the reward was something called nothing!

There is a thin line between superstition and religion. One reads of young Japanese – particularly great men in their childhood – testing taboos just to see if the gods will really punish them, and, likewise for secular superstition. Ôta who began his career as Professor Sleep-in, was, theoretically, the perfect guinea pig for this one. Sure enough, he ended up not doing very well. Then, again, when Japanese say *"nanigoto mo naki"* (anything +emphatic not, i.e. nothing), or simply *nani mo,* they may mean what Russians do with *nichevo* – as, in *"How are you?" "Nothing."* – that is, nothing *bad* has happened, so we have something to be grateful for. In that case, this is a poem of Taoist wisdom, too, is it not?

Taking it One World at a Time: Japanese Epicureans

極楽も地獄も活て居るうちぞ　死ての後は何か有べし　空翠　一茶全集 3-43
gokuraku mo jigoku mo ikiteiru uchi zo shinde no ato wa nani ga arubeshi　kûsûi d.1763
paradise/heaven & hell too living-are during! // dying-after-as-for what? is-ought

Heaven or hell, one thing is true:
You cannot take them with you!

Looking for my own haiku scribbled here and there in the books I was reading (some books have a handful, some hundreds) in early 2008, I came across an impromptu translation of a *kyôka* Issa copied from something and stuck right into his haiku journal. While impressed with the original for including Hell in the *present*, I was more astounded yet with my translation. I had completely forgotten it; reading myself as a stranger, I could see it was one of the best sense-translations 意訳 I had ever read. When I did it, I did not yet know that *kyôka* commonly borrowed phrases yet I naturally adopted an old English aphorism to create a paraverse of the original that can only be called delightfully mad in translation. I tried to match it with things like, *"If you would seek out Heaven or Hell, / You had better enjoy them when well!"* and *"Heaven & Hell? They are mine while I live! / Death may well promise, but what can it give?"* and *"Even heaven and hell / are fleeting: enjoy them / while your heart is beating."* But, all seem dead by comparison w/ the aphorism-based reading. But, to return to the poem, Kûsûi (宝暦 13 没), was an Edo (蔵前) *haijin* and sign-maker. Issa found it on a five-foot long grave-marker (同).

極楽でのらむより只いつまでも　しなで詠る蓮ともかな　貞徳百首狂歌
gokuraku de noramu yori tada itsumade mo shina de nagamuru hachisu to mo kana
paradise-at sit-on would more-than just forever dying-not poeticize=view lotus would!

I'd rather be *alive composing poems* *to this lotus,* *than sitting on its leaf* *in paradise, deceased!*	*Thanks, but* *no thanks for the dais* *in paradise;* *Let others die, I'd stay* *alive to view the lotus.*

I'd rather be
forever here viewing
lotus leaves
for praising them beats
sitting pretty in heaven!

People in paradise in the Sinosphere are shown seated on lotus dais. I could not keep the pun on composing=viewing (*nagamuru*), hence the second reading; and "forever" would not fit in either, hence the third. All translations failed to keep the order of the first and last halves of the poem. With *"more/less than ~,"* like the numerator and denominator of fractions, on contrary sides of the sentence in English and Japanese, restoring order in translation often requires more space than a short poem allows. I crossed out the first two readings for, while they are better explanations, they are boring. The *kyôka* is by Teitoku, the *haikai* poet most often belittled for relying too much upon wordplay. I can think of nothing more harmless than wordplay, but this poem with little of it reflects Teitoku's gentle sanity that, to the masses, crazy for the next life – the grass is always greener on the other side of the grave? – might indeed have seemed mad.

我はたゝ後世のをしへをしらぬなり あうんの二字のあるにまかせて 一休
ware wa tada yo no oshie o shiranu nari aun no ni ji no aru ni makasete ikkyû 15c
i-as-4 just world's teaching+acc know-not alpha-omega's 2 letters exist-on relying

*I have no idea
of what's to come when this
World is done*

*Happy in my Bodega
I put my trust in A & Ω*

Zen is rational religion and well represented by crazy Ikkyû (1394-1481), who wrote the best known pre-Edo *kyôka*, though it is hard to tell which are his and which were written for the stories about his escapades, which generally climax in what we may call *comic rationalization*. I realize that *bodega* is odd here, but Ikkyû did drink a lot and who can resist a rhyme that may help some readers read the "two letters" mentioned in the original? Of course, the *two* letters are not あうん (3 letters/syllabets), but the Chinese characters 阿吽, and not really them but the Sanskrit seed-letters they represent. *Alpha & Omega*, the Beginning & End.

*Who cares what they say about the World to come;
Trust Alpha and Omega, then we all can have fun!*

As we saw with the New Year's gate-pine haiku by Zuigen (p.37), *a-un* generally meant the *in* and the *out* of breath and energy. Using it to sum up our life in this world is brilliant. This poem deserves more readings. So does the next, not because it is as clever but because it provides a fine window on the free-thinking called Zen. One story has it that Ikkyû wrote it for the father of a disciple.

ひとり来てひとり帰るも我なるを 道をおしへんといふぞおかしき 一休
hitori kite hitori kaeru mo ware naru o michi o oshien to iu zo okashiki ikkyû
alone coming alone returning too i/self be yet road+acc teach-would say+emph strange

*We come alone,
and we return alone,
this much is known!*

*How odd to even think
I could teach you the way!*

*Solo we come;
Solo we go; so how can
another know?*

*You would ask me to talk
about the way? Just walk!*

Life After Death, Death After Death, & Doubt

この世にて慈悲も悪事もせぬ人は　さぞや閻魔もこまりたまわん　一休
kono yo nite jihi mo akuji mo senu hito wa sazo ya enma mo komari tamawan ikkyû
this year/times-as-for mercy-and bad-things do not person-as-for yep, yama even troubled

In this world, those who do neither good deeds nor evil,
How they must bedevil the Ruler of Hades!

◆　◆　◆　◆　◆

There are people in this world, who do ne'er good nor bad.
Yama, Judge of Hades, they must drive that Devil mad!

This was taken from a long series of queries, replies and take-offs dwelling on matters of religious significance attributed to Ikkyû (d.1481) and link-verse master and fellow in Zen, Chikamasa 親当 (蜷川新右衛門 d.1448). In 17-14 syllabet format, these *dôka* 道歌, literally songs of the way, usually translated as "moral poems" are sometimes defined as pedagogical or religious *kyôka*, perhaps because the best tickle or jolt the mind as they preach, but most are too humdrum to be fun, much less mad. The above *is*, for it is pure fun made at the expense of popular Buddhist belief. The kind King of Hades, a muscular demon who looks terrifying as he is red from drinking molten metal to punish himself for inflicting punishment (though done for justice) uses a large magnifying glass, to search out new arrivals for every merciful or cruel thing they might have done and charging his lackeys to mete out the fair (and, as depicted by Japanese artists, extremely creative) punishment. To put the poem into 20-21c Usanian slang, one might say the do-nothings were driving poor Enma (Yama in Sanskrit) *postal*. The poem before, by Chikamasa, is this: *"Fooled into thinking that Heaven and Hell exist, / Some find bliss on earth, others only fear"* (極楽や地獄があるとだまされてよろこぶ人におじる人々 親当 *gokuraku ya jigoku ga aru to damasarete yorokobu hito ojiru hitobito*). Many of my readers will have read one of the most-translated of all *senryû*, where a Buddhist priest tells his mistress that Hell is a fiction, presumably to allay her worry of being penalized heavily by sleeping with a man of the cloth. Well, that priest was not necessarily lying, for Zen Buddhists were not true-believers. I cannot recall a poem as good as Chikamasa's at describing how such belief affects people and, therefore, fiction or not, is useful (a common idea among Japanese Confucians, too). Still, it is too damn sober. *As a mad poem*, Ikkyû's chuckling envoi wins. Now, let's see one where Ikkyû goes first:

死んでから　仏というもなにゆえぞ / 小言もいわず邪魔にならねば　一休
shinde kara hotoke to iu mo nani yue zo kogoto mo iwazu jama ni naraneba ikkyû
die-from buddha say/call+emph what reason+exclam complaint say-not & bother be-not-if

Why do they call us buddhas after we die? I cannot say,
Unless it's because none complains or gets in the way

◆　◆　◆　◆　◆

So, why is it that they call us buddhas after we die?
You don't complain or get in the way, that's why!

I have mixed feelings about calling the deceased "buddhas" – translation is hard enough without having to guess whether a fly is on a corpse or a statue – but this poem by Ikkyû is the first time I knew Japanese to think about this. The first translation is closest to the original syntax, but I prefer my looser reading. Ikkyû reminds me of late 20c Japan's most outrageous metaphor, *sôdai gomi*, "sundry large trash," originally a term for sorting garbage for collection, but applied to retired good-for-nothing husbands who were so busy at work that they cannot do any domestic chores and only get in the way of their far healthier and confident wives. We can imagine the complaints and back-seat driving by the bed-ridden old man called a buddha – in the vernacular, *a kind person* – after he dies. As with the last exchange, though in the reverse order, where Ikkyû gives us wit – *though my respondent feels that with this one I may well have invented most of it* – Chikamasa's gives us undeniable wisdom: *"Becoming a buddha after you die is a worthless trick; / Become a good person while still among the quick!"* (死んでから仏になるはいらぬもの 活きたるうちによき人となれ 親当 *shinde kara hotoke ni naru wa iranu mono ikitaru uchi ni yoki hito to nare*). The poem is good and read with knowledge of the common use of "buddha" witty, but, again, it makes too much sense to be mad by any account. Ikkyû, himself, envoi'ed w/ something tamer: *"Coming alone and leaving alone we equally stray. / I'd teach a way we do not come and do not know"* ひとり来てひとりかえるも迷いなり / きたらず知らぬ道をおしえん 一休 *hitori kite hitori kaeru mo mayoi nari kitarazu shiranu michi o oshien*).

極楽は十万億士はるかなり/ とてもゆかれぬわらじ一足 一休
gokuraku wa jûmanokudo haruka nari totemo yukarenu waraji issoku ikkyû
paradise-as-for 100,000x100,000,000 lands distant is, at-all go-cannot sandals 1-pair

Paradise lies a million leagues yonder – that's far away
Fat chance you'll make it, with one pair of straw sandals!

◆ ◆ ◆ ◆ ◆

Paradise lies a trillion countries over – even a gambler
Would say 'no dice', with but one pair of straw sandals!

歳々に悪魔外道のながさるる / その西方にゆきたくもなし 親当
toshidoshi ni akuma gaidô no nagasaruru sono nishikata ni yukitaku mo nashi
year-year-in/by demon/s outer-road flow/go, this westward go-want-not! chikamasa

~~Year after year, that is the way those demons always flee;~~
Year after year, that is where those bad men find fraternity;
'Go West, old man!' they say, but it's no place I would be!

Poem 1. A dead-man is buried with a pair of macramé straw sandals. Standard for foot travel, pilgrims bought new ones every day and equestrians had footmen whose job was keeping their horses outfitted with the same. My "league" and "countries" are *Buddhist lands* and the distance to Paradise, in popular Buddhism, West. *Poem 2*. I assumed Chikamasa referred to native ideas of demons fleeing beans on the Spring equinox, but my respondent thinks he jokes at sects of Buddhism which claim bad men go to Paradise *with particular ease* (it is fun to think of why that is so). I crossed out my reading for he is almost certainly right.

Nothing Sacred: Buddha, Gods, Heaven & Hell

ねさめにも思ひ出して床しきは 彼極楽を恋の病か　正恵　銀葉夷歌集
nezame ni mo omoidashite tokoshiki wa ano gokuraku o koi no yamai ka shôe 1679
waking-up-while-even thinking-of bed-as-for that paradise+acc love/longing disease?

So you awaken thinking of it as you lie alone in bed –
Could paradise, like being lovesick, be all in the head!
～～～～～～～～～～～～～～～～～～～
If you lie awake thinking about it in the darkness
Does that make paradise a type of love-sickness?

The second reading is closest to the original. Though the beauty of the idea struck me immediately, on slowing down to translate, I found the equation of a condition with a place too abrupt: "all in the head" is a child of rhyme and reason.

ねがはくは我後の世は鬼となりて 地獄におつる人をたすけむ　藤原貞因
negawakuba waga ato no yo wa oni to narite jigoku ni otsuru hito o tasukemu tein 同
wish-could-if my aftr/nxt wrld-as4 demon-to becmng hell-into fallng people+acc help-wld
..

This is my wish: to turn into a demon in the next world,
So I can save lost souls in hell where they are hurled.
～～～～～～～～～～～～～～～～～～～
My wish, this: that in the next world I can be a devil,
Born in hell to help the many fallen ones be well.

I found little of interest in the religious part of anthologies of "savage" or "mad" poems that didn't jump out grab me by the throat, until happening across the above two in a 1679 anthology. The specialized vocabulary, including many words of the worst sort to pun upon in translation, names is off-putting.

むつかしく説いたり又はやはらけつ一味のあめをねふらされけり　言因　銀葉夷歌集
muzukashiku toitari mata wa yawaraketsu hitomi no ame o neburasarekeri genin 1679
difficultly explaining also-as-for soften, one-taste of heaven/sweet/sucker+acc lick-have

Rather than trying to explain what's hard or make it easy
Give them Heaven on a Stick: it will soften as they lick!
～～～～～～～～～～～～～～～～～～～
Rather than explain what is arcane or make it explicit,
Give them a taste of heaven, a pun to help them lick it!

It so happens that heaven, *ame* is homophonous with a *sweet*, a sucker. *Sucker* has no bad connotations in Japanese, but without the magical just-so rationale of the pun binding *heaven* to a *sucker*, any translation sucks in the English sense of the word. I will not even *try* for another favorite from the same anthology that has *the Buddha ladling bad people out of the cauldrons of hell* (see pg. 109 and 602) It is stunning for the simple power of the puns on Shaka, the personal name of Buddha – ladle is *shakushi* and *shi* a polite word for mr, like, say, "sir," so we have Sir Shaku 釈氏 (it works for orthographic reasons I will skip) – and the verb *scoop*, homophonous with *"save."* 悪人の地こくの釜へ落行を 中にすくふ は釈しなりけり 克明 同 *akunin no jigoku no kama e ochiyuku o naka ni sukuu wa shakushi narikeri* yoshiakira? (10c). Then, again, this 1679 collection has something not found in many *kyôka* collections, a variety of *dirty* religious poems, all too much to do more than briefly explain here. One expresses thanks for the gift of dark *mame,* or bean/s, from a nun ある尼の豆得させしに in a prayer where "namu-amidabutsu" becomes "*mame*-amidabutsu" and plays on the bean of the prayer beads and that on the nun あまこせのつまくるすゝの玉にに た まめあみだふつ／＼ 沢庵和尚 銀葉夷歌集 *amagoze no tsumakuru susu no tama ni nita mame-amidabutsu x2* Takuan d.1645 (蛇足：似た・煮た？). The poet a famous maverick monk we saw in the lampoon chapters was just having his fun and probably got nothing more than the real thing (beans).

やねとやね谷の隣に声はるはうぐひすならでほゝうほけ経　天保川成
yane to yane tani no tonari ni koe haru wa uguisu nara de hohôhokekyô tenpô no kawanari
 roof and roof valley-in/from voice/s spring-as4 warbler is-not-as hohô...(sutra-words)
..

      Out from the dales between the blue roofs, voices spring;
      No, no warbler, this – just neighbors *ho-hô-hoke-kyôing!*

On finding this many fun religious *kyôka* in the 1679 book, I returned to the first book I read, the 1785 *Tokuwa* anthology by Yomo no Akara et al. to see if I missed any good ones in the religious section (or rather *sections*, for it was divided into Buddhism-related 釈教 and Gods(Shinto)-related 神紙 poems. It turned out I missed little of value that could be translated – there were few poems interesting *conceptually*. There were many good puns. A carter praying for deliverance in the face of repeated heavy sins committed by punning on his work. The implicit (old) idea – people who work animals hurt their karma by it – is too little. 車力念仏　明くれにつみかさねたる車引身をうしとてや願ふ念仏　北向左武喜 徳和歌後萬載集 *akekure ni tsumi-kasanetaru kurumahiki mi o ushi tote ya* . . . Kitamuki Sabuki. The above nightingale/warbler poem is better for reversing the vector of the metaphor. But it is still largely lost in translation. Though I may have saved the pun on *spring*, "voices" do not belong to birds as well as humans in English. I thought of *chuckling, calling* and *murmuring*, but none work for a sutra, do they? Style and translatability aside, the poems – including the grape and lice prayer beads we have seen elsewhere – are tamer than the old ones. None poke fun at religious ideas. The Shintô chapter does have one risqué take on Heaven's Cave: *"Pulling aside the august reed blind for the Cavern Door – Out comes a white face . . . If it's not the crossroads whore!"* (とこやみのよし簾の岩戸ひき明て面しろくもいづる辻君 奈間川野等人 同 *tokoyami no yoshizu no iwato* . . *namakawa norabito*). It is really a triple conflation of dancing Goddess outside the cave, Sun Goddess within and the harlot, but it is still a poem of little import. The best *kyôka* in the section applies the equation of *gods/paper* ⇒ *trash* attributed to Shikibu (p.94) to an old *waka* requesting the Milky Way to supply water to transplanted rice seedlings (天の河苗代水にせきくだせあま降ります神ならばかみ　野因 金葉 c.1126 *amanokawa naedai mizu ni* . . .) and works its way down to *a waste basket*. Japanese readers ⇒ はらひ給ひきよめて給ふさいはいにあま下りますかみ屑の籠 久壽根兼満 *harai tamai kiyomete tamau saiwai ni amakudarimasu kamikuzu no kago* kusune kanemitsu.

Lotus Jewels – or Foolish Philosophical Questions

蓮飯・めしはみなくひつくしたる蓮葉にのこれる粒や露とあざむく 瓠のから酒 徳和
meshi wa mina kuitsukushitaru hachisuha ni nokoreru tsubu ya tsuyu to azamuku hisago no karazake
meal-as-for all eat-exhausted lotus-leaves-on remaining grains: dew-as deceive/resemble

*The grains of rice
stuck to the lotus leaf
after you've eaten*

*I guess they're trying
to pass for dew drops.*

*After a good meal
some grains of rice stay
on your lotus leaf*

*Trying to make you think
they are nothing but dew.*

This mad poem titled "Lotus-rice/lunch," *Hasuhan,* by Hisago no Karazake from the single most famous anthology of *kyôka* has no wordplay in it. *None.* Hamada, the Iwanami annotator says unkindly, *"it is just a poem that has rice grains stand for dew drops."* How misleading! The poem throws a monkey wrench into hundreds of years of poems about lotus-hood and dew-drops, both of which symbolize purity, though one relates more to the eternal, and one to the ephemeral. It also alludes to a famous *Kokinshû waka* by Archbishop Henjô (816-90) that may have thrown the first wrench in jest,

(Mad Poem, or Not?)

*Lotus risen up
from mud, so pure of heart
how* dare *you!*

Or, rather, why do *you
make jewels, with art?*

*Lotus leaves,
pure of soul, unstained
by the mud below*

*How is it, even you could
pass your dew for pearls?*

はちす葉のにごりにしまぬ心もてなにかは露を玉とあざむく 遍照
hachisu-ha no nigori ni shimanu kokoro mote nanika wa tsuyu no tama to azamuku
lotus leaf/s' muddiness-in stain-not heart having what/why-so dew's gem as defraud/pretend

Were this a haiku, the poem would be a back-handed celebration of the beauty of dew on lotus leaves; but the verb *azamuku* suggesting dew deliberately mis-represents itself is *outrageous*. The resemblance of dew-drops to *tama* (gem/jewel/ball/pearl) was a commonplace, but Henjô surely knew *Manyôshû* poem #3837, which notes prosaically – the poem was an impromptu response to a request for a lotus leaf poem because the party was eating off them – that there was "water gathered on the lotus leaves resembling *tama"* despite no rain being around. Henjô takes his first fifteen syllabets are straight from the *Lotus Sutra* 法華経の湧出品. The only argument for not calling Henjô's *waka* a *kyôka* is that a Zen priest is *expected* to be a wise guy and poke fun at religious symbols. It gave rise to numerous prodigy (parody is too limited), most too boring to report much less translate. The exceptions are by the 17c *kyôka* poet Mitoku, and the late-18c scholar of ancient Japanese and nationalist Motoori Norinaga:

見事にて 手にはとられす 白露のきえやすきこそ玉に疵なれ 未得　吾吟我集
migoto nite te ni wa torarezu shiratsuyu no kieyasuki koso tama ni kizu nare mitoku 1649
beautiful-as hand-in-as for taking/holding-cannot white-dew's vanish-easiling esp. gem-on flaw is

> *So beautiful I would pick them up, these dewy pearls!*
> *'Tis a flaw in perfection to break as easily as they do.*

~~~~~~~~~~~~~~~~~~

> *So damn beautiful, yet I cannot pick up the luminous dew,*
> *'Tis said perfection always has a flaw: you break, it's true.*

風こえてちるぞ涼しき蓮葉になにかは露を玉とのみ見む　本居宣長
kaze koete chiruzo suzushiki hachisuha ni nani ka wa tsuyu o tama to nomi mimu
wind crossing scatter+emph. cool lotus leaf-by/in what-as-for dew+acc. gem as only see

> *Winds pass over*
> *and off they go: that's cool.*
> *So what makes us*
>
> *want to see the dew drops*
> *on lotus pads as jewels?*

> *How cool it is*
> *when they skate about*
> *with the wind!*
>
> *What in the lotus pad makes*
> *us see dew drops as gems?*

Mitoku's poem seems trite until you recall that the fragility and short-life of dew is what makes it a precious metaphor. ♪Norinaga's is harder. Is it 1) refreshing that dew scatters rather than staying as a real gem/pearl would? 2) cool watching them slide about (lotus dew is a summer phenomenon)? or 3), is the leaf, or pad, itself cool from the evaporated dew drops? (*What is there in a lotus pad, so cool when wind scatters the dew drops, to make us see them only as jewels?*). The inclusion of a chunk of Henjô's poem and that extraordinarily rational question – all fresh questions are, to most people, who never ask them, mad – makes this a *kyôka* of sorts. The chapter lead by Hisago no Karazake is very different. Call it an indirect, deliberately naive criticism of metaphor-mongering, accomplished by *reversing* the metaphor rather than questioning it: instead of the dew pretending to be something substantial, something substantial pretend to be dew. Its madness, then, lies not in having rice grains stand for dew-drops (maggots could do that better), but in the discovery that metaphor itself is double-edged sword.

~~~~~~~~~~~~~~~~~~

白露のてれん偽なき世哉　一茶　文化九
shiratsuya no teren itsuwari naki yo kana issa
white-dew's sleight-of-hand deception not world!

> *White dew drops, this much I understand –*
> *No fraud is involved in your sleight of hand*

~~~~~~~~~~~~~~~~~~

> *The magic of pearly dew drops is for real.*

~~~~~~~~~~~~~~~~~~

> *This dew works magic that we might realize*
> *the real world > lies < before our eyes!*

If Dew Drops Were Delicious, Men Being Men

白露に味のなきこそうれしけれ 甘くば人の集まりやせん 一茶 文政三
shiratsuyu ni aji no naki koso ureshikere amakuba hito no atsumariyasen Issa 1823
white-dew-in flavor/taste's not +emph. happy-be sweet-if peoples' gather-not-do?

The Treasure Hunt

We should be
grateful that dew drops
have no taste;

For, if they did, not a one
would long remain in place!

Beauty for Free

That dew drops
are not sweet is something
to be thankful for:

No one will try to rob
the poor of their eye treat.

Issa has definitely written a mad poem here. For a poor man in particular, dew is something rare and valuable: beauty to be had on the cheap, though the second reading which makes that explicit is, obviously (see the gloss) my paraverse. I suspect there was already some old poem or proverb or story noting dew's lack of flavor, but, who knows. Issa did read enough that he probably thought of Tao-master Zhuang-zhi's good-for-nothing and therefore long-lived tree. Applying that principle to dew took some doing! Many if not most of Issa's *kyôka*, are preceded or followed by haiku, or, since the content is similar, *kyôku*. Here are two *ku*-length versions of the above:

味あらば喧嘩の種ぞ露の玉 一茶
aji araba kenka no tane zo tsuyu no tama
flavor have-if quarrels' seed/s +emph. dew drops

*if they had taste
they would cause quarrels
pretty dew drops*

*the dew drops
would surely brew fights if
they tasted good*

*sure as hell
if dew tasted good, we'd
fight over it*

*if sweet, it would
surely be "my dew"
and your dew*

*if sweet, it would
be "my dew" to me
& yours to you*

sweet-if yep my dew people/other's dew
amakaraba sazo oraga tsuyu hito no tsuyu
甘からばさぞおらが露人の露

*if sweet the dew
would be divided into
mine and thine*

This pessimistic – or, just realistic? – view of animal nature was not confined to humans. Years earlier, Issa noted how one could not feed chickens without causing a fight between them. Because of his extraordinary interest in dew drops, the ideas were bound to merge. Issa's hundreds of dew *ku* range from sublime to peevish, hard-boiled to maudlin, joyous to tortured. Dozens are idea-centric *kyôku* or near-*kyôku*. I hesitate to introduce more as I plan to do a book on nothing but *dew*, but as I write, looking over dozens of pages of Issa's dew *ku* in my 3000 page manuscript, the first thing I ever did on a computer, I cannot resist.

小便の露のたし也小金原　一茶
shôben no tsuyu no tashi naru kogane hara
piss's dew's addition becoms small-money fld

Small-Change Field
Pissing, I add my two-bits
to the fresh dew.

福の神見たまへ露が玉になる
fukunokami mitamae tsuyu ga tama ni naru
fortune/happinss-god look! dew ball/gem becms

God of fortune,
observe: Dew becomes
Pearl & Gem.

門の露玉などになる智恵もなし
kado no tsuyu tama nado ni naru chie mo nashi
gate's dew gem/ball-into become knowlege even not

dew by my gate
lacks the savoir faire
to make jewels

玉となる欲はある也草の露
tama to naru yoku wa aru nari kusa no tsuyu
gem-into become greed-as-for has is grass/weed's dew

It does *desire*
to become a polished gem
dew in the weeds

我庵が玉にきずかよ草の露
waga io ga tama ni kizu ka yo kusa no tsuyu
my hut/hermitage gem-on flaw? grass/weed's dew

My hermitage,
a scratch upon a jewel!
Dew on the grass

小便も玉と成りけり芋畠 文政6
shôben mo tama to narikeri imobatake
piss/urine even ball/gem as becom! taro-patch

Even my pee
has become jewels!
A taro patch

Even your piss
can turn into jewels!
The taro patch

The first poem is madder in translation thanks to the *two-bit* idiom. The second is a half-stated charm working the gem metaphor in a novel way. The third plays Issa blues on an old saw. The fourth, clearly *kyôku,* is damaged in translation for lack of a *tama*=ball+gem word. Would "smooth and round" beat "polished gem"? But for the cheap connotation *bead* would be good. Other *ku* describe dew as busily trying to become *tama*. It recalls Henjô's dew-drops passed off as gems and Hisho no Karazake's rice pretending to be dew. The fifth, a self-deprecatory *kyôku,* is better in numberless Japanese so one need not think of dew as a singularity. The taro patch *ku* is often encountered. I should add that Issa *also* has poems showing he really looked closely at dew. Eg. *When you actually / go out to collect the dew / bent-gems, long-gems*(いざ拾へ露の曲玉長い玉 *iza hiroe . . .*).

Witty Words of Wisdom or Weighing the Way Song

貧乏の棒もかせげばおのずから　振り回しよくなるも世の中
binbô no bô mo kasegeba onozukara furimawashi yoku naru yo no naka proverb dictionary
poverty=binbô's bô=pole+emph work-if, self-from swing-around=affluent become world/times tk1

If just the bô in binbô, that means a stick,
were put to good use, poverty would not.

As I do not yet have the dictionary with 1,300 *dôka*, I do not know what percent are no-preach Zen, as opposed to pontification such as the above, which nonetheless plays upon one common writing of poverty/*binbô*, 貧棒, with a stick 棒 in it. Sticks, or rather *poles*, were used for displaying and carrying things, including people in Japan. The poem *also* uses one idiom for the resulting affluence to punfully allude to another where swinging poles is *fiddling around* doing nothing.

その昔喧嘩すきしたとろ房や　棒振虫と生れきぬらん　愛宗　銀葉夷 tk
sono mukashi kenkazuki shita dorobô ya bôfurimushi to umarekinuran aisô 1679
once longago quarrel/fight-loving-did robber [was]! pole-swinging=mosq.larv. as born came!

Once upon a time there was a robber who loved to fight.
A mosquito larva, now, his cudgel swings til he takes flight.

If you believe in reincarnation this is a caveat. It is a mismatch for the chapter – *too good* – but I have no chapter for moral *kyôka,*' and the 'squito larvae chapter is full. Were we talking *cells*, flagellates might have shared something w/ stick-swingers. I had to re-create the humor with a 2-step developmental metaphor.

福の神　祈る間あらば　働いて　貧乏神を　追い出せかし
fukunokami inoru ma araba hataraite binbôgami o oidasekashi
prosperity-god/s (-to) pray time is-if, working, povertygod+acc drive-off-might

'Ye god of wealth' – Have you time to pray? Then, work
And you can drive your own god, Poverty, away!

火の車　つくる大工は　なけれども　おのがつくりて　おのが乗りゆく
hinokuruma tsukuru daiku wa nakeredomo onoga tsukurite noriyuku
fire-cart making carpenter-as-for not-but, self made, riding-go

No carter a fire-cart can make, but thee, thyself,
Who must then ride upon it with all thy wealth!

In 1972, I overheard a door-to-door make-up saleslady I sowed some wild oats with praying to the God of Wealth, and myself admit to being the proud owner of that fictive reification of poverty, *a fire-cart*. I wonder how many of us who towed about little red wagons as children grew up to be paupers! These paternalistic *dôka*, unlike the chapter lead, are not creative enough to be called *kyôka*.

世の中にあると思うな親と金　ないと思うな運と天罰
yononaka ni aru to omou na oya to kane   nai to omou na un to tenbatsu
world-in are think not! parents & money; (are)-not think not, luck & punishment

Think not that they will be there, your parents & money.
Nor think that karma's not there, for fate can be funny!

母のちち父のすねこそ恋しけれ ひとりでくらふ事のならねば　つぶり光 才蔵
haha no chichi chichi no sune koso koishikere hitori de kurau koto no naraneba tsumuri no hikaru
mother's breasts/milk father's calves esp. dear! alone eat/live-thing become-not-if 1787

How you miss your mama's paps and pappy's money bags
When you cannot make a living and life drags on!

The first, somewhat mad in the play between positive and negative is too didactic to be anything but a *dôka*. I dropped *divine retribution* for *karma* and added the *funny* rhyme. The second, by Tsumuri no Hikaru (lit. "(his) head shines) is not a *dôka* as it has no moral instruction but just tells it as it is. The odd coupling of mother's breasts and father's *calves* is *kyôka*. The latter is what full grown dependents are said to chew on. Father and breasts/milk are both *chichi*.

迷いぞと知る心こそ悟りなれ 悟りと知るは迷いなるべし 無名？
mayoi zo to shiru kokoro koso satori nare satori to shiru wa mayoi narubeshi anon?
wandering/lost+emph as knowing heart/mind+emph enlightenment be
satori as knowing-as-for wandering/lost ought[to be called]

The heart that knows it wanders lost has found the light,
While one that sees the light, wanders ever in the night.

A standard *dôka*. In the original, a witless Zen paradox. I replaced the *satori*, or enlightenment, with *light,* then added the *night* to make both significant.

おく山へかくれんよりは亀を見て をのれにかくせをのが手足を 蜀山人
okuyama e kakuren yori wa kame o mite onore ni kakuse onoga teashi o shokusanjin
interior mountains-in hide-try rather-than, turtle+acc see, self-in hide! own limbs+acc d.1823

Why head for the hills to become a sage? Go within.
Let Tortoise be your teacher & withdraw your limbs.

Because this poem by our main *kyôka* master seems less mad than some haiku on copying the sea cucumber (*Rise Ye Sea Slugs!* 2003), I first did a jazzed up version, *Rather than retire back in the hills, look at the turtle! / Pull into your self and hide: Live less, be more fertile!* Context might change this. Accompanying a picture of a turtle *as intended* (亀の画に題して隠居の心を), it might amuse more without Ogden's "fertile." I first found Shokusanjin's poem squeezed into page 176 wishing we could be like (Japanese) coins, *square on the inside and round without* in a collection of moral poems and found it so and so, but cracked up reading it following the title *"In Praise of Coins"* 銭の賛, which makes one waver between it and the text wondering which is facetious ⇒ ずれにこそ狂あり。

Less Witty Wisdom, or Weighing Way Poems II

世の中を 恥じぬ人こそ 恥となり 恥ずる人には 恥ぞ少なき
yo no naka o hajinu hito koso haji to nari hajizuru hito ni wa haji zo sukunaki
world-in ashamed-nt person esp. shameful is, ashmd-nt persn-as4 shame's little

If you feel no shame before the world, brother, you should
If you feel ashamed, you're not that bad – you're good

欲深き人の心と降る雪は 積もるにつけて道を忘るる
yokubukaki hito no kokoro to furu yuki wa tsumoru ni tsukete michi o wasureru
desire-deep person's heart/mind and falling snow-as4 piles-up and road+acc forgotten

How is the heart of a greedy man just like the falling snow?
Want upon want piles up until the Way is lost below!

There are books with nothing but "way-songs" *dôka*, but I have none and can only hope the examples I netted for the last chapter were a fair sampling. My impression is that most tend to resemble the above, *i.e.,* pure paradox and mild metaphor, with no saving grace (other than the rhyme, added in translation); but, checking about a 31-syllabet poem (家の風ふかぬ物ゆへはづかしの森のことの葉ちらしはて<u>ぬる</u> ie no kaze fukanu mono yue hazukashi no mori no koto no ha 親が時々怒らないとむしろやばいことになる？) in Tokugen's *Mottomo no Sôshi*, a 17c book of listing (*monowazukushi*), I found variations on that untranslatable pun-filled advice for life in two books, one of which was clearly a collection of punning *waka*, "Similar Letter Famous Place Waka Collection" (『類字名所和歌集』には「ちらしはて<u>つる</u>」). That is when I learned of whole books of *dôka,* presented, as you might guess – morals must be look-up-able – as *dictionaries of ~. That* suggests I have yet to scratch the surface of the genre. With no ready access to such a book in the woods of Florida, I hoped to convince my respondent to peek at such a dictionary and scoop out a witty selection but he was not terribly interested. Who can blame him! With a world of better poems out there . . . and I knew *I* could read the religious parts of *waka* and *kyôka* collections I already had and ferret out some myself. Doing just that I found some good, i.e. mad, ones in the 1666 *Kokin Ebisu-kyokushû* that prove the mating of moral & mad was even greater than I had imagined. Be that as it may, I find the taxonomy tricky to work out. Not all religious poems are didactic, not all didactic poems are religious, not all moral poems are either, nor vice-versa, and there are philosophical poems that seem to fit none of these categories (like most of Piet Hein's grooks). Here are three hard to categorize examples. First, from the 1312 *Gyokuyô wakashû*. Nichibun withheld the poet's name.

たのもしな ひかりをちりに ましへつつ あとをたるてふ くにつもろかみ 玉葉集
tanomoshina hikari o chiri ni majie-tsutsu ato o taru chô kunitsu morokami　ng　p.1312
wonderfl light+acc trash-w/in mxing-while aftr-hanging-buttrfly/ies country's many-gods

A delight to find light consorting with trash, Gods of our land
Butterflies on fallen bloom, among the Boddhisattva!

~~~~~~
Hope is finding light informing trash, staying behind
Butterflies on fallen bloom, boddhisattva in our midst!
~~~~~~
Hope is light informing trash, a band of little butterflies
remaining w/ the fallen bloom, boddhisattva in our land!

The "hope is" readings bring out the didactic feeling. The words *ato o taru* remind me of modern Novelist Natsume Sôseki describing his sorry bowel movements, but mean *a being that, while it could except Enlightenment and be out of here, kindly decides to stay around and help us*. This may be in a *waka* collection, but butterfly boddhisattvas are definitely mad. *Kunitsu* is the land of Japan in the local and, therefore, deep sense one feels with a tutelary deity, among which (and many/sundry are specified) the butterfly seems to be included, thereby bridging not only this world and the next but Buddhism, Shintô and Nature. The second is from another collection of medieval (11-14c – Vague, for I lost a day's work including more, thanks to a Microsoft update ambush) *waka,* found at Nichibun:

いつかたに－ゆきかくれなむ－よのなかに－みのあれはこそ－ひともつらけれ
izukata ni yukikakurenamu yononaka ni mi no areba koso hito mo tsurakere anon 13c?
where-to going-hide-would wrld/society-in bdy/substnce is/hve-if+emph person pained

Where in the world can a human hide without going insane?
We need our bodies to remain yet they insist we live in pain!
~~~~~~
Where in the world can a man go to hide and remain,
When the body life demands also keep us all in pain?
~~~~~~
Where, oh, where, can a man go in a world gone mad,
When life is even harder for a gentleman than his cad?

Mi can mean a body in the concrete sense – taken that way, the wit grows – but it may also mean someone of substance, and it was true that the nobles, especially relatives of the Imperial family risked assassination, etc.. Either way, there is no moral message *per se*, unless it is the Buddhist tenet that life on earth means suffering. The poem rings like a popular song, which maybe it was. And, finally, the most different of my examples. It is from Tokugen's 17c *Mottomo no Sôshi:*
..
物の名もところによりてかはりけり難破の芦は伊勢のはま荻　尤之 双紙
mono no na mo tokoro ni yorite kawarikeri naniwa no ashi wa ise no hama-ogi
thing's nms' evn place-on depndng, change+emph naniwa's reeds-as4 ise's beach-fan

The names of things change from place to place;
Naniwa's famous Cane is Ise's waving Beach Fan.

Various earlier versions have the names of *plants* 草の名, but Tokugen, as a man of *haikai* and *kyôka,* improved it by not giving away the "plants" up front. He presents the young shôgun a lesson: relativism = localism. The plant is really a *miscanthus,* reed. Be that as it may, my point is that there is a whole world of didactic poetry out there I need to see more of before coming to any conclusions.

The 40 year-old Chickadee & other Capped Kyôka

四十からはおいの中にぞ入りにける 若狭にかへる道が知りたい
Youth: *shijûkara wa oi no naka ni zo irinikeri* ・ Old man: *wakasa ni kaeru michi ga shiritai*
chickadee-as-for (travel)casket-within+emph. went ・ wakasa-to return road-the know-want
forty-as-for old-age-within+emph entered ・ youthfulness-to return road/way-the know-want

Young man to old pilgrim

*A chickadee
has gone into your
travel casket*

Old pilgrim to young man

*So, please let me ask it,
The way back to Wakasa!*

Young man to old pilgrim

*From age forty
Sir, you're on the road
to being old*

Old pilgrim to young man

*If so, I shall be so bold
To ask the way back to youth!*

An old capped *kyôka* probably born of a medieval tale. In Japanese, my two readings are one poem, but to so translate it would require changing the bird to, say, a *heron* to pun with *"hair on,"* a *robin* with *"robbing,"* etc. and creating a new story. According to Hiroaki Sato, who only gives one version (*"A chickadee has gone into the travel casket"* / *"I'd like to know the road to Wakasa"*), it is one of "two episodes showing how *renga* in its pristine form may have been composed." (*One Hundred Frogs:* 1983) He takes the anecdote from Fukui Kyûzô (1867-1951), a *renga* (link-verse) scholar, who recalled hearing it from his mother. To sum a long recounting, the youth saw the old man stopped at a "fork" in the road and, noting what the chickadee did, *"gave it a moment's thought, then looked quite pleased with himself. He said to himself, 'Isn't this fun!' and loudly to the pilgrim:"* Then, after the pilgrim, who pretended to refuse to cap the chickadee verse, asked the way to Wakasa, we learn *"At this, the young man clapped his hands and delightedly exclaimed, 'That's it! That's it! Now we have a wonderful renga!"* I am delighted with Sato's prose translation, but think his reading of the poem – he later explains that "the young man, presumes that the sight of a chickadee going into a travel casket fuels the desire to go home" – does not even come *close* to warranting that young man's excitement. *How* did he miss it? Sato also writes *"The relative independence of each part is vital because in linked poetry the sense of linking must be maintained and that is greatly enhanced by the element of unexpectedness in transition,"* and that *"the pilgrim's response is accidental."* Did Sato the puns escape Sato because he anticipated surreal disjunction? There was one tell-tale speed-bump that should have slowed him down. The pilgrim's home-town was *not* Wakasa, but Obama. Wakasa may well be on the way to Obama, but both are 3-syllabets (yielding the same 7-7); *there is no reason for a second name to be brought into the poem if not for the pun.* So, if the exchange is a prototype for link-verse (*renga*), it is for the sort of *haikai-no-renga* that shares much of the spirit of the stand-alone poem that came to be called *kyôka*. And, I would not be surprised to find this story the *renga* scholar's mother told him was invented by someone familiar with *kyôka* in the 16-18c. (See ♪s at book-end!)

(Shrine Master to Shikibu)

*Would you wrap
almighty gods like paper
around your feet!*

(Shikibu to Shrine Master)

*Isn't this shrine the one
called nether? It's neat!*

ちはやぶるかみをば 足にまく物か 神主 忠頼
これをぞ下の社とはいふ 和泉式部連歌　巻十雑部下#658 12c
chihayaburu kami oba ashi ni maku mono ka ・ kore o zo shimo no yajiro to wa iu
all-powerful god/s=paper+acc. feet-on wrap thing?   this+emph lower/dirty? shrine may say

This humdrum two-part *kyôka* is worth introducing because we have already seen the better known Shikibu legend that inspired it. A preface has Shikibu visiting the Kamo 賀茂 Shrine. The rough macramé straw sandals 藁沓: わらうづ, standard-fare for pilgrimage, ate into her bare feet so she wrapped them with *paper*, which is, as you may recall, homophonous with *god/s*. The original does not use simile but this two-words-in-one written once with phonetic letters, かみ(*kami*). Shikibu of the quick wit picks up on a third meaning of *kami* (above/upper) by retorting with its reverse, *shimo*, or "below/lower, implying she is yet in a zone where the presence of the gods is questionable and that base behavior is appropriate (『金葉和歌集』(源俊頼 1055-1129 撰者, 1126-7 年頃成立 第五勅撰集にて).

命知らずとよし言はば言へ ・ 君故に腎虚せんこそ望みなれ 新撰 犬筑波集
inochi shirazu to yoshi iwaba ie ・ kimi yue ni jinkyô sen koso nozomi nare   inu-tsukuba
life-know-not (u say) reason say-if say! ・ you because of kidney-dry do+emph wish is

*A fool-hardy man, you say?
Tell me, then, in what way?*

   *Because, for you
I've come to pray I end up
    with dry-kidney*

*My baby the dare-devil?
Do tell the world why!*

   *For your sake
my aim in life is to die
   of dry kidney!*

*A dare-devil, you?
Explain if you may!*

   *Because for you
I'd gladly pass away
   of dry-kidney*

Most *haikai* link-verse is one person after another, but the draw-verse or *maeku* is not generally a question-and-answer, or challenge. This 17c *haikai* (whether a real link or a one-man show) is such an exchange. *Dry-kidney* is a wasting disease caused by a man's spending too much, usually on his own pretty wife. Eventually, he becomes bedridden and ends up/down with only *it* still standing.

Mad Debates – Varieties of *Kyôka* versus *Kyôka*

corners had-if things-on catch-would ⇔ round-if just-round-if human-heart/s ⇔ too round-if tumble easily

丸かれやたゝまるかれや人こゝろ
marukareya tada marukareya hitogokoro
かとのあるにはものゝかゝるに
kado no aru ni wa mono no kakaru ni

丸くともひとかどあれや人こゝろ
maruku to mo hitokado areya hitogokoro
あまりまろきはころひやすきに
amari maroki wa korobi yasuki ni

The Chamber Maid
○ 女中＝竹斎 ○

The Captious Man
□ 理屈者＝竹斎 □

Round we must be,
just as round as possibly!
The human heart
If it came w/ corners
would catch on things

Round though we
may be, let some corner be!
The human heart
Were it overly round
would tumble too easily

Chikusai, the famous early-17c fictional quack doctor and professor of mad poems, is credited (杉揚枝　狂歌大観２) with this exchange, where the second does not so much refute the first as provide an additional, equally astute observation on geometrical psychology. Together they comprise a lecture of soft philosophy. Shokusanjin would later do a corollary when describing a picture of a "female geisha (performer)," *Curved soles are fine but keep a corner clean; / Pony geta too round tumble easily, I mean*" 女芸者の絵　丸くとも一ト角あれな駒下駄のあまりまろきはころびやすきに　蜀山人歌集 *maruku to mo hito-kado are na komageta amari maroki wa korobi yasuki ni*). In the original, which only alters the second poem above by a few words in the middle, the "human heart" is changed to the beveled-front pony-*geta* worn by dancers whose *tumbling* was often deliberate, i.e., sleeping with a customer. Shokusanjin's original round/square poems, part of a "Praising Square Picture" 四角画の自賛 series, include *"This is what I wish for the hearts/minds of all men! / A coin with a hole, round outside & square within"* (銭の賛　是を人の心ともがな銭の穴おもては丸くうらは四角に 蜀山人歌集 *kore o hito no kokoro to . . .*), and *"A cat's eye changing tells the time & the times they are a changing; / This print of his mistress is a perfect way to catch them* (女の猫を愛する四角画 – 猫の目のかはるにつけて時々のはやりとも見よ身をばかく袖 *neko no me no kawaru ni tsukete . . .*). A cat's pupil can seem rectangular. Geometrical metaphor went deep in Japan:

歌妓おかつの丸髷にゆひしをみて　　蜀山人歌集
さゞれ石の　いはほとなれる　寿は　よもぎが島　田丸くなるまで
sazare-ishi no iwa hodo nareru kotobuki wa yomogi-ga-shima ta maruku naru made
pebble's boulder becomes longevity-as-for mugwort-isle field round (shimada) become until

We celebrate the hoary boulder once but a pebble's dream,
Our isle of mugwort green until the fields turn round!

いく千代も経たるいはほの角とれて苔の衣をきるもしほらし　筆成　狂歌一万
iku chiyo mo hetaru iwao no kado torete koke no koromo o kiru mo shiorashi fudenari

How many eons pass before its hard edge comes off,
And a boulder wearing a robe of moss looks gentle?

Rectangularity vs. roundness in Japanese poetry could fill a book. These poems combine such with pebble-to-boulder and/or moss-growing conceits. Mugwort, a fragrant green grass, evokes Hôrai, the isle of eternal youth; farmed fields 田 that will never be round pun into the new round *Shimada* hairdo Ôta's favorite entertainer wore (accord. to an untrans. preface), and Japan itself becomes the boulder. Fudenari's *edge* 角 is "corners/angularity." Back to our dueling *kyôka*:

われ死なば備前伊部の土となり 徳利となりて酒を入れたい（爺） *ware shinaba bizen-irube . . . tokuri . . .*	我死なば備前伊部の土となり 尿瓶となりてちんぽ入れたい（婆） *ware shinaba bizen-irube . . . shibin . . .*
♪ Grandpa's Will ♪	♪ Grandma's Will ♪
When I die, I'd become Bizen Irube clay *Made into a flask & filled up with wine!*	*When I die, I'd become Bizen Irube clay* *Made into a urinal & filled with cocks!*

The grandpa's wish harkens back to a *Manyô* drinking poem (see pp.97,488) you need not read if you are familiar with Omar Khayyam. I'd call it a public *kyôka*. Grandma more commonly pipes up that she'd be a mortar (*suribachi*). Hers is the sort of thing common in folk music before it was bourgeoisied. The above version was netted. The next, probably 17c, is a favorite.

かたふちにみをなけんとはおもへとも *kata-fuchi ni mi o naken to wa omoedomo* remote-pool-into body+acc throw-would think but	身をすてゝ諸国をめくる執行じやの *mi o sutete shokoku o meguru shugyô ja no* self+acc aband. various countries+ travel training
さすか命のおしきなるらん *sasuga inochi no oshiki naruran* sure-enough, life's dear is+exclam	何に命のおしきなるらん *nani ni inochi no oshiki naruran* what/why life's dear becomes+exclam
西行法師 by Monk Saigyô	女 by a Woman
I think I'll just *throw myself into a deep* *bend of the river*	*You who left* *yourself behind traveling* *for discipline*
No, life is just too dear *for me to let it end!*	*Why whine that 'life's* *too dear to let it end'?*

About Saigyô, Carter writes, "his consistent adoption of this guise of the reluctant recluse who has left the world but still finds himself drawn by it can be seen as one of Saigyô's major artistic accomplishments." This pair of *kyôka* in *Kasanu Sôshi* (かさぬ草紙 tk2) brings out this contradiction and pokes fun at it.

㊤ A Mad Dissing Debate: Drinker *vs.* Teetotaler ㊤

一斗のむ人だにあるを杯の　作法も知らぬ下戸のつたなさ　沸斉
itto nomu hito dani aru o sakazuki no sahô mo shiranu geko no tsutanasa　bussai 17c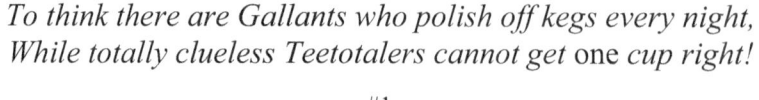
one *to*(4.8 US gals) drinks/ing person/s even is/are !/while etiquette even knows-not teetotaler's' clumsiness

> *To think there are Gallants who polish off kegs every night,*
> *While totally clueless Teetotalers cannot get* one *cup right!*

~~~~~~~~~~~~~~~~ #1 ~~~~~~~~~~~~~~~~

> *The wages of wine are a mistaken life – especially hideous*
> *For those who, drinking, pity us, know not* they *are piteous!*

one/whole life+acc. mistake/ing sake/wine's side-effect+emph.-as-for knowing-not likes person+emph. pitiful
isshô o ayamaru sake no toga zo to wa shira de konomeru hito zo hakanaki　nakarai bokuyô 17c 同
一生を誤る酒のとがぞとは　知らで好める人ぞ　はかなき　卜養　同

> *Irony*. After drinking out the last chapter, I netted *this* at a drink culture website while googling for more about the physician-poet Bokuyô (1607-78). Infuriated at another poet's 10-point counting-song 数え歌 attack on teetotalers – he did not drink – he retaliated against heavy-drinkers. The originals, more similar than my re-creations, start with "1" and end in adjectives. *Tsutanasa* means social clumsiness to the extent of being wretched and *hakanaki,* vain in the sense of being hopelessly short-lived. I translated 8 of each of the 10 distiches, of these 7 are the same #'s. I skipped #2 which says *you must drink for the gods' sake* and *drinking parties are followed by fights,* respectively(二間に酒の飲まれぬいはれなし　神酒を嫌へる神のなければ　*futatsu ma ni sake no* . . 二ぎやかに酒宴のあとは袖の梅　さます小間物けんか口論 *nigiyaka ni shûen* . .). Here are #3 and #4:
> . .

　　　三三の九度の固めの始まりは　神代も今も酒にこそあれ
sansan-no-ku-do no katame no hajimari wa kami yo mo ima mo sake ni koso are
three-three's nine times' hardening's start-as-for gods' age and now wine-in esp. is

> *Thrice thrice makes nine, man & woman bound by a vine —*
> *From the Age of the Gods to ours today all begins with wine.*

~~~~~~~~~~~~~~~~ #3 ~~~~~~~~~~~~~~~~

> *Those who chew out those of us who choose not to drink —*
> *Drunken by their own brew end up bums too drunk to think!*

horribly abstainers+acc scold drinker/s-as-for wine-by drunken end-up lives
sanzan ni geko o shikareru sakenomi wa sake ni nomarete hatasu minoue
三三に下戸を叱れる酒のみは　酒にのまれて果す身上

~~~~~~~~~~~~~~~~~~~~~~~~~~~~~~~~

　　　四海波目出度などと歌へども　不吉に見ゆるげ孤の顔付
<u>*shikai nami*</u> *medetai nado to utaedomo fukichi ni miyuru geko no kaotsuki*　bussai
4-seas waves cheerful/hurrah etc singing but, unlucky-as appear teettlr's face-expression

> *We sing Four Seas, to celebrate waves meeting at our place*
> *— What bad luck to have to see a teetotaler's lonely face!*

~~~~~~~~~~~~~~~~~~~~~ #4 ~~~~~~~~~~~~~~~~~~~~~

*The upright man, even his good character floating in a cup
reflects the ugliness of not knowing when enough is enough.*

四かるべき其人がらも杯に 向へば変わる人の面影 bokuyô
shikarubeki sono hitogara mo sakazuki ni mukaeba kawaru hito no omokage
proper that personal-character even sakecup-to face-when changes person's face

#3. The marriage ceremony with its 3x exchange of drinks recapitulates the mythic quickening of the nation. *Three* is the Taoist foundation. Vine is obviously out of place for a rice-wine culture. *Mea culpa, mea culpa, mea culpa!* Bokuyô uses the 三 character where it is usually not used for the adverb and appeals to a proverb about *how drink comes to drink us* for his feisty rebuttal. In #4, Bussai replaces the 戸 character in *geko* 下戸 teetotaler (lit. low-gate) with 孤, meaning *solitary* or *lonesome*. Bussai's #5 kids about how just a sip on the five main festivals leaves *geko* pale and wilted. 五節句は尚あっさりと飲むうちに 青くしぼめる下戸のはかなさ *go sekku wa* .. . While Japanese who drink little for philosophical reasons – Confucian sobriety – or because they destroyed their health by being a heavy drinker too long and decided to quit for their own good (*i.e.,* alcoholics) could be called *geko,* so could those who turned bright red (about half of Japanese!), those who feel like they were afire (usually the same ones) and those who pass out almost immediately. The last are the ones who turn pale. They also tend to puke most quickly. They were indeed pitiful in a society where drink was more or less de rigor, and I can well imagine how poem #5 must have *infuriated* Bokuyô, who, as a doctor, knew only too well how hard it was on the weak. Here is his retaliatory #5, followed by Bussai's rather telling #6:

五無理とは口に言へど嬉しさを 包みかねた意地の汚さ 卜養
go-muri to wa kuchi ni iedo ureshisa o tsutsumikaneta iji no kitanasa bokuyô
honorific(you)/5-as4 mouth-by say-but glee cram-in-cannot pushiness' dirtiness

*They may say, "Please do not overdo it!" But filthy Glee
is what we see when drinkers push drinks on you and me!*

~~~~~~

*They make everything so damn difficult, then, most turn tail
on us drinkers, those stinkers, non-drinkers' brains are stale!*

..
convolutedly screwng back, heavy-drinkrs-to-as4 backs show teetotalrs'+emph many
muzukashiku nejikaeritaru jôgo ni wa ushiro o misetaru geko zo ôkaru bussai
六かしくねじ返りたる上戸には　うしろを見せる下戸ぞ多かる

Other than admitting my *stinkers* and *stale brains* may exceed the limit of poetic license, no comments are needed for either of the above. Bokuyô's response to #6 points out that most good-for-nothings are punch-drunk; they got that way beating themselves with too many stiff ones. 六でなき人ときいては大方に 酒で身をうつたぐひ多さよ *rokudenaki hito to* . . . Plainer than my metaphor, most of the wit is in the initial pun incorporating the number *six* – Issa's later use of the same *rokudenashi* good-for-nothing to describe *himself* in a properly self-deprecatory yet comic fashion on his sixtieth birthday (*i.e.,* New Year's) is better.

下 A Mad Dissing Debate: Drinker *vs.* Teetotaler 下

八景の中に入りたる酒はやし 餅屋の店は絵にもかかれず 沸斉 日本酒仙伝
hakkei no naka ni iritaru sakabayashi mochiya no mise wa e ni mo kakarezu bussai 17c
8-views' within included sake-woods sweetrice-shop-as-for picture-as-even draw-cannot

Among the Eight Views it is to Cedar Wood I doff my hat!
A sweet-rice shop? Who would want to picture that!

~~~~~~~~~~~~~~~~~~~~~ #8 ~~~~~~~~~~~~~~~~~~~~

Among the Eight Views, it is to Cedar Wood I doff my hat.
Men passed out from food? Who would want to picture that!

8-views' w/in included sake-woods eat-collapse-as-for picture-as-even draw-cannot
hakkei no naka ni iritaru sakabayashi kuidaore wa e ni mo kakarezu bokuyô
八景の中に入りたる酒ばやし 喰い倒れは絵にもかかれず 卜養

I almost wrote Eight *Wonders* of the world, but every locality in Japan has its eight best (or 5 or 7) best sights. Call it a Sinosphere convention born in 瀟湘 of an aesthetic eye for landscape and multiplied as a commercial one for tourism (including pilgrimages). Cedar wood, or forest, refers to a wheel-like arrangement of cedar sprigs hung as the shingle of a drinking establishment and standing for the whole thing. I imagine the interior of a large drinking hall with better-looking drunks than the louts pictured by "our" Flemish painters, but who knows! Sweet-rice cake, for lack of a better word for *mochi*, was synonymous with non-drinkers. It was almost as if Japanese chose from among two highs: alcohol or gluten! Bokuyô's retort uses the sort of conceptual twist that even one well-read in classic rhetoric might have trouble naming. Japanese, as long noted, were more likely to doff their shoes than their hat, but what the hell!

七宝の杯は世に多かるに 名だにも聞かぬ玉の菓子盆 沸斉
shichihô no sakazuki wa yo ni ôkaru ni na dani mo kikanu tama no kashibon bussai
7-treasurs' winecup-as4 world-in many-though, name-evn hear-not precious sweets-tray

For sake's sake, seven-treasure cups make a beautiful treat;
But is precious material ever wasted on trays of sweets?

~~~~~~~~~~~~~~~~~~~~~~ #7 ~~~~~~~~~~~~~~~~~~~~

Seven-treasures, sure; but rice gone, your bowl is but a dirty dish
And the dredge drained from the copper kettles? Sordid.

7-treasurs too rice/food+emph gone-as-4 soup-bowl-sake see depressing empty hot kettle
shichihô mo meshi mo nakushite wa chawanzake miru mo utate no chirori kan nabe
七宝も飯もなくしては茶碗酒 見るもうたてのチロリ燗鍋　卜養 bokuyô

..
I put #8 first because #7 needs illustrations to be fully appreciated. Seven Treasures means various precious materials, mineral, wood or metal. 16-17c European observers spent pages describing the trays, often landscapes, and cups. Today, Japanese-style sweets shops have the most beautiful trays, so something has changed! Re. drinking from dirty dishes, see *Topsy-turvy 1585* (item 6-32, 2004).

公事和談皆何事も酒の世に　わびてや独り下戸のさびしさ　沸斉
kuji wadan mina nanigoto mo sake no yo ni wabite ya hitori geko no sabishisa yo bussai
lawsuits chattng all everythng+emph wine's world in/though miserbly alone ttlr's loneliness

Public matters, conciliation, all talk loves the world of wine;
By himself, sad Sober sits – He knows only mine *and* thine.

~~~~~~~~~~~~~~~~~~ #9 ~~~~~~~~~~~~~~~~~~

What repetition as drunken thoughts circulate cart before horse!
Proverbial flax-spinning spools, they're not just fools but bores.

repeating drunken circling after-before's worthless things+acc humble flax spindle
kurikaeshi ei no mawarite atosaki no kudaranu koto o shizu no odamaki bokuyô
九りかへし酔のまはりて後先の　下らぬ事を賎のおだまき　卜養

Here the *nine* (*ku*) at each poem's head becomes part of a noun and a verb, respectively. I have long thought we need *an ugly* to match *a beauty*. Translating these poems on drinking, I realized we need *a* sober, too. "Mine and thine" was born in rhyme. Flaxen spools in old waka were what one would rewind back to olden-times and later came to be used for repeating oneself in the manner of the senile. *Kudaranu koto* means worthless stuff and that, to me, means *bores*.

十分の上にも　酒は飲めもせん　餅の過ぎたる後は　食傷　沸斉
jûbun no ue ni mo sake wa nome mo sen mochi no sugitaru ato wa shokushô bussai
enough beyond even sake-as4 drink even do-would sweetrice surpassing after as4 cloy

~~*Feeling full, we cannot drink more when it comes our turn;*~~
~~*But after over-eating sweet-rice cake, look out heart-burn!*~~

Having had enough, a drinker would drink more sake yet;
With sweet-rice cake, overeat and sick of it is all we get!

~~~~~~~~~~~~~~~~~~ #10 ~~~~~~~~~~~~~~~~~~

Drinking until full, and then some, decimates a man inside;
Done over and over, it leaves you no body in which to hide!

enuf beyond evn aftr continue ske-drinkng-as4 oft repeatd-if aftr-as4 internal-damage
jûbun no ue ni ato hiku sakenomi wa dô kasanareba ato wa naison bokuyô
十分の上に跡ひく酒のみは　度重なれば後は内損　卜養

..
I first assumed "food-wounds" meant *heart-burn* (see pg. 98 for rice-cake doing *that*), but the OJD tells me it means *food-poisoning* or *getting cloyed* or *tired of something*. Then, looking more closely at the (to me) odd old *nome mo sen*, realized it was drinking-do-*would* positive, not negative, blessed my lucky stars for checking my dictionary, and shivered to think how many other mistakes remain to be found in this book. Note that the web-site I found the debate in (the only one with it) claimed mistakenly these (17c) poets were Shokusanjin's contemporaries, thus crediting Tenmei (late-18c) *kyôka* for it. 天明ばかりじゃないぜ！ The source given was the book on *sake* (篠原文雄『日本酒仙伝』) that inspired psychiatrist Nada Inada to look into *kyôka*. I doubt it made that mistake.

A *Wit*-ness of Salutes, Salutations & Warnings

七くさの花はあれども をみなへし たゞひともとに かつものはなし 蜀山人
nanakusa no hana wa aredomo ominaeshi tada hitomoto ni katsu mono wa nashi shokusanjin
seven grasses/plants' flowers-as-for are but maiden-flower just one plant beat thing-as-for not

花やしきの秋の七草みにまかりけるに、歌妓おかつもきたりければ、

Singer-dancer Beatrice came along when I visited
♪ a Flower-Inn to view the wild flowers of fall ♪

There is a rainbow of bloom but none can Beatrice best,
Just one maiden flower can triumph over all the rest!

Flowering trees owned the Spring in Japan. The archetypal flower of the Occident, those that bloom on small plants without trunks to speak of, especially out in the fields, have their heyday in August in Japan. Of course, "Beatrice" was not the name of the Singer-dancer who, as a sole *Patrinia scabiosaefolia,* routed her competition; it was Okatsu, and *katsu* means "beat," *i.e.,* to win out in a contest over another. It was *her* new hairdo that was fit into a charming poem for *longevity* in the last chapter. Ôta, the wit, has at least half a dozen poems mentioning her. One even mentions her not coming because of her menses and calls a teashop no real teashop without her. I cannot imagine Ôta leaving alone the words of a popular song; and imagine Okatsu picking up on his witty changes and perhaps adding her own. If I ever wanted to be a fly on the wall, it would be for this pair. Then again, with all those eyes, who says a fly has space for ears?

冷えたばかり味がよかろうというはすいくはっと打ち割って見てきこしめせ 月洞軒
hieta bakari aji ga yokarô to iu wa sui//katto uchiwatte mite kikoshimese getsudôken 大団
cooled just flavor-the good-shld say-as-4 wtr//mln/activly hit/cut-splittng seeng eat+hon. c1700

Just cool it in the well to take care of the flavor
Then, dive in, part that watermelon and savor!

◆

Just cool it, for that will take care of the water/
melon flavor; then use karate, or your sabre!

These are readings of a poem sent with the gift of a watermelon. I have seen them carried up mountains to give to temples. If effort counts, the *karma* points gained must be huge. But, here, the poet stayed home. His effort went into the poem sent to a buddy (板垣善兵衛方へ西瓜をくる). The original *ka'to* splits the *suika* (watermelon) in two, as shown by my double slash, and the last half of the melon adverbs into the sudden resolution that goes into the violent act. I was stymied for a proper translation and first brought in the well for drama, then, added *karate* and *sabre* (the slight bend in the Japanese sword does make it one) as a punning allusion to *savor* . . . Another failed attempt: *Chilled alone, good to the bone: just bust or cut this wah! / Termelon in two and splattered by the juice: dig in Mista!* If you can do a better translation, please!

お小袖はいくつめすともとにかくにかりにも妻を重ね給ふな 重勝妻 1679
okosode wa ikutsu mesu to mo tonikaku ni kari ni mo tsuma o kasane tamau na 銀葉夷歌集
hon+small-sleeve-as-4 many wear even whatever hypothetically-even hems+acc double do not!

With a present to her husband, departing on a long trip

Dear, you can wear as many of my light robes as you please,
But though you're bare don't ever dare try on any but these!

Tsuma, or "spouse," puns with a robe's "lapel/hem." Hubbie is warned not to let them overlap, *i.e.* commit polygamy. The correct character is 褄, which differs from spouse/mate 妻 by a thread 衤. A purposeful Freudian slip? *Kari ni mo,* "by no means," hints at the homophone *kari,* "borrow," an allusion to the justification of adultery as just borrowing clothing (pg.136). A much older *Manyôshû* poem (#2829) says that wearing lots of clothing, i.e., chasing ass, is fine, but 'not if you change so much you forget my face,' i.e., no longer love me (*koromo shi mo ôku aranamu torikaete kireba ya kimi ga omo wasuretaru*); but it lacks the pun and the language is so different I doubt it was known by the later poet, who, as the "Wife of Shigekatsu (重勝妻)," or "Overlap-win/beat-wife," chose the perfect pun, one based on her husband's name, for what might be called talis*manic* protection from adultery by sympathetic word power. This *tsuma* pun is first found in a poem in Tale #9 of *Ise Monogatari,* with an entirely different plot. A traveling man expresses his longing for his wife who he identifies with the worn hem of his long-worn, beloved brocade robe. His poem so touched the travelers that all *"wept onto their dried rice until it swelled with the moisture."* (McCullough: 1968)

世の中に人の来るこそうるさけれとはいふものヽお前ではなし 蜀山人
yononaka ni hito no kuru koso urusakere to wa iu mono no omae de wa nashi shokusanjin

♪ *Of all things I hate to have people knocking on my gate*
So saying, I am not talking about you: *Please wait!* ♪

世の中に人の来るこそうれしけれとはいふものヽお前ではなし 亭主
yononaka ni hito no kuru koso ureshi*kere to wa iu mono no omae de wa nashi* the master

♪ *Of all things I love to have people knocking on my gate*
So saying, I am not talking about you: Don't wait! ♪

According to psychologist-essayist Nada Inada (江戸狂歌: 1986), in 1955, an eccentric by the name of Professor Hyakuma 百間先生 hung a mad poem by Shokusanjin by his doorbell, followed by one of his own. *"Please / Don't wait"* are mine. Otherwise, the translation is so close a verbatim gloss was unnecessary.
..

We have seen a variety of *aisatsu* poems in this chapter. *Aisatsu* is usually translated as *greeting,* but really it is a salutation *of any type.* Perhaps a majority of Japanese traditional poems concerned social relations. This was even true for the *ku* of the saint of *haikai,* Bashô. Eg. a *ku* where a bee leaves a peony laden with riches is Bashô, grateful for help received, thanking his hosts as he departs.

Three Superb Mad Exchanges Found in Cranston

小夜更けて今はねぶたくなりにけり + 夢に逢ふべき人や待つらん 拾遺集
sayo fukete ima wa nebutaki narinikeri + yume ni aubeki hiyo ya matsuran   emperor murakami
small-night deepening now-as-for tired become/became +dream-in meet-ought person/s waiting! sis #1183

宵に久しう大殿籠らで、仰せられける　天暦御製
His majesty came up with this when he stayed up late

*The night grows   It grows late
late, somehow drowsiness   and I fear We are now
has found me: growing sleepy:*

御前にさぶらひて、奏しける
Serving in his presence (the Shigeno handmaid) presented

*Could this be the reason why –   Could someone be waiting
Someone's waiting in a dream?   for my Lord in his dreams?*

This is one of an extraordinary mini-chapter in the *Shûishû* (c.1005) with only six *tan-renga,* or "short-linked verses," all of which are introduced and translated by Cranston (*Waka Anthology* v2a). The *drowsiness* and the reply on the left are borrowed from him. The Japanese original has no pronouns but, translating, can easily bear three four or even five. I also followed him in keeping them to a minimum, making it possible to read the poem as a one-person opus, as it could be in Japanese were the prefaces removed and the 31 syllabets united. For the second reading, I borrowed the royal "We" from the English and allowed the 14-syllabet cap to differ. It bears repeating that Japanese held that people made appearances in dreams by their (not the dreamer's) volition. The handmaid takes that idea a step further and imagines that such would-be dream-callers could, like the sandman make us tired when they are kept waiting. Cranston conservatively has it as "slightly wittier" than the poem preceding it, another exchange where 10c Emperor Murakami gets the cap, but I think that, unless an antecedent for the idea of *dream-callers-waiting-bringing-sleepiness* can be found, it is a *masterpiece,* and deserves to be famous (I say "deserves to be" for it is not. I have not found a single mention of it outside of Cranston's book and googling the Japanese brings zero hits!). And this is followed by another, more clever if less conceptually interesting, exchange dating to the reign (833-50) of Ninmyô hundred years earlier. I was tempted to introduce it (SIS #1184) in full, but the animal-hours and the punning requires a considerable introduction and, were I to include it, I would be borrowing half of Cranston's chapter, rather than only a third (笑); and, we will have one more on the next page. Let me just say it was included in the *Tales of Yamato* (大和物語#168), credited to Yoshimune no Munesada, soon to become monk, then Archbishop, Henjô, who famously fell on maiden flowers (pg.216), and the puns foreshadow those in later *kyôka*. The woman complains he failed to meet her in the hour of the cow, *ushimitsu,* punfully *miserable* (*ushi*), to which he replies he dozed off in the hour of the rat, *ne,* which is homophonous with sleep because he wanted a dream preview. The original puns are Shakespearean in their artlessness and I must confess it great fun to see Cranston's heroic efforts to save them. His *'drat it all'* for the rodent is as mad as anything in this book and suggests he is in fine form for upcoming volumes which should include many more wild *waka*.

春はもえ秋はこがるる竈山・霞も霧も煙とぞ見る　清原元輔　拾遺集 #1180
haru wa moe aki wa kogaruru kamadoyama · kasumi mo kiri mo keburi to zo miru　motosuke
spring-as4 smolders fall-as4 burns oven-mountain // mist and fog smoke-as+emph appear

筑紫へまかりける時に、竈山のもとに宿りて侍けるに、
道つらに侍ける木に古く書き付けて侍ける

Heading to Tsukushi, spending the night at the foot of Mt Kamado,
a tree was found where someone had long ago carved these words:

Smoldering in spring,　　　　　　　*Smoldering in spring*
Charring dark in the fall,　　　　　*and burning through the fall,*
Cookstove Mountain:　　　　　　　　*our great Mt Stove!*

元輔 e.c.tr.　　　　　　　　　　　　元輔 r.d.g.
Motosuke　　　　　　　　　　　　　　Motosuke

Vernal haze, autumnal mist,　　　*Fine mist and fog, equally,*
Both look like smoke from here.　　*look just like smoke to me!*

Sei Shonagon's father Kiyohara Motosuke (908-990) was on his way to what is now Kyûshû to assume the governorship when this supposedly happened. *Supposedly*, because Cranston, whose translation is the more responsible reading on the left, points out that another account has it as a single poem by another man. It makes much more sense as dead-cap link-verse (just made up that term for a poem by a dead man finished by a live man). Cranston notes the "predictable plays" on "budding/burning" (*moe*) and "roasting red" (*kogaruru*) and opines that idea-wise, Motosuke in 986, "simply added smoke." I would call it *masterful buffoonery*. This man in a high position has assumed the persona of a hayseed, countering lyrical rustic trope (the *smoldering* usually applies to the new shoots of delicate young herbs and the burning the beautiful maple foliage of fall) in the 17-syllabet verse with a plain, *'Dunno, looks-like-smoke-to-little-ole-me!'* 14-syllabet verse that better fits the name of the mountain to boot. Japanese *love* toponymical poems. Many collections of *haikai* and *kyôka* have hundreds of poems, sometimes scores of them in a row, playing with the names of cities, fiefdoms, mountains, rivers, moors, and other places boasting proper names. Almost *all* bore the hell out of me, perhaps because they are incomprehensible to one ignorant of local history, and the few that do not seldom pan out in translation. Excluding Arima (pp.414-23), they are under-represented in this book.

The Naughty Nightingale Went *"Fufû, Fufû!"*

のきちかくふふうとつくる一声ハ我恋中をみたかうぐひす 則水由 百千鳥
noki chikaku fufû to tsuguru hitokoe wa waga koinaka o mita ka uguisu nori no suiyû 1779
eaves near fufu-w/ warbling one-voice-as-for /// my/our love-within+acc. saw? warbler/nightingale

Bird Watching   *Eavesdropper*

Is that a song   Oh, nightingale,
of envy we hear coming   what is that snicker
from the eaves?   in your song?

Warbler! Could it be –   Have you been spying
you *watched* him & me?   on our love for long?

Usually, I follow the tradition of translating the little yellowish brown bird called an *uguisu,* that the fastidious call a yellow *bush warbler,* as "nightingale," for it is celebrated for song in Japan (though a Florida mockingbird can out-sing it in his sleep) and was thought to be the soul-spouse of the flowering plum, or *ume* the fastidious call an *apricot;* but, here, I made one translation the most common current rendering "warbler" for the alliteration with "watched." *Fufû* is a mimetic adverb, to a laugh what a grin or smirk is to a smile, which is to say, a *chuckle* or *snicker.* While that might include a nervous laugh, such a reading is so unlikely that I doubt I would ever have come up with "envy," which in retrospect works well, by myself. Indeed, I did not. I found the poem, together with the Romanized Japanese, in a Sunday, March 04, 2007 online review (by M. Kei, author of *"Slow Motion: The Log of a Chesapeake Bay Skipjack"*) of the first book of translated *kyôka,* albeit surimono (see pgs 424-51), that I encountered.

> *Kyôka* also ventured into territory that was a little risqué compared to the restraints of *waka.* The poem below has a titillating quality that would have been considered vulgar and unacceptable in courtly *waka.*
>
> Near the eaves
> I hear the warbler
> Sing a song of envy:
> He must be watching us
> My lover and me.
>
> – Nori no Suiyu

Utamaro: A Chorus of Birds. Metropolitan Museum of Art. Akamatsu no Kinkei, ed. Kitagawa Utamaro, illus. James T. Kenny, trans. New York: Viking Press, 1981 [Tokyo, 1790]. Accordion-fold art book, color interiors, unpaginated.

The original poem ends in a question – *so did you see our loving, uguisu?* – that for reasons I cannot explain sounds touching, even *adorable.* The translator,

James T. Kenny, apparently gave up on Englishing it. While I miss the direct address, the phrase he came up with – "~ *us / My lover and me*" – is equivalent in feeling, brilliant and indirectly shows he, too, felt the voice of the poet was female. Still, the "envy," though it, too, feels right, is probably wrong. Hence, after doing one mad improvement of Kenny in case I am wrong, I made a second reading which is my best guess. Perhaps I should add that I am very familiar with this bird, whatever you call it, for it is one that I have often heard. And, I have listened, carefully. Its voice for the first week or so after arrival is to sound what wobbly is to a wheel. Unlike the mockingbird, its call is pretty much the same every year. Yet, the lead-in note is enchanting as it wavers creating a more fluid, or liquid quality while the bird tunes up for the season. Once the uguisu hits its mark and stays with it, I get bored; but who can ever tire of the tenuous? If you would mimic this delicate sound, you must learn to begin each call by whistling *in* (sucking, not blowing, air), for *that* is when the magic happens.

To a Naughty Nightingale

*Is that chuckling
in your warble by the eaves?*

*I'll bet you have
been spying while we heave,
you, dirty little bird!*

This reading, inspired by M. Kei's observation that the poem had "a titillating quality that would have been considered vulgar and unacceptable in courtly *waka*," is conservative in one way: it restores the bird to the tail of the poem. Later, I would find Getsudôken's *kyôka* (pg. 334) which took our bird for a gurgling onanist! So long as we are *uguisu*ing, here is a 17c haiku I'd call a *kyôku* followed by an 1823 *surimono* kyôka that lead into the next chapter.

鶯の羽風や花を味かたうち 茂次鷹つくば
uguisu no hakaze ya hana o mikata-uchi moji 1642
(nightingale[bush-warbler]'s wing-breeze: blossom[acc.]ally-shot)

blown away	*acceptable casualties*
wind from the wings of the warbler! blossoms felled by friendlies	*blossoms dropped by friendly fire: wind from nightingale's wing*

羽風をハいとひながらもさく花にとりのあし痕つけし短冊　不老庵長生久美?
hakaze o ba itoinagara mo saku hana ni tori no ashi ato tsukeshi tanzaku nagaiki hisami

*There among the Blossoms that hate even the wind from their wings –
Have we not left the tracks of birds? Our poem cards plum is wearing.*

The *kyôku* weds ancient trope to a medieval war term. The *kyôka*, one of 11 on a five-picture set (in McKee: 2008) plays the Chinese conceit of writing = bird-track.

A Violent Nightingale & Mimesis With Meaning

心から花のしづくにそぼちつつうくひずとのみ鳥のなくらむ　藤原としゆき
kokoro kara hana no shizuku ni sobochi tsutsu　uku hizu to nomi tori no naku ran　toshiyuki 905
heart-from blossom's drops-by drenched-while troubled/excited=warb=dry-not=ler only bird cries!

Willfully he rips
thru the blossoms, then, drenched
by their nectar

Flying from tree to
tree, with wingborn wind, he
knocks off blossoms

Why does our Thrush Hector cry?
Because his feathers will not dry!

All the while crying up a storm,
He blames others for the deed!

treelimbtip-traveling own wing-wind-in/from scatter blossms+acc who blaming here-there cries!
kozutaeba onoga hakaze ni chiru hana o tare ni ôsete kokora nakuran　monk sosei 905
こづたへばおのがはかぜにちる花をたれにおほせてここらなくらむ　そせい

True, the first poem, a wordplay (literally 物名, or *thing-name*) poem from bk 10 of the *Kokinshû* by Fujiwara no Toshiyuki does not use a name like Hector, but it has something else, a pun: the name of the bird, *uguisu*, serves as two words, *uku hizu*, where *uku* means *feel sad* and *hizu* not to dry. It may be the best example yet of wit that *only works on paper* – that is, *visually* – due to the *nigori,* or muddy-marks, being left up to the reader to supply or leave blank. I say "may" because it is possible that people in an age where such ambiguity was common in writing might have been able to hear the *uguisu* in *uku hizu* and I mention "remove" because in the version I have, at least, the muddy marks are supplied for the s=>z sound. Usually, once the marks are there, the reading is not optional. So I imagine either there was a hick pronunciation of the bird allowing the "z" sound, uguizu, or the said muddy-marks can be considered to be the wetness on the bird. Still, the fancy split-word punning and ridiculous but not exceptionally vulgar content makes this *Kokinshû* "word-play" an excellent example of what would come to be called a *kyôka.* The second poem, from the same anthology, does not engage in such clever wordplay, but, in my opinion, attributing the bird's cry/song to *that* is pretty damn mad, even if less cleverly expressed than in the haiku ending the last chapter. The bird was in a caption.

梅の花見にこそきつれ鶯の人く人くといとひしもをる　古今集
ume no hana mi ni koso kitsure uguisu no hito ku hito ku　to ii shi mo oru　anon 905
plum(apricot) blossom-viewing-for esp. come, thrush's "human comes x2" says even is

Hitoku Alarum

I came here only
to see the plums in bloom
but still the thrush

has changed his tune: ♪*People,*
♪ *People!* ♪*People come!* ♪

One *uguisu* with a personality calls for another. This, too, is from the *Kokinshû*, but a different chapter with *haikai,* comic or ridiculous poems not necessarily name-related. With both the facetious personal affront and the novel onomatopoeia, I would call it a *kyôka*. It also rings true as a possible personal observation. Almost a millennium later Issa has a number of haiku lamenting birds' distrust of "human devils." Even Japanese did not live in the garden of Eden and never did. In case you wonder how the same *uguisu* could be a *warbler*, *nightingale* and now, perhaps for the first time in the book, a *thrush*, see the notes. Here, I wanted just one syllable. If we are going for numbers, which is to say pre-modern verse that was meant to entertain, the more names for one thing the better both for rhyme and syllable-count. Even if a name were to be wrong, so long as other people recognize what it is supposed to be, why not take advantage of it?

只一夜あけのからすと市川のかほ／＼はいさぎよひもの　桜川慈悲成
tada hitoyo ake no karasu to ichikawa no kono kaho kaho wa isagiyoi mono   jihinari
'just one night^dawn/'s crow/s(=flee-let/delay?) ichikawa's this face face as4 gallant!

After just one night / at this sight of Ichikawa's / bold and splendid visage / the crows of dawn / "Caw! Caw!" for more (*Colored in the Year's New Light,* pl.130).

The most common talking bird was the crow. You may recall Kisshû's splendid poem ending *yo ga aketakaa hi ga kuretakaa* where a happy-crow drinker wonders aloud *"Has dawn/dusk caw caw come?"* (pg.100) My translation was just cawful! Consonants may be bent for a pun or rhyme, but vowels, it seems, cannot; at least, not with one syllable words (*caw/come*). By contrast, the above translation of a cawsome 1820's *kyôka* by Sakuragawa Jihinari by Daniel McKee is, at least in part, something to crow about: It is on a *surimono* showing kabuki star Danjûrô VII in the play *"Shibaraku!"* (*Just One Minute!*), named for the phrase – one adverb in Japanese – the hero boldly shouts out to stay an execution. For something *not* worth raven about, see my ♪ bilinguals may enjoy concerning a *possibly* – my respondent does not buy it – lost pun (in parethesis of the gloss).

鐘鳴や蚊の国に来よ／＼／＼と　一茶　文化七
kane naru ya ka no kuni ni koyo-koyo-koyo to   issa d.1827
bell rings!/: mosquitoes' country-to 'come-come-come'

..

The vespers sound
♪ Welcome, come: koyo koyo
to Mosquito Country! ♪

Like Issa's silverfish *kyôka,* we have one part of speech turned into another with Chinese characters to prove it. The onomatopoeia of the huge temple bell (such were licensed to tell time) is written with the Chinese character for "Come!" *Koyo-koyo* sounds just right to me – better than "ring" (to high), "clang" (too harsh), toll (too much like an Occidental bell with a clapper inside) – but Issa would seem to have invented it for the poem, which I would call a *kyôku*. The most famous *kyôka* working onomatopoeia is an anonymous squib featuring the *bunbu* hum of mosquitoes credited to Ôta Nanpô (*yononaka ni ka hodo . . .* pg.108).

If Only There Were No ~~Cherry Blossoms~~ Women?
世の中にたへて女(桜)のなかりせばをとこ(春)の心(は)のどけからまし 蜀山人(業平)
yo no naka ni taete onna (sakura) no nakariseba otoko(haru) no kokoro (wa) nodokekaramashi
world-among completely/end women not-if males' minds/hearts placid (be) would

If cherry trees
would only vanish
from the world

Our hearts might be
serene each spring!

Ariwara no Narihira. Kokinshû (905) waka #84

If all women
would only vanish
from the world

Men's hearts might be
happy and serene.

Kyôka by Shokusan (19c) 蜀山先生

Because this is a book of *kyôka*, I usually put the *kyôka*, though written later, first (left), but, here, the older *waka* might seem crazier to many readers, so I put it first. Before explaining why cherry trees trouble people, or at least poets, and why the parody fits so well, let me give another pair of translations –

If cherry blossoms
were to vanish completely
from this earth

The mind of spring would be
a study in serenity

Ariwara no Narihira. KKS waka #84

If womankind
were to vanish completely
from this earth

The mind of men like me
would always be serene

Kyôka by Shokusanjin 蜀山先生

Poets from the time of the *Manyôshû*, when cherry blossoms in poetry were still fresh – the less magnificent but earlier blooming *ume*, or flowering *plum* (really *apricot*), beloved by Chinese had the first poems – worried lest they come into bloom, stay in bloom long enough to be enjoyed, or suffer wind or rain damage before being shared with others. If this *waka* were written by a notably iconoclastic poet, I would take *it* for a mad poem roasting generations of worrying poets. There is a tendency for parodies, like euphemisms that in time became what they cover, to end up taken for gospel and, themselves, parodied. Narihira's *waka* may be an example of this. He also may have been referring to how busy the host of a blossom-viewing event was. But it is easiest to imagine this famously handsome man, almost as promiscuous as his namesake in *The Tales of Ise*, like many men who conquer and leave one woman after another, blaming his itch on the prey he could not resist, in which case the allegory Shôkusanjin made explicit was intended. But, this may be unfair; Narihira did not author "his" romantic *Tales* (which include this poem) and we do not know for sure he was a lifelong Don Juan, only that he was handsome. The early 17c *Fake Ise* 仁勢物語 beat Shôkusanjin to the punch, changing *sakura*/cherry to 妻子 wife+child/ren and *spring* to *now*. Considering Yamanoue Okura's *Manyôshû* poems, *children*, the ultimate attachment, seem as appropriate as women.

花やちるらんて女中をこわがらせ　柳多留 12
hana ya chiruran de jochû o kowagarase　yanagidaru 1777
blossoms+emph fall+excl with(saying) maid/s+acc frighten

blossoms, you know
end up falling: he says
scaring the maid

Blossom-as-woman is not woman-as-blossom but, but the maid is made to think the metaphor an allegory. This exceptionally translatable *senryû* is borrowed from *Cherry Blossom Epiphany, the poetry and philosophy of a flowering tree,* my book with 3000 translated haiku and senryu and waka . Most poems dealing with women as blossoms or blossoms as women are not so instantly comprehensible. Readers who would learn more about how cherry blossom blossoms could stand for women and vice-versa and the relationship of that to Japanese sexuality should see that book, where I pursue the metaphor from multiple angles in a dozen or so chapters.

世の中のこゝろ絶たる櫻哉　汀躬
yononaka no kokoro taetaru sakura kana　teikyû
world-among's heart/s run/s-out cherry(blossoms)!

..

the whole world
loses its mind when
cherries bloom

This old *ku* sums up what cherry blossoms do to Japanese so well that I gave it seven translations in the above-mentioned book, one for each day of the standard lifetime of a blossom. The blossom high – and it helped that poets like others in the bloomshade drank like fish – was such that I would not be surprised if a tenth of all *sakura*-related *haiku* and *waka* could be called *mad*, in spirit if not form. And, since I am a sucker for novelty, my selection probably boasts twice that percentage, *i.e.,* 600 mad poems. That may be more than all such hitherto translated into English combined (Unless we include the early 19c *kyôka* in books of surimono – beautiful artwork and kyôka duets, so to speak – which I only recently discovered). So, please forgive me if I borrow some of them for this book. It is hard not to! Here is one more. Note before reading: a sleeve is the equivalent of a handkerchief for holding tears.

花をけふつみてしほれぬ袖もなし　紹巴 1523-1602
hana o kyô tsumite-shiborenu sode mo nashi　jôha
blossom/s+acc today stuffing-wring-not sleeve-even-not

lacrima cerasum

today, all of us
wring our sleeves, stuffed
with cherry petals

How Can Cherry Blossoms be Stopped from Falling?

勅とかや下す帝のいませかし　さらばおそれて花や散らぬと　西行　山家集
choku to ka ya kudasu mikado no imasekashi saraba osorete hana ya chiranu to saigyô -1190
edict or something! proclaiming emperor being-let if-so fearing blossoms fall-not

Thou Shalt Not Blow!

*If only we had
a Mikado who'd make
a Blossom Bull*

*In august dread they
wouldn't dare to fall!*

Most Japanese would never connect Saigyô, renowned for elegant *waka*, with *kyôka*. But when it comes to *tear* and *heart* metaphor, as we have seen, and what might be called the drama of cherry blossoms, he has written scores of poems madder than some so called. This one works the way Shokusanjin's *kyôka* would, by being simple and absurd. My bold translation of *choku* as "Blossom Bull" is meant to convey that spirit. Cranston's translation of a delightful early-11c poem, perhaps by (*Kokinshû* editor) Tsurayuki's daughter, starts with the same word: *"An Imperial Edict – / What could be more awesome! / But if the warbler / Should inquire for its house, / How should we reply?"* (*choku naraba ito mo kashikoshi uguisu no yado wa to towaba ikaga kotaemu* shûishû #531 c1010 ♪I would, and did, change three things: imp. ed. => Imp. Ed., Nothing => What, ; => !). This poem saved a red plum requisitioned by the palace from being dug up. *Choku*, Cranston points out, is a sino-japanese word, "as such exceptional in waka." I would say it marks the *waka* as a *wild waka* of the type that might be called a mad poem.

*Nothing can bend
the mind of the wind blowing
through cherries!*

*How i hate the blossoms,
then, for giving in!*

*For the will
of the wind nothing
can be done*

*We begrudge blossoms
for letting him have fun*

*Lust is given:
what would you do
about the wind?*

*What hurts is to see it –
how blossoms go along!*

梢ふく風の心はいかがせんしたがふ花のうらめしきかな　西行　山家集
kozue fuku kaze no kokoro wa ikaga sen shitagau hana no urameshiki kana saigyô 12c
treetops blowing wind's/s' heart-as-for how do-would? obey flower/s begrudge!/?

If "a man is just a man," which is to say an animal of instinct, as the country number *Stand By Your Man* put it, only women can be held responsible for their actions. The *waka* explains why men resent women rather than their competition. Yet, Saigyô also wrote to the contrary, probably on the same day.

I have got it!
From now on i'm taking
a single course:

Not blaming blossoms
I shall hate the wind!

心得つただ一筋に今よりは花を惜しまで風をいとはん 西行#131
kokoro etsu tada hitosuji ni ima yori wa hana o oshima de kaze o itowan   saigyô

How he got there, I cannot say. Because it is better to hate what cannot be helped as such hate is more superficial and hence harmless?

散らば散れ櫻ばかりの花もなし 宗祇 大発句帳
chiraba chire sakura bakari no hana mo nashi   sôgi d. 1502
fall/scatter-if fall! cherry only's blossom-even not

If you'd fall
then, fall! Cherry is not
the only blossom!

Link-verse *hokku* were not supposed to be about *koi* (love and longing), but can we read the above without recalling the old lyric *"There are more pretty girls than one"*? Cherry did that to poets. The link-verse master I call the father of haiku, Sôgi, like Saigyô, considered the epitome of elegant, also let his hair down for cherry blossoms. He, too, wrote scores of *ku* about cherry blossoms that include contradictory but are always passionate messages. The above *ku* is madder than Saigyô's *kyôka;* it contradicts an idea rather than stop an action. Yet, neither is half as mad as many of the *haikai* written by the kooky poets of the 16 and 17c. Here is one with an outrageous new take on an old *waka* theme, namely, the blossom that falls though no wind is blowing, thus proving "she" does so from "her" own free will or bountiful heart. I call this a *kyôku:*

我と花の散は貧乏ゆるぎ哉　無記名 崑山集
ware to hana no chiraba binbô yurugi kana anon.1651
self-by blossom's/s' fall-if/when poverty-jiggling!/?

blossoms falling   *below the cherry*
all by themselves, i wonder   *petals fell and i noticed*
if it's the shakes!   *i had the shakes!*

I, personally, have been *warned* about letting my legs jiggle. In Japanese, it is called "poverty-trembling," as it was thought to bring the same. If the *ku* were written in the 20c, where observation was 90% of haiku, the second reading would be the more likely, but at this time, ideas came first.

A Good Defense for the Blossom-Ravishing Wind

花と見ばさすが情をかけましを 雲とて風のはらふなるべし　西行　山家集
hana to miba sasuga nasake o kakemashi o kumo tote kaze no harau-narubeshi saigyô 12c
blossom-as see-when yep kindness does? "clouds (as-if2say)"wind blows/dissipates-ought

Dutiful Blast

Seeing blossoms,
how could the wind not
want to help!

It is, after all, supposed to
clear away clouds, right?

Saigyô is famous as a lover of *sakura*, but what is not well known is that he *also* had kind words for the villain in the cherry blossom drama. A dozen or so of his *waka* look at things from the Wind's point of view.

立ちまがふ峯の雲をばはらふとも花を散らさぬ嵐なりせば　西行　同
tachimagau mine no kumo oba harau to mo hana o chirasanu arashi nariseba saigyô

It would be nice
to have storm winds free
to clean our peaks
of those loitering clouds
yet let the blossoms be!

Waka asking the wind to blast view-blocking clouds or lay off blossoms were old hat. Combining them is new. The poem is mad for sure, but less clever than his later work chosen for the lead poem. The logic in the next poem, perhaps, in part a response to a fine poem by Izumi Shikibu (d.1030) – *"If at least the wind / Did not sweep it all away, / The garden cherry / Might scatter, and yet all spring / Remain here for my gazing."* Trans. Cranston (*kaze dani mo fukiharawazu wa niwazakura chiru to mo haru no hodo wa mitemashi* Goshûishû #148) – is more clever yet, but I prefer the lead poem's naive rationalization of natural violence.

あながちに庭をさへはく嵐かな さこそ心に花をまかせめ　西行同
anagachi ni niwa o sae haku arashi kana sakoso kokoro ni hana o makaseme saigyô
probably/altogether garden even sweep storm!/?/: so heart/will-to blossoms+acc entrust-not?

I'll bet this gale	*The gale even*
has strength enough	*insists upon sweeping*
to sweep the yard!	*my garden!*
We must, then, give him	*How can I not entrust*
his will with the bloom.	*him with the bloom?*

We can't fight the wind's libido; and he does, after all, clean up afterwards. Before I was capable of reading, much less translating Saigyô on my own, I found a silly 10c *Kokinshû* poem and rendered it into terribly Learical English:

花ちらす風のやどりはたれかしれ 我にをしへよ行きてうらみむ そせい法し
hana chirasu kaze no yadori-wa tare ga shiru ware ni oshieyo yukite uramimu monk sosei 9c

Someone, pray tell me where to find
the dwelling place of Master Wind!
I'll give him a piece of my mind, I will,
that Spoiler of Flowers, the Wind!

Japanese classics scholar Hitaku Kyûsojin, in his standard pocketbook edition of the *Kokinshû*, righteously complains that despite the flowers "falling without regret," the poem resorts to anthropomorphism and reeks of artifice (*gikô* 技巧). Actually, *falling without regret* is, *itself*, an anthropomorphism. Moreover, an untimely blow *can* hurt the blossoms' chance for fertilization. Might not a tree, in its own way, want to enjoy a good bloom? Not, that this matters. The poet has every right to be upset with the wind for perfectly human, indeed, selfish reasons, such as wanting to see or show the blossoms to someone. As the wind was legendarily tied to wind-caves up mountains, playful metaphor served to express chagrin. People must have chuckled at it. What's the big problem? Why have I never read similar unkind words for Saigyô who, as we have seen, did likewise?

まちてちれ花にかこたん風もなし 宗祇
machite chire hana ni kakotan kaze mo nashi sôgi -1502
wait! fall! blossoms-to complain-would wind-even-not

flowers, wait   *blossoms, wait!*
to fall! how can i rant   *who do i blame if you fall*
without the wind?   *without the wind?*

don't scatter yet
we need a fall-guy, blossoms
wait for the wind!

Again, I end up capping Saigyô's *kyôka* with what I would call a *kyôku* by Sôgi. If you like Sôgi, scores of his *ku* may be found in *Cherry Blossom Epiphany*. And, now, we will finish this windy conversation with a *haikai ku* of the sort that might have been called a *senryû* a hundred years later, which, in spirit, is definitely as mad as anything in 31 syllabets.

あらけなや風車売る花の時 薄芝 あらの
arakenaya kazeguruma uru hana no toki hakushi 1689
loutishness! wind[pin]-wheels sells/ing blossom-time

Of all the gall!
A man selling pin-wheels
in cherry time

Cuckoo, Headache, Tabby Cat & Confucius

郭公来べき宵也頭痛持 在色 #301・高まくらにて夏山の月 松意 #302 談林十百韻
hototogisu kubeki yoi nari zûtsu-mochi zaishiki; *takamakura nite natsuyama no tsuki* shôi 1675
cuckoo come-should evening become headache-having; high-pillow-on summer-mountain's moon

Tonight's the night
a cuckoo should come soon
says his headache;

From a high pillow, the moon
rises over summer hills.

Combine this two-man link-verse sequence for a fine haikai-style *kyôka*. Cuckoo were thought to explode into song when a late-spring/early-summer humid low was followed by a dry high. The former brought headaches to migraine sufferers waiting to hear the first cuckoo for relief. Yet, there are poems that suggest the bird itself could drive you cuckoo. One such by Sôkan (1465-1553):

かしましや此里過よほととぎす みやこのうつけ いかに待らん 山崎宗鑑
kashimashi ya kono sato sugiyo hototogisu miyako no utsuke ika ni matsuran sôkan
noisy! this country/village pass+emph., cuckoo, capital's idiots how-much waiting+emph.

You noisy bird, *fly this country town!* *Go, cuckoo, go!* *The airheads in Kyôto* *Await your first sound.*	*What a ruckus!* *Hurry it up, pass through* *this town, cuckoo!* *The fools in the Capital* *breathlessly await you.*

At first, I misread *utsuke*, empty-headed, as *depressed* (*u*, a vowel of depression) and put the poem here to follow the headache. Sôkan does not exaggerate. I recall thinking *Enough whipping poor Will already!* when a certain bird drove me crazier than even loud Katy did. Link-verse master Sôchô (1448-1532) finally snapped after cuckoo kept calling day and night well into fall out in the hills where he was on retreat, *"Hearing you, nausea comes to roost,* hototogisu! *To me, your name is* hedotogisu (*puke-cur* (or *to* gizu *katydid/ geezer*))!" 聞くたびにむねわろければほとゝぎすへとゝぎすとこそいふべかりけれ *kiku tabi ni mune warokereba hototogisu hedotogisu to koso iu bekarikere.* ♪ The pun does not English. Issa sometimes echoed this sentiment, but also took the classic view. Pardon my added rhyme line:

時鳥なけや頭痛の抜る程 一茶 1819
hototogisu nake ya zutsû no nukeru hodo
cuckoo cry/call! headache drill-out amount

Call, cuckoo, call!
Enough to drive out my headache
Once and for all!

Katô Ikuya made the first 17-syllabet *ku* of our lead poem one of three examples of the ingenious way comic (*kokkei*) *haikai* played with ancient *waka*. The old *Nihonshôki* 日本書紀 poem by Sotôri-hime (a princess whose name records beauty *visible through her clothes*) has the line *waga seko ga kubeki yoi nari,* or "Tonight my boyfriend should be coming" and her reason for so believing is reflected in another comic *ku*: "Tonight, mosquitoes should come to be caught: a spider's web" (かゝる蚊の来べき宵なり蛛の糸　正甫　ゆめみ草 *kakaru ka no kubeki yoi nari kumo no ito*　seihô 1656). The Princess's omen, a spider dangling from its web was recast from a nature-centered perspective (mosquitoes *sasu=stab* as do lovers: see next chapter). Katô points out that Ôsaka Danrin school *haikai* had a bent for re-casting old love poems. I would expect to find many *hai-ryû kyôka*.

妻をおもふ恋ぞつもりてふちの猫　幸之 桜川
tsuma o omou koi zo tsumorite f⇒buchi no neko　kôshi 1674
mate+acc longing love+emph. builds-up tabby cat/s

Lusting for mates
love built until too late:
these motley kittens!

All that longing
for its mate amounted
to a tabby cat!

This, Katô's third example, plays with a classic *waka* by Saigyô (that in the *Hundred Poets One Poem* collection) where his longing builds up to form a deep spot, a *fuchi* 淵, or wet gulch, usually in the bend of a river. Poetry for the ears alone could hardly change *fuchi* into *buchi,* a cat with an irregular splotchy pattern, (a tabby, or, maybe a calico, but with the connotations of a *mutt* if a cat can be so called); but, thanks to the arbitrary use of diacritical marks, the mind's eye can. Katô also gave two examples of what *haikai* can do to *sayings,* as well.

夕には死すとも蚊なり夏の虫 宗朋 1642　　　　　薛の夕死すとも可なり 呑水 1715
yûbe ni wa shisu to mo ka nari natsu no mushi　sôbô　　*asagao no yûbe shisu to mo ka narikeri*　tonsui
evening-in-as-4 die even mosquito is, summer-bugs　　morning glory's evening die even possib.+emph.

I coo-could die
to night – summer's cumen in
as I be goin' out!

A morning glory
could become history
in the evening

◆

♪ "You could ask the road/way (Tao) in the morning and die before night." ♪
(朝に道を聞けば夕に死すとも可なり 「論語」 Analects of Confucius
asa ni michi o kikeba yûbe ni shisu to mo ka nari　Kôshi 孔子

I was not eager to present these *ku*. How can parody of the (to us) unfamiliar be interesting? But Katô claimed these *ku* show *haikai* had an unpredictability *kyôka* and *kyôshi* could not match (孔子の教えがこうしたかたちで出る意外性は、狂歌や狂詩の比ではなかった). While not too sure, I agree, I felt obliged to at least *try* to present his case. The *cuckoo* who has ever marked the start of summer in Japan and England (though a different species) replaced the *mosquito* – call it *analogous translation* – because the wit of the original, where *mosquito=ka* puns into *possible=ka-nari*, was impossible to English. A m.g. is *also* an early-riser.

A Touché of Mosquito Makes All Men Kin?

ひつしゃりと蚊こそ哀におもほゆれ 誰ふとも〻を喰し血なるそ
pisshari to ka koso aware ni omôyure daga futomomo o kuishi chi naruzo   teiryû II
slap=mimesis & mosquito esp. pitiful-as think, whose inner thigh+acc eating blood is!

貞柳二世 d.1735 狂歌活玉集 1740

Splat! That's that.
But, lo, the poor mosquito!
It's sad to know

Just whose fat inner thigh
he, stabbing, drank to die!

Splat! Why'd you
have to kill that mosquito?
Did you not know

whose juicy inner thigh he
stabbing drank only to die?

The mosquito
I just swatted leaves me
feeling guilty

Guess whose inner thigh
He drank before he died!

I have dreamed of what a mosquito saw flying through the bamboo grove with my blood and imagined its larvae as my progeny of sorts. There are haiku with less elaborate thought about the relationship between blood donor & recipient, but a *kyôka* requires something *more*. I hinted at it in the first two readings. Gouging flesh from the tender inner thigh was a way to pledge homosexual devotion (see Gary P. Leupp: *Male Colors*). Now, we know mosquitoes who suck blood are female; and I personally think they do males a service, for phlebotomy removes excess iron and increases our statistical longevity more than the risk of rare disease – I refer to encephalitis, if yellow fever were in my neighborhood, I might not be so grateful – lessens it; but mosquitoes in Japanese poetry were metaphorically male, as they *stabbed*, and paired with snakes, female as they swallowed, served as phallic symbols in dirty *senryû* and bawdy ballads.

Teiryû 貞柳 (1654-1735) 置みやけ

人を網へ入たやうなる蚊屋の内は赤貝も有蛸章も有けり
hito o ami e ireta yô naru kaya no uchi wa   akagai mo ari tako mo arikeri
people+acc net/s-to put-in like is mosquito-net's/s'-within-as for red-shell too is/are octopus too is/are

Mosquito nets
make all men fish and each
a different dish:

Some boast red ark shells &
others the beloved devilfish!

The original is less dramatic. Japanese readers knew what the seafood meant. The metaphor was sexy enough by itself. The red shell here was a common term for a mature woman's private part (there was an uncanny superficial resemblance to the vulva) and the devilfish the rare and highly desirable vagina that could cling to a man like an octopus in a narrow-mouthed octopus pot did to the hand of one who reached in for it. This *kyôka* is not exceptionally witty – though it improves if you know the hot and humid summer of Japan – and I put it here partly because it is the earliest use of *that* octopus I know, antedating *senryû* by decades and partly to advertize my book *Octopussy, Dry Kidney & Blue Spots* (2007) to anyone who might like to become further acquainted with these concepts, for there are dozens of *senryû* about said "octopussy" alone.

蚊は冨士の山ほと多き裏屋小屋ならぬ思ひのもゆる大鋸屑 1734
ka wa fuji no yama hodo ôki urayakôya naranu omoi no moyuru okakuzu teiryû
squitoes-as-4 mountain amount many backstreet small-flat become-not longing's sawdust

*Back-alley shacks
with mosquitoes abundant
as Mount Fujis*

*Burning saw-dust – what a joke:
Hopeless love goes up in smoke!*

*No back-alley flat
with mosquitoes as thick
as Fuji is high,*

*Love's labor lost, I burn within
Smudge enough to sting my eyes!*

Modifying a discrete quantity with size reverses the practice common in traditional Japanese poetry of describing the intensity of love as countless waves or grains of sand. I.e., *many* described *much*, here *much* does *many*. Such a reading of the first part anticipates the second, but Fuji could also be read as *Fujis*. Climbing Fuji as a spiritual exercise was common at this time and (small-scale) model Fujis were found in scores of cities around Japan; so the reference to the number of Fujis can be seen as a novel sort of hyperbole where not the target of the hyperbole but the hyperbole *itself* is hyperbolic (as many Fuji models as mosquitoes!?). The last two 7-7 *ku* take the *love-as-burning* trope, usually likened to burning-off salt for the bitter tear connection, and combines it with saw-dust, a cheap smudge. The *"un-fulfilled"* pegged on the "longing/love" puns as "hum-not," making readers imagine the noise made by the mosquitoes. I thought of turning the *kyôka* into something more English, like, say, *"Had we but smudge / enough and wine, mosquitoes, / lady, would be fine*, but even with the present of saw-*dust* and *lust,* I could not finish morphing it into Marvel's sleek appeal to his *Coy Mistress* without exceeding the proper length of the poem. The *naranu* in mid-poem first disclaims the preceding, ♪ then means *unfulfilled* (love).

時をあけよせくる蚊をや待ぬらん しつは蚊やりのさきおそろへて 潤甫和尚玉吟抄
toki o ake yose-kuru ka o ya machinuran jitsu wa kayari no saki o soroete junpo 1532

This poem by monk Junpo gives us that hushed moment just before pitched battle – the smudge fires mustered on the one side and the spear tips of the massing mosquito hoards on the other! *Ka* is *mosquito,* the smudge is *kayari,* and *yari* homophonic w/ *spear*. But, if the last was untranslatable, this one is utterly so.

The Bright and Dirty Tails of the Fireflies

色好みあっぱれそなたは日本一 matsui・蛍をあつめ千話文をかく ittetsu
irogonomi appare sonata wa nippon ichi matsui ・ *hotaru o atsume chiwabumi o kaku* ittetsu
color/eros-liking hurrah! you-as-for japan one! ・ fireflies+acc. gathering bawdy-tales+acc write

Bravo to you!
So gloriously horny,
Nippon Ichi!
++++++++++++++++
Gath'ring fireflies in pails
To write your dirty tales.

When it comes to
being horny, you're #1
in all Japan
+++++++++++++
Gath'ring those fireflies
to write your dirty tales!

When it comes to love
& loving it, you're the one
the primo of Japan
++++++++++++++
Gath'ring fireflies to write
dirty tales is quite a scam!

This is a found *kyôka*, i.e. a snippet of a 16c *haikai* link-verse sequence snipped from a lively context. Before explaining, a word on the *firefly*. It was popular enough a theme to boast multiple tropes including: 1) use by poor but diligent scholars for reading in the summer – as snow was piled by the window to reflect moonlight in the winter – an idea from China, as Japanese were more likely to make such a lantern for night-crawling, *i.e.,* calling on a lover; 2) symbolizing the ephemeral, as the light is faint, unsteady and soon gone, evoking our tenuous hold on life, or the lover so wretched s/he thinks of death; 3) a plaintive (small and in the dark) symbol of ardent longing, as burning within was linked to desire by the *hi* pun (*hi* in *omohi* and *kohi*), and Japan is what has been called a pun (as opposed to rhyme) culture. 4) the *butt* of jokes, for having lights on that part of their anatomy. What makes the above *haikai* sequence from a 1675 Osaka Danrin school link-verse jam so delightfully mad is that it parodies the classic trope with that of desire in its lowest form of pure horniness. And, it is even better when you know that the first part is preceded by, which is to say inspired by a 7-7 of brightly blushing young lovers coming together. Because "you" has no singular or plural in English – as is generally true for nouns and pronouns in Japanese – my 5-7-5 is not wrong and fits what follows, for one imagines someone writing dirty tales by firefly-light is alone. Well, not quite. "Dirty tales" is bent for a pun on *tail*. *Chiwabumi,* properly written 痴話文 are letters that spell out the desires of lovers. At any rate, they are no longer blushing. Note how the implied light of the fireflies in the 7-7 part, while making mad sense together with the previous 5-7-5, relates more directly to the previous 7-7. Because associations leap-frogged in this manner *as a rule* in the Danrin school, it is hard to harvest *kyôka* from it. Only exceptional links such as the above work, barely. So we have a paradox. The literature that may well have the most healthily mad *spirit*, yields the least easily harvested individual *kyôka*. Most *haikai did* flow directly from one stanza to another, but the ones with more closely linked associations generally had a 14-syllabet lead (*mae-ku*) and a 17 syllabet response. *While kyôka* (and *waka*) are usually the reverse, that matters less than the nature of the link, whether or not it creates one 31-syllabet poem. Diligent scholars do, however, find some of these early *haikai* links that work as stand-alones. The first of the following, from the *Inu Tsukuba-shû,* is in Steven D. Carter's *Traditional Japanese Poetry* (his translation, my deparsing). The second, from the *Enoko-shû,* is all mine.

あらぬ所に火をともしけり・いかにしてほたるのしりはひかるらん 犬筑波集 1539
aranu tokoro ni hi o tomoshikeri; ika ni shite hotaru no shiri wa hikaruran ng

What an unlikely place to be lighting a lamp!
Just how is it that a firefly's behind can be made to glow!

尻のかげにて名をやとる覧　蛍火を絶さでしたる学文者　重頼 犬子 1633
shiri no kage nite na o yadoru ran   hotarubi o taesa de shitaru gakumonja shigeyori

His name yet remains in the light of a behind;
A scholar made by not letting firefly fires go out!

Carter's selection resembles the naive style of *kyôka* and mine, alluding to the 4c Chinese scholar 車胤 Che Yin (Shain in Japanese), the satirical. I could not translate puns on *"light=thanks-to"*(*kage*) or *"knowledge=behind"* (*shiri*). Compare their nonchalance – a mark of early *haikai* and almost all *kyôka* – to the more serious older *waka*, such as these two well-known ones I give in loose translation, and even Issa's firefly *ku*, a country blues masterpiece *en su generis*.

"The firefly silently burning up from its passion / is a far sadder sight than bugs that cry all night" (音もせで思ひに燃ゆる。。*oto mo se de*. . . Minamoto no Shigeyuki 源重之 後拾遺集巻二夏)

"Longing for him, even fireflies on the moor seemed to be / sparks of burning passion, embers of my soul, of me!" (もの思へば沢の蛍もわが身より。。*mono omoeba sawa no hotaru mo* . . . Izumi Shikibu fl. c970-1030 和泉式部　同巻二十神紙雑六　My translation is very loose for there are many others you can find). Finally a *kyôka* from the 1730 anthology 狂歌乗合船 (*kyôka* joint-readership?) and a *kyôku* by Issa for comparison.

螢をはあつめて学ふいにしへの　人をひじりといふは尤　永井走帆
hotaru o ba atsumete manabu inishie no hito o hijiri to iu wa motomo sôho
firefly/ies+emph. gathering learn ancient people+acc. sage(=firebutt)-as say natural

Gathering fireflies to study with – no wonder we the men of old
Call "hijiri," or, sages of the burning butt, not cold!

~~~~~~

Dirt Farm

the poor soil	*who'd ever think*
belied by all that oil	*w/ soil here so thin to see*
what fireflies	*those fireflies!*

悪土の国とも見えぬ蛍哉 一茶 文化七
warutsuchi no kuni to mo mienu hotaru kana issa
bad-earth-country as+emph. appears-not, firefly/ies!

The *kyôka* is a delightful just-so etymology of 聖 *hijiri*, a saint, sage or maestro in any field of learning or sport: *fire=hi* 火＋尻=*jiri=ass*. Issa does not mention "oil."

Unnatural Love & Buried Souls, or More Fireflies

さかさまに恋もなる世の蛍かな　胸にはもえて尻そこかるゝ　玉吟抄
sakasama ni koi mo naru yo no hotaru kana mune ni wa moete shiri zo kogaruru   1532
reversed love+emph becomes world's fireflies!/?/: breast-in-as-for smoldering butt+emph burned

Left	*Right*
Even love is	*Torches, lamps,*
upside down in this	*we hold out in front,*
firefly world	*to walk w/out fear*
The breast is inflamed	*So what's with fireflies,*
but the arse, it burns!	*why light up the rear?*

人の行前はちやうちん明松や　ほたるは尻をなと照らん　玉吟抄
hito no yuku mae wa chôchin taimatsu ya hotaru wa shiri o na to tereruran
person goes before-as-for lantern, torch and/: firefly-as-for butt why(?) shines?/!

The 16c *Gyokuginshû* collection features two poems per subject, a judgment and comments. Usually one is favored, but these by 釈三卜 & 山蒼斎 Junpo (潤甫和尚 who, for all I know may have written them, too) judged equal, as both put the cart before the horse 前後顛倒の作法同科. I favor the first: jumping from the metaphor of burning passion in the chest to *the consequences of combustion in relation to the vertical human body to that of the horizontal bug* is harder than a mere front-back reversal. A later *kyôka*, only alluding to the *contrary-to-nature* vector of the burning, improves the "left" poem even further:

若衆を思ひのたまかほたる火の　むねはこかれで/て?しりそこかるゝ　入安 1610
wakashû o omohi no tama ka hotarubi no mune wa kogare de/te? shiri zo kogaruru   nyûan
young-crowd=gay+longing soul/s? firefly-fire's breast-as4 burns-w/ butt+emph chars ~狂歌百首

Could those souls	*Could those souls*
be born of passion for a gay?	*be longing of a gay fashion?*
Behold the firefly	*Behold the firefly*
Breasts may burn, but, hey,	*Breasts may burn from passion,*
The butt is what gets fried!	*But when the ass burns you cry*

Could those souls
be longing for gay boys?

Firefly passion

Burning in the breast annoys
But the buttocks are consumed!

Izumi Shikibu's *waka*, (*mono omoeba sawa no hotaru . . .*) translated loosely, but with all my (he)art, in the last chapter, is one of the most beautiful *waka* ever written and was so well known (as one of the hundred used in card games) I think it safe to say the above *kyôka* are inspired by it or parodies of it, as you prefer. At any rate, that is why I write "*those* souls." I am afraid, however, that without a similar *longing=fire* metaphorical pun tradition in English, no cleverness can prevent loss in translation. The following from the 1310 *Fubokuwakashô*:

むもれ木の心もしらす名とり川さもあらはれてとふほたるかな 民部爵 夫木
mumoregi no kokoro mo shirazu natorikawa samo arawarete tobu hotaru kana minobe tameie?
buried trees' heart+emph know/s-not name-take-river!/: hoh, appearing fly fireflies!/?

*Rumor River, you
know not the hidden mind
of the buried trees.*

*Or do the flying fireflies
reveal it to you and me?*

*Who knows what
love lies in the buried trees
of Rumor River*

*Unless – Does it come out?
Behold the host of fireflies!*

A Name-takes-river (Natorigawa) is a local fixture we might call *The River*, but this one near Kyôto is famous for semi-petrified trees dug from the river-bed by craftsmen. It plays upon well-known older *waka* (mys#1385, kks#650) where the river name implies gossip, name-spreading, something lovers feared so much they suffered their longing in silence. But who knows. A story could make it the soul of a worthy whose name vanished from history without ever blooming . . .

おとは河せゝのいはなみ玉ちりてもゆるほたるも影そすゝしき 隆信朝臣 夫木
otowa kawa sese no iwanami tama chirite moyuru hotaru mo kage zo suzushiki takanobu d.1205
otowa river shoals/murmuring's stone-waves gem scattering burns fireflies even form+emph cool

*How cool the sight of fireflies burning the souls,
the drops that fly from the sybillant flow of the River Otowa!*

*River of Sound
Even the sight of sparks, of
fireflies from stones*

*struck by a hissing flow
of white-hot water is cool*

*The Otowa River,
where even water hisses
as if white hot,*

*striking rocks, sowing sparks
of burning fireflies, is cool.*

Cool reflections of fire in water (punned in the *kage*) are old hat, water hitting rocks, soul/beads strewn about by broken heart-strings – shades of Humpty Dumpty fallen from his wall – and yet the original flows along transforming here and parodoxing there so gracefully that if it were not for the "even" it might be an exemplar of the beauty of *waka*. To me, that "even" makes this an idea-first poem and fair game for mad translation; but the line between straight and mad *waka* can be arbitrated, not settled. Here is one *wild waka* from *Fuboku* the metaphor of which is so beautiful any translation will do: *With the dawn, all the burning fireflies had vanished / and only their smoke remains on the water.* あけ行はもゆるほたるも影きえてけふりを水にのこすなりけり 喜多院入道 夫木 *ake yukeba moyuru hotaru mo kage kiete kemuri o mizu ni nokosu narikeri* kita-in d.1202?

Mostly Fireflies from the 1313 Gem Leaf Collection

いにしへの のもりのかかみ あとたえて とふひはよはの ほたるなりけり 寂蓮家集
inishie no nomori no kagami ato taete tobuhi wa yowa no hotaru narikeri monk jakuren 家集
ancient field-guards' sight/reflction aftr dying/fadng flyng-fires-as-4 late-night ffs are! d.1202

>   *The mirrored souls of the guardians of old fade before my eyes;*
>   *Our signal-lights in the wee hours of the night . . . are fireflies.*

In the 7c, a system of smoke signals by day and fire by night from a web of hilltop, or otherwise raised, platforms was started to guard against invasion by sea. It did not last a hundred years in most parts, but the name "flying-fire" for the stations and the guards captured the romantic imagination. (Oddly, *stepping stones* in gardens, also "fly/leaping (rocks)," are *tobi-ishi*, not *tobu~*.) Poems from a Jakuren anthology start and end this chapter, otherwise all but one are *waka* culled from the relatively wit-friendly 1312/13 *Gyokuyôshû* 玉葉集 anthology.

かきくらす さつきのさよの あまくもに かくれぬほしは ほたるなりけり 番号外作者
kakikurasu satsuki no sayo no amakumo ni kakurenu hoshi wa hotaru narikeri ng 1313
so dark fifthmonth night's rain/sky(?)clouds-by hidden-not stars-as-for fireflies are!

>   *All of the Stars on this dismally dark monsoon night*
>   *not hidden by the rain clouds are them: lightning bugs*

ゆふまくれ かせにつれなき しらつゆは しのふにすかる ほたるなりけり 惟明親王
yûmagure kaze ni tsurenaki shiratsuyu wa shinobu ni sugaru hotaru narikeri prince tadaaki
eveningtide wind-in pitiful(=accompany-not?) white-dew-as-for remembering holds-on ffs are!

>   *As night falls, the shiny dew that leaves not with the wind*
>   *still holding on for dear life, turns out to be . . . fireflies!*

~~~~~~

>   *That shiny dew the wind could not make yield – after dark*
>   *Still holding on, those drops became a field of fireflies!*

~~~~~~

>   *At nightfall when the fireflies go wild in every thicket,*
>   *It comes time for the light in dewdrops to end its visit.*

grass/bush-clumps-in fireflies wilding evening-as-for dew-light+emph leaves-must! 玉葉集
kusamura ni hotaru midaruru yûgure wa tsuyu no hikari zo wakarezarikeri ng (name not given)
くさむらに ほたるみたるる ゆふくれは つゆのひかりそ わかれさりける 番号外作者

~~~~~~

ふくかせになひくさはへのくさのはにこほれぬつゆやほたるなるらむ 実房 d.1225
fuku kaze ni nabiku sawabe no kusanoha ni koborenu tsuyu ya hotaru naruramu sanefusa
blowing wind/s-in bend-over bog-sides'grass/weed-blades/leaves-on tumble-not-dew!/?/: ffs are!

>   *On blades of grass in the bogs, bent by a strong wind,*
>   *The dew that does not spill – It is them, your fireflies!*

With firefly one of the easiest bugs to spot, it is interesting to see so many methods of identification. Light in the dark must ask for comparison and contrast.

ゆくほたる おのれもえそふかけみえて ひとのおもひも さそとつけこせ 番号外作者
yuku hotaru onore moe (339) *toritsuke* or 徳化する うせろ。ゆきやがれ。玉葉集 1313
going ff/s your-own burning accomp. shadow/light seeing person's thoughts(+fire) too　ng

Fireflies in motion can see in the light of their own burning,
Why can't we, too, use loving thoughts to lamp our learning?

くれをまつ おもひはたれもあるものを ほたるはかりや みにあまるへき 隆房 同
kure o matsu omo(h)i wa dare mo aru mono o hotaru bakari ya mi ni amaru beki takafusa?
dusk+acc awaitng longng(+fire)-as-4 anyone has but+contrad. ffs amount+emph. body-to exceed-ought

Who doesn't have passionate thoughts that await the night?
But if you glow like a firefly, methinks you burn too bright!
~~~~~~
We all have them, passionate thoughts that await the dark –
True love should burn like a firefly and overflow the heart!

のきしろき つきのひかりに やまかけの やみをしたひてゆくほたるかな 後鳥羽院
noki shiroki tsuki no hikari ni yamagake no yami o shitaite yuku hotaru kana go toba 木夫集
eaves whitely lunar light-in mountain-ridge's/s' dark longing-go/leave fireflies! 1333

In bright light from the white moonlit eaves, craving darkness
They pass by heading for the mountain shade . . . fireflies.

To think this flowing *waka* (all before *hotaru* modifies it) is by the retired Emperor who revived the Poetry Bureau and commissioned the *Shinkokinshû*! Almost 600 years would pass before Issa also thought from the firefly's point of view. The above 1333 *Fubokushû* find is high-contrast, but no *kyôka*. It is reality.

このまより みゆるはたにの ほたるかも いさりにあまの うみへゆくかも 喜撰
ko no ma yori miyuru wa tani no hotaru ka mo isari ni ama no umi e yuku ka mo kisen 1313
trees-between-from appear-as-4 valley's ffs maybe, lights-as fisherfolks' sea-to going maybe

Are those fireflies down in the vale we spy through the trees
taking their light to the sea to help the fisherfolk, maybe?

This delightful wacky *waka* is doubly *kyôka*. Tiny glowing bug-butts helping out night-fishermen is a crazy idea, and it plays in a good-humored way – facetious sarcasm? – with a *Tales of Ise* poem where the anti-hero's visit to a seaside inn gave rise to a rustic poem conflating fireflies, stars in the river and distant fishing fires. Jakuren (or, Shunzei?), a century earlier, made one of those untranslatable quicksilver *waka* Waley lamented, the word-order of which I must juggle to keep the modification and the modified fireflies together, though both may well apply to those fires. No *kyôka*, this allusive variation is higher poetry than its original:

たのむへき ゆくへとみるそ あはれなる ほたるはかりの あまのいさりひ
tanomu beki yukue to miru zo / awarenaru hotaru bakari no ama no isaribi jakuren d.1203
desirable(from faith) destination as see+emph.! beautiful/sad ff-amount's fisherfolk's lights

No larger they than fireflies so beautiful and sad that show
The way all of us must go . . . The fires of the fisherfolk.

Burning Moths and Burning People

白玉と見えし涙も年ふればから紅にうつろひにけり　つらゆき
shiratama to mieshi namida mo toshi fureba kara-kurenai ni utsuroinikeri
white/bright-gems-as appear tears even years pass/falling chinese-crimson-into change

Even my teardrops,
once so pearly white,
have turned to red

Like in China, but dyed
by the downpour of years!

~~~~~~

Even those teardrops / which seemed like white jewels / with the swift passing / years　have changed to Chinese red / freshly dyed by burning hearts: R&H

The poet, Tsurayuki, editor of the *Kokinshû*, so enjoyed trope-arrangement that when there were gaps in the sequence he bridged them himself. All of which is to say that if R&H did not add the "burning hearts" because the *"i"* in *kurenai* (crimson) is written *"hi,"* which puns with *fire*, it was because the poem *after* it, the next, below, is about *flaming love*. The only problem is they forget the link to the *previous* poem, also by Tsurayuki, with *sleeves dyed by tears*. As it happens, *that* is where the cleverest pun lies: namely, years "pass" with the same verb used for rain "falling" (*furu/fureba*), allowing Tsurayuki to invent a Japanese just-so for a Chinese conceit of *bloody* red tears. The years "falling" dye his tears as rain does leaves, which turn crimson in Japan as in New England. That process is one of gradual accretion, so "swift" and "freshly" are *wrong*.

夏虫をなにかいひけむ心から我も思ひにもえぬべらなり　みつね 古今集
natsumushi o nani ka iikemu kokoro kara ware mo omoi ni moenu beranari mitsune kks
summer bugs+acc what say/call-did heart-from i too longing/flames-by burning+emph.

Oh, Luna moth　　　　　　　　　　　*What lunatics!*
Could I have roasted you?　　　　*I called the moths names.*

If I, now aflame　　　　　　　　　*But look at me, now*
with desire for him but knew　　*burning up from the flames*
I'd burn up from within!　　　　*of my very own passion!*

"Summer insect" means 1) all bugs drawn to flames at night and/or 2) the huge pale green moths that most beautifully and, therefore, tragically immolate themselves. Specifying the "luna moth" makes sense to me because a single species makes better sense for *name*-calling. The original (and translations I lost thanks to Microsoft) mentions the *heart*, but taking "from the heart/mind" here as meaning *from within* or *from one's own,* I dropped it the second time around, the better to hint at what the mention of the moths meant: getting burnt from *without*. Another, less complex, purely metaphorical "summer insect" poem by Shikibu (970-1030) is more commonly encountered (in Japanese or in translation):

人の身も恋にはかへつ夏蟲のあらはに燃ゆとみえぬ計ぞ 式部 後拾遺集
hito no mi mo koi ni wa kaetsu natsumushi no arawa ni moyu to mienu bakari zo   shikibu
persn's self/body also lve-for xchng smmrbugs' patently burn appear-amount/see-not-just only!

    We may give up our lives for love, and that in plain sight
    as the luna moth that burns without, lighting up the night

    People, too, for love will pine away, you would think
    We had never seen moths burn or smelled that stink!

    That a human may give up her life for love is just as plain
    As the luna moth that flies openly into a flame.

Chances are any translation of this poem will be flawed. Why? The original trades our *body/self* for love, and we, lacking both in one word, must exchange *body* for *heart,* and the idea of trading *hearts* for *koi* (*love, longing* or *lust*) distances us from the metaphor, suicidal bugs. Also, as an amateur, I am unsure of the old grammar (*mieru hodo* or *mienai bakari?*). Regardless, Shikibu's observation is not as good as a *waka,* or a possible *kyôka,* as Mitsune's before-and-after, with its confession of kidding or bad-mouthing. Simplicity sounds good, but the connoisseur seeks something more. Obviously, the "stink" is mine!

夏蟲はうらやましくやおもふらんおのか思ひにもえぬほたるを 能因法師 夫木
natsumushi wa urayamashiku ya omouran onoga omoi ni moenu hotaru o   monk nôin
moths-as-for enviously think-would: self's longing/flame-in burn-not fireflies d.1050?

    How luna moths must envy lightning bugs who are not burnt,
    But burn alive from the fire of love within their own hearts!

    ~~*The summer bugs must be envious as hell at those fireflies,*~~
    ~~*Who, burning from within, turn their yearning into light.*~~

    How the Moths must with envy burn to see the Fireflies
    Ignite themselves from within, whenever they desire!

    To luna moths, nothing is more envious than a firefly,
    Who can himself annihilate in the flames of his desire!

    How the Moth must burn with envy for the Firefly;
    Lit up by his own passion he need not fly to fry!

いたつらに身をたきすつる蛍かなのりのためとは思はさるらん 中務爵みこ 御集蛍
itazura ni mi o takitsuru hotaru kana nori no tame to wa omowazaru-ran nakatsukasa 夫木
frivolously body+acc burn-doing firefly/ies!/?/: (holy)law-for-as-for think-not!!!

    'Shadows of the Divine' you say? (in reply to Jonathon Edwards)

    The fireflies light up their bodies for the hell of it, right?
    I doubt they illuminate anything but the night!

Third-rate Poet, or First-rate Mad Poem Mistress?
この傑作の原文をば求む　資料に暇のあるお方　よろしくお願いします
kono kesaku no genbun o ba motomu. shiryô ni hima no aru okata, yoroshiku onegaishimasu

< Credit Given Where Credit Is Due. >

Thanks, my dear,
for the moon light shining
on my sleeves!

I would not have known it
Had you not made me cry.

This moonlight
shining bright on my sleeves
tonight, I view

Because you made me cry;
Yes, it is all thanks to you!

Lady Daibu (Kenreimon-in Ukyo no Daibu) 建礼門院右京大夫集 家集にも見当たらず

I forget where I read the words, but I am sure I read that Lady Daibu was considered "a third-rate *waka* poet." And, I suspect, she is still considered second-rate by those who expect more finesse and enlightenment(?) in a *waka*. But, to my mind, it depends what you want. The hyperbolic complaints that make a champion of conventional *waka* look down his nose at the Lady, should make her a patron saint of *kyôka*, or at least of the self-deprecating variety. There are plenty of poems about moonlight reflected on teary sleeves, but this *thank you* (原文はきっと君の「おかげで」であろう) is novel; if it is not mad, no *waka* is! If scholars did not tend to stick to their own genre, I believe the above poem, which I read about twenty years ago but could not relocate – hence no original is given – would be very famous.   The next poem is harder to call:

There Is No Question

To think that we
in that same world can be,
Yet you no longer

are with me! Sadly, now
I see: To be is not to be!

おなじ世となほ思ふこそかなしけれあるがあるにもあらぬこの世に
onaji yo to nao omou koso kanashikere aru ga aru ni mo aranu kono yo ni
same world still [i] think +emph. sad // am but am despite am-not this world in

This wit differs from the last example, as it depends on word play: that *aru+aru +aranu* sequence. Written when her husband extended his stay – exile, military duties or a second wife 西国に落ち延びて「死んだも同然」と言っている資盛, I'm sure historians know, but I do not care – on the Western front, and she was forced to resign herself to the possibility of never again seeing him alive, it is far from cheerful, but "the same world," tells me – perhaps wrongly, as I've not checked – that at least they were on the winning side of something.

物思へば心の春もしらぬ身に何うぐひすの告げに来つらむ　家集67
mono-omoeba kokoro no haru mo shiranu mi ni nani uguisu no tsuge ni kitsuramu
longing/worrying heart's spring even know-not body/self-to what/why warbler informing comes!?

*What business
has a nightingale to come
and tell a girl*

*spring's here, when her heart
in the winter of love, is not?*

*There is no spring
in my heart, still shivering
from love's misery*

*Is that why, Nightingale,
you'd announce it to me?*

"Nightingale" may not be correct for the bush-warbler in question, but the history of translation and the romantic connotations of the name probably make it the best choice. The first reading seems more likely. Either way, criticizing or explaining a bird's behavior in terms of a human's love life is, in itself, mad.

今や夢昔や夢とまよは(たどら)れていかに思へどうつつとぞなき　右京大夫　家集
ima ya yume mukashi ya yume to mayowa[todara]rete ikani omoedo utsutsu to zo naki
now is dream longago is dream and/so wandered/lost, nomatterhowmuch think-if reality+emph. not

*Now is a dream,
long ago and far away
was a dream;*

*Lost myself, I came to see
there is no reality.*

*Life is but a dream,
they say, whether long ago
or now, you know,*

*If nothing's real, anyway
How, then, can we stray?*

To tell the truth, the second reading reveals what *I* wished Lady Daibu wrote rather than what she did, which was, unfortunately closer to the first reading, the second line of which marks the second time I have borrowed the title of the autobiography of one of my favorite nature/travel essayists, W.H. Hudson (the other is in *Cherry Blossom Epiphany*). Then, again, I see a note that the distraught lady did indeed get half-way to my idea (詞書は「建礼門院大原におはしましける比まゐりたるに、夢の心ちのみして侍りければ、思ひつづけ侍りける」); and another version follows it (風雅集 17-1915 で、第三句は「たどられて」).

*If you would but visit me in my dreams to show you care!
Why not just tell me to die for Love I never see you there.*

It is as hard to differentiate mad and "normal" poems as it is to negotiate reality and dream. The above is *not* another by Lady Daibu, but one of 8c *Manyôshû* editor Ôtomo Yakamochi's many poems to the Elder Maiden of Sakanoue (*ime ni dani mieba koso are kakubakari miezu shi aru wa koite shine to ka* 万葉 #749). When you consider the fact people were held responsible for appearing in other's dreams, it is not that odd to blame someone for not appearing, but combining that with the second charge of wanting someone to pine away is mad, in the sense that few poems in the straight anthologies allow cause-effect-cause-effect chains of logic. It leads me to believe that Yakamochi would not only not have minded Tsurayuki's much denigrated cleverness with the *Kokinshû*, but welcomed it.

Loving Stars on the Seventh Month, Seventh Night

Oh, my! Ought I
stare up at the stars like this
when they meet

but once a year, should we
not let them be discreet?

I will not watch
the sky tonight – not a wink
for a rendezvous

but once a year, I think,
some privacy would do!

Lady Daibu
~ maybe ~

My memories are clearing. Even her translator agreed Lady Daibu was a third-rate poet, which makes us wonder *why* she was translated, for you can bet said translator did not bring out her wit as I, who like her more, do. Could the fact late-20c publishers favored obscure women explain it? Recently, I found scores of her *waka* about Tanabata, or the Meeting of the Herder and Weaver Stars across the Milky Way on the Seventh Night of the Seventh Month of the old calendar (making it late summer or early fall) on the web. Many I had never seen and all I *had* seen and vaguely recalled were included but the above, which is, of course, the one that is most clearly akin to a *kyôka* if not the thing itself. (*Found it!* But, it won't fit here. See the ♪!) The second maddest one *was* included:

How I'd like to
hear their sweet nothings
while we spy

in tubs of cool water
☆ *The Loving Stars!* ☆

God, I'd love it
if the water in this tub
would but reflect

their sweet nothings, too:
☆*the stellar rendezvous.*☆

きかばやな ふたつの星の ものがたり たらひの水に うつらましかば 277
kikabaya na futatsu no hoshi no monogatari tarai no mizu ni utsuramashikaba
hear-would+emph. two stars' tale/s tub's water-in/on/by reflect-not?+emph

I have yet to learn *how* the stars would be more visible reflected on water. Or, was a mirror placed below the water to create a refractive lens to enlarge the lover stars? Whatever, it would surely make what Lady Daibu makes me call *voyeuristic star-gazing* less of a pain in the neck! Some Japanese really looked. Issa has what I would call a *kyôku* about gazing so hard he opened a hole in the Milky Way (穴の明程見たりけり天の川 *ana no aku hodo mitarikeri amanokawa*). I am no star-gazer. Even a playful star 遊星, i.e. a planet, is less interesting than an ant. It takes a major meteor shower to raise my eyes to the sky. What makes this star festival sweet are the strips of colored paper with wishes written on them tied to lithe branches of bamboo. And it looks better today than it could have back then because the earlier solar date of the festival (the numbers 7-7 were too good to change) means that the new bamboo shot up only a month or two before.

女郎花もっとくねれよ星迎ひ sic 一茶　　　　　　ふんどしに笛つゝさして星迎 一茶
ominaeshi motto kunere yo hoshi mukae issa　　*fundoshi ni fue tsutsusashite hoshi mukae* issa
maiden flowers more wiggle+exclam. star-greet　　loin-cloth-into flute stickx2/sticking star-greet

Maiden Flowers,　　　　　　　　　　　　　　　　*sticking my flute*
Let me see you bump & grind!　　　　　　　　　*into my loin-cloth, i'm off*
The stars won't mind　　　　　　　　　　　　　*to greet the stars*

Patrinia scabiosaefolia, the only English (?) my dictionary gives, fails for *ominaeshi*, meaning a *girl* or *wench* (including *tarts*), so I think the conventional translation, *maiden flower* good enough. Old Issa – the first *ku* above was written months before he died (1827), his third wife pregnant with his only child that would live to adulthood – was rude enough that I am not too embarrassed about my outrageous reading for what would more responsibly be translated:

Maiden flowers, squirm more, now, squirm! The Stars come.

The Iwanami standard Issa only mentions the *ku* in a note to an earlier version where *"kachi-zûmo," i.e.,* wrestling engaged in with a winning attitude, was where the Stars came to be. The editor failed to note a contemporary play called *Winning-sumô-floating(woebegotten)-name-flower-touch*勝相撲浮名花触*Kachi-zumôukinanohanabure*, which *might* help explain what Issa was driving at. Said flower, though perennial, was recognized as an Autumn field flower by *haikai*. *Now* they are divorced from the Festival of the Stars which is in July (still, it can be warm in late August and the second of Issa's ku, above, proves it). But, to return to the maiden flowers, I must confess to missing the allusion in Issa's *ku* and only catching it by sheer luck in the foreword to Kato Ikuya's collection of comic haiku (滑稽俳句大全) when he gives a *ku* by Gendô (17c) *"That's where song-poets really twist their words: maiden flowers"* (哥をよむ人も句ねるや女郎花　元藤 *uta o yomu hito mo ku neru ya ominaeshi*) as an example of new humor far from Bashô-like and explains that the foreword to the *Kokinshû* (c905) tells how songs *uta* (*waka*) can console *kuneru*=twisting/wiggling/ writh-ing *ominaeshi*. So, Issa plays with the *Kokinshû*. That is *mad*. But, there is more. I still did not really *get it* until reading a *kyôka* by Bokuyô, which is on page 357 – I had to come back here to rewrite as it makes it clear to me that Issa probably wanted the maiden flowers to show that they are uncomfortable – properly, or adorably shy – about, or less likely, envious of, what the loving Stars were about to do.

浦やまし恋に堪へたる星なれや とし に一夜と契る心は　大夫　lady
urayamashi koi ni taetaru hoshi nare ya toshi ni hitoyo to chigiru kokoro wa daibu
envious! love+dat. endure stars are! year-in one-night tryst/vow heart-as-for

You stars so lucky
not to mind one fucking
night each year,

I'm so envious to hear
of self-control in love!

Who Needs Magpie Bridges in the Sky!

天の川羽衣着たら飛び越えん げに空事ぞかささぎの橋 貞徳 百首狂歌
amanogawa hagoromo kitara tobikoen ge ni soragoto zo kasasagi no hashi   teitoku 1571-1653
heaven's river feather-robe worn-if flying-cross-would really sky-thing/fiction+emph magpie-bridge

◎ Star-crossed Logic ◎

*The Milky Way
is easily crossed, I bet
in a feather robe*

*Magpie bridges in the sky?
How silly can you get!*

*Heaven's River
Don't they all have wings
to get across it?*

*Feather bridges? My, my,
That* is *magpie in the sky!*

This, like Teitoku's *have-nots with something* (pg.280), is idea-first, and only shored up with word-play. It is a prototype for the best of the Tenmei *kyôka*. Teitoku takes a general mythical concept to challenge a particular one, and puns with a term for a "tall-tale," *soragoto*, literally meaning "sky-thing." There are any number of contradictions in various versions of the tale. Rain on this night is often explained as splashing oars from the herder's *boat*, something that would also make the magpie wings redundant. The *Hagoromo* are feathered robes worn by sky-dwellers, mostly beautiful maidens, who figure in some *Manyôshû* poems and the most interesting of all falling cherry-blossom *waka*, in a later anthology SKKS #131, which I borrow from *Cherry Blossom Epiphany* 2007, and give below. I had not known that Sotoku-in (1119-64) was retired Emperor #75.

山たかみ岩根の櫻散る時はあまの羽ごろも撫づるとぞ見る 崇徳院御歌
yama takami iwane no sakura chiru toki wa ama no hagoromo nazuru to zo miru sotoku-in 1205
mountain heights boulderbases' cherries/petals fall time-as-for heaven's feather-robes brush yes see

*when petals fall
from the rocky heights
of the mountains*

*i see down rubbed off
the wings of angels*

*when petals float
down from rocky heights
in the mountains*

*i can see it: those wings
of angels brushing earth*

*when petals fall
from the rocky heights
of the mountains*

*i almost see them brush
the wings of angels*

Only the middle reading is correct – though "earth" should be "stone" – though the others would be as good of a guess as any *if you did not know*, as I did not when I first read it, that "the rub/stroke/brush of heavenly feather-robes" refers to something happening slowly, *"longer than the time required to wear down boulders covering 40 square leagues brushed once every 100 years by an angel's wing,"* i.e., one Kalpa. At any rate, Sutoku-in's poem shows that *waka* could be literally fantastic without being mad or nonsensical. Now, a page more of Lady Daibu's *waka*, for I repeat, I feel kinship between her use of logic to play with a sad love life and that of the mad monks who used it for other things. The first two or three, I believe, are novel and free enough they *might* be called *kyôka*.

たぐひなき なげきにしづむ 人ぞとて このことの葉を星やいとはん *tagui naki . . .*

*Sunk in grief
vast beyond belief, alas
i write things*

*I do not mean, like i
simply hate the stars!*

*What's to be done
with people sunk in grief
sad beyond belief?*

*How the stars, our betters
must hate to read our letters!*

あはれとや思ひもすると 七夕に身のなげきをも うれへつるかな *aware to ya omoi . .*

*So do we send
our laments to the stars
because we feel*

*They who have suffered
will hear our appeal?*

*Feeling sorry
for the stars, what brings us
to burden them*

*with details of our plight
on their only happy night?*

七夕に心はかしてなげくとも かゝる思ひをえしもかたらぬ *tanabata ni kokoro . . .*

*My laments that
go out to the stars tonight
are nothing i want*

*to share, nothing i dare
put into poetry – So there!*

*Dreams freed
from my sleeves, shared
with the stars*

*Well, if they ever came true
I could share nothing w/ you!*

~~~~~~

さまざまに思ひやりつつ よそながら ながめかねぬる 星合の空 *samazama ni omoiyari . . .*

*Many thoughts arise as i gaze into the skies, and though 'tis not
my affair – how can i help it, when those Stars are there!*

なげきてもあふせをたのむ天の河 このわたりこそかなしかりけれ *nagekite mo . . .*

*Of course, it's sad; but they, at least, still cross the Milky Way
They rendezvous – but, you and I . . . we never do!*

引く糸のたゞ一筋に恋ひこひて こよひあふせも うらやまれつゝ *hiku ito no tada . . .*

*Love, oh, love, an unbroken thread – envious, we go to bed,
As they on that stream bed meet, the Stars live, we're dead.*

七夕の契りなげきし身のはては あふせをよそにきゝわたりつゝ *tanabata no chigiri . . .*

*I used to feel for the stars, who met but once a year . . .
Now, with no one seeing me, I'm afraid I'm out of tears!*

世の中は見しにもあらず なりぬるに おもがはりせぬ星合の空 *yononaka wa mishi . . .*

*Our world is no longer. Of what was, only the love
of the stars is far from cold: in Heaven all is as of old..*

From Ox Slobber to Angel Hair to the Amazon

彦星のひくてふ牛のよだれより このちぎりこそ長たらしけれ 蜀山家集
hikoboshi no hiku teu (to iu) ushi no yodare yori kono chigiri koso nagatarashikeri shokusanjin
herder star pulling said ox's/oxen's drool-from this vow especially long-has-been+emph. d.1823

Long kept – longer by far than the slobber of the Oxen led
by our Cowboy Star – their wedding vows and bed.

One of a cluster of seven Tanabata festival poems by the star of *kyôka*, prefaced with a paragraph-long complaint about maudlin *waka* worrying about choppy water the herder must cross, sympathizing with the plight of the lonely weaver, and so forth, reminding readers that *kyôka* must, first of all, be funny. Since Teitoku pretty much owned (year of the) *cow slobber* (see pg.44), I find myself reminded of New Year's poems, some of which compare that time with the Star Festival: both are once-a-year. Another of Shokusanjin's poems recalls Teitoku's skepticism about the magpie wing bridge: *What, with a bridge / of magpie wings and fall leaves / filling the streams // Why leave your ox to find / A boat to reach your wife?* (かさゝぎの はしも紅葉のはしもあるを 猶おいとまの妻むかへ舟 *kasasagi ni hashi mo momiji no hashi mo aru o nao oitoma no tsuma-mukae fune*). The fall *leaves* are *also* a *bridge* and pun on *frost* on the leaves, etc.

..

七夕の ひよくの鳥の 玉子酒 れんりの枝の 豆やくふらん 同
tanabata no hiyoku no tori no tamagozake renri no eda no mame ya kuu ran
seventh-night's half-wing birds egg sake together-branch's beans+emph eat!

On the Seventh, wine
with eggs from birds that fly
tandem: one wing each,

And what beans we pop to eat
from the welded limbs of trees!

Shokusanjin turned everything into food and drink, but the particulars are still romantic and the wit less nonsense than pun. The birds, we have seen (pg.72), *hiyoko* 比翼鳥, are symbols of romantic union so close each mate has but one of their pair of wings (*United we fly!*), while the fused limbs stand for lovers so close they grow together. With the Stars *apart* for 364 days and nights per year, the metaphor is odd, but fits the larger romance of the night that includes *wishing*, where the united birds represent heaven and fused limbs earth (在天願作比翼鳥在地願為連理枝, 白居易, 長恨歌). Wine w/ an egg/s (in the bottle) is a fortifier. When old Issa was working on fatherhood with his younger wife, he was often presented bottles of it by his students. Also, lover stars, unified bird and fused limbs are already found together in an old passage of prose (源平盛衰記・25 日本国語大辞典で比翼か連理枝を引けば). The unique and funniest part of the original – what really makes the poem – is the way the limb of the tree (*renri no eda*) converts to a common *hors' de oeuvre*, perhaps the only Japanese vegetable to make it frozen into Usanian supermarkets: *eda (no) mame* (branch-beans)!

七夕を思へば遠きあめりかのあまさうねんの事にや有けん 蜀山人
tanabata o omoeba tôki amerika no amasônen no koto ni ya ari ken
seventh-eve+acc think-when america's amazon's thing re.!+hypoth.

When I think about this seventh night, I cannot help
Seeing them in America, crossing the Amasônen!

~~~~~~~~~~~~~~~~~~~~~~~~~~~~~~~~~~~~~

The two Stars, I imagine them far off – in America;
Ama-no-kawa, Heaven's River as the Ama-zone!

Who would guess the Japanese, after 200 years of isolation, were so conversant with the New World! The Milky Way is "heaven's river" in the Sinosphere; *Amerika* and *Amasônen* include two Japanese pronunciations of "heaven," *ame* and *ama*. Some years earlier, a Shiba Kôkan map called Argentina's La Plata *Ginga* 銀河, "silver-river," a synonym for the Galaxy, and pronounced Amazon in the North European manner, *Amasonen* アマソテン, while the *Unkonshi* 雲根志 encyclopedia of natural history followed the shorter Chinese adoption *Amason* 亞馬孫(河) but wrote it 天孫河 or *Heaven-Descendents-River*. The jump to 天河 =Galaxy=Amazon was, thus, a natural. Soon, the blue *Amazonenstein* would be Japanesed as 天河石 "Milky Way Stone!" The long "ô" is a puzzle (no precedent yet). Shokusanjin may have coined *Amasônen* for the *sônen* 想念 "thoughts," of a loving, shall we say, heavenly nature. But it is more likely a loose pun (rare in Japanese) on the thin white noodles called *sômen* eaten on that day as a metaphor for the *hosonagai*, or *love me slender love me long* thread of lasting romance. Viz, this earlier *kyôka* by Ôsaka's great *kyôka* master, Teiryû, that turns the spider thread in Saigyô's 7-7 *waka* (*amanogawa nagarete* p.132) into the same:

ひこほしの来へき宵なりさゝかにの蜘の糸より細きそうめん 貞柳 置みやけ 貞柳
hikoboshi no kubeki yoi nari sasagani no kumo no ito yori hosoki sômen teiryû d.1735
herderstar's come-should eve becoming spider's thread-more-than thin noodles

The herder star will come tonight, for only a spider could spin
noodles as thin as these we prepared while she waits for him.

Like Saigyô's, the original *ends* on the ostensible subject. Shokusanjin would later write several 7-7 poems explicitly mentioning *sômen*. My favorite, a cold noodle goodbye, is untranslatable; in English, neither *sobbing* and *slurping* nor long thin cold noodles and such a separation can be equated : 七夕もすゝりては なきたまふらん ひや索麺の ながきわかれを 蜀山家集 *tanabata mo susurite wa naki-tamauran hiyasômen no nagaki wakare o*. The second best *can* be Englished, albeit minus the noodles=*somen* turning into the verb for "to dye" or "to color"!

七月七夕官女 黒がみもいつか素麺としどしの七夕のうたよむとせしまに 蜀山 家集
kurogami mo itsu ka sômen toshidoshi no tanabata no uta yomu to seshi ma ni shokusanjin
dark-hair too/emph! when? somen/noodles year-year's seventh-eve's poems read-do while

~ The Woman in Charge of the Palace Weaving Festival ~

Year after year, when did her black locks turn sômen *white,*
As she did her duty reading poems about the seventh night?

The Maiden Flowers & the Monk (went plunk!)

色/名をめで折れるばかりぞ 女郎花 われ落ちにきと人にかたるな　遍昭
iro/na o mede oreru bakari zo ominaeshi ware ochi ni ki to hito ni kataru na henjô 9c
color celebrating break only+exclam. maidenflower I fell-for came/happened people-to tell-not

*I only plucked you
to keep your lovely bloom,
oh, maiden flower,*

*Don't you go telling the world
how I fell from my high horse!*

*Your charming name!
I could not help but make you
my maiden flower –*

*So please tell not a soul,
It was beyond my power!*

This is one of the most famous *waka* not among the *100 Poet 1 Poem* selection. Indeed, it is more famous than most of them. According to a preface, the monk, later arch-bishop, Henjô (816-890), spotted the flowers while on horseback and reaching down to pluck some, fell (a loose saddle?) and, right then, as he lay there (*fushinagara*), composed the poem. The contradiction between his request and what he *did* — namely, *tell* the whole world by broadcasting his poem — is deliciously mad. Can we help wondering if it is allegorical? The 905 *Kokinshû* version starts with "name" (*na ni medete* 名にめでて) rather than "color," as in the *Henjôshû* (遍昭集) version I first used. Rodd and Henkenius' translation – "*I plucked you only / because your name entranced me / oh maiden flower / please do not tell all the world / that I have broken my vows.*" is perfect meaning-wise, and lacks only the poetry. The *Kokinshû* has dozens of maiden flower *waka*, most silly enough to be mad. Some are in the Autumn book and others in miscellaneous. Here is one of the former, immediately after that of Henjô's. It is by Furu no Imamichi.

おみなへしうしと見つつぞゆきすぐるをとこ山にしたてりと思へば　ふるのいまみち
ominaeshi ushi to mitsutsu zo yukisuguru otoko-yama ni shi tateri to omoeba kks #227
m-fls depressing-as seeing-while+exclam. pass man-mountain-at+emph standing re.think-if

On seeing maiden flowers on Mt. Otoko on my way to Nara to visit Archbishop Henjô

*Thinking, oh my
what a depressing sight!
I passed right by*

*All those Maiden Flowers
standing on Man Mountain.*

Chasing syllables as intently as I do rhyme, Rodd and Henkenius, give this poem, one of a number designated as *haikai* in the *Kokinshû*, a Victorian bustle: "*I passed by the sweet / maiden flowers   wretchedly / I but looked at them / thinking that they grow in gay / array on slopes of Mount Man.*" Women were not supposed to be up such mountains, home to esoteric Buddhist sects. Almost nine-hundred years later, *senryû* would worry about the asses of boys, or even men, who ventured to visit such a mountain (see my senryu book). Be that as it may, the Kokinshû maiden-flower *waka* go on and on. One poet worries about his group's good name if they camp-out in a field with the flowers (kks#229); another claims it odd to meet them but once a year, in the Fall, though they are not growing by the Milky Way – ludicrous, as the Stars met but one night a year while the flowers bloom for much of the fall (kks#231). The *haikai* poems include bolder attitudes yet. Archbishop Henjô – talk about Erasmus Darwin and his *Loves of Plants* – describes them standing out there in the field voluptuous and flirtatious (*namameki*) charmers, clamoring (*kashigamashi*) for his attention (kks#1016), Anonymous questions whether *anyone* can look upon them without plucking them (kks#1017) and this, my favorite, also Anonymous, plays on that:

花と見て 折らむとすれば おみなへし うたた あるさまの 名にこそ有りけれ
hana to mite oran to sureba ominaeshi utata aru sama no na ni koso arikere kks #1019
blossom/beauty-as seeing break-would-do-if/when maiden-flower forbiding style name+emph. have

Lovely blossoms
i could not help reaching out
to pluck one

Only to recall their name
& stop: Maiden Flowers!

My yellow beauty,
i almost plucked you, when –
a maiden flower!

Your name came to mind, just
in time to check my hand

What makes all of these doubly mad to me is that we are not talking about a voluptuous peony or magnolia, but a raw-boned, skinny weed – what Cranston calls a "yellow-flowering autumn grass" – nothing to get excited about. I wish I knew if Saigyô was part of the silliness or parodying it when he wrote: *That maiden flower w/ a stalk in the pond has the wet-sleeve look of one lost in longing* (をみなへし池のさ波に枝ひぢて物思ふ袖のぬるるがほなる 西行 *ominaeshi ike no sanami ni eda hijite mono omou sode no nururugao naru* 12c). This silliness first blossomed in the *Manyôshû*, where Yakamochi kids his old friend Ikenushi about being a lover-boy who dallied with the maiden flowers while supposedly checking the ripe rice (mys #3943), to which Ikenushi seems to reply that he maneuvered around them to get to the banquet (see Cranston #1174-5).

転ぶなら女郎花よりこの白妻　敬愚
korobu nara ominaeshi yori kono hakusai keigu
fall-if maiden-flower-more-than this bok-choy=white-wife

If you would fall,
a maiden flower's half the joy
of this bok-choy!

If you would fall,
maiden flowers can't compare
to this white rape!

In my poem diary, I generally replaced the character for greens 菜 with one for wife 妻, for the pronunciation was the same and if any vegetable is sexy it is the full-hipped, yet not cabbage-hard or round, *hakusai,* or bok-choy. The brainy daughter of the woman whose garden it was noticed the pun, and knowing I appreciated her (happily married) mother's curves, said *"yabai!"* I guess it *was*.

More Maiden Flowers & Prematurely Mad Poetry

白露を玉にぬくとや ささがにの 花にも葉にもいとをみなへし とものり 古今集
shiratsuyu o tama ni nuku to ya sasagani no hana ni mo ha ni mo ito o mina heshi ki no tomonori 905
white-dew+acc gem/soul-in pierces!/? spider's/s' blossom-to too leaf-to too thread/string+acc all warped

The Game is Flora's Name

..

Spiders, you left
no bloom or leaf unstrung
Plan you to make
Pearl necklaces of the dew
that each maiden has one?

The word for spider/s here, *sasagani*, literally "small-crab," but that is no matter, it is the standard poetic term – indeed, we have already seen it several times – and could be replaced with, say, "Arachne." The caption of the original, from the "Thing Name," *i.e.,* word-play chapter (10) of the *Kokinshû*, is "maiden flower (*ominaeshi*)," indicating that word is somewhere in the text. Otherwise, I would have made the "maiden" *Flora*.

Little spider, threading pearls of dew, have you made
A necklace for each maiden flower & her young blade?

Made in the changeling hours, strings of dew drops, spider pray,
would you pearl-loin the souls of every leaf and flower?

Even if you parse the first to gently split the *maiden* from the *flower*, the first of my minor readings fails to approach the mad brilliance of Ki no Tomonori's original where the name *ominaheshi* – in old spelling, today it is *ominaeshi* – is simply spelled out while, camouflaged as an accusative postposition *o* + noun *mina*, "all/every-one," + past-tense verb *heshi*, for *to warp* in the sense of creating the taut longitudinal lines across which something can be woven. The poem defies translation because it has two complex metaphors in addition to the wordplay. I sacrificed the weaving, or fabric idea – not easy, for my grandmother, following an Amerindian practice, just happened to do far more with the warp than most Usanian weavers do and wove in various objects including heads of wheat and rabbit fur, though no dew-drops that I know of – to keep the *tama o nuku,* or "piercing/passing-through/ stringing drops/gems/pearls," meaning the pearl or bead necklaces symbolizing the *love* (*heart-strings*) and *soul* of lovers in ancient times, for that already trite trope serves as a foil for what really is interesting: *the poet's wonder at the spider's or spiders' thoroughness* that has him playfully needling Arachne with a question. *Would you ply every single leaf and flower with pearl necklaces, or fabric woven with such splendor?* With part of the poem *past* (marvel at what has been seen) and part *future* (subjective/intent, at least), it would be hard to English with the brevity required even without the excessive metaphor and wordplay. You might note, I had to reverse the first and last part of the poem just to come up with the sorry stuff I probably should have erased, as I just *did* an equally bad attempt to re-create *what* another Maiden Flower Thing-name *waka* by the editor of the *Kokinshû*, Ki no Tsurayuki, coming only two poems later, did. Instead, I had to settle for content, alone:

おぐら山 みねたちならし なくしかの へにけむ秋を しる人ぞなき つらゆき
ogura yama mine tachinarashi naku shika no he ni ken aki o shiru hito zo naki kks 439
ogura mt. peak standing used-to=level calling deer's/s' passed+emph autumn+acc know person+emph not

Could he wear down　　　　　　　　　　　*Could they wear down*
Mt Ogura? Such pacing and　　　　　　　*Mt Ogura? Such pacing and*
bellowing above,　　　　　　　　　　　　　*bellowing above,*

Who knows how many falls　　　　　　　　*Who knows how many falls*
that buck has cried for love!　　　　　　　*those stags have cried for love!*

As the underlined syllabets show, the original is an anagram. Obviously, doing that in English with *maiden flower* would take twelve lines and *ominaeshi*, nine. Rather than do that, it would be easier to dump the maiden for a *rose*. I did so. But, fearing my ROSE, while easily as entertaining as most translations from Japanese, failed to rise to the level of numerous existent acronymic roses (any metaphysical or cavalier poet worth his salt did one), for once, I exercised good judgment. Here, I bet, with Rodd and Henkenius, that a homophonic pun on *narashi* (used to) as *leveling* deserves translation, but most Japanese annotators do not even recognize it. Unfortunately, the bold translators follow the annotator I have (Kyûsojin) in *not* explaining – not catching? – a *definitely* intended pun that allows us to understand *why* Ki no Tsurayuki squeezed this poem out of the maiden flower. It is found in the last ten syllabets: ~ *aki o shiru hito zo naki*, "there is no one who knows the *autumn/s* ~," which, from the sound of it, can *also* mean "there is no one who ever *wearies* of (them, the maiden flowers)!.." That is *it;* the *aki,* written 秋 (autumn), but suggestive of 飽き (losing interest in), is the homophone that counts. The rest of the poem, appropriate for featuring unrelenting male interest, though of a more animal sort, is but an elaborate pillow for that concluding pun to lie its light head on. To my mind, the combination of internal polysemy and allusive puns make this far crazier than your usual acronym play. I cannot wait to find Japanese scholars who agree with my – apparently not so apparent as it is to me – reading, for I feel this is as good a mad poem as any *kyôka* in the late-18c. Because of the tendency to belittle cleverness on the part of the literary critics of Japan, it seems to me that cleverness itself is often overlooked by the broader body of poem-tasters, perhaps for the kindest of reasons, as finding it would only make the poet look worse!

オマケ　拙句です　女郎花くねるが菊もよくくねる

＜蛇足 枝の長い野菊のそよぎ方の美しさは見物ですよ＞

Deer Who Write Sutra & Larvae Who Dance Them

峰に起き臥すだにも仏に成ることいと易し己が上毛を整へ筆に結ひ 一乗妙法書いたんなる功徳に
hô ni oki-fusu dani mo hotoke ni naru koto ito yasushi onoga uwage o soroe fude ni yui ichijômyôhô kaitan-naru kudoku ni
ridge/peak -on waking lying even buddha-into become thing extremely easy own hair/fur+acc
arranging brush-into binding ichijômyôhô(sutra)+acc wrote pious deed-from 梁塵秘抄

壱 乗 妙 法
EVEN A DEER

♪ *Lying in the hills, you can become a buddha still,*
Just bind your hair into a brush & write a sutra then & there ♪

If this poem which does not actually mention the deer but uses a verb associated with deer or boar seems longer in the original, it is because it *is*. Neither *kyôka* nor *waka* nor even *haikai* with the 17-14 reversed, Even A Deer – actually titled something closer to *Mahayana Magic* – is one of the somewhat longer, popular religious songs from the 11-12 century called *imayô*, or now-style 今様, found in the early-13c *Ryôjinhishô*. It is absurd enough to be a *near-kyôka*. A later *Rice Planting Book* 田植草紙 includes a song where hair is plucked from the belly of deer by people to make a brush so all could write sutras and be saved. Either it is a more sensible (?) version of the above, or both come from a common source.

あはれなり 筆になりても しかのけの りやうしのうへて つゐにはてぬる
aware nari fude ni narite mo shika no ke no ryôshi no ue de tsui ni hatenuru 新旧狂歌
pitiful is! brush-into became even deer's hair's/s' paper-upon finally end/s 俳諧聞書 TK

筆のふるくきれたるを見て

Death, too, is unfair.	*Alas, poor deer,*
You, deer, became a brush,	*for even your hair, living*
But, now your hair	*as a brush, I fear*
sheds on my paper – Again,	*Will pass away in a blink:*
prepare to meet thy maker!	*It sheds hair and loses ink.*

Mad poets could not ignore sutra-writing deer; but how to treat what was already mad? The deer dies *twice* and the paper is a type homophonous with *hunter*. A version by the 16c *kyôka* master Yûchôrô specifies that its *suffering* ceases not even after its hair becomes a brush (ふる筆といふ題にて 鹿の毛は筆になりても苦はやまず つゐにれうしのうへてはてけり 雄長老 新撰狂歌集 tk *shika no ke wa fude* . . .).

子子の念仏おどりや墓の水 一茶 文政四
bôfuri no nenbutsu-odori ya haka no mizu
(mosq.) larvae's prayers/sutra-dance!/?/: grave-water

子子も御経の拍子とりにけり 文化十二
bôfuri mo okyô no hyôshi torinikeri issa
(mosq.) larvae even polite+sutra's beat take+emph.

Bôfuri dancing	*even bôfuri*
sutras to save the dead?	*are dancing to the beat*
Water on a grave.	*of our sutra*

English lacks *a* word for mosquito larvae; hence, *bôfuri,* as is. But, why *Issa, here?* Because the *Ryôjinhishô* songs reminded me that he was often folksier in 17-syllabets than "folk-song" in more. One *imayo* has the wind, waves and birds all singing the song of Buddhist Law (極楽浄土のめでたさは. . .). A Buddhist take-off on the *Kokinshû* introduction or just sutra-dancing evangelical Buddhism? Still, that seems too tame to be mad. Issa, on the other hand, ... Here are more of old man Issa's *bôfuri ku* (下記の年順は、文政二、四、四、五年):

けふの日も棒ふり虫と暮にけり
kyô no hi mo bôfuri mushi to kurenikeri
today's day/sun too mosq.larvae-with nightfalls

today, too, ends
fiddled away by me
and the bôfuri

the night falls
on another day, just
me & the bôfuri

Bôfuri (larvae), written 子子 in other *ku,* is written oddly to show the homophonic pun by putting the *stick=bô* character 棒 before the *waving=furi* to yield the idiom *fiddling around* or *fritting away* or *wasting time.* Issa adds the "*mushi*=bug" because such redundancy helps bring out the otherwise hard to catch pun.

子子の一人遊びやぬり盥
bôfuri no hitori asobi ya nuridarai
mos.larvae' alone-play! glazed/colored pot

子子もふれ御祭ぞやれこらさ
bôfuri mo fure omatsuri zo yare kora sa
m.larvae too shake! hon.+festival! exclams.

in a china pot,
all the bôfuri playing
by themselves

The party's on!
Bôfuri, too, pick it up!
yare! kora sa!

Wow, old Issa says to himself, *they even dance without accompaniment!* When you think about it, we have no word for *dancing sans music* as we do for singing unaccompanied. A china pot means a pattern, mostly blue on white. The first *ku* seems more haiku than *kyôku*; the second concerns a festival, where thunderous drums and shrill flutes echo through town. Another first line: *There's a matsuri!* Then, we'd have Japanese in every line! *Yare, kora, sa* is an *ándale!* (sp) type call of encouragement. *"Go! Go! Go!"* does not do it. The penultimate *ku* below refers to *Bon-odori,* the All-souls Day dance, usually a fall phenomenon, while larvae are summer; the last is a cross between his older *ku* demanding a captain spare the floating moon and the famous fly rubbing=praying w/ its arms and legs not to be swatted. In any case, the anthropomorphism is pleasantly mad. *Issa'ssa!*

子子よせい出してふれ翌は盆
bôfuri yo sei dashite fure asu wa bon
m.l., vigor put-out! move! tmw's bon

子子や小便無用／＼とて
bôfuri ya shôben muyô muyô tote
ms.lrvae!/: urination forbddn as-if

Hey, you larvae!
Better getta move on!
Tomorrow's Bon!

Bôfuri wriggling
as if to say this:
"Don't piss!"

Hairy Monster Cricket Legs & a New Old Chestnut

化けものゝすむ野の薄穂に出て 一朝 ・ 毛のはへた手のきり／＼す鳴 松意 shôi 17c
bakemono no sumu no no susuki ho ni idete icchô – ke no haeta te no kirigirisu naku shôi 17c
changelings-live-moor's susuki plume-as out-coming – hair-sprouted hands' cricket/s cry

Near the dark river
where the monsters appear
in saw-grass plume,

Crickets bare their hairy arms
and legs, crying to the moon.

狂 歌 不 飛, 談 林 十 百 韻

A tall grass called *susuki* lives in the low lands, especially the greater part of the river bed only covered with water when it floods. Moved by wind, its plumes are seen as beckoning rather than waving, as Japanese call people by motioning *downward* with arm and hand. More melancholy than the bloom of what we call *pampas*, these *miscanthus* do indeed seem spooky, especially at night, though it is hard to tell if that is intrinsic or the result of the way such landscapes are used in Japanese movies. Kurosawa *et al* did not, however, invent that image. Artists and writers did that. Monsters alone would not make this *haikai* sequence a candidate for honorary madness, neither does the leap from phantoms produced by the plumes and their moon-cast shadows to the micro level of the crickets (♪ *kirigirisu* is katydid today, but was what is now *kôrogi,* cricket). That is accomplished by those hairy legs (*hands* in the original). Suddenly, insects whose plaintive call made them beloved of classic poets and all sensitive people, are turned into monsters. Tropic parody. Haikai that I would not call *kyôka* concentrate on their more obvious feelers, which earned them the *haikai* sobriquet *hige-dono,* Sir Whiskers. Besides adding an old saw, the moon (and a river) to set the proper mood, I added a new one, a real *saw*. It took a while for the high-art poets to find that one, as they tended to ride with covered legs. Issa, who did his own walking and lived on what in 20c Usania would be called the wrong side of the tracks in the water-city of Edo, left some fine *kyôku*:

我庵の太刀より切る芒かな 一茶 文化十
waga io no tachi yori kiruru susuki kana issa
my hut's great-sword more-than cuts susuki is/!/?

向ふずねざぶと切たる芒かな 一茶 政三
mukôzune zabu to kittaru susuki kana issa
shin/s *zabu*(mimesis)-with cutting susuki is/!/?

They do cut,
better than my old sword,
those susuki!

And they slice
deep into your shins those
bloody susuki!

The teeth are not so obvious as that on Florida saw-grass, but that is not to belittle them. I can attest to the sharpness of their blades, as I only discovered my lacerations when I waded into a brackish river and felt the stings.

手にとれは人をさすてふいかくりのえみの内なる刀おそろし公朝 後撰夷曲集
te ni toreba hito o sasu to iu igakuri no emi no uchinaru katana osoroshi kôchô pre-1672
hand-in take-if person+acc stab said spike-chestnut's smile-within sword/s scary #483

See Medusa, turn to stone, but chestnuts are best left alone,
For when one cracks a smile, it can pierce you to the bone!

~~~~~~

'He'll be stabbed
who picks up a chestnut
from the ground;

Most dreadful of daggers
within a smile are found!

~~~~~~

The Chestnut has a pleasant smile but beware its tricks,
When you reach for its nuts, you find a beard of pricks!

This *kyôka* was originally from priest Kôchô's fifty *kyôka* anthology (権僧正公朝家集五十首). I hope to read it some day, for this illustration of an aphorism with a natural observation – when chestnuts grow ripe they crack a smile, but when you try to pinch the nuts you still get poked – suggests more goodies within. A line from the 14c *Taihei-ki,* popular tales of the Warring Era is alluded to: *"In those times, it was typical for men to hone one's sword while one laughed/smiled"* (笑いの内に刀を研ぐは此頃の人の心也　太平記16). In Japanese, the honing is within the friendly mannerism, temporarily speaking, *and* tooth=blade (*ha*). Pardon paraverses fore and aft of the proper translation. When I like something, I like to dress it up. Today, I had the house to myself – my sister, the owner, is away for chemo – so rather than crossing the tracks for the paper I don't read at the crack of dawn or weeding 'round *her* chestnut trees, I could ease myself out of my dreams with Medusa and that beard intact. *If I had a place of my own, this book would have many more such mad translations, as my shriveled brain needs time and space to do whatever it can only do when half-awake to work its wonders.*

里の子に追ひかけられて毬栗の地に逃げまはるかせの激しさ 朱楽かん江
sato no ko ni oikakerarete igakuri no chi o nigemawaru kaze no hageshisa akera kankô d.1800
country-kid/s-by-chased-spiked/burred-chestnut's-earth+acc-flee-circling-wind's strength
..

The strength of the wind where prickly chestnuts fly on the ground
Beyond the reach of the village urchins chasing them around.

The above chestnut is the new one and this later Tenmei era *kyôka* the old one, *in English*. Steven D. Carter's is superb: *So strong it can help / a fallen chestnut get away / from a village urchin / running along in pursuit – / that's how strong the wind is!* The gloss tells you how much work he put into it. But note also 1) it examples Japanese-style content: a poem nothing but a chain of modification (of the wind's *strength*); 2) the hyperbole is typical *haikai*; 3) It is barely a *kyôka*. Unless. *Unless* prefaced so the *kaze* 風= wind became a *kaze* = 風邪 (I have) a cold.

Bug-song, Morning Glory, Mum-wine & Star-babies

夜鳴くは珍しからず昼の野へ虫のねごとをきゝにこそゆけ　白鯉館卯雲 徳和
yoru naku wa mezurashikarazu hiru no no e mushi no negoto o kiki ni koso yuke bôun 1785
night cry as-for rare/attractive-is-not day's field/s-to bugs' sound-each hear-to espec. go!

Crying at night is hardly rare enough to make one weep;
Go out and catch those bugs by day, talking in their sleep.

~~~~~~~~~~~~~~~~~~~~~~~

Crying at night is what they do, too boring, I say, to listen to:
But daylight fields when bugs talk in their sleep – that's new!

~~~~~~~~~~~~~~~~~~~~~~~

Crying at night is old hat. – Get thee out to the fields by day;
There the bugs talk in their sleep; go catch them if you may!

Negoto, "sleep-talk" puns as *root-by-root*, that is each bug's dwelling. Even losing that, Hakurikan Bôun's classic Tenmei *kyôka* scans. Most bug *kyôka*, dependent on bug names, do not work in English. Eg. 星合の過に(sic?)し夜半も牛をひく草に来て鳴機をりむし　無染　一万 (*hoshiai no sugishi yahan mo ushi o hiku kusa ni kite naku hataorimushi* musen), where *bugs that pull oxen, i.e.,* the *kutsuwamushi,* or "bit" bugs, visit weaver-bugs (a sort of grasshopper) even after the night of Star love. Eg. 土手馬の昔覚へて虫売りが鈴にくつわを添ふる　吉原浅草庵　一万(*doteuma no mukashi . . .asakusa-an*) where memories of operating a taxi-horse to Yoshiwara result in a bug-seller's pairing a bell and a bit (both abbrev. bug names; the horses had bells to warn people out of the way) when selling them there. Eg. 大原や虫も雑魚寝の歌枕馬追もありはた織もあり　京博　一万 (*ôhara ya mushi mo zakkone no utamakura . . kyôhaku*) where the herder becomes a horse-chaser (long-horned grasshopper), the weaver again appears and the promiscuous sleep of various bugs is called *mixed-fish-sleep* a term usually reserved for human (crudely put) free-sex festivals and tied into an epithet or "pillow" of the toponym Ôhara, itself punning as *broad belly* . . . None of these 18-19c *kyôka* are masterpieces – well, maybe the last – but unless you feel that only the loves of humans are real poetry, all are, in the original, not without a certain charm and certainly better than run-of-the-mill *waka*.

ひと夜をば百夜と契る織姫になぜお子たちが出来はなされぬ　楚泉 1785
hitoyo o ba momoyo to chigiru orihime ni naze okotachi ga deki wa nasarenu sosen
1-nght+emph 100/many nght as vow/tryst weavng-princss-to y childrn have-as4 do-not?
..

With one fall night worth a hundred, I just do not get why
the Weaver's little children do not completely fill the sky!

The fall night idea may be from ancient China, but most Japanese know it from #22 of *The Tales of Ise*. One lover says, *One night in fall may be a thousand of the other kind / but our love would not jade though we met eight-thousand times!* 秋の夜の千夜を一夜になぞらへて　八千夜し寝ばやあく時のあらむ *aki no yo no chiyo o* . . . and the other responds *Though one night in fall may be a thousand, after all, / we still have more to say when rooster crows the breaking day.* The hyperbole covered both quantity (nights rapidly growing longer), and quality (low-humidity + big moon). Many *Tale of Ise* poems, like these, are themselves near-*kyôka*; Sôsen's poem equating said 1000x night with opportunity for becoming impregnated demonstrates the extra step taken by Tenmei *kyôka*. It also beats old *waka* wondering why there are no offspring unless it is Star-dust. ♪

早起のたねともなれば朝顔の花みるばかりめでたきはなし　蜀山家集
hayaoki no tane to mo nareba asagao no hana miru bakari medetaki wa nashi shokusanjin
early-rising-seeds as even be-if, morning-glory's bloom/s see extent happy-as-for not

..

"Seeds to make us early risers"? Who needs Morning Glory?
Flowers good for sleeping in – that might be another story!
~~~~~~
"Buy these seeds to help you rise early!" An Asagao beauty:
What's so great about bloom for the eyes, but not for duty?
~~~~~~
Morning glories! The very sight of flowers said to wake us
bright and early – What a fright if they should make us!
~~~~~~
To plant the seeds of early rising? Not in me! A happy
camper I shall be, the less I see of Morning Glory?
~~~~~~
Eye-candy to help us rise in the morning? Glory be!
I'd rather a pretty thing to hold than these we see!
~~~~~~
A flower said to befriend early risers is not for me:
Happy I am the less I must see of Morning Glory!
~~~~~~
A flower good for getting up at an ungodly hour?
Unhappy me, the more I see of Morning Glory!
~~~~~~
Let others win morning glory, I'd rather stay in bed
As for that water bucket, fuck it: I drink wine instead!
~~~~~~

今日酒に菊もひたさぬ不性もの中ゝ命なかく有へき　辰巳
kyô sake ni kiku mo hitasanu fujômono nakanaka inochi nagaku arubeki tatsunomi
today sake/wine-to chrysanthemum steep no-energy-person very life long has-ought

He who today lacks even the drive to steep 'mums in wine
Will probably be the one to keep alive a long, long time!

Pardon my mad translation spree with Shokusanjin's morning glory! I used up space better spent introducing said blossom and early wakers (early-bird Bashô and late-sleeper Kikaku exchanged words on it). The sex is all mine. The original is the *kyôka* of an unrepentant night-owl, period. The second *kyôka,* by Tatsunomi, milks truth from irony. Taoism has long taught that doing nothing is the way to live long; but it *also* has an alchemic side, albeit more interested in elixirs of youth than gold. The contradiction in the two endeavors, or rather the *do-nothing* and *do-something* approaches, is beautifully brought out in the *kyôka,* which, I feel, guesses right re. the man too inert to engage in a ritual for longevity.

Maple Leaf Macaque & Homowisteria Rumps

おく山の 紅葉と見てや 猿まろが尻をも鹿の ふみわけてゆく 蜀山先生
okuyama no momiji to mite ya sarumaro ga shiri o mo shika no fumiwakete-yuku shokusanjin
inner mountains' colored-leaves-as seeing!/: sarumaro's ass+acc also deer tread-split-goes ↓

Deep in the Hills

'Tis when I hear	*Thinking what*
the mating deer bleating	*he sees is fall foliage*
softly as they go	*The buck stops*
Parting the crimson leaves	*not here but, treading, parts*
that autumn does feel sad.	*Monkeyman's red buttocks.*

↑ inner mountain-in red-leaves tread-parting cry/call deers' voice hear time+emph. fall-as-for sad
okuyama ni momiji fumiwake naku shika no koe kiku toki zo aki wa kanashiki sarumaru 9c
奥山に紅葉ふみわけ鳴く鹿の声きくときぞ 秋はかなしき 猿丸大夫

This take on a Hundred Poets' poem attributed to 9c Sarumaru plays on his name, *Monkey-guy*. Japanese 'monkeys' are really *macaque*, bright red of face and rump. The mountains in the old capital (Kyôto and Nara) area are largely maple, like New England, fiery in the fall. Both poems began with my title, *okuyama*, mountains deep in the interior, embodying a concept of central rather than the peripheral remoteness. While purely perverted in translation, parting the foliage to progress is so common an expression in Japanese literature that, buttocks aside, the original feels almost *natural*. Still, the less outlandish parody in Shokusanjin's *Mad Hundred Poets One Poem* 狂歌百人一首 is, I think, better:

なく鹿の声聞くたびに涙ぐみさる丸太夫いかい愁たん 蜀山 狂歌百人一首
naku shika no koe kiku tabi ni namida-gumi sarumaru-tayû ikai shûtan shokusanjin
cry/calling deers' voice's hear time-each tear-bleary monkeyman mighty maudlin c.1800

Each time a deer bleat
strikes his ear, I fear his eyes,
poor Monkey Man!
How they overflow with tears
now the maudlin Fall is here!

At first, I thought our mad poet from a macho era of peace pokes fun at men from a more heroic time who did not mind crying; but the *waka* dates not to the heroic but the Heian era, a peaceful and precious time, and Shokusanjin includes Sarumaru/o's bureaucratic rank, Tayû (lit. "bold husband") for it had become the title for a top-ranking courtesan and they could be, to use a Usanian vulgarity, *drama queens*. At last minute, I found yet another parody which strikes me as true and every bit as sincere as the original *waka*: "To hear the voices of crimson leaf-viewing drunks, deep in the hills, even the autumn can be quite funny."(奥山に紅葉見の客生酔の声聞く時ぞ秋もおかしき *okuyama ni momijimi no kyaku namayoi no koe kiku toki zo aki mo okashiki*.). If I but knew who wrote it!

女郎花なまめきたてる前よりも　うしろめたしやふじばかま腰　蜀山人
ominaeshi namameki tateru mae yorimo ushirometashi ya fuji-bakama-koshi shokusanjin
mdn-flwr charmingly stand-front morethan backsad/shameful, wisteria trouser-hip/rear

男色の心をよみ侍る
On the Homo-erotic

*Comparison is
odorous, but if maiden
flowers forward be,*

*A darkness lurks behind
the purple mum wisteria!*

*Maiden flowers
put on such a charming face,
while wisteria*

*Hakama of jutting butt
tell a sad, disgraceful tale*

*Darker in mood
than maiden flower coquets
of flashing front,*

*The droopsy bloom & bouquet
of the aster wisteria*

1) "Front" refers to its rhyme-sake. 2) *"Ushiro*=rear," locus of male love, fits into "*ushirometasa*=lingering guilt." 3) The *fuji*=wisteria=*bakama* pantaloons puff out creating big buttocks (a mark of disgusting "animal maids" but thought sexy on a youth, and compared to a brilliant mound of gleaming white salt!) or bent-over form. 4) *Fujibakama* is *also* a light purple aster (chrysanthemum), hence identified with the ass, also called *Mum Gate* (*kiku no mon*), and the Way of the Gay. Finally, 5) the wisteria immediately follows the maiden flower in *Manyôshû* song #1538. I introduce what is a lost case, for so sad a portrayal of male color is rare. It follows a crackdown by the government on what had been gay, in both meanings of the word, for centuries if not a millennium. For a glimpse back to when *male color* was haute culture, read Sôchô and friends' *Haikai at Year's End at Takigi*, in 1523, in Mack Horton's fine *Journal of Sôchô* translation. The flow of association is also so fine I hate to pick anything out, but after *"Nothing but asters where the temple boys are. / The autumn wind / wafts a fragrance / from the doorway,"* (yes, the asters got their asterisk in the rear of the book) we have, a rare, inadvertently mad translation: *"The young temple boy with / the tight ass passed wind. // And for an extra treat / you could also hear / his belly rumble!"* In Japanese, *tight-ass* does not have the metaphorical meaning that would double with a bribe to get more. Then, later in this sequence, right after the often cited stanza *"The boy I propositioned / was so terribly unkind! // Would we could grapple, with me stabbing into him, then / dying from the thrust"* (Such mutuality was rare, and not all translators have caught what is happening. Horton notes that t/his was "after Keene."), we are treated to what I would call a *kyôka:*

*He waits & waits for the lad Seitaka, taller than himself.
Does even Fudô, that unmoving god, burn for his love?*

My translation of *ware yori mo seitaka wakashu machiwabite / fudô mo koi ni kogara-kasu mi ka* partly follows Horton, who, 195 pgs later, explains that Seitaka (Cetaka), a name punning on tall-stature, was an attendant of Fudô, (Acala, God of mountains, fire & smithies) with a childish mien, and the verb for burning puns on the name of another attendant Kinkara (Kongara). The God's "nimbus of flame," solved!

The Leaves of Fall, Blushing, Dyed or Just Drunk?

おはしたの 龍田がしりを もみぢばの うすくこく屁に さらす赤はぢ 蜀山人
ohashita no tatsuda ga shiri o momijiba no usuku koku he ni sarasu aka haji shokusan
menial tatsuda's ass+acc kneading:maplecolorleaves' light/dark:cut fart-by expose red-shame

A Mountain of Shame

Kneading her nates
The pot wench Tatsuda,
Her maple yeast

Swelling cuts a crusty fart
Worthy of a scarlet mark!

Tatsuda is the name of a mountain near Kyôto famous for fall foliage (Japan is as red as the reddest part of New England). It is also the name for the Goddess of Autumn and *haikai* liked to spin just-so stories about how she dyed the mountain.

竜田姫たやをやこぼす下紅葉 犬子集
tatsudabime taya o ya kobosu shita-momiji enokoshû
tatsuda princess menses+acc+emph. spill under-redleaves

Princess Tatsuda
spills her menses & voila
fresh red leaves

This *Enokoshû ku* is definitely what I would call a *kyôku*. The later *Konzanshû* (1651), with a different word for the menses, attributes it to Teitoku. It is not as good as a couple more that *are* attributed to Teitoku in the *Enokoshû*.

酒や時雨のめば紅葉ぬ人もなし 貞徳
sake ya shigure nomeba momojinu hito mo nashi teitoku
sake+emph/conjunct rain drink-if/when crimson-leafing-not person+emph not

Sake's a shigure   *A shower of wine*
No man drinks it but turns   *No soul can so imbibe and*
maple leaf red   *not turn crimson*

While the *shigure*, usually written "time-rain," is only a metaphor, the *ku* retains a proper seasonal element, for *momiji*, colored leaves, especially the maple, also meant *venison* and alluded to the Japanese barbeque, a rare occasion when meat from four-legged creatures was deemed proper, and a good excuse for men to go drinking though that might seem to contradict the purpose implicit in the name of these late fall or early winter parties, "medicine-eating" (*kusuri-gui*)! This is why Princess Tatsuda's metamorphosis into a menial associated with disgusting work (anything meat-related) in Shokusanjin's later *kyôka* is a natural. That much can be *explained*, but Shokusanjin's use of the colored leaves as a verb for *kneading* and punning on *koku*, a modifier meaning *deep* (esp. used for hues), as *cutting* a fart, was unEnglishable. Only a scatological wordsmith such as Jonathon Swift could possible resurrect it. Shokusanjin prefaced it with the (fictional?) claim it was in a collection of 100 fart poems 放屁百首歌の中に, but who knows . . .

火と見ゆる紅葉の雨は油かな 貞徳
hi to miyuru momiji no ame wa abura kana
fire-as appear crimson-leaves' rain-as-for oil! teitoku

That cold rain *on crimson autumn foliage?* *I'd call it oil!*	*The rain falling* *on the flaming red leaves?* *Pure rock oil*

立田姫尿かけたまふ紅葉哉　一茶
tatsuda-hime shito kake-tamau momiji kana
tatsuda princess piss sprinkle/s red-leaves!/?

Princess Tatsuda *Is your piss what dyes this?* *red fall foliage*	*Princess Tatsuda* *your leaves are aflame, for this* *you'd better piss!*

Teitoku's masterpiss (I plagiarize Hogarth's *Frontispiss,* where a witch is depicted urinating from her lunar seat down upon Newton's *Treatise on Gravity*) encouraged my bogus second reading of Issa's *ku*, written about the same time as Shokusan's *kyôka*. Shokusanjin had his head full trying to come up with something crazier than had already been done by Sôkan, Teitoku et al in linkverse *haikai*. Hence his outrageous blushing farter.

やよ時雨もの思ふ袖のなかりせば 木の葉の後に何を染めまし 前大僧正慈圓
ya yo shigure mono omou sode no nakariseba konoha no ato ni nani o somemashi jien
hey, shigure! thing-thinking sleeves' not-if/when leaves' after what dye-would? skks 1005

Tell me, Shigure
without the sleeves of lovers,
What would you dye

after the colorful leaves
of Fall abandon ye sky?

Farmers see rain in terms of their crops, so the idea of rain dyeing flowers or fall foliage was probably a noble rather than folk invention. Be that as it may, the logic of this 13c? *waka* seems too simple for a mad poem, but, with that charming *"ya yo,"* a familiar way for a prelate to address the rain, it comes close.

♪ One note here. *Shigure* the time-rain or chilly shower is said to dye leaves in the fall, yet to come at the start of winter. It would seem the fall *shigure* is short for *mura-shigure*, quickly moving showers, and the winter one, the real *shigure* is intermittent cold drizzle.

The Honest Rain That Came In With the Cold

神〴〵の留守をあづかる月なれば 馬鹿正直に時雨ふるなり 蜀山人百首
kamigami no rusu o azukaru tsuki nareba baka-shôjiki ni shigure furu nari   shokusanjin d.1823
gods' absence+acc keeping month is/become-when fool-honestly/honest-fool-on time-rain falls is

> *When that month*
> *comes and our gods leave,*
> *the time-rain falls;*
>
> *Right on schedule, even*
> *nature honest to a fault!*

> *This is the month*
> *our kami stay away but still*
> *a cold rain falls*
>
> *Upon the godless heads*
> *of all men honest to a fault*

There is an old saying: "god resides in the honest head," (正直の頭に神宿る). *Baka shôjiki* is "foolishly-honest" *or* a person who is. The first reading addresses the character of the *shigure*, literally "time-rain," the cold showers said to start with Month-Ten, the first of the winter, also called Gods-gone-month. The second reading, which takes *baka-shôjiki* as a noun, is absurd. I could no more create a unified translation of this poem than theoretical physicists have . . . .

> *Gods gone, a cold rain falls on all honest crowns –*
> *Emptied of the gods, how loudly each drop sounds!*

That is a paraverse, how *I* might have written the poem. But where did the idea lying between the lines that I brought out in my first reading come from?

偽りのなき世なりけり神無月 たが誠より しぐれそめけん 続後拾遺：定家
itsuwari no naki yo narikeri kaminazuki taga makoto yori shigure someken   teika d.1241
falsehood's not world become-has! gods-not-month whose sincerity-from *shigure* started?

> *Today, for once,*
> *this world is not false.*
> *As the gods leave,*
>
> *Whose faith brings us*
> *the cold rain right on time?*

> *Gods-gone month.*
> *And, what, has falsehood*
> *fled the earth?*
>
> *Who is so true that cold*
> *time-rain should start on cue?*

This 13c *waka* by Fujiwara Teika (the only reference for Shokusanjin's *kyôka* noted by Iwanami) Englishes poorly, for we do not rhetorically contrast the names or reputed properties of things with their reality. The *makoto*, or *sincerity/truth/faith* – opposite of falseness – is what becomes *baka-shôjiki* or *foolish-honesty* in Shokusanjin's *kyôka*. The "who" in Teika's *waka*, unlike the grammar-born "it" in Watt's "What is this *it* that rains?" has significance; but *what*? In the *Tales of Genji, shigure* is dead Aoi's soul. More commonly it was a projection of a live woman wishing the rain to stay a lover. There may be some romantic allusion here, picking up on kks#146, to imply *"who in these times where so many are false?"* And, since Teika composed the song at his home named *Time-rain Arbor* (Shigure Tei 時雨亭), the *who/se* may be Teika himself, and his concern solely for the reputation of the *shigure*, though, not knowing Teika better, I dare not guess whether that affection is aesthetic or ascetic, i.e. for rain that dyes leaves and hearts, or rain that, being cold, provides trial/succor. If the latter element is paramount, the "who/se" might be the Law/Buddha, in which case, the Gods-gone Month comes to mean more. Not that any of this solves the parody. Shokusanjin's poem *may* suggest that when the gods of Japan caucus in Izumo, even the figurative one, the godliness found in an honest person's head takes off, leaving him at the mercy of the elements no longer divinely controlled.

正直の頭もいたし神無月 あまり時雨の誠すきるで 栗柯亭木端 1735
shôjiki no atama mo itashi kaminazuki amari shigure no makoto sugiru de bokutan
honest head even hurts gods-out-month too-much shigure's sincere-excess-from TK 狂歌ますかがみ

Our most honest heads are hurting this gods-gone month,
With the time-rains too earnestly living up to their name!

A preface notes days of solid drizzle 神無月霖雨ふり続きければ. Ritsukatei Bokutan, who followed Teiryû as the leading *kyôka* master of the mid-18c, wrote this in his early twenties and presented it to his master, who responded,

神無月 あまり時雨は誠すきた ちと偽りて日和なれかし 由縁斎=貞柳
kaminazuki amari shigure wa makoto sugita chito itsuwarite hiyori naregashi teiryû
gods-not-month too-much time-rain-as-4 sincere-overly, slightly deceiving clear-day flow-want

Gods-gone month, I'd say these time-rains were too damn earnest.
Would they might prove just a little bit more false!

Bokutan's "honest heads" alludes to the same idiom Shokusanjin's later poem does; *itashi* or "hurt/ache" may double for "were god/s" in said head. Over time, we go from *sincere→ too sincere/honest→ foolishly honest*. A different mad take:

鬼ならぬ神の御留守は時雨して洗濯すべき日和だになし 業枝 一万週
oni naranu kami no on rusu wa shigure shite sentaku subeki hiyori dani nashi gyôshi?
demon/s is/are-not gods' hon.+absence-as-4 time-rain doing, laundry do-ought clearday +emph. not!

When the devil's out – but today,   The gods and not the demons
   it is the gods who are away;   are out to play, but dirty laundry
And, damn, if the time-rain leaves   needs at least one sunny day
   one clear day for us to play!   – all we get is shi-gu-re!

Proverbs like *waka* are fair game for *kyôka*. One is: "(life's) Laundry is washed when the demon/devil (boss? spouse?) is out." We may have a poet who really would do his or her laundry but for the damn rain. For more contrast yet, here is a graceful celebratory *kyôka* by Teiryû: *Among men there are no demons at all, in God-gone month, / Coins fly by crocodile jaws faster than the time-rain falls!"* (人におにはなき世なりけり神無月 時雨より猶ふるは散銭 狂歌ますかがみ *hito no oni wa naki yo narikeri kaminazuki shigure yori nao furu wa chirizeni*). I *added* a *crocodile mouth*, the gong struck close to the offertory at a Buddhist temple, for the drama.

Three Takes on Snow: Dick, Swellfish & Fools!

Lost to this world,
I feel my own body
is no longer me

But on days when it snows
I find I still get cold!

        saigyô (1110-90)

Lost to this world,
I feel my own body
is no longer me

But on days my dick rises
I find I still wanna do it!

        gennai (1728-80)

⇐ 捨果て身はなき物とおもへとも　雪のふる日はさむくこそあれ　西行
sutehatete mi wa naki mono to omoedomo yuki no furu hi wa samuku koso are
捨果て身はなき物とおもへとも 魔羅の怒日はしたくこそあれ　源内 ⇒
sutehatete mi wa naki mono to omoedomo mara no tatsu hi wa shitaku koso are

I like to think
the world & I no longer
hang together

But when it snows, I feel
ev'ry bit as cold as ever!

I like to think
the world & I no longer
hang together

But when my dick rises
to the occasion, so would I!

The *waka* by Saigyô is included in some *kyôka* anthologies and played with by the encyclopedist Hiraga Gennai (1728-1779) in his *Biographies of Limp Dicks in Seclusion* (痿陰隠逸傳 *Naemara in'itsu den* 1768). The above is followed by a warning to always 'shoot your wad' lest you get gonorrhea and *really* come to hate the world. Gennai was nothing if not *au courant*. Such clap-catching scenarios were common to *senryû* of the time (see the *Menses* chapter of my *Octopussy*). The way the well-known *waka* is minimally altered – compare and you will see he does much better than me – reminds us of the most translated poet in this book, the mad poem master Ôta Nanpo (Yomo no Akara, Shoku-sanjin 1749-1823), who, as it turns out, some credit Gennai with discovering! The *Biographies*, which starts with a children's ditty 童一謠曰 advising us,

> *If you're really gonna do it,*
>   *Then big is how you oughta;*
> *Stick it up the buttocks*
>   *Of the Great Buddha at Nara!*

如做出事來　做得大則個、穿寧樂盧舍 那佛屁眼則個
suru nara ôki na koto shiyare, nara no daibutsu no ketsu shiyare - trans. Marceau

– may be found, in lively translation by Lawrence E. Marceau, in an episodic festschrift for Howard Hibbett published by John Solt's Highmoonoon Press (2001). Maybe we oughta call the above a *mad ditty,* 狂謠 kyôyô! (又 狂訓歌？)

（雪の日，友人のもとよりふくと汁たべにこよ，とありければ）一萬集
命こそ 鵞毛に似たれ なんのその いざ鰒食ひに ゆきの振舞 唐衣橘洲
inochi koso umo ni nitare nan no sono iza fugu kui ni yuki no furumai karagoromo kisshû
life espec. down/feather-to resemble, what's that!/? pushcomestoshove swellfish eating go=snow's behavior

◆ on being invited by a friend to eat swellfish on a snowy day ◆

"Life's as light as goose-down"? My ass! But, is this fake?
As we go out for swellfish, look what falls . . . snowflakes!
~~~~~~
"Life is as light as goose down"? – I doubt it; but, here goes!
We're off to eat your swellfish treat, aquiver like the falling snow.

There would be more poems by Kisshû in this book, but most, like this, have too subtle allusions and complex wordplay to fit into one translation. 1) Questioning the idea of *Life as light*, a warrior's credo (referring to one's *own* life, not that of others) popularized in minstrel tales such as *Heike Monogatari* is appropriate not only because of A) the risk associated with eating the fish with poisonous organs requiring a licensed chef, but because B), it was illegal for samurai to eat, as the authorities did not want their lives risked for pleasure, C) *down* is suggestive of snow D) and worn to keep warm, something swellfish (esp. soup) was said to do for the body. 2) *Yuki* ゆき is A) a homophone for *go* 行き and *snow* 雪 (another version actually has that character) and B) the latter is what thinly sliced swellfish was said to resemble and called. Finally, 3) *furumai* means A) *behavior/ mannerisms* 振る舞い, B) being *treated* 饗応 to something (here, the *snow* = slices of swellfish), and C), the first part "furu" links with the snow to mean *fall* 降る.

われがちに争ふてくふふぐと汁 もりかへのある命ならねど 山手白人
waregachi ni arasoute kuu fugutojiru morikae no aru inochi naranedo yamate no shirohito
me-win-as struggling eat swellfish-soup heaping-seconds is life is-not but 徳和 1785

Fighting others to get a second dish of swellfish soup
Not that we will ever get another serving of life . . .

All Japanese know the saying *"You are a fool if you eat swellfish and a fool if you do not."* Anyone would think the first line of this *kyôka* should also have become an aphorism but, as far as I know, Shirohito's great poem went nowhere!

雪見とはいつの世よりのたはけぞと謗るはいつのよの痴ぞや 馬屋まや輔
yukimi to wa itsu no yo yori no tawake zo to soshiru wa itsu no yo no tawake zo ya 徳和
snow-viewing-as-4 when-era-from's fool/ishness! revile-as-4 when-era-from's fool/ishness+!

So when in the world did a fool first revile it, wanting to know
Just when in the world a fool first snow-viewing happened to go?

Umaya no Mayasuke's original, which plays upon the Chinese conceit of a fool who fished with a willow limb/string, *en situ*, watched by yet a greater fool, is funny for there was quite a tradition of poking fun at aesthete snow-viewers.

Kicking the Year in its Miserable Rear

今さらに何かおしまん神武より 二千年来くれてゆくとし 蜀山百首
ima sara ni nani ga oshiman tenmu yori nisen nenrai kurete yuku toshi shokusanjin
now more-so what+emph. lament-would? shintake-from 2000 years setting-go years c.1800

♪ Auld Lang Syne is doing fine ♪

Why do I still waste my tears
On yet another passing Year!

Haven't thousands, all the same,
Left us since great Tenmu reigned?

If the New Year's was a time for foolish but, excepting mixed feelings about aging, always joyful poems as not to deform the still forming world, the end of the year was mourned and kicked around. The most common lament was for the demise of the year and its loss (where have all my years gone?) for the man. Shokusanjin plays with the former, as does Issa, who takes the welfare of the leaving year for granted while he gamely chuckles about his approaching end:

行くとしはどこで爺を置去に 一茶
yuku toshi wa doko de jiiji o okizari ni issa
going year-as-for where-at uncle+acc place-leave-as

the years go on   *the years drive on*
when will they drop   *just when will the geezer*
this old man off   *be left behind!*

In the post-classical world of Edo, such abstract seasonal concerns took second seat to money. Most *haikai* on the end of the year emphasize it being the busy and trying time for settling accounts. So, too, with *kyôka*. One of the best known is by Shokusanjin's friend, Akera Kankô (1740-1800) 和文は再現:

しゃく金も今は包むに包まれずやぶれかぶれのふんとしのくれ 朱楽かん江
shakkin mo ima wa tsutsumu ni tsutsumarezu yaburekabure no fundoshi no kure
balls/debts too now-as-for stuff-in stuff-cannot torn/desperate loin-cloth/[y]ears eve

The money I owe
I can no more hide than
the fam'ly jewels

Barely in my loincloth rent
as the old year's arrears.

As Shirane notes, this oft-Englished *kyôka* begins and ends with a pun. "Debts= *shakkin*" doubles as "balls" (*shaku*gan+*kin*tama). As the first character for *balls* is different than for *debts*, phonetic letters are used. The second half of "loincloth=fun*doshi*," doubling for the *year*, becomes *toshi*-no-kure, or Year's End.

> *The year's end:*
> *when Poverty overtakes*
> *our earnings*

行としやかせぐに追つく貧乏神
yuku toshi ya kasegu ni oitsuku binbôgami
leaving year!/: earn-by overtake poverty god

羽生へて銭がとぶ也としの暮 一茶
hane haete zeni ga tobunari toshinokure
wings growing change-the fly-does year-end

> *Money grows wings*
> *and as it flies off sings*
> *"Happy New Year!"*

Year-end haiku tend to be exciting, perhaps because the poets are sleep-deprived from running about settling accounts and attending Year Forget Parties. The above *ku* by old Issa are as mad in their own simple way as *kyôka* and tend to hit harder for coming from the heart. I confess to adding *"sings ~"* to the second *ku*.

歳暮 雪ふらず天気もよくて火事もなしひまさへあればよい年の暮 蜀山人
yuki furazu tenki mo yokute kaji mo nashi hima sae areba yoi toshinokure shokusanjin
snow falls-not weather too good (house-)fire/s not free-time+emph have-if good year's-end

> *No snow falls, the weather is fine, even fires rest tonight;*
> *Had I but time to spare, this Year might have ended right.*

> *No snow falls, the sky is clear and nothing is burning down;*
> *Had I but free time on New Year's Eve I'd paint the town!*

The first time I read this *kyôka* I did not see anything in it other than the observation that there were no fires – Edo was famous for them, and the winter in Japan is the driest and most dangerous time of the year (even today, sound-trucks drive around warning people to be careful with their heaters) – but, later, after learning that Shokusanjin (Ôta) was condemned to work as a minor official, I can see a genuine complaint here. Three years before Issa died, the year he wondered when he would be "dropped off," he also wrote this totally depressing *kyôka*:

煤ほこりはかで此世を古家に只身に添ふは月日也けり 一茶 文政七
susu hokori haka de kono yo o furu ie ni tada mi ni sou wa tsukibi narikeri issa
ashes dust sweep-not-w/ this world old house-as/in only body-with accomp.-as-4 months-days not+

> *This world is like*
> *an old house, hardly worth*
> *sweeping out –*
>
> *When all that stays with me*
> *are the months and days.*

Five Seasons Mad or Almost Mad, Depending

岩戸あけし神代のまゝのひかりにてちつともさびぬあら玉の春　網雑魚巻一
iwato akeshi kamiyo no mama no hikari nite chittomo sabinu aratama no haru　網雑魚巻一
boulder door opened gods' age's justhesame's light-in abit rust/corrode-not newgem-spring

◆ The New Year ◆

A cave-door cracks
The Age of the Gods is back,
it's the same shine!

Spring, our precious jewel
Tarnished not a whit in time!

Oh, say can you see
thru the Cave Door that shine,
ne'er aged nor odd

For the Land of The Sun
and the Home of the Gods!

Is Retiree Red Pine Gold Rooster, 隠士赤松金鶏 a sobriquet for this poem, among others is in the *Shokusan(jin)* anthology? *Why not!* Yes, I fused it with the cock-a-doodle-doo *Star Spangled Banner*. Otherwise, the *kyôka* would not be half so mad as many *haiku* in *The Fifth Season* (2007), as the New Year is itself . .

◆ Spring (Coming & Leaving) ◆

題しらず網雑魚巻一　春之部　蜀山家集　隠士赤松金鶏著 立春
みとれては つゐに前後を忘じけり 梅にうぐひす うぐひすにうめ
mitorete wa tsui ni zengo o wasurejikeri ume ni uguisu uguisu ni ume ditto
enthralled-as4 finally before-after+acc forget+emph.; plum then warbler, wblr-th pl

When you fall hard,
who recalls which the cart
& which the horse!

Did the warbler beat the plum?
Did plum bloom w/ warbler dumb?

Whenever we are
just crazy about something,
mem'ry has no room:

Did warbler sing-out first,
or plum burst into bloom?

心には たれもおもへど かはづほど 春のわかれを なくものはなし 同
kokoro ni wa tare mo omoedo kawazu hodo haru no wakare o naku mono wa nashi ditto
heart/s-in-as-for anyone thinks-but, frog extent spring's separation+acc sing/cry one-as4 not

In our hearts, we all know it is no joke,
that none so mourn spring's passing
as they, who crying, always croak.

The bird is credited with awakening the bloom & the bloom w/ attracting the bird. As love for nature came to compete w/ love between humans in Japanese poetry, we find kidding going both ways. Someone *as* smitten with nature as with human love or using the former to express the latter so oddly seems mad. Spring's departure amused nature-loving *haikai* poets who found laments conflating the end of spring & aging in old *waka* maudlin (See *The Cherry Blossom Epiphany*. Esp.

the chapter on late-bloomers). Rooster Shokusanjin's second *kyôka,* is good both for its first half, recalling Piet Hein on Charlie Chaplin (pg. 32), and because *it is true*, frogs are *very* loud in the paddies at the end of Spring. In Japanese, *naku* means both "cry" and "croak." I could drop the *frog* and improve the poem in the last line because "croak," ravens excepted, is frog-specific in English.

◆ Summer ◆

天の川底のぬけしと疑のはるゝまもなくふれる五月雨 高丸 18c?
amanogawa soko no nukeshi to utagai no haruru ma monaku fureru samidare
heaven's river bottom-pass suspicion clear-up period even not, falls 5month-rain

Who can doubt the floor of the Milky Way's dropped out,
Otherwise, how could this monsoon rain keep falling?

◆ Autumn ◆

大菊をめづる狂歌ははなかみの小菊を折てかくもはづかし 蜀山家集
ôgiku o mezuru kyôka wa hanakami no ogiku o orite kaku mo hazukashi shokusanjin
big chrysanthemum+acc treat mad-song-as-for nose-paper Small-mum folding write embarrassing

It Beats Blowing Your Nose On It!

A mad poem about a giant mum?
I blush for knowing it was done
upon the tissue of a smaller one.

The "blush" is mine. Though unlikely that *hanakami*, i.e. tissue-paper, punned with *hanikami*, i.e., *blushing /shy,* I wanted compensation for a major pun lost in translation: "folding" (name-brand Small Mum tissue) + "plucking," both *orite*. While the seasonal chrysanthemum was a theme in *haikai*, this 狂大菊 poem is utterly *kyôka*, as we feel no connection whatsoever with the natural world as one might were the flower used for what "Small Mum" was usually used for.

◆ Winter ◆

老いぬとも(れど)又も逢はむと行く年に涙の玉を手向けつるかな 俊成 新古今集
oinu to mo (redo) mata mo awamu to yuku toshi ni namida no tama o tamuketsuru kana
aging am(when) again+emph. meet-not-w/, lvg-year-to teardrops/gems+acc offer   shunzei

Aging fast, what hope
have I to meet you again?

So, Leaving Year

Do accept my presents,
these baubles called tears.

Feeling my age,
not knowing if ever we
shall meet again

I send off the Old Year,
My parting gift – tears!

The year's end is in winter, but barely, as spring-the-New-Year, is right around the corner. Another Shunzei (1114-1204) year-end *waka*, a bit less madly, admits to living to greet the Day he always thought would be his last one of the same. ♪

㊤ Another Round of Five Seasons, Mixed Tenmei ㊤

又ひとつ年はよるとも玉手箱あけてうれしき今朝のはつ春　もとの木網　徳和一万
mata hitotsu toshi wa yoru to mo tamatebako akete ureshiki kesa no hatsu haru　moto no mokuami
again one year-as-for approaches yet gem-hand-box opening happy this morn's first spring 1785

Another one! A new year comes to make us older yet
We delight to open up that legendary treasure chest!

It is easy to explain that, in the Sinosphere, people aged collectively at the start of the year (see *The Fifth Season:* 2007), but the "treasure chest" is another matter. It refers to one opened by Japan's Rip Van Winkle, Urashima Tarô, after the fisherman, returning from the Sea Dragon's Palace, found everyone he knew long dead and grew lonely. I will not give away the end of the tale – but, in this context, perhaps you can guess. Unfortunately, Pandora's box will not do for even a mad translation as it lacks the focus on *aging*. The poet, Mokuami, had the closest thing to the sea in Edo. He owned a bath-house. His wife Chie no Naishi, Little Ignoramus, the most popular woman in *kyôka,* had the next poem in the *Tokuwa Kago Kyôkashû* (通りますと岩戸の関のこなたより春へふみ出すけさの日の足　智恵内子 *tôrimasu to iwato no seki no konata yori haru e fumidasu kesa no hi no ashi*). The best I can do with it – *"Coming through! From without the cavern's checkpoint gate / The Sun on beaming legs passes into Spring immaculate!* – is not good enough. What makes her poem a breath of fresh air is the Sun=Day shouting out as people passing through checkpoints were supposed to. It is also natural because sun beams, like distant rain falling from clouds, are idiomatically "*ashi*=legs;" and what is idiomatic does not seem idiotic, which is to say anthropomorphic, even if it is. All people who have read much Japanese poetry know of Yomo no Akera's *Spring zig-zagging up the road in the person of a drunken calle*r (a *kyôka* in so many books, including one of mine that I skipped it here) but, *in Japanese*, Little Ignoramus' is, in its own way, just as good!

御簾ほどになかば霞みのかゝる時　さくらや花の王と見ゆらん　尻焼猿人
on-sudare hodo ni nakaba-kasumi no kakaru toki sakura ya hana no ô to miyuran
hon.screen amount half-hazy(long-culotte) sets time, cherry+emph flowers' king-as appears

Behind the mists, like royal rattan blinds, that half-conceal it,
Our cherry tree's the King of Flowers, Ô, his identity explicit.

..
Since readers taken with Shiriyake no Sarundo's name (Butt-burnt Monkey) might be curious and no other of his poems are in this book, I decided to translate the above, content-wise a Spring Poem, from the 1786 *Azuma Bunko*. In China and Japan, unlike Europe with the Kings seated on thrones before all gathered, divine rulers remained concealed behind screens, so, by mad logic, if one is concealed, one is a king. But that metaphor is not all that makes the poem mad. I believe the *nagabakama*, long cumbersome culottes an Imperial audience had to wear (see item #1-6+ in *Topsy-turvy 1585*), are punned (the *k* sound could be *g* as diacritical marks were rarely used) into the half-hazy *nakaba-kasumi,* and that the Chinese pronunciation of cherry, *ô,* the same as *king* in Japanese is being played,

for the cherry was generally *not* the "king" of flowers, as the peony was so called. Pardon my poli-syllabic Poundism at the end! Obviously, Japanese poets did not write that way. So much for *New Year* and *Spring*. Now, Summer –

再現いずれ負けいずれ勝つをとほとゞきす共に初ねの高こう聞こゆる 橘洲
izure make izure katsu o to hototogisu tomo ni hatsune no takô kikoyuru   karagoromo kisshû
which loses which wins? = bonito & cuckoo both first sound=price's highly sound 1739-1802

Will Bonito beat
Cuckoo or Cuckoo defeat
Bonito? First, I fear
Those bids and calls will burst
both my eardrums & my purse!

What bids & calls!
Will bonito beat cuckoo
& break my purse?
Or, cuckoo the bonito
& my eardrums burst first?

After his singularly uninspired reading (*"Which one will lose / And which one will be the winner? / The bonito or the cuckoo? / The first notes of both of them / Sound awfully high."*) Donald Keene rightly called this a good example of a poem that loses everything in translation and mentioned the *win/beat=katsu*+ accusative *o* ⇒*katsuo=bonito*, and the *sound=ne=price*. That is true, "notes" alone does not do it and my desperate multiplication and addition only slightly better. If only Keene were less intent to put down a genre he was evidently incapable of translating by statements such as *"Puns and verbal dexterity were also valid excuses for writing a kyôka"* (!). Would Keene say that about *English* poetry? Is rhyme (a sort of pun) and the ability to turn a word an "excuse" for, say, Shakespeare's sonnets, or, for that matter any witty poetry? That is not *criticism* but *bullying*. Or, maybe it is just sour grapes from one with a tin ear for poetry (I see him claiming a certain translator has Englished the *Kokinshû* "with its grace and elegance unimpaired" when, on the whole, that is so far from the truth that I know two people who actually claim to have thrown that book out the window). For the record, if I drop the *beating* and *losing* – in the original, so vernacular, one thinks of the Usanian schoolyard of the mid-20c: *"Fight! Fight! Fight!"* – introduce a pun that only works in English and trade in a *banana* idiom for a *bird* and *fish* – we *can* still have a poem:

Bonito bidding goes so high it drives me cuckoo, that I know –
But cuckoos are themselves so loud they're driving me bonito!

Our pleasure writing and delight reading such does not come from the wordplay Keene calls an "excuse" for poetry, alone, but from how it works *the existing image* of hysteria accompanying the first sales of, and first efforts to hear the respective creatures. Competition between *haikai, senryû* and *kyôka* poets to outdo one another's tropes is what is *really* sky high! Tenmei *kyôka* managed to do a good job of keeping the dense information and expanding the wordplay of haiku and senryû, while using the extra 14 syllabets to fill out or contradict narratives. For example, the two puns in the bonito+cuckoo poem can be squeezed into 17-syllabets, but the subtle *kikoyuru,* or "can/may be heard," at the end, which accents the apples-and-oranges incongruity would not fit. Wordplay is not an excuse for poetry but part of it.

Another Round of Five Seasons, Mixed Tenmei 下

吹きまくるすそのゝ風に仙人もおつるばかりの白はぎの花　加陪仲塗　徳和歌後
fukimakuru susono no kaze ni sennin mo otsuru bakari no shiro-haginohana kabe no nakanuri 1785
blow-about/circling hem-field's wind-in/by saint/wizard even fall-amount white-clover=calve/s=bloom

> *When the wind blows around the meadow hem, look out below!*
> *That saint might fall again to see clover/calves so whitely glow.*

> *When wind blows up sweet Clover's skirt around the meadow hem,*
> *Her bloomers so white just might drop an old sage from heaven!*

Clover, as an Autumn flower, was long a symbol of a fair-skinned aging beauty – even Bashô could not resist composing a haiku for old harlots at a 'Clover Inn' – and most appreciated wet with dew especially when the wind, pushing back the foliage above, revealed more blossoms below as it scattered the dew. The poet uses vocabulary for nature, that part found in Japanese poetry at any rate, that might *also* apply to clothing and alludes to the legend of the old sage who fell off his cloud into a river on seeing the white thighs of a washer woman to praise the brilliance of the blossoms.   If Japanese were breast-lovers and the clover a pear, we might have had a workable pun there, but as it *is*, I could only try to show and tell what was smoothly accomplished by the original. And yet, I could still come *closer* to translating that poem than I could one by Akera Kankô giving a nonsensical just-so-story to what had been a mere metaphor for a millennium.

紅葉ばは千しほ百しほしほじみて　からにしきとや人のみるらん　朱楽管江
momijiba wa chishio momoshio shioji mite kara-nishiki to ya hito no miruran kankô
red-leaves-as4 1000-salts/tides 100-salts/tides seeing from=chinese=salty-brocade as people see

> *These leaves of reddish hue, dyed in salt a thousand times anew*
> *No wonder pickled/Chinese brocade is how people look at you!*

That is, the Autumnal hills covered with bright orange and red and yellow leaves were likened to an expensive Chinese brocade. Chinese was *kara* and that means "bitter/salty/picante" or a strong pickle (such as, say, namako or squid guts). The *momi* in the *momiji* (red-leaf/maple) hints at kneading (done to some pickles), "thousand" in the *chi* pronunciation evokes fall emotions as expressed in teary waka conceits and the "hundred" (not translated) in the *momo* pronunciation evokes unsettled butts *momojiri* often punned with the colored leaves *momiji* but meaningless here. Salt washes were used to deepen colors as well as to fix them in cloth by Japanese (and, I would guess, Chinese). And now, the winter:

ふみなんはおしきにもりて聞しめせ足駄の歯になかけそ初雪　平鉄東作
fuminan wa oshiki ni tsumorite kikoshimese ashida no ha ni na kake so hatsuyuki tôsaku
treading-as-4 regretfl=fancydish-on piling eat+elegant longstilt-geta teeth-on put-not, first-snw!

> *Don't tread on her! Pile her high upon a dish, and say a grace.*
> *Save the teeth on your choppine; she's the first snow of her race!*

Yes, the gendering, grace and race are all added, but I was at loss for a fancy serving plate *in a word* that also meant "regretful" before morphing into said dish, or words to warn someone not to leave stilted-shoe prints on the first-snow, while bringing "teeth" into the picture and hinting at the heap with the verb (*kake*) that followed. And how to English *kikomeshite,* or "eat up," in words elegant enough for an Emperor (and possibly chosen for the *gikogiko* tooth-reply of the snow)?

It would be a shame to tread, so pile it on a plate;
Kick off your clods & eat the snow before it is too late!

Moreover, the way "tread" is treated (Japanese verbs have dozens of grammatical options), combined with the following particle it might be read *Nanpa*, a place associated with reeds=*ashi* homophonous with the first part of the *ashida* geta (choppine) chosen! Some might say that is a coincidence, but I doubt it.

The first snow is not water; do not tread, but go ahead –
Heap a helping on a plate and royally you will be fed!

So with all that going on or possibly going on, how could I not add alot to make up for the huge losses in translation? This last try surrenders the shoes, only in the poem for their teeth, and, in *tread*, finds an English coincidence to work and, well, you can see! One reason I was eager to introduce this poem was that it provides good contrast to what haiku do. Issa has a well-known *ku* that goes like this, "A yummy-looking snow is this: *fuuwari fuwari!*" むまさうな雪がふうはりふはり哉 *mumasô na yuki ga fuuwari fuwari kana*). *Mumai* is a childish word for delicious. ♪ *Fuuwari fuwari* would be *fuluffy, fluffy*. Need we say more?

除夜　借金は首たけつもる大晦日門のゝ雪さへはらひかねたり 加陪仲塗
shakkin wa kubi dake tsumoru ômisoka kado no yuki sae haraekanetari kabe no nakanuri
debt-as4 neck/head up to buried last-day gate's snow even dispel/shovel-off cannot 1785

Up to my neck in debt, I fear it's the last day of the year;
Unable to go out to shovel snow, I'm buried in here!

While translating this, I began to doubt my choice of poems. There may be charm in the juxtaposition of sinking in debt and snow when a causal relationship exists between the two, but even a sympathetic pauper can grow tired of year-end debt poems! And, so, it seems, was Akara, though a postword to his poem casts . . . ..

金はありかけもはらふて置炬燵とろ／＼ねいりつかん年の夜　赤良
kane wa ari kake mo harôte okikotatsu torotoro neiri tsukan toshinokure yomo no akara
money-as-for have bills+emph. paid portable kotatsu heater drowsily sleep-into falls year-end

It could be the end of any year, but –

Money to spare after paying our bills, 'round the table-stove
Men sit and warmly wait for sleep, on this, the Eve we love!

Someone attributed this to Anonymous

A Final Round of Five Seasons Mostly Yûchôrô

病つきて野辺に初寝をせし春は 小まつはひかて風やひきけん 雄長老 16c
yamitsuki de nobe ni hatsune o seshi haru wa komatsu o hika de kaze ya hikiken yûchôrô 狂歌百首
can'tstop=sickcomingdown-from field-in first-sleep-do spring small-pine pull-cannot-from cold-pull(catch)

◆ An Old Man's New Year ◆

Caught up in it, I spent my first night in the fields of spring
Not a pine did I make mine, but I sure did catch a cold!

Yamitsuki means coming down with a disease or so engrossed in something one cannot quit. Little pines were ritually *pulled* (*hiku/ hiki*) up, and the same went for "catching" a cold. Yûchôrô only made it to 56 but Bashô, died an elder at 50.

◆ Spring (Present & Leaving) ◆

巣をは跡に残し出たる 谷川の魚にはけつゝ うくひなくなり 雄長老
su o ba ato ni nokoshi idetaru tanikawa no sakana ni haketsutsu ukui nakunari yûchôrô
nest+emph behind leaving depart valley-river's fish-divulge-while ugui dies/sings

~~*The only war-fish left uncaught swims in my memory a blur*~~
~~*But by the mountain stream I heard what I sought, that bird!*~~

~~*Nighting fish nowhere, I was left high and dry in the vale*~~
~~*Until it gave me the bird I heard and now toast with ale!*~~

Ale w/ tears flow side by side as nighting swim and cry
Spilling out their guts, until, like that bird, they die.

Yûchôrô was asked to combine a fish called *ugui,* said to cry/sing, w/ the song of the *uguisu* (warbler/nightingale). *War+blur* & *nighting+ ale* mimic the split-name, but only my last reading (minus the *ale* & *tears*) catches the gist of the meaning. In the original, the *ugui* leaves its (mountain brook) nest, or *su,* to address other fish in the vale. The homophones *sing* and *die* (*naku*) are effective at poem's end. This untranslatable 16c *kyôka* does things only late-18c *kyôka* are supposed to.

..

暮れ行くといへばどふやらよけれどもなにもくれずにげて行春 鶯 摺江
kure yuku to ieba dôyara yokeredomo nani mo kurezu nigete yuku haru uguisu no surie
dusking as call-it someway OK-but nothing giving fleeing goes spring 徳和 1785

To call this time
"the twilight of the Spring"
makes sense, but 'leaves'?

No, she leaves us nothing,
I'd say, rather, she flees!

English cannot punfully equate *dusk,* or season's *end,* with *giving something* to another (both *kure*), but, luckily, "leave" means either *departing* or *giving*. While such puns are in themselves worthless, or, should we say have no more reason than rhyme, here, they do help bring to life one perspective on the end of spring.

◆ The Voice of Summer ◆

きばさみをほとゝぎすまし夏木立刈透しても聞かんとぞ思ふ　星屋光次 1785
kibasami o hototogisu mashi natsu kodachi karisukashite mo kikan to zo omou　hoshiya mitsuji
tree-shears+ cuckoo is/are summer-bosque clipping-transparent even hear-would think

> *Pruning shears?*
> *I'd thin the summer bosque*
> *where cuckoo hides*
>
> *The better to hear him call*
> *when I am sitting inside!*

This may owe something to the wish to level mountain the better to see the moon in the 9c *Tales of Ise* (pg.70). My favorite cuckoo *kyôka* is by Shokusanjin: *"Though I came I did not see the bird but I have proof / A cuckoo's what I heard in the ghostly dawn moon"* ほととぎす鳴きつる影はみへねども　きいた証拠は有明の月 *hototogisu nakitsuru kage wa mienedomo kiita shôko wa ariake no tsuki*). Unfortunately, the wit rests upon a pun that won't English. The "have=*ari*" in "have proof," morphs effortlessly into the chop/stamp-like "dawn-moon=*ariake*."

◆ Autumn ◆

めをと中にたゝ二つもつ衣をばかへあひてけふのはつやあはせん　雄長老
meoto naka ni tada futatsu motsu koromo o ba kae-aite kyô no hatsu ya awasen　yûchôrô 16c
wifehusbnd just two have dress+emph. exchnge tdy's first would meet(requiremnts)　～狂歌百

> *W/ two pairs of dress between them, a man & wife use reason:*
> *Exchanging robes today, they, too, change with the season!*

The original puns on the name of the clothing. An *awase* means something *joined* or *combined*. The *awase* ritually worn for the first time in the year in the first week of the Ninth Month, the last of fall, is a robe with a lining. Yûchôrô splits *awase* from *hatsu-awase,* or First-*Awase,* to verb it as *trying to make ends meet.*

◆ Winter ◆

よし人は犬といふともふる雪にわがあとつけていでんとぞ思ふ　蜀山人
yoshi hito wa inu to iu to mo furu yuki ni waga ato tsukete-iden to zo omou　shokusanjin
good person-as-for dog-as say even fall/old snow-in my trail making go-out+emph think

> *The cultured folk may call me a dog, but out I will go,*
> *To make and leave my trail, blazoned in the fallen snow.*

Iwanami notes that *dogs like to play in the snow*, but snow-viewing by Bashô *et al* was already well known and that does not explain why "good" or "cultured" people had to be specified. Could Shokusanjin look back to the complaints by house owners about virginal snowfall violated by rude souls? If "dog" can pun with "not in" (*inu*) the poet may mean both that though aesthetes are not around, he will go snow-viewing, *and* that he will also, like it or not, piss on the snow, a favorite practice and theme for Issa, self-proclaimed enemy of cold things.

Just Geese Coming In – or Run-of-the-Mill *Kyôka*

烏ほど あほらしくは みへぬなり 月に浮るゝ 初雁のつら 鹿都部真顔 狂歌一万集
karasu hodo ahôrashiku wa mienu nari tsuki ni ukururu hatsukari no tsura (shikatsube) magao d.1829
crow/s amount foolish-as-for appear-is moon-to/with floating/excited first-goose/geese' face/s

Not half so stupid a sight as crows high on moonshine,
The long faces of the first geese flying in look just fine.

While I cannot find enough good seasonal *kyôka* poems, I still feel I have done well enough to favorably misrepresent the mean. So, here let me introduce as many *kyôka* as I can easily translate from a small selection in a mediocre book. These are half of the eighteen geese in the *Autumn* chapter of *Kyôka Ichiman Shû*, published in 1894, and containing mostly late-18c and early-19c poems. Magao, author of the lead, was the leading conservative mad poet, reputedly coming to meetings dressed formally, unlike the others dressed for fun. Did *he* look out of place, like the foolish crow, a fixture in *haikai*?

秋はまた越路の海の浪の花見捨てわたる雁金の棹 加保茶 元成 同
aki wa mata echiji no umi no nami no hana misutete wataru karigane no sao motonari
fall-as4 again echi road's sea's waves' blossoms abandoning crossing goose-pole(=line)

In Fall, again, they turn their backs (make that tails) on the bloom
(in English, 'spume') of the waves to cross the Echigo sea, geese.

That geese turned their back on the bloom to head home in the Spring was well-known in *haikai*. Issa found the perfect adjective for it, *shibutoi* or *head-strong*. *Spume* being "wave-*blossoms*," spring is pulled (or *poled*) into the fall.

おくれたる一羽の雁は雲の海 投筆をせし文字にやあらん 頼益 一万
okuretaru ichiwa no kari wa kumo no umi nagefude o seshi moji ni ya aran yorimasu?
lagging one-goose-as-for cloud-ocean thrown/ing-brush+acc doing letters-as4 not

Unpunctual Punctuation?

One lagging goose against a billowing sea of paper-white cloud:
That's the thrown-brush trick – hardly a letter for crying aloud!

From a distance, it is too hard to make out, but the message
of the first flight of geese seems to read something like ら!

遠目にはさだかならぬと初雁のら と読める玉章 桂
tôme ni wa sadaka naranu to hatsukari no ら to yomeru tamazusa katsura sp?
distant-eye-to-as-for settled-not is and first-goose/geese's as ら reads precious-letter

Flights of geese were thought to resemble writing. The thrown-brush was a technique that a *senryû* reminds us no one used but the originator, Kûkai (Kôbô-daishi) who, being told he did not punctuate a large calligraphy at a temple, did so by throwing the brush against the paper. Hence the title, my doing. I cannot read the letter in the second poem, myself. The original is god knows what. It is hand-drawn and may be a Sanskrit seed-letter or may be pure nonsense, a doodle. Thinking it too hard to paste in a one letter picture I looked for a squiggle I could not read in the "insert" choices in my Times New Roman and found a letter in the language our numbers come from (If it is True-type and embeds you will see it, if not, not 又、意味の知らない字ですから、怖い。「字ハッド」を起さないように祈っております). That "letter" is actually a love letter or other valuable epistle with which geese were identified at least since the building of the Great Wall (or *Long Castle* as it is called in the Sinosphere), when a woman whose husband was drafted to work on it used them to try to contact him (I won't give away the rest of the story, but it is a real weeper), or from before the song about it was composed, anyway. A couple more such letters:

雁かねの夜も厭はぬは 公けの文もて急くたくひならまし　無染 同
karigane no yo mo itowanu wa kuge no fumi mote isogu tagui naramashi musen sp?
geese's night even hate-not-as-for nobles' letter/s-carrying hurry ilk be-would

I guess those geese belong to the ilk happy to work all night
Rushing about with letters for our nobles decked in silk.

Do they come bringing letters? O'er the distant hills, squinting
Would that be sealed rims? ⁒ ⁒ ⁒   Yes, indeed, the first geese!
(Is that the fall's first goose, or a seal ⁒ upon the rim?)

文をもて来たるか遠の山の端に封〆程に見ゆる初雁　風来山人 fûrai
fumi o mote-kitaru ka tô no yama no ha ni fû shime hodo ni miyuru hatsukari sanjin
letter bringing? far mountain's/s' peak/s-on lapel seal-amount seem first-goose/ese

Noble Japanese were night owls. I imagine the men who wandered around engaging in poetry or love-making usually saw the sunrise before going to sleep. After lovers parted in the early hours of the dawn, one reads of poems and their replies being promptly written. Behind that, we must imagine a cadre of messengers dashing about in the dark to humor these people with their important affairs. The *kuge,* or nobles, were not highly regarded at this time in history. I am delighted the seal mark many Japanese even today make where the edge of the envelope glued to the rest so some of it touches both is part of the normal body of letters that may be called up in writing without having to search *inserts* or *symbols*. It suggests the figure of a single goose, and perhaps an eye squinting.

友鳥も楽しからすや初雁の千里の道を遠しともせす　松雄
tomo tori mo tanoshikarazu ya hatsukari no senri no michi o tôshi to mo sezu matsuo sp?
friend-birds+emph fun-must-be!/: first goose/geese's 1000-ri road+acc distant as do-not
..

The First Goose finds his road of a thousand leagues short,
Unless his mate's a bore, in which case, he'd feel it more!

First geese, were your flying mates not all of good cheer,
How could you make a thousand leagues seem so near?

The first geese, did they not fly in good company,
A thousand leagues would seem a thousand leagues.

If you, dear reader, are a readress, please do redress the first reading. The original has no number much less person or gender. Make the first goose a *gander*, if you can uncook it, that is. The two remaining poems are in the ♪s, in Japanese only.

One for the Birds! Or, Saigyô *Kyôka* Master.

色にしみ香もなつかしき梅が枝に折しもあれや うぐひすの声　西行
iro ni shimi ka mo natsukashiki ume ga eda ni orishi mo are ya   uguisu no koe saigyô
color/s-in/by stained scent too dear/familiar plum's branch-with breaking if-could, warbler's' voice/s

With this plum spray
so beautiful in bloom and
memory's scent,
I would break off the songs
of warblers for your present.

The scent of bloom
steeped in beauty and dear,
that I would take
With the warbler's song, if it
but w/ this plum would break!

The original, among supplementary poems to the *Sankashû*, gives no indication whether Saigyô (d.1190) wanted to take the branch inside or send it to someone. This is the sort of witty *waka* that *could* be a *kyôka* were it but called one.

枯野うづむ雪に心をまかすればあたりの原にきぎす鳴くなり
kareno uzumu yuki ni kokoro o makasureba atari no hara ni kigisu nakunari
withered-field burying snow-in heart+acc allow-if/when's area's meadow-in pheasant sings

Giving my mind leave to play in the snow-bound barren field
Wouldn't you know, I found it: a pheasant called out, life!

The idea of letting a *heart/mind* do what it likes – like a horse released to graze – makes this a good creative *waka* concerning the nature of observation, but the meadow, *hara*, as well as the barren field *kare-no*, where one would suffice, suggests a pun on *belly=hara* and a near-*kyôka*. Losing the pun in translation, I added "I found it" and "life." N.Y. spring, cold spring, now middle-late spring:

いかでわれ常世の花のさかり 見てことわりしらむ帰るかりがね
ika de ware tokoyo no hana no sakari mite kotowari shiramu kaeru karigane
how i everworld's blossoms' fullbloom seeing refuse knownot returning geese

How can this goose the full bloom of the everworld refuse
like those who seeing beauty can leave her without blues?

Here, your translator may well be a traitor. I am unsure if this Everworld is Buddhist paradise or the full bloom Saigyô so loved, if the *ware = I/self* is he, himself, or a goose to whom he directs the question, or if the poem starts with the former and ends up the latter. *I.e.*, is this a Japanese-style serial modification of the subject, the returning geese at the very tail, or does it address them? And, the extent of *kyôka-ness* depends on understanding. On to late-spring to summer:

帰る雁にちがふ雲路のつばくらめこまかにこれや書ける玉づさ　西行
kaeru kari ni chigau kumoji no tsubakurame komaka ni kore ya kakeru tamazusa
returning geese-with differng cloud-road's swallw/s finely/detaild this+emph writing letter

On a cloud-path in-bound while the Anserine's out, Swallows near,
Their letters too damn fine to read, until they're almost here!

From ancient times, "goose-swallow" in Chinese meant two (usually people or groups of people or messages) that pass one another, coming and going. But, until reading this poem, I have not read of "reading" any birds but geese.

ほととぎす谷のまにまに音づれてあはれに見ゆる峰つづきかな　西行
hototogisu tani no ma ni ma ni oto-zurete aware ni miyuru mine tsuzuki kana saigyô
 cuckoo valley's between/space-in valley's b/s-in sound-accmpnying=visitng sad seemng ridges

> *Taking their call with them, the cuckoo sail from vale to vale;*
> *The crests behind, so high and lonesome, almost seem to sigh.*

The *sound=oto* ⇒ *visit=otozure* pun includes a fine punning philology: *oto= sound-bringing=tsure*. The *lonely/sad* ridges justified *"seem to sigh."* The poem before (*hototogisu naki-watarunaru . . .*) has cuckoo song double up on choppy waves against the wind. Could it be what started clever descriptions of the cuckoo's voice in *haikai* that continued for centuries? Three poems later,

時鳥こゑのさかりになりにけりたづねぬ人にさかりつぐらし
hototogisu koe no sakari ni narinikeri tazunenu hito ni sakari tsugurashi
 cuckoo voice's acme becomes+emph, visiting people-by excitement/rut catch-seems

> *The cuckoo calls and calls – could we call it 'rutting'?*
> *And all those who visit me find it can be catching!*

While supposedly just meaning full bloom or flourishing, *sakari* sometimes seems more like coming into heat. With Saigyô mentioning the *sakari* as "catching," I felt "rutting" would work. *Excitement* might have been enough. With this, Saigyô's Supplement is out of birds. However, I just happen to have autumn geese, by someone else in a contemporary *waka* anthology.

かりかねの もみちにかけし たまつさを はなにつけてや もてかへるらむ　千載集1188
karigane no momiji ni kakeshi tamatsusa o hana ni tsukete ya motekaeruramu ng 番号外作者
 geese's red-leaves=maple-in written gem-letter+acc blossom/nose-to putting!/: carrying return

> *Red it was, as the epistle came in with ye maple leaf;*
> *And the anserine letter, writ in bloom? Sakura serif.*

..
The original has a named author, but the only open source for the anthology, Nichibun, has yet to enter the names of most poets (if you are a *waka*-lover with money, *please* pay them to hire a secretary to add names!), so I cannot share it with you. No matter, by the time you see it in English, the work is largely mine. The original poem ends in a pun on *blossoms=hana=nose* with what may be a snooty idiom (鼻につけて) I did not mind losing in translation, though it is fine in the original which pushes the envelope on the goose-as-messenger far enough to make it a *kyôka*. With few homophones, compensatory high-frequency punning in English requires arcane words. If you do not know *anserine*, rest assured that neither did I before translating the poem led me to search for an adjectival goose that turned out to be not far from the *aubergine* horse I first encountered in Prof. Crump's translations from Chinese almost two decades ago. I found an adjective for *eggplant* useful and hope this may prove equally useful to you goose-lovers. Thanks to the punning context of this poem, you will never forget it, either!

Cranes, Turtles & Composite Characters & a Charm

つるかめの いのちくらへの かちまけを 君こそしらめ 萬代をへて　源仲正　夫木
tsuru kame no inochi kurae no kachimake o kimi koso shirame manyô o hete minamoto no naka-
crane turtle's life-amount's win-lose+acc you/lord espec. know-should 10,000 ages passing　-masa

Who should know
who wins the match between
The turtle & the crane,

If not he whose ken extends
for eons: my Sovereign!

For a democrat, there is something fulsome here, yet playing with the Chinese conceit of a debate between the two animals about their longevity and the slangy *win-loss* (*kachi-make*) vocabulary says *kyôka*. The only ground to deny that to this *waka* from the *Fuboku* anthology (c1310), is that the New Year was a time for celebration, when considerable freedom was tolerated in the canon.

千年の鶴のたまごを常盤なるまつの十かへりかへすめでたさ　蜀山人
chitose no tsuru no tamago o tokiwa naru matsu no jû kaeri kaesu medetasa shokusanjin
10,000-year-crane's egg/s+acc permanent-base-become pine 10-returns hatch luckiness

As lucky as Crane eggs a thousand years old hatching
In the pine of ten-returns to brood upon the rock of ages!

This, by *kyôka's* first man, puts half a dozen lucky themes into a single poem. Let us skip the details. What matters is that all are seamlessly linked, though not quite as I have them for flow and order are at odds in translation. To a modern Japanese reader this nonsense would not satisfy, but in Edo at this time (c.1800) people were familiar with composite Chinese meta-characters, i.e. letter charms devised by fusing many characters into a super-lucky ones. Before we had *cargo* cults, we had *character cults*. In all of the Sino-sphere, people found magical properties in characters, which were incorporated into charms used even in illiterate cultures – no, *especially*, in illiterate cultures. In literate Japan, despite talk about the "soul of words" going back a thousand years, one does not find this belief *that* strong. Once one has used the written language a lot, most people conclude that word magic is subtle and psychological rather than obvious and material. Still, look at the celebratory poems in this book – not just in this chapter – and you will find good examples of combined puns and metaphor that have something in common with composite characters.

..
年徳の神のおまへの鰐口に かけ鯛をこそ見るへかりけれ 貞富 後撰夷曲集
toshitoku no kami no omae no waniguchi ni kaketai o koso mirubekarikere teifu? 1666
year-morals/benefit-god's before's crocodile-mouth-in decorative-snapper+acc see'd like tk1

A sea-bream offering, I'd make the god of Goodyear smile!
What could be better for the mouth of a crocodile?

The Crocodile Mouth is the gong hanging above long rectangular offertory box at temples and shrines. People wave a rope-knot into it to make a wish. There is a slit partially circumscribing it. This broad grin makes *it* a croc and links back to the jungle beginnings of Buddhism, while the sea bream, or red snapper seems to represent the island nation. The god in question, the *toshitokujin*, is always placed facing the lucky direction for the year, and one was supposed to approach the god from that direction, so one did not always visit the nearest shrine first thing in the year. But, why do I put this here, pegged onto the composite charms of the New Year? It is because the poem, like a composite character, invents a charming combination of items. The sea bream is a New Year staple as its color is lucky and its large eyes a pun-derived symbol of joy (*ô/omedetai*).

あつらへの兎の毛なる筆とれは上るも早し手習の山　庵住　一万 19c
atsurae no usagi no ke naru fude to nareba noboru mo hayashi tenarai no yama anjû
ordered/special hare's hair is brush-as become-if climbing too fast penmanship mountain

Take up this brush   *'Tis hare for thee!*
of hare and you will climb   *With it, your special brush*
Calligraphy Hill   *by leaps & bounds*

As fast as if you, too, had   *I trust you'll scale the heights*
Long hind-legs to fill the bill! *of Mount Calligraphy!*

While not New Year-related, this poem playing on a proverb about hare legs and people born in The Year of the Hare, is an exercise in *charm*. Did the poet order a brush of rabbit hair and give it to some young person with this poem or offer it to a friend with a stationary shop to use? The last charm examples, also not New Year, are rain-prayers. The first, by a friend of Kisshû, an early participant in Tenmei *kyôka,* is a bit hard to follow. The second, by an 18c (1723-1801) *waka* poet is clear and shows exactly where *waka* and *kyôka* would soon meet in *tanka*.

雨の祈りとてたはぶれに人々哥をよむついでに tobuchiri no batei
夕立や古きためしもありの穴堤をくづせ天の川水　飛塵馬蹄 c.1780
yûdachi ya furuki tameshi mo ari no ana tsutsumi o kuzuse amanokawa-mizu
evening shower!/: old try+emph. is=ant/s' hole/s dike+acc break! heavn-river h2o

There's an old way   *There's the old way*
to pray for rain, uncle   *to call for rain, through*
& ant holes, they say   *an ant hole may*
Can drop a dike: are you   *we undermine the banks*
ready for the Milky Way?   *of Heaven's River today!*

tsuchi sakete teru hi ni nureshi tami no sode kawaku bakari no ame mo furanan
earth crckng shines sun-by soakd folks' sleevs dry enuf rain too fall-would! ozawa roan

With the earth cracked by sunlight that has showered our people in heat,
I pray for just enough rain to dry their tear-drenched sleeves. tr.carter
~~~~~~~~~~~~~~~~~~~~~~~~~~~
That just enough rain will fall to dry our peoples' sleeves
soaked by the earth-cracking rays of the summer sun!

Playing with Spring 春 Radicals & 壽 Wrinkles

三すぢまで山のひたひに春がすみ か〻るところへ出づる朝日奈　真顔
san suji made yama no hitai ni harugasumi kakaru tokoro e izuru asahina　magao d.1829
three lines/sinews-until mountain's brow-on spring-mist sets place-to/while appear morning-sun

春　Asahina New Year　春

*At the moment
three lines of spring haze
form on its brow
The mountain, smiling, greets
the rising morning sun*

---

*Just when spring haze has drawn three lines that rest upon
The brow of a hill in Asahina, somehow, up comes the sun!*

I added "smiling" after a Japanese conceit not found in this particular poem, a clever description of the character for Spring 春, also meaning the New Year of which haze is a prime symbol. A big smile would, after all wrinkle one's brow, and a poet noting three such lines might himself smile. Horizontal lines resembling *three* 三 and the *sun* 日 may be found in the character. Mountain 山 is not in the character, except, perhaps, in a more triangular ancient form, but needed to complete the standard scene for spying Spring haze. The number of lines make charming sense, for New Year's Day is sometimes called the *"start of three,"* referring to the new/first day, month and year. The "morning sun," 朝日 *asahi* is punned into a toponym, Asahina 朝比奈, by the addition of one character 奈 pronounced *na* at the very end. As you can see, the *hi* 比 in the middle of the name is not the same character as the *hi* for sun; common poetic license in Japanese. Both readings take considerable liberty with the syntax, for the original flow (not order) is "Asahina's morning sun comes out right at the point when three lines of spring haze have settled on the brow of the mountain."(岩波古典の「川柳狂歌集」の狂歌解説の中)
..

八十とセの春や皺手に寿の一字　一蓉　春山集
yaso tose no haru ya shiwate ni ju no hitoji　ichiyô 1811
eighty-years' spring/b.day!/: wrinkled hand-on longevity single letter

Longevity in Hand

*The eightieth bar
for her star: her palm, too
is well-crossed:* 寿

The above was one of many celebratory *ku* written for Seifu-ni (Starcloth-nun) on her eightieth birthday. Neither *kyôka* nor *kyôku*, it is a genuine haiku as the

Spring, which I failed to squeeze into the above when I added *for her star* to go with the *bar* (a sand bar or reef that rises close to the surface) punned into the *se* of the *tose*, or "year," is both a birthday and season, here, the New Year. My source used the simple character for "longevity," but the original might have been the older, even more wrinkled one, which I shall enlarge:

Crossing Spring's shoal for the eightieth time!
The wrinkles on her palms spell "longevity is mine."

Just as I was translating these visual antics, or, rather charmed poetry, my mother had a major birthday I was fortunate to attend (it was my only trip longer than 30 miles in two-and-a-half a years too!). The result was a series of playful poems.

Of all the numbers, only two go on without end!
Lucky you, to be blessed with both of them!
Wonder of wonders.   Amen.

That is one of two versions of a lucky riddle. The other was made for my mom, herself to read. See if you can guess her age before proceeding to the next poem, a general wish for well-being hinting at her achievements which gives it.

To a Literatae   *Carpe annum!*

If you think vowel-rhyme not only has its uses,
  but is, of all, the type most favored by the muses,
Then you will surely agree when I say
  that we have just cause to celebrate today –
The very best time in the world for a *Lady*
  must be the Venerable Bede Age of *Eighty!*

The title plays with *Carpe Diem*, "Live for the *day!"* Bede was a saint and 'first historian of England.' My mom, an angel but no saint, is the historian of Key Biscayne. Bede, always "venerable," serves as a Japanese-style pillow word for old age though, if truth be told, he did not even make it to seventy. If the riddle still escapes you, look closely at the numbers 8 and O (vs. 1, 2, 3, 4, 5, 6, 7, 9).
..

To an Activist Counseling Moderation

There are wrongs to be righted,
  keep writing, you matter;
But forget not at eighty
  your duty to yourself: get fatter!
You still have the touch –
  by all means, *write on,* but not too much!

These, my attempts at mad verse on an appropriate occasion, my mom's birthday, show you why I should stick to translation for anything longer than haiku.

A Roly-Poly Maybe & other Affirmations of Old Age

よねにあふてたはらころびでぬれそめた 三浦みさきのなまこならねど 黒田月洞軒
yone ni aute tawarakorobi de nuresometa miuramisaki no namako naranedo kuroda getsudôken
whore/rice/88-w/ meeting sack-tumbling-by wet-start/stained miura-cape's seaslug be/become-not-but

寄　俵　恋
Roly-Poly Love

Meeting a tart,
we tumbled around, soaked
to the gills, not

That lying on the ground
made us Miura sea slugs!

Making it clean
to my big Eighty Eight
a fling in the mud!

Like a tumbler, up again
though no spring sea slug.

I first introduced this poem in a footnote to the *Protean Sea Slug* chapter of *Rise, Ye Sea Slugs!* (2003). With the date 1688-1703, the "*first* soaked" in the poem suggests it was written by a young man who just lost his virginity, but if he *flourished* as a poet in such period, he may have lived to the age which puns into my second reading. If the former is right, Ôda and the Tenmei *kyôka* crew were lucky, for the teenager, had he lived, would surely have pre-empted them and taken *kyôka* as far as it could go.

So, I wrote a half-year ago. Since that time, I found the date was the period when the poet, Getsudôken, kept a *kyôka* journal. We will see half-a-dozen chapters from it later. He was not young, but he did not live to be 88 either. Only 63. Either old (fifty-on was *old*) Getsudôken recalled *his* first time or it was a first whoring for the year. At this point, we really should toss this sea slug into another chapter, but what the hell. We will be back on track by the next page.

Tawara, with *korobi=roll*, a *tumble/r* (like a *roly-poly*) that pops back up, literally means a *bale* or *sack*, and in a somewhat rarer usage, common during the New Year for the propitious association with wealth measured in rice bales, means *dried sea cucumber*, or *trepang*. *Yone* can mean "a pretty-whore" a "cunt," or "rice" which, by its character 米 suggests the age 八十八, the celebration of which is so called. This 88 year-old or *tart* "rice," links to the bale or sack (*tawara*), which not only suggests *trepang* and *tumbling* as mentioned, but is a synonym for a harlot. Indeed, the roly-poly, self-righting daruma, usually paper meche, was a common slang for *harlot*, or, quoting my dictionary, a "drab." The *wetness* is tricky. The New Year allusion suggests "spilling rice" (*yone kobosu*), like *tawara* for trepang, a taboo term – which does not mean a taboo'ed word , but one acceptable for use in an enchanted time when words matter – for "tears," in this case, tears of happiness for getting screwed or making it to infinity (in Japanese *eight* meant everything; there was even an eight-based numerical system)! When I put add "*spring"* to sea slug in my birthday reading, I pun on our ~ *chicken* idiom, but note that fresh sea cucumber is generally not eaten in and, therefore, not associated with the season we call Spring. *Namako,* the very word of the creature includes *nama*, or "raw," is a Winter delicacy and theme.

年寄もまた食ふべきと思ひきや 命成けりよねのまんぢう　元の木阿弥 (物語)
toshiyori mo mata kuu beki to omoiki ya inochi narikeri yone no manjû   motonomokuami
elderly too also eat ought-to (I) think!/: life becomes(costs/takes)+emph. rice-dumpling 1680

> *Though it may Kill you,*
> (get yours before you die!)
>
> *I think old folk, too, should get a taste of these, I do!*
> *Though yoni-rice dumplings may take my life, it's true.*

This old *kyôka* by the fictional Moto no Mokuami 木阿弥 (What a story! Look it up!), not the Tenmei poet Moto no Mokuami 木網, is another instance of *yone* (rice) as whore. Since *manjû*, or dumpling can, by itself, mean a cunt or, combined with "boat" (*funa*), a whore who plies her trade from the same, etc., we have an unmistakably sexy intent here. Indeed, the second meaning of the *yonemanjû*, or rice-dumpling (for the skin, which can be thick, is made from rice, rather than wheat flour) in the dictionary is such. Though "eating" itself has sexual overtones, the word used for "also" is not the most common one, but *mata*, a *crotch* homophone, so we have a hint of oral sex. Whores were known to carry dreaded diseases and nicknamed the same thing as blowfish were, *teppô*, or "musket" for that reason, but such deadliness alone provides little if any humor. You need to know that the rice used for dumplings was not your ordinary rice, but the sweet and extremely glutinous, which is to say sticky, variety used for *mochi*, often translated rice "cake" that was infamous for causing old folk to choke and, in that era when no one knew to strike the solar plexus, kill.

祝歌　箒たて 草履へ灸をすゆるとも 千秋万歳 われは長尻　蜀山人
hôki tatete zôri e kyû o suyuru to mo senshû-banzei ware wa nagajiri   shokusanjin
broom+acc stand, sandal-to moxa+acc burn even 1000-falls-10000years I-as-4 long-butt

♪ One More to Celebrate ♪

Though the moxa	*Burn my old soles*
burns my sandal soles and	*and rake me over the coals,*
brooms stand high,	*1000 falls are good!*
A thousand falls will pass	*Stand a broom upon its butt*
before I'll say good-bye!	*I'm staying put: Understood?*

~~~~~~~~~~~~~~~~~~~~~~~~~~~~~

Banzei! I'm Still Here!

Burn that moxa on my sandal soles, stand up that old broom –
'A Thousand Falls!' – I'll be damned if I leave the room at all!

A "thousand autumns ten-thousand years" is a New Year's wish for a long life. I chose *banzei* rather than *banzai* because it sounds more brazen. The broom and moxa are, respectively, obvious and magical charms to get a visitor to move on. In a land where even a countryman like Issa often expressed guilt for living too long, it is refreshing to hear someone of warrior breeding choose life!

Making Light of Age, One's Own & Others

人も見ぬ宿に櫻を植えたれば 花もて寠す身とぞ成りぬる　式部　後拾遺集
hito mo minu yado ni sakura o uetareba hana mote yatsusu mi to zo narinikeri   shikibu   d.1030
people+emph see-not lodge-by cherries+ac planted-if blossoms-having wasting self/body+emp become+fin.

♪ Beauty: Who Says You Can't Take It With You? ♪

*I'd ring my room
With cherry trees that none
will come to view!*

*I'll go to seed w/ my bloom.
Now, that's something new!*

Ringing my cottage   *I plant cherries*
no one calls with cherries   *no man comes to view*
for none to view   *by my cottage*

I'll lose my looks but find   *Something odd, but true –*
my dotage blooms anew!   *In full bloom, I pine away!*

*I ring my hut
With flowering cherries
none will see*

*Merry it is to go to seed
yet keep myself in bloom*

Compare my translation with that by Thomas McAuley and students at Sheffield, the only one I could find on line: *No one at all sees / This house with cherries / Planted so / The blossoms must / Have made me seedy* GSIS #101. It was a *good* guess – without a "yet" or "but" in the original, the relationship between having a bloom and wasting away is not explicit, so it was also necessary – but, I think the *wrong* one. Beautiful blossoms, as a foil, could help bring out the wasted appearance of an old woman, but that adds nothing to the first part of the *waka*, while my readings, two of which borrow the *seed* from McAuley, do. While the larger subject of attractiveness and love and living alone are standard *waka* fare, I believe the paradoxical wit in Shikibu's *waka* make her one of the mothers of mad poems. I added the title and the ♪'s to further bring out the joy wit brings to otherwise dismal subjects. She wrote dozens I, at least, consider mad. We have seen some in this book. I think I read and lost one where she claims to tend a fire so at least the smoke won't desert her – no matter, a *flame* would make a better friend (*hito to hi to*) – a good way to bear the low barometer, for smoke rises straight away and doesn't hang around in clear weather. Then, there is this:

空になる人の心はささ蟹のいかにけふ又かくてくらさむ 式部 同
sora ni naru hito no kokoro wa sasagani no ika ni kyô mata kakute kurasamu
sky/empty-as be man's heart/mind-as-4 spider's how today again hanging live-shall?

> *A man whose mind*
> *is as vacuous as the sky?*
> *He's a Spider:*
> *'Say . . . where might I*
> *spin my little web today?'*

Don't quote me on this one. Empty-hearted is not necessarily the equivalent of vanity with bad implications. Usually, it is more sad-hearted than heartless and implies being in an anxious state for not knowing what to do because of hopeless love or grief or change of circumstance.

> *When you are out of it and your heart is empty as the sky*
> *You just hang on like a spider waiting for what comes by.*

Moreover, while *hito* tends to refer to another person, it may be used as "you" is in English, to refer to anyone, including the poet. McCauley is non-committal, as most translators are: *"An airy / Man's heart is as / A spider's / Web; how should I today / Pass my time?"* Let me assume that "man" generic and apply it to the poet: *When the heart of a woman is empty and floats in the sky // A spider she wonders "How, / today, should I pass my while?"* I will not settle on a reading until I read the comments by Japanese annotators in books I do not have. Regardless, the talking spider is a pretty mad metaphor.

An old woman looks back
老　女　懐　旧

How, overnight,	*Oh, when did my*
did my vernal locks become	*willowy young hips become*
a snowy fright	*locked in a hump*
& the lithe hips of a willow	*While my vernal locks took on*
a hunch-backed old widow?	*too much snow for salt to melt?*

いつのまにみどりの髪も雪つみで柳ごしさへかくかゞみぬる 宿屋めし盛
itsu no ma ni midori no kami mo yuki tsumi de yanagigoshi sae kagaminuru 徳和 1785
some time-in green/dark hair too snow-piled-with willow-hips even bent-over-become

Were this poem by Yado no Meshimori not in a collection of *kyôka*, would it be mad? Male poets often wrote as women and there are accepted *waka* combining two willow metaphors. Perhaps the hips and the hair together did it. If you will pardon an advertisement for a 740-page book that has found less than a hundred readers in its first year of life, readers interested in mad poems about old women might do better to read the crazy old haiku – some I'd call *kyôku* – in the *ubazakura* (Babushka Cherry) chapter of my *Cherry Blossom Epiphany* (2007).

Is Old Age Minutely Described Mad In Itself?

皺はよる ほくろはできる 背はかがむ あたまははげる 毛は白うなる　横井也有
shiwa wa yoru hokuro wa dekiru se wa kagamu atama wa hageru ke wa shirô naru yayû
wrinkles-as4 gather warts-as4 appear back-as4 bends head-as4 balds hair-as4 white becomes 1702-83
..

Wrinkles gather, while moles swarm down bent backs,
hair turns white or falls out: your head looks waxed!

◎　◎　◎　◎　◎　◎　◎　◎

手は震う 足はよろつく 歯はぬける 耳は聞こえず 目はうとうなる　同
te wa furuu ashi wa yorotsuku ha wa nukeru mimi wa kikoezu me wa utô naru ditto
hnds-as4 shake lgs-as4 wobble teeth as4 slipout ears-as4 hear-cn't eyes-as4 dim becme

Hands shake, legs wobble, teeth fall out & your ears
no longer work, while eyes now catch little but tears.

◎　◎　◎　◎　◎　◎　◎　◎

よだれたらす 目しるはたえず 鼻たらす とりはずしては小便もする　同
yodare tarasu mejiru wa taezu hana tarasu torihazushite wa shôben mo suru ditto
drool drips eyesoup-as4 ends-not nose drips let-one-out-when-as4 pissing too

Your mouth drools, your eyes water and your nose runs on;
No sooner is a fart let out, when it's time to take a piss.

◎　◎　◎　◎　◎　◎　◎　◎

又しても同じ噂に 孫じまん 達者じまんに若きしゃれ言
mata shite mo onaji uwasa ni mago jiman tassha jiman ni wakaki sharekoto
again doing even same gossip & grandson boastng hale boastng & young cooltalk

Again & again, the same small talk, boasts about grandsons,
your health and on your tongue the cool slang of the young!

◎　◎　◎　◎　◎　◎　◎　◎

くどうなる 気短になる 愚痴になる 思いつく事皆古うなる
kudô naru kimijika ni naru guchi ni naru omoitsuku koto mina furuu naru
long-winded/boring become tmpr-shrt bc cmplainng bc think-up things all old bc

You grow long-winded, short-tempered, full of complaint,
and all that comes to mind you think is new – it ain't!

◎　◎　◎　◎　◎　◎　◎　◎

身にそうは頭巾襟巻杖眼鏡たんぽ温石しゅびん孫の手

mi ni sou wa zukin erimaki tsue megane tanpo onjaku shubin magonote
bdy-w/ accompny-as4 hd-wrp scrf cane eyeglsss hotwtrbttle warmstone peepot bckscrtchr

Your body has a retinue: head-scarf, muffler, cane, eye-glasses,
hot water bottles, heated stones, chamber pots, back-scratchers.

◎　◎　◎　◎　◎　◎　◎　◎

宵寝朝寝昼寝ものぐさ物わすれそれこそよけれ世にあらぬ身は
yoine asane hirune monogusa monowasure sore koso yokere yo ni aranu mi wa yayû
evning sleep noonsleep sloth forgtflness tht esp. (is) good wrld-in-not self/body-as4

Naps before & after noon, sloth & forgetting what you do;
All of this is quite alright, for the world forgets us, too!

These seven 31-syllabet didactic poems for old people (「老人へ教訓の歌の事」) in Yayû's *Ear Bag* (耳袋 not his well-known *Quail Bag* 鶉衣) written at the behest of an aged acquaintance (望月老人がもたらした狂歌) were netted while searching for *kyôka* by this *haikai* poet with a warm and always wise wit. I hoped to find more of his *kyôka*, but had to make do with these marginally mad examples. To my mind, only the last is a full-blown *kyôka*, though I worked to make others *seem* mad/der. Compare the gloss to the translation, you'll see. A note re. items in the penultimate poem: the "back-scratcher" is a "grandchild's hand" (*mago-no-te*) and the heated stone (*onjaku*) was a portable heater.

温石のさめぬうち也わかなつみ　一茶
onjaku no samenu uchi nari wakanatsumi issa 文政一
warmingstone's cool-not-while becomes, youngreen picking

I'll keep plucking　　　　　　　　　　*My plucking rules*
'til the heater-stone cools:　　　　　*Young greens, look out until*
my na-tsumi rules　　　　　　　　　　*my heat-stone cools!*

なかいきは恥おほけれと孫彦を かかむせなかにおひの幸　未得　吾吟我集
nagaiki wa haji ôkeredo magohiko o kagamu senaka ni oi no sachi   mitoku 1649
long-life-as-for shames many but grdchld/ren+acc bent bck-on ages/piggyback happiness

A long life may bring much shame, but don't tell my back,
Bent for the happiest burden of age – a grandchild in fact!

Issa tried to be cheerful but he was less fortunate than Mitoku.

負けて立れぬ程のとしを拾ふ哉　一茶
makete tatarenu hodo no toshi o hirou kana issa 文政 6.11
losing/bearing stand-cannot amount years+acc gather!

I've picked up so many years of late,
I cannot bear my own weight!

Love it or Leave it, You Better Believe it: *Old Age*.

朝な夕な 杖にも物をくはすべし つかふとなれば 子にはまされり 本阿弥光悦
asa na yû na tsue ni mo mono o kuwasu beshi tsukau to nareba ko ni wa masareri honami kôetsu d.1637
morn evry eve evry cane-to thing+acc feed-ought usng-whenitcomesto child-to-as4 exceeds 狂歌五十人一首

The Honest Patriarch

Morning & night
my cane, just like the rest,
deserves a treat!

When it comes to usefulness,
it beats my kids hands down.

Morning & night
my cane deserves to be fed
just like the rest

No, more! It's a damn sight
more useful than you kiddo!

"Just like the rest" suggests the poet fed not only his children but relatives. Were not Japanese famously gentle with children – in the 16c, the Jesuits, themselves progressive educators, noted how Japanese spared the rod with good results – I might have given the cane *a taste of their hides* as there is a hint of "beating" in the verb *kuwasu*, "have eat." Here are a couple by the delightful monk Ryôkan.

竹森の星彦左衛門方へ杖を忘れて
老が身のあはれを誰に語らまし 杖を忘れて帰る夕 良寛 1758-
rô ga mi no aware o dare ni kataramaji tsue o wasurete kaeru yube ryôkan -1831
aged body's wretchedness+acc who-to speak-ought cane+acc forgetting return evening

To whom can I
relate the woeful state
of growing old

Returning at nightfall, late
because you lost your cane!

Oh, where to find
someone to share the pain
old geezers know!

Like losing your damn cane
and limping home alone!

老いらくを誰がはじめけん教へてよいざなひ行きてうらみましものを
oiraku o da ga hajimeken oshiete yo izanai yukite uramimashi mono o ryôkan
old-age/leisurely-age+acc started? teach! leading-going complain/begrudge would! d.1831

Our dotage –
Who kindly invented it?
Teach me,

So I can go give him
a piece of my mind!

Who came up
with the sage idea of
easy old age?

Someone, tell me and he
soon shall hear from me!

The second is wittier than the first *if* you recognize it as a take-off of the *Kokinshû waka* by Monk Sosei wishing to know the whereabouts of the *Wind* (p.195). Still, my favorite takes on old age in Japanese literature are 1) Issa gnawing a block of *tôfu* with his sole remaining tooth – or was he down to 100% gum? on Tooth-hardening Day and 2) Yayû's gracious *haibun* (essay in a *haikai* – pun-filled, hyperlogical – style) in *Uzuragoromo*, or *Quail Robe*, on the bright side of senile dementia, such as making do with few books, for they may be reread over and over with equal pleasure once your memory is shot.

除夜 鬼はうち福をは外へ出すとも 年ひとつゝよらせすもかな 雄長老
oni wa uchi fuku o ba soto e dasu to mo toshi hitotsu zutsu yorasezu mo gana yûchôrô 16c
devil-as4 strike⇒within happiness-outside putout even year one-by-one approach do-not wish

(New Year's Eve)
<u>Who needs another?</u>
vene mal, sale bene

Could it but keep   *Could it but keep*
one year from being added   *one year from being added*
to my own, I would   *to mine, by my troth*
Welcome the bad & chuck   *I'd call in the bad spirits*
good luck from my home!   *& the good I'd send off!*

Could it prevent
one year meant for me
from getting here,
I'd have the demons stay
& send happiness away!

Yet another outrageous idea from the pre-Edo *kyôka* master, Yûchôrô. The ritual, throwing parched beans out windows and doors to take the bad with them, or bean costumed *demons* to keep them out, and tossing others, sometimes eaten, inside to keep the 福*luck/wealth/happiness*, was performed on the Japanese solar Spring, or year's end – it varied over the centuries. Here, it is the latter. Better bad luck than no ~~luck~~ life at all! Another with said beans *and* a cane:

鳩の杖つくまていろハかわらじな たがひに年乃まめハくふとも 園胡蝶
hato no tsue tsuku made iro wa kawarajina tagai ni toshi no mame wa kuu to mo sono no kochô
dove-cane use/poke/peck-until color/love change-not each-other-w/ year-beans eat-even

Cooing about w/ dove-handled cane, my love for you won't change,
Though we may both eat pecks of those lucky New Year beans.

A cane with a handle carved into a *hato* (dove/pigeon) is *the* typical old (as opposed to a blind or a crippled)-person's cane. Why *this* bird? Probably, because the verb for using a cane, *tsuku,* also means "poke" or "peck," as a bird pecks at feed. And, last but not least, an 18 or 19c *kyôka* about "cane-bamboo" (*tsue-dake*).

降つもる雪の重荷に引かえて人のこしをものはす杖竹 真萩 一萬集
furitsumoru yuki no omoni hikkaete hito no koshi o mo nobasu tsuedake mahagi? c1800
falling-builds snow's weight flipping-back human's hips/back+acc also stretches cane-bamboo

After shaking off the heavy weight of all that snow, the Cane
Springs back to life to help us, white-haired, erect *our* backs!

'Always Young'? Rewind the Spool for the Moon!

いつ見てもさてお若いと口々に　ほめそやさるる年ぞくやしき　朱楽漢江
itsu mite mo sate owakai to kuchiguchi ni homeso ya saruru toshi zo kuyashiki akera kankô
when see ever hey hon+young so mouthsmouths-on praise leaving years regretful d.1800

*Hearing them say, "You look young as ever!" compounds my regret
At giving up another year for a new one, older yet!*

いつ見てもさてお若いとわれは老　朱愚
itsu mite mo sate owakai to ware wa oi

*Hearing them say,
"You look young as ever!"
I feel old today*

I was tempted to put the next poem first, for it is older, but I *like* this one, even though it could be done as a *senryû* with no loss but the season – a big loss if one is a traditionalist, I suppose – as I did.

来んと知りて　はじめ四十路のかとささば　八十路にいたる　老ひ嘆かじ　宗長
↑再現 *kon to shirite hajime yosoji no kado sasaba yasoji ni itaru oi wa nagekaji* sôchô 16c
coming if knew fromthestart 40-xroad's gate barred-if 80x-roads-to reach oldage-as4 lament-not

Had I but barred the gate when forty told me he was on his way I would not be eighty and putting up Old Age today	*Had I locked the door at forty when first I knew it was bound to come, I would not be eighty now and lamenting my old age.*

The responsible translation (right) is by H. Mack Horton (2002). Forty, as we have seen, is the cross-roads of life, when a man officially crosses the ridge to head downhill (pg.174). Link-verse master Sôchô's poem is a take-off on *Kokinshû* (905) poem #895, which I parse to reflect the original:

おいらくのこむとしりせばかどさしてなしとことへてあはざらましを　古今集
oiraku no kon to shiriseba kado sashite nashi to kotaete awazaramashi o anon
old-age's come-would known-if gate barring 'not(in)' replied, met-would-not!

*Had I but known Old Age was coming,
locked the door and said I was out,
You bet, we'd have never met!*

Should we call *O/old A/age* "he" or "it"? R & H go for *"he,"* Horton for *"it"* and, this time, I avoided choice with *"we're."* Sôchô's lead poem is the penultimate of a series of ten lamenting old age. Many *waka* do, not because

Japanese enjoy complaining – a Chinese *forté* – but because a long life makes one seem to be avoiding death, and *that* is embarrassing for a self-consciously brave people. Only the last poem of Sôchô's series strikes me as extraordinary.

繰りかへし同じことのみ老ひぬればしづのをたまき／＼　宗長 再現
kurikaeshi onaji koto nomi oinureba shizu no odamaki shizu no odamaki
repeating same thing/s only age-when/if crude/flax (thread) bobbin/spool

Repeating ourselves	*When one grows old*
we age until we're dead;	*one repeats oneself*
Grow old and e'vry	*over and over*
man spins his thread of flax	*like a spool of flaxen thread*
'the bobbin, the bobbin, the ~'	*like a spool of flaxen thread*

The second translation is Horton's. It is good, so mine is not. He follows his translation of *Tales of Ise* poem #41 (*inishie no shizu no odamaki kurikaeshi mukashi o ima ni nasu yoshi mogana*), mentioned in his notes for another of Sôchô's poems that starts "Like a spool of flaxen thread." I might have translated that *Ise* poem,

In Olden times, spools of flaxen thread spun round & round,
& would a way were found to bring the Past around today!

Two things make Sôchô's poem as mad as the best *kyôka* of the Tenmei era. First, he puts the nostalgic conceit for the (g)olden days (cloth before Chinese brought silkworms?) to use for senile déjà vu (my reading), or the forgetfulness called dementia (Horton's reading), and second, he examples the condition in a sort of verbal concrete poetry. Now, an aesthetic rational 17c old man's *kyôka*.

月故にいとと此世に居たきかな 土の中ては見えしと思へは 貞徳百首狂歌
tsuki yue ni itodo kono yo ni itaki kana tsuchi no naka de wa mieji to omoeba　teitoku
moon because-of more this world-in be-want!/?/: earth-within-as-for see-not so think-when

Because of Luna	*Thanks to the Moon*
I find myself now wanting	*I only want all the more*
to stay around	*not to leave soon*
When I think I won't be	*When I'm buried the earth*
viewing her underground.	*will only come between us.*

Moon-viewing was de rigor at temples because the moon, *not* of this world, stood for non-attachment, the merciful light/law of Buddha and, partly from Shintô, a mirror of self-reflection & the serenity of a pure mind without greed. Old people who were ready to go, so to speak, were particularly close to it. What could be more perverse than for this to change to affection that shackled the moon-viewer to this earth? ♪ One paradox does not a mad poem make, but there is more. Teitoku plays with ancient poetic trope, *waka* where sad lovers profess a strong desire to be put out of their misery, but for the fact that doing so would remove all possibility of ever winning the would-be lover or meeting again.

Displeasure in the Pleasure Quarters *De Arinsu*

しばらくも 夜床に尻をすえざるは わが妻ならぬ いな妻ぞかし　朱楽かん江
shibaraku mo yotoko ni shiri o suezaru wa waga tsuma naranu inazuma zokashi　akera kankô 1785
awhile+emph nightbed-in butt+acc set-not-as-for my wife/lover-becomes-not lightning/no-wife 徳和

(No wonder I thunder!)

*Ne'er in my bed
long enuf to sleep, the girl
called Lightning;*

*Here I am for a screw,
And all she does is bolt!*

The original, unEnglishable though relying on only one pun, describes a popular woman in the pleasure quarter moving back and forth between rooms with two customers not as a *tsuma*, or *mate/wife*, but *ina-zuma*, meaning *lightning* and usually written 稲妻 the first character, meaning *"rice"* (when still on the plant), the second "wife," but, here, with the former written phonetically the *ina* could mean not/none and the lightning becomes "non-mate/lover." There are many prefaces of negation in Japanese, but this is most fitting here because the woman appearing and disappearing evokes the game of peek-a-boo, *ina ina boh!* in Japanese! I tried an extended metaphor: *"She is no mate / of mine who fast as lightning / bolts my bed // Leaving me and my thunder / without even a rain date"* a slang end run: *To a Popular Harlot // Do your duty / move your booty but don't go / room to room // I'm talking, it's good to be hot! / But, don't go walking, it's not!* wordplay of a type closer to the original *Quick as a bolt / from the blue – she'll do me / She'll do you // Eighty percent of lover / is* over: *we are through!* All bore. Sometimes, one pun beats a hat trick. To match the poet, one must forget details.
..

*Will, my Beau
my gigolo, why must you
so quickly go?*

*Slow down, give me a Kiss!
I'll not pay Will o' the Wisp.*

Sex change and all, a clever *aka* is not as fresh as a good pun. I was almost ready to ditch the damn poem when that *bolt*, doubling as noun+verb, came from the blue and gave me my admittedly flawed, but at least *fun* lead translation. The reader might wonder how a grown man could waste so much time on one punning poem. *I do.* It is because I find Akera Kankô's puns the most effective in all *kyôka* and wondered *why* (See his year's end poem, p.234). I think it comes down to relaxing the reader's guard with a combination of easy language and familiar stereotypes and only then finishing him off with a knock-out pun as slick and unexpected as an upper-cut to the chin in the last *ku*. Here is a mad poem charming for it puts the Pleasure Quarter into the mind's ear:

いぎりすも ふらんすも 皆 里なまり 度々来るは いやでありんす 筒井蠻渓
igirisu mo furansu mo mina sato namari tabitabi kuru wa iya de arinsu tsutsui 1788-1859
english & french & all (their)country's dialect sometimes coming-as-4=brothel yucky is+ rankei

Displeasure in the Pleasure Quarters

The Igirisu and the Furansu all have accents they'd share
What nerve to dare talk to us like that de arinsu!

This is one of those poems that ensure translation *never* fully replaces learning the language yourself. I lost the best pun, *come* ⇒*brothel* (*kuru wa* = *kuruwa*), and had no choice but to keep the superb ending, *arinsu,* a variation on the formal way to say "is/are," *arimasu,* unique to the women in the Yoshiwara Pleasure Quarters. The women had not just an argot, but special endings for verbs of which this is the best known. The poem, made by the old man who served as administrator of Nagasaki when Japan was opened by Perry, pokes fun at the women, themselves noted for unique ways of speaking, supposedly upset to be visited by foreigners with *their* odd speech. Tsutsui Rankei probably got the idea from the similarity between the end of the word *Furansu* (France/French) and the Courtesan's *arinsu.* After all, he also dealt with the Dutch and Russians and they are not mentioned. In the late-16c and early-17c, some of the foreign men in Japan – especially the English and the Dutch who were there for trade rather than religion, played around as far as the authorities let them, but there were no English or French around in the heyday of mad poetry. This mid-19c mad poem comes as a tail wind. Because Japanese had long studied Dutch, they had their work cut-out for them to learn the other European "dialects" – when you consider the difference between Indo-European and Ural-Altaic language, dialect is not far from the truth! The word used in the poem *sato-namari*, means *country/town /local pronunciation* or *accent*. It can include the nuances of dialect, too, but the focus being on *sound* here, I felt *accent* better than *dialect*. English lacks the right generic term for a popular sound-centered local lingo, as our good words for such are all specific to *particular* dialects, eg. Scottish *brogue*, Southern *drawl* and Midwest *twang*. Ah, the *de* before the *arinsu*. It is a part of speech that is meaningless but comes before is/are proper or dialectal and, to those of us who speak Japanese, it would sound wrong to drop it, so I left it in my translation.
..

~~~~~~

We do not always recall when we learn words. But I clearly recall learning *arinsu* very late in my studies, after I had already written half a dozen books in Japanese. Coming across it in disconnected references from time to time, I was caught by its similarity to "Alice" (*Arisu* in Japanese) and thought it stood for a fantasy-induced way of speaking by teenage girls who liked *Alice in Wonderland!* Absurd? Well, *yes* and *no*. They have pig Latin in Japan. And, the magazines were full of stories about the verbal inventiveness of teenage *gyaruzu* who ran circles around the less gifted *adorutozu* and *boizu*. These girls were considered to be the avant-garde of language in Japan (an interesting contrast to Usania, where black English bad boys seem to pioneer tongue and body language). My ignorance has indeed brought me much bliss.

Women of Pleasure in a Mad Poem Portrait Gallery

天の戸もしばしなあけそきぬ／＼のこのあかつきをとこやみにして　遊女はた巻
amanoto mo shibashi na ake so kinuginu no kono akatsuki o tokoyami ni shite yûjo hatamaki 1786
heaven's door too while not-open-not (lovers')parting's this dawn+acc. permanent-dark/bed-into make

Must we part! Open not, not for a while, O Heaven's Door!
Let this dawn stay dark and us in bed for evermore!

This poem accompanied a picture of Yûjo, or Courtesan, Hatamaki, one of 50 poets in the *Azuma Song Kyôka Pocketbook* 吾妻曲狂歌文庫. Hamada's notes say she was real and worked in 大文字屋 The Big Letter, a house owned by a *kyôka* enthusiast and that Yomo no Akara even signed a poem for her, suggesting they met, yet he adds and I concur, the poem seems a bit too fitting to be true and may be *a ringer*. There are two more courtesans in the book. Yûjo Utahime 遊女歌姫, better known as a writer than Hatamaki, laments that she would not have responded to the appeal to donate her old mirror to make a temple bell had she known how hard its absence would strike her heart. The poem is competent, but aside from one pun using a bell term is boring. As her name is Courtesan Singing Princess, I suppose the words would not make much difference if they were sung. The third courtesan depicted may be fictional. Tamago no Kakujo, literally reads Egg-scent-a-while-woman and sounds like *Egg-squaring woman*, which makes her dangerously beautiful, for the proverb the editors call a riddle (too easy if you ask me) calls sincerity coming from such a beauty a square egg. The poem:

染めるやらちるやら木々はらちもない　いかに葉守の神無月とて　玉子香久女
someru yara chiru yara kigi wa rachi mo nai ikani hamori no kannazuki tote tamago no kakujo
dye? fall? tree-tree-as-for unsettled, how leaf guards/guarding's gods-not-month+emph.

Should I get dyed? Will I fall? Just what is each tree to do?
Who keeps the leaves until God-gone month is through?

Is more dyeing, or falling in store? How unsettling for the trees!
In this month the gods are out, I guess there are no leaf gillies.

I suppose if we thought of the leaf-keepers as *pimps*, if such a name can be used for men in the employ of pleasure quarter *brothels*, if such a name can be used for a place far more cultured than anything we are familiar with, this may have something to do with the life of a *courtesan*. Who knows. Regardless, it is a good take on the sloppy disarray of early winter, found both between and within trees – which are, after all, super-organisms, only seeming to be individuals, as first pointed out by Erasmus Darwin – when some leaves are still turning while others take the dive. But, to return to the Azuma Pocketbook, there was a picture of what I first thought a Heian era woman, for her tiny piglet of a nose and scalp-high eyebrows. But, no, she was only the mask of pudendic ugly Happiness Otafuku お多福 worn by a male Usurious Scalper,高利刈主. The *kari* meaning prune/shave/ mow/scalp is a homophone for "borrower." We shall skip *his* poem.

And, finally, we find one real woman who is *not* a courtesan, Tonajo 圖南女. She is pictured with a sweet poem on a clam pearl-like moon, sea/see-weed and clam-soup of the sipping type served at wedding receptions. The sipping may hint at kissing. What strikes us as odd is that the two best Tenmei era female poets are missing. One is poet-editor Akera Kankô's better half, Fushimatsu no Kaka, the Unkempt Wife. Here is her representative poem:

よしや又うちは野となれ山桜 ちらずはねにもかへらざらなん　節松嫁嫁
<u>yoshi</u> ya mata uchi wa <u>no</u> to nare yama-zakura chirazu wa ne ni mo kaerazaranan kaka
stop/enuf!/fine again home-as4 field becums mt-chrry falls-not-as4 root=sleep-2 retrn-not

After the deluge, cherry petals find their roots: Sow your wild oats
But remember where you reap: Dear, come home to sleep!

~~~~~~

After the deluge, cherry petals find their roots: So, too, you
May sow your wild oats but, dear, come home to sleep!

..
One could not imagine a more tolerant yet pointed and witty way to remind hubby it was high time to return from the Pleasure Quarters. The most complex yet effective multiple-style word-play *kyôka* by a woman I know of, *After the Deluge* equals the same by any of the top male *kyôka* masters. Even a creative re-creation cannot capture most of the following: 1) *Yoshino*, famed for cherry blossom-viewing and hence the "pillow" or epithet for the same, is split to be reconstituted by the reader. 2) *Yoshi* in the toponym is *fine* or *lucky*, but, here, means *"Whoa, there!"* 3) *mata uchi-wa* first means *"again, our house ~ 又、家は,"* suggesting this is not the first time Kankô holed up in the Quarters, *and* is *matauchi* 又内, a retainer for an important personage, *i.e.,* the poetess in respect to her husband. 4) The courtesans in Yoshiwara were called *sakura* (cherries = the blossoms). 5) The *~no* ending the split Yoshino, means *field,* which, with the *mountain* forms an idiom, *no to nare, yama to nare,* literally, *become fields and become mountains, i.e. desert* or *wilderness* in the metaphorical (*desolate*) sense of the words. Usually meaning "after me/us the deluge," here it means "Do *you* mean to abandon and hence devastate my heart and our home?" The second *nare (become)* in the proverb is skipped, as 6) the mountain turns into a *mountain-cherry* clarifying what Yoshino only suggested, her husband was with courtesans and, then 7), the mountain as a mountain falls moot and we have *cherry-blossoms* saying: *falling, they return to their roots*, with *root* a homophone of *sleep,* both *ne,* giving us the punch-line of her message, which we might loosely translate as *"Save the last dance for me!"* 8) And, finally, the poem echoes the sentiment of a Chinese poem. ♪ Mind you, with all this, the poem reads naturally in Japanese. It seems neither childish nor outlandish as my sorry translation makes it. Let me add that the Pleasure Quarters was not only a place to screw. Men went there for entertainment. In literate Japan, this meant poets were in high-demand. Despite the poem in the last chapter, Kankô probably husbanded his privates for his brilliant *Unkempt Wife* while exhibiting his talent to all.

★ W/in the year, a supplement to Azuma added the other brilliant & better known female *kyôka* master, Chie no Naishi, *Little Ignoramus* & her spouse Moto no Mokuami. They were out of town. Her picture is the coolest in the anthology. The Unkempt Wife? *Still not in it.*

Lice Rosaries Were No More Sorobans than Flies

世をいとふ身にもしらみはすみ染の衣のたまご数珠つなぎ也　良村安世 1785
yo o itou mi ni mo shirami wa sumizome no koromo no tamago juzu tsunagi nari　yoshimura yasuyo
world+acc hating self/body-to-even lice-as-4 charcoal-robes' eggs rosary-link is 徳和後哥萬歳集

寄虱　　　　　　　　　　*Nitpicking Catechism*　　　　　　　　　釈教
　　　　　　　　　　　　(for our lousy monks)

*Even those men
who leave the world behind
keep their lice:*

*Tiny eggs on charcoal sleeves
make the perfect prayer beads.*

The original by Goodtown Peaceworld has a pun on lice *living=sumi* and *charcoal=sumi* which I dropped, instead coming up with *keep* to better oppose the *leave*, which in the original is *hate*. It also benefits by closing with an idiom. *Juzu-tsunagi*, or prayerbead-connection can mean that *all are tied together*, like prayerbeads on their string or wire. And, this being tied together alludes to being attached, which is, of course, the opposite of the Buddhist ideal of nonattachment.

Men & Lice

*Even our monks
who abandon the world
are knit together*

*Seam by seam, how nice –
prayer-beads, eggs of lice!*

Lacking space for the *charcoal* – a *grey*, cheaper to dye than black, hence not a luxury, and suitable for funerals (for a long discussion, see item #1-30 in *Topsy-turvy 1585* (2004)) – robes because I added "seam by seam," I substituted the wearer: "monks." *Prayer beads,* a description, not word, *is* lousy. If the Christian word *rosary* is not *noli me tangere* for you in Buddhist translation, use it. So why, when good translation is nigh impossible, did I do this poem? Because I first misread, or rather imagined the lines of nits meant a *soroban, i.e.,* abacus, and mistranslated accordingly. Then, not wishing to let my effort go to waste (In that, I follow Mother Nature's evolution), I redid the translation *and,* now, will show you my mistranslations, the first of which was titled *Nitpicking Catechism* (for our lousy monks) and went *Even those men / who leave the world behind / keep their lice // Tiny eggs on charcoal sleeves / remind us of abacus beads*. It was followed by yet another mistranslation with a neat explanation:
..

*In Japan, every household had an abacus and it pretty much stood
for keeping one's secular accounts. Unlike the case in the Occident,*

the wife was usually the treasurer and the accountant. Some Buddhist temples, like some Christian monasteries, prospered, so there must have been monks wielding sorobans –

Buddhist Economics

Even the monks who hate the whole world love their lice
Lined up like counter beads upon their robes, very nice!

One thing that drew me to lousy poems was a memory of a New Year's *ku*, by Issa that is about as mad as a *kyôku* can be. It has the gem, or egg-like spring, *i.e.,* New Year, rise and rebound like a breaker – *shirami* sounds a lot like *shira-nami*, "white-caps" – or a raw gem in a tumbler, yet hatch like or, rather *into* lice, or maybe, by another pun, *breed* lice (あら玉のとし立かへる虱哉 *aratama no toshi tachikaeru shirami kana*). While I cannot come up with a decent translation, I cannot get that *ku* out of my mind, as it was the first *extremely* odd one – what I now call a *kyôku* – I encountered. Because nonsense needs space to rationalize itself – by rhyme or reason – it is harder to do well in 17-syllabets than 31 and much harder to translate, though all my books of translated haiku include *some* that work in English. A naturalized translation of the chapter lead:

Natural Rosaries?

Even old monks who spurn the world of woe
keep nit-picking while they live here below
fingering those tiny eggs

There is something intrinsically comical about people pushing or pulling their rosaries (details in item #5-18, *Topsy-turvy 1585* ibid). Involving less clearly human qualities than prayer, Issa, living in a country without raccoons (who would love the real thing the most) even associated them with the busy hands of flies:

堂の蠅数珠する人の手をまねる 一茶
dô no hae juzu suru hito no te o maneru issa
prayer-hall fly/ies rosary-rubbing peoples' hands+acc copy

Temple flies
copy the hands of people
rubbing rosaries.

So many *nice* flies and lice! Here is something *meaner* from the 16c mad-poet Yûchôrô. The *biku* in the *bikuni* (harlot "nuns") explodes in an allusive triple pun:
..
そり落しかしら虱はなきとても臍より下はいかにお比丘尼 雄長老 古今夷曲集
soriotoshi kashira shirami wa naki totemo heso yori shita wa ikani obikuni yûchôrô d.1602
shaved off head lice-as-for not even navel morethan below-as-for howmuch wear/fear/many=bikuni

Though your head was shaved of lice, I shake, bikuni nun,
For down below your navel . . . . I'll bet you have a ton!

Pleasing Fleas, Nice Lice, Lousy Translation.

洗濯せんを案じこそすれ・慣れぬれば 衣の蟲もかはゆくて　新撰犬筑波
sentaku sen o anji koso sure / narenureba koromo no mushi mo kawayukute anon? sôkan?
washing-do+acc considerng accustomd-become-if clothing/robe's bugs evn dear 1667

Humanitarian Dilemma

To wash or not to wash *my clothes: what shall I do?*	*Yes, even your laundry* *presents a real problem;*
You grow used to *even the lice on your robe* *and find them cute!*	*Living with bugs* *in his robes, a monk can* *come to love them*

This is early *haikai,* perhaps by Sôkan (16c). Unlike *kyôka,* usually printed in a single line, the lines are separate. While the form suggests poems by two poets, it could be a one-man mock link-verse (*hitori-renga*). The first part poses what amounts to a question: *What is the problem? Is someone too poor to pay?* Being *used to clothing* is trope for growing fond of one's lover/wife that goes back to ancient Japanese poetry, so the switch to *bugs*, i.e. lice, make this a parody not of a specific poem but of the romantic tradition. Did 14-17 *haikai* love riddles more than 17-14 *kyôka* because more space is needed to answer than to ask? Or was it more because *haikai* teachers used them to solicit replies/students? Regardless, they work well enough in standard *kyôka* format:

Yes, even laundry *puts us in a quandary* *w/ monkish robes!*	*Washing clothes:* *'Tis a dilemma when you* *grow used to 'em.*
As familiarity breeds *Only love for our lice!*	*Yes, with time, some do* *come to adore their lice!*

Note the variety of pronouns in these and the other translations. I recently came across a know-it-all blogger pontificating about pronouns in *hokku. Avoid first-person pronouns! It would not be objective!* That is nonsense, for if we have learned anything from relativity, it is that objectivity is *always* subjective; but, philosophy aside, the closest English can come to the unstated subject of Japanese is "one," which sounds *pretentious*, "you" which sounds *slangy*, passive voice, which *kills poetry*, or no subject, which *sounds like pijin*. The only way to capture all the persons natural to the Japanese language gracefully – unless we go Whitman! – is with multiple translations specifying them. This is not to say all *my* translations are graceful, but to explain that I am no more taking liberties with the original than one who mimics the standard Japanese practice in English, where pronouns are the norm. *There is no accurate translation between exotic tongues.* Anyone who insists *his* or *her* way is *the* way is lost.

庵の蚤かはいや我といぬる也 一茶 文化九
io no nomi kawai ya ware to inuru nari issa d.1827
hut's flea/s cute/dear!/: me-with sleep being/become

My flat's fleas
are sweet because, because
they sleep w /me!

What sweety-pies
the fleas in my flat, viz
they sleep w/ me!

Every time I translate this *ku*, I do so differently. The folksy *kawai*, or *cute, loveable*, is one reason and the other is the way the *ku* is split right up the middle by the *exclamation cum caesura, "ya!"* The implication is that the second half makes sense of the first. Issa may well have read earlier *haikai* on similarly defined lice, but his apparent *kyôku* is a *bona fide* haiku because he combines a seasonal phenomenon (fleas in late summer and early fall) with his miserable life as a lonely single man. This was less than two years from his return to his hometown to inherit half-a-house and what soon followed, gaining a spouse. People who accuse him of anthropomorphism or being maudlin about bugs do not know what it is to be poor and lonely (they come together) for a long time: they do not *get* the blues. Unless they, like me, have lived with cats in a room built into damp ground with *tatami* unreplaced for many years toward the end of a hot summer, they think he is kidding about fleas *jumping out to "greet" him by the door* (something mentioned in another *ku*). I can attest to it *all*. Day after day, my most sensitive cat friend would not even approach the front door until I walked in and took the assault on stinky socks I quickly tossed into soapy water with the most ravenous fleas, opened the windows wide and got the fans going.

部屋渡る竹馬もがな蚤地獄

Flee Flea Hell?
I'd take a pair of stilts
to cross my room!

蚤虱器用さ生んだ人の親

Lice and fleas,
Godparents of a species
dexterity bore!

Perhaps, some day, I will find time to collect (and edit) the thousands, or tens of thousands of *ku* I have written in Japanese. Hundreds concern fleas. I have not had the good fortune to experience *lice*, but a friend recently wrote me of his assault by bedbugs, endemic in New York, and when I told my mother, who has a large, unpublished corpus of body words, including what was in the 15c called a *bodelouse*, she sent me the following anonymous ditty, dated 1700. It is remarkably close to Issa's take on fleas. It is in a section of her book in-progress, *In Bed With Shakespeare*, called *Love Bugs:*

There's no friend
like a bosome friend,
said the old man when
he pulled out a louse.

Things to Show Off, Things to Lose, Things to . . .
しる人にひけらかしてもよき物は 軍場でとる大将のくび 読人不知 私可多咄
shiru hito ni hikerakashite mo yoki mono wa ikusaba de toru taishô no kubi anon. tk 参 34
know-person-to show-off even good thing-as-for battle-place-at take captain's head 1659

Things that are
fine to show-off to all
that you know –

If taken in battle,
The head of a foe.

This is a parody not of a poem but of a genre of literature. We are talking about what might be described as *editorial listing*, the tasteful description and grouping of things, as an exercise of aesthetic discrimination found in *The Pillow Book* (c.1000) of *Sei Shônagon*. Chinese literati spiced up their historical anecdotes and criticism with occasional lists of types of things, usually of a pedagogical or moral value, but until this brilliant, sassy woman – seeing the way she criticized rich men for marrying ugly women, declared that only handsome men should preach because if women failed to pay attention to the catechism they might sin, or that hairy dark-skinned people should not nap in the daytime in the summer time lest they disturb the eyes of anyone who happened by, etc. – some would call her *a diva* – until this brilliant, sassy woman laced her beautifully written miscellany with scores of these charming lists, the practice of listing, 物は尽くし *mono wa tsukushi* in Japanese, was not a genre, or since it would be centuries before books of nothing but listing appeared, a *potential* genre. I have quoted much from Sei Shônagon's listing in a number of books (most recently, in the extended foreword of *The Woman Without a Hole*, where I relate it to the psychology of collecting as it relates to the attraction and appreciation of hyper-short-form poetry), so I will not repeat here, other than to say that we feel a woman's sensibilities at work, whether in the *adorable things* (eg., "a face drawn on a melon") or *dirty things* (eg., "the inside of a cat's ear"). While the category of thing given in the *kyôka* matches Sei Shônagon's style, the thing mentioned is another matter.

"Uncomfortably Gross Things"
むさき物のしな／＼ より

If you check out
what this thing called love
really consists of

Two holes is all you'll see:
One for shit & one for pee.

恋といふそのみなかみを尋ぬれば はりくそ穴の二つなりけり 尤之草紙
koi to iu sono mi nakami o tazunureba bari kuso ana no futatsu narikeri tokugen?
love/desire as say its body/realness content+acc visit/ask-if piss shit holes two are/become!

"Our" dear potty-mouth Saint Augustine did better to put our birth-place *between* those likewise described places, as that implies a *third* hole. But Japanese have long given all humans *nine* holes. For a woman, this requires the vagina and urethra to be conflated, or defined to start with the labia and encompass both. Personally, I go with the metaphysical poets who would have women "put on perfection," *i.e.,* add "0" for a 10. Be that as it may, the awful poem is here because 1) It is found in a Pseudo-Pillowbook尤之草紙 (*Mottomo no Sôshi,* the name puns *visually* on an earlier parody of Shônagon's *Pillow Book*, 犬枕, *Inu Makura,* or *Dog Pillow;* 2) It may be by Teitoku's disciple Tokugen, the writer+editor of said book which was presented to the 14 year-old prince of Japan; but 3) the poem later appeared in Akara's first *kyôka* anthology 満載狂歌集as "possibly by Ikkyû." While it is an in-your-face epigram in the shocking style of Ikkyû, I doubt it is, for he was, shall we say, at home below the belt. Here is another Pseudo-Pillow-book poem found at the tail of the listing of *"Things that deceive"* (偽る物のしなじな). Title it *In Praise of Deception:*

こゝろざしある方よりの偽りはよの誠よりうれしかりけり tokugen?
kokorozashi aru kata yori no itsuwari wa yo no makoto yori ureshikarikeri
solicitude has party-from's deception-as-for sincerity-more-than delightful+emp

..

Trickery & lies devised w/ good intent are far from Troy:
All the Truths in the World bring us but Half the Joy!
~~~~~~~~~~~~~~~~~~~~~~~~~~~~~~~~~
From one who does so from kind intent, Trickery & Lies
Stand to make us happier than Truth without Surprise.

I tried to improve this poem, which is more a moral or instructive *waka* (道歌&教訓歌, respectively) than a mad poem, by working in some clever angles, but, truth be said, the fact it teaches what none need to learn dooms it from the start. Here is a *haikai* example of a type of listing we may call *"While X, Y,~"* things:

無念ながらもうれしかりけり さりかぬる老妻を人にぬすまれて 16c
munen nagara mo ureshikarikeri sarikanuru rôsai o hito ni nusumarete inu-tsukuba
chagrin/fury while even happy+emph // leave-cannot old-wife+acc person-by stolen

A thing that brings regret, but greater joy:
The old wife you'd divorce flees w/ a boy!

No "thing" is found in the original, also translatable, *"It makes me furious, yet also makes me glad / My old wife who wouldn't leave, stolen by a younger lad!"* (*lad* and *boy* were born of rhyme, *hito* means *another person*). I wrote "thing" because the *mae-ku,* or first half, is of a type that solicits many possible *tsuke-ku,* or caps. The best-known example (Blyth, Carter, etc.) of such, from the same Inu (Dog) Tsukuba anthology (1539), is the *"You want to cut; you want not to cut" mae-ku,* followed by replies such as *"Catching the thief, you take a good look & it's your son,"* or, *"A cherry tree's / branch of bloom blocks / the clear moon."* Many of the more general *mae-ku + tsuke-ku* create what amounts to mad listings.

Painful but Funny Things: Riddles & Natural Wit

苦々しくもおかしかりけり・我が親の死ぬる時にも屁をこきて　宗鑑？犬筑波集
kurukurushiku mo okashikarikeri・waga oya no shinuru toki ni mo he o kokite   sôkan?
distressing but funny+emph. – my/your-own parent's dying time-at-even fart cutting

Distressing, yes, distressing, yet it really is a blast –
For a fart to escape you while dad breathes his last!

If the *"want to cut / not to cut"* poem is the most *translated* of the *Inu (Dog) Tsukubashû* (c.1536/9) *haikai*, the most controversial is the above. Why? Because Teitoku (1571-1653) was to take it up and use it to rake dead Sôkan, the editor of the *Inu Tsukubashû* (it is not clear if he actually wrote the poem), over the coals for joking about unfilial behavior at such a time, in the commentary he made for an enlarged reprint of the book. Either, Teitoku, who was broad-minded in most ways, was fixated on the concept of proper filial behavior, or he felt this was a good way to score brownie points with the censors to ensure he could get away with murder in his own *haikai*. Among the eleven more decent responses to the *"upsetting, but funny, too"* (H. Sato) – my *distressing/blast* is forced by the needs of rhyme – draw-verse offered by Teitoku, we have *"A woman falls in public revealing her privates"* (*hitonaka de korobu onago no mae dashite*). But to return to the in/famous fart, we may have a critical disconnect here, with Teitoku imagining a stink, which would indeed be a shame and not at all funny at this time, while Sôkan heard something high-pitched and musical, which *would* crack up people *anywhere*. Moreover, as the distress is heightened by the gravity of the scene, the poem could be read as *demonstrating* rather than *contradicting* filial propriety. So, I repeat, Teitoku was full of beans on this one. More from 1536/9:
..

我が身ながらも貴かりけり・目に佛かゝらに神を戴きて
waga mi nagara mo tôtokarikeri // me ni hotoke kakara ni kami o itadakite
my/own body being-while noble+emph // eye/s-in buddha head-on god/s+acc receive

Though only my body, it is precious even bare –
With Buddha/s for my pupil/s and Gods for my ha/eir!

ふぐりのあたりよくぞあらはん・昔より玉みがかざれバ光なし
fuguri no atari yoku zo arawan // mukashi yori tama migakazareba hikari nashi
balls/gonads about well+emph. wash-let's / olden-times-from ball/gems polish-not shine none

Let us scrub real well around our cojones, men!
From olden times, it's said, jewels unpolished don't glisten!

In Japanese, the *pupils* are called Buddhas and, as we have seen, *hair* and *god* are homophones. The balls are called gold-gems. When draw-verses are as specific as the above, the first of which comes right after the controversial fart in the *Dog Tsukuba-shû*, it would be hard to come up with a response even if it were not in poetry. That makes such a draw-verse a riddle rather than a prompt. Now, 1499:

小さけれどもかがみこそすれ・えびの子は生まるるよりも親に似て
chiisakeredomo kagami koso sure // ebinoko wa umaruru yori mo oya ni nite 15c
small but bent-over+emph. is // shrimp-child-as-4 born-from even parents resembling

◆ *That things so small could be so bent!* ◆

Like their parents from their birth,
Little shrimps are cause for mirth!

◆ *Thy bending done, an elder from day one!* ◆

My little shrimp, it is so damn apparent –
You're the spitting image of your parent!

まくらの上の駒の足音・宇治橋の下に今夜は泊り舟 竹馬狂吟集
makura no ue no koma no ashi oto // ujibashi no shita ni konya wa tomaribune
pillow/s-above's ponies' foot-sound // uji-bridge's below-at tonight-as-4 mooring-boat

◆ *Do ponies clip-clop o'er my pillow?* ◆   ◆ *Plainly they split, yet stay attached* ◆

Below the Ujibashi Bridge, afloat,   *From head to hoof, don't you know*
Tonight, we're sleeping on a boat!   *how all calves their parents match?*

split even splits etc attached even attached // cow-children's feet-nails-until parents resembling
ware mo waretari tsuki mo tsuitari // ushi no ko no ashi no tsume made oya ni nite
割れも割れたり付きも付いたり・牛の子の足の爪まで親に似て

These three anonymous riddle-like *haikai* (14-17 syllabets in the original) and the next, come from the *Chikuma Kyôginshû* 竹馬狂吟集 (明応八年) a 1499 collection sometimes called the start of *haikai* as a genre. Re. the *first*. In the Sinosphere, *shrimp* – a word Roger Pulvers noted in *The Japanese Inside-out* (1982) beautifully embodies the built-in onomatopoeia of English – because of its rosy color, bent back and snappy movement, symbolizes healthy longevity, the spry elder, fit as a fiddle and as jolly as a tinker rather than shrimpy (see Chaucer's Host to Monk regarding such *shrimpes!*). Re. the *third*, in Japanese, nail and hoof are one word and the 7-7 fakes a hint at sexual matters (*attached* and *thrust*, both *tsuki*).

阿弥陀は波の底にこそあれ・南無といふ声のうちより身を投げて
amida wa nami no soko ni koso are // namu to iu koe no uchi yori mi o nagete 同
amida-as-for waves' bottom-on +emph. is // namu-sez-voice/s'-within-from body+acc throwing

◆ *Amida found on the bed of the sea?* ◆

With the sound 'Namu' still in the air,
They threw themselves into the water.

Namu-amida-butsu, a long name for the Buddha, is how many sutras start. The Jesuits wrote about such suicides where believers in the reality of another world, a paradise, not held back by the rules against suicide found in some religions, filled their sleeves with rocks and merrily stepped off boats into the sea.

㊤ Spooky Creatures – Long Tongue, Rubber Neck ㊤

雨ふりて ふり出だしたる 一つ目の 小僧はろくろ首のうら目か ひかる 百鬼夜狂
#57 ame furite furidashitaru hitotsume no kozô wa rokurokubi no urame ka hikaru 1785
rain falling falling-popsout one-eyed boy-as-for turnery/rubber-neck's other-side? hyakki yakyô

一 つ 目 小 僧

Rain clouds on a jelly roll a one-eyed boy whose tongue feels nice,
Better get a licking than wait for the girl on the far side of the dice!

Before explaining the poem and its translation, a word of background. Japanese, like most people who have not lost their cultural memes to religious or scientific fundamentalism have abundant stories of supernatural creatures, some ancient, some new. Uniquely, perhaps, the relentless drive to *season* culture eventually made ghost-story telling, like fireworks, *a summer activity*, good for a chill! By the 18c, large numbers of people gathered on summer nights to tell scary tales at mansions or temples where, ideally, a hundred candles might be lit and snuffed out one by one after each tale was told. *Why* a hundred, I do not know, but there were a hundred-card sets of monsters and most collections of ghost tale *kyôka* featured the same number (sometimes 100 poems, less monsters; sometimes 100 monsters & more poems). I have read only 60 of the poems in the 1785 *Hundred Goblin/spook/etc. Night Madness* 百鬼夜狂 or *Hyakki Yakyô* (punning 余興 *yokyô*, a *side-show,* as 夜 may also be pronounced) as the person who put it on-line stopped after strange things happened to him! ♪Originally published in 1785, the plates got burned in 1806, but jinxed or not, popular acclaim got it reprinted in 1820.

This one-eyed (often one-legged to boot) boy, studied to death by the great folklorist Yanagita Kunio, behaved differently in different parts of Japan, but was generally thought to have a tongue that could dangle down from his perch in a tree – preferably an old pine – and lick the face of the unwary passerby. While sometimes said to emit a pale light, which may suggest electric activity, that does not explain the *rain* here. Rain, *ame,* is homophonous with all candies that are licked or sucked and presumably draw the boy, though the verb for rain's falling *furi* suggest shaking+dropping something, as done for *dice* (Should I have made him a *snake*-eye boy?), which were utterly unrelated to him until the poet recalled another supernatural creature with a stretching body part – the long-neck woman who could walk up behind you and raise her head up and over and turning face you at the end of a neck as long as a python – had a name with the *sound* for "six" in it. That *rokurokubi*, or turnery-neck 轆轤首 (折々「飛頭蛮」とも) whose pedigree goes way back, boasts a fine idiom for something *long ad nauseum*: 轆轤首の反吐 *rokurokubi no hedo,* or "a turnery-neck's vomit." No *kyôka* can match *that,* but I did manage to squeeze in the second meaning for a "turnery-neck," which is *waiting for something,* as people are said to wait "with their necks outstretched" in Japan. As "wait" is pronounced *matsu* as is the *pine* such boys tended to wait in . . . I go too far; but the above explains *why* I compensated for the loss of pun and background with the explicit *tongue, licking* and *waiting*.

頭なき化物なりとろくろ首みて驚かん おのが体を 再現 狂歌百物語
atama naki bakemono nari to rokurokubi mite odorokan onoga karada wo   ng kyôka -
headless changeling is turnery-neck seeing-surprise-would own body+acc - hyakumono19c
..

> *A headless spook? What in the world comes after me!*
> *Looking back, a long-neck is terrified to see . . . herself.*

This came from a collection with *hundreds* of *kyôka*, including twenty for this *rokuro-kubi*, alone, according to Lafcadio Hearn, who introduced a handful of which only this was at all witty. While Hearn was well aware that his *Goblin Poetry* was the pioneering introduction of "a class of poetry about which nothing little or nothing has been written in English," and he made a game effort to explain the puns in the *kyôka* he translated, his basis for selection was less the poem's wit than its value for explaining his themes/goblins, generally major ones, chosen for their high cultural significance in Japan and China. Rokuro-Kubi, Hearn writes, "is either (i) a person whose neck lengthens prodigiously during sleep, so that the head can wander about in all directions, seeking what it may devour, or (2) a person able to detach his or her head completely from the body, and to rejoin it to the neck afterwards." And, in a footnote, adds "In Chinese mythology the being whose neck is so constructed as to allow of the head being completely detached belongs to a special class; but in Japanese folk-tale this distinction is not always maintained." His translation of the above poem, *"Will not the Rokuro-Kubi, viewing with astonishment her own body (left behind) cry out, 'Oh, what a headless goblin have you become!'"* suggests he put it into the second category, but I think otherwise, in part, because I have yet to find a separate head called a *rokurokubi* (the poem below may be separate but it is not called a *rokurokubi*) and in part because it is more interesting to imagine her scare coming from the perspective making her body seem headless. Hearn, explaining why "whirling neck" and "rotating-neck" are unsatisfactory translations, notes, that this creature has "a neck which revolves, and lengthens or retracts according to the direction of the revolution." Such a spiral would make the neck connecting her body less obvious to her than a straight one she could follow back to her body.

女の首 首ばかり出だす女の髪の毛によれば冷たき象のさしぐし 四方赤良
kubi bakari idasu onna no kami no ke ni yoreba tsumetaki kisa no sashigushi yomo no akara
head only stickout woman's headhair-to approach-if cold ivory's hairpin/shiskabob 夜狂#4

> *A head without shoulders to break her hair looks oddly demure*
> *But you'll miss her limbs up close & her ivory pin? A skewer!*

~~~~~~

> *Just a head is there, a white neck with long hair. Beware!*
> *She nears, you feel a chill . . . her ivory pin could kill.*

Kami suffices for *head-hair,* but young Ôta, Yomo no Akara, stretches it into *kaminoke,* perhaps to add the individual hair character 毛 to aim at the elephant 象 in *ivory* and allude to a saying: *"One woman's hair can pull an elephant,"* having little to do with the plot. Be that as it may, Akara's poem is clearly not as good as the previous one, whose author Hearn (or the original) fails to give.

㊥ Spooky – Bad Trees, Charm-peelers, Doppelgs. ㊥

死ね死ね榎　行人をしねとすすむる古榎これや冥土の一里塚かも　さんわ 百鬼夜狂#45
yuku hito o shine to susumuru furu-enoki kore ya meidô no ichirizuka kamo　sanwa　1785
going people+acc "die!" recommend old hackberry this+emph. afterworld's mile-marker/s

The *"Die! Die! Hackberry,"* or *Shine Shine Enoki.*

The old hackberries whispering "Die! Die!" to the passerby
Do they, like gate-pines, mark our final route and why?

~~~~~~

Are old Enoki that whisper we should 'Die!' really Dutch?
Why else would they want us in the Netherlands that much!

Were old Enoki, a tree I have no image for that my dictionary calls *hackberries*, in out-of-the-way places really so spooky they could be made to say what Issa more understandably puts in the mouth of a raven? Or, is this specter an artificial construction fusing Ikkyû's famous mad poem calling the New Year gate-pines (*kadomatsu*) road-marks to the Nether world (p.36) with *enoki,* later adopted for mile-markers on the highways of Japan? Since, English cannot evoke Ikkyû's poem, my second, mad reading takes one of *our* old names for an Other World neither Paradise nor Hell, nor so Catholic as Purgatory, to create a poem that can not back-translate because Dutch, while synonymous for all Europeans in Japan, were called Hollanders (*orandajin*) and placed in Holland (*Oranda*) rather than the low-lands, the *nether* of which is also North, as north was once *down* in European maps. *Stylewise,* however, my mad reading feels closer to this 'Night Madness' *kyôka* than the more explanatory respectable one.

借錢は化物よりもおそろしき 強催促の壁坐頭かな　搔安　夜狂＃27
shakkin wa bakemono yori mo osoroshiki kowasaisoku no kabezatô kana　kakuyasu
owed-change-as-for changeling morethan terrifying dunning wall troupeboss!

Our petty debts terrify more than any goblins or ghosts –
The strongest one of all? That blind-boss stuck on the wall!

Blind men in Japan were given ranks and licenses, including the monopoly right to lend money. In short, they were loan-sharks, feared not only for their cudgels and supposed short tempers, but the backing of the authorities, who took a cut. As they headed troops of blind women who offered music, massage+extras, they were called troupe-leaders. The reference is to a dunning notice pasted by the outside gate of the borrower's house, where normally one might expect to find charms against bad spirits: "Wall-Troop-Leader." *"Blind-boss"* is my coinage. Some of those charms were talisman depicting fearsome protectors such as dagger demons, but none compared to the *zatô,* as townsmen, especially samurai, were awash in debt in the last quarter of the 18c. The poem itself is barely a *kyôka,* but the inclusion of the dunning notice in a book of spooks is, itself, a fine mad choice, which reflects well on the editing of *Night Madness.* There is also a *spook vs. spook* aspect underlying Kakuyasu's *kyôka,* for there was a well-known goblin called a *fuda-hegashi,* or sticker-peeler, or, considering that most pasted-up notices it removed were talismanic spells or pictures of saints and gods and protective demons, a *charm-peeler.* However, were also pasted up in public places (lavatories, cross-road message-boards, etc.) and they included the advertisement most often addressed by senryû. *Night Madness* #38, 札へがし, *The Charm-peeler,* makes it a matter for *kyôka:*

子おろしの女房と見えて 辻門のこの世の札を へがしぬるかな うら住 同#38
ko-oroshi no nyôbô to miete sujikado no kono yo no fuda o hegashinuru kana   urazumi
child/fetus-dropping wife/lady as seems crossroad's gate's this world's stickers strip!

Like lady aborters who take away our tickets to enter this world
Even at the crossroad gates, the charms are dropped or curled.

Lafcadio Hearn can give you more on charms and these peelers – or *strippers* if you are not afraid of conflating them with clothing-removers – but the example poem he gave was utterly boring, while the above, if I have not unwittingly conjured up a new poem in translation, is a fascinating side-long simile.

離魂病 目の前に 二つの姿 あらはすは水にも月のかげのわづらひ 宿屋めし盛
me no mae ni futatsu no sugata arawasu wa mizu ni mo tsukinokage no wazurai 夜狂#5
eye/s –before two-forms appear-as-4 water-in too moon's affliction meshimori 1785

<u>Doppelgangers</u>

Before your I's, behold, a W appears, & loh!
In the dark water, the moon, too, is not alone.

― ― ― ― ― ― ― ― ― ― ― ― ― ― ― ― ―

Mirror before, mirror behind, the nape in back, she cannot find:
Do her mirrors sees doppel, too? Or, are both faces in her mind!

玉くしけ二つの姿見せぬるは合せ鏡のかげのわずらひ 狂歌百物語 和文再現
tamakushige futatsu no sugata misenuru wa awase-kagami no kage no wazurai ng hyakumono
gem/pretty-comb(box) two forms show-as4 combined mirrors' reflection afflicted   19c
L.H.: *If, when seated before her toilet-stand, she sees two faces reflected in her mirror – that might be caused by the mirror doubling itself under the influence of the Shadow-Sickness.*

Lafcadio Hearn's reading of the second is followed by an apology for the "multiplicity of suggestion impossible to render in translation." He explains that while making her toilet, the Japanese woman uses two mirrors (*awase-kagami*)", one a hand-mirror to show the back of her coiffure – I would add the carefully outlined nape of the neck – upon the larger stationary mirror. Suffering from *rikonbyô*, lit. "separated-soul disease," the woman sees something else. Hearn gives a dozen poems showing the progress of this malady marked by the soul's leaving the body to animate a phantom of a women hurt in love, as it is a vital concept for understanding Japanese literature. He also notes "a suggestion of ghostly sympathy said to exist between a mirror and the soul of its possessor." I would add that both *kage* (*reflection* or *countenance* rather than "shadow" in mod. English) and *wazurai* (a dread disease) are associated with a lunar eclipse.

㊦ Spooky – House-moaners, Mermen, Oil-lickers ㊦

床の間に活けし立ち木も倒れけり屋鳴に山のうごく掛物 狂歌百物語 再現
tokonoma ni ikeshi tachiki mo taorekeri yanari ni yama no ugoku kakemono ng *hyakumono*
alcove-in arranged stand-trees even fell+emph house/roof-groaner-by mt. moving hung pic.

Even the tree in the alcove could not stand the groaning house
While the painted mountain swang and trembled like a mouse!

~~~~~~

Even a fake grove may timber in the alcove when yanari calls
Making the house move mountains, albeit hanging on the wall!

Literally meaning the sound a house makes in an earthquake, *yanari*, in the context of scary stories, means the malevolent gremlin or spirit behind other inexplicable, creaks and groans some houses make at night. The "alcove" is the *space for art* built into all traditional Japanese houses called a *tokonoma*. I hold it in higher account than all Occidental architecture, classical, gothic or modern, combined. *Tachigi* is a standing tree or a stand of trees and combined by *ikeshi* means either cuttings stood up to resemble trees or a miniature bonsai grove which we imagine below the hanging black ink drawing of (probably Chinese) mountain peaks. While the poem is ostensibly about the gremlin, its genius lies in the reversal of the house from a victim to a cause of natural disaster.

板一重下は地獄にすみぞめの坊主の海にでるも怪しな 狂歌百物語 再現
ita hitoe shita wa jigoku ni sumizome no bôzu no umi ni deru mo ayashina! ng *hyakumono*
planks-one-layer below-as-for hades-in charcoal-robed monk's sea-in appearing suspicious
..

With nothing but a plank betwixt us & swimming hell below,
Why should a monk in grey arise from the swelling billows!

Buddhism had its Calvinist side. Hearn mentions the "Buddhist proverb: *Funa-ita ichi-mai shita wa Jigoku* ("under the thickness of a single ship's-plank is Hell"); There are many variants. Issa was able to sit an inch above Hell blossom-viewing in one haiku ("See my *Gleanings in Buddha-Fields*" writes Hearn; see my *Cherry Blossom Epiphany* says I). The *sumi* in charcoal-dyed *sumizome* puns as "living" in hell, like the ocean, hardly the place for clergy. The *ayashii* at the end means dubious and suspicious if not threatening. How so, threatening? Hearn:

> PLACE a large cuttlefish on a table, body upwards and tentacles downwards — and you will have before you the grotesque reality that first suggested the fancy of the Umi-Bôzu, or Priest of the Sea. For the great bald body in this position, with the staring eyes below, bears a distorted resemblance to the shaven head of a priest; while the crawling tentacles underneath (which are in some species united by a dark web) suggest the wavering motion of the priest's upper robe. . . . The Umi-Bôzu figures a good deal in the literature of Japanese goblinry, and in the old-fashioned picture-books. He rises from the deep in foul weather to seize his prey.

Hearn seems to describe a type of *merman* found (and sold, dried) in Japan and some other South-east Asian countries. The reality is various. The sea-monk is more commonly a human head on a marsh-turtle-like creature (not a devilfish). There is also a blind-boss (*zatô*) variety with a moon-lute on his back. Most are depicted not as scary creatures after prey but as spooky but harmless ones that pop up or sink suddenly upon encountering ships. Akara wrote a *kyôka* about them for *Night Madness* (湯錢とは いへども深い 海坊主 成佛してや うかみいづらん 赤良 夜狂 #53 *yusen to wa iedomo fukai umibôzu seibutsu-shite ya ukami-izuran*). I am unsure of the first half and will not translate it (though all too few translators hesitate to translate what they cannot read!), but the second part, *"Who floats up only when you could swear he sunk"* ("swear" is mine) is superb, for it plays on a religious term for death, becoming a Buddha, and an idiomatic pun on a floating=receiving body as becoming enlightened.

..
から傘のあばら骨のみ殘りけり あら肉吸ひの夜の嵐や 光 夜狂#34
karakasa no abarabone nomi nokorikeri arashishi sui no yoru no arashi ya hikaru
chinese umbrella's ribs only remain!/: raw-meat sucking night's storm! *yakkyô* 1785

Chinese umbrellas their bare ribs drying in the fetid air,
Left by a flesh-sucking whirl, a night gale . . . a girl!

This terrifying Night Madness changeling is clearly no goblin; I would call it a *ghoul*. The *shishi-sui,* or meat-sucker, was said to appear in the mountains=wild in the form of a laughing seventeen or eighteen year-old girl who might ask for a light, then, if you let your guard down, bite into you and hold on until she had sucked up all of your flesh. Think of that umbrella as the bones of the victim of a one-girl piranha attack on land. Two metaphors alone a *kyôka* does not make but combined with the alliteration probably took it there.

行灯のあぶらなめてふ化け物の はつと消えたるもゝんがはらけ めしもり
andon no abura-name to iu bakemono no hatto kietaru momongawarake meshimori
lanterns' oil-licker called changeling's poof vanished flying-squirrels 同#21

Oil-lickers so named because they have that trick, vanish quick
As the boogie-man or flames sucked from a lamp wick.

~~~~~~

The oil-lickers lick your lamp, then, oil gone, they vanish, too.
Quick as flying squirrels, poof! Like flames on a dry wick do.

Meshimori describes the 油なめ abura-name, oil or grease-licker, a creature common to all lamp-using people. Even hungry mice could not explain the varying oil consumption. The wit of the original lies in dovetailing a boogieman named for holding the hands together and pretending to swoop in to attack small children while yelling *momonga,* or "flying-squirrel!" with a *kawarake*, an unglazed vessel sometimes used to hold oil. Do both vanish at once? Japanese were familiar with ghost stories where old utensils thrown out in winter cleaning took blood-thirsty revenge on humans! (I wish I could share the illustrations!) Who knows but the oil-licker may be in cahoots with an old oil-pot! While the sudden disappearance is spooky, this was mild for *Night Madness*.

オマケ Spooky – Changeling Clams & Toads オマケ

妻去りも はや潮どきと なりぬれば　二見かなわぬ 湯のなかの貝　出典失名
tsuma sari mo haya shiodoki to nari-nureba futami kanawanu yu no naka no kai l.s.
wife left already already tide-time (it) became-when two-looks stood-not soup-within shell

【蛤女房】

♪ The Clam Wife ♪

His bride's gone.
The time came: they say the tide
waits for no man;

But he should have – looking
at the broth, he lost his clam!

~~The tide came in and he got wet thinking of her, his wife on the lamb~~
~~Two glances toward the broth were two too much – He saw the clam!~~

..
The second translation was my first, made before I read a tale which, in short, goes as follows. *Long ago, there was a man who, fishing one day found a huge clam, which he let go after considering how hard it must have been to grow so long, and not long after a beautiful maiden came and offered to be his bride and she made heavenly soup, never allowing anyone near the kitchen when she made it, but curiosity got the better of the man who peeked and saw her squatting over the pot pissing into it and kicked her out of the house.* A better version of the tale might note that clam soup was sipped at the wedding feast before the groom would dive into his bride's clam, so to speak. But maybe that was taken for granted. According to the explanation at the website where I found this *kyôka* and the tale, an envoi, if that term works for a tale, was eventually added where the man found a huge clam in the soup she had left behind, sacrificing herself for the flavor so to speak. Be that as it may, animals turning into humans out of gratitude are common in Japanese supernatural folklore and the up-until-then happy relationship always end abruptly because a man just cannot help *looking*. The "second glance" (in my crossed out reading, "two glances") is a pun most famously made by Bashô in a leaving poem, a haiku, for hosts in Futami-ura, a place well-known for clams. It also puns on the shell and the content/body as *futa*=cover and *mi*=body. The *kyôka* puts the clam *in* the broth which seemingly normalizes it. Note that this clam-wife, unlike the other goblins, ghouls, phantoms and changelings we have seen, is not a *class* but a singular instance. There *is* a class of supernatural clams, or perhaps a potential behavior (?) of all clams, but it is not a clam-bride or wife or anything sexual (as per the metaphor so beloved of senryû) one might expect. It is something larger and far stranger. The clam is credited for the *fata morgana*, the incredible otherworldly mirages seen near the shore. They are often drawn with big bubbles coming from them. In Japanese art, such balloons are also used to depict sleep and dreams. In both cases, it extends from the nose. I have no source for the next poem (20c?), too.

うそじゃない いつかかならず かえすよと 出世払いの 酒はうましき
uso ja nai itsuka kanarazu kaesu yo to shussebarai no sake wa umashiki l.s.
lie is not sometime definitely return will, yes, success-paying's sake-as-for delicious

【出世螺】

♪ A Triton For Making It ♪

How delicious the sake we drink, swearing that some day,
When we've made it in the world (a sure thing), *we'll pay!*

This, too, would seem a play on an idiom or one-time invention rather than a supernatural *type*. The conch, or triton was blown by the mountain wizards. Like the clam, but more rarely, they were also credited with creating mirages at sea (See the drawing of one sprouting the magical mountain of youth in the pre-matter of *The Fifth Season*: 2007). The shell was called either a *rappagai, trumpet-shell*, or a *horagai, tall-tale/exaggeration/fib-shell*. Here, it would seem the second meaning, perhaps deriving from the wizards' reputation as monteblancs – blow-ing such shells (*hora o fuku*) means telling tales/lies – was combined with *shusse-barai*, the concept of accepting gifts with the promise of paying the other back once one has made it. Unfortunately, English has no good word for being successful, much less for the practice of banking on it ahead of time, so the name of this shell, *shusse-hora*, can only be described and not translated. Again, the netted story is fascinating. The 『絵本百物語』 or "picture-book hundred (supernatural) thing-tales" (by 桃山人 Peach(longevity)-Mountain) mentions such a *shusse* conch that spent three thousand years in the mountains, three thousand in the (hollars?) towns and three thousand in the sea. As that conch, like a hermit crab moves from one world to another, perhaps that helps explain why *shusse* is literally "exit/appear(in)-world," and news of this *longevity* got people to try eating conch to live longer. As that did not work, the name became *hora*, or *lie/tall-tale*. Or so goes the alternate folk etymology! Another from *Hyakumono*:

眼は鏡口は盥のほどにあく蝦蟇も化生のものとこそ知れ 狂歌百物語
me wa kagami kuchi wa tarai no hodo ni aku gama mo keshô no mono to koso shire
eyes-as-for mirrors mouth-as-for tub-amount open toad too changeling/make-up thing know!
..
Looking-glass eyes, & a mouth that opens like a basin,
A toad's a goblin you can look and wash your face in!

Or, in Hearn's words, *"The eye of it, widely open, like a (round) mirror; the mouth of it opening like a wash-basin — by these things you may know that the Toad is a goblin-thing (or, that the Toad is a toilet article)."* The common word for any sort of ghost or changeling is *bakemono* 化け物, but here the toad is called a *keshô* 化生. That is for the homophonic make-up 化粧 (literally change-powder) or toiletry. A parallel translation was tempting but I dropped the pun for a double-verb plus rhyme.

That is all the spooks we have room for. A word on fox possession is in the ♪s.

What the Have-nots Always Have Plenty of

借銭も 病もちくとある物をものもたぬ身と誰かいふらん 松永貞徳
shakkin mo yamai mo chiku to aru mono o   mono no motanu mi to dare ga iu ran
debt/s & disease carry-round so have/ things+contrad.interog. things have-not-body-as who says!

Debt and Disease
Would you call them Nothing!
Who has the gall

To call me and my kind
The Have-nots of the World?

Never poor, the compassionate Teitoku lived from 1570-1653. Many *haikai* poets of his good-natured school lived into their eighties. I don't know if that was true for Lightning Slim who sang that *if it weren't for bad luck* he *wouldn't have no luck at all*, but with that attitude, you can bet that if nothing killed him he would have lived until he died at a ripe old age.

（まづしき人のしたしきにもうとまれければよみてつかはしける）
軒近き隣にだにもとはれねば 貧ほど深き隠家はなし 無銭法師 1636
noki chikaki tonari ni dani mo towareneba bin hodo fukaki kakureya wa nashi musen
eaves-close neighbors'-by even call-not-if poverty as-much deeply hidden house-as-for not

When you're down, you're out.

Even neighbors never call when poverty comes to stay
No mountain retreat keeps the world half so far away!

~~~~~~~~~~~~~~~~~~~~~~~~~~~~~~~~~~~~

Even old neighbors
call and knock no more
upon your door –

No hermitage hides you
like simply being poor.

Even neighbors
take great care pretending
not to notice me:

No hermit lies so deep
in the hills as poverty!

If the second half of this *kyôka* is not an aphorism, it should be. The adverb deeply makes poverty deeply hidden, then the house makes hidden an adjective rather than a verb but aside from that there is no word play and the wit lies solely in the way a concrete, or rather, wooden object is compared to a condition.

住吉と人はいへとも住みにくし 銭さへあればどこも住よし 一休 15c
sumiyoshi to hito wa iedomo sumi-nikushi   zeni sae areba doko mo sumiyoshi ikkyû
☆ Sumiyoshi, literally "living-lucky" is homophonic w/ "living-well" ☆

People call it Easytown but it can be Hardtown;
If you have money, any place at all is Easytown!

Is this only about where we *live?* Ikkyû's nominal but nonetheless meaningful complaint allusively plays upon an old saying that wherever one *dies* is Aoyama (a vernal hill). The *kyôka* would not be out of place in a book of Tenmei *kyôka*. It may postdate Ikkyû (be apocryphal).

偽のある世なりけり神無月ひんほう神は身をもはなれぬ 雄長老 狂歌百首
itsuwari no aru yo narikeri kaminazuki binbôgami wa mi o mo hanarenu yûchôrô 16c
falsehoods are world is+emph gods-gone-world poverty-gods-as-for me/body+acc leave-not

> *No, it is indeed*
> *a world of falsehood, this*
> *Gods-gone Month,*
>
> *The God of Poverty*
> *just won't let me be!*

The poet, who had a temple, observed in a preface that the offerings were down in early winter when the Gods were supposed to be caucusing in Izumo. If Poverty stayed behind, it proves Gods-gone month is not what it should be. I write "No ~," for I feel this plays on Teika's famous *shigure* poem playing on kks poem #712 (p.230). Yûchôrô seems the Samuel Butler of Japan, though he is not so well known. He made at least a dozen mad poems about the Poverty God.

とき／＼はよそへもおしやれひんほ神　　　ひむホムの神とてさらににくからす
いちこのうちとやくそくはせす　　　　　このとしまてのなしみとおもへは
tokidoki wa yoso e mo ojare binbôgami　　*binbon no kami tote sara ni nikukarazu*
ichigo no uchi to yakusoku wa sezu　　　*kono toshi made mo najimi to omoeba*
sometimes-as4 elswhere-to+emph play pvtygd　poverty-god re., any more hateful-not
fated while/house as promise-as-for do-not　this year upto acquaintance as think-if

> *Once in a while,*　　　　　　　　　*God Poverty?*
> *why not enjoy yourself*　　　　　*No, I can't bring myself*
> *elsewhere, Poverty?*　　　　　　*to hate the bloke,*
>
> *You need not keep all*　　　　　*Not considering how long*
> *your promises to me!*　　　　　*we have been close!*

Many of Issa's score of *ku* mentioning Poverty echo Yûchôrô's *kyôka*. I include most in a chapter of a book in-progress, HIC! (*Haiku In Context*). Here is one:

よい連ぞ貧乏神も立給へ 一茶 文化十二
yoi tsure zo binbôgami mo tachi tamae issa
good companion+emph poverty-god too depart deign to

> *The Gods Are Off!*
>
> *Poverty, my pal,*
> *it's time you, too,*
> *hit the road!*

On the Prosperity of Poverty & How It Keeps Itself

福の神我が身に金をたび給へ 貧も富みつゝ有るべき物を　仁勢物語 c.1640
fuku-no-kami waga mi ni kane o tabi-tamae hin mo tomi-tsutsu arubeki mono o　nise-monogatari
wealth-god myself–to money give please poverty too prosper-while exist-ought+rhetorical-complaint
(fuku kaze ni waga mi o nasaba tamasudare hima motometsutsu irubeki mono o ise-monogatari c 900)

*God of Wealth,
please give some money
to little ole me!*

*Should not poverty, too
thrive in prosperity?*

This is poem #115 of 208 in the 17c *Nise Monogatari*, 仁勢物語 or "fake" *Ise Monogatari* (the "fake," usually 偽, is itself punned 仁勢 in a way to include part of the original name). The *Tales of Ise* – an *uta-monogatari,* or song/poem-tale where it is hard to tell if the tales are for the poems or vice-versa – was, with the *Tale of Genji*, much later *Tales of Heike*, and *Hundred Poets One Poem* collection, one of the four most widely read books in Japan. As each of the 125 short tales of the original all have one or more poems, many of which were themselves pretty crazy, if not parody, mad poets could not resist it. The fake *Ise*, or *Nise*, is as inconsistent as the original. Some tales play closely with the content of the original, while some, like this one barely echo it. In *Ise* tale #64, a man who wanted to see a lady wished he were the wind to slip through her blinds. The woman in Ise replies that wind or not, he wouldn't slip through and, in Nise, the God replies that even he cannot give someone wealth they are not born with: poverty can prosper only becoming a cheapskate. There is, however considerable *phonetic* resemblance between the poems. Look closely at the Romanization.

目には見て手には取られぬ月の中の　桂の如き君/金にぞ有ける　仁勢
me ni wa mite te ni wa torarenu tsuki no uchi no katsura no gotoki kimi/kane ni zo arikeru
eyes-by-as-4 seeing hands-by-as-4 take-can't moon-within's katsura-like you/money+emph is+emph.

Ise #73	*Nise #73*

*Though we see it,
we just can't reach
the katsuragi;*

*That tree in the moon
is what you are to me!*

*Though we see it,
we just can't reach
the katsuragi;*

*That tree in the moon
is what money is to me!*

Said tree in the moon – one explanatory myth for moon phases has it cut down by the man in the moon and growing back, but, generally speaking, a man hoped to take a sprig and decorate his crown – was a standard conceit for hard-to-reach love. The *Ise* poem is a slightly revised version of *Manyôshû* #632. Only the last *ku* is different (妹をいかにせむ *imo o ikani semu*) and means "*What shall I do with my girl/dear* (who is like the tree . . . ?)" Such borrowing is humorous but too normal to be mad; Changing love for *money*, i.e., the treatment of money as seriously as love in the Fake tale *is*. And the metaphor is good, though neither it nor any *kyôka* ever put the problem into hyperlogical perspective half so well as Piet Hein did: *"Sure money's all wrong, / and the Devil decreed it! / It doesn't belong / to the people who need it."* (*Viking Vistas* Short Grooks II)

神々は出雲の国へ寄ると聞く
貧乏神ばか何故ここにをる
kamigami wa izumo no kuni e yoru to kiku
binbôgami baka naze koko ni oru edo3

酒は飲む博奕はこくし朝寝する
仕方なければ定宿にする
sake wa nomu bakuchi wa kokushi asane
-suru shikata nakereba teijû ni suru

怠け者の貧乏をかこちて
Lazy Bones Complains

貧乏神の答へて
God Poverty Explains

With all the gods
gathering in Izumo,
or, so they say,
What I do not know is why
Poverty's still here, today!

I drink my wine
gamble away what's mine,
and sleep till noon
Tell me, does it look like
I can afford to leave soon?

A gloss of this netted pair of *dôka*, or didactic *kyôka*, probably 18-19c Edo, was not needed as, aside from the rhymes (today/soon), the translations closely match the original. As one who is dirt poor and, despite working almost non-stop, has been so for a decade, now, I find the poems insulting. Because successful creators (and those who steal from them) tend to *become* wealthy, wealth is credited, *ipso facto* for everything, and few realize that most creative work as well as labor is done by *us*. Some of us could earn more, so our poverty is voluntary, but that does not make us happy. We have the *nerves* to go without the medical care, variety of diet, etc. others take for granted. But it hurts that the work we feel obliged to do that keeps us poor is itself handicapped by poverty and that we must endure the insults of those who refuse to consider writing, painting and invention as work unless it brings in money immediately. You should know that Ôta Nanpô (Yomo no Akara, Shokusanjin), the genius who made mad poems fashionable was one of us – I identify more with my poverty than my country – and, in the end, poverty hurt his ability to work more than his drinking. Coming from a poor samurai family, when conservative oppression forced him to retire from the mad-poem movement, which had become his source of income, he had to take a test to become a government bureaucrat. With wealth, he could have written all day for decades, as Charles Darwin, thanks to an arranged marriage with a wealthy wife could do. Since posts had little to do with brilliance and everything to do with connection, despite a high score, Japan's top creator was ordered to put in order decades (or centuries?) of records for one bridge. His despair with his job left us one of the most depressing yet still funny *kyôka* ever written. Unfortunately, the pun on the "falling" (in a vernacular/dialectal conjugation expressing the undesirability of the action) of the unceasing, dreary monsoon rains with the old note-pads (both *furuchô*) he worked with is untranslatable (pg. 542).

The More Poverty The Merrier? I Wish!

かみそりのはよりもうすきゑりをきて くひのきれぬはふしきなりけり 竹斎
kamisori no ha yori mo usuki eri o kite kubi no kirenu wa fushigi narikeri chikusai
razor's blade morethan thin collar+acc wearing, neck cut-not-as-for strange is! 1623?

Wearing a collar
worn thinner than the edge
of a razor blade

It's a wonder my head
still sits on my neck!

With my collar
thinner than a razor blade
This news of note

It's nothing but miraculous
I have yet to cut my throat.

If you are poor in time and money, you learn things. How to keep up stretched underwear? A cord tied *twice* about the waist. *Once* does not work. No barber visit for seven years? An electric clipper does the trick. Clothing? I still have a few decent shirts (all with 18c or 19c old-fashioned collars) but almost all are missing buttons and none have been ironed since who knows when. No matter! Poverty, as we saw (p.282), has no visitors. Which is to say, I can identify with the legendary Chikusai, above, and the real Yûchôrô, below!

ひんほうの神をいれしと戸をたてゝ よく／\みれは我身なりけり 雄長老
binbô no kami o ireshi to to o tatete yokuyoku mireba waga mi narikeri yûchôrô 16c
poor god+acc enter-let and door+acc closing, carefully look-if/when my self was!

Letting my god
back in, on Poverty
I shut the door

& taking a good look,
discovered he was me!

Issa's haiku version, pictures himself with a faded old bandana (winter wear), *announcing* (*nanori* ala samurai) his entry into the fray: *God Poverty c'est moi!* Lacking a tradition and words for calling out one's own name, I'll improvise: *"A rag on my head; / I am a god, just call / me Poverty!"* (古頭巾貧乏神と名のりけり *furuzukin binbôgami to nanorikeri*). The "it was me" idea also reminds me of one Issa *ku* that should be famous both in Japan and in translation *for its humanism:*

来て見ればこちらが鬼也蝦夷が島　文政五
kite mireba kochira ga oni ya ezo-ga-shima Issa
coming-see-when this/we-the devil/s!/: ezo island

discovery

coming we saw
the devil was us
on ainu isle

Issa, like most Japanese, was proud of his country and wrote many poems reflecting that, so it was delightful to find him reflective with respect to the indigenous people of the archipelago. The devil or demon (*we were the demons* might be a better, though less poetic translation) called *oni*, was the one children ran or hid from in their games and Issa has other poems regretting the fear of birds who thought of humans, himself included, as demons. His two other Ainu-related *ku* mention traders spreading lies and Edo wind is being blown upon this/these "barbarian isle/s" (what the Chinese called the Japanese, the Japanese called Ainu). That *wind* may refer to the fashions and customs, or allude to another sort of influence, *influenza*. Because trade winds decide when the isles are visited, the *ku* could be put in its proper season, but Issa's editors place it under *miscellaneous*. Please note the *ku* is not *senryû*, traditionally neither retrospective nor first-person, but a *kyôku*, in the comic yet wise spirit of Walt Kelly's Pogo possum, who spying trash in Okefenokee Swamp made the immortal announcement: *"We have met the enemy and he is us."* He, or she, *still* is!

出雲への路銭はいかに貧乏神　貞徳
izumo-e-no rosen-wa ikani binbôgami
izumo-to road-coins-as-for how? poverty-god

おお寒し貧乏神の御帰か　一茶
oo samushi binbôgami no okaeri ka
oh, cold! poverty-god's honorific+return?

Highway Tolls

How will he ever
pay his way to Izumo?
The Poverty God

Shiver of Recognition

Whoa, it's cold!
Has our god Poverty
come back home?

Teitoku's sympathetic treatment of Poverty (崑山集), left, does not talk down on the poor like that pair of *kyôka* in the last chapter contrasts with the 1539 *ku* by Anon. *"Now, don't you come back Poverty, this is Gods-gone Month!"* (*kaeruna yo waga binbô no kaminazuki* (犬筑波集) but is still beaten by Issa's 19c *kyôku* welcoming the god back that combines realism with his trademark respectfulness for all. Playful treatment of Poverty abounds in *haikai*: I may do a book of nothing else. Now, let us see a *kyôka* so free that it makes *haikai* seem confined.

『ぐるりと家を取り巻く貧乏神』『七福神は外へ出られず』仙厓義梵
gururi to ie o torimaku binbôgami // shichifuku<u>k</u>ami wa soto e derarezu　Sengai
circling house+acc taking-wrap poverty-god // seven happy/wealthy gods-as-for outside-to leave-cannot

Asked for a benediction for a new house, Monk Sengai (1751-1837) sang out:

*God Poverty
encircles this house
like a sleeve!*

*God Poverty
encircles this home
like a wall!*

Then, after the shocked owner complained of the apparent malediction,

*So the Seven Gods of
Good Fortune cannot leave!*

*The 7 Gods of Fortune,
They cannot leave at all!*

♪ *Bor-row, row, row your boat, . . . !* ♪

もとよりもかりの世なればかるもよし 夢の世なればねるもまたよし ネット?
moto yori mo kari no yo nareba karu mo yoshi　yume no yo nareba neru mo mata yoshi たはれぐさ
start-from+emph temp./borrowed-world is-if borrow+emph. ok / dream-world is-if sleep+emph too ok/fine anon?

If the World's but
a fiction lent, borrowing
is meant to be!

And if Life is but a dream,
sleep is good for you & me

If our World
is but a borrowed stage
Then, I'll borrow!

And if Life is but a dream,
I'll sleep until tomorrow!

If this world is
something lent, why should
anyone pay rent?

And if it is nothing but
a dream, sleep is heaven sent!

I was tempted to title this poem, titled *Debts* 借債, the *Stay in Bed Manifesto*. It reminds me of *Be Merry Friends,* a poem (*The loss of wealth is loss of dirt, / As sages in all times assert; / The happy man's without a shirt. /. . .*) by John Heywood (who, Wiki tells us is a grandfather of Donne!) that might be called the *Internationalle of Mad Verse*. Here is a reparsing of my favorite lines:

A fig for care
and a fig for woe!
If I can't pay,
Why I can owe, and death
makes equal the high & low ♪

Heywood (1497-1580?) died in Low Land exile after the English outlawed Catholicism. If Edo *kyôka* postdates Heywood, he, in turn, lags Ikkyû (1394-1481). The next *kyôka* is found in a book of Ikkyû tales (一休ばなし#42), shortly after a set of poems composed after his monastery was partially lost to flood and landslide, when someone asked how he was getting on. His first reply:

我が宿は 柱も立てず 葺きもせず 雨にもぬれず 風もあたらず 一休
waga yado wa hashira mo tatezu fuki mo sezu ame ni mo nurezu kaze mo atarazu
my dwelling-as-for pillar even stand not thatch-do-not rain-by-even wets-not wind strikes-not

My dwelling?
No pillar stands within it,
no thatch is on it;
Rain cannot wet it, and
The wind cannot get it!

In Japan, where walls were secondary, the pillars and roof were pretty much *it*. When Mr. Nosey asked where that phantom dwelling might be, Ikkyû, rather than going metaphysical, quoted *Kokinshû* poem #983 about living on a Mountain with a name that punned for "woe" but was not woeful because of its deer, only to be rudely informed that rumors had it he lived with Monk Joy-draw (喜撰) and was reduced, *ha ha ha*, to being a renter. To this, Ikkyû replied:

かりの世に貸したる主も借り主も貸すと思はず借ると思はず 一休
kari no yo ni kashitaru nushi mo karinushi mo kasu to omowazu karu to omowazu
temporary-world-in lending owner and borrowing-owner lend-as think-not borrow-as think-not

When all the world's　　　　　　　　　　　*Living in Maya*
on loan, nor can we lenders　　　　　*The renter and the rentee*
or borrowers be –　　　　　　　　　　　*happen to agree*

What is borrowed, call it rent;　　　*No landlord's rightly landed,*
And what is lent, Heaven sent.　　　*& rent commanded cannot be*

The second reading, depicting the relation between Ikkyû and his Landlord, is closest to the original. The first *"kari"* is written phonetically; the second in character: 借, meaning "to rent/borrow" or, as a noun, a *debt*. The first, were it written in character, would be 仮, "temporary." Without this pun uniting the Buddhist concept of the world with renting, the poem does not work. In the original, where less extraneous verbiage is needed, the contradictions fly by so quickly one feels that the crafty monk has somehow performed negative multiplication where minus $-1 \times -1 = 1$! I so not mean this critically. After all, by adding a "stage" to one world, turning another into "life" (as per the original) and alluding to the familiar *Row, Row, Row, Your Boat,* didn't I play even faster to save the lead poem, otherwise lost in translation?

世の中のちりし積もりて山とならば 山ごもりせんちりのこの身も 大根太木
yo no naka no chiri shi tsumorite yama to naraba yama-gomori sen chiri no kono mi mo
world-within's dust+emph piling mountain becomes-if mt.-hide-do-would dust's this-body/me too

◆ POSTED ON THE DOOR PILLAR OF ÔNE-NO-FUTOKI ◆

If plain trash grows into mountains, I'm a sage!
& this my hermitage, paper-hidden, is the rage!

As Nada Inada points out, Shokusanjin had once written that the real hermit hid in the (bustling) morning market, while the dewy fields were good for relieving oneself (大隠は朝市にあり、雪隠は露次にあり). Here was a famously messy man (「ちりも積もって山田室」と称) in cramped urban quarters, laughing about it.

Trash builds up & mountains make & that leaves me
Hidden in my hermitage in the middle of this city.

That was the end of the chapter, until I found another poverty-proud *kyôka* in Nada Inada's book so charming I had to squeeze all three readings of the lead poem in parallel to fit it in. This friend of Shokusanjin was a large man living in a tiny rented house. His *kyôka* compares it to an inexhaustible fire-striking box, as he kept striking his head on the lintel so sparks flew from his eyes. Unfortunately, it won't English unless we turn that house into a closet observatory, for when *our* heads strike things we do not see *sparks,* but *stars* (此家はたとへのふしの火打箱 かまちで打て目から火が出る　大家裏住　*kono ie wa tatoe no fuji no hi-uchi-bako kamachi de utte me kara hi ga deru* ôya urazumi d. 1810 ふし：富士：不尽)

A Sampling of Shokusanjin's Mad 100 Poets: その一

001 秋の田のかりほの庵の歌がるた とりぞこなつて雪は降りつつ　蜀山人
aki no ta no kariho no io no utagaruta torizokonatte yuki wa furitsutsu shokusanjin 18-19c
autumn field's harvested-rice-ears' cottage's poem-card take-mistaking snow-as4 falls-on

The hut for ears of grain from autumn fields, I sought – oh, no!
That song card was wrong, so, now I pluck in the falling snow.
~~~~~~

秋の田のかりほの廬の苫をあらみ 我が衣手は露にぬれつつ　天智天皇
aki no ta no kariho no io no toma o arami waga koromode wa tsuyu ni nuretsutsu emp. tenji 7c
autumn field's harvested ears' hut's matting (made) rough my sleeves-as-for dew-w/ wetting

Coarse the rush-mat roof, sheltering the harvest-hut of the autumn rice-field;
And my sleeves are growing wet with the moisture dripping through.

The second translation, the first poem of the Ogura *Hundred Poets One Poem* Collection, is by Clay MacCauley (1907). There is debate whether the hut was for storing grain or simply a temporary hut and whether the Emperor wrote the poem *as* a peasant or *imagining* a peasant. But, fine nuance may be left for notes; here, MacCauley will do, so long as you note that while our translations bear little in common, *waka* and *kyôka* start *identically* in the original. Shokusanjin's first *Hundred Poets'* take-off refers to the popular 100 *Hyakunin-isshu* card matching game, where speed is of essence so people often snatched up the wrong one. The mistake (*"that song card was wrong"*) mentioned was common because both song #1 and #15 begin *"my (long) sleeves ~"* (*waga koromode*), though the sleeves get soaked in *dew* in the *second half* of the former, while *snow* is braved to pluck young greens in the latter. We have already seen Shokusanjin's take on poem #2 (p.140), where the Empress describes white robes drying on a mountain. That poem is also referred to in a fine *senryû* – one with a mad poem spirit – about the poem #1: *"Your wet robe? / Take it over to dry on / the neighbor's mountain"* 濡れた御衣隣の山で干したまふ *nureta miso tonari no yama de hoshi-tamau*). For song #3, I'll give Kakimoto Hitomaro's very famous original 8c first, followed by Shokusanjin, late-18c, Teiryû, early-18c, & anonymous, undated.

003 足引の山鳥の尾のしだり尾の長々し夜を獨りかも寝ん　柿本人丸 7c
ashihiki no yamadori no o no shidario no naganagashi yo o hitori ka mo nen hitomaro
leg-drag-mt.-bird's tail's trailing-tail's longx2 night+acc/! alone maybe/emph. sleep-will

This night that I seem bound to sleep alone will be longer still
than the tails trailing pheasants through the wild foot-drag hills.

..
あし引の 山鳥のお したりがほ 人丸ばかり 歌よみでなし　蜀山人
ashihiki no yamadori no o no shitarigao hitomaru bakari uta yomi de nashi shokusanjin
leg-drag-mt.-bird's tail's trailing⇒boastful-face hitomaru alone poem-composer's not

The tails that trail the wild pheasants drag on long enough;
& I'm fed up with centuries of "Waka is Hitomaru" stuff!

光陰は山鳥の矢のことし　長／＼敷も長寝せんかも 貞柳　犬百 in 活玉 tk
kôgen wa yamadori no ya no gotoshi naganagashiku mo nagane sen ka mo　teiryû
light-shade-as4 mt.bird arrow resembling longlongly+emph longsleep do-would !

Light & shade as long as the shaft on pheasant-hunting arrow-heads.
I, too, would be very long, long indeed, asleep in bed!

あしひきの山屋がうどん汁もよし長々しきをひとりすすらん ng
ashihiki no yamaya ga udon-jiru mo yoshi naganagashiki o hitori susuran
leg-draggng mountn shop's udon (noodle) soup/stock+emph good, singly slurp-would.
..

Good, too, is the noodle stock at this foot-drag mountain shop –
Long, indeed, we slurp alone and hope the slurping never stops!

Hitomaro was often called Hitomaru. Shokusanjin used the customary name to better express, or pretend to express, dissatisfaction with the ancient bard often credited even for old poems he did not write. Most of his work is long, so the original says *uta,* not *waka* and, for once, the terms are not really interchangeable. The second spoof by Teiryû, whose popularity in his day was as phenomenal as Shokusanjin in his, observes reality up a mountain hollar and introduces the arrow partly because it was a symbol of how time flew in the Sinosphere as well as the Occident. *If you know who did the last take-off, please tell me.* For more *slurping*, find the *konowata* (fermented sea cucumber) in *Rise, Ye Sea Slugs!* (2003). Let's skip #4. We did #5 of the plaintive deer call (p.226).

Shokusanjin's take-off of #6 is pure play. The original has *the sight of frost lying white upon the magpie bridge night proving the night has grown late* 鵲のわたせる橋におく霜の白きをみれば夜ぞ更けにける 中納言家持 *kasasagi no wataseru hashi ni oku . . .* That is, *the Milky Way is visible.* Taking the *shimo*=frost 霜 to mean its homophone "lower=下," or *the second half of the poem,* the poet declares he will "*kari*=borrow 借り," i.e. *keep* as is, and does so by fixing it to the *hashi*=bridge where it morphs into "temporary 仮" as was, indeed, the magpie bridge itself (其のままにをくしもの句をかり橋の白きをみれば夜ぞ更けにける *sono mama ni oku shimo no ku o karibashi no shiroki*). Such robustly constructed utter nonsense will not translate, but I explained it, as it shows why the term "parody" fails to do Shokusanjin's genius justice. A *senryû* parody of the same notes that frost never settles on *another* bridge, Nihonbashi (おく霜の白きは見せぬ日本橋 *oku shimo no shiroki wa misenu nihonbashi*). Japan's central hub, it is too well-traveled day and night to let anything come between sole and bridge.

Shokusanjin's #7 facetiously misreads the original's mention of a moon-rise (天の原ふりさけみれば春日なる三笠の山に出でし月かも 安倍仲麿 *ama-no-hara furisake mireba . . .*), pretending to take the old exclamation *kamo* to mean *trying to bite/chew,* and guffaws that the poet, Abe no Nakamaro must have strong teeth and gums to munch the moon (仲麿はいかい歯ぶしの達者もの三笠の山にいでし月かむ *nakamaro wa ikai habushi no tasshamono mikasa no yama ni ideshi tsuki kamu!* Shokusanjin). Coincidentally or not, the earlier *Dog Hundred Poets* parody (犬百人一首 1669) also turns the landscape into a victual reality by taking the also acceptable *ame* pronunciation of heaven (*ama*), thus making it *a sweet.* ♪

A Sampling of Shokusanjin's Mad 100 Poets: その二

009 衣通の歌の流義にをのづからうつりにけりな女どしゆへ 蜀山人 狂歌百人一首
sotôri no uta no ryûgi ni onozukara utsurinikeri-na onna do(ô?)shi yue shokusanjin late-19c
(princess) sotôri=dress-pass's poems' style/school-to self-from transfering women-fellows ergo

It did not fade, but passed on by shining through the dress
of Princess Sotôri – the female style. Oh, no! Komachi? Yes!

~~~~~~

My flower faded as its beauty was wasted on idle concerns
Gazing at the rain, life passed me by – too late, I learned.

花の色はうつりにけりないたづらに我が身よにふるながめせしまに 小野小町
hana no iro wa utsurinikeri na itazura ni waga mi yo ni furu nagame seshi ma ni   ono no komachi 9c
blossom's/s' beauty-as4 transfered/lost idly/wastefully my self/body world-in age gazing do while

Japanese men had mixed feelings about the Japanese women known as the poetess of love (see her chapter in *The Woman Without a Hole:* 2007) so I feel justified with my *Oh, no!* admittedly a far cry from Shokusanjin's pun which puts the *ono* into *onozukara,* or "of its own." I borrowed a bit from Carter for the Ono no Komachi (sometimes just called Ono Komachi) translation of which the last four words were added mainly for the rhyme. The original puns *rain* (*ame*) into "gazing" and has it "fall" (*furu*) with the homophonous aging. Rather than trying to outpun Komachi, or beat up on her as many did, Shokusanjin linked her poetic style, or the poetess school, to the ancient Princess Sotôri, so gorgeous her naked beauty was said to shine right through her clothing (yes, that even beats the liquefaction of Julia's clothes that so turned on Herrick). The idea works better in Japanese than English because the verb used for *fading* or *falling* blossoms in Komachi's poem, *utsuri,* includes connotations of "transferring" and "imaging."

010 四の緒のことをばいはずせみ丸のお歌の中にもの字四ところ
yotsu no o no koto oba iwazu semimaru no outa no naka ni mo no ji shi dokoro shokusanjin
4 string thing even says-not semimaru's hon. song/poem-within "mo" letter 4 though

Four strings! To think Semimaru failed to note them!
It makes me fret to see his song w/ four mo も *letters.*

ORIG.これやこの行くも帰るも別れては 知るも知らぬも逢坂の関 蝉丸 10c?
koreya kono yuku mo kaeru mo wakarete wa shiru mo shiranu mo auzaka no seki semimaru
Hey/here!/: this going & returnng seperatng-as-4 knowng & unknowng meet-slope's checkpoint

This is the Gate on Meeting Slope where all who come or go
Must part from other Men they do or do not know!

Semimaru's name has a cicada in it. Stands to reason, he was a singer-songwriter who played a four-string *biwa,* or moon-lute. His poem, which, as you can see, is not even echoed by the "parody," is a unique old *waka* for two things. As a *senryû* notes, it is exceptionally *jovial* for a *waka*. The first phrase, *koreya kono,* sounds like a folk-song chorus (歌道では明るく見えるこれやこの). *Here,* all you need note is that both readings have nothing in common w/ Shokusanjin's *kyôka* and those four emphatic *mo* syllabets within the first 24-syllabets of the original. If music is your thing, Shokusanjin jokes, then why not four "*o*=strings=緒" rather than four "*mo*=も" sounds? To demonstrate how novel his take-off is, here is an example of a more common(?) *usage* of this *waka*, a *rakushu*, or broadside, occasioned by a land boom 蝦夷地開拓ブーム in the Northern "barbarian" isles:

これやこの行くも帰るも蝦夷咄知るも知らぬも大方は嘘 anon.19c
koreya kono yuku mo kaeru mo ebisu-banashi shiru mo shiranu mo ôkata wa uso
hey this going & returnng, ebisu/savage talk knowing & knowing-not, most-as4 lies

Hey, hey, whether off to the Ainu isles or back, they rib:
Most of the tales you caught or missed are equally a fib!

Borrowing parts of poems does not make a poem *kyôka*, or parody, as this is clearly neither. So, why borrow? I am not sure, but recognizing it is pleasurable.

012 あまつ風雲のかよひ路 吹きとぢよ 乙女の姿 しばしとどめむ 僧正遍照 9c
amatsukaze kumo no kayoiji fukitojiyo otome no sugata shibashi todomen archbishop henjô
heaven-wind/s' clouds' commuting-trail blow closed! maidens' form forawhile detain!

Celestial winds, blow the lanes closed by which they came!
I would see more, detain these young angels for a while.

~~~~~~

Blow 'em shut, keep those celestial maidens here for a while?
The passion yet in master Munesada's breast makes us smile.

012 吹きとぢよ 乙女のすがたしばしとは まだみれんなるむねさだのぬし 蜀山人
fukitojiyo otome no sugata shibashi towa mada miren naru munesada no nushi shokusanjin
blow-close! maiden's/s' form a-while-as-for longing munesada=breast-settled-not master

"Makes us smile" is my meta-reading of Shokusanjin, in *his* style. Remember, this *is* Monk Henjô, who famously fell off his high horse upon the maiden flowers. Like many nobles in danger of assassination, Munesada (his lay-name) took his vows, but his heart was still attached to the *world*, as society was called and, in the Japanese, given the context, his old name puns into being an unsettled breast. There *is* something that makes us smile about this monk's manner of confession. The angels in question were dancing maidens in a play 五節の舞の舞姫. A *senryû* covers both famous *waka* with admirable economy: *"Not adverse to falling off his horse or detaining maidens"* 落馬にもこりず乙女をとめたがり *rakuba ni mo korizu otome o tometagari*. One reason Shokusanjin played with the poet rather than the poem is that, Henjô's *waka* is, for all intents and purposes, already a *kyôka*. Shokusanjin and others themselves had witty poems for dancing girls. Song #2646 of the minor, though large 985 *waka* anthology, *Kokinwaka-rokujô* (in Cranston v2a, w/ some debt in translation), has the more usual (sincere) *waka* message: *"What use have I for an angel from the sky, though she parts / A thousand clouds to get here, if she's not you, sweetheart!"* (*amagumo o chie ni kakiwake amakudaru hito mo nani sen imo ni shi arazu wa*).

A Sampling of Shokusanjin's Mad 100 Poets: その三

020 わびぬれば鯉のかはりによき鮒のみをつくりてものまんとぞ思ふ 蜀山人
wabinureba koi no kawari ni yoki funa no mi o tsukurite mo noman to zo omou shokusanjin
humble being carp insteadof good-roach+acc prepare+emph drink-will so (i) think

Why carp for lack of koi, when on the road a roach will do
for your pupu – I think, enough, my boy – Let's drink!

A *reference* rather than parody of #20, Prince Motoyoshi's *"Like a channel buoy / bobbing off Naniwa strand, / my name is tossed about. / But still I will come to see you – / though it will be death to proceed.?"* = trans. Carter わびぬれば今はた同じ難波なる身をつくしても逢はむとぞ思ふ 元良親王 890-943 *wabinureba ima hata onaji naniwa naru mi o tsukushite mo awamu to zo omou* gss #960). The poems in the original start and end more or less identically: with *wabinureba, feeling forlorn* or *suffering privation* and ~ *zo omou,* "(emphatically) *I think.*" *Naniwa*, written "rough waves," or, "floating flower/seaplant," evokes a shipwreck or drifting off but, here, puns out as "*whatever* (becomes of me)," followed by that *mi* (body/me) which, with its *o* postposition becomes *mio,* or "current," and, joining *tsukushi* (*exhaust/obliterate*=the death of me), creates *miotsukushi,* or "channel marker." Carter quietly catches the punning in simile. As this *waka* out-puns most *kyôka*, Shokusanjin went another way and borrowed bits of it to express his *eat, drink & be merry* philosophy, a healthy foil to the desperate lover. The old adverb *hata* sounds like a *grouper*, but the choice for a stand-in fish was borrowed from a famous old travelogue (「鯉はなくて、鮒よりはじめて…」土左日記). A *roach* resembles a *carp* in all but whiskers. Unlike the insect by its name, it has none. But, as they say, good wine needs no bush.

↓ 024 このたびは幣もとりあへず手向山 紅葉の錦神のまにまに 菅家 9c
kono tabi wa nusa mo toriaezu tamukeyama momiji no nishiki kami no ma ni ma ni michizane
this occasion/travel-as4 prayerstrip even for now offering-hill red-leave-brocade, gods as is x2

Travel is travail!
I brought no votive poems
Mount Offering

Wears a fall brocade, ye gods   *On top of that, as you see,*
I pray, accept it all, as is!   *I have no change with me!*

このたびはぬさも取敢へず手向山まだ 其上にさい銭もなし 蜀山人↑
kono tabi wa nusa mo toriaezu tamukeyama mada sonoue ni saizeni mo nashi shokusanjin
this occasn/trvl-as4 pryrstrp evn for now offering-hill also that-above smallchange even not

The first line should be *"On this occasion/trip."* The *waka* Englishes better with the Mountain last, but I wanted to keep the first half of the poems as they are in Japanese: *identical*. Poem #024, written in 898 when Sugawara no Michizane, one of the "gods of ancient Japanese poetry," visited Tamukeyama, literally Offering-mountain, with a retired Emperor, is in many anthologies. The penultimate poem in the *Kokinshû's* book 9, *Travel Poems*, it is followed by Monk Sosei: *"I ought to tear a strip from my patched robe for an offering / But the gods, jaded from the colored leaves, might return it.*" (たむけにはつづりの袖もきるべきにもみぢにあける神かへさむ　素性法師　古今集 #421 *tamuke ni wa tsuzuri no sode mo kiru beki ni momiji ni akeru kami ya kaesan*). #024 was already crazy, so Shokusanjin simply added a chuckle for readers knew that *the stereotypical noble, unlike a commoner, carried no small change as he had no need for it.*

059　やすらはで寝なましものをさ夜ふけてかたぶくまでの月を見しかな　赤染衛門
yasurawa de nenamashi mono o sayo fukete katabuku made no tsuki o mishi kana akazome emon
wondering-not sleeping-could have! night grows late capsize-until moon-viewed! 11c

I would just as well have slept, but, no, I stayed up late!
The moon turned upside before my eyes; we had a date.

~~~~~~

Akazome viewed the moon a'waiting for her lover –
She would still be up had her noggin not turned over!

akazome dozed off doing/did, head too tilts/capsizes-until moon+acc saw late-18c
akazome ga ineburi o shite tsumuri mo katabuku made no tsuki o mishi　shokusanjin
赤染がゐねふりをしておつむりもかたぶくまでの月をみし　哉　蜀山人 ↑
下戸ならは寝なましものを酒樽のかたふく迄の月そ淋しき　貞柳 early-18c ↓
geko naraba nenamashi mono o sakedaru no katabuku made no tsuki zo kanashiki teiryû
teetotaler is-if sleep-would thing+contra. wine-barrel tips-over-until's moon+emph sad

A teetotaler who would be fast asleep, could never see;
The moon when the keg of wine tips o'er, looks lonely.

"We had a date" in the first is not just for the rhyme but to fill in between the lines. Shokusanjin does not seem to realize that Akazome wrote the poem on behalf for her sister. No matter, that. What counts is the sweet word used for "head" *tsumuri,* which "noggin" mimics well. 蛇足　転ぶまでの雪見句の真似か？ Teiryû doubts one could wait up that long for a lover. But if one had a good supply of . . .

065　うらみ侘びほさぬ袖だにあるものを 此の四五日は雨の日ぐらし　蜀 山 人
urami wabi hosanu sode dani aru mono o kono shi go nichi wa ame no hi-gurashi shokusanjin
grudging, misery, dry-not sleeves even are despite/yet, these four or five days-as-for, rainy-living ↓
..

Anger & Grief
It's bad enough my sleeves
will not dry

What really hurts is Love　　　　　*These past four or five days*
has even stained my name!　　　　*It's been raining non-stop!*

↑恨みわびほさぬ袖だにあるものを 恋にくちなん名こそ惜しけれ　相模
urami wabi hosanu sode dani aru mono o koi ni kuchinan na koso oshikere lady sagami 11c
grudging, misery, dry-not sleeves even are despite/yet, longing-by rotted name esp. regretable

In the *waka* original the name "rots." Shokusanjin's rainy weather preventing drying is a good parody of all weepers; but the *senryû*: *"Two or three days / for a Sagami suffice / to infuriate"* (二三日間がありや相模うらみわび　*ni san nichi ma ga ariya sagami urami wabi*) is far sharper.　Maids from Sagami (same as the poetess's name) were reputedly insatiable (see a dozen egs. in my dirty senryû bk).

A Sampling of Shokusanjin's Mad 100 Poets: その四

066　もろともにあはれと思へ 山桜花 よりほかに知る人もなし 大僧正行尊 12c
morotomo ni aware to omoe yamazakura hana yori hoka ni shiru hito mo nashi　abbot gyôson
each-other-re. compassionately think, mt.-cherry, blossom (you) other-than know person even not

> *Shall we agree to care for one another mountain cherries?*
> *Outside of your blossoms, not a soul here knows me.*

~~~~~~

> *If our eyes, mouth, ears and eyebrows, were all to go,*
> *Outside of our noses, not a soul would know us!*

眼と口と耳と眉毛の なかりせば はなより外に しる人もなし　蜀山人
me to kuchi to mimi to mayuge no nakariseba hana yori hoka ni shiru hito mo nashi shokusanjin
eye & mouth & ear & eyebrows not-if blossoms morethan otherwise know men+emph not

The *pronunciation* of the last half of the poems is identical, yet one word differs. The original *blossoms* become *nose/s* in the *kyôka*. Deliberate puns on *blossom=hana=nose* are old hat (from which *flower-wind* 花風＝鼻風邪 *nose-cold,* both *hanakaze,* are usually pulled out), but elaborating child-style misreadings like this is always fresh. Had I not wanted to compare the *kyôka* and original, *nose* would have been the last word in my *kyôka* translation. When you think about it, the original *waka* is, itself, rather odd; *senryû* too prosaic to fully romanize or parse chuckle, *"So Gyôson held conversation with a wild cherry tree?"* (行尊の咄相手は山桜 *gyôson no hanashi...*). *"Blossoms say nothing; If Gyôson was talking, it was to himself!"* (花物言はず行尊はひとりごと *hana mono iwazu..*). Other #66 *kyôka*:

丸裸哀とおもへ寒垢離は 鼻より外にすゝる物なし 大鹿相行人 犬百 1669
maru hadaka aware to omoe kangori wa hana yori hoka ni susuru mono nashi　daiso sôgyônin
completly naked pitiful-as thnk! cold crud-seperate-as4 nose/s beside slurp(=do?)ing thing not

> *Pity the naked, in winter cold washing away impurity*
> *With nothing to slurp but their noses, drippy, drippy!*

~~~~~~

> *Pity the naked on a cold day scouring what's dirty!*
> *Outside of their noses, nothing's good and slurpy.*

淋しさを哀とおもへ山桜 下戸より外にとふ人もなし 貞柳 狂歌犬百
sabishisa o aware to omoe yamazakura geko yori hoka ni tou hito mo nashi　teiryû
loneliness+acc pitiful think! mt. cherry teetotalrs beside visitng people not　early-18c

> *Loneliness deserves pity – You poor Mountain Cherry!*
> *If only teetotalers called on me, I'd commit harry-kerry.*

With such *kyôka* parodies already out there, we can see why Shokusanjin took a different tack! The first, focusing on a seasonal rite and gleefully making it gross, comes across as a particularly *haikai*-style parody, which it *was*. It may also bring out the cold by pun-stuttering nothing to *d-do* (*su-suru*). ♪ As Japanese loudly slurp down soup and noodles, familiarity from childhood makes slurping a mouth-watering sound, hence reading two. While self-evisceration in plays was often accompanied by flurries of cherry petals, the hyperbole is mine. Yes, it is properly written and pronounced *harakiri*, but I accepted the popular Usanian butchery this time, and this time alone, for the only forgivable reason: *rhyme*.

もろともにあはれと思へお月さま国のなじみはお前ばかりぢや 失出典
morotomo ni aware to omoe otsukisama kuni no najimi wa omae bakari ja lost source
together pitiful-as think! o moon! country's buddies-as-for you only are (+colloquial)!

Join the party formed to pity me, oh, moon above earth!
Yours is the only familiar face in the land of my birth!

Here, what is plaintive becomes downright pathetic. This was the best *straight parody* of just-me-and-mountain-cherry #66, if I can coin a phrase for working faithfully on the main sentiment in a poem. I wish I at least knew whether it ante- or post-dated Shokusanjin's surreal nose version.

068 友もなく酒をもなしにながめなばいやになるべき夜はの月かな
tomo mo naku sake o mo nashi ni nagamenaba iya ni narubeki yowa no tsuki kana shokusanjin
friend too not *sake*+acc. sake too not-w/ viewing-if fed-up become-ought latenight moon! ↓

Should I live on	*If without friends*
if only because my heart	*and without drink, I were*
is not in the world,	*to stay and view it,*
How fondly I shall recall	*How fed-up I should be w/*
this after-midnight moon!	*this after-midnight moon!*

↑心にもあらでこの世にながらへば恋しかるべき夜半の月かな 　三条院
kokoro ni mo ara de ukiyo ni nagaraeba koishikaru beki yowa no tsuki kana emp. sanjo
heart-in am-not-from woeful-world-in survive-if cherish-ought latenight moon! 1016

I had a rhyme of *"though I don't care (for the world)"* and *"this midnight moon we share,"* but, reading Carter's note that the Emperor *"saw the moon . . . around the time he decided to retire . . . because of illness,"* had to drop the "share" and re-translate. "If only because" is pushing the envelope. As it turned out, disinterest in this world did not keep the retired Emperor in it: he would die the next year. The basic idea in the *kyôka* is old – *haikai* poets, who vied at being outrageous, often dwelled on the importance of drink to moon-viewing. Fusing that with *this* top 100 poem may be new. Still, Shokusanjin's play is less novel than this simple *senryû*, ending in a verb form unique to the Yoshiwara Pleasure Quarter dialect: *"'A heart's-not-in-it' / What's this? How good to see / you came here!"* 心にもあらでおや良く来なんした *kokoro ni mo ara de oya yoku kinan shita*). I.e., a retiree who wears a monk's robes calls. You may note that the first 8 syllabets of the 17-syllabet poem match the old *waka*, but I am afraid the pleasure of reading it is reserved for Japanese readers only, as it is not so much the logic as the *style* which makes the poem. In the *kyôka*, too, half the fun is in the colloquial *iya ni naru,* which, luckily, is well-matched by "fed-up with."

A Sampling of Shokusanjin's Mad 100 Poets: その五

083 世の中よ道こそなけれ 思ひ入る山の奥にも 鹿ぞなくなる 皇太后宮大夫 俊成
yo no naka yo michi koso nakere omoi iru yama no oku ni mo shika zo naku naru shunzei 1114-1204
world-among+emph way+emph (is)not, longed-for entering mountain's recess-in even deer+emph cry-are

*There is no way to escape from our world, even deep
back in the mountains, I hear lonely harts bleat!*

~~~~~~

*Over-hunted for hide to make footballs and brush hair,
Back in the mountains, the bleating harts . . . aren't there!*

鞠の皮筆毛の用にとりつくし 山の奥にも 鹿ぞなくなる 蜀山人 狂歌百人一首
kemari no kawa fude mo no yô ni toritsukushi yama no oku ni mo shika zo nakunaru shokusanjin
football's hide brush-hair's use taking-exhausted mountain recesses-in even deer die-out late-18c

I am very happy with my *bleating harts*, but must confess that while Fujiwara no Shunzei wrote many witty poems, this was not one of them. Please consider it a *gain* in translation to make up for losses elsewhere. The *kyôka* depends on *cry* and *die* being the same sound, *naku*. Shokusanjin first used the pun in his far more famous, and indeed, better *kyôka* about overhunted quail (p.369). Still, to my mind, it beats Teiryû's early 18c take:

二つよい事こそなけれ思ひ入る山の奥には花のおそさよ　貞柳
futatsu yoi koto koso nakere omoiiru yama no oku ni wa hana no ososa yo teiryû
two good things esp. not, think-enter/love mtn-recesses-in-as4 blossoms' lateness!
..

*Two good things are never found together – the hills you love
are great, but the cherry blossoms always bloom too late!*

The first phrase is a proverb. ♪ I, like Issa, think late-bloom is good for stretching Spring, so Teiryû's parody does not take me. However, translators might note the *"love."* That side of *omoiiri* is lost in most translations of Shunzei's poem. Now, back to #70. I forgot it. Besides, it would have made a less novel chapter lead. The original, Teiryû, Anon., Shokusanjin, respectively:

070 さびしさに宿をたち出でてながむればいづくもおなじ秋の夕暮 良暹法師
sabishisa ni yado o tachiidete nagamureba izuko mo onaji aki no yugure monk ryôzen 11c
loneliness-from lodging leaving, gazing-when everywhere same autumn evening

*Feeling lonely, I left my lodge and looked around,
But everywhere the same fall dusk was all I found!*

さひしさに書物とり出て詠むれは 昔も同し秋の夕暮 貞柳 狂歌犬百
sabishisa ni shomotsu toridete nagamureba mukashi mo onaji aki no yûgure teiryû
loneliness-from book taking-out read-when longago too same fall evening p.1740

*Feeling lonely, I took out a book to read and wouldn't you know
I found fall evenings were just the same a long time ago!*

070 さびしさよ秋の夕めしたく頃はいづこも同じすりばちの音 失出典
sabishisa yo aki no meshi taku koro wa izuko mo onaji suribachi no oto lost source
loneliness! fall evening/s meals cook time-as-for everywhere same mortar sound

>*What loneliness, this, our supper-cooking time in Fall!*
>*When the same sound of mortar grind surrounds us all!*

さびしさに宿を立ち出てながめたり煙草呑んだり茶をせんじたり 蜀山人
sabishisa ni yado o tachidete nagametari tabako nondari cha o senjitari shokusanjin
loneliness-from lodge+acc upleaving gazing&stuff smoking&stff tea-steeping&stuff

>*Feeling lonely, I left my lodge and looked around,*
>*had a smoke, steeped some tea, sipped it down &*

Teiryû's is a solid take-off. Was the book the *Hundred Poets* with this poem? Despite my dramatic "surrounds us," you may note the lost-source parody is less witty than the original! There is a synonym for the evening hour in *haikai* called *suribachidoki*, or "(earthenware)mortar-time." I suppose all that braying (sesame, chestnut, &?) would be dismaying – mortifying? – if you hear the whole world grinding its teeth or recall metaphor of taxes as seed-grinding and squeezing. The ~ *tari* conjugation, suffix or whatever you-call-it on the verb in Shokusanjin's take makes it but one of a number of things done. *What better way to indirectly express the unsettled mindset of the poet!?* Unlike a pun which may be re-created in a different word, English is lost for words. *"And stuff"* does not hack it.

096 花さそふ 嵐の庭の 雪ならで ふりゆくものは 我が身なりけり 公経
hana sasô arashi no niwa no yuki nara de furiyuku mono wa wagami narikeri kintsune
blossm seducng gale's gardn's snow is not so fallng-goes thng-as4 myslf/bdy is! 1171-1244

>*My garden where the wind woos cherry petals is free of snow,*
>*and what just keeps falling and piling up is age, my woe!*

>*My garden where the wind woos cherry petals is free of snow,*
>*and the ox's jewels are what keeps swinging to and fro!*

花さそふあらしの庭の雪ならで ふり行ものは うしの金玉 蜀山人 shoku-
hana sasou arashi no niwa no yuki nara de furiyuku mono wa ushi no kintama -sanjin
blossm seducing gale's garden's snow is not so fallng⇒swaying-goes sad⇒ox/en's balls

Is this surreal disjunction of ex-chancellor-monk Fujiwara no Kintsune's lament not one of the most cheerful parodies of a melancholy poem ever made? The original has two crucial puns and the kyôka three that will not English. In the original, *yuki*, or "snow=going=leaving=dying" – rhetorically, at least, preferred to growing old. It "falls-continually"=*furi-yuku*= "old-grows." I kept the ideas but lost the wit. I could only translate enough to demonstrate, the wit in the juxtaposition of the two poems. While only the last seven syllabets in the two poems differ in pronunciation, Shokusanjin's *furi* is neither fall 降り nor age 古り as in the original, but becomes 振り or *swing* after the last word, "*kintama* = gold gem," i.e., *balls* testify. Note the poet's name Kintsune hints of the same. At first, the phonetically written *ushi*=bull/ox seems to mean 憂し, sad. Shokusanjin keeps the creature a surprise until those balls, at the very end. The balls, themselves, are neither outlandish nor lonely. They were a common sight on the ox that drew the recreational carts, i.e. carriages, palace women rode to festivities.

A Sampling of Shokusanjin's Mad 100 Poets: その六

099 後鳥羽どのことばつづきのおもしろく世を思ふゆへにものおもふみは 蜀山人
go toba-dono no kotoba-tsuzuki no omoshiroku yo o omou yue ni mono omou mi wa
go toba sir's word-chain's interesting, world+acc caring ergo worry self-as-for ↓

People are kind,
people are cruel no matter,
what you'd do

Sir Go Toba's
kotoba – interesting
if they're true

'I worried about the world,
So, now, I'm in a stew!'

↑人もをし人もうらめしあぢきなく世を思ふゆゑに物思ふ身は 後鳥羽院
hito mo oshi hito mo urameshi ajikinaku yo o omou yue ni mono omou mi wa   go toba
people missed/dear, people grudge/spiteful, futilely world+acc care, ergo worry self-as-for

The *kotoba* in the *kyôka* means "words." I kept it for the echo of the beloved (good ruler + patron of poetry) Emperor's name and added the third line for the rhyme to come. I, too, was touched by Go Toba's 7-7 words, but Shokusanjin's *interest* in the "*tsuzuki=sequence,*" which I failed to translate, implies the causal connection between the 5-7 and 5, as well. Mizukaki, the *waka* lover who put Shokusanjin's *Kyôka Hyakunin Isshû* on-line for all to access, comments: "Even Professor Shokusan, who pulled no punches while ridiculing the big-name *waka* poets, did not mock Retired Emperor Go Toba. さんざん大歌人をからかい続けた蜀山先生ですが、さすがに後鳥羽院を茶化し申し上げることはしませんでした。" I am not so sure. "Interesting" can mean *puzzling*, as in *hard to swallow*. Shokusanjin knew *ajikinaku* meant "futilely" in the original, but pretended it meant "uninteresting" for his reversal. Carter's "seem/when" reading (*"People can seem kind, / and people can seem cruel – / when quite foolishly / I wear myself out worrying / over the world and its ways."*) seems a safer bet than mine.

ひるもうしひらぬもつらし嫁すかし
hiru mo ushi hiranu mo tsurashi yome sukashi
cut(it) depressing cut(it)-not painful, bride slips(it out)

Holding it in hurts
but release is depressing
a bride slips one by

Not all those who played with Go Toba's poem were polite. When I translated the above for my book of dirty *senryû* (*Octopussy, Dry-kidney and Blue Spots*), I had no idea it played with Go Toba's poem which I had not read enough times to recall (I can not even remember my *own* poems!). Here are the first twelve syllabets of each. Only the *mo's* (and) are identical, but . . . See what you think –

The *senryû* starts: *hiru mo ushi hiranu mo tsurashi*   ひるもうしひらぬもつらし
& Go Toba's *waka*:   *hito mo oshi hito mo urameshi*   ひともおしひともつらめし

My point? Unless one has a photographic memory and extraordinary fuzzy pattern recognition, only close familiarity with a poem could make so loose a phonetic resemblance recognizable to a popular audience. In other words, such parody owes its existence to the card game of matching the first and second half of the 100 poems played thousands of times over by most readers.

100 百敷や古き軒端のしのぶにもなほあまりある昔なりけり 順徳院 13c
momoshiki ya furuki nokiba no shinobu ni mo nao amari aru mukashi nari keri r. emp juntoku
hundred-stone/palace old eaves-edge bear=memory-fern-for-even still excess has past is!

The memory fern on ye old eaves of this hundred-stone palace
cannot hold it all, not here – there is just too much past!
~~~~~~
W/ this august poem of a hundred hues, all is bound & wrapt;
A hundred-stone palace: what could sound more oddly apt!

百色の御歌のとんとおしまいにももしきやとは妙に出あつた 蜀山人
momoshiki no onka no tonto oshimai ni momoshiki ya to wa myô ni deatta shokusanjin
hundred-hues' hon.poem/s proper ending-to momoshiki/palace+emph-as4 subtely/oddly fitting

Nokiba no shinobu, or "eaves' remembering" is a general nostalgia of place and alludes to *noki-shinobu,* or *eave-remember,* a variety of *shinobu-gusa,* memory (holding/keeping) fern, a *polypody* (no vernacular given) Englished as a *hare's foot fern.* As a hundred-lays/paves=*momoshiki* just means walls made of large stones, "stone palace" would have sufficed, but that would have missed the point, namely, poem #100 has a *hundred* in it. Shokusanjin noticed that, and tipped his hat to the editor, while also bringing out a possible pun on a "hundred *colors/ styles.*" Yet, once again, the brevity of the oft-maligned *senryû* wins. To wit,

百の字があるでしまいのお歌也
hyaku no ji ga aru de shimai no outa nari

It has a 'hundred'
just the right character
for the last poem.

Were the best part of the *kyôka, tonto,* colloquial for "proper," been Englishable, it might have been a tie. And were Shokusanjin as lowbrow as yours truly, he would have turned *momoshiki* into *momohiki,* and come up with, say, 股引や古き置き場に女中とさ 形見にあまる百滲みじみと. I apologize for keeping the poem, if it is one, in Japanese, but it really is bad enough to justify discretion. There are other, cleaner mad poems playing with this *waka.* Teiryû (p.1740) uses a homophone of *momoshiki* meaning *a hundred (many) different colors* to marvel at the colorful printings of the many editions of the *Ogura Hundred Poets* (ももしきや古き哥人しのぶには猶あまりある小倉色紙ぞ *momoshiki ya furuki utabito....*).Had Teiryû not done that, Shokusanjin might well have done the same, for it is the sort of meta-parody he preferred. And a classy *senryû* notes the collection starts in *knowledge,* or *wisdom* and ends in *morality,* as the first poem is by an Emperor with the former, 智, in his name, and the last by an Emperor with the latter 徳 in it (智で始め徳でおさめる小倉山 *chi de hajime toku de osameru...*)

In Praise of *Kyôka*, or Why Blyth Beats Keene

雀どのおやどはどこかしらねどもちょっちょとござれさゝの相手に　蜀山人
suzume-dono no oyado wa doko ka shiranedomo choccho to gozare sasa no aite ni shokusanjin
sparrow-sir's dwelling-as-for where know-not but a bit/a nip have+pol. drink=bamboo companion-as

My dear Mr. Sparrow
though I have no idea
where you reside;
Won't you join me here
for a drink or come inside?

You hungry titmice,
Stop cheeping for more;
don't quarrel, be nice!
Cheep! Cheep? Not quite!
Birdfeed just went up in price!

I re-worked Blyth's translation (*My dear Mr. Sparrow, / I have no idea / Where you reside, / But won't you just come / And have a drink with me?*) for rhyme, imagining Shokusanjin sitting on the thin veranda that skirts much of most old Japanese houses. The *sasa* in the original means 1) "a drink," one of the etymologies of which has it mean *"Come on!"* – echoing the *cho'cho, i.e.*, "just a moment" and "just a wee bit," as well as soliciting someone for a drink (another etymology has *sa* short for *"sake,"* repeated), and 2) the tiny bamboo sometimes translated as *sasa* grass, where this bird was typically depicted (seemingly pun-answering what the poet supposedly does not know). Needless to say, the English is lame by comparison. Here is an analogous translation:

My dear Mr. Fox, I've no idea at all where lies your den;
But, do join me for a nip! And, why not bring the Vixen?

Artificial? Not, really. A *tanuki* (racoon-faced fox) once jumped through my window landing upon my desk, so it seems perfectly normal to *me*. What counts, however, is the "nip." *That,* like the "cheep/cheap" in my poem, is the sort of gentle pun found in the original Japanese. *Cho'cho to* is also mimetic, for it evokes the small jerky movements and *chi'chi* chirps of the sparrow in particular. A crow can mean an old gentleman dressed in black, but a crow would never be invited to drink *cho'cho to*. (A *kyôka* would use – have used – an interrogatory *~ka* expanded to a *~kaa!*) Now, back to Blyth. Though he forgot to mention the *sound-sense* of the poem, I love how he frames it. He put it right after another Shokusanjin poem noting others had business before him by the footprints on the bridge: *"He got up early to do some business one cold frosty morning and found there were still earlier birds, or worms. Humour and poetry and the feeling of human toil and trouble are here combined."* I'd say what gives the poem its mad touch is the existence of older haiku where the footprints of others who went *snow-viewing* or *blossom-viewing* first are observed with chagrin (see *Cherry Blossom Epiphany* (2007) for many by Chiyojo). The mention of *work* is what made it a sort of working man's parody of the aesthete. But, I could be wrong. Regardless, Blyth's tongue-in-cheek *what-about-the-early-worms?!* made a pleasant link (a *haikai/kyôka*-style surreal link) to the *sparrow* poem. Most of all, I am delighted to find Blyth (1959), contrary to Keene, recognizes the goodness that is in *kyôka*. The devil may be in the details, and Keene may err less, but the angel is in the larger picture and Blyth, looking into *kyôka* and especially

Shokusanjin, with a sympathetic eye does the more valuable work here. Had Keene not written his pages on *kyôka*, someone else could have. Perhaps not so elegantly, for Keene, in prose, is a fine stylist. Still, I am sure the historical detail could be found easily enough in Japan. It would have been little loss. But no one could do or will do what Blyth did. Had I read Blyth's introduction to *kyôka* in *Oriental Humor* decades ago, I probably would have become interested in mad poems then, rather than only nine months (on re-proofing, sixteen months) ago! Reading Keene would only have made me reach for my ten-foot pole.

あらそはぬ風の柳の糸にこそ堪忍袋縫ふべかりけり 真兒 d.1829
arasowanu kaze no yanagi no ito ni koso kanninbukuro nuubekarikeri magao
struggle-not wind's willow's thread-with +emph patience-bag sew-ought!

..
    Our proverbial bags of patience should be sewn with string
    Made from whips of willow that always give in to the wind.

Blyth, again, changed the syntax to save the flow: *"The bag of patience / Should be sewn / With the strings / Of willow branches, / Which do not resist the wind."* I have done the same, *i.e.*, starting with the *bag* and ending with the *wind*. In Japanese "willow thread/string" is the standard term for those lithe branches (and *ito* is used for sewing and flying kites) but in English, the term does not exist, while "branches" sound too stiff, limbs too thick and twigs too short, spray would not be an individual string . . . My "whips" is dangerously close to perverting the message, but seems to work. Blyth writes that "the idea of this, by Magao, comes from a moralistic haiku by Ryôta: *'When I come home moody, a — / The willow tree / In the garden!'"* And then introduces two stanzas from Keble's April. I'll give two lines: *"Thus I learn contentment's power / From the slighted willow bower."* Then, he notes that *kyôka* tends to be *"in a way more moral than both haiku and senryû.* I would rather say it encompasses more variety, and moral poems are included, provided they are witty. I doubt the *kyôka* was just seconding Ryôta. There are *many* poems about bags of patience – *kanninbukuro* or *koraebukuro*. Issa wrote a *kyôka* describing *a gale as the wind god busting his* and there is a fine *Takatsukuba* (1642) haiku I translated for *Cherry Blossom Epiphany* (2007), *"She can no longer / contain herself! The late / cherry blossoms."* And, there are many *waka* with willow-string sewn items. What Magao did was stitch the two ideas, the bag and willow together with that thread. His use of the word *"arasowanu"* tells me there probably is *another* poem – not Ryôta's *ku* – being played, probably a classic *waka,* for they were full of *arasoi* and *arasoi-kanete,* that is "fighting" and "being unable to fight," *i.e.* giving in – if you doubt that, see the chapter on the *Wind and the Cherries* in CBE. There are large *waka* data bases that could be searched – hopefully, for the presence of more than one word/phrase in a poem; not having the privilege to use them I do not know. Be that as it may, the poem is charming, as metaphors elaborated become a sort of fantasy, or make-believe world. Others who introduce *kyôka* may mention that Magao was a conservative who quarreled with Akera Kankô and was responsible for making *kyôka* so boring the genre died. Blyth does not mess much with history, which is, for the most part, politics in the arts, but blesses us with a sample of the poet's better work.

Puffing Pictures, or The White Heron's Message

しら鷺は むかひにきたか たゞきたか しばしやすらへ 煙草一ぷく 蜀山人
shira-sagi wa mukai ni kita ka tada kita ka shibashi yasurae tabako ippuku shokusanjin 家集
white heron-as-for pick-me-up-for came? just came? a-while rest tobacco one puff/smoke

煙草入に鷺をかきたる絵に狂歌をかけといふに

< On being told to write a mad poem
for a tobacco-pouch with a picture of a heron >

White heron – coming to carry me off, or just to joke?
No matter, stay . . . rest a while, we'll have a smoke!

This, pulled from the large online "house-collection" of Shokusanjin's poems, is the sort of poem found in selections of poetry. I assume the person with the tobacco pouch, case, hanging box or whatever was, like the poet, over sixty.

Great white egret, have you come for me, or simply come?
Rest your wings a while, we'll talk when my smoke is done.

Sages were carried off into the cloud-hidden eternal reaches by big white birds, cranes, herons, egrets . . . When you consider how tobacco was credited with seeding clouds, a bird linking us to the same is a natural. Still, the simple poem is not what anyone would write. We feel the easy genius of the master. Because of that, perhaps, it set me to thinking about some of the other picture-accompanying poems in this book. Two more by Shokusanjin immediately come to mind. That small denomination coin, with its square hole and round outside (pg.176) and a caption pretending to praise the coin, while describing the ideal human character. The straw sandals with a description of palace maids having sex, playing on another poem, if I was not mistaken (pg.65). The variety of ways in which *kyôka* associates with pictures is truly astounding. If enough pictures could be found, I would love to do *a whole book of them*, provided a publisher with editors to do the s__t work could save me from rounding up the permissions. That is not the same as reproducing *surimono* with *kyôka*, for the poems created by request for sundry individual pictures would be wilder than those made collectively, on order or commissioned.

ふし見の西行の絵に 西行のたはこの煙空に消てはなの穴より出しふしのね
saigyô no tabako no kemuri sora ni kiete hana no ana yori ideshi fuji no ne   teiryû
saigyô's tobacco's smoke sky-in disappearing nose-hole-from departing fuji's peak=sleep

♪ *On a Painting of Saigyô Viewing Fuji* ♪
..

While smoke from Saigyô's tobacco fades into the sky,
Out from a nostril comes Mount Fuji on high!

The picture that comes to mind has Saigyô drawn large with Fuji in the sky near but not necessarily really touching the bottom of the great poet's nose. If you recall, most pictures of Fuji only show the white tip, and for good reason, the lower reaches usually vanish in the thick lower atmosphere. Teiryû wrote in the 17-18c. Smoking was a hit in *haikai* almost the moment tobacco jumped ship with the Portuguese sailors and Jesuits in the 16c. Saigyô belongs to the 12c. I have seen *haikai* or *zappai* making Mount Fuji the nose of the nation, in which case, the crater is its nostril and, as Japanese depict sleeping and reveries as coming out the same, we have a volcano dreaming itself. I write "we" but have no idea how many if any readers join me in such reveries. In marked contrast to the lyrical but humorous clouds of smoke common to most *haikai* and *kyôka* playing with tobacco, I found a fascinating set of counting (1-10) *kyôka* by "some-one" (ある人 *aruhito*) who may have chuckled but clearly took it seriously in bk #31 (百物語 1659) of *Broadview* 参. I translated three of them (#1, 9, 10), but could not do decent readings and keep the *number* puns except for the first.

一まちに火事のゆくもたはこゆへ わか身のうへと をしはかるへし
hito-machi ni kaji no yuku mo tabako yue waga mi no ue to oshihakarubeshi someone one=entire town-in fire goes too tobacco because, myself/body-re forcing-consider-ought

> *ONE town burns down & tobacco was to blame;*
> *What about your body, won't it suffer the same?*
> ~~~~~~~~~~~~~~~~~~~~~~~~~~~~~~~~~
> *Our town burns up and tobacco was the cause!*
> *Reason enough, I think between puffs, to pause.*

九せとしてたはこにすける人ことに われは持病のなをりたといふ
kuse to shite tabako ni sugeru hito goto ni ware wa jibyô no naorita to iu nine=habit-as do tobacco-on depend person-each-w/ me-as-4 chronic-disease cured say

..

> *All addicts of tobacco make the same damn claim*
> *Smoking is the only cure for what-ever ails them.*

十そんのありとはしりてのむからは たはこにまさるなくさみはなし
jûson no ari to wa shirite nomu kara wa tabako ni masaru nagusami wa nashi ten-losses are that-as-4 knowng smoke-frm-as-4 tobacco-over excel relief-as-4 not

> *To smoke however high the cost is simply wacko;*
> *which only goes to prove, no relief beats tobacco!*

Considering Bokuyô's anti-drinking *kyôka*, I wonder if he is "someone." According to Captain Golownin, held in Japan from 1811-13, talk about varieties of tobacco dragged on for hours *and was the most frequent topic of conversation* (Shades of potheads talking weed in Usania)! Japanese themselves realized this. A *kyôka* puns on the folic etymology of *kotoba=language* and homophony of *sun=hi=fire*: *Fresh tobacco, our leaf words never leave off discussing you; / Verbal pupus w/ each puff in the land of the rising "(u gotta) light?"* わか煙草のむ 言の葉はよもつきじ きせるのさらの日もとの人 参 45 貝田露程 諸国落首咄 *waka-tabako nomu kotonoha wa yo mo tsukiji kiseru no sara no hinomoto no hito* kaida rotei? 17-19c.

Play Pictures and Play Words, or Illuminated Kyôka

油だんなくかせぐ其身のあせ水は 金のなる木のこやしなるらん 一礼斎芳信?
yûdan naku kasegu sono mi no ase mizu wa kane no naru ki no koyashi naruran yoshinobu c.1850
caution(oil)-stop-not earn that persn/body's sweat-water-as-for money-bearng-tree's fertilzr becomes!

Sweat from a body who works with one eye peeled, pure honey,
Or, rather, good manure be . . . for the Money-bearing Tree!

This is a barely mad *dôka*, moral, or didactic poem pasted by doors as a charm. The sweat-as-fertilizer (more interesting as sweat wasted on martial exercise in peaceful times: あせ水をながして習ふ剣術のやくにもたゝぬ御代ぞめでたき もとの木網 *ase mizu o nagashite* Moto no Mokuami 1785) only glistens because it is on a print of said tree displaying five branches of commonplaces – "having a good plan だんどりのよ木" "good perseverance しんぼうのよ木" & so forth – per side, where each commonplace ends on a homophone of *tree* written with the *tree* character (よ木、ゆだんな木、かないむつまし木、等), the saving grace. Two fat gods of prosperity sit below this Money Tree, the Japanese Ebisu on a huge red snapper and the Chinese Hotei on two bails of rice. The artist, Yoshinobu *may* be the poet, too. The tree bore more than money. Its take-offs (trees split into *how-to-bear* and *how-not-to-bear* sides, the lucky *red-snapper* becomes a *giant catfish* and its earthquake brings money to carpenters, etc.) could fill a book. I have seen no *kyôka* with them, perhaps because they are funnier than the original. Indeed, they are the visual equivalent of the *Hundred Poets One Poem* parodies by *kyôka*.

焼亡がかきの本まで来たれどもあかしと 云へばここに火とまる 白隠
jômô ga kaki no moto made kitaredomo akashi to ieba koko ni hi tomaru hakuin d.1768
burn-death/fire-the fence's-base (=poet's name)-up-to came-if-even red/proof/light (of dawn & toponym in his famus poem) said-if here-at/by fire-stops=hitomaru (poet's name)

Though conflagration licks your fence and sparks persimmon spit
high into the sky, a poet's name may Fire Stop – Hitomaru, *to wit.*

~~~~~~~~~~~~~~~~~~~~~~~~~~~~~~~

Though conflagration licked the Kaki fence, dawn brings proof
This is where the fire stopped – Hitomaru saved our roof.

~~~~~~~~~~~~~~~~~~~~~~~~~~~~~~~

Though flames may lick this Kakinomoto, dawn bring proof
That this is where the fire stops – Hitomaru save our roof!

~~~~~~~~~~~~~~~~~~~~~~~~~~~~~~~

K A K I N O M O T O   H I T O M A R U
Though all beyond this fence is left in ashes and the flame
red as persimmon, the fire will stop if you read his name!

Unlike the chapter lead, this is *more* than witty enough to be a *kyôka*; but does it translate? The name puns split, surname in the first part, personal name in the second. Zen Monk Hakuin put the poem by a picture of *waka* "god" Kakinomoto Hitomaru (fl. c.680-700) drawn *with* letters spelling his best known poem that Hakuin's contemporaries used for an alarm clock (read half at night, you'll wake up on time to finish it). A boat disappears in the morning fog off Akashi, which in Hakuin's Fire Charm *kyôka* has three homophonic pun possibilities (red/light/proof 又かきのもとまでが、足の元の掛けであかし?). The Kaki in his name,柿, or *persimmon,* here means a *fence* or wall. Hitomaro, colloquially Hitomaru, puns as *fire+hi+tomaru =stop*. Most of the poem is borrowed from fellow monk Hannya-bô's poem:

わが宿の牆のもとまで焼け来るを般若棒にて打てば火とまる般若坊 般若房宗熙
waga yado no kaki no moto made yake-kuru o hannyaku bô nite uteba hi tomaru hannya
my dwelling's wall's base(kakinomoto)-'til burn-coming+obj hannya-monk-by hit-if fire stops

When the flames reach the base of the wall of my dwelling
Hannya thumps his staff and, lo, the fire stops, no telling!

Hannya punning his "monk" suffix *bô* into a staff is clever and his name meaning *prajna* also has power, but such detail works against the poem as a charm.

愛敬は己に鳥なきさとまでも人のこころに叶蝠助 桜川慈悲成 1830
aikei wa onore ni tori naki sato made mo hito no kokoro ni haku fukunosuke sakuragawa jihinari
revere-as4 self-to bird (=take/portion)less country until+emph people's heart fulfills prosperityguy

Born to please, Boy Prosperity leaves behind
The Land of No Birds to help us, humankind.

This accompanied a picture of big-headed Boy Prosperity – picture, doll, statue popular as a charm in the first decades of the 19c – that uses *bats* to depict all of his features and dress. These are not dingbats but the bats said to be kings in a land of no birds that were good-luck in the Sinosphere. Here, the "birds-not = *torinaki*" initially puns as *take-not*, i.e., "with no benefit to himself." The poem does not actually mention a bat but, besides the half-a-proverb, the "fu" sound in "福*fuku*=prosperity" is identified with one of the characters used for writing bat 蝙蝠. Still, without the picture, the poem would not work as Boy Prosperity is no bat. And yet, in its fine pun and proverbial take-off, it is a good *kyôka*.

人おほき人の中にも人ぞなき人になる人人になせ人 弘法大師 d. 776
hito ôki hito no naka ni mo hito zo naki hito ni nare hito hito ni nase hito kobo daishi
people many pple amng pple+emph not ppl-into becmng ppl-as makng/do-onto/serve ppl

So many humans, but among them not one human being!
Just human becomings and human-making humans.

Kuniyoshi 一勇斎国芳 c.1850 did a fine series of tastefully designed pictures of humans constructed from many humans. The knee for a nose and feet for lips engaged in talk, doubtless a homily, on the one titled "People clumping together become people (a person) 人かたまって人になる" accompanied by this poem beats all others I have seen. The poem, itself, usually attributed to the founder of Esoteric Buddhism in Japan teaches that humans beings are something to be nurtured. *It* is not mad; but *in combination with* the picture seems so! English number, divorcing the *one* and *many,* and lack of an active verb for "becoming" (hence "making") prevents a mad translation. Even today, explanations of "human" 人間 (how man 人 only exists *among* 間) are common in Japan/ese.

Wacky Waka Twisting Tongues & Crossing Sashes

よき人のよしとよく見て よしといひし 吉野よく見よ よき人よく見　天武天皇
yoki hito no yoshi to yoku mite yoshi to iishi yoshino yoku miyo yoki hito yoku mi emp. tenmu
good people good-as good looking good-as said goodfield(yoshino) good look good people good look

By the Emperor when He Blessed the Goodfield Shrine

Good people took a good look, and found it was good:
Take a good look at Goodfield, good people, look good.

~~~~~~

good men took a good look and finding it good called it so
take a good look at goodfield good people look good yo

Tenmu Tennô ruled from 672-694. I usually translate the rolling hills that would become the cherry blossom capital of Japan *Finefield* or just leave Yoshino. "Blessed" is a literal translation of the verb used for an Imperial Visit. It is a fact that an Imperial visit anywhere raised the stock of that place forever and ever, but this was, I think, Imperial property on Cloud Nine, so that is not why I was ridiculously literal. It is because the poem is obviously meant to be a blessing or charm for the facilities and the visitors. In that sense, it is an early example of the literally charming *kyôka*, though not mad for an Emperor was performing his role. And, note how the poem was transcribed: the scribe, counting those *goods,* wanted to make good on them. *Here* is the original transcription (the above is the *yomikudashi* (read-down) or *gloss* (all most read today) of *Manyôshû* poem #27:

淑人乃　良跡吉見而　好常言師　芳野吉見与　良人四来三

There are eight – suggestive of *plentiful* – repetitions of "good" in its adjectival and adverbial (*well/very/closely*) forms, pronounced *yoshi, yoki* or *yoku,* of which seven are single character (5 different and 2 repeated) and one two-character, "four-come" (good people coming from four directions, good luck coming?) the number of which, added to the three following it gives us the lucky number of seven! The five characters each include an aspect of the *good* in the broadest sense: *gentle/graceful* as in a gentleman or noblewoman, *good* as in plain old good, *lucky, likeable,* and *aromatic.* The plain old *good* 良 and the *lucky* 吉 are the ones repeated. We might note the latter doubled is a common propitious mark, or charm in the Sinosphere. There is also something not too common; I call it *stereo transcription.* The characters *sounding* out *yoshi to iishi* (good-as said) or "called it good," literally *mean* "likeable ordinary/usual word-master/s!" Praise for past wordsmiths? The Emperor? Or the oral 伝承詞人 folk poet who sang a poem (*miyoshino o yoshi to* . . . 中西注が詳しい) of which this may be a variation? Together with the first poem in the *Manyôshû,* where name-asking by an Emperor is glossed as desire for marriage by clever choice of a way to spell out "beautiful scoop holding" as "wishing to have a beautiful spouse" (美夫君志持), also in the third clump of characters, this is a good example of the audio-visual fun/puns Japanese have enjoyed with their writing from the get-go. Unlike the first poem, however, this one is 31-syllabet. So, too, the next, *Manyôshû* #527:

来むといふも来ぬときあるを来じといふを来むとは待たじ来じといふものを 万葉
komu to iu mo konu toki aru o koji to iu o komu to wa mataji koji to iu mono o manyô
come-wld say evn cme-not times r though, cm-nt sy-as4 thgh cm-wld–as4 wait-nt cm-nt though 8c

> *Sometimes when you say you'll come you can't & that's no fun:*
> *Why not tell me when you can't so I won't wait for you to come!*

"& that's no fun" replaces five positive and negative "comes" lost in translation.

われを思ふ人を思はぬむくいにやわが思ふ人のわれを思はぬ 古今#1041
ware o omou hito o omowanu mukui ni ya waga omou hito no ware o omowanu 10c
i+acc. love person+acc lve-not retributn-as?/! my lovng prsn's i+acc lve-not anon. kks

> *As I love not he who longs for me, karma this must be*
> *That the one whom I love, My Love, does not love me!*

Imagining the poem to be written for the beloved, I added "My Love," which the reader may remove or replace with "you see," or "I see." I would be surprised if Ovid never wrote this, and recall that Cervantes did. It was easy enough to translate. (思ふ人思はぬ人の思ふ人思はざらなむ思ひしるべく(後撰)と、忘られず思はましかば忘れぬを忘るるものを思はましやは（玉葉) を他人にお任せします。 A few poems away, I also found a superb near-*kyôka* metaphor:

ごとならば思はずとやはいひはてぬなぞ世の中のたまだすきなる kks #1037
goto naraba omowazu to ya wa iihatenu nazo yononaka no tamadasuki naru anon. 10c
identical if love-not-as4+emph say-exhaust-not why? world-among/condition's gem-tasuki

> *Why not just spit it out if you no longer think of me,*
> *For we alike differ in this: our love is like a* tasuki!

A *tasuki* is a thin sash criss-crossing the torso to keep a kimono from touching things and getting soiled when one works. The implication, as Kyûsojin notes, is that the poet may also may have someone interested in him or her. With *clothing* the ruling metaphor in love-poems, the *tasuki* may also imply the poet does not want things to get messy. *Yo no naka* here means *that's the way things are*, i.e. criss-crossing relationships (similar to 1041), but I loosely made it "our love." The original modifies the *tasuki* with *tama*=gems, idiomatically meaning precious/pretty and pun-evoking souls, what English might call hearts of lovers.

世の中を思ふもくるし思はじと思ふも身には思ひなりけり 本院侍従 玉葉
yononaka o omou mo kurushi omowaji to omou mo mi ni wa omoinarikeri _____ 1312
wrld/society+acc thnk/long/lve+emph painful t/l/l-not-of thnkng+emph self-to-as4 heavy/thnk

> *In this world, loving brings us pain but thinking not to*
> *love is a burden so we are blue no matter what we do!*

The four 思 do not translate as wit because one word in English will not *think*, *long* and *love*. I hope enjambing and half-nouning a verb (love) made the translation as witty as the original, itself not very, but enough. Not *kyôka*, these *waka* from Imperial anthologies still suggest Japanese enjoyed playing with logic.

Wishing for Nothing? Or, Nothing to Wish for?

天の下ありとある物なくもがな ほしやおしさやつくるとおもへば 宗長
amanoshita ari to aru mono naku mogana hoshi ya oshisa ya tsukuru to omoeba sôchô 1448-
heaven below every/all thing/s not wish! wanting and regretting! disappear think-if   -1532

How I wish
everything under the sun
would vanish,

So I'd no longer long
for what I wouldn't miss!

I vaguely recall an Indian philosopher telling an English physicist that we have but to say *"I want.."* and it is too late. Desire is unleashed; objects, like the tails of Bo-peep's sheep, will naturally follow. I laughed to read it, for it was amusing to find Indo-European syntax used to explain all human desire. Japanese and Koreans, who, rarely use "I" and almost always start with the *object* and end with the verb – as do most sign-languages – should, by this measure, all be saints. Monk Sôchô's *kyôka* (unintentionally) challenges that Indo-European bias by representing what a philosopher coming from a OV, rather than VO tongue might argue. Of course, blaming *what* we want for our wants is like charging others for what they do in our dreams and as silly a half-truth as pure Indo wantism. While the poet was a serious and comic *renga* link-verse master and not a mad poem poet *per se*, his *waka* included many so wild the reference volume of the TK *kyôka* roots anthology saw fit to include 56 of which this was one. Still, the original I tried to dress up with "no longer long" is pretty plain. In straight translation (*How I wish / that everything on earth / did not exist / To think of how our desire / & regret would just vanish!*) it seems boring, partly because I cannot help comparing it to Piet Hein's grook *"The universe may / be as great as they say. / But it wouldn't be missed / if it didn't exist."* where subject and object are in the same boat of non/being. H. Mack Horton (*The Journal of Sôchô*) translated a slightly different (there is an exclamatory *sate ya* but no "*oshisa* = regret") version of the same: *"How I wish / that everything under heaven / simply did not exist, / for if that were so / then all my wants would disappear."* In either version, this poem, following prosaic misgivings about the small thoughts of old age that autumn, seems too heart-felt to be *kyôka* or *haikai*, i.e. comic, but too off-the-wall for a proper *waka*. It is followed by a poem more clearly *kyôka* in style for pun-dove-tailing *hands clapped together* (*te o utsu*) into the name of the mountain, Utsunoyama, where Sôchô living in retirement, heard of events in the capital and provinces from passing pilgrims and travelers.

再現 度ごとにさても手をのみうつの山うつゝともなきことを聞くかな 宗長
tabi goto ni sate mo te o nomi utsuno-yama utsutsu to mo naki koto o kiku kana sôchô
each time-in hey again hand+acc only hit=utsuno mountain dream/false+emph. not things+acc hear!

Each time they call, I clap my hands and laugh, when I should snore
To hear what on the Mountain of Dreams seems real no more!

This poem was not among the 56 Sôchô poems in my roots of *kyôka* book (tk). Thank goodness for H. Mack Horton doing *The Journal!* You might be surprised to learn his translation is *"Every time they come / to Reality Mountain, / I just clap and say, "Really?" / though there is nothing real / in anything they tell me!"* Obviously, I took more liberty with the original, but the big difference between us is the name of the mountain. How can one Utsunoyama be Reality Mountain *and* the Mountain of Dreams? Well, *utsu* as an adjective generally means "empty," and the empty or vain world was synonymous with *maya*, the false world of dreams, while *utsusu* means "real/ity." *Utsu* was punned into *utsutsu* in the *Tales of Ise* poem (tale #9), which Horton cites, itself a fine *kyôka,* lamenting that though Mount Utsu is in a location with a name containing "do" (*Suruga*), the lovers fail to *do it,* meeting in neither reality or dream (*utsutsu ni mo yume ni mo*). Thus, both reality and dream unite on this mountain. Still, the pun seems a bit weak as a justification for the English name, as it seems to me more a matter of putting *utsu* and *utsutsu* next to each other rather than conflating them, but when we consider the sobering reality of retirement living, a psychological case can be made for Horton's choice, though the score of references to Mt. *Reality* in his index suggest it was chosen pragmatically, with broader translation needs in mind. My needs were to translate one poem, so I chose differently, but I respect his choice (not clearly explained, as such is the pernicious custom for translations into English). That both translations are possible in itself seems fitting, as the usual context for poems about dream and reality posits the difficulty of telling them apart. But, to return to the first of the two poems, what I want to know is something neither Horton nor the editor of the *kyôka* roots book (it has no notes) tell me: *Is this the first poem in Japanese, or better yet, including Chinese, to clearly wish for all things to vanish as a way to vanquish desire?* I can vaguely recall lovers wishing the non-existence of the object of their hopeless longing, but has anyone wished the same for *things?* If not, the poem should be famous whatever be its genre, for making history as a new poetic *meme*. On the other hand, if it is old hat, then I have already given it far too much attention. Why can't a university start up a web of poetic invention? We might call it *The Web of Trope,* more humbly, the Web of Tripe, after the Web of Life, or more grandiosely the *Memome Project* after the Genome one. Without such a bank of organized data, even expert literary criticism can only be bunk.

足ることを知るこそ人の宝舟 もののかずかず積みおかずとも
taru koto o shiru koso hito no takarabune mono no kazukazu tsumi okazu to mo
sufficiency+acc knowing+emph person's treasure-ship things'numerous piling place-not yet

> To know that you have enough is to own a Treasure Ship;
> Not that many goods must be piled high – that is never it!

..
Found at a website with some uncredited Shokusanjin poems, I suspect this is 18-19c. It is a *dôka*, moral rather than mad, but the unnecessary qualification of the metaphor – treasure ships are depicted low in the water from a mountain of magical things and riches, but the metaphor is, after all, psychological – and the combination of two idioms (重ね歌), one about knowing when you have enough and the other about not cluttering in the original makes its spirit kosher *kyôka*.

One Almost Flew Over the Cuckoo's Nest: Sanekata! 上

都人待つほどしるくほとゝぎす 月のこなたに今日は鳴かなむ　藤原実方
miyakobito matsu hodo shiruku hototogisu tsuki no konata ni kyô wa nakanamu　sanekata
capital-people wait+emph. know cuckoo? month-within/moon-this-side-in tday callnot!/? 958?-98

The Haut Monde is here awaiting you, so do hear what I say,
Cuckoo! These hills may be below the Moon, but call today!

Cuckoo! We may be on the wrong side of the month, but call today!

A near-*kyôka* by one who probably cuckolded as many men as any cuckoo did a bird. McAuley's Waka 2001 site provides the Japanese for the 10c Casanova's poem, but not for the preface, translated, *"On the last day of the Fourth Month, when at a mountain estate with a group of courtiers to listen for cuckoos."* His (or one of his students') translation of the poem is *"Capital folk / Are simply waiting for you, / O, cuckoo: / This side of the month, / Today, I would have you sing!"* The cuckoo should bring in the summer at the start of the fourth *moonth*. *Moon* and *month* being the same moonth 月 in Japanese, Sanekata was also joking about the location below (outside) the heavenly firmament of the Imperial Court (Like Milton, the Japanese had the moon dividing the higher and lower realms, much as the navel does our body).

誰がために惜しき扇のつまならん　実方
ta ga tame ni oshiki ôgi no tsumanaran sanekata
whose sake-for regretful(of losing) fan pinch-must?

When one of the ladies of the palace carried off my fan,

For whose sake dust thou cling for life to a purloined fan?

取れかし虎の伏せる野邊かは
torekashi tora no fuseru nobe ka wa
take-return, tiger crouches field is it?

and her reply:

Come and get it! Am I a tigress who'd pounce on a man?

"Come and get it" was too purrfect not to borrow from McAuley et al. Sanekata loved wit and did not mind women giving him his come-uppance. 「～は」もいい！

天の戸を我ためにとは鎖さねども あやしくあかぬ心地のみして 実方 10c
ama no to o waga tame ni to wa sasanedomo ayashiku akanu kokochi nomi shite sanekata
heaven's door+acc my sake-for-as4, barred-not but oddly cloyed(=open)-not feeling only have!

Heaven's Portal
was for my sake left ajar;
But odd to say,
I'm still far from through
longing for you, today.

Lest you get the wrong, or is it right, idea, the poem had a preface: *"When I was openly with the same lady in the northern hall, towards dawn we opened the shutters as the sky looked particularly fine; so, too, did my lady"* (McAuley et al). This stylistically is a *kyôka,* for the poet seems to say that though the portal was left unbarred, it did not open 開かぬ, but *akanu* could be, and with the following *feeling,* clearly means 飽かぬ, the active verb for *insatiate.* I wish I could re-find a *senryû,* once read, noting a c__t (*sane*) in this poet's name, for he did love it!

..
ささがにのくものいがきの絶えしより 來べき宵とも君は知らじな　実方
sasagani no kumo no igaki no taeshi yori kubeki yoi tomo kimi wa shiraji na sanekata 10c
fine/bamboogrss-crab-spider's spinnng ceased-frm come-ought eve evn you-as4 knew-not

– after talking with a woman upon parting for good –

So that spider, wee crab of the whisper-cane, spins no more
– You didn't know it was me until I knocked upon your door!

Here the second half translation by McAuley et al *"Though 'tis a night when I should come, / You know nothing of it!"* is closer to the original. This is the most puzzling spider-predictor poem I know. The colloquial *humph* of the *shiraji na,* the elegantly named spider married, or rather divorced, from the message, a sort of parting snub I'd guess came after he made a surprise visit to someone he had not seen in a while are improper enough to make this "waka" a demi-*kyôka*.

..
たなばたのこゝちこそすれあやめの草年にひとたびつまとみゆれば　同
tanabata no kokochi koso sure ayame no kusa toshi ni hito tabi tsuma to miyureba
seventh-eve/starfestival's mood+emph has iris's yearly once mate/eaves-by/as seen-when

She must feel like the Weaver at her rendevouz,
When, once a year, Iris gets to meet me & you!
~~~~~~
They must feel like the loving Stars – Iris spouses
But once a year adorn the eaves of all our houses!
~~~~~~
She must feel like the Weaver w/ her stellar spouse:
The honor comes but once a year: Iris in the house!
~~~~~~
Like Star Weaver on the Seventh eve, she feels alive
Once a year when Iris has her eave. Today's Five-five!
~~~~~~
Like the Weaver Maid it feels, I'm sure, when Cowboy fords
the Milky Way but once a year: The Iris under eaves adored!

We have seen poems punning 妻/棲 or, *wife/hem* but, here, the same *tsuma* is 妻/端 or, *wife/fringe* (of the roof), for Irises were hung from the eaves on the date slipped into the fourth try. As the purpose was to ward off disease, and the Iris probably preferred to be left in the ground. If the Edo era *kyôka* masters turned whatever they touched into food, Sanekata turned it into romance.

One Almost Flew Over the Cuckoo's Nest: Sanekata! 下

織女のもろてにいそぐさゝがにのくもの衣は風や裁つらむ 小大君 実方集
tanabata no morote ni isogu sasagani no kumo no koromo wa kaze ya tatsuramu ko'ôigimi 10c
weaver's/tanabata-festival's both/all-hands hurry/ing fine/cane-crab's spider=cloud-robe-as4 wind rend-would

On seeing a spider spinning a web on the thread laid out on
the Seventh Day of the Seventh Month, Ko'ôigimi composed:

Yes, the Wind's bent on renting her robes of gossamer cloud,
The Weaver can use some help – nice to see the spiders out!

Again, this is a poem not by Sanekata but a woman, a Lady-in-waiting for the Empress. McAuley, whose preface I borrowed, gives a matter-of-fact, *i.e., gloss*, translation: *"The Weaver Maid / Keeps both hands busy; / A tiny crab, / The spider's garb of cloud / Might by a breeze be rent."* Yes, my "spiders" is the same *sasagani* rendered "*spider, wee crab of the whisper-cane*" a few poems ago. But let's not worry about trifles. What makes this *waka* a *kyôka* is the crazy pivot on the redundant spider/s following its/their literary name "cane/fine-crabs." After specifying the *kumo* in question as a *fine-crab*, making it not only a spider but a spider *for sure* (Japanese poems clarify homophones w/ redundancy in the same way talking drums do: see Peter Farb's *Word Play*), said *kumo* modifies the *robe/s* the wind would rend so we learn it is really/also another *kumo* altogether, *cloud/s!* I tried closer readings that explained what the wind was about: *The Seventh nears, and she could use eight hands to weave her Star / His robe of gossamer cloud the Wind keeps renting (it's not for him).* & *The Seventh nears, and how the jealous Wind doth shred the clouds! / Spiders work overtime lest the Weaver have no robe for her spouse.* But none *sound* poetic. Ko'ôigimi's *waka* or *kyôka*, if you, like me, would call it so, is one of those quick-silver-in-a-groove beauties Waley despaired of. *So do I.* I am afraid the paraverse I used in place of a translation was the best I could do. The reason pretty weaving thread and cloth was laid out on this day was because the Weaver would bring her Herder a robe. The noble-women in Japan were not only literate. They helped raise silk-worms, spun and wove cloth for garments to give their lovers. Now Sanekata, again:

別るれど待ては頼もしたなばたのこのよに逢はぬ仲をいかにせむ
wakaruredo mateba tanomoshi tanabata no kono yo ni awanu naka o ikani semu sanekata
parting can but waitng if-as4 trust 7ᵗʰeve/stars' tonight-on meet-not relat. how do-should?
..

Though part they must,
the Stars trust they'll meet again;

But, if this night,
You and I come not together,
will we ever get it right?

The romance of the Stars as a solicitation. While McAuley et alia's *"Though they must part / If she but waits, trust can / The Weaver Maid; / Unmet this night, / What is to become of us…"* is, on the whole, *awful*, the last line makes up for it.

津の國のたれとふしやのふしかへりそのはらさへやたかくなりしぞ　実方
tsunokuni no tare to fushiya no fushikaeri sono hara sae ya takakunarishi zo sanekata 10c
tsunoland's who-w/ shack-in layng-camebck tht field(exper.)/belly+emph high(price) becme!

In the land of Tsu, who knew you on that moor not less
Than when you left so now your belly, too, is in the air?
~~~~~~
In the land of Tsu, who was it on the moor that left you
w/ something there besides your snoot so high in the air?

The preface suggests Sanekata was working on a woman someone got to first and was pissed off because she concealed it. The *field=belly* pun is easy to spot, but it is hard to guess exactly why "became high" is so emphasized. Was she snotty (High *nose* as *conceited*) or dumped by a high-ranking man (Sanekata was all too aware of his low rank)? Who knows! McAuley et al., took it in a more literal way: *"In the land of Tsu, / With whom have you lain down / So well? That / E'en the meadows—like your belly— / Have been rucked up!"* I have met one Rudy Rucker, but I never . . . (seriously, it is a heck of a translation).

わかきこが袴の股の絶えしより　そのひさかたのみえぬひぞなき　実方
wakaki ko ga hakama no mata no taeshi yori sono hisakata no mienu hi zo naki
young child's trousers' crotch ceases-from that faroff/knees see-not day+emph not.

Since the culottes of my young maiden came to lose their crotch . . .
Not a day have I not watched her legs as one might a star. From afar.

Again, I cannot *not* introduce McAuley et al's take: *A young maiden's / Trousers at the crotch / Did split, and ever since, / Upon her remote knees has / My gaze been bent!* On the one hand, this is a totally innocent poem. Girls graduate from trousers to robes, and this could be a kind statement of concern for a niece. But *hisa* ⇒ *hiza* – which puns from *hisakata,* or *afar* (and possibly *beyond*) – means not only "knees" but "lap" and all between, and even facetiously playing with that makes this outrageous, humorous or both. Yet it was not *this* poem that made me think of Casanova (Frank Harris spared the details), but scores of *waka* aimed at gaining his way with various women in his anthology. Some of them seem of the sort *not* usually kept. We may have them only because he had friends in high places. McAuley explains Sanekata had "close relationships with many of the great men of his time and was often called upon to compose poetry for members of the imperial family." That might do it. A last near-*kyôka (sis = my dear)* –

妹と寝ば岩戸の空もさし曇りその夜ばかりはあけずもあらむ　実方
imo to neba iwato no sora mo sashikumori sono yo bakari wa akezu mo aramu sanekata
sis/lvr-w/ sleep-whn cave-door's sky cloudover tht-nght extnt open=tire-not would-not!

Sleeping with Sis, I've come to wish Heaven's doors would stay shut,
With the sky too dark for day to break, tonight, I cannot get enough!

Sashi, or "barred" becomes *sashikumori,* or "clouding over," a term used in a Hitomaro poem on staying someone, *and* puns with a term found in the *Record of Ancient Matters (Kojiki* 712), sashikomori, meaning *to hole-up* somewhere.

上 Ye Olde & Now *Savage Songs*, or Mad in 1666 上

たはこのむうちより 春は来にけらし 烟も霞む はなのさき哉 正長 古今夷曲集
tabako nomu uchi yori haru wa kinikerashi kemuri mo kasumu hana no saki kana shôchô?
tobacco smoking within-from spring-as-for comes!/?/: smoke even mists nose (=blossoms)-before!

Spring came, when I was taking a smoke – And the proof?
Behold the haze that hangs thick as pudding from my nose!

I only just saw the index volume of my main source, the *Broadview* (*Kyôka Taikan:* TK) thanks to interlibrary loan; the poet index quickly showed me that some of my favorite poets were heavily represented in the 1061-poem, 17c *Kokin Ikyoku-shû*, or *Old-now Savage Songs Anthology*. Examining it, I found a dozen poems by Ikkyû, Yûchôrô, Teitoku and others already in the text, and a score or two I *wish* were. I thought to squeeze them into the appropriate chapters, but with most chapter already a tight two pages, it would take much work, and with no income to speak of, I could not afford the time. They almost went into the Notes, but, on second thought, I decided to grant them a few chapters of their own as these early *kyôka* were under-represented in comparison with earlier *wild waka* and later Tenmei era *kyôka* in this book. Explanations will be extremely short. Eg., the above starts with a take-off on Spring-within-the-year (p.34), plays on the proverbial haze and ends with punning nose-tip = blossoms-before.

めでたいといへはめでたいといふこそ 口真ねこまね正月の礼 宜斉 古今 同
medetai to ieba medetai to iu koso kuchi-maneko mane shôgatsu no rei   gisai 1666
joyful/lucky say-if joyful/lucky say espec. mimicker realsleepng(=mimic) ny greetings

Happy New Year! Say it, & it is a Happy New Year, indeed,
To Spend this Day in bed, parroting greetings half-asleep!

年こえて花のかゞみとなる餅は 黴かゝるをや曇るといふらん 保友
toshi koete hana no kagami to naru mochi wa kabi kakaru o ya kumoru to iu ran   hoyû 1666
year passing blossoms' mirror becoming sweetrice-cake-as-for molds hey! clouds-as say

The mirror mochi we made last year blooms in the new:
Mold has formed, or, should we say aloud, "It clouds?"

銭かねでねをさすならは 鶯の法々華経も一ぶ八くわん 貞徳 同
zenigane de ne o sasu naraba uguisu no hôhôkekyô mo ichibu hakkan   teitoku
coins w/ sleep=/⇒sound+acc make if warbler's *hôhôkekyô/sutra* even one bu eight kan

♪   In Praise of Uguisu Call Vendors   ♪

Even a chick may be had for a song, so just buy that song
of a bird for a buck an' eight cents you can't go wrong!

~~~~~~

Were we to set a Price upon Warbler's first song, good sense
would fix his "Hôhôkekyô!" at, say, one shilling, eight pence.

W/ the first poem, my *parrot* is a copy-*cat* that puns into a "sleep(ing)New-Year." The second is witty partly because the New Year is full of taboo words, *i.e.*, charming words replacing the usual one, but "overcast?" *never!* Even old eyes must more lyrically *haze* or *mist-over*. Wait! It also puns on *blossoms as "clouds."* The third, by Teitoku, combines the old idea about this bird's song-as-sutra with an actual fee (1 & 8 with nuances of New Year & infinite, but haikai for concreteness) demanded by monks for the same and/or a popular bird-call device and starts by punning, "if you are making/demanding/buying ね *ne* = sleep/sex 寝" into ね *ne* = sound 音, *i.e.*, the bird's call. I could not fit it all into one translation. The first ditches the sutra for the titillation giving poetic form to the *ne ne* pun. Presuming it referred to calls sold by vendors at this time of year, I added a title. Waiting is what makes hearing the first-call significant, but if it is a sutra, . . .

水にすむ蛙が歌をよくきけば　とかく卑下なり愚意／＼といふ　満永
mizu ni sumu kaeru ga uta o yoku kikeba tokaku hige nari guigui to iu   manei? 1666
water-in livng frog/s'song+acc closely listn-whn asithappens selfdeprecating foolish-thoughtx2 say
..

  When I really cocked my ears to hear those paddy frogs;
  No demand or boast was there – just gui gui humility!

衣がへの今日しもわたをぬかるゝは　魚の腹もやう月なるらん　貞徳 1666
koromogae no kyô shi mo wata o nukaruru wa uo no hara moyô tsuki naruran   teitoku
dress-changing's today+emph cotton(=guts)+acc removing-as-for fish-belly-pattern moon is!

  Today of all days when we de-gut our dress & put on spring
  Is this not a mackerel sky, in which the moon is swimming?

Really *listening* to frogs. Is that mad? No boasting to the bog, here. These bull-frogs croak *imho! imho!* Or, is it *Imso! Imso!* (s=stupid)? The dress-change would English better with a common word such as *wata* for *cotton stuffing* and *guts*. So, fish-guts may now be added to Teitoku's cow-slobber! Second poem *below:* an *Apologia* for mosquitoes!? Last: ivy is used for *japanning* (lacquer).

やるまいぞやるまいものを時鳥　きいたか／＼今の一こゑ　宗鋪 1666
yarumai zo yarumai mono o hototogisu kiita ka kiita ka ima no hitogoe sôhô see ♪
do-won't! do-won't think but cuckoo   heard? heard? now's one(=people?) voice

  It won't said I, it won't! But by and by, that cuckoo bird!
  Now, man rings out – Have you heard? Have you heard?

罪あるもあらぬ人をも生きながら　鬼はかほとによもやくふへき　宗朋
tsumi aru mo aranu hito o mo ikinagara oni wa ka-hodo ni yo mo ya kuu beki   sôbô 1666
sin/crime have have-not people live while, devils-as4 mosquito-amount+emph eat-ought

  Some humans sin, while others do not, but I have this notion
  That demons live, too, & must eat at least a 'squito portion!

やよ時雨猶うはぬりをたのむそや　まだ色薄き漆紅葉に　みとく 古今夷曲集
yayo shigure ame nao ueanuri o tanomu zo ya mada iro usuki urushi-momiji ni   mitoku 1666
Hey, time-rain still outer-coat depend (on u)!/: still color-pale ivy-maples-on (see p.115)

  Hey there, Shigure, when do you plan to apply the final varnish?
  The lacquer-maples still look dull, your reputation will be tarnished!

㊥ Ye Olde & Now *Savage Songs*, or Mad in 1666 ㊤

寒き夜は いかなる歌も よみつべし あまりかゞめば 人丸になる　宗也　古今夷曲集
samuki yo wa ikanaru uta mo yomitsubeshi amari kagameba hitomaru ni naru　sôya/munenari
cold-night-as-for whatsortof song+emph read-should too-much curling-if hitomaru=man-round becomes

On a cold night, what old poems should a person read?
With arms & legs pulled in, I'd keep Hitomaru around!

This winter poem is corny but heart-warming. If you know the ancient poet Hitomaru's name literally means *person+round*, no further explanation is needed.

鉄砲もそこのけ程に一年を 大晦日迄打くらしけり民部少輔喜隆 後撰夷曲集
teppô mo soko noke hodo ni ichinen o omisoka made uchi-kurashikeri　yoshitaka 1672
musket/gun even getoutoftheway amount one-year! ny-eve-upto emphatically(=shot)-lived!

This year passed faster than a musket ball can fly
I went off half-cocked & all the months shot by.
~~~~~~~~~~~~~~~~~~~~~~~~~
Faster than even a musket ball can fly, the last day
of this year I shot to hell and gone is already here!

Pardon this poem, from another selection of *Savage Songs* published six years later. I wanted a year-end poem to properly close the seasonal sequence. *My* idiom is forced, but *the original* is a fine example of vernacular metaphor and artless idiomatic pun. Now, back to 1666.　From a section on 恋, love:

若衆もたゞ我しりのことくにてみむとすれ共みられされけり貞徳 古今夷曲集
不見恋 *wakashu mo tada waga shiri no gotoku nite mimu to suredomo miraresarekeri*
youngcrowd+emph just my buttocks resemble, see-would do but seen-cannot-be!

Young-crowd love's another thing just like my nates: I mean,
Though I'd like a good look, I'm afraid they can't be seen!

Young-crowd are fashionable gays associated with kabuki but not beneath selling their favors. They and their salty white butts were a common theme in haikai and in pre-Tenmei *kyôka* such as these *savage poems*. Though unsure of the last part of Teitoku's poem, I am intrigued. Only a master could make a simile of his own ass! A less novel poem in the same 1666 collection: *Young-crowd bathing in the sea, their salt-white butts a-shine; / Molten desire grows within – Mount Fuji's dwarfed by mine!* 海て水あぶる若衆のしほじりをみるに思ひは富士の山程　玄康 同 *umi de mizu aburu wakashu no shiojiri o miru ni omoi wa fujinoyama hodo* genkô. The Kalpa, below, is a huge stone mountain of time (see pgs. 143, 212)!

寄亀恋 万年もはなれはせじな石亀のかうとやくそくかたき契りは　夏虫妻 同
mannen mo hanare wa sejina ishigame no kô to yakusoku kataki chigiri wa kachû no tsuma?
10,000 yrs + emph. separate-do-not' stone-turtle's kalpa with promise-firm vow/s-as-for

"Though ten thousand years come to pass," the Tortoise of Stone
promises to keep his vows so the Kalpa will never be alone.

此ほとはうち絶けるにたんほゝを　たまはりてくふ　したつゝみかな
kore hodo wa uchitaekeru ni tanpopo o tamawarite kuu shitatsutsumi kana ng 1636
this amount-as4 exhaust=drum-attenuatingstop! dandelion+acc receiving-eat tongue-drum!

♪ Read when someone received dandelions from someone ♪

Dandy, indeed! Your dandelions' pride, decimated just for me!
I humbly accept your gift and lick my chops ferociously.

◆　　◆　　◆　　♪ The Reply ♪　　◆　　◆　　◆

My pride is bigger than you think; don't worry, the number sent
'Tis but a small part, there will be more dandelions to present!

たんほゝを とたんたんとは やりもせて ちちつちつとそ をくりこそすれ
tanpopo o to tantan to wa yari mo se de chichi'chi'tto zo okuri koso sure ng 1636
dandelion+acc much=drumming-mimesis send-not so a-bit=tapping-mimesis+emph do/send

The preface was not in the 1666 anthology, but a smaller 1636 anthology called the New Selection of Kyôka 新撰狂歌集 from which I also take *the order* of the two poems. Since the usual practice is to send a poem w/ a gift and get a reply to that, it seemed odd to get the thanks first, then a reply to that, so the editor of the 1666 anthology dropped the preface and reversed the order and has the above reply sent w/ the gift of "drum-grass" – in the Japanese, there are no giant felines, and the mimesis and idiomatic play is a percussive tour de force, the *tanpopo* itself and *tantan-to* (*tan to* = many) sounding like a small drum beat and the *chichi'chi-to* (a bit) like tapping the rim, not to mention beating/clicking (*uchi*) tongues and a possible enjambed *hayari* chorus. I think it reads better in the original order. If I accepted the 1666 order, I would have to change the reading:

Couldn't find enough of these dandy lion teeth, but bit by bit
I'll send you more as I pull them, until you tell me "Quit!"

◆　　◆　　◆　　◆　　◆

Not to worry! I will cook, chew & swallow, then when done
With happy scalded tongue, lick my lips for ev'ry last one!

When you read between the lines, there is *that* much difference (minus my many obviously added details and interpretation), depending on the order of the poems.
..
尾も白しかしらもしろし庭鳥のひよこかふじは時しらぬ雪　卜養　古今夷曲集
o mo shiroshi kashira mo shiroshi niwatori no hiyoko ka fuji wa toki shiranu yuki bokuyô 1666
tail+emph white head +emph white chicken's chick? fuji-as-for time-knows-not snow

A baby chick out in my garden white of head and tail?
No, it's Mount Fuji's out-of-season snowy sight!

Fuji in the sky is often white above and below (ending in mid-sky). A short rainbow is called a rain-dog. So is Fuji in the distance a snow-chick!?

A Dandelion Break. 1636, Shokusanjin, Issa, Nenten

舌つゞみうつほどたんと出ずともちゝとなりともちゝ出よかし 蜀山人 家集
shita tsuzumi utsu hodo tanto idezu tomo chichi to nari to mo chichi ideyokashi shokusanjin
tongue-drum hit amount alot come-out-not even wee-bit become even milk come-out! late-18c

Even if the yield fails to match the drumming of her tongue,
A breast is a breast & milk should come out: at least some!

I found this Shokusanjin poem in Nada Inada's *Edo Kyôka*. I had skimmed over but not fully appreciated it before reading the 1636 dandelion gift-exchange poems for a second time in the 1666 book. Indeed, even Nada Inada did not know it almost surely borrowed from those poems. My translation does not reflect, or should I say *echo* it, but look back one page at the Romanization of the originals and you can see it. We find in biology puzzles of taxonomy, which only a jumping gene – presumably piggybacked upon a virus – would seem to (possibly) explain. I think of such, when I find memes from one poem popping up in another like this, under completely, which is to say comically despite the tragedy – different circumstances. As a member of the lowest echelon of samurai, Shokusanjin could not afford to hire a wet-nurse, so the best he could do is this lament cum-prayer for his wife's breasts to do their duty. Unfortunately, his first daughter died before the year was out. There is a *kyôbun* prose accompaniment to the poem: *"When we've no rice, we can eat buckwheat (noodles); when we've no tissue, a hand can blow a nose; when we've no money, we can charge to account; but like the proverbial landlord a crying baby is a crying baby, and nothing is so sad as having no milk."* (a proverb says *one cannot win with a landlord or a crying baby*). When I read this in Nada Inada's book, I recalled the nightmare that Issa, who at age 60 or there-about could finally afford to pay for a wet-nurse cum nanny to keep his baby boy when his wife became deathly ill, went through only decades later. I had forgotten to check Issa's letters for *kyôka* that might have slipped his *Journal* and sure enough, pay dirt!

ものいはぬおさな口を赤渋の水責とは鬼もしらじな　一茶　文政六年
mono iwanu osana-kuchi o akashibu no mizu-zeme to wa oni mo shiraji na issa
thing sayng-not infantile mouth+acc akashibu's water-pressing-as4 demons-evn know-not 1823

To force water down the throat of a wordless babe! I was a sucker,
For not even a devil could behave like Red-pucker.

~~~~~~~~~~~~~~~~~~~~~~~~~

Water torture applied to wordless babes? Why, even in hell,
No demon could excell in what Akashibu does so well!

The father of this wetnurse named "red-astringent" 赤渋 (*akashibu* – today, a disease afflicting mulberry leaves) claimed she was plump, fed on rice cake and whiter than snow, boasting milk that gushed out like *sake* from a just unstopped keg; but when Issa met his hitherto healthy son at his wife's funeral, he was a bag of bones. It turned out Akashibu's breasts were flat as a man's. She faked milking babies while giving them water. I added "I was a sucker," for Issa was taken in by a family of hucksters. The plain forcing of water (*mizu o hameru*) was in the first version of the poem. He used a technical term for punishment in the revised version that I printed and this "water torture" metaphor improves the poem as a *kyôka*. There was another:

乳恋し／＼とやみの虫のなき明かし泣きくらしけん　一茶
chichi koishi koishi to ya minomushi no naki-akashi naki-kurashiken
'papa dear/missing/want!' x2 bagworm's/s' crying dawns crying dusks

Bagworms cry as is their wont "Chichi koishi!"(Where is papa?)"
Mine the same cried night and day for papa & mama's paps.

Bagworms, also faggot worms, do not cry out as far as I know, but they do look a bit like the hampers farmers sometimes kept babies in, so the odd idea – not Issa's, but a literary conceit and possibly superstition common in haikai – may be a metaphor come full circle. Issa's fury and relative lack of finesse contrasts with Shokusanjin's cool and sophistication, but he had better reason to be mad.

をとにきくつゝみの滝をうちみれはさはへにちゝとたんほゝの花 新撰狂歌集
oto ni kiku tsutsumi no taki o uchimireba sawabe ni chichi'to tanpopo no hana 1636
sound-as/aloud hear Tsutsumi(prop. name)=drum's waterfall+acc go=beat-see-when bogside-by a little-bit=drummingwoodsound=of dandelion-blossoms

Provided one knows that dandelion was nicknamed *tomtom-grass*, any reader of Japanese can easily enjoy the above description of a visit to Tomtom Falls. But, it just cannot be enjoyed in English. That is why we have few mimesis-centered poems in this book. We can do a bit better with haiku, because we can use the relevant Japanese as-is. In a short poem, the words seem like well-set gems:

tanpopo no popo no atari ga kaji desuyo tsubouchi nenten
tanpopo=dandelion's popo area/surrounding-the housefire is+emph. 20c

<table>
<tr><td>

the *popo* part
of the tanpopo, *that's*
a house-fire!

</td><td>

The white mane
of your dandylion, *that's*
the house burning.

</td></tr>
</table>

Poppo, as an adverb mimics the popping and puffing of rising fire, steam or smoke. As a noun, it is what we call a *choochoo* train. The word also sounds puffy+round, as train-smoke is drawn in Japan. To me, the *popo* is clearly the globe of white seeds and I think of the bare stem standing after the "fire" (and "golden lads and girls must as chimney sweepers come to dust"), but four Japanese respondents split evenly on whether the poem depicts the smoky white seed-ball or the burning yellow flowers. We can agree that "the popo is where the tanpopo is really burning" but not on what the *popo* is. One felt it described a winter field with dandelion flowers bursting out *popo-popo* in clusters here and there. If that be the case, *I* will see them growing on land with burnt ruins beneath and make the poem a *just-so:*
..

Where the tanpopo grow, po! po! po!
That is the scene of a fire, you know!

Sooner or later I will do for this *ku* what I did with one by Buson, survey a hundred Japanese – or maybe *two* hundred: 100 haikuists and 100 random subjects – to get an objective reading on what is going on in readers' heads, *i.e.,* how the haiku works, as opposed to how we *think* it works, based on our own understanding. But, my point here is that whether we comprehend a poem correctly or not, or whether a correct and incorrect reading is possible – Nenten explains little, for he feels that whatever a reader makes it *is* it – polysemy is easier to comprehend in 17 syllables than 31.

㊥ Ye Olde & Now *Savage Songs*, or Mad in 1666 ㊥

虱ほと世をへつらはぬものはなし むさき人には殊に近づく 尾長老 古今夷曲集
shirami hodo yo o hetsurawanu mono wa nashi musaki hito ni wa koto ni chikazuku yûchôrô 16c
lice as-much/extent world fawn-upon one/being-as-for not, filthy people-as-for especially approaches

> *None suck up*
> *to the World less than*
> *they do, the Lice:*

> *Who's further*
> *from the toad-eater*
> *than a louse,*

> *No toad-eaters, they suck up*
> *to the mean and not the nice!*

> *Currying favor mostly*
> *in the meanest house!*

The sort of mad poem found in any culture with a bluesy sense of humor. Indeed, it is in a 1623 book of comic stories (*Laughs*) I'll bet the same has been written in English. If the data-base of old English poems were available to independent scholars and paupers – mostly the same thing – I might have settled that bet.

湯島の天神別当喜見院か許へまかりけるに兼て狂歌の頓作聞及ひ侍り所望といへれは
我歌に作意の自由しま(為増?)するを さらは申てきけんゐん哉 信海 1666
waga uta ni sakui no jiyû shimasuru o saraba môshite kiken in? kana   shinkai
my poem-in make-heart/aim's freedom do+acc then tell, ask! (?) !/?

On visiting Yujima's Tenjin attached-hall and being asked about composing *kyôka*.

> *To show the freedom of my poems to create greater yet*
> *Ask me for anything you want, and that you will get!*

かくよみければ狂歌とても自慢はいかにそやちと卑下ありてもよかるへしと傍なる人のいへは

On reading the above, an onlooker said *"Kyôka* sure seem boastful! It might be nice if they had a wee bit of self-denigration." Again –

> *Kyôka has it all, our vanity fills heaven, our hearts are free,*
> *And, as the Sky-god's whiskers talk, we balk not at humility!*

狂歌には自慢天満大自在　天神ひげをしてもよけれと 同
kyôka ni wa jiman tenman dai-jizai tenjin hige o shite mo yokeredo
mad-poems-to-as-for boastful heaven-filling-great-existence skygod's

Shinkei's second poem is a masterpiece *in the original*. The dynamic Chinese or Ikkyû Zen style boast in the first half gives it rhetorical legitimacy. Tenjin, the "Sky-god" in the toponym – at least his Noh mask – sports a moustache, or *hige*, which allographically written 卑下 means *self-denigration*. Using phonetic syllabary, the poet graciously allows Tenjin to wear one *and* simultaneously for *kyôka* to be humble. Dozens of poems in this collection treat poetry itself. One, dubiously attributed to Teitoku (ていとく) calls link-verse masters "girls" for reasons involving technical terms too arcane for this book but a must-see for some readers: 連歌師はをんな子なりと覚えたり さしあひもあり妊み句もあり 同
rengashi wa onnago nari to oboetari, sashiai mo ari haramiku mo ari).

負子よりだく子に乳をばのますれど 親の慈悲には前うしろなし 未得同
ouko yori daku ko ni chichi o ba nomasuredo oya no jihi ni wa mae ushiro nashi mitoku
piggybck-child more thn huggd child-to milk/breast+emph drink-allow-but parent's mercy-as4 frnt bck not

> *The child she holds drinks more than the one who rides,*
> *Yet a parent's love before and after takes no sides?*
> ~~~~~~~~~~~~~~~~~~~~~~~~~~~~~
> *Piggyback gets less at nana's breast, than cradled baby,*
> *but a parent's heart knows not before or after – maybe.*

The second line in the original is a proverb, the direction implied in *time* (order of childbirth) rather than space. The classic emphatic *o ba* may be a punning allusion, a homophone for a wet-nurse, *uba* sometimes *oba,* hence the Nana in the second reading. In Japan, two children were often carried at the same time. Since the one in back faced forward, the breasts might be reached from under the arm, but such a child would be at a nursing-disadvantage to the cradled one.

庭訓の往来よりも道遠き たびならはせよいとふしき子に　正長 同
teikin no ôrai yori mo michi tôki tabi naraba seyo itôshiki ko ni shôchô
garden/home-lesson's commute morethan road far travel do-if dear-child-to

> *Rather than tripping to & fro the garden class, send 'em far away*
> *Travel's good for your dear child – Isn't that what they say?*

子どもをは鮨にする程持たれど いひがなければひぼしにぞする
kodomo o ba sushi ni suru hodo mochitaredo ihi ga nakereba hiboshi ni suru anon
children+emph sushi-into make amount have but channel not-if dried pilchards-into make

貧しき人の子おほくもたるをみて　よみ人しらす
On seeing poor people with many children

> *Not to kid, but they have enough of them to make sushi!*
> *Or, lacking rice, sun-dried might do, though less juicy!*
> ~~~~~~~~~~~~~~~~~~~~~~~~~~~~~
> *They have kids enough to make sushi and still are not done?*
> *When rice runs out, they may need to cure them in the sun!*

..
借銭の淵程あるをたいらかに なせるは金の砂子なりけり　友知
shakkin no fuchi hodo aru o tairaka ni naseru wa kin no sunago narikeri yûchi
debts' deepwaterhole amount are+acc level make-as-for gold-sand is+emph.

> *There is only one way to fill up a hole of debt*
> *You must dig until you hit pay dirt and use it!*

Poem 1: The "garden lessons" recommended by Confucius run up against a popular saying. *Poem 2:* The idiom has a "packed like a sardines" feeling. Rice was used to ferment the old-style *sushi,* which was often slept on for the warmth and pressure. Poor people often had little if any rice, but provided they had some access to sunlight . . . . This almost *Modest Proposal* expanded the *sushi* idiom into two ways of preserving large catches. *Poem 3:* Compare reading to gloss.

Ye Olde & Now *Savage Songs*, or Mad in 1666 ㊦

世間は拍子ちがひになり果て　舌鼓のみうつゝなの身や　入安　古今夷曲集
sekken wa byôshi-chigai ni narihatete shitazutsumi nomi utsutsuna no mi ya   nyûan
society-as-for beat-different-as became tongue-tomtom only clicking=blue self/body!

The whole world
hears a different drummer.
I am no fun –

An empty head like mine
can only click his tongue

The whole world
marches to a different beat,
Leaving just one:

This out-of-touch body
dares to click his tongue

~~~~~~~~~~~~~~~~~~~~~~~~~~~~~~~~~

With the world now dancing to more than one drum,
I can only shake my empty head & click my tongue!

I wish I knew the right reading. An anthology of Nyûan's *kyôka* was published in 1610; they may span the tumultuous time when the capital moved from Kyôto to Edo. That, and the *"wa"* (not *"to"* after *seken*) favors the second: we might call heralding a new world; but the way he describes himself favors the first reading, chosen largely because *ususuna* (empty-headed, including *senile dementia*) includes *utsu*, or "beat," i.e., for the pun which flows from the "tongue-drum."

着る物はとても角てもよこれぬる　心のあかの洗濯もがな　従四位源　忠次
kiru mono wa totemo kakutemo yogorenuru kokoro no aka no sentaku mogana   tadatsugu
wearing thing-as-for completelypletely soils/ing heart's crud's cleaning wish!

What men wear will soil no matter what we do: Why start?
I only wish for a way to wash the crap out of my heart!

祖父祖母ひうばひ祖父こと／＼く　死なずに居ては何をくはせん　雄長老
ôji uba hiuba hiôji kotogotoku shinazu ni ite wa nani o kuwasen   yûchôrô　古今夷曲
grndpa grndma grt gma grtgpa evrybdy die-not-w/ being-as4 wht+acc eat-let-not 16c

Grandpa Grandma Great-grandma Great-grandpa, if all were then
Not to die and chose to stay – What the hell would we feed them?

~~~~~~~~~~~~~~~~~~~~~~~~~~~~~~~~~

Grandpa Grandma Great-grandma Great-grandpa, R.I.P. Amen!
If they all living hung around, what would we feed them, then?

みな人のもし成仏をするならは　地獄の鬼やかつへ死なまし　行好
minabito no moshi seibutsu o suru naraba jigoku no oni ya katsueji namashi   kôkô
all peopls+emph becme-bddha/enlightnd-becom-if hell's demons+emph starvedeath wuld

If everyone were to become buddhas with their last breath
Wouldn't the poor devils in Hades slowly starve to death?

Was the first poet a hidden Christian? The Jesuits constantly compared the extraordinary neatness of the Japanese clerics with their dirtiness within! A lax, even approving attitude toward pederasty was the main problem. Most Jesuits who spent time in Japan admitted that even infanticide was done from kind motives. Because the Japanese and Chinese worked harder and fought less than Europeans, they had denser populations. They, who adored children, made hard choices; while we chose to kill others for our "right to life" through colonialization and war. Remember that Japanese 'devils' only do their duty punishing sinners. Part of that, according to popular artwork involved cutting up, stewing and eating us.

仏にはまだなまなりの魚の鮨　菩薩界までをしかゝりたや 長好 chôkô
hotoke ni wa mada namanari no uo no sushi bosatsu-kai made oshikakaritaya
buddha-as-as4 still raw-style fish's sushi saint's-world until/upto pressure-want!

釈教魚といふ事を
On a Buddha-fish

Still far too raw
too fresh for Buddhahood
a sushi acolyte

I want pressure, yes push it,
My fish, right into Paradise!

For a dead man,
I'd offer some sushi still
on the raw side:

Until he reaches the saints
You want pressure applied

A *hotoke* is Buddha, enlightenment or the polite term for any corpse. If we are really talking about a *fish* theme within the Buddhism section, and not a *Buddha-fish*, it should be specified with a 寄. So perhaps there *was* such a fish, but my OJD dictionary has none, so the first reading assumes an allegory for making heavenly fermented *sushi*. The second posits a dead man *hotoke* and adds the "offer" to make that guess explicit. The "he" is regrettable. English demanded it. Shakkyô, another word for Buddhism, short for "Shaka's teachings" is what books of *waka, haikai* or *kyôka* call chapters for poems touching sincerely or not upon Buddhism. We started that chapter of the *Savage Songs* two poems ago with those merciful thoughts for starving devils. It is easy not to translate the more boring moral songs, but hard to give up on great ones depending on untranslatable puns such as Nyûan's wish to turn into a ladle=*shakushi*=Shakha to dip into herbal soup to save= *sukuu*=scoop-out his dying girl (いもが子に限りしもせじしるのみをしゃくしと成て救ひあげばや 入安 *imogako ni kagiri shi mo seji shiru no mi o shakushi to narite sukui-agebaya*). Luckily, many *kyôka,* even in this age of haikai, played with ideas as well as words. But, they too, are not easy. Even my indefatigable respondent was unsure about which reading fit the next:

極楽の金座敷は尻ひえん　只行べきは地獄釜ぞこ　理西 risai
gokuraku no kogane zashiki wa shiri hien tada yukubeki wa jigoku kamazoko
paradse's goldn parlor-as4 buttcks chill-would but go-ought-as4 hell's cauldren-bottm

I'd cool my butt upon the golden dais in paradise;
But the bed of hell's cauldron is what comes to my eyes.

~~~~~~~~~~

The metal dais of paradise will freeze my derriere
Better to sit at the bottom of a pot in Hades, bare!

⑦ Ye Olde & Now *Savage Songs*, or Mad in 1666 ⑦

西むきにせなかをくふと観ずれば 東じらみに夜は明にけり 夢窓国師 古今夷曲集
nishi muki ni senaka o kû to kanzureba higashijirami ni yo wa akenikeri mûsô kokushi
west-facing-as back+acc eating saw-if/then eastern-lice-to night-as-for brightens/dawns

*Facing the West, they ate my back – "Eureka!" thought I:
These are Eastern Lice that brighten with the pre-dawn sky!*

This is the only poem utterly lost in translation I nonetheless used as the lead. Perhaps, it should have been exiled to ♪land. The exception was made because it was the next poem marked – I have tried to follow the order in which the poems appeared in *Savage Songs* – and because it demonstrates *utter inanity* of a type often identified exclusively with Tenmei *kyôka* a hundred years later. The lightening of the sky before sunrise is called *shirami,* or "whitening." Lice, too, are *shirami.* Combined with *higashi-* or "Eastern," we get the pronunciation you see above, *higashijirami.* One hopes the advent of the idea and composition of the poem made the poet so happy he forgot his itching for a while! *Akenikeri* or "becomes bright," written with *~nikeri* finality *also* alludes to *surrender*, while *Yo* 夜, or "night," could imply *yo* the first-person pronoun 予 or *yo* the world 世. Between the lines, the poet would seem to be, like this translator, overwhelmed.

紀貫之か雨により田蓑の島とよめるを思ひ出て
雨により田蓑の嶋の見物に　笠をめさいでぬれつらゆき　藤原兼定卿
ame ni yori tamino no shima no kenbutsu ni kasa o mesai de nure tsurayuki
rain-by fields straw-raincoat-islands' sightseeing-for umbr.hat+acc wear-not so gets-wet tsurayuki=face-goes. by Fujiwara Kanesada *Kokin Ikyoku-shû*

Recalling Tsurayuki's waka about seeing straw-raincoats in the rain as islands
..
*Playing the tourist out observing islands made by raincoats in the rain
Not wearing his umbrella hat, there our wet face=Tsurayuki=goes!*

蛇足。ぬれつらゆき(ぬれつ⇒らゆき)＝濡れ面行き！さて1666年
以前のこのしゃれ。洗練を天明狂歌に待つ云々諸君、どうだい？

With the previous poem, my survey of the 1061-poem *Savage Song* anthology ended. This, I left out as English has no word for or image of a *mino* straw raincoat and the pun on the great poet-editor's name goes nowhere. Like the last poem, though, it is a fine example of what Shokusanjin would do a hundred years later. The poem of Tsurayuki's referred to is not in the *Hundred Poets*, but the gentle take-off + subtle poem-closing name pun, *i.e.,* the style, foreshadows some of Shokusanjin's *Hundred Poet* parodies. I apologize to English-only readers, but felt a point needed to be made even if it was untranslatable. ◎Re. what follows: a score more poems from this 1666 anthology are found scattered throughout the book. I thought I would put all the death poems – including many I considered the best – at one point there are four of my favorites in a row – into the *Mad*

Goodbye chapters. But, checking, I find I dropped one of my four favorites despite discussing it with my respondent at some length. I will introduce it now, then move the discussion to other things the *Savage Song* anthology taught me.

大坂に又太夫といふ舞太夫ありしが臨終によみ侍る歌 1666
来世にて又太夫とやなりぬべき死ぬる時にもめこそまひまひ 古今夷曲集
kuruyo nite mata dayû to ya narinu-beki shinuru toki ni mo me koso maimai courtesan
coming world-in again top-courtesan as becme-ought, dying time evn eyes+emph dance

Read at the/her deathbed for/by a top dancing courtesan in Ôsaka

~~In the next world~~ ~~again, you can bet she'll be~~ ~~a harlot of parts:~~ ~~Even on her death bed, we~~ ~~see the dancing eyes of art~~	In the next world I bet I've another chance at top courtesan! As I lie dying even now, My eyes would still dance!	~~In the next world~~ ~~once again, I bet I'll be~~ ~~a top courtesan~~ ~~Whenever I die, you see,~~ ~~My pussy keeps dancing~~

The woman is a *dayû*, top rank among organized courtesans and her full title "dancing dayû 舞太夫" means she was a great performer on her feet as well as her back. She has been experiencing dizziness, *memai* 目眩, which is deftly choreographed into *me koso(emphatic) mai mai* 目こそ眩ひ眩ひ which, in turn, puns into its homophone 目こそ舞ひ舞ひ allowing the eyes to literally (yet facetiously) dance. I forgot the poem because, first, I had a moratorium on the meaning after visitation by a probably unintended pun reading – parsing *mekosomaimai* as *meko zo maimai*, rather than *me koso mai mai,* I fused it to the *petit mort* (a theme in my dirty senryû book) – and second, because I failed to fully appreciate the dizzy⇒dancing pun and thought, *"Now how can she know her eyes are dancing, whatever that is . . ."* My mind spinning with the possibilities crossed out above, I set the poem aside. Now, recalling the legendary verbal alacrity of courtesans, and considering that such a poem would be a kind goodbye to all gathered to send her off, I settled on one reading. Yoshioka, introducing these poems on-line, also notes something I missed about the death poem after it, the one with a *go* move called *kô* (pg.384). The poet was the first truly famous *go* player in Japan and ancestor to the *go* prodigy 本因坊家 (1558-1623). This poem was followed by the dying haikai master who punned link-verse terms into going out with a puff, lit from his underarm hair (p.690). So, dancing harlot, go player and haikai master, all left death-poems that *testify their love for their trade.* Had I caught that earlier, all three poems would have been together in this book, too! Seeing the death poems together also set me to thinking beyond individual poems to the larger pattern. Prince Ôtsu (d.686) wrote a witty death poem (p.392) for himself a century before the 8c *Manyôshû* which does not give us any, or none I recall. Rather, we see scores of fulsome, though often beautiful eulogies, as we find in Europe (where there are volumes of death poems to gain laughs, which are always for the other guy, *i.e. epitaphs*). Only, later, do we find witty death poems, mostly by warriors or priests, each death-defying and service=entertainment-minded in their own way. And, where were these and later ones by poets published? Mostly, in collections of *kyôka.* ♪

Savage Song Mistakes: On Gathering Gays, Keeping Corn

若衆の尻つきをみて はなれえぬ 念者や桂男なるらん 貞富 後撰夷曲集 1672
wakashu no shiritsuki o mite hanareenu nenja ya katsura otoko naruran　teifu later savage select.
young-crowd's rump-build =moon+acc seeing separate-cannot admirer!/?/: katsura-tree-man is!

A wakashu lover must be him, the mythic man in the katsura tree,
How he swoons when a pale youth moons is something to see!

~~~~~~

The gay youth's heart is as hard to grasp as sand on the shore;
With pick-up lines as many as those grains, I could not score!

若衆の心はよそにありそ海の浜の真砂の数くとけとも 原通勝卿 後撰夷曲集
wakashu no kokoro wa yoso ni ariso-umi no hama no masago no kazu kudoketomo michikatsu
young-crowd's heart-as-for elsewhere is-seems=ariso(name)sea's beach-sand's # approach-even

The 1666 anthology's larger 1687-poem follow-up 後撰夷曲集 *Gosen Ikkyoku-shû* (1672) has half-a-dozen young-crowd=*wakashu*=youth-love (not *pederasty*, another theme, more common in *haikai* and *senryû*) of which two were so good, that, in combination with those we saw from the 1666 collection, they merit a separate chapter – as I had for 恋 basically, heterosexual love – on the theme that I wrongly assumed from later *kyôka* collections could not be well filled. My mistake. The first, above, is infinitely punnier in the original. If you recall, said Katsura tree grows on the moon and the Katsurao is the Japanese equivalent of our *Man in the Moon*. Crudely put, the implication is that he cannot leave the moon/buttocks because it attracts him: a wondrous newly coined just-so myth. For the second, *"Oh, shun the gay youth"* would have been a better start, pun-wise, as "seeming (distant)" morphs into a toponym, the Ariso Sea, that leads to the shore with its metaphorical sand, but, I failed to finish it. The original is conceptually good for taking an old saw used to quantify the quality of love and, instead quantify attempts at seduction to fit the stereotype of the fashionable gay-youth-as-coquette, playing hard to get and loving it, the game, rather than the would-be lover. I also failed to give examples of some of the corniest stuff:

父母にかりてぞきたる皮衣 破れて後はもとの塊 読人しらす anon.
chichihaha ni karite zo kitaru kawakoromo yaburete ato wa moto no tsuchikure
father mother-from borrowed! came leather/skin-robe torn after-as-for orig. dirt-clump

法 界 体 性 智 の 心 を
On the Mindset for Wisdom in the World of Buddhism

This robe of skin our parents give us, we wear from birth,
It breaks and then once again, we're but a clump of earth!

While I regret that the editor of *Savage Songs*, Kôfû, religiously adhered to Teitoku's line on avoiding squibs (*rakushu*) as inherently mean-spirited, it does not much bother me that he included some rather bathetic catechism. I do not say this because he was, after all, a monk, and had a right to, but because it is useful for making us think. Is not the absurdity of religious metaphor only matched and possibly beaten by love metaphor? If one is a free thinker as most *kyôka* poets were, how could religious metaphor not strike them as amusing? Yes, the above is a humdrum reminder of out mortality of the same sort found in a million ditties written in English and pushed on school children for centuries. But there is something delightful to the mind in leather sacks and clumps of earth. We are brought back to the material world, the literally good one that has nothing whatsoever with materialism that spits on material – such as the gold it would hoard rather than craft – as essayed so beautifully by Alan Watt's in his wisest work, *Does It Matter?* The above was the penultimate poem of the 1061 poems in the main text of *Savage Songs*, the last was the next, probably by the same anonymous and possibly intended to be included under the same title:

空は皃月日はまなこ風は息　山野海川我身なりけり　読人しらす？
sora wa kao tsuki hi wa manako kaze wa iki yama no umi kawa waga mi narikeri anon.
sky-as4 face moon sun-as4 eyes wind-as4 breath mountain field sea river my/your self

The sky our face, the sun & moon our eyes, the wind our breath,
the mountains, fields, sea & rivers, all are us in life, in death.

Again, corny. As art-poetry, anyone would prefer the famous haiku about the naked beggar clothed by a magnificent blue sky. But, then, you think. Is this describing us? Or is it the Buddha? Or is it both? And how would you, in a short poem sum up the identity of the micro and macro-cosmos? Most of us might start with the grass or plants as the hair – did you notice it missing? Of course it is implied in the landscapes, but for shaven monks it is convenient not to have it mentioned directly, in your 'clean' face so to speak. This list of correspondence may not be great poetry, but it is a great way to end a book of poetry, is it not? But – the buts go on, sorry! – the anthology is not completely over. After the above poem, Kôfû notes each poet and the number of poems contributed, starting with Shôtoku-taishi, the wise Prince and Regent credited with getting the young nation off on a good foot (a relativist, he noted people saw things differently), then the various Emperors, their ministers, the warriors starting with the Shôgun Hideyoshi, then high-ranking men of cloth, then others, such as himself. And, this is followed by a short seasonal note which includes news about his writing and gathering waka as well! Some day, I would like to see what he collected, but for now, let us just note he added nine more poems of his own of which one was:

金竜寺にて 入相の鐘よりさきもちりぬめり 花やあたなる世をいさむらん
iriai no kane yori saki mo chirinumeri hana ya adanaru yo o isamuran 行風 kôfû 1666
dusk bell-from after=bloom even fallng, (cherry)blossm/s!/as4 false/vain-world encourage
蛇足：春駒を思わせる「勇ル」のよさを伝える為、又英訳やり直したい

After the Vespers,	*After vespers do*
They still bloom & fall, that	*the cherry blossoms bloom*
all those Blossoms	*and fall in vain?*
never give up on this	*Not if they bring cheer*
False World is awesome!	*to all who must remain!*

Getsudôken – a *Kyôka* Master in Bashô's Time 上

棒ほどな涙ながして今ははや 恋のをも荷をになふ斗ぞ 黒田月洞軒 大団 c.1700
bô hodo na namida nagashite ima wa haya koi no omoni o ninau bakari zo kuroda getsudôken
pole amount of tears flowing/ed now-as-for already love/blues burden+acc bear amount+emph.

From mine Eyes
stream Tears like Poles,
& they grow thick
Enough to bear the Burden
of a Love no longer quick.

The tears flowing
from my eyes made poles
thick enough now
To bear a sedan in which
my lovesick blues can sit!

Tears from my eyes
flowed down like sticks, a pair!
Now, grown to poles,
They're thick enough to bear
Love's blue burden of despair.

I have seen *manga* where tears did not so much flow as drool, hanging in the air like the slobber of a cow. But this may be the oldest *pole* of tears. Japanese today depict a crying face with two capital T's but this poem never became famous (as it should have), and I doubt they think of the vertical part as a pole. Thanks to poles being used for carrying things in the Sinosphere, one metaphor became a cartoon (maybe we could have firemen slide down them!). Pretty crazy for a hundred years before Shokusanjin et al, huh? You might recall meeting Getsudôken before. He is the sea-slug who rolled in the mud with a tart (p.252).

わが宿の軒端のつまと見たばかり だひてねられぬあやめ草かな 月洞軒
waga yado no nokiba no tsuma to mita bakari daite nerarenu ayame kusa kana
my dwelling's eaves' wife-as see only, holding sleep-cannot iris tis!/? getsudôken

I only saw her in the eaves, I looked right up her nooky
But never got to hold and sleep with my blooming Iris!
~~~~~~~~~~~~~~~~~~~~~~~
I only saw her as my wife of the eave: I did not hold 'er;
For I did believe she was an Iris, though I never told 'er.

Composed for the 端午 rite Sanekata played upon in the last chapter, 800 years earlier. Same pun on *tsuma*, eave-edge=mate. Thinking the poem might be allegory *nooky* popped into my head. Do I think too much? Sixty poems before:

死にますといふて夜すがらだひてねて今朝のわかれはよみぢがへりか
別 *shinimasu to iute yosugara daite-nete kesa no wakare wa yomijigaeri ka*
dying saying, all-night hug-sleeping this-morning's separation-as4 yellowspring-return?

A night spent in embrace 'dying! dying!' dawn is, instead
of just a parting, a return from the Land of the Dead!

瞿麦 妹とわがぬる夜たがみに目があけばへそのあたりをなでしこの花
imo to waga nuru yo tagai ni me ga akeba heso no atari o nadeshiko no hana 月洞軒
litl-sis=sweethrt & i sleep night echothr eys opn-whn navl-area wld-pnks(=stroke-pee-bloom?)

On nights my love & I awake and look into each other's eyes
Unblinking past the navel, down we go – wild pinking!

The night she & I slept together we awoke and looking down
by our navels, what is this? Wild pink bloom lies all around!

The "dying" on the last page explains itself. Getsudôken is eroticomic. *Dianthus superbus* is usually 撫子, *stroke-ling* (who can refrain?). That might give away the game, so the caption is 瞿麦. The poet may react to a poem by Katsuho 且保 in the second *Savage Song collection* (後撰夷曲集 1672), where wild pink "lips" moved by the wind's ministrations (lit. *hand-application* ⇒fingering) become an *ahaha* happening (撫子の花の口ひるうこくこそ風の手あててあははなりけれ *nadeshiko no hana no kuchibiru ugoku koso kaze no te atete ahaha narikere*). *Laughs* and *sex* cross-over, porn being *laughing pictures* and strumpets *laugh-women* (giglets). My second reading guesses the caryophyllaceous corolla evokes the crumpled tissue paper equated with heavy spendings and that the paper, being the responsibility of a woman, was identified with her.

秋の夜の月のかつらの長かもじ　女とも見えつ男なりひら　月洞軒
aki no yo no tsuki no katsura no naga-kamoji onna to mo mietsu otoko narihira getsudôken
autmn night's moon's *katsura-tree*/wig's long false-tress woman-as-evn appears man is/narihra

Toupee or not toupee? That's a question for a Whig. But wearing a tress!
I guess Mr. Moon is really Narihira! – What girlishness!

The original is great. The tree identified with Katsurao, the man in the moon, is a *katsura*: so is a *wig*. Getsudôken affirms that with a redundant *naga-kamoji*, or "long false tress," simultaneously corrupting it, for men may wear toupees but only women *wear tresses*, especially *long* ones. I do not recall if Narihira ever resorted to costume, but do know that a 18c *senryû* would equate a sea-cucumber with the old-fashioned man (*mukashi otoko*) of the *Tales of Ise,* modeled on Narihira. With Japan at peace, the samurai class competed to be more macho than thou. A man whose *raison d' être* was skirt-chasing, who would submit to doing anything to conquer a woman's heart, was despised as *spineless*. The way *nari* (is/become) works as a verb, then puns into *Narihira* to clinch it would become *the* classic Tenmei *kyôka* trick eighty or ninety years later.

寄笠恋　はら／\と涙の雨のふるからに目よりうへなる笠もものうき　月洞軒
harahara to namida no ame no furu kara ni me yori ue naru kasa mo mono uki getsudôken
flurrying(mimesis) tear-rain's falling from eyes-above hat's quite depressing/floats

With flurries of teardrops showering down – I wonder why
I wear a damn rain-hat that floats above my eyes!

In the original, the hat is just a hat but they are umbrella-like in fact and sound – *kasa* 傘 vs. *kasa* 笠 – so I had to modify it, and all modification that is not hyperbole is boring. Also, the hat is "*uki*=depressing," while homophonically *floating*.

㊥ Getsudôken – Some Tanka, or Soft-boiled *Kyôka* ㊤

月日星うやまひながらさらば又 天へのぼろといふ人もなし　黒田月洞軒　大団
tsuki hi hoshi uyamainagara saraba mata ten e noboro to iu hito mo nashi　getsudôken
moon, sun, stars revering-while still again heaven-to/toward climb-would person+emph not 16-17c

While we revere the moon, the sun and stars, when all is said and done,
Has anyone tried to climb to heaven? — No, not one!

Were there not mountain-top sages in China who literally aimed high? I guess Getsudôken gave no more credence to legends than we do. But I wish I knew what prompted him to compose this *kyôka* that today would be a *tanka*.

The Moon

The way it starts
from that mountain there,
soft and round,
timorously peeking out –
Could it really be a hare?

丸て／＼あんな山からちよと出るをちやつとすいしたこれも兎じや 月洞軒
marukute marukute anna yama kara chotto deru o chatto suishita kore mo usagi ja
roundly-roundly that mountain-from a-bit exit/ing a-bit wondered this too moon is

I knew there was a hare in the moon that is always rightside up when the moon rises. And, its light dancing on wave tops or the floor of a wood on a windy day are rightly seen as white rabbits. But, the moon itself? That is a new mad touch. Speaking of which, do you know what the hare/rabbit does in the moon?

春を待餅をつく／＼とおもふにも臼と棹 sic とはとゝかゝのごと 月洞軒
haru o matsu mochi o tsukuzuku to omou ni mo usu to kine to wa toto kaka no goto
sprng+acc waitng ricecake+acc pound-x2 thghts-to-evn mortr&pstle-as4 dad-mom resemble

正 月 の 餅 つ く を 見 て よ め る
Composed upon seeing mochi pounded for the New Year.

Pounding sweet-rice to prime the Spring pounds it into me:
The mortar and the pestle are ma and pa, it has to be!

The punning is spring=haru=swell, possibly, and tsukuz(ts)uku=keenly=strike, definitely. The hare is usually shown pounding sweet-rice into *mochi*, a white, smooth glutinous substance that rapidly balloons when toasting and is usually called cake for lack of a better word. It is touching to watch an old couple pounding mochi together – usually the man swings the long-headed unstable mallet (pestle is not quite right, neither the 棹, or "pole," in the original) and the woman moves the huge glob of rice about to keep it from sticking – one cannot help but have such thoughts, though one can help expressing them.

水ちかくあそぶ家鴨を我は見ん 腰をふらねばしほがないもの 月洞軒
mizu chikaku asobu ahiru o ware wa min koshi o furaneba shô ga nai mono getsudôken
water nearby playing ducks+acc I-as-4 see, hips shaking cant-help-it-thing

> *By the water side I saw the ducks at play: they made me see*
> *Why I can't help shaking my hips when running out of pee!*
> ~~~~~~~~~~~~~~~~~~~~~~~~~~~~~~~~~~~~~~~
> *By the water I saw ducks at play*
> *When we must shake our hips,*
> *we must, they seemed to say.*

My first reading assumes that the *shô-ga-nai*, "can't be helped / can't help it" puns into running out of piss, because *shô* could be short for *shôben*, "urine." But, I could be wrong. Maybe I am influenced by having read Issa's haiku about shaking off his while a cricket's (or was it a chiming cicada, *higurashi?*) tremulous voice shivered along with him. Getsudôken may simply be excited to notice that ducks cannot help wagging their tails, "hips." And, there is a great idiom comparing the walk of a squat, ungainly woman to a duck visiting the scene of a fire (家鴨の火事見舞い). Be that as it may, even my short reading is too long: "they seemed to say" is not explicit in the original.

ふとももしろきにむかしを思ふかな 早苗取女の尻からげして
futomomo no shiroki ni mukashi o omou kana sanaetori onna no shirikarage shite
thigh's whteness-by longago+acc recall!/: early-seedlng-takng womns' butt-raised (hems) doing

> *In the whiteness of their thighs, I see the world of long ago.*
> *Hems into belts up-tucked, women planting rice bend low.*
> ~~~~~~~~~~~~~~~~~~~~~~~~~~~~~~~~~~~~~~~
> *In the whiteness of their thighs and the blackness of their pelts*
> *The ancient world appears. Rice plants moved w/ hem in belt.*

This is no masterpiece, but literate Japanese knew the legendary Saint fell from the cloud because of a flash of tender white and boys of well-off warrior-class families spent their early childhood with women, so it is less dirty than *nostalgic*.

かくばかりそめてくやしき筆の道 もとのしら紙ずんどましでんす
kaku bakari somete kuyashiki fude no michi moto no shirakami zundo mashi densu
writing only starting regretful brush's way's original white-paper much better is!

雪 風 へ 歌 書 て つ か は す と て
Asked to compose a poem for the Snow and Wind

> *Writing like this, the Way of the Brush – Did I get life wrong?*
> *The blank page at the start was by far the better song!*

The message is only as mad as Taoism is. Were it not for the duet of title and content, I would judge it less successful than a grook by Piet Hein confessing that "We writers have a *lot to* / learn from those bright enough *not to*." (I cite from memory and parse only for the salient rhyme, as good as O. Nash's *that / cat*.)

㊥ Getsudôken – Talk about Hard-boiled *Kyôka!* ㊥

初声はせんずりこゑかしはがれて内所の庭にきなく鶯　黒田月洞軒大団 c1700
hatsu koe wa senzuri koe ka shiwagarete naisho no niwa ni ki naku uguisu getsudôken
first-voice-as-4 masturbate voice? wrinkling inner garden-in coming sing cuckoo

Is the first song of the warbler something like jacking off?
What strange gurgling sounds in a corner of our bosque!

A hard-boiled *kyôka* take on a New Year or spring subject. The *uguisu* is no mockingbird and lacks even the house wren's variety. It just repeats its *hokekkyô* sutra over and over. Still, the first calls involve much initial sucking (for good imitation learn to whistle *in* as well as out) and seem particularly liquid, perhaps because it wavers, as if the throat is not yet grooved. I prefer it to the later call which, to me, seems mechanical. That this should be likened to a noisy onanist is so mad no wordplay was needed.

ほとゝぎすなれがほそ首ひつとらへころさぬほどの初声もがな
hototogisu nare ga hosokubi hittorae korosanu hodo no hatsukoe mo gana
cuckoo your narrow neck strain kill-not amount's first-voice wish! c.1700

Cuckoo may you wring your skinny neck & blast from your head
The loudest first 'Cuckoo!' you can . . . without dropping dead!

蚊遣火　おもひ出るおりたけぬかの夕煙むせぶもうれし蚊めがをらねば
omoi-izuru ori-takenu ga no yû kemuri musebu mo ureshi ka-me ga oraneba getsudôken
think-exitng faggot-burnng-not tht's evnng smoke chokng evn happy 'squitos-damn r-not-if

I recall that for the firewood not to burn would bring more smoke:
If that means no mosquitoes this evening, then let me choke!

The second *kyôka* is a close cover of a *Shinkokin-wakashû* (1205) poem by retired Emperor Go Toba (後鳥羽院 *omoi-izuru oritaku shiba no yû kemuri musebu mo ureshi wasure-gatami ni.*) I recall how I choked on the brushwood fire smoke that evening / and was delighted for it fixed your memory in me – The two seem quite different from my translations – but you can see by the romanization how close they are. Perhaps, I should add that *choking* was connected with pleasurable passion and not an altogether bad sensation. So much for summer, now for fall. The following has a great pun the verb *"hit,"* utsu + semi (cicada) playing with *vanity* or *mortality*, and is, I believe, a true report.

軒にきて鳴音やかまし長さほでてうどうつせみうちころせかし
noki ni kite naku ne yakamashi naga sao de chôdo utsu semi uchigorosekashi
eaves-to coming singing sound noisy long pole-w/ whack cicada hitting-kill-would

It came to the eaves, crying in a voice so shrill I took a long stick
And whacking the short-lived cicada made its life shorter still

~~~~~~

It came to the eaves and cried up a storm until, growing deaf
I picked up a stick and beat that damn cicada to death

A cicada up close is so damn shrill, I too have thought, *Kill! Kill! Kill!*

鬼今宵鼻をふさぎてにげにけり まかでもいもがまめのくさゝに 黒田月洞軒
oni koyoi hana o fusagite nigenikeri maka de mo imo ga mame no kusasa ni 大団 c1700
demon/s this eve nose+acc stoppng-up fled+final. scatter-not evn sis/girl's bean/s' stnk-frm

除 New Year's Eve 夜

See the demon
pinch his nose, blink
& quickly flee.

See the devil
pinch his nose, turn tail
and run like hell.

Her beans still in hand,
must really pack a stink!

Yet untossed, her beans:
It must be from the smell!

The title refers to the year-end, when beans were (now it is the Japanese solar spring) thrown in or eaten to retain the good and out to keep bad out , or at the personification of the same by a man (now, usually the husband) wearing a demon mask. If you recall (pg. 214, 259), bean/s is/are the female sex, but let's *nattô* go there! Getsudôken's poems have enough male color that one might think of him as a *woman-hater* as gays were called, but other poems showed he had a wife, kids and loved sex with women. So, he was just being clever, here. A later bean-the-demon poem is better balanced but depends on too many puns to English poetically. Laughing in a sexy way my respondent connects with *Otafuku* Goddess of *good-luck/happiness* those things *come-in/enter= iri = parched* (beans) causing the demon, or bad things to *run = hashiri*, but the old-fashioned intensifier *ana* sounds like *hole* so *hashiri* becomes ~ *wa shiri (demon)as-for butts/asses'*, and the two in one (demon and his ass) are struck on the fly (あははんとわらひて福はいりまめに鬼めはしりのあなうたれゆく *ahahan to waraite fuku wa iri mame ni oni-me hashiri=wa+shiri no ana utareyuku*.) If you would translate it, *be my guest!* I'll rest. At any rate, Getsudôken inherited the tendency to make everything bawdy from *haikai* & folksong. Speaking of the latter, he even noted one of his poems *was* a bawdy ballad. The content? He roasts a monk who died of too much sex (for details about *jinkyô*, or "dry-kidney" see that chapter in *Octopussy, Dry Kidney & Blue Spots:* 2007) on, of all times, the (death) anniversary of Saint Nichiren. Why that date? Because it is called omeiko/ô = 御命講 a word homophonous with "cunt." And how is the act described? By turning another common word for the same, *bobo,* into a verb! That was common enough, but he also punned "cock," or *mara,* into the last *verb!* (をめいこにぼぼしたばちやあたりけんつゐにじむきよで死なれまらつた *omeiko ni bobo shita bachi ya atariken tsui ni jinkyô de shinare maratta*). For all that, the poet was a good family man:

節分廿一日 まく豆を祝ひおさめて其後に きこしめさるゝよるのまめ哉
maku mame o iwai osamete sono nochi ni kikoshimesaruru yoru no mame kana c1700
scattering beans+acc celebration-finishing that-afterward eat night's bean/s(cunt)!/?

The beans thrown, then, let us not forget to finish this rite!
I'm partaking in some beans myself with the wife tonight.

㊥ Getsudôken – The Spirit of Casual *Kyôka!* ㊦

金玉のさだまりかねて火事以後は ちうにぶらつくまらのかりやぞ 月洞軒
kintama no sadamari kanete kaji igo wa chû ni buratsuku mara no kariya zo getsudôken
balls' settling cannot housefire since-as-for space-in dangling cock's glans/tempor.house! c.1700

Since the Fire, our poor balls, unsettled, never go to bed,
which leaves no pillow for Dick to lay his tired head.

This apparent mini-ballad of the aftermath of a fire adds the central member to the old saw of balls as barometers of anxiety/tranquility that I example in detail in *The Woman Without a Hole*. The added rhyme for head and the "pillow" to go with it does not make up for the loss of the natural pun on *kari,* the glans penis that puns into a *kariya,* or rented dwelling, which, hanging precariously out in space over the nervous retracted balls, allegorizes the post-fire circumstances of the newly homeless victims. Claims that *kyôka* are only parodies or criticism of Japanese poetry based on single measures of judgment seem meaningless in the face of a poem so patently worthless yet interesting (I think) in its own way.

大枝を切て奉る山桜 風にのみやはちらしはつへき 月洞軒 大団
ô-eda o kirite tatematsuru yamazakura kaze ni nomi ya wa chirashi hazu beki
bigbranch+acc cutting give mountain-cherry wind-in only!/as-for fell/scattered would

This big branch I cut to give to you? It's mountain cherry.
'Twould but have caught the wind & scattered harry-kerry!

花の名はよしやともいへ をくられし 人ぞなふよき うばざくらかな 同
hana no na wa yoshi ya to mo ie okurareshi hito zo nao yoki ubazakura kana
blossom's name-as-4 good!/+emph saying sent person even better gramma-cherry!

This bloom's name is so damn good I had to send you some!
Ubazakura – And better yet the old dame who is one!

An old monk received the first gift. He replied that a branch the size of a mountain could only have been sent by you! The Usanianized *hara-kiri* is not in the original, but the poem is mad in *another* way not readily perceived by most English readers. Buddhist injunctions against taking life did not favor lopping off big branches of bloom. Japanese typically disclaimed their gift as "not much," but this rational apologia that forgets the tree by concentrating on the life of the flowers is novel. The second gift to a nun (probably a widow) was a gnarl-branched spray of cherry blossoms from an old tree. *Ubazakura* is usually translated as "grandma cherry" but includes a wee touch of witchy attraction, that of a beautiful woman grown old who keeps her charm. Getsudôken's poems for gifts are all so simple I feel I might well have written them, yet so appropriate, I marvel. One accompanying a *daikon* (large phallic radish) does not read like a poem at all, but is still on target as it promises a mortar and pestle song (unfortunately, that was not copied into the journal) as well (大根をみわらひぐさのつとにして　うすひき歌をそへてさゝぐる *daikon o miwaraigusa . . .*).

わがはらのうへにのせたるわきも子や　是を茶麿といふには有らん
waga hara no ue ni nosetaru wagimoko wa kore o chamaro to iu ni wa aran
my belly upon place/boarded my-girl-as-for this tea-guy to say-as-for is-not

去人の望にて寄茶麿恋
Love and Tea Pillows

What boards my belly is my girl and she is no tea-pillow boy
You do yours and I'll do mine, you can guess what is my toy!

There were pillows, *cha-makura,* packed with parched tea leaves. *Chamaro* is not in the OJD, but I bet what we have is the suffix *Maro*, a term of endearment used for a boy, applied to the un-named pillow generally used by men. If the bamboo-baskets were called *hug-wives* by woman-loving haikai poets (see the end note to ch.11 of *Topsy-turvy 1585* for *dakikago ku* galore), a monk with a taste for boys might have called his tea-pillow just so. While the poet was, like most upper class Japanese of his day bisexual, he loved women most. What Usanian pornophiles call "reverse cowgirl" was, and still is, called tea-mortar (*cha-usu*) in Japanese, for tea was frothed up and tended to overflow and sex in this position . . . *That* is the word the poem implies is more to the poet's interest. Poems on request are a gift, so the poet – as the one asked – felt freer to give crazy responses, such as this, than was the case with other gifts. Likewise for requests for sympathy. A monk friend evidently sad from splitting up with a *young-crowd* (gay boy) wanted a reaction? It was *"Dug up again & again & tossed away, the ass is a fool! / Round and round like flaxen spool: old man, don't drool."*(ほりかへし又くりかへしなげくらししづの小手巻ふかきおいどを *hori-kaeshi mata kuri-kaeshi nage-kurashi shizu-no-odamaki fukaki oido o*). Combining the ancient flaxen spool of turning back time with vulgarity, punning *oi*=old into an *oido*=ass, etc. reminds us of the epigrams of Martial: many dwell on the same part of the anatomy.　And, speaking of anatomy, G's *Big Fan* includes a Seventh Eve poem by a friend, Jizori, or Self-shave, with a term I first met in Issa's dialect dictionary. It translates as *"ant-door(to door)-crossing."* Can you guess what it means? The untranslatable masterpiece may be glossed "If we were to poeticize 'dew that falls upon oneself' it would be the female/weaver-star's ant-cross(dripp)ing geese=glans(penis's) drops." For all who read Japanese, it makes more sense in it わがうへの露とよみしは女七夕のありのとわたるかりの雫か 自剃　*waga ue no tsuyu to yomishi wa metanabata no ari no towataru kari no shizuka ka*.（蛇足：女七夕は女星、我上の星が見えぬ、雁の涙は露、かりは亀頭). The answer is the minute seam that runs from the vagina to the anus. Dew was said to be goose-tears, . . . G. replied (とありしあいさつに)as follows: 狂歌よみのさねとやいはん女七夕のありのとわたるかりの作意は *kyôka-yomi no sane to ya iwan* . . .) With the chapter running out of space, one more typical G.-style poem. No clever puns or metaphors to speak of, just the vigor one finds in folk songs.

びんぼ神まりけるやうにけていなせ ありはどつこひよきとしのくれ
binbôgami mari keru yô ni kete inase ari wa dokkoi yoki toshinokure

Just give Poverty a big kick in the ass like you would a ball:
Send that god off w/ a bang: the year will end well after all!

Hard-boiled Fuji Mountain Madness – Getsudôken ㊦

むさし野にはばかるほどの団がなあふぎてのけむふじのむら雲 富士真行草 元禄3
musashino ni habakaru hodo no uchiwa gana aogite nokemu fuji no murakumo getsudôken
musashi moor-with extend amount's fan wish(for), fanning drive-off fuji's flocking-clouds

Give me a fan as wide as Musashi, the more to move the air!
You see Mount Fuji's clouds? I'd blast them out of there!

This, Getsudôken's test-brush 試筆, or first-writing of 1691, is the poem behind the title of his book with over 2,000 of his *kyôka* written from 1691-1703. If you recall, Japanese desired to start off the year ambitiously by seeing Fuji, if only in a dream, and this moor from where it could be seen on a clear day, was famous for being the most open space in Japan, one from which no celestial object is blocked from view. An Issa *kyôku* points out that not one dog poo is not stabbed by a moon-beam むさしのや犬のこふ家も月さして. The title of the book reflects the poet's unabashed love for hyperbole and, perhaps his aim to think lofty and live large. But that did not stop him from making Fuji literally the butt of his joking poems. Where his teacher Shinkai 信海, called it a *kara* 伽羅 meaning vacuous or, possibly, Chinese, Getsudôken one-upped him by turning it into a top kabuki actor who impersonates a top courtesan both of whom are called an *oyama*, or "honorable mountain," he describes using terms usually reserved for young-crowd, *i.e.* high-fashion gay youth, we have seen before and works that into the syllabary song-poem composed by the founder of one sect of esoteric Buddhism in Japan and alleged introducer of male color. 双方とも『大団』にて。

三国の山のうちでもふじは伽羅じや あのそらだきのけぶりみるにも 信海
sangoku no yama no uchi demo fuji wa kara ja ano soradaki no keburi miru ni mo

Of ye mountains of the three countries of Japan, Fuji's the airhead.
To see its disembodied smoke – is it for real, or a joke?

美しきふじのおやまにほの字哉　雪のはだえのしほ尻のなり 月洞軒
utsukushiki fuji no oyama niho no ji =nochi kana yuki no hadae no shiojiri no nari

Beautiful Fuji, kabuki woman, see the letters 'knee-oh' glow!
The next, I will not say, rent ye salty butt as white as snow!

Soradaki, in Shinkai's poem, is a fascinating word, meaning someone or thing projecting a scent (perfume in the original smoky nuance of the word) *elsewhere*, as some ventriloquists have the uncanny ability to do with their voice. Since Fuji often disappears foot-first, sometimes leaving only the tip, or even *nothing* from which the smoke may flow out from visibly, the description is perfect *and*, here is where *kyôka* shine, a homophone for "sky-peak!" I added the rhyming question to bring out the mood as well as rhyme *smoke*.. Getsudôken's Fuji does not top his teacher's in English. Let me just say that the letter pronounced like what cows eat in the winter is a *fart*, and the original only puns the *toot* of the fart because *nari* also means form, or appearance. That is, the mountain is praised as the acme of beauty *or* kidded for being a volcano full of beans. "I will not say" is not said.

雪おれのふじの大だけ 筒にして 残らずいけてみよし野の花　月洞軒
yukiore no fuji no ôdake tsutsu nishite nokorazu ikete miyoshino no hana　getsudôken
snow-broken uji's big-bmboo vase-as makng/mde remain-nt arrnged yoshno's blssms

> *The bamboo snapped by snow on Fuji, cut, might be the basis*
> *For every blossom in Yoshino to be displayed in vases!*

What a *horrid* idea! Yoshino, the capital of wild cherries. Well, at least this Japanese Gilgamesh is aesthetic and only word-acting. I added "cut" for clarity. Actually, blizzard-broken bamboo usually shatters and even *shreds*. I suppose if something to hold water were inserted in naturalistic vessels made from sections of such bamboo, we would have a beautiful study in violence that might be good to liven up the overly static *ikebana* designs, but that is me now, not the poet then.

雲となりめぐりて春はたちかへる　ふじは世界の雪のふる郷　月洞軒
kumo to nari megurite haru wa tachikaeru fuji wa sekai no yuki no furusato getsudôken
cloud-as becomng wander/circultng spring-as4 bound-back fuji-as4, wrld'snow's hmetwn

> *As clouds, it wanders here & there but, come spring, heads back.*
> *For all the snow in the world, Fuji is home. It's a fact.*
> ~~~~~~~~~~~~~~~~~~~~~~~~~~~~~~~
> *It becomes cloud and drifts around, but every spring the Snow*
> *Heads back to its home. Where? Mount Fuji, don't you know!*

This is a good just-so story for Fuji kept some snow all summer (no longer true). We saw the (snow) *falls=old/home-town* pun in Issa's silverfish poem (pg.29).

行衛しらぬ時しらぬとて　しら雪をひつかぶりふるふじのいたゞき
yukue shiranu toki shiranu tote shirayuki o hikkaburi furu fuji no itadaki getsudôken
destination know-not time know-not!/: white-snow pull-down-falling fuji's peak

> *From where it comes and goes and when, nobody knows:*
> *Old Fuji's crown just seems to draw it down: the Snow.*
> ~~~~~~~~~~~~~~~~~~~~~~~~~~~~~~~
> *No longer knowing when or where, just bringing down*
> *the snow upon his crown, Old Man Fuji, senile saint.*

My first reading was *Where does it go? Is this the time for it? How so? He doesn't know. / His old crown attracts the snow, but Fuji only draws a blank.* Fuji may be senile here, but the verb *hikkaburi* is *active*. If the snow-magnet reading is wrong, Fuji would have to be undergoing a tortuous purification ritual – typically, dashing cold water from pails upon the head but, here, snow.

~~~~~~

The last Fuji poem in the collection pairs the mighty mountain and moor once again, concluding that the former resembled the tall phallic hat and the latter the broad skirts of noble dress (むさしのゝ末広がりにはるかすみ たてた烏帽子とみるふじの山 *musashino no suehirogari ni harugasumi tateta eboshi to miru fujinoyama*.). Judging from pictures of the 100 Poets, dimension-wise, I think the skirts have it.

Getsudôken W-extra – or, Buttering up the Salt-butts.

高砂のぢいもむかしは若衆とて かがみし腰のしほらしく見ゆ 月洞軒 大団
takasago no jii mo mukashi wa wakashu tote　kagamishi koshi no shiorashiku miyu　getsudôken
high-sand's oldman even oldays-as4 wakashu!/: bent/doubled hips/back's salty/sweetly seen c.1700

The faithful old man, even he was once a gallant wakashu
In his hips now bent, I see an adorable view.

This beautiful *kyôka* was written for Jizori, the man who wrote the punning masterpiece of surreality featuring goose allusions and seminal dripping on the ants' door-to-door path on the perineum of the stellar Weaver on her yearly meeting with her Cow-herd. That was an amazingly close view of heterosexual love-making for a gay man. Getsudôken sent him the above with a lucky (but boring) New Year poem identifying his family name Fukuyama 福山 literally happiness/prosperity mountain with Hôrai, or Merhu the mountain of longevity, if not everlasting youth. The "high-sands" I made "faithful" to capture the metaphorical allusion from a drama sets up the snapper at the end, where the traditional conceit for beautiful homosexual asses, *shio*, or "salt (for big piles of the white crystal glistened in the sun)," was dovetailed into the adverb *shiorashiku*, or *dearly/adorably*, modifying the last word, the verb *"seen."* I added gallant, for the smart dress they were known for. Another poem shows compassion for what may be the difficult circumstances of the aged male beauty:

今こそあれ我もむかしは若衆也　あふたら君はこはものであろ
ima koso are ware mo mukashi wa wakashu nari autara kimi wa kowamono de aro
now esp. be I too longago-as4 wakashu being met-if you-as4 strong-one-as be-would

What is, is – once, the wakashu might have been me;
And, if we met, my macho man would have been thee!

This is not a mad poem to my way of thinking, for there is no wordplay or conceptual surprises. But, it is a *kyôka* in the sense that it is 31-syllabets, stand-alone and not a waka. In other words, it is what we now call a *tanka*. Likewise for the next.

気こんよく若衆ぐるひの春あそび　めでたし老のやれ恥しらず
ki konyoku wakashu-gurui no haru asobi medetashi rô no yare haji shirazu
spirit persistently wkshu-crazinss/frenzy's sprng play jyfl/propitus age's hooray shame knws-nt

又春毎に自剃を祝てつかはしければ
♪ *My annual New Year Toast to Jizori* ♪

What could bring more joy to spring than having a wakashu fling!
Old age knows no shame, hooray! So, party on, persist, be gay!
～～～～～～～～～～～
Let's keep it up – that wakashu frenzy we call spring play!
Be joyful & free (be thee): old Age knows no shame, I say!

Wakashu-gurui is a fine expression. A ~ *gurui* is a sort of frenzy or fit which is not necessarily bad. Here, we imagine a raucous yet jubilant atmosphere with some of the same craziness – or freedom? – that marks gay festivities even today. Linking that with the old saying about old age gives wisdom with a mad touch.

いく春かこえし白髪の松ふぐり　それで若衆をすくもまれ人
iku haru ga koeshi shiraga no matsu fuguri sore de wakashu o suku mo marebito
howmany sprngs/nys passd white-haired cojones then/that-w/ wakashu-loving rareman

♪ 又当年七十歳に成たるとて歌こされければ ♪
And I sent him a poem about turning seventy

How many springs have passed since the hair on your balls turned white?
To still love the wakashu makes you out of this world, all right!

Lacking background information, I cannot tell if the balls are only "your" or should be "our," (though Getsudôken's dying at 63 makes that unlikely), or if the *wakashu*-lover "you" "me" or "us," and whether Getsudôken refers to Jizori's love-life or his w/ him. The "white" *shira* puns as "know-not," the word for *balls* used, "pine-cones (like Spanish *cojones*)" puns as "waiting" (years of longing). Nothing like a close-up shot of the balls to give a plaintive quality to a poem!

あら玉のとしも若衆といくちよも　そひねの春のしりはじめせよ
aratama no toshi mo wakashu to iku-chiyo mo soine no haru no shirihajime seyo
nw gem yr evn wkshu-w/ hw-many 1000-eras even togthr-sleepng sprng's butt-frst do-let's

♪ 福山自剃方へかく云やりける ♪
I had this to say to Fukuyama Jizori

With wakashu, too, they slept for all ages, each New Year.
So let's not forget to do it up right, the spring's First Rear!

The first time I came across a certain seasonal topic in haiku, my eyes opened wide: *hime-hajime* = "princess-beginning," the first-sex of the New Year, also called the Spring. The above poem, inventing first-sex for homosexual love, did not need to mention both Year *and* Spring, but the latter has a sexier connotation (pornographic pictures are *spring prints*, prostitutes are *spring-selling-women*, etc.) while the former is modified by "gem," which can allude to balls. The butt, *shiri*, is in phonetic syllabary to include the homophonic meaning of "knowing." That is, the "rear-beginning" is more properly the "first-knowing."

自剃かたより迸術をせんにんならば瓢箪から駒出す手間で若衆だせかし と云こしける返し
へふたんととてもうかれば若しゆうの 尻から駒をほり出しにせよ　月洞幹
hyôtan to totemo ukareba wakashû no shiri kara koma o horidashi ni se yo getsudôken
gourd with very excited/carried-away-if youngcrowd's butt-from pony dig-up do! c.1700

When Jizori wrote that if monteblancs could charm ponies from gourds
with magic, the same effort should bring him a *wakashu*, I replied

So long as we're thinking out of the gourd, wouldn't you
rather have that pony dug from the ass of a wakashu?

Getsudôken W(omen)-extra II – Love & Libido

さむき夜に着あたゝめぬる心地して恋の衣はぬがれざれけり 月洞軒 大団
samuki yo ni ki-atatamenuru kokochi shite koi no koromo wa nugarezarekeri   getsudôken
cold night-on wear-warming feeling-having love's robe/clothing-as-for strip-cannot! c.1700

寄　　衣　　恋
Love & Clothing

You get a warm, warm feeling wearing it on a cold night;
Love's a robe you can't take off even if you might!

The last chapter surprised me. I thought I had enough *male color* in my book of dirty *senryû* (3 of 30 chapters) to last a lifetime. The big salt-mound ass of Japanese *wakashu* culture is utterly alien to me. While I do not mind what others do, so long as they have no more than two children so the already excessive population of the world does not grow and hasten the developing tragedy that already brings great suffering to our species and has exterminated many others, I am revolted by sodomy. Though I appreciate a large rump on a woman, it is not because I want to get into it so to speak but because that bounty hides something I would prefer not to see. Getsudôken, who was apparently grossed out by nothing, had a side I cannot appreciate, as where he expanded fold-counting detail (usually applied to the vagina) to the anus and used it to account for farts as numerous as prayer-beads: 尻のひだかず／＼のびつかゞめるやひる百八の数珠べ成らん *shiri no hida kazukazu nobitsu kagameru ya . . .*(obviously there is a name, probably that of a fundamentalist musician punned in here, but if that interests you, *you* can do the research). So saying, I still appreciate his treatment of love of many types that is always witty but never mean like, say, Martial.

ひくうしの鼻毛にとんぼつなぐとも ねがいの糸はかけぬふた道 月洞軒
hiku-ushi no hanage ni tonbo tsunagu to mo negai no ito wa kakenu futa-michi
pulling-cow (herder star)'s nstrl-hair-to drgnfly tie evn wshng-thread-as4 hang-not forkd-rd

On Hanging One's Wish Out for the Stars

Though I could tie a dragonfly to a hair in the Cowherd's nose,
The split-ends of my desire's thread, forking, goes nowhere!

Pulling the nose hair out of some big fast animal was a mark of agility and speed, tying up a dragonfly to the nostril hair of Hikoboshi the Star might be even harder. ♪   Wishes aimed at the Star Lovers were written on colored paper and hung by threads from green branches. But the poet either doesn't know what he wants, or wants more than one thing. A boy and a girl? Or his wife and a courtesan? Or, . . . who knows! Is he afraid of them being read, or was there a "one wish" rule?   Every year, Getsudôken got a lot of pleasure out of the Tanabata festival and has poems touching upon both of its stars . My favorite is a fine physical foil to the sentimental ones of Lady Daibu.

千夜をひと夜弓矢鉄砲よひお中 だいてねてよりそこがほし／\
chiyo o hitoyo yumiya teppô yoi onaka daite nete yori soko ga hoshi hoshi
thousand-nights+acc one-night bow-arrow gun good relation
hugging sleeping rather than there/it-the want want

> A Thousand Nights compressed in One,
> They, who are close as Arrow and Gun:
> No bundling sleep for them, but *it!* – *It*
> Is what they wanna *Star+Star-start: it!*

Unfortunately, it depends on a word, *star=hoshi,* being a homophone for "want."

年久しき望ありまの山／\ぞ 入て入れたき湯女の湯つぼゞ 月洞軒 大団
*toshi hisashiki nozomi ari*ma *no yama-yama zo haite iretaki yuna no yutsu bobo* ca.1700
year a-while, view/hope have=arima mt.mt.!/: entering enter-want bathgirl's bathing pussy

> *After years, I'd still love the view at Arima, I'd fit right in,*
> *Into those hills and into a hot-spring girl's warm quim!*

One of five topographical sex *kyôka* Getsudôken sent to his *wakashu* friend Jizori. We will pursue the *Ari*ma name pun, one-syllabet word for *hot-water* (*yu*) and *yuna,* here translated "hot-spring girl" later with Kôfû (p.414-). G. looks forward to being inside of something warm within something warm while enjoying the voluptuous mountain view. This may seem awfully shallow to the modern mind that would dress up country matters with romance; It is. Upper class men in Japan, as in most societies, enjoyed varied partners as well as love. Readers who would fault him need only read the tell-it-all diaries of pre-20c European diaries by well-off men. Getsudôken's poems are his diary and he includes wishes as well as fulfillments. The original could be a song. Country or urban, most were once "dirty." Still, some were funnier than others. Getsudôken loved his "enemy" who could "kill" him with her "little-songs" (*kouta,* ditties sung by professional entertainers) 三味線のこまかに御手のきゝました 小うたでころすいとし御てきじや *shamisen no komaka ni . . .*). The only poem that struck me as *truly outrageous* is this next one boasting about what he did with his baby (imo=sis=girl/lover/wife) on the eve of a river-bath purification, when chastity might have been proper:

みそぎしてそこできのふの夜もすがら いもと色しる今朝の初秋
misogi shite soko de kinô no yo mo sugara imo to iro shiru kesa no hatsuaki
purfctn(in a rivr) doing there-by ystrdy night-thru lovr-w/ color/sex knowng fall mornng

> *I went down to the river. Yes, I did my ablutions rite;*
> *On the first day of Autumn, after we fucked all night!*

Still, Wittgenstein would have loved the logic. It makes as much sense to get down and dirty before such a rite as to fast and stay clean for it. And now, the closer. It sums up this aging poet w/ a young libido. Unfortunately, the seasonal puns do not translate (立春 身の程をくはんして) とし若きしるし也けり朝霞 よくたちおゆるわが春べの子 *toshi wakaki shirushi narikeri asagasumi yoku tachi oeru . . .*). Suffice it to say, he is proud to start another year *standing* on his back. 蛇足:へのこ

One T's *Kyôka* ㊤ Dirty Bird, Raspy Heart & Cactus

老楽の重る年はかくすとも　頭の霜に現れにけり　一茶　文化 1 – 11　2-252
oiraku no kasanaru toshi wa kakusu to mo atama no shimo ni arawarenikeri issa -1827
old-age's compounding years-as-for hide though head's frost-in appear/ed+finality/emph.

> *Though I try to keep my age under my hat, the damn years*
> *Come out as Jack sneaks in and frosts about my ears!*

Am I *making* a mad poem where none is intended? It all depends on how or whether we pun the *kasa* in *kasanaru*, "build-up." Using the Chinese character suggests no pun was intended, but the poem seems to call for one. The grammar allows that *kasa* to be a *halo* or a *scab*, but I went for a more questionable *hat*. Issa, whose name translates as "one-tea," was in his early forties and already white-haired. Alopecia. Issa has earlier 31-syllabet poems that are clearly not *kyôka*. Issa did not write many 31-syllabet poems in his forties. Here is one of the first, written a couple years earlier than the above, at age 41,

淹 ニハクナブリのいとまなみ立と思へば又あさるみゆ 享和三 11
niwatazumi niwakunaburi no itomanami tatsu to omoeba mata asaru miyu issa
garden-puddle wagtail's business⇒waves raise think-when again grubbing appears

A garden puddle,	*Busy Maggy*
there the wagtail does it,	*has rippled up the puddle*
making waves,	*with her tail,*
Then, it's back to grubbing	*So, is she in a fuddle,*
as if he never misbehaved.	*or fishing for a whale?*

The caption is 背令 = 鶺鴒, *sekirei,* the bird that taught us sex by flitting its tail up and down (pg.158). Some etymologies of its classic name *niwakunaburi*, include what Usanians now call *shaking your booty*. *Itomanami,* or "leisureless," may hide *itonami,* or "marital duties" and, definitely, *~nami,* followed by *tatsu,* or "stands," morphs into "making waves/ripples." My translations are too mad. Clare's less intellectual *Little Trotty Wagtail* is better than Issa or me. Issa was exploring 31-syllabets. A page earlier, he wrote two happy travel poems neither *kyôka* nor *waka* but, I believe, modern 31-syllabet poems, or *tanka* (see ♪), followed by a death poem by 秀次公, Hideyoshi's nephew Hidetsugu, forced to kill himself at a commoner's house 民家 in Takano, 1601. Like many death poems, it seems remarkably cool, or mad, for being so witty under such circumstances. Unfortunately, it is one of those *kyôka* which refuse to English. Day Fifteen of the Seventh Month was the first full moon of fall, so he pointed out this was not the *sky-well*, or window on the heavens, meaning the exalted quarters *above the clouds* of the nobility, but a bamboo-woven window through which to view the same, and chose a conjugation of the verb for viewing that punned with *folk*, that is, the commoner's house where he was to die. (思ひきや雲井の秋の空ならで竹あむ窓の月を見んとは 2-170 甫道 *omoiki ya kumoi no aki no sora nara de take amu mado no tsuki o min to wa* hôdô). Why introduce it here? I guess to show that Issa lived in a culture where mad poems were the accepted product of duress.

うらめしや人の心のあらやすり ひがきめにだにのぞかれぬ哉 文化 2/10
urameshi ya hito no kokoro no arayasuri higakime ni dani nozokarenu kana 2-314
hateful/a-shame!/: person's heart's (a)rough-file rasp-marks-w/ even remove-not!

What a shame! A heart that roughly filed is absurd
With every rasp toothmark forever preserved.

This epigram with the sort of off-the-wall metaphor that might be called mad dates from the same year he wrote the lead poem, The editors of *Issa Zenshû* think the rough file-marks, *higakime* puns *higame*, prejudicial or twisted views on things. *Perhaps.*

おのがねにつらき別のありとだに しらでやひとり鳥の鳴らん 2-574
onoga ne ni tsuraki wakare no ari to dani shira de ya hitori tori no nakuran 文化 3~8
myown sound-from painful separations are even know-not-from! single rooster crows!

Ignorant of the sad partings that follow his call, that's bliss.
All by himself, a rooster crowing, knows naught about this!

I *know*. My *"ignorance is bliss"* is madder than the original which recalls a once-read but forgotten old *waka*. The only mad touch is the *hitori tori*, where *hitori*, usually reserved for humans, makes the rooster a "lone" bird. Another of Issa's near-misses plays on the literary name of a month sounding like *tread* or *step*, puns a verb for tugging at the dancing maiden's sleeves into pulling-close and crossing from night to dawn, 文月をふみ／＼踊る娘（子）のも引袖引夜明わたる *fumizuki o fumifumi odoru musume no mo hiki sode hiki yoru ake-wataru* 2-509). A lot of puns, but it seems to me a mere exercise: the would-be *kyôka* just does not hold together as a poem. It is hard for someone like me, with a far from perfect control of old Japanese grammar to say for sure what is wrong, but if you put it thus, that even a foreigner with no real training in Japanese literature can sense it is off, you can understand why I am glad Issa stuck to his haiku, only writing a score of 31 syllabet poems in his forties (we have almost nothing from his thirties). At age 48, only a few months into his *Seventh Journal*, famous for containing most of his best work, Issa *finally* recorded a *kyôka* clearly "marked" as a *kyôka*. That would be Kûsui's brilliant epigram about heaven and hell being reserved for the living (p.160). The following page has a mad poem attributed to Ikkyû that tells his pot not to tell people he is eating gruel, the wit of which escapes me (doubtless, it comes with a story). And, on the next, yet another 31-syllabet Issa poem which fails to fly: *"A nightingale in the new year sings out to greet what? / The spring is buck-naked, just like my cactus!"* The original (あら玉のうぐひすなけどさぼてんの真裸なる春に逢ふ哉 *aratama no uguisu nakedo saboten no mappadaka naru haru ni au kana*) is worse. The idea of expressing frustration with weather not behaving ideally is, conceptually speaking, a masterpiece; Issa just does not work the poem enough. I added the "my," for a personal touch turns a mere metaphor into a complex image. Issa did keep potted plants. Decades later, he made a simple *ku* of a cactus put on a high shelf for the winter solstice. Symbolically it sings *infinitely* better, even without that nightingale. But Issa's *kyôka* also improves, so we go on.

One T's *Kyôka* ⊕ Conchs & Leeches for Cuckoo

世の中をすくふ心や山伏の祈るかひある夕立の雲　一茶　文化 7-8　全集 3-81
yononaka o sukuu kokoro ya yamabushi no inoru kai aru yûdachi no kumo issa d.1762-1827
world/society+acc save heart/intent!/?/: mountain-wizard's pray shell/worth have evening clouds

♪ *Cloud Sent By a Mountain Wizard Ends Drought* ♪

A heart that would save the whole wide world with prayer,
This evening shower was born of a conch blast in the air!

This time (five months later), he got it right. Issa smoothly puns together the *value* of praying with a *shell* – both *kai* – which means the *conch trumpet* all Japanese associate with mountain wizards. While not spectacular, *this* is a real *kyôka*. Both "cloud" and "wizard" are in the original text and I guess on that drought. The next fall, Issa wrote half a dozen more 31-syllabet poems. One, with prayer as it is supposed to sound coming from a mouth missing a tooth was a good idea but poorly done (歯がぬけてあなた頼むもあもあみだ　アモアミダ仏あもだ仏哉 *ha ga nukete anata tanomu mo amo-amida amo-amidabutsu amodabutsu kana* 文化 8/7). Two others on *flies* would have been a good *kyôka* had Issa managed to combine them. One (*hisakata no mochi . . .*) has the flies praying to the sky while stuck fast to a cake of *mochi*=sweet-rice, while another has the flies shitting on the face of either a Buddha statue or a recently deceased person, likewise stuck on sweet-rice (*mihotoke no kao ni . . .*). I get the idea that Issa cannot concentrate long enough to work and rework a long (compared to haiku) poem on paper. These poems include one I failed to find for my book *Fly-ku!* Namely, a prototype for part of his famous *"Don't swat!"* *fly-ku*. Mountain *bees* also rub both their hands and feet together, begging for mercy from the honey-gatherer! (*mitsutori ni yuruse . . .*). Again, I do not give it as there is too little wit for it to be 'mad.'

時鳥なく空もちし山里は蛭の降る木も又有りにけり　一茶　文化 9.4
hototogisu naku sora mochishi yamazato wa hiru no furu ki mo mata ari ni keri issa
cuckoo/s-cry/ies-sky-has mountain country/town/s-asfor leach-showering trees also have!

Mountain reaches boasting skies that echo with "cuckoo!"
Also boast clouds of trees that rain down leaches.

Our Emerson pointed out that the cost for a walk in the woods was feeding the mosquitoes, but leeches dropping from trees? Here Issa, who had probably not yet read many mad poems comes very close to *kyôka* I vaguely recall pointing out the cost of being able to hear the cuckoo is living miles from a bar, a *tôfu* shop, etc.. Similar things were written by ancient Chinese poets. A month later,

天人や人見おろさばむさしのゝ草葉にすだく虫とこそ思へ　文化 9.5
tenjin ya hito miorosaba musashi-no no kusaha ni sudaku mushi to koso omoe issa
heaven-pple, pple lk-dwn-on-when musashi-field's grss-blades-to cling bugs+emph think

The sky-dwellers, when they look down must think of us
like bugs clinging fast to blades of Musashino grass

Musashino, the largest moor of Japan, shrinks us. Lacking tree cover – Issa has a haiku claiming every dog-shit on it is struck by moon-beams. The above may be less *kyôka* than *dôka,* a moral poem. Over a decade later, 59 year-old Issa would improve it into what is either a good seasonal *waka,* or a *kyôka:*

七夕の人見たまはばむさしのゝ草葉の虫とおぼしめすらん 一茶 文政 4.7
tanabata no hito mitamawaba musashino no kusaha no mushi to oboshimesuran issa
7th-eve/lovingstars people look(at)deign-if musashino's grassblades' bugs as perceive

Should the Loving Stars deign to look upon us humans, alas,
We might well be taken for bugs on blades of grass!

Pardon my "alas." Since humans wrote wishes for the trysting Stars to read and grant, unlike the earlier version of the *kyôka,* there is reason for gods up there to look down. Issa's judgment improved with age. Back to the present. He is 50. This is the year his blues exploded in haiku. He wished to be a *mummy*(!) on New Year's, showed a frog his *waterfall of piss,* mimetically recorded *horse shit dropping on blossoms* and a woman *blowing her nose on a morning glory,* called *fleas sweet for sleeping with him* (pg.269) and, looking at the Milky Way, wondered where *his* star was . . . and complained,

世(の)中はくねり法度ぞ女郎花 一茶
yononaka wa kuneri hatto zo ominaeshi issa
world-within-as4 wriggle free! maidenflower

Wench-flowers, here,   *Wild Pink (girl flowers)*
we serve out our terms,
obeying one law: 'Squirm!'   *Above my shack the stars meet;*
                                       My only solace blooms at my feet!

星迎庵はなでしこさくのみぞ
hoshimukae io wa nadeshiko saku nomi zo
stars greeting hut-as4 wildpink bloom only!

The first also plays on a mention of squirming maiden flowers in the *Kokinshû*. Many of these *ku* are what I call *kyôku* (Not *senryû,* as wild haiku are often, but wrongly, called). He also wrote an unseasonal haiku, *tanka* in mood: "*My dead mother! / Whenever I see the sea, / whenever I see . . .*" (亡母や海見る度に見る度に *naki-haha ya umi miru tabi ni miru tabi ni*). In early winter, a 31-syllabet poem observes *"Ask and you shall receive"* – *When they heard, / Down from heaven flew some hungry birds."* Well, actually, it does not mention *heaven,* specifies flocks of *sparrows* – hungry urchins? – begging for rice as sutras are said for the a friend's soul and, more subdued, is as tanka as *kyôka*. And, then, in the 11th month, *it happens:* we find not one but two *kyôka* by Shokusanjin right in the middle of his haiku! They are excellent ones, too. Do you recall Ôta's *time-rain,* or cold-showers called *shigure,* falling on the honest fool's head (p.230) and his sixtieth birthday declaration that he had no desire to be a long-lived crane, turtle or pine, but was happy to die human? Within a year of reading these *kyôka* – and, I would bet, a book of them – we have Issa's masterful *Silverfish*.

One T's *Kyôka* ㊦ Springs from Stones, Stylish Hills

新家賀　雨おちの石の凹に泉湧て 汲ども尽ぬ御住居哉　一茶 文化 10/3
amaochi no ishi no hekomi ni izumi wakite kumudomo tsukinu onsumai kana issa d.1827
rain-fall-stone's indention-in spring bubbles-up ladle though exhaust-not hon. dwelling!

♪ New House Celebration ♪

May a sweet-water spring bubble from the rain-catch stone
Filling ladles and never running dry at this, your home!

One of a score of 31-syllabet poems composed five months after Issa read Shokusanjin. On the whole, less successful than his haiku, the above is a masterpiece that would have been in selections of top *kyôka* had Issa been in the loop. The stones stop rain falling from the roof from eating away at the house's foundations and, over time, indent the stone. A few more passable ones.

月代の中ずり程に山やけて 山の額のうつくしき哉　一茶 10/3
tsukiyaki no nakazuri hodo ni yama yakete yama no hitai no utsukushiki kana
moon-rep.'s middle-shaved amount mountain burning mountain's brow's beauty!

Burnt off as clean as our shaven pates, and cool,
The mountain's round brow looks just beautiful!

いくばくのなげきこりつむ小車の 下り坂なる我よはひ哉 一茶 10/3
ikubaku no nageki koritsumu koguruma no kudarizaka naru waga yowai kana
some firewood/laments piled on small-cart's downhill becomes my age issa

Laments like firewood are cut and stacked on a small cart
Heading down hill, at least, my old age has an easy start!

みよし野の吉野ゝ山にぬるてふは からの桜や夢に見るらん 一茶 10/3
miyoshino no yoshino no yama ni nuru chô wa kara no sakura ya yume ni miruran
miyoshino-field's yshno-mtn-on sleeping butterfly/ies-as4 china's cherries dream-in see!

Spending the night up Mount Yoshino of the Yoshino fields,
Chinese cherries must yet be what blooms in papillion dreams!

The *first* admires the mountain, burnt like the shaved front of a Japanese crown, the *sakayaki,* for farming, every year. Lacking *sakayaki,* English is at a disadvantage, but the original was poorly written, repeating *mountain* twice; the added *cool* actually improves it. The *second,* excellent *in the original,* combines an old *waka* pun of *nageki= firewood* and *troubles/laments* with an *over the hill* idiom. The *third* is tricky. Was the cherry forest hyperbolized as extending to China because said dreaming sage/butterfly is a Chinese story? A dozen the following month included only one worthy of mention. "*As if to say, 'I'd entertain Sir Cuckoo,' a mountain cherry / Just one tree blooms, / it's blooming late!*" (時鳥もてなすとてや山桜一木おくれて花のさく哉 *hototogisu motenasu* tote ya . . .). But, even it should be compressed into a haiku. Then, in mid-fall, Issa is hit bad by the shakes (*okori=ague*) and crippled for a few days. He punned his disease into the leg-dragging pillow-word for mountains by taking advantage of the homophonic overlap of mountain, *yama,* and disease, *yamai* and pegged on a secondary pun I leave to Japanese readers: けふも又きのふのころよ足引の病の責やあはれいつ迄 *kyô mo mata kinô no koro yo ashi-hiki no yamai no seki ya aware itsu made*). It is a genuine *kyôka*. Then, thirty poems later, the *silverfish* (p.29). At year's end, Issa has a scarecrow guard the moon until it rots (*sarashi naya yamada ni . . .*). At the start of the second month of winter the following year, he has two *kyôka* metaphorically express his disappointment with borrowed money lost to some scheme. Neither borrower nor lender be – I am unsure which was he. Maybe his wife, Kiku was the perpetrator; later, she would lose a lot in a lottery. In the fifth month of the next year, 31-syllabets describe one baby bamboo that fled to a wee corner of a big thicket where it hid (大藪の隅の小すみ *ôyabu no sumi no kosumi . . .*) and another that breaches the border of a hated neighbor (にくまる〻隣境 *nikumaruru tonarizakai...*). That month, Issa tries to attract fireflies with a tourist attraction he also used on frogs, *a waterfall of piss* (小便の滝を見せうぞ来よ蛍 *shôben no taki o miseo zo koyo hotaru*). Crude, yes; but his *kyôku* still beat most of his *kyôka*. The next month, the heat must have gotten to Issa. He usually likes children, but he complains in *kyôka* about the game of *ishinago,* where pebbles are tossed in holes, starting what *seems* a counting song up to seven, then turning the eight *ya(tsu)* into *yakamashi,* meaning *boisterous* or *noisy* and sometimes shouted to mean *"Shut-up!"*

石なごのおちくる玉の一二三四五ッ　六七やかましの世や　一茶
ishinago no ochikuru tama no hi fu mi yo itsutsu mutsu nanatsu yakamashi no yo ya
stone-child's falling ball/gem's one two three four five six zeven eight=noisy world+emph.

In the time a jackstone takes to fall?
"One!" "Two!" "Three!" I hear them bawl,
"Four!" "Five!" "Six!" Why must they yell?
"Seven!" rhymes heaven but noise is hell!

Fall's second poem explains in 31-syllabets that a melon he kept on the vine by claiming it was poison survived to become a steed for the Japanese All Souls Day (毒／＼とおどした *dokudoku to odoshita . .*), when chopstick-legged cucumber, eggplant and melon horses may be found around the neighborhood. But, again, the 17-syllabet follow-up is far more lively. While it is a haiku, I will give it a mad translation befitting its spirit. Indeed, it has been patiently waiting over a dozen years for me at pasture in the margin of Issa's Journal.

蜋のふいと乗けり茄子馬 文化 12.7
kôrogi fuito norikeri nasubi-uma　issa d.1827
cricket suddenly/flicks mounts+emph. eggplant-horse

A cricket, leaping, lands, of course –
Right on the back of an aubergine horse!

One T's *Kyôka* ㊦の㊦ Sweet Dew Turns Bird Doo

甘い露降か／＼と口明て待 程もなき鳥のふん哉　一茶　文化 12.8
amai tsuyu furuka furuka to kuchi akete matsu hodo mo naki tori no fun kana issa
sweet dew fall? fall? and mouth opening wait/ing period even not bird-shit!

Sweet dew, his due, was bound to fall – and so his mouth,
Trusting, opened wide only to find bird doo come south!

From the original, one might think this autobiographical, but Yaba Katsuyuki's *Encyclopedia of Issa* mentions a friend who, after waiting years to become the owner of a temple, finally learned of his good fortune only to be felled by a sudden illness. So, I made it third-person. Though far from as clever as the *silverfish*, with so many poems treating bird-shit as something good, it is good to find something more down to earth in this most assuredly a mad (and sad) poem. The following spring, Issa composed what may, with the silverfish, be his best *kyôka*, where plum bouquet and farts mix in his grass/smelly hut (pg.52). On the same page, we find the surprising *al fresco* relief for a lengthening day *ku* (pg.148). That summer we find *"Opening the door to my hut when I return late, a roar: / The flies, buzzing up a storm, swarm in ahead!"* (庵の戸を明るおそしとむれ蠅の我より先にさはぎ入哉 *io no to o akaru ososhi . .* 文化 13.7) and two months later, *"After the gale, bitter persimmons still fast on the branches; / upright to a fault yet dripping with rain* (木がらしの梢にシヤント渋柿の下手律儀にもしぐれける哉 *kogarashi no kozue ni . . .*). In the mid-winter month, Issa wrote a true *kyôka* on the only thing poverty collects, *age*. We saw it on page 235 (*susu hokori haka de*). A year later, he wrote *In fall's world of wind that's prickly cold, deep within / the spikes of a large chestnut, are those bugs at home?* (吹風のとが／＼し世 *fuku kaze no togatogashi . . .*). There is a *prickly* adverb, but not so good the nut could not have been better presented in a haiku, as, Issa did a half-page later. The same happened with the flies storming his door, above. In other words, many of Issa's *kyôka* seem mere notes for distillation into haiku. Perhaps that is why the good ones have been lost (I have never read a thing about them). The best *kyôka* that winter, plays upon the name of his region, Shinano, as "do-nothing," applying it to a fly playing in the ashtray べん／＼と何もしなのゝ冬（の）蠅　灰（に）まぶれて這歩く哉　文化 14.1. *benben to nani mo shinano no hae hai ni maburete hai-aruku kana.*). Neither that pun nor the ones on *fly* (*hai*) as *ashes* (*hae*) and crawling (*hai*) English. Issa may allude to himself, as a nearby *ku* has someone, writing letters in the (stove?) ashes and a well-known *ku* by 17c Kikaku compared the existence of an old man to a winter-fly. Issa's next *kyôka*, a couple years later, is equally unEnglishable, but I'll try:

世に住ば手をすり足をすりこ木にしてかけ廻る年の暮哉　一茶　文政 2.5
yo ni sumaba te o suri ashi o suri-kogi ni shite kakemawaru toshinokure kana issa
world-in live-if hands+acc rub/pray legs rub/pray=pestle-into making go round year-end!

To live in the world of men, our hands rub together, that is we beg,
While worn down to pestles by year's end, around go our legs!

This hand and leg/foot rubbing=*suri* with the significance of supplicating for mercy – debts to ber paid at the end of the year, here – is the same found in Issa's famous *fly-ku*, but with the surprising addition of *~kogi*, that verb becomes a pestle=*surikogi* and another connotation of *suri*=rubbing, namely, *wearing down* and, if I am not mistaken, *toshinokure* is used rather than the human-activity stressing *shiwasu* to signify the end of the year so *kure* may pun on the begging of an old man. The following year's *kyôka* declaring what would happen if dew tasted good does translate and is elsewhere in this book (pg.168).

借金の淵におのれとしづみつゝうき世をうらむとしの暮哉 同文政 5-3
shakkin no fuchi ni onore to shizumitsutsu ukiyo o uramu toshinokure kana issa d.1827
debt's depths-in self-from sinking-while floating/woeful-world+acc begrudge year-end!

Knowing I myself dove into debt, as I sink, I still hate
The floating world at year's end: creditors won't wait.

Debt's hole, *fuchi*, that deep spot in a river English has no word for, which we have met before, was ellipsed and "creditors ~ wait" added to explain the significance of the end of the year. The floating world is both the world of woe and late-night entertainment. The original is a fine play of idiomatic paradox, but we may also imagine how a poor man suffers knowing all that unaffordable entertainment is out there.

老の身は寒さまけして何ひとつ まなばぬ窓に雪はつみツゝ 文政七.2
rô no mi wa samusa make-shite nani hitotsu manabanu mado ni yuki wa tsumi tsutsu issa
aged body/self-as4 cold-defeat-doing whatever learn-not window-on snow piling-while

The cold has got	*An old body*
this old man beat:	*can't take this cold;*
The reading window	*No study for me*
is bright with snow:	*though the window still*
I sit in the heat!	*reflects the snow*

~~~~~~~~~~~~~~~~~~~~~~~~~~~~~~~~~~

This aged body, bowing out to the cold, now studies
Nothing, though habit by the window still piles snow.

This poem, referencing a diligent Chinese scholar, is clearly a *kyôka* and, being personal, also a *tanka*. The first two readings were written into my Issa book in 1995. The "bowing out to the cold" and "through habit" in the last betray the frank words of Issa, but, unlike the case with for the older readings, capture every nuance of the meaning. This is one of many good poems (including haiku) written by old Issa that deserve to be known by more Japanese. It could also use more translations, but I will leave that to others and use this last line to explain why I introduced so many of Issa's mad poems. In a word, it is this: because I happen to have Issa's *Zenshû* (all works), generally only found in large libraries, on hand, and know that few mad poems by poets not known as mad poem poets are published as such, I thought it behooved me to share them with my readers.

Real & Fake: Why I Must Wait to Translate N/Ise 上

八 信濃なる浅間の嶽にたつ煙 遠近人の見やはとがめぬ　伊勢物語
shinano naru asama no take ni tatsu keburi ochikochibito no mi ya wa togamenu ise #8
shinano becmes(place of) asama's peak-frm rising smoke farnear pple seeng+emph blame-not

> むかし、男ありけり。京や住み憂かりけん、東の方に行きて、住み所求むとて、
> 友とする人ひとりふたりして行きけり。信濃国、浅間の嶽に煙の立つを見て、

> Long ago, there was a man. Tired of life in the capital, he and
> a friend left to look for a place to stay in Azuma. In the
> country of Shinano, seeing smoke rising from Mount Asano,

> *Who can blame people far and near who stop to view,*
> *When smoke from Mount Asama in Shinano spews!*

白髪なる頭の鉢に立つけぶり不動と人の見やはとがめぬ　仁勢
shiraga naru atama no hachi ni tatsu keburi fudô to hito no mi ya wa togamenu nise #9
white-hair/s become head's crown-from rises smoke. acala-as people see-as4 blame-couldn't

> をかし、山伏あり。京や住み憂かりけん、東の方に行きて、旦那求むとて、
> 徒歩にて行ければ、汗も流れけり。白髪なる頭の鉢に、湯気の立ちければ、

> Odd to know, there was a monteblanc. Tired of life in the
> capital, he went to Azuma. Wandering in search of a patron,
> sweat poured down and steam rose from his white-haired head,

> *Who can blame people who see Acala the unmoving,*
> *When my white-haired crown starts really smoking!*

The *Tales of Ise*, like the *Decameron* or *Canterbury Tales* is, on the whole, comical. Unsure of how much of that ancient wit I get, I only introduce them and their take-off tentatively. Our authority, McCullough translates this *Ise* poem *"Surely no one / Far or near / But marvels to see / The smoke rising from the peak / Of Asama in Shinano." Togamenu* or "blame-not" can mean *incredible*, hence "marvels" is not *wrong*, but *what would such a poem add to the story?* My reading, though only a guess and, hence, less reliable than McCullough's, assumes there was a proverb (or, statute?) against watching fires, or people were exhorted not to waste time sight-seeing, so this volcano justified something the anti-hero champions, *play*. I assume *tales* are not like *plays* in Usanian football, where boring up-the-middles are necessary now and then to keep the defensive side bunched together rather than fully covering passes and outside runs. Diverse chapters, some slapstick and some sophisticated, some entertaining us above the navel, some below, I could also understand. But what benefit is there in *boring* chapters, however short? Each and every tale in *Ise* should have something that is at least mildly witty. That is why I do not trust the translations I have seen. The "fake," or *nise* Ise, substitutes a *yamabushi*, or mountain wizard for the dandy, and Acala is the fiery God of Fire, patron saint of sword-smiths, and as God of mountains literally "unmoving" 不動. His sword 利剣 has some resemblance to a *yamabushi*'s iron staff 金剛杖. *Mountain* ⇒ *mountain god* ⇒ *mountain man*.

Ise #27　我許物思人は又もあらじとおもへば水のしたにもありけり　伊勢
ware bakari mono-omou hito wa mata mo araji to omoeba mizu no shita ni mo arikeri
みなくちにわれや見ゆらむかはづさへ水のしたにてもろゐになく
minakuchi ni ware ya miyuramu kawazu sae mizu no shita nite morogoe ni naku

Once, a man who paid a night-call on a woman did not call again. When she was about to wash up in her basin and saw her reflection, she recited to herself –

"Here I thought no other could be so lost in thoughts of love;
But, in the water, I can see one as blue as me, above!"

And what she recited, that man who didn't call, secretly he heard it all –

Can't you see me in your little basin? Why even frogs
In the water cry au pair to make their little pollywogs!
~~~~~~~~~~~~~~~~~~~~~~~~~~~~~~~~~~~~
Can't you see me in your little basin? This is about us!
Even frogs in the water, crying always cry in chorus!

Nise #27 我ばかりものあらふ人はまたあらじととおもへば水の下にもありけり
ware bakari mono arau hito wa mada araji to omoeba mizu no shita ni mo arikeri　仁勢
i/me amount/only thing/genitals washing person-as-for yet is-not as think-when water-under even is!

水底にものや見ゆらん　馬さへもまめだらひをはのぞきてぞなく　同
minasoko ni mono ya miyuran   uma sae mo mame-darai o ba nozokite zo naku!
water-bottom-on/at thing! visible! horse even bean(vulva)-tub+emph peeking+emph cries

Oddly, a man who paid a night-call on a woman did not call again, When she was about to wash up her thing and saw its reflection, she recited to herself –

"Here I thought no one could so wash & wash their thing;
But, in the water I can see another yin is watching!"

And what she recited, that man who didn't call had secretly heard it all –

Do I too see not a thing in the water? Hey, even a horse
Will neigh=cry for a peek at a tub of beans, of course!

To us, reflections are seen *on* the water, but Japanese have always seen them *under* it. I translated idiom for idiom. McCullough does not: *"No one else / I had thought / Could be so miserable as I – / Yet there is another / Under water."* The second poem of Ise #27 bothers me, for I cannot seem to rule out another reading: *Don't even frogs when they see themselves in a basin / underwater, cry like you? In chorus, it's amazin'!* (I.e.,, the man insulting the woman by saying frogs, too, cry while looking at their reflections.) As for the *Nise* poems, turning the Ise abstraction of the *mono-omou*, or "thing-thinking" of the love-sick into the graphic and concrete *mono-arau*, or "thing-washing," and then using the common *bean* slang for the vulva – and *mame* also means *diligent*. Horse stands for the male thing and *may* allude to its appearance underwater, but definitely helps the *o ba* emphatic later, as it has a horse (*ba*) sound in it and, while a *naku* would be a whinny (how about a *ninny/whinny* reading!), such a "cry" also implies tears, such as a member of long-standing exudes.

Real & Fake: Why I Must Wait to Translate N/Ise 下

三四 言へば得に 言はねば胸に騒がれて 心一つに嘆くころかな 伊勢物語
ieba e ni iwaneba mune ni sawagarete   kokoro hitotsu ni nageku koro kana   ise #34
say/said-if benefit-to, say/said-not-if breast-in clamoring heart/mind single-as lament time is!
前置き：昔、おとこ、つれなかりける人のもとに   後置き：おもなくていへるなるべし。

Our man of old, calling on a heartless lover,

Had you but told me, girl! But saying naught, this breast
Is solid commotion – Now my heart rails without rest.

Something more subtle might have been said.

Nise/Fake 生鯛の背骨は胸に挟まりて 心一つに嘆くころかな 仁勢物語
namadai no sebone wa mune ni hasamarite kokoro hitotsu ni nageku koro kana   nise 34
raw seabream's bck-bone/s-as4 breast-in sandwchng hrt/mnd one-as lament time is!
前置き：をかし、男、魚の骨を喉に立てて、後置き：術なくて言へるなるべし。

Our man so odd, stalling on a red-snapper,

Eating raw fish a bone has come to lodge in my throat.
Now, I am of but one heart – for all I can do is choke!

What else if anything could one have said?

The second half of the originals are identical, but I could not do that and rhyme. Trying to make sense of the take-off leads to re-appraising the wit of the original. The above is a good example in point. I only came to think the original might have it after working on the fake. Both, again:

Our Old-fashioned Man, calling on heartless Corva,

Had you but told me, girl! But saying naught, this breast
Tormented, at least is whole again in suffering sans rest!

Pretty shamelessly put, right?

~~~~~~

Our Odd-fashioned Man, fish bone stuck in his craw,

A raw snapper's backbone has come to rest in my breast,
Now of single mind I fret, in a way, it means I'm blest!

No other way to put it, right?

This time I may have caught the wit of *Ise*, but it is more likely my invention. Likewise for the take-off. Until I can find commentary by someone well versed in the 10c Japan *and* more attentive to wit than most scholars, I expect to get things wrong. The take-off plays *back* against *breast,* so I made an effort to incorporate that in the above reading, then added the blessed idea, my guess.

うら若みねよげに見ゆる若草をひとのむすばむことをしぞ思ふ ise #49
urawaka mi neyoge ni miyuru wakakusa o hito no musubamu koto oshizo omou
pretty young body sleep/sex-good-as looking yungrass+acc other binds thing regretful think
はつくさの　などめづらしき　ことのはぞ　うらなくものを　おもひけるかな
hatsukusa no nado mezurashiki kotonoha zo uranaku mono o omoikeru kana 伊勢 #49
first-grass's etc. rare/sexy wordleaves+emph. backless/heartless things+acc think-have-been!/?

Once, a man, seeing that his sister had grown very attractive, said,

Sweet & tender lass, you look like you'll be good in bed
– It hurts to think another will tie Young-grass, instead!

to which she replied,

Why not 'first-grass!' That, too, is old, even for a platitude!
If words are leaves, leave me be, brother rude in attitude!

つらあかみくさげに見ゆる若草を人の笑はんことをしぞ思ふ nise #49
tsura akami kusage ni miyuru wakakusa o hito no warawan koto oshizo omou
face red smelly-as seen younggrass-at people laugh-would thing regretfully+emph think
はづかしやなどあてことの言の葉ぞ面目くなくもおもひけるかな 仁勢
hazukashi ya nado atekoto no kotonoha zo menbokunaku mo omoikeru kana
embarrassing how! etc/sayingsuch insinuating words shameless even think! #49

Odd man, seeing his sister had a very red face, said

Beet red face, alas, it means that you'll be stinky there –
It hurts to think some grin about it: Young-grass, I care!

to which she replied,

How embarrassing to have to hear such rude insinuation –
If words are leaves, it's fall: you should be the blushing one!

another try ~~~~~~ same reading

Sweet and tender Sis, that she'll be good in bed is easy to see;
It hurts to think another blade will swive young-grass, not me!
vs.
What is this old and dirty talk? 'First grass?' – Good grief!
If words are leaves, leave yours unsaid – this is beyond belief!

real 10c ↑ ~~~~~~ ↓ 17c fake

A beet red face makes it apparent you'll be stinky in another place
It hurts to think some grin about it – Young-grass, 'tis a disgrace!
vs.
How can you pass such lewd insinuations if you are not an ass?
Words are leaves but yours leave nothing to say. They're trash!

McCullough reads the *Ise* sister's reply as, *"Why do you speak of me / in words novel as the first / grasses of spring? / Have I not always loved you / quite without reserve?"* This *may* be a first-class translation, and mine (following a gloss 初草なんて陳腐なこといって、露骨なことをまあ by Fuji Masaharu 富士正晴) wrong. *Ura naku* is problematic. Until I see far more readings of *Ise*, I must bow out.

The Untranslatable Lightness *of* Nakarai Bokuyô㊤

またと世にある物でない過去未来げんざへもんがまひのなりふり　半井卜養 1670
mata to yo ni aru mono de nai kako mirai genzaemon ga mai no narifuri bokuyô 卜養狂歌拾遺
again world-in exist thing-as4 not, past future genzae=present=mon's dancing/acting's appearance/moves

女かとみれば男なりけり業平のおもかげはむかし男なればいまは見ず当世はやりし源左衛門おもしろ
の海道くだりやなにとかたるとつきせじとおもへば／＼絵にかきて歌よみ侍れとのたまひければ

*"Genzaemon's appearance is something extraordinarily special that would never be seen
in the past, in the future, and in the present."* — Takanashi's working translation.

Narihira could pass for a woman in writing, but
who could pass in person like our kabuki star!

*There never was
and never a Genzaemon's
likes we'll see –*

*Mannerisms trés bon,
he's soi-disant it cannot be!*

*Will there ever
a genzaemon be, and was
there ever one
whose dance soi disant
was un, dos, trés . . bon!*

This extraordinary poem by Nakarai Bokuyô (1607-1687), a medical doctor and Osaka-born poet of the Teimon (Teitoku) school who saw this kabuki in Edo because he was drafted to doctor there, is the first example of a *kanji pun* in the analysis section of a paper by linguist Takanashi Hiroko about the relationship of orthography (in Japanese, various scripts for writing words), and the cognition of puns (see the ♪). Checking this poem in my source, I saw I had marked it already but failing to find a good translation, abandoned it. I had also pretty much abandoned the poet because I found his long prefaces difficult. My reading of prose is not up to my reading of poetry and I can only hope my interpretive summary above fell within the bounds of poetic license extended to a prose accompaniment! Re-reading Bokuyô, I saw much that struck me as charming, and delayed publication to add these chapters. Now, addressing the specifics of the poem. 1) The "present" hiding in the Genzaemon's name is properly *genzai,* but *i* and *e* sounds were blurred – in some regions, utterly indistinguishable – so the pun is tighter than it seems. 2) The traditional expression for an exceptional skill or event in the Sinosphere was and still is 空前絶後 *kûzenzetsugo,* or *air/vacuum-before extinct-after.* Like the arrow of time we have already discussed, it shows the idea of directional rather than cyclic time was not unique to the West. Bokuyô paradoxically put that concept back into shockingly prosaic vocabulary to relate with the word *present* in the actor's name and create poetry. 3) Needless to say (?), my pun on "again" (*a genzaemon*) did not translate but *replace* the original. Perhaps we should call it "lost & found in translation." 4) While *mai* means dances, it is dance as a performance (as opposed to the *odori,* religious/social dancing such as *bon* or *sutra* dances). The whole of the *kabuki* performance is stylized movement, which could with equal justice be called acting or dance. Since *mai* is movement-oriented, I compromised with *mannerisms* for my first reading. The second reading maintained the continuous flow of the original but ended up making up its own poor pun. 5) No foreign words are in this poem but Bokuyô uses them sometimes, so . . .

こされとてすゝきのほてゝまねけともいやとてくねりくねる女郎花 卜養
gozare tote susuki no ho dete manekedomo iya tote kuneri kuneru ominaeshi bokuyô
have say/as-if miscanthus plume-in showng beckonng but yuck sy/as-if wriggle x2 mdflws

♪ Read when a group of men went for an outing on the Autumn moor ♪

'See, we have them!' beckon the waving plumes of the miscanthus;
How they squirm in dismay! The maiden flowers cannot stand us.

The "yuck" in this poem made me realize I had to rethink what Issa meant when he requested maiden flowers *wriggle* more (pg.211). I was thinking physical charms, when he may have meant he wanted to see more *bashfulness* (*attractive* in most cultures)! Or, maybe not. Change the "wiggle" to squirm *if you wish*. A generation earlier, another poet's *100 kyôka* collection included the following:

いとすゝきたれとねてさてはらむらん そはてしめちかはらそたちける 入安
ito susuki tare to nete sate haramu ran soba de shimeji ga hara zo tachikeru nyûan 1710
string=child-miscanthus who w/ sleepng/slpt well conceive-will! side-by champignon . . .

Little Miss Canthus, with whom did you sleep? It will show!
Nearby, your champ Pignon erect, looks like one angry beau!

The last part of Nyûan's poem needs explanation. The mushroom on the neighboring field=*hara*=belly-*stands;* usually this means *get angry,* but here alludes to a standing male member. Nyûan may have been a model for Bokuyô as he was a versatile punster. Here is one on early-bracken that combines the old trope about their fists to fill the field with fights (手をにきりあたまをはるの野には又　喧嘩多みやいてゝさわらひ *te o nigiri atama o haru no no ni wa mata kenka* . . .) Spring as a verb *whacking heads* is a pun to die for, but I cannot English it. His number puns are inane. Like modern nonsense (聞恋　かきこしにしゝする音の聞るは　かの十六になる人やらん *kagigoshi ni shishi suru oto* . . .). Japanese readers, do you get it? The sound of pissing, *shishi,* puns as 44, so it is the 16 year-old girl he hears. Or, meeting someone on the 23rd night, pockmarks look like dimples (廿三夜の月にむかへはむしくしの　えくほに見ゆるいもかけ *nijusanyo no tsuki ni mukaeba mushikushi no ekubo ni* . . .) because pockmarks, *mushikushi,* pun as 6494. In the one poem you *multiply*, in another you *add!* According to my respondent, Bokuyô himself admitted to being a light poet, but compared to Nyûan, I cannot help but think he was *more*. Still, he was a 17c poet and could be gross in the artless medieval way of Yûchôrô and Getsudôken. Prefactory note. Japanese thought *green chestnuts*, then, *yams* airy. These are the first indigestible *mame,* or beans, I know of! It is a pun-driven invention, as *kusaya,* or stinky food was eaten to scare-off demons on that day.

ふくはうち鬼はそとへとうつまめの はらにあたりてあらくさやふん 卜養
fuku wa uchi oni wa soto e to utsu mame no hara ni atarite ara kusa ya fun bokuyô
happnss/prosprty in, devil-as4 outside-to throw beans'belly-in food-poisonng, oh stinky shit

Visiting someone, shown a picture of a demon taking a shit
robe hiked up over his arse, I was asked for a suitable poem,

Luck comes in with the beans we throw, but demons go out,
Eaten, they backfire and, in the end, stink beyond doubt!

The Untranslatable Lightness *of* Nakarai Bokuyô㊦

うつくしき花のした葉を見るからに　くちすいせんと人やいふらん　半井卜養
utsukushiki hana no shitaba o miru kara ni kuchisuisen to hito ya iuran bokuyô　1607-1678

Seeing a beautiful flower's lower leaves, entrance narcissus is what people say.
＋＋＋＋＋＋＋＋＋＋＋＋＋＋＋＋＋＋＋＋＋＋＋＋＋＋＋＋＋＋＋＋＋＋＋＋＋
Seeing a beautiful wife in her bloom, I'd kiss her is what other men say!

水仙花をいけて歌よめと有けれは
~ asked for a poem about posing a narcissus ~

This beautiful flower has no limbs to hold, but leaves below
to the imagination and Narcissus may be kissed, you know!

Wow! I lucked out on that translation! Thank you, Black Swan, Guinness Stout and the week's only hour of blues on the radio. Of course, my wrong sex re-creation differs from the original, which gracefully puns together the lines separated by plus signs (蛇足「したば」は江戸時代、町民の妻の事), pulling it along by a string of facial feature = plant homophones taking us from the nose to the teeth and finally the mouth, which fuses with the biggest pun on the flower's name: "*kuchi= mouth-narcissus=suisen=sucking-do-would*. Note that *sucking-mouths* was the common word for *kissing* Japanese, to whom "suck" is not a bad word. I am unsure whether the *mouth* in the original has other meanings such as the alcove by the entrance, etc. (下口をとる＝尻取り句、一口ないし小型、出入口の略等？)

極楽のうちに塵をすてはこそそとはなにかはくるしかるへき
gokuraku no uchi ni chiri o suteba koso soto wa nani ga wa kurushikarubeki

境にありし時極楽寺といふ寺の門前に町人とも塵をすてけれは
寺の出家て散々にしかり悪口し侍けれはよみてつかはしける
composed after townsmen were chewed out for dumping trash in front of
the gate of the Time Paradise Temple in Sakai by the resident retirees

Now, if we dumped our trash inside of Paradise – maybe:
But outside? Who cares about what falls out there, baby!

A mouthful of wine, a mouthful of beer, and now whistles: the 2:00 AM train is here. The above may be one of the most inconsequential real-life *kyôka* ever written; but how charming to imagine a patient complaining about being told-off and asking the good doctor for a come-uppance in 31-syllabets! While the poem is in a book by the poet, we may imagine the patient copying and posting it somewhere as an anonymous drop-head (*rakushû*), squib. Simple, it does the trick. My *baby* rhyme is poor consolation for losing the mad association with the famous poem allegedly by a God in Shikibu's dream responding to her question poem about entering temples or shrines while menstruating. It ended with *nani ga kurushiki,* literally, *"What's so difficult/ painful?"* I say "mad" association, for the content of the poems is so different – one about entering, another not – that a waka would not seek to make it. Yet, having it made is oddly satisfying.

釈迦さまにみくしは落てねはん像　是そまことの地震成物　卜養　同
shaka-sama ni migushi wa ochite nehanzô kore zo makoto no jishin-seibutsu bokuyô
shakya-master-to reverend-head-as-for falling dead/recumbent/enlightened(buddha)statue
this+emph. true earthquake(=self? self-belief?)becoming-buddha/buddhafication

大地震に上野の大仏みくし落けれは
On the rev. Head of Ueno's Colossal Buddha falling in the Great Earthquake

Shakya lost his reverend crown, it lies enlightened on the ground;
Why not celebrate this case of self-awakening in a quake!

A reporting poem. And what beats finding something cheerful in a catastrophe? Nehanzô is the just dead-Shakyamuni, in translation to Nirvana, something celebrated on Nehan day. An enlightened death, or final awakening, is called *becoming-buddha*, but here we have Buddha becoming himself. What a fine mad synecdoche: a recumbent Buddha found in a head on the ground!

入てみん大公ぼうの海中へつりを のもとのふらりきん玉　卜養
irete min daikôbô no kaichû e tsuri-o no moto no burari kintama bokuyô d.1678
insert-try fisherman's sea-in fishing-line=man's basis/around's dangling gold/metal-ball/s

魚釣に出されうた所望あれは
asked for a sporty song to go fishing

If you're just hanging 'round and so are they, let them dangle
in the sea – float or sinker – a man needs balls to angle!

A day has passed. Strong coffee followed by strong cabernét did this one, too. My first tries failed. Until the above flowed from my fingers, I thought the poem lost in translation. I almost shifted it to the notes as a Japanese-only offering.

まふでする道にてあわをふくの神これそまことのべんざいてんかん
môde suru michi nite awa o fuku no kami kore zo makoto no benzaitenkan
pilgrimage-doing-road-on, foam+acc. spew ⇒ fortune/wealth-god/dess
this+emph. true benzaiten(goddess of wealth)⇒epilepsy (& exhibit?)

べんざいてんへまふでする道にててんかんやみあわをふきけるをみてよみける
benzaiten e môde-suru michi nite tenkanyami awa o fukikeru o mite yomikeru
Read after meeting up with a foaming epileptic on the road
of my pilgrimage to the Goddess of Wealth

♪　The Power of Kyôka, or How a *Grand Mal* becomes a *Petit Bon!*　♪

On the road to the shrine of the Goddess of Wealth, a sign of plenty:
Foam that overflows a mouth – a charm we have, in epilepsy!

This robust re-creation came to mind after I switched to Guinness Stout, a beer associated with health partly because of the charm inherent to its *name*, as what is now called *fitness* was called *stoutness* (work-outs were called *stoutness exercise*) back in the day when Tinkerbelle was described as *embonpoint*. The original morphs the verb for *spewing* into its homophone *wealth* and fuses that to the Goddess whose name, Benzaiten, partially overlaps the disease, *tenkan*, phonetically speaking. There may also be a pun on exhibit, but I am unsure. The title is *mine* and reflects my respect for what this physician, who knew epilepsy was not a jinx or otherwise bad, and may have helped the sufferer, managed to do.

After Issa & Ryôkan, Wordway's Wacky Waka

かくれゐて我があと去らぬ影法師ゐならびてだに月を見よかし 大隈言道
kakureite waga ato saranu kagebôshi   inarabete dani tsuki o miyogashi kotomichi 19c
hidden-is my-behind leave-not shadow/form-monk sits-lined-up+emph. moon+acc see-would

独・居・月
Up with the moon, alone

Always hiding behind me, shadow-monk, I wish you could
Come out to see this moon, sit by my side, if you would.

Japanese with their paper walls had more fun with shadow-play than any other people on earth. I doubt there was so much paper in Saigyô's day but he too had shadow-monks lined up (*moro tomo ni kage . . .*) – my "beside me" is "sit lined up" (*inarabete*) – in a *waka*, and Issa played with his shadow-monk more than his sparrows, but it took Ôkuma Kotomichi=wordway (1798-1868) to *address* his shadow-monk as Ryôkan did his reflection in the gruel. The manner is more *kyôka* for the absurdity of the description of what a shadow *does* – conveyed as bold, not at all pathetic "fallacy" – and the light touch of his solicitation. Similar:

春暮れて永き日さびし山彦も　独りごちだに今日はせよかし　同
haru kurete nagaki hi sabishi yamahiko mo hitorigochi dani kyô wa seyogashi
spring darkened long day/s lonely echo too alone-talk+emph. tody-as4 do-would!

Spring is old, the hours of sunlight long and lonely
Echo, might not today be a good time to try soliloquy?

~~~~~~~~~~~~~~~~~~~~~

Summer nears, the days grow long and lonely – Echo, say,
You, too, might do well to talk to yourself today!

~~~~~~~~~~~~~~~~~~~~~

Viewing blossoms, I am viewed by the blossoms, too, I ken
I cut not quite the figure they might want to be their friend.

blssms see-when blssms-by too myself seen!/: friend-as becme-ought figre+emph do not
hana mireba hana ni mo waga mi mirarekeri tomo to narubeki sugata o mo se de
花見れば花にも我が身見られけり友となるべき姿をもせで 言道 戊午集

~~~~~~~~~~~~~~~~~~~~~

朝顔を何はかなしと思ひけん人をも花はさこそ見るらめ 藤原道信拾遺集
asagao o nani wa kanashi to omoiken hito o mo hana wa sakoso mirurame michinobu
mornngface+acc what-as4 sad-as think-would? pple+acc too flwr-as4 likewse see-must

Why do we think the fate of morning glories so damn piteous?
The blossoms, on their part, must find ours the more hideous!

~~~~~~~~~~~~~~~~~~~~~

What makes us think of a morning glory's life as sad,
when flowers, seeing us, must find ours just as bad?

The blossom-viewing reversal. Shokusanjin's envious moon. Piet Hein's grass hushing to hear *us* grow. The spirit is deeply *kyôka*-compatible, whereas young Fujiwara Michinobu's 10c *waka* about the morning glory conveying Buddhist catechism – we, not dying in a day, suffer longer in this illusory world of woe – is but superficially so. Sincerity does not ruin a poem; it is just that a good *kyôka* is something higher than, say, a prayer. Call it the chuckle of the free-thinker that percolates up to heaven through the blossoms looking down on him.

春を待つ人にや見せむ灘の浦の雪の中なる花さくら鯛　言道
haru o matsu hito ni ya misemu nada no ura no yuki no uchi naru hana-sakuradai
spring-waitng persn-to+emph. show would nada's bay's snw's withn is/are chrry-snppr

To all who cannot wait for spring to bloom – Unwrap her!
Below the snow on Nada Bay, behold the cherry snapper!

I grew up by the sea. We called what English call red sea bream "snappers." Unless rhyme demands it, I cannot bream them. Still "unwrap her" is pushing it. Luckily, a *reason* can be found. The poem was the last in his book 草径集 . Annotator 穴山健 wrote it was decorative and celebratory, expressing the poet's confidence that people awaiting a breath of fresh air would appreciate the presentation of his hitherto buried poems. Also, the "blooming" embedded in the word *sakura* (cherry), following the *hana* (first a blossom in the snow, then pivoting to modify cherry-snapper as *beautiful* or *luscious*), together with that blossom means "to flourish." All that is lost in translation: I had to do *something*. Cherry snapper was in its prime during *sakuradoki,* or cherry-bloom time. Most haiku about it are definitely droll and prove that only the length of the poems separate many *ku* I would call *kyôku* from *kyôka.* Among the 30-odd *ku* in the *Cherry Snappers* chapter (44) in my *Cherry Blossom Epiphany* (2007), two (*could we fish / using willow for string? / cherry snapper* and *at the touch / of my knife, a gale / cherry snapper*) are by Mitoku, whom I *now* recognize to be a top 17c *kyôka*-master.

衾さへいと重げなる老の身の寝るがうへにも寝る猫まかな　　言道
fusuma sae ito omogenaru oi no mi no nuru ga ue ni mo nuru nekoma kana kotomichi
futon even very heavy becomes aged body/self's sleeping-above even sleeps cat-tom!

Here my body is so old even a futon feels heavy,
and the tom cat comes to sleep on sleeping me!

~~~~~~~~~~~~~~~~~~~~~~~~~~~~~~~

To think my life until now was spent in utter ignorance
of microscopes, or rather, the presence of bugs in water

いたづらに我が身フルゴロオトガラス水に虫あることも知らずて
itazura ni waga mi furugorootogarasu mizu ni mushi aru koto mo shirazu de
play-for my body/self microscope ♪ water-in bug is thing even knows-not

The creative grumbling of the first poem is *kyôka light*, the second punning time's passing/aging (*furu*) into an old name for microscope and playing on Ono no-komachi's *waka* regretting a life wasted is *kyôka* heavy *and* a modern *tanka*. Had I known of Kotomichi in 2008, more of him would be in this book!

Prayer for Buddhist Grapes & Persecuted X'tians

仏道にちかきぶどうのたなごゝろあはせてたのめ数珠の一房　へづゝ東作

butsudô ni chikaki budô no tanagokoro awasete tanome juzu no hitofusa tôsaku 徳和 1785
buddhist-way-to close grape/buddha-hall's altar/trellis/palm/s uniting request rosary's one-cluster/tuft

ある家に葡萄のよくなりたるを見にまかりしにあるじ同行のよしかたられければ

Composed upon seeing Ripening grapes
♪ at the home of a fellow believer ♪

~~Nearby your altar~~
~~red grapes close to slaughter~~

~~Brother could you~~
~~spare a vine? Or, at least~~
~~a cluster for my rosary!~~

This is one of the seven Tenmei era *kyôka* included in Steven D. Carter's *Traditional Japanese Poetry*. His translation *"Wine being so close / to something quite divine, / why not join your hands / and pray for a cluster of grapes / rich as the beads of your rosary!"* beats what I crossed out, but without an accompanying note – there is none – readers unfamiliar with Buddhist prayer beads might well wonder if we have an underground Christian cult here. And how many would know that *budô no tana* means a whole *trellis*, or *arbor*, notice the pun on a small Buddhist shrine, or *butsudô*, hop to the grapes, *budô*, step to the *tana*, or "trellis" and jump to *tanagokoro*, or "palm/s" joined in prayer, holding the looped string of beads ending in a *tuft* or *fusa* homophonic with a *cluster* of grapes, thus proving by the sympathetic magic of repeated coincidence *why* grapes are Buddhist? Tôsaku's punning is indeed a miraculous, but while sayings about wine's divinity went back thousands of years – as maintained in Tabito's series in praise of wine in the 8c *Manyôshû* – *grape* wine was not common in Japan. I thought the poet might be cleverly asking for a bunch of grapes about the size of a crumpled up rosary, presumably to eat, but my respondent points out that if one of the readings – critics differ – of the preface is right, namely, that the two are setting off on a pilgrimage, it is more likely the welfare of the grapes in the owner's absence is indeed what is being prayed for and, besides, the verb endings make my first-person reading unlikely (another reason I crossed it out).

To a Brother With a Trellis
(~~of whose arbor I am jealous~~)

Wine, they say	*Holy Buddha,*
*hides in div*in*e: let's pray*	*next to your vine, a banyan*
for your grapes:	*root looks thin!*
May they please our tongues	*Grapes like coconuts, so pray*
Like rosaries our thumbs!	*for an elephant to crush them!*

♪ *As Pilgrims Leave the Arbor* ♪

Wine is divine,
so palm to palm let's pray
the grapes grow

As big as coconuts
while we're away!

Perhaps an errant sequence of translation in quest of the untranslatable is not only futile but mad but, surely, playing at poetry is a more productive exercise than, say, working on a crossword puzzle! Yet, who has ever been criticized for doing the latter? While I generally try to keep close to the original, I sometimes give in to temptation and stray. My lead effort in this chapter is a good example. Rhyme led to *slaughter* and our sinking economy brought *"brother can you spare a vine."* All my new readings directly or indirectly retained the fiction of wine. For the first, I took Carter's "wine/divine," dropped the altar for lack of space (most readers would have no image of a Buddhist altar, anyway) and turned the rosary into a sensual simile. The coconuts in the second reading, a paraverse, grew naturally – I grew up in "the Matheson Estate," a coconut plantation – from the human "palms" in the original while the rosaries were exchanged for an elephant to extend the nutty simile within the limited space. You can, of course, drop my coconuts and render that penultimate line, "Bigger than our rosaries," or "As lustrous as rosaries," etc.. I found it hard to keep them for "rosaries" seems less generic, i.e., *catholic* than *Catholic* while calling them "prayer beads" would not do for not only would such a description lack poetry but it would be redundant with the other "prayer" or "praying" in the poem.   Religion-related translation is hell to do. Take, for example, this 17c parody of a 10c poem:

武蔵野は今日はな焼きそ浅草や夫もころべり我もころべり 仁勢物語#12
musashino wa kyô wa na yaki so asakusa ya tsuma mo koroberi ware mo koroberi nise.
musashi moor-as-for today-as-for not-burn! low-grass!/: husband roll/recants i too roll/rec. ↓

No, not, today!	*Burn not, today,*
Burn not Musashi moor!	*Musashi – the grass is low*
Soft spring grass	*Our sin is light!*
Lies hidden there, no less,	*My mate rolls, an apostate;*
my sweet young blade & I.	*I, too, roll below my weight.*

↑むさしのはけふはなやきそわかくさのつまもこもれり我もこもれり 伊勢#12
musashino wa kyô wa na yakiso wakakusa no tsuma mo komoreri ware mo komoreri ise
musashi moor-as-for today-as-for burn-not young-grass-spouse hidden I too hidden

We have seen the fire in the *Tales of Ise* poem on the left (p.98) morph into *heartburn;* here, in the 17c *Fake Ise*, the absconding couple become *Christians!* "Low grass," is *shallow* and implies what English might call, with respect to the sin/crime (of being Christian), *light*, while *"rolling"(coitus)* means treading upon or otherwise disrespecting a Christian image to prove one has left the Faith. ♪

Marine Metaphor Meets Land-locked Culture (ours)

あまのすむさとのしるべにあらなくに 怨みむとのみ人のいふらむ　小野小町
ama no sumu sato no shirube ni aranaku ni uramin to nomi hito no iuran ono no komachi kks727
fisher/sea-harvesters live country/village's guide-as am-not though begrudge is only/all people say

A Littoral Complaint About Complaints

I am no guide to the seafolk hamlets – so why such rancor,
When they ask, and I don't show them a way to the shore?

Who knows if Komachi was what Usanians call a *prick-teaser* or, like the English *Virgin Queen*, a hole short. Regardless, it hurts not to lose the fine yet simply expressed wit of someone called the Sappho of Japan. The wit depends upon the untranslatable 4-syllabet homophonic pun where *uramin* means both 浦見ん＝*bay-see-would* [like to see the bay] and 怨みん＝*begrudge-would*. She laments *that* is "all a *hito*=person/ people say about/tell" her. The translations I have read make *hito*, *"you"* (Cr.) or *"my love/. . . him"* (R&H). Such details matter little compared to the fact that the main message, that she is fed up with the resentment of her allegedly numerous yet never indulged suitors (or, if one who stands for others is better, change *they/them* to *you*) is no longer expressed as a witty pun. I followed the others in changing the *bay* into the *shore*, because the male heart, like a mangrove pen (my metaphor) hopes to land upon and root into the female shore and, in English, the *ulterior/backside/wrong-side-of-the tracks* sense of the Japanese bay is missing, anyway (*Am I a guide to the seafolk hamlets! Why keep crying / that I'll pay for not showing you the clam-bake bay?*). While Komachi's *waka* is among the *Kokinshû love poems* and not in the dedicated *haikai* chapter, with other "eccentric poems" (Cr), many of which have the *kyôka* feeling, *if* only I could mimic the way she turns a noun and verb into another verb after the feisty denial which builds up the complex metaphor in English, you would see this is as good an example of mad poem *technique* as any by *kyôka* master Shokusanjin.

あしのうらのいと汚くも見ゆる哉 浪は寄りても洗はざりけり 後拾遺集
ashi no ura no ito kitanaku mo miyuru kana nami wa yorite mo arawazarikeri. anon gss 1262
foot/feet backside/sole's very dirty even seem!/?/: waves-as4 approaching even washed-not!

    Acquaintances on retreat at a temple had adjoining rooms. On leaving at dawn after the New Year observances, the author discovered a pair of dirty stockings that had been dropped and left on the floor. Picking them up and sending them [to the owner].   Pref. & poem trans. Cranston.

Dirty indeed
Looks to be the Bay of Reeds
  (Read sole of your foot);
For all that the waves keep rolling in,
  It's never had a washing!

Bay of Reeds (my caps) = Reed-bay=葦の浦=*ashi-no-ura* = 脚の裏=Foot/feet-soul. In the 16c, the Jesuits were surprised to note how Japanese noblemen took pride in cleaning up – even sweeping – their own inn rooms. This poem suggested to me that such fastidiousness went back centuries; but my respondent believes we have palace women, and the point was *not* kidding the other, as I had assumed, but concern lest she get her feet dirty without the stockings/socks, and reminded me that such a bay, unlike the ocean, does indeed get pretty dirty. The pun may be an old sawfish, but the application is as fresh as anything found in later classic *kyôka*. I could not resist introducing Cranston's translation. Failing to capture the salient pun, he heroically meta-punned those "reeds=feet" into his parenthetical explanation. I was at wit's end myself, considering a story about someone who left a reed instrument that was so dirty I could bring in the Bay of Pigs, etcetera.

あふまでのかたみとてこそとどめけめ 涙に浮ぶもくづなりけり おきかぜ
au made no katami tote koso todomekeme namida ni ukabu mokuzu narikeri okikaze
meet-until's namesake for kept, tears in floating seaweed/algae became! kks #745

Dallying with a closely guarded daughter, someone came out to say her parents were calling. She rushed inside leaving behind the overskirt she had taken off. Returning it,

this souvenir left	*The silky train*
behind "till we meet again"	*you left behind – 'Until*
it seems this trailing	*we meet again,'*
skirt has become a rope of	*Became an algal trail,*
seaweed in a sea of tears	*floating on a sea of tears.*

The translation on the left (in my centering.) is by Rodd and Henkenius from whom I borrowed the term "overskirt" for the ornate and bulky train that we can well imagine a woman taking off to be at ease. The *"rope of seaweed"* is brilliant. I have eaten *mo*, which is sold soaking in light rice-vinegar. It does seem to link in a somewhat rope-like manner. I use *algal*, for *mo* doesn't make me think of the "duck" in the dictionary's first offering, and *trail* fits the idea of a train well. If you wish to make it a *duckweed* trail, instead, please change "afloat" to *bobbing* and it will add some humor to the metaphor. Regardless, we see here both a outlandish *kyôka*-class *tear+memento* hyperbole and marine metaphor utterly exotic to English, despite its father or motherland being an island. Seriously, I never cease to be amazed with the degree to which Japanese poetry, even while the capital of culture was in Nara and Kyoto, both inland cities, kept the sea. While the desert religions of North Africa and continental influence removed the same from England, neither jungle-born Buddhism nor Chinese literature did anything similar to Japan. In English literature, the sea is all about foreign lands. It is an outside rather than internal or domestic presence. But, to return to the poem in question, I imagine the garment was not intended to be left with the man, but the young woman had no time to waste if she was to avoid detection and so it became *ipso facto* a memento. As the annotator of my edition of the *Kokinshû*, Kyûsojin, puts it, this poem is a window open to courtship among Heian nobles. It is followed by one where a memento becomes a *foe*, as it keeps one who would forget from forgetting. Perhaps that suggests Tsurayuki, the editor of the *Kokinshû*, felt the overskirt returned by courier rather than in person indicated a romance that was not to be.

Marine Metaphor Meets Land-locked Culture II

わたつうみの かざしにさすと いはふもゝ きみがためには おしまざりけり 伊勢話 87
わたつうみの かざしにさすと いはふ藻も 君がためには くらげなりけり 仁勢話 87
watatsumi no kazashi ni sasu to iwau mo mo kimi ga tame ni wa oshimazarikeri   Tales of Ise 9c
watatsumi no kazashi ni sasu to iwau mo mo kimi ga tame ni wa kurage narikeri   Fake Ise 18c?
mighty-ocean=jupiter's laurels/crown-as place duckweed even you-for-as4 regret-not! // jellyfish-is!

After the maids safely gathered seaweed despite the high seas
♪ for a banquet, the lady of the house recited this for her visitors ♪

For my Lords' sake   *For my Lords' sake*
The mighty God of the Sea   *The mighty God of the Sea*
gladly gave it up –   *kept his crown:*

This celebrated duckweed   *The duckweed on your heads*
once crowning his head!   *will be jellyfish, instead!*

I abbreviated the introductory prose for the *Tales of Ise waka* and skipped that for the *Fake Ise*. The original *waka*, itself quite mad, is represents the ludicrous thing a rustic attempting to be elegant might write. McCullough may do a better job of showing that with her translation *"For these lords / The god of the sea / Has gladly relinquished / The seaweed he treasures / To adorn his head.,"* but it is unclear whether *we* celebrate the seaweed being served, or the sea god himself treasures it. I favor the first as words suitable to serving up food, but, by making it the god, his "relinquishing" the prize is nicely accented, so I do not mean that as a criticism. The original shows a fine sense of propriety in one of the details. This seaweed of a variety called *duckweed*, here followed by another *mo*, meaning "even," sounds auspicious (for longevity) by evoking *momo,* the peach, a hundred, or myriad, and the epithet for things palatial (百敷 *momoshiki*). The true mad poem from the parody literally changes nothing but the last seven syllabets – I had to change more in translation – exchanging the *duckweed* for *jellyfish*, getting back at rather than bending over backwards for the uppity visitors. But what makes it especially delightful is the way changing to jellyfish alters the meaning, or adds a second meaning to the verb *sasu*, which, until we got to said jellyfish only meant *placing* the seaweed on the crown, to, *in retrospect*, become a homophone meaning *to sting*.

The above is, despite the unnatural vocabulary, do-able. But, the thick use of marine metaphor and punning in the *Tales of Ise* itself – before we even get to the parodies of it – may be one reason why we do not have cheap pocket-book translations of the droll classic. Take, for example, the poems in episode #75, which starts with, *"Long ago, a man said "Let's go and live in Ise!"* and the woman replied,

おほよどのはまにおふてふ見るからにこゝろはなぎぬかたらはねども
ôyodo no hama ni ou to iu miru kara ni kokoro wa naginu katarawanedomo
ôyodo's beach-by cover they say, seeing-from heart bends/content meeting-not though

Looking does it for me – like seaweed on the seabed off Ôyodo's shore
Rooted, I still sway, but see no need to get to know you more.

McCullough translates *"Though we have not exchanged vows, / The pleasure of seeing you / Has made me quite content."* I like the last two lines, but to find an explanation for the truncated lines she makes us thumb a hundred pages to the back of the book! I do not have her book on hand, so I just write what I know but the seaweed would be *mirume* as it was called *miru* and that is a homophone of "see" and any seaweed pushed over in the current (but still rooted) stands for, or rather, lies for contentment. Harris, by the way, translates this *"Say you that there grow / at the Ôyodo Strand / seaweeds dark and deep? – / My heart cannot blossom out / in your fresh water haven."* I do not know where the "fresh" water came from, but this translation is imaginative to say the least. After such a cruelly indifferent response, the man replied,

> 袖ぬれてあまのかりほすわたつうみのみるをあふにてやまむとやする
> *sode nurete ama no karihosu watatsûmi no miru o au nite yamamu to ya suru*
> sleeves wetting fishergirls hunt & dry ocean's sea-pine=see for meeting-as stop would do!?

> *So you prefer we, like the **sea**weed ama wet their robes to reap,*
> *Stop short by the shore and never actually go to sea?*

Here it is fun to contrast McCullough's dry minimalism *"Do you propose / To substitute / Seeing / For meeting?"* (+ info on the sea-puns a 100 pages later) with Harris's exuberant *"Sleeves drenched with the waves / goes he scything through the weeds / great god of the sea -- / Having seen me but this once / you dry up like the desert?"* The combination of Victorian drama and Yiddish rhetoric is fun, but I cannot imagine any Japanese reader conjuring up Jove! OK, it's the lady again:

> いはまよりおふるみるめしつれなくはしほひしほみちかひもありなむ
> *iwama yori ouru mirume shi tsurenaku wa shiohi shiomichi kai mo arinamu*
> crags-'tween frm cover sea=see=weed vainly-as4 ebbtide hightide value/shells evn are!?

> *Out on the reef, who can say but seaweed may prove hard to get.*
> *Still, tides rise and fall, a man might find some shellfish yet!*

I am unsure of Mc.'s reading *"Who is to say? / If we continue / To see one another, / Something may come of it."* (+info. *ditto*), which I follow, but sure H. is too negative: *"To the murky weeds / growing in among the crags / nothing seems worthwhile: / Ebbing tides nor high tides full / bring no presents from the sea!"* The man again:

> なみだにぞぬれつゝしぼる世の人のつらき心はそでのしづくか
> *namida ni zo nuretsutsu shiboru yo no hito no tsuraki kokoro wa sode no shizuku ka*
> tears-by soaking-while wring world's people's hurting hearts-as-for sleeves' drops?

> *So are these tears from a suffering heart that soak my sleeves*
> *Just so many drops of brine – Wring 'em out and all is fine?*

Mc. finally jumps to life here, *"Wringing my tear-drenched sleeves, / I wonder if perhaps / Your icy heart / Has been transformed / Into those drops of moisture."* H., as always, *"So great are my tears / that no wringing drives them out: / Should the bitterness / that you brew within your heart / flow in drops from off my sleeve?"* Let me put in a word for *the sea*. *Namida*, tears, begins with a homophone of waves, *nami,* creating a link to the earlier chain of associations. Hence my *brine*. The original may deserve a more aphoristic reading: *So would the pangs of love that humans feel be but this – / Drops of brine, wrung from sleeves soaked by our tears?* – & translation, what is *it*?

Two Lousy Translations & Two Lousier Ones!

頭に遊ぶは頭虱　頂の窪をぞ極めて食ふ
櫛の歯より天降る　麻笥の蓋にて命終はる　梁塵秘抄
kôbe ni asobu wa kashirajirami onaji no kubo o zo kimete kuu
head-on play-as-for head-lice summit-depression+emph select eating
kushi no ha yori amakudaru ogoke no futa nite mei owaru
comb's teeth from heaven-descend *ogoke*-box's lid-on life ends

♪ Swing Low, Sweet
Chariot (with teeth?)

Up from her nape,
Head Louse rides a shiny comb
through her locks

To his final resting place
within a lacquered box ♪

This 53-syllabet 12c "now-style," or *imayo* song (#410 *Ryôjin Hishô*), makes the head louse a *boss* lice and has him descend to the nape of the neck to graze where he is caught in said comb's teeth and spirited off *from* paradise, namely, some beauty's beautiful hair, to pass away – a death-bed scene – on the lid of said box. I reversed it by taking him up *to* paradise, for English has no simple recognized term like *amakudaru* for descending *from* it. Even my *lacquered* is wrong, but simpler than translating the truth – the *ogoke* is some combination of wood and hempen cloth etc.. None of that would make this mad by Tenmei era *kyôka* standards. It is just third-person nonsense like a nursery verse and, indeed, is found only one song apart from the famous verse threatening a snail (pg.146). In summary, only the title makes my shortened version mad, or, at any rate, closer to a *kyôka* than a real *kyôka* translated without such inexcusable additions might be. Perhaps, I am too strict. Here is a poem that *is* in a bona fide *kyôka* selection (かさぬ草紙: tk2 17c?), the title of which Englishes as "A Book Not to Lend,"

しらみ子の身のゆくすゑを尋れば　つめのさきこそはかところなれ
shirami-ko no mi no yukusue o tazunereba tsume no saki koso haka-dokoro nare
louse-child's body/self's destination/location+acc ask-if nail-tip+emph grave-place is

Would thou inquire just where that little Louse may now be found?
On my dirty finger nail His final resting ground.

~~~~~~~~~~~~~~~~~~~~~~~~~~~~~~~~~~~~~~

If you would ask where in the world he went, it wasn't to jail:
That little louse got into a pinch, was fingered & ended up nailed.

The original, *taken alone,* is less witty than the previous "Now Style Song." My first attempt at translation – the second reading above – overcompensated with English idiom and rhyme. The original's fingernail grave *may* allude to a *tsumebako,* or "nail box," a small container for the picks used to play *koto* (zither), but that is about it for word play. Format aside, what makes this simple poem mad is that it plays with the line *"If you would inquire where so and so went,"* found in Sôkan's famous death poem (pg.382), itself a parody of poems about cheating Old Age; and, if I am not mistaken, gives us a low-life parody of the lyrical Now-style song, something I hint at with the adjective *dirty*.

So much for lice. More lousy translations. I tried but failed to resist Englishing two *kyôka* that embody bold wordplay and caught my eye so many times, I would guess they must be among the top 10 most famous *kyôka* of all time.

夕されば野辺の秋風身にしみて鶉鳴くなり深草の里　俊成　千載集　*yû sareba nobe no akikaze mi ni shimite uzura nakunari fukukusa no sato*　shunzei 1114-1204
↓ night falls-when fields' fall-wind-in soaking quail call/cry-becoms deepgrass cuntry

   At dusk, the wind   *Shoot one mud-hen,*
  brings the autumn fields   *shoot two, roast 'em for a treat,*
   within to me –   *'tis what they are for!*

 When the quails cry, we're blest   *With each cry, there are less*
  to live in Deepgrass county.   *living on Deep-grass Moor.*

ひとつとりふたつとりては焼いて食ひくひななくなる深草の里　蜀山人 ↑
hitotsu tori futatsu torite wa yaite kui kuina nakunaru fukukusa no sato shokusanjin
1 bird/catching 2-birds/ctchng-as-4 roastng eatng mud-hen calls/cries=dies deepgrass cuntry

 Shoot one mud hen, shoot two, roast them all before they fly,
  No petit mort, when they cry, they're shot and really die!
~~~~~~
 One mud hen, two! How easy to catch, cook & chew those birds!
 When no more remain for food, we may have to eat our words!

Shokusanjin's *kyôka* starts like a counting song, but stops counting *up* . . . Unfortunately, not only is *cry* not a homophone with *die* in English but much of the pleasure of the switch from the expected former to the later that makes the conceit of presence turn into one of absence, lies in the jump from the allusion to birds that were lyrical props to birds going extinct to satisfy lower appetites. The *kuina*, was chosen for being homophonous with "eat" or "eat-not" (accord. to the inflect.). My *moor* pun is not bad, but even altering the *waka* slightly to improve the resemblance with the take-off could not save it. Cleverness cannot match the original pun where "cry" artlessly becomes "die." The poem deserves its fame.

この世をばどりやお暇と線香の煙と共にはいさやうなら　十返舎一九
kono yo oba doriya ohima to senko no kemuri to tomo ni hai sayônara　ikku d.1831
this world+emph whatever take-leave-when joss's smoke-w/ together ashes=yes, goodbye

I tried to English this lively death-poem (*Enough already, world, with incense smoke wafting, I take /my leave laughing my ash off – and, w/ yours, say onara!* And, *Goodbye dear world, a cloud of smoke, we're off – for what it's worth! / My joss and I are sky-bound but our ashes stay on earth.*) but, as UC, they're DOA.

Spiteful Kyôka Without even one Silverfish

女院の御前のひろくなる事は暁月坊が私地の入るゆへ　暁月坊 新撰狂歌集
nyôin no gozen no hiroku naru koto wa kyôgetsu-bô ga shiji no iru yue　kyôgetsu-bô d.1328
Empress's hon.+front's wide become thing-as-for A.-monk's private-land's enter/acquire because

A) *The Empress's Garden is wider by acquiring Monk K's private grounds.*
B) *Her Majesty's Vagina is wider by Monk K's privates having entered It.*

~~~~~~

The Queen whose garden took in his, messed with the wrong monk-bard:
Kyôgetsu left hers so wide she'll never take another yard!

The original, which has an honorific before the garden, ostensibly means A) but insinuates B). It is an example of a *kyôka* that is clean or obscene *depending*. The poet refers to himself in the third-person. A little preface accompanying it explains that the Empress found her "front" (garden) too narrow and confiscated land from her neighbor to enlarge it. There is record of an earlier Empress asking for a huge cherry tree and behaving magnanimously once she learned of a brave protest movement against it (see the 8-fold blossom chapter in *Cherry Blossom Epiphany*), but who knows whether this less considerate behavior is authentic. If it *is* a true story and the Empress behaved inconsiderately to the neighbor – especially if it really was Monk Kyôgetsu – possible, for he was said to be a heir to the Imperial Fujiwara family until his father had two more boys with his wife – then, a mad poem which gives her pun-ishment is poetic justice and the *kyôka* a masterpiece. If, however, the little preface is pure bunk, and there was no Empress to redress, this is just school-boy humor. Technical points: "Front" in Japanese is common slang for a vagina; the syllabic spelling of *private land* 私地 is シヂ while the punned *penis* 似指 literally, *resemble-finger*, a Chinese term, is properly シジ and "yard," like *shiji,* is an obsolete term for the male member punning on the privated grounds. Shokusanjin again:

やうやうと　来てもぐり込む　冷たさは　君が心と　鼻と雨脚　蜀山人
yôyô to kite moguri-komu tsumetasa wa kimi ga kokoro to hana to ameashi　shokusanjin
at-last came snuggle-in coldness-as-for your heart and nose and rain-legs/feet/foot

◎青　楼　四　季　歌　冬◎
The Pleasure Quarters in Season (winter)

When you finally came, and snuggled into bed, I felt the cold –
Next to your heart the rain and the tip of my nose feel warm.

I mistranslated this in the reading copy with something corny like *"when I finally came to snuggle with you, sweet-heart: / Cold as the tip of my nose, or a foot of winter rain, I found thou art."* But, on second thought, recalling how a man may have to wait until a courtesan says goodbye to another man or temporarily leaves him in one room to give some attention to a second (or third) man in another. Regardless, this is milder come-uppance than Issa's ugly silverfish or Kyôgetsu's ugly boast. Shokusanjin expressed discontent with his treatment by a popular courtesan in the pleasure quarters, or as Kaneko put it, *"bothered the enemy (object of one's love) courtesan with piquant sarcasm"* (随分穿つた皮肉に敵娼を

困らせたりする). In the original, the nose *hana* probably puns on the abbreviation for the "flower-fee," or *hana-dai,* paid to a courtesan. The *rain-legs/feet/foot* was lost in trans-lation. As we noted before, rain seen falling from clouds in the distance is called a *leg*. Here, what matters is that *leg* in Japanese includes *foot* in the range of connotations – convenient: for what feels colder in bed than a foot? Shokusanjin's poem could seed a parlor pop spong, a *ko-uta*. The original simply sets her heart next to the nose and rain-legs/foot.

うらめしやわがかくれ家は雪隠か 来る人ごとに紙おいていく 仙厓和尚
urameshi ya waga kakurega wa settchin ka kuru hitogoto ni kami oite-iku sengai
hateful!/: my hidden-house-as-for toilet? coming people-each paper-leaving go 1750-1837

> *How I do hate it!*
> *Should my abode become*
> *a common commode?*
>
> *Everybody visits leaving*
> *whatever paper they bring!*

> *How I hate to see*
> *my hermitage turned into*
> *a water closet!*
>
> *One person after another*
> *Brings and leaves paper!*

Monk Sengai once told-off a boastful local parvenu in his favorite mode of expression, a *kyôku*: "Don't be proud / Even the moon is round / but one night" おごるなよ 月の丸さも ただ一夜 *ogoru na yo tsuki no marusa mo tada hitoyo*. His blunt humor often expressed in *haiga* (poem+picture) made him many fans in Hakata and, paper in hand, they streamed to his hermitage hoping for artistic handouts. Needless to say, this could become irksome for the resident. This *kyôka* teaches us that people generally carried their own toilet paper and they tended to leave paper for the monk to fill rather than hang-around while he worked. I feel his poem, for borrowing its rhetoric from the following *Manyôshû* (8c) *waka* #3129 or, I would guess, one even more similar I haven't found, is more a classic *kyôka* than Issa's, Monk Kyôgetsu's or Shokusanjin's.

桜花咲きかも散ると見るまでに誰かも此処に見えて散り行く 万葉
sakurabana saki ka mo chiru to miru made ni tare ka mo koko ni miete chiriyuku
cherry-blossoms/tree bloom?-if falling see-until who?here-at seing fall/scattering-go/leave

> *Am I human or*
> *a cherry tree that blooming*
> *soon scatters?*
>
> *The way people come here*
> *see me, then up and leave!*

My title for this chapter expresses my belief that, in Japanese, at least, Issa's *shimijimi* intense *silverfish* is the gold standard for poems by furious poets. Were Issa a *kyôka* master rather than a *haikai* master, you can bet that poem would be considered a masterpiece and included in all Japanese anthologies of *kyôka* (not too many, I am afraid). As such, it demonstrates what is wrong about conven-tional study and anthologizing of poetry, does it not?

Near-kyôka by Sosei who didn't fall far from the 木

Coming across Monk Sosei's *waka* Kaneko cited as a *Kokinshû* (905) *haikai*-style *kyôka* when proofing my short & broad history of *kyôka* at the end of this book, I decided to check up on him. I found I already had three Sosei poems in the book: the woman-style intent to chide the wind, the vow not to plant another flowering example of inconstancy, and the idea of cutting off his sleeve for an offering. Then, I added a fourth, a thrush berating others for petals he knocked off himself. I also learned he was the son of Henjô, *the* Henjô who fell on the maiden flowers and that many if not most of his poems outside of the comic chapters of the KKS are mad enough that he deserved a chapter. As all poems are from the easily accessible *Kokinshû*, I will, just this once, skip the Japanese and the word-for-word glosses. The explanations are on the next page, in order.

haru tateba hana to ya miran shirayuki no kakareru eda ni uguisu zo naku kks #6

Did he see blossoms on the plum tree because it's spring?
On its snow-covered bough, a mountain thrush sings now.

chiru to mite aru beki mono o ume no hana utate nioi no sode ni tomareru kks #47

Seeing them fall, that should be all to the Plum Blossoms;
But, damn if their sweet scent does not stay with me anon!

oshi to omou kokoro wa ito ni yorarenan chiru hana goto ni nukite todomen kks #81

They fall! Could my heartstring be a million threads,
that I might transfixing fix every blossom to its limb!

koyoi kon hito ni wa awaji tanabata no hisashiki hodo ni machi mo koso sure kks #181

Tanabata Star Love Poem

I shall not meet the one who comes tonight for my wish
Is not to have to wait . . . . a year for every date!

nushi shiranu ka koso nioere aki no no ni ta ga nugikakeshi fujibakama zo mo kks #241

I smell perfume, coming from that autumn field, but where
is he who shucked and hung his purple boneset trousers there?

nurete hosu yamaji no kiku no tsuyu no ma ni itsuka chitose o ware wa heniken kks #273

On a person approaching a sage's hermitage through the chrysanthemums

In the drying of a dew-drop that spilled from 'mum to me
A thousand years passed on that mountain path: my reverie.

ima kon to iishi bakari ni nagatsuki no ariake no tsuki o machiidetsuru kana kks #691

I'll be right there you said, so I waited and waited . . . but, instead
The longest moon of the year I saw, right there in the morning sky!

omou to mo karenan hito o ikaga sen   akazu chirinuru hana to koso mime kks #799

No matter how true my love, his for me will soon have faded.
So, what shall I do? I'll view him as bloom that drops before one's jaded.

Though my love's deep, what shall I do with him whose will not keep?
Think him a flower that falls before I tire of the treat.

wasuregusa   nani o ka tane to   omoishi wa tsurenaki hito no kokoro narikeri kks #802

Asked to compose and write a poem upon a screen for Emperor Uda

Plant of Forgetting – where in the world do their seeds come from?
Of course, it has to be! From the hearts of lovers grown cold.

#6: Humans usually cannot tell the difference between snow and blossoms viewed on a distant mountain and are influenced to see the latter by the knowledge that it is calendrical spring. Having the bird-harbinger of spring doubly human is mad. #47: The usual desire is to retain at least the scent after the blossoms fall or one leaves the blossoms. Editor Tsurayuki placed the poem between two such. While it is said his father pretty much forced him to become a monk, Sosei's being an unattached man of the cloth makes the poem appropriate even if novel. #81: Threads and romantic hearts go together in Japanese. Here, the thread, *o,* holding one's soul/s together – pardon my making the English heartstring one's own rather than one's sweetheart – is pun-alluded by the initial *oshi,* or "lamentable." (unimportant, but how can I *not* mention where the poem was composed: "at the home of the Middle Captain Lady of the Bedchamber" (R&H)). #181: The Tanabata (Seventh Night) poem is not titled in the original as it is in the poem. I removed it to make room to add specifics: "a year for every date." The usually romanticized ageless love of the Stars is given a mad treatment. Since men did the visiting in Japan, this is another of Sosei's as-a-woman poems. #241: Noblemen traditionally walked about with sleeves so well perfumed, often by their own patented blends of smoke, that one could guess who called even if he was not seen. The *fujibakama* was, I always thought, trousers named after purple wisteria, but looking it up I found an *ague* or *boneset* weed (R&H: *Eupatorium strechadosmum,* or Chinese agrimony). One ancient Chinese list of extremely *vulgar things to do* included hanging out your trousers to dry on flowers, so I found it particularly amusing for the flowers themselves to become the same. #273: Chrysanthemum dew found up the right mountain allowed one to live forever. For an enlightened sage an instant – the twinkling of an eye being a "dew-moment" in Japanese – might well be a millennium. Kyûsojin explains that Sosei was viewing a *suhama* 州浜, or tray-sized landscape, and became one with the tiny figurine. My translation is looser than I like. Somewhere in that moment, *I* pass 1000 years. #691: The *nagatsuki* or long-moon was the last month of fall. Apparently, the full moon hangs around longer than usual. The as-a-woman poem is not mad, but close. #799: The "what shall I do with inconstant lovers?" complaint was usually female; so was the flower metaphor (until hundreds of years later the blossom metaphor was drafted to serve as warriors willing to sacrifice their lives). Putting the two together meant one or the other of these ideas had to be flipped. #802: *Kusa* is usually Englished as *grass,* sometimes as *herb* or *weed,* but rarely as *plant* or *flower*. It can be all of them, but never a tree. ◎ To me, the *I shall not meet, perfume trousers,* and *forgetfulness seed* source poems were most clearly *kyôka*. ◎ Some of Sosei's *waka* were, like some *kyôka,* too pun-proud to English. Eg. おとにのみきくの白露よるはおきてひるは思ひにあへずけぬべし *oto ni nomi kiku . .* #470 sound only hear=kiku⇒chrysanthemum's white-dew=not-knowing(the real story)-gathers⇒night-as-for awake, day-as-for longing/worrying=omohi⇒hi=sun-to meeting-not vanish-ought/will.

Lady Ise's somewhat-*kyôka waka* in Mad Transl.
かすかのの わかなのかすは のこしてむ ちとせのはるも きみそつむへき
kasuga no no wakana no kazu wa nokoshitemu chitose no haru mo kimi (ware) zo tsumubeki
kasuga meadow's young-green's numbr-as4 remaining 1000 year's spring+emph lord+emph pck-ought

東三条の宮す所の御賀を、中務宮したまふに、屏風に、若菜摘みたるところ
For a folding screen given to the Mikado with a scene of young green picking

Do leave a good number of young greens in Kasuga meadow,
That we may still be plucking a thousand springs from now!

In Kasuga's field, leave a goodly number of the young greens
That your Lord may still pluck away after a thousand springs!

We, who pick them, end up with our old backs bent over double:
Young greens we hunt to age less are bringing us more trouble!

Picking them, just look and see how we get bent in half,
Young greens in the field to stop aging? What a laugh!

つむひとは こしもふたへに なりにけり おいせぬのへのわかななれとも 寂蓮
tsumu hito wa koshi mo futae ni narinikeri oisenu nobe no wakana naredomo jakuren
pickng persn/s-as-4 back+emph doubled-as become+final. age-let-not field's yungreens is but

Young green plucking was a New Year ritual, so time-hyperbole was not beyond the pale. In the 10c, *kyôka* and other *waka* were yet to be differentiated – but there is a certain charming novelty in bringing a long future to young greens. The first version I saw has *kimi* (ruler or lover) as the plucker, but others make it *ware*, or "I" 春日野の若菜の種は残してむ千歳の春もわれぞつむべき. Did Lady Ise (fl. 930) write one version from her point of view and one from that of the Emperor who would live with the folding screen? For contrast, I added a *waka* of young greens with an incontestably mad flavor by 12c monk Jakuren (出典：寂蓮百歌集). Note how it (*maybe*) played upon the visual bend of the syllabet へ.

ゆめならて あふことかたき よのなかは おほかたとこを おきすやあらまし
yume nara de au koto gataki yononaka wa ôkata toko o okiyasu ya aramashi
dream not-by meeting is difficult world/society/times-as-for, most/ly bed awake-not!
..

~~Nowadays, when, outside of dreams it is so hard to meet,~~
~~Most people in their beds must try to go to sleep, instead.~~

~~So most girls no longer wait up in bed, but sleep? It seems~~
~~that, nowadays, it's hard to rendezvous except in dreams!~~

Living in a time, when love in the flesh is frowned upon,
and we must dream to meet: I'm pretty much bed-bound.

Nowadays, it's hard to take a booty call except in a dream
So here I am, bed-bound, hoping you will come around!

My first readings based on the mistaken belief that *ôkata*, "mostly/ generally" meant "most people," as per the modern reading made the poem seem a social commentary, closer to what would be called a *kyôka*. Searching for the comic, I found such mistakes all too easy to make. Mad in translation, indeed! Dream visits were proof one was desired, but Lady Ise wants her man to find a way to meet her. *In such a time, when it is hard to meet outside of dreams / I find myself bed-bound: have you no means?* I know too little about the times to talk morals (penultimate reading), and apologize for bringing slang into the palace in the last!

なくこゑに そひてなみたは のほらねと くものうちより あめとふるらむ
naku koe ni soide namida wa noboranedo kumo no uchi yori ame to fururamu lady ise
crying voice accompanied tears-as4 ascend but cloud-from rain as fall-would

> *Though the tears, that accompany my sobs, may not rise up,*
> *from within those clouds, they do fall down from the skies!*
> ~~~~~~
> *I guess it's me! I must be brooding yet within the clouds.*
> *Rain is falling with my tears: they pour for crying aloud!*
> ~~~~~~
> *Are they like me? Those clouds must be troubled as hell.*
> *Falling with my tears, this rain; I guess it's just as well.*

わかことや くものなかにも おもふらむ あめもなみたも ふりにこそふれ
waga koto ya kumo no naka ni mo omouramu ame mo namida mo furi koso fure lady ise
my thing-as-for clouds within even think not? rains' tears even falling+emph fall

A modern annotation favors the second reading (minus my *"I guess ~ well"*) of the second poem; *I* favor a sympathetic, *morai-naki*, cloud reading, for I recall a fall, the rainiest in the recorded history of Japan, when I felt *my* hopeless love was the cause of it (Don't call for a straight-jacket, this was almost twenty years ago!).

なつむしの みをむしはてて たましあらは われもまねはむ ひとめもるみそ
natsumushi no mi o mushi-hatete tamashi araba ware mo manebamu hitome moru mi zo
smmr bugs(moths)' bdy/self/s cook-up, soul/s is/r-if i too learn-wld pple's eys leak slf/bdy is

> *Were it true that the souls of summer moths survive a fire,*
> *I would likewise do to be near you, unseen by other eyes.*

A perfect example of a love poem mad as a *kyôka*. "You" could be "him," but the lack of a pronoun in the original allows a choice. I lost a poor pun on *bug=mushi=boil-to-mush* (poor both for redundancy and because bugs *burnt* up).

きくのうへに おきゐるへくも あらなくに ちとせのみをも つゆになすかな
kiku no ue ni okiiru beku mo aranaku ni chitose no mi o mo tsuyu ni nasu kana lady ise
chrysnthmm-above place-ought even is-not thousand-yrs' body+acc even dew-as bcm!/?

九月九日ぞこの鶴は死にける
On the Ninth month Ninth day a Crane died

> *Impossible, I say! On Chrysanthemum Day, how can it be*
> *that a Crane trades in for dew a thousand-years longevity!*

The dead went to paradise on a lotus leaf, not a mum's, and the date was one when mum wine was drunken for a long life, so Lady Ise felt obliged to share the sad coincidence with the world. And she does so in a way that made me, at least think about the simpler irony of dew, symbol of transience upon a longevity herb.

Kyôka as Bad as its Detractors Think it is, Yet . .

よき価ひを待てうらめやと親や思ふ 玉のやうなるはこいり娘　栗柯亭木端
yoki atai o matte urameya to oya ya omou tama no yô naru hakoiri-musume　kihashi 1740
good price+acc waitng sell-not? so parent thnks gem-like becoms box-entrd-daughtr　狂歌続ますかゝみ

> Waiting to sell when their treasure will fetch a good price:
> The parents of a proverbial girl-in-a-box are not very nice.

Kihashi was editor of the collection. In countries where chastity was a fetish, girls were not allowed out w/out chaperones. Japanese girls over the centuries were pretty much free to come and go as they liked (see items 2-34, 2-35 in *Topsy-turvy 1585*). Daughters closely watched by parents who tended to keep them in, were, and still are called "box-entered-daughters" *hako-iri-musume*. They are typically an only child, or a beauty whose good match will provide political benefits or social security for her aging parents. This *kyôka*, plays up the *gem* as equivalent to precious, both *tama* to make the box a treasure chest and the daughter nothing but a crass investment. "~ are not very nice" is my read between the lines. The poem is the second of 350 in this 1740 book published in Ôsaka, on the whole, the most low-brow I have read.

こぶりよき花の娘にそろ／＼と　ほころひ初よとそよぐこひかぜ　東華堂栗芳
koburi yoki hana no musume ni sorosoro to hokorobisome yo to soyogu koikaze　richibô
small-grain good/prtty floral daughter/grl-to abouttime unravel-strt-would-as blowng love-wnd

> When pretty girls, tight little bundles bloom, there lies our chance:
> To undo their petals and blow them away in a wind of romance!

~~~~~~

> When you forget to go home though the cherries are not in bloom,
> It's a dead give away, the girl you called on was a real beauty.

花下ならで帰る事をば忘るゝは美形の娘のところによりて　馮虚楼嘯雲
hanashita nara de kaeru koto o ba wasururu wa bikei no mususme no tokoro ni yorite
blossm-below is-not-frm return-thing+emph. forgt-as4 beautifl-shapedgirl's place-at callng

The smart vernacular of the first lewdly couples with the lyrical trope of classical libido. The second, by Shôun, plays upon a Chinese poem – the same Akera Kankô's Unkempt Wife, Fushidara no Kaka, did (pg.265) would fifty years later – about flowers in bloom retaining a man. The contradiction is clever, but I still prefer a *senryû* saying only "a beautiful face makes a conversation long." It is enough.

品やつて来るはいづくのよめ 遠目みつちやに白粉ぬり笠の内　冬之
shina yatte-kuru wa izuku no yome tôme micchya ni oshiro nuri kasa no uchi　tôshi
goods=china=features come-as-for someplace/where's bride=night-eye, far-eyes seeing=thickly-coated-with white-powder-applying=painted-hat-within!

> From China, a face for somebody's bride. She'll shine tonight,
> Viewed from afar, below a lacquered hat, her powder so white!

~~~~~~

> White powder covers her face but the flaws come out after all.
> Welcome to the garbage dump – a day after the snowfall.

white-powdr-w/ hiding evn straw(flaws) appear face-as4 dump–on falls snow is+emph
oshiroi de kakushite mo wara no deru kao wa gomokuba ni furu yuki de koso are
おしろいでかくしてもわらの出る顔はごもく場にふる雪でこそあれ 之信 sukenobu

The cosmetic wit is layered pun. China was the source of white powder for make-up, a large make-up item especially for brides who plastered it on (see item #'s 2-15, 2-66 in *Topsy-turvy 1585*) and *shina* is a triple homophone for *goods*, *China* or *features/qualities* of a face! Proverb has it that what is seen afar, under a hat or at night is beautiful, and "night-eyes" puns with bride, both *yome*. A lacquered hat is not wedding wear. We may have a one-night bride, if you get what I mean. The *make-up/ugly face:snowfall/dump* simile needs no explanation.

見とれてはよだれをながすうしろ帯　ちょい／\といふて誰も袖ひく　迎月楼暮新嵐/百
mitorete wa yodare o nagasu ushiro obi choichoi to iute dare mo sode hiku bôshin? 1740
enthralld-as4 drool+acc slobberng cow=rear(tying)-sash justabit-x2 saying evryon sleeve pulls/ tries

This is not even close to translatable. Attraction to a drooling degree takes us to a cow or ox, *ushi*, which morphs into the *ushiro*, or *back*-tying *obi* sash marking a maiden, or woman of the street masquerading as one. Was the come-on expression *choichoi* also used to get a cow to move? Pulling (her) sleeve – trying to pick her up – is the same *pull=hiku*, used for leading a cow and the *mo* emphatic evokes a cow's *moo*. We are being introduced to a mindscape of eros in early-18c Ôsaka.

◎おもふのも思はぬのも情あり原の　業平ならで扨も性わる　栗芳 *omou no mo omowanu no mo nasake ariwara . .*   A good pun into the name Ariwara no Narihira helps a poem about not/being sympathetic whether in love or not. ◎愛でちきりかしこで落す色好み　悪性さらにやまざるのわざ　之信 *koko de chigiri kashiko. . . Unable to quit (yamazaru).* An addiction to sex is punned into a mountain monkey's antics. Mountain monkey was slang for monteblancs or public bath tarts (or, human washcloths, for they scrubbed people).　◎見る程のおとこに思ひつくま祭り　なべての数をこえたいたづら　洗鬢 *miru hodo no otoko ni omoitsuku . .* A great pun into the name Tsukuma Festival and on the pots women wore, one for each lover that year, with a hint of a joke where someone may have carried more pots than lovers. ◎たそかれにためらふ恋の筒もたせ　暗に鉄砲はなしかけけり　如挙　*tasogare ni tamerau . . .* ★ Take note. The *Tsutsumotase*, today, usually written 美人局 or *beauty dept.(!)*, was a shakedown team of husband/pimp & woman. I am not sure if the gun used for a threat or is a metaphor for the woman who was the bait. The lyrical language (other than that one term) makes this a good example of a silk sash on a hempen robe. ◎ 徳利のやうにふられてもしたふのは　むまいなさけがうけたさ一はい 冬之 *tokuri no yô furarete mo shitau no wa mumai nasake ga uketa sa ippai* Fuyusuke. I got a rhyme out of this *"Shook off the way you shake for the last drop from that flask. / Looks like good sake to me – Another round! Must we ask?"* but English (esp. the mandatory pronouns) cannot reproduce the seamless flow from being shaken off in a relationship but still yearning to proof of good sake. *The poem is a masterpiece of the sort Ôta would mass-produce half-a-century later.* The same Fuyusuke also did the triple-pun+double-pun Chinese make-up poem. ◎ 上ばくや下ぢきのよねとちがへども　皆かね次第でまゝにこそなれ　全 *jôbaku ya gejiki (kejiki? for kechigiri?) no yone to chigae domo mina kane shidai de mama ni koso nare.* I tried to do this one up, too: *Some pieces of tail are high and classy others low n' sassy, / But if you've got the do re mi, they'll all get down & nasty!* But, the wit, here, is in the argot used for fancy mistress and cheap lay. This collection spells out the entire eros of Ôsaka, from *musume* to mistress much as the *zappai Mutamagawa* and Senyrû would for Edo decades later. To my mind, the shorter forms fits the subject better – read The Woman Without a Hole & see what you think – but, that does not excuse overlooking such *kyôka* collections – I missed them completely when writing the above-mentioned book of dirty *senryû*. ◎ 虫名十　かあいひ気の身にしみてうきあふまでは　あひたき外に苦もなかったに *kawaii ki no mi ni . . .* ◎ さけのゑひあぶないあぢなあゆみぶり　さはったらばもうとちえぞこけう *sake no ei abunai . . .* Ten bugs and ten fish, respectively, from scores of such!

A Sorry Woman's Song & A Sorry Man's Waka

鏡曇りては わが身こそやつれける わが身やつれては男退け引く 梁塵秘抄
kagami kumorite wa waga mi koso yatsurekeru waga mi yatsurete wa otoko nokehiku
mirror clouding-as-for my self+emph worn-down my self worn-down-as-for men stay away

A Reflection

*My, my mirror
grows cloudy and I know
it is me because*

*If I am not looking old
where have all the men gone?*

anon. 12c *Ryôjinhishô* #409

The above is an 8-5-5-8-7 (33 syllabet) *imayo*, or now-style song, a bit off the right length for that genre or for *kyôka*. But I wanted more poems by women, for they are sadly lacking in *kyôka*. Eventually, I expect to find examples by female haikai masters some of whom had the playful mindset that tells me they *had to* write them. Chiyo, for example, had the intellectual horse-power to have written more and better ones than Issa. Be that as it may, here are my first tries to make the original of the song, which could have been composed by a man, for Japanese men did not mind writing from a female perspective, madder:

*My mirror grows cloudier and that's
proof I'm losing my looks;
As my ship goes down,
men leave like rats.*
~~~~~~~~~~
*My mirror clouds;
I'm losing my looks.
I could fool myself &
blame my eyes; but
All the men I see
gladly leave me
to my books!*

But, when I managed to come up with a rhetorical question for my translation, I knew I did not need to be so inventive. What strikes me as odd though, is that if I follow the original and do not make it a rhetorical question, the *imayo* seems too humdrum to belong in a book of mad poems. I never fail to be amazed on how a bit of tinkering with words creates wit where none seemed to be before. The hint that it *might* be there lay entirely in that one post-position (or article or whatever grammarians want to call it) *wa*, the one you must hate seeing in the glosses, for "~as-for" (or, in abbrev. as4) is not just awkward but awful, though unavoidable because the equivalent part of speech does not exist in English. Among its other qualities, one feels an open-endedness, and that may imply a *question*. I do not know how the reader feels about this small talk that does not address mad poems per se. For me, it is part of what working under extremely limited circumstances for better or worse brings. Were I at a university with on-line privileges to a broader data base (すくなくても岩波体系！) or in Japan with access to bountiful resources, I probably would not have even bothered with that poem, as abundant examples more obviously central to my interests, would have occupied my time. As is, what can I do but try to discover new things in what I have at hand to justify *my* sorry circumstances as, in some way, productive. Speaking of which, here is our sorry man:

わがごとくもの思ふ人は古も 今ゆくすへも あらじとぞ思ふ 拾遺集 1005
waga gotoku mono omou hito wa inishie mo ima yukusue mo araji to zo omou anon sis #965
I-like resemble things-thinking person-as4 ancient times & now go? even not so (I) think

Never of old
not now, nor ever
will there be

Another man by half
as melancholy as me.

Cranston, who translates, *"There has never been / Is not now, and never will / Be another / Who could be compared with me / In my melancholy mood,"* writes, "This flat, unembellished bit of prosaic prosody serves as a rest between more engaging and interactive sequences." *I agree.* My rhyming verse gains far too much in translation! The original is every bit as *blah* as his faithful translation. However, it does one interesting thing. Longing and suffering from blue thoughts is "thing-thinking" in Japanese; Anonymous did well to end the poem, if it is a poem, with a second *think* indirectly illustrating this frame of mind. And, more interesting yet is the fact that this poem was included not only in the *Shûishû* but another anthology, the *Shûishô*. Like the *Manyôshû* poem boasting of getting Yasumiko, *Little Miss Easy-on-the-Eyes* (p.106), this poem is entertaining for, so long as they do not take too much of our time, we all love simpletons, right? It was thoughtful of Cranston to include it in his anthology (2a).
..
「百年の孤独」のボトル海鼠かむ　白山羊 contemp.
"hyakunen no kodoku" no botoru namako kana hakusanyô?
One Hundred Years of Solitutude bottle sea-cucumber chew

chewing sea slug
my bottle "a hundred
years of solitude"

The mention of *melancholy* took me straight to the chapter on melancholy sea cucumbers in *Rise, Ye Sea Slugs!* (2003). The above was one of my favorite *ku*. The existence of such haiku, both natural *and* so symbolically fitting (read the book!) as to seem mad, probably explains why I am not *that* interested in *kyôka*.

The Straight Ones Die: Lamentable Laments

すぐなるは まつきりたをす そまやまの ゆがむはのこる うき世なりけり 竹斎 17c
sugu naru wa makkiri-taosu soma-yama no yugamu wa nokoru ukiyo narikeri chikusai
straight-be/are-as4 cutting-tumble timber-mountain's distort(ed)-as-for remain sad-world is!

All the straight ones
get chopped down right away
on timber mountain.

What a sad and woeful world
Where only the crooked stay!

What sad and woeful times!
The crooked R allowed to be

while the straight
are felled like trees! Do we
live in timberland?

Aside from exceptions playing with ways to block the path to the other world, most "pitiful hurting songs" 哀傷歌, or laments, in tame traditional *waka* bore me. So I tend to ignore chapters with such poems. *Wild waka* are another matter. This one, perhaps mourning the untimely death of a good man is by the fictional beggar saint Chikusai, who wandered about spouting mad poems and was the first to be called (at least in print) a "mad poem *master*," or 狂歌師 *kyôka-shi*. It parodies Zhuang-ze (Lao-tse)'s gnarled old tree that explains it outlived others by being good for nothing. Such Taoist wisdom does seem a bit odd, or at least removed from the reality of a farming people, where inferior plants are culled. Since trees on a "timber mountain" or *somayama* 杣山, are grown to be cut, the metaphor itself is misplaced, making the poem all the more delightfully mad.

はゝの七めぐりの忌日になむあみだぶつのもじをかしらにをきてよめる哥の中にあの文字
あとまでも袖の涙のかはかぬはぬらせし膝のむくひなるらん 濱邊黒人
ato made mo sode no namida no kawakanu wa nuraseshi hiza no mukui naruran kurohito
after until (preface says 7 yrs) even sleeves' tears dry-not-as4 wet lap's karma is!1785

あ *for My Late Mother*

After seven years
my sleeves are yet to dry, but
Why such tears?

It must be Karma, for all
the times I wet her lap!

Why do the tears
not dry upon my sleeves
after all these years?

It must be this: Payback
for the times I wet her lap!

This is Tenmei *kyôka* at its best. A lachrymal morass of personal grief has been transformed into pleasant humor through comic rather than cosmic karma. The original word is *mukui, retribution* or *just desert.* The long preface explain-ing this was for the seventh anniversary of his mother's passing notes that the poem is one of seven each starting with one of the following letters なむあみだぶつ, *na-mu-a-mi-da-bu-tsu,* the appeal to the merciful Amitabha Buddha starting the Lotus Sutra of the Supreme Law. I have not seen the other six. I would like to, but considering the fact that facetious prefaces were common with mad poems, who knows if they exist!

物ごとうときが好みてからやまとの文どもよみけるがみな月ばかりに身まかりければ
あつめつる窓の蛍の影きえて涙や文のしみとなるらん 智恵内子 chie no naishi
atsumetsuru mado no hotaru no kage kiete namida ya fumi no shimi to naruran 徳和
gathered window's light vanishing tears writing/paper's stain/silverfish become! 1785

♪ *Stardust Memories* ♪

as he so loved the melancholy, i read some old
yamato passages and, because he died in july –

As the light faded
from the fireflies I caught
my teardrops on the page
turn from stain to silverfish
and swiftly steal away

The Chinese scholar who first wrote about reading – or, was it writing? – by light of firefly mentioned a *window*, perhaps because another scholar had one by which he stacked up mountains of snow the better to read by moonlight. Or, maybe the space between the double (paper) windows was ideal for turning into a firefly lamp. Or, maybe, Japanese, like me, always put their desks by windows, so that was where a lantern full of fireflies might best be set. *Whatever*. I traded in that window for *other* words, such as spelling-out both the *stain* and the *silverfish* that in the original are, phonetically speaking, one and the same *shimi,* and the last line, *entirely* my invention. It also involves a guess. Were fireflies not mentioned and this not in a collection of *kyôka, shimi* might only have been a *stain*; but, here, why not bet on the additional bug? There may also have been a pun in the preface, for the poetic name of the sixth month, *minazuki,* or "water month" sounds like "see-not," and the stain may well be a witty association with that water. Regardless, this poem by Little Ignoramus, the diva of kyôka, is enchanting. It makes it easy for us to understand why Tenmei *kyôka* became so popular. There are no "stardust memories," but when I think of the dust of a silverfish that allies it to moths and butterflies and the sweetness of an ancient kingdom that was identified with poetry and loving rather than arms . . .

知るしらぬ人を狂歌に笑わせし其返報に泣てたまはれ 貞峨 1734
shiru shiranu hito o kyôka ni warawaseshi sono henpô ni naite tamaware teiga
know know-not people+acc kyôka-by laughd this payback-for cry+hon.! 置みやけ

You who knew or didn't know he who made you laugh & died:
Now, if you would pay him back, laugh again, until you cry!
~~~~~~~~~~~~~~~~~~~~
Whether or not you met, if his mad poems made you laugh,
You know what you owe him – Now, it's your turn to cry!

This is a lament, or rather eulogy, for the most popular pre-Tenmei era mad poet, Teiryû, by his brother Teiga. I wish it were a death poem, for it reads best in the first-person (see the ♪). The "laugh until you cry" in the first reading is mine.

Poems for Bowing & Otherwise Going Out of Life

宗鑑はどこへと人の問ならばちと用あってあの世へといへ 宗鑑 一萬集
sôkan wa doko e to hito no tou naraba chito yô atte ano yo e to ie sôkan d.1540
sôkan-as-for where-to people ask-if, 'a bit business is/having that world-to' say/tell[them].

> *If anyone asks*
> *where old Sôkan went,*
> *we may just say*
>
> *"He had some business*
> *in the other world."*

This, the first of the "Retiring (from the) World" poems in the 19c *Kyôka Ichiman Shû* is, with Saigyô's *waka* wishing to die below a cherry in full bloom below a full moon and Bashô's *ku* about wandering the moor, among the three most famous death poems 辞世. It is so good, it scans with neither rhyme nor pun. There were witty *waka* treating the death of *others,* or rather one's grief for them, in the *Manyôshû* and *Kokinshû*. One example of each,

> *How I wish for arms strong enough to bust the cavern door,*
> *But arm-weak woman that I am, can think of nothing more!*

> *Oh, to be Armstrong prying rocks away from caves, instead*
> *An armweak woman! – How could I bring back the dead?*

岩戸破る手力もがも手弱き女にしあれば術の知らなく 万葉集419 手持女王?
iwato yaburu tajikara mogamo teyowaki onna ni shi areba sube no shiranaku tamochi no ôkimi
cavern door break arm-power wish-for arm-weak woman as am-if method know-not 8c

なく涙雨とふらなむわたり河 水まさりなばかへりくるがに kks 10c
naku namida ame to furanan watarigawa mizu masarinaba kaeri-kuru ga ni ono no -
crying tears rain-as falling-should crossing-river water rising-if return ! - takamura

May my tears fall *like rain to flood that river* *all must cross and* *Overflowing, stop my wife* *and send her back to life!*	*May my tears fall* *like rain to flood the River* *all must cross and* *Be not an indian giver,* *Life – Return my wife!*

But as absurd as relating the arm of the god who held the stone door open to keep the Sun Goddess from hiding to one's gender – and *name,* for the *Manyôshû* calls the poet a Queen with Arms 手持女王 *Tamochi no Ôkimi* – and that to helplessness before death, or of flooding the River Styx (crossed on the seventh day of the dead soul's journey to the nether world) with one's tears might be, these ancient poems seem less mad than Sôkan's far less contrived work. Only my mad additions ("bring back the dead" "indian giver") make them *seem* bonafide *kyôka*. I think this is because we play best with our *own* lives. As laughing off one's death is the ultimate proof of good character and many Japanese had it, many if not most poems written for dying are delightfully mad. But, some are more so than others.

<table>
<tr><td>

How striking
when you see them from
outside Creation
Sky & earth aren't worth
even a box of matches!

</td><td>

Oh, the elation!
When you see them from
outside Creation
Our world's less striking
than a box of matches!

</td></tr>
</table>

けんこんの外よりうち見れば火打ち箱にも足らぬ天地　布施弥次郎
kenkon no soto yori uchi mireba hiuchi-bako ni mo taranu ametsuchi   fuse yajirô
cosmos' without-from emph.=strike see-if fire-strike-box-to even suffice-not heaven-earth

The "worth" is a bit off but "of less significance than" won't scan. This, the *second* death-poem of a samurai (among dozens of *kyôka* and hundreds of *kyôku* in Yoel Hoffmann's *Japanese Death Poems*), appears to reflect a near-death experience. Fuse Yajirô demonstrates his witty intent by using a literally *striking* (*uchi*) word for an emphatic that primes us for the match-box to come already foreshadowed by a cosmos box, kenkon-no-*hako* 乾坤の箱 (the lid was heaven, bottom earth), and, if the original was written in phonetic syllabary as I imagine, the *kenkon* might *also* pun with *genkon*, meaning what is *right before one's eyes*. Even if the last pun is only in my head, this is a mad poem of the first rank. The attitude may *seem* pedagogical, but considering the prevalence of larger metaphors such as the lightning-strike in death poems, I sense novelty if not iconoclastic intent in something as humble as personal fire-making equipment (not really a matchbox but a box w/ a fire-striking piece of flint & iron, etc.: see *Topsy-turvy 1585*, #14-1).

<table>
<tr><td>

'Til now I thought
for sure, dying was purely
for nincompoops
When talents die, though fewer,
I'll bet we make better manure!

</td><td>

'Til now I thought
this dying stuff beneath
a man of parts
but when we die we are still
the ones who do it with art!

</td></tr>
</table>

今までは 下手が死ぬぞとおもひしに 上手も死ねば 糞上手かな　許六 -1715
ima made wa heta ga shinu zo to omoishi ni jôzu mo shineba kuso jôzu kana kyoriku
now-'til-as4 incompetents die+emph thought but competents too die-when good shit!

I always thought dying was just something the untalented do;
– but when talent dies, we are . . . damn good at dying, too!

The *manure* is from Hoffman. Shit=*kuso* may be fertilizer; but it is first of all an emphatic adverb, like "damn." Not taking one's own death gravely is the ultimate act of a wise guy, in this case, a well-known haikai poet. The best death poems may be *haikai*. Hoffman introduces my favorite, a *kyôku* by 歌成 Kasei (d.1859-2-2), a kabuki "artist" who, dying *the day moxabustion was ritually endured for good health*, equated his ashes with *moxa* and hinted at a memento/scar (灰に成る名残も灸の二日哉 *hai ni naru na-nokori mo kyû no futsuka kana*). *Kyôka* are more clever, but this natural marriage with the world even in death makes haiku eternal.

Death (Or, Is it Life?) Takes An Encore!

餓死にも又酔死にもうち死にも恋死も いやしなは空死 山蒼斎 称名
gashi ni mo mata eishi ni mo uchijini mo koishi mo iya shinaba sorajini sansôsai? 院三条西殿
starving death & also drunk-death & battle-death & love/longing-death too yuck, die-if fake-death 玉吟抄 1608

Starving or drinking myself to death, getting shot or pining away
Are not my bag: If I must die, let me . . . playing possum!

親も無し妻無し子無し版木無し金も無けれど 死にたくも無し 林子平 1738-93
oya mo nashi tsuma nashi ko nashi hanki nashi kane mo nakeredo shinitaku mo nashi hayashi shihei
parents not, wife not, children not, galley-plates not, money not, die-want-not

I've no parents   *That I have not*
no wife, no kids, no plates   *welcomed death is funny*
to print my books

and no money: but mate,   *For I have ne'er*
I also do not want to die   *parents, a wife, kids, galley*
     blocks or money!

親もなし子もなし跡に銭もなしからだ斗はからりちん也 成安 後撰夷曲集
oya mo nashi ko mo nashi ato ni zeni mo nashi karada bakari wa karari-chin nari seian
parents not, children not, remain money not, body only-as-for karari-rattle is/become p.1672

I've no parents, no children and no dough to leave behind
At least this bag of bones should make a good rattle

碁なりせばこうをたてても生くべきに死ぬる道には手もなかりけり 本因坊算砂
go nariseba kô tatete mo iku beki ni shinuru michi ni wa te mo nakarikeri honin-bô sansa
go(game) is-if koh making live ought though dying path-for as4 a move evn not+emph 1558-1623

If this were go
I could set up some koh
and stay alive

But, going down death's road,
I haven't found one good move.

Uchi-shi in the first poem probably means dying sword in hand but Japan did have more guns than any other nation at the time. The *possum* compensates for loss in translation due to lack of terms for types of dying in English. The *no/t this and that* poems improve when you know the poet remained single and spent four years carving out the blocks, illustrations and all, for 16 volumes of argument to promote his politics – getting isolated Japan to improve its weaponry, build up its defenses and go out and get outposts for defense (including the Bonin Islands, which Japan would later go and get and, as the Ogasawaras, keep to this day), etc. – without bringing collective punishment to others, only to have them confiscated when he announced publication. The shock was too much, he wasted away and died under house-arrest within a year. English cannot pun the "body" into "is empty" (*karada, kara da*) or jump from the mimesis *chin* to a Buddhist instrument between a bell and a rattle, sounded during the wake with which the body was punned. And note the poem has more rhyme than my translation to boot! Finally, *go* beats *chess* hands down as the premier intellectual game; our ignorance of it proves the Occident has yet to treat the true Orient seriously. *Kô* is a move, or rather a series of moves, that is more satisfying than any other board game move, but you must play *go* decently to appreciate it. The poet was a great go-master.

ほつくりと死なは脇より火を付けて あとはいかいになして給はれ　宗朋
p/hokkuri to shinaba waki yori hi o tsukete ato haikai ni nashite tamuware　sôbô p.1666
sudden[hokku]ly die-if underarm[waki]-from fire+acc set, after hai[ashes]kai-as make+polite

俳諧師なれば臨終に

Let my death be *hokku*
&, when I go in a blink,
be my Second, cap me
w/ a *waki*, light my fire:
Turned to ash, I shall be
Off upon my last *haikai!*

a haikai master's deathbed

If I should up &　　　　　　　　　　　　　　　　　　*if I should pass*
die, mates, use the hair　　　　　　　　　　　*away tonight, just light*
below my arms　　　　　　　　　　　　　　　　*me armpit first*
for kindling: Set me afire,　　　　　　　　　　*& what is left you might*
& let me go – pure haikai.　　　　　　　　　　*sell it to the ash-man!*

Hair is not mentioned, but if you recall the *Manyôshû waka* about *mowing* a man's armpit, it is clearly the tinder in this untranslatable *kyôka* with not only *hokku,* the lead-off *ku* in link-verse from the honored guest, but *tsuke,* i.e., *tsuke-ku,* or seconding *ku* by the *waki* or seconder, usually the host, and *haikai* punned into the text, itself ambiguous. I first favored punning the penultimate 7 as *"ato wa ikai ni,"* where *ikai* means "big" or "many" and, idiomatically, *lots of work for you guys, thanks!* (i.e., お世話になり) but my respondents favor *ato haikai ni nashite,* punning *ato, hai ni nashite,* or "afterward, (I/it) become/s ashes." *Haikai* is also a homophone of a *derelict* to be thrown away 廃壊 and the *ash-man* 灰買, who would be perfect here *if* there were a chance the *nashite (becoming) tamuware* were *dashite (putting out or selling) tamuware*. A handwritten な and た are damn close and such would surely make a good mad ending! One could even write an in-between letter on purpose. But such is highly unlikely. As my respondent argues, the idea of making the poet turn into *haikai* includes the nuance of putting his life *into* a linked sequence, not tossing it out and evokes the endlessness quality of link-verse *haikai*, which is, after all, homophonous with *wandering* . . . and what the newly dead first do.

Dying for more Haikai: Death takes a Second Encore

かり置し地水風火もかへすなり 何ももたねば残念もなし 松堅 1726 ネット
kariokishi chisuifûka mo kaesu nari nanimo motaneba zannen mo nashi   shôken 96歳
borrow-kept earthwaterwindfire+emph return-becomes anything have-not-if left-over-thoughts-not

I return the earth,
water, fire and air, borrowed
for all those years.

To have naught is to have
no regrets and no fears.

This chapter that started as one that was to end the book has multiplied again and again and unlike *Death Be Not Proud*, will not be done. I already mentioned the poems by haikai poets, or *haijin* in Yoel Hoffman's fine book of *Japanese Death Poems*. I thought that would do it, but finding some more on the web where I was innocently searching for something else, I could not resist. I cannot justify adding the lack of *fear* for rhyme's sake because I *also* added those *years*. In the original "air" is *wind*. That is standard. The order is not, for *fire* should come *before* the *wind*. In this poem, it sounds better coming after, so the poet put it there, and I, for the same reason, restored it to its standard order.

世の中はたゞ瓢箪の大鯰 おさへおさへてにげて往にけり 宗旦58歳
yononaka wa tada hyôtan no ô-namazu osae osaete nigeteyukinikeri   sôtan 1693
world-within-as4 just gourd's big catfish hold-holding-down fleeing-goes+finality

The world is just
a big Catfish and I am
a little Gourd:

I tried and tried to keep it,
but it jumped overboard!

A little Gourd
for a big Catfish – life
just won't stay;

You try your best to keep it,
but it slips and gets away.

This might seem hum-drum at a glance, for most of us have seen the image of a monk (or Zen patriarch) standing in a stream – rarely sitting on a boat. But on second thought, to make that catfish a symbol of life is about as mad as we can get; it was supposed to represent the hard-to-grasp Tao, or Way of ways, the way that is always not *a* way. Because of this, the futility captured by the poem is not sad. I bet the poet chuckled as he wrote it. ~~The next~~ (also from 辞世さまざまby 色田幹雄) ~~is by a haikai poet I have often translated, but though I like the language,~~

~~今までは目見へせねども主人公 八八といひし年もあきけり 貞室 64歳~~
~~*ima made wa memiesenedomo shujinkô yayya? to iishi toshi mo akikeri* teishitsu 1673~~

~~*Never until now, have I had the honor to meet my master:*~~
~~*Eight times eight is not too late, I had thought to die faster.*~~

~~I *do not get it*. I know 8x8=64, his age. But is 八八 *yayya*? And does it pun as~~

~~*inviting*, or *scolding*? Did the Shôgun visit him on his death bed? I hope a better reader than I can solve it for me before the next edition. Finally, the last netted poem I did not have. I had seen it in Hoffman's book and skipped it because I had already borrowed too much. But now that it popped up again *on its own* . . .~~

来山は生れた咎で死ぬるなり それで恨みも何もかもなし 来山 63歳
raizan wa umareta toga de shinurunari sore de urami mo nanimo ka mo nashi raizan 1716
raizan-as4, born offense-from die-am/becoming that-from grudge+emph anythingatall not

      Raizan has died   *Raizan is dying;*
   to pay for the mistake   *call it just punishment*
     of being born: *for being born.*

for this he blames no one,   *The fault is his, he leaves*
  and bears no grudge.   *in peace – Don't mourn!*

    tr. Yoel Hoffman   & my paraverse

Hoffman's original justifies left. I erased my first readings, closer to Hoffman's than the above with its added advice, because *"pay for the mistake"* is *brilliant*. *Toga* is an *offense*, not necessarily criminal but likely to incur punishment. For example, a hang-over would be the wages of the *toga* of overdrinking, or a woman might not be able to become enlightened because of her *toga* of being a woman (according to some Buddhist sects). This is *misbehavior* or *karmic sin*, i.e. a *fault*, perhaps, but not *mistake*, yet making it that infinitely improves the last half of the poem. When something works that well, rhyme is moot.

生くること難しと知れど死すること また易からず思ほゆるかな　良寛
ikuru koto muzukashii to shiredo shisuru koto mata yoikarazu omowayuru kana ryôkan
living thing difficult knowing but die-doing thing also easy-not think-can 19c

    Living is hard, that I already knew – but dying, too
    I've come to know, is not an easy thing to do!

Hoffman put Ryôkan with the haiku poets rather than the monks because he was a well-known poet, and gave his haiku death-poem. As he was better known for 31-syllabet poems, I add the above. The good man had a long, I dare say *running*, battle with the trots. With outhouses, in the dead of the night, it was sheer torture.

公事喧嘩地震雷火事晦日 飢勤煩ひなき国へ行く 一陽如酔　狂歌師藤根堂
kuji kenka jishin kaminari kaji misoka ki kin urusainaki kuni e yuku ichiyô josui?

  Suing, fighting, earthquakes, lightning, fires and the month-end,
  Hunger, work and other troubles, vanish just around the bend!
  ~~~~~~
  The land where I go has no work, debt, or hunger to keep you awake,
  No lightning, lawsuits, fires or fights, no trouble and no earthquakes!

Had Ryôkan written the above, it would have included *his* affliction, which is surely not in paradise. *Diarrhea, die! Diarrhea, you or I, one of us must die!*

Death Haiku as Kyôku – Death takes a Third Encore

極楽に誕生日は今日なれや　再現　丈石　八十五歳
gokuraku ni tanjônichi wa kyô nare ya   jôseki   1779   (age 85)
paradise-in birthday-as-for today becomes+emphatic/question!/?

> *This must be*
> *my birthday there*
> *in paradise.*

> *In paradise,*
> *I guess my birthday*
> *will be today.*

Hoffman's translation is on the left. The *ku* includes no *season*, i.e., reason, to call this a haiku. Yet, it is *personal*, hence, no *senryû*, for that form was, until the 20c, not even implicitly first-person. Like most black humor, it was about stereotypes. Of course, the *ku* is a death poem. The conceptual wit is compatible with *kyôka* and, were it 31-syllabet, it would surely be called one. And, so, I think, we should call it and other such a *kyôku*. In a sense, however, *all* true 17-syllabet death poems are haiku because they fall on a date, whether or not the poet takes advantage of it. After all, one can open up a *saijiki*, or haiku almanac, and find scores of death-days shared by haiku-lovers. Despite Jôseki's observation, it is this *deathday* that is celebrated right here on earth by others.

夢一つ破れて蝶の行衛かな　一夢 51歳
yume hitotsu yaburete chô no yukue kana   ichimu 1854
dream one, broken, butterfly's destination!/?

> *A broken dream –*
> *where do they go*
> *the butterflies?*

> *When your dream*
> *breaks off, that butterfly*
> *Where does it go?*

Hoffman (trans. left) devotes a page to this *ku*, written just before winter, when the last butterflies, torn wings (same *yaburete* for *broken* dream of life) and all, *do* vanish. Still, the allusion to Chuang-tzu's (Zhuangzi's) dreaming butterfly dream and pun on the poet's name, "One Dream," makes this as much *kyôku* as a haiku.

書いてみたり消したり果てはけしのはな　北枝
kaite mitari keshitari hate wa keshi no hana   hokushi 1718 8/12
write trying erase-trying end-as4 erase=poppy's blossom=!/?

> *We write and blot,*
> *write and blot, until poem*
> *and poet are not.*

> *I puff, I pop, I*
> *puff, I pop my words until*
> *I drop – poppy!*

> *I write and blot*
> *write and blot: much ado*
> *about a poppy!*

> *I write and blot,*
> *write and blot and finally*
> *blot the whole damn lot.*

Hoffman, who translates, *"I write, erase, rewrite, / erase again, and then / a poppy blooms."* explains that the poem is "built around a pun," where "*keshi* means "to erase" as well as a "poppy," so the poem may be read, *"I write, erase, rewrite, / erase again, and then / a flower erases,"* then concludes that "however the poem is read, the poem's intent remains the same – that nature eventually overwhelms culture." I would, rather, say that mortality, in the Buddhist sense of life as a brief presence on the palimpsest of dreams is sketched in terms of *writing* with the poppy, *a symbol of a fragile one-day bloom* (typically used for young catamites in city brothels or acolytes who easily caught cold(風＝風邪) and died in the mountain temples), uniting poetry, life and death. Hokushi died in mid-fall. Too late for poppies. If he wanted to emphasize *nature*, he would have used the right leaf (一葉). Reading the poem, first, I recalled John Clare's wish to have been able to edit his life, and thought of it as an allegory for life; but on second thought, realized it was better as a splendid impromptu, a confession of trying over and over to compose a death poem until, like country singer-songwriter Tom T. Hall, who concluded a visit to a place in search of material for a song with *"I guess there wasn't a song here after-all,"* he settled on a simple description of what was what though it was naught. The last line may be glossed, *~ and then* / "the erasing wins," or the triumph of the bloom of death, "the flower of snuff," which is to say, all is snuffed out (*keshi* = erase/ extinguish/etc), or better yet "/ *nothing* blooms!" Hokushi was better known for his response to a personal disaster that was praised to high heaven by Bashô:

焼けにけりされども花は散りすまし 北枝 *yakenikeri saredomo hana wa chirisumashi* – hokushi (burned down, nonetheless blossoms-as-for scatter-done)

So, it burned down!	*My home, ashes,*	*In the ashes I sing,*
My cherry had finished	*but what the hell, the blossoms*	*The cherry had already*
blooming this year.	*they already fell!*	*done her thing.*

I elaborate on this *ku* titled "Homeless but Happy" and translated simply *"burnt down / but my cherry was done / blooming"* in *Cherry Blossom Epiphany* (2007). It is *here* for Hoffman oddly blew it (*"~ but look, the flowers droop / unknowing"*) so it begs for correction, and because it shows the equanimity and good humor common in death poems is not an anomaly but *part of the broader culture of life*, as best expressed in the haiku I call *kyôku*, which resemble *kyôka* at heart.

再現 笑ひくさ残さんよりもつね／＼に挾持おきつれ今はくもなし 十口 69歳
waraigusa nokosan yori mo tsunezune ni kyôji okitsure ima wa ku mo nashi jikko 1791
laughngstock leave-would rather thn always keepng have now-as-4 pain=(hai)ku+emph. not!

Rather than leave a poem that people would laugh at I wrote
This one early and set it aside, so now I can die – composed.

Hoffman gave the fine death-ku Jikko came up with, perhaps because "he had already paid due respect to tradition" by preparing the above *kyôka* he claimed to have heard somewhere but probably wrote himself to cap a prose piece on death-poems. The orig. ends "now, I have no *ku*!" where *ku* = 句 = *haiku* &/or *pain* = 苦.

Death Where Is Thy Sting? – A Fourth Encore!

祝の心を 鶴もいや亀もいや松竹もいや ただの人にて死ぬぞめでたき 四方赤良
tsuru mo iya kame mo iya matsu take mo iya tada no hito nite shinu zo medetaki yomo no akera
crane even yuck, turtle even yuck, pine bamboo even yuck: person-as die+emph.! joyful 1749-1823

A crane? Not me!
Turtle, pine or bamboo
Not for eternity!

To live & die a human
Is reason to be happy!

A crane? Yuck!
A turtle? Yuck! Pine, bamboo
Yuck, yuck, too!

I think I've luck enough
if I can but die a man!

We may say we'd love to be reborn an otter, but most of us know damn well we are lucky to be born human whether or not we believe in humanity being a condition for enlightenment or going to heaven. In this sad age, with so many vain souls wishing for long lives not to accomplish something but simply to live, where fighting the crab of cancer makes one a "hero" while dying for one's art makes one a fool, a poem challenging longevity as the ultimate value is valuable.

何事も皆偽りの世の中に 死ぬるといふぞ誠なりける 一休 ikkyû
nanigoto mo mina itsuwari no yononaka ni shinuru to iu zo makoto narikeru
anything even all falsehood/trick's world-in die that+emph. real/sincere is!

In this world where everything's a sham, dying is real:
You can count on death, not to leave you on the lamb!
～～～～～～
In this world, where nothing is for real, do not despair:
When your time comes to die, old Death will be there!
～～～～～～
In this world where all is falsehood we must cling
to what we know: death, by god, is the real thing!
～～～～～～
In this world of trickery and lying just one thing
Is sincerity itself: death and people dying.

This is by the Zen monk Ikkyû (1394-1481). As already mentioned, he enjoyed shocking people by carrying a skull around on the New Year. But, death is also full of surprises and Ikkyû, himself, is said to have gone down with protest. While Akara (Ôta / Shokusanjin) eventually accepted that death would not wait for a heavy drinker, he, too, more than once expressed reticence:

冥途から もしも迎いが 来たならば 九十九まで 留守と断れ 蜀山人
meidô kara moshimo mukai ga kita naraba kyûjûkyû made rusu to kotoware shokusanjin
hades/purgatory-from if guide-the came-is-when ninety-nine-until absent (saying) refuse

If anyone from Hades should come for me and mine, I'm 'not in'
And won't be until the year after I turn Ninety Nine!

The original says "until I'm ninety-nine," but in Japanese, "until" is inclusive. So I added "after" to reflect the poet's wish to live to die a hundred years old. Ninety-nine is celebrated as "white-longevity" – why? Because white is 白 and that is but a stroke short of 百, a hundred! A Buddhist prelate's internet homily suggests the mad poem either borrowed from the folk or, itself, gave birth to more stories. He has Shokusanjin producing a number of these poems, first saying that when death comes for you, to say you won't go until you're (past) 88 (冥土からもしも迎えにきたならば八十八まで行かぬと答えよ *meidô kara moshimo mukae ni*...), then, when you exceed 88, to say you are out until (past) 99 (八十八を越して迎えにきたならば九十九までは留守と答えよ *yasohachi o koshite*...), and if they reply that they will wait for you to come home, then just tell it like it is, you aren't going!(留守ならば帰りを待つと言ったらばいっそ行かぬと言い切ってやれ *rusu naraba kaeri*..). All works much better in Japanese where "you" could also refer to the third-person, i.e., "he's not in!" Translating around *that* problem, was almost as hard as staving off death. More Shokusanjin play with longevity signs:

つる九百九十九ねんめ亀九千九百九十九あゝ尚歯会 蜀山百首
tsuru kyûhyaku-kyûjûkyû nenme kame kyûsen-kyûhyaku-kyûjûkyû aa nao ha-kai
crane 999th year-on turtle 9,999th aah, still tooth-meeting(pre-death eulogy-party)

*Nine hundred ninety-nine for crane & turtle nine thousand plus the same
Years pass and still they blubber – Alas, he will not have another!*

Death is relative. To reverse a Piet Hein grook on catching trains without being vexed – you'll always make your last year and miss the next. The original's "tooth-meeting," (*ha-kai* 歯会), is a social gathering to fill up on laughs to hold their grief while toasting one soon to depart this world. Ideally, it included the one bound to die. Lacking such a word/event, I had to substitute bathetic words and rhyme for it. The general idea of death *at any age* being something to regret was expressed before in a 1752 *Mutamagawa zappai* and repeated shortly after Shokusanjin wrote his poem by a *Yanagidaru senryû*, respectfully:

ninety-nine-at died-life even pitiful is
kyûjuku de shinuru inochi mo aware-nari
九十九で死ぬる命もあはれ也　無玉四

'Tis still a pity, though a life may end at nine and ninety!
~~~~~~
1 year can be cause for much regret: death at ninety nine

九十九で死んで一年をしがられ　柳拾九
kyûjuku de shinde ichi-nen oshigarare
ninety-nine-at dying, one year regretted

I have mislead you ever so slightly. These *ku* are only superficially relative, for it is not so much an old person dying as failing to reach that magical number of 100. Only the *kyôka*, by putting 99 next to 999 and 9999 brought that out.

Death Scene *Machismo* takes a Fifth Encore!

わんざくれ ふんばるべいか 今日ばかり明日は烏がかつ齧るべい 山中源左衛門
wanzakure funbaru beika kyô bakari ashita wa karasu ga kakkajiru bei yamanaka genzaemon d.1645
(desperate words) struggle(hold out)do=dialect? today only tomorrow-as-4 crows-the emph+munch is=dial.

" *Wanzakure! Funbaru bei ka!* "

The devil may care, but who gives a damn! Man will play!
The crows can gouge my eyes tomorrow but I rule today!

◆

Come on, try me! You might as well make my day, your last, too!
The bloody crows already wait. Tomorrow will be late for you!

◆

Make my day! Bring it on! I'm ready and can hardly wait!
Watch me fall upon my blade: tomorrow, crows, don't be late!

◆

Live it up, boys! Paint the town! Do it while you're still around;
All we have, we have today, tomorrow,we'll have hell to pay!

..

This – the Japanese – was spoken or written on the day Yamanaka Genzaemon had to commit *seppuku*. Usually, the condemned made a bit of a show of cutting his belly at which time his head was struck off by whoever had that honor, sometimes a friend with an arm good enough to ensure no suffering was involved. By doing oneself in, the condemned could keep his possessions from being confiscated, enabling his family to survive. Naturally, this made untoward scenes rare, for a man would not want to risk upsetting the authorities. I do not know if Genzaemon had no family to care about or just didn't give a damn, but he was clearly one bad dude. Psychologist Nada Inada marvels at this devil-may-care attitude, the in-your-face cool bravado that became popular in Edo a century later already expressed full-blown. This was no Socrates. Here is your first rebel without a cause: gangster punk. The details, likewise, are hardly romantic: a low-rank soldier of the palace guard charged with neglecting his duty for years by feigning illness and behaving like a ruffian while spending his sick leave in town. Guts are good, but it's too bad this exemplar of cool – the poem has been well-known for centuries – had to be a jerk who threw his weight around. Whenever I read the death poem of young Prince Ôtsu (663-86), who was tricked into participating in a plot and executed, my eyes wet. His punning on the name of the location, homophonic allusion of the *crying* mallards in the pond by which he would *not be* (both *naku*) when his soul disappeared into the clouds (*momo-zutau iware-no-ike ni naku kamo o kyô nomi mite ya kumogakuri namu* see #270 in Cranston: *The Gem Glistening Cup*) is so masterful – ahead of his time, sensitive and subtly witty – that I cannot help but think that had he only lived to become emperor, the history of poetry in Japan would have been different. Haute culture, from an early time, would have appreciated complex wit as something more than a tool for kidding others or for self-denigration, and the segregation of serious and witty poems would never have occurred. But, *damn*, the wording of that bad man Genzaemon's mad poem is good! The nitty-gritty servant-class Edo area dialect 六方詞 (*roppô-kotoba*) is so powerful, *I bet it even survives in the romanization*. No even remotely close translation is possible, for Japanese does not rely on words like *God* or *damn* or *devil*, *bloody*; or *fuck*. It gets down in grammatical ways – call it *dirty grammar*, if you will. Still, we can get closer. If any reader can reproduce the dialect of a low-class 17c English soldier from the scrappiest part of greater London, please, another reading!

夕顔の下がりふすべや老ひの秋　昨日は槿 今日は蕣にて暮らしけり 尚白
yûgao no sagari fusube ya oi no aki kinô wa mukuge kyô wa asagao nite kurashikeri shohaku
evening glory's hanging gourd: oldage's autumn   yesterday roseofsharon   d.1722-7-19

Shohaku's gnosis, dia- and pro-

*Fall comes to age
in that dangling gourd,
an evening glory!*

*Yesterday's one-day bloom
Is a morning glory, today.*

This doctor and pupil of Bashô had a swelling in throat that resembled a bottle gourd. It burst and he died, but not before leaving the above death-poem. The plant is called an evening-*face,* whereas a morning glory is called a morning-*face*, so I made it an *evening glory* to maintain the symmetry. The one-day bloom is the *mukuge*, usually translated as the Rose of Sharon and famous for being eaten by Bashô's horse: note that the conceptual felicity of Bashô's *ku* – a proverbial one-day bloom meeting up with an accident – is seldom noted by our translators. Here, the doctor, who indicates he had already been well aware of his mortality, finds he is even more so, and switches to the symbol of a quicker doom, the morning glory, which happens to contrast nicely with his seasonally grounded (7-19 was mid-fall) – *kyôka* or not, the haiku mentality is there – symptom. We feel a quiet courage here surpassing that of the raving *wanzakure funbaru bei ka.*

百のうちたらぬこの身もおとしには不足なしとや人の云らん 鹿成　一萬集 19c?
hyaku no uchi taranu kono mi mo otoshi ni wa fusoku nashi to ya hito no iu-ran shikanari?
hundred-within this body/me+emph drops/put-down-as-for dissatisfaction-not so others say!

*Though I have yet
to reach a hundred, hey,
I've had my share
of life & might as well just
pass away – Or, so* they *say.*

*They said 'get a life!'
I never had one – no health
no wealth, no wife . . .
No matter! But dreams unshared
make death a worse nightmare.*

The ironic protest on the left is the last death-poem in a 18-19c *kyôka* collection. The poem on the right is not translated. I *just* wrote it. Should I find a way, no, a *place*, where I can pass on my dreams to others, I will die happy & be more than happy to die. Otherwise, there you have it: the death verse I would live to rewrite.

Sick of Living Dying Poems! . . . A Sixth Encore.

食へばへる眠ればさむる世中に ちとめづらしく死ぬも慰み　白鯉館卯雲 徳和/萬載集
kueba heru nemureba samuru yononaka ni chito mezurashiku shinu mo nagusami　hakurikan-bôun
eating-if/when (grow)thin, sleeping if/when wake midnight-in somewhat rare dying even (a) relief　1785

♪ 辞 Leaving the World 世 ♪

Eating makes me thin, and Sleeping keeps me up: Good grief!
So what in the World is odd about my calling Death relief?

~~~~~~~~~~~~~~~~~~~~~~~~~~~~~~

Eating, I lose weight;　　　　　　　　　*Food makes me thin*
Sleeping makes me tired　　　　　　*while sleep wakes me up*

With such my fate　　　　　　　　　　*Such is my world*

I suppose it's rare, but I　　　　　　*that odd or not, I think*
for death can hardly wait!　　　　*death comes to console me!*

~~~~~~~~~~~~~~~~~~~~~~~~~~~~~~

Food thins me, sleep tires me: my life lacks renovation.
Believe it or not, death for me will be a consolation!

~~~~~~~~~~~~~~~~~~~~~~~~~~~~~~

Eating, I waste,
Sleeping, I lose my breath,
since that's the case,

Life, you're fired! I'd taste
Something sweeter, Death!

Pity fat people? No, I envy them. The fat can be thin, fat, soft or muscular, while most thin people are not free to choose. They, or we, can eat all we want, but a body cannot be forced to absorb food. Discipline is worthless. Calorie counts mean nothing. Eating more only makes such a literally revolting body bloat, heat up, backfire and otherwise waste what should build it up so it ends up thinner and more tired than ever. This ostensibly paradoxical death poem with one pun on the *"yo"* of the world as "night," from the representative Tenmei *kyôka* collection, strikes those of us who are involuntarily thin, or have experienced such torture – hence "fat and happy," rather than "thin & happy" – as awfully true.

再現 あるときは花の数にはたらぬども散るには洩れぬ 友田金平
aru toki wa hana no kazu ni wa taranu domo chiru ni wa morenu tomoda kinpei
one time-as4 flowers number-in-as4 inadequate but falling-as-for leak-not yep+his-name

In life I never was　　　　　　　　　　*Alive, I was*
among the well-known flowers　*not among the bloomers*
and yet, in withering　　　　　　　　*of our world;*

I am most certainly　　　　　　　　　*But blown I am, today,*
Tomoda Kimpei.　　　　　　　　　　　*Tomoda Kinpei*

Part of Kimpei's family name Tomoda, *to mo,* functions as rhetoric meaning "I do believe" what came just before it! Yoel Hoffman, (trans. on left), ended his 87-page introduction to *Japanese Death Poems* with this gem by "a certain little-known poet" from a late-18c book (百井塘雨「笈埃随筆」c1789). Not wishing to replace the tip of his essay's beautiful tail with inferior paraphrase, I will only explain something Hoffman may not have known: the poem has a *pre-history.* Consider the death poem of Terazaka Kichiuemon (d. 1747), a samurai:

咲く時は花の数には入らねども散るには同じ山桜かな 寺坂吉右衛門
saku toki wa hana no kazu ni wa hairane domo chiru ni wa onaji yamazakura
blooming time as for flowers number-in-as4 enter-not but falling-as4 same mtn chy

> *When we/I bloom, we/I hardly count in the world of flowers,*
> *But when it comes to falling, a mountain cherry has its hour.*

The humble beauty of the wild flower known only to those who seek it out . . . The romanizations+glosses show this and Tomoda's poem are, despite my translations, nearly identical. But, wait, there is a death poem by yet another samurai called Yabe Toranosuke 駿河宰相頼宣の家臣矢部虎之助 Kinpei & Kichiuemon *must* have known. Like Kinpei, the name is in the poem. *Ya* is emphatic here:

咲く頃は花の数にも足らざれど散るには洩れぬ 矢部虎之助
saku koro wa hana no kazu ni mo tarazaredo chiru ni wa morenu yabé toranosuke
blooming time-as4 flowers number-in-as4 inadequate but falling-as-for!+his-name

> *When the flowers bloomed, I was not in their number,*
> *But falling, I'll join them, Yabe Toranosuke*

Then, I discovered what the poems were *really* about. Toranosuke was a gigantic samurai. Called up, he sallied forth to join the Osaka summer campaign of 1615, when Tokugawa Ieyasu would finally destroy his last rival's family line. This battle ended hundreds of years of war and, excluding the Christian+anti-tax rebellion of Shimabara in 1637, was the last battle for centuries to come. But, owing to the weight of his numerous and enormous weapons, by the time Toranosuke's horse finally staggered into Ôsaka, the battle was over, and he missed his last chance for glory and spoils. So great was his chagrin, the mighty warrior sat down and refused food or drink. Twenty days later, he died, leaving this poem. Knowing that, I made the "leak-not" as "join them." But, again, look at the romanization: the verb is the same *morenu* found in Tomoda Kinpei's poem. As unlikely as it may seem, the lyrical mountain cherry variation that followed in 1747 has an even bigger story behind it! Kichiuemon was one of 48 men who were to have the honor of participating in the most famous vendetta in Japanese history, which ended with 47 belly-cuttings. As the lowest ranking member, he was ordered not to take part, but publicize the act and aid members of the bereaved families, both of which he faithfully did until he died forty-five years later, at age 83, leaving that fine death poem, adding mountain cherry trope to the chagrin at missing the glory found in the earlier poem. Neither of these samurai's poems are *kyôka.* But, *if* Hoffman's Kinpei was indeed a poet who, for whatever reason, had to give up his chance for literary fame, his poem is a *kyôka.*

A Celebration of Dying? . . . A Seventh Encore.

幾世経し うさもつらさも けふあすと おもへばやすく しのばれにけり 無能上人
iku yo heshi usa mo tsurasa mo kyô asu to omoeba yasuku shinobarenikeri munô jônin
many worlds/ages spanning blues and pains today tomorrow re. think-when easily born

I'll shake my blues!
Worlds of trouble I shall lose,
Today or tomorrow:

How easy they are to bear,
knowing soon I will not care!

That slightly unsure "today *or* tomorrow" really brings home the reality of what this man faced. This "fifth encore" was the result of my search, or rather my and my respondent's searches for the context of the poem by Tomoda Kinpei who was not lionized or even recognized when he was alive. Yoshioka found the book Hoffman cited, 百井塘雨著『笈埃随筆』吉川弘文館『日本随筆大成 第二期12』. It turned out to contain other interesting death poems I had not seen elsewhere. I was particularly taken with the above by "His Divinity Good-for-nothing," and one by the Zen monk Hakuin (1685-1768) that was not a death poem *per se* yet, I was disappointed to see (I hate having to play second fiddle; at least it beats rhythm guitar), was nonetheless in Hoffman's book, the frontispiece, no less, accompanying a single massive calligraphic character 死 = *death*. Here it is in Hoffman's spare but perfect translation, with my two line parsing and centering:

若い衆や死ぬがいやなら今死にやれ 一たび死ねばもう死なぬぞや 白隠
wakai shu ya shinu ga iya nara ima shini yare hito-tabi shineba mô shinanu zo ya
young crowd!/: dying dislike-if now die-do! one-time die-if again die-not+emph!
..

O young folk – if you fear death, die now!
Having died once, you won't die again.

(Hoffman: *Japanese Death Poems* 1986)

This poem, one of ten about the proper mindset for facing death a group of young samurai requested of Hakuin is a fine example of a Zen *kyôka*, so rational it's mad, a manifestation of Zen Carpe Diemism, with life/death as two sides of the same coin. Here is a death poem by someone you may know:

死んでゆく地獄の沙汰はともかくも あとの始末は金次第なれ 広重
shindeyuku jigoku no sata wa tomokaku mo ato no shimatsu wa kane shidai nare
dyng-go hell's sifting-as4 regardlss+emph. after(death)'s disposl-as4 money-dependng-is

~~It's not enough death makes us settle our accounts in hell:~~
~~Our mortal remains on earth depend upon money as well!~~

Passing through Hell? I don't know about that – but, first
You'll need some money to dispose of me on earth!

An alternate second line: *Money is what will decide my disposal here on earth!* Who has not seen that pictorial Baedeker of the Eastern Seaboard (Tôkaidô), the prints of Hiroshige (d.1858)? The poem plays upon an old line going back at least to the *Inu-tsukubashû* (c.1536). Japanese Hell was more like purgatory than the Christian one, but there were similar "indulgences" as we have already discussed. I happened upon this poem while trying to find *kyôka* in *Shank's Mare*. Supposedly, it is close to one of them. I never did find *Shank's Mare* on line, so I cannot say. I also cannot recall what brought me to the following poem that dates to 1003, not as old as the Prince Ôtsu's death-poem, but filled with far more puns and good humor (as we would expect from someone fortunate enough to live a long life). That makes it the earliest clearly *kyôka* death poem that I can recall seeing, and suitable to end this long, long string of encores.

みずはさすやそじあまりの老いの波くらげの骨にあうぞうれしき　増賀 僧侶
*mizuha sasu yasoji amari no oi no nami kurage no hone ni au zo ureshiki   zôga shônin 917-
seenot?tooth-sprout 80-over aged waves/ripples/wrinkles jllyfish-bones-w/ meet thrilld! -1003*

> *Past that age we grow new teeth and crinkled as the wind-blown sea*
> *Happy as a jellyfish that finds its bones, in Paradise, I'll be!*
> ~~~~~~
> *Past that age we grow new teeth and crinkled as the wind-blown sea*
> *To find a jellyfish with bones! Heaven knows, I'm so happy!*
> ~~~~~~
> *Past eighty, the world grows weighty, what a joy to float away!*
> *A jellyfish with bones . . . Ahoy! I see it – Paradise Bay.*

Mizuha sasu was a standard epithet for an octogenarian, and either refers to the new tooth they sometimes grow or to something as rare as that. It also may be punned into "see-not-as-for sting (what you don't see, stings you)" or, less ambitiously, contains the sound of "water" (*mizu*) and "stings" (*sasu*) in it. That foreshadows the jellyfish early on, but, first, we get the "*nami*=waves/ripples," standard idiom for *wrinkles* of old age. To *meet up with jellyfish bones* is to encounter something extremely unlikely, even miraculous. While the Japanese is somewhat ambiguous, the saying does *not* concern a happy jellyfish, so the first reading is *bogus*. I did it as a bow to the haiku-length English paraverse of the poem at the site where I first found it. The old monk counted himself among the extremely lucky. Of all the millions of creatures, to be born human and, among men, to become a monk and live long enough to prepare for a good death that seemed a ticket to Paradise was like finding a peanut butter and jellyfish . . . The last reading does not regain the lost puns but does at least restore a natural flow of metaphor by dropping the tooth/teeth that, minus the puns, has little poetic value, anyway. What this poem tells me is that the sort of cleverness found in the *Kokinshû haikai* waka was indeed out there, and not restricted to acceptable *waka* subjects. The only problem, for us, at any rate, is that it was not thought worthy to collect and pass down unless the poet was extremely high-ranking, had friends in the elite, as was the case with Sanekata, or it was a death poem, for they were more likely to be kept. Or, so I imagine. (念のため。The 今昔 12-33 version given in 小学館ことわざ大辞典 uses difficult characters from a sutra to spell out this poem. It was too much trouble to type in.)

Hey, Hey, Hey for *he-no-he* . . . & Poo, Pooh, too!

ある人の放屁しけるをかたへの人わらふあまりに廻文の哥よめといひければ

へゝゝゝゝへゝゝゝゝゝへゝゝゝゝへゝゝゝゝゝへゝゝゝゝゝ

hehehehehe hehehehehehe hehehehehe hehehehehehe hehehehehehe

加保茶元成 Kabocha-no-Motonari 徳和歌後萬載集 1785

Some one asked me to compose a palindromic poem
for those who laugh too much at others' eructations.

fart fart fart	har, har, har!
fart fart fart fart	har, har, har, har!
fart fart fart	har, har, har!
fart fart fart fart	har, har, har, har!
fart fart fart fart	har, har, har, har!

Imagine these two readings as one *he*. If fart were but *he* in English, we might *eh heh, heh* it all the way! The always insightful Blyth had a *"high opinion of this verse, both as poetry* (onomatopoeia) *and as philosophy,"* but later annotators, quick to flee the *farts* and neglect *laughing,* tend to agree with Keene, who called it "childish." after Hamada, who, introducing another poem (in the headnotes), wrote *"It was an era when such worthless antics were common,"* respecting a picture of a hundred scrolls scattered about with a painting of peaches on a lap: *momo momo mo / mata momo mo mata / momo mo momo / momo momo momo no / moji mo kumudomo* Tegara no Okamochi 1735-1813 (百もゝも股もゝも又桃もゝも百股桃の文字もこもこも). *Hundred* 百, *thighs* 股 and *peach* 桃 all pronounced *momo*. *Crotch* 股 and *again* 又 both *mata*. It is not worth translating, but good to put *he he he* into perspective (properly understood, *he he he* has it by far.). To be frank, even finding *he he he* in Keene's *World Within Walls* bothered me. Why? Because, failing to give enough examples of good *kyôka* to show *why* the genre became *the* most popular literature in Edo, I felt he only used it to fart on something he failed to study long enough to appreciate.

The alert reader might think a line of *he he he*'s no true palindrome. That is because *he* へ is *two* letters *to us*. To Japanese, it is *one*, visually symmetrical, as much a palindrome as our *I* or *eye* (soundwise, *ai* reverses as *ia*). What is ironic about this inane "poem" is to find it in what may be the world's best language for palindromes (coupling limited phonemes with a syllabary makes palindromic words a dime a dozen and sentences, while not that cheap are easy to come up with. If there are not many *kaibun*, literally *turning-letters*, as they were called, in the Tenmei era heyday of *kyôka* as a popular art form, it is because they tend to be a bit difficult to understand and were better suited to early *haikai* which, as rowdy and often juvenile as it was, catered to the egg-heads who cracked them (See two examples by Mitoku in the *Short & Inadequate Broad History*). Airy as it is, let us keep on subject. In the same canonical anthology with the *he he he* poem, the editor, Akara affirms the farts importance to *kyôka* by describing a man who abandoned the world with vocabulary filled with fart and airy parts:

山ざとにしりごみしつゝ入しより うき世の事は屁とも思はず 四方赤良 1785
yamazato ni shirigomi shi-tsutsu irishi yori ukiyo no koto wa he to mo omowazu akara
mountain home/town-to flinching-while entered-from woeful/floating-world-things-as-4 fart even think-not

> *Since retiring in the hills with mixed feelings, God was kind –*
> *You would think he never gave a shit for what he left behind!*
> ~~~~~~
> *He sadly up & headed for the hills holding in a broken heart;*
> *It came to pass that for the world he no longer gave a fart.*
> ~~~~~~
> *Since it came to pass that I had to back into the hills,*
> *This old fart gives not a shit for man & all his ills!*
> ~~~~~~
> *Since heading for the hills tight-assed as I could be,*
> *I found I could already fart upon my old amenities!*

山家屁　山住みは屁をひるのみか夜はなほくさきの風の音ばかりなる 智恵内子 c1800
yama-zumi wa he o hiru nomi ka yoru wa nao kusaki no kaze no oto bakari naru chie-no-naishi
mountn living-as4 fart cut=day only nope night-as4 also grass-trees'=stinky wind/s' sound just is=blasts

> *Life at land's end stinks w/ naught to do all day but fart & fart again,*
> *While all night long you listen to the stunted trees pass wind!*
> ~~~~~~
> *Mountain hollars are bad enough by day you want to hollar back;*
> *But night is worse: the wind howls each time you'd hit the sack!*

The idea of cognitive dissonance and God (*i.e.* nature/mind) in this Aire for a Buddhist Hermit by *kyôka* grand-master Yomo no Akara are mine, as is the *broken heart* in the second reading. I could match the idiom (think not a fart for) but not the punning *shirigomi*, literally *retreat,* figuratively (and primarily) *reticent,* including the "buttocks" (*shiri*). The last is by Lawrobinence. The parody of farty hill poems, by top female kyôka master, Chie no Naishi, or the Little Ignoramus, with three unmatchable puns (each " = "), is the madder of the two poems, but neither match the simple brilliance of the following *senryû*.   ○   ○
○   ○

雪隠の尾根ハ大かたへの字形
setchin no one wa ôkata he no jigata
w.c.'s tail-root-as-for most へ letter shape

○   ○

Our water closets
for the most part
roofed with a fart

This *Yanagidaru* bk.1 *senryû* is also in Chapter 26, *Held in, Sadly Passed, Properly Cut,* of *Octopussy, Dry Kidney & Blue Spots*. Chinese, with their "fart-forks," own this theme. Yet, only Japanese boasts a funny fart-face (see pg.634)!

The Last, Really Last, 'Last Minute' Addition
Three more from the Broadview Reference Volume

> By the time that an author has writ out a book, he and his readers are become old acquaintances, and grow very loth to part; so that I have sometimes known it to be in writing, as in visiting, where the ceremony of taking leave has employed more time than the whole conversation before. The conclusion of a treatise resembles the conclusion of human life, which hath sometimes been compared to the end of a feast; where few are satisfied to depart, *ut plenus vite conviva* . . .
>
> – Jonathon Swift from the conclusion of *A Tale of a Tub.*

Never have I had half so hard a time ending a book, even knowing the end was but a break and writing could always be resumed for the next edition, as with this one. That is because I have never conceived and executed a book about something I hitherto knew nothing within the short space of a year, and every time I thought I had enough to do justice, not perfect justice but rough justice to my subject, told friends it would be *two weeks more* and started to count up the pages and proof, the boundaries of the field would shift as something else came into my unblinkered but sadly limited purview. As a result, depending upon his or her personality, the reader will either have been humored or annoyed to find the author claiming over and over and over again to have added so many things at "the last moment" or "after finishing," etc.. as to have made over half of what turned out to be yet another of my huge books a last-minute production, something physically – for I am a slow typist – and logically – for *the* last moment can hardly be not just plural but plentiful – impossible. Aside from a paragraph or two that will be added to the *Short & Broad History* of Kyôka in the After-matter to accommodate my yet broader perspective, this is *it.*

Now, let me explain *how* it happened. Because there were no dates, no authors and, often, poems snatched from the stories in which they originally appeared, I paid scant attention to many of the books (or pickings from books) in the Reference Volume 参考編 of *Kyôka Broadview* 狂歌大観 at least, in comparison to what was in the first 本篇 Main Volume. I did carefully read a few books in it that caught my attention – it is where I found the *Nise-monogatari*, or *Fake Tales of Ise* and a collection of one *kyôka* each for 50 poets where the eye of the un-named editor is uncannily close to mine (over half of the selected poems were already in this book by the time I read it!) – but assuming that anything really good would magically retain my eye, I skipped so lightly over most that, not surprisingly, it turned out that I missed something. Then, it happened. While nearly finished proofing, prior to indexing, I checked the source of *haikai* and *kyôka* included in stories translated by H. Mack Horton in his tiny but sweet sampling of 醒睡草 *Laughs To Banish Sleep* (2002), and with the book's title firmly in mind, I discovered that I already *had* all the *kyôka* in that huge and famous anthology of comic stories among the books in that Reference Volume. When I examined them, I found enough of interest in this book that significantly antedated the first good *kyôka* collections, to feel compelled to fill three chapters, despite my not having the accompanying prose (or annotations, for there are modern printings, that might prove my readings wrong – it is never a good idea to translate without referring to such, but there is always my on-line *Errata*). A year ago, even if I had checked, I doubt if I could have made sense of the material as quickly for my reading was adjusted to shorter poems and I had forgotten most of the *waka* I had

read that might be referenced. Wondering if I might not have unfairly slighted other books as well, I checked some I presumed from their placement in the book might be older yet, and found two with interesting mixtures of old *waka*, including not a few I had independently found and considered to be *near-kyôka* or *proto-kyôka*, and a stimulating variety of *kyôka*. One, 遠近草 *Enkinsô*, or *Ochikochigusa* (1574-89) had so much in it I needed two chapters just to give a digest. Its *wackiest waka* provide a good start for 17c *kyôka* and, perhaps, a few hints for *senryû!* I do not know its editor, but my respondent *just* put its *date* up at his site, so I have *it* (Those who sell books, libraries and researchers often give the year of a modern annotated reprint while failing to supply basic information (original author/editor + date)). I *do* know the author of the last, the oldest collection of *kyôka* I have seen and consider interesting. It is someone whose *kyôka* was translated in Horton's sampling of *Laughs . . .* , the man in the bath who turned out to be *the* leading *waka* poet and expert – apprenticed to and entrusted with the secret teachings of *waka* by Sôgi – of the 16c, Sanetaka 実隆. His Poem Journal 歌日記 the Saishô-sô, 再昌草, dated (printed? finished?) in 1536, brings back together the supposedly divorced genre of *waka* and *kyôka* centuries before they met again (though, this time, with *kyôka* unrecognized) in modern tanka. Only some poems are prefaced *"kyôka"* – usually, I think, for self-deprecatory reasons associated with the poem's use, i.e. accompanying a gift; but many, or at least many of the 283 poems given by the *Kyôka Broadview*, clearly *are* such.
..

~~~~~~

Having finished the above-mentioned three books filling three, two and one chapter/s, respectively, late at night, I was ready to paginate and index the next day. But yesterday turned out to be Sunday. Christian or not, I thought, hell if I am going to do *that* excruciating work better left for young eyes and get worked up over the faults of writing software made by and for people who are not writers on *this* Day of Rest! So, between feeding the cows, helping roll off hay bales from a truck and whatnot – poverty cannot rest – I gave the Reference volume one last glance. Among hundreds or thousands of *kyôka* on places with almost no marks made in my initial desultory reading, I noticed a name with whom I had, in the meantime, become familiar. It was 行風 Kôfû, monk editor of the first great (1016-poem) *kyôka* anthology, the *Kokinikyoku-shû* or Old & Now Savage Songs. Toponymic poetry goes right by me as I neither travel much nor have a head for names (in English, much less Japanese). But, I knew Kôfû wrote and selected interesting poems, so I plunked my eyes down upon that page and slowly looked about. And, as it happens, I was in what may have been the most interesting place for *kyôka* in all Japan: Arima. Literally "have-horse" or "are-horses" the first part of the name *is ideal for punning as a verb* – so ideal, in fact, it was almost *de rigor*. And the name was just for starts. Besides the *yuna*, or (hot)water-girls and the cures expected of a hot spring resort, it had everything, everything a 17c tourist mecca needed and some extras of which my favorite is 私雨 *my-rain*. That and, perhaps, Arima's being a favorite place to meet for poetry jams, may explain why poems #331-985, that is 654 poems out of the 1,654 *kyôka* in this anthology of *"Selections of Kyôka from Local Magazines"* 地誌所載狂歌少 concern this one resort (unless the editors of Broadview are responsible for that) favored by nobles. Yes, I found enough to stretch this edition one last time (★Later: Actually, pages of squibs from Bunzaemon's *Parrot Cage* and Mitoku's *kyôka* were still to be added to the *History,* while Prince Munenaga was crammed into the *Mad Bios.* And, *newly* discovered work was not the only problem. I kept finding poems I read before and left that, thanks to my improvement in reading, had to be rescued. The book only "ended" when it reached the 740-pg limit for my printer, Lightning Source.).

Addition from 358 *kyôka* in *Laughs 2 Banish Sleep* 上
ひとつをも千鳥といへる名のあれは三つをもてふといふへかりけり 安楽庵策伝?
hitotsu o mo chidori to ieru na no are wa mitsu o mote chô to iu bekarikeri anrakuan sakuden?
one though plover=1000-bird-as saying name's such-as-for 3+acc bring even-as say ought-not 1623

If to you, a doe's 'a Dear,' although she eats your garden up,
You might as well call the Mother-in-law your 'sweet-heart!'

This is probably the first and last time in the world that a plover is translated into a deer and the number on a dice into a mother-in-law. The original means "If *one* can be a *thousand*-bird/s than why not call (the) *three* (on my dice) an even number?" The plover has a "thousand" in its name, *chidori,* apt both for its flock-movement and *chi-, chee, cheepy* calls. If any reader knows an English animal with a number in its name to bring us closer to the original, by all means tell me (And please pardon the mother-in-law stereotype: I am sure most are nice.) Meanwhile, here is another untranslatable plover: 思ふかた二つありその浜千鳥ふみちかへたる跡とこそみれ〔御台〕 *omou kata futatsu ari sono hama-chidori* .... With a *lover* in every p*lover,* one might think a poem about a lover of two would be simple to come-up with, but lacking the bird-track-as-letter (*fumi*=踏み⇒文) and their idiomatic meaning of drunken (zigzag) walking, it just won't work. These plovers are two of 358 poems taken from the 1000+ anecdote collection 醒睡笑 of comic stories H. Mack Horton, who did a sampling of 28 stories, artfully translates as "Laughs to Banish Sleep." I do not have the massive volume, but only the *kyôka,* given with no context or info whatsoever on the authorship of the poems (hence "~?") by the *Broadview* reference volume. The *haikai* I borrowed from Horton as *kyôka* at heart, are not among them, so they are evidently not all the poems in the book. But, looking at them is a sobering experience. I can see over a score that I found elsewhere and translated in this book. Among them are a number of *kyôka* by Ikkyû and Yûchôrô, the latter of which boasts an even score of named poems, not a few of the same *waka* I felt were comic mostly by Saigyô (some uncredited) but also Izumi Shikibu, Teika and most delightful of all, we find Ariwara no Motokata's much maligned calendrical dilemma that heads the 905 *Kokinshû* (oddly credited to an old person of ancient times 古老の人). Unlike the otherwise splendid 1666 *Kokin-ikyokushû,* usually credited with being the first major collection of *kyôka,* we even find good *rakushu* including Nobunaga's parade and Hideyoshi's castle-building, the latter my favorite of all the squibs. The 1623 date and variety of content make this book, an early and definitely the largest *hanashibon,* or talk-book – some consider the first rakugo (comic story-telling) collection – possibly the first decent collection of *kyôka!*

身をかくす庵の軒の朽ぬれば いきても苔の下にこそあれ　一路
mi o kakusu iori no noki no kuchinureba ikite mo koke no shita ni koso are ichiro
body+acc hide studio/hut's eave's rotten-if living even moss-below+emph. am

The old eaves are rotten at this cottage, where I hide;
I guess my fate is to be moss-covered while still alive.

The moss is also the robe of a man of the faith, as the editor/author was. His poems include an exchange between what some make "a lovely boy" and others an acolyte 児, and his older monk 師の坊主. I am unsure if I get all of it, but in the end the boy, not shy, expresses delight to find spring under the moss: 去年の けふ花ゆへうせし児のため いまうちならす 鐘の一声 *kyonen no kyô hana* . . . 花ゆへにとはるゝ事のうれしさよ 苔の下にも春は来にけり *hana yue ni towaruru* . . . . Working the *moss* metaphor to bring in things other than subterrenean spring rain or tear-rivers is what says *kyôka* for sure. A complex and impossible-to-translate, much classier *kyôka* – as sophisticated Shokusanjin's best – depicts a less repulsive aspect of monkish life, a "spring talk-meet" at a mountain temple. As the bell sounds announcing the start, he feels hungry. The term, a shrinking belly, combined with the vespers=*iriai* pun-inferred by the assembly=*yoriai* bell, evokes a Chinese poem of falling blossoms (and thinning beauty – famously picked up on by Buson) which, in turn makes the talk-meet *dangô* echo its near-homophone, *dango*=dumpling because it is proverbially paired with blossoms as a one-or-the-other choice, as we have seen! Talking takes little energy, but when it flowers we do get hungry. 山寺の春の談合来てみ れは よりあひのかねに腹やへるらん 安楽庵作伝? *yamadera no haru no dangô kite mireba yoriai no kane ni hara ya heruran*. Now, one I can do something with:

身ひとつは山の奥にもありぬべし すまぬこゝろそをき所なき 安楽庵作伝?
mi hitotsu wa yama no oku ni mo arinubeshi sumanu kokoro zo okidokoro naki sakuden
body-one-as4 mountains' recess-in even is-ought live=be-clear-not heart ! stayplace not

> *No one should live alone back in the hills, out of the way*
> *Unhappy with your Self where can you send him to stay?*

The original is one of thousands of poems playing with the *sumi* homophone of the verb for living (residing) and being pure (clear), none of which translate well, but this is the first time I have seen the impure, i.e. restless heart punned into one without a place to stay. Because English does not allow the heart/mind to separate from the body as clearly as Japanese does (as we saw with Saigyô's poems), I had to make it a "self" and then give a pronoun to "him." Shortly after this poem, we find the wonderful lice-praising poem (*shirami hodo* . . .) the 1666 Savage Poem anthology attributed to Yûchôrô. Since Sakuden included a score of Yûchôrô in this 1623 book, it makes me wonder . . . A few poems later we get,

ひんほうの神も出雲に行ならは 十月はかり物は思はし 安楽庵作伝? 同
binbô no kami mo izumo ni yuku naraba jûgatsu bakari mono wa omowaji 同
poverty's god/s too izumo-to go-if/when tenth-month only things-as-for worry-not

> *If the God of Poverty also goes to the Izumo Caucus,*
> *In the tenth month our trouble should up and leave us*

Again, I assumed Yûchôrô owned Poverty, but this takes the idea of the god's or gods' absence a step further. It is followed by one of Yûchôrô's best poems, where he reverses the *Happiness-in Demons-out* ritual if it would gain him a year of life (*oni wa uchi fuku o ba* . . .). I think Yûchôrô is the first *kyôka master,* as Kyôgetsu has too few good poems to deserve the title. Anrakuan Sakuden's *Laughs to Banish Sleep* may be the first printed matter to make that clear, as Yûchôrô's Hundred Poem collection is not that good.   More in the next chapter!

Addition from 358 *kyôka* in *Laughs 2 Banish Sleep* ㊥

朱をませて 漆ぬるての紅葉はも まつ秋風にまけてちるらん　雄長老 醒睡笑
shu o mazete urushi nurute no momiji ha mo mazu akikaze ni makete chiru ran　yûchôrô seisuishô
vermilion+acc mixing/ed lacquer painted red/maple –leaves even first , autumn-wind-to losing fall!　1623

Even shiny leaves coated with lacquer mixed with vermillion,
Surrendering, fall the moment the Autumn wind hits them!

~~~~~~

So how has that Shigurain come to fall upon just one tree?
Maple in my garden, yonder mountain's beat by thee!

いかにしてこの一本のしぐれけん　山にさきたつ庭の紅葉ゝ
ika ni shite kono ippon no shigure ken yama ni sakitatsu niwa no momiji-ji
how-by doing this one tree's shigure? mountain-before precedes garden's maple

These are not great *kyôka*, but taking the coloration-as-painting-and-varnishing trope seriously, and having the leaves which should be fixed to their twigs with all those layers done in by the Autumn wind is in some fundamental way more purely *kyôka* in the way that would eventually become canonical than Mitoku's *Yayo shigure* poem, with its *primer* vs. *finishing coats* published in 1666, which seems only moderately crazy in a *haikai* sort of way by comparison. And, with respect to the second – pardon my *shigure*+rain! – even though the mura-shigure showers of fall were credited with considerable finesse in hitting their marks – Bashô turned one into the *kake-bari* (peeing on something) of a wandering male dog in one of his *kyôku* – a single tree is indeed an anomaly. The great expert on things comic, Anrakuan Sakuden knew well what he was looking for, and it was ridiculous! After Yûchôrô, he appreciated the milder Ichiji with his Bokuyô-style light puns such as the plovers I had to make deer leading off the last chapter and the one that followed it: 月は見ん月には見えしなからへて うきよをめくる 影もはづかし 一路 *tsuki wa min tsuki niwa mieji nagaraete . . .* No translation is possible. *Mother Goose* may be morphed into "I see the Moon *but* the Moon sees not me," but English can no more pun the moon into good luck or opportunity than Japanese, even with its punning advantage, can save *"one good tern deserves an author,"* the punch-line building upon another pun that ends an expertly-crafted comic story by Lewis Turco about a certain ornithologist who observed an exceptionally altruistic bird. He also had over a half-a-dozen poems by a poet named Muan, or Dream-hut. As long as we are on fall poems,

さひしさの種とはしらて秋風を植てくやしき荻の一もと　夢庵
sabishisa no tane to wa shira de akikaze o uete kuyashiki　ogi no hitomoto　muan
loneliness's seed/s/cause knowng-not, autmn-wnd/s plantd, regret Miscanth. s. 1 clump

Miscanthus sacchariflorus: Planting the Seeds of Loneliness

Had I but known that they would bear the winds of fall,
This clump of reeds would not be growing here at all!

~~~~~~

Not knowing I had the seeds of loneliness – ipso facto chagrin:
I planted Fan-miscanthus, this clump of autumn wind!

Someday, I must read the story framing this and see if I can come up with a better translation for the untitled original, combining a beautiful figure of speech – seeds of loneliness – figuratively and literally with a double synecdoche for wind (tall fall grass and this grass, *ogi*, close to "fan," *ôgi*) while, perhaps, alluding to *waka* on planting *sakura* whose bloom taught inconstancy to lovers. . .

年よらは飯やはらかにそつとくへ　酒は過とも独ねをせよ　夢庵
toshi yoraba meshi yawaraka ni sotto kue sake wa sugu tomo hitorine o seyo muan
year comes-if rice softly quietly eating sake/drink-as-for excessive even lone-sleep do!

Not to grow old? The way is this: to eat soft rice quietly at home
And even when you drink too much, take care you sleep alone!

Just three poems after this sweet little piece of advice, we get Ikkyû's fine toponymic pun on Sumiyoshi (Good-living) as a matter of whether or not you have do re mi (*sumiyoshi to hito wa iedomo*). Five poems later we have Saigyô's cane evoking the stilts of childhood (*takeuma o tsue ni mo*), in a slightly different version (*takeuma o ima wa tsue . . .*) credited to no one (was it that famous?) and that is followed by what seems to be a take-off on a *waka* about leveling valleys if every sad lover were to jump off a peak (I think I translated it, if not, you will still find it somewhere): *I would throw myself off a peak for your sake, but not when I think / Of the deep impression rocks in the valley would make on my brow* (君ゆへに身を投けんとは思へとも　底なる石に額あふなし　或者 *kimi yue ni mi o nagen to omoedomo soko naru ishi ni hitai abunashi* someone). On second thought, if the story has a pond reflecting a mountain: *I would throw myself into the pond for your sake . . . .* No matter. The madness is in the close-up on the potential damage which is just not found in "sane" poems. This is followed by a lament about the worthlessness of continuing a link-verse jam session because neither the poems or the poet's/character's knees are holding up (Japanese formal sitting is little better than kneeling on uncushioned church knee-rests at an old church): 今よりは望もなしやこの御会　連歌も膝もむりやりにして *ima yori wa nozomi mo nashi ya . . . .* No poet's name is given, so I do not know if it is the editor, who scribbled stories, presumably with their poems, upon scraps of paper or note pads since childhood, or "Someone" whose name he failed to catch. What I find intriguing is that the poem seems a perfect example of the sort of *kyôka* that were thrown away (言い捨て) by a millennium of oh-so-serious poets.

日のもとの名にあふとてや照すらん　ふらざらば又あめか下かは〔泉式部〕
hinomoto no na ni au tote ya terasu-ran furazaraba mata amegashita ka wa i. shikibu
sun-source's name-w/ fit so ! shine+emph. (rain) falls-not-if again rain=heaven-below?

Of course, you shine, for if not this would not be the home of the sun,
And if it didn't rain then how could we be under heaven?

This poem (if genuine), I may not get, is old. Another seems to refer to an immigrant: *"How lonely the tips of the limbs of a tree / reaching the land of the rising sun whose mother / like an autumn leaf falls, dyed beautifully."* (もろこしのこすえもさひし日本の　はゝその紅葉ちりやしぬらん　千光祖師 *morokoshi no kosue mo sabishi hinomoto no haha sono momiji chiri ya shinuran* chikô sôshi). Before the next edition, I promise to find the context to both these poems playing upon the ethnocentric and Sinospheric identity of Japan.

Addition from 358 *kyôka* in *Laughs 2 Banish Sleep* 下

待宵の更行まゝのねふたさに 児のかへるさしりもせぬかな　亭坊 醒睡笑
matsu yoi no fukeyuku mama ni nebutasa ni chigo no kaerusa shiri mo senu kana teibô
waited evening's deepened as sleepiness-in boy's returning knowing+emph. did-not!

The much awaited night but, alas, I nodded off and now I see:
My acolyte has left his monk behind . . . it dawns on me.

~~~~~~~~~~~~~~~~~~~~~~~~~~~~~~~~~~~~~~~

Bliss is leaving without being missed and it suits me just fine:
Had I not left him & his behind, I would be sad about mine!

returning+acc known-not thing's delightfulness! behind known-as-for depressing-would
kaerusa o shirarenu koto no ureshisa yo shiri shirarete wa mono ukarubeshi chigo
帰るさをしられぬ事の嬉しさよ　しりしられては物うかるへし　児

Again, I am afraid, I have translated a pair of poems about a repulsive subject. It cannot be helped. 15c-17c Japan was a veritable Greece. One of the eight sections of this book was largely about these lovely boys. The contemporaneous, or slightly earlier Dog-Pillow, likewise, is full of them. At least the poems that treated the subject were, on the whole (*senryû* are another story) less obscene than the epigrams of Martial! The above seems almost sweet, doesn't it? I was more surprised to find a take-off on the ancient *waka* about a ship disappearing in the mist among the islands off Akashi bay that seems to treat a female butt doing likewise with affection: ほの／＼とあかねの小袖ひつかさね　島かくれ行尻をしそおもふ *honobono to akane no kosode hikkasanete shimagakure-yuku shiri oshi zo omou*. The clothing and pronunciation the editors glossed the shiri= butt with, namely *oido,* suggest a woman, but until I read the story . . . Of course, the body does not always mean sex. One attributed to Sôgi mentions drinking nettle and wetting a bed: 我物とほしきのまゝにたてのみて　夜尿しの田の森の茶坊主　宗祇 *wagamono to hoshiki? toboshiki no mama ni tade nomite yobari shi* (see his *Mad Bios* entry!). And, there are poems rising above the body through drugs:

我門に目さまし草のあるなへに 恋しき人は夢にたに見す
waga kado ni mezamashi kusa no aru nabe ni koishiki hito wa yume ni dani mizu
my gate-by eye-opening-herb-has-stew-by dear person-as4 dream-in even see-not

With a kettle full of eye-opening herb in my home
I cannot even dream about my love (I am alone).

~~~~~~~~~~~~~~~~~~~~~~~~~~~~~~~~~~~~~~~

Living as I do with tea can really test one's mettle
Not even my love reflects in a cup filled from a kettle.

Eye opening, or "wake-up grass/herb" meant tea, and the clergy drank more of it than anyone. When the Jesuits decided to practice cultural Accommodation in the late 16c, they were careful to create a special parlour for drinking tea at all their compounds. Part of the problem is that, drinking tea, one does not sleep and, hence, not dream. But, why *a kettle* rather than other details? Does it imply an ascetic life, where tea was not sipped from fine cups reflecting pretty things but poured into a pot or kettle that was eaten out of at the end of the meal?

何事も心のまゝとねかふこそ　つくりやまふよ満足はせし
nanigoto mo kokoro no mama to negau koso tsukuri yamau yo manzoku seji
whatevrthng heart's as-is wish especlly made-up-be-ill+emph. satisfaction do-not

To wish for whatever your heart decides you need
Is to make yourself sick – dissatisfaction guaranteed!

~~~~~~

To wish all could be according to the dictates of your mind
Is to invent complaints the end of which you'll never find!

Yes, like most *kyôka* anthologies to come, *Laughs to Banish Sleep* included some didactic poems. Also, like most early *kyôka* anthologies, there is no shortage of meta-verse, or poems about poetry:

昔よりきとくありまの湯ときけと腰おれ歌はなをらざりけり　西三条道遥院殿
mukashi yori kitoku arima no yu to kikedo koshi ore uta wa naozarikeri　nishi sanjô (sanetaka)
oldtimes-frm benefts are/arima's hotsprings-as heard-but back-broken song-as4 fix-cannt

I hear Arima's hot springs from old are famed for their healing,
But can poems' with broken backs ever be restored to feeling?

Broken backs, or hips (the lower back+hips are *koshi*) are idiomatic for *waka* where the central pivot, usually in the middle 5-*ku*, slips-up. But even explained, the poem does not work because the metaphor only makes us think *"So what!"* Then, I checked Horton's sampling (2001) and sure enough this was one of the 28 stories in it. A noble poet soaking in the water was accosted by a man who –

presented some poems of his own for judgment. There wasn't a good one in the lot, so Sanetaka composed this: *Arima's hot springs / have performed miracles / since ages past, they say, / but your fractured verses / are beyond remedy!"* (Horton: *Laughs to Banish Sleep*)

In such a context, Sanetaka's poem comes alive, doesn't it? And English needs to know the context more than Japanese does because it is harder for us to leave the poem open to an aphoristic or personal meaning, especially if we would keep the immediacy of the latter. We need *your* or *yours*.

They say there's no malady Arima's springs cannot restore
Neither is there a remedy for verses as fractured as yours!

Here, I kept the general idea about fractured *waka* Horton gave up for the personal, but lost space for the miracle (奇特 *kitoku*, or *kidoku*) and, obviously, overworked the logic. But, again, none of that matters nearly so much as the way such a poem works in context and what that means for our theories about what makes for good and bad poems. I.e., *if a poem that requires explanation is not a good one, what about one that requires a story?* The above is #108 in the tk 参 list of 醒睡笑 *kyôka*. #256, by Sôgi, would seem to have primed the pump for it: 音に聞有馬の出湯は薬にて　こしをれ歌のあつまりそする　宗祇 *oto ni kiku arima . . .* I am unsure what he means by advocating "a gathering of broken back poems" at that Spring, but I suspect it is self-deprecatory and I *like* it.

Diversions Near & Far, or late 16c Witty Waka 上

ふるさとへかへるもいまははちならす　にしきにまさるすみ染めそて　法然上人 遠近草
furusato e kaeru mo ima wa haji narazu nishiki ni masaru sumizome sode hônen-jônin 遠近草
hometown-to return-evn now-as4 shame becoms-not brocade exceeds light-charcoal-dyed sleeves

Returning home, there is no shame for now my bowl rings out
Charcoal robes can always put Chinese brocade to rout.

Bridges were burnt and coming home means you must wade;
But there is no shame if you wear ash it even beats brocade!

Though bridges were burnt, no shame follows in this poem:
Wearing a robe of ash beats brocade for coming home.

This is the third "charcoal sleeves/robe" *waka* in *Enkinsô*, or *Ochikochigusa*, as I prefer to read 遠近草 (1574-89). The second: *They threaten but a black pelt is nothing to fear, by Jove / Even armor is defenseless before light ashen robes* (おとすともおそろしからし黒かはの　よろひにまさるすみそめのそて *odosu to mo osoroshi-karazu . . .*). And first: *His holiness in ashen robes, balsa prayer beads worn of duty / Eyes cloud over but no rain, just words hollow as blue sky* (上人のうすすみ衣きりのしゆす　あまけはなれぬそら念仏かな *jônin no ususumi-goromo kiri no juzu amake wa narenu zo sora nenbutsu kana.*) Charcoal robes mean a monk, mourning, or both. Only an *usu-zumi,* or light sumi is definitely mourning, but both are, shall we say, sober. If I read correctly the lead poem has the best pun. *Hachi narasu* はちならす＝鉢鳴らす is to ring out a begging kettle (after *hachi-tataki,* wandering kettle-beating monks), while imagined "muddy" diachronic marks give us *haji narazu* はじならず＝羞じ成らず *no shame.* I added "Chinese" because bright brocade worn home by those who made good was a Chinese conceit and, to the extent it became reality in Japan, such robes often were of imported Chinese cloth. Black pelt may have been armor, for Japanese armor was extremely creative. The pluvial promise evaporating into the blue *amake wa naranu* probably puns as *amake hanarenu*, or failure to separate from his secret mistress. Perhaps the editor of this anthology was a monk himself, for monkish poems are not segregated from the rest and natural: *Though I chant my prayers day and night, something is wrong / Why this drowsiness that will not let me stay awake for long?* (よるひるの念仏してさへおほつかな　ねふりをりてはいかゝあるへき　一反上人 *yoru hiru no nenbutsu shite sae obotsukana neburi orite wa ikaga arubeki* ichihan jôjin.) I do not get it and, for now, can only guess the *nen* in *nenbutsu* lulls the man asleep like a *nenkororon* lullaby.   Now, for a rare mock parody:

おとゝしも去年もことしもおとゝいもきのふもけふもわれこふる君　柿本人麿
ototoshi mo kozo mo kotoshi mo ototoi mo kinô mo kyô mo ware kôru kimi

Two years ago, last year and this year, too, the day before
Yesterday, yesterday and today – My adored Lord!

Two years ago, last year, and this year, too, a poet isn't bored;
The day before yesterday, yester & today, busy adoring my Lord!

But the most notable thing about *Ochikochigusa* is how it starts off with one *waka* after another supposedly *by* ancient well-known poets but really poking fun at them. After two 'by' Tsurayuki, editor of the *Kokinshû*, there are three 'by' the semi-legendary exemplar of ancient court poetry Kakimoto no Hitomaro, of which *Two years ago . . .* is the first. Personally, I *loath* poetry written in honor of rulers and find this apparent snub at the fulsome side of this poet who made Japanese sing like no other well-taken. And, who knows. The above (no gloss for my first reading is accurate) might actually be his envoi. The poem following it, the fourth in *Ochikochigusa*, is a real *Manyôshû* poem (*waga yado no kemomo no shita no tsukiyo sashi shitakokoro yoshi utate kono koro* #1889). Moonlight illuminates the bottom of peaches in front of a house and, oh, how good it feels! That is all. But the *Manyôshû* specifies the poem as *allegorical* 譬喩歌. Of what? The delight felt by a mother at her daughter's coming of age (the peach is literally hairy=fuzzy=毛桃 and the moon, well, you know) is the usual reading. I think it that makes sense, for the Chinese characters specify the front of the house, where the fruit might have been hung (rather than growing in a tree), the *kanji* used for "good" (*yoshi*) is 吉 *propitious* , proper to a rite of passage and the poem is put at the end of sundry poems of spring just before exchanges including love poems. But some, find in the *yado*, or *lodging* – rather than *ie*, or house, the residence of a nobleman's wife, note possible puns on penetration and thrusting, and claim it celebrates a marital visit. Regardless, the allegorical nature of this poem would seem to make it a source of amusement. Further down the page after poems from the *Tales of Ise* and Izumi Shikibu, we find the *Shûi-wakashû* (1005) poem by a Casanova who would be boss of Pure Land that puzzled Cranston and me (*koi o shite nochi wa hotoke . . .*). And a few poems later, #18 and #19, we find a charming exchange that I had found in a book of *kyôka* or on-line (somewhere) attributed to Shunzei 俊成 the great poet and patron of poetry and his even more famous poet-editor (The *Shin-kokin-shû*, *Hundred Poets*, etc.) son 定家 Teika, who was, according to my other source, age 6.

霜月にしものふるこそたうりなれ　なと十月はじうはふらぬそ
shimozuki ni shimo no furu koso tôri nare nado jûgatsu wa jû wa furanu zo

In the Frost Month, the frost really falls: it is abundant –
But what jû=ten falls in this, the so-called Tenth Month?

Who told you no jû=ten falls in the Tenth=Jû-Month, my son!
When shigure the time-rain, falls, think ji+u and it is done!

十月に十のふらぬとたれかいふ　時雨はしうとよまぬものかは
jûgatsu ni jû no furanu to dare ga iu shigure wa jiu to yomanu mono ka wa
十月に十雨のふらぬと誰かいし　時雨ふるこそ時雨のふるなれ
jûgatsu ni jû no furanu to dare ga ishi shigure furu koso jiu no furu nare

I confess, I first thought of the sound of pouring rain *jû~jû~;* but what we have is the Chinese reading of a combined character usually read in a unique Japanese way. If you get it, you get it: that is all I can say. I do not know which version above is oldest. The second belongs to this book. It does *not* mention Shunzei and Teika but credits it to "a person" and "again, a person." I so liked the poem I wanted it to be true, but my respondent says it is indeed of dubious attribution.

Diversions Near & Far, or late-16c Witty Waka 下

盲目とひんなるものは花も見す　さくもしらねはちるもおほえす 宗鑑 遠近草
mômoku to hin naru mono wa hana mo mizu saku mo shiraneba chiru mo oboezu sôkan 1465-1553
blind and poor-are people-as-for blossoms even see-not bloom+emph. know-not-if fall too know-not

Men who are blind or poor from birth see no flowers on the earth;
Having never known their bloom, neither do they mind their doom.

―――――

The blind and the poor do not get to see the flowers like we do
Wanting experience of their bloom, they miss their falling, too.

月影のいたらぬさとはなけれとも　なかむる人のこゝろにそすむ 源空上人
tsukikage no itaranu sato wa nakeredo mo nagamuru hito no kokoro ni zo sumu minamoto sora?
moon/moon-light reaches-not hometown/land-as-for not-but gazing person's heart-in+emph lives

There is no land, no locality the moonshine does not visit,
But its pure light only lives in those who really witness it.

The 190 poems from the *Ochikochigusa* (1574 ~ 89) in *Broadview* include a bit of everything. We will sample the most easy-reading stand-alones. I would have translated more if the stories that must be with them were. There are modern printings with the stories and annotated, so I or someone else – *anyone?* – should be able to do a better job on all than I can with neither. This would seem to be historically valuable both as a model for the early 17c comic stories with *kyôka* and I wish I could wait to see the stories, but I must finish and publish this book. I have been at work on it for a year and made only $1000, at most, and that barely covers the satellite reception I need for the internet stuck as I am out in the boondocks. Monolingual readers, please pardon the largely bilingual presentation.

There are the old *waka* as we have already mentioned. I was most impressed to find a version (わかいゑのひつにちやうさしおさめたる *waga ie no hitsu ni* . . .) of the poem by the 8c Emperor who tried to confine the blues in a box (*ie ni arishi hitsu ni* . . .), and there are plays on old waka such as when a poem by "a samurai," playing on a poem of Saigyô's punning a skinny horse and the eighth shoal (both *yatsuse*) of a river being the one that crosses the Styx so to speak expresses concern for the sixth shoal for crossing a river, as six is *mutsu* and warrior is *mu* ◎しなの川なゝせわたるときゝつるに　こゝなほすはむせわたるかな *shinanogawa nanase wataru to kikitsuru ni koko na hosu wa muse* . .) . . .

★There are vulgar poems in *waka* 57577, but content-wise *haikai*, such as the blind-troupe-leader (*zatô*) with one-eye open for business, his wife's, girls with faces as ugly as a particularly warty type of taro but still edible, and literally ballsy humor: ◎ざとのはうみめは女男かわろけれとせめて一目はあきのまへかな　ある曲者 *zatô-no-bô mime wa meoto ga* . . . by a twisted soul. ◎ 手にいれて見てこそ秋のいもかつら　きめのわろさを君にみせはや　坂井次郎大夫 *te ni irete mite koso aki no imo-kazura* (today, imogashira) . . . vs. いもかかほきめはわろくとあちはひのえくたになくはこらふへしやは　喜田監物 *imo ga kao kime wa waroku to ajiwai no egu dani* . . . ◎大ふくりくらの前輪にかゝるをは　きんふくりんと人やみるらん　桂外記 *ôfuguri kura no maewa ni kakaru o ba kinfukurin to hito ya*

miruran). ★ There is at least one *reporting poem*, a poem about subjects not touched upon in *waka* proper, but not particularly vulgar, such as *a boss-woman (aruji onna) pliant as a willow to the eye, but actually thorny as a briar.* ◎あるし女はすかたかたちはやなきやそ たをやかなれとこゝろいはらき よみびとしらず *aruji ona wa sugata katachi wa yanagi ya zo . . .* anon. ★ There is a *Manyôshû*-style begging, or rather, dog-like howling for love ◎のそむをはおしむこゝろはいぬなりと おもへは君にほえ／＼そやる 和多利石州 *nozomu o ba oshimu kokoro wa inu nari to . . .*) and creative solicitation of the same (if I get it right) by a metaphor split as far apart as a shaggy dog's head is from its tail: ◎ 牛ならてにほいをやるそたきものゝ けふりはそてにつなきとめよと 柳意軒 *ryûiken ushi nara de . . . tsunagi tome yo*). ★ There is an exchange about collecting lint from robes to serve up with a seaweed = starch (both *nori*) at a temple: ◎東堂のころものあかをふりすゝきあまのりつけはやくめさせよ 甘数たゝよし *tôdô no koromo no aka o furisusuki . . .* VS. あかなしと思へるころもふりすゝき あまのりつけはけかれやはせん 東堂 *akanashi to omoeru koromo . . .* . A town in a story in a mid-20c Japanese book of navel lore collects navel lint to make soup for an orphan thunder-godling. That I understand. But this I do not get. ★ There is *wisdom* served up in new – a learned annotator might demure – metaphors, such as water used to keep *ikebana* (cut and arranged flowers) alive equated with the floating world in which we live: いけ花のうき世の水につなかれて いのちはきれてしなれさりけり ある人 *ikebana no ukiyo no mizu ni tsunagarete . . .* I like this but put off translation because the 活 *ike* in *ikebana* actually means *en-livened*, not *arranged* – think of the only half tongue-in-cheek depiction of the cruel doctor of flowers who kept his 'victims' alive in Okakura Tenshin's beautiful essay (with his Book of Tea, if I recall correctly) and, besides, I am unsure of the reading/s of *shinare* (撓れ・死なれ・し慣れ). ★ There are two moon-in-the-water poems by one 教之. The more obviously *kyôka* – with floating weeds punfully depressing (*uki*) seen as a lid better removed from a pond that is the moon's mirror – is a bore. A haiku would more than suffice for *that*. The other intrigues: *I wished to go see the moon in the marsh, the great marsh / For the moon's sake how / I rush around this night!* ねかわしゝいさゝはゆかんひろさはの月のためとていそく夜すから *negawashishi iza sawa yukan hirosawa no tsuki no tame tote isogu yosugara*. I could be wrong. It could be that the entire night passed quickly because of moon-viewing. But the mention of the great (actually wide) marsh suggests to me that he circled it trying to capture the best angles for the reflection and because of its size . . . Could Bashô's well-known haiku *"The harvest moon, around the pond we go, the whole night long"* (*meigetsu ya ike o megurite yomosugara*) reflect this in any way?
..
> *To the marsh I wished to go and did – so, now I rush from rush*
> *to rush to view the great marsh moon the whole night through!*

Sorry, I could not help doing that though it does not help us catch what I thought to be the main point of the original. ★ &, *meta-poems about language & poetry itself* of the sort I so wish a top scholar would take up and turn into a splendid book for all the literate and not just academics: 和哥のうらは家にもあらす人なみに 名をかけすともよしやうらみん 正徹 *waka no ura wa ie ni mo arazu hitonami ni na o kakesu to mo yoshi ya uramin* shôtetsu (1381-1459). I know *waka no ura* or the Bay of Waka is a pillow word for some place and "like everybody" (*hitonami*) puns on wave, but do not get it. If *you* do – Please . . *do!*

Kyôka in a Waka Master's 16c Poem Journal 歌日記

馬さうな菓子をはをきていかなれは 牛をくひける鼠なるらん 実隆 再昌草
mumasôna kashi o ba okite ikanareba ushi o kuikeru nezumi naruran sanetaka 1536
yummy=horsey cake+emph.=horse leaving goes-if cow+acc eating mouse is!/?

On night-duty at the temple, I traded fans with Chûnogon & seeing a picture of cake crumbs on one side & a mouse eating a cow on the other, I wrote this ditty on a piece of thin wrapping paper and left it for him folded inside the fan.

*And what could make a mouse so hungry he could eat a horse
leave his cake to eat a cow before wolfing down his course?*

◆   ◆   The Reply   ◆   ◆

*The horns of this dilemma grasped shrink from the touch.
Cake is sweet but mice have other loves – a slug is such.*

返事 すいするにあまくや思ふ菓子よりも あめうしをなをくらふ鼠は 同
sui suru ni amaku ya omou kashi yori mo ameushi o nao kurau nezumi wa 同
guessng=suckng easy=sweet cake morethn slug(=rain⇒sucker-cow)+acc eatng mouse-as4
..

These are poems #9 and #10 of 283, most of which are exchanges – hard for me to translate as I cannot tell genuine from invented, who initiates, etc.. I skipped the original #9, poem #8, the same riddle without the horsey puns (w/ mouse & cow to span the night-shift hours?), though I found his honesty – "Later," he writes, prefacing #9, "I thought that was pretty bad. Here, is how it *should* go." – endearing. Yes, the editor (and likely author) is a kindred soul. Admittedly, such a poem does make me recall Keene's description of *kyôka* in the Warring Age as the manifestation of a desperate frivolity. But, that is not all to be said. The Jesuits, reaching Japan in the 1540's, described men more gutsy than any met elsewhere in the world. And, more individualistic, as could be seen in the diversity of their facial hair as opposed to the conventionally limited patterns of the Europeans. *Kyôka* also manifested their strong personalities. Sanjônishi Sanetaka (1455-1537), advisor to three emperors despite a low (but still noble) ranking, was the leading *waka* master – even passed a decade-long apprentice-ship to gain the sacred secrets of the *Kokinshû* from Sôgi – tea expert and incense expert of his time. He was, in other words, Mr. Culture of war-torn Japan. True, like many nobles, including the Emperor who, Keene notes, hung out his calligraphy to sell for cash, he had to work hard to make a living, and work almost always means compromise; but Japan was a tolerant society, so he could be his own man at heart and write boldly for poetic freedom. Take, for example, the following poem that boldly exaggerates a saying 歌には鬼神も納受ある that already exaggerates the *Kokinshû* preface's claim that *waka* can influence demons & gods:

目にみえぬ鬼神をたにおとすへし かへの耳をはなにかおそれん 実隆?
me ni mienu oni kami o dani otosubeshi kabe no mimi o ba nani ga osoren sanetaka
eyes-by see-cnt demns gds+acc evn knock-down-ought, wall's ears+emph what fear-to

*Songs beat gods and demons even though we cannot see them;
Why should we fear what a 'wall with ears' might hear, then?*

This followed two poems by others, written for the theme *white wall* (good for graffiti?), urging us not to put people down in poems because walls have ears (a proverb) and we all have faults (a visual pun: compare *fault* = 癖 to 壁 = *wall*). But, as we have seen with older *waka* exchanges, the free language of the medieval is most felt in their gift exchanges. My favorite is a gift of boiled cod, "boiled" *visually* punned as 親栄鱈 "(a)parent nourishment" and the cod=*tara,* with Anokanon Boddhivista associated with Kudara (a part of greater Korea from which Buddhism came) and safety at sea とく法のその巻々のあのく鱈　仏もこれをこのむとそきく *tokuhô no sono maki maki no anokudara hotoke mo kore o konomu to zo kiku* 返し　おもしろき 此ことの葉もとく法の阿糠たらとそ腹にあちはふ *omoshiroki kono kotonoha mo toku hô no ano tara to zo hara ni ajiwau.* The くだらなくもない puns built on boldly broken words (又鱈⇒雪⇒面白き) show what is often credited to late-18c Edo already existed in the journal of the leading *waka* poet before Edo existed. And, there are three poems in a row. The first, a 回文 palindrome, the second, a *haikai* on a katydid (きり／＼すを俳諧に), possibly a proto-*senryû* and a third, a last-day *kyôka* 除日狂歌, puns on the Old Year's leaving, as contemporary Sôkan does* and late-18c *kyôka* will.

理なくともりのはし／＼にこゝはとこゝにしはしのりもとくなり
ri na ku to mo ri no ha shi ha shi ni ko ko wa to wa ko ko ni shi h/ba shi no ri mo to ku na ri
人みえぬふるさとさひし秋風に　つまときり／＼すたれさら／＼
hito mienu furusato sabishi akikaze ni tsuma to kirigirisu sut(d)are zarazara
年はたゝくれう／＼といひなから　手にとるものはけふまてもなし
toshi wa tada kureo kureo to iinagara te ni toru mono wa kyô made mo nashi

The year leaves, the year leaves, it is what we always say
But what does it ever leave? Not a thing as of today!

I need help to crack the palindrome! If *tsuma to* puns as *tsumado,* or wife's door, the *haikai* may be the first to equate the katydid with noisy urination(!), common trope hundreds of years later. Only the last translates. Another poem, prefaced "*kyôka,*" plays on a *Kokinshû* (905) *waka* about suicides filling valleys (pg. 483):

よる夜中酔たひことに身をなけは　深き谷こそあさくなりなめ
yoru yonaka yoitai koto ni mi o nageba fukaki tani koso asaku nariname anon.
comng/night midnght-each-w/ body/self throw/jump-if deep vlly evn shallow be-would

If with midnight, wanting to be drunk we all into wine should leap,
All the valleys would be filled, or at least none would be deep.

So love complaints becoming drunk did not wait for Edo. This next, too, was titled simply *kyôka.* I can only *guess* what it means. *Our skinny monk hides his wrinkles because he does not think / How happy he should be to have a thing that doesn't shrink!* is almost surely wrong. This is only *slightly* more likely:

やせほうのしはをかくすもあしからす へらぬかほにてよしやこらへん
yasebô no shiwa o kakusu mo ashikarazu heranu kao nite yoshi ya koraen sanetaka?
skinny monk's wrinkles+acc hide+emph bad-not reduce-not face good! endure-would

Our thin monk hides his wrinkles and that is just fine
A fat face makes his fasting easier on we who dine.

㊤ Horsing Around With *My Rain* & the *Yu-girls* ㊤

箱根山いやその外に有馬なる 私雨もはれの言の葉 行風 地誌所載狂歌抄
hakone yama iya sono hoka ni arima naru watakushi-ame mo hare no kotonoha kôfû
hakone mountain no this otherwise/outside arima is my-rain too clear/happy word

Out of Box Mountain – in Arima, too, they are we've heard
'My Rain,' is no migraine, but a fair-weather word!

According to Kôfû's note, the above was written for the 1666 *Savage Song* collection. The first Arima section of the "Selections of Kyôka from Local Magazines," which included it, is dated 1672. It follows a just-so poem for that rain (which we shall return to) I am unsure I get. 天道これはれぬふしんや有馬私雨のはしまりはいつ　行重 *ama no michi kore harenu fushin ya (+shinya?) ari . . . koe?*) And that follows Sanetaka's put-down of the broken-back poems he was asked to judge in the bath, and that follows an odd poem that seems to be a request to replace someone in a bath (with the poet?) where the *yuna* (English lacks a word for "hot water" so I will use the economical Japanese word for a *hot-water-woman*) is whooping it up 有馬山湯女のわめける声きけは　いてそよ人をいれかゆるかな　貞林 *arima yama yuna no wamekeru . . . teirin?* And that follows one with two sets of puns by a nun with the Naniwa *sawgrass=bad=feet* healed for the good (opp. bad) by Arima's having hot-water: 難波江のあしの痛みも有馬なる　湯に入てこそよしとなりけれ　妙祐尼 *naniwa-e no ashi no itami mo ari . . . saû-ni*). And going back about a dozen poems to the second in the collection, the one by Kôfû that caught my eye: むせかへる匂ひありまや花ならぬ　ゆわうの花の出湯故かも　行風 *musekaeru nioi ari . . . kôfû.* Punning on *nose* and *blossom* (both *hana*) he turns *sulfur* (硫黄 *iou*, once *yuô*) into the melancholy white blossom of the *u* flower, deftly setting up a run on medical problems treated there.

有馬山高きは湯女の声のみか　二階住居におさかなの代　読人不知
arima yama takaki wa yuna no koe nomi ka nikai sumai ni osakana no dai anon
arima-mt high-as-for, yuna's voice only? second-fl living-in entertainmt charge

Up Mount Arima, the voices of the Yuna rise into the sky;
But entertainment on the second floor goes twice as high.

湯女共に 心有馬の逗留は恋の病やなをりかねぬる 貞因
*yunadomo ni kokoro ari*ma *no tôryû wa koi no yamai ya naorikanenuru* tein
hotwatrwomen-4 heart/feelngs are=arima's stay-as4 love-sicknss+emph cure-cant

Staying longer at an Arima Spa because you love the yuna
Will not cure a broken heart: you might as well leave soona

有馬山湯女恋忍ふ袖にふる　わたくし雨は涙也けり 貞富 teifu
arima yama yuna koi shinobu sode ni furu watakushi ame wa namida narikeri
arima-mt. yuna love bears/hides sleeve/s-on falls my-rain-as-for tears-become

On Mount Arima her wet sleeves are wet thinking of her dear
My rain in his absence would have to be the yuna's tears!

The phenomenological mismatch of high(loud) voices and high prices by itself is weak, but bringing in two physically high places, a mountain and a second-floor makes up for it. We also get a panorama of open spas where voices literally rise into the air and some of the architecture in the town. Losing the awful pun in the second, I added an awful rhyme. The *watakushi-ame,* or "my rain" might also be translated "private rain" or "personal rain." Certain types of rains in Japan were known to fall precisely upon tiny targets, or arbitrarily wet one sleeve but not the other, etc., but this is different. It is a tiny spot of precipitation sometimes found on misty mountains. *My rain* is to *a rain-cloud* what a *rain-dog* is to a *rainbow*. I will always owe my knowledge of *watakushi-ame* to this *kyôka* collection as I owe rain-dogs to Twain (traveling in the Pacific). The next discovery is less exciting. It would seem that the local brand of toothpaste, or rather "polishing sand" (pumice, I bet) was a favorite gift. Following another's poem about it, Kôfû, having received a gift of it replied that ideally one came down Have-horse Mountain with polished words as well as teeth – in Japanese where "teeth" (*ha*) are homophones with part of "words" (kotono*ha*) and having a heart alludes to the feeling that accompanies language and puns with *have*-horse . . . the poem works: 言の葉も磨砂とて給はるは心ありまの山つとよなふ　行風 *kotonoha mo migakisuna tote . . . .* I thought to try translating with a gift-horse-in-the-mouth, but it only turns into Mr Ed (for readers a hundred years hence: a talking horse, star of a 1960's Usanian TV program). This, next, titled *Biroku* 麋鹿 or, *Venison,* is also informative: *The big bad wolf is nowhere to be seen but there is wild boar / Sold by the slice that may be nice though some claim it's horse.* をそろしき狼ならぬ切売の　しゝも有馬といふはまことか　行風 *osoroshiki ôkami naranu kireuri no shishi mo ari uma . . .* Kôfû's deft touch reminds me of his contemporary Bokuyô. I cannot match the Arima pun that leaves open two readings, one where horse puns as "delicious," and one where it becomes what is eaten. The "*osoroshiki*=terrifying" modifier for the wolf in the original probably relates to the slice, or "cuts" sold. I had thought that selling things – watermelon being the most common example – by the slice was an invention of Edo with its enormously lopsided population of single-men fifty or a hundred years later. About this point, I started to see how valuable collections of *kyôka* could be for historians. Next we find some poems on lathe-masters and other handicrafts none of which seemed too interesting except for the fact they were written at all. Details, such as people buying goods late into the night, abound.

..
　　よからさるうつは物をもあちはひに いひまけてうる竹細工哉　貞富
　　yokarazaru utsuwa-mono o mo ajiwai ni ii-makete-uru takesaiku kana　teifu
　　good-not vessel+acc taste/sample-4 says-losing(comingdwn)-sells bamboo hdycraft

　　　　Selling a vessel that could not hold water "to give you a taste"
　　　　a bamboo craftsman drops his price to make a sale with grace.

This may seem just a detail but the fact there were Japanese willing to part with less than perfect work is remarkable. In the Japan I know even green-grocers hate to sell less-than-mint condition goods. As an etcher, I have sold my *prueba de estado,* or "proofs," cheaply. I recall delighting people who had little money but liked my work. To think there were Japanese who once thought, no, *behaved* like me! Hence, I *blessed* the uncommitted original – the poet may have thought it simply *odd* – "with grace."

㊥ Horsing Around With *My Rain* & the *Yu-girls* 上

からくりの糸ひくならて糸まきし 人形筆をつかふ面白　行風　地誌所載狂歌少
karakuri no ito hiku nara de ito makishi ningyôfude (ningyô fude?) o tsukau menpaku   kôfû
automata's string/s pull-not-with string/thread wrapped doll-brushes/doll brush+acc use interesting

Hidden strings pulling ala automaton are not to be found:
Doll-brush strings wrap around, but used can still astound.

Who'd have thought a doll could use a brush with pretty strings
wrapped around, not pulled like those fancy automaton things!

Unless Kôfû had readers who had not heard of a *ningyôfude,* or "doll-pen," allowing my second 'trick' reading, the only wit in the poem is the pull vs. wrap, and this may be, after the 8c "I got Miss Easy-on-the-eyes!" (*ware wa mo ya* ...), the worst lead poem in the book. But, even if that be the case, Kôfû was right to have it in his book. It functions as preliminary explanation – a description of what visually marks the pens, namely, the colored threads wrapped about the handle criss-crossing to make hundreds of cheerful patterns – and indicates that something *happened.* No place is mentioned because Arima was, and still is today, the only place with these brushes. Legend has the brush invented to celebrate the birth of a son for a visiting Emperor. The brushes were popular for both the pretty and propitious color combinations and for helping ensure little children fall in love with brushes and want to practice writing around the clock. They mesmerize children because when picked up and turned vertically a tiny doll (mostly just a head) pops up from the butt of the brush. A string (and bamboo) mechanism *is* involved and for that reason the brush-tips must be of substantial size – not doll-size. Kôfû's poem set up a less informative but much better poem by Tein (1620-1700), father of top kyôka master of the early 18c, Teiryû confirming the brush, indeed doll-like, can surprise human eyes; the long literary tail on the verb (*odorokashinuru,* surprise) morphs into a sleeping bird's wake which evokes a *Shinkokinshû* (1205) poem about being left up in the air so to speak by the lack of a trail made by birds floating in the water.: 名にしおふ人形筆は人の目も おとろかしぬる鳥の跡かな　貞因 *na ni shi ou ningyôfude wa hito no me mo odorokashinuru tori no ato kana.* Many allusions gently play as bird *tracks,* also *"tori no ato,"* relate to the invention of writing in Chinese mythology and are commonly used to refer to childish or messy writing . . .

すすくろき染楊枝さへ紅葉せり口紅粉や此時雨なるらん　松意
susu-kuroki someyôji sae momijiseri kuchibeni ya kore shigurenaru ran   shôi
soot black dyed toothpick/s even maple/redleaf-doing liprouge! this shigure(rain) is!

Dyed black as soot yet crimson-tinged as fall: tooth-pick
What might be thy color-bringing Shigure? Lip-stick!

The next subject to get a handful of poems, *toothpicks*, was also framed by Kôfû: *How novel of Arima and Miwa, both mountains, to present dyed toothpicks not made of cedar* (which grew there and does not change color) めつらしく三輪も有馬の山つとは杉の木ならぬ染楊枝 *mezurashiku miwa mo arima* . . . .This was followed by Shôi's turning fall showers into lipstick and that by something more

romantic by Taikyoku where a glance at the beautiful mouth of a young *yuna* who polishes her teeth has him falling in love, where the falling, or beginning is a homophone of dyed and takes us to the toothpick　若湯女の歯をはみかきし口本を見てこそ思ひ染やうしなれ　太極 *waka-yuna no ha o ba hamigakishi (hamikakishi?)* . . . I suspect he also puns on the toothpick left protruding from her mouth, as Japanese toothpicks were longer than Occidental ones, though "we" also went through a period where they were sported by dandies (see item #6-37 in *Topsy-turvy 1585:* paraverse press 2004). Regardless, the only good pun I could come up with in English *bones to pick* ⇒ *picking bones* was too vulgar. The final toothpick *kyôka* warns: *They are good for damaging your mouth if you overdo it; / So let your toothpick work, not you . . . or you will rue it!* 口中のいたむにそよき精気をは　つかはてつかへといひそめやうし　俊佐 *kuchi-naka no itamu ni zo yoki* . . . The original "says first" (which I took for a caveat) morphs into the object, which I might add archeologists recognize in tooth-scarring (Ibid).
..

世の中の人を人魚とおほしめし すくふ阿弥陀の極楽寺哉　宣恒
yo no naka no hito o ningyô to oboshimeshi sukuu amida no gokuraku-ji kana
world-within's people+acc merman/maid-as thinking scoop amida's paradise!

Thinking of all men as fish, not flesh or foul, Amida
nets us as we swim to take us to Paradise (temple) with Him!

With "person-fish" as *mermaid/man* in English, even the Christian "fisher of men" idea would not save the metaphor. Luckily, I recalled the dying Rochester, (or was it Heywood?) chastising the priest: *Would you prefer we were made of fish rather than flesh!* The topic is Gokuraku-ji, Paradise Temple. *Scoop-up* and *save* are both *sukuu* (and fish are scooped up with paper nets by children in festivals and, perhaps around the year in some temple towns). The net is phonetically embedded in the name for the merciful Buddha, *Ami*da. I have had to skip scores of poems touching upon the various shrines and temples and semi-religious places either because I did not get them or I thought they would take too much explaining for you to get them. I will slip a few into the notes in Japanese only.

鳥地獄 鶯の法々花経の功力にて みなうかむへき鳥ちこく哉 行順
uguisu no hô-hôkei-kyô no kôryoku nite mina ukamu beki torijigoku kana　kôjun
warblr/nightngale's *hô-hôkei-kyô*(sutra/call)'s effects-frm all float/rise-ought bird-hades

Thanks to the working of the Hô!hô!ke!kyô! sung by Thrush
All that sink in Bird Hell, surely will come bubbling up!

You have already been subjected to many poems on the sutra of the thrush (or, often translated, nightingale) because my ability to do a fair imitation of the call disposes me favorably toward them. This has no puns – unless the old conceit of a call being a sutra is itself so considered – but is the first such poem I recall bound conceptually to a place. Shortly after this, Kôfû has a more surprising Bug Hell poem with foam on the water and a crab (written in Chinese with a bug-虫 radical) frothing over with epilepsy: 虫ちこくへ落ても水のあはふくや　そはてんかんの病ある蟹　行風 *mushi-jigoku e ochite mo mizu no awa fuku ya* . . . I have not yet figured out the *sowa* before the *tenkan* (epilepsy), so I let that poem go. I also confess to skipping the more famous Jealousy Baths and Hell's Valley. ♪

㊥ Horsing Around With *My Rain* & the *Yu-girls* ㊥

猫のこと飛上りつゝ取てこよ　それそこ山のねすみ茸をは　地誌所載狂歌少
neko no goto tobiagaritsutsu totte koyo sore soko yama no nezumi take o ba 行風 kôfû
cat-like jump-up-while taking come/return hey there mountain's mice-mushrooms+acc+emph

> *Be a cat, spring! And, what you catch on the fly bring home!*
> *Up Mt. Thaire, mouse mushroom are hiding in the gloam.*

~~~~~~

> *Leap like a cat and what you catch up there, bring back!*
> *On Mt Thaire, there! there! Mouse mushrooms everywhere!*

I recall another usage of this *sore soko* about a 150 years after this. Old Issa, who as a younger man in one of his least attractive more-Bashôite-than-thou moments, attacked Chiyo-ni for being overly precious about borrowing a well bucket to let the morning glory have its way, himself, warned cherry petals (or the blossoms or the trees) not to fall upon *sore soko*, i.e., *that there,* which is to say emphatically located dog shit! In this case, Kôfû plays upon the name of a mountain Soko-yama, homophonous (and heterographic: 塞山, hence my different orthography) with *there.* Not a great poem – the gloam is mine, for mouse implies grey in Japanese and that made me think of the gloaming hours – but it will surely make the presence of such mushrooms on such mountain easy to remember, and is that not one of the best things a poet can do? Please do not ask *me* where in the greater Arima mountain (or mountains?) this one is. A scholar – or amateur with leisure – may translate all the poems with their scores of places in a book with a fold-out map and places numbered for reference in explanations. All I know is that as this is in the Arima section it must be somewhere *there.* I also should confess that while Kôfû only wrote about ten percent of these poems, about half of those selected are his. I am not sure that merit justifies it. On the whole, I think it is that they tend to be written in simple language and have a simple concept at heart. I can read them. Take this one, about a certain waterfall:

> ♪ An Ônagashi Number, here? ♪

> *'Tan-tan-tan! Ta'tta 'tta 'tta! Tan to' – the beating goes:*
> *At Tom-tom Drum Falls how the kabuki tension grows!*

たん／＼／＼たったったったんとうつ　鼓の滝は大なかしかも　行風

The apostrophes emphasize a pause+explosion. The second half of the original is *"Is Tom-tom Falls (doing) an Ônagashi (big-flow)?"* That would be a certain style of drumming suggesting powerful characters are about to fight (movie and tv music was foreshadowed by kabuki centuries ago). Here Kôfû went smack in the middle of a dozen poems and his idea echoes a *ku* by Shinshô published in the *Kebukisô* saijiki (haikai almanac) thirty years earlier 五月雨や鼓の滝の大ながし 信勝 *samidare ya tsuzumi no taki no ônagashi*). The properly seasonal haikai credits the monsoon rains with creating the *ônagashi* effect. Kôfû's poem is preceded by one which introduced only a *tan-tan*'s worth of mimesis and hints at a threat made to the boulders. I think Kôfû thought it failed to do what only *kyôka* can do and, nodding to the old haikai, let the onomatopoeia rip!

天満天神 砂糖よりあまみつ神のいますこそ 山蜂多く有馬なるらめ 行風
satô yori amamitsu kami no imasu koso yamabachi ôku arima naru rame kôfû
sugar-more-than sweet-water=heaven-filling gods' are esp. hornet many have=arima is

Tenman Tenjin (Sugawara no Michizane) Shrine

*Sweeter than sugar our Heaven-filling Honey-God must be why
deep in the Arima hills we see so many hornets in the sky.*

The preface's Tenmantenjin 天満天神 Heaven-Filling-Heaven-God is the 心霊 *divine-spirit* of Sugawara no Michizane, a 9c poet-scholar and minister of state and short for his shrine, or one of the many found throughout Japan. One must like a poet who liked Taoism (his very name, Michizane 道真 is literally "road-truth" and began one poem *"To avoid noisy places is my nature, / yet I love the gurgling of a stream"* (Carter trans.) and regret his death from a broken heart at age 53, very young for someone of such taste. His legendary reputation as an ill-used but loyal minister and fear of his vengeful spirit because many who conspired to get him as good as banished had a bad time of it after his death gained him extraordinary posthumous honors and numerous shrines out of proportion to anything he accomplished. His spirit and shrine name was pronounced in the Chinese manner, but Kôfû chose to give it a Japanese pronunciation to gain the pun on *sky-filling=amamitsu=sweet-honey* to explain the hornets oddly apt for his vengeful spirit, too!

有馬冨士 又こゝに有馬のふしの人穴や いるよりくらき湯壷成らん 行風
mata koko ni arima no fuji no hitoana ya iru yori kuraki yutsubo naruran kôfû
also here-in arima's fuji's person-hole: enter darkly hotwater-tub is

Arima Fuji

*Also here, 'man-holes' may be found on Arima's Fuji,
When you enter the bath tubs . . . darkness does its duty.*

Public baths gradually warmed in the Edo period and this was economical because entrances (pomegranate mouths) were kept low and small to retain heat. That should not be true for a natural sauna. I imagine an artificial grotto in the Arima copy of Mount Fuji with a dark bathing experience for those who could pay for it. Perhaps the next edition will cast light on this, but here and now I switch to one of the last score of poems on sundry small themes by which the 1672 Arima section of the topo-*kyôka* pitters out. Re. a pass? called Yamaguchi:
..
山口の両方にはゆる村草を　みれはさなからつりひけにこそ　行風
yamaguchi no ryôhô ni hayuru murakusa o mireba sanagara tsurihige ni koso kôfû
mt-mouth(place-name)'s both-sides-on grow clump-grass+acc see-if/whn risng 'stache+emph

*Mountain-mouth, both sides boast profuse growths of grass
You'd think you found a dandy with a huge turned up 'stache!*

Or would Kôfû suggest it be 'made up' to look like such a moustache? *Nichevo* doing but *da, da,* I had a hard time not putting Salvador Dali into the translation!

中 Horsing Around With *My Rain* & the *Yu-girls* 下

有馬山高きはかりは徳もなし　湯あるをもつて世にそ貴ふ　重友 1678
arima yama takaki wa bakari wa toku mo nashi yu aru o motte yo ni koso totô shigetomo
arima mt. high-as-for only-as-for worth+emph. not, hotwater have+acc world in/to esp. valuable

Mount Arima!
Who says the only measure
of worth is height?
Having hot water is noble
if your head is screwed on right.

Mount Arima!
Who thinks your highness
measures your worth?
To have hot water must count
as much as boasting noble birth!

~~~~~~~~~~~~~~~~~~~~~~~~~~~~

Mt Arima, I know you're not so tall, but is height everything?
Having hot water is what makes this poet want to sing!

~~~~~~~~~~~~~~~~~~~~~~~~~~~~

What the people indeed find odd is that salt should boil up
with the water in the hills where there should be naught.

世間よふしきこそあれ思ひいる 山のおくにも塩湯わく也　重香
sekken yo fushigi koso are omoiiru yama no oku ni mo shioyu wakunari shigeka?
society/opinion+emph strange+emph is assuming mtn-recesses-in salt-hotwater boil-be

These are the third and first of the opening poems in the 1678 follow-up to the 1672 Arima *kyôka,* respectively. Bringing up the salt is unique and deserves the first spot, but one needs a feeling for the scarcity value of salty food back in the hills to really appreciate it. I recall that it only really sunk into my hard head when researching a haiku on trepan brought up there in *Rise, Ye Sea Slugs!* My screwy idiom is a bit too much for one emphatic *zo,* and my allusion to birth owes more to rhyme than to any reason (in fact, the *last* Arima section ended with a bow toward Japan's ruler by Kôfû, though it is a novel *kyôka* bow for pointing out that rather than wishing for the standard *man,* or ten-thousand, years, he hoped the reign would last a hundred like the Pine on Long-slope 万年かそれより御代は長坂の一本松のよはひ百ほと　行風　*mannen ka sore yori miyo wa* .... Well, if realism shows sincerity...) The second of the three opening poems, not given, states baldly that for cures Arima's name was higher than Fuji's. Though I guess it was mad to claim *anything* higher than Fuji, even metaphorically, I found more advertisement than poetry in the words; on the following page, some "poems" were little more than testimonials, i.e., the man on his last legs who throws away his cane: 入まてはよろ／＼めけるやまひとの　杖をもつかす出湯奇妙や　永利　*iru made wa yoroyoro* .... That set me to thinking. Might not this gang of largely poor and largely aristocratic poets have written many of these poems solely for the purpose of obtaining free lodging and food and other perks at the Arima spa inns and restaurants? Imagine a party of them dropping in on some place and saying, *"Do you want to be in a book? It will be good publicity* . . . Say, for example, there is an Inn called Takeya, or Bamboo-house. A party of poets rides or walks up while competing with each other for a good ditty, or rather *copy.* They come in and offer the owner the best: *Is that a bird? / The first visitor heard / in Bamboo-ya; / A thrush, rushes in to sing the Hô-hô-ke-kyô sutra!* 竹屋　鶯か竹やにやとる初客のほう法花経の声のきこゆる　守辰　*uguisu ka takeya ni* . . .

These "ads" could even wed the name of the particular establishment with the testimonial, as when a place called *Tsuitachi-ya,* The First Day 朔日屋 was punned so someone off his pillowed feet with hips that were out could come in and end up *tsui tachi ya suru,* or, *standing at last,* in a fine poem that defies translation: 難波江のあし腰ぬけし人たにも　有馬の湯てはついたちやする　太女 *naniwa-e no ashi koshi nukeshi* . . . *futome*. The same poet – whose name might mean "fat-lady" – even blurbs the hot-water women of an establishment called Wakasa-ya 若狭屋, or Young Channel, a homophone for *youthfulness:*

有馬山私雨のぬれものは　是第いちそ若さやの湯女　太女
arima-yama watakushi-ame no nuremono wa kore daiichi zo wakasaya no yuna

On Mt. Arima, if you would get wet by 'my rain,' come!
Youthfulness and the yuna, a sure bet for Number One!

Wet scenes, even today, have lubricious connotations. Next, even the names of the yuna get play. At a place called the 下大坊 Shitaôbô we find the (sex-crazed) crowd from Ise trying to taste a yuna named Nabe, or Pot (*nabe* is also *stew* & were it not a common name for maids I would call her a stewpot) with the *shita* in the name bringing them below her navel 湯女の名のなへの臍より下大坊　さくりたいとは伊勢衆かそも　友和 *yuna no na no nabe no heso yori* . . . Reading the poem that follows, I guess the establishment's name might stand for a big oven below a bath for it is: *Even the yuna who bubbles over whom we all call 'Pot' – / Has no fire below her navel: none of the girls are that hot!* わき出る湯女の名によふなへにたに　へその下にはひこそ有らめ　酒粕 *wakiideru yuna no na ni yobu nabe dani* . . . Or, maybe, all the girls at this shop were called Nabe. I do not know. Let us move on to 川野屋 Kawano-ya, or Riverfield. The first poem notes that nibblies were sold by vendors on the second floor, since *nibblies* were homophonous with seafood, we have a proverbial case of fish climbing trees: 川の屋の二階に通うり魚木にのほるけしき也けり　松緑 *kawa no ya no nikai ni* . . . This is followed by several poems where *yuna*, or *a* yuna, named Mizu, Water, received the most lugubrious treatment yet. The first is a pitiful plaint where the river *kawa* turns to skin and bones of the love-sick one who is also a raw cod, *koi*, a homophone for *longing*, and I am not even going to try to English it: 湯女こふる身は生鯉となりはて〻 水の哀れに骨とかはのや　宗定 *yuna kouru mi wa nama-koi* . . . The second goes something like *Dripping and dear from her depths if you do not get wet thinking her adorable you lie about Riverfield's Mizu/Water*, and may have a hint of an *otter* (*kawa-uso*) in it. Too fluid for me to match, the purely phonetic characters emphasize the poem's euphonious aim. I will give you the Japanese and throw in the towel: しつほりとそこからいとしかはゆいと ぬらすはうそのかはのやのみつ 太女 *shippori to soko kara itoshi kawayui to nurazu wa uso no kawanoya no mizu futome.* Now, one I think I *can* handle:

ねかはくは我はへちまのかはのやのおみつ女郎のゆてとなりたし 行豊 *kôhô*
negawaku wa ware wa hechima no kawanoya no omizu jorô no yude to naritashi
wishng-as4 I-as4 squash/loofa's rivrfld-house's hon.+water wench's bathtool-into becme-want

What is my wish? It is this: that I could, myself, a loofa be
So Water the wench of Riverfield bathes while holding me!

㊦ Horsing around with *My Rain* & the *Yu-girls* ㊦

有馬山私雨のふるよりも 湯女にふらるゝ身こそつらけれ　正房 地誌所載狂歌少
arima yama watakushi-ame no furu yori mo yuna ni furaruru mi koso tsurakere　shôbô? 1678
arima mt. my/private-rain's falling more-thn hotwaterwomn's by shaken-off body/self +emph painful

When my rain falls on Mount Arima, who turns blue?
What hurts is when a yuna does not fall for you.

~~~~~~

On Mt Arima the pine mushrooms raise their domes
Umbrellas for this rain that falling falls on each alone.

有馬山私雨に松茸の 笠をひらいてさし出にけり　富由
arimayama　watakushi-ame ni matsudake no kasa o hiraite sashiidenikeri
arima mtn my/private rain-for pine-mshrm/s' corolla/umbrella+acc. opennng thrusts out
つくねんと有馬の山に立そふは あやしや御身誰をまつ茸　光正
tsukunen to arima no yama ni tachisou wa ayashi ya on-mi dare o matsu-dake
blankly ari(are)ma's mtn-on stnd tgthr-as4 sspicious!/: hon.+body whm waits=pine-mshrm

Just standing there on Mount Arima, what are they up to?
(In Japanese, pine-mushrooms don't 'pine' but 'wait' for you).

~~~~~~

Suspicious under covered crowns, silently they stand their ground
Up on Mount Arima, beware, the mushrooms don't sit down!

The poets keep coming back to *my rain,* but the second poem is with a colony of mushrooms. I added "on each alone" and changed "my" to "this" to compensate. The Chinese character is *hat* 笠 not *umbrella* 傘 but they are shaped similarly and used to ward of rain. Only the latter opened up, but if you can imagine a mushroom in slow motion. Both mushroom poems pun the *matsudake*, or pine-mushroom's *matsu=pine* into "wait." The last also puns the *ari* in Arima. We cannot tell if its mushrooms are under suspicion for waiting to meet someone and hatch up a plot or to assassinate someone. I had to pretty much invent something new to keep the wit, or should I say the measure of it. A separate mushroom poem (re. Arima Mikasa) manages to get all of Arima into a pun, with the first part noting that *matsudake* "are (found)" and the second, supplying the startled exclamation "*Ma!*" (Oh, my!)　木の葉をはかき分見れは有馬なる　三笠の山に出し松茸　衆甫 *konoha o ba kakiwakemireba arima* . . . . Haikai played up the phallic symbolism and some of Issa's best *kyôku* have women express surprise to find *them* growing wild (For such, see *The Woman Without a Hole* 2007)
..

妬湯 妬の湯にはねたみの有馬なら 女ふたりの中男かも　光重
uwanari no yu ni wa netami no arima nara onna futari no naka otoko ka mo kôchô?
jealousy/envy hotwater/bath-in envy has=arima if women two between man maybe

Not 嫐, but 嬲 in the baths!

Here at Envy Spa if jealousy in Arima indeed is found:
Look for a man between two women, bumped around!

The poem alludes to a character with woman 女 radicals surrounding a man 男 meaning to toy around with or even physically "pick-on" or knock-about. I imagine two or more *yuna* competing for the favors of one guest at his expense. Until now, I did not know said character existed. Only its homonymic heterograph, one woman between two men, was registered in my mind's dictionary. So I first thought the poet invented it. But, what a name! I imagine natural rock outdoor baths and *yuna* prompted the owner to use a character combining both . . . The simple frivolity of the poem recalls Kôfû, who six poems later laments a missing commemorative stone erected for Shigemori, a compassionate warrior whose loyalty and love clashed tragically in an ancient war between clans. It was supposed to have been in Iwakura, meaning a *boulder-storage*, one would think a safe place. Kôfû puns on Iwakura by placing it after *nani*, or "what," for *"nani o I/iwakura?" What might he say!"* 岩倉　重盛といまさら何をいはくらや　其石塔の跡かたもなし　行風　*shigemori to imasara nani o* . . . I introduce it though space runs short, because it provides a precedent for the mid-19c squib about the Iwakura Mission *jôyaku wa musubu* . . . with its *nan to I/iwakura!* The following is for what I guess to be a small ridge, Nomi-ga-se, or Flea-back.

蚤ヶ背 山人の昼ねすれともねられぬは 蚤か背中にやすむゆへかも 重貞
yamabito no hirune suredomo nerarenu wa nomi-ga-senaka ni yasumu yue ka mo shigesada?
mntn-people's noon/day-nap do but sleep-cannot-as-for? flea-back-on rest because?/!

Why do the folk on this mountain nap without sleeping a wink?
Because they lay flat upon the back of a flea, I think.

Names like that may be found in the Usanian badlands, but what about the next, Tsuru-uchi-ga-hana, or String-hitting-Nose? *Tsuru*=bow-string + *uchi*=striking/er, i.e., exorcist/ism? Short for *tsuru-uchi-ya*, a cotton spinner (a similar *twanging* is heard)? So, is the exorcist a long-nose goblin? Did cotton-spinners boast snow-tipped noses? Or, did a folk-musician play his musical bow with his nose for a pick? Who knows? 弦打ヶ鼻：弦うちかはなより出る弓張の月のいるさや星を見当か　光友 *tsuru-uchi-ga-hana yori ideru yumibari no tsuki* . . . The poem does not English; but *how* it gets from the nose to the bow of the moon that aims at the evening stars fascinates me for it opens up the possibility that what I had assumed to be a later idea, visualizing dreams within *chôchin* or lantern-like bubbles coming from the nose, was already in the air (弓張りの月が提灯に取り変わるって発想). And, finally, we come to an end of our sampling with my favorite place name 多舞保々能城山 Tanpopo-no-shiroyama or Dandelion Fort Mountain. As we have seen, the dandelion was associated with *drumming* rather than *lion-teeth* in Japan. *Tummy-drumming* goes back to ancient China as a symbol of contentment. This is an early example of the *"Aren't we peaceful now!"* poem:

太刀は鞘に治る御代は腹つゝみ　うつやうたすやたんほゝの城　友易
tachi wa saya ni osameru miyo wa hara tsuzumi utsu ya utazu ya tanpoponoshiro tomoyô
thick-sword-as4 scabbrd-in contrl hon.reign-as4 belly-tomtom beat or beat-nt dndln-frt

Beating our tumtums full of meat, swords rusting in their sheaths,
We're off to Fort Dandelion to shoot, or not to shoot, the breeze!

My warrior's pride safely sheathed, this full tum-tum is all I beat –
Dandy times indeed when visiting Ft. Dandelion is dubbed a feat.

Our Star the Shrimp, Our Sun the Crab: *Surimono!*

再現 勇ましき皃はお江戸の飾り海老おんめの正月と団十郎に 桜川慈悲成 d.1833
isamashiki kao wa o-edo no kazari-ebi onme no shogatsu to danjûrô mi ni sakuragawa jihinari
gallant face-as-for hon.+edo's decorative-shrimp hon.+eyes' new-years and danjûrô see-to (go)

Two faces of Edo bring joy to my eyes, dauntless, they laugh at Age.
What's one year to a Grand Shrimp? I'm catching Danjûrô on stage!

~~~~~~

In Edo are two
fearless faces to see:
the New Year's lobster,
a feast to the eyes,
and Danjûrô.

tr. Noah Braunen

:

Googling last minute to see if I may have overlooked writing in English about 16c *kyôka* – nothing. But I did find two items regarding *surimono*, a picture and poem combination that was a big part of early-19c *kyôka* but under-represented in this book because things of beauty end up with the rich – your poor author had to be satisfied with what could be netted on the web. One was a $147. book just out by John T. Carpenter called *Reading Surimono: The Interplay of Text and Image in Japanese Prints*. It was second only to this book as the largest selection of translated *kyôka*, hundreds accompanied by 400 color illustrations and *"contributions from a distinguished roster of Edo art and literary specialists."* The publicity had no examples of the *translation* (a must, for even the cooperation of a hundred scholars each paid as much per hour by their grants as your author makes in a week is no guarantee of the literary worth of one poem but it looked promising (★ *later:* we will see the poems in a few chapters). The other item of interest was an article by Noah Braunen titled *"'Mad Poems' from Japan's Unknown Surimono"* in the "Rutgers Painted Bride Quarterly" (#40/41). Banzai to Braunen! *Examples!* The above (pardon my centering) is how he redid a poem from a Hiroshige *surimono* in the collection of Sidney C. Ward, who had tried without luck to get the *kyôka* translated before: *That fierce red face / Belongs to none other than / The New Year's lobster display in Edo; / Seeing Danjûrô is / A feast to my eyes*. I do not know if that is "misleading," but it is indeed far from poetic, while Braunen's is about as good as one can do with-out getting explanatory. Why is his *lobster* my *shrimp?* The reference is to the Ise 'Shrimp,' which resembles a Florida crawfish. It is lobster large but clawless. All *shrimp,* however small, stand for longevity in the Sinosphere, where one is *spry as a shrimp*. Age 老 is built into the name *shrimp* 海老 = sea-elder. Its back may be bent, but it is snappy in sound and movement when alive and, cooked, boasts a ruddy red or pretty pink complexion. I realize a *shrimpy* and a dauntless image clash, but with a lobster, the huge claws, rather than the grandiose elder-style 'whiskers,' dominate and that puts the image at odds with the aging aspect of the New-Year-as-collective birthday. There is more. I am sitting here looking at a picture of said kabuki star Danjûrô VII in the rare expensive book *Moji no Shukusai* 文字の祝祭 I own (as the translator, I got some free copies) and, guess what? The fan splayed across his midriff is decorated with one large abstract design which, depending on how your mind works might first be recognized as the character meaning *longevity* or a stylized sketch of a shrimp. And a big red shrimp, it turns out, was the emblem for generations of Ichikawa Danjûrô's, a line of actors specializing in being gallants and ruffians. Edoites were proud to be in your face so to speak and these "Shrimp-guy 海老蔵" actors were indeed the face of Edo. Loving *kyôka*, Danjûrô on tour and *via* his fan clubs helped spread it outside of Edo when it was faddish there in the 19c (See *The Fifth Season* (2007) for more on the expression 'New Year for the eyes.' It would not fit here).

aratama no haru no gyoyû ni mesarete ya ume ga sasôte ki-naku uguisu sakuragawa
    new-gem's spring (the n y)'s party-to invitd? plum/s invtd coming-sings warbler   jihinari

> *'Was he invited to the New Year's party?' 'Sure, he's no bum.*
> *This bush warbler came to sing at the behest of our plum.*
> ~~~~~~~~~~~~~~~~~~~~~~~~~~~~~
> *Has he crashed our New Year's party? No, he's a guest*
> *This uguisu came to sing at the plum blossoms' request.*

Braunen points out that this may have been the swan song for the poet, a famed raconteur and comic who died before the book was published, uniting with the quickly rising star of Hiroshige, last and most famous of the ukiyoe masters. His translation (*Was he invited / to this New Year's party? / The bush warbler sings / at the prompting / of the plum blossoms*) is precise. I dressed it up a bit, for as he notes (before another poem not this one), "the poems of Ward's surimono collection, though kyôka in form, are not what we would normally term "comic" or "mad" in the West." It is true. With the pictures counting so much, *surimono kyôka* tend to be understated, but some, including two more Braunen introduces, are excellent and deserve to be read by more than a few scholars and collectors of art books.
:

kesa to nareba kasumi no umi o ôgani no ito-yuttari to ayumu hi no ashi
    dawn (of new year) becoming-if mist-ocean in/through big-crab's so-slow/loose

> *And come the dawn, how slow and easy the Sun-beams,*
> *Long legs of a great crab, move through the sea of mist.*

This poem reworks the tenuous yet majestic rising of the first sun of the year which a famous haiku by Kikaku metaphors as the (very slow) ambulation of a *crane* (*tsuru no ayumi*) using a common idiom of *legs* for what we call *sun-beams* or *rays*. I love it but I am afraid I forgot to note the poet's name and that our fine young translator was mistaken with: *This morning / how slowly, / the great crab, / with pincers of fire, / crawls in a sea of mist*. Not having the original, I cannot know for certain, but chances are 'sun' was written with a phonetic character that allowed "fire" and the *pincers*, while poetic, would hardly do for this peaceful day. The other extraordinarily mad poem (*nanakusa no kayui tokoro e te no todoku niwa no wakana o mago ni tsumasemu*) means more or less *What a relief to have all seven herbs for charm-broth in my garden, at hand so my grandchild can pick them as easily as his namesake can scratch my itch*, but one cannot even start to translate the way *broth=kayu* pun-pivots into *itchy=kayui* and *te*=hand stretches unseen from near the front of the poem to the back where it follows and mentally combines with *mago*=grandchild to make a back-scratcher (*mago no te*=grandchild's hand)! *Merci!*

Japanese Poetry Prints: Spring Comes in Tiger Eyes?

氷とく風の手かひのとらの目の時もたがわてくる玉の春　ひゃくていさかい？
kôri toku kaze no tegai no tora no me no toki mo tagawa de kuru tama no haru   hakyutei sakai?
ice-meltng-wind's hand-raisd/pet tiger's eyes' time+emph. mistake-not-so comes gem/preciousspring

Winds melt the ice without, within, on the tip of every tongue
We find our tiger's eyes & just in time, her spring has sprung!

~~~~~~

Winds melt the ice without, within, the eyes of Tiger never dumb
Say it is time and, loh, behold, Belle Spring, indeed, has come!

This poem from a surimono commissioned for 1806, a Year of the Tiger, is lively in the original but damn hard to keep alive in translation. *First*, in English, wind no more has *hands* than rain *legs*. McKee tried with *"The hands of warm breezes,"* but even if he had the ice melted by "the warm hand of the wind" (surely better) or something altogether different like, say, "windy hands tease apart the ice," not linked to what followed with more than *"and,"* it would still be good as dead. In the original, the pun takes that *hand* and, adding *kai*, makes it "hand-raised," i.e. a "pet" tiger. The best link I could make was a *without/within* contrast. *Second*, all educated people in the Sinosphere know cat's eyes tell time. And, *third*, the original takes advantage of the common epithet for Spring when it means the New Year, *tama* (gem/jewel/ball/ precious), to say it is the cat's year, for Tama was probably the most common name for a female cat. The best development of this happy coincidence I know of is not in *kyôka* but haiku. To wit, one of Shiki's many unsung masterpieces:
:

猫の顔もみがきあげたり玉の春　子規　明治二四
neko no kao mo migaki-agetari tama no haru shiki 1891
cat's face+emph/even polishes-up/gives tama's spring

    Tama the Cat   *Bright New Year*

    Our Gem, too   *Even our cat*
pretties up her face –   *polishes her face: this gem*
    Spring-shine.   *of a spring day.*

さほ姫の手飼成らし虎の年　定時　鷹つくば
sao hime no tegai naru rashi tora no toshi teiji 1642
sao-princess's hand-raised/pet seems tiger's year

Raised by none
other than Princess Sao
Annus Tigris

No mere elaboration of a metaphor, Shiki's *ku* captures the ambience of the day perfectly. As cats do not do their toilets in order to look attractive but when they feel good, we know that love is in the air and a gift, perhaps, in Tama's bowl. I substituted a bell/e for the *gem* in the second reading because a bell *is* a *tama* when round, and the one on the cat in the surimono picture, attached tooth & claw to an expensive half of smoked bonito (shaved for soup and noodle stock) – as McKee noted, its tooth-hardening rite – Toothless Issa's *ku* had him hardening his gums on a block of tôfu – is indeed round. My *Belle* refers to someone nowhere in the *surimono*, Princess Sao, whom I have seen pictured riding in upon her tame tiger on the Year of the same.

初空や煙草吹輪の中の比枝　言水 d. 1719
hatsuzora ya tabako fuku wa no naka no hie gonsui
first-sky!/: tobacco-blowing-ring-within's (mt.) hie (hieizan)

♪ *a pale blue haiku* ♪

~ *the first sky* ~   ~ *my first sky* ~
i blow a ring of smoke   *mount cool within*
around mt. cool   *a smoke ring*

Mt. Hiei may be seen from Kyôto and sounds like "chilly." My title and trimmings are for the season. This was in *The Fifth Season* opposite to Shiki's *ku,* for which it lay open when my sister called about a dolphin on TV. I saw it not only blow bubble rings but snip them to various diameters and blow a second ring carefully within the first that fused and instantaneously expanded enough to swim through! At that time, I was considering whether or not to introduce a picture calendar for 1798, Year of the Horse (like our Tiger Year chapter lead from Daniel McKee's *Japanese Poetry Prints:* 2006) titled *Courtesan with a Client Blowing a Horse of Smoke* with four poems, including one McKee translates *"For one night, till dawn / My heart like a colt / Stirred up and lively / Riding in rings of / Exhaled tobacco" hitoya akete kokoro no koma isamitsutsu fukeru tabako no wanori o zo suru* sanyôdô 山陽堂. I would prefer "all night long" replace the literal first line but will spare you a mad translation with heart racing *wacko* because of *tobacco* and only point out two things *not* mentioned in the explanation of the series which introduced me to two Chinese eccentrics I had missed or forgotten, one accompanied by a horse that could be kept in a wallet or gourd when not ridden and one who could blow his soul out of his mouth to travel anywhere. They are this: 1) *Kokoro no koma* or "heart/mind's horse" is a Sinosphere conceit for what Freud would call the Id ♪ and it meets a metaphysically perfect match in 2) the *ring,* for it is homophonic with *harmony* (*wa*): think *peace pipe.*

Across Your fortunate Realm the Spring Sun stretches out his beams
Even the wrinkled face of the Sea, smoothes out and, like us, gleams.

～～～～～～～～～～～～～～～～

Well ruled and prosperous Your Realm, Spring Sun stretching lazily
His lucent limbs to smooth the ripples = wrinkles from the sea, too.

:

That dolphin also took me back to my childhood by the sea and settled the matter of whether or not to introduce the above (*osamareru miyo wa yutaka ni nami no shiwa mo uchi-nobashitaru haru no hi no ashi* chôchôtei somabito 1820). It is not because I fell for the poem. Sunrise almost *never* smoothes the sea. Night does that, and the sun for whatever meteorological reasons, stirs it up. New Years may be enchanted, but my memories . . . No, it was the accompanying print, one of the most elegant I have ever seen, of two graceful sea-horses floating within a softly rounded ground-swell at the moment the red dawn sun kisses the sea goodbye. McKee, who translates *"The well-ruled imperial realm / Rests in comfort / Legs of spring sunbeams / Run gently over / Wrinkles of waves,"* does a fine job of explaining the larger context, even adding that "the earliest model for surimono may be found in the New Year *kisshô,* felicitous writings ritually presented to the emperor at the New Year" and hazarding a guess that continuing to do so might be seen as a challenge to Tokugawa shôgunal authority by exalting the Emperor "as an alternative and deserving source [?] of fealty" under the guise of tradition. But catching the wit of the poem itself evidently required more knowledge of the New Year in poetry (especially *haikai*) than he had at that time. Sun-legs and sea-wrinkles, both common conceits, are wed by the concept of *stretching out* when relaxed on the New Year (his "run" came from confusing "*nobashiri*" for "*no hashiri*"), and the beauty of the poem is in the sea, *too* – that is, *like us* – relaxing its brow as part of the expanding sphere of peace. ♪

㊤ Coloring in the New Year with a Straight Face ㊤

白赤とまじれる梅の花麹 みそのになりて 遊ふ鶯　狂歌堂＝真顔
shiro-aka to majireru ume no hana-kôji mi-sono (kôji miso) ni narite asobu uguisu kyôkadô
white-redly mixing plum-blossom/fine-malt/curd yr-garden/cultured-miso-to accustomed plays/relaxing warbler/nightingale. *"With red and white / mixed in its malt base / of plum blossoms / the frolicking warbler / has grown accustomed to your garden."* mckee trans.

Red and white, the flowering plum seems a room of starter malt
If Warbler gets too high to hold a tune, your garden is at fault!

~~~~~~

Red and white plum blossoms mix, a culture that is to our taste:
The warbler looks right at home in a garden full of bean paste!

The picture (pl.21) the poem accompanies is on the cover of *Colored in the Year's New Light* (2008), and I agree with Daniel McKee: it *is* a masterpiece. Were it here for you to see, I might have added the following reading mostly for the first line: *A warbler so rosy about the gills fits right into this plum bloom / Red & white and packed so tight your garden is a malt room!* I also agree with McKee that this poem by "straight-face" Magao – under his second *aka* Kyôkadô, *i.e.,* Hall (or temple) of Kyôka – is complex. Indeed, it is. 1) *Shiro-aka*, white-red, reverses the usual order of these propitious New Year colors, hinting at things being mixed up 2) Plum being 'mixed up' is a *haikai* conceit, though it is usually with other things not their own bloom 3) ume, or "plum" (flowering apricot according to some fastidious souls) can pun as *delicious* 4) the plum's blossom, *hana*, can mean "fine/fancy/ precious" and/or describe the fermenting bloom of the *kôji*, a fermenting culture of steamed soybeans mixed with steamed rice and/or barley, that if reversed to *kôji's* blossom (*kôji no hana*) means *sake*, or rice wine; 5) but kôji can also make soy-sauce or bean-paste (fermented bean curd) used for making soups or dressings, and here it is followed by *miso*, suggesting the latter; 6) Then the addition of *no* for *misono*, turns said bean-paste into *mi-sono*, a garden modified by an honorific meaning it belongs to another, but homophonically associating with *beauty* as well; 7) *Narite* means "grown used to" or tame, but despite the grammatically incongruent *no* between it and the *miso* seems to second the *kôji's becoming miso* (not *sake*). 8) The *uguisu* may or may not allude to a singer. About half of these were pointed out by McKee. While the intoxicating mood of the New Year and the fact people did drink led me there first, Magao was a noted teetotaler and *miso* has ever been proverbial to Japanese in the way apple pie was until recently to Usanians – so, while I lean toward my second reading, I would qualify it: the *miso* metaphor not only pivots into the garden toward the harbinger but makes the mood *domestic* and *familiar*. Yet,

..

The first mixer of the year yet the warbler looks used to being here
Malty red & white plum bloom, the fragrant scent of garden beer!

~~~~~~

Red and white and packed so tight a plum blossom malt room,
The ice broken by the liquid voice of a warbler high on bloom.

Here, my respondent (see ♪) *warns I go too far*, but I feel that not only blossoms but the bird may be mixing it up, for even though the first half of the poem may be read as a clever metaphor ending with the modification of the garden, the mixing it up can *also* be tele-syntaxically gerunded to the bird. Since those colors may stand for the respective sexes (today, New Year features a red-white, or girl-boy team song contest on TV), we may have an allusion to a professional singer – or, less likely, a Hokekyô monk (belonging to the sect whose sutra the bird-song resembles) – at a garden party who feels right at home and mixes with guests of both sexes. And there is more: *kôji* has too many homophones to shake a stick at, but one seems so damn apt I cannot help but wonder if it was intended: 香餌 *scented feed*. These birds do not just come to sing but to eat and I imagine bugs dusted by the pollen would be a treat. By now, even McKee, who never fails to mention the complexity of Magao's poems and explains more about each poem than anyone else I have read – and, not only that, goes back to fill in the background, such as mentioning "the poems composed for Ōtomo's plum gathering in the first month of 730," where the bird too appeared – must be doing one or more of the following: clicking his tongue, stamping his feet, scratching his head, or rolling his eyes. *But why stop?* No museum is printing *this* book. I am, on my own money (only the $150. set-up fee for my printer-distributor – actually publishing no longer requires money up front). *Miso*, as it so happens, is proverbially (*miso mo kuso mo isshô* 味噌も糞も一緒) equated with *shit*, and that, despite another proverb discovering there are *grades* (段) of *miso* and *kuso*, is not a negative thing; rather, it evokes the oneness of all in time and space in the dreamtime of the Japanese New Year. That pun improves the "becoming" half of the becoming/accustoming pun, does it not? And this bird is, after all, the harbinger of spring in a culture whose cosmos is less created by fiat than grown organically – much from various organs, at any rate – which might be said to revere fertility in the sense of the natural birth of things or ideas. For farm fertility, poop is not the end-product but something fundamental for new growth. In a culture with this worldview, there is something of 'the chicken or the egg' question in the eater and the shitter, or the food and the excrement. How much of this is in the poem and how much in my head, I do not know. But, it is a fact that Japanese were ever attentive to the shit of *this particular bird*, the same whose by-product, as we have seen, was used to cultivate "the garden on your face" (though, with cosmetics the old translation "nightingale" is *always* used – nightingale poop, *yes*, warbler shit, *no* – modern poetry may throw away elegance but the beauty business cannot) or, rather, keep the skin smooth and white as rice-cake, the *mochi* upon which Bashô's *uguisu* happened to deposit . . .

とし／\にあたまは光源氏にて春の若菜の色好む也　櫻川慈悲成 1805?
toshidoshi ni atama wa hikaru genji nite haru no wakana no iro konomu nari jihinari
year-x2-w/ head-as4 hikaru=shiny genji resmblng, spring's yungreens' color like becomng

> *My head that with the years has come to gleam like Genji, also came*
> *to love those young herbs of spring – so, in the end, we are the same.*

This frisky confession by Sakuragawa Jihinari, whom we just met in Braunen's article, was among a score of poems on a single surimono *"Symbols of Good Fortune to Overcome a Period of Danger"* (Ibid. pl.30). McKee, without a rhyme-guided opinion about what the poet drove at beyond the allusion translated: *"With the passing years/ my head, like Prince Genji, / shining brightly, has like him, too, / developed a taste for the color / of the young spring herbs."* Haikai was full of young greens sought by old men (see chapter 19 in *The Fifth Season* (2007)). These would be maids past puberty, but Prince Genji lived in an age when a real little girl could be groomed to become a noble's second or later wife, so we had grown men paying closer attention to them than might otherwise be the case. Jihinari was barely middle-aged, so he must have suffered from premature baldness. Genji did not, but his first name "Shining" coming after the poet's head implies just that.

㊥ Coloring in the New Year with a Straight Face ㊤

ますら男に追ふはるゝ鬼の姿みる　笑ひそめたる春の山姥　東光園源撰僊
masurao ni owaruru oni no sugata miru warai sometaru haru no yamanba　tôkôen gensen
stout-man-by chased demon's/s' form/s seeing smile-starting spring's mountain-hag c.1830

Seeing a demon flee for his life with a tough guy on the tail o' him,
The mountain cracks its first smile – or is it that witch's first grin?

~~~~~~~~~~~~~~~~~~~~~~

Seeing a demon flee for his life from a gallant with a bean bag,
The first smile of spring comes to the face of the mountain hag!

~~~~~~~~~~~~~~~~~~~~~~

Seeing the figure of a demon / brought to his knees / by a man of power /
oh, how she laughs / Yamamba in springtime.　trans McKee (2008)

This is an unusually simple poem any Japanese could read and get immediately but very good nonetheless because its single *pun*ch comes right where it should and is so smooth you do not see it coming until *the very last character* of the poem before which we have nothing but the usual conceit of a mountain smiling or laughing – *warau* means both – in the spring (covered with shiny new *leaves* homophonic with *teeth*). Then, suddenly, mountain=*yama*⇒*yamanba*=mountain *hag!* Two things are happening here. First, we have smiling mountain/s, already a personification, given an actual *persona*, that of the hag, whose inclusion fits the *we-are-all-happy-together* concept of the season. *We* laugh, *the mountains* laugh; nay, even the wild witch participates in *our* cosmos. Second, we have a new twist for that day when good luck is tossed in and bad out – charm and exorcism united in a single rite as is true with the Latin tradition of *Veni bene Fugit mala* or something like that – with those beans once on or near New Year (on solar Springrise). We have seen how much dirty fun 17c *kyôka* poets had with those beans. This surimono comes from ca.1830, a cleaner time. The new twist is that Yamanba was the mother of "legendary strongboy Kintoki," a sort of Jack the Giant-Killer, as all such children are. She has seen demons knocked around. The print, also on the back cover of *Colored in the Year's New Light*, shows Kintoki a gigantic red boy, towering over a green demon on all fours amid the scattered beans looking as weak as Superman with Kryptonite: *Kintoki Exorcising a Demon with Beans* (pl.32, by Totoya Hokkei). McKee writes,

> *The pleasure of the image is in entering fully into the literal, simplified framework of a child's mind, in which demons are actual monsters, not psychological issues, and good and evil are clearly divided.*

..
Exactly. And, I would add, that follows the Season's ideal of returning to, or reviving, one's natural first (infantile) mind, though it clashes with another ideal, that of inclusiveness, which really should include even demons. McKee hits the nail on the head again when he observes that the poem improves the picture (grim-faced boy and piteous demon) by letting us imagine the boy's mother watching and laughing. But, I am less happy about his translation, for *"brought to his knees"* loses the polyphonic or stereo effect of the original harmony by effectively uniting picture and poem. We should *also* be able to imagine a man – *not* Kintoki – chasing the demon/s. Should I add that children in Japan today beaning their fleeing fathers who wear demon masks enjoy themselves even more than those meeting Santa Claus?

For once, prefatory remarks are called for. The picture (pl.55) the following two poems go with is titled *a Deer with Her Fawn* and puzzling because the doe, if it is not a hornless yearling, is speckled like the fawn. The 七宝連 print was for a late-1820s New Year. The first poem is perhaps the most surprising as even if the ancient location, Kasugano, is worthy of celebration, written with the Chinese characters meaning Spring-Sun-Field and famous for wild deer, there is no Year of the Deer and while "first-princessing" is a New Year season rite, this seems beyond the pale:

春日野や妻もこもれるわか草になきて根よけに見ゆる小男しか　米成
kasugano ya tsuma mo komoreru wakakusa ni nakite neyoge ni miyuru saojika　yonenari
kasugano: mate+emph. hiding youngrass-in/frm crying sleep/sex-good-for looks yearling

> *Ho, Kasuga Moor! Hiding in the new grass, with his doe*
> *A young buck – to hear him bleat, he'll be a good ____!*

Englishmen? How about *stag/shag*? Perhaps the reader can recall both *Tales of Ise* waka parodied in this *kyôka*. One (also in the *Kokinshû*) was itself parodied at least twice in this book – the *field*-burn becoming *heart*-burn was the best; and the other was so outrageous in the original – the man of old sizing up his sister and claiming to envy whoever gets her first – that it is hard to forget. Making both more natural in combination or, perhaps, unnatural in a totally droll and I think wholesome way – was a stroke of genius. The character who drooled over his sister seems put in his place better by this travesty than by his sister's retort (in my reading or McCullough's: pg.355); this one of the few take-offs in *kyôka* that I would call a bonafide parody. One small point. *Neyoge*, or apparently-good-to-sleep-with (looks like a good lay) is written with the character 根 *root* and originally meant someone of good character, *good to the bone*, so to speak, but *root* being homophonic with *sleep* (both *ne*) . . . It is usually applied to a female, but here, applied to a male, I can think of *another* meaning of root that works better than "sleep." Be that as it may, that root also serves to carry the poem from the grass 草 in the first take-off to the second by association. In retrospect, I suppose it *is* a New Year's poem as it would trigger the first-laugh of the year in anyone who read it, and partakes of the Taoist mindset of that time by regressing beyond discrimination 無分別 and being utterly playful 無心 .
..
わか水をけさくみ初めと春日野に去年の星をも見ゆる小男鹿　外成
waka mizu o kesa kumizome to kasugano ni kozo no hoshi o mo miyuru saojika　sotonari
young-watr+acc thismorn scoop-strtng & kasugano's lstyear's stars+emph appear yrling

> *Cupping young water for the first time at the cusp of a new spring dawn*
> *On Kasuga Moor we spot last year's stars on the fur of a fawn.*

~~~~~~~~~~~~~~~~~~~~~~~~~~~

> *Young water scooped up for the first time at the dawn of spring*
> *On Kasuga Moor, behold remnant stars on a yearling.*

For the *Fifth Season*, I translated many old haiku mentioning these reflecting stars, always wondering just how visible stars were in water. Can you recall seeing any? Than again, I can't recall ever looking for them. This gentle *waka* – for if you allow *waka* some play for coincidence, it *is* a *waka* – with the scent of 17-18c haikai humor is a fine complement for the double parody and, I forgot to write one thing: the picture of a doe with her fawn is part of Hokkei's *"Thirty-Six Birds"* series. As I was wondering whether deer counters like hares' were ever "wings 羽," McKee to the rescue: *Birds* stood for birds & *flowers*, which stood for nature – a Sinosphere thing.

㊥ Coloring in the New Year with a Straight Face ㊦

春駒の はミ出す雪の下若菜 残こるを 我も はミ出してつむ　四方歌垣 真顔
harugoma no hamidasu yuki no shita wakana　nokoru o ware mo hamidashite tsumu　magao 1822?
spring-colts protrudng/eat-start snow-belw yungreens/herbs remaing+acc i+emph/too protrude/eating-pluck

~~Spring ponies munching as you go young greens together with the snow~~
~~Those you missed I'll try to find . . . . . better plucked than left behind!~~

What young greens spring colts grazing leave above the snow
I would pluck lest they and I be left out in the cold!

I failed to catch the wit for this poem by surimono's number one poet, Magao. Likewise, I think, for McKee, whose reading, *"The spring horses / eat the young herbs / that push up the snow / and from what remains, / sticking out, I will pluck my meal"* (*Colored in the Years New Light*, pl.117), did not amuse me. Puns on *hamidasu* (*"stick out = start eating"*) and the "comedy" of a man lower on the food chain than a horse do not suffice. Still, my first reading followed his, dropping the fine pivot from *herbs* to *poet sticking out* for this: *The spring horses eat the young herbs that stick up from the snow / & me, I don't care if I do stick out – I'm picking some to go!* But, that, too, was but dressing weak wit. I wondered if the second *hamidashite* might not be *ha midashite, i.e.,* "spying out leaves" (the *kana* looked a bit like leaf 葉 to me) and re-translated: *"What young herbs spring ponies leave below the snow they munch, / I shall find and pluck those leaves for my seventh lunch!"* The 7-herb soup rite *was* on the day 7 of the New Year; but, again, no added information can hide weak wit. I felt there had to be *more,* for Magao was a good poet, as demonstrated by his many poems explained well by McKee. Second, Magao had to have known Kikaku's haiku (copy below from *Fifth Season* 2007), and would have felt obliged to add a better new twist to *man-and-horse-get-greens* than just puns.

土手の馬くはんを無下に菜摘哉　其角
dote no uma kuwan o muge ni natsumi kana kikaku d. 1707
bank's horse/s eat-not (or, would) +emph. contrad.? directly greenplucking!/?

~~what the horses~~	~~green plucking~~	~~going straight~~
~~would not eat on the bank~~	~~i snatch one up from under~~	~~for what the horses leave~~
~~green plucking~~	~~my horse's nose~~	~~green-plucking~~

In retrospect, only the middle reading is even close. I failed to imagine the possibility of many horses needing to munch while traveling through or resting with their teamster, did not appreciate the drastic tone of *muge* and should have known the fact there were better ways to phrase a people eating what horses turn their noses up at reading, should have ditched it for the "would eat" one. Kikaku's poem should be:

Though horses would eat, why must man
rob this bank of all its greens to beat?

Pardon the "beat," which is one way to describe the ritual chopping – with a song – that would follow the plucking. I cannot help translating to fit a context and that context is this book. At any rate, the idea was 1) Complaining that humans were hogging the herbs, and 2) Describing (and possibly but not probably, celebrating in a warped way) the crowds of people out plucking around. Not knowing Kikaku well, unlike the case with Issa, I can never tell. Now, back to Magao. . . . . Typing in the Japanese, I paused. Why *nokoru o,* and not the more common *nokori,* or remnant? Could the *o* after the verb be a slightly archaic contradictory or lamenting emphatic *o?* That *had* to be it. Facetiously lamenting greens left by the horses would play well with Kikaku's *ku* and be equally good with the first *kyôka* on the surimono, which tastefully, yet outrageously parodies *Kokinshû* poem #18 where a Prince summons a signal-keeper on Kasuga to go out to check how many days it should be before the greens are ready for plucking into a suggestion that he stew up a pot of them for himself while they are still fresh. ♪ So I made the poem crossed-out above and rosy about the gills wrote "I have no reason for changing the third-person horses/ponies into the second. When it works poetic license needs no excuse, and when it doesn't none will do." Then, I bounced my brilliant reading off my respondent and . . . he did *not* buy it. Yoshioka did what McKee and I should have done, looked at all the meanings of *harukoma* in a big dictionary. If we had, we would have found it not only meant ponies let out to graze in the spring but *door-to-door performers who danced riding toy ponies, masks,* etc.. Far from home, these outsiders would not have access to proper places to pluck the young plants (some rarely eaten, I would call herbs, others such as turnip and rape are staple food) for the rite. Such a reading makes the second "me-too" *hamidashi* really work, as a word proper to a horse or cow grazing is perfect for someone who plays the part of such an animal. Also it fits better with the other poem than either of our readings.

角もしのいせ海老うしとおもわねど 旅ハ心のあとに引るゝ 一声亭群鳥 c.1800
tsuno-moji no ise-ebi ushi to omowanedo tabi wa kokoro no ato ni hikaruru isseitei muretori
horn-lettrd Ise-shrmp ox=depressng-as think-not-but travl-as4 heart aftr-to/frm pulld/ing

The cornute letter in Ise's shrimp makes it neither blue nor bovine,
But this trip does keep pulling on my heart-strings from behind.

~~~~~~~~~~~~~~~~~~

Though an Ise crawfish is no ox despite its cornute letter,
On the return trip my heart must be pulled along like one

..
We have already encountered the "horn-letter" い standing for *affection,* including *missing* someone or thing (pgs. 147, 433). Starting a poem with an association, then contradicting it in one respect while continuing to milk something from it was common in the 8c *Manyôshû,* and gives the poem an archaic feel. The horny feelers on a crawfish do curve back as do the horns on many *ushi,* or oxen but, here, *ushi* becomes its more significant homophone, "depressed," so the poem means that travel does not make the poet feel low, but he does miss places he saw, like horn-letter いせ Ise. Oxen not *pulling* a cart themselves were typically *pulled* along. I am unsure whether the intended metaphor is trip-as-ox or heart-as-ox. The ambiguous grammar allows for the heart to be in the body and pulled from behind or for the heart itself to be dragging behind. McKee favors the former ("this journey hooks and tugs at / the feelings in my heart"), which I follow in my first reading as a way to use one of my favorite metaphors, heartstrings, though I strongly favor the latter, a heart after Saigyô's, which was often left behind or, like the tails of Bo-peep's sheep, strayed off. I quizzed my respondent on that and got no response. Unless one is translating and must re-create things, metaphorical reification seems silly. But, he did note something McKee and I both missed. The first part of the poem alludes to a proverb 旅は憂いもの辛いもの *Travel is depressing and painful.* The *ui* being a different case of *ushi*. While that overstates it, as the poet writes, it is not completely untrue; being away from one's friends and unfamiliar with the customs is not easy. But, in retrospect, that travail is precisely what makes us look so fondly back at our travels.

㊦ Coloring in the New Year with a Straight Face ㊦
烟をき 磯の潮干のおかしさは いもにとらはるゝ蛸の粗相さ　久堅屋　寛政
kemuru oki iso no shiohi no okashisa wa imo ni toraruru tako no sosôsa hisakataya c.1830
smoking sea shore's lowtide/collecting's funniness-as4 girlfriend=taro-by caught octpsy's slownss

*What has them all laughing / on the shore at low tide / against the misty offing /
is the clumbsiness of this octopus / snagged by my girlfriend* – trans. mckee

*What is so funny on this shore at low tide by the misty sea?
An octopus caught by a mouse he should catch, what a pussy!*

*Low tide on the shore by the misty sea: why laugh? The question begs
How a pussy with eight has been caught by one with only two legs!*

*What cracks them up at low tide on the seashore? To see my mate
with but four limbs pin down another octopus with eight!*

This, one of ten poems in a late-1820's 5-print set "Gathering the Bounty of the Sea at Ebb Tide" painted by Kuniyoshi is one of the more erotic New Year surimono I have seen. When the seashore is involved it cannot be helped, for almost everything on it has romantic and/or sexual significance. However, unlike the bawdier *kyôka* of the 16, 17c and even 18c, this is much less obvious. So much so, in fact that McKee (who caught an allusion in another of the poems) missed it and, I am afraid, the funniest, and to a contemporary Japanese, easiest part of the poem, that was not sexual: it is the inversion of the girl and the octopus. My translation catches it only in its broadest sense, as the inversion in the original is based upon a combination of pun, argot and commonplace, none of which cross the linguistic divide. *Imo* 妹, a girlfriend, darling, mate and an affectionate name for a harlot from the pleasure quarters here puns as its homophone 芋 meaning a taro or potato in the broadest sense of the word. These taro *imo* were said to be a favorite food of the octopus that enough natural history and folk legends had climbing out of the sea to eat them in the full moon of the Fall that they are even found in the fields of old haiku (eg. 蛸追へば蟹も走るや芋畠　太祇) and came to gain the nickname 芋泥棒 *imo-dorobô*, or "potato thief." So, to have the *imo* catch the octopus rather than vice-versa was funny. And it was suggestive because women with prehensile snatches were called *tako*, short for octopus pot (takotsubo) as the octopus grabs hands that are put into them, but most people not knowing that just conflated such women with the creature itself (for details read *Octopussy, Dry Kidney & Blue Spots:* 2007), and the picture showed a woman squatting to hold down the squirming octopus with both knees and one arm (the other is raised signaling for someone to come help her) looking pretty sexy. The eroticism is further brought out by the word used for "slow" (in a stupid and clumsy way) *sosôsa,* which echoes *soso,* the vulva we met in Teitoku's beautiful soft-country (pg. 48). The *clumsiness* at the end of the poem also reveals by counter-point the slang meaning of the *oki,* or sea offshore, at its start; to be offshore, or *oki,* was to be very *skillful*, or manifest deep talent, for which reason it also came to mean a top-level courtesan, a *tayû* (the derivation of this meaning of *oki* is downright Cockney: the area by the beach was called the *heta,* and as that was synonymous with *poor/unskillful* 下手, offshore became *jôzu* 上手 or *skillful*). It is possible the "smoky" mist is meant to evoke the hairiness of the true geisha as opposed to the courtesans who shaved down there, but I would need to know more about clothing and whatnot to make that call. Granted, my "mouse" is opaque to anyone who is not Swedish or has not worked on a Swedish ship (as I have: our *pussy* is their *mouse*). For readers who are not Usanian, *"what a pussy!"* is an insult to the octopus accusing it of being weak. It is not an expression your author would use, nor a sentiment he shares. Puns, like rhyme have their own reason which sane people do not mind. If I used a bit too much translator's license in the re-creations, it was to do proper tribute to the original, which even incompletely read seems beautifully crafted.

ふくハ内おにハの松も色まして みとりめでたき 春の装ひ 亀屋一丸 kameya
fuku wa uchi o-niwa no matsu mo iro mashite midori medetaki haru no yosôi ichimaru
fortune-as4 in, demon=garden's pine too color strengthns green joyous spring's costume

Dressing the Year of the Dog	*A Dog Turns the Corner*
Good Fortune, in! Demons,	*Good Fortune, in! Demons,*
Out in the garden, Old pine	*out in the garden, mind the Fir*
Looks a million $'s – Green;	*Looks a million dollars, green:*
Dressing up is part of Spring.	*Spring will dress an old cur.*

If you recall, *old kyôka* treating the *"Fortune in! Demons out!"* rite of season-parting *setsubun* (generally set on Springrise), played with the parched beans tossed back in over the shoulder or out to symbolize both the bad going out and striking the demons to cause them to flee. That play was sexy, stinky and, even worse – for what can be worse than the runs! While I cannot rule out dirty *surimono* that I have not seen, my impression of the *surimono* poems touching upon this rite in this book is that they are, for better or worse, suitable in tone to serve as a gift for the season and therefore far less outrageous. This one, from an 1800 *surimono* "Dressed up for the Parting of the Seasons" (*Ibid* pl.31) beats the devil-chasing one we saw two chapters ago for punning the slightly truncated charm/exorcism (*fuku wa uchi oni wa soto*) itself into the *oniwa* = hon. garden. "Good fortune ~ garden," with enjambment to both separate and not separate *demon* and *out,* is borrowed from McKee, who explains how or "the poet cleverly bridges the exorcism formula to a description of nature around a house in springtime." I would add that the *garden* being outside also reminds us that *uchi, inside*, is a homophone of *house*. But the poem loses to the devil-chasing one because nothing trumps a pun on, or rather made *by*, the very last syllable of a poem. Turning the mountain, *yama* into the hag *yamamba* was a brilliant example of stopping when you're ahead. Be that as it may, the above is much better than our translations of it. Not only is my *million dollars* anacultural, but 1800 was *not* the Year of the Dog. The bold pivot in the original, which reminds one of those made by surrealists folding a piece of paper for another to continue a picture, is the sort of thing that makes *kyôka* in the original such a thrill to read. I would guess the "green" *midori* alludes to *midorigo,* for the "infant" spring reified by pine seedlings in the picture, and wonder if the *yosôi* either puns on *yoroi*, armor, or *yoso*, outside, as the usual "out" in the charm/exorcism, *soto*, was not in the poem.

~~~~~~

With McKee and his publisher's permission, I would hope to fill a chapter or two with nothing but one or two plates-worth – one, unedited would fill a chapter – of translation+explanation in the next edition. Because the poems that catch my attention are so often those most easily misread – and I treat some of the problematic areas because I happen to find them stimulating and because no permission is needed to reproduce things one is correcting (I have not checked the law, but if it is not so, it surely *should be*, and *that* is enough for me), the easy way to go; but I am afraid this may mislead the reader into thinking I know it all and McKee does not. *That is not true*. McKee has much to teach me and most of us. Please see the Annotated Biblio. entry for balance!

㊤ Snowball to White Snake, McKee to Carpenter ㊤

壺折を水になさしとわらわへのまろめあけたる春のあハ雪　旭 佐?易?方 c1830?
tsubo-ori o mizu ni nasaji to warawabe no marome ag=ketaru haru no awayuki asahi no sajubô
bottle-fold+acc water into get/become-not to/so/and children roll-up=open spring's fluffy/light-snow

With hems tucked up, their dress stays dry but maidens still will not let go:
To stop it from melting, they roll up the fluffy new spring snow.

~~~~~~~~~~~~~~~~~~~~~~~~~~~~~~~~~~~~~~~

With their kimono's tucked up / so as not to get ruined by water / these
young maids / roll it up to open the year / spring's powdery snow – mckee 2008

Who knows why raising one's hem by cinching up the fabric of a robe, or kimono if you would so call it, under an *obi*, wide belt, should be called "jar-fold" *tsubo-ori*, but as McKee notes the idea was to keep it dry – also *water* is an *engo*/association of *bottle* – and to pick up on the pun on "open the year," which, as you can see, failed to fit into my translation. He also provided a passage from *The Tales of Genji* from the *"Twilight Snow of the Asagao Chapter"* (the title of the picture by Gakutei 1786-1855) where the idea of maidens rolling up a huge snowball came from (the *surimono* with three poems of which this, in the middle, was the sweetest, is part of a series, *Eight Views of Genji* by the Fundarika ren, or White Lotus (*kyôka*) Club). Unfortunately, with all this going on, Mckee missed the larger pun, one that makes the poem conceptually comic. *That it does not become water* (*mizu ni nasaji to*) pivots from concern for the kimono to the activity. Now, I may be writing in Florida, but I recall from years 'up North' (Washington D.C. and Tokyo) that snow*balls* last a hell of a lot longer than snow*fall*. The snow here is specifically *that which fell on/in the New Year* and not in the Old one: the girls naturally want to keep it around. So, they make it round, the proper harmonious shape of that season anyway . . .

子宝のつちをも?た?けて早蕨のてうち／＼も愛?らしき春　秋長堂物築?
kodakara no tsuchi o motagete sawarabi no teuchi teuchi mo airashiki haru s.monoyana
child-treasure/s' mallet hold-raising=dirt-lift-up brackn hand-strike x2 evn adorable spring

Our treasure, children	*A child, a treasure,*	*Baby treasures breaking*
raise their magic mallets high	*raises a mallet high up*	*raise the surface of the earth*
with bracken hands	*to pound it down*	*up come clenched fists*
& though they pound away	*Upon the little bracken*	*Even the pushy bracken*
in spring we don't dismay	*Sweet little things in spring*	*adorable in spring birth.*

One of the pleasures museum-published books of surimono bring is the opportunity to work with old script. While Mckee studied it and had others to consult, I can only appeal to my mind's eye, guided by *haikai*-based knowledge. I read *teuchi teuchi* for the above; McKee (2008) has *"teura teura."* Translating *"Raising up / the treasured child's mallet / the young mountain vegetables / pop up fresh and pure / this spring is adorably cute,"* he explains *"The spring is . . . transformed into a young child, the popping up of its warabi, a type of mountain vegetable with a crook at its top, described in terms that would be used for an adorable infant."* Still, he (like everyone but Makoto Ueda and me) provides no word-for-word gloss, so I could only *guess* what *teura* meant to him. A contraction of *te no ura*, the back of the hand? *Fortune-telling by observation of the entire hand?* My respondent, who has not seen the original, trusts an art-person (McKee) more than me – I admit to lack of experience reading script – here, and goes with the fortune-telling *teura*「手占」(手の指をかわるがわる屈伸し、伸ばしたのを陰、屈したのを陽として、易の八卦(け)に当てて占うこと。てうらない) はワラビの先端の形の、これも見立てです。 While plentiful precedents for both bracken fist-striking and fortune-telling may be found, I bet against McKee *and* my respondent on this one. ♪   I first put the poem in the notes, but realizing it was an extraordinarily good one transferred it to the text. What is most impressive is how it starts with children, pivots the raised mallet into dirt-raising (popping up) baby bracken, which, then, pivots back to being children's hands (*sawarabi*, pretty/young-bracken, was common literary idiom for slender hands+fore-arms) when they strike. Such a pivot followed by a second reverse pivot is quite rare.

Our little Treasures with bracken hands their mallets raise – Horrible Indeed, to see them pound away – and, yet, in Spring it is Adorable!

~~~~~~

How Spring delights when bracken bairne, her treasures, push up earth and open their little hands to wave and clap away in mirth!

The first reading above is identical to the first of my previous three. The second extends the third, taking an improbable reading of the Spring at the end of the original composed by the poet whose (family) name happens to began with Autumn. We may imagine something even less likely, such as Spring's Princess Sao with the magic toy mallet in her hand striking the mountain here, there and everywhere causing things to pop up, but it might be better to wait until I find a poem that actual writes that before making that reading, which would seem to be McKee's. The surimono, commissioned by Magao's Four-Directions group, dated 1822, features a picture of children's toys on a lacquered tray by Katsushika Hokusai. It is one of the enormous number of fine still-lives Japan's artists so excelled in. The poem is one of three.

　　立ツ春はをさなきなから梅柳めはな立ちよく見ゆるめでたさ　　窓乃屋
tatsu haru wa osanaki nagara ume yanagi mehanadachi yoku miyuru medetasa madonoya
arriving/standing spring-as-for←infantile-while →plum willow bud=eye-blossom=nose-standing/features   good/beautiful appear/seen-can-be joyfulness/auspiciousness

♪ *Something to Celebrate* ♪

*Spring in her cradle stands and though still in their infancy
the lovely features of the willow and plum are plain to see!*

~~~~~~

*With freshly risen spring / Still young / The fine features of buds and flowers /
Of plums and willows rise up / a fortunate sight to see*   – trans. mckee 2006
*While spring arrives / still in the bud of youth, / the plum and willow /
reveal their lovely features, / bringing joy all around.*   – trans. carpenter

This is one of two poems with an 1834 Utagawa Kunisada print of Okane the strong woman of Ômi calmly stepping on the lead of a run-away horse, stopping it in its tracks while holding her tub of laundry with one arm and keeping her hem closed with the other. McKee notes Kunisada's teacher did one in 1822 and variations by rivals such as Kuniyoshi or students, one of which by Taito II (undated) shows her as a courtesan stepping on the string of a horse *kite*, which Hokusai includes in a still life. In other words, *surimono* built a visual and poetic vocabulary. Carpenter's translation is better, but feeling the conceptual wit was still too subtle to catch, I spelled it out, losing space for the *joy* (hence, the title). The poem may be a generic greeting for the Year of the Horse print, but I bet Okane showed her power as an infant.= 平行

㊦ Snowball to White Snake, McKee to Carpenter ㊦

弁才のめくミや 口をあきの方に うたも はくしやの あらたなる春? 森羅亭萬象
benzai no megumi ya kuchi o akinokata ni uta mo haku ja no aratanaru haru   shinratei manzô II ♪
benzai's blessng/s!/?/:/, mouth+acc open⇒lucky=sunrise-directn-in spit/disgrge⇒white snake's re/newng sprng

♪ Watershed Year for an Old Man with Hair the Color of his Muse's Snake ♪

Blessed by Benzai, I face the right way to see her Snake and spit
Out this verse – Has Spring spoken through my old mouth, or its?

~~~~~~
The blessings of Benzaiten -- / Even the mouth / Of this old body /
Opens and spits out poems / In the new spring of the snake – trans. mckee 2006
~~~~~~

With Goddess Benzai's blessing, / I open my mouth to utter poems / in this year's auspicious direction, / just as the white serpent / appears anew in spring – tr. carpen.

It is not so lonely translating *kyôka* with company. This was the last of my double company, i.e., poems spotted in both Carpenter and McKee, before having to return the latter to the library. Here, Carpenter pretty much pegged it. The entire message of the original – minus the wit, lost in the explication – is there, and only the initial line, which McKee caught, is a bit off. McKee seems to have missed something else and I think I know why because he, like me, is so intent to read meaning into everything – crediting the poets with creating a cornucopia in each poem – that, also like me, he sometimes finds what is not really there, or is but only in a vestigial rather than active mode, and stops too soon to find the actually intended wit. Since this sort of imagination, or creative reading, as Emerson called it, finds much more wit that was indeed intended than a plodding scholar could, and much faster, which is what counts most for museum catalogues where one cannot give a world of time to each wild poem, I do not in the least think the attendant errors diminish the larger accomplishment and, in the long run, because we are more likely to remember something learned after the embarrassment of erring, he, or she, who errs and errs again – this was in his 2008 book which had proportionately less errors than the 2006 book – will, as Piet Hein once put in a grook, end up learning more and erring less and less (though I am not sure I am getting to the less and less part yet as I cannot help biting-off more than I can chew). In other words, McKee did not seem to recognize that *aki no kata* meant the auspicious direction for that year. Issa used it alot:
..

大雪や出入の穴も明の方　一茶
ôyuki ya deiri no ana mo akinokata

Heavy snow, the mouth
Of our tunnel facing out
Opens ye Lucky Way!

Snow may have been auspicious, but Issa lived in Snow Country where they often had to tunnel out of their homes. Here, we imagine a turn in the tunnel to bring Issa out in the most propitious direction to start the year. Here, as in the *kyôka,* the 明 light and/or opening of the New Year is first readable as opening up. Also the use of "hole" rather than the more common "mouth" in the original brings to mind the primal birth and a cavern dwelling. But, perhaps the more clearly *kyôku* of Issa's *akinokata ku* never actually says that word. It alludes to the bright/light connotation of the Chinese character in it by referring to its contrary "dark" (though *kurai*, as it is pronounced, is not a perfect antonym as it does not also mean *closed*): *New Year's Shelf / from the darkside out comes / a lucky mouse* とし棚や闇い方より福鼠 *toshidana ya kurai kata yori fuku-nezumi*). But, as I was saying, McKee knew about and explained the concept of the lucky direction of the year – usually called *ehô* – as it was in the preface of the poem which also noted the poet was celebrating his sixtieth birthday, but did not recognize the less used *akinokata* as a word that might have been looked up. Instead, he found *aki* homonyms, such as *growing weary of* and *autumn* which reflected the poet's growing old and which contrasted nicely with the *arata naru* renewal, which he associated with the snake's ability to shed its skin. He also points out something Carpenter, in the smaller space given to the poem, does not mention: Benzaiten was the Muse of Music and Poetry. I only recalled her as the Goddess of Prosperity and Beauty whose albino snake symbolized the good luck, or supernatural, element involved, still reflected today in the reports of various albino creatures every New Year in the Sinosphere (for white sea cucumbers, see the Sundry section of *Rise Ye Sea Slugs!* 2003) and – hey, males outnumbered females two, three or even four to one in Edo! – bred a bevy of Benzai performers who stripped and let snakes have access to their privates as they were often mentioned in *senryû*. Yet, for all my awareness of Benzaiten and the image in my head which includes her biwa (moon-lute), I had forgotten she was a Muse, and hence owe more to McKee than Carpenter for my translation, even if Carpenter's is closer. McKee is right to see the Muse has renewed the poet's creativity, helped him shed and thus, overcome, the burdens of old age. And note the poetry in McKee's reading. He has the poem go from old to new, from age to rebirth and that, in a broad sense, is correct.

One thing was missing from *both* explanations. As most *surimono* are meant for gifts, there were few birthday celebrations/thanksgivings of this sort – or at least no others *I* recall in the three books of theirs I read – and presumably for that reason neither author picks up on *the significance of that 60th birthday*. Completing 12 full-cycles of the New Year animal zodiac made it ritually the year of one's rebirth and return to what Taoism thought of as the original foolishness, which is something akin to the naive (in the good sense of *naive*, which Japanese even today use when they use it as an imported foreign word, *naibu*) "first-heart," 初心 shoshin, one was supposed to return to every New Year, which McKee did a fine job of introducing in his overall introduction. In haikai poetry, that was marked by foolish poems that year or the following one – Japanese poets faced the same problem the West did with its Millennium: whether the 00 year was the new start or the 01 year (See my *Fifth Season* (2007) for examples of which Issa's are the best known). This *kyôka,* punning a sacred *white snake* with a rude *spitting/uttering* is a fine example of the extreme license allowed the poet in his year to be (or at least start) foolish. And, he was indeed one with the snake, as he was born in the Year thereof 60 years before.

The picture for the print shows a white snake wrapped around a pine tree. While Benzaiten was a sort of St Christopher for sailors and McKee mentions a white sea serpent, it looks like a harmless species. Carpenter identifies it, or rather the tree as a famous one ("the Yôgo matsu at the Myôkendô in the Yanagishima district of Edo"). I would point out that from the placement of the red rising sun just over the snake's right shoulder – if snakes had shoulders – the snake faces North-North-west, which seems to suggest the poem before it and the poet, presumably in front– where he would have to be to write the poems – faces southeast or south, which was the lucky direction for that year.

㊤ Reading Surimono – Literature Over the Radar ㊤
青柳をつゝらこにして鶯乃桜に寝よきとくらくれはや　四方歌垣真顔
aoyagi o tsuzurako ni shite uguisu no sakura ni ne yoki togura kurebaya yomonoutagaki magao
green-willow+acc wickerbasket-into making warbler's cherry-in sleep-easy den give-wish

> *Would I could weave a green willow into a basket, a nest to keep*
> *This warbler in the cherry bloomshade happy to sing and sleep.*

~~~~~~

> *Of some green willow a basket I would make for a nest to keep*
> *The warbler in a cherry tree where it could get some sleep!*

My second reading follows the translation in *Reading Surimono*, "I should like to place / a wicker basket, woven / from green willow branches, / in a cherry tree as a nest / for the warbler to take a nap," minus *branches* that a willow no more has than a woman does, and with *my* image of a single young willow made into a basket. The explanation puzzles me: *"Magao offered a more typical New Year's kyôka, suggesting that he would like to see a warbler in a cherry tree instead of a plum tree, its normal home by poetic convention."* Typical because overturning a convention is more common in that genre than allusions to things Chinese? The comparison was to the previous poem with clouds stopped by the *uguisu's* song that would have gone right past me were it not explained as I did not know of Qin Qing's "cloud-halting song" from the Daoist classic *Book of Liezi*. But does the bird need a nap because it is exhausted from its cloud-stopping concert? Does Magao think the song repetitive – as noted before, this bird is no mockingbird – and want some quiet? My first reading is altogether different. Since cherry in Japanese usually refers to one in bloom, and that would not happen while the plum bloomed, we may have the wish to keep the joyous song alive once the New Year's season ends by passing it on to the mid-to-late Spring cherry blossoms. As the willow's new green starts to come out while the plum blooms and is fully leaved by the time the cherries do, it provides a temporal bridge. Also, Magao may play on Bashô's *ku* wondering if the bird was not the soul of the sleeping beauty of a tree (*uguisu o tama ni nemuru ka taoyanagi*) – Bashô alluded to the butterfly about when Chuang-tzu slept and, as Ueda (1992) points out, may have coined the word *taoyanagi*, for *taoyame*, or "graceful lady."

Without some explanation, I feel the poem dies. My respondent, who has not seen the original guesses the poem should end not *togura kurebaya* とくらくれはや but とくれくれはや(暮れか暮ればや). Though this is not settled, I could not help putting my two-bits into the reading of the above poem as it was the third poem – the clean-up batter – on the very first plate of the 294 in the Catalog and I had seen enough of Magao thanks to McKee's books to expect more from him. The print, a classic *shikishi*, or square one, by Takashima Chiharu depicts a masked *gagaku* dancer whom I would have taken for a Javanese shadow-puppet character. Actually he is Kitoku (C. Gui de) a Xiongnu (western nomad) noble who surrendered to the Chinese in 61 BCE. There are barely recognizable plum blossom crests on his sleeves and train, but no warbler. The first poem cleverly hides "noble Kitoku" in a poem that gets the scent of the first in before the sound of the second which the second poem picks up and turns into a cloud-stopper which the third, Magao's, if my second reading gets it right, passes into the future. Carpenter notes the second poet who made much of his Kyôto court connections was showing off his knowledge of Chinese classics. Elsewhere in *Reading Surimono*, we learn he was dubbed (?) a *kyôka master* by a noble who claimed descent from the ancient Under-the-Chestnut

(Kurinomoto) line of *kyôka* (see my Broad Short History, pg. 608). But reader, can you guess why *this* particular *suriban* got first billing? Perhaps someone familiar with museum catalogues might, but I could not. Neither date, theme, size, shape, picture type or poet-*surimono* commissioner mattered one iota. . . It follows the alphabetic order of the names by which the *artists* usually went, from (Takashima) *Chiharu* to (Ukiyo) *Utayoshi*. To me, that is odd, but I, who have put together *this* book, can hardly criticize it! So, where to *now?* I love willows, so –

ふく風の手をもてよりやかけつらん柳のいとに春雨の糸 天馬楼和吉住 1820
fuku kaze no te o mote   yori ya kaketsuran yanagi no ito ni harusame no ito   tenmarô
blowng wnd's hands+acc bringng braid+emph wllw-thred-w/ springrain-threads wakizumi

Will the deft hands of the wind come to braid them again?
The threads of the willow with the threads of spring rain!

Here, the picture by Kyôichi shows a man with a Heian period hat and Edo period *geta* walking under a willow. Carpenter provides the legend: Ono no Tôfu deciding to persevere and become a great calligrapher after watching a frog try over and over to leap up to a willow hanging over a pond, finally succeed. The cross-dressing, he notes, may come from a kabuki play of the same. The translation *As the breeze blows, / will the hands of the wind / caress the willow branches / that are now entangled / with the strands of rain?* was a bit off. Too bad, for the poet would seem to be cheerfully going along with the *hybrid* motif Carpenter further elaborates elsewhere in the book where the left-hand plate (in another museum) is also introduced. It includes a poem which would instigate a song/poem match between said frog and warbler, which takes us back to the preface of the *Ancient and Now Anthology*, i.e., the 905 *Kokinshû*, and provides a clear New Year link. And, now, let us follow that *ito,* the thread/string/strands, to a *surimono* with a Shigenobu II print:

咲花の木陰によりて春雨の糸に心の駒つなくかも 護心亭三猿 goshintei san'en
saku hana no kokage ni yorite harusame no ito ni kokoro no koma tsunagu kamo
bloomng blossms' treeshade-to approachng sprngrain's thread/s-by heart's-colt/s tie

Finding shelter below this cherry tree in bloom, she stands – but will
the strands of spring-rain hitch her heart's horses and keep them still?

~~~~~~

How beautiful she looks soaked in the rain, standing in a sea of bloom,
The Princess of the Dragon Realm must be feeling ecstasy not gloom

harusame ni nureshi sugata zo utsukushiki hana no namima ni tatsunomiyahime bokubokutei kineo
nodoka naru hinata yori nao harusame ni nurete ureshiki hana no kagemon shinryûtei harukaze

Here, there were *three* poems for 1834, Year of the Horse, but I combined the last two into one to save space and drop what only works with the picture. All the translations were fine and the first includes a fine adaption of the metaphor: *"strong enough to rein in the colt of unbridled passion."* Had the poet not signed another poem with a Shigenobu print, I would have thought Goshintei San'en a pseudonym, for the name includes protect-heart and monkey; if you recall, the monkey was the ego that controlled the horse, the id. But why a dragon woman in the Year of the Horse? Perhaps because women who morphed into dragons tended to be slaves of passion, so too vice-versa. Be that as it may, bringing the Dragon Princess into the old poetic conceit of 'waves of bloom' was *brilliant* and I wish I had found the poems for my *Cherry Blossom Epiphany*. But what I really *want* to know is whether the idea of a strings of spring-rain came from the noodles *harusame* or those prints ♪

㊤ Reading Surimono – Literature Over the Radar ㊦

幾春も かわらぬ御代は うら嶋の 明て若やく新玉手箱　梅花堂煉方
iku haru mo kawaranu miyo wa urashima no akete wakayagu aratama tebako baikadô nerikata
howmany springs unchanging reign-as4 urashima's opening juvenates new-gem notionsbox   late-1820's

This year again unchanged for countless springs Your Rule we know
Will ever be a Youth-restoring treasure box of Urashima Tarô!

How many Springs	*How many Springs*
unchanged Your Realm	*unchanged our august age*
Where every year	*Where each new year*
Tarô's box opens to restore	*Urashima's box unlocks*
not age but youthful cheer!	*to bring youth back here!*

Each year once more for countless springs Your Rule, we know
Unchanged, a Youth-restoring treasure box of Urashima Tarô!

The first of three poems on a surimono dated late-1820's – maybe 1826, because it would put the Year of the Dragon upside-down, as is the effect of opening said precious box Japan's Rip Van Winkled Fisherman brought back from the Dragon Palace. The Utagawa Toyohiro print shows the happy fisherman heading home on a huge turtle (like most such, with a mossy cape expressing hoary age and claws on its feet rather than fins!) with the jet black box. Urashima Tarô would open the "not-to-be-opened" box when grief-stricken to find his family dead for generations, and quickly age to join them, while, in the poem, the box opens bringing youth – hence, my respondent thinks the *ara* (new) may pun as an exclamation of surprise and, as I made explicit, good cheer. The *Reading Surimono* (2008) translation is, *"In a never-changing realm, / spring after spring / Urashima Tarô / opens the jeweled box / to bring youth again."* It is beautiful but, I feel, a bit off. Though the only link between the first and second half of the original is the suffix, ~ *wa,* usually romanized for lack of a better word, "as for," so it is hard to prove what it means but I avoided "in ~ " because I felt that, while a fairy tale was involved and evoked an enchanted mood suitable for the New Year, the poem was, first of all, meant to celebrate the benevolent reign as that was not only suitable but almost de rigor. The second poem:

年なミのかへる手箱を浦嶋も明てめでたき玉の初春　万流亭　世冨
toshinami no kaeru tebako o urashima mo akete medetaki tama no hatsuharu manryûtei
year-wave's retrning handbx/cskt+acc urashma evn opnng joyful gem's first-spring   yotomi ↑

A magic casket to turn back the waves of time that even the ghost
of Urashima might open with joy, such is the new spring we toast!

Here, contrary to the first poem, I bring in the fisherman more than the *Reading Surimono* translation, *"Returning on the waves / of time, the handbox of Urashima is opened / to bring good fortune / in this jewel-like spring."* Though I added *ghost* and *toast*, my reading is closer to the original, describing the subject, the "gem/precious/beautiful first-spring," *i.e.,* the New Year, *as* said box miraculously slowing rather than speeding time. It plays with the rebounding *tachi-kaeru* wave, one metaphor of New Year's arrival and an even more common trope, wrinkles as waves and vice versa. Actually, there was some call for the ghost. The "jewel-like" (gem/precious/beautiful) *tama* is a homophone for *soul* or *spirit*, and setting things right for ghosts was a major theme for Japanese drama. The third poem (*kokoro ni mo norishi keshiki zo kame no se ni hinode medetaki haru no urashima* shinratei), then, had all of us, or our *kokoro* (heart/mind/spirit) watching that joyous sunrise while riding on the turtle with Urashima, whose name, meaning Bay Island, gives us a faint alternative view of the sun rising over the top of a turtle island. The second plate in the Catalog also intrigues me for it exhibits two impeccably well-done types of *kyôka* both of which lose all their wit in translation. The first is by Momonoya Nagatane:

桃の弓芦の矢はよしとらずともいるぞめでたき年の夜の豆　桃の屋永胤
momo no yumi ashi no ya wa yoshi torazu to mo iru zo medetaki toshi no yo no mame
peach bw reed arrw-as4 fine, take/catch-not evn shoot=parch! joyous/lucky year-night's beans

> *A peach wood bow & reed arrow may not kill but they can still*
> *Harrow demons on New Year's Eve as good as any beans will.*

Such bows were used at Year End exorcisms called *tsuina* or *oni-yarai, "drive out the demons"* at the Imperial palace which got the idea from China, then spread to shrines and temples where men wearing demon masks were "shot." Not knowing that, I first imagined a familiar talisman against bad luck, the dinky *hamaya* bow simply kept until returned to the Shrine, *"A peach wood bow w/ arrow of reed though never drawn still charms /But shoot=parch your beans for New Year's Eve keep you from harm."* when we reach the *mame*=beans at the end, the *iru* in *iru zo,* or, *"(they/we still) shoot!"* retrospectively evokes its homophone "parch." The ceremony was eventually combined with bean throwing on the *setsubun*. The *iru* pun is not mentioned by Carpenter. No matter, the poem defies translation anyway! The second poem, by Edanoya Chitoyo 枝屋千豊 addresses the subject of the picture, the God of Prosperity/happiness), Fuku-no-Kami, who dances in a Kyôgen drama by that name. The Romanization reveals the wit. Each *ku* starts with a syllabet of the name:

FUji no ne no KUmo ni toyosaka NOboru hi mo KAsumu ka kesa wa MIe-gakure suru
fuji's peak's clouds in poshly climbng sun evn hazing? thismorn-as4 seeing-hidden does

> *This morning is even the Sun who shined through clouds to climb Fuji*
> *haze-hidden? Now and then it's peek-a-boo – I'd say that all is buji!*

> *The brilliant Sun that climbs Mt Fuji lighting up those lucky clouds;*
> *Even he is blessed w/ so much haze we hardly get to see him now.*

The poem itself is not bad. The translation, *"As the sun climbs / the peak of Mt. Fuji this morning, / it's hidden and then appears / amidst abundant clouds"* conflates the clouds mentioned early-on with the hazing over symbolic of the date, New Year's. My first reading is ridiculous (a gift for loony bilinguals!); the second makes explicit the subtle wit. Next, a misplaced (dm:2006?8? jc:2008?) poem re. bird-tracks=writing:

hakaze o ba itoinagara mo saku hana ni tori no ashi ato tsukeshi tanzaku nagaiki hisami
wing-breeze+emph. hating still bloom blossms-to bird's footprints' placed poemcards

> *There among the blossoms that so hate the wind of their wings*
> *Are those not the tracks of birds upon our new poem hangings?*

㊥ Reading Surimono – Literature Over the Radar ㊤
佐保姫の衣の浦に春たちて　かすみの袖をぬふ沖の舟　　南枝春告 1799
saohime no koromo no ura ni haru tachite kasumi no sode o nuu oki no fune　nanshi no harutsugu

Spring comes to Princess Sao's Robe-within Bay to cut the fabric for
Her sleeves of mist loosely sewn by the tacking boats offshore.

~~~~~~~~~~~~~~~~~~~~~~~~~~~~~

As the New Year arrives / at the Bay of Koromo, / Saohime, goddess of spring,
wears robes woven with mist / covering boats in the offing. – trans. carpenter

The Hokusai picture from *An Array of Beauties for the Year of the Sheep* shows a girl pulling a piece of red tie-died fabric taut between her delicate little mouth on the one side and her delicate little fingers on the other while her free hand seems to pinch or pin a crease. Carpenter evidently added a description of Sao, "goddess of spring" to obtain something rare in Japanese-English translation, a rhyme. The humor in the original is conceptual, for there are a handful of fabric and sewing-related words worked into the original, with the wittiest *making boat/s do the actual sewing* (*nuu*). I added "tacking" to clarify the metaphor, for, if I am not mistaken, it was overlooked. Still, Carpenter improves the poem by uniting the Goddess with her Spring, so an ideal translation might start with his and replace his "covering" with "sewn by" or "tacked by." Most stitching for traditional Japanese fine clothing is no more than basting or tacking which is easily pulled out and re-sewn each time the garment is washed. Don't get me wrong. I am cheating from an illustrated reverse dictionary. I have crocheted and woven things, but my knowledge of sewing terms is so poor that I did not even try to translate the many sartorial *kyôka* by 19c female poets and only the boat-as-needle metaphor excited me enough to do the above. Trying them now, it is *still* hopeless. Take these two by the most elegant poetess ever, anywhere (judging from one print of her fully clothed shown seated from behind!) Chie no Naishi 智恵内子 or, the Little Ignoramus: 1) *Over the winter, even a Mountain princess has her needlework to do – / Tall-Back Falls marks what she sews; Cloth-stretch Falls keeps it true* (山姫も冬は氷のはりしごと瀧津せぬひやとづる布引 吾妻曲 *yamahime mo fuyu wa* . . . 1786) and *Princess Sao's robe of mist so newly done – Would you see Basting- / Ville come before it pulls out – there is no time for wasting!* さほ姫の霞の衣ぬひたてにかゝるしつけのをがは町哉　徳和 1785 *saho hime no kasumi no* . . .). With the first, the needlework is for small-sales/change which pivots from the homophonous "ice," the Takitsuse Falls which puns in the measure of the back also alludes to Tagitsuhimenomigoto, a goddess, and the second fall need not be called a fall because the proper name was known. My rhyme could not keep what was a good poem alive. With the second, the basting is not in *the name of the town* but the thread for the basting puns with small in Ogawa, or "Smallstream/ brooksville. In retrospect, both of these, like the tacking boat poem, were toponym dependent. Places, especially when unknown to foreign readers, do not translate, much less pun. On the opposite page to Hokusai's maiden sewing, another a woman holds an open fan and,
..

かゆ杖にふりむく妹が身ハよれて糸の柳の腰にめも付く　　浅草庵
kayuzue ni furimuku imo ga mi wa yorete ito no yanagi no koshi ni me mo tsuku asakusa an
gruel-stck-to turnng-faces girl's body-as4 twstng thread-wllw-hip/waist-to buds/eyes attach

Turning to face the gruel stick the girl's slim body twists
And all our eyes are drawn to the willow's budding hips.

~~~~~~~~~~~~~~~~~~~~~~~~~~~~~

Turning to face the gruel stick how the maiden's body twists
Eyes braiding with its strands are drawn to pussy willow hips.

Carpenter's translation, *"During 'gruel-stick' rites, a young girl looks back as she twists and turns, with hips as slender as boughs of budding willow"* is fine except for making "rite" explicit, which is wrong. His explanation was invaluable for I would not have recognized the woman was *a samurai wife* by her hat, and that matters because her buttocks were wacked so she would bear a boy, something particularly important to samurai families. Without that information, one could not connect the poem and picture. Gruel usually means the Seventh Day seven greens/herbs, but this is a second rite that takes place on the so-called "Small New Year" or "Woman's New Year" on the Fifteenth Day, *i.e.,* the full-moon. The *hips* are where the willow limbs bend over and *twisting* naturally puns with *braiding* because the slender pendulant limbs are called *threads* in Japanese; but what makes the poem worthy is not that simple confluence of terms, but the artless pun on *"me* め*"* meaning either " *bud* 芽 " or " *(human) eyes* 目 " in the last *ku*. As this Small New Year is in my yet unwritten second volume of *The Fifth Season*, it was my first time to learn of this rite. Luckily, I have some old haiku almanacs (*saijiki*) with me out here in the woods of Florida, so when I read of "playfully tapping women's buttocks with sticks of wood used to stoke the fire heating azuki-bean gruel" (Carpenter), when I had imagined a stick used to *stir* said gruel (which I bet includes the lunar part of the broken mirror *mochi* rice-cake), I could immediately check about this important matter. What did I discover? We are *both* right. The stick came from those gathered to heat the gruel and it was shaved on one end, which was burnt – probably used to light the fire (I'll check out such detail for that book, but not now) – and used to stir the pot with the other end. Since one haiku mentions the scent of citron known by a woman's behind (粥杖や柚の香にうしろ(後？) 知られたり 綾足 *kayuzue ya yuzu no ka ni ushiro (ato?)shiraretari* ryôsoku? rinsoku? 18c? 講談社大歳時記ですが、「柚」が「袖」と誤字！又「うしろ」だと七に珍し字余り、それも後の読み違いから？), it would seem that was the end used for whacking. Another haiku, also probably predating the *kyôka,* has "A woman hit / while *pretending* to flee / the gruel stick!" (粥杖に逃ぐるふりしてうたれけり 三敲 *kayuzue ni niguru furi shite utarekeri* sankyô?)
..
新玉のふミ初むる時影さした鳥の跡より客乃来るらし 花実亭常盤
aratama no fumi-somuru toki kage sashita tori no ato yori kyaku no kuru rashi
new-gem/year/sun's step=writing/letter-starting time/when shadow/silhouette cast,
    bird's/s' track/s more than guest's coming seems   kajitsutei tokiwa ca. 1822

Writing the first love letter / of the New Year, rather than words / that look like footprints of birds / better that she see the shadow / of a patron on the paper door. – trans. Carpenter

Just as brush to paper goes for her First Letter of the Year,
She must fly and bird-prints wait – Her first guest is here!

Bird tracks mean *writing.* Carpenter notes the play upon a saying that a bird's shadow on a paper door/window means a guest will come and, continuing the train of thought from the poem preceding this one, makes the neutral original clearly happy, while I, looking at Kunisada's print showing a courtesan, pen in one hand, paper in the other, just about to write what the length of paper suggests will be a long letter, *glaring* over her shoulder with a *pronounced* scowl, instead feel that the poet meant she was disturbed by having to meet a client so early with no time off at the start of the year, just when she was writing the one she loved. As "a guest is a *kami,* god" (*okyaku wa kamisan*), she will have to drop the *kami*=paper she is about to write on and allow him to brush her. But, *note that I may well be wrong*. My respondent, a poet, finds the poem is awkward at best, and feels that, picture aside, this courtesan probably writes and fires off letter after letter (collective first-letters) and a client coming that fast shows she is a one busy harlot! (で、らし)

㊥ Reading Surimono – Literature Over the Radar ㊦

天の戸を秘？らく扇に君か代をあふく要裳！玉乃初春　麻屋直成 late-1820's
amanoto o hiraku ôgi ni kimigayo o augu kaname mo tama no hatsuharu asanoya naonari
heaven's door+acc. opens/ing (=secret ch., visual pun) fan=deepwisdom/skill your-realm/age revere=fans(vb.) !=fulcrum=eye even(=robe-train ch.visual pun!) ball/gem/precious first-spring

& the pivot of her fan is the jewel of our new Spring,
Opening the door of Heaven's Cave to bless our Lord

Out comes the spring, this fan that opens from its pivot hidden
in her sleeve fans the desire of our lord and does as it is bidden.

As her fan opens a new Spring shines out the door of Heaven's Cave:
May our Reverence keep You cool and evermore Your Kingdom save!

As the rock door of the cave / opened, ushering in / a new imperial realm, the fan / pivots on its jeweled pin, / precious as the onset of spring. – trans. carpenter 2008

I might not come up with a good re-creation of this poem though I had a whole night – it would definitely require some help from one's dreams – and day to spare. That is the very reason I introduce it. After all, isn't this whole book about poems hitherto impossible to translate? Well, here, there is no "hitherto." I failed. Carpenter, by explicating the more obvious pivots and puns for their information, does somewhat better, aside from his "new imperial realm" which seems to indicate a change of Emperor when there was none between 1819 and 1848. There are three pivots of which one is one of the three standard (sound-based) puns, and two rare visual puns, if I read correctly. Re. the visual puns, I doubted my eyes about whether I really saw a 秘 or *secret/precious* where 開 is usual for "open" (and odd for being used in an *onyomi* reading for a *kunyomi* verb) until I saw an even clearer character 裳 meaning a complex multilayered and creased outer kimono train worn by women in the Imperial palace – exactly what the woman wore in the picture – for *mo*, which is simply an emphatic and/or "even" usually written with one phonetic letter も. The first pivot is the *hiraku,* which first serves to "open" the cave-door, then, as is, attach to the fan as a gerund (English cannot do so without adding an "ing") and simultaneously lets the *ôgi* 扇 seem to be the cause of the door's opening by a pun, a homophone that is hard to catch (奥義), but not *too* hard, for even my vocabulary-handicapped MS-Word software had it on the tip of its keys: it means the *arcana, penetralia*, the deep inner secrets of things or, less grandiosely, alludes to the dance and song of the goddess Umezume that got the Sun Goddess to open the door a crack and the ability of the strong-hand God to get that rock moved and hold it open so life had the light it needed to dawn. That brings us to *Kimigayo,* which could mean the Emperor, his rule, his age or any man's age (if reverently mentioned), which is worshipped or revered, *aogu* but even that is read one is reminded of the fan for rather than the clear 仰ぐ it is written in phonetic letters making it very easy to think of its homophone, meaning to fan or encourage 扇ぐ・煽ぐ. This verb does seem a bit odd gerunded to the *kaname,* or literal pivot (of the fan) that follows and, I think, is only justified by a mock punned caesura, the *kana*, which, helps bring-out the *me* part of the word, which, sounding like "eye" (the etymology of *kaname* includes crab-eye *kani no me,* deer & mosquito eye, both *ka no me*), pivots to eye-*ball*, with that *ball* then pivoting into gem/jewel/precious, the standard epithet for the New Spring or Year, which concludes the poem which began only 31 syllabets before with *Heaven*. In the meantime, as I unsuccessfully sought a magical translation, which is to say, *solution*, I looked up "pivot" in the OED, hoping there might be *something* to help me. Finding *pivilo* was of unsure derivation, maybe a *pin*, *dibble* or *penis*, etc. did not help, but I was *delighted* to find an early description of, and judgment upon, the word *as it applied to Japanese poetry* (!). Both are by Basil H Chamberlain: *Trans. of Asiatic Society, Japan* V 86 (1877); & *Class. Poetry Japanese* (1880), respectively:

> A more complicated species of pun, occurring when a word with two meanings is used only once as a sort of pivot on which two wheels turn. In this case, the first part of the poetical phrase has no logical end, and the latter part no logical beginning.

> The 'pivot' is a more complicated device, and one which in any European language, would be not only unsupportable, but impossible, resting as it does, on a most peculiar type of *jeu de mots*.

紅くまの初日めてたく市川に鯰のかゝる凧の釣糸 文桜舎直樹 bunôsha naoki
beniguma no hatsuhi medetaku ichikawa ni namazu no kakaru tako no tsuri-ito
red-shading's first- day = sun's joyous ichi-river-in/at catfish's catching kite's fishing line/tail

The actor's first makeup is brilliant / as the first sunrise of the year / shines over the Ichikawa stream / where the catfish is caught / by a fishing line tied to a kite. jtc.

*The fishing string of a kite, dangles a hooked catfish merrily
o'er the Ichikawa with Edo's first sun in red make-up verily*

*A catfish hangs from a kite over the Ichikawa – Thrilling
to see against a kabuki-red first sun, ahoy, that string!*

*Danjûrô's first makeup red as sun rise over the river
Ichikawa where catfish pull on lines tied to kites*

*First Make-up, First Play, we celebrate
The First Sun, red in rising may it stay
on the Ichikawa where Catfish pulls
the tail of a kite, the tail of a kite*

The Utagawa Kuniyasu print accompanying this poem shows the awesome red striped – I would call it *war-paint* for lack of a better term in English – *Shibaraku* face of Danjûrô VII painted on a huge kite with the *Namako Bôzu*, or catfish monk, standing in front of him facing away from us but, judging from the body language, taken aback. Carpenter explains that the catfish monk was played by Danjûrô's boy who would later become Danjûrô VIII and that this young man, awed by and failing to measure up to his larger-than-life dad, ended up committing suicide in his early thirties. But, kite fishing? Do we imagine the kite D.VII lifting D.VIII up, up, and away? Did Japanese, like some Oceanic folk, use kites for fishing? My respondent notes the character *river* 川 resembles the strings on the giant kite . . . The poem caught my attention as a prime example of a Japanese-style poem where everything modifies the noun at poem's end. The *string/line* only flows smoothly into everything by being placed at the poem's head in English or demoted to a mere part-player (*by* a fishing line). Carpenter does well to get pretty much everything into his reading though even his elegantly pivoting second line cannot completely save the poetry.

㊦ Reading Surimono – Literature Over the Radar ㊤
角文字のいそがぬ春の日のあしをたのミて牛にのる人はたそ　百囀舎梅鳥 1821-2
tsuno moji no isoganu haru no hi no ashi o tanomite ushi ni noru hito wa ta so　hyakutensha baichô
horn-lttr's hurry-not spring-day's/sun's legs/pace/beams+acc asking ox-on mounts person-as4 who?

> *Who is it that would ride upon an ox to put the cornute 'U'*
> *into 'unhurried' and travel like sunlight on a spring day?*　haft.+*au*.

> *Who is it that won't blow his horn but rides cornute while the sun*
> *moves slowly as his lettered ox until spring's day is done?*

The first reading is by Haft (in Carp. 2008) except I changed "that mounted" to "is it that would ride," "on" to "upon," "so he can" to "to," "horned" to "cornute" and "i" to "U," though "U" is of course wrong, since い is *i*. With that last change, I felt my doctored Haft beat my overly convoluted rhymed verse. In Japanese, the *i* is the first letter of *isoganu*, "unhurried," as is *u* in English, *and* the English *U* does look like horns! In the delightful picture by Hokkei, *"The intinerant renga poet Botanka Shôhaku"* sits upon an ox that not only is slow but lies on his belly, head cocked to the side as if to listen to what the poet is reads though his mouth is not open. As Haft notes, the horn-letter idea is said to have come from a 31-syllabet poem one might call a *kyôka* sent as a message from a lonely Princess Esshi (1259-1332) to her father, the Emperor Go Saga, whom she was not getting to see much of:

ふたつ文字牛の角文字直ぐな文字歪み文字とぞ君は覚ゆる
futatsu moji ushi no tsuno moji sugu no moji yugamu moji to zo kimi wa oboyuru
two-lttr, cow/ox's horn-lttr straight-lttr bendng lttr+emph. you/lord-as4 remembr/long4

> *One letter is two*
> *One is like ox horns*
> *One straight and true*
> *One is bent, your last clue*
> *My message is* 'I miss you!'

Here is half of the Japanese syllabary, あいえおうかきくけこさしすせそたちつてとなにぬねの — Can you find the four letters and make the word? (Hints for a non-Japanese reader: the number 2 is written 二; one must imagine which letter might straighten within a vertical line of flowing script). For comparison, Keene translates the above: *"The letter in two strokes, / The letter like an ox's horns, / The straight letter, / And the crooked letter, too / All spell my love for you."* (from the 14c *Essays in Idleness,* the *Tsurezure-gusa* of Kenkô (1967)) It is a fine translation. The word "letter" is indeed repeated in the original and *"All spell my love for you"* is bold and creative. Only the first line is a problem: there are many letters written with two strokes. Be that as it may, here is the solution, the four letters, or syllabets as I call them: こいしく. *Koishiku* means "beloved," or signed on a letter, "lovingly" or "affectionately yours." That is also true for the "thinking of" or "remembering" Keene translated as "I love you" (more appropriate now than in 1967, as "I love you" is now mandatory, when emotions were held to be cheapened by too much talk). Because Japanese have no specific word for *missing* someone, I believe these words mean that and may be the most accurate translation of *oboyuru*. One aside: At the time Princess and Kenkô lived, *koishiku* was correctly written こひしく (*kohishiku*). That suggests it was already pronounced in the modern way (or some other possibilities we'll skip).

折よくは申させ給へふたつ文字　牛の角もし奉るなり　佐川田昌俊
oriyoku wa môsase-tamae futatsu moji ushi no tsuno moji tatematsuru nari akitoshi

前関白信尋公へ淀鯉奉るにそへて Accompanying Carp sent to the Prince

At a good time, please convey what I sent to his Highness
One two letter and the horn for him to do as he deignest!

反し Reply from Imperial Prince 後陽成天皇の皇子

魚の名のそれにはあらずひまのおり ちと二文字牛の角もし 前関白信尋公
uo no na no sore ni wa arazu hima no ori chito futa-moji ushi no tsuno moji shinjin?

Now don't let them just stand for the name of some fish!
When you've time, two-letter horn-letter: Mark my wish.

"Carp" and the imperative "come!" are both *koi/kohi*. The poet, a warrior skilled in the art of the tea ceremony, had to be circumspect as it was out-of-line to directly address a member of the Imperial family, but the Prince wrote back that he wanted to see him in person. There were scores of *kyôka* about the horn letter between the 14c and 19c. I like this artless personal exchange recorded in the 1666 *kyôka* collection 古今夷曲集 better than the arcane riddle about some old renga poet in the *surimono*.

元日は牛の角文字尽きぬ世のすぐなる文字の御代ぞめでたき 続春駒狂歌集
ganjitsu wa ushi no tsuno moji tsukinu yo no sugunaru moji no miyo zo medetaki 1721

丑の年亥の元日なり... When the Year of the Ox fell on a certain day

The New Year comes on a cornute letter and hurrah, what is more,
It takes us straight to a world without end: Day of the Boar!

The boar is first 亥 or い = *i,* or 猪(いのしし = *inoshishi*), both horn-letters appropriate for the Year of the Ox, and as that happens right away, *i.e.,* "straight" away, implying the straight-letter, which is actually found in the colloquial word for "boar" *shishi* しし. This is hard to explain, much less translate. The best pun is the literary "stab" that comes naturally off the horn invisible for being written "exhaust-not (i.e. last forever)," the modifier for *world* it turns into. This next is from the *Tokuwashû*.

無筆誦経 角文字も書くことならで般若経読むのはうはの空覚えなり 堂伴白主 徳和
tsuno moji mo kaku koto nara de hannya kyô yomu no wa uwa no sora oboenari 1785
horn-letter even write-thing cannot-w/ prajna sutra reads-as4 rote learning-is   Dôtomo Shironushi

An Illiterate Chanting Sutra: The Prajñā Parrot Paramitā

He reads the Sutra of Wisdom when even the horn letter
Is beyond his ken? Rote memory says it all much better.

..
This seems inane but is funny because the clever conceptualization of these letters is betrayed by the attention given to the horn-letter い *as one of the simplest of all letters to write.* For all the difference, one thing is common to all these *kyôka*: the historical way 角文字 *tsuno moji* or horn letter/s are treated. With *haikai* and *senryû* one finds the horn letter identified almost entirely with romantic love's *itoshiku* (like "dear" on a letter). *Kyôka* may play but it remains aware of where it came from.

㊦ Reading Surimono – Literature Over the Radar ㊦

小松にハあらて祢のよきさミせんにひかれて千代やのへに出けん 金地亭砂子
komatsu ni wa ara de ne no yoki samisen ni hikarete chiyo ya nobe ni ideken kinjitei sunago
small-pine/s-as-for are-not-so root=tone's good shamisen(player)by plucked/led,1000yo field-to go!

*The realm will succeed / through a thousand generations / if, out in the fields, we pluck /
not pines but the resonant strings / of the sweet-toned shamisen.* – trans. AH in Carp. 2008

*This realm will last a thousand years if, for good luck, in fields, today,
We leave the pines to grow, and follow a good shami girl out to play!*

The above from *Woman with a White Rat*, a c. 1825 *surimono* print by Gakutei, was not my first reading. Though pulling up pine saplings was partly a show of strength, "pluck" is not really suitable, Alfred Haft's pun was too good not to borrow:

*Though little pines bring a thousand years of life and luck,
Out to the fields we head to pluck our shamisens, instead.*

As he noted, the original not only plays on "pulling" the pine and playing the instruments (both are *hiku*) which *pluck* recovers, but puns *root* and *sound* both *ne*, though the characters 根 and 音 respectively, are different. Unfortunately, my short ditty failed to note the phrase modifying the shamisen where that pun was: *"ne no yoki,"* or, "(having a) good tone." Still, I liked it more than Haft's "sweet-toned," as that is a word to describe the mousy high-notes on a Chinese fiddle and not what is, in essence, a banjo and attracted Japanese by its crisp percussive sound. I thought of an envoi for my lacking re-creation: *May the sound be bold and clear as the One they mirror.* Then, re-reading the original for inspiration, I noticed that no one was plucking or picking a shamisen: it was *being* plucked or picked, *hikarete* (lit. "pulled"), *i.e., pulled along* or *led by* (hence "shamisen *ni*") by said instrument with a good tone, and that, in turn, meant by a professional musician. "Sound" is written with what seems a cross between the character for "root," associating with the pines to be pulled and possibly hinting at the phrase "looking good to sleep with" (*neyogi*) and a fancy phonetic writing for "ne," 祢. The second poem in the *surimono*, part of a series of women as the seven gods of good fortune (*ne* also means "rat/mouse," this was the day of the same, familiar of Daikoku, god of grain and riches) began *utaime no koe mo nodoka ni* . . . ("The entertainer's /gentle voice expands in song . . ." tr. Alfred Haft). An *utaime*, or "singing woman," though a group usually had a shamisen player or a fiddler. So, I delayed publication until I got my *shami girl* translation, which is to say, for another half an hour.

から人の髯ほとのひし姫小松根ことひかはや千代のためしに 石唐楼苔蒸
karabito no hige hodo nobishi hime komatsu negoto hikabaya chiyo no tameshi ni
chinaprsn's beard amount growng prncess-smll-pine root&all pull-wish 1000 yr/reign test-as

*Grown as big as a Chinaman's beard, little Princess Pine
I'd pull you up roots and all, leave my name a thousand years!*

*We pluck the roots / of princess pines, / which stretch out as long /
as a chinese beard, / part of an ancient custom.* – trans. carp.

The Chinaman's whiskers provide an interesting measure of *length* that indirectly hints at longevity, as the long-lived mountain saints had particularly long hair (and nails) of all types. I also like to imagine the poet, Sekitôrô Kokemushi, started with the "roots and all" *negoto*, recalled the homophonic "(Chinaman's) sleep-talk," and introduced his beard as a measure because the expression means, "it's all Greek to me." That has nothing to do with the rite, but I cannot help wondering whether the poet, like me – had Carpenter not explained it – could not read the *picture*, where a courtesan and her child-assistant parody Chinese hero Guan Yu – the wee kamuro holds up a broom instead of a halberd (I wonder if that means to get a guest to leave or is a symbol of cleaning up the world – the Dutch had them tied to their masts when they said they were cleaning up the seven seas of their rivals and I imagine explained to the Japanese in Nagasaki what those brooms were doing up there) and only vaguely suspected it was about something Chinese . . . . The pines are pulled up roots and all and the one difficult part of the poem is the final *tameshi ni,* lit. *"as a test."* It could mean *as an attempt to live* 1,000 years, but that seemed too obvious, so I tested my respondent and he came up with 長く語り継がれるだろう事柄として.

~~~~~~

Let me stop with the examples and add an *apologia* of sorts. The best translations and explanations are not in *this* book because I had little to add and would prefer to introduce them whole in a future edition. I also felt some qualms about asking *"what about this?" "what about that?"* and adding things, for I realize an art book has limited space and the pictures, which often hold more information and need more explaining than the poems – are rightly given preference, even though many poems get more attention than literary translators give them. One may have a difference of opinion as to what counts most. To *me*, it is communicating what makes the poem witty, but that is not the priority of catalog translation. Be that as it may, I cannot imagine any better way to teach a class of advanced Japanese than to introduce a selection from one of these *surimono* collections. True, most translations are not *that* entertaining; but couldn't the same be said for most poems in most collections of translated Japanese literature? And, with *surimono* catalog books, producing a stand-alone poem in translation was not the aim, anyway. They are meant to enhance the experience of looking at the picture. And, it is my opinion that each page of McKee and Carpenter's surimono books offers most readers who do not know much about Japan more than entire chapters of literary translation with little background information (as they are aimed at scholars) do. Finally, with the pictures and originals to look at, anyone who can read the Japanese and think they can do better can try themselves. A teacher might even take the tentative nature of many of the translations as an opportunity to see if he or she or their students can do better. With pictures and poems full of allusions and puns playing back and forth and elsewhere, we have in *surimono* a cornucopia of culture-riddles unlike anything else I know of. McKee wrote of how *surimono* were often distributed by the poet (who commissioned them, most likely as good pr for his group of poetry) in person, doubtless to enjoy watching the other party trying to figure it out or, when necessary, help out. Would these not be fine classroom aids?

It was hard for me to read *surimono* and not write more, for almost every picture has things that interest me. One of the last things I saw in Carpenter 2008, was a removable-neck shamisen w/ eight dots in two rows that indicated it was a *yatsu chichi*, or eight-tit (cat-skin) *shamisen* – or a fake 8-tit cat-skin *shamisen*, for they were usually burnt on – it took me back to my experimental instrument-building days and how my discovery of the 8-tit led me to check where the cat's navel was in relation to its 8-tits . . . But, I had never seen a *picture*. Earlier, in one surimono (p.286), I noted a 3-string *kokyû* with strings seemingly horse-hair – something I had seen (and played) only on the Mongolian 2-string fiddle, while the Japanese fiddle string was, I thought silk – called "the only traditional Japanese instrument played with a bow" and a square-bodied 4-string *kokyû* played by a standing *utaime* (singing-girl/entertainer) in another (p.396). Could two instruments so different both be a *kokyû* Japan's only fiddle? Here, too, is a riddle.

Finally, "100 Poets 1 Poem" Parsed as Poetry!

This was supposed to be a blank page making the transition from main text to aftermatter clear to the eye of anyone thumbing quickly through the book and so it *was* until the day after the pagination ended which was the day before the index was started. Checking out English translations of *A Hundred Poets One Poem* in order to disambiguate two M(ac)cAuleys 90 years apart who fused into one because of my sloppy spelling, I found Peter McMillan's recent *One Hundred Poets, One Poem Each – a translation of the Ogura Hyakunin Isshu* (Columbia University Press) which I had heard of from the author and from the PMJS mailing list but not yet seen because poverty kept me from buying a copy and I doubted it had enough relevant for this book to compensate for the trouble of working out an interlibrary loan. Google book-search only let me see three or four of the translations – all in Keene's foreword – yet they were enough to make me recall the Japanese expression *me kara uroko* (like scales falling from my eyes)."

> *Like water*
> *rushing down*
> *the river rapids*
> *we may be parted*
> *by a rock,*
> *but in the end*
> *we will be one again.*

Keene notes how "we," not specified in the original, brings the poem to life. *Amen*. I might have said an allusive metaphor became a sure simile, but what matters is that out of the multitude of possible readings the original offers, McMillan *chose* one. This is something Japanese-to-English (or vice-versa) translators should do *all* the time, but few *ever* do. And, just as important, there are *seven* lines. Another of the sampling that starts *"So this is the place!"* and ends *"Ôsaka Barrier"* has seventeen words parsed into *eleven* lines (!) of which the first has, as you see, five. Now, you might think that readings with such prolific parsing, or tiny lines, would be antithetical to mine, which, for *waka* and *kyôka* tend to favor two-lines, some of which, were it not for the rhyme, might even be considered one-line; but – and here is the *me kara uroko* moment – they immediately felt *closer* to what I was doing than the usual five-liners! *Why?* Long lines encourage readers to gather or break words on their own more than medium-length lines that willy-nilly force long syllabet clumps upon us allow. That usually means a better read because most translators are not good enough poets to deliberately parse lines as well as we all do naturally, without realizing what we do. They follow what they feel are the rules, are patted on the head for it, and that is that. What McMillan has done is utterly different. He simply followed his heart, doing *what comes naturally in English*. And that, for a translator, is not only hard but, bucking the dominant syllable and/or line-counting tradition/s, took a hell of a lot of courage. This did not make all the poems look long. Some required *less* lines. The foreword included a four-line eighteen-word translation starting with the two-word line "For you" (endearing in a Yiddish way!), and the phonetic length depends on beat, not line – or, syllable – anyway.

While Keene has hyped undeserving books in the past, this time his praise is, itself, worth praising. And, if I ever do not feel compelled to squeeze lots of poems in little space, I shall adopt McMillan's peter-perfect free parsing. Delicate nuances demand a fretless instrument.

After
  matter

This picture from the 1786 *Azuma-kyoku-kyôka bunkô* is Chie no Naishi, the "little ignoramus," one of the two top female *kyôka* masters of the late-18 to early-19c. Hopefully an ugly line between these words and the picture that came from nowhere and cannot be moved, removed or adjusted to match any margins (it is neither in the picture nor markable, i.e. in the text) can be removed with a tool, that is ridiculously hard to identify and use in my Acrobat pdf'er. It is one of the countless things Microsoft mysteriously does to make amateurs cry and waste time rather than create, perhaps in order to help their token rival, Mac, whom I cannot afford to support (also no Macs have that ergonomic clit on the keyboard).

Meaningless Postscript, On Expecting the Unexpected

すかし屁の消え易きこそあはれなれ　みはなき物と思ひながらも　紀定麿　徳和
sukashi-he no kie-yasuki koso aware nare　mi wa nakimono to omoinagara mo　ki-no-sadamaru
slip[silent]fart's vanish-easily espec. sad is: substance-as-for not-thing knowing-while　1785

> ~~How sad a thing~~
> ~~the silent fart, so quick~~
> ~~to disappear!~~
>
> ~~I get no cheer in knowing~~
> ~~'twas nothing from the start.~~

In traditional *waka*, those suffering unrequited love were said to "easily vanish," a quick sort of *pining away*. Hence, I read the above as a metaphor for such love that did not come to fruition. As it turned out, my reading, likewise, failed to make it, and I crossed it out for missing the point, which, *patience*, we will soon get to. Still, the translation had a certain charm, so change was not easy. Since this problem is not unique to this poem, I leave it as is and explain how I ended up with the correct reading, despite myself. While no longer as thrilled by pure logic and besotted with metaphysical poets as in my salad, or, rather, pimple days, if a poem more concept than picture catches me in my wine time (11~12AM, 5~6 & 11~12PM), I cannot help but jump in and make it mine or, to paraphrase Cranston, lie back and let it rewrite itself (*"I have tended to let the poems rewrite themselves in ways that sometimes are no doubt not strictly excusable on the grounds given above"* (*Waka,* vol 2a)). This taking in or letting go – oddly, they amount to pretty much the same thing – is exactly what AI translation cannot do and why computers may *write* some sorts of poetry (the simple and the surreal) well enough but never *translate* it well. Here is my *wine time* reading:

> *Pity the silent fart,*
> *vanishing without a trace,*
> *though nothing of substance*
> *in the first place*
> *– Who is? –*

You may note the form varies from the original enough to be a different sort of animal, what I call a *paraverse*; but, as it turns out, my wine had more verity than I did. This mad translation, rhetorical question and all, that I assumed to be my invention, actually got it right, while my less creative, acceptable one that I eventually had to cross-out did not. Why did *I* get it wrong, while my wine was right? *Unrequited love* – the metaphor implicit to my first (mis)translation – was born of my reading or, rather, the union of countless sad lovers bemoaning or welcoming the vanishing of their souls in the *Manyôshû* and the word *Fart* as exampled by Suckling's *"Love is the fart / Of every heart; / It pains when 'tis kept close; / It pains a man when 'tis kept close; / And others doth offend, when 'tis let loose"* in Samuel Johnson's *Dictionary!* As it turns out, this *kyôka* is generally explained as *a parody of corny death poems*, and the *mi,* i.e., the *substance,* puns on the *body* or the *self,* not *love.* I missed that intent because when I read and translated it in the mid-1990's, I failed to notice it was in a chapter of the classic 1785 *kyôka* anthology *Tokuwa Kago Manzaishû* titled 哀傷歌 *aishôka*, or *laments*, the sub-context of which means "other than for love, as those complaints are in the love-poem chapters" and I missed a small-font preface to the effect that said fart was being applied to *impermanence* 寄屁無常, and that particular word for impermanence, *mujô,* was one seldom applied to love. Burton Watson (read in Shirane+Brandon: 2002) , as far as I know, got it correct the first time with a good straight translation made by reversing the word order and turning the allusive pun into a clear simile.

> Though this body, I know,
> is a thing of no substance,
> must it fade, alas,
> so swiftly,
> like a soundless fart?

Of course, there still is a problem with the *logic*. Not Watson's, or mine, but the original's. It may hurt for one to pass away unheralded, but nothing stinks like a silent fart, usually modified, for good reason, as "deadly." Speaking of which, *kyôka* is itself a good example of a literary form tending to flatulence that has not received much attention yet is nonetheless said to stink. Modernologist and Tokyo University phd. student (Department of Contemporary Literary Studies), Ryan Morrison, notes in his web magazine/blog *Behold My Swarthy Face* that,

> Donald Keene, perhaps the most conspicuous of the previous generation of scholars, apparently was not too fond of kyōka, calling it a "minor form of poetry." In his *World Within Walls*, Keene wrote that "their [i.e., the kyōka poets'] fascination with trivialities . . . was clearly the result of a disinclination or inability to face the world seriously." "We are apt to form the impression," he continues, "that the kyōka poets lacked subjects of their own; that was why they so often resorted to parody."

He subtly suggests by further discussion and example that Keene undervalues the genre. Let me be blunt. Keene's charge against *kyôka* poets could be made for most *waka* poets and not a few *haijin* (*haikai* poets) too. No, it could be made for *most poets anywhere.* How many have "subjects of their own?" I would say very, very few, and even those extraordinarily inventive souls, for the most part, write on whatever has always been written about *in their culture.* And, the fact the poems might be personal is no help. Feelings, like other opinions, may be sincere and newly-hatched from the individual's point of view, but totally boring for one who has read much of the same going back millennia. So, we might better ask: *Which is more boring, poems repeating things that go back forever or poems parodying – though the question is unfair for if you have read this book carefully you now know that "parody" encompasses many sorts of take-offs and allusions for which we have no better word – such poems?* To my mind, those so-called parodies, or at least the better ones, tend to be the poems that do *not* repeat history but add something new to it. I recall reading about the First Chinese Emperor, he who had all books burned so he would become known as the first emperor of all time, when I was still a boy and thinking *Ripley's Believe It or Not* sure found something outlandish that week; but, *now*, I think that Emperor represents the modern view of the poet-as-creator, one who composes *ex nihilo*. In other words, our ability to forget the past is so great we hardly need destroy it deliberately to pretend to originality. Don't get me wrong, anyone who has read my books on old haiku knows how much I appreciate variations on hoary old themes that are *not* parodies by any name. I am also a Keene fan. I like most of his translations and envy his material, some of which I would have preferred first dibs on. He *does*, however, short-change humor, of which *kyôka* would be the prime example. Is it possible he does this because it is especially hard to translate and believing the genre to be inferior helps him rationalize his choice not to? Even the great are not exempt from cognitive dissonance.

Be that as it may – and I hope I have been fair to Donald Keene, as he is certainly not alone in overlooking *kyôka* – I, who consider taking the world with a grain of salt a mark of sanity, would like to end this book as I began my book on the dream time of the Japanese New Year, *The Fifth Season* (2007), with a quote from G.K. Chesterton's *Heretics*. It is not the same quote. The last one championed the cosmic contentment of staying home rather than globe-trotting *ala* Kipling and lamented how the automobile shrank rather than enlarged the world. I used it because the enchanted season I introduced bore and was born of a culture that Chesterton, had he come to know it from within, would have loved, as surely as we who know it love Chesterton whether or not we are Christian. This one, from chapter 16, "On Mr. McCabe and a Divine Frivolity" explains why *wit* is not merely a spice to sprinkle on otherwise bland ideas to make them palatable, but just what we seek, the thing that, whether we know it or not, makes us pick up a book. After the preliminaries (*"Mr. McCabe thinks that I am not serious but only funny, because Mr. McCabe thinks that funny is the opposite of serious,"* while, in reality, *"Funny is the opposite of not funny, and of nothing else,"* *"Whether a man chooses to tell the truth in long sentences or short jokes is a problem analogous to whether he chooses to tell the truth in French or German"* etc.), we find this enlightening passage:

> . . . the only serious reason which I can imagine inducing any one person to listen to any other is, that the first person looks to the second person with an ardent faith and a fixed attention, expecting him to say what he does not expect him to say. It may be a paradox, but that is because paradoxes are true. It may not be rational, but that is because rationalism is wrong. But clearly it is quite true that whenever we go to hear a prophet or teacher we may or may not expect wit, we may or may not expect eloquence, but we do expect what we do not expect. We may not expect the true, we may not even expect the wise, but we do expect the unexpected. If we do not expect the unexpected, why do we go there at all? If we expect the expected, why do we not sit at home and expect it by ourselves?

その①狂訳

On Mad Translation

"Anything that works justifies itself, ipso facto."
Edwin A Cranston, on translation (in *Waka* vol.1)

I tried to keep my translations translations. Though I took extraordinary license, in this book, I did not, on the whole, paraverse, which is to say, create alternative poems based on but not following the original, as I do in *A Dolphin in the Woods*. For an example of what I did *not* do – at least, not often – here is *Manyôshû* (8c) song #3810:

味飯乎 水尓釀成 吾待之 代者曽無<无> 直尓之不有者 # 3810
味飯を水に釀みなしわが待ちし 代はさね＜かつて＞なし直にしあらねば
umai-hi o mizu ni kaminashi waga machishi kai wa sane-nashi tada ni shi araneba
(tasty-rice+acc water-w/ chewed/fermented i waited value-as-for not directly is-not-if)

*To Think I Could've
Given It to Someone Else*
(or even drunken it myself)
―――――――――――――
What a waste of good saliva,
rice and water chewed for you
while I waited, it turned sour
And *now* you tell me
we are through!

Now that certainly *seems* like a mad poem – and you may see even madder paraverses in *A Dolphin* (2008), but the original, I am afraid, is closer to Cranston's *"It did me no good / To ferment the tasty rice, / Brewing with water, / Waiting for you – none at all. / For you're not here to have it."* Since *kamu* can mean chew as well as ferment, and women in old Japan did chew sweet-rice and spit it into vats to start the fermentation, mentioning *chewing* is conservative enough. What takes my translation beyond the pale, besides the unique length of the lines, is the misleadingly risqué title, "good saliva" to accent the waste, souring wine alluding to the relationship (English, not Japanese idiom), and the last two sentences turning an editor's note into the punch-line. In *this* book, I resisted the urge to explain within the poems, preferring outside glosses to give readers the pleasure of rereading poems while making the connections themselves; but I often went as far as any modern translator to make sense of what I translated, and farther, for, as I have declared in all my books of translation, my policy is that *if I am to err, I prefer to err on the side of wit*, for, speaking as one who has also been translated, it is preferable to be misread yet thought witty than turned into a bore by a cowardly translator. Perhaps I mistakenly made some poems mad that were not in the original, but in most cases, I only did what I had to do to ensure they were *still* mad (in one way or another) in translation.

That was supposed to be it for my second soliloquy on mad translation, but looking through an old file, I found a poem to make one of my favorite points. The example is, again, not a recognized mad poem but a plain *waka* from a major collection.

> あらを田をあらすきかへしても人の心を見てこそやまめ　古今集
> *araoda o arasuki kaeshi kaeshite mo hito no kokoro o mite koso yamame* kks 817
> new-plot/paddy+acc mattock turn turning-even person's heart+acc see +emph. quit!

Here are translations by Cranston and Rodd+Henkenius, respectively. Note how different they are.

> *To make new paddy / Sink your mattock in the soil / Over and over / Turn the heart of a lover, / Look close – and love will wilt.*   = Cranston

> *in newly opened / fields they turn the earth again / and again   I'll not / give up until I've seen his / heart laid open as often*   = Rodd & Henkenius

This poem first appeared in the Sarumaru anthology (猿丸集) with a preface about his calling on a fickle or unfaithful woman in the spring, but according to Kyûsojin, said anthology is not trustworthy, so we cannot fault R & H for "*his* heart." But, what does *"see his heart laid open"* mean? Cranston, who plays safe with the genderless "lover," has the poem express "contemptuous disillusion," but is that clear from his good but impersonal translation? It only makes me recall Ovid and his prescriptions for falling out of love by having us look close, real close, at the human body and its various functions. And I wonder *why* anyone would write a stand-alone poem to tell people that looking inside(?) under(?) a lover's heart will make love wilt. Kyûsojin's reading (歌意) is: *After trying time again to ascertain that person's real intentions, I'm going to cleanly quit (loving?calling?)*. He also writes the conjugation of "quit" shows "intent." Unfortunately, the tenses and intentions just do not jive. I know little grammar, but I do know awkward logic when I see it. ◎ **My point:** for *waka* or *kyôka* to be interesting, *we must be bold enough to create clear meaning*. Eg.:

> *With a new plot, you must turn the soil over and over;*
> *We may part, but first I'll sink my mattock in her heart!*

> *With a new plot, we turn the soil over & over; but try*
> *That with a human heart and you'll watch love die.*

> *With a new plot, you turn the earth over & over; I'd try*
> *That with her fickle heart – Is love a weed? Let it die!*

> *Turn o'er the soil the more times the better for a new paddy,*
> *Try that with a lover's heart & you'll lose your sugar-daddy.*

> *With a new plot, we may turn the earth over again and again;*
> *But if you saw the underside of his heart, he's dirt: ditch him!*

> *With a new plot, we turn the earth o'er & o'er – Give up?*
> *Until I've seen his heart laid bare as often, no, I will not!*

And *I* will not give up on trying to re-create wit in translation. "Translation" includes Japanese modern translations (現代訳,歌意) meant to explain poems, which often do little better than your usual English readings. Let me give two more examples of poems witty enough to be mad, but, dealing with love, remain bonafide *waka*.

wagimoko ga kozarishi yoi no uchiwabite waga tamakura o ware zo shite neshi
my sis/girlfrnd came-not night's miserable my gem-pllw I+emph. doing slept kkrj #3250

<table>
<tr><td>

On that evening,
when my dear girl did not come,
utter was my grief;
It was mine that was the arm
I used as a pillow for my sleep.

</td><td>

On that night,
my baby failed to show
I was so upset,
I laid my head upon my arm,
and, with *myself*, I slept!

</td></tr>
</table>

I apologize for not justifying C's translation, left, with each line capitalized. For comparison, I wanted the same format. Unquestionably, Cranston's translation has more life to it than most. It boasts an interesting emphatic phrase in *"It was mine that was the arm"* and a good vowel end-rhyme in *"grief/sleep."* That is *much* more service than one usually gets from a translator in a world that expects so little of a translation. But, I still could not help but feel *the original was more risqué*. *Tamamakura*, or gem (precious/ beautiful)-pillow, has erotic implications that do not come through in *pillow* alone (unless, like David Allen Coe's cuntry song where said pillow is stained). So, I dropped the *pillow* for space to allow the poet to sleep *with himself*, an obvious allusion to perverting the normal behavior of sleeping with *another*. Because Japanese does not specify second-person, my first reading had "you failed to show, girl" for the second line, but the "girl" upset my mother, so I slyly rewrote with a gender-neutral but even more diminutive term of endearment.

hiru wa naki yoru wa moete zo nagarauru hotaru mo semi mo wa ga mi narikeri tsurayuki
day-as-for crying night-as-for burning! flowing firefly and cicada+emph. myself become/s kkrj 4015

Crying in the day, Burning in the night I go Down the endless years;
Firefly and cicada are Embodiments of myself. trans. Cranston

Crying by day and burning by night, I drift along;
The fireflies and cicada are me, so, too, this song.

Crying by day & burning by night, I float I flame;
Firefly and cicada, in me, one and the same.

Crying by day, burning by night, always astream
Both firefly and cicada, my life is but a dream.

Crying by day, burning by night, I have come to see
Both firefly and cicada, are ultimately me!

Here, the flowing in the original does allude to the poet's life as Cranston elaborates, but Tsurayuki deserves credit for combining a bug that cries thereby alluding to tears that float the crier and lightning bugs who were strongly associated with streams in Japan. So he cries himself a river and floating burns on it. I could not communicate that in my mad translations either, but by getting rid of a big word and working rhymes, I could improve the wit . . . if only a bit.

One way to allow the monolingual reader to appreciate at least part of what translation entails – many choices – is to play with reducing long poems to *kyôka*-length mad ones. Here is Donne (1573-1631), redone:

Absent Love

Her absence, my gain,
when in a corner of my brain
unseen, we meet;

None miss her, none complain,
Though I kiss her head to feet!

Her absence, my gain.
None miss her, none complain
when, now, we meet

in a corner of my brain,
I can kiss her head to feet!

I am afraid, however, neither is as interesting as his longer original, titled *That Time and Absence proves Rather helps than hurts to loves*. See what you think:

ABSENCE, hear thou my protestation
    Against thy strength,
    Distance and length:
Do what thou canst for alteration,
    For hearts of truest mettle
    Absence doth join and Time doth settle.

Who loves a mistress of such quality,
    His mind hath found
    Affection's ground
Beyond time, place, and all mortality.
    To hearts that cannot vary
    Absence is present, Time doth tarry.

My senses want their outward motion
    Which now within
    Reason doth win,
Redoubled by her secret notion:
    Like rich men that take pleasure
    In hiding more than handling treasure.

By Absence this good means I gain,
    That I can catch her
    Where none can watch her,
In some close corner of my brain:
    There I embrace and kiss her,
    And so enjoy her and none miss her.

My shortened versions seem flat. Apparently, the teasing foreplay was needed. And the complex metaphor describing the rich man's pleasure is so good, it hurts to lose it. In most translation of dense poetry such as Japanese *kyôka*, the loss can feel much the same as this. Even with a decent translation, there is always that loss. Not that Donne's poem is *that* good. At least, it falls short in the category of conceptual brilliance when compared to Piet Hein's grook called "Address to my Beloved." The grook has three stanzas, the first two of which treat women who attract more from afar than up-close vs. those who charm more up-close than afar and concludes:

But you, alone, my love, I love, wherever you may be
So you can stay, or go away, it's all the same to me.

That is, content-wise, what is wanted in a good *kyôka*. With the other stanzas it is a masterpiece: I have tried and tried and cannot reduce it to the standard *kyôka* length. If the Nobel Prize Committee had any scientific minds among their judges of literature, Piet Hein would have received the prize he surely earned. But, let me present another Donne. This time, we will start with the original so the reader, if he or she so wishes, may try to make a *kyôka* of his poem before seeing how *I* did. You might hold a piece of paper over mine, below it.

> DEATH, be not proud, though some have called thee
> Mighty and dreadful, for thou art not so:
> For those whom thou think'st thou dost overthrow
> Die not, poor Death; nor yet canst thou kill me.
> From Rest and Sleep, which but thy picture be,
> Much pleasure, then from thee much more must flow;
> And soonest our best men with thee do go –
> Rest of their bones and souls' delivery!
> Thou'rt slave to fate, chance, kings, and desperate men,
> And dost with poison, war, and sickness dwell;
> And poppy or charms can make us sleep as well
> And better than thy stroke. Why swell'st thou then?
>   One short sleep past, we wake eternally,
>   And Death shall be no more: Death, thou shalt die!

My *kyôka-length* rendition telescopes the original, so only the ends remain –

> *Death be not proud!*
> *One short sleep past, we wake*
> *eternally. Doubt not*
>
> *Who shall be no more: Death,*
> *For His sake, thou shalt die!*

"For His sake" was added both to fill in between the lines and to improve the wit by presenting the reverse side of the coin (Christ dying that we should enjoy eternal life). On the other hand, we lost the expression of death-as-pleasure. Perhaps a reader who tried his or her hand at *kyôkafication* gave that more attention, but I thought Don Quixote, no, Cervantes, did that better (pp. 571-2) so I concentrated, for better or worse, on the message/wit I thought may have been done first by Donne.

~~~~~~

I am unsure exactly what I am up to with all these additions on translation. One voice in me says "Go ahead!" Another says "Stop while you're ahead!" Well, I will stop now, probably too late to still be ahead, with some genuflection about *why* I explain so much.

Who doesn't want one's line of work to be appreciated? It is *lonely* translating into English, so I feel the need to let others know what we who do it, or at least I, *do*. In Japan, translators always get their names on books covers, write *Translator's Afterwords* or *Explanations* and often, becoming famous, are interviewed, paid for magazine contributions, etc.. A large *vocabulary-of-translation* in the public domain makes it easy to explain things (eg., in English, *literal translation* has no commonly known opposite, so I must use a direct translation from Japanese: "sense translation"). In other words, my *selfish explanation* is that *I crave a translation-literate readership that can appreciate our art so much that, if I cannot find one, by God, I'll make one!* The *altruistic explanation* is that lacking a good vocabulary and sufficient variety in phrasing, and worse, sufficient expertise in reading old Japanese, I am all too aware of my limitations as a translator and hope that by showing others what I can nonetheless do, I would hope to encourage *them* to do better. I can do this because my only native gift is my strong imagination that makes me overachieve myself in reading and re-creating poetry or prose. For decades, I was fortunate enough to correct translators (English ⇒ Japanese), many of whom were better wordsmiths than I was. I found I could push them to do better by showing examples of more creative solutions. If this book can encourage – or shame – my betters to do better translation to share with all of us, I will be happy. And, finally, all of the above may be mere rationalization. From nursery school, I have *loved* show & tell.

その②解釈

On Understanding

此歌の心をいかにがてんじやか
いはずと作もとをりものめは

黒　田　月　洞　軒

& Explaining

So tell me just what This Poem means,
You who say a work speaks for itself!

Translated Poetry
Kuroda Getsudôken c.1700

There is a school of thought that holds poetry to be above explanation and feels the proper thing to do is simply read what is on the page. I have encountered that opinion, or prejudice against explanation in English and in Japanese. The roots of this belief differ. The Japanese tend to stress the import of reading something *sunao ni,* or meekly taking it as is, without putting any of your self into it as a matter of etiquette or respect to the original, whereas English tend to dwell upon the idea of poetry, as a special sort of artwork apt to be ruined by explanation. That difference may stem from the shortness of Japanese poetry, for Japanese poets often did preface their poems to an extent that might be considered explanatory in English as it was needed for the reader to make out the meaning of the poem. Thus they realize that explanation and poetry are not mutually exclusive fields.

I agree with both party's *ideals*, but feel we need to remember that an ideal is an ideal, something to aim for but not necessarily to do. Considering our different life experiences, cultural background, linguistic skills and personal sensibilities, it is debatable whether reading a poem "as it is" is possible for any one but the poet him or herself; and, when a foreign language is involved, it is not debatable even rhetorically. It is *impossible*. And, while a poem, like a picture, looks beautiful surrounded by blank-space for contemplation, I have heard no one claim that explanation harms our enjoyment of a picture. Is that because most scholars know that they do not know the symbolism of much that they see – note how heavily semiology skews toward pictures and treats poetry lightly if at all – or is it because the English poem is so much less dense than the Japanese that there is little need to dig much for the full meaning?

Most educated Japanese are aware there is more than meets most eyes in poetry. There is a tradition of editors providing short comments about poems, as often or not before the poem as after. The only problem is that the often cryptic hints pointing out only the sort of thing a well-educated reader might miss in a manner so subtle, even poetic, as to heighten the aesthetic experience of reading, go right over the heads of most Japanese and nearly all foreign readers. The glosses are elegant, even beautiful partly because they are so short and sweet. But, that means leaving out more basic information many of us need. That, by itself, is nothing to criticize. All good readers want to read up, rather than down. Who am I to request highly cultured writers to come down a bit for me?

All I can do is point out that there would be many more readers of old poetry in Japanese, and for that matter, English, were it properly introduced, i.e., explained in more detail to the masses. But, I can validly complain that because of the reticence of the Japanese to put themselves into a poem, editor-annotators are all too-often afraid to share with us their educated guess as to its meaning/s and wit. As one who wants more help understanding, yet all too often find myself catching what these editors miss, this is a problem. I should not be getting more than they do. Indeed, their not mentioning what I think obvious makes me doubt myself. It makes me wonder if I am not finding more in the poetry than is actually there. Yet, to put something I have already written more than once in this book into new metaphor: I would rather make 99 poems wittier than they deserve to be than to make 1 witty poem dull in translation. An academic friend of high learning who found I had read too much wit into the poem of one he knew to studiously avoid it warned me that some poets in the fuddy-duddy Nijô school of *waka* avoid wit like the plague. So, I realize I am bound to make mistakes, but to me, all pre-modern Japanese poets are witty until proven to be bores and not the vice-versa.

Returning to the perspective from English, I cannot help wondering whether lack of explanation and lack of witty translation are related. Anyone who has written a patent knows that numerous discoveries are made *in the process of explaining one's invention*. Translating and explaining poems allows otherwise overlooked wit to manifest itself when you are ready to see it. There is no small irony here if it is true, for explanation, far from killing wit, becomes its savior.

In the end, the desirability of explanation is not explainable, but testable. I cannot tell whether you my readers are the scientists or the guinea pigs, but if you have read this or any of my books you know well what explaining translated poetry is and whether it adds or detracts from *your* reading experience. As a writer, I know that sometimes I may complicate things too much – Piet Hein offers to do just that in a grook for readers convinced "real" poets should be impossible to fully comprehend who find his poems lamentably clear – other times, I may run out of space and, giving in to my book-design side, fail to give information that would enhance the reading experience. So, I have my beliefs; but I also have regrets all around and, after five years of publishing in English, still lack sufficient feedback to know what is working and what is not. Despite my habit of constantly running off the track, I do wish to please. I am eager to hear your opinions about the ratio of poem to explanation, and the ideal amount of redundancy (assuming most readers will not read through my books at a sitting, I repeat myself more than I would with a short book), and what exactly you would have more of and less of.

This book being so full of w/it, includes more explanation per poem, translatable or not, than any of my previous books. That makes it an ideal book for, with your help, testing the limits of the art.

その③道草

♪ Snake-legs, or Grass by the Road ♪

> *. . . the sane majority find the language provided for them by their country's traditions vastly in excess of their needs, while the insane minority are for ever discontent with their native tongue because of its total insufficiency to express what they feel and know . . .*

To hide at the end of chapter or, worse, book, information needed for most readers to appreciate what is on the page simply because footnotes are thought unseemly is as silly as hiding chair legs behind skirts, a practice we once thought not only normal but necessary for our mental health. Most of what you will find here is unneeded *omake,* or *extras,* that may be enjoyed without referring to the text. By "snake-legs" 蛇足 I admit to some *redundancy*, and "grass by the road" 道草 *entertainment* not directly linked to the destination. The lead quote, from Greville MacDonald, M.D.'s *The Sanity of William Blake* (1907. George Allen & Unwin. Ruskin House London, 1920) is a good example of the latter. Readers will differ on the value of such. Some notes supply material found too late to squeeze into a tiny chapter. Some add details of possible interest only to the scholar, but most should be considered the just desert for all who have enjoyed the book. Some is in Japanese, because translation would have been futile or too much work. Monolinguals ought not complain. Languages exotic to one's own take longer to learn than the most specialized medicine yet bring not one tenth of the income (in my case, not a hundredth or thousandth!). Exotic bilinguals deserve some reward for decades of hard work. And, finally, there are notes intended to stimulate further research and elicit e-mails with glosses and marginalia for the next, expanded edition, and for new books, such as mentioned in the first ♪, below. Nonetheless, I would have put these notes after their respective chapters were it not bound to make the book much longer and more expensive.

~~~~~~

Silverfish Adverbs of Spitefulness.   27頁

♪*I Seek Personal Mad Poems* such as Issa's infuriating silverfish faces or Ryôkan's happier wingless *tôfu* for a second volume, but they will not be easy to find as editors interested in *haikai, waka* or *kyôka* generally ignore them. Work by the star 16c *haikai* link-verse master, Sôchô is an exception. Take this lament for example, *"So how do I write now, with my right hand out of commission, when even holding chopsticks is a pain in something hard to wipe?"* (いかにせんものかきすさむ手はおきてはしとる事と尻のごふ事 *ika ni sen monokaki susamu te wa okite hashi toru koto to shiri no gô koto* 『狂歌大観』の参考篇の9「宗長手記・日記」). Sôchô fell off a horse. His situation is sad; his poem is "mad," because of the things mentioned in it; unlike Issa's masterpiece, however, the wit is mine. Later, however, Sôchô would quip in another poem that he was afraid of one locality since "horse" was in its name. In Sôchô's case, the poems were picked up by the editors of the massive *Kyôka Taikan* (tk in this book) because they were in a journal that had itself been treated as a literary work (and well Englished by Mack Horton). That is usually not the case; only sleuthing in Japan can dig up most personal *kyôka*.

♪   **Style-wise, Issa's technique (puns in unlikely parts of speech) is not unique**. Even *waka* not considered particularly comic do it. Here are two from the 1312 *Gyokuyôshû* 玉葉集 for Japanese readers なけきつつ あめもなみたも ふるさとの むくらのかとの いて

かたきかな 斎宮女 *nagekitsutsu ame mo* . . . and, ゆきてみむーいまははるさめーふるさとにーはなのひもとくーころもきにけり 高倉 *yukite mimu* . . . Both run the verb for fall (降る *furu*) into the "*furusato*=hometown." A more spectacular example, from *haikai*, again, for readers of Japanese, turns *"say not"* into *sardines!*「さらなる魚ぞあまりちいさき　何事もいハじ／＼とおもへども」（檀王法林寺本　俳諧連歌）。なるほど、従来の＜鰯＞語源説 1）弱し、2）卑し、3）祝しもある。無論、一茶の紙魚／＼とした有心狂歌は、この『犬筑波集』の無心俳諧に勝つは勝つが、後者の鰯々もなかなかの pun じゃ！

♪ **Spiteful Poems.** **I exaggerated the uniqueness of a truly "mad" *kyôka* a bit.** Kyôgetsu, sometimes considered the first *kyôka* master, uses dirty wordplay to tell off an Empress (pg.370). Edo *kyôka's* first man, Shokusanjin, likened a certain woman's cold, cold heart to a cold cold nose and feet, the latter of rain, for viewed falling from a distant cloud it is so called:「やうやうと 来てもぐり込む 冷たさは 君が心と 鼻と雨脚」*yôyô to kite mo* . . .と言ふ様に、随分穿つた皮肉に敵娼を困らせたりする。　But word-play and spite outside of the disgruntled lover or vitriolic (Buddhist) inter-sect insult tradition (in which case the poem would be in Chinese-style) was indeed rare. *

♪ 念のため。**Issa repeated the idea of his 1813 silverfish poem in 1824**, three years before his death, I. The 31-syllabet poem is angry but, unfortunately, not mad. It calls his countrymen *devils* who eat and tear up bequeathed documents: 我みだのゆづりの状をくひ裂て世を故郷の人は鬼ぞも *waga mida no yuzuri* . . .

~~~~~~

Why good poems are dangerous – on not *moving heaven and earth*   32 頁

♪ **Please Do Not Think of My Translations as Final.** Eg. the second line, *"Who wants to see Heaven and the Earth disturbed?* could also end *"~ and Earth become disturbed."* Feedback is always welcome. Readers are encouraged to try and do better with their favorite poems. Note that the main break in the original (*uta-yomi wa heta koso yokere // ametsuchi no ugoki-idashite / tamaru mono ka wa*) is clearly between the 5-7 and the 5-7-5, itself actually 12-5) rather than the common, but far from requisite 5-7-5 // 7-7. If most of my readings give more beats to the first half, it is only because that is how the content fit best. Japanese *kyôka* poets did the same (The percentage of poems straying from the convention varies by genre – more in *kyôka* than mainstream *waka* – and by book, i.e., editor. If you know of a thorough survey of this please tell me. All I know is that 8c *Manyôshû waka* often broke after the 5-7 though most, like almost all in the 905 *Kokinshû*, after the 5-7-5, 16-c haikai link-verse after a 7-7 start, and *kyôka*, as *waka*, tended to follow *waka*.) To give a concrete idea of the possibilities, just this once, we have many, many readings, three of mine and two by others in the text, five by me below, and one by Keene, on the next page:

Nothing is better
than being a poet of little worth.
What a mess if we moved heaven & earth!

~~~~~~~~~~~~~~~~~~~~~~

Nothing beats being a poet (like *me*) of little worth:
Who the hell *wants* poems to move Heaven & Earth!

~~~~~~~~~~~~~~~~~~~~~~

Nothing is better than being a poet, Sir, of little worth –
What a mess if our poems moved them, heaven & earth!

~~~~~~~~~~~~~~~~~~~~~~

How Good a thing it is
to be a Bad Poet!

What a disaster
for the firmament to move
before you know it!

~~~~~~~~~~~~~~~~~~~~~~

The composition of a poet, to my mind, should be infirm:
Was the firmament not meant to have a permanent term?

The second line of the last reading, born entirely of pun and rhyme, is beyond the pale.

♪ *A Dangerous Poem about Dangerous Poems?* Keene, who translates *"It's best for a poet / To be clumsy: / If heaven and earth / Started to move in sympathy, / Do you suppose we could stand it?"* (I *guess* it his translation: the note was on an inaccessible page on Googlebooks. Whether he did it or found it, "clumsy" is, to say the least, a clumsy translation and only pardonable as a clumsy attempt at *abcbd* rhyme), makes an intriguing unsubstantiated, but certainly likely, claim that the poem "incurred the wrath of Hirata Atsune and other Shinto zealots." As these nativists believed *waka* had unique persuasive powers due to Japanese being a divine language, such a claim makes sense. The poet, Yadoya no Meshimori, himself a student of national studies (*kokugaku*), wrote books in the field, so I would *expect* interesting debate. If anyone can find this and write it up, it will be added to the notes of the next edition. As far as possible, I want the quotes not summary.

♪ *How Poetry Affects to Effect.* Any thorough cross-cultural study of the alleged effects of poetry, or words beautifully or persuasively expressed? Now, all I know of besides the broad claims of the ancient Chinese *Book of Songs* and Japan's *Kokinshû*, are bits and pieces: Irish poets so feared they were banished as Plato had once thought good for his republic, a curse aimed at a pet sparrow-eating cat in England, an execution-ordering emperor's hand stayed in Japan (see pg.598) . . . etc. Claims about the powers of poetry can be made in hilarious ways. Take this sentence from Trifaldi, a Countess who as the keeper of a Princess in *Don Quixote* was seduced into opening the way to her mistress by poetry:

> *"instead of composing Lamentable Verses . . . that make Women and Children cry by the Fireside, they try their utmost Skill on such soft Strokes as enter the Soul, and wound it, like that Thunder which hurts and consumes all within, yet leaves the Garment sound."* Moreover, she writes, *"Love-Madrigals and Roundelays . . . are no sooner heard, but they presently produce a Dancing of Souls, Tickling of Fancies, Emotions of Spirits, and, in short, a pleasing distemper in the whole Body, as if Quicksilver shook it in every Part. . . I pronounce these poets very dangerous, and fit to be banished to the Isles of Lizards."* (Cervantes 1547-1616, Ozell's revision of the translation of Peter Motteux).

While the thunder sounds *kyôka*, indeed, it is not so grandiose as the *Kokinshû* and *Book of Songs* 詩経 claim that oddly seems more concrete in Meshimori's denial of its desirability than in the original, for who would warn against an impossibility?

★オマケ ものゝふのこゝろなぐさむ歌よみの蛙はいかで軍するらん 腹藁？ 失典 失礼

♪ *Piet Hein's Grook.* The first two lines of THE COMMON WELL (To Charles Chaplin) are: *The well you invite us to drink of / is one that no drop may be bought of.* And, speaking of rare things, how often have you read two *think-of/drink-of, bought-of/thought-of* style rhymes ending in pre-positions in a row? (*Grooks VI*, w/ the assist. of Jens Arup. Borgen's pocket books. Narayana press 1978)

♪ *So Long as So Long.* We will see little more of fine *kyôka* poet Tegara no Okamochi (1735-1813) because most of his poems depend too much on untranslatable multiple related puns. *'So long as so long'* was an exception – I could work with the bare bones – for the concept did not depend upon that punning relationship but was only polished by it.

Calendar Conundrums and the Right to be Silly 34 頁

♪ **KKS#1** 尽くし。 I knew I could not expect great things from R& H's translations of Ariwara no Motokata's KKS#1 poem when they not only cited a critic on Shiki calling it a "mere grinding away at logic" (理屈をこねただけ) but added an insult of their own: "This poem is a good example of the disingenuous reasoning that often appears in *Kokinshû* waka." *Tondemonai!* As I wrote, the poem is no literary masterpiece, but to call a paradox that plain – if anything simplistic – "disingenuous" is even further from the truth than Shiki's claim. I was delighted to discover in Cranston (1996) that the same poem was used to start an "enormous handbook of *waka* topics" that served as a reference for Sei Shônagon and Murasaki Shikibu. That collection, the *Kokinwakarokujô*

(古今和歌六帖 c.985), *Kokinrokujô,* or kkrj, has 4,499 poems presented in 25 classes and 517 topics. Its unknown editor, like *Kokinshû* editor Tsurayuki, was no fool. The even larger *Fuboku-shû* (1310) skips *that* poem but has a number of poems playing on it, some too literally (あら玉のことしとやいはん立かへり春よりさきに春はきにけり、*aratama no kotoshi to ya . . .,* 等) to be worth translating, and some conceptually, for example –

くれはてぬとしのをはりに春立てさためかねたる我よはひかな 光俊 夫木集 1310
kurehatenu toshi no owari ni haru tachite sadamekanetaru waga yowai kana mitsutoshi
setting/ending-exhausting-not?-year-end-on spring arriving settle-cannot my age 'tis!

> *Spring is here before the end of the year – I, no sage,*
> *confess that now I cannot figure out . . . my own age!*
> ~~~~~~~~~~~~~~~~~~~
> *Before the year has rightly ended I am struck dumb;*
> *How can I tell my age, now that spring has come?*
> ~~~~~~~~~~~~~~~~~~~
> *That spring came before year's end is no secret;*
> *but now I really can no longer tell my own age!*

I must admit to dressing that one up good. The common denominator of the three readings is what is in the original which conceptually speaking is probably wacky enough of a waka to be a *kyôka,* yet stylistically a bit plain. This, from the same collection, is more involved:

ひとゝせにふたゝひ春は立ぬれと老木のはなはいかゝさくへき 仲実朝臣
hito tose ni futatabi haru wa tachinuredo rôki no hana wa ikaga sakubeki nakasane
1 year-in twice spring/s-as4 coming-but oldtree's/s' blossoms-as4 how bloom-ought

> *What means it to have the Spring come in one year twice:*
> *How now can an Old Tree bloom in the winter of its life?*

Next, we find a fine take-off (*toshinouchi ni mochi wa . . .* see pg.609) of Motokata's *waka* as the first poem of what may be the earliest totally elegant *kyôka* opus (20 poems+prose commentary), Nijô Nyôbô's late-14c *Rice-cake Wine Poem Match* (*Mochi Sake Uta-awase*). And, not long after, we find the *liveliest* take-off. It is link-verse master Sôchô's first *Journal* entry in 1524! His fine *kyôka* borrows Motokata's language to haze someone begging admission to the temple. The last two lines are, in H. Mack Horton's translation, *"should we call him last year's scamp, / or should we call him this year's novice?"* (*aratama no hatsumotoi kiri hitotose ni kozo to ya iwan koshami to ya iwan*). In the original, the last year and the scamp are punderfully one and the new year and novice punfully close. Not all treatments of the old *waka* are direct. Some simply treat the broader subject of the Spring starting in the New Year. Speaking of which, I have not done enough research to know if Motokata's poem began the tradition of starting seasonally arranged anthologies with the early Spring, but I'll bet it helped make it an institution. The best single collection of Tenmei era *kyôka,* selected by Yomo no Akara (Ôta), the 1785 *Tokuwakagomanzaishû,* starts with a charming but untranslatable *kyôka* punning on the name of types of pine and bamboo used in New Year decorations to combine rather than confront the double-date (初はると歳暮をいはふ門かざりわか松もありくれ竹もあり 紀春長 徳和歌後萬載集 *hatsu haru to toshikure o iwau kado kazari wakamatsu mo ari kuretake mo ari* Ki-no-Harunaga 1785). And, going back to the 17c, how about the first poem of Iwanami's classic Bashô poem collection? Yes, the 19 year-old future Saint of haiku did a dynamic rewrite of Ariwara no Motokata's *waka* using verbs rather than nouns and compressing it into 17-syllabets. It is Englished and explained in my book of New Year haiku, *The Fifth Season* (2007). Bashô may have changed his style later, but who is to say that such play – thinking about the arbitrary nature of cultural devices and how we interpret time – did not help him develop? And most interesting of all from the point of view of this book, Arakata's poem appears with only the slightest change (the addition of one *"i"* twice) – which is what makes the take-off so fine – as #202 of 360 *kyôka*, or *near-kyôka* in the 1623 *Seisuisho* selected for the reference volume of the *Kyôka Taikan* attributed to 古老の人, an old person of long ago. As I do not have a copy of the book, I wrote H. Mack Horton, who translated twenty-eight of the thousand-odd comic stories from the *Suiseisho* as *Laughs to Banish Sleep*, for the framing, which he was kind enough to provide:

> . . . the poem appears in an anecdote under *jôgo*, "heavy drinker." It's framed in a story about how when the solar New Year falls during the lunar old year it's celebratory, so the domestics are given a treat. Each person gets one rice bowl filled with *sake*, but an old man (古老) takes two. He is challenged to defend his effrontery, and he answers with the KKS poem that in this year the new year has come before the old one is out – so are we to call it "this year" or "last year?" It happens that *iiwan* "rice bowl" is a near-homophone of *iwan*, "call." So set up, the original might be heard to mean something like *"This may be one year, but the old one calls for a bowl and the new one calls for a bowl [so I was just being cautious]!"* Everybody laughed. (personal correspondence with some changes and bracketed addition.)

Bowls were commonly filled and drunken after meals by the well-off at the time *Laughs* was written. Half a century earlier, Luis Frois and other Occidental visitors were disgusted by the practice (see items #6-32, 36 *Topsy-turvy 1585*). To my mind, the enormous number of take-offs – including this last one– reaped from this much reviled *waka* speaks in its honor; but I can understand how those who *hate* it could take the same for proof of how much *harm* it has done! And, I would beg to respectfully, but strongly, disagree.

♪ ***Miracle: Someone Appreciated Ariwara Motokata's Poem!*** When I finally discovered the presence of three books with more *kyôka* translated than all together done to that time and got them from Library loan, The first I saw, Daniel McKee's *Colored in the Year's New Light: Japanese Surimono from the Becker Collection*, had Motokata's poem up front in the first big essay of the catalogue, on *Time*. It was used to kick-off the sub-essay, the "Seasons of the New Year." McKee's translation was the usual – maybe a wee bit snappier but still boring for lack of words rather than descriptions of years and by comparison with his scintillating prose; but the fact not a single disparaging word was said made me shout, *Hooray!* Only someone from the Art side of scholarship rather than the Literary side would be so kind. I had mixed feelings, however, about his explanation,

> "the calendar says it's still the same year, but according to the markings of the natural world, with melting snow and blossoming plums, a new life cycle has begun. If nature is held superior to calendar, then shouldn't the New Year – which is supposed to correspond with nature's renewal in spring – be celebrated right away, not waiting for its official recognition? . . . "Spring" . . . is often synonymous with "New Year" . . . This correspondence does not imply, as Motokata imagines, that the year can be adjusted to the weather cycle." (Ibid. 2008)

Reading this, I heard music: Loretta Lynn singing *If Loving You Is Wrong* (I don't want to be right) where the truth of burning love left doubt about that of conventional ties (chains of marriage to a love grown cold). Calendar *versus* Nature. It was the same thing. But, as it happens, *all* readings I knew of to date have assumed Motokata's poem referred to something more cosmic yet less natural: not nature vs. calendar, or artificial vs. natural, but calendar vs. calendar, or artificial vs artificial: *two dates*. There is the coming of the Lunisolar New Year 正月 the first day 元日 of which is always the first day 朔 of the first month=moon 一月 which wanders back and forth between bounds set by Sun (1/21 ~ 2/22 according to one source 1/22~2/20 according to another, and 1/8 ~ 2/20, another probably wrong*), and there is the date we might call Springrise 立春 *risshun* which is about Feb 4. McKee knows about these things and describes most of them more elaborately than I do in *The Fifth Season* (2007) but does not seem to have realized that the vocabulary in the old poem and its prefacing phrase rule out any reading but date vs. date. In the absence of the mention of specific phenomenon (eg. Princess Sao wetting her hem or Issa's cats in heat!), when spring's "comes within the year" or "stands/rises," the theme was calendrical discrepancy not calendar vs nature. That is not to say that poems written on Springrise would not be influenced by the weather of that particular year. Some were, and in the much older *Manyôshû* poem #4482 we have one that challenges the lunar date for the New Year, which was supposedly the start of Spring and does indeed seem to conflate but not mistake Springrise and natural spring.   Here is another crack at the poem dedicated to gutsy McKee, though the core of the reading and title are conventional:

♪ *Do we honor the Sun, or honor the Moon?* ♪

With Spring so soon, what about the Year we're in, if Truth be told
Before the Moon, I cannot tell if we should we call it New or Old!

♪ **The Wonderful Yamato-uta Website of Mizukaki** provides a dozen or so poems influenced by Ariwara Motokata's KKS #1. Some already found their way into this book. A quick mad translation of four that did *not*:

年のうちに春立ちぬとや吉野山霞かかれる峰のしら雲　藤原俊成 shunzei d.1204
toshi no uchi ni haru tachinu to ya yoshino yama kasumi kakareru mine no shirakumo

Haze wraps around below the white clouds of Winter unknowing still
Upon the hoary peaks of Mount Yoshino within the Old Year, Spring!

雪のうちに春は来にけりよしの山雲とやいはむ霞とやいはむ　慈円 jien d.1225
yuki no uchi ni haru wa kinikeri yoshino yama kumo to ya iwamu kasumi to ya iwamu

Spring has come to Mt. Yoshino covered with snow
So, are those banners mist, or clouds? Who knows!

鶯もまだ出でやらぬ春の雲ことし(こち?)ともいはず山風ぞ吹く　定家 teika d.1241
uguisu mo mada ideyaranu haru no kumo ~~kotoshi~~ *kochi to mo iwazu yamakaze zo fuku*

Spring clouds from which no Robin has yet appeared –
This cold mountain wind can hardly be called an Easter.

野も山もまだ雪深き年の内に霞ぞおそき春は来にけり　宗尊親王 munetaka
no mo yama mo mada yuki fukaki toshi no uchi ni kasumi zo osoki haru wa kinikeri

In both the fields and the mountain the snowfall's still waist deep;
Spring's here, but her hazy train has yet to visit Winter's keep.

The first, I think, puns on within the year as within the house of, and I think of the white clouds as hair. I added "those banners" for padding in the second. The third is an uguisu (warbler/thrush/nightingale) not robin, but *I wanted a harbinger*. I bet the *kotoshi* was a mistake for the *kochi*, the *East* or *Come-hither* warm wind of spring. Why not call it an *Easter? Waist* and *train* in the last are an exaggeration.   Note too that the third and fourth poem are actually more Springrise *vs. Natural/meteorological* Spring – along the line that McKee described for Motokata's poem – than Springrise *vs.* the *Lunisolar* New Year per se.   I suspect that in years when Springrise came before that New Year, there was an excuse to notice the discrepancy, so such poems were more likely. Note that old haiku were so witty on this *Springrise before the New Year* (*toshinouchinoharu*) that in *The Fifth Season* (2007) I did not have to hyperbolize as I sometimes do with translations of *waka*.

* McKee gives the 1/8~2/20 date, 1729, when it occurred that early, while nothing I find online mentions such a possibility. One blogger notes that normal year New Years fall between 2/3~2/20 so that Springrise (2/4 or 5) almost always precedes it, while the New Years for the 7 of 19 years with intercalary months fell on 1/22~2/2 and thus always preceded Springrise. I suspect McKee's date is mistaken, but who knows. Maybe there was some anomaly I have yet to learn about.

* A top Usanian *waka* scholar found my delight with McKee for quoting Motokata's poem without prejudice surprising, as *"It is merely a shallow modern, Shiki-inspired heresy, a failure to read KKS as it was - on all available evidence - expected by its compilers to be read, that condemns Motokata's poem as in need of recuperation of some sort."* Perhaps, but all the commentary in English *I* recall follows Shiki on this, and, I repeat, the fact Carter, Keene and others *do not include this poem* that launched a thousand take-offs in *their* anthologies of traditional Japanese poetry suggests to me it is not appreciated; and that, I feel, may be representative of the larger lack of appreciation for the Japanese equivalent of English's light verse, which is to say, the subject of this book. Googled: *"Sterile wit distinguishes the works of Narihira's grandson Motokata. He often professes to be astonished by paradoxical situations"* – McCullough (*Brocade by Night:* 1985); *"Motokata's cleverness, witty paradox, and pose of elegant confusion were extravagantly admired by an age enthusiastically adapting to Japanese poetry the conceits, artifices, and intellectual posturings of the Chinese "oblique" (i-p'ang) style of the Six Dynasties period"* – Brower & Miner (*Fujiwara Teika's Superior Poems of Our Time* 1967). The former, which was one book I *had* seen, gives Motokata's worst poem KKS#261 to make him an exemplar of inanity. The latter, which I had not read before, shows rare appreciation of him while still pointing out . . .).

New Years – More Laurels or Nails in your Casket?   36 頁

♪**Another Version of Ikkyû's Poem** ends less catechistically: *"The gate pines? But mile-markers for that ultimate trip, / Sans horse, sans sedan and sans ye comfy roadside inns."* 門松はめいどのたびの一里塚 馬かごもなくとまりやもなし *kado-matsu wa meido no tabi no ichirizuka uma kago mo naku tomariya mo nashi.* If you wish, make the "ultimate trip" a *permanent vacation* and "ye comfy inn" that isn't, a *way station*. Despite the different *English* phrasing, the first half of the poem is identical to that of the lead poem of the chapter. Ikkyû's friend Chikamasa 親当 follows w/ something madder, making the annual crossroads a sort of hub-station for trips to the Underworld, where Month & Day runners/carriers were in constant movement 年越はめいどの旅の問屋場か 月日の飛脚 あしをとどめず *toshikoshi wa meido no tabi no toiyaba ka tsukibi no biyaku ashi o todomezu.*

♪ **New Year Metaphor and Urashima's Chest.** I introduced haiku about the gate-pine rather than my favorite *kyôka* expressing mixed feelings for the gift/burden of another year because the key word did not translate: *"Yet another year is here but nonetheless, how we delight to open that fateful treasure chest"* 又ひとつ年はよるとも玉手箱あけてうれしき今朝のはつ春　もとの木網　徳和一万 *mata hitotsu toshi wa yoru to mo tamatebako akete ureshiki kesa no hatsu haru* Moto-no-Mokuami. The "chest" is the problem. The original *gem-hand-box* was opened by Japan's Rip Van Winkle, Urashima Tarô, after the fisherman came back from the Sea Dragon's Palace to find everyone he knew long dead and grew lonely. I will not say what happened to him – read the tale – but, in this context, perhaps you can guess. Unfortunately, Pandora's box, though ambivalent, was *not* focused on aging, so even a classical allusion fails. 玉手箱と遊ぶ好例は蜀山人の「浦島太郎の画に」「乙姫の吸つけざしも のまれねば あけてくやしき 玉煙草かな」 蜀山人家集 (*otohime no suitsukezashi . . .*). つまり、遊女がキセルの用意すれば、吸わなくてもお支払い付けに出てしまうも、朝まで待たせたのも、双方とも悔しい。

♪ **Kisshû's Masterpiece?** There was one poem I was unsure of when I first read it, but feel I get it now. Literally it means: *"the more (you) take the more loss (you) run=pass/leaving year/s, give(me)! give (me) (them)! such thinking stupidity."* To wit:

とれば又とるほど損の行く年をくるゝくるゝと思ふおろかさ 橘洲 岩波の解説より
toreba mata toru hodo son no yuku toshi o kururu-kururu to omou orokasa kisshû c.1785

The more you get, the more you lose, year after year –
Why do we always think the new one brings us cheer?

The more you keep the more you weep, so why worry
at the end of one year, and why hurry into the next?

The more we get, the less we've left, so why do we cheer?
What fools we are to beg like this for yet another year!

Kururu is *kureru* "give me," or, taking the "o" as an emphatic "despite," may *also* mean the new one is *coming*, but before it pivots to mean *toshi o kururu* (give (me/us) a year/s), it "sends off" the old year, *toshi okuru*. The repetition gives a frantic quality to the poem inappropriate for that solemn season where the world is re-created or consecrated, but true as an expression of the excitement. All three readings are closer to and further from the original in one way or another. A somewhat related *Azuma-kyoku* 吾妻曲 poem has *Each Year's gift from the sea left by the tide as a line upon our brows* とし波のよするひたひのしはみよりくるゝはいたゞくをしまれにけり　手柄岡持 1786 *toshinami no hitai no shiwami yori kururu wa itadaku oshimarenikeri* tegara-no-okamochi The lack of a wave-related metaphors for the New Year and the ripple/wrinkle union dooms translation from the start. One cannot make a whole poem of new fabric unless it goes Jabberwocky, all the way. Wit needs familiar ground to work: *Each year Father Time plows yet another furrow into our brow until all who live become like Mother Earth, . . . etc..*

~~~~~~

New Year Zen+Zaniness, or, Dao and How!　　　　　　　　　　　　　　　38 頁

♪　**The Arcane Bow.** Can anyone read Teitoku's circular bow? Another of his bow poems, titled "Spring within the year" (年内立春 early solar spring: see pgs. 34-5):

    The Year's dart has not yet flown but, hark, a catalpa bow!
    Spindle tree, Spring is strung, zelkova, too, with arrow!

年の矢はいまたゆかねとあつさゆみ まゆみ月弓はるはきにけり　貞徳 *toshi no ya wa mada yukanedo azusayumi mayumi tsukiyumi haru wa kinikeri* (貞徳狂歌抄 tk1、自筆詠草みて). The catalpa has a "real-bow" in the name of the tree from which it is made and contrasts with the bow of the waning moon that would be seen a few days before the lunar New Year in the early morning which was character 月-punned into the zelkova or keyaki, also called tsuku/tsuki(moon)-bow. I put a *hark* before the catalpa, or azuza bow (*azusa yumi*), not just for the hidden arc, but because the string of this "round" (made of a whole branch rather than split and lamenated as the serious? bows were) bow was struck by miko (shamanesses) and, reading Teitoku's *kyôka* (the one in the main text), I felt the verb *naru* was intended to pun that hum. Teitoku's father was the owner (?) of a castle and most nobles had such a catalpa bow myth originated in Japan's first human ruler, Emperor Jimmu, great grandson of the Sun Goddess, whose bow came to dispel evil with a pluck (if there is a particular note or tone I do not know it) after a golden bird perched upon it. None of this can save Teitoku's good poem in translation. *Senryû* brought the catalpa bow as used by a shamaness down to earth: *"A soul of one who was dumb speaks up: Azusa miko!"* (世を去りし瘂も物いふ梓神女 *yo o sarishi oshi mo mono iu azusa miko* y 74). My favorite shamaness story, from *A Korean Story-teller's Miscellany* (trans. Peter Lee), comes to mind: the deceased, speaking through a medium chastises his family for visiting her when they knew he felt communication with spirits was bogus!

♪ ***For balance, a Not-so Arcane Bow.*** The following *kyôka* by Tenmei *kyôka* grand-master Akera Kankô's brilliant *Unkempt Wife* includes puns on archery-related terms. *Yatake,* modifying heart, means a tough unbending mindset and is homophonous with cane used for arrow shafts. *Willow* modifies a true-bow *mayumi, not* made of the same, because it *was* the standard simile for beautiful eyebrows, *mayu.*

ものゝふのやたけ心のひかるゝは妹が柳のまゆみなりけり　ふし松嫁ゝ　徳和 1785 *mononô no yatakegokoro no hikaruru wa imo-ga-yanagi-no mayumi narikeri* fushimatsu no kaka warrior's arrow-bamboo-heart shines-as-for lil-sis (girlfriend)-willow's real-bow=eyebrows is!

    The unbowed warrior finds his heartstrings drawn by a dart
    From the eye of a maiden with eyebrows like a willow's arc!

~~~~~~

Growing the Rock of Ages from a Pebble　　　　　　　　　　　　　　　　40 頁

♪ ***Japanese also get a kick from this subject***. In a book of Bierce-inspired humor, under the heading *"Boulder,"* Gunshi Gaishi (本名トシオ。元筑波大図書館長) writes:

> According to those who have followed rivers from their mouths to their founts and observed boulders growing from rocks which grew from pebbles, the way the sand on the seashore grows into boulders as it ascends the rivers is plain as day to see. Moreover, this natural law is manifest in the words of our national anthem: *". . . until pebbles grow into boulders and grow mossy.* 郡司外史著『迷解 笑辞苑』1981

And, one finds *waka* probably post-dating said *waka* but predating the use of it as an anthem. I fished these from the 1310 *Fuboku Wakashô* 夫木和歌抄,

ふかみとりいはねか上にむす苔や空にのほらぬけふりなるらん　前中納言匡房卿
fukamidori iwane ga ue ni musu koke ya sora ni noboranu keburi naru ran   masafusa

> *Can boulders bubble-over and smoke rise,*
> *but not into sky? Ask the dark green moss.*

としへたるいはほか上に雪ふりておひにけらしな苔のしらひけ　源仲正　同
toshi hetaru iwao ga ue ni yuki furite oi ni kerashi-na koke no shira-hige   nakamasa

> *Snow falling upon an august boulder shows its age;*
> *The white-whiskered moss recalls a Chinese sage.*

The original source of the second, which I like, is a book with a hundred *waka* on moss 堀河院御時 百首苔. No sage is mentioned in the original. A *kyôka*, probably 18-19c:

さゝれ石の岩となれる山川に育ちの早き春の若鮎　栗花園 一万 rikkaen?
sazare-ishi no iwa to nareru yamakawa ni sodachi no hayaki haru no waka-ayu
pebbles' boulder-into become mount. river-in grow-up quickly spring's young sweetfish

> *In the mountain stream, where rocks become boulders before you know,*
> *How quickly they, too, grow – the young sweetfish of spring!*

Growing rocks, or rather, *boulders* is an enchanting subject. For the hell of it, I googled "pebble grows." Two hits were interesting. The bracketed remarks are mine:

1) *"Deutschland Uber What Now?, Part 4 Notes: Very short and uncontroversial anthem voices desire for emperor to reign until tiny pebble grows into huge moss-covered mountain...."* [As it happens, there *has* been controversy over the Japanese anthem. Besides the anti-Emperor radicals who object to the mention of his reign (*kimi ga yo*) and jokes about pebbles "growing," we have one unique critique. Korean essayist Lee Oh Young opined that the anthem reflected the optimism and aggressive growth-orientation connected with Japanese imperialism, in contrast to the pessimistic Korean anthem where Mt. Paekche wears down to dust as, according to the laws of entropy it should (*In This Earth and In that Wind*: 1967. Transl. by David I. Steinberg). Lee later wrote a best-seller about the Japanese tendency to shrink things down (「縮み」志向の日本人).]

2) *"To the people that claim that Barack is a racist... it hurts like a pebble in the shoe but that pebble grows into a rock, then a brick wall & eventually the whole building falls down on you."* [Now that is someone who truly knows how to work a metaphor!]

「祝」そよ、君が代は千代に一度ゐる塵の白雲かかる山となるまで　梁塵秘抄
kimigayo wa chiyo ni hitotabi iru chiri no shirakumo kakaru yama to naru made
lord's reign/times-as-for, thousand-reigns/generations/ages-in once is dust
white-clouds touching/positioned mountain-as/into become until

> *Until fine dust, each thousandth year adding but one grain*
> *Builds a lofty cloud-covered mountain – may you reign!*

This is the first item in the *Ryôjinhisshô*, an anthology of 11-13c popular poetry and song. At first, I put too much effort into wording and too little into reading: *May you reign until dust makes a mountain crowned with sages / and white clouds as happens but once in a thousand ages!* I love those sages and volcanoes do indeed sprout up in Japan about once every milennium, but the poem was far more hyperbolic than reality! It is a cross between a *kalpa* (an immense unit of time measured by minute actions: see pg. xxx) and a Chinese saying elaborated in the preface to the *Kokinshû* where dust and dirt rise up from the *fumoto* (base, or skirts) to build a lofty cloud-covered mountain (How a yet-to-be mountain has a *fumoto* to grow from is beyond me, but anyway). Still, I wonder whether this poem (credited to Ôe Yoshitoki 大江喜言 in the 1086 *Goshûishû* 後拾遺集) might not have something more hidden between the lines, such as I make explicit here:

> May my Lord's Reign so free of dust that only one grain
> appears in a thousand years, last until a mountain rises
> high into the clouds from an accumulation of the same!

In other words, might not the mention of dust, a dirty thing sullying the clean shining mirror of Shintô or sinful desire clouding the bright moon of Buddhist Law in a poem serving as a benediction, call for a reframingt, namely *"if you grant we find but one speck of impure matter once per every thousand years in your brilliant realm"* and, then pivot to build the cloud-covered hyperbolic blessing using the "once in a ~" *kalpa* style of rhetoric? That would be a sublime trick of rhetoric. So clever, I am afraid, that no one I know of even considers such a reading . . . . *Am I nuts?* The following from *Tales of Eika* is translated sketchily in the text. Space permitting, I would free it up as follows –

わたつ海の亀の背中に居る塵の山となるべき君が御代かな　栄花物語
watatsumi no kame no senaka ni iru chiri no yama to naru beki kimigayo kana

> Like the chiri on the back of the turtle afloat on the main
> that became the Mountain of Youth, so, too, Your Reign!

Eiga-monogatari (1024-28) shows why it's fun. *Chiri* is between *dust* and *trash*, but not as clean as moss – make it *mire* if you want a more enchanted word. The folk, bless them, played with the idea in the hyperlogical manner of *kyôka* poets and asked in song:

万劫亀の背中をば　沖の波こそ洗ふらめ　いかなる塵の積もりゐて　蓬莱山と高からん

> The back of that Calpa Turtle out at sea
> must be washed by waves, and constantly!
> What dust or trash would stick and build up so
> that into a high Mount Merhu it could grow?

From the *Ryôjinhisshô* 梁塵秘抄 *mangô kame no senaka o ba* . . Note that Kalpa, a Buddhist term for a phenomenally long time, generally refers to how long it takes for something to wear *down* (pg.143). It is intriguing to see it modify growing turtle island!

~~~~~~

Did the Icicle Tears Begat the Slobber of Ye Cow?　　　　44 頁

♪ **Was I a bit harsh on Shunzei's 12c Icicle Tears?** My aim was more to show how good Teitoku was than to put down Shunzei, whose originality I admire. I should add that because Teitoku was a learned man, he definitely knew Shunzei's poem.

♪ **Why am I so upset about the treatment of Teitoku and alleged slobberal** that I complained in both *The Fifth Season* (2007) and now in this book? Because it is smug and wrong. Henderson writes of Teitoku "wishing to celebrate a New Year's Day which happened to be the beginning of the 'cow year'" and, noting the mimesis of *taruru tsurara* and the verb *taruru* meaning both *drip* and *hang*, calls the *ku* a "trick work emphatically 'not haiku' while Yasuda, who quotes him with clear approval, gratuitously adds, "*Icicles* is of course the seasonal word, and in itself has seasonal values, keenly suggesting a sense of winter – none of which is utilized in the poem." As for Henderson's remarks, Bashô was right to discourage beginners from relying upon mimesis and coincidence, but this hardly makes poems with them 'trick' works and unworthy of haiku. And Yasuda? He is so far off-base, I must tag him out. As I showed with *waka* and *haiku* examples, the melting icicle is a sign of spring. To insist the icicle belongs to winter alone is silly and seems to forget that the Japanese New Year marked the start of Spring. It is true that the date fell within the range of what today might be considered the tail of winter and that is often the coldest part. But, that New Year was also an enchanted mini-season and looking forward to Spring as we know it was part of the charm. If there was snow, that was considered good for it furnished a blank sheet from which life might spring or write itself anew. If it were warm and icicles dripped, that was proof Spring had properly come, on time . . . I will bet that if a historian can ascertain the exact date when Teitoku's ku was written and find information about the weather from other sources, that we will find that it was a relatively warm New Year. 在日暇人諸君よ！貞徳の名句が作られた、あの元日の天気は、氷柱が「涎」しそうな暖かいものであったかどうか、調べてくれませんか？再版にその、ご研究の結果を感謝しながら載せます。 Let me add that there is much good in Yasuda's *The Japanese Haiku*. The numerous otherwise untranslated arguments presented in the "haiku experience and length" section of the "Haiku Nature" chapter brings the reader something not found elsewhere though, at times, Yasuda errs in his analysis of what he presents (eg. a passage by Yamamoto Kenkichi on the way in which the words in a haiku only become significant simultaneously once the total meaning is grasped is twisted to show that "every word is an experience," another matter altogether), the thinking reader can still enjoy the book. Differently put, I like Yasuda's work for it is full of something rare in criticism, ideas, even if many are, imho, wrong.

♪お口直し。 **The idea of tears, being frozen extrapolated even to bird-song:**

たにかけの こほりもゆきも きえなくに まつうちとくる うぐひすのこゑ 千載集 1187
tanigake no kôri mo yuki mo kienaku ni matsuuchi tokuru uguisu no koe ng 番号外作者
valleys-peak's ice & snow too melting-not, pine(firstweek of NY)-within thaws warbler's voice

> *Why is it, that while both ice and snow have yet to go,*
> *The first thing to thaw would be the warbler's yodel?*

A soft celebration of Princess Sao's country matters　　　　　　　　48 頁

♪ ***What makes Teitoku's erotic pastel particularly interesting to me.*** In a word, I, like Hearn, was amazed at the absence of "the Eternal Feminine" in Japan. True, we have Benten, the patron goddess of art & letters, also goddess of feminine beauty (for courtesans and strippers – especially if they played with snakes – alike) and wealth. But her presence, physical or spiritual is hardly felt. Hearn wrote, "through all the centuries Western fancy has been making Nature more and more feminine" and that "out of simple human passion, through influences and transformations innumerable, we have evolved a cosmic emotion, a feminine pantheism." Indeed, Sam Gill has documented how Occidentals with background in Classic mythology even colored Amerindian worldviews with our Earth Mother concept. With such references rolling about in my noggin, when I read Teitoku's *kyôka*, both "dirty" *and* more exalted than the usual *waka* or *haikai* about a mountain wearing a cloud sash, I was thrilled at such country matters writ large. ♪ *Was Sôkan et al's Goddess with piss-wet clothing a partial take-off?* 宗鑑の裾を小便で濡らす佐保姫の名句＋句＝首は　気持ち悪い俳諧というより、「霞立つ天の川原に君待つといゆきかへるに裳の裾ぬれぬ」*kasumi tatsu amanogawa*. . . 万葉＃1528のロマンと霞の新年歌を交じり笑う、半ばパロデイ型狂歌と考えてもいいかもしれない。

Old Issa cuts farts into plum scent　　　　　　　　52 頁

♪ **Mixing It Up Bad.** While I knew when I wrote the chapter that farting+mixing were not Issa's invention, I had not yet found the following precedent he may or may not have seen, a *kyôka* by the 16c wild man of *kyôka*, Yûchôrô, includes in the 1666 *Kokin Ebisu Kyoku-shû,* or *Old-new Savage Song Anthology* that mixes potted, or rather boxed (square pots?) willows with cherry, while bringing in farts, shit, and if willow-branches were already synonymous with young or drunken male al fresco pissing, perhaps that, too. 桜にはあらぬはるべをこきませて　枝をたれたるはこ柳哉　雄長老 *sakura ni wa aranu harube o kokimazete* . . .. It is too juvenile to waste time on. Issa's, though *kyôka*, has soul, it is *ushin* 有心, coming from within as it describes his situation, *i.e.*, a geezer with a comparatively young wife. ♪ **More Fun with Farts.** The artless fartful essay beginning ありなし草 *Arinashigusa*, the compilation with one of Issa's (fartless) *ku* must be read in the original. Here is about 5% of the total of 「微席が屁にこたふる弁」

いふ事なかれ、放屁一声服薬千貼にむかふと。。。。妹がりさむみ冬の夜も屁をもつて風流とせざれば 　。。。ひそかに掌握するものを握り屁と号す。。。。馬の屁は四ツ谷につゞくべし。牛の小便は品川に長し。。。はしご屁はおかるをおびやかし、炬燵屁は九太夫を驚かす。。。。たとへ喰かくしする和尚はあれども、ひりかくしする若衆の移香は後朝もいかにいぶせくやありなん。。。。ぶつと放つ屁は仏陀のめうかんにいたるもうれしと尻をほつたてゝ微席なるものいふ事屁の如し。一茶全集8巻545頁 (蛇足。おかる＝二階・泥棒、めうかんは妙感)

The editors of *Issa Zenshû* point out that this came on the tail of a fad of fartology kicked off by Hirata Gennai's *Fartology* 放屁論 and including better known work by others such as 屁放大神大御伝、or Farting Great God's Great Message and 放屁百首 *Farting Hundred Poems*. Gennai was the great editor-writer-artist at home in ideas and possessing a genius for subtly surreal associations, who first recognized Shokusanjin – it takes one to know one – and is thus partly to be credited for the Tenmei *kyôka* boom. The hundred poems would be *kyôka*, thagt is, if they and their editor 蒙々斎牛貫 existed.

~~~~~~

Volcanic Hearts, or Burning Passion as the Fashion　　　　　　58 頁

♪ ***Did You Note the Author of the tears putting out the burning red dress?*** It was Ki no Tsurayuki (-946?), editor of the *Kokinshû* (c.1005). Japanese men of his time wrote as women when it tickled their fancy to do so. Tsurayuki wrote an entire travel diary, the *Tosa Nikki*, as a woman! This may have been partly because women first developed and used a flowing script with many lovely native words while men, with more formal studies, remained with the stiff Chinese (Japanese Chinese, not Chinese itself!) written style, and partly because the gender gap widened in the centuries since the *Manyôshû* (c.760-70), so that what would have been acceptable back then (a male poet wishing to be literally underfoot of his unreachable love) would be thought effeminate, so a man who would express such feelings had to do so as a woman. Even today, Japanese are more willing to cross-sing: men, stars and karaoke amateurs, sing *enka* (the song genre that started karaoke) where a woman is the protagonist and vice-versa, whereas, in Usanian country music, the words must be changed. There is no small irony in this, when you consider the way that Japanese would later call the *Manyôshû* manly and the *Kokinshû* effeminate.

♪ *Literally Lonely+Sad Love.* When I mention the 孤悲 *solitary+sadness* characters often used when the *koi=longing* was more lonely than passionate in the *Manyôshû*, most Japanese either draw a complete blank or shrug it off as the meaningless old orthographic system rendering Japanese completely into characters which everyone knows is called *Manyôgana* (万葉仮名). *Duh, you don't say!* They forget there are many ways to write *koi*, and whether the choice is the poet's or a scribe's, meaningful choice in a largely phonetic system demonstrates how visual information was never thrown completely away for the auditory. A French semiologist could probably write a whole book on it.

♪ *Fire in the West*. Even without the *omo(h)i* pun putting *fire* into all love, English, too, were perfect pyromaniacs of passion. Here are two *kyôka*-class examples from Butler's *Hudibras*. Frustration puts an interesting negative twist on that fire in the first and adds a physical justification to a common metaphor in the second.

Love in your heart as icily burns / As fire in antique Roman urns,
To warm the dead, and vainly light / Those only that see nothing by't.

Love is a fire, that burns and sparkles / In men as nat'rally as in charcoals,
Which sooty chymists stop in holes   /   When out of wood they extract coals:
So lovers should their passions choak, That, tho' they burn, they may not smoak.

Hudibras c. line 310 above; 425, right. Thanks, Gutenberg Project!

That was all of it and enough English examples in a book of Japanese poetry, but when I looked for the *Shinkokinshû* to read on the john and maybe find more wit than usually ascribed to it (I was just coming to it in the short history of *kyôka* later in the appendix), I could not find it and instead took Saintsbury's *Loci Critici*. There, reading Addison's essay of *True and False Wit*, I found a summary of passionate fire by just one poet that was so impressive that I just had to introduce it. After noting the true wit of ideas and the false wit of resemblances (later Addison adds *contraries*), or punning, after Locke, Addison, evidently recalling the joy he got from Cowley's poems, allowed that puns and concepts were not mutually exclusive and blessed their congress with a term: *"mixt wit."*

> Out of the innumerable branches of *mixt Wit*, I shall choose one instance which may be met with in all the writers of this class. The passion of love in its nature has been thought to resemble fire; for which reason the words fire and flame are made use of to signify love. The witty poets therefore have taken an advantage from the double meaning of the word fire, to make an infinite number of witticisms. Cowley observing the cold regard of his mistress's eyes, and at the same time their power of producing love in him, considers them as burning-glasses made of ice; and finding himself able to live in the greatest extremities of love, concludes the torrid zone to be habitable. When his mistress had read his letter written in juice of lemon, by holding it to the fire, he desires her to read it over a second time by love's flame. When she weeps, he wishes it were inward heat that distilled those drops from the limbes. When she is absent, he is beyond eighty, that is, thirty degrees nearer the pole than when she is with him. His ambitious love is a fire that naturally mounts upwards; his happy love is the beams of heaven, and his unhappy love flames of hell. When it does not let him sleep, it is a flame that sends up no smoke; when it is opposed by counsel and advice, it is a fire that rages the more by the winds blowing upon it. Upon the dying of a tree, in which he had cut his loves, he observed that his written flames had burnt up and withered the tree. When he resolves to give over his passion, he tells us, that one burnt like him for ever dreads the fire. His heart is an Etna, that instead of Vulcan's shop, encloses Cupid's forge in it. His endeavouring to drown his love in wine, is throwing oil upon the fire. He would insinuate to his mistress, that the fire of love, like that of the sun (which produces so many living creatures,) should not only warm, but beget. Love in another place cooks pleasure at his fire. Sometimes the poet's heart is frozen in every breast, and sometimes scorched in every eye. Sometimes he is drowned in tears, and burnt in love, like a ship set on fire in the middle of the sea. The reader may observe in every one of these instances, that the poet mixes the qualities of fire with those of love; and in the same sentence, speaking of it both as a passion and as real fire, surprises the reader with those seeming resemblances or contradictions, that make up all the wit in this kind of writing. Mixt wit, therefore, is a composition of pun and true wit, and is more or less perfect, as the resemblance lies in the ideas or in the words. Its foundations are laid partly in falsehood and partly in truth: reason puts in her claim for one half of it, and extravagance for the other. The only province therefore for this kind of wit, is epigram, or those little occasional poems, that in their own nature are nothing else but a tissue of epigrams.

You will note that despite giving grudging admission to mixt wit as valid wit, he none-the-less qualifies it (without giving any reason) as only acceptable for epigrams. Since most *kyôka* wit is *mixed* and all *kyôka* are short enough to be epigrams or the occasional poems Addison allows, one might say that the mad poems in this book have the great English essayist's mark of approval. And to think I found it on the john! (If your John is a place, it is "in;" if the device, then it is like no man, an island, and best preceded by "on.")

Yam Lovers Turn to Eel and Get Split & Roasted   60 頁

♪**While being *split* like eels and *roasted* is metaphorically sad**, I could not help adding a sexier metaphor, namely *spit*. For the eel *are* skewered to keep them from curling-up as they roast. The only *spit* metaphor I happened across, however, was in an old *Nihonshoki* (   ) Song by a satisfied Prince to his Princess as translated by Edwin A Cranston (#167 in his anthology): *" . . . Two glorious vines, / We lie embraced and intertwined, / Game flesh on a spit, / We are sleeping sweetly when . . ."* The word for the game on the skewer part is *shishikushiro*. The double metaphor is impressive, but the most powerful vine allegory I know is a longer song in the 12c *Ryôjinhishô*, *"Whenever I see a beauty, I would turn into a vine and wrap around her from my roots to my tip and though I may be cut up or chopped to bits, I was born to never let go"* (美女うち見れば一本蔓にもなりなばやとぞ思ふ　本より末まで縒らればや切るとも刻むともも　離れがたきはわが宿世　梁塵秘抄 *binjô uchi mireba* . . .).

♪ Re.: **Stories of Long-Yams/Taro Turning Eel**. I found a reference in a book of *kyôka* that were largely reporting and complaining: 参考　1) 山の芋の半分はうななぎのよふに見へけるを《半分はうなぎに成し薯蕷有生非生もしれぬ世の中》長崎一見狂歌集 *hanbun wa unagi ni narishi imogashira* . . . c1700 。2) 鯉をえさせける人の書札に扁を誤りてヲ扁に書こしける返事に《山芋うなきに化する証拠もて　鯉をたぬきにする扁もあり》宗吟　古今夷曲集 tk1 . . . Sôgin 1666。蛇足。え＝得させける、犭扁＝けだものへん、化する＝けする。

The King of Siam: Love so mad it is ~~almost~~ impossible to translate.   64 頁

♪**Cranston's translation of SIS 1188** (*Who is lost in love / Finds himself become Buddha: / If you tell me this, / I reply that I am then /The Lord of the Pure Land*) almost *allows* a reading where suffering gains one brownie points in the next world. I was *relieved* to see Cranston, too, call the poem "ambiguous." Does becoming a *hotoke*/buddha mean "to die," or "die of love," as now? Is it "plausible" people believed in "an imaginary hierarchy of passion.: if lovers are ordinary buddhas, then I am Amida himself?" The Japanese editor 小町谷照彦氏 wonders whether a lost proverb is behind the poem, if love might have been considered hell, etc.. Many guesses; no solution.

♪**The *Broadview* version** starts *koi shite*; Cranston's *koi suru ni*, another (ls) *koi suru to*.

♪ **Only Hurt That Way Again.** On the whole, I prefer my reading to Cranston's, from which I borrowed the first line, *"If every heartbreak / Can be endured in silence / At the fracture point / Even pain becomes at last / A sad souvenir of love."* But, his "love" in the last line may beat my "thee," chosen largely for the rhyme.

Putting the Furious Loving of Cats into a Season   66 頁

Most people dislike being kept awake in the wee hours of the night and whether they admit it or not find the preternatural energy and appetite of these cold-defying all-night lovers hard to take. Only the poet burning the night oil who vicariously enters the fray can properly appreciate them. Here is the greater part of Peter Pindar's AN ODE TO EIGHT CATS *Belonging to Israel Mendez, A Jew*. SCENE: The street in a country town; The Time: Midnight – The poet at his chamber window. After Carl Van Vechten (*The Tiger in the House*. 1922), I will omit "the four moralizing verses:"

> *Singers of Israel, O ye singers sweet,*
>   *Who, with your gentle mouths from ear to ear,*
> *Pour forth rich symphonies from street to street,*
>   *And to the sleepless wretch the night endear!*
> *Lo! In my shirt, on you these eyes I fix,*
>   *Admiring much the quaintness of your tricks;*

Your friskings, crawlings, squalls, I much approve;
Your spittings, pawings, high-rais'd rumps,
Swell'd-tails and merry-andrew jumps,
  With the wild ministrelsy of rapt'rous love.

How sweetly roll your gooseb'rry eyes,
As loud you tune your am'rous cries,
  And loving, scratch each other black and blue!
No boys in wantonness now bang your backs,
No curs, nor fiercer mastiffs, tear your flax,
  But all the moon-light world seems made for you.

Good gods! Ye sweet love-chanting rams!
How nimble are you with your hams
  To mount a house, to scale a chimney top,
And peeping from that chimney hole,
Pour in a doleful cry, th' impassion'd soul,
  Inviting Miss Grimalkin to come up:

Who, sweet obliging female, far from coy,
Answers your invitation note with joy,
  And scorning 'midst the ashes more to mope;
Lo! borne on Love's all-daring wing
She mounteth with a pickle-herring spring,
  Without the assistance of a rope.

Dear mousing tribe, my limbs are waxing cold—
  Singers of Israel sweet, adieu, adieu!
I do suppose you need now to be told
  How much I wish that I was one of you.

For readers not lucky enough to own a full set of Peter Pindar poems, here are the missing verses: *Singers of Israel, you no parsons want / To tie the matrimonial cord; / You call the matrimonial service, cant – / Like our first parents, take each other's word: / On no one ceremony pleas'd to fix – / To jump not even o'er two sticks.* 狂 *You want no furniture, alas! / Spit, spoom, dish, frying-pan, nor ladle; / No iron, pewter, copper, tin or brass; / No nurses, wet or dry, nor cradle, / Which custom, for our Christian babes, enjoins, / To rock the staring offspring of your loins.* 狂 *Nor of the lawyers have you need, / Ye males, before you seek your bed, / To settle pin-money on madam: / No fears of cuckoldom, heav'n bless ye, / Are ever harbour'd to distress ye, / Tormenting people since the days of Adam.* 狂 *No schools you want for fine behaving, / No powdering, painting, washing, shaving, / No nightcaps snug – no trouble in undressing / Before you seek your strawy nest / Pleas'd in each other's arms to rest, / To feast on love, heav'n's greatest blessing.*

～～～～～～～～～～～～～～～～

Leveling Mountains for Love of the Moon & Sex　　　　　　　70 頁

♪ **Old-fashioned War Against Nature**. Even before the *Manyôshû* – in the *Kojiki* (c.710) – we find desire endangering topography when an Emperor wished for "five hundred iron mattocks" (Cranston) to dig up and chuck aside a hill where a maiden was "a-hiding" from him (*otome no ikakuru oka o . . .*). Books could be written on deliberate attacks on the landscape. Herodotus records in detail how a General had his soldiers take time off from a campaign to demolish a river that drowned his favorite horse. Better to make a mad poem than act out!

♪ **The Most Spectacular Prayer for the Destruction of Topography** in Japanese poetry is in the *Manyôshû* and specifies a *road* rather than mountains. A woman lamenting the pending assignment/exile of her lover/husband, wished for it to be *pulled in, folded-up and burned by heaven's fire*. A tricky poem. More is in *A Dolphin in the Woods* (2009).

♪ ***Compare my Explicit & Snappy idea-centered translations of the Kokinshû poems*** (kks 877, 880, 881) in this chapter with those of others to see how what is *potentially* read as a *kyôka* in the original may become clearly mad Englished.

♪ ***Tsurayuki, Pretending to have been disillusioned by the moon*** being so public (kks #880) may play on adult matters, but *some people can actually recall their shock at learning from others that the moon, which seems to a small children to follow them about like a pet, did not follow only them.* Zora Neale Hurston did (*Dust Tracks on a Road*: 1942); Tsurayuki might have. But triggered by a childhood memory or not, the poem is not *nostalgia*. It is a purely facetious complaint, a splendid example of *mushin* 無心.

♪ ***"Leg-dragging" Mountain.*** 足引山は葦引!? Did you notice the usual 足 *leg* character is, instead, 葦 *reed* in this poem? Checking my OJD, I found 9 etymologies for this epithet for mountains so common the mountain need not be mentioned. Sure enough, one explains the use of "reed" in the *Kokinshû* by an origin tale: *the gods pulled up reeds/cane to make rivers and the discard created as a side-effect became mountains!*

~~~~~~

But will it Fly in Translation? — Love Sundry & Typed 72 頁

♪ ***Some definitely do NOT fly***. 早乙女恋 早乙女の笠の下紐とけそめてあひみん秋をたのみかけ水 季保 同 *saotome no kasa no shita . . . Kihô?* This *Love for Maidens* engaged in spring rice planting looking forward to fall has hat ties replace the usual undergarment ones and primes the pump with an agricultural term. I may try, say, *When the hats of the girls planting rice come off for keeps in fall, / I'll be there to reap what I see and see what I can reap!* But, it does not *work*. Neither does this 雑恋 sundry love poem: 海豚ならぬ妹か五たひのいかなれは命にかへて我は恋しき 雄左丸 同 *Iruka naranu Imo ga gotai no Ika nareba Inochi no kaete Ware wa koishiki* osamaru?). I can try, *My doll no dolphin to me – no joke! / l would gladly give my life for you, my pig in a poke.* Hopeless! Dolphin (*iruka*) sounds like *"is (she here)?"* – modern poet Tanikawa Shuntarô made his name with a nonsense verse playing with *iruka*: Is/are/exist it/you/we/he/she/they? – but the characters read "sea-pig." Pig implies fat, which she is not. One of half-a-dozen etymologies for *iruka* in the OJD derives it from *popping up + sinking down*, both love-related terms. The acrostic "Ii ii wa" means "it's fine," my reading of the poem is not.

♪ 未解読首も一例：あな恋し恋に心もまめ蟹の逢ぬ夜半をも中にはさめり 中栗 同 隔恋 *ana koishi koishi ni kokoro mo mame kani no awanu yahan o mo naka ni wa sameri/hasameri*. 穴小石蟹の泡挟めりなどの掛けはわかったが、大意に自信ない。

♪ **I tried my own *iruka*-style poem *in English*.** Long as the tail of a shaggy dog, it may be summed in a line: *Poor puss on purpose jumped on a porpoise that turned out to be a shark whose bite unlike said dog's was worse than his bark, not that he had one.*

~~~~~~

Approaching Love by Fire, Rain, Roads, Stars, etc. – both chapters. 74 頁

♪ **Far from Mediocre, Good Love Kyôka?** We have seen many examples of so and so poems. Some may have improved *in English* because I felt no compunction to translate well; dealing with what can only be improved, the terror is less. The 1785 *Tokuwa-shû* has some better love-related poems, but they tend to be much harder to English. My favorite is by Tegara no Okamochi and as masterful as any by Shokusanjin. The puns are too tightly woven into the flow of the idea to be translated. Japanese readers, enjoy: 片思ちぎられぬ物とはいまぞしるこ餅一本箸のかた思ひにて 手柄岡もち *chigirarenu mono to wa ima zo shiruko-mochi . . . .* 蛇足無用！And the first three in *Tokuwa's Love* 恋歌上 section: 初恋 こは／＼も人のみるめ目をぬき足にふみそめてけり恋の道芝 銀杏満門 *kowagowa mo hito no . .* 蛇足：目と足を抜く慣用語に浦のみるめ、葦をかさねてもままの首 ◎寄山初恋 くるしともいはで心に納太刀これやわけ入恋の初山 唐衣橘洲 *kurushi to mo iwa . . .kisshû* 蛇足：岩に大山詣で志願をたて木製太刀を納める秀歌 ◎忍恋 うき涙しのぶに心ありの穴つゝみがきれて袖をもるやと 加陪仲塗 *uki namida shinobu ni kokoro ari . . .* kabe no nakanuri 蛇足脱帽：こころ有りの破壊原因蟻への変身は旨いし、諺の前後の部分、用心「あり（の穴）つつ」のかけながら飛び繋ぐ妙もありましたーぴす。

♪ **Thunder & Lightning *Kyôka*.** My favorite, explainable yet utterly untranslatable thunder *kyôka* is by Chinese and waka studies teacher cum mad-poem abettor (?) of the first stars of the Tenmei *kyôka* movement, Uchiyama Gatei 賀邸: 天のはら鳴りて時々下るならきうすえてやれ雷のへそ *amanohara narite tokidoki kudaru nara kyû suete yare kaminare no heso* (なだいなだ著：江戸狂歌より). Heaven's fields become the sky's belly which growling sometimes descends, that is suffers diarrhea, when mugwort might be burnt on the thunder(ing) site, i.e., the navel, a part of the anatomy thunder demons were thought to steal if left uncovered. One could start, with say, heavenly firmament and have it emit thunderous eructations before dropping cataracts of rain, but without the navel lore and mugwort all we are left with is the foul weather.

♪ **The Isle with a Hole in its Belly?** This poem was *first* read differently by my respondent who noted pleasure quarters could be called an island and a belly with a hole could refer to Yoshiwara, the quarters near Edo because "people-holes," meaning caves with people, could be found on the "belly" of Mt. Fuji overlooking it. 『柳樽十六篇』に「人穴は富士権現のうしろなり」があります。浅草の富士浅間社の後ろにあるのが吉原です。この場合の「人穴」は卑猥ですが富士権現と繋がります。富士信仰は江戸時代に盛んで人穴は浄土と見なされたようです。*Wow!* To that, I can add a *senryû*: "*Making her name with a man-hole, the mistress boasts a Fuji(widow's)peak*" 人穴で出世妾の不二額 柳多留 88 *hitoana de shusse mekake..*). And it got sexier yet with wind-holes in the belly (as caverns were so credited on mountains) standing for the vulva: 「吉原→人穴→風→どてっ腹に風→腹にあなある島」. But, what does this mean for the reading? Does the poet, suffering heart-ache alone in the private world of love, miss the hole he may buy? Or, have I missed something? While intrigued with my respondent's observation, I still favor an allusion to the fictive island. ★*Later*. When material referencing the poem and its loose phrasing of a hole in the belly to the legendary island was called to the attention of my respondent, he took back the above reading. But, I enjoyed it too much not to share it with you and if he reads this I apologize for mentioning it. I always introduce my own mistakes, for they are the best part of translating for those of us who enjoy our fallibility.

How to Escape from the Love-sick Blues at Home   80 頁

♪**Love Anthropomorphized in English.** If I had English and Japanese-reading students and access to both the old English poetry data bases and the waka data bases, I might collect and compare the personified Loves/*koi* over the centuries. Here are a couple from Butler's Hudibras that have that *kyôka* touch (as I write this, I recall Blyth finding Zen in English literature and feel simultaneously glad to have a precedent and silly):

'Tis like that sturdy thief that stole
And dragg'd beasts backwards into's hole:
So Love does lovers, and us men
Draws by the tails into his den,
That no impression may discover,
And trace t' his cave, the wary lover, . . .

He that will win his dame, must do
As Love does when he bends his bow;
With one hand thrust the lady from,
And with the other pull her home.

Hudibras 429-34, 449-52. Thanks Gutenberg!

The second is not so much *about* Love as learning from his metaphor. The bow-as-lover metaphor was common in classical Japanese love poems. I vaguely recall but cannot pin down one close to this and hope someone will find it for me.

♪**Englishing *Koi*: the main problem** is 恋 is much broader than "love" – except for the way *love* is applied to all sorts of things that are *liked*, a usage not found in Japanese – which is but a segment on its continuum of meaning/s. It often means "wanting," the condition of both desiring *and* lacking. The English *longing* is close, but too narrow. *Desire,* too, and not colloquial enough. If we only had a *noun* for *missing!* (Don't feel bad, the Japanese have no *verb* for it, as *koishigaru* is too lovey-dovey and *sabishigaru* too plain lonely). The *blues* will do in a pinch, but *blues* lacks the positive side of *koi* and is not restricted to matters of love unless modified with "love-sick." Despite these many problems, *koi* seems like such a simple word that translators usually fail to explain it. That is not to say that words that *are* usually explained can be translated any better.

Aware, for example, is almost *always* noted and explained at least once, then put into the glossary, as well. Translated as "Alas!" it is identified with "pity," as an aesthetic term, it is a sort of *melancholy beauty*. Even so, depending on the poem and translator, it can be almost anything! Take the translation of KKS #939 (*aware chô(to iu) koto koso utate yo no naka o omoi-hanarenu hodashi narekere*). McCullough and Rodd & Henkenius, respectively, make it, *"What men call* love */ Is simply / A chain / Preventing escape / From this world of care."* and, *"each murmur of joy / and sorrow   agitates my / heart and binds me more / tightly   shackles me to this / sad life I had hoped to leave."* Calling it *love* and what *in so many words* amounts to *emotions* is not wrong, but I would probably translate it *altogether differently*, say,   *What's called* beauty *binds me to this world of woe / Preventing my thoughts from ever rising up to go.* Or, maybe, *Beauty is what keeps us shackled to this world of woe; / Without it, I would have left it long ago!* Sometimes *aware* meant just "beauty;" but as *matter* is never *just* matter but includes gravity, *beauty* is never *just* beauty, but a force that attracts and holds us to it.

~~~~~~

My love is an otter & other dreams. 82 頁

Could the otter play with a slightly earlier anon. wacky waka in the *Kokinshû* (*namida-gawa makura nagaruru ukine ni wa yume mo sadaka ni miezu arikeru* kks#527)? In Cranston's translation, *"In this floating sleep, / Pillow bobbing in the current / Of my river of tears, / I cannot see you steadily / Admist my swirling dreams"* and R&H *"even in sleep the / swift currents of this river / of tears buffet my / pillow   keeping me from rest – / not even my dreams are spared."* You might think the/ odd enjambment reflects that buffeting, but, no, most R&H poems are parsed & spaced by a machine, and one not too bright to boot! I'll have to try my own translation of this some day!

~~~~~~

To pluck a sleeping zither 84 頁

♪**Real Erotic Poems**. I would like to find more good, especially *personal* or, at least naturally-born *kyôka* about love, desire and sex – as opposed to those written on-order for inclusion among other poems on such – but lack the resources or time to do so alone. In the final stages of the book, checking on something else ★, I came upon two poems in the *Nagasaki Ikken Kyôka-shû*, which, in combination with Shokusanjin's more elegant and sophisticated sleeping zither, give an idea of what I am looking for. The pseudonym Nagasaki Ikken was doubtless made for the book which observes life in Nagasaki. I do not know the date. *Broadview* has no information; my respondent has not yet listed it.

女の洗濯するを見て　　長崎一見狂歌集 tk1 c.1700?
雪のはたへそゝくたといのみつからも　浅くは思ひまいらせず候
yuki no hada e sosogu tatoi no mizukara mo asaku wa omoi mairasezu soro
snowy skin-to pour proverbial water-from⇒by-itself+emph. shallow-as4 thinking-goes.

Seeing a Woman Bathing

The water poured flows naturally down her snowy skin
For my thoughts to stop shallow would be a mortal sin!

~~~~~~

Water, like a proverb, finds its own way down her snowy skin,
while my thoughts of themselves likewise find they go within.

見るに心ひかれて胸もおとり子かあらほんのふのきつなとそなる
miru ni kokoro hikarete mune mo odori-ko ga ara-honnô no kizuna to zo naru 同 tk1
seeing-by heart drawn breast too dances⇒dancng-grls raw/new pssions' tie+emph. becom

To see them is to have one's heartstrings drawn in fashion
My breast dances with the girls, and I recall raw passion!

*By my heart-strings tugged about, my breast is wildly Dancing
Girls, when they move, form a bond 'tween me and passion!*

The first alludes to the effect of a white skin touched by water that had saints falling from clouds, puns on the proverbial water finding its own level and shape into a broader self-actualization of the poet's thoughts and, indirectly flips over the usual idea of sexual urges as shallow, though in a delightful polite-speak I could not imitate. Instead, I went fishing between the lines and pulled up some fish only nibbling in the original. The second uses the first part of the "dancingirl," one word in Japanese, as a verb and is honest in the manner of the modern *waka*, the *tanka*, about how the dancing affects the poet. If you have not seen a performer up-close for a long time, it does strike one as a revelation. As one who has retired from society for long stretches and experienced just that, *I* am moved by the testimony. "Raw" here is "rough" as an unpolished gem, and in Japanese, good for being one with the original source (The spiritual value of crude things, of bare material, in Japan is explained at length in *The Fifth Season* and in T*opsy-turvy 1585*). We are talking *primal passion* and *religio,* without the lingo! 要するに「恋」という項目すらない狂歌集からこそ恋を釣り、狂歌を狂歌集でない一茶の日記など俳書に漁る。おもえば「有心狂歌」とでも言える類に出会う好方法にもなりうる。ところで、『長崎一見狂歌集』の上記の首々の間、少数ながらあった俳句の中、*Rise, Ye Sea Slugs!* に入れたい一句を取った「黄瓜もやなまこのゆうれいあらわれたり」。海鼠がもともと海胡瓜（sea cucumber）という英語では、幽霊の奇瓜は当然過ぎるで翻訳しても面白くないが。。。

★ **This book has many "final stages,"** as every time I started to proof, I would find out something new and interesting as I checked for something else. Before the final "final," I discovered quite a cache of personal eroticism among the 2000 or so *kyôka* by Getsudôken (c.1700) that was in TK1, so this note will be partly contradicted in later chapters. 二ヶ月で書き下ろしたりと思へば　やはり挙句は馬鹿の一年.

What! No Pockmarks on the Bare-faced Moon? 88頁

♪ **Saigyô's poem appreciating some clouds with the moon** may have another more anthropocentric interpretation. Years ago, it was my first reading. I chickened out for, grammatically, it's harder to support, and tricky, for the English "entertain" is not quite as broad as *motenasu*. It can mean serving *pupus* to moon-viewers or offering dancing girls for a banquet. So saying, here are two more translations just in case I was right:

nakanaka ni tokidoki kumo no kakaru koso tsuki o motenasu kagiri narikere

Sometimes it's much better with clouds enough for hors d'oeuvre's with the moon!

Many times, for sure, I could use some clouds – enough to entertain me & the moon!

♪ **Make-up for Modesty.** Readers of my *Topsy-turvy 1585* will already have read this in far more detail, but let me point out that Edward Morse observed young Japanese women applying white powder despite being exceedingly white themselves because *not* doing so would make them seem boastful of their light skin. As most of us must read things at least twice to remember them, I do not feel bad about occasional redundancy.

♪ **A Rudely Bare Moon.** There is a 17c *kyôka* about a bare moon but it is not her face but her entire person, and involuntary.

かつらおとこ雲の衣をふんぬいて丸はたかなる月のなりかな卜養
katsura-otoko kumo no koromo o bun-nuite maruhadaka naru tsuki no nari kana
katsura-tree man cloud-clothing/robes+acc jerk(rudely)-stripped/ing round/completely nude becomes moons appearance.　bokuyô

*The Man in the Moon's stripped off all her cloud-wear: how rude!
Look at Luna: Can you not see? – She is now buck-naked, nude!*

The original expresses rudeness by the *bun* prefixed to the verb meaning "stripped", indicating it was done quickly by force. A far simpler poem than my translation and more juvenile than Sharaku's bare face concept, another rhyme comes to mind: *crude*. An unneeded preface says the moon was full.   ★ As I proceeded to proof, ten minutes later – two notes down – an NPR review of some jazz/world fusion ambient – make that boring – music release mentioned what may have been the title of a song or the album itself and it was: *"last night the moon came dropping her clothes in the street/"* The critic said it was taken from the Sufi poet Rumi. So, if the reader knows any Rumi fans . . .

~~~~~~

Moon Envy – Parody? Yes. *Facetious?* Maybe.   90 頁

♪ ***Reversing the Vector, or Extreme Anthropomorphism.*** Ôta's envious moon reverses the usual trope in two ways. First, *the envied* becomes *the envious*. Second, the *object of thought* becomes *the thinker*. "I see the moon" has become "and the moon sees me." This sort of reversal is found among the *haikai* poems in a chapter 19 of the *Kokinshû*. The poet, none other than Ariwara no Motokata, is the same who wrote the much maligned first poem in the collection which plays with the arbitrary nature of the calendar, or our perception of time. Here it is, in a translation that splits the single verb *uramirarureba* into "bitter" and "hate" despite being absurdly short:

よのなかはいかにくるしと思ふらむここらのの人にうらみらるれば　元方
yononaka wa ika ni kurushi to omouran kokora no hito ni uramirarureba motokata
world-withn-as-fr painfully thinkng!/?/: many/masses of people-by begrudgd/hated

> *How it must pain the world to know*
> *that many bitter people hate it so!*

Perhaps I should add that it immediately follows an Anon. poem that laments *yononaka no uki tabigoto ni mi o nageba fukaki tani koso asaku nariname*. This one comes out too long:

> *Were we whenever the world brought pain to throw ourselves off peaks*
> *Even the deepest valleys would become shallow indeed!*

No one followed Motokata and took pity on the *world*. Three centuries later, in the *Gyokuyôshû* (1312) we find,

みもつらくよもうらめしきふしふしを わすれぬものは なみたなりけり　実雄
mi mo tsuraku yo mo urameshiki fushi fushi o wasurenu mono wa namida narikeri saneo
body/self painfl world too hated jointx2 (sad episode?) forgets-not thing/one-as4 tear/s is/r

> *Even bodies hurt, the world's a hateful place where*
> *Not a single thing forgotten, but turns into tears!*

~~~~~~

> *Tears are what do not forget every little thing*
> *that we hate about the world, like our bodies hurting.*

The second reading reverses the word order but maintains the flow better than the first and is wrong only in making the hurting body an example ("like"). The "tears" not the "world" are the subject, and, in English that makes them come first. Note how convenient it was for me to keep the world where it was to make it seem the subject and thereby relate better to Motokata's reversal. *With word-order and their semantic relations often at odds in translation between Japanese and English*, we have an excuse to make things come out as we wish. The only question is how often translators are aware of it!

♪ ***Was Ôta Seriously Feeling Blessed?*** When young Ôta, Yomo no Akara, wrote *"What tranquil times! But too many blessings has a cost: / Live long and you will come to bear a heavy cross!"* (長生をすれば苦しき責を受く めでた過ぎたる御代の静けさ　四方赤良 *nagaiki o sureba kurushiki seki o uku medeta-sugitaru miyo no shizukesa*), he may have represented someone suffering the ravages of old age, but my point is that, even as a young man, he was familiar with the stereotypical nation-view expressed in *zappai* and *senryû* by relaxed hanging balls and played with it. A typical, less reflective view, similar to that found in *senryû* but with more clever, paradoxical metaphor was expressed by Akera Kankô's "Slovenly Wife," Fushimatsu-no-Kaka, in her 1785 *kyôka* "Celebrating With Swords" 寄刀祝. It is too dependent on Japanese sword terms to English, but for the reference of Japanese readers: いにしへの乱れ焼刃もしら鞘にうちをさまれる御世ぞやす國　節松嫁々　徳和 *inishie no midare yakiba mo shira-saya ni uchi-osamareru miyo zo yasukuni* Fushimatsu no Kaka. Pounding the sword into the scabbard, she makes peace seem downright erotic! Poems grateful for peace appeared within decades of the closing of Japan. Here is a *kyôka* from the 17c *Savage Songs*:

A paper robe in place of ancient armor, still a man of parts,
Can rest, safely protected from the cold wind's chilly darts!

いにしへのよろひに替る紙子さへ風のいる矢は通さざりけり 蓮生法し 古今夷曲集
inishie no yoroi ni kawaru kamiko sae kaze no iru ya wa tosazarikeri   renshô?   p.1666
long-ago/ancient-times' armor-w/ exchanging paperobe even wind shoots arrows-as4 pass-not

Amazingly, armor was already considered a thing of long ago. You can imagine thoughts a hundred years later! That is why I feel the moon *kyôka* is a parody that cuts two ways and not just a totally positive take on his society as Edo expert Tanaka Yuko suggested. But Ôta could have been pretty content before he was forced to censor himself and may indeed have agreed with Tanaka's reading and Robert Herrick's assertion:

THE PRESENT TIME BEST PLEASETH.

PRAISE they that will times past ; I joy to see
Myself now live : this age best pleaseth me.

♪ **More Contentment in the 19c.** The next poem is brushed in front and slightly above the face of a formally smiling – grinning with a slight grimace suggesting being ever so properly awed – *monkey* dressed up in propitious New Year robe with a Sacred Shintô hat and a stick with paper folded in a holy way on an 1824 surimono. Issa had observed the same in 1816, *In my country even the monkeys wear top hats* (*waga kuni wa saru mo eboshi . . .*) Well, an *eboshi* hat, at any rate; and in case that did not explain what was what, he had a second haiku specifying the monkey performed holy rites 祈祷. I recall seeing that picture by Hokkei (1780-1850) before, as the rich colors of the bold black and gold stripes behind a red rising sun contrast with the overall soft tone and the papers make an abstract rectangular chain for an effect that I find exquisite and unforgettable. At that time I must not have been able to read Suigan's poem. Now I can, so –

ゆたかなる御代の恵ミやまわさなくさるにもおよふ千金の春　晴雪楼翠巖
yutakanaru miyo no megumi ya mawasanaku saru ni mo oyobu senkin no haru suigan
affluent-becme hon.reign's blessngs sent-round-not monky-to-evn reaches 1000gold-spring

Blessed be these wealthy times when a thousand gold-piece Spring,
Comes to a monkey who waits with a smile doing nothing.

The beautiful 2008 book *Colored in the Year's New Light* has the picture (pl.12) and more explanation about the monkey and what he wore, but I am afraid the poem, itself, was misread: *The blessings of this beautiful realm! / We reach out to the monkey, who, / even without going round to perform / carries with him a spring / worth one thousand gold pieces*. The first and third line are more precise than my reading, but the larger idea was lost. Only 5 years before this, Issa writes of a Buddha who just lying there is showered with petals and coins. When I included it in my *Cherry Blossom Epiphany* only a couple years ago I had not yet learned about colossal wickerwork lying-Buddhas that were the rage at that time, but luckily that did not affect my translation. McKee was not so lucky. A reader of my *Fifth Season* might notice that two major concepts are fused in this *kyôka*. One is the celebration of how fortunate a time in which we live – why I put it in the Jealous Moon note. The other is how good fortune is shown and it has to sub-categories: one is to enjoy the kingly luxury of not moving and having things come to you and the other is for the fortune to be so large that it extends to cover everyone and everything, including monkeys, of course. Haiku by people from 17c Bashô to 18-9c Issa mention foreigners coming to greet, or rather pay obsequeence to the Emperor on New Years. And a nativist (Hirata Atsune), while admitting those foreigners sure got around in the world, added that such only went to show that Japan was the head and they were the arms and feet – in other words, *gravitas* means they come to you. Of course, people must be tossing coins somewhere, though it is not shown in the picture, but the real wealth is in being alive another spring without having to gad about to survive. Here is a conceptually related *surimono*, likewise a masterpiece-class work of art, from *Colored in the Year's New Light* (pl.146), dated "ca. 1830" –

なみまより浦嶋太郎月龍宮までも春や立らん　史喬
namima yori urashima tarôzuki ryûgu made mo haru ya tatsuran shikyô 1832?
waves-amng-frm urashima=lee/bay-isle tarô-moon dragn-palace untl spring/ny-arrives

Mist, up from the sea, covers the Leeward Isle: it's Turtle Moon,
To even Dragon Palace undersea Spring brings her boon!

Context turns the otherwise taken-for-granted name of the Japanese Rip Van Winkle, Urashima Tarô's name into a Leeward Island and Turtle (Tarô or first son was also slang for a marsh turtle) which, followed by *tsuki* becomes the Tarôzuki, a poetic name for the first moon, the month of the New Year. Since a turtle (different type, for sure) saved by the fisherman originally took him to that enchanted palace (and returned him with hexagrams printed on his butt according to *senryû*), said moon is particularly suitable for Spring's trip, though any moon includes the nuance of reaching all parts of the world, and thus opens up the horizon for Japanese New Year, which tends to be more vertically-oriented in time. The heading said the surimono was for "a" New Year. I would say it must have been for 1832, as the poem is definitely Year of the Dragon. The *tatsu* ("standing" or showing itself of the Spring) is a homophone for one of the two most used pronunciations of "dragon," the one used for the Year, *Tatsu*-doshi. Since "spring" also means the New Year, the end of the poem puns as "This Spring/N.Y.? It's the Dragon!" This is one of the best haikai-style *kyôka* I have seen. Finally, again in the same book of surimono (pl. 71), we find Spring blooming within Seven-Plum Wine: 七ツ梅ともよふ酒の中にまで開くやはるそめてたき　桂香舎成益　*nanatsu ume to mo yobu* c 1810　蛇足：濁りもない「よぶ」で「酔ふ」の視的掛けも？「ぞ　めでたき」に「そめ」？「酔い初め」とまで想像してしまえば、狂読？Adding the above examples of contentment from *surimono* I see that the next note demonstrates why the Japanese ought to be printed, too.

♪『尤之双紙』(1634)の中で徳元は、拾遺集の「かくばかり経がたく。。。」の和歌の「羨ましく」を「うら山しく」と綴る。十四歳なる若宮に裏読みを教えるためであろう。

♪ **A Typical Moon-viewing Kyôka**. While *kyôka* as novel poems are not supposed to be typical, here is a pre-Tenmei *kyôka* that struck me as such. It is wordplay, plain and simple, that justifies getting drunk on the night the moon starts to wane by finding that message in the name of that moon, written with characters meaning the *sixteenth night* 十六夜, but pronounced *izayoi*, (mis)construed as *iza yoi*, いざ、酔い why-not-drunk!? 盃の数をかさねて酔ばよへ月も今宵はいざよひの月　元信　華紅葉 *sakazuki no kazu o kasanete yowaba yoe tsuki mo koyoi wa izayoi no tsuki* genshin 1729). On second thought, stylewise, it is exceptional, as most *kyôka* appealed more to the mind's eye while classic waka appealed more to the mind's ear. This appeals to both equally.

〜〜〜

Bald Mountains & Nostril Hairs by Moonlight　　　　　　　　　　92 頁

♪ ***Six Ways To Read the Unkempt Wife's Night With the Moon***, if it was her night and not her husband's and his buddies' night with the same, maybe in fair company . . . I bounced my readings off my respondent, who is almost always right (though the hole-in-the-*belly* that was a hole-in-the-*chest* threw him for a loop), and he favored the Moon-as-Katsurao, which is to say the handsome Katsuragi man reading. As you may have noted, it was my first reading, not because I thought it was likely to be right, but because the author-as-designer wanted the readings arranged beautifully (in order of size).

♪ The "laurel" is one conventional translation. The *katsuragi* (according to Wiki) has but two species, the sole members of the monotypic family native to Japan and China. In other words, it is no "laurel." It has similar leaves but they are opposite not alternate, and boasts bright autumn colour, *"a mix of bright yellow, pink and orange-red."* Since the moon usually meant the harvest moon, such beauty would bring it into the purview (Wiki). And, the leaves at that time emit a scent *"resembling burnt brown sugar or cotton candy"* (ditto). I mention this because color and scent were *the* words of traditional Japanese eros. (To confess, until I checked, I only knew the katsura wood was good for handicraft, as a *senryû* Blyth translated has a craftsman moon-viewing with a different – shall we say, more interested? – expression on his face from the usual. As long as I am confessing, every time I read *uka-uka,* the words I translate as "forgetting myself," I think of Issa, saying he cannot be *uka-uka* (careless) when taking a piss New Year's morning, perhaps because he might meet and have to greet his neighbor, perhaps because he reads something into it, or, perhaps, simply because he puts on New Year's Dress when he wakes up). Yet Rokuo Tanaka, like my respondent, is quite the scholar. When he writes,

> "Men may spend the whole night gazing absently at the full moon. This looks as though the moon is teasing them, just as women can tease them."

I must acknowledge that another reading is possible. Then, again, I guess, I already have. But when he writes,

> "This interpretation leads the reader to an understanding of Fushimatsu no Kaka's poignant criticism (written from the point of view of a woman who is not free to leave the house at night) of men drifting in the Floating World of pleasure and indulgence all night long" (the poem is on page 265),

I must protest. *This is backwards!* Rather, the Unkempt Wife's protest about her husband's long stay in Yoshiwara makes us tend to read this moon-viewing poem as something similar, which it may, or may not be. True, I have read in an article on Ishikawa Jun or on Nishiyama Matsunosuke of a moon-viewing party held by Moto no Mokuami in 1779 that lasted *five days and five nights,* but, I have also read that wives of *kyôkya* poets, especially those who were poets themself, were present during these parties (in 蜀山家集). Here, by the way, are two *kyôka,* one written almost a hundred years earlier by Getsudôken, a man, for, *i.e.,* in place of a woman(女にかはりてよみて送る), and sent where he does not say, and the other by another Tenmei era female poet, or someone using a female name, for one never knows unless the poet is famous:

あまりじゃの秋の夜毎の色ごのみ　月のかつらの男よけれど 月洞軒 大団
amari ja no aki no yo-goto no irogonomi tsuki no katsura no otoko yokeredo   c.1700
too much is's fall nights-every's color-taste (prurient interst) moon's ktsra man good-but

> *Night after night in fall, there's just too much sex to ignore!*
> *That is not to say Katsura the moon man is not to die for!*
> ～～～～～～～～～～

> *There's too much, just too much sex on the mind these autumn nights*
> *Not that we don't find him, the man in the moon a pretty sight.*
> ～～～～～～～～～～

> *Night after night, you men ruin fall with all your dirty passion,*
> *Though I must say Katsura does turns me on in fashion!*

ひとりねの蚊帳のうちへさよふけて桂男の入るは無遠慮 きし女 徳和 1785
hitori ne no kachô no uchi e sayo fukete katsurao no hairu wa muenryo kishijo
single-sleep's mosquito-net's inside-to night late ktsra man's enterng-as4 impolite

> *Coming right into the mosquito net of one who sleeps alone*
> *and late at night, moon-man Katsurao is most impolite!*

One might hope such precedent would settle the reading on Kaka's poem but I am afraid the first part has room for ambiguity, or rather *tri*guity, if such a word exists, On the whole, the existence of such poems does favor my respondent's reading that has a woman going lala for the man in the moon. This was not always the case. My respondent had to correct me in the other direction for Lady Ise's older Katsurao man poem:

つきのうちに かつらのひとを おもふとや あめになみたの そひてふるらむ
tsuki no uchi ni katsura no hito o omou to ya ame ni namida no soide furamu
moon-within katsura(tree)'s man+acc think-of!/: rain-in tears fall

> *I think of you, my Man in the Moon with his katsura tree –*
> *When it rains I feel your tears, falling with the rain for me.*
> ~~~~~~
> *My Katsura boy, my man in the moon, I think of you –*
> *When it rains, know that my tears are falling, too!*

Lady Ise (fl. 930) had a son with the Emperor and remained in good-standing with the Empress, but her son was sent away to stay to the West of Kyôto. That place was called Katsura. Here, I thought the poem was romantic until my respondent gave me the rest of the story! The annotation 脚注の訳 he found supported the first reading (あなたの涙), but grammar does not forbid the second and, call me sexist if you wish but I favor the crying-mother version (& when I asked my respondent, he agreed with me). Here, in Japanese only, is more information about what must be the place called Katsura: かつらひと つきのひかりのささぬよも のほるうふねにさをはとるらし 実兼 1312 玉葉集 *katsura-hito tsuki no hikari* . . . Sanekane? Here's a witty *katsura* waka *sans* love and location.

てるつきの かけをかつらの えたなから をるここちする よはのうのはな 鴨長明
teru tsuki no kage o katsura no eda nagara oru kokochi suru yowa no unohana kamo-no-chômei
shining moon's light/face/shadow katsura's branch is-while break feel-do late-night's u-blossom

> *While branches of moonlight stretch out from the Katsura tree,*
> *The soft white Unohana bloom, I would, breaking, take for me!*

The plant in question is somewhat bushy, closer to a white crepe myrtle than a "type of sunflower" (Kenkyûsha's J-E dic.)! In Japanese, *"u"* has a depressing but beautiful quality, so its name gives the *u* bloom a melancholy befitting that of the moon. (原典長明集). The above is not a *kyôka*, but a witty *waka* that perhaps could be. Kamo no Chômei (fl. early 13c)? His famous book about life in a mountain hut was first translated as a Japanese answer to Thoreau (by Minakata Kumagusu) but if truth be said, a Buddhist fear of attachment to the beauties of this world killed the journal just when it started to become nature writing. I recall being so upset that I spoke aloud: *Damn Religion!*

♪ オマケ。 **And, finally, there is a Katsura Romance by 17c *kyôka* poet Mitoku** where people do not figure in at all. The autumn rice combines with, or rather puns as lightning to be "country-wives" for said Man in the Moon. We imagine them waving=beckoning the moonman with their full-heads or ears (?) as hands, and none of this odd in the original Japanese: 人間の入る余地のない桂男の狂歌：「よひよひに出あひをそしと月のうちの かつら男をまねく稲つま」未得 吾吟我集 *yoi yoi ni deai* . . .mitoku 1649). 蛇足：月が宵々約一時間送れて出る。稲妻がそれに合わせて出るところが面白い。

♪ **Eating the Moon.** Hamabe-no-Kurobito's rice-cake moon reminds me of the time I discovered one of Issa's haiku moons mistaken for food! I found it in a book of children's haiku published by the Issa-dera (temple of Issa), together with a picture of a frightened cookie-like winter moon, minus a bite from the roof-tile demon (not like griffins, but subtly adorning the end of some tiles)! Assuming the *ku* was by a third-grade child, the editor passed it and the illustrator misinterpreted it. Issa's idea was that the cold moonlight made the demon *look as if* it might bite (not the moon but anyone). In other words, it reflected *the frame of mind* of the painfully cold Issa, who even claimed to have been *born* cold and fused that with the cold way his step-mother and the town treated him. As clear nights tend to be coldest, it is only natural to feel it coming from the winter moon. The poem is not a *kyôku* but a realistic observation of how the cold affects one man. Pure adult haiku. Guessing said *ku* was included by the editor *as a joke*, or a test – something I would love to do! – I wrote him; and was disappointed to get an apology so profuse the page I was reading seemed to blush. Some day, I must try to find whoever pulled off that prank to ask *why* it was done. I doubt a child did it. I suspect a parent. Anyway, I spotted it almost the moment I opened the book and showed it to the librarian before I checked the book out. He expressed doubt at first, then, after I showed the original to him, said, *"Well, Issa has a reputation for being childish . . ."* For your amusement, if you read Japanese, here it is: 寒月や喰いつきさうな鬼かはら *kanzuki ya kuitsukisôna onigawara*. Issa has the same demon glaring malevolently on a terribly hot day. Again, it is hardly mad, if one is aware of how nature alters our perceptions and recognizes the difference between natural and unnatural anthropomorphism; not that the latter is not fine . . . for *kyôka,* that is, not haiku.

Drink in Kyôka & Tabito's Manyôshû   96 頁

♪ *The Manyôshû poems.* I did not do all of Tabito's drinking songs, for many others have – indeed 10 of the 13 are translated in W. G. Aston's 1899 *History of Japanese Literature* – but whenever I reread them I am tempted. One reason why is that what Aston wrote in 1899 still holds true: *"No Edward FitzGerald has yet come to give us an English metrical version of the best Tanka of the Manyoshiu and Kokinshiu. A prose rendering must serve in the meantime."* OK, here's *one* more for Fitzgerald-lovers:

賢しみと物いふよりは酒飲みて酔泣きするしまさりたるらし 万葉341
sakashimi to mono iu yori wa sake nomite einaki-suru shimasaritarurashi
intelligently things say rather than wine drinking drunken-crying do better is

Cleverly talking your way out of the blues – you can try;
But it's surely better to drink until you're drunk and cry!

♪ The following mad death-poem roughly follows Tabito's wish a thousand year's earlier (in one of those 13 drinking songs) to be reborn as a keg of *sake* so he could be soaked by his beloved mead, but adds something that does not translate:

ware shinaba sakaya no kame no shita ni ikeyo moshi ya shizuku no moriyasenan
i-die-if sake-shop's vat's below-at bury maybe drops leak-would moriya sen'an d. 1838

When I die, just bury me below some vats of wine –
If they should on me, Mori=leak, that would be fine!

When I die, bury me with a keg above my head! One thing:
I'll be a grateful dead if it can also be . . . Lee King!

What is added? His name, Moriya Senan, the whole of which ends the final 7-syllabet *ku*, puns into "leak-as-for-do-would," *i.e. "should leak."* One wonders how many years this poet anxiously waited for his impending death to pop out with this poem! There is a chance he read a similar *kyôka* that, lacking his name pun, is little but a vernacularized update off the *Manyôshû* original: 我死なば酒屋の瓶のしたにをけ　われてこぼれて若

かゝるかに　治貞　古今夷曲集 *ware shinaba sakaya no bin no shita ni oke warete koborete moshi kakaru ka ni* jisei? 1666. And I should add that vats of *sake* that could be ladled into smaller kegs were themselves mostly buried in the earth to keep cool, so one can see why he is closer, metaphysically speaking, to the wine than he would be if you imagined kegs sitting on a floor. My fake name "Lee King" does not sound Japanese and loses to the original not only by being too short but by not being at the end of the line.

♪ **It just so happens my wine ran out four days ago** and I have had to get by with a bottle of Guinness Stout a day – half-before lunch and half before dinner, corked in-between w/ aspirin to make up for the missing salicyln – and forgetting to remove the bottle from my room awoke to this:

ゴキブリや旅人の夢もビールに浮く 敬愚
gokiburi ya tabito no yume mo bîru ni uku au

A cockroach! Tabito's dream floats in stale beer.

Cockroaches, like ants, ignore dirty wine glasses. The antibiotic properties in red-wine repel them so long as it is not too sweet. But beer is another thing. Tabito's *waka* indicate he wouldn't mind being reborn a bug and he hoped to end up soaked in alcohol, so when I saw that dead . . . . Beer may be autumn, but this is more *kyôku* than haiku.

オマケ　さかつきのうちにうつりし影みえて 蛇をのむ大蛇おそろしき酒　腹藁？
sakazuki no uchi ni utsurishi . . .　蛇足　逸話に弓が映り蛇かと怖がる者。大蛇＝上戸。

More Drink: Heartburn, Sake as Mead & Octopus　　　　98頁

♪ *The Ise parody.* According to "a generally reliable eleventh century chronicle, Ôkagami," the real Narihira got in trouble for abducting a girl who was to have become an imperial consort and her elder brothers had to fetch her back. He was known to be exceptionally good looking, which is why I used the word "seduced."

♪ *The Octopus Novice:* I am still unclear why the octopus is a novice. I see the word 入道 appended to a giant squid but not an octopus in OJD. It might be that it is the predominance of the head as opposed to having stubby legs. ♪ I cut the following *Kokinshû* (9005) poem by Toshiyuki after I found the more easily translated and marvelous flea companions but, as my own editor, could not bear to part with it:

玉だれのこかめやいづらこよろぎのいその浪わけおきにいでにけり としゆきの朝臣
tamadare no kogame ya izura koyorogi no iso no nami wake oki ni idenikeri kks # 874
　　jeweled small-jug(=turtle)!/: whither koyorogi's beach's waves splitting offshore-to go+emph.

　　　A poem sent to the ladies-in-waiting after a keg of *sake* sent to the Empress,
　　　　with a request for the Emperor's leftover *sake* got no response.

　　　　So where, oh where, has our turtle flask gone if not the beach
　　　　To part the holy sea and disappear from mortal reach?

I shortened the preface and made the main pun, turtle=small-flask explicit for it could no more be translated than Carroll's *tortoise* could have "taught us" in Japanese. In so doing, I ran out of room for *jeweled*. Because offshore=*oki* might be punned with *oku*, the inner reaches of the Palace, I added a Christian "holy" pun on *sea/see* (*mea culpa* ／＼). The other translations I have seen spill the wit by dropping the main pun for separate flasks and turtle/tortoise(sic) metaphor. The "left-over *sake*" (KKS poem's preface) is puzzling. Rice, unlike grape wine, did not age well, so I imagine any not drunken quickly by the Emperor was passed on.) Monk Sôchô would later send a paraverse of the *waka*, with a jug of *sake* to his abbot. The humor in his "usual *haikai*" as he called his *kyôka* (see/sea weed, a bottomless=never-ending-supply hinting, perhaps, at turtles-all-the-way-down for the abbot's long life) is even less successful in translation, though Horton, exiling the

In Praise of Getting Plastered and Puking   100 頁

♪ ***Another reading for two possibly misread poems.*** Let me provide what may be the right translations if the other two are wrong. The first was: *gomuri to wa kuchi ni iedomo ureshisa o tsutsumi-kanetaru ijinowarusa.* If *go-muri* is *you* rather than *you're forcing it.*

Don't force yourself, says he who holds the most: His mouth
hardly tries to hide his glee, tossing yet another south.

As for the flax bobbin one, *kurikaeshi yoi no mawarite atosaki no kudaranu koto o shizu no odamaki,* I took the *mawarite* as round-robin drinking, but it could be this:

Getting drunk over and over, words on the tip of our tongues,
Spin 'round like that bobbin – Baby talk before we're done!

Later. Both of the above are among Bokuyô's series of 10 poems striking back at heavy drinkers from the perspective of the teetotaler attacked by another poet (pg 178-181). On the whole, Japanese were famously nice rather than mean when drunk and that probably helps explain why drinking was not demonized though alcoholism was known. This poem, published in 1740, perhaps by Momoko, indirectly addresses these two points:

酒呑て酒の地獄へ落るとも酔た心は仏なりけり百子？　狂歌餅月夜
sake nonde sake no jigoku e ochiru to mo yotta kokoro wa hotoke narikeri momoko

Though drinking takes me to the depths of Drinker's Hell
As my drunken heart is in Nirvana, 'tis all as well!

Though a man drops into wino hell from drinking,
His mind can float like Buddha – never sinking.

Though wine may make us spend ourselves into living hell
Our minds may be happy as if we were in heaven as well.

Poop as Omen & What It Means in a Dream   102 頁

♪ ***The Poop-Fertilized Garden on Your Face.*** Maybe I should add that this is not misogynistic, for even warriors had their mirrors and used make-up; but, that is not why a note was needed. It is because of a last moment – one of many, for the book is growing out of control – discovery of a much early *face-as-a-garden*. A *kyôka* in the 1679 *Silver Leaf Savage Songs* 銀葉夷歌集 tk1, titled "化粧 make-up," puts it like this:

白粉を皃のはたけにつくるなり　誰恋種のたねを蒔らむ　伯水 hakusui
hakufun o kao no hatake ni tsukuru nari dare koi-moto no tane o makuramu

White powder becomes the garden plot on your mug
Whose seeds are sown for the reaping of love?

Mug is too vernacular. No, too ugly. We should probably imagine a courtesan. More to the point, deliberately or not, "shit" (*fun*) is punfully hidden in that white powder. Either the *senryû* and *kyôka* came from a common folk-song, or the former owes the latter.

More Shit: Snowy Outhouses & Counter-clockwise   104 頁

One wonders what Shokusanjin and friends would have thought about Swift's *Examination Of Certain Abuses Corruptions, And Enormities In The City Of Dublin* 1732:

> "Every person who walks the streets, must needs observe the immense number of human excrements at the doors and steps of waste houses, and at the sides of every dead wall; for which the disaffected party have assigned a very false and malicious cause. They would have it, that these heaps were laid there privately by British fundaments, to make the world believe, that our Irish vulgar do daily eat and drink; and, consequently, that the clamour of poverty among us, must be false, proceeding only from Jacobites and Papists. They would confirm this, by pretending to observe, that a British anus being more narrowly perforated than one of our own country; and that many of these excrements upon a strict view appearing copple crowned, with a point like a cone or pyramid, are easily distinguished from the Hibernian, which lie much flatter, and with lest continuity. I communicated this conjecture to an eminent physician, . . . and at my request was pleased to make trial with each of his fingers, by thrusting them into the anus of several persons of both nations, and professed he could find no such difference between them as those ill-disposed people allege. On the contrary, he assured me, that much the greater number of narrow cavities were of Hibernian origin. This I only mention to shew how ready the Jacobites are to lay hold of any handle to express their malice against the government."

The Good of Bad Poems and the Not So Bad   106 頁

♪ **The Wren & his Princess.** 「みちのしり」という遠国の枕で「未知の尻」を連想するのが小生だけ？ ♪ 道の後木幡嬢子を物にした若き仁徳の第二番目の喜びの首について、勝手にも一語。彼女が「争わず」という。朝鮮半島文化圏では、女性が不本意にも争う真似をするのが作法。で意外だったであろう。♪***Better dead than not wed w/ me.*** 万葉集歌＃2355 は「うつくし」とも「うるわし」とも読めるが、中西の「うつくし」よりCranston の「うるわし」を選んだ。後者の方に情ある。因みに万葉仮名は「恵得」。もともと、そういう万葉仮名をどうやって解読できるという事もよく解らない。魔法使い？

Mosquitoes, Martial Preparedness & Fallen Heads +   108 頁
Steam Boat Tea, Stone Dumplings & Other Concerns

♪ **That Horse Parade.** *Valignano S.J.* has been criticized for the expenses incurred in obtaining great horses for Nobunaga and for going along with his successor Hideyoshi's plan to conquer China. Given the circumstances, neither criticism is just. Nor is the neglect of his role in introducing the far-sighted policy of *cultural accommodation* which was not merely convenient but respected the equality of (advanced, literate) cultures in everything but religion (*Topsy-turvy 1585* (2004)).

♪ ***Some of Rakushu examples*** came from 秋道博一『落首がえぐる江戸の世相』文芸社 2002 , a book that treats 200+ *rakushu* in detail. I was saddened to find not all the poems were on the side of the little-guy. Edo poets showed precious little sympathy for the heroic Ôshio Heihachirô 大塩平八郎 (1793 - 1837), who was executed – or died in prison – for protesting unfair tax policies against rural folk. Making fun of him, they supported the policies strongly favoring the big city, *i.e.,* their own interests.

♪ ***'Rakushu' like the kidding poems of the Manyôshû.*** Later, I learned not all *rakushu* concerned politics. After the fighting monks of Mt. Hieisan wrecked the Mitsui Temple and carried off their bell in June, 1264, one jokes that acolytes at Mitsui would no longer be able to dye their teeth black for lack of the same *kane*: *kane* meaning *bell* 鐘 and 金 *metal*, for scraps were needed to mix with the vinegar and urine and so forth. The poem, resembling the best simple Tenmei *kyôka*, cannot be translated without that pun, one more on *striking* the bell and *applying* the treatment, both *tsuku,* and the new "tooth-white" coinage 三井寺の児は歯白になりぬらん つくべきかねを山へ取られて『寒川入道筆記』 *mitsuidera no chigo wa hajiro ni narinuran tsukubeki kane o yama e torarete*).

♪ **One superb rakushu by the great Yûchôrô I missed.** I marked and forgot the following poem in Nada Inada's *Edo Kyôka* and only found it again because I took it along to read while having a cat that turned out to already have been done, done, if you get what I mean. *What luck!* It is an extraordinary *rakushu* because it is *signed*. I thought the poet, Yûchôrô, unbelievably foolhardy until I found the preface with it (see below) in his *Hundred Kyôka* collection. Nada Inada wrote that *this* was *the* poem that knocked the scales off his eyes with respect to *kyôka.* He happened to come across it right when he had some tax problems and immediately identified with the Yûchôrô's defiant attitude, after which he set about researching *kyôka*, concluding it was "something that shows us history from eyes of the common folk living at the time" (狂歌とは実に庶民の生活者の側から、歴史を見せるものだったのである). Sorry for the long introduction. Here it is:

田家　この歌当時有憚 / 田のはたに家は作らし度々の検地の衆の宿にからるゝ 雄長老
ta no hata ni ie wa tsukuraji tabitabi no kenchi no shû no yado ni kararuru yûchôrô 16c
paddy/plot/s-side-by house-as4 make-not time-time's inspectors' lodging-as rent

Field-houses: This Poem Was Confidential at the Time

*No house shall be built in the lot by a field with crops of mine
Lest tax assessors find a place to stay from time to time!*

Tax assessors (called *surveyors* in Japanese) were hated because they had the legal right to requisition places to stay and things to eat, and not a few evidently did just that. Yûchôrô was upper class, but this is hardly what one might expect from an aristocrat. *Kyôka* is, or *should be*, a major resource for historians for they complicate history. This is particularly true for the more journal-like selections in the *Kyôka Taikan* anthology (*Nagasaki Ikken* being the best example). There is a tremendous amount of documentary information recorded in 31-syllabets. Historians and area studies specialists should take note. The detail is such that a generalist who cannot tell what's what, such as your author, can just go *hmmm*. Hence, such *kyôka* are grossly under-represented in this book.

♪ **Another Bonus for Japanese readers only**. This *rakushu* is pretty well-known for I often came across it: 年号は安く永くとかはれども諸色高くて今に明和九 *nengô wa yasuku nagaku to kawaredomo shoshiki takakute ima ni meiwaku*. This is interesting for the pun in the poem was not invented by the poet but adopted from the public. The reign name Meiwa 明和 means *light-peace*, but because ninth year of the Meiwa reign, *Meiwa-ku,* was a homophone for *nuisance* or *trouble, meiwaku,* many predicted trouble and, sure enough, a leadership and policy change from the New Year brought high inflation that would only grow worse after 2/29 of that year (1772), when a third of Edo burned down with about 15,000 casualties. Before the year finished, the reign name would change to Anei 安永, or Ease-Forever (or *eons* at any rate). The prevalence of puns in Japanese poetry is not only because the language facilitates it but because homophony is so often treated as supernaturally significant. In other words, what the Occident might call superstition or magical belief *about* language is part *of* language in Japan, and so long as it is not taken too seriously – and it rarely is – it is *not* at odds with rationalism.

Saigyô, the Monk who Cried Rivers 　　　　　　　　　　　　　　　　114 頁

♪ *A Chapter of Tears.* Had I gathered enough *kyôka* tears for a chapter on tears, we would have one, but I blew it. They are here, I think, but diluted into many chapters. ♪ **The most novel kyôka tears by far** are found in the Big Fan 大団 journal (c1700) of Getsudôken – *lachrymal poles!* (p.330).　♪ **Closest to Saigyô's trope.** One late-18c? *kyôka* cleverly couples tears trickling like the melted ice below ground and rotted sleeves, both of which Saigyô put into *waka*. But, especially in translation at least it is wretched: "Pluvial Love // The sleeves gone / rotted by tears seeping down / my neck, within; / It's no longer worth a heck, / at least not as a raincoat." 寄雨恋 したとほる涙に袖もくちはてゝきるかひもなきあまころもかな 法橋題昭 六百番歌合 tk *shita tôru namida ni sode...*).　♪**The simplest extension of the oldest tear trope,** that of sympathetic magic *causing rain clouds to dump on and stop a lover from leaving.* It is in the Tokuwa 1785 classic Tenmei *kyôka* anthology and gives details of the stilts of the leaving lover's geta (open-top clogs/choppine): (下駄の歯もたゝぬほどなり別れ路の涙の雨のふりかゝるには　真竹深藪　*geta no ha mo tatanu hodo nari . . .*　madake-no-fukayabu. 蛇足：自分の力を超えた「歯が立たぬ」の掛け.)

♪ **FIRE+WATER.** Searching a large *waka* db for two key words, it would be easy to find many poems combining the *fire* within and *water* without. For example, *Kokinshû* #529: *How can I, no fisherman's torch, yet burn with desire / floating down a river of my tears like a funeral pyre?* (*kagaribi ni aranu . . .*). The *funeral pyre* is my invention, but you get the idea! Or, this translated by Cranston (2a), *"Flames of my longing / Never cease their hovering / About my love, / And surely the falling snowflakes / Must be melting in the sky."* (*waga koi shi kimi ga atari o hanareneba furu shirayuki mo sora ni kiyuran* anon *Goshuishû* 1072/3). If the poem were prefaced with a letter complaining that the snow mentioned in a letter from *him* was not seen by the other party, we would surely have a *kyôka* here.

~~~~~~

The man with a baby in his heart – more Saigyô　　　　　　　　116頁

♪*A Similar Tear River* 涙川あふせもしらぬみをつくしたけこそほとになりにけるかな　慈鎮和尚　六百番歌合 (1193) *namidagawa ause mo shiranu* mio . . *jichin*

♪ *Heart Metaphors, Anyone?* 12c Saigyô gives us the most, and most beautifully expressed heart metaphors, but the 8c *Manyôshû* and other old collections are already full of them. It is the sort of thing that would be fun to collect and categorize/tax as a team – turn students in a seminar into heart-hunters – and turn into a book.

♪ *Ancient Japanese trope and country music.* I planned to do a book-length comparison decades ago. As a result, I know that almost all my generalities are half-truths. For example, when I claimed the heart cannot be "polished" in English, meaning *with respect to common idiom*, in the back of my head, I could hear The Possum singing Billy Joe Shaver's *"I may be just an old lump of coal, but I'm gonna be a diamond some day"* and more vaguely recall that the *heart* was what evolved and was to be polished. Perhaps, I should add that I studied up on classical opera for comparison's sake, and my conclusion was that, for a word-lover, at any rate, country music was far more highly evolved, boasting a more complex pool of metaphor on more themes and excellent meaningful puns. Music-wise, as well, the irregular country vibrato is a far higher art than what the opera machines do (steady pulse is good for maximum volume but not for maximum delicacy) in much the same way that a *shakuhachi's* rich notes makes a piano's simple monotones sound like a toy. For proof of the power of this musical form: there are no small number of songs, called *weepers*, that will wet your eyes in less than two minutes, guaranteed, and some will suddenly chill your spine (eg., *The Green, Green Grass of Home*, seemingly mere nostalgia until the last stanza, when . . .). I think it no wonder that Japanese low-brow humor has been largely ignored by the leading translators in the 20c. I would *bet* most of them think Pavarotti gave the world more than Hank Williams, when the single wavering voice of the latter balanced in mid-yodel – actually, a natural semi-yodel, ala Emmett Miller (nothing like the fancy Swiss ones) – of *The Lovesick Blue*s is infinitely more touching to anyone who listens from the heart than the taurine bellowing of the late opera star. (Pardon my outburst, and, yes, I know much country music today is crap. Much of *everything* is.). オマケ「心からこころに物をおもはせて身をくるしむる我が身なりけり」 *kokoro kara kokoro ni . . .*　とは、西行上人の最も入り込んだ、抽象的心の一首であろう。さて、この英訳＋解説を敢えて行う勇者おられますか？

♪♪ *Country Music and Kyôka-like Waka: Not Just Metaphor but Plot.* This is a note for the above note as I realized the comparison does not stop at the level of metaphor. Months after writing the above, I happened across the words *"Like Garth's song!"* scribbled into the margin of song #1055 in my pocket-book *Kokinshû*. Here is the *waka*:

ねぎ事をさのみききけむやしろこそはてはなげきのもりとなるらめ　さぬき
negi goto ni sa nomi kikiken yashiro koso hate wa nageki no mori to naru rame　sanuki
wish-things all hear-would shrine espec. in-the-end-as-for lament-forest-into become!

> *This shrine, where all our prayers are heard, will in the end*
> *Be the one buried below a pile of hearts that need to mend.*

The original plays on the "*ki*=tree/s" within "*nageki*=laments," and the Forest of the same alludes to a place by that name. Here, for once, I think Rodd and Henkenius beat me: *"this holy precinct / where it seems prayers have been / lavishly answered / will surely become at last / an arbor of repentance."* Changing *nageki* (grief, lament, mourning) into "repentance" is brilliant and arbor is beautiful. The basic idea of the *Kokinshû* poem and Garth Brooks' country music hit called (Sometimes I thank God for) *Unanswered Prayers* is identical, but the latter provides the details behind the title, while in the former you have all of it, except the qualifying *sometimes* in those 31 syllabets.

~~~~~~

Humorous Slobber in a Sober pre-1205 Collection (Shinkokinshû)?　120 頁

♪ **The Anonymous Poem with the Chinese-Junk-Wetting-Sleeves?** As some readers may already know, it is from the #26 *Tale of Ise*, which means it dates back at least two centuries and might be by Narihira. With apologies for not catching it in the text (now, too full to fit more, I offer a take-off on the same from the Fake Tale of Ise, the early 17c *Nise-monogatari*. The original tale is titled 五条わたり Gojô Watari, or Gojô Crossing and concerns a woman who lived in the area of Gojô, *Gojô-atari*, who the anti-hero claimed to miss as much as vice-versa. The *Fake Ise* tale is titled 五十あまり *Gojû Amari*, or *Over Fifty,* and the poem keeps the monster-sized Chinese ship, but rather than having it wet sleeves, the enormous waves it leaves in its wake are used to hyperbolize the ripples=wrinkles on the face of the おかし男 Odd Man: おもほえずひたいに波のさはぐかな もろこし船のよりしばかりに　仁勢物語 *omôezu hitai ni nami no . . .*)

♪ **From Jakuren's Flotsam & Jetsam to Teika's Strands of Black Hair: a Great SKKS Sequence.** While I finished my selection of tear-rivers from ch. 15 of the *Shinkokinshû* with Jakuren's wonderful expanded metaphor, it was actually over a dozen poems later in a sequence of *dream* waka (still within the greater theme of *koi* (love/longing/passion). The sequence seems less mad than the tear-rivers, so we will see only a small sampling. This *waka* immediately follows Jakuren's:

逢ふと見てことぞともなく明けぬなりはかなの夢の忘れ形見や　藤原言家隆
au to mite koto zo to mo naku akenunari hakana yume no wasuregatami ya　kotoietaka?
meet(will) thinking+emph. not, brightens/dawns fleeting dreams forgotten keepsake!

> *You think you'll meet but then you don't and suddenly the dawn*
> *Leaves you only the remnant of a dream, forgotten before long.*

What makes the poem is the last phrase, which, if it is newly minted deserves an award. The poem following that, though awkwardly worded, has the delicacy of a good haiku.

床近しあなかま夜半のきりぎりす夢にも人の見えもこそすれ　藤原基俊
toko chikashi anakama yahan no kirigirisu yume ni mo hito no mie mo koso sure　mototoshi
bed-near hole-stve midnght's cricket/ktydd/s dream-in+emph person+emph appr+emph

> *The sunken stove by my bed, late at night this katydid –*
> *And, in my dreams, someone really did appear.*

The *kirigirisu* may be a *cricket* (later called *kôrogi*), so if French is your native tongue so you are graced with a better word, you might redo this with a *grilloux*. In English, . . . This is followed by a less poetic but remarkably precise linkage of fitful sleep, dreams, long longing and choking up or feeling suffocated by Shunzei and that is followed by an extraordinarily bold poem by his son, Teika, the main editor of the anthology. As if to contrast himself and his father in bold relief, we have concrete detail rather than concept.

The more I press my face into the futon the more I see
Your face – each strand of black hair I parted for thee!

~~~~~~

Her face – each strand of black hair I stroked with glee.

What to do with that hair? I love Carter's treatment of this: *"Those long black tresses / that I <u>roughly pushed aside</u>: / now strand upon strand / they rise in my mind's eye / each night as I lie down."* He keeps the order of the first and last half of the poem; mine reverses it, to clarify the conceptual emphasis of the original. Carter also notes it is "an allusive variation on poem 213 (in his book) of Izumi Shikibu," and that is why I underlined what I did. For *her* poem, Carter translates the same *kakiyarishi* as *"whose hands / have so often <u>brushed it smooth</u>."* With Teika's poem, the implication is that he didn't know what he had when he had it. With Shikibu, perhaps it was the better to contrast with her lying down not giving a thought to her "hair's disarray." I do not write this to criticize Carter's translation, but to let my readers know that the differences – the choices – involved in translation that I show you in this book (and my other books) are not unique to me (or professors Crump and Crandon, both of whom are exceptionally open though rarely *baka-shôjiki* like me). The "poetic license" of the poet is nothing compared to that translator grant themselves. Now, two more teary Jakuren's, one found in a small collection of his *waka* at Nichibun and one more from the *Shinkokinshû*:

おさへても－つつまはしはし－とまれかし－なみたさへこそ－かたおもひなれ
osaete mo tsutsumaba shibashi tomaregashi namida sae koso kataomoi nare jakuren
repressing even pressed-in/wrapped a-while stop-somewhat tears esp. half-love are

Hold them back, keep them under-wrap, stop 'em in their track;
But Tears disowned cannot be – they are *one-sided love in fact.*

~~~~~~

Blue me! I could fill my sleeves with fireflies – fat chance
of notice when not a soul cares to share my sad romance!

longing is/have-when sleeve-in fireflies stuffing even, saying but ask person-as4 not
omoi areba sode ni hotaru o tsutsumite mo iwaba ya mono o tou hito wa nashi
思ひあれば袖に蛍をつつみても 言はばや 物をとふ人はなし 寂連 skks

The *Shinkokinshû* poem is too subtle to be a *kyôka* and too fine not to be largely lost in translation. The insinuation is that tear-drenched sleeves might dampen the light of the fireflies as well as the stated problem of having no one to talk to.

~~~~~~

Silly as Saigyô: pre-1310 waka weepers 4 perspective ㊤   122 頁

♪ **The Dew-as-Bug-Tears Guy**. The tears ran too thick to allow this aside to remain in the text.

But don't think maudlin Yoshitada was harmless. He also left us this:

わきもこか衣うすれて見えしより たはれねせしと思ひなりにき 好忠 恋歌中
wagimoko ga koromo usurete mieshi yori tawarene seji to omoinariniki yoshitada
my-sis(girl/lovr)'s robe thin/nng seemd-frm, sportng-sleep-not do thinkng-be-came 夫木

My girl, since I noticed your dress was thin, I knew
I wanted in – Didn't I want to play in bed with you!

~~~~~~

Since I saw your dress, my girl, was worn down and thin,
Thought of sleeping with you vanished: I want out, not in!

Tawarene is a fine word. This is neither a *kyôka* nor a proper *waka*. Regardless of the reading – the first, mine, the second my respondent's – it is like a *tanka*, a horrid one, either shameless (reading one) or merciless (reading two)! There is a 99% chance my respondent's reading (my Englishing) is the correct one. A mad poem would have made the put-down funny. The original is less witty than my translation.

♪*A Model for Saigyô?*   I crammed in too many teary poems to fit an example more relevant to the chapter's title. Judging from this *waka* by Nôin, an 11c monk, like Saigyô later, known for traveling, and another about burning desire via moths and fireflies (pg. 207), he also provided a model for the passionate man of cloth.

涙川こひよりいてゝなかるれはかくこほるよもさえぬなりけり 能因法師
namidagawa ko(h)i yori idete nagarureba kaku kôru yo mo saenu narikeri nôin d.1050
tear-river love/longing-from leaving-flow-if/when such freezing night even slow-not! 同

> *A river of tears, when it flows out of being passionate,*
> *Even on a freezing night like this does not slow a whit.*

> *A river of tears, flowing as it does from love is always hot,*
> *Tonight may be cold as a witch's tit, but freeze it will not!*

> *Tear River – as it flows from passion – is no matter:*
> *On a freezing night, it never grows cold, just fatter!*

The original plays on the built-in fire=*hi* pun, implying, conversely, that crying for other reasons would slow and the tears would end up frozen into icicles (see Shunzei and others on pgs. 44-5). The poem does not seem as odd as those icicles which Teitoku's Year of the Cow slobber subtly lampooned but, as a response to those icicles, it really *is* odder in the sense of being one step further removed from reality. It works in translation provided the reader accepts the idea of love-as-burning. But, most tear-river poems do not. Eg: *Sleeping clothed, Tear River bridged by logs with bark, / That my lover cannot cross, even in dreams, after-dark.* なみたかは まろねのなかの まろきはし こぬうきせには ゆめもかよはす 基家 *namidagawa marone no naka no maroki-bashi . . .motoie*). The idiomatic link between the clothed sleeper and the logs is lost, and we have that bridge again . . . . Or, how about, *Only my Girl – when my river of tears flows out to Sea, / Mirume, night after night, in* see*weed dreams we meet!* 人をのみ-うみに出たる-なみたかは-さてもよなよな-みるめやはある 家隆 *hito o nomi umi ni idetaru namidagawa . . . ietaka*). Here, the *mirume,* a seaweed, puns on seeing and means to meet. In the original, we have the buds of a riddling (enabled by a complex sort of syntax only a linguist could gloss) folk-song, but for the English to work, we would have to have them *meating* in a stockyard, for, spelling aside, *see* requires an object and that messes things up: *River of Tears, where* do *you flow? My girl suspects you are my cover. / Wet dreams night after night! At least we always get to sea (each other)!*

Silly as Saigyô: pre-1310 waka weepers 4 perspective ㊦   126頁

♪*A Follow-up on Shunzei's Hailstone Tears?* There is a fascinating poem by Retired Emperor Fushimi, who supported the 1313 *Gyokuyôshû* compilation that may touch upon Shunzei's:

こほれおちしひとのなみたをかきつめて われもしをりし よはそわすれぬ 伏見院
kôre-ochishi hito no namida o kaki-tsumete ware mo shiorishi yo wa zo wasurenu fushimi
freezng-fell persn's/s' tears+acc raked-gatherd i too wiltd world-as-for+emph. forget-not

> *Scooping up your tears, that, freezing, fell, to keep them,*
> *I, too, bowed down my head for a world I don't forget.*

My first translation was "Scooping up the tears of the people I'd bag them / And mark them well, lest I should ever forget" because I read こほれ as *kobore,* which combining with *ochishi* makes the "falling" more dramatic; but my respondent thinks 零れ or freezing a more likely reading and said the poem was among those under the heading of 恋 "love/longing." I think that rules out my Emperor-mourning-for-all-the-people take, but it still might refer to Shunzei and his poem, for poems, for various reasons, were not always placed in the appropriate sections. Maybe the Emperor was gathering Shunzei's poems. It is most likely, I think, that he sends it to a third party, a woman who, like him mourns the not so distant past in their troubled time and who may have mentioned Shunzei. Who knows!

♪ **More Tear River Spill-over.** I shifted some *Fuboku Wakashô* (1310) poems that lose too much in translation into the notes that flowed naturally from Noin's poem, above and add more below. They may be removed from the next edition.

よそへゆく おもひのかせの 海ふけは 心のうらに たつなみたかな 慈円
yoso e yuku omoi no kaze no umi fukeba kokoro no ura ni tatsu namida kana   jien
elswhre-to going longng-wind's sea blow-if/whn heart's-back/bay-in rise tears=waves!

When ye Winds of Desire blow o'er distant Seas of Love,
Ground-swells of Tears roll into the Heart's hidden cove.

The unrecoverable loss is *tears* morphing into *waves*, the *nami+da.* and the *ura,* unseeable part of the heart/mind and melancholy *bay as a back-water.* Here is a more hopeless case yet: *Until the River of Tears I cry for you, dear, stops to flow / My blues will cross the bridge of broken sleep in droves.* (君こふる なみたの川の たえせねは なけ きそわたる うたたねのはし 琳賢法師 *kimi kôru namida no kawa no taeseneba nageki zo wataru utatane no hashi* monk rinken.) With multiple metaphor, invention (my *bridge of broken sleep*) kills the original wit, born of dovetailing existent ones to build a metaphorical topography. But metaphorical topography is still better to translate than poems dependent on real topography, which has Proper Names. Saigyô wrote one about separation (for a friend, not necessarily a lover) that I loosely translated *Carried away? We will find a bar someday, a delta seat, / Our tears, flowing, split in two – they, too, as one must meet.* (流れては いつれのせにか とまるへき 涙をわくる ふたかはのせき 西行 *nagarete wa izure no se ni ka . . .*). Whether there is some idea such as tears flowing around the nose ending up at the mouth, I do not know, but there *was* a Futagawa, or Split River which is punned on. Without it, the poem seems lacking.

Silly as Saigyô: pre-1310 Wild Waka w/ Dust & Smoke   128 頁

The poet who wrote my favorite dust *waka* (*kimigayo wa hikari tsukisenu hinomoto ni asa tatsu chiri no kazu mo e-shirazu*) leaves us no family or first name. She was the Kodaishin, a rank I have no ability to translate, in the entourage of Minister of the Left, Hanazono. I was delighted to learn of her sex from my respondent after I mentioned my favorite dust and trash *haiku* are by the great female haikai poet Chiyo (Chiyojo/Chiyo-ni). Translations of her haiku may be found in *The Fifth Season* (2007).

The Man who Troped Transience 4-15   132 頁

♪ **Filamental, Dr. Watson!** After doing my translations, I turned on my satellite and googled for others. I found one by Burton Watson: *"Drops of dew / strung on filaments / of spider web – / such are the trappings / that deck out this world."* (*Saigyô: Poems of a Mountain Home* Columbia UP: 1992). Wow. That *is* a good word; I immediately regretted not using *filament* myself and worried about how overblown some of my translations of the poem might seem next to this austere yet smooth work. At the same time, however, even in the context of adornment, dew drops strung up could not entirely lose their homophonic connotation of being our souls, our very lives, especially with the string and strung-through idea which usually is used in a life-and-death (or romantic) context. *That* and my, at this point utterly unsubstantiated, feeling that the final 8 syllabets (yes, one too long) may be read existentially, not just predicating the nature of the *world* but emphasizing it is *where we are,* mis/informed my readings. Still, Watson's "*this* world" – no "this" in the original – *implies* the same, only it does not foolishly walk the plank. Our different translations also bring out an important point about anthropomorphism in translated poetry. Watson's *"the trappings / that deck out"* turn the world into a horse or a boat or some *thing* – today, we might imagine one of those richly decorated globular Christmas tree ornaments – while my *"necklace,"* obviously cannot help but give us a human Gaia. The original uses vocabulary that could apply equally well to either and, thus, both is and isn't anthropomorphic. For a nuanced discussion of how anthropomorphism only becomes a problem in translation, read ch.1-4 of *Fly-ku!* (2004). Such problems can be insurmountable, as I demonstrated was the case for Issa's famous "Don't swat!" *fly-ku.* With *this* waka, however, the choice was not forced. By using more ambiguous terms an *either/or* translation would be possible (one of mine was such). I chose that necklace, not just because strung up gems were usually worn that way, but in order to *demonstrate without a word how style can make a poem madder than it really is.* This poem is *not* one of Saigyô's mad ones. I hope readers can turn me over and wake up to the fact that *the opposite thing is not only possible but what tends to happen: poems in translation* (at least J-E translations in the last half of the 20c) *tend to become less mad*, which is to say, more staid.

♪ **Why so much Saigyô?** *The Milky-Way-to-spider-web* poem took so much space, I had none left to discuss why I put so much Saigyô into this book. Maybe that was for the better, as I have a lot to say. Saigyô, to me, is an unrecognized anomaly. I am unsure if he is "the most renowned of Japanese poets, rivaled in the minds of Japanese readers only by Bashô" (Carter), as lovers of ancient poetry swear by Kakimoto, lovers of finesse put Buson next to Bashô, and Kyoshi, who, more than Shiki, put modern haiku on its feet, is revered by millions – think of how hard it would be to rank English poets! – but I think it safe to say that, *with Issa*, he is the most *beloved* pre-modern poet. While Saigyô does not have as many small animals to pull at your heart strings, he is the prototypical melancholy man, both appreciating and suffering from solitude, a passionate poet of the heart, a male Sappho if it were, *and,* uniting old age, childhood and Nature, a less wordy Wordsworth, too. As *the* cherry blossom poet, he was so prolific that the *49* (!) *waka* of his I put into *Cherry Blossom Epiphany* (2007) did not suffice. I regret some I missed! But what is the *anomaly?* This: 1) Saigyô is an exceedingly clever poet, unafraid of logic, hyperbole, outrageous metaphors or anthropomorphism. 2) Such cleverness is poorly regarded by most critics of poetry in Japan. 3) Yet, Saigyô is highly respected by all and never, to my knowledge, attacked as other wit-loving poets (and editors) have been. The last *waka* shares much with Ariwara no Motokata's reviled this-year-last-year poem (pg.34) selected by Ki no Tsurayuki, but who bothers to criticize *it!* There is no question that Saigyô's is the more beautifully written and personal (Motokata's is not, unless the experience of pleasure composing the poem counts), yet, I would imagine that Ôta Nanpo, our first-man of *kyôka*, might have preferred Ariwara's for being pure play rather than didactic. I have little doubt that the number of Saigyô's poems in this book are out of proportion to his contribution to what became known as *kyôka*. Doubtless, there are other lesser-known poets who played with paradox and created outrageous metaphor. My reason for offering so much Saigyô is that, as far as I know, no one has ever concentrated upon his *wit* and so, *through* Saigyô's treatment, we see better how *kyôka-like* poems were overlooked to create a falsely tame picture of the greater world of *waka*. Also, I happen to have an old Iwanami pocket-book with thousands of his poems I bought, used, for about 50-cents. I have no such cache of poems for any other ancient *waka* poet. Since it has no notes, I cannot read all of them with assurance (and may have missed good examples), but I can only work with what I have, so Saigyô (and, for the same reason, Issa) it is! With respect to my style of translation, I will admit it is stylistically madder – which is to say, more clearly logical, or explicit – than Saigyô's elegant style. But I am not convinced any of my contemporaries can match *his* style. For that, we would need familiarity with classical literature (equivalent of that of Chinese literature by Japanese poets) and fluency in English styles such as was enjoyed by 19c translators, scholarship beyond mine, something common enough in the 20c, and courage, which has been all too rare in my humble opinion. Though the Penguin classic Englishmen (Brownas and

Thwaite), if they are still alive, and Edwin Cranston who is for sure (a letter last month), sometimes manage it, most poems in translation (even theirs) fail *as poems,* when judged by the standards we demand in native English language poetry. So, *if* my artificial clarity and rhyme reads well, that, *in itself*, is true to the original, for the original, as a rule, reads well, and translations, unfortunately, do not. (Any one, should I cut the last 14 lines?)

An Entire Chapter Removed from the Text, & the Notes for it:

Kyôka by the Arch-bishop Who Fell on the Maiden Flowers

やまかせにさくらふきまき みたれなむ はなのまきれにたちとまるへく 遍昭集
yamakaze ni sakura fukimaki midarenamu hana no magire ni tachitomarubeku henjô 816-90

> ~~The cherry tree wrapped in mountain wind, petals fly about~~
> ~~like lashing hair and I, I would stop and stand right there!~~

Saigyô was not the first nobleman-turned-monk with a wit. I found about four-score of Arch-bishop's Henjô's *waka* at Nichibun. The above enthralled me. Forgetting I once translated a version where *tachi* (stand) was *kimi* (lord) and a preface noted Henjô wanted his lord, the Prince, to tarry a bit when they were together (*Cherry Blossom Epiphany:* 2007), and thinking a woman's disheveled hair – associated with love-making – was implicit in the *midare* that usually modifies one plant, a willow messed up by the wind, I took it elsewhere. It helped that I knew Henjô's maiden-flower poems *and* recalled lying on my back in a bamboo grove during a gale, though *standing* would indeed be the best way to enjoy a pink blizzard. So there I was, thinking I had found an unsung erotic masterpiece, while all I *really* did was misread a well-known poem!

ちりぬれは のちはあくたに なるはなを おもひしらすも まとふてふかな
chirinureba nochi wa akuta ni naru hana o omoishirasu mo madou ~~to iu~~ kana
(♪ See the notes! The *"to iu,"* or "is said" should be *chô*, or butterfly/ies!)

> ~~Holding something against blossoms that falling just become trash~~
> ~~– Now, that is what I would call straying from the righteous path!~~

~~The life-span of Narihira (825-80), who wrote the famous poem about cherry blossoms bringing us worry that kyôka poets out and out made explicitly women, is a subset of Henjô's (816-90). This poem shows who was the more mature of the two and is a great retort to the commonplace of blossoms leading men astray. Who can claim the danger of attachment to something that will soon be blown away or swept up? And, in a roundabout way, it is a retort to those who blame women for leading men astray. Can we really become attached to a mortal body? How I wish I found this poem before I published *Cherry Blossom Epiphany!* Now I *must* find a major publisher, for my printer cannot do a book more than 740 pages and it is already that (Hey, New York Review of Books editor, check it out! Compare it to another book you publish: Burton's *Anatomy of Melancholy*.).~~

みなひとは はなのころもに なりぬなり こけのたもとよ かわきたにせよ
minabito wa hana no koromo ni nari koke no tamoto kawaki dani seyo henjô
all-people-as-for blossomy dress-in becoming, mossy sleeves dry at least do!

> *All the humans are out in their floral dress – me, I'm out of it.*
> *Ah, Mossy Sleeves of mine, at least, dry yourself a bit!*

Floral dress does not mean floral patterns but colorful fine dress worn to celebrate the New Year or go blossom-viewing. A man of the cloth wore mossy green in Japan. *Contentwise*, this is not so mad as Shunzei's lachrymal icicles melting down his mossy sleeves and into the supposedly conservative *Shinkokinshû* edited by his son Teika et al, but *stylewise* it is more so, for the sleeve/s is/are directly addressed.

うつせみは からをみつつも なくさめつ けふりたにたて ふかくさのやま
utsusemi wa kara o mitsutsu mo nagusametsu keburi dani tate fukakusa no yama
empty cicada-as4 shell+acc seeing-while relieve, smoke only raises deepgrss mtn

A cicada slough? No, worse! You can keep one for a memento.
On deep-grass mountain, all we get is smoke when humans go.

The cicada's empty shell is an old symbol of the transience of life and of this world being empty, one of vanity, yet you can keep one. Of course, the shells we see are mostly left by molting cicada – though I have seen and heard a centipede clean out a senile cicada alive – hardly *memento mori*. Henjô knew that, so the hyperlogical *kyôka* style paradox probably alludes to something more. The old capital of Nara (it changed to Heian = Kyôto in 794) would be the slough, but I do not know whom he most lamented the lack of a *memento mori* for.

ささかにの そらにすかくも おなしこと またきやとにも いくよかはふる
sasagani no sora ni su kaku mo onaji koto matagiyado ni mo iku yo wa furu   henjô
spider's sky-in nest hang evn same thinghuntr's lodge-to how many gnrtions pass

When a spider hangs a web across the sky, it is the same:
How many generations does a hunting lodge remain?

The hunting lodge here only makes sense as metaphor for more. Life is a hunt and we tread on something more aethereal than the proverbial Elizabethan stage.

わかやとは みちみえぬまて あれにけり つれなきひとを まつとせしまに
waga yado wa michi mienu made arenikeri tsurenaki hito o matsu   henjô
my hut-as-for road see-not-untl overgrown, faithlss persn+acc waiting

My cottage has become so overgrown, I cannot see the lane,
While I waited and waited for a man who never came.

Written from a female point of view? At a glance, too tame for this book, but taking the usual long night's wait and stretching it into this makes it a novelty.

~~はるるよの ほしかかはへの ほたるかも わかすむかたに あまのたくひか 遍照~~
~~*haruru yo no hoshi ga kawabe no hotaru kamo waga sumu ga tani ama no tagui ka*~~
*

~~*This clear night, the stars in the stream might as well be fireflies*~~
~~*Could this valley where I dwell be part of heaven's skies?*~~

~~I have experienced this with a slope of florescent mushrooms. Fireflies need a meteor shower to make sense.~~ Still, as hyperbole for bright reflection, superb! ♪

♪**My Conflation of Henjô and Narihira and Mad *Mi*stranslation.** The selection of poems I found was far from sufficient to get the measure of this man Carter introduces as follows, "If Ariwara no Narihira is a poet full of questions, his contemporary Yoshimine Munesada, known by his religious name Henjô, seems to be a man with only answers." ~~As the last poem introduced was a favorite of mine and happened to end in a question, here is another reading that would not fit in the text:~~ Note how readings I must cross out as mistranslations tend to be beautiful. It says something about what makes me err.

~~*On a clear night,*~~
~~*the stream bed fills with stars,*~~
~~*as bright as fireflies*~~

Could this valley where I dwell
belong to heaven's firmament?

はるるよの ほしかかはへの ほたるかも わかすむかたに あまのたくひか 遍照
haruru yo no hoshi ga kawabe no hotaru kamo waga sumu ga tani ama no tagui ka

~~This and most of the other poems given were clearly not crazy enough for kyôka, but I can tell the playful mind behind them had to have written wilder poems yet.~~ I have written that pure *hiragana* is confusing, and that not using the diacritical marks allowed for easy punning. Narihira's firefly poem 晴るる夜の星か川辺の蛍かもわが住む方に海人のたく火か　業平 (岩波 skks) was in Henjô's collection without attribution, and I figured two of the か were が and the fires used for attracting fish which in the distance melted in with the fireflies became something heavenly, but wrong. I would not be surprised to find some *kyôka* that originated in mistakes such as mine.   ♪**Another Oops!**

Once they fall, cherry blossoms are but trash – The butterflies
Not knowing that, flutter about with stars in their eyes.

This is the *chinureba nochi wa* poem (the second in this Henjô section) that I misread properly translated – if "stars in their eyes" is alright for *madou*, or *stray from the path*.
♪***Jakuren Playing with Henjô.*** A couple centuries later Monk Jakuren, responded to some of Arch-bishop Henjô's poems. These are from his 寂蓮百歌集 at Nichibun.

はなのいろに こけのころもを ぬきかへて　よをそむきたる そてといはせむ
hana no iro ni koke no koromo o nugikaete yo o somukitaru sode to iwasemu jakuren
blossom-color/s-to mossy robe+acc strip-changing world+acc turnbackon-sleeves-as say-not

Stripping I'll reverse my mossy robe so I become a flower groom:
No one will call me a Goose, who turns his back on bloom!

をみなへし－こけのころもは－からすとも－あきかせさむし－いさふたりねむ
ominaeshi koke no koromo wa karasu (hakarazu?) to mo akikaze samushi iza futari nenu

Q. 苔衣計らずとも＝烏でも秋風がさむい＝のかけことば？

Sleeves of Moss do mean a Monk, but Maiden Flowers do not flee!
The Autumn Wind bites tonight – Why not plunk down with me?

蛇足。 The first alludes to a poem in the chapter, suggesting a different solution to the clothing problem – the "goose" is my *mad* translation – while the second plays with the convention? of *monks and maidens* that Henjô started. The translations are a bit madder than the originals. As I prefer facetious poems to serious ones, I like it more than the famous exchange of Ono no Komachi and Henjô (岩の上に旅寝をすればいと寒し苔の衣をわれに貸さなむ / 世をそむく苔の衣はただひとへかさねばつらしいざふたり寝む).

The Testing of Snipe & Playing With Cherry Clouds   134 頁

A week after discovering the *cherry-stone clam*, I read across a fine mad usage of the separated cherry and its stone by Robert Herrick where, – well, you'll see!

CHERRY-PIT.

JULIA and I did lately sit
Playing for sport at cherry-pit :
She threw ; I cast ; and, having thrown,
I got the pit, and she the stone.

♪ Cherry-pit, a game in which *cherry-stones* were pitched into a small hole. (The poem+ note and so much else, if you like Metaphysical and Cavalier poets may be found at the beautiful yet bountiful website, Luminarium. The italics are mine.)

~~~~~~

Laundry mountain & Takuan's matin itch – play w/ 2 of 100 Poets 140 頁

♪ With respect to the dawn parting in Tadamine's waka (kks #625) that Monk Takuan played with his scabies, of the half-a-dozen translations I have seen, half have the lover looking cold or even heartless and half have the moon looking so. I found a way to leave it ambiguous. In that, I am being faithful to the original, though I readily admit my "of all things in the world" is rhetorical overkill aiming at bringing out the idea more clearly to show (to readers capable of reading the original) the difference between the lyrical and the metaphysical can be a matter of style, and just to entertain.

♪ **The pickled shôgun poem.** Takuan's allegorical *kyôka* bears some resemblance to the superficially nonsensical, supposedly allegorical *wazauta*, ancient children's songs that might be premonitionary *or* retrospective, though the former was the ideal and, I would think, the latter more likely to have been common (see Cranston: *Waka* v1 ?2? #178). If you put the name Takuan right after the poem (which I did not), it being the name of a pickle (if it already was, that is), you feel it fits even with the extra syllabets.

~~~~~~

Things that cannot be – a list a thousand years old   142 頁

♪ **Metaphors for Untrustworthiness. The four poets** are Ki no Tomonori 紀友則 whose poem kkrj #2198 starts it, Ki no Tsurayuki 紀貫之, the great editor and metaphor master, Ariwara no Tokiharu 在原のときはる and Ōshikafuchi no Mitsune 凡河内躬恒. I do not give their names by the individual poems as it matters little *and* to force you to see Edwin Cranston's *Waka* volume 2a (with its treasure for all) if you are really *that* interested! Not only did I find that remarkable (and surprisingly little known in Japan) sequence in Cranston, but the following older poem (新撰万葉集 *Shinsen Manyôshû*, i.e., New Selection MYS 893), elaborating said distrust in the word of a human, or all humans, *before* the *Kokinshû* (905), with its famous anon. poem #712 (*itsuwari no naki yo . . .*).

kotonoha no tanomubeshi ya wa aki kureba izure ka iro no kawarazarikeru smys #155
word-leaves trust-ought?-as-for autumn comes-when ever color's/s' change-must+emph

Now I ask you this: / Can I trust mere leaves of words? / When weary autumn comes,
Where is the land where the colors / Do not change with the season?   tr. Cranston 2a

Pardon my lack of parsing for the professor. It is a good translation. Do not think the "weary" (*i.e.*, jaded, or no longer attracted) a platitude. It is punned into the very word "fall" (*aki*) and in this context clearly intended. I failed to fit it into my mad translations of the same. And, as you see below, when I squeezed it into my third reading, I got blah.

How can we in words, our so-called leaves, believe, when fall
Shows us time and time again: what's colorful always leaves!

~~~~~~

How can we in words, our so-called leaves, believe, when fall
Shows us time again that all color leaves at Nature's call!

~~~~~~

How can we in words, our so-called leaves, believe at all
When out of love we fall, as color flees at winter's call!

♪ **And the originals**. I do not supply much original Japanese for the 4 poet series as all the poems are in phonetic syllabary with but one character, your split radish: 人. ♪ **Re. the fireflies and the thatch-grass**. Translating anything involving *fire* from Japanese into English involves a loss of information because the Japanese vocabulary for fire (much of which probably postdates these poems) is the proverbial Inuit vocabulary for snow. The grass, which I, perhaps wrongly, imagine tied up in bundles on the field, was lit with a verb for lighting 灯 used for lighting lamps, lanterns or candles lit to illuminate rather than to burn up. Cranston's verb *alight* and my *torch* nod to the knowing but mean little to other readers (though we used torches for light, mine is even misleading for that verb came to mean burn-up/down). ♪ ***Near Title***. I first thought to title the chapter *On Top of Old Smokey* for the salient line is *"there ain't one girl in twenty, a poor boy can trust"*). To tell the truth, once, it happened to me. Waiting for my ship to come in, I was indeed a'courtin' too slow and, sure enough, she jumped my ship-to-be for a rich guy that *was*. But, one-in-twenty is a far better chance than that admitted by the ancient poems Cranston presents! They are more along the chance of finding a flying fish in space. But that is not why I ditched Old Smokey for Diogenes. It was because I thought more readers would recall "my poor meat-ball" than the poor boy. In Usania, meatballs may fall on the floor, but poverty is traditionally swept under the table.

♪ ***My Impossible Song.*** When I was not young, but young enough, I wrote a song with many stanzas, each giving four impossibilities. I cannot recall a single stanza, only half-lines – some good: *"When cactus bloom where penguin play;"* some bad: *"and fairies no longer drink dew;"* and some simple: *"and one times one is two,"* *"When the sun comes up in the west"* and *"When the stars no longer shine"* – and the final line of each stanza, *"~ I guess I'll forget about you!"* The challenge was finding rhymes for *you* . . .which brings to mind three more of the last half of the lines: *"and false is always true,"* *"and cows no longer moo"* and *"vegetarians love beef stew."* *Now*, reading the forty impossibilities the four ancient poets came up with, I am delighted to feel totally outclassed. All readers who experience joy in logic probably will take to *meaningful listing*, such as metaphor on a theme (*unlikeliness* in this case). It is a remarkably effective way to help us appreciate how little we humans have changed over the millennia. Like Euclid's proof of negative numbers, it delights all rational souls.

♪ ***Impossibilities in English.*** The context is completely different, but Butler's *Hudibras* (near line 345) has a few fine impossibilities lined up, with a masterful finale:

Quoth he, To bid me not to love, / Is to forbid my pulse to move,
My beard to grow, my ears to prick up, / Or (when I'm in a fit) to hickup:
Command me to piss out the moon, / And 'twill as easily be done.

♪ オマケ **A Great *Kyôka* Curse for the Unfaithful Lover** that would have been in the main text had I come up with a good translation: 恨恋　雷の神に祈しかひあらば踏外しても落よ仇人　俊満？ 狂歌一万集 *kaminari no kami ni inorishi kai araba fumihazushite mo ochiyo adabito* shunman c 1800. 蛇足：甲斐＝法螺貝、恋敵は雲井で、その雲から？ I do have a *bad* translation:

If I only had a Conch, the Thunder Gods, their chief I'd call –
To make you miss-step, so off Cloud Nine, Love, you would fall!

Cloud Nine means the ninth layer of clouds, the *kokonoe* or highest (Imperial) noble circles where, I guess, the lover found another.

Segregated Beaches with Heron and Crow　　　　　　　　　　144頁

We generally pay little attention to the order of poems, but with short, ambiguous work, it can be important both for anthologies, such as the *Kokinshû* where trope is developed, and Journals such as Issa's which did likewise, naturally, for themes by writing half a dozen haiku in a single season *marvelous to read in the order written, but only so-and-so otherwise*. The importance of order for informal journals like Issa's may not be fully appreciated even by specialists. To wit, his annual *ku* on given themes are arranged alphabetically rather than chronologically in the *Issa Zenshû* (一茶全集の第一巻をご覧).

Perverse Nursery Verse = Snails! (pg. 443,448 for more re. horn-letter). 146 頁

Country Wants City Wants Country Life 148 頁

♪ ***Those Day Mice in Shokusanjin's poem***. Usually, the *sun=day* mice are combined with moon mice. How large a leap was made to get to the *pelts* of mice and rabbits? Let us see a typical old (1679 *Silver Leaf Savage Poem*) *kyôka* with them:

月と日の鼠に命かふられて　ことり／＼としぬる人／＼　貞冨　銀葉夷
tsuki to hi no nezumi ni inochi kaburarete kotorikotori to shinuru hitobito teifu
month and day-mice-by life/lives gnawed bitbybit die/dying people

Moment by moment, bit by bit, our lives, they gnaw away
– the rodents called months and days love human clay.

Pardon my replacing the obvious "die" with the Judeo-Christian idea of human clay!

♪ ***A Country to Go Back To.*** Old Shokusanjin who enjoyed the theatre and women of the big city still found his duties so onerous that he dreamed of a country estate with time even if he had no money. Issa, a dozen years after he returned to the country knew well that those who come back with empty pockets are not beloved. He, like Shokusanjin played with the old saying about returning home wearing brocade in this *kyôku*:

虱着て昼中もどる故郷かな　文政 6.9
shirami kite hirunaka modoru furusato kana   issa
lice wearing day-time return/ing hometown/country!

Wearing lice   *Coming home*
in the daytime, I return *in the day, wearing lice;*
to my hometown.   *That's my country!*

This is probably personal but may also be an observation of migrant workers returning in the Spring. Issa played on a version of the saying (衣レ錦昼行) specifying the daytime for leaving dressed in brocade, right after a *ku* where he played on another version where wealth *leaves* the hometown in brocade at night not to return (富貴不帰レ。。。『史記』). That poem, using the hazy moon as a metaphor (its haze is a *kasa*, homophonous with a face-hiding hat, and its clarity or lack thereof a symbol of purity/avarice) is barely a *kyôku*, but worth noting to show how Issa, like the mad poets, played with subjects from various angles: 錦着て夜行く人やおぼろ月 *nishiki kite yoru yuku hito ya oborozuki*. While Issa was conservative when it came to rice-riots and other public action taken against profiteers that got out of hand, his haiku show sympathy for radical Buddhist calls for divine justice resembling Christian millennialism.

♪ ***A Mad Poem that Gets What's Wrong with Living in the Country***. Had I not misplaced this pretty well-known 1796 poem by a student Shokusanjin loved who died at age 43, it would have been in the text:

ほとゝぎす自由自在にきく里は酒屋へ三里豆腐屋へ二里　頭光 万代狂歌集
hototogisu jiyûjizai ni kiku sato wa   sakaya e san ri tôfuya e ni ri   tsumuri no hikaru
cuckoo/s freely hear country-as-for wine-shop/bar-to 3 miles, bean-curd-shop-to 2 miles.

Out in the sticks where you're free to hear as much cuckoo as you may,
    It's three miles to buy wine and two for tofu – Would you stay?

I found Tsumuri no Hikaru's gem among the 20 *kyôka* in the famous poem supplement to my Benesse Old Language (*kogo*) dictionary. As the gloss tells you, "would you stay?"

He Loved Both Women and Chinese Rhyme   150 頁

♪ **Mori's Hand.** The last line is discussed at more length in *A Dolphin In the Woods*.

♪ **Ikkyû's all-character poems**. I read that Iwanami published a more thorough translation and annotation of them in the late 90's than what was in whatever old book I read and copied some pages from around 1990; but I could not afford to buy the volumes then and still do not know how the 難解 *very difficult* and 未解 *unsolved* poems I felt may have been actually censored in the earlier works have fared. (A Piet Hein grook joked about a pastor who puts on his halo to go out. Who knew, it was his horizon! Mine is circumscribed by my empty pockets.)

♪ **Kyôshi is not a parody of Chinese poetry**, though some Chinese poems may be parodied. It is, rather, in part, a reaction to some Chinese poetry, namely, the oh-so-lyrical tipsy sage stuff the Japanese *themselves favored* for a millennia because it was the high-prestige style (in China). A decade ago, I was *astounded* to read Carl Oldenburg's beatnick っぽい travesty of classic Japanese haikai, *Frog Croaks: Haiku Tongue in Cheek* (1975). Why so? Because I knew *haikai* was, itself, full of more pee, poo, sex and drunkenness than Oldenburg could imagine and which might have been translated by anyone at any time but was not. When I read of *kyôshi* being a parody of Chinese poetry, Oldenburg's book is the first thing I think of. Here is the start of the preface to the early 19c kyôshi book 半可山人詩鈔 part of which is reproduced in Hino and Takahashi (1991):

> *Shi* 詩（Chinese poetry）is the sleep-talk of Chinese (sleep ~ Chinese: *Greek to me*). *Kyôshi* is the sleep-talk of Japanese. The sleep-talk of the Chinese is all angle and plane, gibberish on the square 四角四面陳汾漢, too incredible to believe. The sleep talk of the Japanese, on the other hand, from the *sayôshikaraba* on high (samurai formal talk) to the *rinsu-yansu* on low (pleasure quarter dialect) is such that nothing can not be said and (because they say nothing concrete) nothing can be ruled out. . . .

And thus (now, I compress), *"courtesans can make lies the truth and eggs can be made square"* and *that* is what *really* should be called sleep-talk. Indeed, how I 予 pronounce characters as I see fit, writing one thing (劇場) and saying another (しばい), so that only the accompaniment of a phonetic syllabary allows others to follow what is written makes me wonder, he concludes, why it is not "the sleep talk of *Japanese*" (coined above). Then, he goes on to claim rhyming was like *"walking on devil's tongue"* (*konjak*, of a consistency between blubber and jello, i.e. very shaky), and, narrowing our choice, hurts our freedom 狭うして。。。自由ならず. No, *he* would not so restrict *himself* but compose with freedom 我儘勝手次第. With this (mistaken) attitude about rhyme, is it any wonder Japanese failed to discover the wild side of Chinese poetry?

♪ **Kyôshi, only a start.** Until I do a thorough search for pre-mid-18c *kyôshi* in Japan, my opinions in this and the following chapter should be taken with a *cup* of salt. Hino and Takahashi have done much research and mention books by other scholars, so I suppose I should go along with their opinion that *kyôshi* is, for all its predecessors, a genre created by Ôta. But, recalling how 17c *kyôka* is largely forgotten by Tenmei *kyôka* fans and how no one found Issa's *kyôka* I must wonder what old work, published or unpublished, perhaps, like Issa's, from someone belonging to another genre (and therefore ignored by specialists who tend to study work by someone recognized in *kyôka* circles) is out there!

♪ **Re. the content of the *kyôshi* 貧頓行 *The Poor Dull Ayre* (?)** – I had no room to wedge the title into the page – Professor Sleepyhead (Ôta) was probably *not* the first to reverse the proverb that *Earning overtakes Poverty*. Japanese are big on inverse proverbs and this one has some. What is refreshing is his qualification, *"most of the time."* Like his first line, where he pointed out that becoming *dull* would be no help for making ends meet, it neither supports nor contradicts the proverb, but *plays* with it by pretending to take it seriously. Personally, I like reading Ôta by any of his names for he gets me going.

As I read his poem, I found *myself* punning proverbs: "All work and no *pay* makes Jack a dull boy," and expanding idioms *"When they shoot you the bird, pluck it and put it in the oven!"* & cetera. Reading a Japanese saying I read scores of times before, namely, that *even passing through the underworld took money* (*jigoku no sata mo kane shidai*), within the context of his poem made me suddenly come up with *this:*

RICH MEN CANNOT BE KEPT DOWN BUT THEY CAN GET LOST.
IF YOU ARE POOR, PEOPLE ALWAYS TELL YOU WHERE TO GO!

The first line plays with a proverb this old pauper, who does not consider himself a bad man, dislikes, in a manner every bit as twisted as Professor Sleepyhead's, leading to the second with snapper enough to make this a bonafide example of mad-cap a la *Ôta* in English. After that, exhaustion got the better of me, but my brains were still whirling and I had to get up from bed for a pen to write down these words: *"Your money or your after-life!"* Indulgences. (Indulge *yourself.* Put that phrase into a poem and send it to me!)

♪ ***Zen Rhyme that is NOT Ikkyû.*** To get a real handle on *kyôshi,* we cannot just read *kyôshi.* I need the help of readers into Zen, wit and rhyme to give me (and other readers) a better idea of that side of kyôshi. I have vol.4 of Blyth's *Zen and Zen Classics: Mumonkan,* which just surfaced from a cardboard box displaced from its hiding place under a cabinet in my sister's dining room (no room in my room) by a family member visiting for grave matters. I am unsure if Blyth fully grasped the importance of rhyme in Zen poetry – despite having written the best essay on the significance of rhyme I have ever read – I forget the book, but he points out why the *arrow* that killed Cock-robin had to be shot by the *sparrow.* I say this because I never see him try to mimic it. In no particular order, first, Case XXXI and XIII, both about words and their usage. The small font translations are by Blyth (Ibid).

問 既 一 般
答 亦 相 似
飯 裏 有 砂
泥 中 有 刺

識 得 最 初 句
便 會 末 後 句
末 後 與 最 初
不 是 者 一 句

THE A IS THE SAME
AND THE Q IS A DUD
SAND IN THE RICE
THORNS IN THE MUD

IF YOU GOT THE FIRST WORD
YOU QUICKLY GOT THE LAST
BUT TO SAY THE TWO R ONE
IS 2 MAKE THE FUTURE PAST

1.*The question is the same. / The answer is the same. / Sand in the rice, / Thorns in the mud.*
2. *If you understand the first word of Zen / You understand the last; /But these two words / Are not one word.*

I think the first is criticism of worthless questions, but I found both it *and* Blyth's commentary boring (writing *of* Zen, rather than *finding* it elsewhere – in haiku or English literature – Blyth can be as bad as Elvis Presley singing gospel (wretchedly saccharine), and for the same reason) and, besides, I am not interested in anything here but pointing out that lines 2 and 4 end-rhyme and *there is a sort of magic in the crisp form of the original* as well. I crossed out the "is" in Blyth's first translation to give it 4x4-words. I know Q & A seem odd and the "dud" reflects the commentary rather than the original which says *the question is trite and the answer resembles it.* As to the relation between *that* and the final two lines, supposedly, it stands for "the not-to-be-digested intellectual contradictions and paradoxes" and seemingly soft like mud hiding "the thorns of life upon which we fall and bleed" (I should think it painful enough in the sole of the foot), but I feel that even a question must seem convincing and the riddle poem without the rhyme is not. The rhyme is needed just as the pun is needed for a *kyôka* lacking a sufficiently novel concept to delight even in prose. Call that my bias. Case XIII has nothing about the *future* or *past.* Now, Cases XI and XIV, metaphorical and what-if descriptions of the brilliant monk Jôshû. Here, I will stay closer to the original:

```
    眼 流 星         趙 州 若 在
    機 掣 電         倒 行 此 令
    殺 人 刀         奪 卻 刀 子
    活 人 劍         南 泉 乞 命
```

HIS EYES SHOOT STARS,	HAD JÔSHÛ BUT BEEN THERE
LIGHTNING'S HIS WORD.	HE'D SNATCHED THAT KNIFE:
A MAN-KILLING BLADE,	HOW DIFFERENT AN AFFAIR,
HIS LIFE-GIVING SWORD	NANSEN BEGGING 4 HIS LIFE!

1. *His eye is a shooting star; / The movements of his soul are like lightning. / He is a death-dealer, / A life-giving sword.* 2. *If Jôshû had been there, / Everything would have been done the other way round. / He would have snatched away the knife, / And Nansen would have begged for his life.* Both Blyth tr.

I am not happy with my first translation, especially the second line which speaks to the speed and decisiveness of his thought, but how would people know that without words and I did want that rhyme. Zen poetry should snap. No explanations ought to stretch it out. The original is a clear abcb, that is to say a broken couplet. The first character of the second line of the second poem does indeed imply a contrary scenario and Blyth is closer to the original than my "how different an affair" shifted to the third line – but, 13 syllables? One could kill or not kill a whole litter of kittens in that much time. Ah, I forgot to say that when Nansen demanded a brilliant reply to a Zen question or the cat's life, the cat died because none of the disciples came up with anything, after which Jôshû, who had been absent, returned and hearing about what happened immediately put his shoe upon his head at which Nansen lamented that had he been there the cat would still be alive.

```
        聞名不如見面
        見面不如聞名
        雖然救得鼻孔
        爭奈瞎卻眼睛
```

HEARING A NAME BEATS SEEING A FACE
SEEING A FACE BEATS HEARING A NAME
~~BUT SEEKING SALVATION UP A NOSTRIL~~
~~WILL ONLY SERVE TO CLOUD YOUR EYES~~

Rather than hearing the name, seeing the face is better; / Rather than seeing the face, hearing the name is better; / But however much you help the nostrils, – / Look what you've done to the eyes.

The original of Case XXVIII, above end-rhymes lines 2 and 4 but I did the above 4-liner with no rhyme based on what seemed to me the natural reading of lines 3 and 4 before reading Blyth's explanation of this "real monkey-puzzler." His explanation, or Mumon's, starts off well. An old woman finds out the hitherto incognito great Zen scholar and before long more of the town knows of his appearance than his name. Then, we are told *"As for the last two lines, the Sixth Patriarch wanted Emyô to see his real face, – but all of it, not a part. We must not do something pleasant to the nose but disagreeable to the eyes, or vice versa. All the face must be gratified."* So, the parts of the face seem to stand for the senses. I get that, but fail to get the link between the first and second half of the poem. Since the only on-line explanation I found concurred with Blyth's translation on the nostril/s being the object of "help/save," and the original is a rhyming couplet in four lines, again:

HEARING A NAME BEATS SEEING A FACE	A NAME BEATS A FACE
SEEING A FACE BEATS HEARING A NAME	A FACE BEATS A NAME
BURNING INCENSE SAVES THE NOSTRILS	TO PLEASE YOUR NOSE
BUT WILL LEAVE YOUR EYES AFLAME.	YOUR EYES MUST CRY

Since I really do not understand Chinese, much less this Japanese variety, and have no inclination to quote or rephrase stories, I will not comment more except to point out that I must be a monkey as I can only guess this means that normally only one sense can be satisfied at a time, or to vulgarize: *Knowing is one thing or another.* Now, *Mumon* Case XXXII:

劍刃上行
冰稜上走
不涉階梯
懸崖撒手

WE WALK ON SWORD BLADES,
RUN OVER SHARP JAGGED ICE
SCALE CLIFFS WITHOUT HAND
WITHOUT LADDER OR ADVICE

~~~~~~~~~~~~~~~~~

ON SWORD BLADES WE WALK
& O'ER CRACKED ICE WE RUN
HANDLESS WE SCALE WALLS
& OUR LADDERS LACK RUNGS

Walking along the edge of a sword; / Running over jagged ice; / Not using a ladder; / Climbing precipices handless. tr. Blyth

Here, only the first two lines of the original rhyme. My second try is a paraverse, not translation.

X X X I I I

路逢劍客須呈
不遇詩人莫獻
逢人且説三分
未可全施一片

SWORDMASTERS GET THE RIGHT O'WAY
NO POET? KEEP YOUR POEM – SHUT UP!
MEETING OTHERS, GIVE NO QUARTER;
TELL 'EM THREE QUARTERS, AND STOP!

~~~~~~~~~~~~~~~~~

MEETING A SWORD-MASTER, GIVE IN,
SEEING NO POET, HOLD YOUR BRUSH.
AND NEVER TELL ALL TO A STRANGER,
THREE QUARTERS IS MORE THAN ENUF.

If you meet a master-swordsman in the street, give him a sword. / If you meet an unpoetical man, don't offer him a poem. / When you meet someone, tell him three quarters, / Don't on any account let him have the other part. trans. Blyth

Here, I do believe Blyth nodded. While 須 may be a character in one famous sword, here it is an adverb modifying "giving." I guess it was proper not to make another go to Hell for killing you (笑). Be that as it may, look how long Blyth became – if I capitalized his reading like mine, it would be two or three-times as long. I had to drop the "street," no big loss for the first line; but the second line, "not-meet-poet-person-not-dedicate (compose and give a poem to)" was the killer. My first version probably failed to communicate the idea. My second reading reminds me of Francis Bret Harte, who, via *The Cremation of Sam McGee*, always takes me to my dad who had me read the poem shortly before passing away and

Frita Karlo, whose abundant frizzy hair flared up, according to Diego Rivera, turning her into the Sun Goddess during her final – to use a more modern term – installation. The original end-rhymes lines 2 and 4 and is otherwise snappy. As Blyth explains, the first two lines reflect a Chinese prescription to treat each person according to his "condition" (duh). If you have read Sufi tales telling the same, you know that the whole telling is snappier than Blyth's reading of just the poem part of the Case which is, I hate to say, an academic matter. "The Verse," as he calls it, is *not* merely a message, but a gem to be savored: *the final two lines are now in all the proverb dictionaries*. To demonstrate that aphoristic quality a translator must re-create or naturalize the poem, which in the case of the above, Mumon, or not, is a didactic poem of the road, *dôka,* that only becomes a *kyôka,* in my mad translation where the brush becomes a tongue and a sword. And, now the last of this sampling. It is not called the "verse" but the commentary for Case #34, *Nansen's No Way*. In case you did not read the preceding chapters, Blyth introduces the eccentric Zen priest, his *dramatis persona,* like this: "Nansen is the chap who loved his teaching more than cats."

南 泉 可 謂
老 不 識 羞
纔 開 臭 口
家 醜 外 揚

然 雖 如 是
知 恩 者 少

OF OLD NANSEN, I LAMENT:
LOST TO SHAME, INDECENT
HE, OPENS HIS FOUL MOUTH,
'COME INTO MY DIRTY HOUSE!'

THAT SUCH A MONK BOASTS
DEVOTEES IS OPEN TO DOUBT

Nansen, growing old, was lost to shame. Just opening his stinking mouth, he told others about the disgrace of his own house. However. we must say that few are grateful for it.

This was tough. As Blyth's translation is a straight gloss on the original, you can see how much work it took to create something that scanned & squared. The Chinese is neutral, but past-tense, such as Blyth used, might be better. Finally, with respect to all these poems that I translated as madly as I could, I must confess I did not find them as interesting as *kyôka* or *kyôshi*. I did not dare make this long, long note a chapter, for I *also* know next to nothing about Zen. But, when Blyth's *Mumonkan* popped up in my room at an opportune time, I knew I could not just let it go. If anyone has something better, please send it to me.

~~~~~~

Blue Camels & White Swimmers: News in Character   154 頁

♪ **The Camel Poem in the text.** Pardon no citation. It came from Hino and Takahashi, 1991, who took it from 半可山人詩鈔, part of which they reproduce. The camels date the poem well enough for every artist, poet and diarist that saw their tour wrote *something*.

♪ **Best Camel Pun.** It was not in a poem. Asked by a *suribon* (illustrated prints+poems) publisher whether he would contribute a poem to a camel book, Shokusanjin turned down the offer saying that in his old age he found, even with *kyôka,* the most *camel=rakuda= easy(-is)* thing for him was *not* composing them. ことし紅毛の国より来れるもの駱駝をひきて長崎に来れるかたをうつして、狂歌のすりものとなせるよし、五揚舎福富のもとよりいひ おこしければ 老ては狂歌もよまぬが駱駝 と書きつかはしけるもおかし。**オマケ**：「詠まぬながらくだ」の洒落で覚える、楽ではないがなんとなく似たる言葉あそびがある：「蜀山人々々々々とにせ筆の多ければ《書きちらす 筆は蜀山 兀として 阿房の出る にた山師ども》との事。『蜀山家集』より。

♪ ***The great artist Hokusai loved big-bottomed women***, but the only acknowledgement of the attraction of curves I know in a Japanese poem is indirect: *Manyôshû* #1738-9, where a young woman, who slept with all – men visited anytime day or night and never got enough of her – is described as having a thin waist and broad (separated) breasts (胸別=むなわけ=のひろき吾妹 腰細の). To me, *thin-waist* implies *big rump*, but I hope to find an old Japanese poem somewhere that actually mentions, nay, *praises* one belonging to a *woman* (yet there are plenty about big-salt-mound(shiny crystalline) butt gay youth!).

♪***Ladies Bobbling Along Like Gourds, an Earlier Kyôka***. No, we don't have the ladies themselves, but we do have a more general description of humans by the fictional 17c *kyôka*-master Chikusai behaving like rolling and bobbing gourds tossed into the water: 人はけにみづへなけたるひやうたんのぬらりくらりになかれゆくとし　竹斎　(杉楊枝) *hito wa ge ni mizu e nagetaru hyôtan no nurari kurari ni nagareyuku toshi.*

Playing With Myths of Beginnings & Ends　　　　　　　　158頁

♪ ***Birds in bed.*** Speaking of which, once, on a Japanese blog, I read someone argue with tongue only half in cheek that, with a bird for their instructor, it is not surprising some Japanese practiced sodomy from ancient times. I think the bird got the role purely for the twitch in his tail, but if historical phylogeny can recapitulate Freudian ontogeny, some anal stage primal consciousness just might play a role in the choice. I recall dreaming – a real night dream, not a day-dream – of Elena, a Cuban girl who sat on the other side of the room for whom I had a secret crush in grade school: believe it or not, she had a bm that was pure jewels and pearls and all the luminous and sparkly things a child loves. I did not then know that craving such shiny objects, even to the point of wanting to eat them, was called pica, and that comes from the Latin word for . . . a *kasasagi* (magpie)*!*

♪***Mitoku's Heaven as a Cool Place to Go.*** The original poem conflates Paradise with the road going there, as the sutra gowns were sold – *Your money or your After-life!* – to speed the long, long journey. Most were light and worn more as underwear than robes per se; *katabira* were worn alone in the summer (to the disgust of the diva taste-master Sei Shônagon, who professed to retch at the sight of hairy dark-skinned men through the diaphanous fabric, and European visitors who religiously put down all flesh a thousand years later – to paraphrase the dying Rochester or Heywood to a priest, *"Are you saying God should have made us fish?"*). Mitoku's poem is, I think, facetious, yet so delicate a twist in convention as to barely draw a smile, while Tosui's warning of the consequences of praying too much is a hearty laugh. They reflect the breadth of style in *kyôka* satire.

One world at a time – Heaven or Hell one thing is true . . .　　　160頁

♪ Re: **My *"You can't take it with you"* translation.** Decades of providing creative alternative translation possibilities to translators followed by a two-year long chain of experiments creating and playing variable tension string instruments made my thinking in 1994 or 5 *that* flexible. I now read Japanese better, but doubt I'll ever match it (pic.pg. xx).

♪ ***Why I Chose Teitoku's poem.*** I considered cutting my translation down to one reading in order to squeeze this next one into the chapter:

見て涼むまでこそよけれ蓮台にむかへられてはたまるものかは 元信 華紅葉 1729
mite suzumu made koso yokere hachisuha ni mukaerarete wa tamaru mono ka wa　genshin
seeing cool-down-until+emph. good lotus leaves/leaf-on come-for-as-for bear+emph.?!

> *Just to view them is cooling, the floating lotus dais . . .*
> *I can hardly wait to die and have one spirit me away!*

Though a good traditional poem playing up the seasonal aspect of the lotus as a summer flower, the jump from heat relief to relief from this world makes it a fine mad poem as well. Yet, I prefer Teitoku's poem, surely because I, too, believe . . . in *this* world. Here is an example of a similar but less aesthetic expression of Teitoku's worldly attitude:

死んて後とはん万部の経よりも　命の内に壱歩たまはれ　酒粕　銀葉夷歌集 tk1
shinde ato towan manbu no kyô yori mo inochi no uchi ni ichibu tamaware shûhaku? 1679

To Monks Who Would Save My Soul: Suit, I mean, *Sutra* Yourself!

*Afterlife? Who cares! I'll rather feast and gain a pound alive
than fast for fat indulgences that only promise I'll arrive!*

The original pun-equates an enormous distance with the tens of thousands of sutra bought to help one cross it, and contrasts that to *one-step*, also a monetary unit. As those puns were untranslatable, I latched on to a British monetary unit with another meaning and, I hope you didn't mind, re-created a more explanatory poem (and title).

~~~~~~

Life After Death, Death After Death & Doubt　　　　　　　　　　162 頁

♪**Chikamasa** 親当. If the other party in the Zen Mondô *dôka* exchange 道歌問答集 really was Ikkyû's friend, he was a superb punner. Many of his *dôka* are clearly *kyôka* and, unfortunately, even less translatable than those I tried in the text. For example, 欲あかを洗いおとせばさっぱりと　襦袢につけしのりぞとうとき *yokuaka o arai otoseba sappari to juban ni tsukeshi nori zo tôtoki*. This is great. But English has no greed/desire manifesting itself as *yokuaka,* or *crud,* to be cleaned from a clerical singlet, much less *starch* precious for homophony with the *Law* (tenets of the Faith), both *nori*. Reading something like this, we can see why Ikkyû, who had a high opinion of himself, had a higher one yet of his friend Chikamasa, a leading link-verse poet of the time.

~~~~~~

Lotus Jewels – or Foolish Philosophical Questions　　　　　　166 頁

More on Norinaga and Mitoku's poems.　♪***The dew-drops on the lotus leaf*** not only have uniquely heavy metaphorical baggage but share with those found on some gigantic (elephant-ear) taro leaves: when they move and combine and break and recombine, and when doing so are less like round, or nearly round gems than protean creatures. I have not read enough Norinaga to know if he was pointing that out rather than being philosophical. I have observed a single kudzu leaf can host *thousands* of minute dew-drops while taro leaves toss about drops the size of pin-balls (observing them in the rain you think you are playing!) and may combine to make much larger irregular ones, pine-needle-like *tsuguna* may string them up straight and so forth. I hope to do a book on dew someday. So Norinaga scholars, please keep your eyes peeled for me!

♪ ***The Dew-drops' Fault.*** **Mitoku's** *kyôka* holding the unwillingness of dewdrops to hold their form for their admirer who would like to pick them up to be a *flaw on their perfection* is a variation on that commonplace. Elsewhere (the *senryû* book? this one?), I have introduced a marvelous old (early 20c?) party song where the words praise a girl for being beautiful, intelligent, kind, and otherwise absolutely perfect except – this, the last line of the last stanza – for one slight flaw, *"she won't fall for me!"* Mitoku's poem indirectly tells us the idea was already used in the 17c. Not having space to tell that to you, I gave a second reading to suggest it. Here are two readings that were cut for space:

*So damn beautiful yet I cannot pick up the luminous dew,
'Tis said perfection has a flaw: breaking proves it true.*

~~~~~~

*How beautiful, this luminous dew I wish I could hold:
That 'perfect' always has a flaw proves true to mold.*

I cannot not mention a pair of Issa's *ku* composed almost two centuries later. One has a little child try to pinch (and pick up) a dew drop (*tsuyu no tama tsumande mitaru warabe kana*). The other notes that at the moment one pinches it, it is the Buddha/ dead (*tsuyu no tama tsumanda toki mo hotoke kana*). With the lack of pronouns and the past-tense, I think he refers to a memory of his beloved daughter Sato who died that Spring, when she pinched that dew-drop, she, too was already as good as dead. But I could be wrong. Three years later he wrote,

しら露としらぬ子どもが仏かな 一茶
shiratsuyu to shiranu kodomo ga hotoke kana issa
white=unknowing dew knows-not child-the buddha 'tis!/?

A child yet to know that shiny white dew is dew – That, too, is bliss!	*Oh, to be a child not knowing that dew is dew happy as buddha*	*A child yet to know that we like dew all go . . . True bliss is this!*

I would call that a *kyôku* as it equates the innocent white=shira=unknowing dew with the child and plays on a proverb *shiranu ga hotoke* (know-not is buddha), or "ignorance is bliss." So the older poem, which specifies pinching it may mean that even pinching a dew-drop the child only laughs delightedly at being fooled and I ought not have brought Sato into it. Regardless, my motive for bringing in such poems is to show how concepts do not kill but enliven haiku, and that *kyôka* need not be quarantined.

If Dew Drops Were Delicious, Men Being Men 168頁

♪ **Sweet Dew Precedent in Precious Flowers?** The compiler-editor of the first major *kyôka* collection 古今夷曲集 *Kokin-ikyoku-shû* (1666), 行風 Kofu wrote a long essay detailing what he expected, or rather, did not want, in a *kyôka*. One of his 15 *no-no's* was puns with imperfect homophony. For reader who do not know Japanese let me first give the gist of the content: *Were the Keria's bloom really gold, the folk in Wellout town will come out to steal the gilt globes.* As this flower was paired with frogs a lot (Bashô's famous frog was first a globe-flower) as they, too, plopped into water(?), and frogs were in wells, not only is well-out=ide=come-out/appear a pun, but one with a fitting allusion. (山吹の花がまことの金ならば いかにぬすみに井出の里人 *yamabuki no hana ga makoto no kin naraba ikani nusumi ni ide no satobito* anon.) The *i/yi* vowel/s used for the place name *Ide* and coming-out *ide* (いで vs. ゐで), so close that today they are identical, made it a poor pun in Kofu's opinion. I do not have the index volume of tk or I would check to see if this poem was included nonetheless or deep-sixed for its sin. Luckily, later *kyôka* poets and editors were not that strict about slight differences in pronunciation more imagined from proper orthography (which not all poets knew) than real. Many of Kofu's demands are, however, good, so long as one allows for the exception that works nonetheless. (Scholars may find Kofu's treatise in 「生白堂行風の狂歌論：禁制十五項を中心にして」 高橋 喜一(梅花女子大学文学部) "The Essay on Comic Poetry by Seihakudo Kofu, a Poet in 17th Century," by Takahashi Kiichi in Japanese only. Free to see, pdf.)

♪ **Issa's Dew Poems Largely un/Recognized, but . . . .** Reading Issa's *Journals* in the mid-90's, I was *astounded* with Issa's cornucopia of dew *ku* and, then, curious why I had seen so little of them. Now, I think I know. It is because many are *conceptual* and that is not so what people looked for in haiku, much less Issa. Not just modern haiku *saijiki* but even Shiki's *Categorical* (possibly because the journals were not available) missed almost all of them. It delighted me to discover five years later that my favorite early-20c haiku almanac, the *Kaizôsha Haikai Saijiki* – let me be honest, that is one reason *why* it became my favorite – gives Issa the lion's share of (fall) dew. For *general* dew, he boasts 20 *ku* to his nearest competitor Buson's 10; for *white*-dew, he has 5, so, too, Buson; *night* dew, 4 to Onitsura's 1; dew-*drops*, 9, half of the total for all poets; *setting* dew, 3, again, half of all, *scatter/ dropping* dew, 7 of 11, dew-*world*, 2 of 3. But even Kaizôsha's *saijiki* could only show a small part of his dew *ku*. I would not say I am 100% satisfied with Issa's dew for even he failed to pick up on the tremendous differences in how various plants display it. But, here is a *ku* that seems less haiku or *kyôku* than a 17-syllabet *tanka*. I added the title for other of his *ku* dwell on how busy the dew can be.

露はらり／＼大事のうき世哉　一茶
tsuyu harariharari daiji no ukiyo kana

Such Commotion!

Dew-drops in motion
The floating world
is a big thing.

Only one of Issa's dew-*ku* is *always* included in *saijiki:* "This world is a world of dew, of dew, but even then . . ." (露の世は露の世ながらさりながら *tsuyu no yo wa tsuyu no yo nagara sarinagara*). One of the most *painful* haiku ever written, anyone who read his wee biography of his daughter's short life gets wet eyes reading it. But, damn it, Issa had a lot of fun with the dew. Why not introduce *that*, too? (Actually, *one* other dew-ku is often seen. A cricket or a Katydid is involved and everyone knows Issa liked little animals, so . . .). And, note that the dew-drops in motion are serious humour.

Less Witty Wisdom, or Weighing Way Poems II　　　　　170 頁

This chapter was expanded from a note. I was not kidding when I wrote it was preliminary until I did more research on *dôka*, or "way-poems." But they kept turning up, so my note got too long. They are found in all sorts of places. Here is one more yet pulled from a 12c *waka* anthology. I do not have the poet's name:

世のなかのうきはいまこそ うれしけれ おもひしらすはいとはましやは　千載集 1187
yononaka no uki wa ima koso ureshikere omoi shirasu wa itowamashi/ji? ya wa　chisaishû
world-within's woe-as now espec. delighted know-inform-as4 hate-would-not+emph!/?

It makes me very happy, now, our world's so full of woe:
How could you hate something that only let's you know?

This is not so far from the thinking that made a certain New England woman genuinely *thankful* she was kidnapped by native Americans, some of whom she killed to escape. Today, thankfulness for suffering seems paradoxical if not mad, but I realize it was a commonplace at the time. And here is one more moral poem from a 1740 Ôsakan *kyôka* anthology found when I checked for another poem for proofing purposes. The idea of a god that comes when you do *not* pray makes an otherwise moralistic poem decently mad.

月見花見二日酔して朝寝せば いのらぬとても神やあふかん　百子？狂歌餅月夜
tsukimi hanami futsukayoi shite asane seba inoranu to demo kami ya aufukan　momoko

貧 乏 神 の 古 団 も た れ し 絵 に
On a picture of the God of Poverty old fan in hand

If you sleep-in from moon or blossom-viewing, i.e., a hangover,
You will need not pray to meet a god who never rolls in clover!

If moon or blossom-viewing or one too many make sleeping-in rife
No prayers will be needed for this god to enter your life!

Three Mad Exchanges. The Chickadee, for example.　　　　　174 頁

♪ ***In Search of the Chickadee.*** First let us note that dictionaries *also* English this bird as *great tit.* To me, it looks nothing like either! No matter. What counts is the *name in Japanese.* My respondent located the source of Fukui Kyûzô's story of prototypical linked-verse in a book published in 1930 (福井久蔵『連歌の史的研究　前編』（成美堂

書店）昭和五年の「はしがき」）from which I could ascertain the Japanese original is written 四十から and おい so as to leave the two homophones 四十雀・四十から and 笈・老い ambiguous. If one had to choose, however, the ostensible *chickadee* and *casket* would be what to write, so Hiroaki Sato was correct to do so. After the story concludes, Fukui wrote that he was unsure where the tale originated but that he, too, passed the big divide of age 40 and came to publish books on linked-verse thanks to the seeds planted by his mother in his youth. The passage is beautiful, as one might expect from a top tanka poet. (一体これは何に出てゐる説話か私はまだ種本を知らない。唯幼い私の心に母上がみづからうつして下さつた一つの現像である。少年は老い易く、私は彼の青年の謠つた初老といふ四十はとつくの昔に過ぎ去つて、今は暦をまきかへす春を迎へ、頭は半白になつた。生来蒲柳の質而も識浅くこれといふ業績を学海にささげ得ないことを衷心より常に恥かしく嘆いてゐるが、日にまして気性も努力も衰へて、ただ老いゆけばゆくほど幼時の思出が何とも云へないゆかしさ懐しさを増してゆくのを覚えるばかりである。爰に少しの機縁があつて近年少しく連歌に関する書をあさり、連歌の史的研究といふ二巻の書を成すに至つたことを亡き御魂に告げまつると共に、ひからびた連歌の古根に水を注ぎ青い芽をふきかへさせたいと思ふ心は洵に切なるものである。。。）。

♪ ***Another version.*** My respondent *also* located the story in a book of old tales published in 1975「四十雀」in 全国昔話資料集成8『西播磨昔話集』（岩崎美術社）. The pilgrim sits on the veranda of a house where he was going to spend the night, sees the chickadee enter his casket and, *talking to himself*, gives the first part of the verse, which is heard by the elder of the house, who insists the pilgrim must be a master traveling incognito for using the *chickadee* to allude to his years and *travel-casket*, his age, and pack all of this in 5-7-5. The pilgrim had been practicing saying things in 5-7-5 as *haikai* was popular but had no idea what he punned (which is why the Japanese「四十雀が笈の内にぞ入りにけり」specifies *chickadee* and *casket*). His host *insisted* he stay so a *haikai* session could be arranged for all the enthusiasts in the area. The poor pilgrim tried to beg off to no avail, and as he sat alone despairing over the attention he didn't deserve, sadly said to himself "Aaah, *though I say, 'To Wakasa!'" they won't let me go back*."「アーア、若狭へとては帰られもせず」. The elder catches that, too. Minus the *aaah*, it is 7-7 and has the Wakasa =youth pun. As the tale ends we wonder if the reluctant "haikai master" will *ever* escape (ところが、主人がまた物蔭からこれを聞きつけて飛んで出て、「先生ただ今承つておりますれば、まことに結構な脇句ができましたご様子、イヤモウ全く恐れ入りました」）.

♪ ***The pilgrim in each tale*** has the rustic name Rokube 六部、and the first verse is the same, but in one tale it is said by a youth and the other by the pilgrim, while the second verse belonging to the pilgrim in both tales is different, with one asking for the way and the other lamenting the inability to get there. As a tale, the reluctant *haikai* master is the more moving, but, as poetry, the exchange by the youth and pilgrim is best. I suspect that Fukui, as a fine poet in his own right, may have improved upon the story his mother told him but we shall only figure out what is what by examining more variants of the story.

♪ ***Plentiful examples of this Bird***, the *Shijûkara* **punning "From Forty,"** are found in *kyôka*. One example from a surimono book combining Utamarô's prints and *kyôka* has already been Englished by James A. Kenney as *"Seeing my feathers / You think of me / Only as a great tit; / Your cruel reply / Is a little hard for me to take"* (四十雀と君に見えていただきのいろにはちょっとつらき御返事　寶の敦丸　*shijûkara to kimi ni miete ya itadaki no iro ni wa chotto tsuraki gohenji* Takara-no-Atsumaru　百千鳥狂歌合せ c1790 (Utamarô: *A Chorus of Birds* (*momochidori kyôka awase* 1790 (The Metropolitan Museum of Art/Viking Press: 1981). The translator fails to note the *significance of the name*, which in the original is the crux of the poem. The bird/poet is indeed put down, but it is because he is seen as "over the hill" (a great tit) by the girl, whose reply makes it all too clear she has no interest in him. Another *kyôka* in the bird section of the masterful 1643 Four-animal-genre *kyôka* contest (四生の歌合) with dueling poems on the subject of warbled love-making (さゑずりかはすこひ) includes a poem by one "Old Guy from Forty" 四十からおひのすけ which, to me, would have been no more than "a happy warbling exchange around the clock" (あさゆふにちん／＼からりから／＼と　わらうやうにて　なきかはすかな *asa yû ni chinchin karari . . .*) had not the judge/editor explained: *"from forty, one's poems come to reflect one's self and the words just flow out..."* (はんにいはく四十からのうたは をのかすかたに にたる歌なりかる／＼しくや侍らんかゝれども). This Celebration of Forty is rare. Fear of Forty would be more common. Eyesight was said to dim then. Here is a *Yanagidaru senryû* with a fictional touch more common to *kyôka*:

三十九の暮蝋燭をたんと買 *sanjûkyû no kure rôsoku o tanto kai* Y-15 1780
thirty-nine's end-of-year candle/s+acc properly buy (for once the gloss was not needed)

His thirty-ninth year. *As year thirty-nine*
As it ends, how proper! *ends, how proper & fine*
He buys candles. *to purchase candles!*

♪ ***Wakasa Town Name Punning.*** More evidence that a pun was intended from another aspect of the link-verse waka exchange. There is even at least one pair of *kyôka* focusing on age matters snow= white (hair)=unknowing (かさぬ草紙ＴＫ参考 27, supposedly by Izumi Shikibu, where *wakasa*=youth is punned as a town's name. 和泉式部＝白雪をいたゝきながら<u>わかさ</u>とは　しての山路をとははとへかし *shirayuki o itadakinagara . . . /* 老人＝白雪をいたゝけはこそとふそかし　<u>わかさ</u>へ帰る道をしらねは *shirayuki o itadakeba . . .*).

♪ ***Today, My Respondent***, gamely (for they are not to his taste) checking on some moral poems (*dôka*) for me discovered what for this book will be **the final word on the chickadee-in-the-basket poems**. なお『道歌教訓和歌辞典』を見ていたら「四十雀負担の内へぞ入りにける若狭へ去る道ぞ知りたや」六十六部回国上人，生国若狭小濱之者『たとへづくし』）がありました。これも昔話だと思います。「大意」として「四十歳となりいよいよ老境に入った。若さを取り戻す道を知りたいものである」となっています。In a word, the linkverse poem is credited to a book of sayings by someone born in Wakasa and was *an allegory for how we feel turning forty*. Looking back, I am amazed that when I first read Hiroaki Sato's *Hundred Frogs*, five or ten years before *I* was forty, I immediately registered that pun. I probably had thoughts along the line of, *Is there something wrong with me always finding funny meanings in apparently straight-forward poems?* (If you recall, Sato, no dummy, did not mention much less translate the pun). For other wild readers out there, all I can say is, *don't let them tell you that you are making it up!* Sometimes, your imagination must outrun the pros to catch the poetry.

♪ ***Months Later***. *Proof of the Extent of 40-Chickideeism.* I found the following c.1700 poem too late to attempt a reading, but in brief, it is a *seventy* (!) rather than forty year-old chickadee poem on the Year of the Bird. *Shijûkara*⇒*Shichijûkara*. 酉のとし元日七十歳にて　ひやうたんもくるみもいらて飛廻る七十からといふとりのとし　甚久法師狂歌集 *hyôtan mo kurumi mo . . .* Jinkyû. I.e., one added ち made a 70 yr.old Xroads chickadee!

~~~~~~

Mad Debates: Varieties of *Kyôka* versus *Kyôka* 176 頁

The earthy exchange of the old man and woman on what vessel they would be reborn as has variations. Another cited by Nada Inada is identical for the man but instead of a urine flask, the woman more tastefully goes for the symbolic satisfaction of being a mortar.

~~~~~~

The Piss-proud Drunk vs. The Sharp-tongued Teetotaler 178 頁

While Bokuyô takes one side in the put-down contest of drinker and teetotaler, he has one poem bringing them together below the cherry trees: In *Cherry Blossom Epiphany* (2007), I introduce a number of poems where *sake*, the drink and *sake!* meaning "bloom!" are deliberately conflated – Issa does it, for one – but none have this sort of complex wit .

花盛り下戸も上戸ものみたべて開かぬ先にさけさけといふ　卜養狂歌集 1669
hanazakari geko mo jôgo mo nomi-tabete hirakanu saki ni sake sake to iu bokuyô
blossom-acme teetotalers and drinkers drinking eating bloom-not-before 'sake sake' say

Ambiguous Imperative

It's blossom peak,
drinkers and teetotalers
alike now whine –

'Late-blooming cherries, sake!
Sake! Please, don't make us pine!'

It's blossom peak.
Do drinkers & teetotalers
wine together?

"Hurry, cherrý! Sake! Sake!
Bloom now or never! Sake!"

In the original, they do not *whine* but "say," & the imperative suggests both parties, intoxicated by the bloom rudely shout it out. *Bloom! Bloom!* or *Wine! Wine!* is not *Strip! Strip!* but the mood evoked makes me think of it. As I was finishing up the book, I found the following delightful *sake sake* poem by Konomichi Kuraki (this road is dark) in a 1799 print by Hokusai in Carpenter: *Reading Surimono* (2008):

梅の花さけ／＼よりも酒よりもわれハ女房をもちぐミにせん　此道くらき
ume no hana sake sake yori mo sake yori mo ware wa nyôbô o mochi-gumi ni sen
plum-blossoms sake sake more-than sake mor-thn I-as4 wife+acc. mochi-group-as do

Rather than urging / plum blossoms to bloom / so we can drink rice wine, /
I prefer to hold my wife / while enjoying rice cakes! — trans. carpenter

Rather than pushing the plums to bloom so we can drink rice wine,
Put me with the rice cake crowd – I would poke this wife of mine.

Bloom, plums! Bloom for our sake, our sáké! Not me. I'd take
My wife, my sweet honey bun! Put me with those who eat cake.

This is the first of three poems with a picture of a man napping while his wife grills mochi (sweet-rice-cake). As we have already seen, the world was split between the wine-drinkers, or tipplers and the cake-eaters, or teetotalers. The word *~gumi* (from *kumi* 組) means a group such as a gang or a union or tight-nit association. The poem puns from "having" a wife into joining the latter group, as drinkers tended to stay out and he wanted to be home. As *mochi* was poked while it was cooked and poking mochi was idiomatic for coitus I could not resist adding that verb to my paraverse of Carpenter's more tame – responsible? – translation. Seeing a book straddling his face like a slightly curved A-frame roof, I almost wrote "eat" rather than "poke." Why not? As you can see in my book *The Woman Without a Hole* (2007), Japanese were into that.

A Wit-ness of Salutes, Salutations & Warnings 182 頁

There must be a tremendous number of 31-syllabet poems used in and as personal exchanges – especially with and for gifts – outside of *kyôka* anthologies, scattered about the world of print. Here is one exchange between the famous female *kyôka* master Chie no Naishi and Yoshino no Kuzuko, who has almost as many poems (five) in the Tokuwa anthology from which it comes. Both depend on the homophony of *persimmon* and *writing* so I will not even try to translate the poems which are, as the Iwanami editors note, natural (unforced) and reflect the highly cultured female sensitivity. 智恵内子のもとへ大和柿にそへてよみてつかはしける ◎よみならふ哥のたねにとへたながら心ばかりをかき送るなり　吉野葛子 *yominarau uta no tane ni to* . . . Yoshino-no-kuzuko; 返し ◎たまはるは御所にも似たり言のはの花もみもある枝柿のもと　智恵内子 *tamawaru wa* . . . Chie-no-naishi 1785.

A Violent Nightingale & Mimesis Made to Say Something 188 頁

♪**Nightingale=Warbler=Thrush?** I feel more at ease with inconsistent bird names in a book of 31-syllabet poetry than one of 17. With haiku, where the emphasis on catching and sharing the reality of seasonal life demands a higher degree of precision about what is what and people, naturalists one and all, will call you out on names. Over the centuries, we find a fair number of haiku addressing the bothersomeness of names or things that make poetry hard because they have all those names, so I know we who lack hard memories (my fuzzy memory, on the other hand, is second to none) do not suffer alone.

Sweet Uguisu by name,
'Nightingale' had the right feeling
until someone learned it wasn't the same
and, as science allows for no appealing,
You became a 'Warbler' – and, if that
were not enough, horribler, yet,
now it seems there is a rush
to turn all three of you
into something new
a 'Thrush.'

~~~~~~

Open your ears but close your mouth, the plum is blooming – hush!
There is no bliss if you should miss the First Song of the Thrush!

I could not resist making one poem just for the rhyme. It has bilingual allusions for the *bliss* in "Ignorance is bliss" is Japanesed *hotoke* which can mean Buddha and the uguisu's song is said to be a sutra, which is a tool for enlightenment which brings bliss. Be that as it may, in Japanese, the *uguisu* is not the bird with a thousand names; that honor belongs to the *hototogisu* or, cuckoo (whom I have also seen translated nightingale, which is a far cry from his call but close for sharing legends of bleeding themselves to death!) who can boast a dozen or so appellations with scores of orthographies.

♪ *Tada hitoyo / ake no karasu to / Ichikawa no / kono kaho kaho wa / isagi yoi mono*
After just one night / at this sight of Ichikawa's / bold and splendid visage /
the crows of dawn / "Caw! Caw!" for more = McKee trans. ↓

Caw Caw for More! Or, How a Lost Pun Was Found, or Maybe Not: a Story for Translators and/or Bilinguals. Glancing at the romanization of Jihinari's poem in *Colored in the Year's New Light* (above), I was puzzled. I was familiar with an *ake-garasu* or dawn-crow (esp. those that caw then) but had not seen it devolve back into the description *ake no karasu*. I guessed it might be for the sake of making the pivot from "just one night" to the crow more natural (*tada hitoyo* ⇒ *yoake* ⇒ *ake no karasu* vs *hitoyoakegarasu*). Then, putting on my reading glasses to look carefully at the calligraphy to type in the Japanese, I saw or thought I saw the か *ka* for *karasu* was no か *ka* (as the book romanized it) but a *ga* が, which is to say the muddy glotalization usually not written down until the 20c. Still, with *ka* not welded if it were to the preceding noun, it was *odd* to find it glotalized (if indeed the extra squiggle was a way of writing the marks). Noting it was at the top of a line – this poem was exceptionally broken – 9 lines were needed to help it squeeze in between the actor and his lucky bat flying overhead – gave me pause to think: Could this have been done to ensure no one missed the connection to the immediately proceeding *no* (the character I use for lack of choice in my software is not quite right but that is no matter, the point is it was a letter, not character)? I checked my OJD and, sure enough, there *was* a word: *nogarasu*, "field crow." Usually the *no* is written in character, 野. Jihinari, knowing that doing so would hurt his evocation of the New Year – not let 明け breathe – did not use it, but instead put on the glotalization marks in the next line so the reader could get it in retrospect. *Or, so I assumed.* But, wait, it gets better yet. *Nogarasu* is a perfect homophone for a verb that means *exactly* what I thought that first line was driving at 逃らす: *Let flee/escape*, a reference perhaps to the hero not killing the villain, but merely scowling him down and letting him go after he freed the good people the villain planned to execute. The *to* is an indication that what comes before is a quote (short for *tote*)). As I read this, I felt pretty sure I had caught a missed pun, the second best in the poem. But when I asked for my respondent a *kajin,* or tanka poet for his opinion, he thought *akenogarasu* was just "too ugly a clump of sounds" and felt it far more likely that *akegarasu* was split up to gain an extra syllabet in the connecting *no* and the clear *ka* sound: *ake no karasu.* And he thought the verb neither Edo, nor grammatical. On the grammar, *I think he is wrong,* for the verb is not a conjugation of *nogareru* (in which case it would indeed be off) but an archaic (now obsolete) variant the OJD defines as identical to *nigasu,* or let flee. And, it is a fact that there were some who liked to mimic ancient language in 19c *kyôka,* so while it is not probable it is, I still think, possible that the poet did intend a pun. In other words, the mistake I thought I found in McKee may be my own. Perhaps, I should add I also favored *field crows* for they eat the dead and I wrongly thought someone would be executed. I have mixed feelings about the old orthography for face *kaho kaho* carried over into English. *Face* is usually pronounced *kao* – like *cow,* as Japan's leading bath soap manufacturer, Kao, which uses the image of a *cow,* knows well. McKee kept it because he needed to show he caught the pun on Aho/ô meaning *"fool."* Japanese, very attentive to crows, noticed some crows sound stupid and some of them actually admitted it and called the fool-crows "ahôgarasu." The OJD example sentence for such crows had one keeping someone awake with its *"gaa-gaa'ing,"* that is to say, infantilized *cawcaw*ing! (「～あほうがらすのがあがあは」) and not cry *aho-aho*. In other words the *kaho/aho* punning brings to mind the *ahogarasu* thereby seconding the *nogarasu* and giving us two varieties of crows in one poem – or what was two varieties until my respondent squashed the first. That is not to say the *aho-aho* is not also a call. While not the most common sound for a crow's caw in Japanese, it was probably the second most common and Issa used it in a *ku* in 1821:

老踊あほう／＼や夕烏　一茶
oi odoru ahô ahô ya yûgarasu issa

Old me dancing –	*Dancing Age*
Do I hear 'Aho! Aho!'	*'A fool!' 'A fool!' is it?*
The evening crow.	*The evening crow.*

Here, I should add that my respondent also pointed out something I knew, that in Edo a fool was a *baka* not an *aho* so there was not much punniness there. But, I wonder. If they were well aware of that difference then as now, it might have been played with. They have their *aho* and we have our *kaho*. Still, that is only a start on Jihinari's complex *kyôka*. There is a strong wind sometimes proverbially said to follow the dawn-crow, *could there be a hint of the winds of justice, the fight to follow?* The *to* after the crows, meaning "with" also told me there was something McKee – and I – might be missing. My respondent pointed out that the play actually did start at dawn. If so, the crows would "*to*=with" the actor sound well. He also noted that the fact the dawn crow usually was found in poems about lovers parting at dawn may explain the *one night* (that I feel may pun on *one world,* meaning "the whole world is excited about Danjûrô." If I ever do more writing on Sakuragawa Jihinari and come to feel confident I entirely get this poem, I may add my translation, or re-creation to McKee's but I am not ready yet. Let me add two things. First, Jihinari, a bard and stand-up/sit-down comic was close friends with Danjûrô and had two pen names based on the name of the play *Just a Minute!* 暫く *Shibaraku!* namely, *Just a Minute House* 暫亭, and Shibarakutei 芝楽亭 Lawn/play-pleasure-House. He evidently identified with those who stood up for justice. Second, "Just a minute!" – a one-act play – lasted for *centuries*. It was first produced and performed by the first Danjûrô in 1697 and subsequently *year after year* by generations of Danjûrô's. There was considerable variation of detail (such as the hero's identity) until it was fixed – by whose decision I do not know – with the 1878 performance of Danjûrô IX. I should point out to readers who have not seen the prints that Danjûrô VII, despite being fully clothed, looks more powerful than a muscle-bound demon and more terrifying than a giant malevolent alien. One might think the English-speaking world would have a similar straight-forward super-hero who stood up for justice, but all I can think of until Hollywood, where these types abound, is the more human Robin Hood.

If Only There Were No ~~Cherry Blossoms~~ *Women?* 190 頁

Could Narihira's poem have been a *kyôka*? I would like scholars of early *waka* to seriously consider this. When I asked my respondent if he thought I was the only one who felt his *"If cherry trees would only vanish . . . hearts would be serene"* was playing with traditional trope and so hyperbolic, even outrageously expressed (with the woman metaphor tongue-in-cheek to boot), that it and perhaps some more of Narihira's poems in the *Tales of Ise* were, qualitatively speaking *kyôka*, he replied he doubted it, for the world of *waka* and of *kyôka* were completely segregated in the mind of Japanese and nothing by Narihira, a canonical figure of the former, would be read/ appreciated as an example of the latter. 日本人で業平の歌を狂歌として鑑賞する人がいるかと云えば、ちょっと想像しにくいと思います。業平は和歌史の人です。古今伝授で永く和歌史に君臨してきた『古今和歌集』の歌人です。 Of course, he speaks in terms of the current group-mindscape, or to use his word, collective-mesmerization 集団催眠 that understands *kyôka* only from the premise that it is contrary to rather than complementary to or even part of *waka*. Until people awake from that false view of *kyôka*, he does not expect I will find *any* agreement. But he, like me, is not a *waka* specialist. There may be exceptional *waka* scholars out there already, who do not feel that *waka* is *waka* and *kyôka* is *kyôka* and never the twain shall meet, but, like Kipling's poem, have come to conclude the two may be put together. If a reader knows such a scholar, or if you are such a scholar, please write.

A Good Defense for the Blossom-Ravishing Wind 194 頁

When I did my learical translation of monk Sosei's poem over a decade ago, I assumed it was by a woman! Now, it suddenly dawns on me. He may be repeating or rephrasing what he over-heard a woman say. If the poem was intended as such, Kyûsojin's criticism is doubly wrong! At any rate, *I* imagine the voice of an emotional dynamo such as Lady Daibu or Sei Shônagon when I read the poem and not a man. Monk Sosei inherited his wit from his father, Archbishop Henjô, famous for falling on Maiden Flowers. Carter, who notes his mother was "a prominent poet," gives other examples of Sosei's wit, including this one, which, in my translation, at least, is clearly a *kyôka*:

> *I shall dig and I shall plant no more Flowering Trees,*
> *Lest come spring, men should learn from their inconstancy!*

hana no ki mo ima wa horiueji haru tateba utsurou iro ni hito naraikeri sosei late-9c
blssm-trees+emph now-as4 dig-plant-not sprng arriv-when change color/feelngs-by peopl lern

A couple generations later, the great lady's man Fujiwara no Sanetaka attached a poem to a cherry blossom spray to insult a woman at the Palace who must have gotten over him:

植ゑて見る人のこゝろにくらぶれば遅くうつろふ花の色かな 実方 10 c
uete miru hito no kokoro ni kurabureba osoku utsurô hana no iro kana sanekata
plantng-see person's heart-to compare-if slowly changng blossoms' color/feelings!

> *Let's plant it and see if when it blooms the flowers change their hue*
> *and, scattering, leave us men more slowly than you ladies do!*

Needless to say, the 9c poem is far better. It would make an interesting class to have students try to explain exactly *why*.

Cuckoo, Headache, Tabby Cat, & Confucius   196 頁

♪ ***Sôkan as a Master of Parody.*** This example of Sôkan poking fun at cuckoo lyricism should be food for thought, not necessarily for all readers, but for all who recall reading of his being ridiculed for making a fan of the moon. I have long believed that unfair, as he was playing with trope about the cool moon-light and using facetious hyperbole. I have not yet had the opportunity to read enough of Sôkan's poems to find the evidence needed to prove my hypothesis, however.

♪ ***Monk Sôchô's Cuckoo the Puke Cur.*** Pardon the confusion re. the pun. The *hoto*⇒*heto*⇒*hedo* (without diacritical marks, the pun works) *puke* is for sure, but I cannot tell if the remainder is 1) not intended to be punned, 2) *togisu*, a emaciated cur, or 3) *to gisu*, and katydid/ geezer. (出典は tk 参 9). I welcome a scholarly gloss for the next edition. Meanwhile, here's a mad reading of Sôchô exchanging the Japanese pun with a play on English idiom (in Japanese, *cuckoo* does not mean *crazy*) with a caveat added:

> ♪ *Cuckoo! Cuckoo!* ♪ Keep that up and soon, I *will be*, too!
> And watch where you fly for you also make me want to spew!

♪ ***Sumer is i-cumen in!*** Did you notice? My translation plays with the oldest popular song in English, which features the bird my *"coo-could"* implies: *Lhude sing cuckoo!* Reading the introduction to Legman's *The Limerick*, I rediscovered a stanza that has, if not a mad poem quality, at least the earthy feeling of some *wild waka:*

> Ewè bleateth after lamb,
> Low'th after calvè coo;
> Bullock starteth,
> Buckè farteth –
> Merry sing cuck*oo*!

The backwards accents mean the "e" is loud. The cuckoo's italicized *oo* is a new one on me, but, guessing from Japanese, which still has symbols for something to be literally sung out (unfortunately, it is not in the all-too limited symbols in Microsoft Word, so I cannot share them with you), I imagine the reader was supposed to sing-out the *oo!*

♪ ***Comic/Mad Haiku.*** If what Katô Ikuya and the world calls comic *haikai* and what I call *kyôku* interests you, please do not forget to see what I write about his book under *Kokkei Haiku* in the Mad Glossary. I will address his claim that *haikai's off-the-wall creativity blows away that of kyôka and kyôshi there.*

A Touché of Mosquito Makes All Men Kin?   198 頁

♪ ***Something of Importance to Connoisseur's of Japanese poetry.*** The *naranu* in mid-poem (*ka wa fuji no yama hodo ôki urayakôya naranu omoi no moyuru*) first disclaims the preceding, **then** means unfulfilled (love)." In *waka*, it is common to have a long metaphor or stock epithet tacked onto the front of a poem to both set the mood and lighten it by pivoting into the real content of the poem. The *naranu ka wa* can first be taken to mean the actual location of the would-be lover burning with passion *is not* in a back-street tenement. *Then,* it becomes part of an idiom for love that does not come to fruition, *naranu omoi*. If a chain of modification filling an entire poem is the oddest thing commonly encountered in Japanese poetry (and what I call "Japanese style" for it's being unique to Japanese as far as I know), I suppose this is the second oddest. Like the former, it was there from the beginning (the *Manyôshû*, at least). Using such rhetoric fits a poem indirectly poking fun at *waka* lovers and, at the same time, seems a natural for poets self-consciously creative, as disclamatory modification is representative of the surreal associations and disjunctions of flow and meaning that came to make Edo Edo.

Unnatural Love & Recycled Souls, or More Fireflies 202頁

♪ オマケ **A far more imaginative firefly** *kyôka* **by the popular** *kyôka* **master Teiryû** (1654-1735) found *after* writing the firefly chapters. The punning is unEnglishable, but it is too good to let pass. First, the original for Japanese readers: ほたるこひちゝをのまさふ 姥玉の　闇にありくも子共すかしに　貞柳　置みやけ *hotaru koi chichi o nomasô ubatama no yami ni ariku mo kodomo sugashi ni*. It starts with *"Fireflies, come!" hotaru koi,* an age-old call for fireflies to approach that children sang out, and offers them *milk=chichi*, to drink – a bribe, likewise part of children's songs– that, with the *uba,* a nanny or wet-nurse that follows, conjures up the image of *breasts* (the same *chichi* means milk *and* breast). That wet-nurse combines with gem=*tama*, to create the adjective *pitch-black*, *ubatama* which links to a moonless night *yami*. And finally we are told children walking cling to it/them (the light of the fireflies, rather than the missing moon, I guess, though we also think of the breasts evoked by the lure for the fireflies). In other words, we have a surreality, a word, or rather pun-based absurd universe composed in 31-syllabets (but not invented of whole cloth: since writing this I see my respondent found a firefly-attracting charm-ditty where the bug is warned off of bad milk/breasts and told to come for the good stuff!). There must be more firefly *kyôka* out there, which, like this one, are far crazier than the rather predictable romantic *waka* and obscene *haikai* metaphor, but, so far, this is it. I wish I could come up with a translation for this masterpiece, but have not yet.

Burning Moths from Waka to Kyôka to Waka to 206頁

♪ *Filling in the Metaphorical and Metaphysical Gaps with One's Own Poems.* I, too, did just that in my first *exhibit* (展覧 : so called by Tenki-san) of translated haiku, *Rise, Ye Sea Slugs!* (2003), which is chaptered by metaphor. Of the 900+ poems (mostly Edo era haiku and all on the sea cucumber) in the first edition, no less than 100 are mine (敬愚 keigu). I did not then realize the great Tsurayuki beat me out by a thousand years!

♪ *More on Burnt Moths.* As I wrote, Shikibu and Mitsune's summer moths and other things were destroyed forever by a cruel Microsoft update. It included the most lyrical non-rhyming translations I have ever done (I guess the deities meant to inform me that elegance was just not in my cards). *Sorry.* But here is Cranston's translation of Ôshikôchi no Mitsune's fine poem, with a few of stylistic changes (失礼!) I could not resist: *"The Summer insects – / Why should I have mocked at them? / It is 'Tis plain enough / How in love I too have found / A fire in which to burn."* A word more about the Luna Moth resurrected from a Microsoft fire. I saw great numbers of these huge luminous light yellow-green moths swarming hot stage-lights at a mountain-top bluegrass festival near Kamakura and imagine *they*, and not your dingy, everyday moth (or sundry beetle ilk), *must* be what inspired the poets. Shikibu *et al* may have been at home in natural motif, but she/they was/were no Virginia Wolfe (speaking of which, did she dare include any metaphors, or was it straight modernism? I forget).

♪ *Moths Envying Fireflies.* Monk Nôin's delightful poem calls for hundreds of translations, for it is a simple but fun fantastic idea. I crossed out my favorite reading (*The summer bugs must be envious as hell at those fireflies, /Who, burning from within, turn their yearning into light.*) for two reasons. First, with moths supposedly *seeking* a passionate death, the first line does not match the second. Second, because the idea in the last line is so good it deserves a new idea for the first line that would change the poem beyond recognition. I would bet there is already such a *waka* out there to be found, too; so, I will wait ten years before doing more with it myself.

♪ *Shadows of the Divine?* The allusion is to Jonathon Edwards' poetic book by that title. It interpreted natural things as reflections or representations of God's Will (*shadow* in English once mean an image and not just a featureless dark silhouette), or divine instruction. In other words, a rainbow, thunderstorm, toad or oak are all meant to tell us something. They are *signs*. This "reading" of nature, with some Hindi import would grow into the metaphysical beauty of Emerson and Thoreau and the Usanian nature essay.

Loving Stars on the Seventh Month, Seventh Night. 210頁

♪ **Lady** (Kenreimon-in Ukyô no) ***Daibu's Kyôka*. It is possible, no, probable, this is *it***, the poem I read decades ago about embarrassment to be spying on the loves of another!

さまざまに 思ひやりつつ よそながら ながめかねぬる 星合の空　大夫 12-13c
samazama ni omoiyaritsutsu yoso nagara nagamekanenuru hoshiai no sora daibu
variously (vicariously)imagining-while outside/stranger-as gazing-cannot star-meet-sky

Manifold your thoughts go out, but wonder as you may tonight,
The Love stars are too far away to watch them as you might!

~~~~~~~~~~~~~~~~~~~~~~~~

The many things I imagine must be going on – I'd view!
But as a stranger to the Stars, 'tis not a proper thing to do!

~~~~~~~~~~~~~~~~~~~~~~~~

I cannot view those Loving Stars as if they are out there,
when my heart is torn & things that hurt are everywhere!

At first, I felt a physical reading, including the multiple perspectives Japanese allows and English denies (whatever person or number you want) was intended but, thinking out-and-out voyeurism less interesting than oh-so-proper shyness, switched to the second reading, the one I recalled and wrote blind in the text (page 210). But, on further thought, came to wonder whether those reading are not all wrong and the last, a new reading, right. Unlike most waffling translations – which, I am afraid, means most – right or wrong, all are crisp. I read too much Sheridan and Swift and picked up the four-beat eight-syllable line that seems most natural in English for the two wrong readings.

♪ **I apologize for the f__ word** used in translating the last poem of the chapter. The odd thing about Lady Daibu is that I find her *waka* uniquely easy to put into witty English, thus creating a feeling madder than felt when reading the original. Rest assured *she* did not use the adjective I rudely enjambed in the second line!

♪ **Lady Daibu's 'Thanks To You' vs Saigyô's Moon-in-Sleeve poem.** Saigyô's poem *shirazariki kumoi no yoso ni mishi tsuki no kage o tamoto ni yadosu beshi to wa,* which Carter translates: *"I could not have known : / that to the moonlight I saw / far off in the clouds / I would be giving my sleeves / as lodging for the night"* –

Could I have known I'd soon be giving the Moon, whose light
I saw beyond the clouds, my own sleeves to pass the night?

Lodging the moon is old hat, but seen *beyond* or, as per Carter, *in* (from outside) the clouds, provides contrast making the moon/light's presence in/on the sleeve conceptually surprising. Still, Lady Daibu's thanking her man for the gift of the moon in her sleeves is less dependent on contrast and hence more clearly mad. I confess I was tempted to do a mad paraverse where the Man in the Moon ends up snoring upon Saigyô's sleeve.

~~~~~~~~~~~~~~~~~~~~~~~~

Who Needs Magpie Bridges in the Sky! More for Milky Way Lovers. 212頁

Shokusanjin left us a set of seven *kyôka* on the 7-7 festival that I cannot help introducing because they let us see how *kyôka* covered much the same ground that English light-verse did. Each is written after the style/content of a different Chinese poet. I recognize most of the styles/poets of Kipling's anti-automobile poems, but my Chinese is not up to this:

星合の天の戸口にかく文字は 凡鳥ならぬかさゝぎのはし　蜀山人
hoshiai no amanoto ni kaku moji wa bonchô naranu kasasagi no hashi

The letters found on Heaven's Gate when Stars meet?
No avis vulgaris there but Pica pica passion's heat!

For Chinese poetry aficionados, the above is "after 呂安." As noted elsewhere, bird-tracks looking like writing and perhaps being the origin of script was a Chinese idea for thousands of years. A 凡鳥 means a plain bird and by extension a plain person and by pun a *plain style* 凡調, perhaps hinting at Sanskrit 凡字, too. The magpie bridge at the end of the original was lost in translation as only its pun, where *hashi* is assumed to be shorthand for 端書, *hashigaki,* a short impassioned scribble (otherwise it would have been *Pica pica neat*) preface to the Stars big night written on Heaven's Gate. Pardon all the Latin, but "ordinary birds" and "magpies" just would not hack it. Even with them, I am afraid that I was unable to do justice to the original. One more poem (折からの桃も林檎もありのみに苦き李は星に手向じ 蜀山人 家集 *ori kara no momo mo ringo mo arinomi ni muzukashiki ki wa hoshi ni tamukaji*), after 王戎 , seems interesting with its *peaches, apples* and *pears* – the 有の実 is elegant slang for the last – but I am not sure I get it – maybe a pun on not drinking?

From Ox Slobber to Angel Hair to the Amazon (and to Tamagawa)   214 頁

♪**Many, Many More Milky Way Kyôka**.   Having seen as many Star Lover poems as there are stars, I was jaded before I began to read *kyôka* about the festival. But as the book progressed, I could not not introduce the interesting ones that still managed to pop up. My favorite are among Getsudôken's *kyôka*. Here is one more, from a 1740 book published in Ôsaka. As the editor is 塘藩山堂 百子, I guess the poet is.

逢ふ時は笠や脱らん 天の川 年に一度はぬれ過すとも 狂歌餅月夜 tk1
au toki wa kasa ya nuguran amanogawa toshi ni ichido wa nuresugosu to mo momoko
meeting time-as4 hat!/: take off hey, heaven's river, year in once-as4 soaking-spend though!

七 On the Seventh Eve 夕

While they meet, let's doff our hats the better the Stars to fete:
It happens but once a year — why not let ourselves get wet!

The night they meet, I'd remove my hat and fete the Stars,
When it happens once a year, I do not mind getting wet.

The hats serve as umbrellas. This is a fine example of a conceptual rather than pun-made *kyôka,* unless you consider taking account of a common idiomatic connotation of *wet* in Japanese, *sex*, is such. It also has the natural popular touch soon to be relearned in Edo.

♪ オマケ　イ）蜀山人のモノですが。。。「七夕のうた らしきものをよみてのち、例のざれごとうたもふみつき七日といふ文字を上にして 《 ふんどしをさらすとやみん 珍宝の青とふがらし星にたむけば 》 *fundoshi o sarasu to ya min chinpô no ao tôgarashi hoshi ni tamukeba   shokusanjin*」 （蜀山歌集）。これを敢えて英訳しない。唐辛子とは小さい男根のことでしょうが、褌を神棚にして、それで初心に戻れとか？。。。未解読です. 一方、この玉葉集の和歌は、わかりやすい。天の河ではないが、「うのはなのつゆにひかりをさしそへて　つきにみかけるたまかはのさと」。我輩も手作りのカヤックで多摩川の白水を（台風一過中か直後）愉しんだ。そのとき多摩川にも、あまそうねんにも負けない勢いをみせた。尾花の上を飛んだ感じ。かの肉食小魚こそなかったが、岸を抱きながら川上へ戻らんとすれば、羽蟻の類がいきなり飛びついて脇の下を刺したから、結局カヤックを担いで生田へ帰りました。　ロ）手柄岡持の素朴な傑作。前置きは「文月六日人のもとより竹をおくらんとありしに」。歌：「くれ竹ときけばこなたはほし合の空時宜なしにもらひ申さん」 *kuretake to kikeba konata . . . okamochi*。これは解かりやすいが、英訳は。。。

Deer Who Write Sutra & Larvae Who Dance Them   220 頁

♪ **Dirty Folk Songs?** Or, there may be a common older source. As Takenaka Rô (たけなかろう著『にっぽん情哥行』1986) has documented, moderns often assume that older clean songs generally *precede* dirty changed-songs (*kae-uta*), while, in truth, it often is the other way around. Many originally dirty old songs were cleaned up in early modern times, and it is only poetic justice for some of them to be returned to their earthy beginnings. For translated examples, see my *senryû* book *The Woman Without a Hole*.

♪ **Sutra-Dancing Larvae?** Why dancing as well as chanting? There were Buddhist sects that traveled about with covered stages they set them up for dancing sutras. From the picture records, they would seem something between rock festivals and Christian revivals in Usania, minus the rattlesnakes. And, for the record, larvae do indeed keep remarkably busy, though unlike most Japanese folk-dancing, they tend to move up and down as they dance rather than around and around.

~~~~~~

Fall, or Monsters, Crickets and a New Chestnut   222 頁

♪ **Hairy Cricket Legs** may *look* ugly but, to me the *voice* of the *grilloux* (As Hearn pointed out, French have the good aesthetic sense to appreciate it and give it a sweet-sounding name) is akin to that of a young nanny singing a plaintive lullaby. The real monsters are nowhere in nature; they are on stage in the opera house. I recently posted this poorly worded but sincere haiku: 日本にもオペラありけり蝉あらし *Opera even in Japan! From the trees, a cicada storm.* At least the original breaks in the right places! The smiling chestnut poem source: 権僧正公朝　家集五十首の中に.

♪ **The Wind as a Cold.** My explanation as to how the strength-of-the-wind poem would be a far better *kyôka* if read as a clever message suffered for space. Japanese call the disease we call a *cold*, a *wind*. Written 風邪 rather than 風, the puns went back at least as far as 12c *waka*, and possibly earlier. It was so common in early *haikai* that the disease was sometimes written with the character of wind 風 alone. I have not read enough of Akera Kanko to feel confident of his intentions, but had that poem of urchin chasing chestnut been by Shokusanjin, I would *know* it was originally intended to inform someone he had a bad cold. That unexpected twist from weather to within (which might be accompanied by a preface saying, "turning down an invitation to go snow-viewing with a bad cough and a runny nose" or something), would turn the *haikai*-style comic hyperbole into the higher humor called wit. The fact that the wind is not written with Chinese characters increases the likelihood a punning use was intended and the preface misplaced. Perhaps I should add that colds were not all of it. Japanese blamed the wind for everything the Europeans blamed the air for. As their proverb put it, "The Wind is the Fount of All Disease" 風は万病の本.

♪ **One 17c fall-to-winter poem with a Supernatural touch.** This last-minute find (from my respondent's site), a *kyôka* by Mitoku, would not fit between the leaves and cold rain and snow, so, with a bit of help from *the Lady on the Flying Trapeze:*

吹風の手にやははきをつかふらん　山を木の葉のちり塚にして　未得 吾吟我集
fukukaze no te ni ya hôki o tsukau ran　yama o konoha no chirizuka ni shite mitoku 1649
blowing wind's/s' hand-in-as-for broom/s+acc. use?/! mountain+acc leaves' trashpile-into-make

> *Do the winds have brooms that with the greatest of ease,*
> *They can turn whole mountains into trash-piles of leaves!*

♪ **The Susuki, Obana, Japanese low-land Pampas Grass, or Sawgrass.** To give you an idea how fresh Issa's shin-cutting *miscanthus* was, let me give a few examples of the trope that was common from the 9c to the 19c. First, one by Lady Ise (fl.930):

ひともきぬ をはなかそても まねかれはいととあたなる なをやたちなむ 伊勢集
hito mo kinu obana ga sode mo manekareba itodo ada naru na o ya tachinamu

> *No one calls though pampas waves 'Hither!' with plume-sleeves;*
> *It doesn't live up to its name – I don't deserve mine as a tease.*

My translation is part guesswork: it is hard to tell the miscanthus (*susuki*) from the miss. Called *obana*, or "tail flower" when its plume is emphasized, coming out (tail protrudes) can mean a love-affair becoming public knowledge, and, as Japanese beckon by moving the fingers *down* instead of up, plumes nodding as they wave in the wind seem to say "Come here!"Lady Ise's contemporary but slightly older Ariwara no Muneyama, son of Narihira the famous poet-playboy, wrote *"Are they the sleeves of fall's wild flowers, that grass in plume that seem to boldly wave us over to meet them?"* (aki no no no kusa no tamoto ka hanasusuki ho ni idete maneku sode to miyuran kks 243). He may have been the first to take that "sleeve" out of popular song (where I bet it was), but Lady Ise and her Empress first found ways to facetiously question the worth of the supposed beckoning. The "o" in the *obana* above may also serve as a grammatical sign of contradiction and disappointment as the plant fails to live up to its reputation while her name is none-the-less sullied (unsubstantiated gossip about her seeing someone, not being a "tease" which rhyme demanded). Two or three centuries later, Fujiwara Teika wrote

maneku tote kusa no tamoto mo kai mo araji towarenu sato no furuki magaki wa (sgs)
beckon say grassy sleeves even value+emph have-not visit-not village's old fence-as4

Miscanthus in a Quiet Garden

Beckon they may, but those grass plumes waving make no sense
Out in the hills, who would call on one with a rundown fence?

I borrowed the title as is from Carter's translation, which has "can do no good" where my rhyme found "make no sense." His is closer to the original on that count. Teika, who probably began his *waka* studies before he could walk, was doubtless familiar with all of the above-mentioned poems. He takes the old saw and plays on it so naturally that it sings. I would call the poem an example of what Bashô called *karumi,* or lightness, in *waka*. And, because it is not about love, it seems all the more *kyôka*, too.

Bug-song, morning Glory, mum-wine & star-babies. 224 頁

♪ **Seventh Night Star Babies?** If poverty did not separate me from the bulk of my library (for ten years now), I could give you specific *waka* or *haikai* about Star babies. I could even give you a translation of a *Manyôshû* Milky Way poem – one by Yamanoue Okura – by a Korean woman that is delightfully obscene. In one of her best selling books, she described standing sex, from behind that that ends in graphic coitus interruptus, which, to my mind (not hers) could be read as a just-so story for the lack of children. Reading that poem in her translation brought to mind Lucretius, who opined that women of the oldest profession tended not to bear children because they wriggled around so much that the seed did not stay in the furrow. Had he only dwelled on the matter a bit longer, he might have discovered centrifugal force and, by contrast, centripetal, in which case, he might have become father of force as well as atomic physics. Be that as it may, the Korean woman's translation of no little part of the *Manyôshû* (if you recall, it is written in Chinese characters) based upon ancient Korean as she understood it – the editor for the business section of a major South Korean newspaper, she was an amateur linguist, whose readings seem to me to have been worked out in an acrostic manner – is itself *the maddest exploit in the history of folk-linguistics* (compared to her achievement, Psalmanazar, with his 'Formosan,' was a *rank* amateur); I do not know how much if any truth is in her readings, but they captured the attention of some top Japanese publishers and won her supporters partly because she was *not* a fraud. She may well have been *wrong*, as many linguists expert in ancient Japanese and Korean claimed, but, unlike Psalmanazar, she was sincere. I should confess I had dinner with her and her daughter and suggested she might consider a third possibility, that many of the *Manyôshû* poems were written by bilinguals who intended more than one reading, for neither the originals nor her largely obscene readings (which bore some resemblance to earthy Japanese folksong about which she claimed to know nothing) are, in themselves terribly interesting – not a few are downright boring – but read together, A-side *and* B-side, we feel the poets were quite witty guys. For that reason, I hoped there was something to her studies, though I had and still do not have the ability to judge it myself. I do not know what if anything came of my suggestions to consider bilingual games rather than choosing one or the other.

♪ ***The Man Too Lazy To Make Mum Wine: Taoist Exemplar of Do Nothingism.*** Toward the end of the 20c, scientists finally proved that the lazy man probably does add to his life because alot of activity demands a high caloric intake while a low caloric intake was *the* biggest factor associated with longevity. Drinking wine with chrysanthemums steeped in it was part of a ritual for longevity, but . . . this note is to mention that 1) Japanese added an interesting twist to Taoism by selecting the sea cucumber to be the exemplar of it. Bashô's most outrageous disciple, Shikô, wrote a haibun, or haiku essay identifying the sea cucumber with hermit sages and, still not knowing sea cucumbers work hard all night cleaning dirty sand, the haiku poets of the 19c lauded their unmoving nature, and gave them ridiculously long lives. Shiki pretty much treated them as immortal primordials. And 2) see my *Rise, Ye Sea Slugs!* (2003) if such interests you. Like this book, you will find it takes so long to read that it will keep you out of trouble and ensure your longevity.

~~~~~~

From maple fall to red fannies & wisteria buns　　　　　　　　　　226 頁

♪ **"Sarumaru's"** *waka* **and the** *kyôka***. Seeing the poem attributed to Sarumaru** in the 13c *Hundred Poets One Poem* collection was by Anonymous in the 10c *Kokinshû* #215, in the absence of proof for the 100-poets attribution, I cannot help wonder if Sarumaru was *chosen to be the author* for his nominally red face and butt, in which case there is no little irony in the *kyôka* going right back there! Maple leaves and buttocks also have a subtle sound relationship I did not mention: *momiji*=red-maple-leaves vs, *momojiri*= peach-buttocks, a type that cannot stay in the saddle or otherwise stay put. Regardless, not all *kyôka* looked that low. One predating Shokusanjin, *has red faces scattering the colored maple leaves, with Sarumaru roaring ferociously:* 奥山に紅葉をちらす赤つらや声もすさまし猿丸太夫　長崎一見狂歌集 tk1 *okuyama ni momiji o chirasu akazura koe mo susamashi sarumaru dayû* nagasaki-ikken. Drunks are loud, but why he should be *that* loud, I do not know. Another has no monkey man and is just beautiful:

奥山に紅葉詠めて酒呑んて　たのしむ時そ秋はうれしき　失出典、御免！
okuyama ni momiji nagamete sake nonde tanoshimu toki zo aki wa ureshiki mid-18c?
interior mntn-in red-leaves poeticizng sake drinkng, enjoyng time+emph. fall-as4 delightful

Deep in the hills, poeticizing fall leaves and drinking wine . . .
When you enjoy yourself, Autumn is a happy time!

This was worth enlarging to size 10.5 font because it provides a reasonable challenge to the Fall-as-the-beginning-of-the-end-is-melancholy stereotype that dominated *waka* and *haikai*. I lost the source, but am pretty sure it was mid-18c because Teiryû (d.1833) wrote something similar in his *Hundred Poets One Poem* parody:

Deep in the hills, breaking limbs w/ colored leaves & burning them,
We, within the drunken din, forget the fall and lonely yearning!

奥山に紅葉おりたきざゞんざの声きく時そ秋をわするゝ　狂歌活玉集 1740. *okuyama ni momiji ori taki zazanza no koe kiku toki zo aki o wasururu.* "And yearning!" is compensation for losing the pun "we forget the fall = we are never fed-up (w/ partying))."

♪ **Little on men loving men or boys.** *Haikai*, with its bawdy exuberance and *senryû*, with its urban black-humor are full of homo-eroticism, but *kyôka*, at least the Tenmei era "*Kyôka*," has relatively little of it (thousands of poems could probably be found, but I mean as a percentage of the whole). It may be less competitive exclusion than timing, for government crackdowns on male-prostitution picked up about the time *kyôka* became popular. See my *Octopussy, Dry Kidney & Blue Spots*: 2007 for more on Japanese homoerotic love in poetry (three of thirty chapters). ★ After writing the above, I did find more of it in 17c *kyôka*, especially Getsudôken's poems.

The Honest Rain That Came In With the Cold   230 頁

♪ ***Honest Heads with Gods in Them, Just-so.*** A 1679 *kyôka* has a simple fun explanation for why gods are in the head that contradicts the proverb of gods in the heads of the honest-to-a-fault folk by explaining by pun why gods are in the heads of *all* men and women but the bald (though nothing was said about the bald): 男女みな正直のかうへやらはへぬる毛をもかみと社いへ　重香　銀葉夷歌集 *otoko onna mina shôjiki no kôbe yara haenuru ke o mo kami to koso ie* chôka??? 蛇足：「毛＝け」に穢れを込め。

♪ ***Gods-gone Waka.*** It is always pointed out that the famous *waka* by Fujiwara Teika (1162-1241) references the anonymous *Kokinshû* (905) poem #146, *itsuwari no naki yo nariseba ika bakari hito no koto no ha ureshikaramashi*:

> *If only this world of ours was a world without lies*
> *The words of another, Lover, would bring delight!*

~~~~~~~~~~~~~~~~~~~~~~~~~~~~~~~~~~~~~

> *If only this were a world without falsehood*
> *A lover's words would make me feel so good!*

The first third is virtually identical; but I would like more discussion about why Gods-gone month was in Teika's poem（偽りのなき世なりけり神無月　たが誠よりしぐれそめけん *itsuwari no naki . . .*）神無月に時雨降り初めることくらいは、知ってる。で、なぜ、わざわざ「神無月」を？蛇足ではないか？第三句に神無月しかなかったはづはない。偽りなきと神無月を併せたかったではないでしょうか。たとえば、よその神頼みからではなく、自分の暗い心から？それとも、冷たい雨の教訓？価値を認める仏教信心から？

> *What you see is what you get, this month, when the gods are gone –*
> *Whose faith brought the Shigure, & at the right time not the wrong!*

♪ ***Gods-gone Kyôka.*** The earliest clear-cut *kyôka* of Gods-gone-month I know is an exchange recorded in the diary of Monk Sôchô (d.1532). Both poems are too punderful to re-create, but the here is the gist of it: first, Takachika 小原兵庫頭(高親) replies to Sôchô's unrecorded letter: 神無月文も無益のことの葉の　そむきがたくてかき絶にけり (宗長日記) *kaminazuki fumi mo muyaku no kotonoha no somukigatakute kakitaenikeri —*

> *Gods=paper-gone month, letters are to no avail when leaves=letters fail;*
> *It is hard to stop, but my writing=persimmon brush is gone.*

God/s puns with *paper* (*kami*), *persimmon* with *writing* (*kaki*) – I added "brush," though unsure whether said variety (resembling the head of a large brush) already existed. Then, Sôchô wrote a reply to the reply: かきかはす爰もかしこも紙な月　文こそあらめ牛蒡大根 *kaki-kawasu koko mo kashiko mo kami-nazuki fumi koso arame gobô daikon —*

> *Drying-persimmons=exchanging-letters, I, too, would be pleased to write little*
> *In gods=paper-gone month: stamping's for ruffians, burdocks & big radishes!*

Fumi or letters may pun with *stamping down* hard when pulling edible burdock and daikon radishes. The former was just harvested, but the latter would grow and be pulled by *big louts* (the verb for "should not be," *arame*, is homophonous with such) all winter. Sôchô, who has many male-color poems, may also joke on what was in stock on the mountain, older men w/ thick-roots=*daikon*" and acolytes w/ thin ones, metaphorically burdocks (a boy with a large women, was said to "wash a burdock in the sea"). Note, too, that the pronunciation of the month, *kaminazuki,* was in the process of turning to *kannazuki*, thus killing the paper (*kami*) pun. I would guess such ubiquitous puns have played a larger role in Japanese than rhyme in English to help retain old spellings and pronunciations longer than they would have otherwise.

♪ ***Gods Gone but Buddha . . . is here.*** I guessed this concept lay behind Issa's haiku part of which became the title of my first book in English, *Rise, Ye Sea Slugs!* I wanted to follow it in *waka* and *kyôka* but found myself needing more guidance than I had time to beg.   Here is one *kyôka* clearly celebrating the Gods *and* Buddha:

出雲路へ集り給ふ留主なれは 我神国に仏あり月　則本太山　狂歌餅月夜
izumoji e atsumari-tamau rusu nareba waga shinkoku ni hotoke ari tsuki daisan? 1740
izumo road-to gathering-do(respect.) absent-be-when our-godsland-in bddha-is-mnth

They leave for their caucus in Izumo, we merrily say 'Adieu!'
In our land of all the Gods, this is Buddha's-here month, too.

When they leave us to caucus in Izumo, we are still blest:
This month in Gods' Country, the Buddha is manifest.

♪ **Bokutan's Gods-gone Month+ Honest Head + Shigure**. Iwanami's annotation of Shokusanjin's famous *kyôka* did *not* mention Bokutan's *kyôka* with three of four major elements in it. The editors probably did not know of it. Japanese poems may be short but there are so many even specialists cannot know all. For literary criticism beyond guessing based on narrow selections reflecting another's taste we must put a *vast* body of poetry on the web. Like SETI, this intellectual property must not be hoarded by wealthy universities and other privileged parties. Not only should it be open to all, but *enlist the help of a broader public.* Nichibun and J-text are good starts, but much remains to be done. The situation with English is worse. Luminarium (metaphysical & cavalier poetry) and Gutenberg are great, but the larger searchable body of old English poetry is only available at a small number of wealthy libraries. Considered public, it is anything but. (*Come on, Google! Redeem those digitized old poems for all of us! Work with Gutenberg and the poems may even get some good bio notes, etc. pegged on!*)

♪時雨の亭のオマケ。　狂歌乗合船 tk1（1730）に「亭」にかけたあほな一首、「ばら／＼にちよっと傘かす其礼をうくるは時雨の賃といふへき」流水 (*barabara ni chotto kasa kasu sono rei o ukuru wa shigure no chin to iu beki* ryûsui). 蛇足無用。又同書に貞柳は「神無月そりやこそしくれ偽りの　なき世はみえたさつとやめかし」*kaminazuki sorya koso shigure itsuwari no* ....。蛇足よりまだ未解決.
♪梁塵秘抄のオマケ。「そよ　神無月降りみ降らずみ定めなき時雨ぞ冬の初めなりける」*kaminazuki furimi* ...こうして、時雨の定めなきを、冬の到来の定めなきと一体化する事は、偉い。ただ「素直に歌われている」（小学館の編集者）と思いません。

Three takes on the snow: dick, swell-fish & fools 232頁

♪ **One blowfish and Two Muskets for Japanese readers only**. オマケ：魚の名をむざと話すな けふの雪 に身をあたゝむる種が島ぞや　帆南西太　徳和 1785 *uo no na o muza to hanasuna kyô no yuki ni mi o atatamuru tanegashima zo ya* Honami Nishita. 蛇足　—鉄砲＝毒で危ない河豚の称を忌みながら「放すな」も掛け、十六世紀半ば鉄砲が上陸した島名の含む「種」を、身を暖める河豚肉の特色と結んでもって遊ぶ、小傑作。その種の種といえば、恐らく 1666 年の「古今夷曲集」に出た未得の種子島一首である。即ち「来不逢恋」がその題で、「鉄砲のたま／＼きてもはなさぬは　結局おもひのたねか嶋哉」*teppô no tama-tama kite mo hanasanu wa kekkyoku tanegashima.* さて歌が未解く（「はなさぬ」とは？）ですが、おもしろそう。「たまたま来ても」のスタイルが、天明狂歌にもまけない、かるくて微笑ましい創り枕。

♪ **Two Fascinating Creatures.** While I ended up introducing some *swellfish soup* against my better judgment, as that will be the name of a book thirty percent done for five years now, I did manage to refrain from introducing *kyôka* on the subject of another book-to-be, the *tanuki*, or racoon-fox, a masked canine mistakenly translated as *badger* and unwisely (following dictionaries) called a *racoon dog* (Japanese-English dictionaries must lack Southern editors or whoever named them had not seen how delicate their snouts and how thin the ankles of their paws are: they are *foxes*, damn it, foxes!). Because most of the *kyôka* touch upon their belly-drumming and many of those combine with *dandelions* which do not drum in English, the translation requires a longer framework incompatible with a book such as this anyway. But, here is one mad poem by Teitoku, as adorable as the animal itself about tongue-drumming good *tanuki soup*, which, as might be expected from a trickster (poet and animal, alike), turns out to have been purely vegetarian! 腹までもまだ入り足らずうましとて 舌つゞみ打つ狸汁かな 貞徳 *hara made mo mada iri-tarazu umashi tote shitazutsumi utsu tanukijiru kana*. If you cannot wait for my *tanuki* book to learn more about their oddest (fictional) property, which is *not* their belly-drumming, please see the chapter on *Balls* in my dirty *senryû* book of two names.

Kicking the year in the rear – Mixed feelings about sending off . . . 234 頁

♪ **Ole Dang Zine?** Not knowing how to spell the title of the old song English-speakers use to sing-out the year and Japanese use to close bars, I came up with a new one, a *zine* of 365 pages. It did not make the final reading, so this is its memento mori. The poem need not be first-person singular. I changed "we/our" to "I/me" for visual balance, you can change them back if you wish.

♪ **Ragged Loincloth.** Why did *I* note that *"Shirane notes"* something I easily noticed myself? Because Shirane, who used Watson's translation from *Eight Islands*, had the necessary notes on the puns on the same page, something laudable for a university press book. Carter, whose translation (*The money I owe / is no easier to conceal / than what's behind / the holes and tears in my loincloth / at the end of the year*), excepting the long penultimate line, is fine, but after mentioning "wordplay so complicated that it can only be suggested in translation" in his introduction to the comic verse chapter of his book, made the metaphor a smooth simile and pocketed the puns: the regrettable, but usual practice of the 20c's invisible translator. オマケ （日本語でしか面白くない師走の狂歌） 霜月に雷鳴を聞て 時しらぬ師走の末に鳴神は臍くりかねやつかみにそ来る 泉墨 狂歌戎の鯛1737 *toki shiranu shiwasu* . . . senboku?

♪ **In the Rear?** I made up the phrase "kicking the year in the rear," but, before finishing the book found a *kyôka* by Getsudôken (c.1700) that comes close to suggesting the same (*binbôgami mari keru* . . . pg.337). I say "close" because it is unclear if Poverty or the departing rear of the year or both are being given the boot. That may not seem like much, but every time that sort of thing happens I do not so much feel scooped as validated, for it shows my mind is on the same wave-length with the poets and that my mad translations may hit the larger target even when they miss the details of the individual poem.

Five Seasons Mad or almost Mad, depending. Mostly Shokusanjin. 236 頁

Fighting Mad Maiden Ferns (and haikai connection) Left Out. I left out a poem representative of Shokusanjin's early work as Yomo no Akara from the Spring selection because it would be best enjoyed together with chapter III, "The Frightened Young Bracken" of *Fly-ku!* (2004). It features maiden-hair ferns – bracken, now considered mildly carcinogenic – shaking their little fists at the spring wind/s which is/are, with the help of a pun, *slapping* (haru=spring= slapping) the face of the mountain where they grow. For Japanese readers, the original: さわらびが握りこぶしを振り上げて 山の横面はる風ぞ吹く 四方赤良 巴人集 *sawarabi ga nigirikobushi o furiagete yama no yokozura haru kaze zo fuku*). The bracken's "hands" and the bracken's plight (to be broken off and eaten) was a favorite theme of haikai for *centuries*. The reason they got a whole chapter in *Fly-ku!* was because I wanted to show how the fact that the word *te,* or "hand" was broader in Japanese than in English made what *in translation* evokes the phrase "pathetic fallacy" was not at all fulsome in the original. Moreover, some of the details (begging for life, praying) were inherited by Issa's fly acting as if it desired not to be swatted. To understand where Issa's famous fly-ku or Shokusanjin's bracken come from, you really need to read the old *haikai*. Here is one of my *kyôku* from a page-long sidetrack to that chapter reinventing Japanese bracken within contemporary Usanian culture. I took a swipe at the detestable habit of using fists rather than open palms for celebration:

冬に勝ちガッツポーズの蕨哉　敬愚

fuyu ni kachi gahtsu-pohzu no warabi kana
winter-over winning, gut's-pose's bracken 'tis!/?

Spring Triumphant

*winter's back
broken, the wee bracken
pumps its fist*

A Japanese wrestler independently invented fist-raising for in-your-face triumph and it was called *gattsu pozu*, or, "gut's pose." Guts Takahashi is alright by me. Japanese had an inferiority complex with respect to whites and he helped fight that. But there is no excuse for Hollywood putting those damn fists (& fatuous exclamations of *"Yes!"*) of our pushy civil?ization into movies about pre-1970's events. It is defamation of character.

♪ **The Leaving Year *vs* Last Day.** Shunzei's last-*day* poem, found in Carter (I only mention it), seems more natural than a leaving-*year* poem because surprise at greeting the same *day* again Englishes far better than concern for the leaving year that/who will probably not be seen again. This is because we see each departing *year* as a separate entity, not to be confused with the previous or the next one, while we see the *day* as identical to that in other years. Japanese have less trouble with the *year*, both because of the lack of singular/plural person and because of a vaguely felt entity that might be called the end-of-the-year god that seems to make each departing year the same as well as different. Issa's *ku* in the last chapter or Shunzei's in this are records of how one translator who hopes to entertain readers coped with this problem. (Re.: Shunzei's last-*day* poem. On further thought, it may be madder than that present of tears to the leaving Year (p.237). *If* no one previously treated the last *day* of the year as the *first* one generally was – expressing amazement to still be here – it was a hell of a novelty!)

~~~~~~

Another Round of Five Seasons, Mixed Tenmei 上   238 頁

Puns on High Sound/Price Karagoromo Kisshû vs. Shokusanjin. Kisshû's *bonito/cuckoo* high sound/price pun (*izure make izure katsu* . . . pg. 239) is famous. **Reginald H. Blyth** translates a less well-known *kyôka* depending on this common pun in his 14-page presentation of *kyôka* in *Oriental Humour* (1959). By Yomo no Akara (Shokusanjin), it is "an example of pathos and humor mixed," and helps bring home Blyth's point that "*kyôka* was not mere trifling; it was an arduous task to include all kinds of meanings in one short verse." To demonstrate, Blyth used something I have not seen him use elsewhere: *a multiple reading*, one for each meaning (Damn! Beaten to the punch again!).

舞ひ雲雀籠の鳥屋が手に落ちてかふ値も高くあがりこそすれ　四方赤良
mai hibari kago no toriya ga te ni ochite kô ne mo takaku agari koso sure yomo no akara
dancing skylark/s caged bird-shop/seller's hands-into falling high price/sound even rises!

Dancing skylarks	*Dancing skylarks*
in cages: they have fallen	*kept in cages have come*
into the hands	*down to earth,*
of the bird-shop-man,	*but the voice of their song*
and the price is high.	*rises high in the sky*

To display them side-by-side as the two facets of the composite translation they are (Blyth had them in serial split by a paragraph of prose), I reparsed two lines in each (Orig.: *In their cages; / They have fallen into the hands;* & *"Have come down to earth, / But the voice of their song*) and removed *"their,"* too. I am unsure about those calls to heaven. I recall them singing *from* high. Though I have heard them peep once in the gorse before shooting up, I think it may allude to their calls as they rose high in the sky. Since Blyth did multiple readings, I will turn things about and hazard a mono-translation:

Sky-dancing Larks
fallen into bird-shop hands
kept caged so long,

The high price they demand
Soars like their exalted Song!

In other words, I find Shokusanjin's poem a bit closer to Karagoromo Kisshû's than Blyth does (or, would if he compared them). But I could well be wrong. And, it does not matter. Even if Blyth were a bit off, in my opinion, he would still be much keener than Keene in his more sympathetic understanding of what was what with *kyôka*.

♪ **Cheep! Cheep!** Somewhere else in this book, we have 2 more cheep/cheap bird puns.

Another Round of Five Seasons, Mixed Tenmei ㊦   240 頁

♪ ***From Yummy Snow to?*** *Mumai* or "yummy," is usually *umai* today. Likewise, "horse," *uma* today, used to be *muma* as well. An early *kyôka* you would have to be out of your gourd not to love put *yummy* and *horsey* together beautifully: へうたんの内より 出る酒なれと　駒とはいはてむまいとそいふ　信澄　銀葉夷歌集 tk1 *hyôtan no uchi yori ideru sake naredo koma to wa iwa de mumai to zo iu* shinjô? 1679. A pony, *koma*, came out of a gourd in an old Chinese wizard/sage tale, but for a gourd full of sake what comes out is a *horse*, which is to say it is *yummy!* I suppose it could be done in English if –

♪ on presenting a gift of *sake* with some nibblies ♪

Just wine within – no *pony* will pop out of this gourd.
But, what have we here? Why it's an *horse* d'oeuvre!

I know we got off-subject – *ie,* lost our seasons here – but this 17c poem had to be fit into the book somewhere and it was either in the notes for the *Silver Leaf Barbarian Songs* or here, after Issa's *mumai* snow. Or I should have replaced Issa's *yummy snow* with the following in the main text but, then, the *horse d'oeuvre,* above, would have no place to go.

♪ **One Good or Bad Overloooked Tenmei Winter Kyôka.** Here is the big radish, a *daikon* from the winter section of the 1785 *Tokuwa* anthology I could not help but champion because Sugimoto and Hamada (the Iwanami editors) put it down as a *hopeless concept* (「表現はともかく無理の発想である。」):

たがたねをこゝへこぼして大根のちを離れてもかく育ちけん　其筈琴成
ta ga tane o koko e koboshite daikon no chi o hanarete mogaku sodachiken sonohazu no kotonari
whose seed+acc here-to spilled daikon's earth/tit-from separating struggle grows up right?

Whose seed here spilled to create huge roots who pulling themselves
apart from the bosom of earth, would strive to forget their birth?

I once had a similar feeling about a type of large daikon with pale green-necks that you – if you, like me, tend to see things in slow motion – might imagine leaping up from the crests of their furrows like flying fish, attempting to flee the field to avoid being eaten, or, perhaps, aiming for the moon (if you recall, large rockets lift-off *very* slowly). I wrote many haiku of such fantasies which are scribbled into some book where they will eventually die like silverfish that never find a mate or, if lucky, be typed into a computer and published. The "seed" may allude to a *tane-daikon*, one left to keep growing and flower; but, to tell the truth, I do think the *kyôka* could be better done. I also see in rows of cabbages with the heads cut off and some leaves left neatly framing the "necks" Spanish or Portuguese conquistadors decapitated just above their fancy large collars. Because Japanese did not have that type of cabbage or collar no such *kyôka* will be found.

Just Geese Coming In   240頁

♪ ***Kuge* spoiled and wasteful?** I think not. Their world was not ours. They did not know what was what. We *do*. We cannot pretend to believe in a world without limits. Most Usanians and our/their fellow jet-setters around the world fly about in airplanes or cars at the drop of a hat and think it their *right* to do so though they may talk up ecology and, worse yet, force it on others living far more frugally. By comparison, *kuge,* who lived off their peasants, were angels. Mencius once told a King in a time of famine that keeping a stable of fat horses was worse than being a cannibal. Why? Because His Highness was, in essence, feeding people to beasts. Today, we feed people (and the diverse creatures of the biosphere) to our *machines*. Private jets should be *outlawed*. No one should be allowed to attend more than one long-distance conference a year in person.   The computer and worldwide web permit us to remain close to one another without actually moving. Flying more should cost more and not be rewarded. People who travel to space to satisfy their ego should be shunned as the psychopaths they are. . . .   Enough for this book. Re. *nobles as night-owls*, see *Topsy-turvy 1585* (2004). On a more pertinent note, that *kuge* poop poem came from a Japanese university website with hundreds of Edo *kyôka* that does not specify sources, so I cannot date it. Within Ôta's lifetime (not when he was Yomo no Akara), a *kuge* would actually try to assert authority over *kyôka* (see pg. 632)!

♪ オマケ。 **The Last Two Geese Arriving from the** 狂歌一万集．「入月に心あるかな山かたを崩しておつる夜半の雁金」　寝顔 (*irizuki ni kokoro aru kana . .* 　 negao) 蛇足：雁が落ちるという慣用語をみごとに遊ばす一首です。「日暮の里の眺めにあかぬなり 投る土器落る雁金」　仲塗 (*nippori no sato no . . .* nakanuri) 蛇足：土器投げ遊びの名所で、それも落ちるは落ちるが。。。

♪ **The Best Waka that is a Kyôka on Geese Leaving Japan** is not in any chapter. It is from the early-14c *Gyokuyôshû* 玉葉集 *waka* collection and evokes the marvel of the geese returning to a still snowy homeland while playing on proverbial success-as-returning-to-one's-hometown-wearing-brocade. It has far too many puns to English:

はるもなほ ゆきふるさとに かへるとや はなのにしきの ころもかりかね
haru mo nao yuki furusato ni kaeru to ya hana no nishiki no koro mo karigane ng

Spring nonetheless/still going=yuki=snow falls=furu ⇒*furusato=homeland-to-returning! /?/: blossoms'=fancy-brocade's-time=koro* ⇒*koromo =clothing borrowed-money=karigane=geese*. Nichibun does not give the poet's name, but the anthology definitely has it. This "waka" is a fine example of why it is insufficient to define *kyôka* as a *tanka* with many more puns than *waka* have. This out-puns 90% of *kyôka* but if we think it is about nature, it is as a light *waka*. If we find out the poet had to return home in the Spring, so it is an allegory, than I would call it a *kyôka*, despite being in a *waka* anthology. 再版迄、情報乞！

♪ ***Two More Conceptual Poems by Saigyô.*** No birds, just no other place for them:

月のゆく山に心をおくり入れて やみなるあとの身をいかにせむ
tsuki no yuku yama ni kokoro o okuri irete yami naru ato no mi o ika ni semu
moon-goes mountain-to heart/mind+acc sent to set (too) dark is later self+acc how to do?

*I sent my heart after the moon over the mountain's arc
Now, what can I do with just a body in the dark?*

In *Cherry Blossom Epiphany*, a chapter on *heart/mind* was 99% Saigyô. No poet I know of has played half so much with the literally roving heart. To think the separation of mind/heart and body is, stereotypically, an Occidental concept (actually, it is found in many cultures and some do so far more thoroughly than any Indo-European culture)! In retrospect, many of those mind/heart vs body *waka* have a *kyôka* 'mad' touch to them.

道とぢて人とはずなる山ざとのあはれは雪にうづもれにけり 西行
michi tojite hito towazu naru yamazato no aware wa yuki ni uzumorenikeri saigyô

The sad beauty of the mountain village where none go;
The road closed, it lies buried deep beneath the snow.

The "it" is not the village but its sad beauty. That, too, is conceptual and close to a *kyôka*.

Celebratory Characters: 'Spring' 春 and 'Longevity' 壽　　　248 頁

♪ ***Examples of Composite Characters.*** Call them 寄せ文字 or 重ね文字 *assembled* or *compounded* letters, respectively. Unlike 吉書 lucky writing burnt on the 15th as a sort of offering, these were stuck on the gate/door as a charm. This was more a Chinese than Japanese practice. They were generally printed in gilt lettering on a red diamond. One common example combines 日日有財見 or *day+day+have+wealth +see* into a compound character far simpler than many single characters by making single radicals serve in more than one way. It is the visual equivalent of a pivot word with a homophonic pun! Another is a more complex assemblage of treasure+progress+wealth+ invite 寶進財招 which I feel may have once been meant to mimic the Treasure Ship.

♪ ***Play With Character.*** Eventually I hope to add a chapter or two of poems about characters and words that are not only New Year-related. At present, I do not have enough gathered. Here are two samples that demonstrate the problems faced in doing this: 1) *"Depending upon how you draw that line on the letter* ト *= to,* / *A fortune can be raised right up =上, or put down just 下=so!"* 片仮名のトの字に棒の引きようで　上になったり下になったり 無名 *katakana no to no ji ni bô no hikiyô de ue ni nattari shita ni nattari.* Is there a message, such as, say, the arbitrary nature of *drawing lines* or judging a glass half-empty/full? Could the *katakana* letter ト (*to*) imply *prognosticating,* ト？ I cannot yet judge whether or not it is a keeper. My favorite treats 'diacritical marks' and is lost even to mad translation: "In this world, the clear and cloudy are different as can be / *hake* is full of *ke* and *hage* has no *ke* to see!" 世の中はすむとにごるで大違い　はけに毛がありハゲに毛がなし *yononaka wa sumu to nigoru de ôchigai hake ni ke ga ari hage ni ke ga nashi.* Hake 刷毛 is a brush-stroke that clearly shows the mark left by the individual hairs of the brush. The effect common in *sumie* but reproduced in some printed work, is exceedingly clean/crisp compared to the cloying *nihonga* and daubing of oils (other than Turner's understudies!) or even the floods of washes, yet *ke* け, despite being a clear/clean sound, is not only "hair" but *filth,* while the cloudy or dirty sound *ge* written げ with those two cloudy or muddy marks is part of *hage*, meaning bald, bereft of *ke, hair,* or, filth, though some feel baldness itself is unclean while heads are shaven for purification . . . In a word, the poem brings out the contradictions in *the language of clean and dirty* that was sometimes put to polemical use (eg. by Norinaga).

♪ ***Carnal Metaphor.*** From the example of "Ikkyû's" Erotic *Mondô* (witty debate in this case) which I found in an encyclopedia of *Cuntology* (女陰万考), the work (一休　禅師諸色問答　は、凸凹笑艸　第一輯　愛貝老漁編　太平書屋　1980　にあるらしい) may be worth a chapter or two in a future edition. Meanwhile, if you would learn more about the rich vocabulary for describing good and bad sundry male and female genitalia in Edo era Japan, see *Octopussy, Dry Kidney &Blue Spots* (2007), my book of dirty *senryû*.

♪ ***Poems as Charms.*** Waka have ever been written and intoned to wish people well and pray for this or that. The generally given reasons for it are the belief in the efficacy of the word-soul (*kotodama*) and the hypnotic charm of 5 or 7-syllabet clusters. I see no need to make specifically Japanese arguments for what is common to most traditional cultures; charms, spells and prayers are universal, or were, before the rude assault of monotheism and scientism. I have introduced Issa's many *ku* about the flower of happiness and riches, the peony, some of which were clearly intended as charms. (See *Peon and Peony*, one of my irregular columns, among the back-issues of the web magazine "Simply Haiku," or wait for my book, *Haiku In Context*.). Until now I have not written or read about the parallel of composite metaphor and composite characters.

♪ ***Asobi-e and Kyôka***. A parallel with the lucky word/item-filled poem may be found in the visual genre called 遊び絵 *asobi-e*, or "play picture," particularly, those combining elements of letter- (mostly character), assembled- and riddle-pictures (*moji-e, yose-e* and *nazo-e*, respectively). As Daniel McKee has eloquently noted in his online introduction of the genre, the prime descriptions of play-pictures are *kokkei* and *share,* the former of which *"may include humor based on the disruption of social conventions, such as low or scatological subject matter, or just plain silliness for its own sake"* and the latter of which *"suggests a creative intelligence playing with the material of society and convention in an imaginative and fashionably unexpected manner."* He further notes that *"In the case of complex riddle pictures, we can easily imagine a group of people gathered around the same print, competing to be the first to solve a new area of the work."* He goes on to ask rhetorically: *"asobi-e are delightful and full of witty breakthroughs, but are they not shallow and short-lived? Once the riddle has been understood or the joke told, is the print still of interest?"* The answer is *yes*. I would say the same is true for good *kyôka*. As one reads one solves, or tries to solve a riddle and *if it is good,* you may enjoy it more than once. When Mckee writes that the pictures *"are also one of the few areas of Japanese prints where success did not bring about endless repetition. As the goal of the asobi-e was to be unusual and surprising, the "share"* 洒落 *could only be repeated so often, making most asobi-e unique."* To the *degree* this is true, I would say the same for *kyôka* as opposed to other areas of Japanese poetry (later, I found McKee's translations of 19c *surimono kyôka* – they were, on the whole, not as free as older *kyôka*, so I am not sure the same could be said). But I think most *asobie* and *kyôka* are like most work found in *any genre:* too boring to merit a second viewing/reading. McKee's best line requires no caveat. All I can do is clap my hands:

"The 'play' of asobi-e is the freedom to make the impossible happen."

And that, too, is exactly what the more surreal *kyôka* are all about. However, I think there is a contradiction in the claim that, *"Endlessly inventive and entertaining, asobi-e are not only expressions of the wit and imagination of individual artists, but also reflections of Edo culture and style."* Neither *asobi-e* nor *kyôka* are endlessly inventive *because* they are indeed reflections of a given culture, which, however fecund and marvelous, was limited, as are all cultures. But, pontificate as I may, I wish the foreword of this book were half so well-written as McKee's online introduction to *asobi-e!*

♪ ***Prayers for Rain.*** The second poem (*tsuchi sakete . . .*) has a preface Carter, from whom I borrowed it, translates: *"An expression of concern written when he heard men and women of the area had gathered to consider what to do against the drought."*

Is Old Age Minutely Described Mad In Itself? 256 頁

About Those Naps. Until I found Mitoku to end the chapter right, I finished it with Issa's naps, for he featured them more than any poet I know. Most of these *kyôku* – I use the term as a compliment and recognize all have a seasonal element making them bonafide haiku, too – do not directly concern old age. The best known concerns the single life and sleeping literally "large" (the letter 大) : *"Sleeping exactly how I please, loneliness in bed with ease!"* (Actually, it starts with said *ease*, which is actually *coolness* (大の字に寝て涼しさよ ... *dai no ji ni nete suzushisa ...*) but what the hell! Then there is his guilt trip about sleeping while others work and create what he will eat: *"A nap, what nerve! / Enjoying rice planting songs / I don't deserve!"* (もたひなや昼寝して聞田うへ唄 *motainaya hirune shite kiku taue-uta*), and my favorite, the far less encountered:

あらあつし／＼と寝るを仕事哉　一茶　文政6
ara atsushi x2 to neru o shigoto kana issa-over-sixty
hey, hot, hot! and (saying) sleeping+acc. work 'tis/!/?

Damn it's hot!
Hot! I say – sleeping
is my work, today!

I highlight the last as one of the most pure old-person haiku ever written and perhaps his best use of the idea of life's various activities as "work," which he often applied to various animals in an affectionate way.

~~~~~~

The Cane, or Coping with Old Age. 258 頁

♪ **Canes + Pigeons**. I was already familiar with canes+pigeons+beans+poking or pecking when I read this *kyôka* in a book of bird *kyôka* selection dating to 1790 (Utamarô pictures pigeons). The combination is common in *senryû* about dirty old men attempting sex with little girls (see my dirty *senryû* book, *Octopussy, Dry Kidney & Blue Spots:* 2007) as the "bean" means either the clitoris or the whole female sex. 又 Long shot ですが「かわらじな」とは「かわらけ＋品」つまり若きときから愛した妻も掛けて？

♪ **Beans or Peas? Which do Pigeons go for?**   Beans outside of their shells are sometimes peas. Soy-beans in their pods are served up looking like peas, yet chick peas are garbanzo beans . . . Unlike the pigeon, literature picks one or the other, and coming across two passages from *Love's Labor Lost* (4-1, 5-2) this morning I found I may have been wrong to give women *beans* rather than *peas*.

This fellow pecks up wit, as pigeons peas,
And utters it again when God doth please.

~~~~~~

Children pick of words as pigeons peas,
& utter them again as God shall please.

They were in Peter Milford's 動物植物辞典 (Encyclopedia of Fauna and Flora). その翻訳について、念のため後者は「時が来ると再びそれを吐き出す」ではなく「時知らず～」でしょう。子供は、そういう者だから可愛い。又は怖い。(ああ、どこ見ても誤訳天国じゃ)

♪ **Bamboo in the snow**. Tips once fifty feet in the sky poke their noses into your window. A bamboo forest entire turns into a village of igloos! Almost all of the bamboo recover, but by piling their snowy heads upon tree forks, they do break and topple competitors!

♪ **This Cane is not for an Old Man** but too good to toss away for not fitting the chapter,

たくりほくりはきて座頭の行かふる　杖や海月の海老のめならん　友和　銀葉夷歌集
takuri-hokuri wa kite zatô no yuki-kouru tsue ya kurage no ebi no me naran yûwa 1679

The Troupe Head 座頭 I.e., Blind Man

Clickity-pop down the street, the blind troupe leader glides;
As a jellyfish, his cane would be the shrimp – its eyes!

Shrimp are sometimes found hanging out (symbiosing?) between jellyfish tentacles. Shogakukan's OJD (日本国語大辞典) defines 'the jellyfish's shrimp' as a metaphor for the blind leading the blind, but that I believe is wrong; Shogakukan's large proverb dictionary, including the same example, correctly defines it as individuals of different abilities combining to make do. The *kyôka*, obviously, followed the correct interpretation. Jellyfish (*kurage*) was homophonous with *darkness* and idiomatic for *being blind*. See *Rise, Ye Sea Slugs!* (2003) for some *waka* on *darkness* and the moon jellyfish.

'Always Young'? Rewind the Spool. 260頁

♪ ***The first poem, "Young as ever"*** is much harder than it looks. I am happy with both my long and short translations, and like to think they are right, but Akera Kankô was vague as to what he meant by regret for leaving years; I really had to guess. A paraverse:

"Young as ever!" I think of my youthful years, long fled;
You're kind – but, hey, were I any older, I'd be dead!

♪ ***It is Good, so Mine is Not***. At first, I only dropped the "like a" from Horton's *"~ spool of flaxen thread,"* and replaced it with *the* or *that*, but could not resist trying something different so as not to be a copycat. He *does* seem to have come up with the best way to translate it, so mine comes up short. Thank goodness so many of the poems in *this* book are untranslated – or, at least, untranslated *as poems* – to date! With books engaged in retranslating (probably *most*), it is common to find lack of credit for all but complete borrowing and translations slightly but *oddly* – because there is an obviously better word any good translator would have on the tip of his or her tongue – *off-target* because he or she, out of pride, fear (of copyright infringement or being thought unoriginal), or from misguided consistency (one translator) that insists upon rewording when none is called for.

Displeasure in the Pleasure Quarters De Arinsu 262頁

I regret not introducing more kyôka of the pleasure quarters, but Yoshiwara was a world of its own and most poems on it would only be entertaining if presented as part of a longer treatment of the subject than I wished to write. But the following, captioned *Love via Plants* 寄植物恋, might have been in the text had I come up with the rhyme earlier:

我思ふひと枝手折者ならば指をも切りてやり梅の花　天地玄黄 一万
waga omou hito eda ta-oru mono naraba yubi o mo kiriteyari ume-no-hana
my loving person branch hand-break one is-if, finger+acc even cuting give plum blossom

If the one I love should break a blooming limb for me, his point
known, I'll be his sugar plum and pledge my baby finger joint!

Most of my readers will know courtesans sometimes gave clients the last joint of their baby finger as pledges, some will know breaking off blooming branches was standard idiom for taking a spray for viewing back at home or presenting. Tenchi Genkô's Tenmei *kyôka* improves further if you catch the final pun: the *yari*=*giving* also sounds like *spear* which, together with plum, *ume*, is a variety of the same. Believe it or not, we have a mad poem about the loss of a finger in English, too. It is by Robert Herrick,

UPON THE LOSS OF HIS FINGER.

ONE of the five straight branches of my hand
Is lop'd already, and the rest but stand
Expecting when to fall, which soon will be ;
First dies the leaf, the bough next, next the tree

I bet that some day, I will find a *kyôka* saying the same, though it will start with the loss of a *tooth* because "tooth" (*ha*) is homophonous with *leaf;* but, to return to the broader problem. Another reason Pleasure Quarter poems do not please in translation is that their appeal often lies in the language itself. *Eg.*,「おいらんに さういひんすよ 過ぎんすよ 酔なんしたら たゞおきんせん」早鞆和布刈（盲目の大学者、塙保己一？）*oiran ni sô ihinsu yo suginsu yo yoi nanshitara tada okinsen* hayatomo？岩波体系 57 狂歌の解説より）。禿の花魁を苛める酔った客さんを叱るこの言葉は、なんと楽しい！が、英訳では...Not even a great novelist could English the adorable protective voice of the little girl helper, the *kamuro,* telling a customer he had better not say such (bad) things about the (her) *oiran* (high-rank courtesan) or else! If you, like me, can imagine the scene, that simple poem seems a masterpiece. Similar masterpieces of dialect may be found in *senryû*. Here are two from *Yoshiwara: The Glittering World of the Japanese Courtesan* by Cecilia Segawa Seigle in her translation: *Anone moshi mata midomo-ra ga kinshitayo* (*Excuse me, Miss, / those "We the Samurai" / are here again*) & *Odoreme to ieba kamuro wa waraidashi* (*Thou pipsqueak! / the samurai shouts and / the kamuro starts to laugh*). "The *kamuro,*" she explains, "are amused by the stiff and countrified language of the samurai and take a conspiratorial mocking attitude" (Ibid, U. of Hawaii: 1993). Wow! *"Thou pipsqueek!"* deserves a translation prize. I think I'd prefer "We *your* samurai" but what can be done with *midomora!?* The way these poems differ from *kyôka* is not so much that *senryû* have 17 not 31 syllabets, but that the focus is on stereotypes, here the *samurai*. While we are on Yoshiwara, another *kyôka*, almost translatable, by 銀杏満門 1785. It refers to the parade where the women gracefully strut their stuff – on eight-inch stilted geta while wearing robes all aligned with the crack in front so they can show theirs.

Writing 八's & ハ's And Yet . . .

On stilted shoes, she shows her '8' and rights herself when she tips:
Who would guess that by herself she cannot write a bit?

傾城無筆　思はずよ世にうかれめの八文字その駒下駄もふみかゝぬとは
omowazu yo yo ni ukareme no hachi no moji sono koma mo fumi kakame to wa

Damn, I wish we had left-handed italics so I could make someone teeter back & forth! The eight 八 refers to both the separated hem-lapels and separated legs (& the Arabic numeral can show what they show if you look). The main pun is on the manner of *stepping*, the *fumi,* which they do so well (their shaky high-stilts make our longest stiletto heels a cake walk by comparison), for *fumi* is a homophone for "writing." I had read of Courtesan's who wrote well and used that talent to milk money from their clients; evidently, not all were literate. But, perhaps the best influence of the Pleasure Quarter, or, at least, Courtesans with their finger-lopping ways, on literature was indirect. Here is the most clearly *kyôka,* as opposed to *haikkai,* demonstration of what I am talking about:

東寺なる瓜実顔の君ならは指はさら也腕も切らはや　百子 momoko
tôji-naru urizanegao no kimi naraba yubi wa sara nari ude mo kirabaya

　　　　Love & Melons　　　　　　　　　　　　　　寄　瓜　恋

Melon-seed face of Temple East, with solstice coming, something begs;
Forget the fingers, in your case, I'd lop off my arms and legs!

A melon-seed face was oval, a type of beauty. No solstice is mentioned directly, but the temple name, Tôji ("East Temple, a nickname for Kyôto's 教王護国寺 Kyôôgokoku-ji) is synonymous with the winter solstice and hence we have a *tôji-kabocha,* or winter-solstice squash/pumpkin/melon. We feel a symbolic honing down to the spiritual core of the solstice and the identification of beauty with roundness in the Sinosphere taken to its hyperlogical conclusion. I would also suspect, though I have no proof yet that there might have been dolls on sale at said temple, as Japanese dolls tend to be limbless.

吉原のオマケ未英訳：そしてまた おまへいつ　きなさるの尻あかつきばかりうき物はなし
東作 *soshite mata omae itsu ki-nasaru no shiri akatsuki bakari uki mono wa nashi*
Tôsaku c.1790. A complaint. Holding his horses while a courtesan did not see him though he waited until the bright red rear of the night, the dawn made a monkey of him.

Women of Pleasure in a Mad Poem Portrait Gallery　264 頁

After the Deluge and a Chinese Poem. Rokuo Tanaka translates: *"After us the deluge!" / You don't care for my house / Unless the cherry blossoms fall / Even to sleep / You will not return home"*). I like the way we go from "fall" to "to sleep," but "After us the deluge" – the standard translation for the idiom woven into, rather than patched on to, the Japanese – just does not fit. But, looking back at my own try, I see that my turning the deluge proverb into cherry petals did not work. How about the following?

> *Though 'home sweet home' be blown to hell, you stay, while blossoms also blow, you play . . . Forget not even they rejoin their roots to sleep!*

Tanaka adds something I missed. There may be an allusion to a poem by Po Chüi in the *Wakan Rôeishû* 和漢朗詠集 (Japanese and Chinese Poems to Sing, ca. 1012) that starts *"Beneath the flowers / Forgetting / To return home / Because of the lovely scene/ . . ."* (花の下を帰えらむことをわするるは美景に困てなり... from Tanaka: 2006)

♪ **What I found after I learned the Singer/courtesan Hatamaki and Ôta were acquainted.** Hamada Giichirô gives evidence they knew each other. Searching the on-line 嘱山家集 collection of Ôta's work, I also found a possible mention of Hatamaki in a series of poems in the memory of Oshizu, the courtesan Ôta redeemed to be his mistress. Like his wife, she died all too soon. Temple records 浄栄寺過去帳 show he visited the temple, sometimes with a group for poetry parties, on her death anniversary *for thirty years*. Does one of five poems offered in her memory one year, くりかへす暦の数もはたまきに ちうたばかりの手向とぞなる *kurikaesu koyomi no kazu mo hatamaki ni . . .*, have Hatamaki singing a *jiuta*, or ballad, for her? I cannot tell. But another of those poems is noteworthy even without Hatamaki.

しづやしづしづのをだ巻はてしなくなど物思ふ夏のひぐらし 蜀山人
shizu ya shizu shizu no odamaki hateshi-naku nado mono-omou natsu no higurashi
shizu! oh, shizu! shizu/flax-spinning-spool end-not etc thing-think/long summer chime-cicada

日本人読者諸君！上記のお賤に対する悲しみの表現は完璧ではないか。一茶の「露の世は露の世ながらさりながら」が有名で、大田の「しづやしづしづのをだ巻」が全く無名であることは、いけない。確かに、さと女は、御妾より可愛い。惜しい。けれど、物思うときの蜩が果てしなき賤の苧環と組む妙味も、広く認められてもいいと思いませんか？機知と感慨がこんなに深く寄り合う例は他にあるまいぞ。（夏の日暮らしでおわる名歌もあるという事、知っているが、ここでは蜩も活かしている）

I will not give a poor translation. Let me just say, for those who read some but not a lot of Japanese, that Shokusanjin morphs Oshizu's name, first repeated over and over (without the honorific "o") into the flaxen spool (*shizu no odamaki*) that symbolized winding back time and remembering (or forgetting) over and over (pp 101.181.261.337.490) with endless longing that gerunds right into summer evening cicadas – identified with fall, but often heard in late-summer at dawn and dusk – no bug I know of has so clear and cyclic a tune or contains time itself (the *higurashi* mimics the Doppler effect from the initial coming to the final going). The *chiming cicada*, as *I* call it, is the only animal that has ever drawn my tears without biting or stinging me (The setting: early dawn, I in hopeless love, not one but a chorus of them cutting in and out). ♪ The poem also alludes to a lament that has the *higurashi* meaning living day-to-day – call it a lovesick or lost-love summertime blues – and I am just not up to translating all of that. I will go out on a limb and say I think the poem one of the finest short laments ever written, and would add that it proves once and for all that puns and deep feeling *can* mix. *Shizu ya Shizu* should be famous in Japan, but I am afraid that most serious poetry-lovers do not look for expressions of grief from a *kyôka* master. Now, as compensation to my readers for not translating that poem, let me present you with another in English that is witty, magical and sad for all who, like me, are fortunately or unfortunately unable to forget the possibilities that life kills.

A Song by G.K. Chesterton

There's a sound of the flutes and the lutes tonight
In the island of Nevercometrue;
In a fire-lit isle in the seas of night
Black with depth of blue;
And the man that might have been I shall dance
With woman that might have been you:
Under the world where a man remembers
More than he ever knew.

There's a noise of songs in the gongs tonight,
In the garden of Nevercometrue;
Under the trees of the terrible flowers
That bloom when the moon is blue;
And the man that never was I is wed
To the woman that never was you -
O nothing nearer than all that is,
In Nevercometrue come true.

(参考 6/19/1793・浄栄寺で加療中・大田南畝の妾 お賤・死亡、三十歳。法名 晴雲妙閑信女)
♪ ♪*A Few More Words on the Sound of the Higurashi and the Translation of its Name Occasioned by Picking Up a Penguin on the John this Morning.* Wondering how Ariwara Motokata's New Year's conundrum might be translated, I took *The Penguin Book of Japanese Verse* with me into the WC. Oops! Said poem was not in it. As is the case with Donald Keene's *World Within Walls* and Steven Carter's *Traditional Japanese Poetry*, said poem, first in the *Kokinshû* and parent of hundreds or thousands of poem progeny, was apparently in bad odor, for it was not included among the select. But before checking for it, I looked at the Penguin book where *it* chose to open, so I might be presented with whatever fate pleased and it was this: *"It grows dark, it seems, / With the cicada shriek. / But it is the walls / Of the mountain cleft / That make the gloom."* A huge 'X' mark was scribbled next to it that only I could have written, so this was evidently not the first time it shocked me. Here we have what may well be the most beautiful sound in creation and the translators, who evidently have never heard a *higurashi,* make it *shriek!* While the whole reading is ludicrously wrong and recalls a passage from Peter Farb's *Word Play* citing Nabokov's description of the smooth progression of the tongue along the palate creating the euphonious *"Lo-li-ta"* mistranslated into Japanese as *a tortuous back and forth exercise of that organ* required to touch all the proper places that could only reflect the translator's struggle to vocalize L's (ご参考に拙著『誤訳天国』白水社) – that is to say, the misreading was born of prejudice coming from having experienced another sort of cicada – I could guess what it was they mistranslated despite Penguin's unforgivable failure to include even a romanization of the original. Rodd and Henkeníus, whom I immediately checked, read it more or less correctly, as follows: *"I thought the sun set / as the twilight cricket shrilled / but I was quite wrong / for in reality it / was only the mountain's shade"* (higurashi no nakitsuru nae ni hi wa kurenu to omoeba yama no kage ni zo arikeru kks 294). The "less" is because I take umbrage with "shrilled." The call is only *shrill* if you are over-caffeinated in a place too noisy to catch the second half of the call, the decelerating diminuendo. I am fine with "twilight cricket" for the word twilight has the proper delicacy and, as Brownas and Thwaite prove, English speakers are too prejudiced against the cicada to give it a hearing. R & H also properly note the *higurashi* is a cicada and its name can also mean "sun set."

Pleasing Fleas, Nice Lice, Lousy Translation.　　　　　　　　　　　　268頁

♪ **Later Lice**. After finishing the chapter, a lice *kyôka* by Meshimori was pinched from Kaneko Jitsuei's introduction to *Shokusankashû* (一夜寝し妹がかたみと思ふにはうつり虱もつぶされもせず 宿屋飯盛 *hitoyo neshi imo ga katami to omou ni wa utsurijirami mo tsubusare mo sezu*) and, months later, one by Yûchôrô from the *Kyôka Jiten* (別路のかたみの虱取るたびに我が恋衣うらみうらみて　雄長老 *wakareji no katami no shirami toru tabi ni waga koigoromo urami-uramite*). Respectively,

The only keepsake from our one-night stand, how nice –
Thinking of her, I prefer not to pop my pubic lice!

With each parting, I turn my robes inside out – mementos are nice
But I have memories to burn and travel alone: no lice!

Meshimori's lice have more in common with Marvel's flea that mixed the lover and his mistress's blood, than with Issa's familiars. Not squashing them is suitably outrageous, but hardly as novel as Issa's naive *ku*. The content is improved by running into the name Meshimori 宿屋飯盛, literally *Inn wench*. Such a 'wench' could be so helpful (foot-washing, sewing, cooking, massage, and sometimes . . .) travelers might indeed have felt sentimental about one-night stands. Yûchôrô's much older poem plays on "looking at the lining" = *ura mite* = and *resenting/hating* = *uramite*. "*Memories ~ alone*" atones for the loss. ◎オマケ：汗水に成て世渡る人の身の　夏の虱は浮つしつみつ　ある人　狂歌咄 *ase mizu ni natte . . . . On the body of one who makes a living bathed in sweat, / Summer lice may float or sink, but they are always wet.* From "Kyôka Chattering" (1672)

Painful but Funny Things　(fart by fathers death-bed)　　　　　　272頁

♪ **A draw-verse,** or just **draw** is my term for the *maezuke* (or *maetsuke*), half a verse put up to elicit caps. A riddle may have more than one answer, but such are hard to come up with impromptu, so *haikai* link-verse masters could not help but favor simple draws similar to the headings for *lists of things* (*monowazukushi*) if they wanted to attract many students. *Senryû* were born of the easy draw. The longest discussion of *maezuke* I know of may be found in the second half of the foreword to my dirty *senryû* book (gill: 2007).

♪ **Yoshioka Found the Riddles** for me in the *Chikuba Kyôginshû* 竹馬狂吟集, sometimes considered the first anthology of *haikai*. As riddles are often based upon cleverly (mis)construed idiom, the best not uncommonly defy translation. Eg. 足なくて雲の走るはあやしきに / 何をふまへてかすみたつらん (*ashi nakute kumo no hashiru wa . . .*) from the same collection asks *How can clouds run without legs and mist stand upon air.* Rain falling from clouds observed from a distance is called "legs" and mist was said to "rise/stand." In English, clouds might build *banks* before they have *money*, make rain *liquidity;* but, obviously, such would bear little resemblance to the original. Also, experience affects what works or does not. I love (つぶるるもありつぶれぬもあり / 秋風に木ずゑの熟柿また落ちて *tsubururu mo ari tsuburenu mo ari aki no kaze ni kozue . . .*):

♪ *Some Get Squashed, Some Do Not!* ♪

When the Autumn wind hits the persimmon,
A bitter fruit drops now and then: it's given.

Only bitter fruit remains in the tree. Unless you have seen how they squash on impact and, better yet, felt one underfoot (they beat banana peels) you are not really ready for the poem.

Spooky, Creatures (all four chapters).　　　　　　　　　　　　274頁

♪ **Spooky Phenomenon & Wit.** I skipped the large first entry in Hearn's selections from *Kyôka Hyaku-monogatari* (*Goblin Poetry* in the annot. biog.), the *kitsunebi*, lit. *fox-fire*, or

Will-o'-the-Wisp. Hearn's description of that "tongue of pale red flame, hovering in darkness, and shedding no radiance upon the surfaces over which it glides" created by "the goblin fox," foxes turning into beautiful maidens to beguile men and the broader psycho-social idea of possession by foxes is so interesting I wanted to choose some of the poems to give me an excuse to quote more. Unfortunately, none were witty enough to warrant it. Hearn selects for the narrative and folkloric value. To introduce them as *kyôka*, I need to get the original *Kyôka Hyaku-monogatari* to select poems for wit alone.

♪ *A Few More Monsters.* Blyth has some good spook pictures scattered through his *Oriental Humour* (1959). He describes a hair-cutter monster from the last page of *Yôkaizukanshô* 妖怪図巻抄, *"Scroll-Picture of Goblins,* as looking "somehow vindictive and jealous," and asks *"Are not spitefulness and envy comical things?"* (situation comedy thrives on them). Blyth mentions other "more or less humorous monsters" on the fly-leaf. Here are the obviously comic ones w/ one small edit and added glosses:

> *Maikubi* (dancing-heads), heads of people who died fighting and still fight each other, as heads only, in the sea; *Tenjôame* (ceiling-licker), a monster who licks the ceilings of old shrines and houses and leaves marks on them; *Warai-Onna* (laughing-woman), a woman with a hideous face who towers over fences and laughs and laughs; *Kamimai* (paper-dance), a demon which in October makes papers fly up into the air one by one."

It is amazing any *kyôka* written to complement monsters came out well. 1) With monsters, or goblins, that are already fantastic, what can a poem do to make them funnier? 2) And, with so many monsters, most could not possibly be familiar to enough people to permit the allusions needed to make poems playing with their characteristics interesting.

What the Have-nots Have Plenty of   282 頁

What made Teitoku's poem interesting is the way things generally put on the *minus* side of the ledger became *plus* merely by emphasizing the "have," which was there all along. Teitoku could not have dropped *debt* and *disease* for "plenty of nothing" because a colloquial "nothing" does not exist in Japanese (the Zen *mu* is an abstract construct not in common use). Here is a somewhat associated mad poem from *The Id of the Squid* (and other outrageous rhymes about oceanography) by the pseudonymous Arch E. Benthic:

> *I've been smoking like a chimney,*
> *And I feel I should cut back.*
> *The will power's strong within me,*
> *It's the won't power that I lack.*

The title "Maybe I can stop smoking at sea this trip" is enhanced by an illustration, by John C. Holden, showing the poet sitting against and plugged into his ship's chimney.

On the Prosperity of Poverty & How It Keeps Itself   284 頁

♪ **Going from the real Tales of Ise #73 to the Fake Nise Ise # 73**, I had to change *two* words (you/dear=> money, are=> is), where the original only changed *one* (kane=money=> kimi=you/dear). Imagine working from McCullough's translation: *"My love is like / The cinnamon tree / That grows on the moon – / Though one may see her / She is untouchable."* My love => money, her=> it, she=> it. Three changes would be necessary. (Because the man has not gotten a message through to her yet, McCullough chooses third-person, but I assumed that lacking a "my" in the original, a direct address, even if imaginary, made more sense. さて、こう言われば、笑われるにちがいないが、「昔、そこにはありときけど、せうそこをだにいふべくもあらぬ女のあたりを思ひける」とよめば、小野の小町のあそこのない事に触れる歌にしたくなります。無理かもしれないが。。。

♪ **Here is Ôta's Lament about his depressing job** that puns the monsoon's falling (rain) with old logbooks: 五月雨の日も竹橋の反故しらべ　けふもふるちやうあすもふる

ちやう *samidare no hi mo takehashi no hankô shirabe kyô mo furuchô asu mo furuchô*. I first found it in a book by Nada Inada (なだいなだ著：「江戸狂歌」1986), who pointed out that Ôta did such a good job compiling the records for the Takehashi, a bridge between the outer and inner palace in Edo, that some historians today are grateful this brilliant man was forced to be a clerk! His excellent work did eventually get him a slight raise that proved to be enough to live on, but barely (for a married man with children and a mistress who loved the theatre). He became an administrator for some small ward. If my recollection is correct, H.G. Welles portrayed the heroic duty-bound selfless samurai as the international civil servant of his future *Utopia*. Well, Ôta/Shokusanjin was one of them, and here is what he thought of his honorable life: 世の中はさてもせはしき酒のかんちろりの袴きたりぬいだり (*yononaka wa sate mo sewashiki sake no kan chirori no hakama kitari nuidari*). The homophonic pun on *chirori*, a certain type of heating pot and psychological mimesis for flustered rapid movement, that provides the wit fails to English, but, let me try:

> *The world today is so damn busy, just try juggling pots*
> *Of hot wine while pulling on and off your stiff culottes!*

These culottes (hakama) were absurd designs, in their extreme versions so long they covered the feet and, dragging behind seemed to give their wearer a second knee. Stiff and hot, they could not be worn for long by anyone but a masochist (See *Topsy-turvy 1585* (2004)). Officials had to pull them on to do their duties (meet and judge people) then remove them to recuperate in more comfortable and cool non-bifurcated clothing. I suppose one could say no one has the right to drink around the clock, but poor Shokusanjin had to work until dying in his 70's, while anyone with means would retire at 50 or 60.

The more poverty the merrier? 286 頁

♪**Highway Toll for Poverty.** An anthology contemporary to Teitoku also had a Poverty God + road-coin 路銭 combination:

貧乏神出雲へ行てかえるさの 路銭おとしてゐとまりにせよ 且保 銀葉夷歌集
binbôgami izumo e itte kaerusa no rosen otoshite i-tomari ni seyo katsuho? 1679
poverty-god/s izumo-to going-return's road-change dropping stayover-as do!

> *Off goes our god, Poverty, to Izumo – and we can only pray*
> *that losing his pocket money on the way back, he must stay!*

♪**Sengai the mad, mad Zen monk.** The logic Sengai used to terrify the new homeowner into thinking he was being jinxed before turning the seemingly bad words into a charm in the second half of the poem is pure *kyôka*. He did the same with haiku, leaving the final half to be figured out (or explained in prose after he was questioned). For example, he urged *"Young bride / Be alive till they say to you / Die! Die!"* (transl. Yoel Hoffman: *Japanese Death Poems*), which *sounds* far from felicitous to say the least. But, in the stereotypical multi-generational family cycle, the one many wish to die is the aged matriarch who makes things hard on her live-in daughter-in-law, which is what a young-bride is. *In other words*, he is wishing her to have children and become the female boss of the house and live a long, long time!

Bor-row, Row Your Boat, ...! & be merry friends. 288 頁

Matchbox Explanations that did not fit in the text:「ふし」は火の枕の火山の富士のみならず、そのあだな不尽を活かす妙の上に、「かまち」とは「框」(door-frame)ですが、火打には石と鉄が組む。後者には、古い「釜」の刃の欠片がとくに良いとされて、火打ち鉄の同意語として使われたようで、目とは、石の溝みたいな窪みの外端にも掛けている。つまり暗喩はめちゃくちゃ細かいで、英訳不可。Fire-box explan. in *Topsy-turvy 1585*)

Sampling Shokusanjin's Mad 100 Poets: その一　Poems #1 ~ 8

♪ ***While I have no problem with parodies, I hate translating the original 100 poems***, for they have been done so often I feel compelled to do a thorough review of notes on them as anything I do becomes a judgment on other translations (or interpretations by Japanese). That is one reason, I used MacCauley (1917) for the first. That does not mean I agree with his reading. If I were to flat-out guess, I would think the rough thatch of the matting a choice to be at one with nature on the part of the Emperor and rather than "moisture dripping through" (MacCauley) or sleeves "always wet with dew" (Carter), would prefer to imagine *"the dew forming on my sleeves."* Be that as it may, at this point, I feel there are translations enough of the 100 poems. What is needed, rather, is for someone to gather the best critique/appreciations as Makoto Ueda did for Bashô's poems.

♪ **#003 Why 'Fed up with Hitomaro' and Soupy Precedent both in one Haikai!** Among Carter's interesting selection from the 1539 Inu/Dog Tsukubashû, we have, in his translation: *Ah, to savor the good taste / of Hitomaro's poems! // A mountain pheasant / from the foot-wearying hills— / makes a good soup!* (*hitomaro no uta no aji no mumasa yo ashibiki no yamadori no shiru tare mo kue*). Shokusanjin may be riffing on *haikai*.

Time's Arrow in Teiryû's Poem. Does it surprise you to find it in the Orient? The Occident fancies itself the inventor of real Time, by which a progression rather than a cycle is meant; but, the wise, East and West and in-between, all know it is a spiral. Like history, circling, it repeats, yet it changes nonetheless. Metaphorically, what this means is that time may *always* be graded. And, English, though boasting tenses out the wazoo, lacks much of the vocabulary of time expressed by Japanese terms such *kozo-kotoshi,* as seen with New Year poems, or *hatsu* (first) this and that and even *hatsu mukashi* and *nochi-mukashi* that seasonal haikai and witty *kyôka* alone seem to use. Here is Bokuyô, the great late-17c *kyôka* wit's student's student Ôya no Urazumi in the late 18c: *"Those loves of which we talk about become past in the present;/ Who cares what last becomes it, what isn't holds no argument!"* うき事をかたるは今が初昔のちむかしまで別儀あらじな 大屋裏住 *uki koto o kataru wa ima ga hatsumukashi nochimukashi made betsugi arajina.* The original, which I am not sure I got, is titled, *Love by Tea Leaves,* 寄茶恋。 Tea leaves were picked from the eighty-eighth night. They were picked for 21 days. 20 is called *hatsuka* (which is a homophone for the first day of the year when all that came before newly joins the past, as they are now in the old year) on the following day, as they are packed. Hence they are "first-pasts," *hatsu-mukashi.* The loves of which we talk about become "*first*-past" in the original. The following ones though no change is present, become "later-past," *nochi-mukashi,* or "later-past." Tea leaves picked later were called that, but the poet does not want to jump the gun. I am not sure I got that right, but I am sure the explanation of *hatsu-mukashi* I saw in one of the *surimono* book's (mentioned at the end of this one) was even worse. Maybe we can clear things up for another edition!

♪ **#007 The 1669 Dog Hundred parody takes the alternate pronunciation of Heaven's Plain**, Ame-no-hara, and puns it into something sold mostly to children:

> *A bellyful of sweets sounds oh so heavenly, but has no taste;*
> *Suckers from Mount Foxy, perchance, made of dirt and paste!*

(飴の腹味はひ見れば味がない いなりの山にこねし土かも　飴中買 (賀近) 犬百人一首 *ame no hara ajiwai mireba . .* Gakin 1669. The pseudonym *Ame no Nakagai* means what we might loosely call *The Candyman.* Each spoof in this *Dog Hundred Poet's* collection has its own pseudonym, and most feel similar to the pen-names later adopted by Shoku-sanjin *et al* in that they sound somewhat like the names of the old poets and mean something. I will skip further explanation of details in this parody here and only point out that Shokusanjin's poem is funnier as the the childish simplicity of its facetious reading that would require no explanation what-so-ever for Japanese readers seems utterly artless.

♪ **#008, Perhaps the Kookiest Kyôka of All, but I had to let it go:** the wit does not translate, even in part. But Japanese readers who have not seen it should. The original, one of the better known of the 100 poems, roughly says *"I'm content to live in my hut in* the sticks Southeast of the capital, though people may call this Mountain Blue." (*waga io wa miyako no tatsumi shika zo sumu yo o ujiyama to hito wa iu nari*). The direction is called dragon-snake (*tatsumi*) homophonic with the boondocks, a hint of the deer (*shika*) an animal with plaintive calls is punned in, and the Mountain's name sounds like *melancholy* or *depressing*. That is to say, this 9c poem by Monk Kisen (喜撰法師) is, *itself*, what might have been called a *kyôka* centuries later. Shokusanjin did not bother to parody what was already mad. He simply expanded the directional dragon-snake to include all twelve year-animals, ending in such a way to give the name of the mountain while boasting in one character 治 that he got them all: 008 わが庵はみやこの辰巳午ひつじ申酉戌亥子丑寅う治 *waga io wa miyako no tatsumi uma hitsuji saru tori inu i ne ushi tora u ji*. I am unsure what *I* think of it, but Mizukaki, whose website introduces it, writes:「と十二支を全て詠み込んで、しかも「うぢ（宇治）」でオチがついたのは狂歌の神（がいるとしたら）の恩寵かと疑われます。蜀山狂歌の名作と誉れ高い一首です。」

A Sampling of Shokusanjin's Mad 100 Poets: その二 #9, 10, 12   292頁

♪ **#010's author Semimaru is often pictured with a moon-lute** on the poem cards. Seeing the pictures reminded me that he was *blind*, not *mo*, perhaps, but *mô*. If that difference in pronunciation was less important then than now, Shokusanjin may be playing with this, too. The four letters make me wonder if the checkpoint might not have been on a crossroad on that Meeting Slope (逢坂 Ausaka/Ôsaka) the poet was said to live near to. My translation followed Carter. I assume he read previous glosses. Otherwise, I'd have made it something like: *Separation? Hey, whether we are heading off, or coming back, / Whether you know it or not, life always crosses, it's a fact!* Why? Because I have long liked Piet Hein's grook explaining why missing a train should not leave us vexed (we'll always be late for the last train, and always too late for the next).   No matter.

A Sampling of Shokusanjin's Mad 100 Poets: その三 #20, 24, 59   294頁

♪**Poem #20.** *I am unsure of my reading of the 1669 Dog Hundred Poet parody* (あびぬれば湯に肌をなて柔和なる　身を洗てもあらんとそおもふ　眉目よしの聟 (*abinureba yu ni hada o . . .*) by Mimeyoshi no Muko (fine-featured groom), or I might have texted it. Prince Motoyoshi's *wabinureba* bathos becoming *abinureba*=bathing is most amusing. The difference is greater than the one syllabet seen in the romanization, as the former is a simple verb and the latter a compound one (the respective *nureba* completely differ).

♪ **Poem #24 Did Shokusanjin *not* play with the unique usage *ma ni ma ni* in**, where the mountain's beauty was presented to the gods *"as is, as is,"* because so many other parodies *did*? One unidentified *kyôka* pretends the *ma ni ma ni* means 間に間に, "between, between," a homophone, and has a comb pulling lice from *between, between* the hairs (このほどは櫛も取りあへずむさければ虱わくらし髪の間に間に *kono hodo wa kushi mo toriaezu musakereba shirami waku rashi kami no ma ni ma ni*.)! A remarkably graceful *senryû* taking the *ma ni ma ni* as space+ time, imagines the gods among the red maple leaves preparing for their annual Izumo caucus (紅葉せし間に間に神の旅支度 *momiji seshi ma ni ma ni kami no tabijitaku*). The cavalier gift in Poem #24, – *"here, take the autumn mountain's beauty!"* – is brought down to earth yet still sent up to heaven in an epigram by Robert Herrick, not only closer to a *kyôka* than the *Hundred Poet waka* but the very thing in spirit and only a few beats too long,

STEAM IN SACRIFICE.

IF meat the gods give, I the steam
High towering will devote to them,
Whose easy natures like it well,
If we the roast have, they the smell.

Sampling Shokusanjin's Mad 100 Poets: その四　Poem #66　296頁

♪**Slurping Noses and haikai-style parody.** Link-verse *haikai* for most of the 17c was deliberately outrageous. So when the postword to the 1669 Dog Hundred, 犬百人一首 says that the parody comprises *kyôka*-fied *ku* (individual 17-syllabet haiku or 31-syllabet link-verse clusters) you expect more snot than not. (「賀近山庄（佐心子賀近）の句を狂詠に翻転して笑のたね」と幽双庵の後書き tk2)

~~~~~~

Sampling Shokusanjin's Mad 100 Poets: その五　Poem #70, 83 & 96　298頁

♪*For #83. The Naku Pun.* As we saw earlier (pp.220,298), deer disassembling into parts to serve us – still common for cows in Chinese Mother Goose – were an old *waka* tradition. Checking on Carter's translation of the Fujiwara no Shunzei (1114-1204) poem, I found another so charming and clearly mad, that I could not resist Englishing it myself:

mizu no ue ni ika de ka oshi no ukaburan   kuga ni dani koso mi wa shizuminure shunzei
water-on-top-of how is it? mallards float?! dry-land-on even body-as-for sink-becomes

Mandarin ducks – how they float on water I can't understand!
Here we are struggling so hard not to sink upon dry land.

The ducks in question, *oshidori*, are symbols of conjugal felicity common to the Sinosphere, and floating, as we have seen, means unsettled malaise and a low life in this world of woe. While these ducks and love are classic subjects and the poet is probably serious, I feel a kinship with *kyôka* here. Carter also points out that Shunzei's quail poem alludes to two poems by Narihira, which, to tell the truth, I read before and thought to put in this book but forgot. Narihira, the handsome lover sent a goodbye letter to a woman about his leaving Deepgrass and wondering if it would become a wild field in his absence. The anonymous woman's reply is absolutely mad. In my whittled-down Carter translation, *"If it be a field, / I'll spend the years crying / like a quail – / and you at least will come / briefly for some hunting."* (*no to naraba uzura to nakite toshi wa hemu kari ni dani ya wa kimi ka kozaramu.*) A wild field was what Europeans called a "desert" and the idea of the Narihira's poem might be Englished as "after me the deluge," in which case, I suppose the lady's quail must be fish and she must be angled (笑).

♪*About "No two good things," or an association for Teiryû's take-off on Shunzei's #83*. I first heard the proverb in London, when I noticed a phenomenal pair of spheres bippity-boppitying down the street in front of us and sighed aloud that while I feared the centrifugal force might rip them apart, if only I could find a Japanese intellectual with *those*, I would have proposed long ago. It was unwise to let such thoughts escape when my companion to the book-fair, the chief-editor, was female, my boss and single, but in the millisecond I hesitated, I rationalized that she liked astronomy and physics, so the purely physical miracle we could not help but behold in front of us would amaze her, too. She – now the publisher – was just too cool, replying *"Forget it! Two good things never happen and she already has two!"* I was puzzled and asked and learned the proverb.

♪ *Poem #96. More on the ox balls.* I clearly recall *haikai* older than Shokusanjin's parody where balls are seen from an ox-cart and compared to *sake* flasks (no mangoes in Japan) – *tokuri*, the ones used to heat it. Because of these associations, the balls are not dirty but clean and happy and the melancholy mood suddenly warms and cheers up the attentive reader. And, just the other day, I found the 1669 *Dog Hundred* parody of this poem which points out that if this lord (he was a former chancellor) was also *wagging a sake flask* (sharing it with others). Shokusanjin would have seen this and if he also knew the *haikai*, put them together. はなさせぬたらしの意気の君ならて　ふりうく物は徳利也けり　入道酒大上戸大臣 犬百 *hanasasenu tarashi no iki no kimi nara de*...）. 念のため、蜀山人のと、心地の違うが、牛の金玉狂歌又一首オマケ：我心牛のふぐりもさだまらず世をいとはふといひてぶら／＼　元安　古今夷曲集 1666 *waga kokoro ushi no fuguri mo*... 蛇足：火事とかそのほかの理由で引っ越さなければならない場合、家具はこぶ大車を引くに忙しいふぐり殿でしょう。けれど「ぶらぶら」だと、事情が別。

Sampling Shokusanjin's Mad 100 Poets: その六　Poem #99 &100　　300頁

オマケ#100: 百敷やふるき衾をはらふにも　なをあまりある　ほこりと泪　　後撰夷曲集 1672　（或夷歌恋百欧の中に）*momoshiki ya furuki fusuma o harau ni mo* . . . .。平凡は平凡ですが、埃と泪という組み合わせは妙に所得った！

In praise of kyôka, or why Blyth beats Keene.　　　　　　302頁

♪ **Cheep Kyôka.**　When I delayed publication to read *surimono* book translations of *kyôka*, I found another "cheep, cheap" *kyôka,* or rather translation of a *kyôka* by Daniel McKee (*Colored in the Year's New Light:* 2008). Judging from the time of publication, his cheeping warbler and my cheeping titmouse may well have criss-crossed in the sky. Here is his translation of Gosokusai Kabenuri's 1820's poem, with a few improvements (in my opinion), centered and deparsed – it is in 5 lines), and my mad reading:

古路物ハならへて見せ？をはるの日に　鶯の祢もやす／＼ときく　五息斎壁塗
koro mono wa narabete mise o haru no hi ni uguisu no ne mo yasuyasu to kiku　kabenuri

*Arranging my old street goods I set up shop and on this spring day
the soothing sounds of the warbler sound like "cheap! cheap!"*

*On a day in spring, when used-goods vendors line ye street,
Even warbler's priceless song is easy to find on the cheap*

As McKee explains, the *uguisu no ne* can be the sound of or price of the warbler. And, I would add, the warbler might be a warbler-call usually sold on the New Year. He also knew that *yasuyasu* has more to do with relaxation – as opposed to straining to hear the first call – but could not resist the cheep shot, for what I consider the best of reasons:

"Although the above translation's comparison of this to the voice of the bird (cheep, cheep) is not actually in the original, it is in the spirit of *kyôka*."　Ibid

The poem accompanies a Hokuga painting of *A Dealer of Used Goods Making Spring's First Sale* (pl. 111). Even combining our readings you get but half of the original, and that a bit misleading, for, if I am not mistaken, the call, while not "cheep," is not soothing either, but something like its diamond sutra mimetic rendition, *hô-ke-kyô!* and that seems to mellow on this halcyon day when vendors line the Elysian streets of Edo.

♪ **Blyth & Shokusanjin.** The main reason I put this sampling of Blyth on *kyôka* here, after six chapters of Shokusanjin was because Blyth's presentation was so strongly weighted toward Shokusanjin, whom he adored for what we might call his Zen sanity. The last poem Blyth gives claims that if we stop dwelling on this world's transience we might enjoy life more. "The humour by which and in which he lived," writes Blyth, "was of an all-pervading, "organic," natural kind that is hardly to be separated from his daily life and thought." In that sense, I would agree with Blyth that he is like Issa, but more so, for Issa had his faith, while, for Shokusanjin, like Twain, good humour *was* his faith.

♪ **Where Blyth Beat** Me. When we retranslate or discuss poems translated by others, we do not mind pointing out things they missed as it makes us, the follower into the leader. But, inevitably, this exalts us at the expense of the other, even if it is someone we also praise. So, let me put one poem here from *Oriental Humour* that I definitely read, pondered but failed to catch and therefore had not included in this book: *"The Japanese Spirit / Will not creep between the legs / Of the townsman / Standing there in the street, / But will cut him down!"* (Blyth translation 道なかにたつの市人きりすてゝまたはくゞらぬやまとだましひ　蜀山人 *michi naka ni tatsu no* . . .). Shokusanjin's poem is titled *"A Eulogy of a Picture of Kanshin creeping between someone's legs. China is China, Japan is Japan. Do not forget the sword of Japan, while picking up the thrown-away paper of*

China." As poems go, it is one of his worse. But Blyth explains it is a response to "the famous story of . . . a man of the Han Dynasty, born poor, but rising to high rank," who, when forced by town ruffians, crawled under a boy's legs, thinking the ignominy better than bloodshed. Japanese, Shokusanjin notes approvingly, have too much pride for that. Blyth also goes one better here, for he supplies a picture of a fat man crawling under a boy's legs by the monk Sengai (1751-1857) and, on the fly-leaf, the poem that accompanies it: *"Why need Kanshin / Be ashamed? / In this world, / Who does not come / From between the legs?"* (韓信はいかて怯へき 世の中に 股より出てぬ人志なければ 仙崖 *kanshin wa ika de obi-beki yononaka ni mata yori idenu hito shi nakereba* Sengai). I gave the entire roman letter gloss because I *like* Sengai's *kyôka* far better than Shokusanjin's. So Blyth gave and approved of *both* attitudes. So do I.

♪ **On *Arasou/i* or Fighting/competition in Waka.** I give examples enough in *Cherry Blossom Epiphany*, but now, glimpsing at the *Shinkokinshû* (1205), find yet another:

Onto my sleeve spreading the scent of plum bloom, a new display:
leaking in through the eaves, moonlight comes to join the fray

梅の花にほいをうつす袖のうへに軒漏る月のかげぞあらそふ 定家 *ume no hana nioi o utsusu* . . . The original has the moon there to *arasou*, or fight/struggle..

~~~~~~

Puffing pictures: white heron, et. al.   304 頁

♪ **Golownin wrote pages on Tobacco in Japan.** A passage: *"Our interpreter, Teske, . . . was himself a great smoaker; but often said, that the christian priests had not done the Japanese so much injury by the introduction of their faith, which only produced among them internal commotions and civil wars, as by the introduction of tobacco; for the former was only a transitory, long forgotten evil, but the latter diverted, and probably would for centuries to come, large tracts of land and a number of hands from the production of necessary articles, which are now dear, but might otherwise be cheaper. Besides, the workmen could not then so often interrupt their labour, but now they were continually resting themselves in order to smoke their pipes."* As Tex Williams would sing a century and a half later, in a novelty number that shares more than a little of the mad spirit, ♪ *Smoke, smoke, smoke that cigarette!* ♪ *Smoke, smoke, smoke until you smoke yourself to death . . .* ♪ *. . . And when you finally get to the Pearly Gate, just tell St Peter he'll have to wait* ♪ *First, you gotta have another cigarette!* (done from memory: it may be a bit different).

♪ **One More Shokusanjin Picture Poem.** This is the penultimate poem in Blyth's introduction of *kyôka* in *Asian Humour*. My translations:

竹林はやぶ蚊の多き所ともしらでうかうかあそぶ生酔 蜀山人
chikurin wa yabuka no ôki tokoro to mo shira de uka-uka asobu nama-yoi shokusanjin
bamboo grove/s-as-for bush-squitos' many place evn knwng-not-frm carelssly ply tipsies

<div align="center">

七 賢 人 の 絵 に
♪On a painting of the Seven Sages♪

</div>

Not even knowing	*Heedless in their play,*
bamboo groves are full	*or do those sage tipsies*
of big mosquitoes!	*not even know ?*
Seven sages lost in play:	*Bamboo groves are famous*
Those poor tipsy fellows	*for their big mosquitoes.*

Blyth, who called this something more like a *senryû*, the debunking of a favorite subject for Chinese painting, translated *"The half-tipsy fellows / Are thoughtlessly enjoying themselves, / Forgetting / The many mosquitoes / In the bamboo grove."* He did right to reverse the syntax order to preserve the flow as the original, as is often true in mad poems, and sometimes true for the poem does not split in two, unless it is part way through the penultimate 7-syllabets, after *shira-de,* "knowing not from/ because." My second reading may be restored to my original "sage *drunks"* once you have enjoyed the *tipsies* (the gods seem to be here and there like *gypsies*). *Nama*+drunk can be either be partly drunk or plastered, so *tipsy* is one's best bet. Blyth might have put into his translation or explained that Shokusanjin plays with Japanese folk wisdom, knowing it was not necessarily Chinese. In Japan, one cannot mention *bamboo grove* without being asked about the (stripe-legged, so big they clunk when they fall to the *tatami*) *bush mosquitoes,* or vice versa). This is not hearsay. I lived for a decade surrounded on three sides by a bamboo grove. The sages are there because the many joints symbolize longevity and they are also considered a cool place. In other words, it is not just that the sages, being tipsy do not sense they are being eaten alive, but that these wise men did not even know such common folk wisdom. Even the grammar is such to emphasize "they don't even know *that.* Blyth unerringly picks good poems, but his mind sometimes soars over the commonplace elements in the mad poem wit. Still, I sure wish he chose and translated more of it. I had thought to save the above poem for a forthcoming book on/of mosquito haiku (living with cats and no screens, for decades, I have great experience with them and hundreds of haiku of them), but seeing Blyth did it, had to put in my two-bits.

Play Pictures and Play Words, or Illuminated Kyôka 306 頁

♪ **Kyôka in Asobie**. I found all the poems featured in this chapter in *Edo no Asobie*, a book of "play pictures" mostly 18 or 19c (江戸の遊び絵: 稲垣進一 1988). While many but not all of the poems in the pictures are put into print – I am grateful, for the script is hard for me to make out, & as the editor states up front, *pictures were given priority*. Were I to see entire picture-books and make my own selections based upon the quality of the poems, the poems, which I had better add, most play-pictures do *not* have, would improve. The poems with pictures first selected for pictorial significance and quality span two continuums: from 31 syllabets more prosaic than most prose to the poetic, and from hard-to-decipher dense kernels of information to the utterly nonsensical.

♪ **Plainest Poem. Or, not all Asobie poems are Kyôka.** Here, for reference, is the plainest of the 31 syllabet poems: *Blessed be, celebrate! Having seven fu items all together / Is a sign that you will gain good fortune!* うけいわひ七ふの品を揃へてハ 大き福を得る *uke iwai . . .* (by Hiroshige II pic.) The initial word *uke* means to receive something as a blessing and puns on *float*, normally more likely to have blue nuances (in the *uki* form) but, here, with a *funa* (usually *buna*, a big fish) and *fukuro*=bag rising up into a pale white-red (auspicious) sky above the other five *fu* objects, a brush=*fude*, spray of wisteria=*fuji*, a gourd=*fukube*, a scroll of writing=*fumi* and a flute=*fue*.

♪ **An Attractive Fu (Good Luck) Poem, though I Cannot Read it.** What bids to become my favorite *fu* poem has a character not only I, but the editor could not read, so I left it out of the text. ふく／＼とふく女ふき出すさゝきげん ＿能筆のふえるふづくし 宝来舎述 (*fukufuku to fukume fukidasu sasa-kigen ＿yoki fude no fueru fu-zukushi* horai? c.1850. The artist, Kuniyoshi, used only the *hiragana* letter ふ=*fu* to draw Otafuku. Since good luck allowed one to become fat, I would guess the contrary was also thought likely. My 2000-page Kenkyûsha's E-J dictionary could only find room to tells us *otafuku* means a "plain looking" or "homely woman," i.e., "a fright," neglecting to mention such a woman was always chubby, with especially big cheeks (on her face) and more importantly that her name literally translates as "honorable-much-fortune." This matters, not knowing the literal meaning of her name, one who did not know her symbolic or ritual usage might feel as mystified to see this pudgy almost toad-like woman hanging on the wall, as Chinese and Japanese were in the 16c when they were horrified by pictures of a man with a look of intense suffering nailed up to a cross and bleeding and wondered what god-awful sadists these foreigners were to gaze affectionately on *that*. I can believe there are those who would gaze upon the "passion" of Christ and that someone who believed in charm, by which I mean sympathetic magic, might not only paste up a charm picture but even chose to sleep with a bountiful Otafuku at the start of each year, but that is just a guess . . . The poem plays on *fukufuku* as *fortunately/bulging/snorting* and liquids being gulped or sloshed about, the last likely after she *fukidasu* bursts-out or bubbles over, laughter and, perhaps, also her ample flesh from her robe. Followed by *sasakigen,* or her "drinking-limit," we also wonder if she *spews* or . . . and, then, the unreadable character before we learn this *"fu* list" has grown with a __ good brush=*fu*de. 蛇足：さかづきおう けたおたふく ＝題。

♪ ***Visual Lampoon Pun.*** *Asobie* included anonymous lampoons that, like the 31-syllabet *rakushu,* often include a comic punning element. My favorite, dated to 1853, is poemless as far as I can tell (the reproduction is small). It is built around a pun worse/better than anything I have seen in a *kyôka* or, for that matter, Thomas Hood (see *A Dolphin In the Woods*: 2009). *Fugu* ふぐ, or globe-fish, becomes *bugu* ぶぐ, *arms*. Decked out in military and Hachiman Shinto regalia it churns up the sea, while a foreign "black-boat" is shown fleeing with four seamen puking over the side, from eating of the poison fish. The editor forgot to tell readers (99.9% of Japanese today do not know) that the fish was also called a *teppô*, or gun, because it was lethal if you were hit=poisoned (the same *ateru/atari*). As the type of humor found in *asobie* with messages and *kyôka* are similar, it would be fun to do a book combining them.

♪ ***More Fire-stopping Background****.* The ethno-historical roots of anything where Hitomaro/u is involved are countless. The temples being hotspots of literacy it was only natural for the famous poet to be considered an avatar of Buddha. If the following Chinese-style poem is by Hakuin 白隠, who also related the famous *waka* to the apotheosis of its author, something I find amusing as other glosses make the Akashi Ura poem itself a cryptic catechism

身　化　何　神　明　道　歌
神　仏　薩　明　菩　非　是
霧　朝　浦　石　明　今　到
人　其　無　船　有　嶋　有

OUR GOD OF WAKA WAS REBORN
AS THE BUDDHA ON THAT MORN
FOG LIFTS ISLAND IS STILL THERE
BUT THE BOAT OF MAN WAS BARE!

The original AABA rhyme and lines, especially the last line (are *islands* is boat not that person), beat mine – and include the name Akashi Ura – but it is hard to be rectangular in translation. On the folk side, one hypothesis connects Hitomaro/u with safe births through a connection between *menses* and *fire*, the stopping of which was what pregnancy was all about (a miscarriage would have it going again). I am unsure if Hannya-bô's earlier poem intends to invoke Hitomaro and welcome a more thorough study for the notes of a future edition. It was alleged to have been sung-out as a fire came to the monk's house. In Japan, where wooden houses and dry winters invited urban conflagration, people squatted on their roofs, waving off the sparks with big fans while singing out spells to ward off the flames (See item #14-3 in *Topsy-turvy 1585* (2004) for more).

♪ ***People Made By and Making People.*** I first thought the poem was a *kyôka* by the artist, Kuniyoshi, for there was no indication otherwise in *Edo Asobie*. That might have been because the editor knew 99% of his readers knew it as Kobo Daishi's, which made it over 1000 years older! (Kobo Daishi, also known as Kûkai, is credited with inventing the Syllabet Song, unlike our Alphabet Song, a real poem (about transience), in 776. It was translated into a European language by Rodriguez c.1600, but, oddly enough, is left out of all the anthologies of Japanese literature I have seen . . . .) I was *lucky* not to know the *people make/made poem*, for when I googled for it I found lists of tricky-to-pronounce or hyperlogical poems. It was between the two following poems in a list of 比較的知られている教訓歌, or comparatively well-known didactic poems, *kyôkunka* (あっ！「狂訓歌」を探してみよう。もしもなければ創ってみるしかない！).

なせばなるなさねばならぬ何事もならぬは人のなさぬなりけり
naseba naru nasaneba naranu nanigoto mo naranu wa hito no nasanu narikeri
doing-when becomes, do not if/when becomes-not: any(no)thing becomes-not-as-for,
person(someone)'s doing-not becomes (is the reason for it)

*What's done becomes, what isn't doesn't, & whatever doesn't
doesn't become because (who knew it!) someone doesn't do it.*
~~~~~~
*What is done becomes, what is not does not because someone
does not do it, it becomes something that does not become*
~~~~~~
*What is done will be, what is not will not and all because someone
does not do it, something becomes something that doesn't become.*

人の非は非とぞにくみて非とすれど我が非は非とぞ知れど非とせず
hito no hi wa hi to zo nikumite hi to suredo waga hi wa hi to zo shiredo hi to sezu
persons=other's/s' wrong-as-for hating wrong-as do(think) but
my wrong-as-for wrong-as knowing-but wrong-as do(think)-not

*When they are wrong, they are not just wrong but, hatefully so. No, wait
A minute! There is nothing wrong about being wrong when we are in it.*

Elsewhere on the list, I was surprised to find one by the head of the Grand Shrine of Ise whose haiku often head haikai anthologies, Moritake:

世の中にかくべきものは かかずして事をかくなり恥をかくなり　荒木田守武
yononaka ni kaku beki mono wa kakazu shite koto o kaku nari haji o kaku nari moritake
world-within such ought thing/s-as-for lack-not lack-being shameful becomes shame making (?)

*In this world, some things we ought not lack we do for lack of
doing things we ought and so we ought to be ashamed for naught.*

The puns on *kaku* almost lost me, or *maybe they did*. So I hope my English using that word not found in colloquial Japanese, *naught (nothing)* equally loses yet pleases you. Danish Poet Piet Hein has a positive version of this poem that is the better conceptual *kyôka*, for working well with less tricks. This is credited to the Shintô priest sometimes considered the first father of haiku but who knows. I am confused because it appears in Anrakuan's *Laughs to Banish Sleep* (1623) as Chikamasa's, with but one change, the first *kaku*, which I guess was intended to mean *such-and-such,* is written 書く which means "write." That makes it a parody. Anrakuan's comic stories include fiction so he probably made that change. But Chikamasa died before Moritake was born, and when you consider that stories try to contain as much truth as possible to make the fiction plausible, . . .

~~~~~~

Wacky Waka Twisting Tongues & Crossing Sashes　　　　　　　　　308 頁

This chapter was placed here (pg.308) because the material for it was found checking up on a poem with a picture in the previous chapter. The visuality? of written Japanese indirectly relates to the highly intellectual and rich imagery of picture-play and this is brought out by the way the *Manyôshû* tongue-twister was written.

~~~~~~

Wishing for nothing, or, nothing to wish for.　　　　　　　　　310 頁

♪ **Danish poet Piet Hein's grook about the universe is titled** NOTHING IS INDISPENSABLE, and subtitled *"Grook to warn the universe against megalomania."* If Japanese mad poems become popular, I would espect a Piet Hein revival. If Shokusanjin is the Fool mad-poet exemplar, then Piet Hein is the Wiseman mad-poet exemplar.

♪Monk Sôgi (1420-1502) whose haiku were more interesting than most people know (see *Cherry Blossom Epiphany* for scores of them), has what I *thought* an uninteresting *kyôka (?)* in the *Savage Songs* of 1666 (古今夷曲集): 物毎にたらぬ／＼と思ふこそ　まよふ心のつくり病ひよ　宗祇　*monogoto ni taranu taranu to omou koso madou kokoro no tsukuri-yamai yo*. But, as I typed I realized it *is* interesting. As true for his *ku*, Sôgi's wit is so elegantly understated we tend to read right past it! I *just* realized that applying *tsukuri-yamai* or, "made-up illness" to something that is not a physical complaint is witty.

Thinking whatever we come across is never enough
Hypochondria of the heart always finds life tough!

Tsukuriyamai is a feigned disease, but here I feel it means *made-up* in the sense of artificial. "Hypochondria" was the best I could do. Another try: *Thinking you don't have enough is a sickness born of the mind / Wandering lost makes you miss all the things you want to find* – keeps the "wandering lost (*madou*)," but loses the poetry. I must try again another time, another book. The sweet *"yo"* assertion is also lost in translation.

~~~~~~

One Almost Flew Over the Cuckoo's Nest: Sanekata, Casanova I　　312頁

♪**One More Spider *Kyôka*.** 800 years later, Getsudôken would provide new angles on a number of Sanekata's more salient metaphors for the romantic, or if you prefer, salacious. One, their common Iris Wife in the Eaves, will be in the Getsudôken chapters. The *spider*, also held in common, did not fit. So here it is:

間男がくべき宵とて背戸にゆき いたづらおかた蜘の巣をとる　月洞軒　大団
maotoko ga kubeki yoi tote seto ni yuki itazura okata kumo no su o toru　Getsudôken
male-lover/gigolo comes-ought-evening because, backdoor-to going
prank-loving-palace-lady spider-web+acc. removes

That night a lover?
Out the backdoor this joking lady heads
to carefully remove all of her rival's spider webs!

Rather than purloining the message, cut the telegraph lines. Nothing is said about a rival.

♪ **An Iris Bonus a bit beyond me from 1312.** あつまやの－のきはにねさせ－あやめくさ－うゑぬしのふも－おひすやはあらぬ My respondent guesses it is this: 「四阿の軒端に根差せ菖蒲草植ゑ主伸ぶも生ひずやはあらぬ」but I am still unsure what it means. I only know that one writing of Azumaya puns on wife: 吾妻 and I sense a possible allegory. And here is one more by no other than retired Emperor Go Toba: わかこひは－ひとしらぬまの－あやめくさ－あやめぬほとそ－ねをもしのひし 後鳥羽院宮内卿　*waga koi wa hito shiranu ma no ayamegusa ayamenu hodo zo ne o mo shinobishi* My respondent writes,「菖蒲草」で「あや」「ね」に係る枕詞とあります。そこまでは OK ですが、「怪めぬ」＝人が不審がらない程度に泣き声あるいはおしゃべりを、あるいは天皇だったから、夜這いは女の方からで。。。忍んだ、とは？ I think Go Toba is allegorically praising a lover in the same palace for being secretive about their affair, but who knows.

~~~~~~

One Almost Flew Over the Cuckoo's Nest: Sanekata, Casanova II　　314頁

Sanekata's Portal of Heaven *Kyôka* (*imo to neba iwato no sora mo sashikumori sono yo bakari wa akezu mo aramu* pg. 315). If you recall, it is a brilliant poem of the joys of a night of love-making where the poet could never get enough. I confess that it took me quite a while to figure out the poem, if, that is, I did. The website translation was: *"The portal of Heaven, / For my sake was / Shut not, yet - / How strange - endlessly for it to open not / Is all of my longing..."* That makes *no sense* whatsoever! Reading it (and all too many other such, the likes of which I find in *most* books of translation from the original) evoked my usual response to things that should not be: *didactic doggerel.*

> *Translation is funny:* U need
> not always be on the money;
> but unless you are set on *wit,*
> all too often, *U won't get it!*

It is understandable that translators, who on the whole represent those the Bible claims will inherit the earth, often settle for meaningless "direct" translation. To *get something,* which is to say get it *right,* often means *guessing* and one is more likely to be criticized for getting something *wrong* than for *not getting it.* So, the meek pragmatist just translates what seems to be on the page without daring to divine the reading between the lines, which is, in most cases, what the lines are there for! We hear a lot about *poetry* lost in translation, but what about *ideas?* Without them, why the hell do we *need* poetry when one amplified variable tension piano-wire or well-cut piece of bamboo can produce better aural stimulation than all the poems that have ever been read?

~~~~~~

Ye Olde & Now Savage Songs, or Mad in 1666 – all chapters.   316 頁

♪ **I am unsure about that "Didyahear? Didyahear?"** following the cuckoo call the poet did not expect. I translated as if the cuckoo's call (often called "one-voice," *hitogoe*) sounded like that. Making the cuckoo seem as contrary as another animal we know, the cat, works, but had the transcription used phonetic syllabary and left *hito* ambiguous, rather than clarifying it as "one," we might imagine other people in the house who *had* thought the cuckoo would call soon calling out the same in unison. I was unsure of Sôhô's cuckoo (*yarumai zo yarumai mono o hototogisu kiita ka kiita ka ima no hitogoe*) and chose the one of two readings that seemed most fun to read. Another, where the bird's voice seems to say "heard?" "heard?" is just as likely –

> *"No, he won't! No way!" said I; but, then, of course, Cuckoo!*
> *"Didyahear? Didyahear?"– Or, in a word, 'Fooled you!'*

♪ **Ivy⇒Lacquer Maples?** The leaves of the maple are lustrous as well as red, but readers unfamiliar with *Japanning,* as it was called, should know the reddish-orange and black lacquerware is made from ivy, the sap of which is poison. I made the "ivy-maple" a lacquer one because I had no room to explain in the text.

♪ **The Uguisu's Song. One More.** There was another *kyôka* more interesting than Teitoku's, but I was too unsure about its meaning to main-text it.

ほそ／＼と鳴鶯の初音には朝とうまるも及はさりけり 行安 古今夷曲集
hosoboso to naku uguisu no hatsune ni wa asa to umaru mo oyobazarikeri kôan 1666
finely/thinly sings warbler's first-sound-in-as-for morning-with-born even matches-not!

> *The first songs of our Uguisu are so delicate a thing*
> *Confucius sounds crude with 'Born in the morning ~'*

That is, I guess, the delicacy of the wavering beauty of the first voice of the bird announcing the morning of the year is compared to that of the proverbial transience of the Morning Glory (in a well-known saying of Confucius). I could be wrong. Anyone?

~~~~~~

A Dandelion Break. 1636, *Shokusanjin, Issa, Nenten.*   320 頁

Pursuing that Popo in the Tanpopo. With so little information ruled out by a short poem, reading is largely interpretation and a critical understanding of its significance should start with *a survey of readers* to know how it is read. For a better idea of what I mean, see my survey of Buson's poem about two houses by a river (so far, only on the web, eventually in a book-to-be called *HIC,* or *Haiku In Context*). Or, is someone already doing something like this ↓ for Nenten's enigmatic dandelion?

たんぽぽにどこがぽぽかと聞いてみる　樽坊
tanpopo ni doko ga popo ka to kiite-miru　tarubô

I try asking
a *tanpopo* just where
its *popo* is.

I try asking
which part's the *popo*
of a *tanpopo*.

This *ku* was rejected by the *Mainichi Shinbun* Bannô Senryû contest. Grammar *favors* the first reading but allows for the second more relevant reading, where other people are asked. I think the poem is a *kyôku* rather than a *senryû*, as I feel many of Nenten's haiku are better called *kyôku*. Be that as it may, Nenten, like the author of "The Purple Cow," tired of being asked about his ditty, composed a follow-up, himself:

たんぽぽのぽぽのその後は知りません　坪内稔典
tanpopo no popo no sonogo wa shirimasen　nenten

As to what follows
the tanpopo's popo, *that*
I do not know!

~~~~~~

Savage Song Mistakes: On Gathering Gays, Keeping Corn　　328頁

Kôfû's Waka at the End. On deeper thought, I am unsure if *blooming* (先・咲き) was seriously intended to be punned in a sort of epithet for the *falling*. On the main text, I made the (cherry) blossoms *bloom* as well as fall – a more active "scatter" is called for, but too active for a plant without exploding seed pods in English. If the metaphor is one of *cheering on*, sticking to the confetti-like *falling* alone might work better. So, here are a few more translations.

<div align="center">
REPEAT 入相の鐘よりさきもちりぬめり 花やあたなる世をいさむらん
iriai no kane yori saki mo chirinumeri hana ya adanaru yo o isamuran　kôfû 1666
dusk bell-from after=bloom evn fallng, (cherry)blossm/s!/: false/vain-world encourages

*After vespers, still they fall because keeping up the esprit de corps
of this false world of ours is what blossoms live & die for.*
~~~~~~
*After vespers, still they fall, cherry blossoms have no fear;
In a world of vanity we ought to thank them for the cheer!*
~~~~~~
*After vespers, still they fall, these blossoms full of cheer;
In a world of vanity we need confetti right here!*
</div>

I find this poem interesting enough to translate many times because blossoms falling generally become examples of nonattachment, *gracefully* letting go of this vain world; so, having their falling evaluated in this way, while expressed in a smooth *waka* style, is still pretty mad. The verb *isamuru* suggests the bloom has the frisky spirit of spring colts!

~~~~~~

Savage Song 1666 Revisited – or, some Additional Notes for no chapter.

♪ Discoveries made in 古今夷曲集 *Kokin Ikyoku-shû*. On rereading this book, not only did I find some more good poems, both of a "savage" and gentle nature by my haikai-era first-wave *kyôka* favorites (Yûchôrô and Teitoku), but far more *moral* and otherwise didactic poems than I anticipated. While the Buddhism (*shakkyô*) section remains even in Tenmei *kyôka* anthologies, there are less of them and less otherwise moral or mock-moral poems than found in 1666. In other words, 17c *kyôka* seems to have been a catchbag for a greater variety of 31-syllabet poetry than found before or after. I also discovered a poet whose work I already knew, but had not seen enough of to catch my attention, Mitoku 未得(1588-1669). His *kyôka* are simultaneously convoluted yet seem simple if only they could be grasped. When I try to read 物毎にあらばありのみなしとても 求めはせじな世はなり次第 未得 *monogoto ni araba ari nomi nashi totemo motomeba sejina yo wa nari-shidai,* I imagine a native speaker of Japanese trying to read Donne at his best/worse. This one is, at the moment, but I hope not forever, beyond me. Sometimes, he achieves a grace reminiscence of Teitoku's sweet *tanka*-like *kyôka*:

茶をのめばねられぬ老の初むかし 大むかしまで思ふ夜すがら 未得
cha o nomeba nerarenu oi no hatsumukashi ômukashi made omou yo-sugara mitoku
tea+acc drink-when sleep-cannot oldage's first-past, bigpast-until think night-through

When you drink tea and cannot sleep, you first recall the past,
Then, staying up, you're long ago and far away at last.

The original's *"hatsu-mukashi"* or "first long-ago" in *haikai* generally applies to the old year or things from it first encountered or thought of in the new year, but here applies to that only allusively, for it is first of all the term for the first sencha – tea leaves that have been dried to obtain flavors not quite like the fresh leaves (not "second rate" as my J-E dictionary claims) that were first drunken in the 3rd month, 21st day. Mitoku uses it in a new and beautiful way I could not exactly capture in translation so I borrowed the title of W.H. Hudson's autobiography – and, maybe, reversed the order – though we are not talking about drinking *yerba mate* from a silver gourd. A simpler poem from the same collection, by Shinkai (teacher of Teiryû & Getsudôken) discovers a new and convincing use of, or definition for, "first-long-ago." Someone who died yesterday and was put into a pot and buried become "first old-times/past today" きのふ死んで壺に入たる亡者こそ 今日は初昔なれ 信海 *kinô shinde tsubo ni iretaru môja koso kyô wa hatsu-mukashi nare*). I hope to find an anthology of Mitoku's work some day (Oops! See additions from 吾吟我集 pg.613-17). Reading becomes much easier when one becomes familiar with a poet.

♪ *Meta-mad, or, Poems about Poetry.* I wrote there were many in this anthology, but the 1672 follow-up has *more,* literally *by the score* (half-a-dozen mention scoring in *haikai*). Unfortunately for this book, but fortunately for the translator, they are so arcane for those not doing the poetry that he felt no compunction to introduce them. If you like to read poets treating poetry, go to Gutenberg and look at the exchange between The Dean (Swift), Dr. Sheridan and a Preacher Dan. Here are a couple couplets from Swift to Sheridan "Upon His Verses Written in Circles" – *"But now for your verses; we tell you, _imprimis_, /The segment so large 'twixt your reason and rhyme is, / That we walk all about, like a horse in a pound, / And, before we find either, our noddles turn round."* Most of the fun might be comprehensible to Japanese poets, though the diversity of poetic form and the ferociousness of 'our' *ad hominems* would astound them. Here is the last stanza of a rejoinder by Sheridan to Swift: *"I'll write while I have half an eye in my head; / I'll write while I live, and I'll write when you're dead. / Though you call me a goose, you pitiful slave, / I'll feed on the grass that grows on your grave."* (Not long before Sheridan had eye problems, which their circle related to his single versus double rhymes, etc..). If you wish, you may call Japanese poets lacking in strong emotions – the sort that rages in opera – I prefer to think of them as less juvenile (Of course this is stereotyping, hence *unfair,* but read Mendez Pinto's *Peregrinations* to see how not only Jesuits but an adventurer already had Occidentals, himself included, pegged as such in the 16c!).

~~~~~~

Getsudôken 1 – a free-style kyôka master in the era of Bashô.   330 頁

♪*Tear Pole Grammar.* Why *hodo na* rather than the usual *hodo*? An explanation is at the end of this chapter note as it will not interest most readers. ♪**Using or Not Using a Pole to Carry Love's Burden**. Some day I may trace the metaphorical pole in Japanese love-related poetry. For here, let me mention two antecedents of Getsudôken's lachrymal pole. First, we have *Kokinshû's* poem #1058, a *haikai* type that is a *kyôka* in every way:

人こふる事をおもにとになひもてあふごなきこそわびしかりけれ
hito kouru koto o omoni to ninaimote augo naki koso wabishikarikere anon
person yearn-4 thing+acc weight-as carry/shouldrng meet=crryngpole-not esp. miserble

I carried the burden of my yearning for him, a girl without a pole.
It's hard to bear the wait, alone, when someone does not show!

There are many slightly different variations of this poem suggesting it arose from folksong, but the one pun *carrying-pole = augo = rendezvous* is what makes it work. I substituted a *weight=wait* pun, and pretended all my readers knew that women commonly carried water two pails at a time using poles (see *Topsy-turvy* 1585 (2004) item #2-59). Otherwise, I might have had to translate the originally genderless poem as R&H did: *"his yearning love he / bears like a heavy burden / on his shoulders like / a porter without a pole — / no meeting eases his lot."* Actually, I also wanted a poleless *girl* for an obvious reason. It so happens that in the 1679 *Silver Leaf Savage Songs* (銀葉夷歌集 tk1), where we find poems by his teacher Shinkai, we find a *kyôka* pole-bearing love as well!

捨られぬ衆道女道をになひなは　恋の重荷に棒やおれなん　春澄
suterarenu shudô nyodô o ninahinaba koi no omoni ni bô ya orenan shunjô

~~*If you must bear the burden of loving boys and women*~~
~~*Break it off, break the pole which makes you carry them!*~~

If you can give up neither your longing for boys nor for women
Love's twin burden will break the pole by which you carry them!

While a phallic undertone is to some degree unavoidable, misreading the obsolete grammar (sure *looked* imperative) side-tracked my first translation and explanation (~~Unlike China and Italy, Japan was not big on eunuch culture, and almost never went all the way, as Chinese did, by removing the "pole" as well! But, as you can read in my book of dirty senryû, there was *one* example of it and some poets did consider how it affected urination., but one does not speak of breaking off a *pole* from a tree. So, my second, phallic reading stands. Getsudôken who did not wish to be a monk, kept *that* pole, but admitting that love was not free, let his tears as poles bear his burden. Viewed that way, his tears are as *manly* as those coursing down the faces of the macho fools engaged in chili-eating contests, as described in exquisite *poro-poro* mimetic detail by Issa~~).

♪ ***Wild Pink in translation.*** If you immediately thought I should have managed to fit "tickled pink" into the translation or text and have the leisure to work for free, please feel free to be my editor! ♪ ***Ahaha(n).*** Do you find the *ahaha(n)* laughing-as-sex idea odd? Just look at the nonsensical tails (*Nay, Pish! nay fye, You tickle mee! / Fa la la* etc.) on the refrains of many bawdy English ballads – the original slap-stick?) and something similar should tickle your fancy. Unfortunately, the OJD fails to give that definition for *Ahaha*, but only gives it as 1) laughing, and 2) laughing in a particularly mindless way as a dimwit might for nothing in particular. – Well, *hey, nonney, nonney, honey!* ★ 程な？（棒ほどな涙ながして〜）。単に「程の」の誤植かとおもって、歌人・狂歌研究家の吉岡生夫氏（本書の所謂 respondent）に訊いてみたところ、たぶん、その「な」が「の」の誤植ではなく：「《格助詞「に」の音変化。上代東国方言》時間・場所を表す。に。」但し、氏はつづく、別な辞典では「な」が上代語で「限られた語の中にみられるだけである」が「名詞を受け、それが下の名詞に連体修飾語として続くことを示す。格助詞「の」「が」「つ」と同じ用法のもの。」文法音痴の小生の意見に価値もないが、吉岡氏の結論に納得：「しかし歌の解釈では最初の「に」の方言の方が良さそうに思います。ピカソの「泣く女」（？）を思い出しました。」

Getsudôken 2 – Some tanka, or soft-boiled kyôka.

♪ ***The Hare in the Moon.*** Sorry to wander from Getsudôken's *kyôka* about the moon *as* hare, but the English language culture has *a moon-recognition problem*; and, here is as good of a place as any to give my two-bits of advice. I vaguely recall making out the face of the man in the moon but, honestly, it made no lasting impression on me. *Am I alone?* I would guess not. Only avid astronomers recognize the different "face" of the moon at different hours in Usania. But *almost as soon as I learned Japanese and, with it, of the hare, I became able to recognize the hour of the night from any photograph of the moon that referenced the landscape or was assumed to be rightside-up*. Those big ears are so clear to see they can serve for the hour-hand of a clock. *Our culture needs to be re-educated about the moon*. I hope some day to find a *kyôka* giving that hare detailed attention, but in the Sinosphere it is taken for granted. So, I'll do it myself:

耳に立つ白き兎ぞ見たければ　朝まで飲んで見な満月を　敬愚

Have you never seen a hare walk on its ears? Drink until dawn
On a full moon night, look up, and you will before long!

Getsudôken 3 – *A jacking-off bird?*　　　　　　　　　　　　334 頁

♪ **Liquid or gurgling uguisu**. I wish I had a good word for euphonious gurgling. A glissando that softly bubbles? A barely nascent yodel? Aston in his *History of Japanese Literature* (1899) shows that he has heard an *uguisu* in its warm-up period when he writes: "The repertory of the *uguisu* is by no means so varied as that of the nightingale, but *for liquid melody of note* it is unsurpassed by any songster whatever." While Getsudôken was right to hear the sound as wet, it is, in my opinion, also a clean one, and only a hell of a lot of sex on the mind would allow one to hear it differently.

Getsudôken 4 – *The spirit of casual kyôka!*　　　　　　　　　336 頁

♪ ***Private Parts as No Big Thing.*** On Jan.21, 1857, Heusken the brilliant polymath and young man of culture told the American Counsel General Townsend Harris (who put it in his diary) that he was received cordially at a Japanese house and in the presence of *"the mother, wife and daughter"* of his host, *"the man opened his dress and taking his privities in his hand – in sight of all the females – asked the names of the various parts in English."* Japanese acquaintances find this hard to believe, but I have read enough by Heusken and his translator and friend Townsend Harris to know they are trustworthy and I put this here to stress that the introduction of "privities" in the fire aftermath poem does not only does not make it dirty, but would not qualify it as bawdy by the Japanese standards of that day. It would just not be the sort of detail noted in *waka*.

♪ ***The Door-to-Door Ant Path.*** Readers will have to teach me the proper English term for it, unless like the clitoris, it has been ignored, and a medical term, say Latin for "God's last stitches" or, the "Hole-to-Hole seam." I tried my Japanese-English dictionary (Kenkyûsha's), but nothing was between *Arinomi* and *Arinsan*. The latter, though it sounds like Yoshiwara-speak, is *phosphoric acid*, something one expects to find in a dictionary. The former is an elegant word for the pear, which translates as "the fruit of being/having." Why? Because ordinarily it is called a *nashi,* which sounds like "nothing!" (Lest I contradict something I pointed out elsewhere: *nashi*, as *nothing* is used in the context of a reply and is not a general word for it). If English speakers were as pun-fearing souls as the Japanese, upper-class hunters would have to hunt fair rather than fowl, and so forth. For the record, I have come across that *arinotowatari* perineal path a score of times, yet this was my first encounter with the *arinomi* pear. That tells us something about dictionaries, does it not? ♪ ***The Ant-Gate-Crossing a Mistranslation?*** While the phrase is certain, there is a good chance my sexy reading of Getsudôken's friend 自剃 Jizori's *waga-ue no tsuyu* poem is wrong and the *kari* is no glans and just the geese with the ant's/s' pegged on for good measure. To atone for my miss, if it was a miss, here is the stunning goose-tear panorama by Tameie that Jizori played with: 民部爵為家 for Japanese readers: あまのかは とわたるかりの なみたとや もみちのはしも いろにいつらむ (*amanogawa towataru kari no namida . . .* 夫木 pre-1310)

Getsudôken 5 – Fuji, mountain of mad metaphor   338頁

♪ **The Fuji that Almost Got Away.** Another last minute find – and a later last edit to shorten half a page on computer problems which left me unable to access my e-mail with an unread letter re. surimono for which I was delaying publication. Let me just say that I am one of the calmest most patient people in the world about almost anything. Letting the crap of the world that others call life go by is what allows me to do big books alone. Only computer problems ultimately born of the greed of billion-dollar corporations that force one to fiddle around and lose time better spent on productive work get my goat. It does not help being utterly helpless – remember, I am stuck out in the woods. Too furious to need coffee, I skipped it and went right to my second medicine, red wine and decided to dip back into a *kyôka* anthology of 50 poems, 1 each by 50 poets, I think the best selection published, 狂歌五十人一首 (17c? 18c?), and see if I missed anything good and there it was, yet another Getsudôken Fuji:

煙たつふじに雲の手ひつかけて　自ざい天からつり釜にこそ　玉雲軒月洞 (sic)
kemuri tatsu fuji ni kumo no te hikakkete jizai ten kara tsuri kama ni koso   Getsudôken
smoke-rising fuji-to/w/ cloud/s-hand/s catchng freely heavn-frm danglng kettle-as+emph

> *Hand-like clouds reach out and taking hold of smoking Fuji, why,*
> *they hang it like a cooking pot from an unseen hook up in the sky!*

> *Clouds reach out, take hold of steamy Fuji, so it hangs down*
> *From heaven like a kettle, in the air above the ground.*

I suspect the second reading with unmentioned cloud-hands (standard metaphor, not invented by the poet) themselves supporting the smoking/steaming kettle is more likely than the hyper-active first reading. Either way, Fuji's tip, often seen when its skirts vanish in the air was a phenomenon awaiting a good metaphor. Burning mugwort would be the most common one in haikai, but I cannot recall reading this one elsewhere.

♪ **How the Salt-ass Fuji Went over & a Possible Progeny.** Getsudôken sent his outrageous poem to a high-ranking nobleman and the reply seems to have been a mixed review: it might be tasty for someone who had a pickled butt, *but* . . . (其阿上人へ富士の歌を見せて・塩漬をしつけた人にしほ加減　あぢはひさせん　しほ尻の歌　*shiozuke o shitsuketa hito ni shio kagen ajiwai sasen shiojiri no uta* ＃1442 因みに、「大団」の次の歌は、「市川伝六礼に来りしに「男いちかはゆらしきが部屋に居て　尻しよとよべばなぜに出ぬ六」 *otoko ichi kawayurashiki ga* . . .   I am not sure I got it but did not want to bother my respondent with such a saucy exchange. I look forward to being corrected by my betters in reading. And right after the kettle Fuji found because my pc let me down, there was a great drinking poem by one whose name was Wineheart 酒心:

夏の夜はまだよひながら覚めにけり　はらのいづこに酒やどるらん　酒心
natsu no yo wa mada yoi nagara samenikeri hara no izuko ni sake yadoruran   shûshin
smmr-nght-as4 still evnng=drunk(hangovr) while awakn+emph. belly=field where sake lodges?

Hangover Season

> *A summer night, one awakens so quickly dawn seems like twilight –*
> *Where in my windy guts did Wine find an inn to stay the night?*

The pun on evening and drunk *in the original* is superb and the perfect demonstration of how a pun makes rather than opposes conceptual humor. There is no "windy," but guts, *hara*, is a homophone for *moor* or *field* (I imagine the vast Musashino). This Wine or Sake-heart is yet another poet I would like to check out further but have not.

♪ **The Fuji Fallacy.** Likening the mountain to a hat so narrow and tall that it could be used to censor an erection is ridiculous, but as odd as it may seem, such was not *hyperbole* but *perception* in Japan. Mystified by the absurdly steep inclination of the slopes of Fuji found in the illustrations he encountered in the late-19c, Morse (*Japan Day by Day*), carried out a pictorial survey by having Japanese draw the silhouette of the mountain as they actually recalled it, and found they tended to make it much, sometimes several times, steeper than it was in reality.

Getsudôken W-extra – so many wakashu I marked the poems "W." 340 頁

♪ **Close-up of Balls.** Balls, especially human ones, are gross yet plaintive. 居士 Shiki 子規 has a whole series on his hot and sweaty summer balls that convey his bed-ridden years like no other *ku* (see the *Balls* ch. in *The Woman Without a Hole*: 2007).

♪ ***The Kyôka journal Ôuchiwa*** 大団***, or Big Fan, as a sensitive document of early Edo era sexual life.*** Someone interested in these things should go over Getsudôken's poems more slowly than I have. It would be interesting to find out more about Fukuyama Jizori, for Getsudôken clearly regarded him as the coolest person in the world, though I cannot for the life of me figure out why that has him born from the crotch of a transplanted plant: 自剃元?うへ木のまたからうまれたか　本来いかにおしゃれふく山 *jizori?* . . .). There are also poems referring to third parties that are hard for me to fully grasp. For example,

> Again, to Jizori. . . . . . As it is written in the dirty picture book of Seishônagon, it is worthless to laugh at someone for being erect as a piece of wood and not knowing the way of women (*i.e.,* fucking them).

又自剃かたへ　若衆ずきする法師斗うら山しからぬものはあらじまたには木のはしのやうにをやしても女の道をしらぬと人にはわらはれ何のゑきなきものとせいしやなごんがまくら絵のうちに書しを思召やられよとて。

うら山しからぬ法師の若衆ずき　たゞ木のはしのかたひものずき　月洞幹
*urayama*shikaranu *hôshi no wakashuzuki tada no ki no hashi no katai monozuki*
jealous=back-mtn=not priest's yungcrowd-liking just stick-edge-hardthngs liker

> *No one to envy, that wakashu-loving priest up in the hills.*
> *He is just a callous man who clings to hard things.*

> *He just loves those insensible hard things (?)*

There are two major puns. 1) The temple is far from the city with its women, on the backside-of the mountain, and that "back-mountain (*urayama*)" allusion is punned into envying (*urayamashi*) which then is denied. 2) The "piece of a tree" is literally what the porn industry of Usania calls "wood" but idiomatically means "callous" or "unfeeling." I cannot tell if it is meant for the subject or the object and *also* may pun on *ki no bashi,* or psychological relief. I introduce it partly for the introduction. *Who knew?* A dirty parody of Sei Shônagon! I love her wise-ass– or Oscar Wilde – diva aesthetics (eg. it is sinful for a preacher to be ugly as people do not pay attention and risk sinning) and cannot wait to find and read that parody. The *Big Fan* also has poems explaining the choices the poet makes. Here, again, is a poem still beyond my grasp:

若衆こそいみじくなければかねもたば　よね衆に思月の洞めも　月洞幹
wakashu koso imijikunakereba kane motaba yoneshu ni omoi tsuki no horame mo
wakashu esp. excessively-not-if money have-not-if harlots-to longing/
think-of /tsuki=getsu's grotto/hora=dô+self-denigrative me even

> *Wakashu are fun, if not overdone – but moon grotto me,*
> *Lacking money, is thinking to taste a Tart for his honey!*

For this extremely tentative reading, the common word *wakashu* is set against the relatively rare *yoneshu*, women who sold their pleasures, and the moon in his name (*Getsu* in his name but pronounced *tsuki*, here) punned into the thought of buying the favors of the relatively cheaper women, followed by the second character of his name, the topographically low nature of which is accented with the self-demeaning *me* (Or alluding to poor prostitutes living in holes or his having a pock-marked face?). Getsudôken and his wife were from high-ranking samurai families, but did not have all that much money to spare. Affairs with youth and /or boys was considered the more proper and manly behavior for upper-class men (See *The Boor's Tale*, or *Denbu monogatari*, c.1640, in G. Leupp: *Male Colors* (U of Cal. P. 1995/97) for a fictional debate on the morality of loving *men* vs. *women*). I suspect some relationships may have even been of what we might call a domestic nature (eg. an effeminate distant boy relative who lives in to help-out with errands – something I observed in Mexico) rather than encounters when I read poems like 福山自亭へかく云やりける：長生の家に女と若衆置て　いく春祝へ老松ふぐり (*nagaiki no ie ni onna to wakashu oite . . .* Getsudôken) feting a retiree with his "old pine *cojones*" who left behind at home a long-lived woman, or women, and *wakashu*.

~~~~~~

Getsudôken W(omen)-extra II – Love & Libido – back to women.　　342 頁

♪ More **Nostril Hair.** **Again!?** I *know*. It was bad enough to have the man in the moon looking up our noses, but now rhetorically hitching a dragonfly to a star's nostril hair!? If you do not read a lot of Japanese, you may be surprised at its prevalence, and that among a people with nostrils so small the 16c Portuguese Jesuit Luis Frois observed Europeans to pick their noses with the index finger, while Japanese used their pinkies (for the other 610 contrasts, see *Topsy-turvy 1585* (2004)). But, Getsudôken was not through. Here is his most ridiculous nose-hair usage of all, though English cannot help *trunking* it.

其阿へ普賢の讃たのみけるに出来ざりければ　月洞軒 c.1700
法師にてふげんのきゃうかよみかねて　おもへばぞうの鼻毛也けり
hôshi nite fugen no kyôka yomikanete omoeba zô no hanage narikeri Getsudôken
priest-by/as samantabhadra's *kyôka* composng-cant think-whn elephnt's nosehair is+emph

When I could not comply with a request for a Eulogy of Samantabhadra for Goa,

*A mad poem about Sam's white elephant written for a monk
when I could only hope to count the hairs within its trunk?*

As to what this Buddha Elect was, various sects differed, but he is always depicted seated on a lotus dais carried by a huge and very intelligent looking white elephant. Getsudôken has humbly placed himself on the literally lowest level of understanding. So, on a slow reading the looking up the nose as abasement, it is not ridiculous at all. It is a very clever refusal of a difficult request. There is another clever *kyôka* playing on said white elephant's trunk in the 1785 *Tokuwa* anthology. Dropping the hair, it has the trunk/nose *hana* morph into (cherry) blossoms and pities Saigyô the great 12c cherry blossom lover for never having seen such, much less in the middle of the street. Said elephant was the name of a top courtesan who met Saigyô in a popular ballad and Edoites were quite proud of the annual parade of the top courtesans through the street　西行のおめかけたき普賢像はなの中よりはでな道中　浜邊黒人 *saigyô no omekaketaki fugenzô hana no naka yori hadena dôchû*　Hamabe no Kurohito. This white elephant was actually the name of a variety of flowering cherry and has a chapter to itself in the 3,000 haiku *Cherry Blossom Epiphany* (2007). ★ 鼻毛オマケ A poem we may title *The Cherry Host: "Looking way up high to the tip of the blooming limbs of the cherry; / What she sees, looking down, are his nose hairs, long as spring day* 桜さくこするゑをたかくふりあけて　みるは鼻毛のなかき春の日 花のあるじ *sakura saku kozue o . . .* 狂歌咄 1672

~~~~~~

One T's Kyôka ㊤ Dirty Bird, Raspy Heart & Cactus   344 頁

♪ ***Because this Book favors the Mad, I could not afford space for other 31-syllabet poems*** by Issa, but *tanka* lovers might note that Issa *also* wrote some poems that might be called *that*. Eg., these two by a young and happy Issa, *On the road, wheat mochi in the shade of a willow tree;/ In a different place, even the bells make me happy.* 旅めくや柳の かげの小麦餅　所かわれば鐘もうれしき　享和 3.11 (*tabimeku ya . . .*) *Threading a needle together, us two, without / early summer rain;/ Every other day setting off after a morning bath* 針の穴二人で通五月雨一日おきに朝風呂の立　同 2-170 (*hari no ana futari . . .*) . Or, this darker one, when he was having a rough time of it, *As if to say 'Hurry up and die! Die!' the damn raven / croaks "Kurô! Kurô!"(Eat shit and choke).* はやく死ね／＼とや烏めが　食ふ／＼と鳴きにける哉　文化 7-1 (*hayaku shine shine . . .*). The onomatopoeia Issa hears *"kurô! kurô!"* – meaning *"Eat (it)!"* and short for *kuso kurae* or *"Eat shit!"* an expression filled with malice, is remarkably close to the name "crow," while the usual onomatopoeia is *"ka-ka-,"* identical to our *cawing*. If Issa had a cat at that time, I would suspect that would be the target of the crows or ravens' enmity if they had any, which is dubious. Something like say, *"Croak! Croak!"* – *"Raven are you croaking for me to die? / Or are you hungry for a frog and only joke?"* would be a *kyôka*, but Issa's poem seems too serious, hence I kept it in a note.　★**Caw! Caw! Crow Poems.** Were this book in Japanese alone, I would want a whole chapter of crow caw poems. Unfortunately – as you may have already noted and will again – they just do not translate. The best I know is by Ôhe no matagusa (Big-fart Crotch-stinks): 横柄に人の妻戸をあけがらすかゝあ／＼と呼わたるかな　大屁股臭 *ôhei ni hito no tsuma to o akegarasu kakaa kakaa to yobiwataru kana*. A man has the effrontery to shout out at the gate of another man's wife and that is dawn-crowed. But what can be done in English with a dawn=open=ing=crow where *kakaa!* was actually how wives (with a "my old lady" feeling) were addressed? I thought of Orientalized Amerindians: *Squaw! Sq-caw!* but, no, that would not do. When Japanese can do justice to Mississippi John Hurt's *"Red Rooster says Cock-a-doodledoo; Richland Women say any dude'll do!"* I expect English to do likewise for that poem!

~~~~~~

One T's Kyôka ㊥ Conchs & Leeches for Cuckoo   346 頁

♪ **Why Wench Flower?** I translated what I usually translate as *maiden flower* as *wench flower* because the characters 女郎 in 女郎花 that only meant *maiden* a millennium earlier when the priest Henjô fell off his high horse on them had, by Issa's time, come to be used for a *harlot. Wench* seemed to fall in the middle of the broad connotation and fit most of Issa's rough *ku* about them. Here, by the way, is an *omake* or bonus waka (or proto-*kyôka*) for Japanese readers, from the 1312 *Gyokuyôshû* 玉葉集, that shows the maiden flowers becoming wenchy, or rather a poet becoming horny at the thought of them out there: あきののに　いろうつろへるをみなへし　われたにゆきて　をらむとそおもふ　実頼 *aki no no ni iro utsuroeru ominaeshi ware dani yukite oramu to zo omou*. Saneyori.

♪ **Readers of** *Rise, Ye Sea Slugs!* might note the close resemblance of Issa's *Yuck this! Yuck that!* sea cucumber who *would neither a saint nor demon be* to the double "yucks" (*tsuru mo iya, kame mo iya*) in Shokusanjin's *happy to die human* poem! Indeed, that haiku came less than two years after Issa recorded Shokusanjin's *kyôka*. As I had not read most of the 31 syllabet poems in Issa's journals carefully – the silverfish chanced to jump into my eye when I perused Issa's journals in a library prior to buying them for myself! – because my interest was purely haiku, I must confess to missing it entirely.

♪　オマケ。1）「むら雨の古の垣根や野鼠の　穴うの花の盛りのみして」　文化 9.4 *murasame no furu* うす暗い景色はうまく描写している和歌か短歌でしょうが、根＝鼠と「あな」＝穴の掛けだけでは狂歌として機知不足。2）「後の世にもしや住てふ人しあらば　つぎ穂の梅よ花も咲なん」 文化 10/3　*ato no yo ni moshya . . .* 狂歌でしょうが、解釈次第。当分預かっておる。多分、下に生まれるより、あるいは、そうであっても、養子になって花咲くチャンスが欲しかった。と）

~~~~~~

One T's Kyôka ㊦ Springs from Stones, Stylish Hills   348 頁

♪ ***Seeing my old Aubergine Horse translation*** my eyes teared over as I recalled learning that adjective for eggplant from the late J. I. Crump's translations from Chinese which used it for a (black) steed! One of a handful of souls I think of whenever I publish a new book, he had Learical dimensions and would surely break a cucumber's back and need a stout aubergine steed rather than a cucumber nag to visit us upon. To make this real to the reader who has not lived in Japan, here is a copy of a drawing I made surrounded by a dozen or so haiku scribbled inside the jacket of a book of early (*shôki*) *haikai*.

One haiku imagines a stout soul's odd way of dismounting left the 'horse' in that sitting position. お尻より下りたか茄子が腰かけて. Another records the tail being made of corn tassel. I spotted them in Ikuta near the house of a Sumo-san who lived into his 90's.

♪ ***Counting Songs:* Issa vs. Shokusanjin**. We saw Issa's stone-pitching counting song punning on *eight* as *noisy* (ya⇒yakamashi). Blyth introduced another counting song *kyôka* by Shokusanjin that he judged "one of the most technically remarkable *kyôka*" I would have put next to Issa's crotchety masterpiece (*ishinago wa . . .* pg.349) had I found Blyth earlier. Better late than never:

羽根の子のひと子に二子みわたせば娵御にいつかならんむすめご　蜀山人
hane no ko no hito*ko ni* futa*ko mi*wataseba yo*mego ni* itsu*ka naran* musu*mego*

This child one, that child two, battlecock & shuttledore I do see
Sweet little girls who some fine day pretty brides will surely be!

My translation does not even try to pun in the numbers from 1 to 7 that are in the original. Blyth explains that the poet "playfully used the song of the playing children to speak of them" and bestowed the ultimate accolade: "This is poetry." He did not even try to translate its Mother Gooseness so I cooked one up (adding "sweet" and "fine day" and "pretty" for rhythm, mostly). The song is definitely technically more complex than Issa's: the "three" is woven into a compound verb (gaze-spanning), the "four" into a concrete noun (bride), the "five" into an abstract noun (sometime), and so forth through "seven," though it precedes "six" (for a reason I do not know?). The poem is literally charming, as well; but for all that, I like Issa's rant more. Perhaps it is only because I have spent hundreds of hours with Issa and feel his emotions, while dozens of hours with Shokusanjin do not let me know if there is any emotion behind the play. Yet, even as I write that, I am unsure whether that matters one iota; and, I am afraid it may, rather, reflect my trying present living circumstances (pent up frustration so I can share Issa's catharsis). I will be most interested to see how critics react to Issa's *kyôka* – this and the silverfish, especially – which, as far as I know, have never been spotlighted before.

♪ **Issa's *kai=shell=value aru /is* pun.** I failed to note that in bunka 10.9, Issa's fifty-first year, he jotted down a splendid *waka* by Shunzei (1114-1204) that might be called a birthday *kyôka* which takes the waves=wrinkles of early old age (fifty) perhaps expressing envy for someone by the shore and finds value in it punning with the shells there found. (うらやまし五十（路）の波にほ（し？）ほ（た）れて・かひある浦に巡り逢ひけん　俊成卿 *urayamashi isoji no nami ni shio tarete kai aru ura ni meguri-aiken*). Issa, as we saw, took that same shell=*kai*=value into the mountains for a wizard's horn. In other words, Issa learned *kyôka* from *wild waka* as well as recognized *kyôka* poets.

One T's Kyôka 下の下 *Sweet Dew Turns Bird Doo*　　　　　350 頁

♪ **The double 下 in the chapter title** recalls Issa's *ku* about living the *ge no ge no ge,* or *low low low life,* which is not in this book. Here, for your reference: 下／＼も下／＼下々の下国の涼しさよ　文化十 *I.e.,* : *ge ge mo ge ge ge ge no gekoku no suzushisa yo*. And the idea was that the literally low-life (down by the riverside) was literally the *cool* life.

♪ **Untranslatable Issa.** Among old Issa's last *kyôka,* it describes clouds racing to wrap themselves around the 'hips' of a mountain, fixing the underpinnings for fifth-month rain. What makes it good is how the *obi,* or *belt/sash* is put into the adverb, *obitadashiku,* meaning both *vast* (number of clouds) and *tremendous* (speed). (五月雨の下拵へや山のこしをおびたゞしく雲の廻れり　文政 7.5 *samidare no shitagoshirae ya yama no koshi (o) obitadashiku . . .*) The poem is mad for the clouds that threaten rain become a sash that will prevent leakage if a menstrual reading is taken. A Kurohimeyama, or Dark Princess Mountain (in Issa's Shinano) version found the following month makes that likely as the first phrase 雨もよひ, or *liable to rain,* if I recall a note read long ago correctly, suggests the premenstrual in the Shinano dialect (雨もよひ日も黒姫の山のこしに　おびったゞしくも巡る雲哉 同 7.6 *amamoyoi hi mo kurohimenoyama no koshi ni obitadashiku . . .*).

♪ **Unstudious Old Age.** I found something to pair with Issa's self-deprecatory wasted snow-light *kyôka* by the master of creative-*waka*, Kotomichi 言道:

いつよりか開けながらの窓の書(ふみ)風ばかりこそもてあそびけれ
itsu yori ka hirakenagara no mado no fumi kaze bakari koso mote asobikere issa
when-from-as-for? opening-when's window's writing wind only+emph takes plays

Since when has the wind alone come to know them,
The pages of my books lying by the window open?

The moon spying in and the wind leafing through books are old Chinese conceits connected with scholar's studies (inscribed on what might be called window-pane plaques). Here, "only the wind" implies the poet is too tired or blind to read. Both this poem and Issa's have a touch of waka *ushin,* or *heart*, in them. They may be chuckling but are probably true laments. Here is a lighter & better *bonafide* Tenmei *kyôka* by Ôya no Urazumi, the student of Bokuyû, student of the physician who came to Edo from Ôsaka in the 17c, Bokuyô, student of Teitoku, fount of so, so much good humor.

ともし火にせんと思へばたちまちにたちぎえのする窓のあは雪　大屋裏住　吾妻
tomoshibi ni sen to omoeba tachimachi ni tachigie no suru mado no awayuki ôya no urazumi
lamp-as do-would considering-when suddenly up-and-vanishing does window's light-snow

Thinking I would make it my lamp, suddenly, it wasn't there:
The snow flakes falling by my window vanished in the air!

Just when I thought to use it; maybe I would do some writing,
The snow by the window melted . . . There goes my lighting!

♪ *All Issa Chapters. A Retrospective.* ♪

As I perused the 31-syllabet poems in Issa (the index of the *Zenshû* has the character 歌 so it is *easy*), I noticed the large number of what I call *kyôku* (haiku with a *kyôka*-like feeling) nearby. I put some in the text, but there were many that I failed to fit. Here are three favorites that span the period. In 1812, the year Issa read and copied Shokusanjin's *kyôka*, he wrote one I have yet to solve. 火とり虫人は人とてにくむ也 文化 9.4 *hitorimushi hito wa hito tote nikumu nari.* Perhaps it means that we humans dislike moths that swarm fires/light because they, the *hitorimushi*(fire-taking-bugs), trespass upon *our* name, *hito.* *Hito's* many etymologies include 'friends of the sun' and 'party of the light/fire,' so we are as the gods and they Prometheus multiplied a zillion-fold. An 1818 *ku* is easy on the face of it: *"Out of the dark / into the dark it goes! / The love of cats."* 闇より闇に入るや猫の恋 文化 15.1 (文政 1) *yami yori yami e hairu ya neko no koi*). Or, *"~ they go! / Cats in heat."* if you prefer a more English approach. What makes it a *kyôku* is that it takes all but the final line from Izumi Shikibu's famous *waka* summing up her supposedly unenlightened life. Another poet described a sea cucumber's life the same way (see *Rise, Ye Sea Slugs!*), though the human gullet is the dark they go into. If the *ku* is taken as a parody, it is a *senryû*, too. A poem in 1824, three years before he died, describes *"A tea house for geezers with kanko-birds right and left"* 爺茶屋や右に左に閑古鳥 文政 7.5 *jiiji chaya ya migi ni hidari ni kankodori.*) The identity of the bird in question, the *kankodori*, has been debated for hundreds of years (Buson's poems actually address this), but would seem to be a cross between a morning dove that likes quiet hours & places, and a snark, with occasional reference to the 'calling bird' that helps show the way to the other world, though that is more often associated with the *hototogisu* and the main idiomatic meaning of the kankodori is *business being slow*, or *the times being dead*, for which reason, I sometimes translate it as the 'nothing-doing bird,' which makes it right at home in Shinano, according to Issa, capital of the same.

Real & Fake: Why I Must Wait to Translate N/Ise 上   352 頁

♪ 伊勢 **vs** 仁勢 *N/Ise* or, **Visually Punning Titles**. Readers of Japanese or anyone with a careful eye for analogy probably noticed how similar the title of the real and fake tales of Ise are. *Nise*, meaning "fake" is usually written 偽, but here, it is punned with two characters one of which was in the original title and one of which visually mimics the other character. The original *i* of Ise is mostly found in names and I have never even thought about whether it has any "meaning." The *ni* in the fake does have a meaning: *benevolent* or *humane.* Like the pun from a "Dog 犬 Pillow Book" to a "Likely 尤 Pillow Book," it is mostly visual and makes sense! ★注：同様な視覚的な語呂合わせ求む！

♪ **Mukashi vs Okashi**. I could not decide how to translate the initial difference in the fake text, which usually changed, 昔、男＝むかし、おとこ *mukashi, otoko* into おかし男＝おかしおとこ *okashi otoko,* a difference of only one Japanese syllabet. About the best I could do was play *odd* against *old.* The lack of a single word for "Once upon a time" or "Long, long ago" in English makes a simple switch between the two impossible. Perhaps, were I to try to translate all the Fake Tale, I *might* come up with something. Probably not.

伊勢：みちのくのしのぶもぢずりたれゆへにみだれそめにし我ならなくに 10c
仁勢 一話の第二歌　道すがらしどろもぢずり足元は乱れそめにし我奈良酒に 17c
蜀山人/四方赤良：　生酔の礼者を見れば大道をよこすぢかひに春は来にけり 18c

Untranslatable Lightness of Nakarai Bokuyô & Linguistic Bonus.   356 頁

♪ **How These Chapters Came to Be**. I owe it all to linguist Hiroko Takanashi, for as noted, I failed to follow up on this poet until I checked on a poem in her article about the relationship of orthography, puns and cognition. Because all my chapters are based on poetic themes, works or individual poets, and because some of the explanation may be too detailed for general readers, I decided to put poems mentioned in her paper here:

よせぎれと見ゆるお寺の錦かなどこもかしこもはぎだらけにて kankô
yosegire to miyuru otera no nishiki kana dokomokashiko mo hagi darake nite
patchwork/quilt-as appears hon.-temple's brocade(landscape)!/?/:
everywhere clover=patches abundant/plastered in/because

What brocade this!
Your temple grounds display
a new aesthetíque:

Clover patches, every way
Should we call it a pastiche?

The fall brocade
this run-down temple wears
seems more a quilt:

Clover patches here & there,
I guess it beats being bare!

The autumn brocade
this temple boasts, I'd call
poverty-grade.

Clover patches here & there,
the landscape has seen wear!

In *Orthographic puns: The case of Japanese kyoka*, linguist Hiroko Takanashi explores the effect of diverse orthography on the cognition of *puns,* contrasting the semantically ambiguous *kana* (phonograph) pun, where the discovery of the two meanings comes with learning their incompatibility and *kanji* (logographs) puns where one meaning is instantly recognized while another comes later as a surprise. The above by Akera Kankô (d.1800) examples the former. Takanashi's working translation, *"The landscape of the temple looks like gathered cloth because of its abundant hagi* (patch-works / bush clovers)" may be a bit off for reasons none of which matter for her study: 1) *Yosegire, gathered* scraps of fabric, *also* meant *a garment* made of them. That, logically, makes a better counterpoint to the age-old conceit for brilliant autumn scenery in Japan, *nishiki,* (Chinese) brocade. 2) While "brocade" does *refer to* the landscape, it should not be *replaced* by it, for the greater *conceptual* wit (*what the puns serve*) lies in modifying, or, possibly vulgarizing (brocade was proverbially worn home by those who made good) that metaphor – *possibly* because patchwork may have been in fashion for paper robes, *kamiko* (Kankô *should have* made it a *shrine*, not temple, and added a paper=*kami*=*gods* pun!) among the avant-garde of Edo. 3) *"Because of"* at mid-poem is too obvious, as the original, albeit in accord with Japanese syntax, keeps it for the end. And *my* translations? Reading between the lines, they *add* a bit. The last two build upon the negative, or *trashy,* connotation of the word used for "abundant," *darake.* Be that as it may, Takanashi's interest is in *how* the *hagi* (patchworks / bush clovers) pun is "comprehended by readers, and what are the effects of the orthography" when the readers encounter it. To wit,

> since it is *kana [phonogram],* it is interpreted as sound (*hagi*) prior to lexical access. For the resolution of the semantic ambiguity, the garden path effect [a charming linguistic term], which makes the pun attach to the more immediate frame, comes into play. Since the immediately preceding word *dokomokashikomo,"* everywhere," belongs to the non-aesthetic frame because of its colloquial language, it is more straightforward to accept the "patchwork" interpretation. The following word *darake,* "abundant" is related to the same frame. The four words, "gathered cloth," "everywhere," "patchwork" and "abundant" [I skip the Japanese here and some other places] are all compatible with each other, and create a semantic network within that frame" [*Five* words, if we include *nishiki,* "brocade," ignored, perhaps, because "landscape" excluded it from her translation, though it was the subject of the first part of the poem and, as fabric, together with *yosegire* (patchwork), helps predispose us to read *hagi* as "patches" even more than the immediately preceding word. *My* amateur "garden path" has widely placed stepping stones]. At this point, readers may be aware of the two meanings, the choice of which is unclear because of the semantic ambiguity imposed by the kana spelling. Although this kana is the familiar orthography for the meaning of patchwork[patches], familiarity with the orthography contributes little in the case of kana; ambiguity still remains because any kanji words can be transcribed with kana. But because of the garden path effect the meaning "patchwork [patches]" is activated faster than the "bush clover" meaning. (Ibid)

Let us pause for air. With academic papers, an amateur needs a hit of pure oxygen after every paragraph (and my bracketed additions are no help!) This, you should recognize from hundreds of examples we have seen, is part of a complex description of what happens when a pivot word is read. There is more.

> Activation of the latter [bush clover meaning] may be hindered not only by the garden path effect but also by the absence of its familiar orthography 萩(*hagi*). The meaning "bush clover" enters the picture, however, because cultural knowledge associates it with the graceful garden of a temple and the serious tanka-like frame. With *otera no nishiki*, "landscape of the temple" it creates a semantic network within the aesthetic frame. It is the gap produced by the two incompatible frames, one describing the ordinary artifact of common people, and the other aesthetic, that generates the humor.

Brocade was a conventional conceit for brilliant autumnal scenery (maple, cherry, & pine for a foil), while *clover* was typically seen in the moon-light or up-close with dew rather than being included in these color panoramas. We have precedents of *kyôka* and *waka* playing with it. One (kks#56), by monk Sosei, mixed willows with blooming cherries to come up with a hitherto un-invented *Spring* brocade for Kyôto. Kankô's poem further expands the possibilities for fall's landscape-as-brocade and *may* poke fun at a friend's temple for its far-from-kosher, *i.e.* Kyôto, grounds. I must read him more to know. Here is another *kana* pun in Takanashi's example of a conventional *kyôka*:

にっこりと山もわらふてけさは又きげんよし野の春は来にけり　山手白人
nikkori to yama mo warôte kesa wa mata kigen yoshi no ⇒*yoshino no haru wa kinikeri*
broadly mountain/s too smiling, this-morning/newyears-as-for espec. mood good⇒goodfield/field/s-to spring come-has!　yamanote shirohito 1785

The mountain, too, cracks a big smile this morning, it's understood:
We all feel yoshi as the Spring has to Yoshino come for good!

The name Yoshino, *good-field,* was punned since the 8c *Manyôshû* (pg.308); *smiling* was standard conceit for newly verdant mountains glowing in the sun, but, as Takanashi points out, the *broad* smile painted by the adverb *nikkori* and the redundant *being in a good mood* (and, I would add, the *"too"* meaning *like people in good spirits for the New Year or spring's official arrival*) make the conceit positively human. Leaving *yoshi,* normally *kanji* when part of Yoshino, in *kana* (よし野)*,* accents that by allowing the incoming pivot-pun, (*kigen*) *yoshi*, a *good* mood, to remain in play with the smiling mountain slightly longer. I tried to keep the original pun, making Yoshino *Goodfield* (though the character most common is *aromatic*芳野, *not good*) but failed and ended up replacing the singular Japanese pun with two in Japanese and one in English! With *Yoshino* recognized, the poem will not scan as a whole, but only coming *or* going. To read it all the way through, you must mentally switch *good* from modifying *mood* to the generic *field* or *fields*. As Takanashi points out, the "comic book-like world" of Yamanote Shirohito's *kyôka* takes off on a sober, season-sensitive *Shin-kokinshû* (1205) *waka* of spring haze on still snowy Mount Yoshino (*mi yoshino wa yama mo . . .*).

又と世にあるものでない過去未来源左衛門が舞のなりふり　半井卜養 1670
mata to yo ni aru mono de nai kako mirai genzaemon ga mai no narifuri bokuyô
again world-in thing-as-for not past future genzae=present=mon's dancing/acting's appearance

"Genzaemon's appearance is something extraordinarily special that would never be seen in the past, in the future, and in the present." HT's working translation.

This extraordinary poem (my translations, pg. 356) by Nakarai Bokuyô (1607-1687), a medical doctor and Osaka-born poet who saw this kabuki in Edo because he was drafted to practice there, is the first example of a *kanji pun* in the analysis section of Takanashi's paper. The "present" hiding in the kabuki star's name is properly *genzai,* but the *i* and *e* sounds were somewhat blurred – in some regions, utterly indistinguishable – so the pun is tighter than it may seem. Here is the train of cognition in the linguist's words (minus most of the Japanese script, quotes where italics will do, and otherwise trimmed):

> . . . the readers encounter the words *kako,* "the past," and then *mirai,* "the future" before they come to the pun. Both words belong to the same frame, the first to be introduced. Then, the kanji 源左門 activates the sound (Genzaemon), and the particular meaning the kanji stands for, the name of the kabuki actor. . . . Despite the fact that the meaning of "the present" with the sound of *genzai* is the one that would be expected on the basis of "the past" and "the future," the kanji shifts the frame. It is a surprise that the kanji 源左門(Genzaemon) appears here, causing a dramatic frame shift. [Then] the sound *genzae* . . . is conceptually modified to *genzai* and the meaning of "the present" is activated, probably with its corresponding kanji 現在 in mind. After the pun, readers find the word *mai-no-narifuri,*" appearance" that belongs to the kabuki frame. After the hidden meaning in the kanji of the pun is resolved and readers reach the end of the text, the two meanings are sorted into each frame. . . . The incompatibility of the two frames is condensed as in a punch word, in which two frames co-exist.

While *"previous literature has primarily focused on sound play,"* the broader significance here, she adds, is that *"the visual aspect: puns in kyoka also play on orthography. The kanji and kana orthographies have different effects, and by choosing one or the other, kyoka poets manipulate their reader's cognitive processing of the two available meanings."* To that, I would add that not only the poets but scribes and editors may do the choosing. *"When written in kanji, the logographs offer direct access to one meaning, and the discovery of another hidden meaning is a surprise."* With Genzaemon, above, we get a silly surprise in the *"present (genzai);"* with Ueda Akinari's poem (see pg. 675), we sniff out sarcasm when we realize the defender of the *Ancient Chronicles Kojiki* 古事紀 is really, or, rather also being slandered as, a *kojiki* 乞食 beggar. Agreed; but there is a complication. Time again, I have been *astounded* by how common and extensive the orthographical differences are with the same poem in different books. Sometimes it is because the poet left many variants; but, usually an editor favors one style over another for readability, aesthetics or design purposes (fitting the poem on a page with other poems). Unless you have a problem with inconsistency for its own sake, you learn to get used to it, as English readers once did) reading Japanese. But, with particularly witty poems, where the spelling can change the meaning (imagine Joyce), it matters. But it is hard to say just how much, and a far larger number of poems and types/cases of punning affected by orthography will need to be studied. Genzaemon provides a case in point. When I looked up the poem (卜養狂歌集 1669 の一年後の卜養狂歌拾遺、狂歌大観 1 内) in a source that as far as possible relied on primary material, the kabuki actor's name was written in *kana,* げんざへもん. It still works fine in *kana* because it is not a perfect homophone with present. My guess is that an editor wanted to be sure readers who no longer knew of the actor quickly picked up on the name as names tend to be in Chinese characters more often than anything else, and to show them the name's orthography, for, as Takanashi noted, the similarity of the second character of the name 左 with one of the two characters in present 在 visually improves the pun. With Akinari's *kojiki,* we have a perfect homophone. There, the *kanji* was more important for showing all not familiar with his and Norinaga's bitter battle. For one who does not need such help, it might have been more interesting to make it *kana* where, *"the phonographs leave ambiguity"* so *"more of a resolving task is required of the reader."* There is no in/correct here. Some readers like to guess, some want quick resolution. Japanese orthography, being infinitely freer than that of English, can be adjusted to the level or stylistic desire of the reader.

> Since the *kana* orthography does not allow a bias in terms of semantic salience, the discovery of the two meanings is, instead of a surprise, an appreciation of the conceptual merger of the incompatibility that resides in the accidental match of the sound.

While I was delighted Takanishi chose the neglected genre of *kyôka* to example the role of orthography in pun cognition, I wish tanka (waka) puns were also examined as they very commonly used a *third* method of orthographic punning I want studied: the *possibly unfinished phonogram*, which is to say *kana* where unmarked ellipsis of the ditto-like marks that blunt, thicken or give lip to (?) consonant phonemes (k⇒g, s⇒z, t⇒d, ch⇒j, h ⇒b) allows not only the homophonic ambiguity inherent in *kana*, but greater play from the possibility of paraphonic – or nearly homophonous puns that until the 20c would have seemed natural rather than forced because those "muddy-marks" (*nigori-ten*) were left to the mind's eye of the reader to fill in so often that it was, if not correct, at least accepted spelling. We see scores, perhaps hundreds of examples in this book, of which the oddest is probably *Kokinshû* (905) *waka* #422 (心から花のしづくにそぼちつつうくひずとのみ鳥のなくらむ*kokoro kara hana no . . .*pg. 188) with its うくひず*ukuhizu*, where two verbs one positive and one negative, "*uku*憂く *feel blue*" and "*hizu*乾ず*dry not*," and*,* and a species of bird, うぐひす *uguhisu* (possibly *uguisu,* but I am unsure when the sound-shift happened) coexist, or rather, could be born from a single word, with one complication, namely, one of the two *kana* letters that could have muddy-marks *does*. For a clean example of three-from-one, うくひす*ukuhisu* would have been better, but the editor's point was to hide the uguisu inside the two verbs *uku* & *hizu*. In Japanese, the difference is less than in the romanization (*uku hizu*) because words are not separated. That, too, is a way orthography influences punning. Then, both the second verb and the bird would need the mental addition of muddy-marks, rather than both verbs being fine as is and the bird needing one muddy mark added and one removed.   Such complexity is an anomaly possible because a bird otherwise mentioned was the subject, so this *uguisu* (warbler) did not have to immediately fly. Which is good because it doesn't unless *uguisu* is taken as onomatopoeia for the bird's cry (extremely unlikely). It is enough that it serves as an allusive pun, or riddle, that, as in cases where *kanji* mask a homophone, may be *solved*, or *discovered* later. Still, it charms me because, the unwanted muddy-marks reminds us of the wet *uguizu*. Or, do I over-read? (probably)

♪ **Bokuyô's Genzaemon poem.** The *preface* gives the actor's name in Chinese characters, *kanji*. As Bokuyô prefaces almost all of his poems, he would seem to intend for us to read them that way, preface first. Chances are that the poem in the book Takanashi referenced did not give the full preface and, *instead* replaced the *kana* in the poem with the *kanji* one would expect for a name. Be that as it may, the reader would have been prepped for the name, so Takanashi's sequence of cognition would not change.

♪ *Hiroko Takanashi's article.* Much of the article does not directly read *kyôka* but treats linguistic things. In the theoretical background, we encounter the mechanism of puns with terms such as a *script-switch trigger* (Raskin, elaborated by Attardo) to which she can contribute because it lacked anything on the *quality* of the two scripts, and we get an overview of studies/hypotheses about the respective routes and speed of cognition of logographs and logograms. Among the many terms she introduces, I wish I had thought of one, "pseudo plausibility" (Chafe), applicable to *kyôka* playing upon *tanka*, for I sometimes used "facetious" with no intention of criticizing the poem (or poet) and might have used it instead. We learn something about where the "frame" she uses comes from, and so forth. Elsewhere, she gives a brief historical background of the conflicting importance of "cultural knowledge" (which helps build the multiple frames) as "one of the cues for processing kyoka;" that is exactly what I try to share with my readers, but it is nice to have a term for it. I may be more deeply into *waka* and *kyôka* and hence critical about details in some of Takanashi's readings, but her article provides hints on how to discuss the tricks in terms specialists can appreciate, as opposed to my naive approach, or lack thereof. I hope this book will, likewise, provide her with hints for a more complete look at the visual aspect of puns in Japanese comic poetry.   It seems to me that Occidental scholars have failed to appreciate visual information that does not simply signify a word by the vaguely/unconsciously read gestalt or merely represent a sound. In other words, we are not looking at the entire picture. Takanashi is on the track of something very important, if we wish to improve artificial intelligence.

After Issa & Ryôkan, Kotomichi's Wacky Waka   360 頁

Kotomichi's Cherry Snapper Under the Snow at the End of the Book. As with so much in Japan, it had a precedent, or at least something close enough to reference. It is a poem in a kyôka collection of the 17c waka, haikai and kyôka-master Bokuyô that he originally put at the back of a volume of scored *hokku* titled *Sakuradai*, or cherry-snapper, after being requested for a *jare-uta*, or playful, punning song/poem for such a purpose (桜鯛の発句にて点取の巻の奥にされうたよみてやりける). It puns every time you eat=*kuu* with each poem=*ku* and declares the collection is lively=*ikite* and will work=hataraku (is interesting and edifying) simultaneously with the similar but not quite identical connotations of posing=*ikite*, or arrangement of said fish served up still moving=hataraku. (くふことに句毎に味も新しやいきてはたらくこのさくら鯛 卜養狂歌拾遺 tk1 *kuu goto ni ku goto ni aji mo atarashiya ikite hataraku kono sakuradai*). This poem may also have helped the dedicatory poem – snapper, albeit not specifically cherry – starting early-18c Teiryû's memorial collection (pg.703). So we have at least three centuries of literary snappers. For a whole chapter of haiku cherry-snappers, see *Cherry Blossom Epiphany* (2007). *A variation of Bokuyô's poem is explained with a different preface and a challenge poem which it answered, but comprehending the episode would take more time than I have.

~~~~~~

Buddhist grapes & persecuted X'tians   362 頁

Another Try at the *Fake Ise* Translation. If you recall, I kept some of the original's ambiguity. (*Burn not, today, / Musashi moor, the grass is low / Our sin is light! / My mate's rolling, alright; / & I, too, rolling, have left.*). Keene, by skipping the puns on low grass and light sins and the rolling, neither of which he mentions, translates simply: *"Do not today / Set fire to Musashi Field / In Asakusa / My husband has recanted / And I also have recanted."* Aside from the poem taking off from a *Tale of Ise* poem, there is no wit in such a reading, though it might still beat my unclear one. Borrowing his fine word, "recant,"

> *Not today, you can't burn Musashi moor: so, burn it less:*
> *My husband has recanted, and I too have recanted, yes!*

~~~~~~

Literal/figuratively lousy translations – & One Death Poem   368 頁

♪**One More Dead Bug Poem**. There was a wonderful journal of bugs, edited by an entomologist and full of gems of literature. Were it to become active again, I might put out a call for poems on nothing but sending-off bugs. Besides our *imayo* and *kyôka* on lice, we have the old Greek poem/s to a dead pet cricket which Lafcadio Hearn introduced and, . . . here is one more by metaphysical poet Robert Herrick but two beats longer than a *kyôka*:

> THE AMBER BEAD.
>
> I SAW a fly within a bead
> Of amber cleanly buried ;
> The urn was little, but the room
> More rich than Cleopatra's tomb.

♪**One More Try to Translate a Great Death Poem** with punning nothing short of spectacular and vernacular laid on with a trowel.

> 此世をはどりやお暇いせん香の烟りと共に灰左様なら 一九 狂歌一万集
> *kono yo oba doriya oitoma sen-kô no kemuri to tomo ni hai sayônara* jippen ikku
> this world +emph what-the-hell hon+leisure(take-off)-do=
> incense's smoke together with, yes=ashes, goodbye

So light my joss!
The smoke may make you cry
but I won't cough,

It might even cure me (I joke),
& ash your leave, I'm off!

The joss=*senkô*, in the original punned straight off the helper-verb *sen* (*suru* in a would-do conjugation) serving "leisure" to mean "taking leave," the *hai*, sounding like "yes!" written with the Chinese character meaning ashes (*i.e.*, cremation) just before the final *sayônara* are impressive. If the famous novelist Jippensha Ikku really composed this on his death-bed, he must have died a happy man. I added alot to replace what was lost but the translation still seems dead. ♪ **And Another Hopeless Poem** by Kasukusai Yotanbô:

うき涙ふるき屏風の蝶つがい はなれ／＼になるぞかなしき 糟句斎よたん坊
uki namida furuki byôbu no chotsugai hanarebanare ni naru zo kanashiki 吾妻 1786
bluesy tears old folding-screen's butterfly-pair(hinge/s) separate become+emph. sad!

Tears to see these old screens, separated, pane from pane,
(all five seasons lay apart – who can stand a broken heart?)
A butterfly whose wings spanned worlds, flaps one in vane.

And, likewise, can a translation stand where its single wit is split in two? In Japan and, I would imagine the rest of the Sinosphere, even today, a hinge has a butterfly in it. A human Atlas may hold up the Earth, but a butterfly Atlas would hinge Heaven's Gate.

月雪のみたてもあまりしら／＼し しらけていはゞこれは卯花 子子孫彦吾妻 1786
tsuki yuki no mitate mo amari shirajirashi shirakete iwaba kore wa unohana konokonomagohiko

A
The moon & snow will never do for the flower called an u;
But pretend you never saw one, and the simile holds true!

The snow & moon are too damn bright to stand for any u;
Only if you draw a blank can you make the claim they do.

B
If an u in bloom is really as white as the moon and snow,
Why not claim the azure sky is blue in our world of woe?

I am not sure my interpretation is correct. My own opinion is too strong and my grasp of grammar too weak. But, whatever the poem turns out to mean, without a flower name (*u*, or oogh) with a melancholic sound, meaningful translation is impossible.

Spiteful Kyôka that are Not Silverfish 370 頁

♪ **Monk Kyôgetsu's claim** to have enlarged the Empress is found many places. Here is one *kyôka* corollary: 御前の前いかにも致せ制すまじこなたのしじもしどけなければ （沙石集・五・末 *gozen no mae ika ni mo ..*）．つまり、。．．念のために。

♪ **Other Sengai *kyôka* & *kyôku*.** I thought there was another *kyôka* where visitors are stranded in the Sengai's w.c. and must plead for *paper*, which puns into calling on the *gods*. But my memory may be wrong, or decades ago I misread the poem we saw. A writer with a fuzzy memory stranded in the country, too poor to reunite with 99% of his library can do no more. Some day, I hope to add more Sengai to this book. Help, anyone?

Making Kyôka by Mad Reading? – or, the 10c Lady Ise in translation. 374 頁

♪ **Misreading Lady Ise's poems**. While I well know our minds read what they want to, it helps to be reading something that is genuinely beyond your comprehension. I have never really studied old grammar and the still molten syntax sometimes allowed things I never could have imagined. Japanese readers, might try this example of what I was up against. It is a Lady Ise poem: なみたのみ しるみのうさも かたるへく ひとのこころを まくらにも せよ *namida nomi shiru mi no usa mo kataru beku hito no kokoro o makura ni mo seyo*). I first translated it as follows: *I would tell him about the blues only my tears know / If I could but find his heart and use it for my pillow.* But, my respondent assures me that Lady Ise's poem really means "If only I could turn *my* heart into *his* pillow." You figure.

♪ **Not Reading Prefaces and Missing Names**. With short poems, the possibilities for reading are large and the presence or absence of additional information is vital. Yet they are often presented without it. The information about that dead crane on Mum Day was not given by Nichibun, so I first thought I had the plain paradox of clashing symbols of longevity and transience and that seemed more *kyôka* for being all cerebral. The same thing happened with this: われまねく そてとともしらて はなすすき いろかはるとそ おもひわひつる *ware maneku sode to mo shira de hanasusuki iro kawaru to zo omowabitsuru*. I thought it meant *No inkling has susuki that it beckons with its plumes, /& even as we charm, we wave the seed of our doom.* or, ~ */ Nor I that the one I charmed would bring me gloom!* which is, again, aphoristic rather than specific. Here, *what Nichibun's barebone text did not indicate* is that the poem was *not* Lady Ise's, but the Empress's, and meant *No inkling has susuki that it beckons with its plumes, / I am sorry if I led you on and brought you gloom.* I still do not know what it was about. Maybe the Empress had misgivings about setting up her lady-in-waiting with the Emperor whose mistress Lady Ise later became (or already was?). From my respondent → 脚注の訳「（后）（あなたを手招きする）私の袖とは知らないで、心変わりを悩んでいたのですね。」

The Straight Ones Die First: Lamentable Laments 380 頁

♪ **I found the Teiryû Eulogy** 知るしらぬ人を狂歌に笑わせし其返報に泣てたまはれ *shiru shiranu hito o kyôka ni warawaseshi sono henpô ni naite tamaware* in a 19c book and misread it as a death-poem. As I like my first-person mistakes better than the correct third-person translations, I saved them (below). ★Later, I learned that it was even better in the original for alluding to a poem the deceased wrote to his brother on the death of their father. For the whole picture, see the Mad Reader written months after this book).

> *Men I knew, Men I didn't – I made you laugh, before I died:*
> *Now, if you would pay me back, laugh again until you cry!*

> *Whether or not we met, if my mad poems made you laugh,*
> *You know what you owe me – Now, it's your turn to cry!*

♪ Another 18-19c eulogy was skipped because it proved all too well that sometimes rhyme cannot come close to making up for the loss of a fine pun. その人のしるしの塚はありなからはかなく落る我泪かな 時成狂歌一萬集 *sono hito no shirushi no tsuka wa arinagara hakanaku (haka naku) ochiru waga namida kana*)

> *Here is a mound for one once quick and brave – So why*
> *Do I cry? Because my tears fall on grass over no grave.*

In the original, the adverb *hakanaku* is both two words, *grave=haka* and *not=naku*, meaning *without a grave!* and, *after* the following verb/gerund, *falling* modifying "my tears" which follow, also evokes *crying*, then finally morphs into an adverb meaning *despairingly/futilely.* Such puns are more than enough to make a poem, or in translation, break it. I added the "brave" because the dead soul had to have been worthy to have a memorial raised in the absence of a body. You might say that compared to the absent puns, thus translation is an empty mound raised for the poem which is not found within.

♪**What about *Epitaphs*? What *about* epitaphs!** While most Japanese poets and many who were not – even some children – wrote their own death poems, many if not most of which are witty, I have found few witty epitaphs – so few, I made the above-mentioned error, turning a rare epitaph, or rather tribute, into a death-poem! Why? Mostly because there are few epitaphs, period. One cannot go walking through Japanese graveyards searching for humorous ditties. In classic poetry we find many laments, mostly for dead rulers, but they lack the epigram quality we expect in an epitaph. Likewise, in haiku, we find touching remembrances of the dead, but they are not the dry dust of the epitaph but wet, wet as tears. In case you do not recall any epitaphs, here are four:

 1. *Beneath this stone lies Dr John Bigelow,*
 an atheist all dressed up with no place to go.

 2. *Here lies the dust of faithful Marvin Peeper*
 swept up at last by the Great Housekeeper.

 3. *Here lies my wife / in earthy mould / who when she lived / did naught but scold.*
 Good Friends, go softly/ in your walking/ lest she should wake/ and rise up talking.

 4. *Here lies Martin Elginbrod / Have mercy on my soul, Lord God*
 As I would do, were I Lord God / And you were Martin Elginbrod.

The originals of 1, 2 and 4 are four lines. I added the "faithful" to indicate what I assume the man's social position, steward. All four are taken from a book of (Christian) *Holy Humor* by Cal and Rose Samra that is a joy, even if you are not of the faith. All share the spirit of the *kyôka*. The last is extraordinarily good and would have delighted the feisty 16-17c poets of Japan. And, guess what, it comes from a 16c Scottish tombstone! I would like to find out if there the author's name is for real, in which case he may have written it, himself. Elsewhere, I recall seeing epitaphs punning the name into the poem as Japanese death-poems did, but you'll have to dig them up yourself.

♪*A Third Type of Death Poem, or Rather Celebration/Lamentation/Remembering*.
There is a poem, neither death-poem by the dying party, nor an eulogy or roast following soon after death, but one written on the anniversary of a highly respected dead party's passing. Kyôka includes some for the first anniversary, third, seventh, etc., but they tend to be for people they actually knew or for their relatives. What I find remarkable and think deserves a full book are the death poems of haiku that I first became aware of reading Issa's death-day memorial poems for Bashô. Such poems are called Bashô-ki 芭蕉忌。 There are hundreds of such ~ *ki* 忌 poems found in any haiku almanac. Not all of the celebrated souls are called by their name, nor are all of them haiku poets. Novelist Akutagawa's death day is called Kappa-ki, because his writing did much to keep the legendary water creature called a kappa alive. I, like all people writing haiku in Japanese, have written some, including one for Wright who died on my birthday after writing enough haiku to fill a book. If circumstances permit, I may do such a book myself. To me, such poems reflect what makes Japanese culture precious. We will never, I repeat, never, look seven generations ahead, if we so not look at least that far back and *feel* for those who came before us. To live as though there is no tomorrow is not a problem because it ensures we repeat history, but because it ensures we will soon have none. Unless we *know* we are no better than our ancestors, we will not fight to leave something to those who inherit our memes (to hell with genes, we have more than enough of those already! One might even say that our genes are now killing our memes).

Death (Or, Is it Life?) Takes Another Encore! 9-9 386 頁

Don Quixote, as might be expected from one mad in some of the best ways, has a superb poem, titled *A Song*, addressing the god (or whatever you would call him) Death: Ozell's revision of Herschel Brickell transl: 1930; *Death, put on some kind Disguise, / And at once my Heart surprise: / For 'tis such a Curse to live, / And so great a bliss to die; / Should'st thou any Warning give, / I'd relapse to Life for Joy.* I tried to *shorten* it to *kyôka* length, but failed. Instead, it came out five words *longer!*

Death,

in disguise, come
take me by surprise:
'Tis such a curse to live,
And so great a bliss to die –
Should'st thou any warning give,
I'd jump with joy right up from bed
When I'd rather not be alive, but dead!

As touched as our knight was, we should recall that the real ruler of Spain actually slept in a coffin and carried around a skull, not to mention other relics (pieces of saints) in his last years. Not just the ideals of chivalry but Christianity as practiced was satirized here.

~~~~~~

Death Where Is Thy Sting? A Fourth Encore!   390 頁

Contentment, Another Example. Shokusanjin's acceptance of human mortality, or jab at the reverence for longevity over humanity (turtle? crane? not me!) is impressive. So is this earlier *waka*, titled 思来世, or thoughts on the coming world, by Kotomichi (1798-1868):

品たかきことも願はずまたの世はまた我が身にぞなりて来なまし 言道
shina takaki koto mo negawazu mata no yo wa mata waga mi ni zo narite kinamashi
goods high thing even wish-nt again-wrld-as4 agn myslf-into+emph becmng come-wld

    Nobility? No wish have I to attain a higher place in life
    In the next world, I would as soon, once again, be me.

Light talk about being reborn in Japanese poetry goes back at least to the *Manyôshû* where Tabito opined that he would risk becoming a bug to drink. Shokusanjin's contentment with the human lot/mortality in this world and Kotomichi's contentment with his own lot in the *next* one – usually contentment with one's lot in *this* world is dependent on a grade-up in the next one and the self is not thought to keep – are novel.

~~~~~~

The World's Most Macho Death Poem. A fifth encore!   392 頁

わんざくれふんばるべいかけふばかりあすはからすがかつかじるべい『増訂武江年表』I love the poem but the official account of the misbehavior of the man with a macho death-poem is damning._You cannot feel for someone who fakes illness for years and goes about town pushing his weight around. 「累年、病を称して仕えを怠るうへはつつしみて蟄居すべきのところみだりに市中に出不法のふるまひありしむねお聞きに達し・・・・・」「寛政重修諸家譜」続群書類従完成会 ???

~~~~~~

Just Can't Stop Dying Poems! . . . A Sixth & Seventh Encore   394 頁

♪ ***A Death Poem's Mood***. Mountain cherry trope is so fascinating I gave it a chapter in *Cherry Blossom Epiphany* (2007). But the scores of poems I translated do not include a *waka* I just found that brings out the mood of Kichiuemon's death poem: *"I wanted this melancholy for myself – Mountain cherries, / Had I not come, you might have shed your bloom unseen"* Yôgen Hôshi gsis #141 (*kokoro kara mono o koso omoe yamazakura tazunezari-seba chiru o mimashi ya* in Crans. 2a, but my trans.). ↓ *ubatama no yobai* tôshi ♪ オマケ。うは玉の夜這に老の身もかるくくらけも骨にあふの海かな 冬之 狂歌活玉集 1740

~~~~~~

Hey, Hey, Hey for he-no-he... & Poo, Poo, Pooh!   9 last   398 頁

♪ *As 'he he he' runs out of gas in English*, here is a pair of fart *kyôka*, half of which translates. True, they are not high-art and undeniably gross, but still they *are* wittier than most epigrams in Greek or English. The untranslatable lead starts with the syllabary song, unlike our alphabet song, true literature (a medium-length *waka* by Kûkai), having the perpetrator, slovenly Owaka – 'honorable *waka*' punned w/ a maid-servant's name, let something slip, or rather, pass: the unmentioned fart letter "へ *he*." いろはにほとの字の間でしくぢって　私やこの家をちりぬるをわか *i ro ha ni ho to no ji no ai de shikujitte watashiya kono ie o chirinuru owaka*. The translatable follow-up confirms the farter's identity and includes the logical consequence (what maids stereotypically did – see *The Woman Without a Hole* (2007) for examples – while having sex with their masters):

旦那さん私を糞と思ふかな　への出たのちに無理に追出す
dana-san watashi o fun to omou kana he no deta nochi ni muri ni oidasu
master+hon me shit-as think!/?/: fart left afterward forcefully chases-out

I guess my master thinks of me as shit.
After I farted, he pushed me right out!

♪ **Most Famous Palindromic Poem.** If you recall, *he he he* へへへ is a palindrome. As the only one in the *Tokuwa* anthology and captioned (廻文), it may even be a parody of palindromes. Note that the *non-usage of diacritical marks* is critical to the success of most. Only the diacritical mark at the dead-center of the 31-syllabet poem may always be marked without ill effect. The most famous *waka* palindrome, below, demonstrates why:

なかきよのとおのねふりのみなめざめなみのりふねのおとのよきかな
na-g/ka-ki-yo-no-to-o-no-ne-b/fu-ri-no-mi-na-me-za-me-na-mi-no-ri-f/bu-ne-no-o-to-no-yo-ki-k/ga-na

That syllabet is in the middle of "*mezame* = awaken." The poem is a charm written by a picture of a treasure boat that is slept upon on the New Year or the following night (when people stayed up until dawn, NY Eve was impossible) with the hope of seeing pleasant dreams boding well for the year and means roughly, *"How good it is for all to wake from a long sleep on a long night to the good sound of a boat riding in on the waves!"*

♪ ***Repetitive Nonsense ala Chinese (?)***.   Believe it or not, there is at least one minimalist AABA 4x7 character Chinese-style mad verse, or *kyôshi* that is actually at least a bit funny. By Gubutsu* 愚佛, or Silly-buddha, and titled dog-bite-meet 犬咬合, i.e., *The Dog Fight*, it goes *Wan wan wan wan mata wan wan. / Mata mata wan wan mata wan wan / . . .* (狂詩古今狂歌大全).* Princ.Comp credits it to Shokusanjin, almost surely a mistake.

椀々々々亦椀々。　　*Rough! Rough! Rough! Rough! Again, Rough! Rough!*
亦亦椀々又椀々。　　*Again! Again! Rough! Rough! Again, Rough! Rough!*
夜暗何疋頓不分。　　*In the dark of night, I couldn't tell the number of mutts,*
始終只聞椀々々。　　*From start to finish, I just heard Rough! Rough! Rough!*

The Chinese character used for the barking, or ruff-ruffing does not mean "rough" but "bowl." Be that as it may, if the dogs were barking to be fed so the "bowl" became significant as punning mimesis we would at least have doggerel, but this is not even up to mutterel. (♪♪Princeton appraises it higher. Note below.)   With about 15 minutes of work, however, it was easy enough to work the *ruff=rough* idea into a mad exchange:

Tom Cat said, *"Dog, you have such an eeeasy life!*
Your Wives don't scratch, they only bite – Meow!"

"Tom," said Mutt, *"Who is free to play all night?*
I've a Master to obey! I have it rough! Ruff! Ruff!"

The *he-he-he* fartsody and these bow-wow bowls may make us groan, but Piet Hein's description of a train trip he had just made proves repetitive minimalism can be high art:

Tokyotokyotokyotokyotokyotokyotokyotokyo! (private correspondence)

Think about it. You get the name of the stations at each end *and* the sound of rail travel! You might note that it is also a toponymic *kyôku* (this *grooku* is elsewhere in the book because I want to be sure it becomes known). And, that gives me my cue to apologize for yet one more thing that should have a chapter in this book but does not, *toponymic kyôka*. There are thousands, but I – who travel little and find detail about places I do not know very well myself to be trivia – did not even try to translate any. For Japanese readers, here is a simple example from the 1785 *Tokuwa* anthology turning the Sumida River into a drain for the ink(*sumi*)-stone pools of the poets and book-keepers, etc. of Edo: 一ぱいに硯の海をひき出してすりながしたるすみ田川かな　紀定麿　徳和歌後 #629 *ippai ni suzuri no umi* . . . Ki no Sadamaru) . What interests me in this, aside from the possible play on Bashô's Mogamigawa draining away the heat of summer, is the comment by the Iwanami editors: *"At that time, the Sumida River was not muddy like today, so making it flow like ink is way off. This is an example of a failure at establishing an association* [a budding epithet? 縁語構成失敗の一例といえる]." I think such an idea should have been kept for the Seventh Eve when everyone was writing down their wishes – indeed, I have read more than one poem where the entire Milky Way turned into black ink. One published in 1740 in Ôsaka: *Too dark the clouds, we cannot see the lover Stars in rendezvous; / Up there in the Milky Way, would they wash their inkstones too!* (星合も見えぬ斗の黒雲は天の川にも硯洗ふ欤　百子　狂歌餅月夜 *hoshiai mo mienu bakari no kurogumo wa amanogawa ni mo suzuri arau yo* momoko). But, regardless, I wonder about that river. Issa has the rat drinking from it, and I had always thought it was already dark by the end of the 18c. I probably had it wrong and Issa was contrasting the river that stood for clarity and purity with the dirty critter. *"Once, in Sumidagawa River, people enjoyed swimming, or the regatta, and ate Japanese icefish and corbiculae and had scene of peace and quietude that Pon-pon ship were going up and down"* as one comically Englished line on the world wide web puts it. I can only say for sure that there is some fine irony in the reversal by the *kyôka* that the Iwanami editor may have missed. While Sumida, with a name thought to pun on *sumi*, or *clarity*, was good water, a 17c sake maker put the river into his brand name 隅田川諸白 but actually drew the water from a well! With that sort of a reputation, we should perhaps see the *kyôka* as a deliberate squib on a pristine name. However, it is at least *possible* it is hinting at growing pollution. All agree the water was great in the 17c, but I would not be so sure about the down-river side of Edo by 1785. After all, Edo had had a huge population explosion in the 18c that made it the world's largest city. ♪♪ Back to the *Wan Wan* Dog Fight Poem. This poem found its way into the *Princeton Companion to Classical Japanese Literature* where it is called "zany proto-dadaism" (the far-edge of what I have been calling, more loosely "surreal") wrongly attributed to Shokusanjin and used to example his "delightful streak of craziness." Googling to see if Silly Buddha might not be a pen-name of Shokusanjin and, thus, exonerate the *Princeton Companion*, I found something interesting about dog onomatopoeia. Before the Edo period, when most dogs were wild, they tended to go *"biyo-biyo"* or *"byô-byô"* – howling, I guess – rather than *"wan-wan,"* the milder *ruff-ruff* or *bow-wow* of the domestic dog that has it easy. If that be true and if the poet knew it, what could be a better symbol of the new circumstances of dogs that changed the howling to *bow-wow*ing than doing that literally with the bowls they ate from?

My Rain & the Bath-girls, Tourism Kyôka – ♪ *for all 5 chapters* 414 頁

♪The 地誌所載狂歌抄 may not be a name but a description: the 狂歌 or *kyôka* 載 carried in, and 抄 selected from 16 volumes of the 地誌所 or local place magazine, issued over thirty years, from 1657 to 1687. A biography later confirmed what I suspected about the 1672 volume, 有馬私雨 *Arima, My Rain*, that it was indeed edited by Kôfû. He may have had some influence on the 1678 volume 有馬大鑑迎湯抄 too. The rest still does not look very interesting though I did spot *some* poems of interest such as Black Hair Island where male and female waves let their hair come down and get it on *yoru yoru* night after night, just-so because that puns as approaching to the point of contact. 黒髪嶋　うらやまし黒かみさけてよる／＼は女波男波のまくらならへむ　喜雲　*urayamashi kuro kami sagete yoru yoru wa me-nami o-nami* . . kiun 1667 An Englished ku with M & F waves making sea cucumbers is in *Rise, Ye Sea Slugs!* (2003), but the above is better lost in translation.

耳塚　故郷をきかまほしくや思ふらん　そのから人の耳づかの耳　了意
furusato o kikamahoshiku ya omouran sono karabito no mimizuka no mimi ryôi
homeland/town+acc hear-want long!/: those chinese-peoples' earmound's ears

The Ear Mound

*How they must long to hear of their country – all those ears
away from home in this mound of the Chinese peoples' ears!*

~~~~~~

氷室山　我庵は冬そはけしき氷室山　夏のあつさは麹室かも　了意 1677
waga io wa fuyu zo wa keshiki himuroyama natsu no atsusa wa kôjimuro ka mo

*Ice-vault Mountain? Call it my place every winter
that hot as a malthouse becomes every summer*

Broadview gives *no* supplementary information, but the net provides the editor/s of the 1667 & 1677 vols. Most readers will have heard of Mimizuka, the tumulus for trophies of war with the continent. But it may be new to hear sympathy at this date. *Haikai* love ice-rooms on mountains, but Himuro-yama is a mountain so named. Having lived with windows open to the snow in a hot, moist room built into a hill-side so mold grew under a *futon* left on the floor only two days running, I know *exactly* what the poet means! I also can attest to the accuracy of the next poem on the Semi-no-ogawa, or Shoalsee Stream, playing on its homophony with the cicada: 瀬見小川　年よれは絶せす音の聞えけり我耳蝉の小川成らん *toshi yoreba taesezu oto no kikoekeri* . . . as I suffer the condition described and hear not bells (tinnitus) but a stream and sometimes a storm of cicada!

♪ **My Rain,** *which might also be translated* **Personal Rain** *or* **Private Rain**, intrigues me partly because I can recall being astounded at the Japanese practice of prefacing all sorts of things with *mai* from the English "my." *Mai ka* (a private car, or one's own car), *mai kon* (a personal computer), *mai homu* (ones own home, home ownership) etc.. In the 70's and 80's, it hurt my ears to hear ads for *'mai'* this or that in Japanese. In the 90's, the horrid use of this pronoun as an adjective found its way into *English* advertizing . . . How delightful to find this poetic and authentic Japanese "my rain" that I can like! Polling my haiyû (friends in haiku), I find that most are not familiar with it.

♪　**Poems of Commerce in Arima.**　Mitani Kazuma's books have illustrations of hundreds of Edo street vendors and shops, with explanations spiced with *senryû* and *zappai*. Haikai's Kyoriku (d.1715) edited a large collection of *haikai/zappai* on craftsmen. *Broadview* includes collections of *kyôka* by people in various professions: 鶴岡　放生会職人歌合 1767/15c?. Most of the poems either bore or are beyond me, but one strikes me as the pun equivalent of a fine loose rhyme: 日は入て月こそ空にねり出れ　独すまひの心地のみして　*hi wa irite tsuki koso sora ni neri-idere hitorizumai no kokochi* ... Were the poet not 相撲 Sumô, I would have missed it (*hitorizumai* 独りすまひ vs *hitorizumô* 独りすまほ) *living by yourself* vs. *wrestling with yourself*). Still, I bet there are good *kyôka* about professions out there and some already Englished. I stuck to translating what seemed unique observations such as selling imperfect vessels, rare local items, such as the "doll-brush," and skipped weapons, toy or real, probably sold in all tourist towns and only felt sorry later that I did not translate one of the last noting that blacksmiths did such a good business, apprentices walked about outside brandishing weapons for sale as the shop was too packed to allow all the customers in: 買人をあますましとて長刀をふり売にする鍛治の弟子共　宗之　*kaibito o amasumashi tote*. . . That *is* a picture to imagine!

♪ ***A Skipped Poem about Wakasa-ya, the House of Youth   I think I'd like*** if I knew what it said: いちといひて二の湯にあらし若さやの　か〻を頼て文をやらはや　友和 *ichido iite ni no yu ni araji* . . . I guess this is about the rules of the establishment – people had to read so-called *yubumi* or 'bath-letters' and abide by them. It seems as if a mother is being asked to get involved and that *mom=kaka* may pun on *treading heels (kakato)* and that may be either a massage or for a device to stir up the water, etc....

♪ **Bathing Aids.** This word (literally hot-water-hand) was in the loofa poem I translated, but not needed in English. Looking it up in the OJD, I found a *haikai:*姫瓜の湯手にもなるかへちま瓜　友定　俳諧遠近集. *hime-uri no yûde ni mo naru ka hechima uri*　tomosada.

♪*And Here are Some more from Arima Selection* I could not fit but hated to leave. どうせ手元にアリマすから 。。。

```
1 蜘蛛滝　爪琴の手とやきかましさつ／＼と　糸ひく蜘の滝おとし哉　　　尚芳
2 鹿舌山　むかしより爰に有馬を何者か　かした山とは名付初けん　　　　清紙
3 大門　　大もんの袴を着し出ぬるや　公家の湯入のおむかひのため　　　行風
4 惣湯女をよめる　口はしのきいたる湯女の声／＼は有馬山から四十から／＼　重香
5 みめのよき湯女に湯文をよませたら　いよ／＼人かまいらさん銭　　　　行安
6 有馬冨士　山も風ふせく心やありまふし　かふる霞のきぬ頭巾哉　　　　重正
```

tsumekoto no / mukashi yori koko / daimon no hakama / kuchibashi / mime no yoki / yama mo kaze

1) is a droll soundscape description of Spider Falls; 2) a Deer-tongue mountain (both *kashita*) punned into a lent one just-so; 3), not one of Kôfû's wittier poems offers curious information about the treatment of *kuge* (court nobles or peers) in an otherwise laid-back resort; 4) fetes the chirpy voices of the yuna with the chickadees probably meaning older men appreciate the same; 5) has a pretty *yuna* read the bath regulations but hell if I get the last part (maybe about money paid for a no-show); 6) may fuse a *haikai* conceit about mist keeping a mountain warm with Sôgi's concern lest cherry blossoms catch cold and really describes the fake mist on a large model Fuji (diaphanous silk was also used for Hôrai (the magical Mount Merhu): see *The Fifth Season*: 2007);

7 妬湯　春の日もしつ心なく後妻の　湯花ちらしてにへかへるらん　行風
haru no hi mo shizugokoro naku uwanari no yubana chirashite niekaeruran　kôfû

7) The Uwanari-yu or Jealous Bath plays upon the famous poem by Ariwara no Narihira about cherry blossoms making men worry in the spring and is beautiful though I am unsure how to translate it. Do we have a first-wife knocking off and boiling blossoms standing for the second wife? Another on the same place far less elegant but easy to get:

腹たつるけしき有馬の後妻の　湯のふつ／＼はのろひことかも　貞因
hara tatsuru keshiki arima no uwanari no yu no butsubutsu wa noroigoto ka mo　teiin
belly-stand(b angry) lndscpe is/arima's secnd wife's hotwater's butsubutsu-as4 cursing?

*Jealous Springs is one angry landscape – the bubble sputter
of the water boiling up could be the first wife's curses.*

It helps to know that jealousy between the wives of a nobleman was legendary and the angry spirits of love-sick women were greatly feared. This word *uwanari* is itself very odd for it first means *the second wife*, second, *the envy felt by the first wife toward her* – that is, she impersonates the bad spirits laid on her! – and third, *just plain jealousy*. The Chinese character for the name of the establishment 妬 implies the last. Because of the second meaning, I had to make the first rather than second wife implicit in my translation, as we would identify curses with the curser not the cursed. I like to imagine the name comes from either a new establishment presuming itself to arouse the envy of other older bath-houses or as an abbreviation for *uwanari-uchi*, second-wife-beating (by the first wife or her friends), because guests were struck by fragrant switches. Be that as it may –

take my etymology with a cow-lick – there was this dark side to Arima. I don't think it boasted gibbets, but it did include, to borrow the title of one of Yi Fu Tuan's books I once scouted, *landscapes of fear*. Yes, how about this? *When you look over the way, the bath-girls become demons / Arima is not all that far from Hell's Valley* (note: sinners were usually nude and sometimes boiled) 有馬湯女を鬼そと見渡せは あたりに近き地獄谷哉 貞因 *arima yuna o oni zo . . .* Teiin. The springs there are extremely sulfurous. Translating *Hell* was hard. I think I came close with this cheerful retort by Kôfû:

*To grow up here, in Hell's Valley with such a name, I'll be
Damned if it's not funny but – Buddha-dais are all I see!*

But neither that, nor *To grow up here, in Hell's Valley with such a name, no dice! / But I'll be damned if I don't see a gallery of Buddha-dais!* really works in translation. Adding "damned" helped a bit, but there is no substitute for the familiar: the plant referred to, *hotoke-no-za* or Buddha's seat (henbit, bee nettle, *Lamium amplexicaule*), is one of seven lucky ones eaten in New Year's soup. 地獄谷と名にこそたてれ是や此 仏の座のみ立ならひつゝ 行風 *jigoku tani to na ni ko/so/datere kore ya . . .* kôfû (蛇足：こそ・子育て). Only one of the Hell's Valley poems, by Kôfû survives translation.

鳥ちこくにおちしとすれや静なる 暁ことの鴨のかんきん 行風
tori-jigoku ni ochishi to sure ya shizuka naru akatsuki goto no kamo no kankin
bird-hell-into dropping do if/and quiet becomes, daybreak-each's ducks' sutra=joy?

*Down they drop into Bird Hell and, then . . . silence.
Come dawn we always hear them: sutra for the souls of ducks!*
∼∼∼∼∼∼∼∼∼∼∼∼∼∼∼∼∼∼∼∼∼∼∼∼∼∼
*They splash down in Bird Hell and, then, the sound of silence.
Dawn after dawn we wake to sutra for those lucky ducks!*

Kôfû again. As incoming birds were said to "drop" they are indeed metaphysically right to drop into hell and the result is skillfully kept quiet until the last word, *kankin*. 看経 could mean *chanting sutras*, especially for the repose of the soul of the departed; it also could mean 換金 the *exchange for cash* of the dead ducks (vendors supplying the inns at dawn); or, less likely, unless there was a literary tradition of happy noisy birds at dawn, 歓欣 or *joy*. I am unsure of the pun for I also do not know if birds killed by poisoned water could still be eaten (poisoned fish have been eaten in many countries). Regardless what further research reveals, there is something about *ducks* that gives them a head-up in translation. Ducks and only ducks are comical no matter what you do with them.

毒水 諸の病もいゆる湯の山の なかれの末にいかに毒水 宗之
moromoro no yamai mo iyuru yu no yama no nagare no sue ni ika ni dokusui sôno
various/oodles-of diseases+emph. healng htwatr mt's flow's end-at much-so poisn watr

*Diseases of all sorts flow down this mountain where springs heal;
This poison water in the vale is but nature turned full wheel.*
∼∼∼∼∼∼∼∼∼∼∼∼∼∼∼∼∼∼∼∼∼∼∼∼∼∼
*From all disease this hill of springs healed those who sought her
Who can be surprised if her run-off ends up poison water!*

8 落葉山　そちも思案時雨は袖の涙かと　落葉山ほとかはゆなにこそ　　　行風
9 平清盛公石塔　花いけにへいしすへしは清盛の墓さふらふといはぬはかりそ　行風
10 奥院　えてし哉口にはくしゆの我あるは　いかなるかこれ奥のゐん　　　行風

sochi mo shian shigure . . . / hana ike ni . . . / eteshi kana kuchi ni . . . all, Kôfû

Even Borges' Chinese Encyclopedia seems as logical as an insect next to my squeezing translations that work within ones I can not yet do. To finish, 8) with the "river" *kawa* suitable for a mountain modifying while morphing into "cute" bathgirl (*kawa*yuna) to finalize the metaphorical fusing of mountain-*shigure* and bath-girl's *my rain* is a *kyôka* masterpiece and I only wish it could be translated; 9) If you recall, Kôfû made a poem playing on Iwakura (なんと岩倉) that lamented the condition of Shigemori's memorial; this does the same for Kiyomori, another legend. I do not fully understand it but love the mildly expressed but poignant outrage to find his grave untended.   10) This is one I'd rather not try than risk getting wrong, but I can say that punning with a vowel change (*oku-no-in* ⇒ *oku-no-en*) is both rare and, here, well-done.

Crabs, Shrimps and Surimono – from Noah Braunen's article　　　424 頁

♪ **Danjûrô's Lobster – or Ise (Florida) Crawfish – poem. Two more tries:**

> *Two faces of Edo*
> *know no fear – Ise's King Shrimp*
> *heads the New Year.*
> *Feast your eyes then, what an Age,*
> 　*Go catch Danjûrô on stage!*

> *In Edo, new, two*
> *Fearless faces without match*
> *Ise's crawfish*
> *will feast your eyes: then catch*
> 　*Danjûrô for a surprise!*

♪ **Surimono Kyôka.** Before giving one rather plain example, Braunen notes that "the poems of Ward's *surimono* collection, though *kyôka* in form, are not what we would normally term 'comic' or 'mad' in the West." He has a point. The average *surimono kyôka* I have seen *is* less interesting, both linguistically and conceptually, than the average *kyôka* in a book where they do not play second fiddle to the pictures. But the novelty of the crab metaphor – true for rays of sun shining through the Edo skyline I would guess – in one poem and the complex split idiom and puns of the seven herb broth/gruel=itchiness in another are so good that I am more convinced than ever that someone needs to scour *surimono* for good poems which might otherwise not be collected. Of course, *good* is not synonymous with 'mad' or 'comic,' but I think we can agree the aforementioned poems are witty. We owe thanks to the collector Sydney C. Ward and translator Noah Braunen for bringing them to us. After reading the *Painted Bride* article, I made the extra effort required – interlibrary loan arrangement – to see more surimono and though it set back publication by weeks, as the additional chapters show, it was worth it. I discovered enough good kyôka to *know* surimono should not be overlooked by literary critics and learned that, outside of Japan, Art Publishing has given much more attention to *kyôka*, albeit late-18-mid-19c *kyôka* alone, than Literature has!

♪ **Why do I suggest people "see *The Fifth Season* to capture the mood?"** Let me try to explain. My book of 2,000 translated haiku about the New Year, which was until the mid-20c given a section or separate book in haikai almanacs as large as that for the other four seasons, may not include more than a few *kyôka*, but it clarifies some poetic conceits which make reading New Year surimono easier. Even Blyth, very appreciative of the Japanese New Year as a time of enchantment and re-creating the world, gave it not even a tenth of the attention he gave the other seasons, if you count the number of poems he translated for each season, respectively. That was unfortunate because even cultural anthropological studies of New Year customs do not pick up all the *conceptual detail and mixed feelings* that may be mastered by a careful reading of many poems. I hope visually oriented people who buy books of *surimono* will read more of the poetry I have translated and explained and come to appreciate those pictures with a new mind's eye.

Japanese Poetry Prints: Spring Comes in Tiger Eyes? McKee　　　426 頁

♪ ***More Teeth-hardening Poems.*** Issa's tôfu *ku* was but one of many. I once gave a talk about teeth-hardening rite haiku to some dentists and lost my little collection of witty old haiku and *senryû* by failing to get them safely back to the file. Carpenter 2008 has a *kyôka* specifically addressing the topic:

鏡もちかすミ男の歯固にくひかいたやうな春の三日月　青陽館梅世 seiyôkan
kagami mochi kasumi otoko no hagatame ni kui-kaita yô na haru no mikazuki umeyo

♪*What happened to the Round Mirror Mochi in the Sky?* ♪

That crumbly edge of the spring crescent moon – good grief,
It looks like the Mist Man took a big bite to harden his teeth!

~~~~~~~~~~~~~~~~~~~~~~~~~

The crescent moon / on the third day of spring / looks like a round rice cake
chomped on by the Mist Man / to harden his teeth.   – trans. carpenter 2008

Issa mentions a Spring moon that looked like it would wet anything it touched, so I imagined the usual blade-like sharp edge was not seen and added "crumbly" not in the original as well as the *"good grief,"* for this is a Charlie Brown world! Note that I never heard of this "male deity of spring mentioned in ancient Japanese literature" (Ibid). He is not even in my OJD. So surimono taught me something here! I would add that this deity would, like the *katsura otoko*, the usual man in the moon, seem to be very handsome and use mirrors to stay so, as the rice cake here seems a mirror plain and simple until we find out it is the moon. Also, one of the pieces of mirror-mochi stands for the moon (in a stack, the earth on bottom is largest the moon in the middle medium and the sun on top smallest, for the full moon does look a bit larger than the sun and it is between the sun and earth. Having successfully strengthened my nails (for picking stringed instruments) by tapping them, I believe there is something to the belief that teeth may be hardened by use.

♪***Another Danjûrô Lobster/Shrimp.*** Since writing the above, I found McKee has scores of pages about the New Year in the introductions to his books on/of *surimono* (2006, 2008). Still, my book (see biblio) has more detail and especially poetic trope. I also found, in 2008, I believe – it was last minute before returning the book – another New Year shrimp/crawfish/lobster *kyôka* and by the same poet, Sakuragawa Jihinari:

再現四方の春かど松竹に寅のとし江戸ツ子役の海老ハ尾頭　桜川慈悲成
yomonoharu kadomatsu take ni tora no toshi edokko-yaku no ebi wa okashira

New Year's around and from the bamboo within our gate-pines
Out springs the Tiger Year led by King Shrimp, an Edoite

~~~~~~~~~~~~~~~~~~~~~~~~~

Spring is out and all about the gate-pines bamboo Tiger year
crouches below our Shrimp with head and tail, it's Edo Kid!

I did not have time to put in capital letters and forget where the lines are supposed to break in McKee's translation – as a poor typist, capital letters give me trouble so I skip them when tired – but here is what I have: *"Spring in all directions in the gate pine's bamboo a tiger year felicitously lurks and playing "kid of edo," its master, Ebizô, a lobster head to tail."* Again, I cannot picture a "lobster" without big claws and wonder, if Florida crawfish or Ise Shrimp will not do, how about "King Shrimp" (it might mean another species, but who cares!)? More important, McKee points out how this poem captures the Edo espirit. Dauntless Danjûrô, seventh generation Ebizô (king-shrimp-guy) stands for the macho Edoite and at the same time, the fact that most self-respecting Edoites will start the year in debt rather than not buy an Ise *ebi* whole with feelers intact. *Okashira* generally means boss お頭(leader of a festival float or a gang) or head and tail 尾頭. I recall seeing that *tail* 尾 in the script, so while the *boss* was punned, the latter "head and tail" was intended. However, even the enormous OJD does not give a "whole shebang" reading for *okashira*. But, there is a word *okashira-tsuki* or "tail-head-attached" which means just that and is used particularly for whole things used as offerings, though today the *o* is usually wrongly taken for an honorific instead of a tail. In other words, thanks to this *kyôka,* I now know something even my huge dictionary does not: *okashira-tsuki* was sometimes used in the abbreviated form *okashira*. Pardon the minutia.

♪ ***A Different Kind of Shrimp Served Up by Takuan***. Despite the traditionally propitious significance of every feature of the *ebi*=shrimp, embodiment of the most valued of all treasures, longevity, one 17c monk had the freedom of mind to play more objectively with its symbolism. I found this in the 1666 *Savage Songs* anthology edited by Kôfû:

蜆子絵によめる　いかばかりえびを取くふ報ひあらば 終には老の腰やかゞまん　沢庵和尚
ikabakari ebi o tori-kuu mukui araba tsui ni wa oi no koshi ya kagaman

If we must pay for each shrimp we eat, then in the end
Is it any wonder that with age our backs must bend?
~~~~~~~~~~~~~~~~~~~~~~~~~~~~~
One can hardly eat a shrimp without causing any hurt;
After years of eating them a crooked back is just desert!

Here, shrimp are not associated with the good fortune of being blessed with a long life, but with a misfortune accompanying it. Could Takuan have noticed not all old people were bent and, as a monk who reflected on the sin of taking animal life, realized how odd it is that we benefit by eating rather than protecting a symbol of longevity?

~~~~~~

Coloring in the New Year w/ a Straight Face – all McKee chapters 428 頁

♪ **"Straight Face" – *In Case You Missed It*.** As explained somewhere, the name of the top surimono commissioner and poet, Magao, literally means "straight (or, true) face." His wit, which Daniel McKee explains well, though dense with pun and allusion, did, on the face of it, tend to be subtle and understated, so it is not an altogether misleading title.

♪ **The *Harugoma*.** I ought not to have missed the other meaning of the *spring colt/pony*, namely a beggar-performer. I should not have stopped once I found *one* interesting reading but looked up that word, *just in case*. My Japanese respondent wrote 「春駒」にはもう一つの意味があり、辞書から引くと「 門付け芸の一。正月に各戸を回り、馬の首の形をしたものを持ったり、また、これにまたがったりして歌い踊るもの。また、その芸人」です。「春駒」である「我」には「食み出し」（はみだすこと。はみだしたもの。「社会の一者」）という意識があった。それと同時に馬が食べたあとなので雪は取り除かれている。若菜の葉も「食み出して」（おさまりきらずに外に出る。はみでる）いる。それを摘むという情景と思われます。 I put this here partly to show how fortunate I am to have Yoshioka Ikuo's help. Also, because I thought I might mention a similar case with a haiku where *I* looked it up in the dictionary – by *the* dictionary, I always mean the OJD, or, as it is usually called the *Nihonkokugodaijiten* – and found something similar.

福介がちゃんと居てぼたん哉　一茶
fukusuke ga chanto suwatte botan kana issa 1822
luck/happiness-guy properly sits/ting peony/botan 'tisØ!

lucky boy
sits right plumply
a peony

A Lucky Boy　　　　　　　　　　　　　　　　　　*A Lucky Boy*
sitting there properly　　　　　　　　　　　　*sits down as he should*
my peony　　　　　　　　　　　　　　　　　　　*peony, botan!*

My peony blooms
Fat and happy Lucky Boys
always sit down!

Issa's poem caught my attention because I felt he used the peony, *botan*, as psychological mimesis – *gitaigo*, as opposed to *giseigo*, onomatopoeia – describing a heavy flower or a number of heavy flowers pulling the thin limb/s of the plant to the ground or close to it. I already knew the flower was not just the symbol of prosperity but of might and wealth (it was the Sinosphere's "king of flowers") that was admirably modest for keeping close to the ground (see my article, *The Peon and the Peony* at Simply Haiku, summer 2005, on line, or wait for the book, *Haiku In Context*). The original Fukusuke – Fortune-guy, Lucky-boy – was a large-headed model (ceramic or wood) of the Chinese God of Prosperity, invariably seated. I know that and saw it noted in a book on Issa. But, that did not explain the *chanto,* or "as is proper" – a word a parent might use to get a kid to behave better – so I looked up *fukusuke* in the OJD and, sure enough, shortly before Issa wrote his *ku*, there was a fad for – or a plague of – door-to-door salesmen of good luck, i.e., wassailers (?) who danced wearing large masks of Fukusuke until you paid them off. Issa mentions their visit in his journal a couple years before the above poem appears. So Issa praising his peony, criticizes a practice of his time and plays with a saying about ideal beauty standing, walking and sitting like three different flowers, where the "sitting" is identified with the peony – this is only obliquely alluded to in the poem and could not be squeezed into the translation, unless,

Japanese Botany

That Lucky Boy,
sitting just so, is also
a beauty you know.

The original is a simultaneously simple yet complex poem which I would now call a superb *kyôku*. In retrospect, that is for readers who did not experience house-invasions by dancing Lucky Boys, it is also something *kyôka* often were, even for contemporaries, a puzzle, as is my last reading, a paraverse, rather than translation per se. Back to the Spring ponies or colts, if you prefer. You may now note that McKee's translation is not *wrong*. It is a bit more accurate than even my final translation. Only, it seemed lacking without a proper understanding of mind animating the "I." The other poem in that *surimono* was such a fine parody, I feel obliged to give it so students of literature who do not pay much attention to surimono can see that Shokusanjin and gang in the late-18c were not the only ones who did it well: 春日の野の飛火乃野守ゆでてみよ　いまつミたての若菜ひと鍋　百林亭真杉 Compare the romanizations of the 9005 Kokinshû waka #18 by Anonymous and Hayakurintei Masugi's 1822 *kyôka* for yourself:

kasugano no tobihi no nomori idete miyo   ima iku ka arite wakana tsumitemu
kasugano no tobihi no nomori yudete miyo   ima tsumitate no wakana hitonabe

"Go out" becomes "boil" by changing one syllabet い⇒ゆ(*i/yu*)! I should add that the picture shows a beautiful indoor scene of a Genji-like courtier with four two adult ladies in waiting and two children for which the poems about outsiders make a perfect foil. *In case the critical reader wonders how I could write a book on the New Year and still miss the *spring colts/ponies*, it is because my book is the first of two volumes and only covers half of the main themes. *Manzai* and other performer/wassailer/beggars (which would have found *harugoma*), will be in the largely unwritten next volume. Checking now, I see Issa does have five *harugoma,* and *all* are about the beggars: *Spring colts / even the bamboo ones / high spirited!* 春駒は竹でしてさへいさみけり　*harugoma wa take* . . . But, again, I should have caught it because of the *mo* (*even*, or *too*) after the *ware* (I). "I, too" should have told me something more was going on. On the New Year in particular, that *mo* ties everyone together. We translators – yes, I am writing this for the part of my readership who knows the joy of guessing a meaning and the pain of missing it – need to pay more attention to that *mo*. When, we read, say, *tamamushi no hikari nodokeki haru no hi wa kaiba mo isamu nami no hatsu hana*　tsuru no hinako (hokusai:1821 in carpenter 2008), we need to recognize and explain where we cannot fit into the translation (*". . . where the seahorses frolic"* A. Haft) the idea is that *even* the horses of the sea, as those on land, *isamu* – frolic in a gallant manner. *In a common verb, the sea is being reunited with the land.* Or, let me take another, a poem about a Japanese fiddle, *yama mo kasumi nobe wa komatsu no ne no haru ni hikeru kokyû mo yumi hajime kana* shûkyôtei tsuchimaru (hokusai:1822 ibid). Here, again, *". . . the bow of the kokyû / is drawn for the first time"* to be sure, but the thing which makes the New Year spirit felt is that this musical instrument *too* is experiencing its 'first bow' of the year. That is to say, the *kokyû* is included among the other first-bows of the year, i.e., those used for archery. Note that there is nothing wrong with the translations. It is just that the heart of a poem, like its wit, needs something more than just translation. And, in the case of the *kokyû* poem, the most interesting thing to me was that the Japanese original does not have も *mo* but a very clear の *no!* Hokusai or his helper – the four poems are all written by the same hand – must have made a mistake, for the poem is better with the *mo*. Or, maybe not. it is possible the poet did indeed avoid *mo*, for some in post-Bashô haikai preferred to be what I would call *too* subtle, which is to say to leave the "even" unsaid in order to be less obvious. A perfect example of that is a poem by Ryûgaen Isshi found in a ca. 1828 print by Hokkei, *Geisha arriving for a performance:*

ikabakari hana ya chiruramu shamisen no koma no isameru haru no hikizome 柳芽園一枝
how much blssms+emph scatter?/! shamisn's brdge's encourge/livens sprng's frst-pick/playng

> *Her first performance of the spring makes the bridge on her shami dance*
> *Were that bridge its namesake, petals would fly and it would prance!*

> *How quickly / the blossoms will scatter / when the year's first sounds /*
> *of the shamisen / stir the colts to frisky play.* – trans. carpenter 2008

> *How the petals fly as the bridge of her shamisen starts dancing*
> *Wildly as a colt enjoying his first horseplay of the spring!*

Here, as Carpenter points out (and I would surely have missed), the allusion is probably to a passage in a popular folksong wondering why a colt was tied to a blooming cherry where movement might make the blossoms fall; but the poem itself does not mention a colt but only another denotation of *koma,* the bridge of a string instrument, and the connection is made by the verb *isameru,* the transitive form of *isamu,* the high-spirited behavior expected of spring colts, without the *mo,* or "too." However, we can still guess that the bridge of the instrument in its friskiness is joining the larger *koma* community of the New Year. My respondent feels the metaphor alone is more likely than actual colts. Issa has a *ku* where a dancing girl's wood clogs (*bokuri*) knock of petals . . .

♪ **Hands of the Wind.** As I was much more familiar with the "legs" of the sun and the rain than the "hands" of the wind until coming across the latter in abundance in the 19c surimono, I looked it up in the OJD, which had an eg. from a 19c *senryû* relying on the common god=*kami*=hair pun for a nominal just-so explanation as to why trees become bare in the Gods-out Month:

> 風の手で木の葉を削る神無月　柳 120
> *kaze no te de konoha o kezuru kaminazuki*

> god=kami=hair

> *The hands of the wind*
> *help shave leaves off trees*
> *for Kamiless Month.*

♪ ***The Ise Shrimp/Crawfish/Lobster's Ise in Surimono Perspective.*** While the title for the *picture* by Kubo Shunman with the horn-letter lobster poem expressing the mixed feelings about travel was *Poets and Pilgrims on the Road to Ise Shrine*, McKee points out the ca.1800 *surimono* was made to commemorate a pilgrimage of poet friends to Ise Shrine and that the pilgrimages peaked in 1830 with 4.5 million visitors/yr.. 22 poets, many major poets in the *kyôka* movement, contributed poems making this a historically significant surimono as it shows the extent of interest in the mixed genre that would, to some extent, become the centerpiece of the *kyôka* movement after the conservative government clamped down on Shokusanjin and gang. McKee translated and explained 6 of those poems of which the following, by Magao, was the last. The illustration was too small for me to read the lettering so I only give the romanization:

kimi ga kogi nagaku funaji zo   yadogoto no kugutsu wa ikani sode o hiku tomo   magao
you rowng long boat-road+emph. inn-each's pppteer=tarts-as4 howevr sleeve+acc pull though
It's a long road you have to navigate, / rowing your boat – / no matter how at every house / the puppeteer girls / tug at your sleeves.   – trans. daniel mckee 2008

> *'Tis a long road to go if you must row, and lug, and float,*
> *though the pretty puppeteer at ev'ry inn will tug yr. boat.*

I also tried punning "always tug you inn by coat" but settled with the above. Of course, the original mentions "sleeves" and there is no *lugging* or *floating* mentioned. McKee's translation (aside from the "how") is fine, but I just cannot tell if the tug gets back to the boat and lets the wit float or not. Speaking of *tug*, I like to think Magao picks up on the "pull" (same *hiku*) on the heart associated with the ox in the Ise Shrimp poem, but it is hard to tell.

♪Re: ***A Pet Cat with a block of Dried Fish*** in McKee 2006. The image (pl 11) by Teisei Hokuba (1771-1844) of a cat w/ teeth and claws sunk into the bonito was so powerful it was hard to concentrate on the poem. First, I was intrigued by the orange tiger shadow (rounded ears) behind the head of the grayish cat to suggest it was the Year of the Tiger and wondered if such shadow-language was unique or old hat (it was not addressed). Next, the edge of the pupils were thin right-handed* crescent moons the thickness of the three-day moon: that was the day of the first-month when the rite of *hagatame,* or "tooth-hardening" was performed. So, this cat was not just a diurnal but a lunar (and w/ the above-mentioned shadow) annual timepiece! * waxing moons are right-handed, waning, left-.

♪Re: ***The Sea-horses***. The art decor style clean lines of the picture by Aoigaoka Keisei (fl. c. 1818-1835) seems ahead of its time. Both sea-horses and what some today call sea dragons were called "dragon's miscarriages/abandoned babies" (*tatsu-no-otoshi'ko*). Though this was for the 1820 Year of the Dragon, it was closer to what I think of as a sea horse rather than the more ornate, or rather camouflaged variety that *looks like* a sea-dragon. McKee notes Hokusai made sea-horses for the Year of the Horse, which is remarkable if the name connection was not yet made in Japanese.

♪***One Good Poem I Missed.*** Minutes before having to return McKee 2006 to the library I found a poem by Gôshû Hino Ryûjôen Umeyasu in a 1832 surimono print by Tottoya Hokkei too interesting not to introduce:

kama no futa akete medetaki haru wa kyô jigoku mo ukabu kugai jûnen
kettle/s' lid opening joyous spring-as-for today hell even floats/rises painworld 10yrs

> *After ten long years in the water world of woe, she is happy as can be –*
> *Today, w/ Spring, the cauldron lid comes off & Hell herself floats free!*

~~~~~~~~~~~~~~~~~~~~~~~~~~~~~~~~~~~~~~~

> *Today, with happy spring / The lids are lifted / From the cauldrons /*
> *And Jigoku floats free / After ten years in the world of pain* – trans. mckee

McKee explains that Jigoku was tricked away from her family and raised by mountain outlaws and had to make her living selling her beauty – she named herself Hell (Jigoku) and wore clothing showing scenes from it – Japanese artists who enjoyed depicting supernatural monsters naturally did a good job on Hell – which may be seen in Hokkei's print. *Kugai* is a Buddhist word for the world of pain in which we all live in but vernacularly the particularly tortuous circumstances women sold into prostitution had to endure. Jigoku, who convinced herself it was her karma, for something bad she did in another life, met Ikkyû and impressed him by reciting his Gate Pine poem, which we have read in this book. Since Ikkyû's poem was one of the rare, rare ones not treating New Year as a completely joyous occasion, it is fitting that pictures of Hell should be introduced in this New Year's print. McKee also points out that there is a saying that on New Year's the lids are lifted from even the cauldrons of hell. As I explain in detail in *Topsy-turvy 1585* (2004), Hell in Japan was not a place that was bad in itself. Rather, it was a place that served to make the world a better place. Unlike our Devil, the King, or chief judge of the Japanese Hades was carrying out his duty responsibly and torture was not done for sadistic reasons, though some artists showed ghouls who seemed to enjoy their work meting it out.

Snowball to White Snake, McKee to Carpenter 436 頁

♪ ***The Great Teura vs Teuchi Debate***. As another *chi* ち in the same poem sure seemed similar to me and the magic mallet implies such striking, I feel fairly confident on this one, despite both McKee and my respondent feeling the opposite here. How I long for an open debate! More people, more input! McKee wrote the following in his 2008 book:

> "I have no doubt that many mistakes have crept into this catalogue, as they did into our previous effort, Japanese Poetry Prints . . . These errors . . . are entirely my own and I can only hope they will be outweighed by the many positive discoveries we have been able to add to surimono studies. It is my hope . . . to create an online version of such collections, so that viewers can arrange the prints according to different criteria, and corrections can be continually input, not limited by publication deadlines.

All I can say is *amen*, and likewise for mine. I have already thrown up questions at open online forums and want to do more in the future. Anyone who would not limit him or herself to easy things to translate or write about needs such a system to do their best work and grow as a scholar more rapidly than would otherwise be possible. I would only add that it is not a simple matter of "corrections." The forum needs the open bbs system more common in Japan than the top-down blog system typical in the Occident so people can comfortably debate their respective readings rather than simply comment upon authority. By the way, here is one more *teuchi-teuchi* poem by Mitoku 未得:

春風にあひせられてやさわらへの　てうち／＼をするはいくたひ
harukaze ni abiserarete ya sawarabe no teuchi-teuchi o suru wa ikutabi 1649
spring wind/s-by/in showerd!/?/: yung-brackns' fist-shakng-do-as4 howmanytimes?

> *How many Springs have the Young Brackens bashed about
> by gusts of wind shook their fists and all but raised a shout?*

I must admit to being unsure of what is happening. I think *teuchi-teuchi* is what Shokusanjin would later call *nigirikobushi o furiagete, i.e.,* fist-shaking. But it might mean the wind or someone battered by it is killing/plucking bracken hands by hand, as *te-uchi* most commonly means that. Perhaps, we can settle this by the next edition. The final "all but raised a shout" is all mine. Note that warabe is a pronunciation of warabi that happens to be homophonous with "little children."

♪ ***On the Treatment of Bracken***. McKee's "young mountain vegetables" bothered me even if precision with respect to natural phenomena does not much matter to kyôka so it should not matter much to the translator. First, I thought, he saw some dictionaries call the *bracken* or the *maidenhair fern*, as it is also translated, *poisonous*, and thought to set that straight by making *warabi* plain and simple a mountain *vegetable*. On second thought, I would bet a Japanese person whom he asked in person "What's this *warabi*, anyway?" responded, "Well, you've probably seen it in a pack at the store; it is called Sansai, "mountain vegetables." In his 2008 book, I believe he changed it to *fern*. I have only seen Carpenter 2008 and he got it more or less right. Here is the first of six poems, the best lyrical series I think I have seen in surimono, by Rokusekien Meshimochi:

恋しらぬうなゐをとめもさわらひの手をなつかしミにきる春の野　六石園飯持
koi shiranu unai otome mo sawarabi no te o natsukashimi nigiru haru no no meshimochi
romance know-not lttle girl evn young brackn's hand+acc cherishingly squeeze spring-field

> *Even a young girl who has never known love is fondly recalling*
> *How she held hands with maiden hair fern in the fields of spring*
> ~~~~~~
> *Even the maiden who never knew love longs for what she misses,*
> *Holding hands with the bracken in spring fields she so cherished.*

Carpenter's translation, *"Even the young maiden / who has never known love / will have fond memories / of holding hands with fern shoots / in the fields of spring."* is fine and – no, both he and I may be wrong not to try harder to maintain the thing-centered original syntax, though it does require the field to move to the front of the poem –

> *This field of spring, where even a maiden yet to know man,*
> *Once again holds hands with sweetly remembered bracken*

– unless we do something complex such as adding, say, *"Here, where ~"* at the start and then breaking near the end with a dash or dots to end with the field. The poem refers to a Noh play about a priest meeting a 'young local woman' who turned out to be the ghost of Unai-otome, who was courted by two men and, Carpenter explains, *"could not decide which to take as her husband, and ultimately drowned herself out of despair"* and which I recall from the 8c *Manyô-shû* (where there are two poems with long prefaces about her) as the idea of an eight-year-old with such a beautiful mind that she would kill herself to stop men from fighting over her is not something even my poor memory would ever forget. *"The poem suggests,"* continues Carpenter, *"that the young woman who finds true love will still enjoy 'holding hands' with fern shoots, the curled heads of which were traditionally said to resemble closed fists."* When I write that Carpenter had the warabi "more or less right" it was because fists were not the main thing "traditionally." They were synonymous with tiny hands and arms and though they often wringed their little hands for mercy (not to be broken off to be eaten), they also wove, stole things, cheered, were squeezed, scooped up dew, were read by fortune-tellers (!), sweated, held hand-mirrors (dew-drops), and Chiyo, the greatest female haiku poet even had them giving a hand to a party climbing a steep mountain (see *Fly-ku!* for all the poems). The fists and pounding seem to have become especially popular in *surimono* because Shokusanjin had what may be the earliest fist pounding – threatening a fight – bracken (an Edo kid?) in his *kyôka* about the wind slapping around a mountain (*sawarabi ga nigirikobushi . . .*). Also, *natsukashimi* is a pleasant feeling combining memory and the joy of reunion with something absent or missed. I imagine she, the ghost (grown somewhat older?), grips some plucked shoots and fondly recalls the fields of her childhood. Ah, the next of the six lyrical poems in the ca. 1823 lyrical series called *Bizenware wine bottle and a Chinese-style bowl with plum blossoms* pictured by Gakutei reads a strand of mist as a one-string zither. I have spent years experimenting with one-string instruments and will definitely include the poem and the story of the instrument made from a plank from the eaves of the lodgings of an exiled courtier in a book-to-be on my adventure and discoveries. I have read a big fat novel about a one-string koto, but the poem is worth the whole book!

♪ ***The Strong Woman of Ômi.*** McKee, after describing numerous versions of the strong women prints, added the following disclaimer(?): *"As these multiple examples suggest,* *the motif of the strongwoman was a popular one in nineteenth century literature and art, though a fascination with powerful women did not by any means translate into respect for women's rights."* Because *Mad In Translation* focuses upon poetry, I neglect the broader context, but feel obliged to respond as some might infer from this that Japan was not a particularly progressive place for women. Actually, it depends on what country or time is considered and what classes are compared. In the 19c, one can say that low class (most) women in Japan still had more rights vis-à-vis their spouse with regards to divorce and ownership of property, not to mention the household budget, than their counterparts in West Europe, while the samurai women (5%?) who once enjoyed more freedom than women in most of West Europe (see ch. 2 in *Topsy-turvy 1585*) were indeed left behind as women gained more rights in parts of the West over the course of that century.

~~~~~~

Reading Surimono – Literature Over the Radar: all Carpenter   440 頁

♪***Why Is It "Over the Radar?"***   *Kyôka* such as Issa's Silverfish or any number of the obscure *wild waka* in this book fly too low to be picked up by the scholars of literature; but, why have I seen practically nothing of Magao, Jihinari and surimono *kyôka* when, from the bibliographies in the back of McKee and Carpenter's books, it is clear there is a *large* body of translation going back decades? Probably because books related to costly art are only seen by art students and the wealthy. Despite the public face of museums, books sold in the museum gift shops (and some bookstores catering to wealthy urbanites) are never seen by most of us. They fly too high for us to see them. As most scholars are not wealthy, it is a good bet that more high-level drug-dealers, money-market hucksters own books of *surimono* or the thing itself than do those who can really appreciate them. Or, am I only extrapolating my sorry circumstance upon the world?

♪***The Palace Woman with a Fan and Hidden Pivot for the Cave Door.***   The lettering on Shigenobu's print is very faint. I know it is selfish to want more after all the Museum, Carpenter and McKee have done, but it would be wonderful to have the transcription of the Japanese as is (in print) so we could more easily observe orthographic punning. For readers not lucky enough to see *Reading Surimono*, the pivot of the fan is, with the woman's hand, hidden within her sleeve. A butterfly, identified with a hinge, is on her dress. Am I wrong to feel erotic undercurrents here? ★ I bounced my ideas off my respondent. Checking a dictionary of Edo-speak 江戸語の辞典 講談社学術文庫 he found all the sexy undercurrents I felt in the poem under the heading 天の岩戸 Heaven's Gate:

> 「両国辺に出た見世物の一。女が腰かけ、その前から小人形が唄・囃子につれてひょいひょいと首を出し、『やれ出た、それ出た、上見て下見て八丈じゃ』などうたう時、女陰を見せる」云々です。

So, I am not utterly crazy. 「天の戸」（女陰）を小人形の持った「扇」が開く。「君が代をあふぐ」は男性器が屹立する、その要に「玉」（睾丸）がある。こんなふうにも読めます。Detail aside, believe me, there *is* a risqué undercurrent here, though if my respondent saw how utterly innocent the picture is, he might have found it far harder to imagine!

★ ***Sex in Late-18c to early-19c Kyôka***. Perhaps the most risqué in *Reading Surimono* is a Rakuseian poem on a print of "Ichikawa Danjûrô VII and a woman watching a young boy practicing calligraphy," after Kunisada. Carpenter, noting the "distinctively homo-erotic connotation" rose to the occasion with: *"Effortlessly, he takes / the staff of the brush / to do it in the Daishi-style, / revealing lovely ink tones / at the crack of dawn in spring."* (やすらかに筆の志りとる大師やう墨色もよき春のあけほの　楽聖庵 *yasuraka ni fude no shiri toru daishi-yô sumi-iro mo yoki haru no akebono*. Kôbô Daishi (big teacher), creator of the syllabet song and an extraordinary calligrapher – he could write several things at once, throw ink, etc. – introduced esoteric Buddhism and homosexuality (in the temples) from China in the early 9c. While holding the far end of the brush may well be one of Kôbô's styles of writing – it allows for more play in the stroke – "taking the rear of the brush" generally means the wee flourish made as a brush-stroke ends while the tip leaves the paper. That flourish was evidently one mark of the so-called Daishi-*ryû*, or style. So, the poem has a bit more cover than one might assume from Carpenter. So saying, I cannot improve on his translation or explanation of how the children write out certain phrases and offer their writing to the local deities. Tenmei *kyôka* were somewhat more open, but If the 18c was relatively easy(?) when it came to heterosexual sex, it was less approving of homosexual sex than the 17c and pederasty (esp. for sale), in particular, was already on its way out when the *Tokuwa-shû* (1785) sent it off in style with two *osanago-koi* 稚子恋 *kyôka,* one punning the selfish and surreptitious nature of such a love with orphan-child and hide-and-go-seek (いとけなき心に思ふまゝごとの末は人目をかくれん坊かな 鷹羽番 *itokenaki kokoro . . . taka no hatsugai*) and the other has the ties (many and colorful for charm-related reasons) on an infant's robes *not* untied by his lord 稚子の思ひつめたるひとつ身になどつけ紐をとかぬ君かな 紀 定麿 *osanago no omoi . .* Ki no Sadamaru. Then again, maybe they would not need to be untied. The 19c was even more conservative – sex segregated in *senryû* & porn – and *surimono* on the clean side, but some erotic allusion was permitted in language and picture (those scrumptious labial kimono-openings). Seldom, however, are both found united in the same *surimono*.

♪ **A More Complex Lettered Carp** by Shokusanjin *"Try counting scales, 6 times 6 the number's by the text / Read the two-letter first and the horn letter next."* 「鯉画賛 六々の鱗の数を数へみんひとふたつ文字牛の角文字 *rokuroku no iroko no . . .* 千紅万紫」It was said that the こい Carp had 36 scales. I am afraid *senryû* counting vaginal folds are more interesting. He had another *tsuno moji* poem that is much better, so long as you recall the concept of the broken-back poem where the part before and after the pivot at mid-poem do not jive. It is a *meta-poem,* exampling itself by being properly broken, using the great-shrimp of Ise for the horn-letter and the two-letter and straight one for that "back/hip" (こし *koshi*). The unmentioned last letter of the Princess's four is a good picture of the break く. (海老の画に 角文字の伊勢海老を見て二つ文字すぐなる文字の腰折れの歌 蜀山人 *tsuno moji no ise ebi o mite futatsu ...*). It is far better than the previous carp, but not suitable for translation. And the best of all his horn-letter poems, in my opinion, is one of his first, written as Yomo no Akara: 寺子ども引きたる牛の角文字はいろはにほてい和尚なるかな 四方赤良 狂歌若葉集 1783 (*terakodomo hikitaru ushi no tsuno-moji . . .*). The punning from the letters indicating lessons of grammar that start, following the ox, with the い *i* to Hotei the fat god is, in the original, a delight to read.

Postscript – Silent Fart 454 頁

♪ *Silent Fart, Meet the Loud One.* No, we are not getting gross. For *that,* you can read Mark Twain's *1601.* Gutenberg, may it last forever, has it available on-line with excellent notes. Many of us are familiar with Tchaikovsky's 1812 symphony punctuated by West Point canon blasts, but few know what those notes reveal: *West Point first published Twain's Elizabethan farts!* And, no, I am not a devotee of crespulant literature even if I do have a chapter on its poetry in *The Woman Without a Hole* (207). The loud one I refer to here is not Twain's foul blast but a long lost friend, a *kyôka* I read before I even knew what a *kyôka* was and vaguely recalled with affection. I happened to find it as I arranged and edited these notes, the moment I opened Gunshi Gaishi's Ambrose Biercean dictionary 『迷解 笑辞苑』looking for the item on pebbles becoming boulders.

屁なりともあだなるものと思ふなよ ブツといふ字は佛なりけり 仙崖
he nari to mo ada naru mono to omou na yo butsu to iu ji wa hotoke narikeri sengai
fart is even vain/worthless thing-as think-not! butsu-as said letters-as-for buddha are!

Who says a fart is but empty air! Cut one & it goes
"Butsu!" – If that is not our Buddha, who knows!

"Butsu" the noise made by a short eructation (as might escape in bath water?) is one pronunciation of "Buddha." The one pointing this out is the monk, Sengai. That I came so close to missing what must be one of the best 100 *kyôka* of all time only goes to prove something I already knew. This edition is only the start.

Modern Kyôka
Or a short essay on something
I know nothing about.

I do know something about modern *senryû* and, as a whole, find it nothing at all like the classic stuff. Suspecting the same would be true for *kyôka*, especially because modern tanka includes most of what was kyôka, I was not going to say a thing about it, but wouldn't you know that as I read while doing my business before going out to feed the cows, I *found* some in one of a small number of Japanese books that are not dictionaries or haiku-related that I brought with me when I returned to Usania after twenty years abroad a decade ago. The book, titled *The Drool of Pavlov's Dog – the conditioned reflexes of desire* (パブロフの犬のよだれ 1988) is an interview series by the famous underarm hair-flashing porn star and linguaphile (it is not just the words she uses but how she enunciates them) Kuroki Kaori 黒木香. I was up to page 130, reading her interview with Hayashi Amari 林あまり, a singer of sexy songs and the wind-cloud-child 風雲児(between a wunderkind and a soldier of fortune) of *tanka*. After the poet heard some of the porn star's poems, she suggested some changes, noted they tended to be a bit more journalistic and critical than proper to *tanka* and, indeed, were too interesting for her more staid genre and, were, in a praise-worthy sense, "high-class *kyôka*" (誉める意味で高級な狂歌です). The most intriguing example was one she composed for the Italian porn star Ciccholina with whom she co-starred (あしびきの蛇をも飲みこむ聖ヴァギナ　魔性の色な　すたれることなし *ashibiki no hebi o mo . . .*). I am not shy of sexual themes but having seen neither of their movies, I am not even sure I would get the pillow word right, so we shall skip Englishing it in this book. The guest's praise primed Kaori into spilling a set of "tanka" she had prepared: そそり立つ　雄々しきカリの目に涙　夢甘白く　喉元縮む *sosori tatsu . . .* and ぷるぷると震える陰唇　御慈悲あらば　一突きに我れ　昇天せしめよ *purupuru to furue . . .* And, a little later, again, not for this book. 又、突きまくる極太肉棒の犬となり　あなるところも今塞がれむ *tsuki makuru . . .* These are closer to *kyôka* because of the outrageous metaphor and, in the last, a great pun on a type of sex many of us do not care for. The *tanka* star explained that sex was common in *tanka* but usually as part of a loving relationship not just sex for sex's sake, but it was expanding to cover the whole span of reality, at which point the porn star said she much appreciated the observation and feeling that went into a certain work by the tanka poet which I will introduce with another found two paragraphs later. Note that the first is pure *tanka* and the latter can be taken as *kyôka* only briefly, for it really comes from deep down in the ambivalent feelings a woman (and a man who is thinking of paternal possibilities) has about her menses.

生理中のＦＵＣＫは熱し血の海をふたりつくづく眺めてしまう 林あまり
seiri-chû no fuakku wa atsushi chi no umi o futari tsukuzuku nagamete shimau

> *It felt hot fucking when I had my period and*
> *We couldn't help staring at the sea of blood.*

> *Like a murderer, both of his hands are red;*
> *What is my man washing off in the shower!*

satsujinki no gotoku ryôte o akakushite otoko wa shahwah de nani nagashiiru
殺人鬼のごとく両手を赤くして　男はシャワーでなに流しいる 林あまり

Amari found writing tanka to be a form of masochism, as she found agony rather than ecstasy in composition. In other words, as the porn-star put it, she was a slave to words. True, replied the poet, most would be, or fancy themselves to be, a miko (shamaness/medium) of words, but I am content to be their slave. Then, she explained, that no fulfilled person could write tanka, anyway. Psycho-therapists often prescribe writing haiku as it is known to be good for mental health, but proscribe *tanka* as bad for the same. *Tanka*, she continued, was a creature of the shade. The actual composition might be S (somewhat contradicting her earlier statement), but the thing itself was M. Perhaps. But this "slave to words" was no slave to convention. Kaori asked about her tendency to go over the syllabet count at times. Amari replied that it had to do with rhythm and that she had to be alert or her poems degenerated into certain rhythms and by bursting out of rhythm poetry became sex rather than just masturbation. To which, the porn star introduced one of the *tanka* poet's poems that mentioned masturbation while using extra syllabets to create a poem that clearly is not:

亡き母がわたしを見たら殺すでしょう　夫の死後のマスターベーション
naki haha ga watashi o mitara korosu deshô otto no shigo no masutahbehshon

If my dead mother saw me, she would kill me;
Here masturbating after my husband's death!

This is exceptionally good, honest yet not at all sad because Amari uses idiom so fresh the subject is taken not only out of the closet but out of the poet herself. It is not just a matter of rhythm, but speech patterns. Unfortunately, I am unable to replicate or properly explain it. Let me just say that Hayashi Amari's word-sense is so good that when I read the above I recall Bacon on becoming Nature's slave to master her. Kaori, who mixed largely obsolete polite verb forms and archaic vocabulary into her speech, knew exactly which poems to introduce, even as she pretended to be interested in sex, alone. . . But where does all this leave modern *kyôka?* Again, I have no idea, for the porn-star's "high-class *kyôka"* – Kaori's language is more lofty than usual in modern poetry – I did not translate are all I know of it. But, if Hayashi Amari was not kidding about modern tanka, it is obvious to me what modern kyôka *should* be, or rather *do*. (The millennium of *kyôka* I have come to love is more the dream of reason than the nightmare of its sleep – Am I the only one to find the celebrated words, "~ *sueño de la razón,*" in the #43 print – one first intended as a frontispiece – of Goya's *Los Caprichos* (1799) ambiguous?) As *the tanka that are good for you*, "mad poems" should be an ever-growing, ever-giving reservoir of sanity, or free-thinking, in a world that will be destroyed without it, and of good humor for drinking or diving into, as you like.

An Appeal for Help Finding
Novel and Fine Modern Kyôka
To Replace This Temp. Chapter

小生の現在狂歌知識は、皆無しかも、現在狂歌通になる暇もない。若し貴方には、その知識も有り、趣味も本書のとよく似合うかと思えば、是非傑作の首狩りになって下さい.

黒木香のセンスは悪くはないが再版までに現在狂歌の小撰集に取替えいたしたいとおもいます

◆　オマケ　◆

そちが和歌こちがわからぬかなの川　たすけ舟なる漢字のいかだ

そちが和歌こちが馬鹿なるかなの川　かんじなければ心もみずに

生牛糞から牛の屎まで

from paying translation to non-paying translation, or, thirty years as a translator

此のうたのこゝろはしらしをそらくは　ていか家隆もしゃかもたるまも　　宗祇

しゃかたるまていか家隆もしらずせは　歌にはあらてうしのくそかな　　童子

　　明日、狂歌大観の索引篇を二千マイルも離れたる HU の Yenching 図書館へ戻さなければと徹夜の校正調べ。索引には各歌の頭文字が少なすぎて、一首を引いてみるためには、十か廿首も調べなければ済まないということが多かった。そのため、一首を見て戻ることのできない予は、たまたまの出会いが多い。上記も、朝 3 時半の発見。老犬達の目を覚ます程まではいかなかったが、大声で笑ってしまいました。そういえば、解かり易い首もあれば解かり難い首もあるが、歌そのものも、そもそも謎々になってしまう同然の行間もおもしろい。けれど、笑いだすまでには、そうでもない。それは、1978 年、日本で初めての勤め口であった日本翻訳センター㈱の最初の依頼の思い出のため。「うしのくそ」つまり、牛糞がみそとなる。お客さんから注文を受けた若きセールスマン（社長のことをよそ者にむいても、敬語を濃密に使う、ど田舎者の望月君）が、翻訳者の卵の外人さんの我が方へ、にゃにゃとした表情をしながらやって来たところ。事務所の回りにもわかる者皆も、やはり笑わないばかりの変な表情が気になった。さて、手渡してくれた、その依頼書の件名？「なま牛糞」。餌製造者のその商品の消化吸収実験の結果を要略、報告するれっきとした仕事ではあるが、専務がその最初の仕事の依頼書を記念に持ち帰ってもいいと言われては、親切に思い出になる初仕事を選んでくれたでしょう。何年後から、俳諧を読むようになったが、馬糞こそ、山程に出会うことになった一方、唐の女の子の髪型のそれを除けば、牛糞はひっそりとして眠っていた。で、上記の狂歌を読めば、寝不足ながら、笑って、「これでフールサークルが完成！」と勝手に独り踊り。牛糞から牛糞までの翻訳者人生。しかも、ここ、癌と闘中の妹の住む片田舎では、毎日牛糞を踏みながら暮らしている（縁があればと、くそ程ありながら、ふんと呼びたい）。妹が頭が悪くないが、想像力全くない、長い独り暮らし人生で、旱の牛糞にも負ける程カチ／＼と堅苦しくなっている。一緒に居るとやはり、ふむふむと不満なる毎日にはなる。そういう糞真面目な家にいながら狂歌を読み選ぶ　．．．

A Sampling of Tenmei Era Poet Names.

Most are taken from the Tenmei era fifty-poet (& fifty portrait) one-poem mini-anthology *Azumakyoku Kyôka Bunko* 吾妻曲狂歌文庫 put together by Yadoya no Meshimori 宿屋飯盛, whose name, "Lodge's Food Server" usually means women who helped draw travelers into the lodges and took good care of them in every way. Meshimori, a man, actually managed a lodge. Perhaps half again as many names are literally translated here and there in the text, mostly for no other reason than their being so ridiculous or clever it would be a sin not to let the reader share my amusement. In no particular order, but with some favor given to the famous –

• 尻焼猿人 Shiriyake no Sarundo is *Arse-burnt Monkeyman*. Famous classic poets included a Monkeyguy (Sarumaro 猿麿), Redman (Akahito 赤人) and Blackman (Kurohito 黒人). The "man" (人) is pronounced differently, in a way that may give a hunter-like nuance to the name. Such wanton pronunciation is common in *kyôka*, as it was in *haikai*, but more even so.

• 四方赤良 Yomo no Akara is *All-about Redgood*. Soundwise, *akara* is "redness." Yomo is literally "four-directions," but means *all-around*. I read an explanation once, but it must not have been very interesting. I forgot it. As Tenmei *kyôka's* first man, Ôta Nanpô, who was indeed, *read all around,* often went by *Akara* alone. Do not confuse that with *Akera Kankô*, whom, we will see below! Later, Ôta would call himself *Shokusanjin*, a quieter one-piece Chinese scholar of a name. Japanese collections tend to use one or another, so you cannot assume without checking where the poem was first published which name properly applies, with one or the other name are early or late work.

• 朱楽管江 Akera Kankô. *Crimson-pleasure Pipe-inlet* seems erotic though there is doubtlessly a bonafide Chinese connection, but, *soundwise*, it suggests one who sits there *akerakan-to,* with his mouth hanging open, or more pleasantly, some one who is *ridiculously open with everyone* – there is a passage in Shokusanjin's 蜀山家集 praising his character, Akera Kankô edited the 50-poet *Azuma Kyoku* anthology and included a handful of women, but none who were half the poet of his wife who is not in it! Caveat: Because many if not most of the Tenmei poet's names mimic those of ancient waka poets who almost always had the *no* between the names, much like aristocrats in Latin Europe with their *de* (or *del* or *d'*) some-family *de* some-family, but, unlike the Europeans, usually did not actually write it down, translators who must write it out in full sometimes do so when it does not actually exist. This is the case for Akera Kankô who has been mis-Englished more than once as Akera no Kankô, which cannot be right, as the "no" would destroy the pun.

• 節松嫁嫁 Fushimatsu no Kaka is Kankô's wife. Ostensibly, *Knot-pine Bridebride*, soundwise, her name means the *Unkempt Wife* or, maybe, though it makes little sense in English, the *Undone Wife* – I write it anyway, for in Japanese her name seems to echo her husband's. She was the second best-known kyôka poetess and, as you may guess from the above, my favorite, though I have not yet read much of her work.

• 智恵内子 Chie no Naishi is *Wisdom-is-not-child/ling* and I follow the wonderful translation by whoever translated an article by Tanaka Yûko for *Japan Echo* magazine: "Little Ignoramus" (Anyone: *who deserves credit?*) Her husband, Moto no Mokuami, ran a bath-house in central Edo. While he was a well-known *kyôka* poet, she was the best known *kyôka* poetess and her daughter, also a *kyôka* poet came to be known as Hima no Naishi, which the same translates as the "Girl with no time."

• 土師掻安 Haji no Kakiyasu is a name I would never guess how to pronounce. Visually, *dirt-teacher-scratch-easy*, phonetically, he becomes "shame made easy," i.e., or, as the above-mentioned article put it "Easily Embarrassed." The idea is more self-deprecatory: he often does things he should be ashamed of. I am afraid we have only one of his poems translated in this book.

• 加保茶元成 Kabocha no Motonari or *Pumpkin/Squash Source* or *Around the Pumpkin Plant* though the name visually reads Adding-preservation-tea-original whatever that means! An herbal drink! The above pronunciation comes from Sugimoto and Hamada's *Senryû & Kyôka* (Iwanami 大系#57: 1958). Keene has it Kabocha Gennari, or "Fed Up with Pumpkins." While I felt Keene misjudged Motonari/Gennari's fart palindrome, until I read more 18 and 19c books of *kyôka* and find his name phonetically given many times, I withhold judgment on this. *Moto*nari is good for evoking the *below*, or *around the Persimmon* vs *the Chestnut trees* of the past (*kakinomoto vs. kurinomoto* – see pg. 608); but, Gennari, or "fed up with," is not just good but great on the ears, so I would half like Keene to be right. Who knows! Maybe *both* are. Stay tuned to updates (on-line) for solutions to problems like this that cannot be settled by fiat. ("Pumpkin" beings to mind *Peter, Peter Pumpkin Eater* because the wife he "could not keep" was mistranslated in the most popular Japanese version as the wife who escaped from being imprisoned by him! A generation of Japanese children imagining a pumpkin as a jail! Well, maybe that is less frightening than the all too real specter of poverty that keeps millions of men – such as your author – single.) ♪ In *Yoshiwara: The Glittering World of the Japanese Courtesan* (U. of Hawaii: 1993), Cecilia Segawa Seigle makes him the *Original Pumpkin*. I would guess that we would get ten names out of ten translators! At any rate, our Pumpkin was the leader of the Yoshiwara ren (*kyôka* group in the Yoshiwara area), and Seigle adds that his mom was Sôô no Naisho "Quite a Wife," and his wife Akikaze no Nyôbô, literally, Autumn Wind Wife and meaning "Fickle Wife." What does it say about a culture when whole families enjoy poetry together?

• 森羅亭万象 Shinratei Manzô/Manshô/Banzô II (1762-1831), is a slightly different sort of name, taken from the better known Shinratei Manzô I (1754-1808) a bard, creator/economist 物産学, Dutch (Occident) scholar and kyôka master Mori-shima Chûryô, 森羅亭万象 who had another pen-name (for *kyôka*?) I like better: 竹杖為軽 Takezue no sugaru, soundwise meaning "I depend on my bamboo cane" with a character saying it makes him feel *light*. 森羅亭万象 puts a 亭 cottage/studio/ pavilion in the center of a Chinese phrase for "all phenomena" or "all-creation" 森羅万象 that looks like *forest-arhat-ten-thousand-elephants* to me. As befitting a name for all phenomena, it is pronounced in three ways, *shinramanshô, shinramanzô* and *shirabanzô*. Around 1990, I took the first pronunciation and punned it to mean that all phenomena were up for laughs by trading in the elephant character for a homophonic one meaning "laugh," 森羅万笑 which was the name of my column in Japan's top popular science magazine. I think the second Shinratei M/Banz/shô should have come up with what I did so as not confuse people.

• 春恥女 Haru no Hajime. "Spring's Shameful Woman." *Reading Surimono* has only one poem of hers (*Highlighting her eyebrows purple makes Princess Sao look like she is powerful, too – murasaki no kasumi no mayu o hikitatete chikara mo tsuyoku miyuru saohime*) which is not much, but I wanted to introduce that name! The poem accompanies a picture of the strong woman Ôigo pouring sake from a keg for a mighty Chinese warrior. The story *is* interesting.

• 鼻毛延樽 Hanage no Nobitaru (my guess: Hanage Nobitaru?). "(My/His) Nostril Hair Stretches Out." This 19c poet had one poem with a picture by Hokusai in *Reading Surimono* not worth quoting, but after all the attention given to nostril hair in this book, could I *not* mention such a name or give one last poem?　糸よりも鼻毛をのばすいかのほり 河辺の風に親父つられて　貞堂　狂歌活玉集 *ito yori mo hanage* Teidô 1740

四方歌垣真顔　Yomo Utagaki Magao. "Four-directions Song-wall Straight-face." The most well-known 19c kyôka master and king of surimono, his name was part of his publicity. That is the Four Directions, meaning "all-around" came from Yomo no Akara (Shokusanjin) the great *kyôka* master of the 1870's-90's who was forced out by the changing political situation. Song-wall is an ancient practice where youths and maidens sang or poeticized back and forth outdoors with results something like the English May Day and reinforced Magao's claim that *kyôka* went back to the *Kokinshû* if not the *Manyôshû*.

offer

Any reader who would like to introduce more – perhaps a clean 100 names – in the next edition, (or, perhaps, for a different Tenmei-only kyôka book) please volunteer. You may advertise *your* work or co-author in exchange.

P.S. Did I mention *my* pen name for haiku (and *kyôka*) is 敬愚, or "respect-fool(ishness)" ? It is an invented homophone of 敬具 or "respect-tool," i.e. *your respectful tool*, a common way to close a letter. For a pen name in English, I would choose one that sounds beautiful, droll, or otherwise interesting. I have used the alliterative Robin-dobbin, pedagogical Uncool Wabin (first invented as a suitable e-mail address for my nephew). But note that I did *not* mention the *pronunciation* of my Japanese name. That is because, while its being *keigu* is convenient for signing letters, the pleasure of the pun is visual.

A Short & Inadequate yet Extraordinarily Broad History of the Japanese 'Mad Poem*s*' called *Kyôka* or *not* called *Kyôka* but *like* them.

~ *By Any Other Name* ~

I

I *hate* writing history. It pits my *style* side, which would make one thrilling aphorism after another, against my *critical* side, which, hating generalization as unfair to some and misleading to all, would have me drag on and on in an endless sequence of *if-and-buts*. The cost is heavy, too. I mourn the time lost chasing down names and dates when I could be reading, which is to say hunting for treasure, or better yet, writing, which is to say working to share it with others. History is a game best played in leisure by the wealthy or university-affiliated. A poor man cannot sit out in the woods and write it, for even with a connection to the world-wide web, for which we pay out the nose (over $1000./yr.) as the rural 23 bps phone-line outside broadband range necessitates satellite, most resources that are online are private or inaccessible though supposedly public. Those *with* access who read this may feel I exaggerate. I can only ask, how would *you* like to work without access to the main data-bases for your specialty, not to mention the book-reviews and journal articles for all the peripheral fields, squirreled away outside of your perusal (by J-stor, for a start)?

(Circumstances do not allow me to move to a city or drive to a university library. I am stuck on a country property burdened with animals – tax-cows, old dogs and other merciless time-eaters – with my sister (intermittently knocked out by chemo) without money to move or hire help for I am the help, or even for auto-insurance, without which I dare not borrow her old clunker. Moreover, *we should not have to drive for access*. Library policies requiring *physical presence* for data-base use are anti-social and anti-ecological. Why waste fossil fuel for what can be moved on-line at infinitely less cost? Is the computer's fourth reason for existing (after calculating power, storage capacity and search capability) not supposed to be the benefit it could bring to the biosphere by saving paper and keeping us *still?* Perhaps we should link ownership of a computer to reasonable travel restrictions. When monotheist cultists brought down the Twin Towers, we were given a good opportunity to rethink our wasteful mobility. For a while, tele-conferencing took off; but, all too soon, the wealthy world, led by Usanians, including academics who attend far too many physical conferences for a finite world and many if not most liberal souls who preach environmentalism, were back to setting a bad example for all by flying hither and thither at whim. Should I add that not just independents such as me but even scholars associated with fine universities in countries where J-stor is seldom bought (eg. Japan) are shut out, even from articles far past copyright? There are truly public databases, but so much remains inaccessible it is fair to say that for all the hype about sharing, skilled hackers aside, millions of us float in a sea of information, with *data, data all around, but little we may see*. With labor, the tools *are* largely in the hands of the workers, even if they do not own them; with scholarship, however, even the tools of the trade are monopolized.)

And most of the books I need (in Japanese) cannot be found on interlibrary loan. I did spend about $400. to buy used books in Japan; but to cover the field even lightly, I really needed to spend several times that. And I would need almost ten times that (exchanging 100 yen/dollar) to properly cover the margins of the field as well. If access cannot be bought on-line, the *Waka Taikan* CD alone costs several thousand dollars *and* might require a change of computer to use which would cost more . . .

Again, I *hate* writing history. Though my books sold enough for me to afford middle-class perks (bifocals, digital camera, hd and/or satellite radio – only far-right talk on cheap radios – a decent Bordeaux on occasion, etc.), I might still choose to sacrifice a portion of my new-found wealth to hire a scholar in my stead. Any good bilingual would do. How hard would it be to dig up the common denominators out of five or ten histories one might find at a top library. As little as $1000. might suffice for, say, ten-pages. Then, I am afraid, I would infuriate him or her, as I would publish it with objections pegged on, because even if I dislike writing history myself and know damn little about it, what little I *do* see almost always rubs me the wrong way. Oscar Wilde once claimed "the one duty we owe to history is to rewrite it." I feel no such *duty*, for, to me, it is impossible to do *otherwise*. And, that goes even for whatever history I might myself write. That is the problem. I cannot get through writing a history without contradicting it. So saying, I cannot leave you with *no* history, so, I will do my best with what I have. If you are a picky person, please take a drink before reading and keep sipping as you proceed. Make it either red wine, for the calming salicylic acid, or tequila, not so much for the alcohol, as for what comes with it: *more than a grain of salt!*

So much for confession and self-deprecation – the Sinosphere has much better terms for the latter as modesty is *de rigor* – now for some assertion. Even if I were to hire a scholar to do the history for me, I am afraid that if said scholar used the various accounts of *kyôka* written in English I have seen or even most of the Japanese ones cited, the history that might be assembled would almost certainly fail to include, or fail to recognize most of what I consider significant. Despite the fact that the 100-odd books reproduced in *Kyôka Taikan*, or *Broadview* clearly revealed the literary importance of 16-17c *kyôka*, in the absence of a corresponding analytical rethinking of the history – or none energetic enough to blast through the shuttered windows of the Ivory Tower – almost everything written about *kyôka* continues to parrot the scholarship of the 1950's and 60's which, failing to appreciate older kyôka, treated 18-19c Edo *kyôka* as what amounts to the only real thing. And, more recently, this has fused with the trendy homage (largely deserved, especially when international comparison is involved) of the cool culture of Edo. I can understand both the appeal of Tenmei kyôka and of Edo but still, *why, after a quarter of a century are 16-17c kyôka still largely unknown?* Do scholars have to spend so much time teaching, conferencing, and analyzing/writing that they have no time left to *read* the vast amount of primary material now available? Or, is it apprehension lest becoming knowledgeable about material considered of small literary value is not the best way to build a career? Not that one must stop with 16-17c kyôka, either. One must not only dare to tread but wade deeply into the sacred (?) world of *waka* in order to take the history of Japanese comic poetry back to the beginning. Of course, my judgment-calls on the extent to which individual poems share something with *kyôka,* or are the thing itself in everything but name, may be questioned; but I think the hundreds of examples, most by well-known *waka* poets, suffice to prove that *kyôka* and *waka*, though forced apart in public for appearance's sake for a time in history, were never actually divorced. In other words, my history and selection of poems to translate challenge not only the Edo-centric history of *kyôka*, but the token attention – so little as to constitute negligence – given to 31-syllabet comic poetry, whatever it was called, in appreciations, histories and anthologies of traditional Japanese poetry. I cannot prove it, but I feel *kyôka* was not only not an anomaly, but may have been the most common type of poem written for some occasions and it is odd indeed that the world is largely oblivious to its importance in the everyday literary life of Japanese over the ages. This being my understanding, or bias, if you prefer, I feel my history, as incomplete as it must be owing to my rather sorry circumstances, will nonetheless present a far broader and, if I may say so, *fairer* history of *kyôka* than any I know.

With apologies for so long a prologue to a short history, let's start.

II

To do this right, we should go back to China, for the first Japanese to write mad poems doubtless read some Chinese, and the Middle Country literatae were proud to be more rational *and* crazy than anyone else. But I won't go there until I find someone well-versed in Chinese poetry – actually, I did know one scholar who loved wit so long as it wasn't nonsense and would have been perfect to work with to fill this gap, but Professor *Songs-of-Xanadu* Crump is no longer with us and, come to think of it, if that person also read Japanese . . . (Yes, this *is* a proposition, anyone?). Suffice it to say that, from what I found in Liu and Lo's *Sunshine Splendor* (a huge anthology of Chinese poetry from the 12c B.C. to the 20c), we not only have the famed Li-Po (701-762) – much beloved by Japanese – *who saw fermenting grapes in the mallard-green Han River* and *drank with the moon and his shadow*, but Tu-fu (712-70) *advising flower buds to open a petal at a time lest simultaneous bloom attract a despoiler*, presumably *the wind, whom he called "a bully,"* and not *the swallows he did not mind dropping mud on his lute and books when they flew in trailing gnats that whacked him in the face like the tail-wind of a truck* (pardon the anachronism), and, better yet, though late for the first Japanese anthology, the 8c *Manyôshû* – my favorite, Han Yü (768-824), who *questioned the worth of the evergreen in a properly seasonal world*, found *many good things to say about losing his teeth, turned a bowl into a pond of poetry and took pity, perhaps for real, on mosquitoes*. Of course, the presence of a poem or variety of wit in China does not assure us the same made it to Japan. I know Li-Po was well read and Tu-fu not unknown, but I have no idea whether or not Han Yü stimulated the imagination of the *Kokinshû* poets, which is to say, found his way under The Chestnut Tree much less The Persimmon Tree. But, we are getting ahead of ourselves.

III

The first *waka*, called a *kayô* 歌謡 or song that *might*, in my, probably sole opinion, be a prototypical *kyôka* is in Book 15 of the *Record of Ancient Matters*, or *Kojiki* (c.710). Sung by Prince Wren (written 大雀 *big-sparrow*, ridiculous, for other than being small and brown the birds are utterly different), later Emperor Nintoku (r. 394-427) to express his gratitude for having been given an awesome beauty for a wife, by his father who found her while traveling and heroically refrained from swiving her himself, I *believe* it puns on the thunder in her name as it jumps from being overwhelmed to overjoyed in 31-syllabets. It is in this book (p.106), and I hope others will consider my reading. The usually mentioned examples of pre-*Manyôshû* comic poems from the *Kojiki, etc.* are not called *kyôka* but *hinaburi* 夷振, *barbarian* or *rustic measure*. What I saw – not enough to be sure – was not worth introducing.

The first *waka* that obviously could be called a *kyôka* follows shortly after another *kayô* in a narrative in book 14 of the *Nihonshôki* (c.720). The other, 7-syllabets too long to be a 31-syllabet poem, is itself comic, to me anyway. First, *the story:* A carpenter named Inabe-no-mane, finishing lumber set on a stone with an axe, was observed by the dangerously mercurial Emperor Yûryaku (r. 457-89), who thought it odd and questioned him as to whether he ever missed and hurt his tool, to which Inabe replied *"Never."* The Emperor, evidently upset by his confidence, called some young women and had them strip down to their thong-like loincloths and put on an exhibition of sumo in front of the carpenters. Sure enough, the carpenter eventually missed and nicked his blade, at which point the triumphant (?) Emperor, saying *'That's what you get for speaking irresponsibly!'* ordered him taken to a field and executed. At this, point his fellow carpenters, or one of them, maybe, sang out –

あたらしき伊名部の工匠 懸けし墨縄 其が無けば 誰か懸けむよ あたら墨縄
atarashiki inabe no takumi kakeshi suminawa shi ga nakeba tare ka kakemu yo atara suminawa
pitiful inabe-the carpenter stretchng ink-strng/cords he not-if who? stretch! pitiful ink-string

> *Alas, for poor*
> *Inabe the carpenter*
> *& the ink-string he stretched!*
>
> *When he is no more,*
> *Who is going to stretch it,*
> *That poor ink-string?*

The strategy of lamenting for the ink-string – (part of an elegant device used in the Sinosphere to mark lumber for cutting or foundations for digging) that a skilled craftsman can pull-back and twang at an angle to instantly do what Occidental architects require mathematics or cloud-edge rulers for! – is what seems mad. At any rate, *it worked.* Maybe the relationship of carpenter and tool reminded the cruel Emperor Yûryaku of his fanatical love for his hunting hawks or something, for he regretted the possible loss of a skilled craftsman aloud and sent a reprieve that arrived just in the nick of time. When that news came back the Emperor sang out –

ぬば玉の 甲斐の黒駒 鞍着せば 命死なまし 甲斐の黒駒　　雄略天皇
nubatama no kai no kurokoma kura kiseba inochi shinamashi kai no kurokoma
blackbead/gem's kai's blackcolt saddled-if life died-wouldhave kai's blackcolt

> *Black as a berry,*
> *the black colt from Kai –*
>
> *Had we saddled him,*
> *a man would have died,*
> *The black colt from Kai!*

The translation is Cranston's except for the centering, some de/capping and the penultimate line *"Someone's life would have been lost"* (Waka 1). It would not do to lose the opportunity for a *rhyme* to go with the Learical repeat! Note how the *thing* (a horse is living, at least)-*centered* manner in which the relief is expressed matches that of the poem triggering the Emperor's remorse, and how wit is born in the artless way the just-in-time reprieve is alluded to rather than spelled out. There is also no little irony in a poem by *this* Emperor being considered as a candidate for the first recorded *kyôka,* or 31-syllabet mad poem, because he was so erratic and oddly heartless some historians believe he was out of his mind, or, dare I say it . . . *mad!*

IV

Scores of poems that might be considered either predecessors or examples of mad poems are found in the first major collection of poetry in Japan, the 4516-poem *Manyôshû* (ca.760), the first of which is by Emperor Yûryaku and all of which I *have* read. These poems, which unsong scholar Kaneko Jitsuei 金子実英 (正発音すら未証), in his expansive history of *kyôka* 狂歌小史 prefacing a book of poems (蜀山家集) by Shokusanjin, or Ôta Nanpo, the genius *said* to have made *kyôka* a literary genre (*I* think it already *was*), dubbed "dramatically kidding songs" (戯笑(咲)歌 又 戯に嗤へる歌), exhibit two of the three characteristics Hamada Ichirô (annotator of Iwanami's *Tokuwa* . . .) ascribe to the canonical *kyôka*: 1) *imaginative content* (off-the-wall ideas, outrageous hyperbole, ludicrous logic, absurd anthropomorphism) and 2) *word play* (compound puns, serial puns). They lack only 3), *parody,* or take-offs on older poems. But they do sometimes play on what I would call *mythical commonplace*. Eg. a lament where the poet, *as a woman, lacks the hand-power to open the burial cave boulder-door so the deceased may come back* (an allusion to the Strong-hand-*man* a god who helped open the primordial cave the Sun Goddess holed up in: see pg.382). As the *Manyôshû* was born in a country so new to writing it had to use Chinese characters as letters, one might say there was literally no ground for parody.

I exaggerate. There must have been unwritten songs, Chinese writings and probably censorship of the sort to be expected when nobility rules. But, I would grant there is nothing in the *Manyôshû* like the Tenmei era (late-18c) *kyôka* that gives a red butt to Saruhito (a poet with macaque in his name) while playing on his fall foliage poem, or turns the mythical *Cavern* into a *tavern* with a low-class lady of the night (a *tsuji-kimi*, or crossroads-lord, i.e. street-walker) who wears the white powder make-up put on by another goddess who was *outside* said cavern doing a dirty dance, some call the world's first striptease, in the star-light to excite the laughter of the other gods and draw out the curious Sun Goddess (とこやみのよし簀の岩戸ひき明て面しろくもいづる辻君 *tokoyami no yoshizu no iwato* . . . 徳和#861 pg.165).

This is not to say *Manyô* poems behaved themselves. Some, particularly the comic ones in Book 16 (*Storied and Sundry Songs* 有由縁、雑歌) that Kaneko put lock, stock and barrel on the mad side (巻の十六に見える戯咲歌は凡て狂歌), are clearly *noir*, famously poking fun at individuals for red noses, skinniness, hirsute underarms or facial stubble. Here is yet one more (the best known example is on pg. 56) cruel jibe at a thin man, a government minister, no less:

寺々の女餓鬼(めがき)申さく大みわの男餓鬼たばりて其子産まはむ #3840
teradera no megaki môsaku ômiwa no ogaki tabarite sono ko/tane umaha/makamu
temples' female starvng-demons prpose Omiwa's male-starvng-demn doing child/seed bear

Why not propose to all famished female ghouls (each temple has some),
To found a dynasty! Ômiya, are you not a male one?

The *gaki* are all bones except for their horribly distended bellies, have thin necks to make eating very difficult and were said (at least later in the Edo era) to scavenge shit by the road. The character prefacing the subject of many of these cruel poems, 嗤, means laughing in the sense of *ridicule*. The butt of the kidding is not, however, historical figures, but their peers, so it is less parody than picking on people, and some imagine the poems delivered at banquettes as what we might call *roasts*. Some, however, come out of the blue. You might recall the girl taunting a cowardly boy with the promise of sharing a grave (pg.62). Here is another Book 16 example I have *not* yet introduced. The content is not so good, but one must grant it to be creative, as it is a less likely idea. It is the kidding response of an un-named young woman to Crown Prince Niitabe who was so excited about a pond he saw, especially its lotuses, that he hardly knew how to put it into words.

勝間田の池はわれ知る蓮(はちす)無ししかいふ君が鬚無きがごとし #3835
katsumata no ike wa ware shiru hachisu nashi shika iu kimi ga kaminaki ga gotoshi
katsumata pond-as-for i know lotus/es not, and saying you hair(beard)-not alike

Katsumata Pond, yes, I know the place – no lotuses there,
Just like you have no whiskers to speak of, nope, no hair!

Katsumata Pond, I know, and lotuses? No more are there
Than you can boast upon your chin and sideburns hair!

Here scholars divide. Some think there really was no bloom and the Crown Prince, who lacks a full beard, is kidded for having been dazzled by the bright reflection of sunlight on water into seeing it (参考：中西進の注釈 3,6). Others think there *were*, the Crown Prince had ample facial hair and the poet used a rare rhetoric where two false negatives negate each other. It doesn't matter. Either is unexpected, that is, what the *kyôka*-lover wants and expects. I favor the latter reading as it seems madder. Especially with that knowing "I know = *ware shiru*." So did Shiki in 1899. (参考　其実、池には蓮多くあり。其人には鬚多くあるを反対にいへる処滑稽にして面白し). But not all *Manyôshû* wit is ridicule. Consider Ôtomo Tabito's 13 poems about *sake*. Most are, *at heart*, what would later be called *kyôka*. The logical paradoxes are there, but they are not spelled out. Indeed, most English translations suggest the wit was not even picked up. I redid a few in this book to make that clear. Some, such as the one calling non-drinkers *monkeys* could be classified ridicule, though, as I explain (p.96-7), it is a fair response to teetotalers. Others, such as chancing his reincarnation as a bug for joy in this life, are clearly free-style, mad in the best sense by rising above petty concerns. And, rising higher yet, the mere fact that 13 poems about drink are plopped down into a book of poetry that does not have thematic sections on, say, *food* or *riding* or *hawking* or *archery*, etc. gives the *editing* a mad touch, as might be expected for the compiler of the *Manyôshû* was Tabito's son, Yakamochi.

At this point, even your hesitant historian can declare something.: There is no question that comic and vulgar poems rub shoulders with the serious and proper (and even the solemn and majestic) in many books in the *Manyôshû* it. Kaneko, in 1927, wondered how the editors allowed the serious (*majime*) work of the titans of classic Japanese poetry to mix with comic poems, but bailed out without trying to account for *"this truly interesting phenomenon"* (誠に面白い現象である 同): *"The question as to why this should be belongs to philosophy, so we will not discuss it here"* (何故かと言ふ疑問は哲学の問題に属するから、此処では触れないで置く). I think philosophy belongs everywhere or nowhere, but do not find this particular phenomenon difficult to make sense of. Good aesthetics, *i.e.,* editorial sense, suffices for an explanation. *Who wants to read one serious poem after another? Who wants to read one beautiful poem after another?* I translate one *Manyô* poem in this book found among poems by the titans near the front of the *Manyôshû*, which is not only not funny, or at least not intended to be so by its author, but unquestionably *bad* (*I got Yasumiko:* pg.106)*,* because it makes my case better than a good poem would. It is the modern editor who will *not* put a youth's obnoxious boast about winning his cutie-pie together with masterpieces whose judgment puzzles *me*. Who decreed that books of poetry must contain poems of similar style and quality arranged as neatly as eggs in a carton? If you, like me, feel poems are meant to entertain, variety must take priority.

V

While a subtle wit pervades the entire next major anthology, the *Kokinshû* (c 905), so the serious and the comic are still mixed, many of the most playful poems are segregated from the others and *named*. Book 10, titled "Thing-Names 物名," contains *waka* with exceptionally tricky punning, acrostics, and other wordplay. Book 19, "Sundry Forms 雑体," contains various sections with titles based on the form, i.e. number and arrangement of syllabets. The largest section has fifty seven *haikaika* 誹諧歌, or *haikai* songs, about which Kaneko wrote (and I concur), "these are beyond any doubt, what later would come to be called *kyôka.*" (此の俳諧歌はとりもなほさず

後に言ふ所の狂歌である). At the same time, however, he made an important qualification. Because Shunzei, in the 12c, may have said that *"kyôka* are *haikai"* (「俳諧といふは狂歌なり」『和歌肝要』、但し仮託書らしい) before long, *haikai*, or those blowing its horn, came to claim that *haikai* were the only legitimate form of *kyôka* 後世俳諧歌のみを以て真正の狂歌であると主張した一派の人々. That, Kaneko makes clear, is mistaken. If anything, *haikai* are but one form of *kyôka* 併し俳諧歌は狂歌の一体であつて、其の凡てではない. I concur, but hasten to add that here, *haikai* does not mean the entire span of what we *now* call *haikai*, either. To the editors of the *Kokinshû*, for example, it would have meant humorous light verse, mad, perhaps, but lightly so, and written in a language as elegant as any *waka* and concerning accepted natural or cultural themes. Many of my favorites are in the main text (hence, I keep this short), but here is one I skipped, used as an example by Kaneko:

山吹の花色衣主やたれ問へど答へず口なしにして 素性法師 古今集 905
yamabuki no hana-iro-goromo nushi ya tare toedo kotaezu kuchinashi ni shite sosei
keria flwr's colord-robe ownr-as4 who askng-but replyng-not jasmn=mouthlss-as being

> To whom belongs this cape of globe flower's pure gold?
> – It must be Jasmine, for, when I ask, I am not told!

The *owner* (*nushi*) of the globe flower (*keria* or wild rose)-colored robe (*koromo*) is, one assumes, human, but bringing up the *jasmine* in the last half of the poem turns it into a question about the identity of the dye (remember, a flamingo pink garment did not necessarily cost a bird his life), which is answered by silence, as *jasmine* in Japanese is *kuchinashi*, or "mouthless" by name). If you wish, you might replace *Jasmine* with *Chrysanthemum*.

> To whom belongs this Keria colored cape? – Anyone?
> Aster, I'd say, for when I asked her, she stayed mum.

Be that as it may, the poem by monk Sosei (d.909) is indeed a dyed in the wool *kyôka,* or one type of *kyôka*, the elegant artful haikai type, which Kaneko examples with three more of which one more (the onomatopoetic warbler's warning *hitoku-hitoku,* or *People come!* pg. 188) is in this book. I think that the *Kokinshû* has *more* witty poems than are in the *Manyôshû*, but Kaneko's point that they cover a narrower range of topics holds water. Readers who follow evolutionary biology might think of the *Manyôshû* as *This Wonderful Life, i.e.,* pre-Cambrian primary diversity, though it was not meteors or volcanoes but tight-assed editing that lopped off many thick branches of poetic memes from the official tree of Japanese literature (I know, S. J. Gould may have played up the difference a bit too much; the same can be said for comparing the *Manyôshû* and *Kokinshû*. The latter is a bit fresher and full of life than sometimes realized. We may need to see-saw back and forth on this).

To demonstrate his assertion that haikai *kyôka* were not all *kyôka*, Kaneko exampled another sort of *kyôka not* in the *Kokinshû*, bearing more resemblance to the wilder ad-hoc poems found in the *Manyôshû*. The first, found in an instruction manual for composing waka, *Fukuro-zôshi* 袋草子 (the book of bags?), is a studied response from Tadami who tried to get out of an invitation to the Court by pleading lack of proper transportation (now horse or ox cart?) and was told to come even if he had to ride his stilts (in the Sinosphere "bamboo-horse"). The second is an impromptu response, a rationalistic defense from a character in the Tales of Uji 宇治拾遺物語 3-11 (c.1220) to the wife of a subordinate who came back from drawing water to find him in their house sipping some soup from a ladle, as he, evidently, walked in uninvited and could not help himself, and upbraided him for his bad behavior.

竹馬はふしがちにしていと弱し いま夕かげに 乗りて参らむ　壬生忠見
takeuma wa fushi-gachi ni shite ito yowashi ima yûkage ni norite mairan tadami 1157
bmboo-horse/stilts-as-4 joints-win-out being very weak, now evnng-light/shadw-by ridng go

All joints and little meat my bamboo horse is pretty weak;
I'll ride over now with twilight shadows to extend my feat.

Soup for the soul, medicine for this sinner bad from the cradle:
For goodness' sake, did not Buddha make me take the ladle?

昔より阿弥陀ぼとけのちかひにてにゆるものをばすくふとぞしる
mukashi yori amidabotoke no chikai nite niyuru-mono o ba sukuu to zo shiru
oldtimes-frm amidabddha's promise=spoon-by boilng one+emph save=scoop know=soup

Twilight probably refers to the gentle time when the wind dies down, but I pretended the reading of *kage* was 陰 or shadow, and not 影 or light, (when it could be either) for the compensatory pun, my *feat*. Though *our* stilts are not equine (our *brooms* being that) and the *evening-shadow's* allusion to the color of a real horse he chose to ride in to work is lost in translation (as it was lost to me reading the Japanese until my respondent set me straight), the first, nonetheless works in English (So, I hate to say that the Iwanami printing of *Fukurozôshi* does not have *fushigachi* but *fushikage*, another horse color which would reduce the joints to a mere punning allusion and fail to make the horse a bony pony. I hope that version is wrong). The second fails to convince. Nonsense rhymes do not make up for the loss of meaningful puns. The original plays masterfully upon Amitabha's promise. Maybe another translator can do it right. Another try. I think it a bit closer:

The Sutra say He will scoop up sinners from the cauldrons of Hell
I found salvation in your Soup – Buddha told me all was well!

But good translation is not needed, I hope, to make Kaneko's point that even in the era of the *Kokinshû*, when *haikai* became official comic poetry, there were "truly mad/wild/free-style mad-poems on vulgar/folk-matters in vulgar/ folk style"(俗意俗調を以て、ありの儘の滑稽を尽した狂歌らしい狂歌). Yet, while Kaneko called them "*kyôka*-like *kyôka*," he also noted they were thought of as a *kyô* or mad style of *tanka* (short waka) 狂体の短歌, for *haikai* pretty much monopolized comic poetry until the Kamakura era (late-12c) when *kyôka* came to be called *kyôka*.

VI

I go further, further than Kaneko, further even than my respondent who goes further than Kaneko, in that when I try to understand the nature of mad 31-syllabet poetry, I include *waka* on accepted subjects not called or even associated with *kyôka* by anyone but me. I refer especially to love-poems 恋歌 *not* in specific sections for the comic, which nonetheless are conceptually convoluted, metaphorically laughable and boast the same sort of morphing by pivot words and whatnot, sometimes called "elegant confusion" by Western scholars. Viewed objectively, *waka* about, or born of *koi* (longing, love and even love-sickness/blues in a word!) have always comprised the main body of mad poems but, because trope slowly develops so those who use or read it tend to forget how odd it is, the craziness – outlandish and even outrageous metaphors, puns and rationalizing – came to be considered normal rather than novel, the nobility who contributed most of the poems in these anthologies were themselves love-besotted, and love was a time-honored and therefore acceptable theme for *waka*, love poems, as a rule, were not associated with *kyôka*, and still are not. Indeed, *most* love poems are *not* mad, but many are, and there are so many of them I would hold they are one of two categories of *waka* holding the largest cache of unsung *kyôka*. If you want examples, there are hundreds in this book. Because they were gathered in haste, I would expect to have missed most of the good ones. Here's one I happened upon today, that should have been with the tear rivers, though the word is not in it.

はやきせにみるめおひせばわが袖の涙の河にうゑまし物を 古今集 905
hayaki se ni mirume oiseba waga sode no namida ni uemashi mono o anon.
quick(quickly) rapids(lover) in(with) mirume (seaweed name = meet-chance) grew-if my sleeve/s'tears-in plant would but . . .

*If sea-weed (weed to see) but grew in the rapids, I'd sow some
in the river of tears coursing down my sleeve!*

The original works where the translation fails as there is a real seaweed, *mirume*, that puns as *see*, or *meet-chance*, and its long use as trope meant no explanation was needed as to why she wanted to plant it. With the additional punning allusions to "quickly" and "lover" (*se* back from back-carried child, or a baby, the common designation for a male lover), not to mention the facetious attention given to the speed of the tear-flow implying that were tear-river not raging so, maybe . . . we have what would definitely be considered a *kyôka* were the subject any other than love. *Kokinshû* #595, where another anonymous poet laments that no sea/*see*-weed grows, despite a sea of tears beneath the bed, does not attain *kyôka* heights of wit.

The other main category – reading this book, you might guess *death poems*, but, *no,* for they blossomed centuries later (try again!) and we are still in the 10c – would be *social poems*, such as *greeting, thanking, scolding, praising, excusing,* and otherwise *reacting* to others. The stilt horse and unasked soup-sipping poems given by Kaneko, above, and the turtle flask poem (*tamadare no ...* p.489) are good early examples. A large portion of these social poems are about *giving and receiving*, i.e., accompanying or acknowledging gifts. Obviously, humor helps one cope with frustration (like having to go to Court when one wants to stay home) or takes the edge off another's anger (people should ask before sipping your soup). Analyses of the psychology of humor never forget *that* explanation. For those seeking friendship or love – there is considerable overlap in love poems and greeting poems – however, understand, consciously or not, that the other party would enjoy a laugh along with the present – which might be the poem, itself. Even today, in Japan, a gift may be accompanied by the words ご笑納下さい, or please accept this with a laugh/smile. True, those words originated from the self-depreciation common to the Sinosphere, the implication being that something is ridiculous, i.e. of little worth), but I feel they include the wish to delight the other. And, paradoxically, poems sent with gifts and the acknowledgement/thanks permitted just the opposite of self-deprecation, an opportunity to show off one's intelligence and, because it makes others laugh, be forgiven for doing so. In the Sinosphere, where modesty in speech was taken quite seriously, such an opportunity to shine must have been a godsend.

Before reading for this book, I had no idea how rich or interesting this vein was. The only hint I had, oddly enough, came from *haikai*, not old haikai, but Bashô, who put *haikai* on serious footing. As unlikely as this may seem to people who identify haiku with the objective observation of nature, over half of his *ku* are social messages. Unfortunately, such poems remain, as far as I know, ungathered and, on the whole, difficult to understand for an imperfect reader of Japanese. While I do have one chapter in this book, *A witness of salutations & warnings – Complimenting entertainers, giving watermelons, etc.*, most of the dozen or so examples in this book are scattered about and insufficient to prove what I feel to be the case. Since gift-giving and-receiving has always been a hot topic for cultural anthropology, I bet there must be books on it in Japan, and, if nothing else, would expect a chapter on gift-related poems already exists, but even so, chances are it would not concentrate on the most interesting examples, which is to say the *kyôka*. Were a scholar to take up this subject and find enough examples to fill a few chapters, I would be more than happy to help dress up the translations while giving credit where it is due, and balance what I feel to be a bias in favor of poetry for poetry's sake in the histories.

VII

Before preceding to relate the next major anthology and kyôka, let me confess my belief about the relationship of comic poetry to folk culture and how poetry has been treated by critics or scholars – those who present it in anthologies – in Japan. If you disagree with it, I do not mind if you consider it my bias (If you wish to send a rebuttal, please do; but if it is good be prepared to be included in the next edition).

While *wit* in a culture may come and go – Addison described pun cycles in England with the acme, in the realm of King James the First, extreme even by Japanese standards – I believe that in a literate culture, the percent of witty poems probably tends to grow generation by generation, century by century, because the more trope and poems accumulated, the more fun can be had with them. This is not to say that such a trend would be patent to all, especially after centuries have passed. What is written and what gets published and shared with the world are not always the same. One would have to love wit and follow it through documents *other than published anthologies* to prove or disprove such a hypothesis. Such research is probably rare, for the prevailing view has long considered comic poetry full of allusions and play upon older material second-hand and inferior to ancient poems with their fresh material. Otherwise, we would see more of it in anthologies of poetry and on-line.

The *reason* for the comic being slighted are not identical in Japan and in West Europe + Usania. Occidental modernity admits only the individual, supposedly *ex nihilo* or God-given – not surprisingly the same as *Genius* was a God substitute – variety of creativity. Japanese do not speak so religiously of creativity, but rather of the pure or sincere nature of the ancients who wrote from the heart. Yet their respective biases overlap. "Our" critics dropped the witty poetry of old England, that is the light verse engaging in philosophy (and love) as entertainment of the heroic, metaphysical and cavalier poets, for the deep romantics of Germany and the suffering moderns, while critics in Japan holding nativist and romantic ideals borrowed in part from our romanticism, savaged wit in poetry, especially that of 31-syllabets (perhaps because it is the form of their sacred *waka*) calling it *artificial, anthropomorphic,* and *Chinese*. Specifically, they lament poetry's fall from the native grace and simple honesty of the *Manyôshû* to the fancy, often humorous *Kokinshû*. Obviously, such views put the brake on research into the history of *kyôka* before it really got started. That is why reading Kaneko's short history of *kyôka* was a breath of fresh air to me and inspirational to my respondent.

While it is easy to recognize a difference between writing your own plain love songs and playing with those of long dead poets, one must wonder if those plain love songs were not themselves mere echoes of existent oral culture and point out that the clever wording of many folk songs belies the critics' native=simple vs. Chinese=artificial antithesis. Human brains *like* playing with words every bit as much as cats like to chase mice. In Japan, as elsewhere, folk lyrics prove everyman has always enjoyed contrast, paradox, anthropomorphism, and so forth without the help of Chinese (or Greek) rhetoric, thank you. See *Kokinshû* editor Kyûsojin Hitaku's put-down of Monk Sosei's light-hearted poem about reproaching the wind, (kks#76, pg.195) for a typical example of what bothers me. Or, take Tsurayuki's poem: *Year after year, the colored leaves flow down the Tatsuda River / So would its mouth then be Autumn's berth each winter? (toshigoto ni momijiba nagasu tatsudagawa minato ya aki no tomari naruramu* – yes, "each winter" is mine*)*. Even though Kyûsojin admits the poem was skillfully crafted, he cannot help pointing out that it is intellectualism divorced from real feeling 理知的で実感が乏しい. To me, competing with other poets to come up with the first or last signs of a season, or new metaphors to express them is not inferior to direct observation but different. Such ideas help us see nature in a new light, and are by no means antagonistic to reality, either. Why must we put down thought, engine of the most economical travel known to man, the head-trip?

I do not doubt critics are sincere, by which I mean their judgment is, as far as they know, based entirely on aesthetics or whatever criticism is supposed to be based on (Not majoring in literature, I do not know *what* is proper); but demeaning the *artificial* 人工的, *anthropomorphic* 擬人法を用い *contrived* 技巧にすぎった *fart-rationalizing (what I call hyperlogic)* 屁理屈 and identifying them with Chinese 漢, or foreign poetry and intellectualism is not only wrong when the clever intellectual games of folksong are considered, but suspiciously convenient for the power elite, who are threatened by words, the only weapon of the weak. Let me add that I only mention Kyûsojin as I *have* his *Kokinshû*. He is not meant to be taken as a boogie-man. I was more shocked to find Origuchi, a cultural anthropologist, put down Song 16 of the *Manyôshû*, where the Empress declares she prefers Fall mountains to Spring ones for *worthless copying of the Chinese*. ♪ While Chinese may have debated the pros and cons of various seasons, that should hardly ruin the poem which I found remarkable for ending with *ware wa,* or "I/me-as-for," or more figuratively translated "if you ask me." She was judging a match of poems on behalf of each season, but still, this informal expression of self is so rare in Japanese poetry one would think it, and not just the obvious Chinese influence, would merit discussion. The above, more my impression gained from various things read over the years than specific argument, and it is all I can offer in the absence of a suitable library.

Later. Googling something I forget brought me to translator Matt Treyvaud's blog Nosword, where I first met Ôkuma Kotomichi (1798-1868). Impressed by his "riffing off" of older *waka* and the powerful language of one poem about winter clouds that might have something more terrifying behind them than the moon (なにとかや月にはあらでおそろしきものも出るべき冬の夜の雲 言道 *nani toka ya tsuki ni wa*), I googled him and found –

> *Poetry expresses human emotions (ninjô) and does not contain anything else. . . . if the Chinese heart is my true heart (magokoro), there is nothing I can do about it. If the Buddhist heart is my true heart, I cannot help it. If we compose poetry by avoiding the Chinese heart and the Buddhist heart, we may believe we are composing poetry in the style of our country. But our country has used Confucianism and Buddhism since ancient times, and people today have absorbed them since they were born. . .* trans Peter Flueckiger in Shirane+Brandon

Wow! Here was a second-generation nativist poet (with a poem included in a collection of 100 patriotic poems), yet he had the wisdom or humility to recognize when foreign-derived elements were natural. Ueda Akinari had debated Noringa's claims of Japanese superiority (other lands and languages being as false as the Christians usually made other religions) putting Japan and its language into its relative/real place in the world as measured objectively from the outside. What Ôkuma did was to do the same from *within*. More broadly put, he recognized that *sincerity* (note the *makoto* hidden within his name), that is, *true emotion*, could not be defined by one age or one person and forced on all (as Norinaga and other nativists did when they categorically decried foreign elements in Japanese). He recognized what might be called *the objectivity of the heart*. I googled on and found Roger K. Thomas, who kindly sent me his old article. From the title "Macroscopic vs. Microscopic: Spatial Sensibilities in Waka of the Bakumatsu Period (1998)," I hoped to find a Romanization for the old Dutch (?) microscope Kotomichi's poem spelled フルゴロオトガラス(*furugorootogarasu*) – I am only sure about the *glass* – but that poem, included in this book, was not in it. Instead, I found something relevant to the above quote. Kotomichi declared the use of Chinese vocabulary (common in *haikai*) *"according to the poet's feelings"* to be *"the true exclamatory utterance of modern man."* Exactly. The mixing of Yamato words and Chinese-derived compounds had long been colloquial and their exclusion by nativists to keep Japanese natural, as they saw it, was actually an artificial endeavor along the lines of the re-introduction of genuine (?) old English folk dance in Appalachia.

From Thomas, I also learned that early 19c nativist (or neo-Manyôshû) *waka* poet Kagawa Kageki summed up the contrast in terms of the Confucian *ri* 理 or *logic/rationalization* vs the vague concept of a native *shirabe* 調 or *rhythm/song/style*. Let me add that I am *not* entirely anti-nativist. I admire efforts in Japanese *and English* to save the beauty our ancestors produced. My heart is with William Barnes, who tried to preserve native words and newly mint them from clear roots (*wortlore, nipperlings*) to replace Latinisms (*botany, forceps*). I have decried in print (where I forget: I wrote alot in Japanese) the overuse of *kango*, compound Chinese-style words, especially in combination with helper verbs, when native *Yamatokotoba* verbs tend to sound better. And brevity is no excuse: one example I gave was *"sokushin-suru."* Is it shorter than *unagasu?* I was upset because journalists, following textbook news-speak, who neglected euphonious and mimetically meaningful words (built-in onomatopoeia and other mimesis), left me nothing to learn and that hurt *my* writing style. But to find a nativist who was also broad-minded – *why, oh why, had I not heard of Kotomichi earlier?* The man is evidently not as famous as he should be!

I added this aside on criticism because it influences histories, and so far that the critical view of *kyôka* is uniform, creates *a* history both directly, as others cite their analysis, and indirectly by influencing anthologists so that their selection of poems reinforces the accepted history, with perhaps a wee bit of extra attention given to this or that Tenmei era poet who charms the anthologist and allows him or her to feel his selection is also special. That is why I find psychiatrist Nada Inada's understanding of *kyôka* as a tool, or weapon for the little guy refreshing. He does not once denigrate reason or call it shallow or Chinese. He may not offer as broad a panorama as *Mad In Translation*, but literary critics who give poets demerits for cleverness and anthologists who follow what they recommend who do not have time (or skill?) to read the raw material in the *Kyôka Taikan*, should find his naive (in the good sense of the word) pre-Edo-boom *Edo Kyôka* (江戸狂歌　岩波 1986) good rehabilitation.

VIII

The third famous classic *waka* collection, the *Shinkokinshû*, published in 1205 is notable for having neither the artless creativity of the 8c *Manyôshû* nor the delightfully crafted humor of the early 11c *Kokinshû*. Yet this does not mean comic poetry was dead. Based upon the phenomenal amount of it in the one-person anthologies of Izumi Shikibu, Saigyô, Lady Daibu and others active in the 11 and 12c, it was more alive than ever. I translated enough of their poems for this book – three whole chapters for Saigyô, two for Lady Daibu and ten Shikibu+fake-Shikibu poems – that my readers should have their own opinions about just how mad they were. That is not to say the *Shinkokinshû* ignored them. It included much of their work, just little of their more amusing work.

So saying, I do not believe the *Shinkokinshû* to be *as* humorless as some would have it. Reading it through fifteen or so years ago, I recall my joy to find a finely curated exhibit of trope, one rich poem after another creating what might be viewed as a single tropic installation. What is interesting depends where you come from. In my case, I had *just* read the *Kokinshû*. There is pleasure, even wit in the economical elaboration of the broad taxonomy of half a millennium of trope, provided you get it. Re-reading, I found, in book 15, near the end of the fifth and last book (or chapter) on *love=koi*, a cache of *weepers*, including at least a dozen *tear-rivers,* many of which are witty if not risible. Their translations fill a chapter of this book, *Silly as Saigyô: more waka weepers for perspective – from the 1205 Shinkokinshû*. Reading them, we can see how the tradition of love poetry allowed the cleverness, without which we would have no *kyôka*, to survive in even the most proper places.

Of course, when only poems on a limited number of themes composed in certain styles are included in anthologies, poets and readers with imagination suffer for it. While the *Shinkokinshû* is masterfully done, one does sometimes wish the editors got drunk more often. I find myself wondering whether Jakuren, the witty monk with a good sense for folk-song – do you recall his warning to the snail about not butting heads with calves? (pg.146) – who was *supposed to be* one of its editors might not have diversified and lightened the collection had he but lived a little longer. At the same time, we might remember that strict limitations of content and form are not all bad. The same would eventually give birth to serious haiku – a good thing if not overdone – and who can deny that nothing makes a better foil for humor than a straight example. Qualifications aside, however, I concur with my respondent and others who see the *Shinkokinshû* as a watershed, marking the culmination of a haute-culture policy of excluding or segregating the obviously witty and wild from the serious sort of *waka* deemed the only literature worthy of collecting and preserving. Meanwhile, other comic poems must have been composed – and by others than the famous poets mentioned – but they were less likely to be both written down and kept in a form to be passed down for generations. For better or worse, there is a fine compound verb to describe what probably happened to most of the witty poems we might so enjoy seeing if only . . . . My Japanese-English dictionary defines 読み捨てる *yomi-suteru* as *reading books once and tossing them out;* but *yomi* also means *to read-aloud* or *compose*, and the most common form in which the verb is found referring to poetry is the more fluid 詠み捨て *yomisute,* which, modifying or describing the poems, might most meaningfully translated as *read on water*. This would, then, be the *sad* – to all who cannot share the poem – practice of purely consumable poetry (I suppose some, maybe most of the poets were happy enough to enjoy the moment, so this is *our* lament, not theirs, but so be it). We can imagine some connoisseurs of comic poetry keeping notes and compiling little booklets, maybe even large collections, such as was done for bawdy ballads in England. Then, alas, we can also imagine those notes, those poems, suffering fates sadder than not being written down. From water to fire, or rather to fire *for* water . . . Who can doubt that some if not most of the most entertaining poems ever written ended up as many of "our" bawdy ballads did, bath fuel. And, finally, pardon the thought, I know not if paper was ever used to wrap fish in Japan, but it did serve bums.

Still, the difference between the respective fates of the proper/serious and improper/comic poems was not always clear-cut. The treatment accorded each differed by degree. Some less famous anthologies include ridiculous poems that somehow made the cut. Though most of the work in these anthologies might be far from brilliant and owe their inclusion to the poet's identity alone, not a few (often from collections of independent poets like those mentioned) are interesting and novel, even to the point of being "mad" in the best sense of the word. Edwin A. Cranston's *Waka* (2a) has some excellent comic poems in styles not found in the *Kokinshû* (similar to the two cited by Kaneko) from a number of minor (not necessarily in size or interest) anthologies – in that sense, his selections are already part of the history of the history of *kyôka* whether he mentioned *kyôka* or not – and I found a fair sampling of more recent, mostly post-*Kokinshû* poems outside the Imperial canon in the huge thematic 1310 *Fuboku wakashô* anthology, a Meiji period (1868-1912) copy of which I am lucky enough to own. Then, there are a fair number of poems not as dense with wit as the *haikai* in the *Kokinshû* but more personal, which is to say idiosyncratic, in the 1312 *Gyokuyôshû*, which is Imperially sanctioned, but, on the whole, loosely edited. I am afraid, however, the most outrageous, by which I think I mean *exciting,* work tends to be scattered through letters, journals and whatnot (remember, Kaneko found the stilt-horse in a *waka* instruction book!), rarely made permanent by being printed in large numbers. As Japan, with its dry winters and earthquakes, was ever the paradise for the enemy of paper memory, fire, most have doubtless been lost forever and one can only beg private collectors – and those who sell to them – to do their part to preserve the rest by copying (digitalizing) and passing them on to the rest of us.

IX

The first confirmed use of the term *kyôka* in Japan is by Fujiwara no Teika, a 12c poet and literary compiler best known as the editor of The *Ogura Hundred Poets One Poem* collection that we encountered, mostly in parodies, in this book, and the chief editor of the *Shinkokinshû* (a less reliable source has Teika's father Shunzei using it). In 1191, Teika describes a poetry gathering for *kyôka* and a poet, or poets participating, as good at *kyôka*. (「藤原定家の『明月記』建久二年の条に「。。入夜被読上百首。事畢有当座狂歌等。深更相共帰家。（中略）有狂歌合」と。つまり、狂歌の座あり、しかもそれに上手と評される歌人もいた」) Kaneko, judging from that description, imagined the *kyôka* party as a diversion for *renga* (link-verse) poets, as their highly stylized 100-verse or 1000-verse sequences – a far cry from the usually witty ancient 2-man-1-*waka* single linked-verse – were, to quote a lazy Usanian president, *hard work*. But, Kaneko continues, another contemporary source 「井蛙抄」 suggests separate groups of poets, with the serious, or 有心 *ushin=have-heart/mind/meaning/sentiment"* poets called the *Below the Persimmon Tree Crowd* in one garden and the frivolous (art for art's sake), or 無心*=mushin=no-heart/mind/meaning/sentiment* poets called the *Below the Chestnut Tree Crowd* in another. Evidently, the latter's poems tended to be *yomisute,* so what happened below the Chestnut Tree stayed below the Chestnut Tree. Still, I find it hard to believe that some of the witty *waka* found in the minor anthologies did not arise at these garden parties. And, I cannot help thinking that someone with a good memory wrote down a collection – as was done with ballads and limericks in England – that still survives somewhere, waiting to be discovered . . .

While we cannot deny the Persimmon *vs* Chestnut Tree divide between poets or in the work of individual poets existed, it does not follow that *kyôka* must be defined as "waka *beyond* the canon" – *waka* too obviously outrageous (wrong subject, wrong words) to be admitted as elegant art-poetry – and excluded from the history of *waka*. We may also think of *kyôka* as a loose canon *within* the Good Ship Waka, if you will pardon a metaphor that is wrong because unrecognized *kyôka* do not harm the ship but provide the buoyancy needed to keep it afloat. Who knows if *waka* could have survived as long as it did (until modern *tanka*) with so little change as to seem archaic if not obsolete, without good ole *kyôka* tagging along to give the poets respite and chuckles. If, like me, you see the comic at the heart of literature rather than a derivative or mere parody of the serious, you might also agree that *kyôka* by whatever name could have survived without formal *waka*, but not the vice-versa.

With the comic shut out of formal *waka*, *renga*, or link-verse, began to supersede the independent 31-syllabet poem as *the* poetry and increasingly outlandish *haikai* link-verse that would seem to have been squirreled out from under that Chestnut Tree became increasingly popular among some *renga*-masters and their students. This *haikai* tended to be novel, even ridiculous. As it came to be a separate genre from the more elegant but boring *waka* link-verse, the only obvious difference between it and *kyôka* came to be that the latter was composed alone and stood alone, while linked *haikai*, though it was sometimes composed alone, usually showed a clear 17-14 (or 14-17, depending on region and time) split, *as if capped*. *Kyôka*, on the other hand, often continues without break and when it *does* break, usually it is less conclusive. Moreover, because *haikai* really broke, the parts could stand alone. Indeed, that happened earlier than generally acknowledged. As demonstrated with scores of examples from the 20,000 poem *Hokkuchô* (大発句帳 古典文庫 reprint) in *Cherry Blossom Epiphany* (2007), by the 15c, Sôgi and the other link-verse masters wrote thousands of 17-syllabet poems that work beautifully as stand-alone *ku* – and not only as model *hokku* (link-verse starters), but as ordinary *hiraku, tadaku,* etc., many so similar to what we call *haiku* today that no one can tell them apart.

I have not read enough *waka* postdating the above-mentioned early-14c *Fuboku* and *Gyokuyô* to fill in the gap that follows. The best I can do is point out a single 14c work found in the *Broadview* (*Kyôka Taikan*) anthology that suggests the seed for the highly sophisticated *kyôka* of 18c Edo already existed and only awaited the right season to sprout up in abundance. It is the *Cake vs. Wine Poem Match* (*Mochi-Sake Uta-awase*). There are only ten pairs of poems. Not called *kyôka,* they exemplify the best spirit of light verse. The commentary with judgment by p.m. Nijô Nyôbô (二条女房, or ~ Yoshimoto 1320-88) – did he write them? – is *delightful* and aside from one punning passage about falling on his ass (*mochii ni tsuki*) so *gentle* that I, unfamiliar with the use of *nyôbô* as an appellation for one serving in high office, thought *he* was the wife of (Emperor) Nijô! Donald Keene, with not a word respecting the *quality* of the work, much less an example, writes "we can imagine the prime minister might have enjoyed the momentary escape provided by such *kyôka . . .* A kind of desperate frivolity brought solace to men tormented by the unrest of their times." I am sure Keene means well, but his words demean the poet/editor. If I have few translations from it in *this* book, it is only because it is too delicate a work to re-create in part. But, here is one more, the first poem. It nods to Tsurayuki by playing on the first *waka* he selected for the *Kokinshû*:

年のうちにもちはつきけり一年をこそとやくはんことしとやくはん 餅酒歌合
toshi no uchi ni mochi wa tsukikeri hitotose o kozo to ya kuwan kotoshi to ya kuwan

> *Rice cake pounded within the old year – What, then, is true:*
> *Would we roast the last year now or should we toast the new?*

Actually, it says *"eat"* last year and *"eat"* this/new year, but the lost puns had to be made up. *Read* that poem match and you will admire the "prime minister" in editorial capacity not for "desperate frivolity" but for having *the grace to chuckle* in a troubled time and be grateful for his indirectly showing us one route by which *kyôka* came through the Warring Age unscathed (another being Zen monks, below).

X

As Keene and Shirane have done it, I will not detail the formal history, or chain of *begats,* for what was mainly upper-class *kyôka* evolving or, rather, devolving into a popular genre other than to add something about the *content* of the poems written by those mid-16c to early-17c aristocrats who so enjoyed their *kyôka* gatherings. Had their poems only concerned mindless matters of interest to the affluent – as Keene writes and Shirane, by not giving examples to contradict him, lets pass – I, a proper pauper of long-standing, would not have been drawn to them. But, as the Jesuits noted with interest in the 16c, though Japanese aristocrats were often very poor, this did not rob them of their self-respect and they were still respected by others as well (in this, the Jesuits recognized a culture more enlightened than that of Europe, where respect pretty much came and went with money). That would change by the 17 or 18c, when the *kuge* came to be disrespected (see pg.104). I note this because the first multi-author collection (*shû*) of *kyôka* by that name, the 187-poem *Shinsen Kyôka Shû* (1636) has at least half a dozen poems about *poverty* or *poverty gods* (*binbôgami*) by name, and many times that by content. I cannot say if this was because the fall of the old order left many nobles in dire straits or because the theme had been pioneered so attractively in the 16c by Yûchôrô – in my opinion, the first great master of black-humor in *kyôka* – that even the affluent could appreciate it in a more abstract way (like Alexander & the ascetic philosophers of India). What I can say for sure is that poverty poems had to make *kyôka* palatable to a broader audience, as they make them more acceptable to *me* (♪ Your author is even turned off by the affluent yuppies and muppies with their gourmandizing, travel and stock talk on many (not all) National Public Radio stations, and wished that public matters important to poor people with good brains would not be left to the right wing radio as it is where he resides at present).

Teitoku (1571-1653), as the leading literatae of the 16-17c, helped make *kyôka* respectable by doing them and encouraging others, too, but a collection of his *kyôka* awaited his death to be published and was not really that good of a collection (not compared to what would be printed in the *Savage Song Collection*, below), so it is evident his feelings about *kyôka* were complex. At any rate, by his death, composing *kyôka* for the sake of *kyôka* – rather than meeting with friends to play at *kyôka* after the serious business of poetry was over – was established for good. Teitoku's students and their students kept the ball rolling, and it is usually said the first poet who claimed to be a *kyôka*-master and nothing-but was Teiryû (1634-1735) of the third generation after Teitoku. By this time, the *kyôka* parties for impromptu composition and sharing work that originated among the aristocrats in Teitoku's day had become *ren*, large associations open to the masses. While knowledge of *waka* was needed to appreciate some parodies, the rules for composition were less fussy than for *waka* or even *haikai* (already big business), so commoners, often wealthier than well-educated samurai who depended entirely on stipends, had an easier time getting into it. Thousands of people were involved; I think of Teiryû as the operator of *a profitable franchise of wit*. There is no question he wrote some fine poems, too. You saw some in this book. On the whole, however, he bores me next to Getsudôken (who had the same teacher, Shinkai, and was a half-generation older) whose work better reflects the older roots of *kyôka* as a personal yet wild poem – what *tanka* would eventually become. Teiryû despite becoming the central figure of *kyôka* in his time, may have sensed the same, as he did not publish collections of his own work out of deference to Getsudôken, who, he knew, did not entirely approve of it, during his lifetime.

To me, the most notable early-Edo work (an oeuvre, not collection) of *kyôka* is a poem match called The *Four Life* (types) *Poem Match* 四生の歌合, published in 1643, *i.e.*, ten years before Teitoku's death. I wish I knew more about the author, Kinoshita Chôshôshi 木下長嘯子, if he *is* the author, for genius deserves to be known. Fifty-nine pairs of *kyôka* contest the aptness of their romantic complaint or celebration in terms of the respective animal or plant (bugs, birds, fish, beasts) they represent, clearly yet indirectly captioned by pseudonyms of the highest quality of any I know before the late-18c – excepting the parodying pseudonyms of the 1669 *Dog Hundred* 犬百人一首 – including characteristics of the animals or plants in the poem by allegory, allusion and/or pun. The poems themselves are pleasant, fully developed pun-streams of the sort only Japanese (of the languages I know) does gracefully and, in combination with their marvelous pseudonyms, work, again, in a way every bit as sophisticated as the work of Shokusanjin *et al* over a century later! In other words, *this little-mentioned* – had I not found it in *Kyôka Taikan*, I would not have known it existed – *work is a masterpiece.* It proves *kyôka* attained the heights of art-poetry before the later popular development in Ôsaka and the acclaimed Tenmei era Edo. Whatever was needed was already out there. Two pairs are in this book. There would be more, but the complexity of the poems and elegance of the prose required more time than I could spare to do them justice. If a reader *can* give the Four Life Poem Match the attention it deserves, I would love to add more chapters to feature it.

The most novel, if less polished, early-Edo work *with* kyôka – the *kyôka* intersperse and conclude tales – that I have read, is the 1640 anon. *Fake Ise*, or, *Nisemonogatari*. I planned to give it several chapters in this book (rather than just a few poems) because of the extraordinary diverse ways it plays the *Tales of Ise*. Few books can better show the distance between our "parody" and the Japanese equivalent, if it can be called that. The tales of the "*okashi otoko* / funny man" (vs. the original *mukashi otoko,* or "man of old,") and their *kyôka* foreshadow the surreal way Shokusanjin plays the *Hundred Poets One Poem* anthology in his *Kyôka Hundred Poets* over a century later, thereby, proving that editorial finesse was not invented in late-Edo. The small (chintzy?) but nonetheless Rabelaisian character of the main character in this *kanazôshi* (pop. lit in Japanese mixed syllabary+characters as opposed to Chinese character-only hard stuff) and the fact everyone who read was familiar with the real *Tales of Ise* with its lively poems, some of which might themselves be called *kyôka*, made it the best known story-book parody of the time. I ended up settling for a few scattered translations because I came to feel that doing a good job would require me to do more study of the *Tales of Ise* than I had time or money to do. The content includes food for thought, but it is a bit too heavy on food for food's sake, never easy to translate between cultures with mutually exotic palates as well as tongues.

Keene and I see eye-to-eye on two details. First, the comic verses on 100 kinds of liquor attributed to Kyôgetsu-bô (1265-1328) and said to be the oldest extant collection of *kyôka*, is indeed uninteresting. Second, as far as I know, *The Collection of Barbarian Poems Old and New* (my *Old & New Savage Songs*) published in 1666 and edited by Seihakudô Kôfû 生白庵行風 a disciple of a disciple ot Teitoku, is, with the possible exception of the much shorter 1636 *New Selection of Kyôka* (新撰狂歌集), what Keene calls it, the first important selection of *kyôka*. I gave it five full chapters (10 pgs, and, if other poems from it found elsewhere are added, half again that) though unaware until I read Keene that it had that reputation – the *Taikan=Broadview* offers no commentary whatsoever for the material it reproduces – just because the poems were interesting. The fine old selections in it prove respectable *waka* poets (eg. Saigyô 七瀬川やせたる馬に水かへば　九瀬になるとてとをせとそいふ　西行上人 *nanasekawa* . . .) did poems anyone might call *kyôka*, as was true for some of the Zen *dôka* in the religious section (on the whole, too sweet for an otherwise superb anthology) and most of the death poems by a variety of people. Many of the early 17c and contemporary poems selected are also good. I was amazed to find that half a dozen of the 52 by Teitoku were not only witty in a delicate way but as *beautiful* as the best modern *tanka* – which tells me that Keene did not actually read this collection, for if he did, he would surely have paid more respect to Teitoku *as a poet* – while some by Mitoku (see below) exhibited the dense layers of wit and careful self-editing I would not have expected until Tenmei *kyôka*. The editor, to his credit, did not balk at introducing many poems by the bold and outrageous mad poets of the previous century, of whom Yûchôrô, with 32 poems included – likewise, Keene cannot have read this and failed to appreciate Yûchôrô – is the exemplar (eg. that poem worrying about the food supply holding-up if great-grandparents survived, pg.

324; the lice admirably unaffected by social prejudice pg.322, and the older obscene poem for the land-grabbing Empress by Kyôgetsu-bô, pg.370). So, it is easy to imagine the anthology not only sparked broader interest in the genre, but, by introducing both fresh crude ideas and classic beauty in abundance, influenced and encouraged poets such as, the earlier-mentioned Getsudôken and Teiryû. Every time I look at it, I see more poems I'd like to translate. Here is one of 21 poems by the Zen priest Dôgen that just caught my eye: *Neither roundness nor angles do I find: / Indeed it lacks all the primary colors – Would that be my mind?* (円からす又方ならす 長短も五色にもなき我こゝろ哉　道元和尚 *marokarazu mata hô narazu . . .*). While barely a *kyôka,* detailing an abstract thing and turning a poem into a riddles are, in a sense, mad. And here is another, by Teitoku, that I missed:

臓そうで綺麗な物は歌人の口にかゝれる山のは霞　貞徳
musasô de kireina mono wa kajin no kuchi ni kakareru yama no hagasumi teitoku
overdne/dirty & pretty thng-as4 wakapoet's mouth-in touched mt.-ridge(=tooth)-mist

How dare they Miz my Mist!

Something sordid but beautiful creeps about – The mist
Of spring on the ridges touched by the waka poet's lips.

~~~~~~

What is sordid but beautiful? I would say the spring mizt
Modified by waka poets' all too toothy mountain ridges.

The *waka* poet's mouth touches the mountain's ridge/s, *ha,* homophonic with *tooth/teeth,* which coming into contact with *mist,* results in the clean かすみ *kasumi* (mist) sound clouding into がすみ ~ *gasumi* (*ha-gasumi*). Did Teitoku feel the thousands of poems about mist/haze as a mark of Spring and absurd metaphors (eg. steam born of red hot bracken) cheapened it, or that *waka* literally overtaxed it with types such as the above? He may have had a particular *waka* in his scope; I do not know. I give it nonetheless because it shows Teitoku is good even when he's bad. I love the way he starts his poem in the style of *a listing* (*mono-wa-tsukushi,* ala Sei Shônagon. To make that clear – it was lost in my first translation – I added my second less poetic reading. It also shows why literary historians should consider giving *kyôka* more attention. *"I missed it?"* was not quite true. Teitoku's poem was among *scores* of poems *about* poetry – perhaps we should call them "meta-poetry" in the above collection that I *skipped* as I thought they were, on the whole, better left to scholars more familiar with the various genre and interested in their quarrels (和歌対狂歌の歌内喧嘩 集＋注 求む).

When I jumped from Teitoku and his students clear down to Teiryû, naming only his slightly older fellow Shinkai student Getsudôken as an important link to the wild-side of *kyôka,* and admitting only Mitoku as a possible poet of interest, I jumped too fast. I had not yet realized how much Kôfû and Bokuyô, as light poets – in the best sense of the word – offered us. While Kôfû may have received the support of Teitoku when he was alive and later his first and second generation students, his 43 poems in the 1666 *Savage* anthology that he edited are by and large less interesting than the 32 by Yûchôrô and do not even come up to the more uneven 52 by Teitoku. But anyone who reads his more abundant and far more relaxed yet lively poems in the 1672 *Arima My Rain* 有馬私雨 volume of what we might call a huge *baedeker of kyôka* 地誌所載狂歌少, which he also edited, should be able to feel in their lightness the presence of *kyôka* as a solid, definitely existing genre that did not have to wait for late-18c Edo to mature. Old Kôfû is playful as a porpoise. One feels the artless ease of the comic master. And, maybe I am too easy-going a critic, but it also seems to me that Bokuyô, the physician who brought the same light but sure touch from Ôsaka to Edo in the mid-17c, also deserves more of a name – more credit – in literary history. In some ways, he reminds me of Erasmus Darwin, a physician whose poetry (about the lives of plants and his love's cats etc.) was not admired by critics of the next generation *despite their influence* (admitted by Shelly and others), and I hope to do further research on him. Of course, there is room for argument here. My opinion is tentative, based on my reading of a few score poems. Still, I feel that if only Bashô lived to be 80 rather than 50, he would have read and enjoyed these two as aseasonal prophets of his *karumi,* or "lightness." I would guess they, not the later Teiryû or far earlier poets of the *Kokinshû* and *Manyô*, directly or indirectly contributed memes to the evolution of the best of the late-18c 'canonical' *kyôka* poets.

~~~~~~
~~~~~~

★ *More 'Yet-to-Gain' Mitoku, Regrettably Missed Earlier* ★

I did not fully realize how much Mitoku contributed to *kyôka* until it was too late to give him the chapters he deserved (Mad Bios). So, he will be added to, and over-represented in this yet un-paginated section (MS-Word makes re/pagination hell). I do not know if his book, the 658-poem *Gagin Wagashû* 吾吟我集 (c1649), all his – the name of the book with two different "my's" (吾, 我) is in itself unusual – was read as much as the *Old & Now Savage Song Anthology* (in which he had more poems, 63, than anyone else) of 1666, but it includes various kyôka *themes* which most writers on the genre regard as typical that would be popular in the late-18c and *styles* (eg. *kana* 哉 endings) that show how closely linked *haikai* and *kyôka* were, as some poems could be either. He also created charming palindromic *kyôka* (examples in the notes). I slip in his 1649 book *here* rather than before the 1666 *Savage Songs* for the same reason I would discuss Darwin before Wallace. While I would not call Mitoku a disciple of Teitoku, he did write him early on for critiques of his poems and advice and might be considered a leading representative of the Teimon school of haikai in Edo, where he lived, and most of the best poems in the 1666 book actually antedated his 1649 work, though in one way his book seems more modern. Because Kôfû was the consummate gentleman, parody, especially the off-color variety, was under-represented in *Savage Songs*. Mitoku gives us dozens – possibly scores, I may miss some – early in his one-man anthology. Perhaps the most outrageous is a poem おもひつゝぬればや若衆見えつらん夢としりせばさめざらましを 吾吟#25 *omoitsutsu nureba ya* wakashu *mietsuran yume to* shir*iseba samezaramashi o* that plays on 9c poetess Ono no Komachi's famous poem (easily found as *Kokinshû* #552),

> *Did you come because I fell asleep thinking of you, Sweetheart?*
> *Had I known 'twas but a dream I would have skipped the waking part!*

(*"skipped the waking part"* is mad; it should be simply *"would not have awakened"*) Mitoku reproduces the original changing just one word, *hito no* ⇒ *wakashu* (the む⇒ ん is only updated orthography) and when that "you" (the other, one's love), literally "person's," becomes "young-crowd," or gay youth, the *shiri*, or *buttocks* protrudes from an innocent word, if *"knowing=shiriseba"* can be so called. Or, to put it another way, when *shiri* ass*ociates* with wakashu, the conjugal? part of that verb, ~ *seba*, becomes "doing" the same, and, voila, we have the most subtle sodomic dream ever! I suppose one could write "dreaming" "d*reaming*" to convey that idea in English, but even the slightest *change* – as opposed to the pun that comes entirely from the head – ruins the wit. It is followed immediately by dancing girls redefining the idea of *fading/transferring color/eros:* いろ見えてうつろふものはおどり子の このみ／＼の花ぞめの袖 *iro mie de (or, here, miete) utsurô* . . . lamented by another of the famous love poetess's poems, kks #797. A few poems later, we have an almost perfect reproduction of kks #735 by Kuronushi, where a man longing for a woman as he circles her house hears geese crying as they fly over and wonders if she does too, which becomes, with a few small changes someone longing for something which turns out to be geese bound to become the condiment in the soup of others (おもひ出てほしき時にははつかりのなきてわたるを人の汁のみ *omoiidete hoshiki toki ni wa hatsukari no nakite wataru o hito no shiru no mi*). The pun on the verb *know* (*shiru*) that becomes the soup is explicit in the Chinese character and the poem itself is of the utterly nonsensical appetite-driven variety found previously only in the *Fake Nise* of c.1640. Later in the anthology, he has poems that not so much parody as play-off, or rift on others.   Do you recall Izumi Shikibu's supposed defense of menstruating women entering shrines, by linking the gods to trash (through their homophonic affinity with paper)? That link is masterfully deconstructed when brought to bear upon the leaves of the Gods-gone month: おのつから木の葉吹たて塵にのみましはる風の神無月哉 *onozukara konoha fukitate chiri ni nomi majiwaru kaze no kaminazuki kana*.   The way what is assumed to be the Wind God is de-godded so to speak by that God's becoming the Gods in the name of the month they are absent so that the leaves only consort with trash and not gods, or by homophony, *paper* is not even close to translatable. Like the late-18c *kyôka* master Shokusanjin, we have a diverse styles and a deft touch. Moreover, we sometimes have interesting framing of the poems. The young-crowd Komachi is prefaced by a description of pretty youth dancing the Komachi (yes, her very name is a dance-style) "better than so-called beauties . . . maybe the dance should be renamed 'the young-crowd.' " (see ♪). This, content-wise slightly *off* coupling of observations on dance and parody is later found in the surreal, or dadaist associations of Hiranaga Gennai (remember that *Limp Dick* parody of Saigyô's wintering in?) and other extraordinarily limber 18c Edo minds.

河つらのしは〻氷にのびぬれと　冬ことによるわか老のなみ　未得
kawa tsura no shiwa wa kôri ni nobinuredo fuyu goto ni yoru waga oi no nami

> 'Tis wondrous how the ice smoothes out the face of the big river,
> But the wrinkles on mine just grow deeper every winter

亭主とて跡にと〻まる人は誰そ　この世をかりの宿といへるに
teishû tote ato ni todomaru hito wa da zo kono yo o kari no yado to ieru ni

> So who, then, is the owner, the one who gets to stay
> If this world of ours is but a house to let, as they say?

~~~~~~

> If this World of ours really is nothing but a house to let,
> How odd it is the owner and I have not yet met!

But, Mitoku was not all parody. These above two show him being conceptual. With the first, exceptionally easy to read for Mitoku, the translation suffers from *waves* not being *wrinkles* and *face* being narrow of connotation of face or, lacking sufficient synonyms in English;" but, if no one else has connected ice with an unwrinkled face, it is a rare, rare animal, a new conceit.   The second is the sort of facetious naïveté found in Meshimori's poem preferring bad poets. The *kari* is left in phonetic syllabary for a good reason. It should be 仮 "tentative" but here means 借 "rented." The poem is interesting because the homophony-driven logic leads us somewhere Japanese rarely went: metaphysics.   But neither of these poems are particularly poetic to start with. Unfortunately, the most poetic conceptual ones seldom translate. Here, for example, are geese that come lined up as/in a line/pole before they are hunted and carried off the same way: 御狩にもあはぬさきより一さほにつらなりて来る天津雁かね *mikari ni mo awanu saki yori hito-sao ni tsuranarite kuru amatsu karigane*. English cannot get all of that out of *hito-sao,* or "one pole." And the expression *awanu saki yori,* lit. meet-not before-from (found in an old folk song about birds flying in that was sung when chopping, and possibly alluded to) plays on odd grammar recalling our folk song *Rye Whiskey* ("if the whiskey don't kill me, I'll live till I die"). Or, take this masterpiece about cherishing-cherishing someone who (his or her heart) becoming a boulder won't be budged: こなたには 恋し／＼と思へとも 人やうこかぬいはほなるらん *konata ni wa koishi koishi to omoedomo hito ya ugokanu iwao naruran*. Until you reach the *iwao,* or boulder in the last *ku,* the cherishing-cherishing (or loving and missing) is just that, but after reading the boulder they pun "little-stone, little-stone." There is one such pun among the sea cucumber *ku* in *Rise, Ye Sea Slugs!* (2003), but Mitoku invented it hundreds of years earlier. The poem was captioned 寄巌恋 or, *Love* (including lovesickness) *w/ Boulders* and was among 130 poems, each putting some thing with Love. We have seen a fine one "with musket" elsewhere (pg.528). Unfortunately, Mitoku sat down to do up all these *love+things* like someone who has done a daily comic strip for ten years. That is probably why I was turned off and never checked out the author when I skimmed his book before. Most things find decent metaphors but lack the Rabelasian energy of Yûchôrô and personal pathos in Getsudôken's work. Some more I liked include a Tsukuma Festival declaration of being less than happy to find oneself among a pile of *pots* (on a woman's head, each is a lover) with a good pun in each of the last two *ku* 寄鍋恋 あた人のつくま祭にかつくてふ なへての数に入われそうき *ada hito no tsukuma matsuri ni katsugu . . .*) and the gift of a plate with deep colors for affection and an unbearably light pun following a humdrum pivot: 色ふかく人をは思ひそめつけの さらに忘れぬわかこゝろ哉 *iro fukaku hito o ba omoi-some-tsuke.*

猫のはにかみのこされてとふ蚤も虎の尾をふむ心なるらし 未得
neko no ha ni kaminokosarete tobu nomi mo tora no o o fumu kokoro naru rashi

A flea that leaps away from death between a cat's teeth
How life after 'stepping on the tail of a tiger' must feel.

I added the marks about the saying as the poem was in a section with scores of them. As far as I can tell, there is not a pun in the poem! One could feel Mitoku working about a new genre. The first few examples give the proverb *before* the poem, and I am afraid most poems lose as much wit or more from the added words as they gain from their puns. The above works by adding one creative simile (the first line) to define the saying, funny because it does not really need definition. We have seen another that worked before, where equality in nursing and front vs. back carrying were ludicrously combined (pg. 323). Though not well done, having a clear section for playing with sayings clearly demonstrates that there is no reason to restrict parody, or as some call it, "allusive variation," to old poems.

名のみして口にねぶらぬあめうしのいかてかたえぬよだれ成るらん
na nomi shite kuchi ni neburanu ameushi no ika de ka taenu yodare naruran
name alone havng, mouth by lickng ~~slug~~/sucker-ox/'s how runout-nt drool is?!

~~Slugs never run out of ammo as a slug is always a slug:~~
~~But why do we find those trails of slime instead of blood?~~

From their name, you might think they would be good to lick
But never short of slobber? Caramel cows, what's the trick!

The above is the second of Mitoku's rundown of beasts. The beast is an 飴牛 *ame-ushi* cow, or sucker-cow, which is to say a caramel-colored cow as that was the color of most suckers. I first forgot that "heaven-cow" which might also be so pronounced was a bug called a *kamikiri-mushi* and confused it for the *namekuji* 蛞蝓 or "slug" which has the character for "tongue" 舌 right in its name and tried to come up with an equivalent and . . . The poem may have been intended to humor Teitoku or to honor his haiku about cow-slobber icicles – I almost wrote *popsicles!* The first beast in the series was a parody on a *Tale of Ise* poem; so the parodies, not all of which I caught continued. I put aside the third, with a *tanuki* (racoon-fox) tanning his own hide by drumming on it, for a book-to-be on tanuki. The fourth is charming in the original:

糸つけて手かひの猫はしやみせんのかはにかけても人にひかるゝ 未得
ito tsukete tegai no neko wa shamisen no kawa ni kakete mo hito ni hikaruru

> *Just string him up and stretch your pet cat into a banjo skin*
> *He scratched you, so now, you might as well scratch him!*

My reading bends a bit toward one we have seen already about cats that if they die mating can keep up the lascivious sound-making as shamisen (*neko no tsuma moshi koi-shinaba* . . . 後西上皇 pg.69. I am unsure of the priority as I have yet to date the poet (looks imperial or a pseudonym). Both pun on *hikaru* (play/strum), but Mitoku's pun does so with *pulled-about*, i.e. kept on a leash – from that string to the ones played – while the other poem does so with *scratching*. Mitoku's pun was farther from English's span of connotations, so I chose to switch to the other – though *scratch* to *strum* or *pluck* is still a stretch – and then added the karma to gain some fun in translation (又近畿方言の読みでは、「ひかる」「叱る」とも掛ける).

くちなはのをのか針めのほころひを 誰にぬへとてぬけるきぬそも 未得
kuchinawa no ono ga harime no hokorobi o dare ni nue tote nukeru kinu zo mo
serpent's own needle/s'eye/s' deterioration+acc who-to/by sew say strips dress!

> *Needles are something every snake has, but what cloudy eyes!*
> *Who can thread them much less tailor the new suit to his size?*

If my translation seems a bit odd, well, I think the original's jump from fang/needle-eyes to those used to thread them is already odd enough that Kôfû would have disapproved. The question is how much nonsense, associations that do not smoothly dovetail but involve some disjunction should be allowed. Mitoku was exceptionally tolerant of it and that helped make up for the monotony arising when one man tries to exhaust a theme. And, I may repeat, but the odd thing about Mitoku is that his most puzzling poems – especially those I do not get – seem to be his best. That is not because difficulty attracts me. Anyone who has read this book closely knows I am a simpleton at heart. I prefer relatively easy poets and do not like difficulty for difficulty's sake. In that sense, Mitoku is different. Here is a good example of what I mean: 浜見れは真砂に蟹のかうたてゝ はさみきる手をあんしかほする *hama mireba masago ni kani no kô tatete hasami kiru te o anji-gao suru.* We have a crab on the beach, shell 甲 raised high punning with the creation of a decorative stands by cutting and folding paper (*kôdate* 甲立 or 紙立) looking like – lit. with the face of one – pondering how to cut (some paper, *i.e.,* the design of the decoration, by implication) with his scissors/pincer/s. I also *suspect* an allusion to a *go* player using *kô* – a move requiring immediate response from the other player 劫立 that gains one a chance to make another move otherwise lost (see pg. 384) – to try to carry out a sequence of moves to pinch off and prevent another's potential colony (if that is what it is called – I play *go* but do not talk it) from surviving. And crabs with those little eyeballs also raised high, *do* seem to be pondering what to do. ♪

一まいを万枚になすはく屋こそ 金を打出のこつちなりけれ
ichimai o man mai ni nasu hakuya koso kin o uchide no ko-tsuchi narikere
one-sheet+acc 10000-sheets into become gilder esp. gold+acc pound-out small-mallet is

> *It is the gilder who of one sheet makes a thousand-fold,*
> *that is the real thing, a magic mallet to pound out gold!*

Mitoku also has a section for craftsmen. There are older *kyôka* collections of them, but, as mentioned before, I could find little wit in them meriting re-creation. The above plays with the magic mallet we have already seen many times. The homographically identical gold/money (金 can be *kin*=gold or *kane* = money) allows one to imagine gold coins popping out with each pound of the mallet in Japanese. I also love Mitoku's carpenter poem やすらかに軒をつたふて家作る大工をいはゝ蜘のいとなみ *yasuraka ni noki o tsutaute ie tsukuru daiku o iwaba kumo no itonami* but the simple but graceful puns fail to re-create. Here, we might note that, like Teitoku, Mitoku was a big name in *haikai* where Kyoriku would soon be doing a fine craftsman series. I wish I had it here for comparison's sake, but suffice it to say that if one pays attention to content, the split between *kyôka* and *haikai* is not *that* big.

述懐　しろ髪は毎日見るそうかるなる　かうそる道に今は身かろし　未得
shi ro ka mi wa ma i ni chi mi ru zo u ka ru na ru ka u so ru mi chi ni i ma wa mi ka ro shi
white hair-as4 every day see+emph depressed become; this shave road-on self/bdy's light

> *To see my hair, ev'ry day white as snow made me blue*
> *Shaving it, I took the path . . . and now I feel light, too!*

The above, capturing deep feelings 述懐, is one of fifteen palindromic *kyôka* filling the tenth and last chapter of Mitoku's collection. I have always thought the idea of retirement as a time to practice religion beats what I see of it in Usania. I chose to English the poem because it was easy to translate, but I am afraid I do not have time to reproduce its raison d' être. As it must be a hundred times easier to make palindromes in Japanese than English, I have a good excuse not to. The first poem, captioned "Spring," was much more complex as the first letters of the first three *ku* combine to spell out the unnamed blossom mentioned at the end of the third *ku*. It is *mikiko,* short for 御酒古草 *mikikogusa,* literally *"hon.-sake-ancient-herb/flower,"* and meaning the peach, or more specifically either peach in *sake* drunk for longevity – after the Chinese legends of the Blue Queen with her magical peach tree up a mountain – or, sake drunk with peach flowers in it on the third day of the third month: 春　身の留守に　きてはおりとる　このはなは　のこる鳥をは　敵にするのみ *mi no ru su ni ki te h(w)a o ri to ru ko no ha na wa no ko ru to ri o h(b)a te ki ni su ru no mi.* It would seem someone stole a drink while the poet was blinking off and that is metaphored as the breaking and taking of the blossom and that puts said thief, his buddy, in bad odour with the late bird (as they visit blossoms) he then becomes, and that said new "enemy" is the last "drop" (both *teki*) in the bottle, but I could be wrong and, unless you are a better reader than me, we shall let this go for the last of the palindromes: 賀　なかき代は君民の体　たうとし　うたいてのみたみきはよきかな *na g/ka ki yo wa ki mi ta mi no te i . . .* As a poem, this praising "Your long reign" with the corpus of ruler and ruled sung up as precious . . . is very sweet and does not interest me. However, we do feel in it the idea of *kyôka* as sort of tool for celebration of the New Year, which included celebrating the ruler and the reign that would peak in the conservative years of the early-19c in the poems accompanying surimono.

In appraising the influence of any historical figure on a genre, it depends on how we define the genre, what eras are specified, what was reprinted and how many and *who* read it. I would bet Mitoku, like Bokuyô, Getsudôken, Kôfû, Teitoku and Yûchôrô, influenced Shokusanjin. His *Gagin Wagashû* was oft reprinted, but I do not yet know the figures for other books and including the enormously popular comic stories containing *kyôka, etc.,* so I will not guess about their comparative influence.

XI

For all my effort to broaden the picture, I can see how relating *kyôka* to the evolving main lines of poetry – *waka* and *haikai* – misses much of the picture. Any valid taxonomy of *kyôka* would need to include more, seemingly outside genre and complicate the lineage, such that it is, with jumping memes, congruence and possibly, even mutation. To fully understand it would require much more reading, explaining it more space to elaborate (at the cost of the large numbers of poems that make a book like this interesting), and we would probably need what we find in Japanese Old-Language Dictionaries (*kogojiten*): charts. I cannot do that here and now. Let me just declare something my relatively broad reading makes clear: the Edo era *kyôka,* or the main body of what is generally introduced as mad poems today, did not evolve from their immediate past alone. They were not just a sort of anti-*waka*, nor even just a properly improper vehicle for the proudly avant-garde urban literatae to play with or for the *haikai* crowd to enjoy as 31-syllabet stand-alone poetry. Whether Edo and its historians admit it or not there are *various* lines of proto-*kyôka* that trickled down from ancient times to the Tenmei era. While fads and convention (fads being a short-term convention, they are ultimately one) favor certain tendencies in reading, the nature of the written word is such that the literature of any time in history could always be directly referenced in so far as it could be found. Because of that, memes out-jump genes, & taxing literature is never as simple as working out natural history.

There were poems by free-thinking Zen monks of the 14-16c of which Ikkyû's are but the most famous. A number of them are usually included in the religious sections of collections of kyôka, already recognized as part of the world of *kyôka*. I would have given them more space in this book had I the resources at hand to make good selections directly rather than from the few in the aforesaid collections. I think we do need to evaluate their relation to the broader picture. To give but one item of many that interest me – did the seemingly nonsensical Zen koan play any role in bringing nonsense to poetry without rhyme? Or, was there so much in folksong to start with that it was redundant? There are, after all, some utterly nonsensical poems in the famously diverse chapter 16 of the *Manyôshû* that suggest the folk already had it. I did not introduce examples because I do not care for nonsense. Even Lear got too nonsensical for me at times. I want to be tricked by hyperlogical causality and delighted by metaphysical associations. Pure nonsense only works as scat (which is all I like in jazz because I hate the standard jazz scale – not New Orleans jazz, which I like – as much as I love blues notes, especially when they bend). The Zen poems also may relate to *riddle poems*, another type that seem mad to me. There are other reasons I am drawn to Ikkyû. His attention to rhyme in the Chinese style poems gives a new tool to mad poetry in Japan, whether or not it has been recognized to date. But not having the proper books on hand to make my own selections, I had to settle for a regrettably small sample of his *kyôka* and *kyôshi* in this book.

In addition to *haikai* poets engaged in *kyôka*, we have to look at *haikai* that share something with *kyôka*. I have given some examples taken out of context from comic link-verse in this book from the *Enoko-shû* (puppy-collection 1633), and various (Osaka) Danrin link-verse, etc. but more are needed. I did not have sufficient reference material on hand. There are far too many similarities between *haikai* and *kyôka* for this and other early *haikai* anthologies not to be taken into account when working out the history of *kyôka*. The best *kyôka-like* riddle poems I know were in the 1499 *Chikuba Kyôginshû* 竹馬狂吟集, a *saijiki* (almanac)-style – perhaps the first – anthology I have not yet had the good fortune to obtain and read (the wonderful examples on pg. 273 are courtesy of my respondent). The 狂吟 *kyôgin* in its name is, as you may have noted, the same *kyô* as in *kyôka*. While mainly used in a humble (self-deprecating) way to modify the *gin* 吟 (a character usually used to signify *haikai* link-verse sessions) – and *kyôka* – it has an overtone of the comic, perhaps because it was often applied to poems excused for being composed while drunk, or such is my impression. Carter, who does not try to relate them to *kyôka,* has five poems from this anthology – which he parenthetically names *"Crazy Verses on Bamboo Stilts"* – and twice that from the *Inu-tsukubashû,* or Dog-Tsukuba collection, probably by Sôkan (d.1534). His first, from the *Chikuba Kyôginshû,* is a good example of where *haikai* and *kyôka* overlap: *Suu-suu goes the sound / of wind blowing through the reeds. // That bug calling / seems to have lost a front tooth – / giving in to old age.* From Carter's translation, you can see the syllabet split is 14-17, more common with *haikai* than *kyôka*. His individual bug sounds more *haikai,* or rather, haiku, but the original does not specify number and the *"mo," too,* could be interpreted to connect the bug/s with the aging season and/or the poet, himself. So, it could also be, say

> *Suey-suey goes the wind blowing through the Ogi reeds;*
> *To hear the bugs, they, too, lack eye-teeth: we go down hill!*

> *suisui kaze no ogi ni fuku koe // naku mushi mo mukaba ya nukete yowaruran*
> sui-sui wind's/s' blowng voice/s // cryng bug/s too front-teeth+emph/? pulld weakenng!

And, there were anonymous squibs, the so-called *rakushu,* or "fallen-heads" that, Kaneko notes, the 18-19c *kyôka* master Yado no Meshimori wrongly thought *the* fount of *kyôka*. It is possible, Meshimori, as a man who studied politics, gave in to cognitive dissonance. Or, he read little of the *kyôka*-like *Manyôshû* or *Kokinshû* poems, for they were not easily accessed in his day, while the Tales of Battles in Medieval times which included *kyôka* were. A representative example, Kaneko cites is a mean laugh at a greedy man who thought his reward for bringing in the heads of two enemy (killed in an ignoble fashion) was too little and ended up getting nothing, no, worse, tied down and bludgeoned to death on the grave of those he killed. There are *kyôka* for each stage of his come-uppance, both pun on the name of the place he might have become master of. The first suggests that if he had but taken that spit of land, he might not have ended up killed while being spit upon. 落ちければ命ばかりは壱岐の守みのをはりこそ聞かまほしけれ *ochikereba inochi bakari wa . . .* Well, actually there is no spitting – the land pun is on Owari, Tail-spread, which is a homophone for his "ending" – and the poem concerns his fleeing . . . I am not the person to translate these, as war tales do not interest me, so I have no books of reference and am not familiar with the names. Another example he gave shows even better what caught Meshimori's eye. It is from the most famous of all the Tales, the *Tale of Heike* (16c). After a crucial battle was lost by a man whose name puns into "support," which made the position of the commander-in-chief, whose name puns on the ridge on a roof (very important to Japanese architecture: see Edward S. Morse's books!), a poem plays with the Heike clan's name, taking it literally as a level-house:

平屋なるむねもりいかに騒ぐらむ柱と頼むすけを落して　平家物語
hiraya naru munemori ika ni sawaguran hashira to tanomu suke o otoshite
flat(1-story-dwelling) is (fighting on the side of) munemori how agitated+emph
pillar(hold up jpse houses rather than walls)-as depend sidekick losing/fallen

> *The Ridge-pole guardian of the Flat, what agitation –*
> *To look down and see a pillar of the house had fallen!*

Here, Helen McCullough's translation: *The ridge guardian / at the one-story dwelling / must be in disrepair / after seeing the downfall / of the mainstay he trusted* (*Tales of Heike:* 1988) is more accurate except for one thing. I do not think our metaphor is a sail-powered houseboat. There are, evidently, lots of these, and from what little I have seen, I am afraid I must concur with Kaneko that they are mean-spirited as they are invariably pointed at the losers. It is, indeed, unpleasant to see wit used merely for rubbing salt into wounds. The content of these *kyôka-style rakushu* reveal the ugly, back-side of what Benedict would later call a "culture of shame" (I bet Europe has the same and would welcome an example for my notes). But, were all early lampoons directed at losers? ~~*Kyôka Taikan* had all too few *rakushu,* so I will not know until I get to a library in Japan or buy a dictionary (despite the name 落首辞典, it must be an *encyclopedia,* and it exists!) of them~~ – At this point, I had to leave my computer because the dog barked at the armadillo I finally trapped –

how, I do not know, for it had firm lead-in boards running from the mouth of the trap to the hole and it sat there for a week (maybe there is a second hidden entrance!) and, after taking hay to another field to distract the cows, drove the old truck slowly through an overgrown field with sinkholes to get to the far fence, lifted the trap over upon a big log and then opened the door using an old tobacco stake I brought along (it is said armadillos can give you leprosy, so I was careful), and, finally, tossed a broken branch in the fat fleeing armadillo's direction, not to hit it, but to tell it "and don't come back!"

Back, again. I recall that this matter of the relationship of *kyôka* and *rakushu* was one place where I disagreed with Kaneko Jitsue (蜀山家集: 1927). He rightfully regretted the *haikai* world hijacking, or rather, claiming to *be* what *kyôka*, as he saw it *was,* so *kyôka,* no longer having its own identity came to be considered nothing but an anonymous squib. But, in deploring *kyôka's* becoming identified with *rakushû* alone rather than *rakushu* being seen as one form of kyôka – as *haikai-ka* was one form of *kyôka* – he went too far in putting it down as lacking humor and being a sort of cowardly bad-mouthing by people who lacked the guts to stand up to authority. I admire the feelings behind that opinion. Kaneko was doing something we all should do more often, critiquing his own country – I would guess he read and loved Voltaire and wished such bravery could be found in a Japan that was heading into militarism and destroying what had been a good start in democracy (with an Emperor as a figurehead as was the case with kings/queens in England) as he wrote – but it was doubly unfair. One *can* find witty *rakushu* taking on the establishment rather than the fallen and, considering the fact that direct criticism was suicide for much of the Tokugawa era, it was a miracle *anyone* signed criticism. What bothers me is his *"yue ni"* or *because of*, when he wrote that *because* the *rakushu* were nothing but *warufuzake,* or mean-spirited kidding, the authorities outlawed them early on. (. . . 我国にあつてはそんな深い意味を有するのものは、殆ど無いと言つてい〻。人道の為に人の罪悪を諷誡するとか、正義の為に要路の人々の専横を憤るとか言ふ事は絶対に無いのである。只人を誹つて自ら快を遣るとか、或は他人の気付かない社会の欠陥を指摘して、自ら足れりとするのが普通の様である。全くわるふざけに過ぎないものである。故に大宝令にも既に落書を罪する規定がある程度である。) *No!* They were outlawed because they were indeed dangerous to the establishment. The irresponsibility of some only provided the *excuse* to clamp down, and that excuse is what we must not swallow.

★ Squibs & their ilk – Lessons from the Parrot in a cage ★

All those books of *kyôka* in *Broadview* have become the ground that I, a reincarnation of Zeno's tortoise, keep getting half-way across as I near the closer yet ever-receding finish. I added Mitoku and thought that was that – time to spell-check and paginate the After-matter – but, as the automatic Friday morning virus check occupied my computer, I looked *just once more* at the reference volume of *Broadview* and found I had underestimated the amount of *rakushu* in it because the largest 'book' was culled from a journal, that is, presented in a context hard to jump into, and because my concept of *rakushu* was too narrow when I first saw it. Those squibs 落首抄 from the *"Record From a Parrot's Cage* 鸚鵡籠中記 *ômurôchû-ki,"* Asahi Bunzaemon's Journals kept from 1684-1717, show I clearly had more *rakushu* to introduce. They bring a broader perspective yet about what *it, rakushu,* was.

世の中は皆三味線になりにけり　てれん／＼のおとのみそする 江戸の狂歌
yo no naka wa mina shamisen ni narinikeri teren teren no oto nomi zo suru c.1707
world-w/in/society-as4 everyone/all shamisen became: racketX2's sound only!makes

What times are these when the world is nothing but shamisen!
Why strum a cat skin when the real racket is plucking men?

The shamisen has a banjo-like sound but louder because the heavy pick lets not a decibel of sound escape the string. *Teren teren* is not the usual mimesis ascribed to it but *fraud* or *a racket* repeated twice. A *yo-no-naka* complaint as a comment on the times may include self-reflection. Were it not for the Confucian idea of the spirit of the times reflecting the character of the ruler, the poem might have been signed. The poem was well-known and may have influenced a c.1712 squib about the corrupt gold-mine monopoly: からくりの竹田近江が糸切れて　てれん／＼のばち当る也 *karakuri no takeda chikae ga ito kirete teren-teren no bachi ataru nari.* Here, that heavy pick called a *bachi* is homophonic with *just punishment* for the bad guy. The puns do not allow the poem to be Englished and a proper appreciation requires more historical background than I care to give. In more cases, the puns are based upon the names and places and even more impossible: すりこふ木町はあへ物世はからし　上は徳政下は損政　c.1702 *surikôgi-machi wa aemono yo wa karashi . . ..* Though impossibility, like zero, is not ratable, such difference is real to the thinking translator. The example poem mentions moral government above and "loss govern-ment" below, which seems to get around the Confucian equivalence. Still, no author is given; but, Bunzaemon notes the author of a 1704 *kyôka* claiming an earthquake was good for reforming the world that has nothing particularly witty to say as far as I can see 吉方よりさるとし男地震来て　万々歳といはふ世なをし *ehô yori sarudoshi otoko jishin . . .* got a reward for it (松平美濃守中小生狂歌よみ、高聞に達し御褒美等被下と)! That is a new twist. Up until now, all the rewards for poems I have seen have been in stories. And in 1705, we have 10 of a 100 poems about *nuke-mairi* (going on pilgrimages without gaining advance permission or waiting for the proper time for taking vacations – if they return with proof of the visit, employers could not punish them) playing with the famous *Hundred Poets One Song* anthology. The first:

秋の田を植付もせでぬけ参り我きるものは雨にぬれつつ
aki no ta o uetsuke mo se de nuke mairi waga kirumono wa ame ni nuretsutsu

Not bothering to plant the fields this autumn, I am off
on a pilgrimage, robes wet by rain, too happy to cough!

Not even planting the fields this fall off I go without permit.
A pilgrimage – I'm wet by the rain, let dew wet a hermit!

The tails of the translations differ as they are mine. We have seen enough parodies of the famous anthology in this book. Japanese readers will find some easy to read, eg., 春過て夏季にはやるぬけ参り衣ながらあま法師も *haru sugite natsuki ni hayaru . . .* where summer *came* becomes summer-*season* for pilgrimages, *heaven* puns into *nun,* and *drying, priest,* and some tricky, eg., 天の岩戸振袖見ればぬけ参り 浅まの山に七八十四五 *ama no iwato furisode mireba . . ..* Even knowing 七八十四五, *nanaya jûshigo* "seven eight fourteen fifteen" is from a popular song does not solve it, but I will spare you a guess. Let us just note that while pilgrimages were legal, they troubled spouses, employers who suddenly lost their otherwise submissive workforce and social service providers. The hundred poems are, strictly speaking, neither squib from below nor repression from on high; they are more like *"The Fan Exercise"* or *"The Cat Call"* of Addisson, poking fun at social phenomena, but unsigned, I guess for fear lest an authority misunderstand. Be that as it may, all this travel helped news flow around the nation. The following year, we learn of a pine literally flowering somewhere, about which a Babe of Kyôto (unless 京童 was a pseudonym) joked

十の字に蝿がとまれば千年よ　松の花迄ちやかしこそすれ
jûnoji ni hae ga tomareba sennen yo matsu no hana made chakashi koso sure

And if a fly were to sit right on top of the number 十 ten,
A blossom on a pine, why, it would make a 千 thousand!

A pine was said to live a thousand years. But would such nonsense be a *rakushu?* I wouldn't say so. But it surely is a *kyôka.* Then there was talk the next year – now we are once again up to 1707 – of human body parts flowing down rivers after rockfall wiping out villages on the lower slopes of Mt. Fuji followed by this poem: 運上を取りあげられて下部いたみ　治療するがの富士三里焼く *unjô o toriagerarete . . . .* As the punned place names would ruin a translation anyway, I will not try to guess what it means other than to say that it would seem an allegory of drastic medical procedure turns a disaster into a tragicomedy, as broadsides did to the same in olde England. Callous? No, *wise*. What better time to laugh? Still, *some* bad news and *lots of it* are a different matter. The following year, Edo would go through purgatory and Kyôto hell. The former was bathed in volcanic dust; the latter burnt down.

上よりはすなをになれとふる砂に　我等こときは泥坊になる
ue yori wa sunao *ni nare to furu suna ni warera gotoki wa dorobô ni naru*
above-from-as4 "obedient/honest becom" as-if fallng sand-w/by my-likes-as4 thief bcom

Sand from on high says "be sunao!" truthful, admit defeat:
In that case, me and my ilk must call ourselves deadbeat!

~~~~~~

Falling from high, sand says be yourself? Who'd have thunk
That a literal reading would make a 'thief' of this monk!

すなをなる御代のしるしに砂降て槍のふらぬかまたも仕合
sunao naru miyo no shirushi ni suna furite yari no furanu ga mada mo shiawase
obedient/honest/gentle becoms hon.age/reign's sign-as sand fallng, spears fall-not still happy

The sand fall, a sign of this docile age – who locks the door?
It beats a rain of spears, that's something to be thankful for!

I was thankful to find these poems for I have long been intrigued by *sunao,* a word used from at least the late-18c to the late-20c to simultaneously mean *honest* or even *frank* (a word deriving from 'free' I might point out) *and docile* or *unquestioning obedience.* When I consider my fellow Usanians who give no respect to people who really deserve it simply because they were taught pride for the sake of pride, I find something good in that odd combination. Usania could use more *sunao.* But, mostly, I have been horrified to find the word used as a bludgeon by authoritarian types to prevent social inferiors from speaking up. Without the "sand=*suna* and *sunao* pun, the translation lacks the wit that flows naturally from coincidence affecting the main word (I am afraid my rhymes are peripheral). If the original were only a complaint about the nation being lulled to sleep, I could have brought in the *sandman* even if the Japanese eye-lid, as described by Barthes in his *Empire of Signs*, could hardly hold a grain of it. Though sand fell in Edo, I assume the squib was made in Bunzaemon's Kansai where the dorobô born of pun, literally a "mud-monk"? means a do-nothing. If an Edoite wrote it, maybe this would be more accurate a reading: *Falling from high, dust says cover up and meekly kneel?/The lowly likes of such as me, it rather makes us steal!* There was also a Chinese mad-poem giving more details of the sand (volcanic dust, grit, sand, etc.) blown from Fuji followed by a poem playing on the high peak *ne* and prices which does not mention the sand and would seem to have been made simply to make fun of the mountain by someone who was upset at its belching out the dust: 名に高き富士の高根を現金に御料私料もとも二両そ *na ni takaki fuji no takane o genkin ni onryô shiryô mo tomo niryô zo*. Or maybe it is about the high cost of climbing it. Either way, it is fun to read in the original.

摺こう木民のあへ物世はからし　慈悲も下より金も下より
surikôgi tami no aemono yo wa karashi jihi mo shita yori kane mo shita yori

Pestle thin, the sauce of the folk is red pepper, bitter you know,
Mercy & money still flow, but today they flow up from below!

A pestle worn from the daily grind, a symbol of the hard-life, leads to pepper which in Japanese connotes bitter as well as hot. The second line wets my eyes more than chili. I recall Kropotkin, who pointed out that the poor tend to give more than the rich, and think of the good world we could have made in the 20c but did not. Three poems later, a man in Edo complains because the levee he walked to go to the public bath was privatized. The poem is boring (花色をとられにけりないつらに我身よごれて永湯せしまに *hana-iro o torarenikeri . . .*) but finding it in a journal written by a middle-level samurai in Nagoya is not. I guess the dirty body fit the larger theme of sand-in-everything. Indeed, it is followed by another Mt. Fuji report. From the flank of the crater where Fuji belched out that "sand," a baby Fuji 小富士 was born. Bunzaemon points out we should not call it "little," as it was already bigger than such and such a mountain. It is accompanied by a poem. おふじさま雪の肌へに火とまりて小ふじをうんで御代は万年 *ofuji-sama yuki no hada . . . .* Because the dust-covered Edoites – I assume the poem comes from Edo – got compensation for their discomfort in the form of this mountain to mark their Age "for 10,000 years to come (now 'parasite volcano' 宝永山 Hôei-san is 2,700 m. high), the entry is appropriate for the celebratory New Year's Month. *Then it happened.* A fire destroyed much of Kyôto and we get 58 poems. A small collection 少今集 following the first few about fire-fighting carts, starts with what may be a parody and plays with the "child" in spark 火の子 to explain the spread of the fire: 風さそふ姉か小路の火元よりふり行ものは火の子なりけり *kaze sasou ane-ga- . . .* Another plays on Shunzei's New Year poem about the New Year seemingly coming just to the Capital to add relativity: 世の中はちゝに物社悲しけれ京都斗の火事にはあらねど *yononaka wa chichi ni mono koso kanashikere kyôto bakari no kaji ni wa aranedo.* Yes, Kyôto's fire was not just Kyôto's fire. But translating such subtlety will not let me finish this book and, to tell the truth, I prefer bolder examples, such as these two recalling the aftermath of a hurricane.

見渡せばやなみすらりとこもかけて都は春の乞食なりけり
miwataseba ya-nami surari to komo kakete miyako wa haru no kojiki narikeri
see-span-when shop/house wavs/rows lined mats-placd capitl-as4 sprng-bggr/s beca/ome!

I looked around the capital and what sight did my eyes greet?
Rows of shops covered w/ mats like beggars by spring streets!

見渡せば京も田舎に成にけり　加屋の仮寝屋の春の夕暮
miwataseba miyako mo inaka ni narikeri kaya no kari(ne?)ya no haru no yûgure
see-span-when shop/house wavs/rows lined mats-placd capitl-as4 sprng-bggr/s beca/ome!

Looking about, our capital would seem to have become the country
With 'squito nets for bedrooms, spring dusk looks almost funny!

The straw mats mentioned in the first were used as temporary roofs as we use tarps today. I would guess some came from boats because they were used for sails as well! I suppose they were also sat upon. The *"greet"* and the *"funny"* were for the rhyme but, I trust, are on the money. Here is a good one I almost passed up for reading the first two characters "Nippon" rather than "Hi-no-moto." Both mean *Source* or *Origin of the Sun* – meaning, where it comes from and implying some sort of ownership or stewardship, accordingly – but the latter *hi* pronunciation yields a homophone meaning *fire*.

日本のあるじ成べきしるしには　先大焼をしろしめすかな
hi no moto no aruji narubeki shirushi ni wa mazu ôyake o shiroshimesu kana
sun(=fire)'s origin's owner/lord is confirmation-as-for first big-burn+acc show-off!/?

Lords of the Land of the Rising Sun, or are they the Spark of the Earth,
That they must first their mettle prove by burning down so much of it!

A historian might enjoy framing this with the information in the journal. I have trouble even with the little prose provided by *Broadview*. Needless to say, my invention of "Spark of the Earth" is not as good as the simple pun in the original, a fine example of a case where the orthography delays (not facilitates) catching the pun. Were this earlier in the book, I might have found a way to go from the sun to sunburn, instead. Be that as it may, the poem should be a famous *rakushu*, but this is my first time to see it. Either it did not find its way into *any* popular collections or my sense of humor and that of the Japanese literatae who anthologize things is different. As for the *Parrot's Cage*, it was not printed even in part until 1965 (all in 1969). ♪ Though that was 40 years ago, the poem would seem not to be online anywhere and is, in my opinion, good proof that much if not most of the best *kyôka* have yet to be dug up. Less bold but nonetheless telling descriptions were given of the masses fleeing town rather than trying to extinguish the fire-children (sparks) coming from afar: 風むかふ遠き火の子の来ルと見て　消さん先ににぐる諸人 *kaze mukau tôki hi . . .* That was illegal, but making a stand for a tinderbox before the wind would be suicide. Then, in the third month, a respite from the fire: *Here and there, from sunny ground, even in Bunzaemon's own garden, hair some thin as that of an old person's hair and four or five inches long, most shorter and some thick as horse hair was sprouting up! It was reported in various parts of the nation, but never in the shade.*

公家はやけ武家は腰ぬけ町はこけ　土にはゆるはもつけ也けり
kuge wa yake buke wa koshinuke machi wa koge tsuchi ni hayuru wa motsuke narikeri

Nobles roast, while boastful warriors flee: the town's burnt toast
What is growing from the ground can only be a wrathful ghost!

In other words, what seems like harmless gossamer was taken for one more bad omen. Another collection from this era in Broadview, 宝永落書 gives a variation of the above has "fool firemen" (火消はたわけ *hikeshi wa tawake*) rather than "cowardly warriors" and it precedes a note on black, white and red hair growing from a burnt area. Maybe it was not gossamer but a fungus! And, sure enough, there was a fire at the end of the year (12-29), in his Nagoya, I would guess, as only local detail is given. I am going to guess the poem after that notice was by Bunzaemon, for it is hardly the sort of thing anyone would put on a wall or broadside:

年の内に火事は有けりひとやけを　去年とやいはむことしとやいはむ
toshinouchi ni kaji wa arikeri hito-yake o kozo to ya iwamu kotoshi to ya iwamu
year-w/in-in fire-as4 is+emph one-burn/ruin+acc lastyr-as say/call? thisyr-as say/call?

> *Well the fire was in the winter but the ruins are not cold*
> *So, are they new for this year or left-over from the old?*

The original is even worse than mine and I only put it here to give one last example of the incredible influence of the first poem of the *Kokinshû*. And now, we finally get to 1708 when we first see a real *kyôka*, either about or by the abbot of the Pure Light Temple visiting Ueno: 又鯨上野へとられ増上寺　浜ばたに居ていかい御油断 *mata kujira . . .* I do not get part of it, but the final play on the whale's evident failure to be wary using an idiom about a cut-off of oil is brilliant, as whale oil was, of course, used for lamps. With the next entry, we finally get the left hand, or the right (see Rodney Needham: *Exemplars*): from *fire* we go to *flood*: *"Pitiful, indeed, to be in the shoes of a snail with no shell! / And all from a flood from one spring rain – who can tell!"* あはれとも身は家なしのかたつふり　只一時にながす春雨 *aware to mo mi wa ie-nashi no . . .* I can imagine more than one friend will chide me for wasting time not only translating but dressing up doggerel (the shoes are mine). Call me a fool, but I feel such poems often reveal our common humanity better than good ones and will continue to give them their due. And this book was so full of it that not to translate it would be to give a biased (too good?) image of Japanese popular poetry. Here are poems already up at my respondent's website – that is to say poems that a poet and researcher of kyôka sees something in – but not yet explained:

> *See No, Hear No and Speak No What?*
>
> ~ the Three Saru, or *Sanzaru*: Miezaru, Kikazaru & Iwazaru ~
>
> *In this sick world we go from matter to matter deciding what now?*
> *Who cares where that might take us – Monkeys don't see anyhow!*
>
> *What is not done for the sake of our lordship and yet we still bow?*
> *The times may go from bad to worse, Monkey won't hear anyhow!*
>
> *In your heart, you may have this or that idea you would avow,*
> *But once your looks go south, it's monkey don't talk anyhow!*

世の中は其時々のさばきにて　行末のことは見ざるものを　井伊
yononaka wa sono tokidoki no sabaki nite yukusue no koto wa miezaru mono o
何事も御為／＼とせこいれて 世のつまるとはきかざるものを　御勘定方
nanigoto mo otame otame to seko irete yo no tsumaru to wa kikazaru mono o
心にはどふかこふかと思へども　器量なければいわざるものを　御老中
kokoro ni wa dô ka kô ka to omoedomo kiryô nakereba iwazaru mono o

Now, the three monkeys pun into the "(thou) shalt not" ~ *zaru* conjugation of the verbs and in the original proverb mean we should have no part whatsoever with evil. The poems do not incorporate but play with the monkeys. I had many other ideas for each translation. To take the last, for example, *In your heart you may have this or that thought to share / But lacking good looks, you might as well address the air!* I even had *monkey locking the door to your mouth when looks go out the window,* etc., but with all three poems ending identically in the original, such play had to go out the window. The poets are obviously pseudonyms. Bunzaemon's journal shows he was disgusted with the corrupt rulers of his fief and held this sort of view. Who knows but some of the poems are his.

天下取事はきらひで尾張には　家中の物を取るがすき也
tenka toru koto wa kirai de owari ni wa iejû no mono o toru ga suki nari
heavn-below conquer thing-as4 hate-so owari/end-in-as4 homeall-thngs+acc take like

Seizing the whole damn country would be too much hassle,
So our rulers stay home to steal from everyman's castle!

~~~~~~~~~~~~~~~~~~~~~~~~

Owari, the tail of the earth would not be the head of it:
We stay home to empty yours, leaving but the edifice!

~~~~~~~~~~~~~~~~~~~~~~~~

Why go out to conquer and rob the ends of the earth
When loot's close at hand in the land of your birth?

Chances are the intended subject was the corrupt ruler or rulers this middle-level samurai was subject to yet despised, but considering the fact he lead a dissolute life himself (illegal gambling and overdrinking), this poem, if it is his, may have a touch of reflection in it, too. And that is that. I had thought journals by haikai masters would be the best place to find *kyôka* off the beaten, or rather, printed path. But, that may only be true for the best ones. Who knows how many more journals by other samurai are out there and what poems are in them!

Back to the Short & Broad History!

Then we have *kyôka* mixed into stories. We saw one old classic in the form of a chickadee flying into a traveling casket. Thanks to the sleuthing of my respondent, the enormous amount of variation and the difficulty of pinning down the original in such cases became clear. So did the variety of places where *kyôka* turn up. Now I know that before revising this book, I must look everywhere, from popular prose literature to obscure folklore. Perhaps because I did not major (or even *minor*) in Japanese literature, with the exception of the c1640 *Nise-monogatari*, or Fake Tales of Ise (the poems of which are included in *Broadview*), I completely overlooked prose. At the last minute, I found and added a few *kyôka* from the very popular anti-hero travelogue novel, *Hizakurige*, or *Shank's Mare*; but I am afraid I could not find enough on-line to do a chapter and had to settle with a sampling in the Mad Bio entry for the author *Ikku* (十返舎一九 1765-1831). There must be many more stories, from long serial tales to short jokes where *kyôka* serve as the punch line. The first thing I want to see is 醒睡笑 *Seisuishô* (1623), a book of comical short stories and jokes. From the sampling of 28 of "more than a thousand anecdotes" translated by H. Mack Horton (*Laughs to Banish Sleep*, by Anraku Sakuden. Highmoonoon: 2001), I get the feeling there are treasures galore. . . =★= *Whoa!* After writing this, I found 300 *kyôka* from it were already in the reference volume of *Broadview*, minus their stories/context, and added three chapters (pg.402-7)! If I get the whole book stories and all, more may be added to the next edition. Look at its date, 1623! That is 20-odd years before Mitoku's one-man anthology and 40-odd years before the great *Savage Song* anthology. Though not an anthology of poems, *it may well be the largest assembly of interesting kyôka in one book up to that time.* If it were widely read, *Laughs to Banish Sleep* (all of it, not the tiny sampling) may well be far more important to the history of *kyôka* than its absence in the histories suggests. It is one more reason I feel we have only begun to piece together the history of *kyôka.*

Then, we have what can only be called personal poems. A number of these are found in the *Broadview* collections, of which Getsudôken's is the most satisfying. I agree with Kaneko, that personal poems on the unexpected happenings of life, such as getting caught stealing a sip of soup, rather than playing with the topics passed down from *waka* and *haikai* represent the best side of *kyôka* and I tried to include all I saw, understood and managed to translate, but am afraid my search for them has only just begun. We saw a number by Sôchô (fairly well known in English, thanks to Horton's fine translation which includes some but not all of the *kyôka*). Perhaps you recall him burning his robe under the heater and fearing a town because of the horse in its name because . . . . If most such interesting *kyôka* are indeed, only found in journals, letters and odd little books, as I suspect to be the case, even the *Broadview* anthology I have so heavily depended upon may only be scratching the surface of the history of informal Japanese poetry. That most of Sôchô's were in the *Kyôka Taikan* is only because his journal is particularly well-known and on more than one occasion he actually calls his poems *kyôka*. I would not be surprised to find scattered *kyôka,* not necessarily so called, or even treasure troves of them by talented 15-18c *haikai* wits, who, unlike Issa, preceded rather than followed the 1780's heyday of *kyôka*. While wonderful in his own way, Issa lacked the brilliance and intellectual breadth of many of those guys (Buson, Yayû, Shôzan, etc.). Seeing what he nonetheless did, I have great expectations of finding *kyôka* by others. Issa's *kyôka*, which I could introduce to you only because I bought his journals when I still had an income to speak of, show that even a Bashôist (someone striving to keep to the narrow way of haiku), or especially a Bashôist needs the catharsis of writing outrageous poems and that much, much more is out there, scattered in places *kyôka* anthologists do not look. Ryôkan, by the way, with his *tôfu that, thank goodness, could not fly*, was an exception as he is well enough known as a one-of-a-kind poet of interest that a considerable number of his poems could be found on-line. Still, I do want to hunt down his entire collection, for I suspect more should be in this book.

Finally, we come to folk-song, including party songs (*kouta*). I introduced some from *Ryôjinhishô* (12c) that suggest there was plenty of witty material out there. Formally speaking, few song lyrics are 31-syllabet, but that does not mean we should overlook the genre/s. Ideas and styles of rhetoric may be learned from formally different forms of poetry or even prose. Here, too, my studies are insufficient. The only edition of the *Ryôjinhishô* in my possession skips a lot, and I do not know what is missing. I have, however, read considerably on bawdy Japanese folksong (see: *The Woman Without a Hole* 2007) to give me the impression that the rough and rowdy *kyôka* I find particularly fresh in comparison to *waka* and *haikai* probably owe a lot to the popular music of the time. Obviously, a thorough history of *kyôka* would require not just a little but much more study of song. I have a sneaking suspicion that the earthiness of Getsudôken that makes him seem more ancient than Bokuyô and Kôfû, who were actually of the next generation, comes from his drinking and singing songs with his servants (mind you, this is pure guesswork if guessing could be called work). This will be hard to research, not only because less popular song is written down than high-poetry, but because, in Japan, the lines between both the words/term-inology and worlds/actuality of poetry and song are themselves under dispute.

XII

The few histories accompanying selections of late-18c Tenmei era, or, sometimes more broadly Meiwa-Tenmei (1774-1789) *kyôka* of Edo (Tôkyô) that I have read all *mention* earlier mad poems by Aristocrats in 16-17c Kyôto and popular associations, *ren,* presided over by *kyôka* masters in 18c Ôsaka, but they give so few examples of their work as to suggest that Edo *kyôka* owe little or nothing to them. And what is written in Japanese tends to be parroted in English, so this is equally true for writing in Japanese and English. Having read and enjoyed many old *kyôka*, that bothered me so much I ended up expanding this book far more than planned. I felt obliged to introduce enough good examples – not easy in translation where one cannot help favoring the poems that translate best rather than the best poems – that the literary achievements of old *kyôka* could no longer be passed over. Though I have suffered for not having more late-18c and 19c work at hand to select from, as I know it means I have short-changed the talent in this period, the heyday of Edo *kyôka* and I would have loved to read and translate more (and hope to supplement a later edition) I felt no compunction to go into debt to order more used books as I knew that no matter what should happen to me, someone would surely introduce more, because Japanese hold Tenmei *kyôka* in high accord, and what Japanese hold in high regard eventually becomes English. As I did not have equal confidence the older material would *ever* be noticed, that is where my limited resources went. It has, after all, been 25 years since 狂歌大観 *Broadview's* publication yet *even in Japan*, one finds little awareness of *kyôka's* significance for the history of Japanese poetry in general and *kyôka* in particular. This is reflected by the dearth of old *kyôka* on the world-wide web. Aside from my respondent Yoshioka Ikuo's website which has a large and methodologically growing *Broadview* selection with the background information and explanation lacking in the bare-bones original, and the Tokyo University (?) Edo kyôka sampling without annotation, the few exceptions generally come from Nada Inada's *Edo Kyôka*, which, despite its name, includes dozens of older and non-Edo *kyôka*.

~~~~~~

(Months later) As it turned out, my guess about where attention would be focused, turned out to be a bit off. Over the course of the year I researched, read and translated the poems in this book, that is, in 2008, two books of *surimono* were published with a total of a thousand or so translated *kyôka!* And I found out about more published earlier with a total of even more. Surimono 摺り物 are sets of luxurious late 18-c and early-19c woodblock prints most often celebrating the New Year, i.e. propitious themes, but also about various locations, creatures, arts, etc... 1-24 pgs in length, coming with an average of 2-3 mad poems each, usually written right on the space about the pictured subjects where background might go in the West. The odd thing about this is that no one gave me a heads-up. Why? I believe it is because these books are published by Art rather than Literary presses and do not get mentioned by the list I belong to come to the attention of my friends interested in Japanese poetry. Indeed, my J-lit. savvy scholar friends only learned of them from me when I happened upon an announcement for the largest, which was published in November (2008): *Reading Surimono* by John T. Carpenter, who, when I wrote, informed me of two of McKee's books on the same. But what a *shock* to learn *one day before I was set to index this book* of Carpenter's translations which outnumber all *kyôka* translations to date, combined (that I knew of)! Having just found a few *surimono* poems better than any I had seen to date and better than *kyôka* were supposed to be as late as 1835 in an article in *The Painted Bride*, a Rutgers student magazine I googled into (pg.424), my curiosity to see more of these poems evidently well-known by wealthy collectors and my need to know whether or not I still had a patent on their witty translation left me with no choice but to delay putting the book to bed until I managed to get those books by interlibrary loan and learn the quality of the originals and translations. Now, as I wait to see them, *I half want them to be bad and half want them to be good.* For, if they include many really good poems from the 1820's and 30's, the demise of good kyôka would be shown to occur later than usually assumed and my chagrin for not having material from that time period to translate for this book will grow; and if the translations are really good, my initial reason for doing this book, namely, being assured by one brighter than me that I was probably the only person who could translate kyôka with the wit intact, might no longer hold up. My anxiety would be greater had I made this a little book of late-18c *kyôka* as first intended. As is, with half of this now big book concerning wild waka and 16-17c *kyôka*, even translations far better than mine would not negate its value. So, I would not mind being outdone. And I can always return to my first love, haiku.

If you have read this book through, you know how it turned out, for I will slip – have slipped, by the time you read this – the chapters I made based on those books into the text just before the *Afterword*, most of which was written a half year ago. If you read this history first, you are like me right now. You can share my suspense, for I will save my findings for the end of it.

~~~~~~

Even if the teachers of the Tenmei era wunderkind of *kyôka* resided in Edo – the *waka* poet Gatei 賀邸先生 （内山淳, 時椿軒kenchin） who encouraged Kisshû to start the first Edo kyôka group is most commonly mentioned – *they* would have read the older poems from Kansai (Kyôto + Ôsaka) and the first generation of Edo *kyôka* poets. True, the collections published by Teiryû's students are on the whole boring, so the more exciting Tenmei *kyôka* can be seen as a reaction – and, was indeed meant to be and marketed itself as contrary and brand-new – but that does not excuse *our* minimizing or even denying the past. We may see Tenmei *kyôka* as a revival in so far that it picks up the conceptual humor found in the better old *kyôka*. At the same time, what Hamada Giichi (annotator of the 1958 Iwanami reprinting of the 1785 *Tokuwashû*, perhaps the best Tenmei *kyôka* anthology) writes, that *what would become Tenmei kyôka emerged as naturally as pimples from the heads of the young bushi* (warrior, or administrating class) engaged in grueling literary studies from early childhood (いわばにきびとして自然発生的に起こった), is also true. I think of the odd parodies of the classics in translation by the precocious counterparts of these young samurai in London and can understand how studying *waka* and serious *haikai* would provoke a reaction even were there no *kyôka* tradition. Such is real history, more *and/but* than *either/or*. Still, natural as pimples or not, the genre's reinvigoration probably owes much to an accident of history, the convergence of two stars. First, Tanuma Okitsugu Senior Councillor of Japan from 1772-1786. If his rule was not really "lax" but from broadmindedness, he deserves credit for allowing even *kyôka* that were private or anonymous to become personal *and* public (including, cross-class desegregation of letters). Second, Ôta Nanpo, (Akara/Shokusanjin) who, thanks to Okitsugu began writing, mixing and publishing without fear, is, indeed, the greatest all-round *kyôka* master of all time. Many of his *kyôka* are *sui generis*, and his editing ability – more important for tiny poems than long ones – allowed him to select and present his and his fellow poets' most attractive work effectively.

While the personal appeal of Shokusanjin and urban appeal of Edo partly account for the imbalance, there is another reason why old *kyôka* tend to be ignored when scholars introduce Tenmei *kyôka*. It is the same one that has kept Sôgi's 15c *ku* out of most *saijiki* (haiku almanacs) – *the excessive attention given to lineage, rather than content* (the poems) to determine what belongs to one genre or another. Shiki (1867-1902), who was not mislead by traditional scholarship but went straight for the heart of things, included hundreds, possibly thousands of haiku by Sôgi and other pre-Teitoku, pre-Sôkan, pre-Moritake *rengashi* in his monumental (12 vol.) *Categorized Haiku Anthology* (分類俳句全集). The manner in which the poems in Shiki's anthology are categorized leaves much to be desired and there are under-represented poets, but, at least Shiki selected poems for what they were – if it reads like a haiku, it *is* a haiku. *That* took guts. Later, 20c scholars, who should have learned from Shiki's editorial wisdom, put their blinkers back on and used the teacher-disciple-chains, the centuries of begats of Japanese poetry, to rule out Sôgi et al because he and his school did not lead directly to later haiku. Even Bashô's having expressed great admiration for him did not help.

I have read several theories re. the demise of *kyôka* in the 19c, but am not prepared to judge or discuss them in detail until reading more collections of *kyôka* and competing genres of poetry from that period. About all I will venture to say at this point is that I doubt it fair to blame the poets for failing to keep up the good work. My experience has been that there is *always* good work, but it does not necessarily receive attention. And, partly contradicting that, I also wonder whether the modernization from the mid-19c (bourgeoisie energy heading for the Meiji Revolution, in Nada Inada's words) would have left too little leisure for studying and composition thereby making such a complex poetry, depending on a good memory of things past even if just to poke fun at them, less and less viable, after which the Meiji Revolution itself became increasingly authoritarian and wit became dangerous. Then, again, I can repeat what I wrote already in a note to a quote by Shiki in the Fore-matter. Namely, I think that what my respondent Yoshioka Ikuo hypothesizes to have been the final nail in *kyôka's* coffin (my metaphor) is likely to be true: Shiki, by opening the modern 31-syllabet waka, or *tanka*, to all types of content and style, left *waka*, now *tanka*, with no B-side. Mad poems vanished because they no longer had a place or reason to be.

Let me reiterate the last hypothesis. When I wrote "the final nail" I did so without thinking of *final* as a qualification. Finding Kotomichi at the last moment, now I do. The virtually unlimited content and styles Shiki approved of for 31-syllabet poetry already existed in Kotomichi's waka almost a half century earlier. Shiki, who read and loved his work, did not invent or claim to invent the modern *tanka*, he just discovered and put it in a proper context. *Kyôka, waka* and *haikai* were all coming together in the late-18c and early 19c. One can see the reactions of nativist *waka-ism (?)* as similar to that of segregationists becoming more obvious and outrageous only after facing what they felt was the threat of integration. Roger K. Thomas (1998) noted that literary critic Ishiikawa Jun called Shokusanjin's *kyôka* "a haikai-ization of waka not a decline." I cannot entirely buy that, for *haikai* is but part of my broad picture of *kyôka*, but agree that *kyôka* may be seen as a positive development rather than a fallen literature and that genre lines were being crossed in both, or rather many, directions. One can, for example, find many *kyôka*, which is to say poems in *kyôka* collections, and not just by Shokusanjin, that are more *waka*, i.e. elegant and honest, than many alleged *waka*. And, one can find *waka* more *kyôka*, i.e., comic, than many *kyôka*. I have not yet read enough 19c Japanese poetry to judge, but it seems possible the percentage of cross-overs grew and grew until, for better or worse, the respective genres became artifacts, or, if you prefer *ideals*, leaving us with one integrated reality, a body of poetry Shiki dubbed *tanka*.

After Reading Surimono

By the time Interlibrary Loan got me the books and whatnot – a second old dog busy dying, so this book now has a one on each end (I write between time spent digging a grave the hard way (with a short-handled shovel) and the vet's arrival to put Becky the beloved toe-licker to sleep (and now I am back after filling in the grave with two carpfuls of dirt) — checking out McKee and Carpenter's books set me back a month. *Mad In Translation* already missed its chance to be a March Hare, then aimed for

April Fool's. Now that, is tomorrow, and I am thinking May Day . . .

The *surimono* books (McKee 2006, 2008; Carpenter 2008) need three separate discussions, one about the translation, one the poems and one the various essays and articles (by half a dozen people in Carpenter) about *surimono*, especially as they touch upon the world of *kyôka*. The first two were treated indirectly – sufficiently for this book – in the last dozen chapters of the main text and I will only add here what I feel the significance of the poems and the translation is for the general history of kyôka. In a word, I feel the poems prove that kyôka was alive and well into the 1830's even if they were not the riotous disestablishmentarianism found in the 1780's, not that the latter was what it may seem to be either; and the translation is beyond doubt the largest effort ever made to translate poems that cannot be fully translated ever attempted – with *senryû*, there are many puns but they are, on the whole fully translatable, provided the cultural background is provided (see Blyth, Ueda and, especially, my work). To my relief, neither McKee nor Carpenter (and Alfred Haft, who translated some of the poems in the latter) threatened my apparent monopoly of mad translation. They do many competent translations but only rarely dare go out on a limb far enough to really swing. Perhaps they could have done so – all are excellent writers – but with limited time to cover broad catalogues, it would have had to come out of the time spent researching and writing the explanations, most of which are excellent, and, needless to say, there was no demand for it. Unless my books start to sell and *prove* re-created wit has a market, only another fool such as I will even *try* to keep comic poetry comic.

The article with the broadest historical significance, as it holds an important message for literary collectors, critics and historians, is *The Daimyo as a Kabuki Fan and Kyôka Poet – surimono commissioned by Edo no Hananari* – by Tsuda Mayumi. Let me note first that he, ruler of a major domain (Chôshû: way out West close to the top of Kyûshû)) – the equivalent of a small kingdom in Europe – wrote lyrics to be sung to popular tunes and was enamored of the popular culture of kabuki and geisha which he enjoyed in Edo for the law required he spend every other year there. His pen name, as Tsuda notes, shows how close Môri Narimoto was with his friends in Edo (including top Ukiyoe artists and his *kyôka* teacher, Magao), for it means "The Flower of Edo." You may read the article for more about him and of the involvement of daimyôs in surimono. What interests us here is that "historians and specialists in Edo literature" were not aware of the extent of his involvement in commissioning *surimono* because the former do not make literature a priority and the later "have so far devoted little attention to *kyôka surimono*" as evidenced by the absence of the topic 'surimono' in the *Nihon Koten Bungaku Daijiten* (1983), the leading encyclopedia of classical/traditional Japanese literature. But, here is what I want you to see:

> . . . because . . *kyôka* was once considered a 'minor' form of literature, and because a distinction is maintained between literature for public and private occasions, *kyôka*-related documents have been purposefully removed from both the Yamaguchi Prefectural Archives, which preserve vast amounts of material on Chôshû history, and the Mohri Museum, which preserves materials related to the Môri family. Neither institution holds a single *surimono*. Until recently, the current curators did not even know that Narimoto had produced such works. (trans. Alfred Haft, in Carpenter: 2008)

If you recall, *kyôka* as informal poetry was not only considered off-record but literally not recorded, so that it was what might be called a *yomisute,* or "read and throw-away art for much of its history, which is to say, the B-side, which may well be the larger side of 31-syllabet poetry. What went on under the Persimmon Tree was passed down to us while what went on under that Chestnut Tree was left for the squirrels. I *knew* that much. But to find what little did get written down treated so poorly in the 20c was an eye-opener. No wonder the mild-mannered gentleman translators of the mid-twentieth century would not touch *kyôka* with a ten foot pole! They were only following the judgment of their teachers in Japan. Am I wrong?

The most amusing article is *Surimono to Publicize Public Authority – Yomo no Magao and his pupils*, by Kobayashi Fumiko. After introducing surimonos marking the passing of the name Yomo from Akara to Magao and one of Magao's other names to a disciple of his, the treat. Another disciple of Magao's called Shibanoya Sanyô commissioned a *surimono* showing himself receiving a certificate of membership in the Kurinomoto Bureau of Kyôka in Kyôto from an aristocrat. Yes, after nine centuries, we see it again: *Ring around the Chestnut-tree*, Kurinomoto! Kobayashi found a kyôka anthology called *Kyôka Mikuniburi* (Kyôka in the National Style), published in Edo with a preface dated 1816 by Tôi'an Kotowari referring to the editor, Kôto Kyôka-Dokoro Honami Gyôraku-kyô (Lord Honami Gyôraku of the Kyôka Bureau in the Imperial Capital) as *aogeba takaki Kurimoto no Mushin-za* (the exalted *kyôka* school of Kurinomoto). I have passed on the translation of the names, but need to add one thing: the *"mushin-za"* translated as *"kyôka* school*"* is literally "No-heart/mind stage/troupe/location," the ancient term for comic as opposed to serious poetry we discussed before. At any rate, Kobayashi writes that this would seem to make Honami Gyôraku the aristocrat involved. An advertisement for a manuscript (*Noki no Matsukaze*) that may not have been published claims, "This book clarifies the beginnings of *kyôka* in ancient times, and the history of the *kyôka* school of Kurimoto, which had been highly thought of in the elegant court poetry gatherings for generations, but about which now no one knows anything." Another book by said aristocrat, *Kyôka Sanbyakushû*, a collection of 300 *kyôka*, did make it to a library but "was lost in WWII." Unfortunately, it was not in Kyôto but Hiroshima. A number of *kyôka* poets were dubbed Kurinomoto Gozanin (members) and about ten years later the scheming aristocrat decided to hit up the big guns for pr or money. He sent a representative to Magao and Rokujuen Meshimori and *"commanded them to agree to fall under his jurisdiction."* They ignored it, insisting they were under no obligation to obey some aristocrat in Kyôto. Kobayashi left the matter as to whether or not the Honami family had any legitimate claim to being heirs to a school of *kyôka* open.

McKee, looking back on the roots of *surimono*, as he did in his other books in more depth, mentioned the history of poems as New Year gifts to the Emperor or shrines and the significance of the Japanese New Year as a re-creation ritual. But, let me jump back to something he wrote in *Japanese Poetry Prints* (2006) about Ota Nanpô's Treasure Match (*takara-awase*) events, when junk was presented as treasures eulogized in grandiose ways making fun of the monuments of the cultural past: *"Finding the importance of things by looking to the past for precedents, this enlightened early act of performance art revealed, is absurd."* So far so good, but

> "there was a fatal flaw at the heart of Nampo's kyôka movement, which was precisely that the authority of the classical past was constantly required to make the rejection of it have authority, throwing it out through the front door while bringing it in through the back. Kyôka, ultimately, could never fully reject the classical structure, for it relied on it entirely for its very form and oppositional constructions. Without veneration of the past maintained, *kyôka* poems would not only fail to look so learned, indeed, they would have no meaning at all." (McKee 2006)

This is *beautifully* written – English does so much better when not deconstructing in translation but coming right from the author's head – but I must protest that it gives too much stock to Tenmei enlightenment, as we do when we call the 1960's a cultural revolution despite seeing how yippies became yuppies and their vws suvs in a historical blink of the eye. Pardon my cynicism, but I am afraid most people everywhere just dog-paddle with the current. Reports of revolution in art or literary fashion always claim too much. Second, I think the idea of *kyôka* – which follows the view of most Japanese who have written on *kyôka* – is far too narrow for, as we have seen in this book, *kyôka* is for the most part not parody ("oppositional constructions"), nor does it pretend to *want* to "fully reject the classical structure," as, say our "free verse". So why imply it was trying to, and, why call learning that does indeed imply *respect* or *affection* for the past – a normal feeling for us if we read what ancients have written – by the religious/orientalist word *"veneration?"* In other words, I doubt inherent contradictions did in *kyôka*. Yet, I oversimplify. McKee *also* noted that it was conservative politics – a change of government – that forced Nanpô to pass the baton to Magao who "vigorously rejected the satirical elements of his early compositions, insisting that *kyôka* should be an elegant, refined type of poetry." Around 1808, McKee notes, Magao insisted *kyôka* was *haikaika* and fundamentally one with the "unconventional" verses of the *Kokinshû*, and hence, ancient. So far so good. As we have seen, the resemblance is there, though the Kokinshû *haikaika* are but one type of *kyôka*. I know too little about what was in Magao's deepest heart of hearts to go along with McKee's conclusion: *"Kyôka had been transformed from a critical re-evaluation of the past into a classical revival movement."* I would rather say that *kyôka's* wit was justified by the only rhetoric possible in a conservative time, claiming a traditional pedigree. And, McKee provides much information about how Magao in his 1814 *Haikaika Kyôdai Hyakushû* did this by insisting that composing *haikaika* – he stopped calling them *kyôka* – was a means for poets to go back into the past and come to understand and *feel* the ancients through becoming one with their style. In this, he followed the nativist Noringa who wrote the same in 1798, and also in going back further than the *Kokinshû* to refer to the *Manyôshû*. "This conflation of modern *haikaika* with ancient poetry, and the remarkable idea that by composing haikaika one was actually participating in an ancient tradition and bringing it to life in the present," continues McKee, "took its most visceral manifestation in the surimono exchange." Here, I must cut in. In one sense, Magao was right and Nanpô and others who exaggerated the uniqueness of their 18c Edo wit were wrong. As we have seen in this book, witty poetry *did* have a long tradition and writing it does make us – as I write some, I feel that way myself – participants. But, changes also occurred. If the 17c poets were mostly noble administrator-warriors, priests and doctors, the 18c poets were mostly lower-ranking warriors, merchants and monks. And, after the warriors were told not to mix with the merchants, those merchants and other townsmen became the backbone of the 19c *surimono* poets. McKee described what the last group got out of *surimono* at considerable length.

> Through the presentation of surimono merchant commissioners were able to reveal themselves, in explicit opposition to their contemporary political designation, as the masters of the codes of cultural history, while simultaneously reinventing themselves and the world in relation to an older configuration of social distinction, based on cultivation and sensitivity [sensibilities?], rather than official caste with a feudal system.

As he explains, merchants were a despised money-making class while samurai were a respected culture-protecting class, but over the centuries, the former had come to accumulate considerable cultural capital. They were major patrons of the arts in what was perhaps the most literate culture in the world – so it was only natural for them to have shown interest in *kyôka* and pay to print the *surimono* they could give away as publicity for their *kyôka* group; but there does indeed seem to be something new and hard not to chuckle at in Magao et al's first poetry parties of the year, which

> offered a highly polished, historically resonant form that allowed for the projection of the past onto the present , bathing in its idealized glow. . . . the surimono's commissioners became the virtual equivalents of classical courtiers, presenting refined and beautiful poetic greetings . . .

McKee notes that many leaders died in late 20's (Magao 1829, Rokujuen 1830, etc.) and that, followed by wide-scale starvation and disease from 1833-6, pretty much killed *surimono,* which relied on excess resources and room for play. We need to add this to the hypotheses already presented for the demise of *kyôka.* However, until I see many 19c *kyôka* that are *not* related to surimono, I would not venture to guess whether hard times hurt or helped the mad poem. We have, after all, seen the excellent *kyôka* squib about the coming of the black ships and Issa wrote his best mad poems when miserable . . . The only honest way I can end this short, broad and totally inadequate history is with two words: *who knows!*

When discussing the farts and the heavy use of the fart letter へ *he* in Japanese, I mentioned a picture, a "fart-face" made from it. Such a picture, called a へのへのも へじ *henohenomohe-ji* (also, へへののもへ（い）じ), or へのへの *he-no-he-no* for short, generally has seven letters. A second more complex "bungling bonze" is the へマムショ入道. Hemamusho-nyûdô. When it is earless, it is a hemamushi-nyûdô, for it has no ヨ. The first sound of a "bungle" (*hema*) is "he," so they are kin. Needless to say, they look better drawn with a brush but at present, *he he he,* I lack even that!

♪ Notes for a Short & Inadequate History ♪

♪ To readers who might have expected more answers from me in this tentative history based on extremely limited reference material, I can only repeat the words of Lessing (1729-81; in the dictionary, following the *lesser yellowlegs*) explaining that his papers *"For Thoughts"* were not intended to "contain a complete dramatic system," and,

> I am, therefore not obliged to solve all the difficulties I raise. My thoughts may seem to have very little consistency – yea, even to contradict themselves – provided that they are at least matter for thoughts in others. I would here but strew "thoughts of cognition" (fermenta cognitionis). From George Saintsbury: *Loci Critici* (1903).

狂歌にとって不運であったのはインフォーマルな場において行われていた名称をそのまま継承したことであった。その性格からして和歌の対立軸となる資格を持ちながら最後まで「言い捨て」の呪縛から解放されることはなかったのである。しかし時代が移り、連歌が流行り、俳諧が持て囃される。その趨勢に対抗手段を持たなかった和歌に代わって同じ五句三十一音詩である狂歌の果たした役割は、曇りのない目で見るならば、歴然としたものであろう。　吉岡生夫「歌の未来図」より。

あるいは、本書 *Mad In Translation* の中に出てきた、「言い捨て」を無事に生き残ったよき狂歌の数々を御覧になったら、その歌と歌人が文学歴史から外されたことを思えば、良心的な読者のお目も涙で曇るのもおかしくない。

♪ ***Heart/Mind/Feeling/Meaning vs. No Heart/Mind/Feeling/Meaning.*** Some thoughts about the *Mushin* or "no shin" vs *Ushin*, or "have shin" waka. There are many paradoxes that pop up when thinking about the terms in translation, especially the 無心, or *mushin waka*. "Shin," or heart also means *mind* in English, but the poems were often exceedingly clever, so they definitely were not "mindless." Neither does the fact they could be meaningless, or nonsensical make them heartless, as that means *mean*. People who disliked *mushin* poetry took it to mean the poems were composed without putting one's heart into it and that made them insincere, if not *bad*. Aficionados, however, may have found them literally enlightening, for Zen Buddhism valued non-attachment. Moreover, clever or not, some had an *artless* feeling – after all, a*re not puns the very language of dreams?* – that suggested there was a benefit to practicing what we might call light verse even if we forget the obvious, that laughing is good for the heart. Still, this *mushin* was opposed to the have-heart, or 有心 *ushin,* of conventional waka and even today we have people who swear by one and curse the other! I understand that for centuries this segregation of the serious and fun could not be helped as once the ancient link between the sacred and the witty was broken and there were some very fuddy-duddy nobles always ready to throw cold water on people having fun. But it still bothers me, as I believe with the *kyôka-master* of the Occident, Piet Hein (1905 - 1996), that:

Taking fun as simply fun and earnestness in earnest
shows how thoroughly thou none of the two discernest.

(from *Runaway Runes* – short grooks 1: the orig. is 4-lines and titled)

To be fair, the best of the link-verse masters engaged in both genre of *waka* depending upon their host, and *mushin* with its confusing connotations was slowly replaced with *haikai* 俳諧 or 誹諧 a term with positive if not aggressive connotations. I can never exactly recall its etymology, but this much I know, it was synonymous with humor and that humor could bite without apology. Even when they fought, *haikai* factions did so in entertaining ways because *haikai* meant fun, poetry fun to make and fun to read with fun people. *Haikai* prose (*haibun*), even when it is criticism, and *haikai* pictures (*haiga*) are *all* supposed to be entertaining. This does not mean that seriousness was verboten. It remained, and with wit to gain the reader's attention, became all the more touching. In case I forgot to include it earlier, let me add that in the *Kokinshû* days (late 9c – early-10c) when the have-heart and no-heart parties were said to gather round their respective trees (persimmon and chestnut), a representative of the former sent a waka to the latter wondering if those with and without hearts differed in how they heard the wind in the garden pine/s (*kokoro aru to kokoro naki to ga naka ni mata ika ni kike to ya niwa no matsukaze*). The reply was

kokoro nashi to hito wa notamaedo mimi shi areba kikisaburau zo noki no matsukaze
heart/feelings-not so people/others-as-for announce+hon. but ear/s+emph. have-if
hear+self-deprecating/respectful suffix+emph. eave's/s' pine/s-wind/breeze

My lordship declares that we lack hearts but with your leave,
One only needs ears to hear the wind in the pine by the eave.

I borrowed much of the phrasing from Lord Muneyuki's reply to the evidently more exalted Reverend Jichin from Steven D Carter (*Just Living by Ton' a*). The reply was well received – and it set me to thinking about the difference between *listening*, which Carter used and *hearing* which I used (yes, I let the sound settle it), but, regardless the question is not really answered. If the have-heart implication is that sound only means something when colored with emotion, the *no-heart* view should be that without a heart to get in the way, the ears would always hear (objectively in the sound's being heard from the eaves and not from the garden). But that is too obvious to be worth stating, so the only way to respond politely to the question's insinuation was to joke. However, the whole Q & A is misleading for, as we have seen in this book, *kyôka* and real feeling were not generally at odds. If anything, *kyôka* was a way of expressing subjects and feelings shut out by proper *waka*. Most *kyôka,* from time immemorial, were not only *not* parody but *not* purely wordplay. Wordplay is wordplay, whether in *waka*, in *haikai* or in *kyôka*. Where the form it takes are identical, such as, say, palindromes (*kaibun*), or name poems (*butsumei-ka*), we do not so much think of *waka*, *haikai* or *kyôka* but whether the poem is witty and not just the poetic equivalent of umpteen students packed into a phone booth. As puzzles for the sake of puzzles are not my game and translation is hopeless, I have introduced few in this book. But, taking a last look at the 1785 *Tokuwa-shû*, I found two that seem to have meaning enough to be of interest.

鳥名十　かりのとき山からつとひいつるみはときしやさきのあやうからすや
kari no toki yama kara tsudoi-izuru mi wa tok/gishi yasaki no ayaukaras/zu ya 笹麿

Now there are ten birds hidden in here, from the goose, *kari* to the crow, *karasu*, and I, imagining all those "sharpened arrow heads" (*togishi yasaki*) flying about in all directions, tried to read 笹麿 Sasa Marô's poem as 狩の期、山から集どい出る身は研ぎし矢先の危や

うからずや. Japanese readers may note the trouble. Why should the hunting party fear arrows as it leaves the mountain? My respondent saved me. The sharpened arrow-heads like the ten birds are only there for the association and the poem should be read 狩りのとき山から集ひ出づる身は 解きしや先の危うからずや. That the dangerous part of the outing will occur after the hunting party breaks up. A slight difference, but note the arrows are out of the picture. Ah, the point is that the men are in danger of spending too much on drink and women at inns or catching disease from night-hawks (street-walkers), etc.. So, the table is turned and they are the hunted.

きやうとくもせりたてゝなす哥のくはいゆとりのないもおほね口豆　山手白人
気疎くも競り立ててなす歌の会ゆとりのないも大根口まめ　　岩波の注に因んで
kyôtoku mo seritatete-nasu uta no kuwai yutori no nai mo e ône kuchi-mame　iwanami
今日、疾くも迫り立ててなす歌の会ゆとりのないも大根口真似　相談者の読み
ke(f)u toku mo seritatete . . . . ône kuchimane　my respondent

Here, we have 10 edible vegetables 菜菓名十 starting with *udo* (Aralia cordata, underlined as it is hard to spot, the "t" clouds into "d") and *seri* (dropwort), two of my favorites, including another of my favorites, the *kuwai* (arrowhead bulb), thanks to old spelling for what now would be just "kai," and go on to end with the cruder *ône* (big root, i.e., *daikon*) and beans. When it comes to the actual(?) reading, My respondent reads a poet feeling pressured by the rapid onslaught of a poem(waka)-meeting, where the atmosphere is stiffling and copycats are rife, while Iwanami has the poets *kyôtoku mo* + 競り or *depressingly/basely competing* at the same where the poet takes exception with mostly glib people. If I had to referee, I would favor Iwanami as the homophonic idiom tying beans to glib talkers is the only direct tie of the vegetables to the poetry meeting and I want that. Regardless, my respondent saved the poem for me because I had not found the *kai*=meeting in the old spelling *kuwai* (Iwanami does not give a full reading as I fleshed it out above, but just some notes). I think you can now see why I skipped name play, but to return to the real subject here: *did you notice that there was a message which involved feeling – albeit, more re. waka-meetings than about the fate of hunters on the way home – in both?* I suppose that if we defined "have-heart" as having a deep personal interest in something, the poems could be ruled "no-heart" if we knew that the one poet did not go hunting and the other did not attend waka parties. In that case, we might be tempted to call *no-heart* poems those which stick their noses into other people's business. But, we already know that many *kyôka* are personal, so the definition game goes on.

~~~~~~

♪ **The Stilt Horse. Another version.** My respondent notes that the version 『袋草紙』(岩波書店) he found in the library has another horse color playing on the joints, *fushi*, but not the whole *fushigachi:* 竹のむまはふしかげにしていとよわし今夕かげにのりてまゐらん. I am sticking with the one I have. I like it. I also like this sort of poem and, with your help, want to find more. About these,所謂俳諧歌とは多少趣を異にする。狂歌らしい狂歌である。Kaneko wrote 探せばいくらもあらう。I sure hope he is right!

~~~~~~

♪ **Origuchi on MYS#16.** What offended me was a note with Origuchi's reading of the *Manyôshû* (the pb is w/ my library in Japan). Elsewhere (女房文学), he noted something far more interesting about the same poem; namely, that the Empress's poem comes down in favor of one side of a group offering poems on behalf of the respective seasons and as such is the first proof of *mono-arosoi*, or thing-matches in Japan.

~~~~~~

♪ **The Waka Poets' Sordid but Beautiful Mizt.** At first, I thought Teitoku was just bored with the countless poems about Spring = New Year mist, which came to symbolize the teary, bleary, aged eyes of the *waka* poets – note: the stuff in eyes that was not tears in Japanese was usually called *meguso*=eye-shit. Then, I recalled Teitoku's beautiful erotic mist-covered soft cuntry (p.48) and thought, *Aha!* It is literally the way the mist touches the *ha*=ridge=teeth of the mountains! When it is pronounced in combination with *ha* the clean syllabet か *ka* becomes the cloudy or dirty one が *ga* (see those little smudges?).

Teitoku, attentive to the charm of things in the magical first season of the year – the New Year I call *The Fifth Season* because we think we have only four, not because it comes last, which it did not until the 20c – would prefer not to use combinations that fouled up the philologically clean *kasumi*. This, then, would be one Teitoku poem the yet-to-be-born nativist Norinaga, a raving maniac when it came to clean and dirty sounds in his Big Peace language born of the gods, would surely drool over.

♪ **On Wit Pervading the Kokinshû** (905). A precise yet all-encompassing gloss on the *Kokinshû* for the open source J-text at the University of Virginia by Lewis Cook captures the gist of what makes me love the *Kokinshû* and many critics hate it:

> Exceptions abound, ... but it is safe to say that a questioning or plaintive mood prevails, the poet asking why things must be as they are, or why does experience not better agree with either reason or imagination? This has earned Kokinshu (more precisely, the middle and later poems usually taken to typify the anthology) a reputation for ironic wit and ratiocination which in turn has, on a favorable interpretation, been read as evidence of a sophisticated awareness of the discrepancies between language and reality, or, on a less sympathetic reading, as indulgence in sophistry or sheer wordplay.

♪ **The Savage Song Editor's Policies.** Squibs are absent from the 1666 collection. The problem is not that they violate some rule demanding *kyôka* be utterly playful, for the editor includes sections with moralistic poems, of which all too many are seriously weak in wit. As explained elsewhere (pg.512), the editor 行風 Kôfû had many specific ideas about what *kyôka* should and should *not* be – 15 of the latter, one of which is unfortunate, in my opinion: He followed his teacher Teitoku in completely ruling out anonymous squibs, *i.e. rakushu*, which they deemed *by definition* mean-spirited and cowardly. So, it would seem that Kaneko's anti-*rakushu* stance was not pulled from a hat, but indirectly expresses an old idea that honorable people should be willing to sign their opinions and die for them. Scores of poems *about* poetry include many that seem pretty mean to me, but they are, indeed, always signed, so poetry would seem to have been the one area where ferocious argument was allowed (all the more reason for a scholar well-versed in *waka*, *haikai* and *kyôka* to look into this in depth!). Editor 行風 Kôfû also had something interesting to say when pushed by the great *haikai* poet and editor Shigeyori (1601-1680) to hurry up and finish the book. 名にしおはゝいざこれとはん都衆　わか選ふ狂歌ありやなしやと　行風 c.1666 *na ni shi owaba iza kore towan miyako-shû waga erabu kyôka ari ya nashi ya to*. There is an allusion to an old *waka* asking a capital bird for news; but I get the feeling he implies that he is slowed down by being asked by the capital folk whether this or that of their poems are in the book. But that is just a guess; maybe I can settle on a reading by the next edition. That poem was placed between a ferocious putdown of a *haikai* collection by Teitoku and a self-demeaning poem sent to Teitoku by an old and sick poet. The latter:

はいまはる腰おれ歌を筆にのせて　書て送るははゞかりて候　為盛
hai mawaru koshi ore uta o fude ni nosete kaite okuru wa habakarite soro tamemori?

> My lame poem and I crawl on all fours – both so bent –
> As nature calls, the former must by brush alone be sent!

We have seen *broken-hip/back waka* before. As my respondent pointed out – I had missed it – the humble *habakari* a euphemism for a W.C., may or may not mean the poet, suffering the runs, begs off some event. It helps to assume the brush is horse-hair.

♪ **Mitoku's Gay Komachi Dancers.** Here is the full preface to the original。未得の「吾吟我集」　歌♯25、若衆の小町音頭の話ある前置:

うたおほくきこえねば。これかれをかよはしてよくもしらず。をのゝこまちおどりは。外面そともに姫のあつまりなり。あはれなるふりにてつよかれず。いはゞよきおうなよりも。腰なよ／＼として声つよからぬは。若衆のおんどうなればなるへし。「狂歌大観１」より

♪ *More Mitoku*. 未得オマケ。Just spillover, an *omake,* or bonus, for Japanese readers. ◎「かゝみもちいざたちわりて煮てくはん　としへぬる身のおひのいはひに」 *kagami mochi iza . . .* (蛇足：鏡へ老の仇討ちか？餅⇒岩⇒祝うも旨いが、年越した餅と年経るのの掛けは year/years つまり number で英訳しても台無し). 第一章の前の「ざれ歌」中で見つけた。　◎又、第二章の春には、この微笑ましい一首：「冬にたつ霞のきぬはさほ姫のむまれぬさきのむ月さためか」*fuyu ni tatsu kiri . . .* （蛇足：一月の美名で「おむつ」？「うまれぬさき」で七日の菜叩き歌を？）。　◎「たつとても霞の衣ぬひえぬや尻もむすはて乱るいとゆふ」 *tatsu tote mo kasumi no kinu no . . . .* (蛇足：宗鑑の佐保姫＋天明狂歌の女流歌の縫い用語尽し？). ◎ More drumming dandelions!　あまくたる天鞁のあれは打かへて　地からはやせるつゝみ草哉 *ama-kudaru tenko no . . .* (蛇足：タンポポの鼓の歌は無数あるが「革」の当て字で囃し相手は天の河ならユニーク)。

◎　御狩にもあはぬさきより一さほにつらなりて来る天津雁かね　◎
mi-kari ni mo awanu saki yori hito sao ni tsuranarite kuru amatsu karigane

(蛇足：未得には珍しい全く幼きスタイル。が、これこそ素朴な傑作と思う。翻訳不可能は残念。英語では、竿をなして飛ぶことはない。　◎虫「地かたふきてまはれぬ舞や是ならん　岸ねにこけて行くかたつふり *jigata fukite mawarenu*」（蛇足：よく解からないが、大勢の宿狩り貝の毎日、昼丘を登って、夕方になって、ころころと浜辺へ転び戻ったのを見ました）。◎鏡　「人を見て人は人をもたしなめは　人こそ人の人のかゝみよ」　*hito o mite hito wa . . .*　◎腰をいたむ人ふしに度々灸するを見て「時しらぬ病ふじのねいつゝむつ　鹿子またらに灸をする跡 *toki shiranu yamai . . .*」　（蛇足：雪が山に降る月と灸跡の数。注がないから、「ふじ」の濁り点が大観の編集っ子加えた？節・富士の掛けだから視覚てきに曖昧のままにしておいた方がいい）。◎「山桃の選り喰ひなれや年遅し誰が身ひとつ世に残るべき *yama momo no erigui . . .*」（蛇足：借り宿の世の直前の首。食えば長生きする青女王の桃も連想しながら遅く熟する山の桃の実。百年も千年も後一日の日が来る、亀も鶴もいや、人間として、普通に死んでもいい、という蜀山人の達観に通じる心でしょう。）

~~~~~~

♪ *The Man in the Parrot Cage, Spill-overs and General Notes on Asahi Bunzaemon.* Most of the addition, including this note, will be kicked back – or forward, by page number – to the main text in the next edition. In respect to Asahi's given name 文左衛門. I call him Bunzaemon rather than Monzaemon after Roberts (below) and, later, Nenzi (below), because most Japanese do so, though most references are only the result of a popular comic book based on his journal. I also feel *Gen ~* sounds better after *Asahi* and is good to differentiate him from Chikamatsu Monzaemon, the far more famous novelist.

◎*The Focus of His Rage.* There is good reason the journal of over two million words took 250 years to exit the Owari Domain's storage where it was put after family line died out. Luke Roberts, in *A Transgressive Life: The Diary of a Genroku Samuraian* notes:

> In an entry made in 1693 he described his own lord, Tokugawa Tsunanari, in the following way, "Our lord was born with a desire to increase his own wealth. Ever since he was five he has been greedy. Now that he is older he is only more skillful at it." (Adapted from a paper for the 1994 Association for Asian Studies Annual Meeting, UC, Santa Barbara – Let me add, this is one lively essay!)

His or not, some poems reflecting feelings he probably shared about various rulers and nobility were even more bitter than those I translated. *Eg.* a sardonic comment about a forced suicide (execution) on a lucky day 千早振五月晦日は吉日よ 増右親子を成敗ぞする *chihayaburi satsuki misôka wa kichinichi yo . . .*; a pun from *a while* to *scolding* a daimyô called "a fool" for being oblivious to what went on! 君が代の久しかるべきためしには兼ねてぞ知れし大名の馬鹿 *kimi ga yo no hisashikarubeki . . ., Eg.* a plays on a saying about nobles who steal stewpots (wives) warning of such coming from the capital 都より公家がくるげな油断すな 鍋取公家と聞もおそろし *miyako yori kuge ga kuru . . . . Eg.* punning the name 紀, short for 紀伊 Kii, Owari domain's leading family, with a *tree=ki* someone doing monkey business fell from . . .月をとる其ゑんかうの手が折れて 紀よりも落る元の猿楽 *tsuki o toru enkô no te* . . . Eg. a play on the song #2 of *Hundred Poets* having said Kii steal the white garments leaving the mountain (in the original drying not wearing the same) to scratch its head . . .百人一首 春過て夏きに恥を百妙の紀伊へとられてあたまかく山 *haru sugite natsu ki ni haji o . . .* Roberts notes "Monzaemon was not brave enough to criticize the laws and characters of the rulers beyond the privacy of his diary." I am glad he did not, for if he did we would not have his Journal. He also points out that Mon/Bunzaemon participated in illegal gambling. That and other peccadilloes would have given the criticized – who really do seem like bad men – an excuse to exile or even execute him.   Robert's student, Laura Nenzi translates a few of the poems "Monzaemon" took from the *Gosangû Hyakunin-isshu* 御参宮百人一首 with the poems they parody in *To Ise at All Costs Religious and Economic Implications of Early Modern Nukemairi* (Japanese Journal of Religious Studies 33/1 2006). She notes that *nukemairi* is "generally Englished as 'stealing away on pilgrimage' (*Angry Masters, Upset Husbands: Nukemairi as Sites of Contention* Vaporis 1994)." As I am no expert on pilgrimages, I did not realize all were specifically about going to Ise until she set me straight. As for the scale,

> Monzaemon describes entire communities turned upside down by the 1705 pilgrimage frenzy and frantically striving to provide food, fans, hats, umbrellas, lanterns, and free transportation for thousands of pilgrims at a time. Certain shops, he writes, put out barrels filled with money for the pilgrims to grab. . . . each barrel, when filled with cash [sic. *coins*], required the efforts of seven or eight people to be moved outside (Asahi 1968, 41).

And, for all these problems, and for all the lampoons, the pilgrimages did not stop. Sixty six years later,

> In 1771, Kōnoike Zenzaemon, a wealthy Osaka merchant, was still providing generous contributions to the *nukemairi* pilgrims, this time giving alms to some 184,000 people in six days, for a grand total of four hundred and sixty ryō (Shinjō 1960. In Nenzi, Ibid))

For more detail including the reasons given for the pilgrimages in 1705, see the article. I must confess to being astonished that a nation with as many free-thinkers as Japan could be so disrupted by what amounts to religious frenzy. The statistics are astonishing, and might be interesting compared and contrasted with European pilgrimages (and pre-modern Mecca) as Noel Perrin did for the spread of firearms in 16-17c Japan (see *Giving Up the Gun*, a fine book: though NP was no expert on Japan, he understood a subject of general interest and essayed it, as all scholars should, but – speaking as a demanding layman – few do!).

◎ ***One More 3-Monkey Kyôka & Fire in the Breast for Good Measure!*** Not far from the *Parrot Cage* squibs in that *Broadview* reference volume, we have *kyôka* taken from tales of the Zen's beloved bad-boy Ikkyû, his travels: 一休諸国物語.

何事も見ざるいはざるきかざるはたゝほとけにはまさるなりけり 一休
nanigoto mo mizaru iwazaru kikazaru wa tada hotoke ni wa masaru narikeri ikkyû
anything+emph see-not say-not hear-not-as4 just buddha/corpse-to-as4 excell is!

See nothing, say nothing, hear nothing about all things – If
that is the case, it makes you barely better than a stiff!
~~~~~~~~~~~~~~~~~~~~~~~~~
that is the case, you are beat only by Buddha, a stiff!

Ikkyû played the fool because he valued intelligence. If I am not mistaken, either reading is possible, but they both carry the same message. The wit is in the monkey, *saru,* within *masaru* meaning to excell over, or beat, and the traditional idiom for a corpse, Buddha, being framed in a religious discussion to bring out the ambiguity. Among the 33 poems, I also found a good one I missed on trope I gave chapters to, *fire in the breast:*

むねの火のもえたつ時の有ならは心の水をせきとめてけせ　一休
mune no hi no moetatsu toki no aru naraba kokoro no mizu o sekitomete kese
breast's fire's blazing time is become-if heart's water+acc daming-build extinguish

When fire blazes in your breast, don't cry or run about;
Just dam the water in your heart to pour and put it out!
~~~~~~
If fire blazes in your breast, why let it burn your blouse?
Dam the water in your heart and easy it will be to douse.

I added "cry" because external tears are probably imagined, and "blouse" to allude to the burnt Chinese brocade in an old waka (pg.58) probably alluded to here.

◎ **Poems in the Parrot Cage I Do Not Yet Get**. My favorite is 死ますといひし女中はよがり徳　いわれし公方ひとり損霊 *shinimasu to iishi jochû wa yogari-* . . ., I appreciate the love cries but do not yet get the contrasted loss and can only guess the poet thinks the authorities should not only *say* they die but *do* it for the good of all! Then there is 首代出す百姓　田地追放　あきれたりかり物ゆへのとみはやみて我首代に金とられつゝ *akiretari karimono* . . . involving hunting rights, bounties & peasants (Please visit my website, Paraverse.org for a gloss with understanding gained too late as well as errata.)

◎**Rakushu** **Not *in the Parrot Cage* but Found among Other Collections Nearby.** I read much faster than when I started this book, not so much because I learned alot but because I loosened up with respect to what I expected to find in a poem. So I find stuff to share every time I crack *Broadview.* The *rakushu* collections are marvelous for showing us the lower margins of the *kyôka* genre. Here are some examples from one book, 諸国落首咄、 *Sundry Countries' Squib Stories,* two books ahead of the *Parrot's Cage.*

やけ／＼てかきのもと迄きたれども　歌よみなれば愛でひとまる
yakeyakete kaki no moto made kitaredomo uta yominaraba koko de hi tomaru
burned burning fence/hedge-base=Kakinomoto(poet)-until came but
song/poem read/intone-if/when here-with/at fire-stops=Hitomaru

< *Kakinomoto Hitomaru Fire-stopping Charm* >

It burns it may burn, right up to the fence but the poem I intone
Starts 'persimmon,' hence, 'fire-stop' Hitomaru saves our home
~~~~~~
Though it burns to the gate read this poem and it's not too late –
Kakinomoto *and mo' betta yet, say* Hitomaru *& fire will abate!*

Yes, we have seen this before in two versions by the Zen monk Hakuin and by the monk who, perhaps, first came up with it (p.306). This inspired me to try again as it is simpler, and I think, beats both. Interesting that a literally charming poem should be in a collection of squib. Did the mere fact a poem is not in a standard *waka* anthology make it a *'rakushu'?* Or, was it because it was an allusive variation? Or, because it fit in no category (there are not enough out-and-out incantatory *waka* to make them a genre)?

物いはずあんず顔なるつらつきは是を木なりなものといふなり
mono iwazu anzu kao naru tsuratsuki wa kore o ki nari na mono to iu nari

Saying nothing, a face seemingly be deep in thought: I see
That is one man I would guess is what we call a tree!

My mom sent me the *New Yorker* for a few years when I was in Japan. I was not impressed, for I sought ideas, not fancy words, but had I not read a feature on the porno industry – where one porn star was described as a "life-support system for his penis" – I would not have known what "Have we got *wood?*" meant! Later, I learned that men were "tree," implying that *wood*, in the teashops set aside for swiving (I apologize, I cannot recall the newer French), where women were water (lest you think dirty alone, that goes back to Confucius, mind you). If I get the above right, it tells me why *senryû* would soon take over the dirty stuff. The idea would work as well or *better* in 17 syllabets. So saying, I do not mean to diminish the idea that expresses the essence of male libido, visualization, which is to say, imagination. And, what can we say about a poem like this:

あく筆の用にもたらぬいろはがな　てら入はせでろういりぞする
akuhitsu no yô ni mo taranu iroha-gana tera-iri wa se de rô-iri zo suru 17c?
bad brush/writing's usefulness-as suffice-not abc-letters temple-entering-as4

One who writes so poorly is no good for temple letters,
In a dungeon he must go – leave religion to his betters!

I write so poorly, I won't even do for temple letters,
Into jail, I must go and leave religion to my betters!

Temples and shrines are always dispensing this and that dispensation or charm in writing. One wonders what religion did before writing. So, one finds a premium there for good penmanship. As far as the standard language goes *rô-iri* definitely means prison – adultery or something might send both parties to prison but for the alternative, taking the vows – but Tokugawa Japanese were not *that* big on prison and I cannot help feel there may be an unmentioned pun 老入り, or entering old age, though no such word is found. Why become old when you can become a monk, instead? Depending upon how one fills in the unwritten pronouns, one can get a typical self-deprecatory *kyôka,* or a kidding poem, which makes it more of a *rakushu*. But there are still many poems that are altogether beyond me. When I read *"Whether piss goes for one mon or a hundred, in the town where fights break out, they dispense straw"* (小便が一文しやう百しやうといさかひ町でわらをだしける *shôben ga ichi mon . . .*). I am lost. Now, I know straw was supposed to soften up sea cucumbers, but I am missing something needed to 'solve' the poem. Or, *"Whose first-writing made the letter 'he' (へ i.e., fart) seem so sweet? / Leave it to the reckless ones' heaven-bestowed brush!"* (しほらしやへの字成にも書ぞめをするは天筆わやくものども *shiorashiku ya he no ji . . .*). I will have to wait for the story to crack that! (蛇足：有り難い発見だ！無茶という意味の「わやく」！で日本は誤訳天国じゃ！). Teitoku had a fine *kyôku* playing with the idea of a "heaven-brush" meaning something written by a member of the Imperial family:

天筆といふもや月の兎の毛　貞徳
tenpitsu to iu mo ya tsuki no usagi no ke

'Heaven's Brush'
must be a boon, made from hare
hair on the moon!

'Heaven's Brush?'
So is it hair from up there,
the hare on the moon?

The poems include one nonsensical "my love is like" poem, though the love is called a *tsuma,* or "mate" rather than the more usual *koi*. 我夫はおくびのいらぬ小袖やら　いつ来て見てもあはんとぞ思ふ *waga tsuma wa okubi no . . .* I tried a near translation *My love is like a robe without a head-hole, to wit / Though I try to make it fit, I never can get into it.* and a far, *My love a triangle must be for she is not a square / And when I would visit her she is never around.* Neither work. The original, with its simple *wear/visit* pun, and the comfort of playing on an old saw – clothing as mate – does. If such a poem were to be written on a stick outside the girl's house, I guess it would be a squib.

そろ／＼と我は仏にあたまからなりかゝるやらひかりこそすれ
sorosoro to ware wa hotoke ni atama kara nari kakaru yara hikari koso sure
nearing(psycho.mimesis) i-as4 corpse/buddha-into, head-frm becomng? light+emph does

> *The time is near – apotheosis starts above, w/ the crown:*
> *Mine already shines and, then, I guess, it will work down!*

The poet? compiler? so liked this poem that he put it last *and* included it *twice* among the 100 poems! The first one has it by "a man over fifty" and the second (the last of the collection) a hardware store owner, Dôguya Niheibe. And, I might add, I note my very selective respondent just put it online! Baldness does not send men to heaven that fast, but the poem is indeed one of those simple but effective combinations of pun (corpse/buddha) and concept (bald-shine+ buddha glow or halo) that is recognizable, at a glance, as a classic or a *should-be* classic. Even I had found and marked it on first-reading, but failed to get back to it. I hope to read the stories used to frame and reframe this poem by the next edition. They must be delightful. This poem (which really should have been with one of our chapters on aging) teaches us that even a fine poem that would grace any old collection of *kyôka* may be found among the despised *rakushu,* though *rakushu,* itself was sometimes not a squib or a charm, but any poem of 31-syllabets that was not a recognized *waka*. In other words, it became synonymous with *kyôka.* And that is why we must look everywhere for them.

♪ **Kyôka in Stories vs Linkverse in Stories.** As I proofed the After-matter, an announcement on PMJS (premodern japan studies) group mentioned medieval stories, both original and translation on line. I checked out these *otogizôshi* and was delighted to find *Monogusa Tarô,* or *The Lazy Man*. A poem in it, written after the man slipped and fell on the koto (zither) of the woman he hoped to marry, seemed interesting, and I asked for more information and R. Keller Kimbrough at the U. of Col., Boulder, responded "I am particularly fond of Virginia Skord's translation of the koto poem that you mention below. It has been most recently published in Haruo Shirane's *Traditional Japanese Literature: An Anthology, Beginnings to 1600* (p. 1110)." It follows shortly after her translation of the woman's poem, which is more sad than witty and softly end-rhymed:

> *kyô yori wa waga nagusami ni nanika sen*
>
> Whatever can I do now
> To while away my idle hours
>
>
> *kotowari nareba mono mo iwarezu*
>
> The koto's smashed; my hopes are dashed –
> I'm so abashed!

His response is very clever with the instrument *koto* and its breaking *wari* punned into a homophonic *kotowari,* while *koto* also puns on "word" while contrasting with *mono* (both "things," the former abstract, the latter concrete), the things he dares not say. For the Japanese, I had to go to a 1909 book called *Warriors of Old Japan*. It shows the original was a typical early link-verse style, with the woman's 17-syllabets and the man's 14, and did not even try to translate the man's poem but leaving it in the Japanese (which as you can see, echoes the woman's and vowel-rhymes with itself, too!), explained. The online version (I'll skip) was not bad, but Kimbrough is right, Skord's is indeed a charmer. With rhyme and pun (*bash* in abashed is good) the wit is re-created. Because the poems only work as link-verse, but not as a single capped-verse, it cannot be called a *kyôka*. Yet, the man's response is about as *kyôka*-like in spirit as a poem can get. I wish I had a date on it, but all I can find is that it came from the Muromachi period, 1338-1568.

I must see more of such poems, as form is but half of what we need to study to get a full picture of the evolution of a genre. Mad poetry is also a frame of mind.

♪ *All Types of Content in Tanka?* I oversimplified a bit. *Tanka* became diverse, or rather inclusive, as Shiki hoped, but the sickest of black humor and parody, what one *kyôka* enthusiast has called *tanka noir,* remained out of bounds. A good term, *tanka noir*; but it should not be equated with *kyôka*, which boasts a broader content than *waka* proper, while *noir* covers far less. If extraordinarily playful tanka were to be called *kyôka* I would have no complaint, but *kyôka* ought not be reduced to 31-rude or dirty syllabets.

♪ *Novelty Songs, Limericks, etc.* Because of my appreciation for country music (or what country music has been and could be), I was tempted to ignore the term *mad poem*, altogether, and English 狂歌 as *novelty poems*, after *novelty numbers*, as songs such as *"A Boy Named Sue,"* (It makes him grow up tough in his father's absence, but when he meets that no-count who gave it to him . . .) sung by Johnny Cash for number one hit on both country and pop, the poet/lyricist is often over-looked, but Shel Silverstein may have been the closest thing to a mad poet in late-20c Usania, and got away with rhyming in a free-verse age by concentrating on song lyrics where it is not only tolerated but accepted and in children's verse that also delights parents.), *"The Perfect Country Song"* (a trage-comedy cramming in a large number of recognized of country themes of prison, dogs, mama, trains, cheating wives etc.), *"Henry Ford What Have You Done?"* (sung by Jerry Reed who died yesterday(!), bemoans traffic jams, road signs and other such problems – only the most common early-19c complaint – made by Belloc, Chesterton and Kipling, among others – about not being able to piss by the road in peace, is missing) are called. There are many more we never hear because most people owning and operating radio stations are greedy wheeler-dealers thanks to national policies favoring unintelligent people who live for one thing: money. The only reason I did not use that word "novelty" is because *kyôka* came to be a genre with collections of *nothing but* and people coming together to celebrate *nothing but*, while novelty songs, have ever remained novelties in the sense of being one-of-a-kind oddities *played within the broader genre of country music*. One cannot find *novelty* stations.

The *kyôka* shares more with the *limerick* in being short and having one form, though this was not true in its salad days before it was called a limerick: Stephano's sea-song in *The Tempest*, has a double-length couplet of which one line I cannot resist sharing goes: *"Yet a tailor might scratch her where ere she did itch:"*), is collected and appreciated with its own kind, expected to be humorous, and not shy of risqué subjects.

But a limerick is a limerick; and a limerick, clean or dirty, has its stylistic possibilities severely restricted by the droll metrical scheme, while the *kyôka* within its 31-syllabets has as much wriggle-room as a *tanuki* (racoon fox) or a mole within its loose skin. Some *kyôka,* every bit as elegant, even beautiful as a high *waka*, bring to mind a playful sonnet rather than limerick. Contentwise, the proto-limerick examples given by Legman in his introduction to *The Limerick*, share much with *kyôka*. We find the equivalent of the *koi, i.e.,*, *love, longing,* or *the blues,* found in so many of the wittiest ancient *waka*, such as the poem on the left from Robert Jones' *The Muses Gardin for Delights, or the Fifth...*, dated 1610:

Love is a pretty pedlar	*The Indian weed, withered quite,*
Whose pack is fraught with sorrows,	*Green at morn, cut down at night,*
With doubts and fears	*Shows thy decay,*
With sighs and tears,	*All flesh is hay;*
Some joys – but those he borrows.	*Thus think, then drink Tobacco.*

The first A of the AABBA is missing and the rhythm is a bit off for a limerick, but the last line is *kyôka*. Tobacco was also adopted just as fast, with the equivalent of what would be a mad *dôka* (moral-song) by Robert Wisdome dated 1613 on the right, above. Japanese also used "drink" as well as "suck" for what we now call *smoking*, but here, too, the last unrhyming line, with its "think, than drink," is a *kyôka* style closer. You might note, the limerick meter is not there. Like *kyôka,* the meter was diverse. It is in the following from "Mad Tom" or "Tom of Bedlam," which Legman calls "the greatest of the mumpers' songs,' first recorded in a music book printed in 1615. I will two-line it for space:

From the hagg & hungry Goblin, that into raggs would rend yee,
& the spirit that stands by the naked man, in the booke of moones defend yee,

Legman mentions "a tune as haunting as the words." I really must hear it, for it is hard to imagine the limerick meter sounding so! He also dates it to the late-16c about the time when the limerick form reappeared – it *first* appeared in 14c poems such as the stanza of the classic *Sumer Is I-cumen in ...* and an animal warning rhyme (*The lion is wonderliche strong, . . .*) – "*suddenly, in the mad songs of the half-naked wandering beggars, turned out to mump their livelihood after 1536, at the dissolution of the religious almonries under Henry VIII.*" Perhaps they picked it up from the monk's warning rhymes, who knows, but we do have "mad songs," literally identified with the insane. As you can see from *Mad Tom*, the songs of the Bedlams, as they were called, may not have been art-poetry, but they are sure as hell not light either! Without more study I can say no more about that officially mad sub-genre and so return to the matter of where the *kyôka* and limerick agree and differ. In the final event, I suppose that what matters most is not so much form and content as character, and that character reflects the broader culture. When Morris Bishop wrote (again, I reparse for space) that

The limerick is furtive and mean; you must keep her in close quarantine,
Or she sneaks to the slums and promptly becomes disorderly, drunk and obscene.

he not only contrasts limerick to sonnet but demonstrates English-speakers' attitude toward bawdy subjects. In the Japanese case, *kyôka* may have been unacceptable for traditional art-poetry, but socially speaking was not a mean or obscene drunk. With a healthy popular song culture –Confucians cracked down not like Christians – there was no concept of quarantine: sex was so common in rural folksong and, later, the black humor of the shorter *senryû* serving bachelors in a city short of women, that *kyôka* was less compelled to go that way than limerick were, though some dirtier than any in this book may be found (something from the erotic version of the *Tales of Ise* I failed to locate in time, may be added to a future edition). In the end, intelligence given an excuse or place to play does similar things. Some of the good ones, like *kyôka* had authors,

As a beauty I'm not a great star,
There are others more handsome by far,
But my face, I don't mind it,
Because I'm behind it –
'Tis the folks in the front that I jar

This was part of self portrait series by "minor poet" Anthony Euwer called The *Limerotomy*. A *senryû* first translated by Blyth has someone wishing he could see his own face from the side, but it lacks the mad twist, or punch line that makes the above worth reading and thinking about. Or, on a higher level, we have this well-known exchange:

There once was a man who said: "God   *"Dear Sir, Your astonishment's odd;*
Must think it exceedingly odd   *I am always about in the Quad;*
   If he finds that this tree   *And that's why the tree*
   Continues to be   *Will continue to be*
When there's no one about in the Quad."   *Since observed by Yrs. faithfully, God."*

The author is Monsignor Ronald Knox; and, like *kyôka* – or, kyôka-like *waka* – where exchanges were not uncommon, we find this poke at the Berkleian idea that things exist only when they have an observer, evoked an excellent reply, which, again, like *kyôka*, may or may not be the author of the first incognito, but regardless, we *are* amused even if we feel that Berkeley and God are equally odd. Then, there are *parodies* such as *"There was a young student of Johns / Who wanted to bugger the swans, / But the loyal hall porter / Said, "Sir, take my daughter. / Them birds are reserved for the dons"* which, according to William S. Baring-Gould (whose *Lure of the Limerick* is a superb introduction), plays on A.C. Hilton's "Young Gourmand of Johns," which I have yet to read; and moral usages, as found for *kyôka*, such as G.L.P.'s *Limerick Prayer Book*, which honestly confesses *"These rhymes were designed by a priest, /To affect your religion like yeast; / If they help it to grow, / Like the yeast in the dough, / There'll be one better Christian, at least."* (in Ibid). Then, there are comic takes on animals such as Florida newspaperman Dixon Merritt's *Pelican* and rare Japan-class punning such as the anonymous *Ann Heuser:*

A rare old bird is the pelican;	*There was a young girl named Ann Heuser*
His bill holds more than his belican.	*Who swore that no man could surprise her*
He can take in his beak	*But Pabst took a chance*
Enough food for a week	*Found a Schlitz in her pants*
I'm darned if I know how the helican!	*And now she is sadder Budweiser.*

And I find among the limericks gathered by Legman (*Limericks*) examples of what I came to realize I appreciated most about mad poems in the course of writing this book.

There's a man in the Bible portrayed	*A bather whose clothing was strewed*
As one deeply engrossed in his trade.	*By winds that left her quite nude,*
He became quite elated	*Saw a man come along,*
Over things he created,	*And unless we are wrong*
Especially the women he made.	*You expected this line to be lewd.*

The first of these two poems (#'s 1585 and 1587) from his *Weak Sisters* chapter, has no author or note. Picturing God as an obsessed craftsman, it is delightfully warped from the start, but it is what the last word (*made*) does that makes it akin to the best *kyôka*. The second is not so off-the-wall, but pleasant and doing everything it can, considering it was printed in "various service magazines in 1944." *Kyôka*, as we have seen, include such self-referential verses.

★ ***Kyôka as Limerick***. I just googled into a kyôka not given but replaced by a limerick in a Lecture on *21st Century Netsuke* by Robert O. Kinsey for the International Netsuke society Honolulu, Hawaii, 1/28/04. *"This netsuke portrays a scantily clad woman sea diver who has fallen asleep embracing the body of a huge fish."* I wonder, could it be a carp, homophonous with love (*koi*)? "She appears to be having very erotic dreams. There is calligraphy engraved on her posterior. A well known netsuke collector, who understandably insists on anonymity, carefully examined this netsuke and observed that it reminded him of this limerick: *"On the breast of a harlot named Gail/ Was tattooed the price of her tail/ And on her behind/ For the sake of the blind/ Was the same information in Braille."* Legman's version has a "harlot at Yale" but never mind. Kinsey continues,

> "Japan's vast heritage of poetry includes a type of poem called 'Kyoka,' which literally translates as "mad verse." . . . The roots of comic Kyoka can be traced back for more than a thousand years, and it was extremely popular during the Edo period, until the end of 18th century when it was suppressed. It was the custom of feudal lords to keep literary scholars in their entourage, both poets and storytellers. Humorous poetry seems to have originated in salons of these daimyo. After long sessions of composing serious poetry, the poets often found relaxation late in the evening by concocting lighthearted verses to amuse the daimyo and themselves."

While poets wrote *kyôka* among themselves for all those 1000 years and hardly needed said salon, it is true that the daimyô, and, for that matter, the shôgun played a role in all this. Maybe it is worth a chapter in another edition. Anyone?

♪ ***Another Overlooked Category of Kyôka.*** When Captain Golownin was held in Japan, 1811-13 (*Memoirs of a Captivity:* 1824), he noted signs and the use of price tags as part of his more general observation of Japan's being more literate than Europe. Here is an example of that commercial literacy found on the web. Appropriately, I guess, it was at a site selling Edo era fire-making kits reproduced with the cooperation of experimental-archeologists (実験考古学者), available for ￥3,990, shipping separate.

文豪　幸田露伴先生より弊店に贈られた直筆の短歌

贈　伊勢や　詠　燧石狂歌　露伴

石の中に春やありけむ ゆうぐれを うつかねに火の花とちりける rohan
ishi no naka ni haru ya arikemu yûgure o utsu kane ni hi no hana to chirikeru c.1800?
ston-withn spring!/? is: evenng/vespers strike metl=bell-by day=fire-blossm=spark-as fall/fly!

In this Stone, we find the Spring, and with the Vesper Bell,
= Metal's striking, Fire-blossoms = Sparks scatter pell-mell!

I would think this supplied to the owner to hang in the store. Hopefully, someone studying the history of Japan's ad-culture can find me a chapter-worth of store-*kyôka*. The picture for the above "kyôka for a fire-stone" is on page 28. Below find what is on page 29, Issa's odious silverfish *kyôka* as I found it in Issa's reprinted journal (see pg.31). Alas, my Acrobat 6 pdf kept claiming the picture had color space violations despite it being saved as grey scale many times over. As the file itself is long, I have wasted three hours fruitlessly redoing it. My computer feels hot enough to boil over – either it or I will literally get hurt if I do not stop – I would have fiinished the book and sent it to the printers if the software had only behaved itself. Damn, damn, damn! I know how Issa felt! The illustration will be uploaded to paraverse.org., but I will repeat Issa's poem in Japanese alone, below.   There should be diacritical marks by the reverse slash part of the repeat sign which should itself join the forward slash part as a singular mark..

書物も残らず棒にふる郷の
人は紙魚／＼にくきつら哉

MAD BIBLIOS annotated & occasionally critical

Japanese – *Not* alphabetical but in descending order of indebtedness.

Nihon Kokugo Daijiten. 日本国語大辞典（縮刷版）小学館 Shogakukan 1980。 Without this 10 volume (reduced print, 20 vol. if large print) dictionary, there is no way I could have done not just this book but all of my books of translations and explanations of pre-modern literature. It offers more variations of words than others and has ample usages, most of which happen to be just what I can most use, poems! These are heavy books, together they weigh as much as I do, but even if it means buying or making a spinning book-stand you need this buy your desk (or, today, one can subscribe to use it online). When one finds only a small percent of the old words searched for, one tends to stop searching. With this dictionary, and only this dictionary, I get an 80% hit rate. I call it the OJD, ostensibly after the OED, but actually meaning the "Only Japanese Dictionary."

Kyôka Taikan* (tk** or ***Broadview). Meijishôin. vol.1 text. 1982. vol.2 reference 1984. 狂歌大観　狂歌大観刊行会編集　明治書院　本編 1982、参考編 1984 。 捜引編. Edited by the Kyokataikankankokai and published by Meiji Shôin in 1982/4, contains about 23,000 poems from a hundred-odd reproduced books of *kyôka* – including great collected anthologies such as the 1666 *Kokinikyokushû* (Old & New Savage (or, Barbarian) Songs), write-while-you travel collections such as the slightly later *Chishishosaikyôkashô* of which the Arima section edited by Kôfû was superb, personal poem collections such as Getsudôken's *Ôuchiwa*, or Big Fan journal, which gave me scores of poems and even selections of *kyôka* from material of other format such as journals, of which the biggest by far was the *Ômurôchûki or Report from the Parrot Cage's squibs* and books of comic stories of which Anrakuden's *Seisuishô*, or *Laughs to Banish Sleep* cannot be beat – in accord with its name that Englishes as *"kyôka grand(or broad)-view,"* dating from the early-13c. to mid-18c, with late-17c to early-18c particularly well-covered. These major collections are critiqued in passing with translations in the main text or the Short & Broad History, so I will not reiterate here. Almost *all* of the *kyôka* collections I read are from these two volumes. The books in Vol. I (main text) are mostly stand-alone poetry while Vol.II (reference) includes many taken from comic stories or tales and some facsimile reproductions. *"Reference"* or not, *no information other than the bare bones (what the reproduced book offers) is given*. There *is* a large collection of 18-19c Edo *kyôka* published earlier I could not afford – 15 volumes at about $150./each – but, until this *Broad-view* collection was published, almost no 16, 17 and early-18c books, largely from Kansai (Osaka, Kyoto), were in (type-face) print. I wish it gave us rough dates for each work, the date of death for each poet, pronunciation of their names and so forth (dates below mostly come from a chart posted by my respondent Yoshioka Ikuo). Even Vol. 3, which indexes the poems by word-order and poet-name, fails to give that minimal information! Worse, one finds dozens of poems starting identically, where if the blank space were only used to add a few syllabets we could find one without searching all! *Aaaargh!* Still, I wish I could afford the index (seen briefly via interlibrary loan at a cost of $25). Complaints aside, with *Broadview* published, there is no longer any excuse for neglecting *kyôka* in Japanese or in translation. The editors were aware of the significance of their volumes for repairing the bias in favor of Tenmei senryû and the vol. I Preface states that if the older poems were sometimes crude, they were also bold and prolific, overflowing with a primal creativity lost when the Tenmei poets polished the genre:

「一般に、こんにち狂歌と呼ぶものは、所謂天明狂歌とその流れをくむものであるが、天明狂歌の成立によって、いわばその前史と見なされるに至った数百年の狂歌は、まことに骨太であり、豊饒でもあったのだ。豊饒は、ときに粗野であり、洗練を欠くが、天明の江戸狂歌が、洗練のうちに、払い落とし、失って行ったものが、実はそれ以前の狂歌においては、他のさまざまの文芸・芸能の領域と深く力強く結びつけられて存在した」。(『狂歌大観』昭和 59. その Vol.1, 本編の序)

Here is a list of all the books and (in vol.2) selections from books in *Kyôka Taikan*. For more names & dates, visit 吉岡生夫 Yoshioka Ikuo's *kyôka* website. 1 ★ = more than one poem taken,   2 ★★ = a handful,   3 ★★★ = a dozen or more, &   4 ★★★★ = scores!

V.1 本篇：『東北院職人歌合』６９首、『鶴岡放生会職人歌合』４９首、『十二類歌合』１２首、★『狂歌酒百首 1758 (が、伝暁月坊 1265-1328)』９７首、『金言和歌集』２０５首、『三十二番職人歌合』６４首、『永正五年狂歌合』２０首、『調度歌合』２０首、★『玉吟抄 1532』２００首、『七十一番職人歌合』２８４首、『道増誹諧百首』１００首、『詠百首誹諧』１００首、★★『雄長老狂歌百首 1589』１００首、『古今若衆序』６首、『三斎様御筆狂歌』１４首、★★『入安狂歌百首』１００首、★★『四生の歌合 1643』１０８首、★★『新撰狂歌集 1636』１８７首、『関東下向道記』８７首、★『貞徳百首狂歌』１００首、『狂歌之詠草』５５首、★『貞徳狂歌抄』３５首、『職人歌合』３９首、★★★『吾吟我集 1649』６５８首、『東海道各駅狂歌』５０首、『鼻笛集』９８首、★★★★『古今夷曲集 1666』１０６１首、『堀河百首題狂歌合』２０２首、『堀河狂歌集』２９９首、★★『後撰夷曲集 1672』１７２４首、★★『卜養狂歌集 1669』２３０首、★★★『卜養狂歌拾遺』２４９首、『豊蔵坊信海狂歌集』７２５首、『孝雄狂歌集』２９５首、『信海狂歌拾遺』９２首、『類字名所狂歌集』２０２首、★★★『銀葉夷歌集 1679』１１８６首、『狂歌旅枕』２８３首、★長崎一見狂歌集』１７６首、★★★★『大団 c.1700』２２５７首、『春駒狂歌集』１２５首、『甲州紀行狂歌』４５首、★★『続春駒狂歌集 1721』６６首、★★★『甚久法師狂歌集 1722』１７５首、★『家つと 1729』２３９首、★『華紅葉』２７９首、★『狂歌乗合船』３２５首、★『雅筵酔狂集・腹藁』７２９首、『狂歌三十六歌仙』３６首、『続家つと』２２２首、★『置みやけ 1734』３０９首、★★『狂歌糸の錦 1734』２３０首、『狂歌机の塵』２５７首、★『狂歌ますかがみ 1736』２３２首、★『狂歌戎の鯛』２４０首、★『狂歌種ふくべ』３１６首、★★★『狂歌餅月夜 1740』３１５首、★★★『狂歌続ますかがみ 1740』３５０首、★★★『狂歌活玉集 1740』７４３首♪。

V.2 参 「平治・平家物語」４５首、「山門・寺門落首」１１首、「太平記」３０首、★★「餅酒百首 sic? 歌合」２０首、「応仁・応仁別記」２０首、「廻国雑記」１６首、★★★「再昌草 1536」２８３首、「永正落首」１２首、★★「宗長手記・日記 c.1520-30」５６首、「信長記」１２首、「太閤記」２３首、「幽斎道の記」３０首、「長諳道の記」１５首、★「新旧狂歌俳諧聞書」１４９首、★★★★「遠近草 1574-89」１８９首、★★「越後在府日記」９４首、「犬枕并狂歌」１９首、「寒川入道筆記」２８首、★「雄長老狂歌」１５首、「戯言養気集」１３首、「きのふはけふの物語」３３首、★★★★「醒睡笑 1623」３６０首、★「竹斎」８８首、「俳諧狂歌発句」２３首、「策伝和尚送答控」３３３首、★★「仁勢物語 1639」２０８首、★「かさぬ草紙」１５９首、「寛永以前落首」２２首、「長斎狂歌」６４首、「浮世物語」１６首、★★「百物語」４４首、「竹斎狂歌物語」１１首、★「一休はなし」４５首、★「私可多咄」３３首、「狂歌咄」２３５首、「一休関東咄」１０首、★「一休諸国物語」３３首、「秋の夜の友」５７首、「杉楊枝」１１３首、「元の木阿弥」８首、「けんさい物語」１４首、「新竹斎」５４首、「二休物語」２０首、★★★★「地誌所載狂歌抄 1672 (有馬の章)」１６５４首、★★「諸国落首咄」１００首、「宝永落書」１０７首、★★★★「鸚鵡籠中記落首抄 1684-1717」４０８首、★「犬百人一首」１００首♪、「狂遊集」３６首、「古今狂歌仙」３６首、「貞徳狂歌集」１０１首、「江戸名所百人一首」１００首、★★★「狂歌五十人一首」５０首、「絵本御伽品鏡」５６首。

♪   To Avoid Dog 100 Confusion.   犬百　に関して。「犬百人一首」は佐心子賀近。1669。参考篇にある。貞柳の油縁斎狂歌犬百人一首は「狂歌活玉集」中。

~~~~~~~~~~~~~~~~~~~~~~~~~~~~~~~~~~~~~~~

『蜀山家集』ssks 全 附 網雑魚+金鶏の『あみざこ』一冊を附録　歌謡俳書選集十編輯及解説　藤井乙男.冒頭の玉の狂歌小史と蜀山人評伝、金子実英著。昭和二年。京大博士の藤井は監修。金子のエッセイは、狂歌を知る上に不可欠な、しかも楽しい読み物です。狂歌を広く考える大観てきな見解と、蜀山人の人生と芸に深いが暖かい伝記。狂歌研究家でわが文友とよきアドバイザーでもある、吉岡生夫氏は曰く「金子氏の「狂歌史」がなければ私はなかなか前進できなかったと思います。ただ「狂」だけに拘るとこぼれ落ちるものがある。むしろ多いと思っています。」そう。狂歌を、その語からではなく、あくまでもその内容から考える、あるいは認める、というごく当たり前のことは、常識ではなかった。今でもない。金子は偉かった。ちょっと、と思った唯一のところが、落首について、金子が「正面から正々堂々と他人の非行を攻撃したり、為政者の失態を論難したりする勇気をもたない者が、其の不平不満を洩す一つの方法である」という一般論。とんでもない。統制者を批判してそのため殺されては、批判はそれで終わっちゃう。勇気の有無の問題ではない。無名でも、何もいわないよりも、落首を書くには勇気が要る。だって、「大宝令にも既に落書を罪する規定がある程度である」（吉岡）。とは言って、金子万歳！そして、この家集は、毎度拝見すれば新しい発見ある底なしの Cornucopia で、オンラインで見えるのが有難い。感謝。注。網雑魚の首も「家集」となっている場合もある。じっくりと直す暇なかった。どうせ知りたければ、J-text でオンラインです。◎ *Shokusan Kashû* (Shokusanjin's personal collection) with Ami-zakô? (a net of mixed fish). Ed. Fujii Otsuo. With a history of *kyôka* and biography of Shokusanjin by Kaneko Jitsue. 1927. (Jitsue is a guess. We find no indication of the pronunciation). Hundreds, maybe thousands of Shokusanjin's poems (If anyone feels like counting, tell me and I'll add the figure to the next edition). I do not know what percent of his poems it is, but the whole man is indeed here. With poems to dancing girls and his dead wife, we feel we get to know the poet. This is what Blyth had, and probably explains why he concentrated on Shokusanjin to the exclusion of all others in his *Oriental Humour*. Kaneko's essays are wonderful and simultaneously do justice to Shokusanjin *and* the broader (older) history of *kyôka* that was largely ignored until the *Kyôka Taikan* was published in 1982/4. I am so grateful that Kyushu University and, later, J-text saw fit to give us this great volume on-line. May more poets be so published!

～～～～～～～～～～～～～～～～～～～～～～～～～～～

川柳狂歌集　杉本長重+濱田義一郎校注者　岩波の日本古典文学大系 57. 昭和 33. 狂歌「徳和歌後萬載集」「蜀山百首」「我妻曲狂歌文庫」は濱田の方が担当也。たまたま、古本屋で買って、川柳の解説のために米国まで持ってきた本。827 首もある「徳和歌後萬載集」は天明狂歌の代表作であって、どう見てもついていた。解説は、天明狂歌の指導が橘洲の狂歌会から出版、赤良の競作とその勝利がなかなか詳しい。狂歌のタイプ別（本歌取、発想の滑稽、言語の技巧）の分析と実例はなかなかのものです。◎ *Senryû Kyôka Shû* Sugimoto Nagashige + Hamada Giichirô annot.. Nihon Koten Bungaku Taikei 57, Iwanami Shôten: 1958. Hamada is in charge of the *kyôka* part. Includes the representative Tenmei kyôka collection *Tokuwakagomanzaishû* (1785), selected by Yomo no Akara (Ôta/Shokusanjin), *Shokusan Hyakushû*, or 100 poems by Shokusanjin, published in 1818, and the 1786 *Azumakyoku Kyôkabunko*, with one poem each by fifty poets + and some poets who were skipped added later that year. The 1786 book has brief annotations about each poet added by the Iwanami editors. The 827-poem *Tokuwa* anthology is the source of the largest portion of the Tenmei poems by poets other than Shokusanjin in my book. Iwanami Taikei has another book with Tenmei *kyôka*, but unfortunately I have not yet seen it.

～～～～～～～～～～～～～～～～～～～～～～～～～～～

古今狂歌大全　永沢三郎編　強文舘　明治 27（略として「一万」）天明から文政の狂歌が中心の様が、その前後のもある。「狂歌一万集」中にあるかと思ったが、二千首もなかろう。しかも凡作駄作が多い。とりわけ「恋」に何か「寄」首の数々が「月並み狂歌」のみごとな実例となった。それも狂歌の総合的理解のためになるかと、本を買った自分を慰める。狂詩も少しある。狂歌主の名前の発音、年付などない. すべて二字斗りで天明名人でない者の同定は困る。捜索できるオンライン狂歌人人名録がなければ、発音を当てずっぽうする他ない。天明狂歌流

行の口を切り開いた大田軟畝ないし四方赤良編『万歳集』(1783) が部分的には入っているかもしれないが、今のところよく判らない。 *Kokin Kyôka Daizen* Nagasawa Saburô ed. Kyôbunkan: 1894. A "collection of 10,000 mad poems" (*kyôka ichiman-shû*) actually less than 2,000. Less good ones than found in the 827-poem *Tokuwa* anthology. Unfortunately, there are no dates for original sources and I do not recognize most of the names of which only two characters are given. Some may be from the 1783 *Manzaishû* and/or *Wakabashû* – the poets names are late 18c. – but I have no way of knowing. It serves to show what run-of-the-mill *kyôka* were, and some of the poems relating love to this or that thing were interesting enough to seed a couple chapters entire. Of the fifty-odd *kyôshi* (Chinese-style mad poems), only a few were worth translating. I bought it cheaply and, sure enough, in months it broke into a dozen parts!

狂歌百人一首　蜀山人　On-line で見つけて、よかった。字も打ち込まないで済む。水垣久氏の簡単な解説が時々役立ったが、同じ歌の川柳パロデイもそばに入れた面倒見までは、ほんとうにご親切。感謝！◎*Kyôka Hyakunin Isshû,* or *Kyôka Hundred Poets One Poem.* Shokusanjin's parody, or rather rainbow of take-offs on the famous 100 show what a poet with the mind of an editor can do. How fortunate that one kind man, Mizukaki Hisashi, took it upon himself to put all the poems online, with comments and examples of other parodies (from the two other *kyôka 100 Poets* parodies found in TK – I had them, but it saved typing – *and* some senryû for good measure!

『百鬼夜狂』1785. これも上記のと同じ Online 親切屋のお陰で拝見できて、その中のよき例・霊を英訳できた。ものをオンライン化することは、資料手に入りにくい外国にいる方にとって不可欠で、文化庁はその文化的貢献に賞金を与えるべきでしょう。 (*Hyakki yakyô:* hundred demon night frenzy). The same person who put the Shokusanjin's Kyôka Hundred Poets on line, Mizukaki 水垣 久 put a good portion of this book with *kyôka* on spooky supernatural creatures by 16 top *kyôka* poets, including Yomo no Akara, on line, too, but not all. He stopped at 60 (I have yet to see the last 40). Why not all? He writes that spooky things started to happen to him and seeing that people connected with this book had fared ill, decided to bail out. In Mizukaki's words, 四方赤良（大田南畝）を始め、当時活躍してゐた十六人の狂歌師が百物語戯歌を狂作、いや競作、百首を選んで纏めたものです。その後、妖怪をからかつた報いか、文化三年(1806)の火災で版木の大半を失ひました。が、世に再刊を望む聲高く、初版刊行三十五年後の文政三年、恐れを知らぬ蔦屋 . . . I am grateful to him for not yanking the site, for without it, my entire sampling of spooks would have been from Hearn's *Goblin Poetry*, a later, lower quality – poem-wise, but I read the illustrations were good – book.

夫木和歌抄　藤原長清編　1310 年　再版　発行者市島謙吉　明治 40. 大 DB が使えない貧乏たる門外漢としては、このテマ別、しかも索引別本ある、三流和歌集は、せめての者慰め。安く買って、手元にある本はなによりも。探せば、狂歌っぽい、珍首の玉々、石の中におちこち散らばっていて、拾うの疲労だけです。◎ *Fuboku Waka-shô.* Selected by Fujiwara Nagakiyo 1310. Most of the 20,000+ waka are pretty poor stuff. There are hundreds of almost uniformly boring poems by one poet, Toshiyori/Shunrai 俊頼,* but here and there we can find interesting poems of the sort not in the Imperial or even second-rank anthologies, some of which bring us closer to *kyôka*. I got a 1907 reprint for only a hundred bucks　(30x cheaper than the waka taikan cd that might not work in my English OS pc) I did not always note the original source of the poems I found in this book, but they are given in it and the poems may be looked up because there is an index. And, you know if you see the date 1310 that they precede it.

* I am mystified because Carter (1991) writes of a Shunrai/Toshiyori's imaginative handling of topics and gives interesting examples of which "Ah, how it pains me / to see you burn so demurely, / you glowing fireflies! / It should make one sob out loud – / life in this world of ours" (*aware ni mo misao ni moyuru hotaru kana koe taetsu beki kono yo to omou ni*) in his fine translation is my favorite. Either he is a different poet or the *Fuboku* editor dug up a collection of his throw-aways.

江戸狂歌　なだいなだ Nada Inada 。岩波書店 1986. 外国人だけではなく日本国

民も理屈をこね入れた機知をもって、自分のあるいは皆の主張をしてきた。その日本人の、読者の元気な舌を、切り落としたがる文学歴史・評論家たちが書けなかった狂歌の紹介を、革新的精神医がやってくれました。とはいっても、伝統的出版社岩波にも脱帽です。*Edo Kyôka*. Writer-psychiatrist Nada Inada proves even an amateur could understand the importance of *kyôka* when great literary critics writing in Japanese or English could not. While the title might suggest it is limited to the late-18c poets of Edo, and Shokusanjin is indeed most thoroughly treated, Nada Inada respects the earlier *kyôka* masters of Kyôto and Ôsaka by introducing their better poems rather than their worst (as critics intent on building up Tenmei *kyôka* tend to do). I doubt if there are more than 200 poems in the book, but socially significant *kyôka* are well-covered. I found Kankô's hard-working tax collector at year's end and Yûchôrô not building houses lest tax collectors use them and more of interest in this book, as I have indicated here and there. Most of the limited number of *kyôka* found online (outside of a couple large kyôka-related sites), happen to be in this book, and I bet, directly or indirectly taken from it.

日文。Nichibunken. This is not one book but a website with scores or even hundreds on line and open to all that gives those of us not in academia or independently wealthy the only opportunity to peruse great numbers of *waka* that I know of. Unfortunately, the lead-in's and other contextual information as well as *most of the poets' names(!)* are not given. Since the hundreds of thousands of poems were typed in by a single kind man, Professor Seta Katsuhiro 勢田勝郭氏, at the Nara National College of Technology 奈良工業高等専門学校 one cannot complain – but what a shame that no person or institution has seen fit to supply the names (and Chinese characters). Can they find no volunteers?

万葉集 mys は、中西注、岩波文庫。歌によるが、本来の機知がその堅苦しい現代訳に殺されてしまうことは少なくはないが、それでも理解のための注も原文も読み下しも五千ほど用意した中西は偉いし、あのに安く売っている岩波も偉い。感謝。ただし、歌主の名前や歌の年付をはっきりと歌と同じ頁に見たい。作者を各章の前に置くよりも解かり易くなる。◎*Manyôshû* (mys 8c). Annot. by Nakanishi Susumu, published by Iwanami bunko (1983/90). The explanations are minimal, but with about 5000 poems, it is extraordinary just that all receive attention and is available in a cheap pocket book allowing the masses access. The only problem for this foreign reader is that it is very difficult to tell at a glance *who* wrote a particular poem, and *when*. I am afraid that is a shortcoming common to many anthologies published in Japanese.

古今集 kks は、久曽神昇 注 講談社学術文庫。これほど充実したノットを文庫で安く買うのが何よりも。ただし、どうせ大きなスペースがあったら、歌の機知をもう少しうまく説明できたはずとおもったところが多かった。歌意味も鑑賞はいいが、もう少し柔軟性と大胆さがほしかった。◎ My *Kokinshû* (kks c.905) is annotated by Kyûsojin Hitaku and published by Kôdansha gakujutsu bunko (1983/90). The most notes I have ever found in a cheap pocket book, for which I am thankful, though I felt they could have been better – too many that seemed simplistic even for this foreigner who is not a literature major – in particular when it came to the area about which I am most interested, namely finding all of the wit in the original.

山家集。岩波の古い文庫。注など全くないから、編集者の名前もどうでもいい。20世紀後半から、注のある西行の文庫が絶対必要だったが、残念ながら岩波が西行の面白さと注の必要も理解していないみたい。*Sanka-shû*. This old Iwanami pb (1928/78 35th printing!) with *no notes whatsoever* found in a used bookstore & bought for 25-cents let me introduce plentiful *waka* by Saigyô, but I can only pray that most of my interpretative guesses were correct. I have seen an English translation by Honda, but his translations are too sketchy to be of much use for one interested in wit.

新古今和歌集 skks は、岩波の古い文庫。注など全くない。注ある程度あった新古今集を買ったが、まったく役に立ったなかった。*Shinkokinshû* 1205. An old Iwanami pb (1929/92 67th printing!). No notes whatsoever. I have yet to find a fully annotated Japanese skks, much less a translation. This is odd when you consider it is one of the big three classical waka anthologies, but understandable because it built upon the other two and such finesse is not something easy to follow in Japanese, much less English.

パロデイの精神　富士正晴 Fuji Masaharu　平凡社 1974. 残念ながら書名通りではない。伊勢、又「仁勢物語」が平行、それに、幾分の難い表現のすぐ後（文中）に、括弧入り現代訳もあるが、それ以外には、作者となるかもしれない者と公家の事態などの長いエッセイばかり。「仁勢物語」の中でに広げる、種々の実に多様なパロデイの指摘や分析は皆無。 This book *Parodei no Seishin* has the *Tales of Ise* and the early-17c *Nise* or fake one side by side, with some parenthetical help for understanding both inserted in the sentences. The title led me to expect something on the extraordinary variety of take-offs employed by the *Nise* author, but there was none. Still, the long preface about the relationship of the probable author, the young nobleman, or 公家 *kuge,* 光広 Mitsuhiro and older haikai master/judge 幽斎 and circumstances – the romantic intrigues and punishments of the nobles – was worth reading. It helped me understand how *kuge* came to be looked down upon early in the Edo period which helped me make some sense of *kyôka* read elsewhere, such as, say, this ironic early-18c poem:

敷島の道は神より佛よりお公家さまこそたふとかりけれ　海音堂貞峩
shikishima no miichi wa kami yori hotoke yori o-kuge-sama koso tôtogarikere

On this isle, the way of the gods and of the buddha pale
Today, it is the nobles, the mighty kuge, we hail!

Is this land where the Gods and Buddha are loved not feared?
No, it's where the honorable, worthless kuge are revered!

The poet was not as explicit as my second reading, though the honorifics *"O ~"* and *"~ sama"* together do imply disgust. The circumstances that had Teiga 貞峩 riled up are doubtless unlike those a century earlier, but knowing the *kuge* were in bad odor helped me catch the poet's intent. Anyway, don't buy the book for an analysis of parody. Iwanami's ktbgtk #90 仮名草紙集 (found too late to use for this book) has notes on vocabulary but also stops short of the sort of reading needed for us to fully enjoy the humor.

新撰万葉集 893-913, 古今和歌六帖 976-82　(略 kkrj)の歌は先ず Cranston の和歌英訳本 vol.2a（下記）の英訳＋ローマ字化で見つけて、のちに和文を、吉岡氏見つけてくれました。日本にもほとんど相手にされていない両和歌集の宝物を拾って英訳と解釈した Cranston は偉い。氏の本の書評は少なすぎて、困る。十数年前、ある人の退屈な万葉英訳が、日本などでちやほやされていたが、Cranston の貢献はその十倍か百倍も上だ。2007 年の Yamagata Banto Prize を受けたのが、実に well-deserved! The *Shinsen Manyôshû* and *Kokinwakarokujô* are not only important for filling in the period between the Manyôshû (8c) and Kokinshû (early 10c) but, as I trust you saw from examples in this book, interesting in their own right and important for grasping the broader history of Japanese literature that includes *kyôka*. Few Japanese have read them and I would have entirely missed them if not for Cranston 2a, below.

見なければならないがまだ見ていない本無数あり。初期俳諧集『竹馬狂吟集』も、『近世上方狂歌叢書』も、何十万円のお金ださなければ買えない江戸の狂歌何十巻も、岩波体系にもある大田の初期物等等、拝見したかった！わがへんてこな趣味でものを選びたいから、選集は好きではないが、選集であれ単作であれ、解釈もついている狂歌本を沢山読むべきであった。ウエーブ古本で探したら、十、廿冊もあるはずが、日本語の解読力に限界ある不勉強なる外人ながら、そういうお世話になるような本は、上記岩波の古典文学大系 57 の一冊しか手元になかった。そのため、むろん大に損した。名前のローマ字化のために発音を江戸狂歌本なんとか会の人名辞典でしらべたかったが Worldcat によれば米図書館に全くない。

Bayerische Staatsbibliothek 以外に外国にないみたい。派手といえば、サンクトペテルブルグ大の Victor Victorovich Rybin の『知られざる歌麿：「百千鳥狂歌合はせ」の詩的、文法的分析』The unknown Utamaro, a poetic/grammatical analysis of a tournament of comic poems about a multitude of birds（国際日本文化研究センター）って44頁のものまでも、念のため一応参考にしたかったが、状況は状況。

隣ない田舎ながらも春近く　　敬愚

と自分に言い聞かせながら、資料が自由自在に見られないほど辛いことはない。何回も我が為に図書館へ行って来た吉岡生夫氏のお世話がもしもなかったら、無力のあんまりで小生こそ狂ってしまったかもしれない。軽・丸屑曰く「労働者にその生産の道具を」。敬愚も言う、研究者にだって、その資料を！　とは言っても、物がなければそれだけの工夫で誤魔化す。良き歌がなければ、翻訳で悪き歌を改良、傑作にすればいい。あるいは、無理して前後に合えない首も入れてもいい理由こそ捏造したりするうちに、意外な発見もある。解釈のある本を買いかねて、誤訳をばしでかしても限界あるお金・時でいっぱい頑張っては、なぜ恥じる？しない。笑って、正解通りに再び英訳し、本来一つしかなかった首を、二首までも成ったことを、感謝する。場合によって、誤訳の方がむろいい。

隣ない田舎のままに春も去り　　敬愚

◎　二ヶ月経つ。狂歌にも俳諧にも、もっと突っ込んでみたいが、お金も、適切な住まい、何もない身。本書を読んで頂いて、「狂訳」を、もっと見たい、しかも余裕のある個人、出版社ないし機関、ご連絡よろしくお願いします．

◎　又一ヶ月が。初版直し中、鈴木棠三著『狂歌鑑賞辞典』（角川 1984）拝見。拙著と 5%重複か。小話から出たもの、謎々っぽい言葉遊び、道歌、パロデイのタイプが多く。概念の優れたもの、とりわけ 16−7 世紀の狂歌が少なかった。

Suzuki: Suzuki Tôzô's dictionary of *kyôka* appreciation, *Kyôka Kanshô Jiten* (Kadokawa: 1984), was found too late to be of much use. Our poem overlap is about 5%.

~~~~~~
~~~~~~

English
– While my sources are over 90% Japanese, *if* the books within *Kyôka Taikan* (Kyôka Broad-view) are not counted individually, I have looked at more English sources, enough to justify alphabetizing by author below:

~~~~~~

Aston, W.G.   *A History of Japanese Literature* Heinemann: 1899. The description of what is inevitably lost in translation given in the preface is superb and, conceptually speaking, not the least dated. And what honesty! How many of our modern translator-anthologists come out and clearly admit the following? *"In the present volume it has often been necessary to pass over the best and most characteristic passages of an author in favour of others which lent themselves more readily to presentation in an English form."*   His description of *kiôka*, which, as we saw in the front-matter, begins so appreciatively, takes so interesting a turn that I shall quote the entire passage.

Kioka (literally "mad poetry") is a comic and vulgar variety of *Tanka*. There is here an absolute freedom both in respect to language and choice of subject. The *Kioka* must be funny, that is all. In this kind of poetry, of which an immense quantity was produced during the Yedo period, the punning propensity of the Japanese has been allowed full scope. *Share* (rhymes with *sake*) reigns there supreme. *Share* is one of those numerous Japanese words for which there is no exact English equivalent. It may be translated "wit" but in order to express its full meaning a spice of what is comprehended under the terms gaiety, esprit, playful fancy, stylishness, must be added. Japanese wit, like that of other countries, has an element which defies analysis or classification. But the jeu'de-mots predominates. *Share infests not only the Kioka, but the drama and fiction, to an extent well-nigh intolerable to European tastes.* Dr. Florenz, Professor of Philology in the Imperial University of Tokio, has treated this subject with truly German conscientiousness and erudition in a paper read before the German Asiatic Society of Japan in July 1892. Following a native investigator named Tsuchiko Kaneshiro, he classifies *share* under two heads with divisions and subdivisions, making in all twenty different kinds. Our old enemy the *pivot-word* [first defined by Chamberlain] is here, also the pillow-word, and several varieties of the ordinary pun, with various fearfully complicated acrobatic contortions of speech which I shall not attempt to describe. Even the reader who has a competent knowledge of the language requires a special study to understand and appreciate them. He follows these far-eastern waggeries with a halting step, and frequently finds himself in the position of the Scotchman who was heard suddenly to burst into laughter at a joke which had been made half-an-hour before. Nothing testifies more strikingly to the nimbleness of the Japanese apprehension than their delight in these "Taschenspielerkunstchen des sprachlichen Ausdrucks" (linguistic prestidigitations), as Dr. Florenz has aptly called them, whether in conversation or in books. *It may be doubted whether such an excessive fondness for mere verbal wit does not amount to a disease, and whether it has not constituted a serious obstacle to the development of higher qualities in their literature.*

The sentences italicized suggest that while Aston defines *kyôka* more broadly and accurately than most moderns who dwell on parody and the 18c, he did not evaluate it highly. However, that is not all. Aston continues to hypothesize that Japanese *had no choice* but rely on short and punning poetry because their limited phonemes, "open vowels preceded by single consonants or none" made not only end-rhyme impossible (or impossibly boring) but "only within the narrowest limits" allowed the poet to, following Pope, "make the sound an echo to the sense." allowed the crafting of "sound as an echo to the sense." In other words, he invented a negative theory for the genesis of *kyôka*.

Blyth, Reginald H. *Oriental Humour* Hokuseido: 1959. Includes an idiosyncratic 14-page, 24-poem (16 by Yomo no Akara / Shokusanjin) sampling of *kyôka*. The first example given is a parody of Saigyô's blossom-viewing poem (a trail-marker left from the year before is not followed in order to see new sights and that becomes a marker misread getting the poet lost). It is later given by others, I recall (Keene? Shirane?), but not one of my favorites for Saigyô's original idea of looking for his marker so as *not* to see the same thing is more novel than not seeing it and getting lost in the profusion of bloom (a common theme in haikai), so the only merit of the poem is that it only changes one syllabet in the first half of the parody. Otherwise, I was delighted with the choice of poems. *Blyth correctly notes that kyôka "parody" is more a sort of "lightening" of the original than digging at it*, and exampled by one more take-off, where a blossom-viewing poem turns into a blizzard and the sedan-men (I think he used that quaint word, *palaquin*) must be paid more (I wished he pointed out the bonus was like that of the Mexican mariachi, paid in booze 酒代). If I wander describing Blyth's book, it is because his book, all of his books, are full of life and life is mostly the little things in it. Blyth included the three most commonly translated *kyôka* after him, Shokusanjin's drunken Spring zig-zagging up the street (the word zig-zag must be Usanian for he uses much less accurate vocabulary), Teiryû's Mt.-Fuji-is-better-in-a-dream (the only pre-Tenmei example) and Meshimori's bad-poets-are-safer-for-not-moving heaven-&-earth (pg.32). The section is by and large a tribute to the kindness and sanity of Shokusanjin rather than any real attempt to comprehend the field. Blyth had the same anthology of Shokusanjin's work I relied on (it is on-line now, if you are interested), but as mentioned elsewhere, until the Kyôka Taikan (broadview) reprinted many of the 16, 17 and early 18c books in 1982 pre-Teiryû *kyôka* was neglected in Japan, so I cannot fault him for his choice. Today, with the Kyôka-Taikan, there is no excuse to keep giving Tenmei kyôka all of our attention. Blyth (like me, sometimes?) makes some wild assertions. Just before the *kyôka* section starts, he more or less defines *zappai* as "unpoetical senryû." That is ridiculous –

and reflects a Kantô (Edo/Tôkyô) as opposed to Kansai (Kyôto, Ôsaka) bias – but is nothing to discuss here. Yet, while I may quibble with details and do not ascribe to the gender stereotypes (which are neither without a kernel of the truth nor without charm for those with no ax to grind) that flow almost as incessantly as his Zen, who but Blyth will give you a sentence like *"It may be true to say, combining Tertullian and Oscar Wilde, that the only thing we can possibly believe is the impossible."*? That was on page 4. And he is second only to Lafcadio Hearn for giving his readers an education in English literature as he introduces Japan in relatively universal terms. Any book by Blyth is worth reading and it is a pity this one, only available used, is beyond the price range for people of the likes of yours truly. The delightful hyperlogical Chinese humour alone should merit this book a paperback reprint!

Bownas and Thwaite (Geoffrey Brownas, Anthony Thwaite) *The Penguin Book of Japanese Verse*, 1964. Most books of Japanese poetry without the originals to compare and notes are not worth the paper they are on, but these translations are good enough to make it the exception. It has the usual handful of kyôka. Only a handful. And the best comic translation of one of the comic Manyôshû poems I have read.

Braunen, Noah. *"Mad Poems" from Japan's Unknown Surimono.* Article in Rutgers "Painted Bride Quarterly" 40/41 double issue. Some examples of *surimono* poems. The short history (chopped-up Keene) is ludicrous but his translation not bad at all and a few of the poems far better than most *surimono kyôka* I was familiar with.

Carpenter, John T. et alfred Haft and others. *Reading Surimono: the Interplay of Text and Image in Japanese Prints* with a Catalogue of the Marino Lusy Collection. Leiden, 2008. +Hotei Publishing. With 300 surimono (fancy color prints) with two or more kyôka each, all translated and explained this is at least 20x more translated kyôka than I knew existed in any single work other than my book to be and I only found this book the day before I was set to call it quits and start the index. Why? Because it came from the world of art rather than literature. True, the pub says it is of interest for students of literature and its essayists include Edo literary specialists, but the libraries, literature and scholars devoted to literature pay scant attention to books coming from arts publishers, partly because they cost so much and partly because they tend to be poorly written, conceptually weak, or both, probably because authorship goes to those with access rather than to those with knowledge and skill. But, here, we have someone who in an interview confessed he owned no *surimono* himself because he was not wealthy. That, and the specification of "text" in the subtitle suggesting that Carpenter might be one of the exceptions and his "Reading" deep rather than dilettante, so I put publication on hold and got to work on an interlibrary loan (as you might imagine, not a single copy was in Florida). *Did I ever want to see that book!* To be more precise, I half-wanted to find horrid translations as foils for my beauties – or, rather, to *make* them beauties as beauty is relative – and half-wanted to find something so good I, unable to compete, could straightaway return to my first love, *haiku*. And, this was also true for two more books by Daniel McKee that Carpenter alerted me to when I wrote him that I also ordered by interlibrary loan and await with bated breath. If you read this book before reading the bibliography, you know what I found, but let me summarize in case you have not.

The eleven illustrated essays comprising the first quarter of *Reading Surimono* alone would make a fine book and I learned something from each though I only quoted from a few in this book. In the penultimate paragraph of his article *Inventing New Iconographies – Historicist and Nativist Motives in Late-Edo Surimono* the overall editor and main translator of the poems (Allred Haft, who also did many poems, translated some articles from Japanese) Carpenter wrote,

"References to the classics that surimono poets and artists made with such frequency and ease – analogous to references to Greek and Roman legends in English Romantic Poetry – pose an undeniable obstacle to modern readers. Still, the literary and historical references are usually to Japanese and Chinese classics that have become part of world literature through excellent translations. Our enjoyment of surimono would be enhanced by a

greater familiarity with these sources. Conversely, ...a study of surimono could amount to a wide-ranging albeit eclectic, survey of pre-modern Japanese literature and culture."

It not only "could" but *does* become just that in this book about *"the most extraordinarily literate form of printmaking in world history"* (from Carp. intro).The lengthy explanation and explication of the cultural background of the pictures and poems beats anything I have seen other than McKee's work, which does the same. I almost forgot to mention it has an honest-to-god subject index and a comprehensive index of poets as well. In other words, not only have the art folk outdone the lit folk when it comes to kyôka, but they have outdone the lit folk method of presenting Japanese poetry, period. I would recommend these books more highly for courses of Japanese literature than any other anthology of translated Japanese poetry I can think of because they are published with too few notes for readers who are not specialists, who may think they know what is going on but really miss most of it. One article in the book mentioned the average price of a surimono print today to be $4-6,000. If we round off to five thousand dollars and multiply that by the approximate number of prints in the book, 300, we get $1,500,000. The price of the book is about $150 (a much better price than usual for a bilingual book that large – it is huge – not to mention it has good color illustrations). That is 1/10,000th of the cost. Yes, 万が一の値段で御座います。 Some libraries do not catalogue the book under Carpenter but "Corporate-author(ship)" so it is safest to search for it by title.

Carter, Steven D. , *Traditional Japanese Poetry. Stanford University Press:* 1991. Only seven of 1157 poems are *kyôka*. Carter says nothing demeaning about *kyôka*, but notes the emphasis on "wordplay (is) so complicated it can only be suggested in translation." Perhaps that is why he did not translate more, though he is definitely not adverse to humor as he did a good job of finding and translating many witty waka and *haikai*, including some of each I think qualify as *kyôka* so his book is my favorite one-book selection and translation of what its title says. While syllable-padding hurts some translations, many are excellent and some exceptionally creative (eg. the last line to his *honobono to akashi . . .* translation: "my heart following in its wake." その暗喩も旨いぞ)

Cranston, Edwin A. *"A Waka Anthology"* Translated, with Commentary, Appendixes, and Notes by ~, Stanford University Press Vol 1: *The Gem Glistening Cup* (1993), **Vol.2a** and 2b: *Grasses of Remembrance* 2006 (so far). I like Cranston's attitude toward translation – particularly *"Anything that works justifies itself, ipso facto"* – and the readings that *do*. ◎As Cranston writes concerning his Vol.1 (largely the *Manyôshû*), *"there is not a poem in this volume that has not been rendered into English at least once and sometimes several times before,"* but only he gracefully introduces so many of the poems *with their poets,* that even someone who has read them in Japanese gains something. And, *all* of Cranston's books are readable because he explains more on the same page (rather than notes at the volume's end) than any other academic or, for that matter, popular scholar I know (except for yours truly, though I am only nominally popular). The biggest difference between his method and mine is that his explanation precedes the poems, while mine follows. ★ Vol.2a, on the other hand, probably has more *waka* never before rendered into English for the first time than any other book, with the possible exception of Honda's *Manyôshû* translation (so sketchy as to be useless to anyone who reads Japanese). And, as you may have noticed in this book, Cranston's selection includes many *waka* of the type I would call *wild* or even 'mad,' and they come not only from the oft-translated *Kokinshû*, but *from anthologies rarely read by Japanese today.* Most of those are damn hard to English and require a translator to go farther out the limb than most academics, fearful of critics, dare. Cranston, bless him, often does. And, he promises to follow the practice of the Sinosphere and exercise more poetic license, mad abandon, joy de vivre or whatever you call it with each volume to come, as it is not only suitable but *expected* for an elder. In case any of the comparisons of my mad translations and his plain ones did not support my enthusiasm for his work (sometimes I guess I make choices that make me look good), here is an example of a good translation of a *waka* sent to the Emperor by Kiritsubo no Kôi from I forget which anthology: *"Now the end has come, / We part along diverging paths, / And one sad desire / Still lies heavy in my heart: / To live, not leave, our life."* (*Kagiri tote wakuru michi no kanashiki ni ikama hoshiki wa* *inochi narikeri*). That last line is one to die for. I only wish the index for vol 2a were in 2a and not 2b. As the books are too expensive for me to buy, I had to use library loan and never had both books together to re-find things! A scholar friend doubts Cranston himself could buy his books. Everything from the *Shinsen Manyôshû=ssmys*, and most from the *Gosenshû = gss, Shûishû = sis* and *Kokinwakarokujô = kkrj* come from that volume, which the publisher should rush to put out in paperback with its own index at a decent price. With POD printing, there is no excuse for not doing this. ◎ Vol.2b, with all the poems in the *Tale of Genji,* had little for *this* book, but if you would grasp the conceptual and emotional underpinnings of what some consider the world's first true novel . . .

Gill, Robin D.: ◎*Topsy-turvy 1585* (paraverse press: 2005). Luis Frois listed 611 ways Europe and Japan are contrary in Portuguese in the 16c. All are translated and discussed. They are supplemented by hundreds more. This makes the book a one-stop reference for things Japanese and saves me much time otherwise lost searching for citations. ◎ ***The Woman Without a Hole, or Octopussy, Dry Kidney & Blue Spots*** (paraverse press: 2007). The only book in English on and of *dirty senryû*. It is one book with two names and a good reference for sex in the poetry and song of Japan. It complements *this* book, for one fills in the hitherto neglected half of Japanese poetry below the navel and the other that found above the neck. If *senryû* were neglected for being obscene; *kyôka* were neglected for being hyper-rational, or *rikutsuppoi*. ◎ **The Fifth Season** (paraverse press: 2007). Full of Edo period New Year haiku, a big help for reading *surimono* pictures and *kyôka*, for they are largely about that season. ◎ **The Cherry Blossom Epiphany** (paraverse press: 2007). The 3,000 old haiku include over a score of waka by Saigyô, many of which I feel verge on being *kyôka*. ◎ **Rise Ye Sea Slugs!** The *namako,* so common in *haikai,* is so rare in *kyôka* that this book was only cited a two or three times. Since the camel and the elephant do well enough, it is odd that the sea cucumber is so slighted. ★ For more of and on my books, please see the publicity at the end of the book.

Hearn, Lafcadio: *Goblin Poetry* (in 1905 *Romance of the Milky Way*). With scores of poems from Tenmei Rôjin (Takumi Jingoro), i.e., Tenmei (era) Elder ed. *Kyôka Hyaku-Monogatari* 狂歌百怪物語 (1853) translated, this was not only the first introduction of *kyôka* in English but the largest selection Englished until this book (unless scores of Ryôkan's poems translated might be called *kyôka*, but I have not seen them to judge) – with the exception of art books of surimono (luxurious prints+kyôka) I learned of so late I had to insert this qualification – Hearn knew he was breaking new ground and defined it well:

> The word "kyoka" is written with a Chinese character signifying "insane" or "crazy"; and it means a particular and extraordinary variety of comic poetry. The form is that of the classic *tanka* of thirty-one syllables (arranged 57577); — but the subjects are always the extreme reverse of classical; and the artistic effects depend upon methods of verbal jugglery which cannot be explained without the help of numerous examples. The collection published by Takumi includes a good deal of matter in which a Western reader can discover no merit; but the best of it has a distinctly grotesque quality that reminds one of Hood's weird cleverness in playing with grim subjects [♪Hearn is right. See the Thomas Hood cartoons+captions in my book demonstrating composite translation, *A Dolphin In the Woods* (2009).] This quality, and the peculiar Japanese method of mingling the playful with the terrific, can be suggested and explained only by reproducing in Romaji the texts of various kyoka, with translations and notes. The selection which I have made should prove interesting, not merely because it will introduce the reader to a class of Japanese poetry about which little or nothing has yet been written in English, but much more because it will afford some glimpses of a supernatural world which still remains for the most part unexplored. Without knowledge of Far Eastern superstitions and folk-tales, no real understanding of Japanese fiction or drama or poetry will ever become possible."

Hearn also writes

> "From a prefatory note, it appears that Takumi Jingoro published his collection with the hope of reviving interest in a once popular kind of poetry which had fallen into neglect before the middle of the century."

Judging from the examples Hearn gives, there are *some* puns, but they seldom match the wilder *waka*, much less the wild conceptual play of good Tenmei era *kyôka* which made the form so popular. But that may be because Hearn selected for easy translation, so I will withhold judgment on the original until I read it. Like most translators, but more openly, Hearn did not attempt to translate the poems as poems, and uses brackets to indicate that. He also admits to omitting *kyôka* "dealing with fancies too gruesome for Western nerves . . . also those treating of merely local tradition." (Thanks to Google Books + Univ. of California for access to *Goblin Poetry* via Lafcadio Hearn's Writings ed. by Elizabeth Bisland)

Hein, Piet. ***Grooks.*** *All of his collections* (generally "with the assistance of Jens Arup") embody the mind of the conceptual *kyôka*. They were popular in the late-60's and early 70's in English, but are timeless and should still be in every library and bookstore. (See Piet Hein in the Poet Bios, as I dub him an honorary *kyôka* poet). In Luis Untermeyer's words, Hein has "almost miraculous genius for uttering large thoughts in the most condensed space." If you go for logical humor as rhymed epigram, you cannot do better.

Hoffman, Yoel. *Japanese Death Poems – Written by Zen Monks and Haiku Poets on the Verge of Death.* Charles E. Tuttle Company. 1986. This book contains more *kyôka* than any other (excluding *surimono*) in English, for most of the 31-syllabet death-poems – many actually included in kyôka anthologies – could be called kyôka, yet only a couple are so recognized ("a *kyôka*, a satirical tanka" for a poem by Sengai; "a *kyôka* death poem" for one by Kyoriku). Dying Japanese were so good-humored that this may be the finest book of Japanese humor ever written in English. I may redo some poems or point out things that might have been pointed out were I the author, but please do not interpret that as criticism. When I find a gem I want to polish it, and I do so in the hope the book may be expanded and, where necessary improved, and reprinted many times over.

Horton, H. Mack. ***The Journal of Sôchô.*** Translated and annotated by ~ Stanford University Press, 2002. Most of the link-verse master's poems are not *kyôka* but the journal includes the sort of personal exchanges, poems-as-communication where *kyôka* thrive and there are some good ones. This is the rare translation with sufficient notes. More are on the same page as the text than is usually the case for UP press books, but I wish *all* could be on the same page rather than hidden in the back and wish this university and others would reconsider their editing policies to allow large footnotes. © ***Laughs to Banish Sleep.*** Anrakuan Sakuden: 1628. Part of the Highmoonoon episodic festschrift series for Howard Hibbet. This tiny but fine sampling from a huge book of humor includes some poems I consider *kyôka*. If I can get hold of the original, I may add another chapter for it! Or, I would be honored if Horton would, for he is the rare translator willing and able to re-create the wit otherwise lost in translation. (As it turned out, I found 100's of *kyôka* from *Seisuishô* in *Broadview* v.2, & added some chapters myself, albeit sans conte.)

Keene, Donald, ***World Within Walls:*** Japanese Literature of the Pre-modern Era, 1600-1867. Columbia University Press, 1999. The most thorough (though limited) history of *kyôka* I have seen in English. While the perspective is stereotypical, the sort of thing a Japanese scholar of classical literature who knew little about *kyôka* might write, it is well done, for Keene *is* always keen. Unfortunately, the stereotypes are about as far from reality as any stereotypes I know. *Compare the Teitoku and Yûchôrô you have come to know in this book with Keene's disparaging words about them* – and that, despite giving a large chapter to Teitoku, whose talent in every field of letters he intermittently peed on * (Keene's attitude being, he was the leading man of letters for half a century, so I must, *sigh!* give him all this space) – and compare the breadth of poetic device you have found here (even in the Tenmei period, alone) with Keene's idea of *kyôka* as little more than parody, etc. and . . . .. However, when Keene puts *kyôka* into a broader perspective, sometimes, I wonder if I do not over-rate it. To wit, *"Kyôka was a minor form of poetry, but considering how little humor there is in Japanese literature, we should be grateful for the work of some gifted poets who occasionally approached the realm of genuine comic art."* Reading this, half of me thinks of the razor-sharp wit of Seishônagon and the hyper-logical play born of the editorial surrealism in Edo. That half of me says *Keene has lost it.* On the other hand, when I read passages such as the following two from Butler's

Hudibras, I, too, feel myself almost sharing Keene's judgment. There is no question that English poets *have* scaled commanding heights of humor.

As beards the nearer that they tend
To th' earth still grow more reverend;
And cannons shoot the higher pitches,
The lower we let down their breeches;
I'll make this low dejected fate   265
Advance me to a greater height.

Hold, hold, quoth she; no more of this,
Sir Knight; you take your aim amiss:
For you will find it a hard chapter   585
To catch me with poetic rapture,
In which your mastery of art
Doth shew itself, and not your heart:
Nor will you raise in mine combustion
By dint of high heroic fustian.   590 [*fustian*, a sort of pummeling doggerel]
She that with poetry is won,
Is but a desk to write upon;
And what men say of her, they mean
No more than on the thing they lean.   A Million Thanks to the Gutenberg Project!

The first is exactly *kyôka* in spirit, but includes two full metaphors, whereas a *kyôka* could only fit one. The second is indeed a whit too long for Japanese poetry. It would need to be put into witty *prose*, peppered by witty poems boiling it down to 31 syllabets (I have no idea how much prose+poem comic literature is out there. Has anyone really looked?). Who in Japan/ese could created anything like the finely knit wit of our "Will to boot and Will in overplus" (his word) with his sonnets? And, proceeding from the Bard to the Dean, could any Japanese ape Ovid and wax both logically and lyrically for over a page to end up with *"Caelia shits!"*? I imagine Keene's capacious cranium has a large storehouse of Occidental "genuine comic art" – and judges Japanese by comparison to it, while mine, lacking capacity, must pretty much forget English wit to find room for the Japanese, which is more than abundant enough to fill it. So, who am I, with my limited memory and absent library, to doubt him? But, let me say this. Seeing the "episodic festschrift," a series of tiny books translating short work or selections of Edo avant-garde literature, to celebrate the career of Howard S. Hibbett compiled by John Solt and published by his highmoonoon press, it is obvious that *we have barely scratched the surface of Japanese humor*. It may well be that Japan boasts more not less "genuine comic art" that a comparative-sized culture in the West. If a few of the booklets in that series were expanded (not just commentary, but more material translated) and more books on supposedly "minor" popular genre – eg. my dirty senryû (*The Woman Without a Hole*), Adam L. Kern's Edo era literary comics, (*Manga from the Floating World: Comicbook Culture and the Kibyôshi of Edo Japan*. Harvard University Asia Center, 2006.), etc. – we might be able to not only prove Keene wrong, but convince ourselves of it.

★ What I mean when I say Keene *pees* on Teitoku is this: his *haikai* "provides so few flashes of insight or emotion;" his *waka* and *renga* are "depressingly bland and lacking in character;" his prose "gives little pleasure;" his *kyôka* "lacking the sharpness or bite of true wit, consist mainly of ponderous plays on words or frivolous references to the classics;" his "heavy-handed drollery did not suit the genius of *kyôka*;" and "Teitoku failed as a poet." As a Teitoku fan (until recently I thought I was his *only* fan, but the playful haiku poet Tsubouchi Nenten gave a talk to members of his Sendan, or flotilla, that praised, or rather, rehabilitated Teitoku in 2008), I cannot help but feel like retaliating with "Keene failed as a critic." By the way, Keene, quoting a Japanese scholar, called *kibyôshi* "glorified comic books for adults" and claimed "these writings, despite the education of the authors, are almost totally lacking in intellectual content. Readers today seldom find *gesaku* fiction satisfying, even if they can admire the deftness of the style, or the lighthearted humor." I quote from the introduction to Kern's above-noted book. It would seem that if a critic is not favorable to light humor, his disfavor may spread equally between poetry and prose.

Kenney, James A. See Utamarô in Bios

McKee, Daniel. *Colored in the Year's New Light: Surimono from the Becker Collection.* Johnson Museum of Art, Cornell:2008. And *Japanese poetry prints : surimono from the Schoff Collection* Herbert F. Johnson Museum of Art 2006. Please read what I wrote about John T. Carpenter's book for most applies to these, too. In fact, when I wrote Carpenter, he told me about his work. Recalling McKee's ebullient introduction to *asobie,* play or trick drawings – stumbled upon googling – I thought if that translated to poetry, my scholar friend's assumption that I was the only person who could do *kyôka* justice might be wrong. That turned out not to be the case, but, wow! McKee did a beautiful job of introducing the Japanese New Year Season, directly or indirectly the subject of most surimono, and analyzing the world of commissioning *surimono* with particular attention paid to Magao, and translated and explains hundreds of poems. While he sometimes over-writes in the manner of all brilliant young scholars,

In keeping with the bright and reverent tone of this sacred season, in which heightened consciousness of the present as freshly reborn materiality collided with a profound sense of stasis and eternity, New Year kyôka surimono made a game of linking, through layers of words and images, the contingent forms and figures of the moment to those transformed into timeless icon and archetype in cultural memory . . . . . .

his prose at its best is scintillating and he likes ideas. The following, from the acknowledgment, explaining why the "direct and indirect assistance of many" was needed, deserves attention –

"catalogues of collections are often looked down upon as the poor cousins of monographs, but in many respects present a much greater challenge to their authors, as well as a more objective representation of a given field. Rather than working with a chosen set of materials, largely already mastered and selected toward a given end, the cataloguer of a collection is faced with a group of predetermined objects covering a variety of areas, which must somehow be incorporated into a meaningful whole."

Exactly. I think it explains why his and Carpenter's art books may be the best introduction to *kyôka* in English that we have up to this book, *Mad In Translation*. The poems are, however, arranged by broad thematic categories rather than artist –

Time: picture calendars, zodiac, seasons, meanings of spring, exorcisms, . . . Place: poetic places, travel, landscapes, famous goods, . . . Entity: Commoners, Warriors, . . . Celebrities, Nature and Animals, Evocative Objects . . .

which makes for better reading than Carpenter's *Reading Surimono*, arranged by artist. On the other hand, there is no index like RS and perhaps a few more errors, but I was absolutely delighted with his *attitude* toward them and what we can do about them (see the note on pg.___). I would only add that online Errata should also become part of all books with any pretension to intellectual content. If any university presses have them, I do not know of it. *All* should. I seldom read books of translation that do not contain errors and, with the internet there is no excuse for not having corrections easily available. Carpenter has expressed interest to do just that for Carpenter: 2008. And, on a separate note, I would like both authors or publishers to post a few sample pictures+translation+ explanations on-line so more people can see what fine things in literature are going on. And, let me add that Carpenter and McKee's books have large bibliographies of surimono books that taken together mean that thousands of *kyôka* have been introduced!

Satchell, Thomas. See Ikku (Jippensha Ikku) in Bios.

Sato, Hiroaki and Burton Watson. *From the Country of Eight Islands: An Anthology of Japanese Poetry.* Columbia University Press, 1986. This book I searched for because the *kyôka* introduced by Shirane were translated by Watson was a bit too tightly guarded at Googlebooks for me to see enough to judge it. I did learn it had only nine *kyôka,* and saw two. One gave me a shock. *"Dawn Cherries"* by Hezutsu Tôsaku 1726-1789. *"On* *the crest of the hill, / 'Cherry blossoms!' / 'No, no – clouds!' / till the dawn sun rose up / to squelch the argument."* The "squelch" is mad indeed; but the shock came when I opened *Cherry Blossom Epiphany* (2007), to check *my* translation of this poem I recalled doing, and . . . it was not there (circumstances kept me moving so things got lost). Googlebooks rules did not allow me to see the explanation (if it *was*), but plenty more about what the above *kyôka* makes fun of may be found in the *Cloud* chapter of CBE!

Shirane, Haruo and James Brandon, *Early Modern Japanese Literature: An Anthology, 1600-1900.* Columbia University Press, 2002. While not so detailed as Keene, neither is it so prejudiced. Shirane does not put down *kyôka* and notes how popular narratives included it; but he still introduces less than a dozen, mostly borrowed from Burton Watson, and such neglect indirectly suggests a lack of appreciation for the importance of the B-side of 31-syllabet poetry – that this wild *waka* comprised the lion's share of 31-syllabet poetry in the 16 or 19c – or an unwillingness to attempt the translation of wit. Or, I think too much. The reason may be more simply that. Shirane did more gathering than translating and the material was just not yet out there in English. In that case, I hereby give my permission for a dozen, or if so desired, a score of *kyôka* from this book and an equal number of dirty *senryû* from my book on that subject. If I had a copy of this book at hand, I might have refered to it more, but I only glimpsed at parts at Googlebooks.

Takanashi, Hiroko. *Orthographic puns: The case of Japanese kyoka.* International Journal of Humor Research. Volume 20, Issue 3, Pages 235–259. *The paper proposes a cognitive model for processing humor in puns written in kanji (logographs) and kana (phonographs) in kyoka* and *shows how kyoka poets manipulate the use of kanji and kana orthography to trick their readers in different ways, directing readers to different processing routes of kanji and kana puns.* (from abstract). The process of understanding half a dozen or so *kyôka* details her argument. More information is in the notes to the chapter on Bokuyô as it was too arcane to be put into the main text, but still interesting.

Tanaka, Rokuo: "Forgotten Women: Two Kyôka Poets of the Temmei Era" in Jessica Milner Davis ed. *Understanding Humor in Japan.* Wayne State University Press, 2006. * While focusing on two top Tenmei era female kyôka poets – note: no one has ever written up any *male* ones (since the 1980's gender trumps everything for getting things published) – this is by far the best writing on *kyôka* I know, and I only wish it were a book rather than a chapter in one. You saw the lead quote. More: "The basic technique of *kyôka* composition is the skillful use of literary allusion to create an exquisite subterfuge, . . . poetical devices such as *kakekotoba* (掛詞 pivot words), *engo* (縁語 intertextually associated words), and *mitate* (見立 figurative language)." I would not ascribe to every word. Eg. where Tanaka claims *"Kyôka* does not employ the traditional fixed epithets and decorative modifiers (枕詞 *makura kotoba* or pillow words) that were so often integral elements of traditional waka," I would say *kyôka* plays with said elements. But One of the poets (Fushimatsu no Kaka) is a favorite of mine, so I hope a book is in the works. If it is not, some day, I may have to do it. (After writing the above, I wrote Rokuo, with whom I had exchanged some letters prior to my interest in *kyôka,* and received an automated reply: he passed away in December of 2006. As my pc more or less simultaneously destroyed itself (ms-update+mcafee+hughes-satellite-software clash?) and, being stuck in the country, it took months to get up and running again, I had missed announcements of his death. I also just learned he was "old." I thought he was middle-aged if that, for his words were youthful. *Damn!*

* I note that Tanaka also did a thesis on an old *kyôka* anthology about *shokunin* craftsman/workers that I have not seen, as I have not seen a thesis just googled upon in an art history course syllabus that seems even more interesting: "The Mock One Hundred Poets" in word and image: Parody, satire, and mitate in seventeenth-century comic poetry (kyoka) . . . MacDonald, Ian McCullough Stanford University Ph.D. 2005, etc.).

Thomas, Roger K. *Macroscopic vs. Microscopic: Spatial Sensibilities in Waka of the Bakumatsu Period.* 1998 Harvard-Yenching Institute. As explained in more detail elsewhere, I learned more of the debate about what is natural or native and how that related to the language of *waka* from Thomas.

~~~~~~

Ueda, Makoto. *Bashô and His Interpreters.* Stanford University Press 1992. I have quoted only a little from this book but still introduce it *as it is the only book of translated haiku I know other than mine that provides sufficient interpretation to give readers an idea of what goes on in the heads of those who read Japanese haiku in the original* (now I would add the *surimono* books of Carpenter and McKee, though, for me, Ueda's multiple perspective makes it the only one I can recommend without a single reservation to *all* readers. It incidently demonstrates that the multiple readings I bring to poems, while unprecedented, perhaps, from one person – most people have minds that settle on single readings – represent the way poems are read collectively. As such, you may consider it as evidence, or a sort of antedated appendix to my books (笑). I only learned of Ueda's book when dear late William Higginson used it for evidence my multiple readings were valid in a *Modern Haiku* review of *Rise, Ye Sea Slugs!* in 2004.

~~~~~~

Utamarô: *A Chorus of Birds* (momochidori kyôka awase 1790), intro. Julia Meech-Pekarik, note on kyôka and transl. James A Kenney (The Metropolitan Museum of Art/Viking Press: 1981). Total 30 kyôka. The translator's brief note on the history and nature of *kyôka*, called "mad verse" is short and sweet. Some of the translations show extraordinarily good sense. Eg. the poem for the second bird, the shrike: *"I feel as if / My heart were shrinking, / Hung to dry / On a withered branch . . . /,"* Kenney is smart for bringing in the "heart," where the original has *"omoi"* or longing. While I did redo a examples not interesting as translated for this book, I would guess the translator had to let the wit go because "too much" explanation was frowned upon. Until the fiction of translation – as opposed to re-creation – between exotic tongues is shown for what it is, such will continue to be the rule rather than the exception.

~~~~~~

Watson, Burton. *Japanese Literature in Chinese.* Columbia UP 1975. I had hoped there would be scores of them, but I could only find a single *kyôshi* (or kyôshi-as-kyôshi, for one finds kyôshi elsewhere, as one finds kyôka elsewhere than where they are presented as such, so there may be a few more going incognito). His example is by Sûkatan who, he guesses, flourished in the early-19c:

> *Part of the roof blown away, rain pours in;*
> *I dive into the closet, hastily — it is tight.*
> *In a low voice, the children ask me, "Papa,*
> *Is the bill collector coming again tonight?"*

Here is Watson's translation: "Part of the roof blown away, rain pouring in, / I crouch down, hastily squeeze into a corner of the closet. / The children in a low voice query their father: / "Is the bill collector coming again tonight?" I tried to restore the rhyme probably found in the original, but unlike Blyth+Hokuseido (or me+paraverse press), Watson – or his press – failed to provide the all-important original, so I stuck close to him. Granted, it was harder back then. Publishers today should give the original or get out of business.

~~~~~~

Watson, Burton. see Sato, for his *kyôka* translations.

~~~~~~

XYZ All the Books or Papers I missed. As my occasional complaints in the text, notes, biblios and bios make obvious, there is more I still need to see – mostly in Japanese – than what I have seen already. If you know of anything I should see in English or Japanese, please do not hesitate to contact me, but remember that I am not near a library, only rarely can use interlibrary loan, cannot buy anything and must beg for handouts (extra papers or books) until my circumstances change. Also, as I prefer to concentrate on sifting out poems I like from large collections in the original so I can myself grasp the measure of the poets and their books and re-creating them in English to nit-picking analysis based upon the opinion and selection of others, my main need is for primary material (in print, though, not script).

Glossary.

Allusive Variation. A common term for *honkadori,* or a poem "taking an original." I prefer to call such take-offs or, more loosely yet, speak of a poem's "playing" or "riffing off" another, because *variation* implies a kinship often not even alluded to.

&. I use ampersands to shorten lines for design reasons; and I do so *without apology* because I want to English a little of the enormous variation of orthography in Japanese.

As-for. One of the ugliest make-do's in the word-to-word gloss, it has long stood for the "wa" following a subject that is *topical*. Sometimes, I abbreviate it "as4." Maybe I should *always* do that just to show it is an awkward device far from the un-Englishable original.

Bloomshade. One of dozens of words I have invented in translation which probably managed to get into this book. Edwin Cranston uses invented words in his translations, too. A few I recall are *everworld* (tokoyo), *tailflower* (obana) and *seapine* (for a type of seaweed so named). Such words should not need a glossary as they should be obvious in context. So, no more are in this glossary.

c.16c, 17c, etc.. I use c for "century" to save space and for the reason explained for the ampersand, 上, to share Japanese-style active reading w/ English-speakers & save space.

Cloudy Marks. See **diacritical marks.**

Diacritical Marks. かがさざしじただはば。 The first, third, fifth, seventh and ninth syllabets, pronounced *ka, sa, shi, ta,* and *ha,* respectively, do not have them. The second, forth, sixth, eighth, and tenth, pronounced *ga, za, ji, da* and *ba,* do. Japanese call them 濁点 *dakuten,* or "clouded/murky-dots" A linguist informs me the former are *unvoiced* and the latter *voiced*. Orthographically speaking, I suppose the か would be an unvoiced が, but such terms make practical sense only with a language where consonants alone cannot be read outloud but only when a vowel is added. With Japanese where the former (ka) is every bit as pronounceable as the latter (ga), They are simply different syllabets, or *mora,* if you prefer to use an established term. I like "glottalization," literally, *tonguing,* better than *voiced,* for the "g" at least has the right feeling. But not all of the dotted letters are tongued. With h (はひふへほ *hahihuheho*) vs. b (ばびぶべぼ *babibubebo*, for example, it is the *lips* that do or do not touch each other. Others are or are not fricative, etc.. As *glotalization* has come to mean *stopped-up,* and as all these letters are by tongue *or* lip *or* palate somewhat touched in passage, it does loosely fit. But comparing *h* and *b* again, while the lips *do* close for the latter, *when they are released it comes out all the more explosively,* so "stopped up" is but part of the sound and not the whole. Personally, I think that *sharp* vs *blunt, crisp* vs *cloudy, muddy* vs *clean, i.e.,* the original Japanese way of thinking about these diacritical marks better reflects both the phonemic changes and the way Japanese actually think of them, so I usually use something like the Japanese expression, eg. *muddy marks,* or the purely physical *diacritical marks*. Common ellipsis of these marks in *waka* vastly increased the possibilities for punning. I had assumed it was for aesthetic reasons alone, but recently was informed by LC that the ambiguity created an pedagogical opportunity for disciples or heirs who would know when to add or not add the diacritical marks. Needless to say, this creates difficulty for reading poems aloud unless they are read twice, once each way. . .

Haikai. 俳諧・誹諧 1) The comic *waka* section with plentiful word-play found in the *Kokinshû* (905) and other such is 誹諧. Note that the 誹 used in the *Kokinshû* is not the usual hai 俳 used for haikai and haiku. This character implies a sharp wit, for it is also a verb, *soshiru,* that means cursing, though together the meaning is more like *kaigyaku,* or kidding 諧謔. Most of the poems in that section are indeed kidding or complaints, either by or to the poet. They are humorous for the same reason blues lyrics are: unless one is trolling with a snag hook, a barb needs bait. 2) *Waka link-verse* of a frivolous (see *mushin*) rather than serious intent, *haikai no renga* 俳諧の連歌. 3) The increasingly outrageous link-verse that gave birth to collections of 17-syllabet stand-alones that eventually became known as haiku. Its 16-17c flowering was full of obscenity, vulgar language and witty associations of great variety that tend to be too detailed, or local to translate while its 17-18c Bashô-school (Shômon) flowering was relatively dry and subtle. While the *renga,* or link-verse element continued, it came to be called simply *haikai.*

Haiku. All 17-syllabet (or close to that) *ku* with a seasonal note. That includes such poems going back to at least to Sôgi in the early 16c. Shiki realized this in the late-19c.

Hiragana. The softly curved ひらがな variety of phonetic *syllabet* as opposed to the sharp-cornered *katakana* カタカナ. Or, here is *hiragana* in *katakana:* ヒラガナ。 And, here is *katakana* in *hiragana:* かたかな。 See *Syllabet,* and Phonetic Syllabary.

Hokku. A word best not used out of a proper linkverse context. Better to call haikai (3) simply haiku, old haiku or just ku, for most in collections of stand-alone *ku* were not meant to be *hokku* (linkverse whole or section lead poems).

Honka. The extant poem partially incorporated into a new one. With *waka* more than one *honka* is rare, but with *kyôka* two *honka* for one poem is not that rare. See "plays with" for the practice of *honkadôri,* or "original-poem-taking," as it is called.

Hundred Poets. Abbrev. of *Hundred Poets One Poem*, the Ogura *Hyakunin Isshu,* basis for the quick-draw card-matching game that made these waka famous & liable to parody.

Hyper-logical. Without humor, Burke's judgment on Paine (*dat operam ut cum ratione insaniat:* he labors to make his mind unsound by means of his reason) might apply. With humor, the same might be considered therapy. Metaphysical madness?

Japanese style. This, one of my Humpty-Dumpty words, means a poem that is nothing but a chain of modification of the subject that brings the poem to a head at the end, or, has only one verb or emphatic expression after said subject confirming it as the subject that does not supply what is missing according to the conventions of all other world poetry that I know of: namely, *a plot*. This peculiar style is found equally in waka, kyôka and haiku. The Korean essayist Lee Oh Young came close to noticing this style when, in the context of his book on Japan as a culture of miniaturization (縮み志向の日本 1982), he took up tanka with a string of の *no* that took something large down to something small one possessive の no at a time. But, not just *no,* even the verbs which actively still double for gerunds make these chains of modification, and what is interesting is that such could by itself be considered a poem. Perhaps it can be seen as an extension ad absurdum of the *makura-kotoba* = pillow-word, or epithet, or *jo,* a longer preliminary part of the poem that may pun its way into the main message. I await the guidance of linguists as to what I should call this phenomenon that is invisible in translation as translators rewrite the poems giving them plots, not necessarily on purpose but because attempts to match the word order rather than reproduce the connections result in that!

Kakekotoba See **Pivot Word** and **Pun**

Kango 漢語 A word made of two or more characters pronounced in a more or less Chinese (as our "interest" is more or less Latin) way. Conventional *waka* used few of them, *haikai* and *kyôka,* often use them to good effect – they permit new concepts to be compactly expressed, liven up (alter) the syncopation of the poem, serve as a visual stereo for what is really pronounced in the old Japanese manner, etc.

Kamigata kyôka 上方狂歌*.* I try not to use this term for the 16-18 c *kyôka* of Kyôto and thereabouts (including Ôsaka that was near to it compared to Edo and therefor "up," too). Likewise for the later word for greater Ôsaka, *Naniwa,* for this is a general book.

Katakana. カタカナ The stiff-looking phonetic letters, or syllabets, as opposed to the soft *hiragana*. Today is generally used for phonetic rendering of foreign and scientific names. See *phonetic syllabary, syllabets,* and *hiragana*.

Kokkei Haiku 滑稽俳句. Something *kokkei* is "novel" or "outlandish." Some call all such haiku *senryû*, but traditional *senryû* tends to be third-person black-humor playing stereotypes, while the droll but occasionally exhilarating wit scattered throughout classic haiku – most of these *ku* are not *hokku* (lead *ku* in link-verse jams), so I deliberately call them *haiku* – casts a much wider net. Such haiku, I call *kyôku*, are generally *ignored*, which is to say not selected from the original work for haiku anthologies, because their editors love haiku proper, nor for *kyôka* anthologies, because the editors, appreciating their own, do not seek 31-syllabet link-verse *haikai*, much less 17-syllabet examples. The happy exception is the *Kokkei Haiku Daizen* 滑稽俳句大全, a selection by Katô Ikuya 加藤郁乎. I confess to being both sad and happy find it, for I thought I was the only person who collected such (thousands are mixed in with the *ku* categorized by hundreds of seasonal themes in tiny hand-made filing envelopes in a cardboard box I live in fear of losing). I do not, however, separate them from other haiku: you will find hundreds naturally mixing here and there in my books with thousands of translated sea-cucumber, cherry blossom, fly and New Year's *ku*. We would not want too many novelty songs in country music or too many haiku to be mad, but *kyôku* should not be ignored, or worse, put down. They keep us on our toes and improve our relationship with the more standard stuff.

Ku. 句   Either short for haiku and other 17-syllabet poems (*senryû* or *zappai*, too), or a phrase, especially the 5 or 7-syllabet segments of a 17 or 31-syllabet poem. For the latter usage, a *ku* functions something like the numbered line in English poetry for the practical purpose of locating what one is referring to. It is also used for expressions counting 一句、二句 or modifying 佳句(a good ku/ 駄句(a poor = one's own = ku) haiku, or types of haiku in haikai such as 発句 *hokku* (first ku in a link-verse session) 平句 hiraku (ordinary *ku*), etc.

Kubi 首, also **shu**, is one of two counters for **waka** and means a separate "head." 一首 *isshu* would be "one waka," 百首 *hyakushu* would be a *hundred waka*.

Kyôka 狂歌, or mad poem. Formally resembles the most common form of *waka*, the *tanka*, in being stand-alone 31-syllabet(*mora*) in length, ideally pausing or breaking into 5-7-5-7-7 segments, but rarely as completely as lines do in English poetry except at the 17-14 division, with the last 5-syllabets of the first half often becoming the first part of what follows retroactively, by assuming a meaning different from what it did before the last part was reached (see *pivot*), but *kyôka* with no breaks to speak of, link-verse-like major 14-17 breaks or breaks in odd places are not rare (statistics next edition?). The position of the pivot likewise varies but favors the last 7 syllabets to set up a one-word snapper (punch-word, not *line*) where the comic effect is greater. While *kyôka* may be serious, coming straight from the heart, as poetry written and read for the sheer joy of it, lightness is the rule. If laughter is indeed good medicine, this "no-heart" (*mushin*) poetry can, paradoxically be better for said organ than the "have heart" (*ushin*) variety favored by generations of haute culture. Word-play helps keep us where wit would have us, on our toes; but the best sign of a *kyôka* is its freedom of terms and themes as mentioned by Aston and Kaneko. I would call it poetry that pursues logic wherever it might go.

Kyôku, 狂句or **mad haiku.** *Senryû* that are for whatever reason not *senryû* may be called *zappai*, or sundry (17-syllabet), i.e., not inferior, but different, *hai*/comic-verse. So, I reject *kyôku* being used for *senryû* – something started by the 4th generation Senryû四世川柳in a shameless attempt to requisition the character 狂 after *kyôka* made it popular – in favor of that Bashô suggested by so captioning his greeting to his hosts in Nagoya: *Come with the gale, / Look at me, as blustery / as Chikusai!* (*kogarashi no mi wa chikusai ni nitaru kana*). The antihero of a 17c comic novel, a quack doctor from Kyoto who heads to Edo composing *kyôka* on the way, Chikusai had arrived in Nagoya with clothes in tatters (see Shirane for the better written summary I rob and a standard translation) . . . Bashô uses the term *kyôku* hoping others will follow suit and have fun. I use it for comic haiku that some, not knowing classic *senryû*, consider *senryû*, when they are actually 17-syllabet *kyôka* that Bashô, too, might have called *kyôku*.

Kyôshi, 狂詩 or **mad Chinese-style poem.** 詩 or poem is used to indicate pretty much all non-Japanese, usually rhyming poetry, but since the mad poets of Japanese did not write poems in Roman letters, but only in characters, *kyôshi* means Chinese-style. The most common form is 4-line with an AABA end-rhyme, but unlike the case with *kyôka,* any number of lines and rhyme schemes (including no rhyme) were permissable. I argued elsewhere that the form, style and content, may be credited to Ikkyû and other mad monks, but it is a matter of degree. Ôta Nampo, still in his teens, did loosen it up further, sparking the exploration of a broader range of subject matter.

Mad-cap poem. Don't ask me why but it doesn't sound right, so it is rarely used.

Mad-cap verse. Used by Steven D. Carter and some others, I suppose the "-cap" does help by communicating the eccentric nature of the poem more clearly than "mad" alone. Despite my frequent resort to rhyme, I do not care to call unrhymed and unmetered poetry "verse," so I *tried* not to use the term though, liking it, I may have occasionally.

Mad poems. *The Princeton Companion to Japanese Literature* calls *kyôka* or *kyôku,* "mad poems" and defines them as "*waka* with a humorous or witty cast of language or thought," intended for a mass audience. The use of *"kyôku"* (see above) for *kyôka* is, or was occasionally seen in Japan, but should, in my opinion, be reserved for *kyôka*-like haiku, *i.e.* 17-syllabet *ku* which at present, do not have a name but are occasionally described as *kokkei ku* (see above). "Mad poems" seems the simplest term as just plain "comic" will not do when we have other varieties of comic poetry in Japanese as well. If it must be explained, so be it. Most Japanese also need an explanation.

Makura. See *pillow word.*

Mimesis. I use this word and *mimetic* a lot. *Onomatopoeia* is too semantically too small and alphabetically too large. Japanese has less built-in mimesis than English (eg. *stop, shrimp*) but more functioning obviously as adverbs.

Muddy Marks. See **Diacritical Marks.**

Mushin. 無心。Literally "no-heart/mind/feelings." A disinterested poem, composed for the fun of it as purely decorative art might be. The type equated (too simply in the author's opinion) with *kyôka*. The Kurinomoto party, or poets under the proverbial chestnut tree. Light verse as opposed to the serious stuff.

Naniwa kyôka. The first major popularization of *kyôka* as a movement of poetry in the greater Ôsaka area. Peaks under Teiryû's tutelage.

Nativists. The leading nativist – with respect to language and the spirit or worth of humans, a cultural chauvinist – Motoori Norinaga was also the leading student of ancient literature and *waka,* which he believed embodied the spirit of the godly people of old and manifested the word-soul. His influence over generations of historians and literary critics was not all bad – deep study of ancient literature does bring benefit – but by stressing purity and sincerity alone, I am afraid he and his followers not only did not revive but helped bury what drew *me* to ancient Japanese poetry, the humor. If you think me unfair please send a short apologia for Norinaga that I may add to the next edition.

Phonetic Syllabary. In *Oriental Humour*, Blyth gave examples of fine Chinese puns, but it seems to me that the mixture of a phonetic syllabary and the Chinese character (*kanji* in Japanese) in Japanese allows more versatile punning than possible for any single sign writing system. In English, only someone who can use sign language yet still speak and hear can truly appreciate the stereo effect Japanese readers may enjoy. With just that phonetic syllabary, however, Japanese can be very hard to read because words are not separated into neat clusters as in English. If you read Japanese, look up the chapter of Lady Ise's poems and you should see what I mean. As old *waka* are often written in phonetic syllabary alone (and that is all Nichibun supplies for some that actually *did* and *should* include Chinese characters), I was often at a loss for reading them and had to trouble my respondent to confirm (or throw out) my guesses. I wrote a couple *kyôka* of my own to express my feelings on that matter (see pg. 590).

Pillow word, *makura kotoba*. An epithet usually attached to a place, which may be used in full, in part, or not at all, but evoked by said place-name, which, itself may be skipped as obvious if that pillow is used. In *kyôka*, they most commonly evoke a desired mood, or ridiculously contradict it and set up the pivot or some other pun on the name.

Pivot word. A common Englishing for *kakekotoba* 掛詞, a sleight of tongue so common in waka – even one's not considered particularly witty or comic, much like rhyme is not limited to light-verse – that some even make it de rigor. Cranston defines it with a word I am unfamiliar with: "A form of zeugma in which a set of syllables functions in two senses through an exploitation of homophony, or in which the same word serves double syntactical functions." It is one of the many varieties of puns in Japanese that may be exquisitely elegant or so ridiculous that we must groan not in disgust but admiration. In these, a word or part of a word is used in two senses, one that goes with what precedes, the other with what follows. Aston, who credits Chamberlain with the term, gives a droll English example: "Thackeray has something of the kind in *The Newcomes*, where he speaks of the tea-pot presented to Mr. Honeyman by the devotees attending his chapel as the *'devotea-pot.'* Here, the syllable 'tea' is contrived a double debt to pay. It represents at the same time the final syllable of 'devotee' and the first syllable of 'tea-pot.' " Expand that before and after and you have it. Still, not all *kakekotoba* pivot and not all pivot words pun. We might also call *kakekotoba* a "contingent word," as its meaning is contingent upon context and not always only with what preceded it, then what follows it, as is the case for the pivot-word.

Plagiarism. See **Plays With** and **Honkadôri**. Phrases recognized to be from other poems broaden the allusions or add to the information that may be crammed into one poem. We see *kyôka* with but one letter changed from the original. As the wit of such a poem depends upon the original being known, there is no intent to deceive. Hence, despite old and not so old poem-parts everywhere, plagiary is nowhere in the picture here.

Plays With. I use these words often where Japanese might use the verb *kasuru*, or "brush against" or we might loosely say "parody" though no true parody was intended and the poet was merely using parts of another poem for fun. I do *not* use the proper Japanese word *honka* that Cranston translates and defines as "a 'base-poem' whose phrases are reworked into a later poem in a major and persistent form of intertextuality." Japanese poetry is so full of appropriation, allusion, take-off and parody that a word was needed for the poem that was mis/used in one way or another. "Original" rarely works, for the poems using it are not different versions of the same. "A source" is a bit better.

Puns. A pun is a word read in context more than one way, phonologically or semantically. Potential puns abound in Japanese because of the relatively small number of phonemes increasing the probability of homophones and they are further vastly increased in premodern written Japanese by a tendency to forbear the use of the diacritical marks (*nigoriten*=cloudy-marks) diffentiating k, s, t, ch, and h sounds from g, z, d, j and b/p. The large, large number of possible orthographies for any particular word allows for one or the other possibility to be weighted, influencing the order in which the meanings are read. See my discussion of Hiroko Takanashi's article (pg. 356, 563-8). Furthermore, a character may save a pun otherwise almost certainly overlooked. Lewis Cook, explaining why he restored to the Virginia Text Initiative's online *Kokinshû* some of the characters removed by previous editors, notes that *matsu* in poem #777, which had been rendered まつ, was 松 ("pine tree") in the original even though its primary meaning was indisputably the verb 待つ ("to wait"), because the editor, "Teika was deliberately using *kanji* rather than *kana* to leave open the possibility of reading puns, in this instance a pun on "pine tree" behind the verb." This *pine*, syntactically dead wood, adds to the overall picture, as it allusively joins the lonesome fall wind later in the poem. Sometimes, the use of the character was gratuitous and removing it no loss, but "there is room for debate, however, and I have tried to consistently err on the side of caution, leaving Teika's kanji intact in many cases where the Shinpen Kokka Taikan editors for example replace them with kana." I would say *amen* to that, and more rudely give my opinion that the editors, as moderns, tend to hate inconsistency and fail to appreciate how it enables wit not only directly, but indirectly by keeping us on our toes. Even more care is required with the diacritical marks, for the presence or absence of the Chinese character cannot rule out a homophonic pun, while settling the pronunciation kills the possibility of a pun based on pseudo-homophony. Great stylistic variety helps make Japanese puns, like our rhymes, high, low and in-between. Some painfully crawl, some skip and some soar. I would hope to find a typology of Japanese puns (at least a dozen, maybe a score). If I do not find a good one, and no one else promises to get one done – by all means, take advantage of this book, so full of examples – I *will*. As most Japanese are no more aware of how much they take for granted – compared to English, for example – in their own largely pun-aided wit than most of us are with respect to the contributions of rhyme to ours, I would think such an analysis might come from without, but I also get the impression that because the Japanese themselves tend to look down on cleverness in poetry, foreign scholars more adaptable (*sunao*) than yours truly, pick up that attitude.

Respondent. As explained in the acknowledgement, mostly Yoshioka Ikuo, who is trying to comprehend the history of waka with its wit, which means carefully studying *kyôka*. Here is the 帯文 blurb for his book 草食獣（吉岡生夫第四歌集）by essayist (謎の歌集／百人一首 — その構造と成立) and 日本笑い学会理事, 織田正吉：

和歌における新古今集、俳諧における芭蕉。日本の伝統詩は笑いを排除し、隔離することによって芸術的完成を遂げたとみなしてきた。敷島のやまとの国びとは、和歌・狂歌の歴史的分裂関係を今にひきずり、短歌から笑いの排除をつづける。それで現代の感性を詠むことは可能なのか。吉岡生夫は実作によってその疑問を呈する。

Readers are invited to visit and/or contribute to Yoshioka's growing *kyôka* website which examines poems from the various books in *Kyôka Taikan* and provides supplemental information (especially dates and pronunciations). It is a blog so comments are possible.

Rhyme. Unless otherwise indicated, end-rhyme that goes with mad poems in English as surely as puns do in Japanese. I would guess that today most mad poetry in English is by scientists who 1) know that there is plenty of rhyme and other formal restriction in nature and appreciate how that stimulates rather than destroys creativity and 2) are unashamed to really think things through, which makes them hyperlogical fools or wisemen unlike the layman who reins in his or her brains and stops short. Most books of scientific humor show that scientists, unlike most in the humanities who, striving to be the complete captains of their poems, switched to the reliable engine of "free" verse, kept raising the sails of rhyme happy to go with the fickle wind of words – in another book, I quote Hudibras on rhyme and reason taking turns at the tiller; this is a new metaphor as far as I know. Madness in the *kyôka* sense of it, means being humble enough to allow coincidence to have a chance. In Japanese, puns are so easy that anyone creative could make a poem like, say, the following, but better.

♪ *For Melons To Make the Most of Time* ♪

Can't elope? But Katy did, so, please, Honey, do try!
Soon your musk will turn to dust; the birds and bees will fly!

By the way, I once saw rhymed 31-syllabet Japanese poems in a book by Buson, Yayû or Kyoroku. I vaguely recall *kaki* persimmon vs *kaki* oysters and roasted sparrows and their metamorphosis. It may have been in the Shueisha series. It was pegged on to *haibun* or a *saijiki* or something. If you love rhyme, read fast, have access to a good Japanese library and time to waste, I would be very grateful if you could locate these for me!

Savage/Barbarian Songs. 夷曲 Ikyoku. The first great *kyôka* anthology was called the *Kokinikyoku-shû*, or the Ancient (&) Recent *Savage Song* Anthology." Though all previous translations of the title make it *Barbarian,* I favor *"savage"* because 夷 meant a comparatively primitive people without a written language such as the poncho wearing Japanese to the Chinese and, later, the Ainu to the Japanese, while *barbarians* are other, differently civilized people. Also, many of the poems have a savage touch providing good contrast to the sophisticated Tenmei kyôka. Sometimes 夷歌 is used. It may be pronounced either *ebisu uta* or (as *ateji*) *hinaburi,* or "rustic style." as well as *ika* 夷歌.

Senryû. Poems 17-syllabet, like haiku (or shorter, if *Mutamagawa* egs. are included) that largely develop black humor (third-person by implication) stereotypes about life, culture, and things, including types of people. A large portion is bawdy, or obscene and the only full introduction to *that* is my book, in the bibliography under *Octopussy*. It provided an outlet for the part of *haikai* excluded by the Shômon, or Bashô school haiku.

Surimono. 摺物 Literally, block-printed matter. Mostly sumptuous color prints or small set of prints with one to a dozen *kyôka* presented by the commissioner, usually the head of a *kyôka* group to students and patrons for the New Year, a season so rich in ritual as to constitute a season separate but equal to the other four, as elaborated in *The Fifth Season* (2007). The 17c Teitoku school *haikai* poets started the tradition and Ôta and friends improved upon it in the late-18c with the involvement of top artists. Like beautiful women, beautiful books generally go to the wealthy who keep them out of sight, so I was unaware of their existence until recently. While most may be thought of as greeting cards for the culturally literate, some had enough prints to fold into small books, such as Utamarô's *Chorus of Birds*. Luckily, I found the museum catalogue books by Carpenter et al and McKee with hundreds of early-19c *surimono* and perhaps a thousand translated *kyôka* in time to give examples and declare that when it comes to *kyôka*, the art presses have published ten or even a hundred times more translations than literary presses. Is it not amusing that in Japan/ese, surimono *kyôka* constitute but a minor part, perhaps 1%, of the vast body of *kyôka,* while in translation they are at least 90%, maybe 99% of the same? It speaks to the least discussed part of the translation process, selection, and that in turn reflects the character of English language translators and publishing houses.

Syllabet. My coinage for the relatively uniform-length Japanese syllable. Resembles what linguists call a *mora*, except that it may be written with a single letter. English syllables tend to be almost fifty-percent longer, so counting them does not, in my opinion (and Blyth's and an increasing number of knowledgeable folk), bring us as close to matching the original feeling as keeping a *waka* translation down to 13-15 beats. I occasionally go a wee bit over in this book (never, with haiku!) because more words permit more otherwise lost information to be translated and simply because 8-syllable 4-beat lines and comic verse go so well together in English that I could not always resist.

Tanka While referring to classic short (31-syllabet) *waka*, because the vast majority of *waka* were short, they were almost always just called *waka* or *uta* (or *ka* for short, or counting, *kubi*), so *tanka* usually means modern *waka* (see below), a less exclusive form than the classic *waka*. As my respondent Yoshioka Ikuo notes, citing passages such as 安田純生は「用語の面のみに着目すると、狂歌は現代の文語体短歌や話しことば調短歌に近いものを有している。少なくとも江戸時代の正統的な和歌より狂歌のほうが、いっそう現代短歌と近い関係にある」（邑書林『現代短歌用語考』1997）と指摘する, *tanka* includes much that would have been considered *kyôka* for most of the past millennium, but as this is generally not recognized, he further notes, the genre is left without a true history. Because frivolity and wordplay is frowned upon in some *tanka* circles, I do not expect all tankaists to love this book, but I would hope others find something to celebrate in the mixed roots of their literature. Take the title of Tawara Machi's 1988 tanka best-seller, サラダ記念日 *Sarada Kinenbi* (Salad Anniversary). Sarada サラダ is obviously modern and Occidental while *kinenbi* is a stiff *kango*, or Chinese word. A few of her poems:

> *Composite me! Every facet split off and fly away, do!*
> *That means all three hundred and sixty five of you!*

我という三百六十五面対ぶんぶん分裂して飛んでゆけ　俵万智

ware to iu sanbyakurokujûgo-mentai bun bun bunretsu shite tondeyuke tawara machi
i-as called threehundredsixtyfive-hedron/sidedpartpart partsplit doing fly-go/leave!

classroom-in each/one-each/one's time fulfilled-is ninety-two eyeballs and i
kyôshitsu ni sore-zore no toki mitashi-oru kyûjûni ko no medama to watashi
教室にそれぞれの時充たしおる九十二個の目玉と私 俵万智

A happy day in the classroom, how time flies
for me and the pupils of ninety two eyes!

面対 *mentai* following 365 (not 360 as a hyperlogical poet might want) in the first poem makes it a geometrical body as surely as a hexahedron or a heptahedron is. *Composite* is my compensation. The *pupils* gain in translation as Japanese lacks that homophony.

天気予報聞きのがしたる一日は雨でも晴れでも腹が立たない 俵万智
tenki yohô kikinogashitaru ichinichi wa ame demo hare demo hara ga tatanai

The Weather Report, well I missed it today,
So rain or shine, I've no cause for dismay!

It tickles me to watch you before it is heard . . .
Groping in the silence to find that right word.

沈黙ののちの言葉を選びおる君のためらいを楽しんでおり　俵万智
chinmoku no nochi no kotoba o erabi-oru kimi no tamerai o tanoshinde ori

Only the last, added for contrast, could never be taken for a *kyôka* and only the weather report seems absolutely so. Without the rhyme and poetic license I take most tanka from *Salad Anniversary* would not be considered mad at all. I must play more with *tanka* to better understand how much of my mad translations are and are not me.

Tenmei Kyôka. The Tenmei era is, strictly speaking 1781~89, when Ôta Nanpo as Yomo-no-Akara et alia published books with high percentages of novel *kyôka* born in the festive, stimulating atmosphere created by a liberal social mixture of samurai, merchants, physicians, monks, townsmen etc. in what was then the world's biggest city, Edo, now Tôkyô. It is the only period of *kyôka* that gets uniformly favorable press. It deserves the appreciation it receives, but as this book shows, interesting *kyôka* always existed and it is a mistake to give Tenmei era Edo a patent on it. Edoites share something with Usanians, a fault Tocqueville described as inferiority-born cultural boastfulness the last flower of which was an "Edo boom" in the last quarter of the 20c when Tokyo ruled and the apparent success of *Japan As Number One* created an atmosphere favorable to crediting all cool things to Edo. I am sympathetic, but leary. Thanks to *Broadview*, I made sure that Kyôto and Ôsakan mad poets got the attention they merit. But, I want to consider the claims made for Edo being special or even superior with respect to *kyôka* more carefully than I have in this book. To do so, I need to read more *kyôka* published and written in the 1750-83 build-up period and 1889-1835 denouement period. Lacking the resources to do so at present, I must withhold judgment. I also want to to look closely at the *editing skill* of Nanpô et alia. As Picasso once said, an artist does not so much need to know what he likes as what he does not. Perhaps, what Nanpô's greatest service was what he *excluded*.

Usania, Usanians. If the reader, like me, spent time as a teenager in Mexico and learned it was Los Estados Unidos de Mexico, or the United States of Mexico, and knew that the super-power to the North was and is begrudged its usurpation of the continental name, an explanation might not be necessary. But first, a poem by Ogden Nash that has the spirit of a *kyôka* and provides an *itoguchi,* or a clue – or at least an associative handle – to take you back to the beginning. I will skip the unappealing title, *Yes-and-No Man:*

> *Poor Manfred, always in bad odor,*
> *Muddled middle-of-the-roader.*
> *Veering Left toward visions bright,*
> *Leftist jargon drives him Right*
> *Until the Rightist hatchet men*
> *Turn him to the left again,*
> *Searching for a category,*
> *Spo-radical and desul-tory.*

The puns in the last line are like Japanese puns, though the Japanese would not need hyphens and might, instead, bring the pun out by syntactically merging it into something, as we have seen and as can not be explained to non-Japanese readers. But *Manfred* is where we shall start. When Nash wrote, only a half-century ago, most educated readers would have immediately applauded his choice of names. Fred, as all would have known, meant *free*. Some "American" history buffs would have gone back long before Groucho's Fredonia (Duck Soup) to an early-19c poem advocating the name Fredonia for this nation of *Fredes*, or free men, because a South American country had already taken the Proper Name we were supposed to adopt: *Columbia*. When Washington Irving inspired the New York Historical Society to do a survey on the adoption of a Proper National Name decades later, the general opinion was that we were already beginning to usurp the continental name and that was to our credit, for we were destined to rule the "miserable" people to our south and, besides, human nature was such that even were we named *Squash* (this from rev. Gilmore Simms), no one would want to change it, etc.. Well, we did come to more or less own the name, but that does not make it *right*. Call me a ridiculous rationalist, but I would say that I was born on a peninsula in *Usania*, part of Turtle Island (supposedly the Amerindian name) the Northern half of the Americas.

Ushin. 有心。 Literally "have-heart/mind/feelings." An interested or truly personal poem, composed to communicate genuine feelings on subjects considered suitable for them. Equated with *waka* of the sort found in Imperial anthologies. The Kakinomoto party, or poets under the proverbial persimmon tree. The serious stuff of haute culture. The only real poetry to those who belittled *mushin* much like classic music lovers who have the gall to write histories of music which only recognize their particular variety.

Uta or ka. 歌, 哥 Short for *waka*, the character broadly means a Japanese poem rather than a Chinese or Chinese style poem. Later, that came to mean a 31-syllabet poem as opposed to a 17-syllabet one. Literally it means "song." *Waka* was once intoned in such a sing-song voice – examples may be found on the internet – that one understand the usage of "song," but I (and most others) usually translate it as "poem," which makes sense for they were generally *read* in a normal voice or silently, and it makes sense to save "song" for poems with the more clearly musical "melody" (*kyoku*) in their name or for lyrics generally sung rather than read, such as those of *kouta* 小唄.

Visual Reading. Usually I mean what the Chinese character nay suggest in contradiction to the phonological reading. **But** Readers may have noticed that I often make a point of mentioning wit that strikes the eyes alone. Yes, I have a chip on my shoulder. To most Occidental readers – excepting 'concrete poetry,' which is, on the whole, as boring as poodle hairstyles or topiary landscaping – the only role for the eyes in poetry is to embrace the poem tucked in a page within fluffy white margins. Otherwise poems are pretty much for the ears. We waste so much of the far greater capability of the eyes, as compared to the ears, to take in information in the case of humans whose radar capacity is dismal compared to that of bats, that a totally blind person might enjoy almost *all* of our poetry. This may be good for the blind – and if I must continue doing 100% of the proof-reading and editing of my own books, that is how I will probably end up (this book is literally making my eyes blur) – but it severely handicaps not only the deaf, who would be happy to see more visual poetry, but all of us. I think that pure literature should take note of the visual aspects of appreciating Japanese poetry and defend the eye, but to date, most defenses have come from people writing about the visual arts. Looking down on

Edo era comics (*kibyôshi*) that are literally crammed with meaning as 'childish' is not all so different as missing the wit born of what might be called orthographical wordplay. Both can be crude, but they can also be every bit as sophisticated as anything appealing to the ears, and bearing in mind the much vaster amount of information that may be taken in, conventional criticism may even have it backwards.

Voiced and Unvoiced Consonants 濁点. See **diacritical marks** and **puns**.

Waka 和歌 All 5-7-syllabet "Japanese-style" (as opposed to Chinese-style) art-poetry mostly written by nobles in a culture of the court (praising or lamenting life/rites and the rulers) and courtship. Most *waka* was 31-syllabet, or "short-song = *tanka*" length, so the 31-syllabet *waka* became synonymous with *waka*, and the word *tanka* only came to be used at the end of the 19c and is generally not used to refer to older poems. In his long introductory essay to *Shokusankashû* 蜀山家集 (1927), the first modern to take a broad view of *kyôka*, Kaneko Jitsue, gave what might be the standard description of *waka*:

> *Waka is serious. It has no place for play. Whether treating nature, love or death, the koto-strings in the poet's heart are taut. . . . . But the Kyôka master is not like that. His attitude toward nature or life is definitely flexible. To put it kindly, he is broad-minded, to put it critically, he lacks sincerity. Waka aim for elegance and a refined aesthetic; kyôka for the comic and vulgar. If the one is aristocratic and old-fashioned, the other is popular and forward-looking.* 和歌は真面目なものである。其処には遊びがない。自然の歌にしろ、恋愛の歌にしろ、悼亡の歌にしろ、作家の胸奥の琴線はピンと張り詰められている。精一杯に秋を鳴く鈴虫の様に、歌人は満腔の熱と力を以て、喜怒哀楽の情を歌ひ出す。けれども狂歌師はさうではない。彼等が自然とか人生とかに対する態度は確に弛緩して居る。善く言へば余裕があるのだが、悪く言へば不真面目である。

Though traditional *waka* were typically written by men who roamed about like Tom cats chasing new loves or visiting their wives, or by the lonely waiting wives, the sentiments are honest enough – desire, love and loneliness do indeed tend to be sincere – but I think there is more wit than Kaneko admitted or most modern readers imagine. Sure, the trope quickly became repetitive, but old saws can make pretty good, even new, tunes if you know how to play them and as *waka* became a poetry of convention, it also became one of competition, out-troping others, which can be followed with interest by a good reader. There is much seasonal/natural motif by English standards, usually fit to romantic concerns (later *haikai* would reverse that vector). And, last but not least, there is so much punning in *waka* that no one considered *kyôka*, one cannot claim that *waka* and *kyôka* differ on the basis of the presence or absence of puns. Indeed, many *waka* in good standing have more puns than many admitted *kyôka* do. One must consider many factors.

Yamato-uta 大和歌 Same as *waka*, but the pronunciation of the characters follows the native Japanese reading and as such seems more like the thing itself, as *waka* used few Chinese–character combination words, unlike *haikai* and *kyôka* which came to mix them in with Japanese words for more a more varied and interesting rhythms (I think) and novel effects at the cost of losing the musical fluidity of the *yamato-uta*. In that sense, they are or old-fashioned *waka*, a far cry from modern *tanka*, with vocabulary once only found in *kyôka*.

Mad Bios of our poets

♪ The bios favor 17c poets because I have read much of their work and can, thus, speak from direct experience about them as poets. And, I have short-changed the canonical Tenmei poets, with the exception of their leader, for the poems in the resources I could afford (used) were almost all written before they were born and I have learned not to judge poets second-hand. Should more resources come my way, or good fortune bring me out of the woods and into a community, each of the major Tenmei poets will get his or her due. If the quality of the work demands it, I might even give them another book. Meanwhile, please make do with this tentative introduction to the stars of this book, would-be stars but for this or that included as a statement of intent, poets included more for their influence than their presence in this book, and even some honorary *kyôka* poets from the Occident!

Akara (*Yomo no Akara*) ⇒ **Shokusanjin**. Ôta Nanpo's early *kyôka* name. Tenmei *kyôka* names were not abbreviated in the earliest books as they were intended to be read whole for their *meaning*, but the most famous sometimes were because Japanese books of poetry usually squeezed in as many poems as they could into a page. In the 19c all the names were sometimes abbreviated to two characters. That is the case with the *Kokin Kyôka Daizen*. Akara's bio is found under his later *kyômei*, Shokusanjin.

Akera (*Akera Kankô*) ⇒ **Kankô**. The first, or family name, is usually not used in abbreviations, but for Kankô it sometimes happens. Take care not to confuse Akera for Akara.

Akinari. 1734-1809. **Ueda Akinari** is best known for his fiction. I still recall my delight to find his rational and relativistic (but far from dispassionate) argument confuting Norinaga's ethnocentric contrast of live and divine Japanese vs. dead and animalistic foreign (Chinese) sounds in *Sources of Japanese Tradition* by Tsunoda, De Bary & Keene, decades ago. It made me think he would write good *kyôka*, so I checked but, alas, found out too late for this book that there is a book of them! 秋成狂歌集 古典文庫299／上田秋成／古典文庫1972 秋成狂歌集／丸山季夫編. 集別名:万葉体狂歌集(安永4年板) ; 海道狂哥合(文化 8 年板). I am particularly interested in the "other title" of his *kyôka* anthology, which is *Manyôshû*-style *kyôka*. The only *kyôka* of his I have seen are of a type we might call diatribe against his nemesis. I found a one more in time to add it here.

しき島のやまと心のなんとかの　うろんな事を又さくら花　秋成
shikishima no yamatogokoro no nantoka no uron na koto o mata sakurahana akinari
archipelgo of yamato-soul's somthngorother's dubious stuff agn bloomschrryblossms

All this crap about the soul of the Isle of Big Peace
Blooming again, good grief! Let those cherries be!

If asked where lies the soul of the Isle of Big Peace,
Mountain cherry blossoms glowing in the rising sun.

archipelgo of yamato-soul+acc person-frm ask-if/whn morn-sun-in glows chrryblssms
shikishima no yamatogokoro o hito ni towaba　asahi ni niou sakurahana norinaga
しき島のやまと心を人間はば　朝日ににほふやまざくら花　宣長

Looking at the originals, you can see that Akinari kept the first two and last one fifth of Norinaga's waka in his angry poem. Akinari has the first part of the *sakurabana,* or cherry blossom work as *saku,* or "bloom" before finishing. Nada Inada, in whose book, these were found, was amazed that Akinari could be so down on his nemesis years after he died, but I think the "again" makes it clear that he is disgusted with another spike in know-nothing chauvinism that proved his logical rebuttals to Norinaga accomplished nothing (and Norinaga had the guts to publish them with his work). Pardon my extremely loose translation (*cherry blossoms* would have ruined the beat, so I would have English readers see cherry blossoms where most might see fruit in *cherries,* and translating the Chinese characters for Yamato is a bit mad, . . .). Another Akinari *angry poem* says *"Though the truth is twisted to get them, disciples he wants, and indeed people call him Kojiki-denbei!"* ひが事をいふてなりとも弟子ほしや　古事記伝兵衛と人はいふとも *higa koto o iute nari . . .*). The *Kojiki* is the *Ancient Chronicles* and the *den* following it means transmission with annotations, etc. Norinaga might have been thought a warrior from heaven (天兵 *tenpei*) but by putting the extra 衛 after the 兵 we get a name stuck on men in menial jobs, which makes the intended homophone of 古事記 *Kojiki* 乞食, or "beggar." I could not properly translate the poem, but find Akinari's framing of the ideologist as a beggar because he is unable to fairly earn supporters and must instead pander to them fascinating. If enough poems in his book are of interest and translatable, Akinari will get a chapter or two in the next edition. If not, this note will finish him.

Asahi ⇒ *Bunzaemon*

Bashô. 松尾芭蕉 1644-94。This patron saint of haiku, the man credited with making *haikai* a profound genre of poetry, has been used by his followers to bash perfectly good comic or even subtly humorous haiku (such as Chiyojo's borrowing a pail to let the morning glory keep the one it took), but the master himself did not segregate wit from heartfelt content and, as Peipei Qiu (2008) points out "The celebration of eccentricity was a prominent theme of Bashô's poetry." She points out his playful identification with the *kyôka* master anti-hero Chikusai in Toyama Dôya's 1634 comic tale by that name and translates a *ku* from *Minashiguri* (1683) *"Ice – bitter-tasting – / just enough to moisten / the throat of a mole"* (*kôri nigaku enso ga nodo o uruoseri*), alluding to the eccentric refusal of a monarch's offer of a kingdom by a Chinese recluse who notes that a mole drinking at a river needs but a bellyful to be content (Here, I wish she cited my translation of Bashô's student Shikô's long *haibun* in praise of the sea cucumber as an enlightened Chinese sage and exemplar for the haikai master, for outside of a search for Taoism in Japanese letters such as hers, I cannot think of why anyone *else* will ever cite it!). She also introduced Ueda's translation of Bashô's well-known *hokku*, or opening verse for link-verse session at a snow-viewing party in Nagoya *"Now then, let's go out / to enjoy the snow . . . until / I slip and fall! (iza saraba yukimi ni korobu tokoro made)* and notes that "the eccentric gesture here works effectively toward achieving *ga*, for the eccentric persona demonstrates that he "would risk anything for the sake of *fuga.*" (Ueda). Peipei Qiu also shows Ôta Nanpo's *Neboke Sensei,* or Master Sleepy-head, eccentric persona was, like Bashô's wandering aesthete, rooted in Chinese models of eccentricity, and introduced a *kyôka* from the *Neboke Sensei Bunshû* (1767):

iza saraba maromeshi yuki to mi o nashite ukiyo no naka o korogearikan 寝惚先生
now then rounding/ed snow-as self/body making floating-world-among tumbling-go

*Here goes nothing! I'll make myself a snowball, roll on the ground
and just tumble through this world of woe – Yes, I will get around!*

*Let me be off! As a ball of snow, I'll just make myself round
and picking up as I go . . . tumble in to paint the town!*

I translated because PQ's reading *"Now, then, let's do it – / making this body of mine / a rounded snow ball / and let me toss it about / in this fleeting world"* caught the *wrong* snowball. She does note the fleeting world is also the water-world or demimonde of the pleasure quarters and that *korogearikan*=tumbling-walk/move (but not "toss!") had risqué connotations and that this attitude, or aim, while equally eccentric, or *kyô*, was not that of the *haikai* master, as our budding *kyôka* master would "subvert *ga* with *zoku*," i.e., make the elegant vulgar, while Bashô did the contrary. For my part, I am intrigued because Nanpo aka Master Sleepy-head's poem is prescient. Like a snowball rolling along, Nanpo, as Yomo no Akara, would indeed quickly pick-up adherents of his brand of *kyôka* and take a mistress who was an entertainer and who knows where it would have ended up had the conservatives not come to power to torch that snowball . . . But, to return to Bashô and his snow-viewing poem. I would call that *hokku* a *kyôku*. It has a masterful light touch, true *karumi*. If Ueda's (1992) translation is not mistaken, a critic called Shida claimed that "Sanpû's verse: *overcoming the fear / of catching a cold, I go out / to view the snow* (*kakugo shite kaze hiki ni yuku yukimi kana*) may be appreciated alongside this [Bashô's] hokku." I suspect Shida *meant* to say (I have not seen the original, but logic does not need to be spelled out) that we could appreciate the subtlety of *Bashô's hokku* next to this one by Sanpû, which is, nonetheless much wittier than Ueda's translation, which loses it entirely. Something like *"Not wanting to miss / the snow-viewing, I go out / to catch a cold."* or *"Resigning myself / Out I go to catch a cold / – Snow-viewing,"* etc.. But, to return to Bashô, I am unsure how much influence he had on later *kyôka*, but judging by their work, I think the 17c *kyôka* masters (Teitoku, Bokuyô, Getsudôken, Kôfû, etc.) are all already Taoism-influenced eccentrics. Indeed, *kyôka* might be called "eccentric poetry" (Let us see if this book sells in England).

Bokuyô. 半井卜養 Nakarai Bokuyô. 1607-1678 A physician and Teimon (Teitoku) school waka, haikai link-verse, and kyôka poet, one of the five top poets of the 17c. His outrageous wit reflects his Ôsakan roots, but he spent many years attending to his fief's Edo representation (hostage presence). Much of his wordplay is not pun – though he does that well – but *sound for sound's sake*. In that, he seems more modern than other *waka, haikai* or *kyôka* poets (including the mavericks Takuan, Ryôkan or Sengai). Watch him adverb a wine flask, a *tokuri*, before turning it into a medical concoction:

前文省略　とくり／＼ちょく／＼／＼とすいかつらにんたうちうのきのくすり酒
tokuri-tokuri chokochoko to . . .. I am unsure of some things here, but it ends on *kusurizake*.

Like Bashô, most of his poems were made on or for social occasions, greetings or mementos, etc., but I doubt anyone really asked him for many of the poems containing the unlikely combinations of things he *claims* he was requested to squeeze into a poem. I would guess he composed the poems first, *then* wrote the prefaces to properly frame them.

といひける後さかなにたうふしゐたけこんやくふをにしめて
出しこれにもとてもの事に歌よめとむりに所望しければ

こんやくふ さかなに酒をしゐたけや なにそと人のたうふなるらん　卜養
konya kuu(konyaku)sakana ni sake oshiita kya(shiitake ya) nani zo to hito no toô(tôfu) naruran

---

竹に庭鳥を書ひよこのいかにもちいさきを書て歌よめと侍りければ
おやは／＼竹の林の庭鳥の子は ちくりんしやちんちくりんしや　同
oya wa oya take no hayashi no niwatori no ko wa chikurinsha chin chikurinsha bokuyô

But, who cares if they were really made to order or not! The first, above, turns three foods into verbs that make contextual sense – too much for me to translate, sorry! – the psychological mimesis *chikurinsha-chin-chiku-rinsha* for tiny chicks based on a pronunciation of "bamboo grove" in the second cannot be beat, but, he also has the earthiness Getsudôken would inherit (the narcissus kissing) and, say つれなきの君かこゝ

ろはおにゆりのひとくちにかみころせん／＼ *tsurenaki kimi ga kokoro wa oni-yuri no hitokuchi ni kami-korosen-korosen*; and did take-offs of the sort that came to be (excessively, in my opinion) identified with late-18c *kyôka,* such as this sweet take-off on the Bay of Akashi where the persimmon in the ancient poet's family name makes the bed reddish while his first name morphs to eat said persimmon in one bite! ほの／＼とあかしいろつく柿の木の　ひとまるくちにかふりくはゝや *honobono to akashi iro tsuku kaki no ki no hito-maru-kuchi ni kaburi kuwabaya.* It seems odd Bokuyô has not received more attention in Japan. I guarantee that had the last poem been written by Shokusanjin, it would be famous (★　英語あんまり読めない読者諸君！上記のほのぼのと可愛い狂歌は、若しも四方赤良＝蜀山人作であったら、名歌になったと思いませんか？あんなに気持ちいいパロデイは、ざらとある訳ではありません。) Or, there is his reverse-facetious claim, to have thought a fashionable striped (and/or island-made) fabric was woven=Dutch but, no, it was inherited=horse (zebra?) しまぎぬをおらんだものと思いしに　よくよく見ればうまれ付きかな　*shimaginu o oranda mono* . . . that indirectly records the introduction of a striped horse (zebra?). The only one of his poems I recall seeing more than once is 黒こまのかけて出たるもちなれはくふ人ことにあらむまといふ *kurok=g=oma no kakete idetaru mochi nareba kû hito goto ni aramuma to iu.* The play on *sesame=goma* as a near-homophone of pony=koma (relying on the visually ambiguous orthography enabled by the common ellipsis of diacritical marks that homophonically morphs once again into something delicious (*muma=mumai*) after the light pun on *ara* (fresh or *unbroken* horse to a light, exclamation) is as sweet as anything by Issa. (★　これも上記と同じく。軽い狂歌の傑作です。) Because I am not confident about my ability to read many of the prefaces accompanying most of his poems and hate imputing them with my semi-literate Microsoft Word (Japanese software is infinitely more intelligent, and therefore faster, but requires a Japanese operating system) I had only a couple Bokuyô poems in the book and paid little attention to the others until, having to check one of his poems at the last minute, finally saw enough to know I owed it to my readers to delay publication and present more, as best I could. If someone who reads old prose well and can help with imputing wishes to help, I will translate more, including a couple *omake* already in the notes but not translated, for another edition. 卜養には、蜀山歌集あるいは一茶日記の如く、狂歌大観の卜養狂歌集よりうんと大きいな歌集は？もしもあったら、拝見したい。Keene, who credits Bokuyô with promoting a taste for *kyôka* among upper-class samurai, calls his poetry "hardly readable today; the humor consists mainly of puns and plays on words." While I would agree that it is *hard to English*, as we saw in the chapters where I did just that, and the above examples I did not even try to translate, Bokuyô's humor does utilize many puns – as does Shakespeare's – but it was full of ideas, too, and I would add, much of it is as readable today as when it was written, *provided it is read in Japanese.* And if his poems are lacking in strong emotion (a charge brought by Japanese critics, not Keene), I say, *so what!* It only goes to his credit, as it proves this exemplar of *karumi,* or "lightness," is extraordinarily sane.

Shokusanjin probably liked Bokuyô 卜養. He wrote an eulogy for a student of his student Bokuryû 卜柳, and put one of the latter's poems in the 1785 *Tokuwa* anthology: 寄田楽豆腐恋　やる文のかへしもせねば田楽のくし／＼胸をこがす我みそ　卜柳　*yaru fumi no kaeshi mo seneba denraku no kushigushi mune o kogasu waga mi zo.* The food terms do not translate, but this masterpiece born long before the Tenmei *kyôka* heyday makes the perfect complement for Shokusanjin's split-eel lovers! Here, the poet, alone, punned with *miso* (bean-paste), gets burnt. The shishkabobs, repeated, become a classic intensifier of love's pangs and, if Bokuryû wrote it while changing his affiliation, there might even be a hidden message 伝学 in it. The student of the student, Ôya no Urazumi – the name, literally, "The Landlord Lives Out Back" – has 6 poems in *Tokuwa*. Sugimoto and Hamada don't note it, but one of them, the first poem in Fall 立春, *may* refer (we need a date on it) to an ailing Bokuryû: 今朝ひとはちりくる庭のかんな屑柳の枝をけづる秋かぜ　大屋裏住　*kesa hitoha chirikuru* . . . . And what would Bashô have thought of the high *haikai* sense in his Love + Rice-planting Maiden 早乙女恋 *kyôka*? (早乙女の思ひかけ樋の水もれて今は哥にもうたはるゝ恋　同 *saotome no omoi kake hi no mizu . . .*) where we are treated to the panorama of rice planting irrigation conduits and all, hearing even the girls singing about one of their loves that – oops! – like that water, spilled out? In these rice paddies, *waka, haikai, kyôka* and improvised folk-song are all planted and grow together for a fine hybrid harvest. Here is an Ôya no Urazumi poem easy to English:

あけそむる年の要の扇うりよぶ一こえに春は来にけり　大屋裏住
akete somuru toshi no kaname no ôgi uri-yobu hitokoe ni haru wa . . .

Opening his fans to sell upon the pivot of our Old/New Year/s,
This man calls out and all can tell Spring herself is here!

~~~~~~

Bunzaemon. 朝日文左衛門 *Asahi Bunzaemon.* 1674-1718. *Monzaemon,* or *Mon-zaemon* in some Englishings, but Japanese sources on the net all say *Bun~* and not *Mon~*. His famous 2-million letter/character diary, "鸚鵡籠中記 *Ômurôchûki* Record From a Parrot's Cage," first fully published in 1969, gives a middle-level samurai's partly secret life (illegal gambling, foods, etc.) view of the corrupt leaders spiced by hundreds of *kyôka,* many of which are *rakushu,* or squibs, touching upon socio-economic or political matters. *Broadview* 狂歌大観 v2 参 includes 408 poems 鸚鵡籠中記落首抄. While the mostly anonymous poems were gathered from around the country, and the location is often noted, I cannot help wondering how many of the poems touching upon local (尾張藩, Owari domain, including the Nagoya area) figures are actually *by* the diarist. It could be many, or could be none. Hopefully, I will know by the next edition. As most books or shorter selections of *rakushu* tend to favor what might be called professional level work or squib-as-art poetry, the *Broadview* sampling (and it would be better within the diary) is invaluable for providing what we might call a literary-anthropological view, as it includes not a little that groanably bad reminds us that humans are by nurture as well as nature kin.

~~~~~~

Buson. 蕪村。 While I have nothing in this book, I think I have read experimental rhyming poems he did (if not, it was his friend Yayû). Not only his unerring eye for what I would call scenes of primal nostalgia, but his wit was extraordinary – haiku with acupuncture students sticking needles into sea cucumbers for practice, ants in peonies connecting with magical kingdoms, . . . – I expect to find something for another edition, when and if I make it back to Japan or gain the cooperation of a Buson scholar.

~~~~~~

Cavendish, Mary (Duchess of Newcastle). I have nothing of hers in this book, but should, for she was delightfully mad. Let me drop in a third or so of her too-long-to-be *kyôka* (28-lines) but nonetheless perfect example of her genius.

DEATH is the *Cook* of *Nature*; and we find
Meat drest severall waies to please her *Mind.*
Some *Meates shee* rosts with *Feavers,* burning hot,
And some *shee* boiles with *Dropsies* in a *Pot.*
Some for *Gelly* consuming by degrees,
And some with *Ulcers,* Gravie out to squeese. . . .

In *Sweat* sometimes *she stues* with *savoury smell,*
A *Hodge-Podge* of *Diseases* tasteth well.
Braines drest with *Apoplexy* to *Nature's* wish,
Or swimmes with *Sauce* of *Megrimes* in a *Dish.*
& *Tongues* she dries w/ *Smoak* from *St mack's* ill
Which as the *Course* she sends up still. . . . . .

I have seen short poems of hers worth including, but could not find them on-line.

~~~~~~

Chikusai. 竹斎. Like Kyôgetsubô, often called the first *kyôka* master, Chikusai is actually the hero of 富山道冶 Toyama Dôya's 1634 comic tale by that name. Like Bokuyô, our other poet with a particularly good light touch, he was a medical doctor 医師 and used his tales to poke fun at bad medicine, examine various newsworthy things and introduce interesting places – doctors who got to see a lot were good reporters – I am unsure how much is autobiographical, how many poems ascribed to him actually come from that book, etc. not that it matters – a good poem is good whatever the pedigree! Since the *kyôka* master did not need to compose with others, as the link-verse masters (*waka* or *haikai*), wandering Don Quixote-like characters are possible. As we saw before, Bashô was inspired by that image and if only he had lived to be 80 or 90 rather than 50 or 51, I expect he would have played with *kyôka* in his dotage.

***Daibu*, Lady**. Kenreimon-in Ukyô no Daibu was wife of a famous warrior and mother of a boy Emperor who sank in the sea with his grandmother while Daibu was unhappily fished out after attempting to die with the others on losing the Gempei Wars of 1180-5. But we should not allow her understandably melancholy journals to conceal her fine wit.

Fujimoto Yûki 藤本由己 fl.ca.1647-1726 He is in *Broadview*, but the poems in his one-man collection *Harukoma Kyôkashû* 春駒狂歌集 are so boring I neither marked a single one nor looked at the sequel *Zoku* 続〜 volume, much less mention him here until I found *one* fun poem of his about the *tsuno-moji,* or *horn-letter* (added to the notes), while doing last-minute googling about the etymology of the same in that sequel, which I read and learned he wrote some fantastic nonsensical *kyôka*. I am out of time to really read (i.e., do more than guess) translate and explain for this edition. Japanese readers, enjoy:

◎鬼に瘤とられたる処絵かいたるに《黒塚のおにゝこぶをはとられつゝ あとよろこぶといふはまことか》 *kurozuka no oni* 蛇足：英訳は無理が、こぶでよろこぶだけでこれは、名歌になってもおかしくない。◎雷神そは桶をつかみ雲中かたけて行。男とられて提灯やふられこけてゐる処絵かいたるに《夕立のざっと吹ます此夜来客雷につきそはつかみゆく》 *yûdachi no zatto* 蛇足：十八世紀すでに、「お客は神様」ってば？◎狼衣を着て狩人と物かたりの躰を絵かいたるに《おほかみに衣とはかりおほすなよ 此世かりうと後世をねらやれ》 *ôkami ni koromo* 蛇足：英訳を控えますが、「かりうと」を Hollywood にしてもおもくろい。◎茶店暮雪 《床の内のみしらけてのあののもののさののわたりの雪のかけもの》 *toko no uchi no* 蛇足：月ののので のでなく、後に川柳に出てくる「の」の字でユキまくる発想は、すでに尾に出た？◎The last is for Scott who asked about foxes to which I replied that my interest lay with my friends, the tanuki; well, here we have both: 《かれ木をも花にばけさすふるきつね おもしろたぬき雪やこん／＼》 *karegi o mo hana ni bakesasu furu kitsune omoshiro tanuki yuki ya konkon* 蛇足：古木⇒狐⇒常も？

Dropping a watch is said to have little chance of improving it, but did this man have a literal stroke of genius? Do such things happen? Can a teetotaler who starts to drink like a fish unclog fatty capillaries pinching or starving the nerves in his corpus callosum?

Getsudôken. 黒田月洞軒 fl.1688-1703. One of the two top students of Shinkai 信海, who studied under Teitoku. A samurai with a wife related to a daimyô, he could afford to go his own way. Which may be one reason the slightly younger Teiryû inherited the school. Because Getsudôken's *kyôka* are mostly written for personal reasons, they, like Issa's have a poignancy often missing from poems written for themes to be included in anthologies. As personal collections or journal poems are much rarer in print than anthologies, yet represent what must be the larger part of the proverbial iceberg, I felt it best to give his kyôka collection 大団 (tk) more chapters in this book than his small fame would warrant. His unabashed sexuality is refreshing for not being outrageous to be outrageous as in *haikai*, or stereotype-based black humor as in *senryû*, but simply bawdy as folksong once was. I do not know enough about his life and his relationship with his gay friend and fellow poet 自剃, Jizori (pronunciation a guess. No information on him was found).   That hurt my translation.   I even had their ages reversed at first – I thought Getsudôken lived to be at least 88!) and had to do some rewriting. If any reader-sleuth with access to libraries in Japan and an interest in biography could give me a solid page about Getsudôken and a paragraph on his friend for a future edition I would be much obliged! Re. his relationship to Teiryû, his younger fellow student of Shinkai, here are two poems and an explanation from my respondent 吉岡生夫 Yoshioka Ikuo's *kyôka* blog.
男山言葉の花は散りぬれとなを頼みありむさしのゝ月（貞柳） *otoko yama kotoba*...
いや我れはあつまのゑひす歌口も髭もむさむさむさしのゝ月（月洞軒） *iya ware wa*...

黒田月洞軒の『大団』にも登場するが一首目が貞柳、二首目が月洞軒である。詞書に「元禄元年辰九月十三日信海法印遷化ありけれは今より後狂歌の道たとたとしきと浅草大護院へ申し上（げ）けれは月洞子御事豊蔵坊に狂歌おとり給ふましけれはあなたへ添削をこひ申せと仰...(無断で借りて御免！) It is all a bit too complex for this book (and me), but Getsudôken's self portrait as a hairy-faced barbarian of a poet punned into the expansive plain of Musashi is *perfect*. Walt Whitman would have approved. And one last poem that is not great but a perfect reflection of the man, of his earthy expression and honesty. The poem is about playing *go* with a genius so young he had no hair on his lower belly and having to put on some hairy monkey moves just to stay in the game a while. I may try a translation if I ever do a collection of *go* poems.

其阿碁打に出合碁にまけて帰られければ
下腹に毛のなき碁うちに出合て　さるはい手してにげてゆかるゝ
shitabara ni ke no naki go-uchi ni deatte sarubai te shite nigete-yukaruru

蛇足：若き天才はインチキいらぬ（下腹に穢もなきの掛け）大碁を打てば、ケだらけ月洞軒、猿滑かなんかみじめな手で答えざる終えなかった。

I *lied*, for checking the Big Fan for another poem in my notes that seemed to have a typo, I came across two *more* poems I could not help introducing as representative of his style/life and what I suspect may be the greater (lost) part of traditional Japanese poetry. If literary scholars were more alert, the first would surely have become a classic long ago.

納涼の狂歌題に吐かたきと直重方より云こしけるきくひとことに左いふとてかく云やりける
よむ歌をきく人毎にひやされて　ひやあせかけば　爰ぞ納涼　黒田月洞軒
yomu uta o kiku hito goto ni hiyasarete hiya-ase kakeba koko zo nôryô   Getsudôken
read song/pom+acc hear peple-each-by kid=chill=ed cold-sweatng here+emp keep-cool

On being told by Naoshige that he was having trouble writing a *kyôka* on the theme of obtaining the cool [in the heat of mid-summer], I sent him this:

Read a bad poem & ridiculed by all, suffer to become a clown;
The cold sweat upon your skin will surely cool you down!

Whenever I read they laugh at my poems and hating defeat
Cold sweat visits me and then and there I beat the heat!

Each time I read a poem they never fail to laugh at me
And with my own cold sweat I beat the heat ea-si-ly!

Reading a bad poem, ridiculed by one and all who hear:
To chill a mad poet, his own cold sweat beats beer!

さゞれ石のいはほと成て毛がはえて　それをしらがにみよし野の春
sazare-ishi no iwao to narite ke ga haete sore o shiraga ni miyoshino no haru
pebble's boulder-into becomng, hair grows/wn that white-hair-as hon.+yoshino's spring

直清方へはる立歳暮をくるとて

~ Asked by Naokiyo for something on Spring at Year's End ~

The little pebble became boulder and grew hair – obscene,
But that became white crowned mi-Yoshino in the Spring!

Or, *"and grew into a hairy thing."* Yoshino tended to have snow for the New Year so early solar spring was combined with the pebble-to-hoary-boulder-as-Old-Man-Winter. Obviously, "obscene" goes too far. And the "beer" in the previous poem is cold *sake*.

Gyôfû ⇒ *Kôfû*

Henjô (Arch-bishop) 僧正遍照 816-90. The classic poet with a great sense of humor, who got a millennium-long frenzy of maiden flower (*ominaeshi*) poems started by comically confessing to a tumble with them and has the most risqué poem in the *Hundred Poets* – a request to stay the heavenly maidens by closing down their cloud-route (p.293). Let me re-translate a *senryû* touching on the two above-mentioned *wild waka*:

落馬にもこりず 乙女をとめたがり y 64
ochiba ni mo korizu otome o tometagari

He is not shy to fall off his horse,
Or stop angels in their course.

Ikku. 十返舎一九 **Jippensha Ikku** 1765-1831. I should, but do not have more Ikku in this book. We only have one of his *kyôka* in the text, his famously good-natured death poem that ends in *sayonara* (pg.369). I knew he was the author of the famous *Tôkaidô Hizakurige* 東海道中膝栗毛 (1802-9), a comic novel 滑稽本 about the misadventures of two fun-seeking, poor yet pretentious travelers on the Tôkaidô, the main road between Kyoto and Edo with a rarely well-Englished title: *Shank's Mare*, but when I read parts of it standing in a bookstore decades ago, did not know it was full of *kyôka*. I learned too late to do a chapter in this edition. I could find little of the Japanese text on line and will have this book published by the time I could order a copy. If a fan of this book – or a translator of Hizakurige – wishes to select a half dozen poems to present in one chapter or a dozen for two, please try and send me the result. I will give you full credit. Here are a few sundry finds from an hour or so of largely fruitless googling around. First, something recalling the Miller's Daughter in *The Decameron*: anti-heroes who would sleep with a pretty daughter but end up experiencing her ugly mother in the dark. The mistake is discovered when one man kissed his friend who had crept up from the other side of the bed, realized his mistake and made a fuss of it aloud at which the old woman pipes up: *Hush or you'll awaken my daughter!* After one "with a good deal of kicking" managed to escape to the next room, he said to himself,

"By stealth I entered, a witch's love to earn,
But which was which I could not well discern."

'My' translation follows Thomas Satchell. I added only one "a" and re-spelled the second "which," which was "witch" in the Tuttle 1962 printing I saw, as his own text called the daughter *the young witch* and the mother *the old witch*, which made *both* witches (I have not seen the Japanese). Be that as it may, you can see Satchell in 1960 already turned mad poems into rhyming couplets, something I thought I might have started. *Oops!* Another example of his rhyming translations, without the context: *"Fooling the blind he had a little spill, / The current was swift, the punishment swifter still."* Mind you, Satchell is not rhyming these because the original is end-rhymed, but because the original is witty, and rhyme is a vehicle of wit. I do not know if anyone has commented on it, but *good for him!* I get tired of lazy translations, whatever the excuse given. And, it is not just happening in English. The translator/author of a modern *Japanese* "意訳 sense translation" of *Shank's Mare* admits to doing what amounts to the same thing: 「なお、原文中の狂歌は、訳しにくいためほとんど省いております」 ("Also, I have deleted almost all the *kyôka* from the text because they are hard to translate" – Can you believe it! That is *Japanese-Japanese* translation!). One might ask why, in that case, he didn't just leave all the originals! Now, let me try to English one of the few originals I found on-line in Japanese. Hounded by his creditors, one of our anti-heroes lept upon a teamster's horse to flee, with the result you might anticipate, especially, if you know about the extraordinarily vicious Japanese pack-horses (see item 8-2 in *Topsy-turvy 1585* (2004) for details of their behavior in the 19c), and while he lay still his mind kept moving and gained him a poem that is reflective but, as you might expect, far from apologetic:

借銭を負ふたる馬に乗り合わせひんすりゃどんと落とされにけり(喜多八)
shakkin o outaru uma ni noriawase hin suriya don to otosarenikeri ikku: shank's mare dbts+acc carryng hrse-on ride-meetng(tide-ovr) povrty=neigh-doin plunk droppd+finality

Saddled with debts, I jumped bareback upon the old dun horse,
But just one "Nay!" and poverty is thrown without recourse!
~~~~~~
Saddled with debts, I fled on a dun but soon I was undone;
Even horses "Nay!" a pauper: I was thrown on my bun.

I tend to translate a bit longer than Satchell. But, seeing that *which/witch*, I'll bet he finds and uses that same *nay/neigh*, whic,h in the original is *neigh* and *poverty*, both *hin*. That is one damn witty 19c *kyôka*. But, I am afraid that many of the *kyôka* in the novel pun on place names and may not be funny unless the names are changed, which would not please most readers as these picturesque tales are in the form of a travelogue. Eg. Here is one up at a number of sites as it is easy to understand *in Japanese:* 借金は富士の山ほどあるゆへにそこで夜逃を駿河ものかな *shakkin wa fuji no yama . . .* So, it may not be easy to fully sample Ikku – or, where his characters mouth them, should I use his family (pen) name Jippensha? – but I like his style and plan to look for more of his *kyôka*.

Ikkyû 一休 1394-1481 was the son of an Emperor in an age when competing political and hereditary factions put such children's lives at risk. who was sent to a temple at age 6 knowing he had to conceal his identity. From Japanese comic books, I knew him only as that smart aleck boy at the monastery, who could rationalize any misbehavior so delightfully all loved him. Only later, did I learn that, as a monk, he slept with women, and wrote interesting rhyming Chinese-style poems. I have yet to read most of Ikkyû poems and would bet there are more that should be in this book! I almost put his self-portrait here because it shows a man who looks like he would write what he is said to have written. It also seems to show a monk who, most outrageously of all, did not want to die and said so. I did not because I wanted to put the pictures of many of the poets together in order not to create the wrong impression of them. Most of our "mad" poets are mild, not at all like Ikkyû!

Ise, Lady. fl.930 伊勢の御息所 Ise no miyasudokoro. My favorite of her poems is far from a *kyôka: My hometown desolate and overgrown, if only someone / were here with me to view wild flowers in the fall fields* ふるさとの―あれはてにける―あきののに―はなみかてらに―こむひともかな *furusato no arehatenikeru aki no no ni hanami-gatera ni komu hito mogana* 変種: ~あれてなりたる~来る人~). Or, to read between the lines,

My hometown's a fright, but I would not be under the weather
If only you came so we could view the wild flowers together!

Like Izumi Shikibu and Lady Daibu, someone who wrote so naturally and using her brain that I found something mad about her poems which other scholars would doubtless call *waka* plain and simple. I let my readers decide.

Issa. 一茶。 1762-1827. One of the big three haiku poets of the Edo era today, though not that well known in his own time, Issa was a studious and religious country bumpkin who wrote bluesy haiku as one might expect and elegant ones that belie his background and speak to his genius, as well. His journals give us a larger body of haiku neither intended as *hokku* nor even as greetings than found anywhere else I know and the *kyôka* mixed in give us a picture of a more purely private use of *kyôka* than found in the work of *kyôka* poets, for even when they wrote personal *kyôka*, they usually had one eye on their eventual publication. The obscurity of Issa's silverfish-turned-adverb *kyôka* proves that selections of *kyôka* relying on standard anthologies of *kyôka* by *kyôka* poets may well be missing many of the best poems. I hope others with access to the journals of *haikai* poets other than Issa will provide me with additional chapters for a later edition or new book. I would *bet* that Buson, Chiyojo, Yayû, Shôzan and other witty *haikai* poets wrote *kyôka*. Ryôta 蓼太, who gave a poem (高き名のひゞきは四方にわき出て赤良／＼と子どもまで知る *takaki na no hibiki wa* . . .) with a bottle of *sake* to Akara surely did.

Jakuren. 寂蓮法師. 1139?-1202. I have only read a hundred-odd poems by Jakuren (at Nichibun), and most were not even close to being *kyôka*. Yet, judging from the snail poem (pg. 146) and the following, he had a deft touch and *must* have composed many *kyôka*. Hopefully more will turn up somewhere because where there are two masterpieces there must be many.

つむひとは こしもふたへに なりにけり おいせぬのへの わかななれとも 寂蓮百
tsumu hito wa koshi mo futae ni narinikeri oisenu nobe no wakana naredo jakuren d.1202
picking person/s back+emph duble-as becme+emph age-allow-not field's youngreen is but

We who stooping pick them all end up with backs bent double:
Hunting young-green to age less brings old folk more trouble!

Picking them, just look and see our backs are bent in half.
Young greens in the field stop aging? What a laugh!

I trust the shape of the letter へ was considered by the poet, for there are other ways to express bent backs. But even without such a visual pun, *the humor is first-rate*. Had Jakuren only lived a few years longer, so he could have had a major input into the Shinkokinshû (he was supposed to have been one of the editors), I bet it would have ended up with a good deal more comic poetry. And, had he lived decades longer, he may well have become the first father of *kyôka*.

Jihinari. 桜川慈悲成 *Sakuragawa Jihinari* 1762 – 1833/4. Until I came across a dozen or so of his poems in an article and books of *surimono*, I had no idea this famous creator and performer of *rakugo* (comic stories), plays and *kibyôshi* (cartoon-books, of which his story of eye-glasses that made the wearer see a rose-tinted world – even a paradise in one's workplace – is representative) was a *kyôka master*. With not a single 19c collection of *kyôka* with me in my country exile, I had only one of his poems (probably netted on the web) translated. But, judging from those dozen, I would say that percentage-wise, he had as many or more really good poems than Shokusanjin at his best! By good, I mean good concepts, puns and timing. It is possible he was simply extremely selective about the *kyôka* he allowed to be published and there are no books or caches of his *kyôka* to be found, but if there are many more out there, expect a special chapter in the next edition! His sense for drama is felt in his poems, not naive, but well thought-out. In *Otoshibanashi Tsunezune-gusa* (c 1810), he typed rakugo *ochi*, or snappers, as "forced-logic ochi," "simple-minded ochi," "wordplay ochi," etc.. When you think about it, the more narrative variety of *kyôka* might be considered a *rakugo* in 31-syllabets.

Jinkyû 甚久法師 . There are no poems by this late-17c bonze, or, rather prelate, in this book (except one I just added to the chickadee note) for I discovered him in the Kyôka Broadview too late to attempt translation. As they are highly nonsensical and almost entirely pun-based, maybe I was fortunate to miss him! A 1707 introduction to a collection of 175 of his poems 甚久法師狂歌集 put him with Sôkan and Bokuyô as a formidable *kyôka* master (いにしへ山崎宗鑑半井卜養なんと其外狂歌に達したる人／＼. That tells me two things. First, there must be many more such people I have missed and, second, that Sôkan, whom I had only known from *haikai*, may have left many *kyôka*, not just the few found for this book! Here is a sampling of Jinkyû's poems in Japanese: ◎牛の水入を見て・涎たれ人をつくゑの水入は うき世はなれぬうしの角文字 *yodare tare* ◎悟浜和尚七年忌早納豆（納骨？）にて斎有（西遊？）けるに・七年にはや納豆のおしる人

おしむからしてなみとこほるゝ *nana nen ni . .* ◎ ある所にて梨を出し身の上によそへて読給へと云・さむくなしとほしくもなし庵もなし　たゝこのみにてありのみそかし *samuku nashi . .* ◎玉峰和尚甚久か像を絵に書して讃をせよと有折ふし日くらし鳴て立けるを則我身になそらへ・つゐと立その日くらしの身は軽し　おもむくかたにつく／＼法師 *tsui to tatsu . .* ◎六十一の歳旦楽園へ行年を越んと晦日の夜道の川へこけ込ほう／＼の躰・六十は川へなかしてその跡に　また年ひとつ生れ子の春 *rokujû wa kawa e . .* ◎ある人の云所定めすありき寝所はいつくそと問・吾庵はねふたい時にねる所　おきてののちはしらぬ也けり　*waga an wa nebutai toki ni neru tokoro okite no nochi wa shiranu narikeri.* Ah, that last one is purely conceptual. Let me crank out a translation or two:

When asked how one who wanders without fixed abode knows where to sleep –

Wheresoever I sleep when I grow sleepy is my place to keep
As to where I'll go awake . . . there you may have a case!

~~~~~~~~~~~~~~~~~~~~~~~~~~~~~~~~~~~~~~

Where I sleep when I fall asleep you may call my flat:
Don't ask about me awake: I can't tell about that!

◎六十二歳旦・明ぬれは年と歌とをとはれけり　三十字一もし／＼　*ake nureba toshi to . .* ◎常盤氏の宅へ今助と云窂人男あり是に一首と望まれ・今助もむかし男となり平や　くらひたをれて爰に在原 *imasuke mo mukashi . .* ◎腰を病て居ける時読る・今よりは歌もよまれし読とてもみなこしおれと人やいふらん　*ima yori wa* ◎ある女男死して年忌の節髪を剃けれは・女郎花かさりおろして今よりは　僧正遍照男子なるへし *ominaeshi kazari . . .* ◎善人と云題にて・よき人はわかめはまくりありまの湯　このあんはいはとふもいはれぬ *yoki hito wa wakame . . .* ◎　申の年京都へ登り知れる人の云いつくを宿と定めけるそ・飛まはり都のうちのはなちとりとまるところに春は来にけり *tobimawari miyako . . .*　蛇足：浜⇒花千鳥。又、俊成の本歌取り？　◎　京都旅宿へ有馬新介と云人見廻しに風の心地にて対面ならす狂歌にてあいさつ・まれ人はまたも来かしとふり立て　風を引茶のあはてすまする　*marebito wa mata mo . . .* ◎　幡州はりま灘にて・旅ころも あらひなみよる はりまなた　のりつくるほと こはくこそなれ　*tabigoromo arai . . .* ◎　ある人の云よき庵あらは借りて居給へかし・柏寺のなまくさ坊といはりよよりや　あんもちならぬ身こそやすけれ *kashiwadera no namagusa . . .* ◎五十年忌法事去方より御菓子給りて・いたゝくは五十年忌のおもりもの　鶴はせんへい亀はまんちう *itadaku wagojûnen . .* ◎七十一の歳旦・紙袋七十一年はなれぬは　妙なるのりのつよさなりけり　*kamibukuro . .*　蛇足：糊＝法。樽やら皮袋などではなく紙袋という発想、脱帽！◎医王院に火事有て亭坊薬師の尊像出さんとて裸にてかけ廻り其身もしたゝかにやけとなんとしたるよし・とこからか火をつけたけのいわうゐん　へこもからだもみな薬師堂 *doko kara ka hi . . .*　蛇足：からか火＝からかい。「へこ」は褌の卑語。薬師＝焼くし。◎七十二の歳旦・背中にも肩にも物はおかねとも年か七十二になりにけり *senaka ni mo . .*　蛇足：二＝荷が簡単過ぎても効くが英訳は無理。◎ある寺の和尚甚久心得はいかにと尋有ければ・木まもりになるまで残るしぶ柿はわれとじゆくしてあまみをそしる *ki mamori ni naru made . .*　蛇足：これも一種の達観だろうね。

~~~~~~~~~~~~~~~~~~~~~~~~~~~~~~~~~~~~~~

Kaka. 節松嫁嫁 ***Fushimatsu no Kaka***. All but one of the poems by Akera Kankô's "Unkempt Wife" that I have seen are in the 1785 *Tokuwa* anthology. Some are very good, and most show a strong haikai-style wordplay of the sort associated with Kisshû. She would outlive Kankô and inherit leadership of his group or school of *kyôka* that was . . . (see, below). She doubtless merits far more room than I gave her, but until I find an anthology with more of her work, such as the moon-viewing I first found in Nada Inada's book and later in Rokuo Tanaka's translation, I can write no more.

~~~~~~~~~~~~~~~~~~~~~~~~~~~~~~~~~~~~~~

Kankô.朱楽漢江 ***Akera Kankô*** 1740-1800. Often misread in translation as Akera *no* Kankô (there is a pun-reading of the name which guarantees no "no" is added). One of the big four Tenmei era mad poets (Akara, Meshimori and Kisshû being the other three), Akera Kankô's mix of idea and pun is exquisite. When Yomo no Akara (Ôta, later Shokusanjin) had to bow out for political reasons, Akera Kankô tried his best to keep things going for the Akara school of *kyôka,* and after he died, so did his wife, the equally brilliant Fushimatsu no Kaka, above. If I only found a large cache of his poems, as I did (online) for Shokusanjin, he, too, would surely have been a larger presence in this book.

Kisshû. Karagoromo Kisshû. 1743-1802 唐衣橘洲 Instigated by his *waka* teacher, Gatei, who, praising a clever moon-as-menses poem of his (pg.50), said it showed he had a deep sense for *kyôka*, Kisshû was the first to organize a *kyôka* circle, or meetings 狂歌会, in Edo and planned to publish a collection of them by sixty seven authors. Akara, who knew about it because he himself had 44 poems in it (Kisshû, had 107), quickly put together a better book presenting *kyôka* in chapters divided by seasons and subjects, with little of the difficult kyôka of the high *haikai* style which Kisshû excelled in, and Kisshû became a has-been. I exaggerate, for he remained one of the top *kyôka*-masters in his own not-quite-so-popular *haikkai*-influenced style and I, who like *haikai*, probably would have presented many more of them had I only found an anthology with more of his work. I have seen *thousands* by Shokusanjin but only a score by Kisshû. I hope to correct this unbalance in a future edition. Meanwhile, one found in Nada Inada's *Edo Kyôka:*

酒ならぬ薬をのみてみる月は雲よりもうき風の神かな　橘洲
sake naranu kusuri o nomite miru tsuki wa kumo yori mo uki kaze no kami kana
sake's-not-medcne+acc drnkng view moon-as4, clouds mre thn float=sad wind=cold-god=papr!/?

*Drinking medicine other than Wine, the Moon I'd view with you
Is in the grippe of ye Wind, a worse curse than clouds – Adieu!*

"I'd view with you" is not in the original, but Kisshû had a cold, or, as Japanese call it, a *wind*. The language is not full of Chinese as my use of the obsolete *grippe* (influenza) and *adieu* might suggest. It is both extremely simple and full of puns in the original. The party he was begging-off from was held by Shokusanjin on "some year's Eighth-month/moon" and Shokusanjin's poem on the occasion (月をめづる夜のつもりてや茶屋のかゝもつゐに高田のばゝとなるらん 蜀山人　*tsuki o mezuru yo no tsumorite ya chaya no kaka mo tsui ni takada-no-baba to naruran*), punning on the place name, lets us know that women, wives I would think, were there, too. One more poem shows that Kisshû was not all haikai but could, shall we say, get down. This is the sort of thing Issa wrote!

世にたつはくるしかりけり腰屛風まがりなりには折かゞめども　唐衣　吾妻
yo ni tatsu wa kurushikarikeri koshibyôbu magari nari ni wa ori-kagamedomo kisshû
world-in stand-as4 hard+emph hip-high folding-screens become-as4folding-bend-even

*It's getting harder for a man just to stand – although he bends.
A folding screen, waist-high, little privacy, if any, lends!*

OK, *privacy* is mine. Still, coupling the proverbial screen that must be crooked to stand up by itself with the need to bow low to survive in Japan, that is, wedding a formal bow, (done from the waist) to a screen partition that was only that height is a simple stroke of genius not at all like the classic haikai-influenced poems usually offered to show why Kisshû was not as refreshing as Yomo no Akara. Again, I have seen too little to judge him.

Kôfû – 生白堂行風 *Seihakudô Kôfû*. Also *Gyôfû* (there is a Mt. Gyôfû, but at present there is no agreement on the pronunciation, so I chose the shortest). Flourished in the 1660's-70's. When young, he knew and was evidently very highly regarded by Teitoku and his top pupils and was entrusted with much old material they (or Teitoku) had collected which he combined with new material to edit into the first truly great *kyôka* collection, *Kokin Ikyoku-shû* (古今夷曲集 1666). Perhaps he should be credited with doing what Shokusanjin was credited with doing over a hundred years later, making *kyôka* into a genre that nobody could deny. As a poet, he did not particularly shine in the great book he edited, but we can easily see why he was so highly regarded from his charming light celebration-of-place poems in the Arima part (the 1672 half, 有馬私雨 which he edited) of a large toponymic, touristic(?) collection 地誌所載狂歌抄. While

Kôfû may not be a major poet, the combination of classic simplicity with truly artless and often extraordinarily bold puns deserve far more attention than they have hitherto received. They make me recall Shokusanjin and someone Shokusanjin (and I) like: Yokoi Yayû. If a scholar who reads this book likes the examples of his poems that comprise the lion's share of the *Arima My Rain* chapters, and would like to bring more attention to Monk Kôfû, please note that his treatise of 15 things he was *not* looking for in a *kyôka* may be found on the web 生白堂行風の狂歌論：禁制十五項を中心にして *The Essay on Comic Poetry by Seihakudo Kofu, a Poet in 17th Century* (The English of the title is not mine, but found at ci.nii.ac.jp/naid/ 110000973475. Since "mad" without explanation would be misleading, making what is *kyôka* in the original "comic poetry" was a wise choice). The treatise is in an article by Takahashi Kiichi 高橋喜一 of Baika Women's University and is ISSN:13442287. I would be happy to include a glossed translation of the 15 points in the next edition if anyone dares to attempt a full translation (not easy!). Likewise for Kôfû's introduction to the *Ginyô-ikashû* 銀葉夷歌集(1679) that he edited, anyone?

~~~~~~

Kotomichi. *Ôkuma Kotomichi* 大隈言道 1798-1868. *Perhaps* an unrecognized *kyôka* master – I have yet to read more than about 150 of his waka and Keene writes he wrote a hundred waka *a day* in 1849. Keene, who calls him "perhaps the most enjoyable poet of the late Tokugawa period" gives a lengthy introduction and admits his waka "have intelligence, humor, compassion, and charm," but finding "little passion" concludes "this lack alone makes him an interesting second-rate poet rather than a master." Is that why Carter fails to include him among his late-Edo period top-four? From what little I have seen since discovering Kotomichi, I wonder. Do both Keene (and Carter?) love *opera*, which I detest? Not all of his poems that I have seen are well-written, but conceptually and observationally speaking, this poet has it all. Take his Visiting the Blossoms 尋花:

咲く花を尋ねてゆけばいつよりか去年(こぞ)来(こ)し道に道はなりきぬ
saku hana o tazunete yukeba itsu yori ka kozo koshi michi ni michi wa narikinu

Going to view the blossoms at some time I realized here
I was on the very same path I happened to take last year!

Aston, in what may be the first English introduction of *kyôka,* noted how Ki no Sadamaru 紀定丸（1760－1841）took Saigyô's 12c poem (*yoshinoyama kozo no shiori no <u>michi kaete</u> mada minu kata no hana o tazunen*) about changing paths after seeing the trail-mark/s (broken branches) he made the year before to see new cherry trees in bloom, changed one syllabet and reparsed words to make the poet get lost thanks to the abundance of the bloom (*yoshinoyama kozo no shiori no <u>mi chigaete</u> urotsuku hodo no hanazakari kana*). That is fun – and in a *haikai* vein for indirectly praising the bloom – but Saigyô's original is madder in the best sense. Kotomichi's poem is neither traditional *waka* nor *kyôka* but a stunningly natural *tanka.* I think of Issa's old dog leading the way to the cemetery, but find this coming to realize one is on the same path a deeper poem. Likewise for, *Since when did I come to clasp my hands behind my back, / and from whom did I acquire the knack of looking ancient?* いつしかと我がとりなれて後ろ手の老のすがたは誰にならひし *itsushika to waga torinarete ushirote no oi no sugata wa tare ni naraishi*); or, *The lives of fish, countless fish, of each there is a record / The marks left by our knives upon the old cutting board.* (かずしらぬ魚の命は板の上の刀の跡にしるしぬるかな *kazu shiranu uo no inochi wa manaita no ue no ha no ato ni shirushinuru ka na*). That last poem has many fans, but it seems something I might come up with. I was *more* impressed, which, I suppose, means surprised with this:

今はとてうち寝る時は命さへわが身とともに伸ぶかとぞ思ふ 大隈言道
ima wa tote uchi nuru toki wa inochi sae waga mi to tomo ni nobu ka to zo omou

As I lay me down to sleep, I know without doubt
This is the time my body and my life stretch out.

My rhyme "without a doubt" is a creative take on the emphatic *zo*. And, there are the diary-confession sort of poem such as Issa sometimes did. *It is nothing to me, but my poor wife and children, / To see their misery, things are indeed hard.* (*waga mi koso nani to mo omowane me kodomo no ushi chô nabe ni uki kono yo kana*) My translations may be a bit flippant, but I hope you can appreciate Kotomichi's power of observation and honesty (The last poem was found in Keene, who calls it "self caricature"(?/!) *No, no, no!* It describes what it is like to live with others when you are poor but feel your work is worthwhile and you have a duty to the greater world. Those fortunate enough to make money or become well-off by inheritance by middle age fail to understand the limited options of the impoverished old writer or artist.). Combine that with the easy way he played upon old *waka*, as we saw with the microscopic creature poem (pg.361), and I think it more than likely that Kotomichi wrote far more *kyôka* than Issa who left us scores of them; we shall see. Next edition, *maybe*. 「彼の歌風は、構想の洒脱軽妙、観察の微細であつて、かつ斬新奇抜、従来の歌人が詠み出でなかつた境地を自由によみこなし、総じて印象明瞭、生趣溌刺たるものがある。修辞上からいつても、用語の新しく自由であつたこと、好んで擬人法を用ゐて巧であつたこと等、たしかに特色を有してゐた（佐佐木信綱『近世和歌史』*Yes*.)

~~~~~~

Kyôgetsu-bô 暁月坊 also **Gyôgetsu-bô**. 1265-1328. My Iwanami senryû+kyôka book (古典文学大系#57), *The Princeton Companion to Classical Japanese Literature* and most others writing in English spell it the latter way but a comparative search for both spellings in Japanese (*hiragana* with the accepted Chinese characters) gave us 38,400 for Kyôgetsu-bô vs. 3,510 for Gyôgetsu-bô and that is supported by the odd old orthographic varients 教&居. Sometimes called the first *kyôka* master, this monk, like Ikkyû, was of Imperial blood and may have had to play the fool to survive. He is reputed to have written many interesting things, even a hundred *kyôka* about *ants*, but little survives. I was *not* terribly impressed by his hundred *sake* poems and am unsure if the fault is mine or theirs. One of his three most famous poems is the only one I know as angry as Issa's silverfish. I do not know how he could have gotten away with that claim to have enlarged the Empress's privates after she privated his garden without dire consequence and assume said *kyôka* was only published after both parties were dead. An untranslatable putdown of a *waka* sent to him for "points" that plays on weasel sayings (てむまでは及びもなきぞみぞいたち　和歌の道にはまかげさすとも　古今夷曲集 *ten made wa oyobi mo nakizo* . . .) suggests he was at his best when in a bad mood. His other two best known poems:

あまりに狂歌をよみければ定家卿秀歌の一首もよみてさる物なりと人にいはれかしと教訓せられければ：暁月に毛のむく／＼とはへよかし　さる物也と人にいはれん　下と同
kyôgetsu ni ke no muku-muku to hae-yogashi　saru-mono nari to hito ni iwaren
kyôgetsu-on fur shaggy-x2 grows! thusly=monkey-thing is so people-by say

　　　When someone lectured me about how my reading too many *kyôka* will
　　　　make even a great Teika poem seem a spitting image of the same,

　　　Monk Kyôgetsu spits, he spits like a camel, the Filthy Beast!
　　　And this image others have it bothers me not the least.

皆人は死ぬる／＼といひけれと暁月坊はいきとまりけり　越後在府日記
暁月坊の辞世に *minabito wa shinuru shinuru to ii keredo kyôgetsubô wa iki-tomarikeri*
all people-as-for "dying dying" say but kyôgetsu-monk-as-for live-stay/dead-ends+emph

Everyone says　　　　　　　　　　　　　*Everyone says*
'He's dying! He's dying!'　　　　　　　　　*'He's dying! He's dying!'*
but I don't care　　　　　　　　　　　　*Passing away?*

Monk Kyôgetsu knows that　　　　　　　*Kyôgetsu Bô's right here*
he's not going anywhere!　　　　　　　　*and he is going to stay!*

Why do I make a *camel* of the *monkey* in the first poem? I was trying to reproduce the *type* of il/logical leap made between the preface and the poem in the original. As I have yet to read a thorough explanation of the first poem (さるものとはさりとて？), I have no idea if, or if not, I got the big picture – that if one gets too far into *kyôka* they are found everywhere – right for the preface. The second is also puzzling. As Genji uses the expression *ikitomari* for staying on alive in this world, it would be the first reading, but I think the phonetic lettering is used to allow for the alternative as well, a verb meaning to come to a *dead-end*. Regardless, it is an admirably exuberant death poem!

***

Magao. 真顔 1753-1829. Shikatsube no Magao 鹿都部～. Also, 狂歌堂～ Kyôka-dô ～, Kyôka Temple/Shrine-Magao. Head of the Yomo 四方-ren (Four Directions Group). A "sweet bean soup merchant" who became the *honchô* of 19c *kyôka* and had the longest such reign (?) of anyone since Teiryû, as Ôta (Yomo no Akera, later Shokusanjin) was forced out of his leadership position after only about 15 years when national politics enforced a reactionary agenda. Amerigo Vespucci was called "a pickle-dealer" – or, was it "son of a pickle dealer?" – in the war of words between those who thought Columbus should have had his name on the continent and those who thought Amerigo won the honor by knowing he was not visiting India – but, with Magao, it was no insult, as the merchants were the wealthiest class in Japan. Magao is, instead, insulted by those who insinuate his dressing up in a classical manner for some poetry meetings made him less authentic than, say, the earlier Tenmei poets, some of whom were still alive. I would say that the man knew what he was doing and that by linking *kyôka* to the past helped it to maintain a public presence under the nose of a conservative regime. The neat craftsmanship of his layered puns and multiple allusions, ignored by scholars of literature (some of whom accuse him of killing *kyôka*), are thoroughly explained by John T. Carpenter, Daniel McKee and others coming from the art (museum collection catalog) side of the divide. McKee found Magao contributed eight percent of the kyôka on *surimono* (gift-oriented picture+poem books) during the decades of its heyday. That means hundreds, possibly thousands of poems. If most are good but few have the little something that draws one to the poet as well as his wit and make them truly great, I would blame it on his being a busy professional – indeed, he prided himself on being the first real professional *kyôka* poet – writing too much on demand and too little from the heart. But, note that I have not yet seen enough of his 19c poems outside of *surimono* to make the above more than a tentative judgment. Magao also *edited* work I have not seen. One charming poem – not a masterpiece, but an aphorism playing on a proverb worthy of a dictionary of sayings – that I happened to google across while searching Magao:

うなバらによれる鰯のかしらより　光さしそふ初日の出かな　烏亭焉馬
unabara ni yoreru iwashi no kashira yori hikari sashisô hatsu hinode kana

Better than being chief sardine of a school buried under the sea,
I'd be a head stuck on a stick to have the First Sun shine on me!

Maybe I have this wrong, but I think it was a 山陽堂 member poem and it was in 年始物申　どうれ百人一首 *Nenshimonomô Dôre hyakunin-isshû*, a New Year 100-poet-1-poem anthology edited by 狂歌堂 the Mad-poem Temple's Magao 鹿都部真顔. 1793/1835. It is but one of many, many books I need to see before coming to any conclusions about M.

***

Meshimori. Yadoya no Meshimori. 宿屋飯盛 1752-1830. One of the Tenmei big four (w/ Akara, Kankô and Kisshû) and after his cohorts died young or were forced to retire, also one of the four luminaries of the following generation (with Magao, Baba Kinrachi, Tsumuri no Hikaru), two of whom did not live long, so it ended up with him vs. Magao. His poems tend to be simple, solid parodies of well-chosen old poems or misreadings of common-place that delight us in much the same way the innocent misunderstanding of children does (there is a Japanese translation *Kids Say the Darndest Things*). Yet, they are not naive and sometimes meaningful. His facetious wish that all poets were poor so the earth and heavens would not be moved, perhaps the most famous kyôka of all time, may be read as facetiously childish fear or as a message. I would need to study his work more to guess what message. Some see it as a challenge to nationalists who thought of Japanese as the only live, soul-filled divine language and boasted of the magical powers of *waka*. Others, rather, see it as a reflection of the move from the generation of literary titans to petit bourgeoisie, as the aesthetics of the noble samurai gave way to that of the townsmen. Nada Inada, who took the latter view, introduced a telling new-perspective poem by Meshimori. There is one pivotal homophonic pun, *haru*, first *swelling* then *spring* (the New Year) which I must lose in translation:

掛こひの夜あけにをもき革財布かつぎし肩もはるは来にけり 飯盛
kakegoi no yoake ni omoki <u>kawa saifu</u> katsugishi kata mo haru wa kinikeri

The debt-collector, his leather bag heavy as New Year's day breaks.
In his shoulders, he too feels the swelling that Spring's coming makes.

As far as I know, up to this poem, not only poems by commoners but by samurai made the debt-collector the scourge of the end-of-the-year. But Meshimori, who actually owned a lodge, had debts to collect (or, hire someone to collect). And, as Nada Inada points out, the debt-collectors had a hard lot, for with so many poor samurai to collect from, they never knew when one would crack, whip out his sword and . . . The above poem deserves to be not just *as* famous, but *more* famous than Yomo no Akara's much-translated *drunken-Spring-zig-zagging-up-the-street*. Granted, few of Meshimori's poems are masterpieces, but, percentage-wise, I find more good ones than is the case for anyone else, even Akara/ Shokusanjin, with the possible exception of Sakuragawa Jihinari whose poems I have seen but a few of to be sure. I will see more of Meshimori's work soon for I have just found copies of his *Manyôkyokashû* 万代狂歌集 (文化十二 1812) 古典文庫〈第 305/306〉 were reprinted in the 1970's and are available used at a price even I can afford: just 1,400 yen each (it is a two volume set)! Judging from what I have seen in anthologies, I would think that if he had any journals and they survived, they would be as readable as Issa's and contain some real surprises, but I may be just dreaming.

Mitoku. 石田未得 1588-1669. With Bokuyô, one of the two great comic poets of his time. While in Edo, he wrote Teitoku (in Osaka) for his advice when still young. He helped form the Tokugawa era's *kyôka* sensibility and wrote the most charming palindromes I know. My first Mitoku bio must have vanished in one of several automatic update ambushes, for when I came to supplement it, *nothing* was here. In a word, I found that compared to my favorites Yûchôrô and Getsudôken, he was more dependent on puns and less conceptual, but at his best, when he linked the wordplay and the ideas, his wit was so smooth, so subtle, that translation by one such as your author, who, you may have noted, has no truly elegant style, was hopeless. I gave examples of some such but, unfortunately, no longer recall them. And, I wrote that until I found hundreds of his poems, I could not yet judge whether or not he was as great – the best up to Yomo no Akara – as many seem to consider him. Then, . . . as I proofed the Annotated Bibliography, putting one to three stars on the various books in *Broadview* depending upon how much I found in each, I skimmed one *Gaginwagashû* 吾吟我集 (c1649) I was unsure of and immediately found more interesting poems than I had read and marked before. And, it turned out that all 658 poems in it were by Mitoku. Were I not exhausted from fighting Microsoft-word to paginate the text and notes, I would add several chapters to the main text. As is, I am afraid that the easiest thing to do was to cram it into the *Short Broad Inadequate History*, which I did.

Momoko. Hansan? Hanzan? Hanyama? 百子堂藩山・藩山堂百子/土十唐。This man edited two books in *Broadview* but not a word on the pronunciation of his name or date of birth and death could be found on the web. From the occasional もゝこ in one of the books, I guess that is how 百子 which he used more, is pronounced. While both books start with so many tributes to Teiryû (『日本古典文学大辞典』によると百子は（中略）貞柳の弟の娘の婿というわけです＝吉岡。なるほど！) and boring poems that his being overlooked by biographers is understandable, there are poems, probably his, in both books that show us the 17c free-style alive and well in the 1730's. Five are in the text of this book. Had we critics with the nose and will to sniff-out truffles from a seemingly barren landscape, that one where the limbless melon becomes the ad absurdum of finger-loping for love *by itself* should have made him famous long ago. Here are some more poems with no attribution from 狂歌糸の錦 (1734), that should have been in the text, just found while checking each work to decide how many ★'s to give it for the Mad Biblio:

手の不足したる　蛸を見て手なきものに産れてきたる此蛸は兄嫁にぬれ坊主成らん *tako o mite tenaki mono ni . .* 蛇足　坊さんの生れ変る罰。海鼠になったらさらによかろうが　玉子酒を　女夫して箸を逆鉾かきさがし跡はこん／＼とん／＼とねる *meoto shite hashi o . . .* 蛇足　「夫婦」を、うぶにも「女夫」或いは、だから卵酒？　又、狐+狸？　水口　旅やせの足は鷺かも水口へ踏込とはやどどやう汁哉　*tabiyase no ashi . .* 蛇足　泥鰌. 鰻よりも夏瘦せに効く。 17と14の身分けしない方こそいい狂歌だね？
(Ill traveler Thomas Hood wrote of standing in the sea to acquire mussels on his withered calves.)
前置　やことなき御方鮎の鮓まいりけるに石かみあて給ひ御機嫌あしかりけれは　君かよほひ鮓にありたる此砂のいはほと成て押と見るまで　*kimi ga yowai sushi ni aritaru . . .* 蛇足　君が世⇒齢は字余るか、こぼるか？　押し=惜しい？　外人みたい！

There is something utterly amateur about the above that I, a non-Japanese find amusing, though I would suspect my respondent might find it simply bad. And there are worse poems (?) yet, simply noting the plight of an ugly beggar woman in a world where we can not help but look at looks 悪女をあはれふ　門／＼へ顔もて見せに行にこそみともないとは世の人の無理　*kado kado e kao mote mise . . .* (蛇足　見っともない) or responding indignantly to a sudden request for a greeting poem by a client when he was hanging out at a medical-ash (whatever *that* is: the OJD tells me it was mixed with white and black sake for some festival(?))-selling store by pointing out the rule of haikai exchanges, i.e. *You first!* 薬灰を売店に遊ひけるに買人の来りて我に直段のあいさつせよと頼けれは　はいかいに脇から付る法はなし　先そなたから発句出さしやれ *haikai ni waki kara tsukeru . . .*). It is these responses to various situations that remind me of *kyôka* when it was a wonderfully inclusive poetry – before becoming too full of itself – and had all the room in the world!

Monzaemon, or *Mon-zaemon* ⇒ *Bunzaemon*

Munenaga. 宗良親王 1311-85? Prince Munenaga Shinnô Senshû 1377 天台座主. I have no poems by this prince who joined the Tendai Buddhist order at age fifteen and rose to become head priest before fighting for the South Court and Imperial Restoration, spending years in exile, and returning to lead the resistance. While the Southern Court poetry he was associated with is not supposed to be very interesting, I found scores of wild waka among a selection of a 1,000 of his poems 宗良親王千首 dated 1371. Unfortunately, this was after I finished and paginated the text so it must be squeezed in here. Pardon the hard-to-read solid *hiragana*. I give it to you as Nichibun has it online.

New Year's past, and clouds that would have just said 'snow,'
some take for an overcast, others spring haze – they see it so!

はるたてと－おなしゆきけの－そらのくも－くもるとやみむ－かすむとやみむ　*haru tatedo onaji . . .*

いつもたつ－けふりにまかふ－ふしのねは－めつらしけなき－あさかすみかな　*itsumo tatsukeburi . .*

It is there, up Mount Fuji mixed with smoke, always –
So tell me what's so special about this morning haze!

Though cold still in the hills where snow falls, in the New Year/ Our capital is hazy and spring is here, no there! なほさえて－やまはゆきふる－ころなれと－みやこはかすみ－はるそたちける *nao saete yama wa yuki furu . . . Who would know that Spring came here, back in the hills, / where snow is present and the wind still chills?* やまさとは－はるくること

も－たれかしる－のこるゆきけに－かせはさえつつ *yamasato wa haru kuru koto . . .* The "here" or "there" is mine. As one who spent much of his adulthood in the hills outside the capital, the difference described is not academic; such experiences made him sensitive to the arbitrary nature of luni-solar seasons vs. the climate. But the Prince had a robust soul, and enjoyed himself playing with time-worn conceits: *It is not fake. The first sound uguisu makes flows out / with tears once ice and the snow melting leaves no doubt.* いつはりの－はつねならまし－うくひすの－なみたのこほり－とけてなかすは *itsuwari no hats.*

This snow tossed about by the wind from warbler wings?
In parts where no flowers visit, our consolation for spring!

うくひすの－はかせにゆきを－ちらしてや－はななきさとの－なくさめにせむ *uguisu no hakaze . . .*

おもひわひぬ－せめてこてふの－ゆめもかな－こころのはなの－たのしみにせむ *omoiwabinu semete*

Lonely night, at least, let me dream that I am a butterfly
So I may console myself with blossoms born of mind

Flowers are everywhere in Japanese. In snow, in foam from waves (参：宗良の編集した新葉集より：いそのなみ－よせてかへれは－いはほにも－さきたるはなの－ちるかとそみる *iso no nami yosete . . .*) hitting *boulders,* something Munenaga often played with:

つゆしつく－くさのいほりに－かはらぬは－いはやものきに－こけやむすらむ *tsuyu shizuku . . .*

How can a new grass cottage dripping dew, and a solid stone
cavern yet remain the same? Both with moss are overgrown.

This combines the grass cottage in 100 Poets #1 and moss-covered boulder of 8000 reigns we also find in: *Not quite boulders, but in my old home-town the sandy beach / In our garden has grown moss thick enough to shame a peach.* いはほとは－またならねとも－ふるさとは－にはのまさこに－こけそむしける *iwa hodo wa mada . . .* or *Boulders? In my home-town even the sand is fertile; /Our old garden boasts moss sufficient for a turtle.* The same poem in two translations, more bad, I am afraid, than mad. The next is better:

いまさらに－はなとみなれし－やとのうめ－ちれはやゆきに－またまかふらむ *imasara ni hana . . .*

Not again, Plum, after we've come to know your bloom is real!
How can we still tell when, now, blossoms fall upon the snow?

Here, we have an old one edge saw used for anticipated bloom given a double edge to complete the metaphor in a tone cheerfully complaining of the double jeopardy(?).

If I should wake to see my pond Willow has dishevelled hair
I'll make no scene but simply let her go: Wind, see if I care!

いささらは－いけのやなきの－あさねかみ－われはけつらて－かせにまかせむ
わかかとの－はひりにたてる－あをやきの－いとはなひけと－くるひともなし

The willow by my gate lacks thread for designs: too bad!
Then again, that means she cannot be tangled up, or mad.

Those two work. They prove Munenaga or your translator is a mad poet. The next don't English. えたくちし－かはそひやなき－またもえくむ－そのねはかりの－はるをしれとや *eda kuchish kawazoi . . . Oh rotten-limb willow by the river bank, the only thing /about you that is new are your roots that still out-spring.* The next has the poet in a pickle for pickling puns with a misdemeanor for breaking little bracken hands. つまきにも－またをりそへて－かへるさの－わらひやしつか－すさひなるらむ (蛇足　漬物用と美犯罪の掛)

tsumagi ni mo mata ori- . . . And my English reading of this bold observation – *But compare it to Your Realm not dark or overcast in spring, / – the moon, mist-covered, does it not seem a different thing?* くもりなき－みよのひかりに－くらへてや－はるはおほろの－つきとみゆらむ *kumori-naki miyo no hikari ni* . . . does not compare, either. But note that in the original, contrasting the clear ideal – the New Year as spring a looking glass into all ages – with the reality is well done. I also am afraid that his playing with the idea of dyeing from without also seems poor in English: *Spring rain falls on the old grass dead as it's ever been,/ while from below the dyeing starts the change to green.* はるさめの－ふるののくさは－それなから－したよりそむる－みとりなりけり *harusame no furu no no kusa* . . . *Neither showers nor the dew ken to dye it, yet below / its sorry leaves, the Grass waits for the Winter to go.* そむるとは－しくれもしらし－つゆもみし－うへはつれなき－まつのしたくさ *somuru to wa shigure mo* . . . And these are true observations, as is this: わつかなる－くさのわかはに－つなかれて－ところもさらぬ－のへのはるこま *wazuka naru kusa no* . . .

    In mountain villages, an altogether new melancholy, ah!
    — *Today at dawn, the Chorus of the Chiming Cicada!*

やまさとは－いつなくとても－さひしきに－けさよりしつる－ひくらしのこゑ *yamasato wa itsu* . . .

いつしかと－はななきさとに－いそくかり－おのれかへりて－はるやしらする *itsushika to hana* . . .

    Whatever the date, when geese hurry off flowers bloom behind;
    They tell me spring has come: leaving they bring it to my mind!

    When is it, when! The geese all rush to their flowerless loam
    Each would be the one to bring tidings of spring back home.

I hate "ah!" in poetry, but the *higurashi*, literally evening cicada, that I call a chiming cicada needed a rhyme. If you wish, lose that *"melancholy+ah"* for *melancholia*. (蛇足「為連」又「し連る」ないし「しづる」は重ねながら相打ち、蜩でなければ人以外にない、相次いでに鳴く声をうまく描写する例で、『日本国語大辞典』に是非お勧めしたい用例です). One of my returning goose translations is wrong, probably the first. Here is an easier poem: *I think of boats . . . vanishing one by one behind distant isles / Seeing them leave us for their homeland, the returning geese.* はるはると－しまかくれして－ゆくふねや－おのかとこよに－かへるかりかね *harubaru to shimagakure* . . . The original plays with Hitomaro's famous *honobono to* . . . poem. Not all are so fine, but even then a poem like the following one makes us wonder where to draw the line between *waka* and *kyôka*: *Who can stop Spring when none know where she would stay / But checkpoint guard, stop the blossoms from flying away!* めにみえぬ－はるのゆくへは－さもあらはあれ－ちるをはとめよ－はなのせきもり *me ni mienu* . . .

    Spring Wind, I'll bet you think they are still yours to take;
    I beg your pardon, leave the blossoms fallen in my garden!

わかものと－なほこそおもへ－はるのかせ－ちりつむにはの－はななさそひそ *waga mono to nao* . .

ゆくみつの－あはれきえせぬ－おもひゆゑ－よるはみたれて－とふほたるかな *yuku mizu no aware* .

    The water flows on and on, but River of Forgetting it is not:
    To see my passion flying with the fireflies, I'm burning hot.

The first above was later reinvented by *haikai*. I am tempted to do many readings: *Spring wind, I'll bet you think the blossoms are still yours / But I would ask you to ignore those upon my garden floor*. Or, how about a head/(garden)bed rhyme? Fireflies lead us to Munenaga's *koi/love* poems. Fireflies, as we have seen, liked rivers, but bringing in a water-saying is more *kyôka* than *waka*. A less creative firefly poem protests about having them put in his sleeve when his breast is already on fire なにせむに－そてのほたるを－つ

つむらむ－さらてはもえぬ－わかおもひかは *nani sen ni sode no hotaru . . .*　わかそては－
こぬにそぬるる－いかにして－あめをさはりと－ひとのいひけむ *waga sode wa konu ni . . .*

> *Look at my sleeves all wet because someone did not visit;*
> *Yet you think the rain is good reason to stay home – Is it?*

うきひとの－こころよりまく－たねなれは－ふゆもかれせぬ－わすれくさかな *ukihito no kokoro . . .*

> *If hearts of false lovers had seeds to sow (am I bitter)?*
> *'Forgetfulness Grass' so hardy it survives even winter.*

I could not find better examples of where love poems and mad poems are *identical* than the above two which were so good I tried very hard to do them justice adding a wee bit to the second line of the first and first line of the second to perfect the mood and rhyme. I am less satisfied with, but cannot not introduce the following series of tears for comparison sake with the ones in the 1310 *Fuboku* anthology we saw in the text:

たちさわく－なみたのそての－みなとふね－わかこころから－よるへなきかな *tachisawagu namida*
たかなかす－なみたのかはそ－かくはかり－いしとなるまて－かたきあふせに *daga nagasu namida*
なみたかは－せかるるほとは－せきためつ－そてよりほかは－あさせともみよ *namidagawa segaru*

> *Your teary sleeve is a port where boat-made waves are tossing:*
> *my heart would be swamped, it stands not a chance of crossing*

〜〜〜〜〜〜〜〜〜〜〜〜〜〜〜〜〜〜〜〜〜〜〜〜〜〜〜〜〜〜〜〜〜〜

> *Who makes such a terrible torrent of tears? Such flows are known,*
> *With resolution bound to turn from a rapid meeting, to bed of stone.*

〜〜〜〜〜〜〜〜〜〜〜〜〜〜〜〜〜〜〜〜〜〜〜〜〜〜〜〜〜〜〜〜〜〜

> *This stream of tears on my sleeve I would dam to cross to her;*
> *But it seems I must go elsewhere for a shallower river.*

My "Your" may be wrong but it makes more sense that way to me. The second poem is too hard for me. My reading of the last contradicts the first. But to hell with the pronouns and hence the owner of the river – or, it could be we have lovers *both* with rivers . . . the larger metaphorical development is what we are after. And here is one more I just cannot English well: *All night long something keeps falling on your room – it doesn't drip or ooze, / But drops from my sleeves like silent hail with my blues!* よもすから－たまちるそては－ねやのうへに－おとなくてふる－あられなりけり *yomosugara tama chiru sode wa . . .* Be that as it may, I wonder if the idea of tear-drops as "hailstones falling silently" *otonakute furu arare* is Prince Munenaga's invention. That would be quite a patent! And how about his turning the *ogi* in his garden into the sea to float his marine metaphor? うきことの－かきりとせむ－かせのおとに－こころみたるる－にはのをきはら *uki koto no kagiri to . . .* & there is more I do not get, eg., this w/ Ezo: あちきなや－きみにこころを－おくのうみよ－えそなつさはぬ－えそかちしまも *ajikinaya kimi ni kokoro o . . .*

> *The star lovers wait so long I think pie in the sky, how sweet,*
> *though we all know each fall by and by, they really do meet.*

たなはたの－まつまやいかに－ひさかたの－そらたのめせぬ－ちきりなれとも *tanabata no matsu . .*
なのるへき－はなのなならぬ－をみなへし－をちかたひとも－いかかこたへむ *nanoru beki hana no*

> *Maidens (Ominaeshi), you really should declare your unflower name!*
> *Otherwise, how can he who falls on you reply w/ the same?*

I think the next a fine poem for a 7-7 night with a strong wind いつしかも－うらみむとは
た－おもはねと－ころもふきかへす－あきのはつかせ *itsushika mo uramimu to hata* 蛇
足　機の掛　fine but not Englishable. The above only worked thanks to the existence of and my finding that "pie in the sky" to match the otherwise lost *soradanome*. We have

discussed Henjô and the "maiden flowers" enough already. Here let me just point out that I could not use that Englishing because the "flower" in the name would contradict the whole point of the poem. That is to say, *ominaeshi* has no "flower" explicitly in it.

How charming! Who would know this old eave, with Iris in the air
Is once again young Adam's Eve, so long as she is blooming there?

めつらしき－けふののきはの－あやめくさ－ふりにしつまと－たれかみるへき *mezurashiki kyô no . .*
たのめすは－たのまさらまし－ささかにの－いとかくはかり－つらきゆふへを *tanomezu wa tano- . . .*

I do not count I cannot count on news from Arachne.
A web is but a web for me – Tonight is pure misery.

As we have seen, from *waka's* Sanekata to *kyôka's* Getsudôken, the Iris in the eaves and the predicting spider attract poets who favor the comic. As we have seen, Munenaga's poems often have a riddling quality. Here is one last example where that is very clear:

まつもうし－わかれもつらし－きくたひに－こころつきぬる－かねのおとかな *matsu mo ushi waka .*

Waiting, it hurts, separating, it smarts – to hear is hell;
Our poor hearts are wrung . . . by the sound of a bell.

Introducing mostly light poems I fear I may not help Munenaga's reputation. Well, see what you think of how he treats age, death, a year-end metaphor and a meta-metaphor.

あはれてふ－ことにつけつつ－くちのはに－わかたらちねの－かからぬはなし *aware to iu koto ni . .*
てにむすひ－みになつさへは－あちきなく－すすしきみつも－むねをやくなる *te ni musubi mi ni . .*
このころは－なみうついはに－こけふかし－つつみのたきの－おとやきこえぬ *kono koro wa nami .*
たのしみを－そらにきはめて－くものうへに－とひやたつらむ－あまのはころも *tanoshimi o sora . .*
いせのうみに－しつまはしつめ－みのはてよ－つりのうけなる－さまもうらめし *ise no umi ni shi- . .*
ささされいしの－いはほとなれる－こけのうへに－おひそふまつの－はてしやはある *sazare ishi no . .*
やまかつの－たきすさひたる－ほたのひの－のこりすくなく－くるるとしかな *yamagatsu no taki . .*
なにはなる－あしかりをふね－かりそめの－よのことわさも－えにはよらすや *naniwa naru ashi- . .*

~~~~~~

Ogden Nash (near-mad poet) Aug.19, 1902 - May 19, 1971. Unlike Piet Hein, whose grooks are mostly of the hyper-rational variety I would call mad in the best sense of the word, Nash's incredibly wordy and prolific work is only sporadically so. His "Which the Chicken, Which the Egg?" – *"He drinks because she scolds, he thinks: / She thinks she scolds because he drinks, / And neither will admit what's true, / That he's a sot and she's a shrew."* – is a proper hyperlogical epigram, but most of his work I have seen can only be described as *shaggy doggerel*. And, yet, Nash's *style*, especially his outrageous rhymes, depending on bent pronunciation and bent or not often punning to boot, not to mention the often superb associative jumps remind me more of *kyôka* technique than *anyone* who wrote in English. A quick look at the one book I have here (*The Old Dog Barks Backwards*) – if I had more, more Nash would have been in this book – shows things like *"good riddance / you didn'ts"* and *"If the Greeks had never existed who would have been the most annoyed? / Freud."* The last, in "The Slipshod Scholar Gets Around to Greece," ends *"Thus was Agamemnon avenged and his adulterous slayers eradicated. / The Greek words for Electra were Accessory Before the Fact, but Dr. Freud and I think of her as a daughter who was over-daddycated."* Or, from Wiki, After his return from a brief move to New York, he wrote *"I could have loved New York had I not loved Balti-more."* Someday, I hope to skim through all of his work to select short, conceptually interesting pieces. If I have the energy, I may shorten others so they may be appreciated in a less leisurely age. I hope to do many things . . .

~~~~~~

Ôta Nanpo (sometimes Na*m*po) ⇒ Shokusanjin.

~~~~~~

Piet Hein (Honorary Mad Poet) 1905-1996/4/17. Short philosophical rhymes called *gruks* or *grooks* by Piet Hein, Danish scientist/mathematician/designer-poet – best known for his super-eggs as large as the Stockholm traffic circle or as small as the balanceable gold and silver eggs used as ice-cubes and various board games – were popular in English translation in the 1960's and 70's, but, unfortunately, seldom seen today. Unlike Ogden Nash's poems, many dated by detail, grook humor is largely logical and a good selection of them will read as well a thousand years from now as today. The shortest is *"Co-existence, or No existence"* (though it also has an interesting title), and all come with an elegantly simple line-drawing. Hein inscribed the 1979 printing of the 1968 book *Runaway Runes* for me as follows: *I've tried to Haiku, / You, Robin Gill, should try too / With your Hai I.Q.!* The pun is less haiku than *kyôku*, but decades down the road, with my brain considerably shrivelled, I took him up on it. Perhaps the same year – I have misplaced the letter – he informed me he went by train, from the new capital to the old one – *Tokyotokyotokyotokyotokyotokyotokyoto*. That is a masterpiece with both a perfect mimesis of rail-travel and a simple yet surprising wordplay with the snapper saved for the last syllable. It deserves to be at least as famous as Van de Heuvel's one word haiku (*tundra*). At the time, I knew he first became famous writing under a pen name during the German Occupation, but not *how* it worked. Now, I read that *"Losing one glove / is certainly painful, / but nothing / compared to the pain, / of losing one, / throwing away the other, / and finding / the first one again"* was a cryptic message for the Danes not to collaborate, for liberation would come. If I did not catch that, who knows how many Japanese *kyôka* I likewise have failed to pick up on! Piet Hein's *kyôka* sense is felt in his wordplay, such as the above examples or when he confesses about his country Denmark that *". . . we have no raw materials. / We have no power. / We have know how,"* and in his hyper-logical concepts, such as when he finds *no cow a horse* and *no horse a cow* is *"one similarity, anyhow,"* or confesses that *we ought to live each day as if it were our last below,* but as a senior he knows that doing so would have killed him *long ago,* and makes a halo into a horizon (title: *circum-scripture* (!)) . . . Were it not for concern for copyright (I have no time to properly edit now, much less seek permissions*), I would give you a dozen of his grooks entire, right here, for poems that are conceptual rather than descriptive or narrative – except in so far that plotting to keep the snapper at the tail – are all too rare in popular literature today and the grooks would provide a convenient mirror on *kyôka*. I say "convenient" not the "only" because a broad search of meta-physical (I have only pulled some poems from Herrick here) and other 16-19c English poetry, especially anything called "epigram," will provide many more matches but it takes some doing to find enough good short ones, while the grooks are, for the most part, already mad, as I define it. Here is one example of a *kyôka* (epigram) by Swift:

> Behold! a proof of *Irish* sense;
>   Here *Irish* wit is seen!
> When nothing's left that's worth defense,
>   We build a magazine.

A footnote explained that old Swift, driving out with his physician, observed a new building and asked what it was designed for. Told that it "was a magazine for arms and powder," upon which he wrote this into his pocket-book. This reminds me of the *rakushu*, or political lampoon sort of mad poem. Anyone with time and access to the Old English Poetry data base is welcome to try to find English language 'matches' for the *kyôka* in this book.

* Hopefully, with the permission of Piet Hein's estate, a new edition can include a full chapter – or two – with the poems starting: *A bit beyond perception's reach. Everything's either. It ought to be plain. Mere intentions go for naught. Oh, it's grand when the things. Some girls I worship from afar. There's an art of knowing when.* Find and read these and see if you agree that if scientists chose the Noble Prizes for literature, Piet Hein would surely have won it!

Ryôkan 良寛 1758-1831. Ryôkan came from a family rich enough to have helped his talent blossom into a lucrative career as a popular *haikai* master (paid by students for hosting parties and judging, etc.) in the city, but he chose to become a Zen monk and live in a remote village, where he wrote poetry in various traditional and invented styles. While witty, he was remarkably mellow. While my impression is based on the limited number of his poems I could find on-line, I read enough to note that they tend to make us smile. The downside is that we rarely laugh aloud; the upside is that none of his poems leave us with a sour taste. Until I find and read *all* of his poetry, I cannot say whether we will find many more excellent mad poems such as the charming wingless *tôfu* (pg.86). My favorite of his poems seen to date is a *tanka* (one that seems too modern to call a *waka* but too sincere to call a *kyôka*) on plants he evidently neglected to water *"Plucking violets / by the roadside – Ah! / my potted plants! / I forgot all about them, / my poor potted children!"* (道のべの菫つみつつ鉢の子を忘れてぞ來し其の鉢の子を *michinobe no sumire tsumi-tsutsu hachinoko o wasuretezo kishi sono hachinoko o*). He had many versions of this, mentioning they are pitiful in one and there is no one who will take (and care for?) them in another. Such paraversing proves it must have been a favorite of his, too. Here is another bluesy favorite in a style similar to that of Issa:

ware danimo mada kuitaranu shira-gayu no soko ni mo miyuru kagebōshi kana
i/me+emph too still eat-suffices-not clear-soup's bottom-on even see-can shadow-monk!

> *'I, too, have yet to eat my fill!'* – Yes, in my gruel,
> Even my shadow looks so hungry it could drool."

He may have gotten the idea partly from the *Tales of Ise*, where a woman as she is about to wash her face looks into the tub and laments to see another as blue as her, but his wording does not at all reflect that. In other words, the poem has zero intent to be a parody. An overly fine point, perhaps, but I think it neatly sums up Ryôkan's relationship to the world of poetry. He is not alone, but he is independent. Burton Watson writes that Ryôkan *"stands in magnificent isolation from all contemporary schools and poetic theories, drawing inspiration from the eccentric T'ang Buddhist poet Han-shan and writing poetry that blithely ignores many of the technical dictates of traditional Chinese verse."* I would guess he *also* read 17c *kyôka*. Keene writes of his poems that *"all of this is endearing, but Ryôkan's poetry seems to belong to Japan rather than to the world."* Would he write that today, when *sushi* and *tôfu*, even without wings, have made it to the world's supermarkets and haiku has come to be increasingly well-known? The *kyôka*, or should I say, conceptual part of his work seems universal enough to me!

Saigyô 西行 (1118-90). Born into a low-ranking clan, he became a monk in his early twenties, when he spent much of his time in the Capital. Later, he spent most of his life as a traveling ascetic or sage-hermit, remaining in touch with the top high-ranking court poet, Fujiwara no Shunzei (see Shunzei). His confidence, as a powerful man skilled in martial arts and an extraordinarily creative thinker, is reflected in his bold poetry. While he loved poetic conceits and punning – the very first poem in his *Sankashû* anthology takes the question posed by the first song of the *Kokinshû* (905) on what to call the year on the solar spring when it precedes the lunar New Year and, adding *rain* to the mix, makes what on first sight seems only the verb for rain *"falling=furu"* pivot into the adjective *"Old=furu"* (春としもなほおもはれぬ心かな雨ふる年のここちのみして *haru to shi mo nao . . .*) to modify the *Year*. I assume it really rained, too, as from start to finish – Saigyô's poetry is well-grounded in reality, physical or psychological. His world was a large one, and he wore his melancholy on his sleeve with grace: *"When you think / you alone know the blues, / You find another / and want to go to China / to pay him a visit!"* (我ばかりもの思ふ人や又もあると唐土までも尋ねてしがな *ware bakari mono omou hito ya mata mo aru to tôdo made mo tazunete shi gana*). And that world was also small, in the best sense of the word: *"Waking alone from sleep on my straw mat, my tears are drawn by a cricket's song."* (ひとりねの寝ざめの床のさむしろに涙催すきり／＼すかな *hitori-ne no nezame no toko no samushiro ni namida moyôsu kirigirisu kana*). While the cricket's delicate chirp has an irregular grain and plaintive tone that affects me far more deeply than the controlled bellowing and shrieking of opera appreciated by people with a different sensibility than mine, my tears were drawn by a different insect, the bell cricket, whose name, *higurashi,* or "day-darkening" relegated it to evenings in poetry. I very rarely cry for anything but a cold wind and the fact the floodgates were opened by a dawn chorus and Saigyô mentions *waking from sleep* proves to me that he is putting personal *discoveries* (not the same as trope or confessions) into poetry, something all too rare. He has 94 poems in the *Shinkokinshû* (1205), more than any other poet.

~~~~~~

Sanekata. 藤原実方 Fujiwara no ~ 958?-998. His boldness is extraordinary, or at the very least, extraordinary to have come down to us, thanks to his being well-connected; but he is not so unerring a poet as the other Casanova poet, Narihira, for his metaphors are often sloppy. One telling example: 葉をしげみゝやまのかげやまがふらむあくるもしらぬひぐらしの聲　実方歌集 *ha shigemi miyama no kage ya magauramu . . . .* When evening cicada sing at daybreak, he claims it is caused by the thick mountain underbrush keeping them from knowing it ever dawned. Actually, *higurashi*, contrary to their name, *always* cry at dawn as well as dusk. Nobleman who stayed up late would probably fall asleep shortly before they cried and might be pardoned for not knowing that, but considering the fact these evening cicada do not continue singing once it becomes dark, the poem falls apart. Yet, this carelessness – it still beats kks #204! – may be what made a large percent of his work (and I have only seen some online at the site where I first learned of him, there might be more) *kyôka.* I gave him two chapters mostly to hint at the size of the mother lode of *kyôka* by whatever name it was written or published.

~~~~~~

Shikibu 和泉式部 (Izumi Shikibu c.970-1030). Not *Murasaki* Shikibu, author of *The Tale of Genji* whose hundreds of *waka*, while often witty, are so in context of the novel and too subtle for the logic-in-your-face *kyôka*. This Shikibu, who had far more poems, 67, in the Goshuishû (1086), than any other poet – over twice as much as the top male Monk Nôin's 31, plays with logic in ways that make many of her *waka* seem like *kyôka* or something close. "The nameless book" (*Mumyo-zôshi* c1200), probably authored by Shunzei's Daughter (actually grand-daughter), raves "It's hard to believe that, though a woman, Izumi Shikibu composed so many excellent poems. It may be due to some karma she acquired from a previous life, for I can't imagine such talent springing from the present world." (trans. Michele Marra). To my mind, she is to *waka* what Chiyo is to *haikai*. I put dozens of never-before Englished haiku by Chiyo in *Cherry Blossom Epiphany* because I never tire of her wit. In this book, I tried to do the same with Shikibu's *waka*, but I am not as much at home in *waka* as I am in haikai, so I can only cross my fingers and hope I got most right! Most of the examples describe the high boundary of *kyôka,* which is to say they are *waka* with a touch of mad spirit in my opinion. Two I missed that are in Carter make my point. The first (*tsurezure to sora zo miraruru omou hito ama kudarikomu mono naranaku ni*), borrows considerably from his fine translation, the second, only the caption and first word.

My idle eyes turn to the sky,
Though it's not as if the man I wait for
will descend from heaven!

~~~~~~

◎ written when pondering the uncertainty of the world ◎

Being someone not a soul will miss – while I am here,
Should *I* say it? *"Alas, poor Shikibu, I knew her well!"*

shinobu beki hito mo naki mi wa aru ori ni aware aware to ii ya okamashi
miss/mourn-ought people evn not persn/self-as4, is/exist time-in pitifl pitifl say put shuld?

~~~~~~

Shokusanjin 蜀山人 1749-1823. Also, Yomo no Akara, Ôta Nanpo/Nampo. 生名大田長次郎。成人名大田覃（おおた・ふかし）は、雅号を南畝、狂詩号寝惚先生、狂歌号四方赤

良、狂歌第二号、そして長年使ったから首数の多い号は蜀山人で、それで行く。狂歌以外の分野で最も一般的に通用性あるは、大田南畝。Born into a poor samurai family, Ôta Chôjirô, commonly called Ôta Nanpo, his general purpose *nome de plume*, wrote mad *waka*, or *kyôka*, and mad Chinese verse, or *kyôshi* from his teens, first publishing as Yomo no Akara 四方赤良 for the former and Neboke Sensei 寝惚先生, Professor (or Doctor) Sleepy-head, for the latter. As Yomo no Akara, he edited and published the book that started the Tenmei *kyôka* boom at the same time Kisshû (see above), did his. Unlike Kisshû's anthology arranged the easy way, by author, his anthology arranged by season, theme, and *je ne sais quoi* was a resounding success. It was published on New Year of Tenmei 3 and when he held a party for his mother in the third month of that year, celebratory *kyôka* came from more than 180 people! Edo's *kyôka* boom was on! Later, he would adopt the name Shokusanjin. In this book, as a rule, I use the name used by my sources. The baldest and boldest expression of his philosophy of life is probably this:

世の中は色と酒とが敵なり どうぞ敵にめぐりあいたい（述懐）
yononaka wa iro to sake to ga kataki nari dôzo kataki ni meguriaitai
world-as-for color/sex and sake the enemies are, please enemies+dat. meet-want

Sex and sake, our enemies, are what all men must face –
Blessed it is to have such foes I would, instead, embrace!

In this world, sex and drink are said to be man's foes
That I could be so lucky to have such foes in droves!

Had politics not turned conservative and forced him to retire from an active and, as he would put it, *snowballing,* literary career, allegedly because of his being a friend of a man executed for corruption/political reasons and for suspicion of writing lampoons he never admitted to writing – actually, I would guess, to nip-off a potential threat in the bud – he would have become wealthy as a poet-editor, for his wit was intelligent yet open to all and his editorial and inter-class organizational skills extraordinary. I have not seen enough of his *kyôshi* (Chinese style mad poems) to judge, but he is generally credited with making both minor genres of mad poetry into major ones. I think *kyôka* was so popular under Teiryû *et al* in Ôsaka, that it may be more a matter of making it *equally* popular in the capital city, but Shokusanjin's poems are so delightfully fresh – and so many of Teiryû's all too predictable – that it is tempting to credit him with *everything*. While I have published some of Shokusanjin's old-age and poverty complaints in this book, he was not dirt-poor like yours truly. He could afford to enjoy nights out attending plays with his mistresses right up to his death. The real tragedy of his relative lack of wealth was that it forced him to do work work and kept him from retiring, thereby depriving him of the opportunity to concentrate on the arts full time. That poverty was a crime, for considering his high scores on the civil service exams, he deserved a much higher post. But such, like most good ambassadorial assignments in 20c Usania, depended not upon accomplishments but on the pull of the wealth he did not enjoy. 蛇足「たとひ時うつりうまごと去り、楽しみ悲しみ行き交ふとも、天さへ酔へる花の朝、頭もふらつく月の夕、雨の降る日も雪の夜も、日々酔ふて泥の如く、一年三百六十日、一日も此君無かる可けんや」。(蜀山家集の前の経歴の中で金子曰く「四方の留糟」の此君盃の記)。

Shôzan 嘯山 1718-1801. Nothing of his is in this book; but, believe me, *any* haikai master who lives into his 80's wrote plenty of *kyôka*. It is not because they did do so after becoming senile but because people full of good humour live long. His haiku in 律亭集 reveal a mind not shy of conceptual wit and I expect that if I ever get to see his *unedited* poems 律亭贅集 (not yet in print) there will be *kyôku* galore and maybe a cache of *kyôka*. Because haiku researchers discard *kyôka* and *kyôka,* and *kyôka* researchers (such as there are) do not research *haikai* poets not, like Teitoku, officially into *kyôka,* my guess is that most of the best (those *I* would like, at any rate) *kyôka* have not yet to be type-faced!

Shunzei 皇太后宮大夫俊成 1114-1204. This master of the grand empress's household office and father of Fujiwara no Teika famed for choosing the *Hundred Poets One Poem* Collection may well be the greatest kyôka poet before Shokusanjin. I say that judging from the small sampling I have come across here and there that indicate a diverse subject matter and extraordinary wit. I hope to find more of his poems and give him a chapter or two. Meanwhile, here is another of his poems. It is from the "sea" *umi* section of the 1333 *Fuboku* 夫木 collection, every bit as sophisticated a trick as anything Shokusanjin et al came up with. I tried (*Every river has a head, but flowing all end up at sea; Such headless equality, no gods but the Buddhahead!*) but am afraid it cannot be Englished, for the pivotal pun of upriver=*kami*=gods leading us to the ocean, which having no such upriver or *kami* is the Atman or Buddhahead, would be utterly lost in passage (川は皆なかれいりては海なれはうみはかみなきほとけなりけり俊成 紙園社百首川 *kawa wa mina nagare-irite wa umi nareba umi wa kami naki hotoke narikeri* shunzei 蛇足：川上のかみ⇒神。仏を海と見立てるのを、あったかも説話 just-so story!).

~~~~~~

Sôchô 宗長 1448-1532. This monk and link-verse master was student of the witty link-verse master Sôgi. He is, together with Teitoku, the only notable link-verse master included in Kyôka Taikan (Broadview) and, thanks to Mack Horton, his wit is known in the English-speaking world. One particularly sexy sequence Horton translates includes the following 17-14 syllabet poem (which I borrow with changes such as improper enjambment for rhyme, and a hint at one missed pun) shows his skilled wordplay:

ware yori mo seitaka wakashu machiwabite + *fudô mo koi ni kogarasu mi ka*

*How he waits & waits for the lad Seitaka, who stands above
Himself – Fudô, unmoving, burns with his unrequited love!*

Cetaka (sk) an attendant of Acala (sk) is called Seitaka in Japanese. That is homophonous with tall (setaka or seitaka). Acala (sk) is called Fudô, literally "un-moving." That is not explained in the poem, but as it was the one thing (burning for love though not moving – if you recall, men like cats literally moved around for love) overlooked in Horton's otherwise satisfying and generous notes, . . . Horton does point out that this vulcan god is always depicted with a nimbus of flames, which makes this a good facetious just-so. Note that, as this is link-verse, right and left of my hyphen are separate lines by separate poets and the first could only refer to a tall young-crowd (gay youth) and only becomes the name of the attendant with the clever cap, which I guess is by Sôchô, though the link-verse session had six or seven participating and individual lines are not credited. I would bet there are more sources for Sôchô *kyôka* than the collections translated by Horton and given in *Kyôka Taikan*.

~~~~~~

Sôgi 宗祇 1420-1502. Judging from his *hokku*, or haiku, Sôgi has far more wit than the only adjective that ever graces his name, "orthodox," might suggest. That is why my *Cherry Blossom Epiphany* has scores of his haiku. I have not yet read any collections or journals of his and the only 31-syllabet poem of his in this book is one moralistic kyôka. One reason I suspect there are kyôka riches out there to be found is an exchange with Sôchô found in one of the 28 episodes from Anrakuan Sakuden's 1,000+ anecdote *Seisuishô* (1623) or *Laughs to Banish Sleep*, translated by H. Mack Horton. You may find it beautifully laid out over two pages in the booklet published as part of an episodic festschrift for Howard Hibbett by Highmoonoon Press (2001). Here, I'll deparse and despace with slashes and equal signs, but otherwise leave it without my usual interference because it is perfect as is to reveal Sôgi's playfulness:

Strained Etymologies (1.1.5) [Title] // One evening when Sôgi and his disciple Sôchô were walking on the beach, they came upon a fisherman hauling in nets covered with seaweed. // "What do you call that?" they asked. / The fisherman replied, "Some say *me,* some say *mo."* / "That would make a good *renga* link" Sôgi remarked, and he composed this: // *me to mo iu nari / mo to mo iu nari* = *Some say me, Some say mo.* // He then asked Sôchô to provide a rejoinder. Sôchô composed the following: // *hikitsurete / nogai no ushi no / kaerusa ni* = *Leading home / oxen that were / out to pasture.* // Female oxen make the sound *unme* when they low, and male oxen, *unmo*. Sôgi was impressed. // Then Sôchô asked his master for a verse in return. Sôgi composed this: *yomu iroha / oshiyuru yubi no / shita o miyo* = *Look beside the finger / that points to those syllables / in the iroha.* // *Me* comes after the *yu* of *yubi* [finger] in the *iroha* syllabary, and *mo* comes after the *bi*. (Ibid)

Iroha is the famous syllabary poem and, as Horton explains in his notes, the lack of diacritics allows the syllabet (my word) *hi* ひ to also be read *bi* び. Somewhere else in this book I mentioned not borrowing this episode as I quoted Horton's wee booklet too much already, but not imagining any better proof of Sôgi's ability to have written extraordinary *kyôka* than this, could not help myself. This is the sort of odd associative leap that marks the best work of Shokusanjin. If it turns out to have been apocryphal, brewed by "the Kyôto abbot and tea connoisseur Anrakuen Sakuden (1554-1642)" well, so be it. In that case, *his kyôka* need to be ferreted out. And, here, by the way, is #351 of 360 *kyôka* from *Laughs to Banish Sleep* 醒睡笑 collected in *Broadview* 狂歌大観 参編:

我物とほしさのまゝにたてのみて 夜尿しの田の森の茶坊主　宗祇
waga mono to hoshisa no mama ni tade nomite yobari <u>shi no ta</u> no mori no chabôzu　sôgi
my thing so desiring-as nettle drinking night-pissing-doing's plot's woods' tea-monk

Free to drink all the piss-a-bed I wish, and 'tis no crime
to go at anytime for a monk in the woods of Shinoda
if called would love to steep a fox in rhyme!

Tea-toady me!   *It's all mine and*
Out thru' the woods I trip   *yes, I am free as 'some*
at night to pee;   *prefer nettles;'*

Pissabed I chug not sip: *To go out at night & piss*
Even serving, old is free!   *whatever's in the kettle*

Some prefer nettles
I suck a lady's thumb, tea:
so I am free to go
When foxy nature calls me
into the Shinoda woods at night!

Until I read the accompanying story in *Laughs to Banish Sleep*, this is all I can do. "Doing" night-piss puns into a toponym, a place famous for a white fox that became a woman. Thanks to *haikai*, I knew *tade* tea was drunk by men as a diuretic. It made them piss rivers and may have helped with a type lumbago that swelled the balls, flushed kidney stones, relieved the prostate, killed infections or whatever. The dictionary gives over a dozen names in English and Latin, including "a lady's thumb," "gentleman's cane" "kiss-me-over-the-garden-gate" and a "water pepper" (as in W.C.?). The *tade* in idiom suggests "each to his taste," or, "some prefer nettles." I met a Greek on Key Biscayne who says *nettles* make a fine diuretic soup, so that, too matches! It is *not* "a piss-a-bed," as dandelion owns that fine *aka*. Combining such tastes with ideas of free indulgence is masterful. Possible puns: *tade=tada*, i.e. *just drinking*; *yobari=yobare*, i.e., called (to Shinoda). A "tea-monk" served tea in a palace and came to mean "a toady," so it may be meant in a self-deprecatory manner. I was tempted to introduce *monkey* for such a *monk*, but that would be too Humpty-Dumpty even for me. Combining the final self-deprecation with the initial claim to utter freedom is, again, masterful. But, I am sure that, if this really was by Sôgi, we need to try to find whatever remains of his informal poetry, for the top linkverse master may well have been the top *kyôka* master as well!

Sôkan 宗鑑 1458-1546. Monk and haikai master known for bringing link-verse down to the level of folk, he wrote many *ku* that might be called *kyôku*, such as this poorer-than-thou complaint *"No clothes for me / as the year draws to a close / this evening!"* 年くれて人物くれぬ今宵かな *toshi kurete hito mono kurenu koyoi kana*. The original puns on *kure* as "ending" and "giving." Clothing is not specified, but was the most common gift, so I borrowed it for art's sake. Cf., Blyth's syntactically and semantically closer translation: *"The year draws to its close; / Nobody gives me anything / This evening."* HK 1.). Sôkan's single *kyôka* death verse (business in another world #382) tells us more about his down-to-earth wit than all the knee-jerk Bashôite criticism of his supposed worthlessness combined. As the introduction to Jinkyû's work (see above) mentions Sôkan next to Bokuyô as a great *kyôka* wit, I bet more can be found for another edition.

Sosei 素性法師 d. 909. Son of Henjô who fell on the Maiden Flowers. He had almost two score poems in the *Kokinshû*, about twice as many as his more famous father. A good number suggest he was partial to the *kyôka* side of poetry. Over a dozen are in this book.

Takuan 1573-1645. Re. the hundred-odd poems found online, *Wow!* I hope to find more. One of the most likeable poets in history, like Ryôkan, he did not shy away from yucky personal problems, he made entertaining for all of us and, like Ryôkan, he is the rare, truly independent spirit whose waka *must* be novel, which is to say *kyôka*. But he was serious and not all his Zen poems (a handful are in *Savage Songs* 1666) are *that* witty:

布袋絵の賛に　此袋あけてみたればなにもなし　何もなひこそなにも有けれ
kono fukuro akete mitareba nani mo nashi* nani mo nai koso nanimo arikere

On a Picture of Hotei, God of Happiness

If you should open his fat bag you would find nothing;
And nothing, of all things, means it could be anything!

Takuan had a heading in Yoel Hoffman's *Japanese Death Poems* though he never wrote one, or did he? It is a matter of definition. Asked for one he "drew the character for 'dream'." Can 夢 be a poem? Context *says it all*. Were beautiful or otherwise strongly affecting words poems, any Chinese character brushed right can indeed say more than most sonnets. It is why the word "calligraphy" fails to do them justice. But I find it uniquely touching as a death poem, for were it not for the many dreams that would die with me if I cannot get them out and share them, I, too, would be happy to give up my life at any time. Dreams are nothing and they are not only anything but everything that has yet to be. Takuan's death poem flows naturally from his *kyôka*. And the single-character death poem itself could be called a *kyôka*. Why? Because if you pronounce the dream *mu*, rather than the vernacular *yume*, it is homophonic with "nothing." Takuan could not have used the phonetic む because the Zen tradition of spouting off *"mu!* nothing!" would have stopped the reader's imagination in its tracks. But, with the character 夢, a good reader might well read it *"mu"* and consider the homophonic 無 .

* Most 'nothing' *kyôka* use *pears*, also *nashi*. Were this book in Japanese, it would have a chapter with nothing but punned pears. Here are two from the same 1666 古今夷曲集:

前首の前置:'ある人のもとへ柿と梨と送る消息に'。後首の前置:'有空不二の心を'

何事もなしと申さんと斗を 只一ふでに書おくるなり　自曲 *nanigoto mo nashi ...*
ありのみと梨といふ名はかはれども くふに二つの味ひはなし 平時頼朝臣 *ari nomi to*

Teika. 定家 Fujiwara no Teika. 1162-1241. Most famous for selecting the 100 poems. As a young man he competed with his father Shunzei in writing original poems that to my mind seem like *kyôka*. At age 22, he wrote, *"Think of the past!" – / so the moonlight seems to say, / itself a remnant / of autumns long since gone, / that I could never know."* (*shinobe to ya shiranu mukashi no aki o hete onaji katami ni nokoru tsukikage* sgs in Carter, trans. Carter). Carter's translation is beautiful and excellent in so many ways, I hesitate to touch the poem, but let me add one mad, and obviously anachronistic reading to hint at the *fresh* attitude I also feel in it:

> *'Think of the past!' That's easy for the moon, fossil memento*
> *of our ancient times to say about things I do not know!*

A number of poems Carter selected show how young Teika played with convention.

> *"Haze, you ask? Here, when day breaks, I'm held fast*
> *by the Spring, its blossoms, its warblers, its everything!"*

Yes, in my loose translation (*kasumi ka wa hana uguisu ni tojirarete haru ni komoreru yado no akebono* sgs via Carter). Haze was *the* mark of the arrival of spring, but Teika claims to be surrounded and uses terms usually used to describe snow-bound wintering in! One more, the title of which I maintain in Carter's translation, but translate myself (*maneku tote kusa no tamoto mo kai mo araji towarenu sato no furuki magaki wa* ibid).

> Miscanthus in a Quiet Garden
>
> *Beckon they may, but those grass plumes waving make no sense*
> *out in the hills, who would call on me by my rundown fence.*

The poem follows 9c waka by Narihira's son Muneyana (kks 243), and Lady Ise, the latter of which has people calling as well as the sleeve allusion. If I read her right, she is blaming *her* miscanthus for inviting a man in and giving her a bad name (another metaphorical danger of the miscanthus, for coming into plume is making patent and what is patent may be gossiped about . . .) ひともきぬ をはなかそても まねかれは いととあた なる なをやたちなむ 伊勢集 *hito mo kinu obana ga sode mo manekareba*. Carter's "can do no good" is closer than my rhyme-found "make no sense." Note: Japanese beckon by moving the fingers *down* instead of up, hence plumes nodding as they wave in the wind seem to say "Come here!" Teika found a way to facetiously question the worth of the supposed beckoning and he did it so naturally! The way Teika takes old saws and questions them or otherwise makes them sing is delightful. Another poem selected by Carter has him expressing surprise to experience what he had only heard about, difficulty telling snow and blossoms apart, and another picks up on an old argument about where Autumn comes from (or where it is first found) by noting that close observation showed no change in the Heavens/sky (i.e. from above) but the moon-*light* did seem to have something Fall in it. My favorite poem of his looks at clouds in the evening and wonders which is the source of the breeze stirring the blooming *tachibana* 夕暮れは いづれの雲の なごりとて はなたちばなに 風の吹くらむ skks 247 *yûgure wa izure no kumo no nagori tote* . . . (and see his father's #238. The jump in time and space by itself is surreal. The scent released by the blossoms evoke those we loved and clouds were identified with their souls, so the jump is also metaphysically perfect. Teika seems to combine the reasoning of Ki no Tsurayuki with heart-felt observations. If much of young Teika's work was kept – he is said to have been more into sincerity than wit in his old age – and I can obtain access to it, some chapters may have to be added to this book!

~~~~~~

Teiryû 鯛屋貞柳 又 由煙斎 1654-1734. Family name Taiya, or Snapper (sea bream)-shop. One of two top students of Shinkai (the other, the slightly older and wilder Getsudôken), a top student of Teitoku. He made *kyôka* almost as popular in Ôsaka as Ôta would make it in Edo a half century later. Or, to quote the *Princeton Companion to Japanese Literature*, "he affected a larger number of writers and gave *waka* a perverse new life appropriate to an age of *haikai*" (*kyôka* being *"comic waka"*). While, I have not seen a collection of *all* his work, what I have seen is, on the whole, not as novel as Ôta's. Still, they are often clever, beautiful and exquisitely apt for the occasion. One my respondent selected for his *kyôka* blog: *"Drinking I forget winter's cold and though I'm old, the spring / Is what this New Year's wine, with its tonic egg can bring!"* 飲からに冬のさむさも忘られて春の心を あら玉子酒 貞柳 家つと *nomu kara ni fuyu no samusa mo wasurarete haru no kokoro o aratamagozake* (drink-from winter's coldness even forgetting spring-heart+acc revise=new/

unpolished egg-wine). Judging from what I know about a later poet, Issa, egg *sake* was a common gift from students to their older teacher, so I added "though I'm old" for what may be a *thank-you* poem and added the *New Year* because the "new/rude gem/ball" (aratama) that with the *go* morphs into *tamago*, or *egg*, is an epithet for it. Teiryû lived in a more tolerant time than Ôta and was able to spend his long life doing poetry with others. When he died, he was feted in print by hundreds of pupils. This half-Englishable eulogy by his son plays on the literal meaning of his full name *Taiya=snapper-monger Teiryû*:

新しい尾ひれの付た言の葉は 死後迄はねる鯛屋貞柳　柳因 狂歌戒の鯛 tk
atarashii obire no tsuita kotonoha wa shigô made haneru taiya teiryû ryûin 1737
new tail fin/s attached words-as-for death-after even flap/jump snapper-shop teiryû

Those dapper fins & tails he put upon our words have snap,
Like the sea bream in his name, even dead we see them flap.

"Tails and fins" is idiomatic for "flourishes" or "garnishes." Sea bream, or snapper as we call it in Florida, served up whole as *sashimi* arranged where its body *was*, can be seen fins quivering and tail flapping on the plate. The original is better for ending with the play on his family name and speaks well of the lively spirit of Ôsaka *kyôka*. The poem is more poignant if you know that in 1700, Teiryû sent an eulogy for his father Tein, a well-known *kyôka* and *haikai* poet to his younger brother Teiga, also a poet, which said *"I don't know what sort of fish we are, but we need to not let the snapper-shop fins fall!"* 足下とわれ真子か白子かわかねども続く鯛屋の鰭な落しぞ *soko to ware mako ka shirako*.)

Teiryû is the only poet not belonging to the later Tenmei group in the Famous Poems 名歌名句鑑賞辞典 supplement to my ancient words dictionary (*kogo-jiten*, something all college graduates own in Japan). He has the first two of the 20 *kyôka* (vs. 925 *waka*, 402 *haiku,* and (likewise badly under-represented) 20 *senryû*). The second is the oft-translated conceptual *kyôka* favoring Fuji in a propitious dream to climbing the real thing which we have seen (p.46). The first is not Englishable so, as far as I know it hasn't been: 月ならで雲の上までずみのぼるこれはいかなるゆゑんなるらん　*tsuki nara de kumo no ue made sumi-noboru kore wa ikanaru yuen naru ran*. It is a not just a riddle but one with the hints in puns, one double and one triple, and allusion: *"If not the moon, what then rises clearly=sumi=ink above the clouds and how has this come about=yuen=oil-smoke=his-name)?"* Teiryû had adopted a pen-name Yûensai 由縁斎, but after this poem achieved renown, two characters changed to 油煙斎 = "oil-smoke," i.e. *lamp-black* in the new name, is together with animal glue (gelatin), the ingredient for *ink* (*sumi*), which is punned into something "*clearly* rising" above the clouds that is not the moon. That invisible (or punned) *ink* refers to a large piece of ink (people ground their own from these lumps which were rectangular or sculpted – I was given one in the form of a cicada, frosted in gold to someone I sent a real cicada slough spray-painted gold) sent from a Nara ink-maker to the august sovereign, rhetorically placed above the clouds. The poem was supposedly impromptu. ♪*Here are Eight Eulogies for Teiryû.* 7 of 37 included in a book published to mark the seventh year after his death, 狂歌餅月夜　百子編 1740 (Jumped the gun? Seems like 6 years), and 1 of 27 in a book published in the year of his death, 1734 狂歌糸の錦. In Japanese alone, they are an *omake* オマケ, or bonus.

七年忌いさや狂歌の配り物　石をふたつに割てせき半　　則本太山　*nananenki iza ya . .*
言の葉も昔なからの油煙斎　消て其名のすみのほる哉　　八雲軒玉峯　*kotonoha mo . .*
すみ馴て今は浄土に手合の　箔のかたちの油煙斎仏　　備前岡山司喉　*sumi-narete ima wa . .*
唐はしらす日本に又もあらかねの　槌て打ても出まい狂仁　同所風俗子都則　*kara wa shi . .*
照る月は団ならねと七年の　其の人をあふきこそすれ　同所似竺　*teru tsuki wa uchiwa . . .*
寺入の孫に形見の硯海　みるめ悲しや油煙斎なし　　長生亭柳因　*terairi no mago ni . .*
形見こそ仇の月見と内に寝て 七年忌ともしらぬか仏　貞裘関法橋契　*katami koso ada . .*

釣棹のいとうとくも鯛屋翁 仏の御手にかゝり給へは　　永田布声　*tsurizao no ito . .*

All of these are not just interesting, but *fascinating* in different ways that would require a chapter just to explain. The second and fifth are simple masterpieces and the last where a fishing pole string becomes an intensifier enroute to the belated snapper to be pulled up by Buddha . . . (A happy Japanese var. of our 17c *Death is a fisherman, the world we see / His fish pond is, and we the fishes be /. . .*) But, wait, in yet another book 狂歌活玉集 there are 52 more poems marking that Seventh year! Here are a few of them. Most reflect the cognizance of his death-day being on the full moon of fall.

名月に此世さらはと彼岸の玉のうさきととんた貞柳　四弘亭忍阿　*meigetsu ni kono yo*
七年をけふか／＼とよみくらしおつる涙はなにの由縁か　鉤帯堂可笑　*nananen o kyô*
花と見て手毎／＼の家土産も今は浮世に置きみやけ哉　土磔斎寛水　*hana to mite te . .*
なき跡や今宵煮て喰ふ芋にこそすいきの涙流す月影　木原貞椿　*naki ato ya koyoi nite*
しに分れてよりはや七年の月はあれと影法師たに見ぬそ悲しき　西園斎米都　*shini wa . .*
手向たし手向たいやとおもへともろくな狂歌は由縁斎様　如柳　*temukitashi temu . .*
その人は爰に在明まん丸し　七年前に死なれたはうそ　其考　*sono hito wa koko ni . .*

蛇足「家つと」も「置き土産」も貞柳の歌集。後は日本語と想像力で大体解ける。These seven would likewise need a page to explain. The second and third pen-names Kuso Dôkashô and Dorokusai Kansui, seem to pun-read Whatodo Withshit and Stinkofmud Bilgewater. Their puns and conceptual wit reinforce my belief that there are uncelebrated, unprinted collections by such unknown people out there if we were only to hunt for them. The last, while it has a beautiful pun, is a *waka* and a good one. Be that as it may, filling an entry of an annotated bio with death anniversary poems may be the maddest thing I have done in this book, but nothing about Teiryû, in my opinion, is so remarkable as the number of people who loved him. So, these poems, some from Ôsaka, but many (five of the last batch, above) from "other countries" *are* his main bequest to the world of *kyôka*.

★ While star-ing books in *Broadview* for the Biblio, I took one more look at 家つと a collection of Teiryû's work and found four poems too interesting to leave behind:

Asked for a poem in response to the attitude expressed in the following *waka*

世の中はかりの世なれとかりもよし夢の世なれは又寝るもよし　ある人
yononaka wa kari no yo naredo kari mo yoshi yume no yo nareba mata neru mo yoshi

*Is the world of life on loan? I'll just borrow it to reap!
Is the world but a dream? Well, then I guess I'll sleep!*
~~~~~~~~~~~~~~~~~~~~~~ or ~~~~~~~~~~~~~~~~~~~~~~
*This world may only be lent, but I'm happy just to rent.
This world may be a dream; good, sleep sounds pleasant.*
~~~~~~~~~~~~~~~~~~~~~~ vs ~~~~~~~~~~~~~~~~~~~~~~
*This world may be lent, but it's damn hard to actually rent.
This world may be a dream; sleep would be more pleasant.*
~~~~~~~~~~~~~~~~~~~~~~ or ~~~~~~~~~~~~~~~~~~~~~~
*This world may be on loan, but though you pay it will not keep.
The world may be but a dream. Nice, perhaps, if you can sleep.*

世の中はかりの世なれとかりにくし夢の世なれとそうもねられす　貞柳
yononaka wa kari no yo naredo kari-nikushi yume no yo naredo sô mo nerarezu

The second is by Teiryû and both are better in the original for the pun on "temporary" world and "rent/ borrow," both *kari*. The first poem is standard Japanese Epicureanism which we have seen. Teiryû's complaint about the "dream" is brilliant.

草　歯ぬきならで他の国より象ぶらふ　めんよう／＼鼻でまんぢう
hanuki nara de hito no kuni yori kisaburô menyô-menyô hana de manjû

This is my favorite of Teiryû's many poems celebrating the tour of an elephant that started in Nagasaki in 1729. My next favorite is 大象の来るは目出度ことしかな三八 廿四孝みるにも *ôzo no kuru wa . . .* I have not yet to solve either, though I enjoy the components of each. The play on *hana yori dango,* or, "dumplings beat blossoms" to *hana de manjû* or "nose eats dumpling" – "nose" being a homophone of "blossom" and the dumpling a different sort with a Buddhist sound appropriate to the elephant whose punned name puns on "coming" etc. in the first is all exquisite. The second takes numbers 3284 from soroban mathematics (「八に、三を乗ずれば、幾個となるや」とい う問題を「三八、廿四」と計算（暗算九九）していた(?!))。 and 廿四孝 from a *ruri* puppet play and loses me entirely. I did *not* find Bokuyô "hardly readable today" (Keene), but even on second read, I find much by Teiryû, the professional, is. Here, for contrast is an exceptionally prosaic poem, if it is a poem, by Rikyô 李郷 in a book put to bed in 1730 by 走帆, or Running Sail, a student of Teiryû's: *"A live elephant I saw on the twentieth of summer's dawn / And all its hairs and hide were grey like a mouse"* いきた象を見しは卯 月の廿日にて　毛さへ色さへ鼠色なる *ikita zo o mishi wa . . . .* A mouse is as far from the elephant as can be, but grey in Japanese is either "ash-color" or "mouse color" and the little rodent commonly serving for a "lab-rat" today is called a "twenty-day mouse" in Japanese because they reproduce and grow *that* fast. One folk etymology of the Uzuki, or deutzia month, has it related to *birth* and the start of the natural cycle – hence, I made it summer's dawn – but I think the character 卯 looks very elephantine. Such is the poetry of coincidence, but the actual wording is nothing but poor prose! ああ、同じ「狂歌乗合 船」に李郷は「打こけて取乱したる思ひねの夢に逢よはひとり相撲か」も拝見。やはり駄 歌にもそれなりの魅力ある。それに別な本で走帆にもこの戯れ歌：ふりつめは女に化るも ことはりや　雪も狐も同しこん／＼　狂歌種ふくべ　★　抜けた貞柳歌：　たんほゝに手を 打ほとの歌も哉　鼓の趣向聞ふるしけり　*tanpopo ni te o utsu hodo no uta mogana . . .* 狂歌種ふくべ. The last is a dandy poem but I am not sure I got the second half.

~~~~~~

Teitoku 貞徳　又　長頭丸 1571-1653 and his unabashedly playful school of *haikai* composed *kyôka* in their leisure. His students, including Kôfû 行風 editor of the great Kokin-ikyoku savage-song anthology (1666) with many old poems Teitoku probably passed to him, and correspondents not only bore the Teiryû and the Naniwa (Ôsaka school) of *kyôka* but influenced the Tenmei revival more than most Edoites realize. While most of his *kyôka* are less finely crafted than his haiku, his character is so good that not a few belie Keene's plain put-down of his work based on an admittedly boring example. I cannot understand why graphic artists are admired for producing art for art's sake and poets like Teitoku despised for doing the same with words. While I have seen only a small portion of his mad poems, from what I have seen, they deserve more attention. Surely, his witty explanation why the poor are not "have-nots". (pg.282) and his depiction of the soft-country of spring (pg.48) deserve a place among the *kyôka* all-time top hundred, if not top ten. And you will note that the two are completely different styles of *kyôka,* one lyrical erotica and one mock-didactic. And the bow poem I could not solve (pg.38), pun-filled yet mystical, is altogether different! Likewise for this beauty I found in the *Old & Now Savage Song* 古今夷曲集 （1666 anthology where he had 52 poems, second only to Mitoku's 63: 白壁をつけたる宿の庭にさく　花は豆腐のうば桜かな　貞徳 集 *shiro kabe o tsuketaru yado no niwa ni saku hana wa tôfu no ubazakura kana.* This simple and not especially beautifully composed *kyôka* that today might be called a *tanka* by anyone who allows *tanka* a bit of word-play, is as much Teitoku as the shallow name puns and puny (if not punny) wit with which he is identified. And note that the picture is as magically fitting and evocative as any by Buson. Yes, tôfu-making discard is call *u-no-hana*, referring to a bush covered with small soft-white blossoms, and it mostly serves to pun into the *ubazakura*, or grandma cherry (an august, as in old, cherry tree), but that, and the way the *hana,* or blossom, is delicately separated from the barely punable *u*, to call attention to its presence, makes me recall a healthy slightly plump (by Japanese standards) silk-tôfu skinned beauty in her fifties who, with her husband, ran the tôfu shop. I think she is the flower/mistress of the house, or lodge. Like Occidental bakers, *tôfu* shop-keepers are up long before dawn and can use a white wall for the light, while an old gnarled cherry in blossom looks fantastic framed and backdropped by white walls and (traditional Japanese) architecture. I repeat myself, but If I introduce more Yûchôrô,

Teitoku and Teiryû in this book than the modern Edo-exalting scholar would, it is because not only were they good but I think we need to be clear that the wit of Ôta and fellow Edoites did not just drop from the sky. Their *kyôka* would not have been born were it not for the *kyôka* of Western (as Osaka and Kyôto are called) Japan. From what I can gather, the era presided over by Teitoku may well have been the golden age of *kyôka*, though it is generally treated only as juvenilia, i.e., the age of nominal and therefor worthless *haikai* that Bashô the latter day saint of haiku would soon have to clean-up with a mental effort tantamount to the physical heroics of Hercules flushing out the Aegean Stables. While I have nothing against Bashônian haikai, or haiku as we know it – it is my favorite poetry of all – such an idea is horribly unfair. If said horse-shit, or as Bashô would put it, Teitoku's drool (or slobber), were appreciated on its own terms (pg.44), and both the *kyôka* in the link-verse (parsed either 5-7-5-7-7 or 7-7-5-7-5) and shorter 5-7-5 *kyôku* were to be collected and selected half as assiduously as haiku has been, I dare say Teitoku and his Teimon school, much maligned for playing with words rather than seeking the heart of nature, would be celebrated, instead, for creating a deliciously mad zone of happiness in an era only recently torn apart by a hundred years of civil war engaging more firearms than found in all of Europe at the time, that only ended in his lifetime with the unification of all of Japan for the first time in history.

Tsurayuki (Ki no ~) 紀貫之. Editor of the *Kokinshû* (905) who encouraged witty poetry and has been criticized for the same. When you consider that no one criticizes Hokusai and other visual artists for playing with pictures, why is it that poets and other writers are thought poorly of for doing the same? While only a handful of his poems are in this book, he is a major presence nonetheless as the scores of *Kokinshû* poems introduced reflect his taste as an editor.

Ueda Akinari ⇒ Akinari

Yado no Meshimori. See Meshimori.

Yûchôrô 永雄長老 (1547-1602). A nobleman (戦国大名若狭武田家の一族、細川幽斎の甥, or perhaps more interesting, son of a nun who was a kyôka-master and older sister of Hosokawa Yûsai, the top haikai master (just before Teitoku) and abbot of a temple 建仁寺の高僧. I am not sure if I would call him founder of *near-modern* (16-19c) *kyôka* (近世狂歌の祖) or editor of the first "kyôka" 集 (anthology) *Shinsen Kyôka-shû* 新撰狂歌集, (the 1508 永正五年狂歌合 and 1589 雄長老狂歌百首 etc.not being 集). – as some have thought, but I *do* consider him the first poet to write a high percentage of outrageous *kyôka* most of which are not religious. I selected an exceptionally high percentage of the limited amount of his work I have seen for this book because of that. I confess that his poem about Shikibu having a stinky you-know-what (pg.95) *shocked* me, for I had never seen such bald, or rather hairy, obscenity outside of folksong and *senryû*. His *kyôka* are natural, artless in the way of genius. I think of Yûchôrô as a cross between Heywood and Rochester and want to find more of his work than the little in the *Kyôka* Broad-view, if it exists. How ironic that Keene gives one lame poem of his from an anthology admittedly, on the whole, boring to show "the rather pedantic humor of the *kyôka* composed at this time."(!) Compare the *nineteen* examples *in this book*, with that *one* cited by Keene to show a boringly proper aristocrat and you may recall Borges on how selective biography can turn one person into any number of entirely different people.

★ If you happen to have a favorite kyôka poet I missed, failed to give enough space or under-rated, please contribute a chapter to a reprint or additional book of *Mad In Translation*. You may, of course, end it with a couple lines publicizing your own work.

Acknowledgements,

This book happened so fast there was no time to accrue the usual pile of debts. Indeed, 90% of mine belongs to *one* person, Yoshioka Ikuo 吉岡生夫 a tanka poet and fellow researcher of *kyôka*, who, doing his best to keep up with my flood of questions, generously gave me hundreds of hours of his time. Some of my inquiries led to items or thoughts that may have been of help to him as well – and even resulted in a new section at his website – but I am afraid that all too many did not, and am very grateful for his patience. When I write "my respondent," it almost always refers to him. Without his advice, I would not have known to buy the book that made *Mad In Translation* a moderate-sized introduction to a mighty, overlooked genre, instead of a tiny book with a few hundred Tenmei (late 18c) *kyôka* and some old *waka* for comparison's sake. I refer to the *Kyôka Taikan* (1982). At the same time, I had from the start the sneaking suspicion that what is usually called *kyôka* is but the tip of the iceberg of the long-ignored light-side of *waka*, and Yoshioka, working to put the *warai* (laugh/smile) back into *waka*, I knew, felt the same way. As a tanka poet well-versed in *waka*, he did not always agree when I found something *kyôka* in specific *waka*. He has more exacting measures of what is what than I, an outsider, do. But such was a difference of degree. We both felt from the start that the world of *waka* was diminished by the marginalization and exile of the comic, and I came to see his concern that a lack of attention to the same deprived modern tanka of its rich history and indirectly made it all too easy for bores to validate their taste as "traditional." Despite my initial ignorance about details, and lack of reading skills, I was at least able to give moral support to his endeavor (though no scholar, I was once well-published in Japan, even asked for blurbs by prestigious publishers, while my presence in the English language world is so low I cannot even get to agents for leading publishers). As I had a background in *haikai* and not *waka*, one major problem was trying to guess what solid *kana* (no Chinese characters) *waka* meant. Please do not hold him responsible for my numerous mistakes. This book grew so large so fast that I did not find time to ask even half the questions I should have – many translations are uncorroborated guesses – and he did not have time to answer all I *did* ask, though he gallantly tried to do so. I believe I might have prevailed upon him to find the many *ng* (not-given) names and fix the pronunciation of others, but he was already too generous with his time and I felt it would be unkind of me to ask more. (All good readers of Japanese are hereby deputized to find names+dates and search out mistakes and inform me so I can post them in my on-line *Errata* and use them for the second edition. Alternate to that, a grant to pay for help in Japan or an honorary pass # from some library to use the large waka data base which has those names would help.)

L.C., a scholar whose reading ability in Japanese and English vocabulary are light-years ahead of mine, had pressing matters over the year I wrote this book and was unable to answer more than a few short questions about *waka*, but deserves a mention for it was he who inadvertently got me started on this book about a year ago by replying to my question about whether anyone had really translated more than a mere sampling of *kyôka*. *"No,"* he replied, adding that if anyone could do so, *it would have to be me*. Reading *that* did I have a choice? Going back to my e-mail, I see the context was not quite what I recalled. I thought I had suggested *he* do *kyôka*, but his reply was –

> I did once write to you that I think kyouka are more engaging than senryu [I wrote him when I did my book of dirty *senryû*], mainly because they have the volume and density necessary to do serious parody with layers of allusion and multiple puns.

> I don't recall your replying that I should then attempt to translate kyouka. I have a fair amount of material - including the Iwanami vol. you refer to - and some obscure volumes in the vast Koten Bunko series (which is hard to come by . . . . One good

example is volume 426, "Koushoku Isemonogatari" - complete with headnotes explaining key terms, etc. - a parody of course of Ise mg and of Ise mg commentary traditions - and much of the pleasure of reading it depends on knowing Ise mg very well (or having a copy at hand) and knowing the commentary tradition. Which is to say, I never thought it might be possible to _translate_ such verse, because it is so allusive. *But with your approach (paraversing with copious commentary) I expect something could be done, maybe something very effective. . .*

[after mentioning some limited translations] I haven't seen any that work, though. For the obvious reason that a joke, especially a sophisticated and allusive one that depends on innuendo, double-entendre, punning, etc., doesn't work if it needs explaining to be "gotten." Delayed reactions undermine the action, after all. Then again, might not a rich swathe of entertaining commentary and perhaps multiple / optional versions allow the patient reader to go back and get the jokes? I.e., *I'd be delighted to be proven wrong, and you are the one person I know who might be able to do so.*

Needless to say, I took to heart the italicized sentences and that is why you are reading *this*. Yet (damn!), I have yet to see the *kôshoku* (*erotic*) *Tale of Ise* mentioned. Perhaps I can get it and another book from that series I have more recently learned of with *kyôka* by Ueda Akinari in time for the *next* edition. Meanwhile, I do not like to embarrass scholars by naming them, but *if,* despite my mixed success with the translations, asides on my miserable circumstances, imperfect citation, irregular editing, etc., L.C., nonetheless, finds the overall result sufficiently to his liking to write additional chapters or glosses for the notes of the next edition, I will gladly make room and spell out his name!

Mizukaki 水垣 久 of Yamatouta website – a labor of love which has a hundred waka each for a hundred ancient poets (the closest Japanese equivalent to Annina Jokinen's Luminarium) – responded to questions about the honest *shigure waka*. Were I religious, I would say, God bless you. He also contributed indirectly to this book by being the person who put Shokusanjin's parody of the *Hundred Poets* and most of the 1785 Hundred Demon Night Frenzy on line. I could not have shared them with you had he not made them public. As noted in the bibliography, Mizukaki did not finish up-loading the latter book as he experienced some of the bad luck historically associated with it. As one too snake-bit to be scared of snakes, who trusts in the good luck of bad luck, I, hereby, declare his unlucky streak *over,* and hope he will put the last part of the book on line.

Gohongi Hiroko of Taikado, a used-bookstore, helped by doing an efficient, caring job of checking out, paying for and mailing me books I found at various bookshops via the web had more influence than she imagines on this book. Writing non-fiction requires sources. We who are not novelists cannot just make up stuff from our heads.

John T. Carpenter responded rapidly and fully to a query about the content of Reading Surimono – lots of *kyôka* in it – and made sure I knew about Daniel McKee's books as well. I hope I have been fair to their work.

Edwin A. Cranston responded to questions about some *waka* he translated. My greater debt to him, however, is indirect. His books contained much of value for me. In short. Cranston has gathered more fresh material and seems less afraid of humor than any other Japanese-English translator I know. See his entry in the annotated biblio.

Stephen M. Forrest provided a web address for Aston's book of Japanese literature. He did so because I asked a question on PMJS (pre-modern japanese studies). I thank Michael Watson for starting and others for keeping the group alive.

H. Mack Horton responded with good humor and with just the information I needed about the framing of a certain poem in Anrakuden's *Laughs to Banish Sleep*, though it was not in the selection he translated. Another of his translations was also useful. See the annotated biblio.

John Solt (highmoonoon press) published the *episodic festschrift for Howard Hibbet*, a fine sampling of comic writing including *Laughs,* above, and kindly sent it to me.

Takanashi Hiroko at Elon University for responding instantly to my request to see her paper (I could not afford to buy) on orthography and punning as exampled by *kyôka*. Also, I am grateful to her for discovering just how good the 17c kyôka poet Nakarai Bokuyô was – so good, I had to stop the press to add a couple more chapters – when I checked up on the astounding poem of his that she used (pg.356) to example kanji-punning and feel guilty my good fortune was accompanied by the discovery of an orthography-related lacuna in her presentation of his poem too interesting not to mention.

Roger K. Thomas. Learning of his writing about late-18 and 19c *waka* and *kyôka* at last moment, I wrote and he immediately responded with a copy of his article on Kotomichi's understanding of the naturalness of using foreign words. Were J-stor open to all, I would have found him and his work years ago, for it included a note about a sea cucumber that slips from a maid's hands and falls to the floor that is to poetic style what Ben Franklin's haberdashery sign advice was for style in shop shingles. I had it in *Rise, Ye Sea Slugs!*

All my friends in haiku at Satin Doll gave me moral support throughout the year, thus keeping my spirits up. One haiyû, Miyoko, failed to find and send me a sample of the summer-sheets (a waffle-weave) I hoped to convince someone in Usania to sell for they save energy by making us comfortable in sweat, but she, nonetheless found other comfortable sheets of a weave far superior to ours which have made my Fall and, now, Winter, very, very comfortable. When one owns nothing, such little things mean alot. My readers should be grateful to Miyoko, for her contribution helped me sleep and that helped me dream and my dreams helped me translate. She also sent the book with the *ku* I used on the first page.

My mother prepared me for mad translation from childhood by changing the words to Peter Piper to have him picking *plankton*, introducing me to Ogden Nash, *the honorary kyôka poet*, Piet Hein (work and man), and more recently (when I was at work on *Rise, Ye Sea Slugs!*) to *The Id of the Squid* book and the *Bodelouse* poem.

And, Peter Dale, thanks, for offering to read and help edit. Fortunately or unfortunately, I just kept finding stuff to add and it dragged on so long that I decided, wisely or not, to put the book out quickly so I could finally finish up two *other* books (*Han-chan, the Cat Who Thought Too Much,* and *A Dolphin In the Woods*) that have been kept on hold too long. I may still take you up on the offer for the next edition.

Thanks to Interlibrary loan in Alachua County for delivering on half a dozen books from 4-08 ~ 3-09. And special thanks to the Ringling Library for both McKees, N. Texas for offering, Nebraska for sending Carpenter & HU's Yenching for the *Broadview* Index.

And should I mention my AI igo program, 手談 *Handtalk?* I play a quick game with it before starting work each day, just to see if my mind is ready. I owe more to Prof. Chen Zhixing, its creator, than royalties from the purchase of the program could possibly pay.

Finally, a belated toast for William J. Higginson, who passed away during the year this book was written (2008). He was the first person with a name (author of *Haiku World,* etc.) to review a book of mine written in English in a good magazine (*Modern Haiku*). The review did not get the attention of major media, so I never did make it in the English world of letters, but without the encouragement, who knows if I could have persevered long enough to write this book. It is hell to write for oneself alone, and he gave me hope. I wish he could have lived to read this book. Bill could be very strict about what was and wasn't haiku, while *kyôka,* as another kettle of fish, might have let him relax and laugh. And laughter being good medicine. . . He was so kind with his time and so conscientious in his response to questions. And he might have given us even more. If only the small-minded descendents of our Beat poets who wrote haiku had not made reprinting their poems difficult, he would have graced us with a fine book of that history (*We must take care not to allow copyright law to bury our culture*). But, to end on a proper note, let me add that he always signed his letters, as I, a heathen, shall this Acknowledgement – *Bless.*

An Appeal to Academics: Share Your Nô-miso with Me and the World!

ふみしらはめくらもへひにおちつへし しらねはやすき和歌の道かな 盲人 私可多咄
fumi shira wa mekura mo hebi ni ochitsu beshi shiraneba yasuki waka no michi kana   *môjin*
treading know-not-as-for blind+emph.snake-with relax-ought know-not-when easy waka-way! 17c

Ignorance is bliss – *as they who no snakes seeing can relax,*
Knowing naught is why today, The Way of Waka is a snap!

```
         (耳>
         // )
          lL
```

In e-mail, my namesake has a red breast and asterick eye, *this* robin is all ears, or *ear* 耳 at any rate. Ironically, the "L" foot will not allow me to look in the usual direction we draw faces, left. Basic Font effects surely should include a mirror option – and 90-degree turn – which would vastly improve font as a drawing tool, i.e. *fun!*

Ignorance is bliss – *as we who no snakes seeing can relax,*
Knowing naught is why, for me, even waka can be hacked!

Ignorance is bliss – indeed, *seeing no snakes, I can relax*
&, knowing nothing, walk the Way of Waka – me, a hack!

Môjin, *blind-man* is a pseudonym. "Blind-snake" (盲蛇 *mekura hebi*) i.e., *"The blind do not fear things like snakes"* (盲蛇物に怖じず *mekura hebi mono ni ojizu*) is the Sinosphere's version of "ignorance is bliss," that is usually Japanesed *shiranu ga hotoke,* or "not knowing is Buddhahood, which, considered with its equivalent is quite funny (to my warped mind), for if you are bitten by the snake, you might, indeed, become a corpse, commonly called a Buddha, or *hotoke!* Depending on context, the poem could be general self-depreciation for all informally engaged in *kyôka,* (less likely) a caustic put-down of another's sally into waka, or a disclaimer of expertise with respect to *waka* by the author, the last of which is fitting for your translator who dragged out hundreds of *waka* – intertwined with and, perhaps, one with *kyôka* – in *this* book. My books of translated *haikai* got *almost no critical reaction,* which is to say, input from superior readers in the field; but now that I am treading not on snakes but upon sacred *waka* territory, or messing with a genre of poetry many take seriously, I expect and *hope* for plenty of criticism. Do not be shy. *Send it to me,* damn it! *Show me* where I am wrong. *Show me where you can do better.* But, please, take care to write well. If your argument holds water, it will become a gloss – *with your name on it* – in the next edition.

A *kyôka* written upon consideration of the popular etymology
of the Japanese word for 'language' or 'word,' *kotoba,* 言葉.

古も今もかわらぬ羊歯目や心の種をのこす言の葉

If "words are leaves," leaving seeds that sprout in the mind,
We who write are humble ferns and not the flowering kind.

*A*nd final words for my *Readers*,

De/in/con/structive *Critics*
& *Mom* (for once, *please* read the book *first!*)

TO MOMUS.
by Robert Herrick

WHO read'st this book that I have writ,
And can'st not mend but carp at it;
By all the Muses ! thou shalt be
Anathema to it and me.

Once, I was blessed with a poison review from just such a Momus. Proud to have read but one chapter of twenty, chosen at random, he introduced the entire work a more thorough reader had judged my best book yet (personally, I am unsure) by pulling out just one long sentence with a particularly wild chain-of-associations for derision, while failing to note that *most* of my sentences were short and clear. Then, not knowing other more just critics had long lamented *the excessive qualifications and confessions of ignorance ruining my authority*, the obnoxious little man had the gall to claim, *without a single example*, that I was too damn sure of myself! This, mind you, while taking one of my cautious qualifications, namely, that *The Fifth Season* was not a *proper* haiku almanac (*saijiki*) for a number of reasons to mean that it was not a haiku almanac, *period!* You need not know about the ancient Chinese debate about whether or not a *white horse* is a *horse* to sense a problem in *that* logic. I would be lying if I said I do not revile the reviewer. I can forgive a lot but *not* dishonesty. Please don't get me wrong, if you have criticism of substance, *I will thank you by name and gladly eat it up*. If serious mistakes, such as unfair criticism of a fellow translator, were made, I will chase it down with my hat to boot. And, the proof will be seen in the next edition. Constructive criticism is *always* welcome – if violent, I think of it as a windfall, if gentle, a godsend. When Herrick writes,

TO THE GENEROUS READER.

SEE and not see, and if thou chance t'espy
Some aberrations in my poetry,
Wink at small faults ; the greater, ne'ertheless,
Hide, and with them their father's nakedness.
Let's do our best, our watch and ward to keep ;
Homer himself in a long work, may sleep.

– I must demure, though the poem itself is sheer delight. *My* generous reader *will* mark-up my book and *will* find the time to tell me when *I* nod. And, knowing I do so far more than Homer, I openly keep all major, and many minor, errata on-line (as others should). But, when Herrick goes even further, leaving advice –

TO HIS BOOK. (VII).

BE bold, my book, nor be abash'd, or fear
The cutting thumb-nail or the brow severe;
But by the Muses swear all here is good
If but well read, or, ill read, understood.

– I wonder. Could he have been pulling our legs? Regardless, *my* books need only be *absolutely honest*, as honest as the good people of Salem, only executed, God bless them, because they would not confess to being what they were not in order to be spared. Here is my response to '*To Momus,*' and my appeal

TO YOU, MY DEAR READERS

On the other hand, if thou art skilled,
And, yet, have time enough to kill;
Write what's wrong! Send me a letter:
Help make a good book better still.

But there are *some* things I do *not* want to hear. Please do *not* tell me I "need an editor," when what I plainly need is *money* enough to allow me to buy more reference resources or access to them and, more importantly, control my own space and time (basic Maslow stuff) thereby gaining the peace of mind to slow down and edit myself, as I have edited others, or, perhaps, hire someone with a larger vocabulary who is attentive to detail. I even know a few such exacting men of parts, if you will forgive the Elizabethan vocabulary, I could ask.

And, please, do not tell me I "need a publisher." I *am* one. All I lack is liquidity, *money*. My annual income for the past few years, minus some help from my mom for helping the family and a few friends appreciative of my work, has been about $1,000. In Usania, land of mammon, many would sooner confess to murder than to poverty. But, so be it. *That* is why I cannot afford to send out more than a handful of publicity copies to prime the pump, much less hire someone to help with publicity, packing and sending (why I prefer people to buy online and not from me) and why I find it hard to get major reviews, including those for libraries, that generally operate under the mistaken assumption that reading copies are always available months ahead of publishing. It is also why none of my books go to book-fairs which might aid in publicity and why they must be *"no return"* (a good review that results in the wrong sort of bookstores ordering the book would bankrupt me, so I cannot take a chance) which prevents even the right book-stores from stocking Paraverse though their customers might be delighted to know me.

A two-page appeal to potential patrons, publishers and agents may be found at paraverse.org. In short, I can command a large readership if given half a chance.

狂とは *or, More on* Mad *if You have a Magnifying Glass.*

When I asked my respondent, Yoshioka Ikuo, about some nuances of *mad*狂vocabulary, he, who long worked to interest *more* people in *kyôka* was . . . *horrified.* He had just fixed a misleading definition of *kyôka* at the Japanese Wikipedia that relied too heavily on said 狂 character and here I was trying to gave him join me barking up the wrong tree! (Y：私の関心は狂歌に対する関心の底上げ、つまり笑われるかも知れませんがWikipediaの「狂歌」に変更が加えられることです。[いやいや、我輩も英語のWiki の俳句と川柳の定義、あるいはその重なりと境線について、かなり手を入れた、同じお節介者です。嗤ふ立場ではありません])．As Kaneko's broad 1923 definition of *kyôka* along the lines of Aston (1899) including old poems called other things entirely did *not* carry the day against those who would restrict *kyôka* to what was actually called so, excessive interest in the name is, understandably, a touchy matter for a Kaneko supporter. Yoshioka-san had even gone so far to make a name change, calling the greater genre – *kyôka+waka* – 5-part-31-sound-poems. (Y：のちに五句三十一音詩の名称の変化に着目して私は「私の五句三十一音詩」を書くことになったが、「『古事記』の夷振（ひなぶり）、『万葉集』の戯笑歌、『古今和歌集』の俳諧歌、あるいは軍記物の中の落首などに起るとする古人の説には賛しがたい」（岩波書店『日本古典文学大辞典』）の浜田説が大勢であるだけに今も[金子が]百人力であることに変わりはない). I do not much care for the 5-part (or "line," if you prefer the usual Englishing, though the poems are as often as not *not* broken into lines) part of that name because there are, in my opinion, too many 31-syllabet *kyôka* that do *not* break that way, and (to be my usual rude self) look forward to my respondent dropping it. As far as words go, I would rather *redefine* than drop them because others have them wrong. Imagine if we abandoned *black,* as many psychologists thought the wisest course, for a value-neutral word such as, say, *ebony.* Black beauty would still be an oxymoron for all but one storied horse. People with bad eyes should be equally proud to say "I am *blind as a bat"* (magnificently sighted in other ways) rather than resorting to proper uglyisms such as "visually impared." See my long "Apologia for 'Cunt'" in *The W~~o~~man Without a Hole* (2007) for another example of a bad word that could be good. As far as 狂 *mad* goes, I take its bad image as a challenge. Rather than avoiding, minimizing or dropping it, I *enjoy* the opportunity to re-define and defend the character of the character.

After making it clear I was *more* radical than he was about not relying on names and out-Kaneko'ed Kaneko on taking a broad view of *kyôka,* Yoshioka kindly sent definitions from the *Morohashi* dictionary, which I do not have. Here is a condensed translation of the summary for 狂: *1-1: out of one's mind and crazy or losing it and becoming a fool, off the proper path, at any rate; 1-2: having a disordered mind; 1-3: getting mad or clashing with people for no apparent cause; 1-4: behaving erratically; 1-5: ~~hurried or flustered~~; 1-6 luxuriating (behaving extravagantly as a verb); 1-7* ならぶ~~narabu~~? *doing things one after another nonstop; 1-8: going one way and not coming back; 1-9: extremely energetic; 1-10: foolish; 1-11: monomaniacal; 1-12: so idealistic little things are ignored; 1-13: a bird's name (the coot?); 1-14: obsolete* 「古、（漢字なし）に作る」?; *1-15: ~~a proper name~~. 2-1: easy to do, or easily excited; 2-2: confused. 3) How dogs run* 狂狂. *Japanese usages* 邦A: *kuruu. To frolic, or sport.* B: ~~a machine, damaged, does not run right~~. *C: missing a target, off-schedule.*

There is probably *something* of all the above but what I crossed out evident in *kyôka*. We find our main interest among the 160 *kango,* or *character-combinating-words –*

Kyôka 狂歌:

1 ~~Singing in a crazed voice / crazy way~~ 気ちがひじみた声でうたふ（後漢書）；
2 A song with a crazy (insane) feel to it 気ちがひじみた歌（白居易）
3 Songs sung in play; poems composed in play たはむれに歌ふ。又、たはむれて作った詩。強詩（杜甫、白居易）
4 Waka that jest in concept or language. Tanka with a comic aim. Kidding songs. 構想・用語に諧謔の意を含めた和歌。滑稽を旨とした短歌。たはれうた。ざれうた（明月記）

All but the first apply, though it is pleasant to think of a proper poem sung outrageously. A fifth should be added: "a self dennigrating word for one's own *waka*." And, since I noted there was more serious interest in *kyôga* than *kyôka* in English, Yoshioka-san sent that, too:

Kyôgen 狂言:

1 Words that contradict logic, talk without bounds, a humble expression by one whose talk differs from convention. 道理に戻つたことば。取り留めもない話。自己の説の正道に合はないひとの謙辞（荘子ほか）
2 Words that shock people; big things said that violate common sense; grandeloquent claims. 「人を驚かすことば。常識を外れた大きな言。大言壮語。（唐詩紀事　杜牧　ほか）」
3 A) Comic performances inheriting ancient tricks and skills that came to accompany traveling entertainment shows in time evolving into comic skits performed between acts of No drama. イ「古代のわざをぎの遺流で、中世、田楽・散楽等に附属して起つた滑稽な演技。後世、能に対して其のあひまに演ぜられる滑稽な戯」 B). A type of drama; a line or school of drama performed by actors; a kabuki device (?) ロ「芝居。役者の演ずる芝居のすぢみち。歌舞伎のしくみ。（曾根崎心中）」C). A plot, in the sense of a scheme or sham. ハ「企んだ計画。しくんだいつはりごと。（洞房語遠）D」. A joke ニ「ざれごと。（源平盛衰記）」

♪You might note that the first two *kyôgen* definitions here apply to some of the more interesting *kyôka* which likewise indulge in hyperbole and high-falootin language, while the way *kyôgen* came to be an interlude for Noh parallels the way improper poetry under the chestnut tree complemented the proper affair under the persimmon tree (pg.608), while the tricks and jokes make us think of the riddles and sleight of tongue in *kyôka*. One 4-character word, *kyôgen-kigo* 狂言綺語 means embellished words, and by extrapolation, fiction, or a tall story. 文飾した詞。転じて、小説などの文をいふ。（白居易ほか） Such too seems to relate to our mad poems with 狂 giving free license to the imagination, does it not?

Kyôku 狂句 A haiku with a comic sense. To sporting around with a *ku*. " '*Kyôku*' *In from a gale, looking like Chikusai, the mad quack!"* (Bashô) おどけの意を含めた俳句。句に遊び楽しむこともいふ。〔芭蕉、冬の日〕狂句、木枯らしの身は竹斎に似たる哉。

♪ We discuss the fictional Chikusai who roamed about spouting *kyôka* and getting into trouble, elsewhere. I was delighted to find *Morohashi* agreed with *my* usage of *kyôku*, for usually it is 1) defined more broadly to include *all* 狂 poems, most particularly *kyôka* and *kyôshi* (the purely Chinese-character equivalent, see below) and *not*, I repeat, *not* applied to haiku, 2) used to pejoratively refer to 17-syllabet (or shorter) poems deemed neither haiku nor senryû, and 3) used to mean a *senryû*. I dislike all of those usages and hope people will not use them, so they can become obsolete. Let me add that while I am grateful to Morohashi for seeing things my way, I am not sure it was Bashô's. It is likely he played on Chikusai with his *kyôka* to tastefully deprecate his own *ku* with the 狂 *kyô*, as it once was used to humbly refer to one's own *waka*. He generally referred to playful poems as "light" or having *karumi*, and not as "mad."

Kyôshi 狂詩 A type of Chinese poetry with a droll content and style popular in the late-Edo period. A song/poem made in jest. The word "kyôshi" is not very old and apparently arose among the Five Mountain monks. Many are found in Ikkyû's *Kyôunshû* (mad cloud collection). The Chinese have "pole-belly" poems (so funny you must stay your belly with a pole?), but they did not call them this, . . . 江戸末期に流行したおどけの意味・句調を含めた一種の漢詩。ざれてうたった歌。〔喜遊笑覧、三、詩歌〕狂詩といふもの古くは聞えず、五山の僧等がそれより出きしなるべし、一休狂雲集二巻あり、其内狂詩多し、唐人に捧腹すべき詩句あれ共、それを狂詩ともいはず???、云々、（略）。

Kyôbun. 狂文 Writing that is mostly comical or jesting. A literary style begun by kyôka masters and dramatists in the mid-Edo period. Dramatic writing. 滑稽・諧謔を主とする文。江戸中期以後、狂歌師・戯作者等によつて始められた文章の一体。戯文。

Kyôwa 狂話 Playful stories. Jokes. Also lying. たはむれの話。冗談。又うそ。（紅楼夢）

♪ As for *kyôbun*, I would only add there is not much difference between it and much *haibun*, the prose of *haikai* or haiku poets. Humorous *haibun* packs in mad associations and wordplay every bit as wild as *kyôbun*. We might say that much *haibun* is kyôbun. The only connotations including "fibs" it bears mention that the ⇒ difference would be that *haibun* usually contains some *haiku* and *kyôbun* some *kyôka*. And, with *kyôwa*'s blacks who told some of the best tall tales in English – found in Zora Neale Hurston's masterpiece, *Mules and Men* – called their activity "lying."

Yoshioka also sent me some less directly relevant words such as 狂士 ***Kyôshi*** (One with grand ambition but slipshod strategy to accomplish it 志が大で事を為すに疎略な者) and 狂生 ***Kyôsei*** (A crazy man; an out-of-control prolifigate; one who thinks extremely highly of himself 気の違った男。放蕩でしまりのない人。超然と自ら高く持する人（荀子ほか）) and responded to my questions about kyôken 狂狷 and kyôkan 狂簡, respectively, one who in pursuit of ideals is unbending to the extreme, and one who is only interested in a grandiose aim and pays no attention whatsoever to detail. In all of these, I see Don Quixote and, yes, myself – or, at least myself as I might appear to some.   There were *three surprises* in the *Morohashi* material. One you may have noted: the definition of *kyôka* is very broad. Another I have already noted: the definition of *kyôku* is identical to the one I prefer though I cannot justify it on historical grounds. The last is what Yoshioka observed was *not* included by *Morohashi*. It is the term 狂吟 *kyôgin*. The character *gin*, comprised of radicals meaning "mouth" and "now," evokes the image of a live poem-jam and was found in the titles of some early books of *kyôka*.

Later, looking into my *kanji* dictionary, or *kanwa jiten* (漢語林：大修館), I found a number of *kango*, or compound words, I should have introduced in the appropriate chapters together with poems whose content evoked the same. For example, 狂号 *kyôgô*, literally "mad-number," and seemingly – to me, at least – the penname of a mad poet, means *crying up a storm in a manner that might even be judged ludicrous.* We must have seen a score of poems describing just that! Then there is 狂薬, *kyôyaku*, or *mad-medicine*, a drug that makes men go wild. One might think it a good-looking woman for a man or a handsome man for a woman, but it actually means *liquor*. Since drink was long considered fuel for composing poetry and some famous Chinese poets even calculated – or someone rumored they had – their respective ppc or poems per cup drunk, and we have seen some poems about heavy drinking and read of Shoku-sanjin's love affair with *sake* . . . And there is 狂奔 *kyôhon, mad running-about*. This can include hyperactivity in the pursuit of a dream or, better yet, in a happy condition that once would have been called a reverie. I suppose it might be called the active partner of the *other* ideal way to live, floating with the current. I love the word *as a concept*, but have yet to use it in my Japanese writing, perhaps because the sound *hon* does not evoke "running" in me. To be fair, there are also less interesting (expected) compounds such as 狂直 *kyôchoku*, rigidly upholding the right regardless what others feel; then 狂痴 *kyôchi*, mad imbecility, i.e., *dementia*. But such cannot be helped. It would seem that the idea of the mad genius – concocted by the financially and socially successful bore to excuse the poor state of more creative souls – was not *all* hogwash, as the fool and the wiseman are related in their 狂 someness .

Partial Idea & Name Index
Also see *Table of Contents*, *Poet Index*, *Glossary* & search the book on-line!

ADDITIONS not fitting in the *Table of Contents*

Monk Jinkyû 683-4. Mitoku (*kyôka* +palindromes) 613-7.639-40. Prince Munenaga 690-94. Asahi Bunzaemon/Monzaemon's "Parrot Cage Journal" (squibs & *kyôka*) 621-5

Access 528. 595-6 ■ Ainu 286.293.
Al-fresco 148 ■ Alice 10.171.489
Anagram 219.265 ■Angel wings 212
Angry mad 29-20.370-1.569
Anserine letters 246-7.
Ant-crossing (perineal trail) 556
Anthropometamorphosis 75
Aoki Yayoi 136 ■ Arima=>Tourism
Ariwara Motokata's KKS#1 Poem 34-5. progeny 466-70.625
Art books 451
Asahi Bunzaemon/Monzaemon: added to *Short History* pp.620-26
Asobie 534 ■ Aston 10.654-5
Aubergine horse 359.+pic.560-1.
Aun 37.161 ■ Automata 83
Autumn ~ not melancholy 526

Bad poems 34,106-7 ■ Bald 533.643
Balls as a pillow in peace 336. ~ to angle 359. ■ Barnes, William 606
Bashô's bird-shit 103
Bean burglar 137. ~ stink 357.
Beans vs Peas 535
Bell talking 189
Benthic (*Id of the Squid*)Arch E. 541
Bilingual reward (オマケの話) **464**. 479.
Bird/s
~ bridge 212.214.291.522 ■~ Gate -crashing 425 ■~ Hell 417.577. ■ ~ of 1-wing fly 2gether 72.214 ■ ~ sex 158.334.344.510. ■~ sutra 165 ■ ~ talking 188-9.517.531.546.552. 560■~ tracks as writing 187.443.522
Blake, The Sanity of William ~ 464
Blind-bosses 276.535-6
Blowfish 233.528.549
Blyth 11,39,302-3.398.506-9.530.541. 546-7.561. ■ Bokuyo 563
Boulder from pebble 176-7.472-3
Bows 38-9.n471-2

Braunen, Noah 424-5. 578
Bracken hands 436-7. 529-30. 584-5
Bradock & Bradock 78
Breast milk 145. 171. 319. 320. 321. 323. 380. 521
Broadsides => Squib
Brownas & Thwaite (B&T) 33.57. 134. 146.
Brower, Robert 34. & Miner 470
Buddha 587.640. ~ *as a ladle* 164-5
Buddha-fish 325
Butterfly boddhisattvas 172-3.

Cap-verse 174-5. 513-15
Cactus 345.■Cambrian diversity 601
Carpenter, John T. 424.437-451.516. 584-7. 631-2
Carter, Steven 19.33.80.119.134.177. 223.249.294.300.362.419.495.498. 519.522.525.529.534.539.543. 544-5.619.636.
Caterwauling 56
Cats 47.66-9.74.176.197.361.418.426. 477-8.563.573.583.615-6
Cave door 33.165.236.238.264.312. 315.382.446.522.586.599.622
Cavendish, Margaret 19.678.
Chamberlain 447. 655
Charcoal robes 130
Charm poems 534.573
Chaucer's Wife of Bath 136, Host 273
Cherry King 238; snapper 361.568
Cherry stone & ~ pit 501
Chesterton 9. 456. 539
Chestnut *vs* Persimmon 608
Chickadee > Middle-age
Chikamasa 162.511 ■Child poem 409
Chiming Cicada 538-40 ■China 597
Chinese verses => kyôshi
Cicada 334 ■ Clothing puns 183
Clover's white bloomers 240
Coconut 43
Coe, David Allen xxx
Cold-as-*wind* 223.524.
Comic stories w/ kyôka 402-7
Composite character 533
Composite translation 530
Concluding this book. 400-1
Counting Poems 178-81. ~ songs 561
Country life 504. ~ music 493-4.644.
~ matters 48. 474
Crab ~ man 6. ~ leg sun-beams 425

Craftsmen 575
Cranston, Edwin. 59.62-4.71.81.119. 136.142-3.156.184-5.192.293.364-5. 379.392.454.457-9.477.481.493.502. 521.598.608.
Crickets 222.524. ■Croc. mouth 248-9
Cuckoo *vs. Bonito* 239. ~ *Dislike* 520.
Curvaceousness 510. ■Dancing 481-2
Dali 419. ■ Dandelions 319-21. 423
Danrin 197.200.■Daoism 168.225.471? 526. Darwin, Erasmus 613
Death poems 382-397.570-2.603
Deer 62.220.226.298.431.639
Descartes body/mind=heart separation: see Saigyô chapters & 532
Dew-drops *tsuyu* 123.166-9.511-3.
Diacritics (nigoriten) 188,197.573
Didactic poems 170-3. 513
Disclamatory modification 520
Dog fight 573-4 ■ Donne 460
Dream-callers 184.209.374
Drunk but fine 413.490
Dry Kidney 175. ■ Ducks 333

Ear mound 575 ■ Edwards, Jona. 521
Eels morphing 60.477
Emperor Tenmu 308 ■ Enma =>Hades
English vs Japanese comic poetry 660
Epilepsy puns into a blessing 359
Epitaph 380-1.570-2
Erotic 134.315.331!343! 481-2.555.558.
Everglades, the 65
Exorcism light 259.335.357.430.443
Exotic Tongues 268
Explanation & Exotic Poetry 462-3

Fans 72.86.312.338.446.678.703
Fantasy 431
Farts 228.272.339.398.454.475.560.573. 587.642
Fata morgana 280.■Finger lopping 537
Fire 336.623-5. ~stopping charm 306-7.549 ■ Fireflies 142.200-07.349.381. 459.495.501.521.692
First-past 543.554. ■ First-snow 240-1
Fleas 99.423.
Florida crawfish 424. => Shrimp
Fraud in nature 166-7 => dew
Free-thinking 6.19.158-9.163.324.329 332. ■ French Macaroni 356.
Frog 236 ■ Frois 559
Fuji Mt. 1.46-7.128.199.289.304.319.

338-9.419.443.520.557.622-3.682.
Fundamentalism 158
Fused limbs of lovers 214-5
Fushimatsu no Kaka 265
Geese 86.126.142.244-6.337.532.557.
  614!639. ~ as text 130.244-5.246-7
Genji 84.429.436 ■ Gennai 232.475.
614 ■ Getsudôken 330-43. 554-9.
610.627■Ghost poems 274-81. 540-1.
Gift=> Kyôka Exchanges.
Gill,Sam 48 ■ Goblin=>Ghost
Gods = paper 94.175.527
Gods-gone-month 72.229-231.264.
  283.527.582.614
Gourd, out of 341.531. ~ with 386
Guests 183. ■Guns 318.343.528.549
Hades 160.164.278.325.396.
  ~ King of 162.324.583-4
Haft, Alfred. => in Carpenter
Han Yü 597 ■ Hakama 542. ■ Hall,
Tom T. 389 ■Hamada Giichirô 12.22.
88.166.598 ■ Hare to climb 249. ■
Harris 36, 367 ■ Hearn, Lafcadio
11.275.277-8.281.524.541.658-9
Heart 142-3.532 ■ Heartburn 98
Heaven's Gate => Cave Door
Hein, Piet => Piet Hein
Henjô cut 499-501.
Henkenius => R&H.
Herrick 501.544.568. 711-13
Heywood 288.
Hino Tatsuo + Takahashi Keiichi 153.
  505. ■ Hiraga => Gennai
Hoffman, Yoel 383.386-9.395.396
Hogarth 229 ■ Holderlin 12
Homosexualities 152.198.226-7.328.
  340-2.406.510.557.558.
Horn-letter 147.433.448-9.587.683
Horton, H. Mack 227.260-1.310-1.
  402.407.468.626.699-700.
Hundred Poets 118-9.140-1.197.
  226.290-301. 452.526.543-6
Hurston, Zora 479 ■ Ikkyû =>Kyôshi
I Lobster You Flounder 78
Indulgences 510-11 ■ Ink string 598
Interpretation 138.321.584.596.612
Iris (ayame) wife 313.330.551.694
Issa's griffin eating the moon 487-8
Ise & Nise 284.352-5.563.568.611
Ise Lobster => Florida crawfish
Issa kyôka 29-30. 109.344-351.560-2
  kyôku 84.512-3.563.=>Poet/m Index
Japan at peace 90.91.159.316.427.
  483-4.
Japanese anthem => Boulder
Japanese pronunciation. 26
Japanese style 520
Johnson, Josephine 49

Just-so wacky waka 126.205.206.228
Kabuki star/s Danjûrô 424.447.517-8.
  579.Genzaemon 356.565-6
  aka => Fushimatsu no Kaka
Kalpa 143,212,318 ■ Kaneko Jitsue
  10.598.600-2.619-20.650.
Kanji play 141.250.374?422.533.622
Katô Ikuya 197.520.
Katsurao => Man in the Moon
Katydid & Katybit 147,196.494
Kei, M. 53.186-7.
Keillor, Garrison 19,20,
Keene, Donald 239.302-3.398.412.
  452.455-6.466.539.568.611
Kenny, James T. 186-7
Key Biscayne historian 251
Kidding 54-7.599 ■ Kisshû 50.685
Knutson, Roger M. 25■ Kôfû 611
Kotomichi foreign memes genuine 605
Kyô (mad/wild/eccentric/novel) 2.
  10-12.18-20.602-3.665-7.713-4
KYÔKA
  Complex egs. 60.92-3.265.428-9.etc
  Definition of 2-3.10-12.598-9.600-1.
  607.654-5.658.Evaluation of 53.23-4.
  First usage of term 608. History of
  21. 595-647. rules in Kôfû's treatise
  512.638. Re. All => Glossary xxx
  Varieties: As Advertizements 646-7.
  Dueling poems 176-181. 515.
  Exchanges 182-6.516.603-4
  Folk style gross 5.177.232.355.431.
  515.523-4.627. haikai linkverse 200.
  modern 588-9.670-1. Parodies 613-
  4.655 => parody, 100poets. Riddle
  540. Squibs 108-11.328.491-2.549.
  619-626.638-42. Stories, in 352-5.
  402- 7.626- 7.643 Surimono, on
  424-451.578-87.628-34.
Kyôku 45.512.666
Kyôshi 22. 150-7.505-9.573-4.666-7
Kyûsojin Hitaku 141.195.365.605
Lacking things 87
Lakoff 124. Laments 380-2
Lampoon => Kyôka ~ squib
Lanoue, David 39 Lark 530
Learical 195.258. ■ Lee, Peter 471.
Lessing 635. ■ Leupp, G. 559.
Lice 266-7.322.326.368.504.540.44
Lightning 262.480. ■. ~ Slim 282
Limericks 105.520.644-646
Listing (imposs. things) 142-3.503.540
Literary criticism 302-3.398.
Longevity 250-1
Lotus dais 160.325?510.
Love Bugs 269
Long ago and far away 209,554
Love 309

Love & Love-sick blues 80.480.
MacCauley, Clay 290.543
Machismo 392.572
Mad => kyô. As angry 30-1
Maezuke, or draws 540. ■ Magao 633
Maiden-flowers 211.347.357!501.560.
Maidenhair fern => Bracken
Man in the Moon 92-3.284.328.331!
  482!486-7
Manyôgana 475.491.
Manyôshû 54-7. 62-3.137-8. Tabito's
  drinking poems in rhyme 488. 525.
Marceau, Lawrence E. 232
Materialism 329
McAuley, Thomas 254-5.312-13.314.
McMillan, Peter 452
McCullough 34.352-5.366-7.470.481.
541.619.
McKee, Daniel 187.188-9.426-439.
  468-9.517. 534.546.5.579-86. 628-34
Meiji 110 ■ Memome Project 311.
Merman 278-9
Meshimori's Moving Heaven & Earth.
  32-3. 465-6 (more translations)
METAPHOR 58-9
1. Passion as Fire. Omohi 61.122.199.
   206-7.318.334.495.520.613.677.
   Mune yaku/kogare 58!72. 98.202.
   641.677. Koi 493 . See Firefly and
   Moth. Fire in the West (Hudibras,
   Addison on Cowley) 476. Fire+
   Water 493.
2. Tears as Rivers 60.115!116.119-24.
   127.130.481.493.496-7.603.693. as
   Ocean 115.120.122-5. as Harbor
   121.123.693. as Pond 114!115.126.
   as Artesian flow 125.492. as Dew
   120.123.131 as Jewels 127.131.237
   496. as Rain 120.331.375.382.414.
   487. as Dye 115.130.206. as Icicles
   44-5.126. as Hail 126. as Poles 330.
   554-5
Metaphysics of Dew. 512-3
Metaverse 32.113.211.237.290.292.
  317-8.322.407.462.465. 407.
  411-2.516.591.612.637-8. 680
Michizane as honey 419
Middle-age (shijûkara) 174-5.513-15
Milkyway => Star Lovers
Miscanthus 222.524-5. ■Mitoku 613-7
Mizukaki Hisashi 300.469.544.651
Monkeys 625 ■ Monkey-man 226
Moon 50.332 ■Morrison, Ryan 455
Morse, Edward. 1. 6. 482. 557-8
Mosquitoes 197.547-8. ~ Larvae
  221.524 ~ smudge 128.334
Moth 375.521. ■ Mumon 506-9
"My rain" 414.421-2. 574-5

My mistakes 266-7 ■ Mysogeny? 190
Myths 158-9 => Free-thinkers
Nada Inada 67.101.183.289.480.541
  606. ■ Nakanishi 137-8
Names of things 111.377.414-24.636-7
Nansen 509 ■ Nash, Ogden 171
Nature 346.521
Nelson, Willie 59. Nenzi Laura 640
Nevercometrue 539
New Year themes 34-46.236.238.240.
  242.248-50.466-71.578-9
Nightingale => Uguisu
Ninomiya Chûhachi 41
Nobles 532.632.653 ■ Nobunaga 111
Nonsense 618 ■ Nose-blowing 236
Nose hair 92.342.486.559.594
Now-styles 146-7
Obama 174
Octopus 99.198.434.690
Odd Japanese usage 540 ■Old age 131
Oldenburg, Carl (Frog Croaks) 505
Old Smokey 501-2
Order of Poems 503 ■Origuchi 605.637
Orthography+punning 188.356.563-8
Ôta Nanpo 10. 21. 85.182. 505.541-2.
  546.629
Over-population 323.324
Ozawa Roan 10
Palindrome 398.573.617
Pampass => miscanthus ■ Parker 129
Parody 408.431. ~ unrecognized 520
  => *kyôka variety*
People w/ Holes through them. 74.480
Peony 580-1 ■ Perrin, Noel 640.
Parsing 609■Personal Mad 464.601-2
Petit Morte 139.327?330!
Piet Hein 19.20.32.285.310.333.391.
  460.466.544.550-1.574.636
Pictures + *kyôka* 304-7.547-8
Pilgrimage 583.640. ■ Pimples 629
Pindar, Peter 477-8. ■ Pissing. 49.
Poetry's *Effect* 32-3.466.552
Pogo 287. ■ Pooh, Winnie 3
Poverty 4.170.193.282-9.350.506.
  541-2.610 ■ ~ god 283.403.542
Praying *for house* 348, *for rain* 249.
  534.
Prince Ôtsu 392. ■ Privities 556
Pulvers, Roger 24.273
Pun/s 24.26.94.105.326.356.358.447.
  515-6.527. 532.541-2. ~ Addison's
  cycles 604.654-5.668-9.
Qui, Peipei 2. ■Quixote 571-2
Racoon-fox=tanuki 528-9
R&H or, Rodd & Henkenius 36,59,
  141.206.216.219.364-5.458.481.
  494. 539

Rhyme 27-8.50-1.505-6.669. ~*on a
Japanese word in English* 415.443
Richland Woman 560. River cut 142.
Roberts, Luke 639-40■Rodd=>R&H
Round vs square 86,176
Rosary problem 362. ■ Ryôkan 86
Saigyô vs Motokata 498
Saint (*hijiri*) just-so 201
Sakura serif 247
Salad Anniversary 670-1
Sato, Hiroaki 174.272.513-15
Sea cucumber 379.526.560
Sei Shônagon 270
Sengai's best 287.542. ~ appeal 569
Senryû & kyôka 641-2
Sequence 206.521
Sewing metaphor 444
Shamisen 69.343.450.582.616.621
Shellfish as women 198-9
Shi-ching/Shijing 32
Shigure 229-231.404.527-8
Shiki 10.34.600 ■ Shirane, Haruo 2.
  33. 605.630
  ■ Shokusanjin => Ôta Nanpo
Shrimp 273.579-80.
Silk sash on hempen robe 377
Silverfsh 29-30.381.465■SKKS 606-7
Slobberal 44-5.473-4 => *Icicles*
Smiling Mountains 430.565
Smoke signals 204 ■Snowball 436.675
Snow-reading 562 ■ Sogawa 545
Sôkan 520. Soot 51
Spider 87, 132-3.197.215.218.255.
  313-4.500.552.576. 617.
Spring colts 432.441.581.329.553.581-2
Star Lovers 210-5.314.342-3.347.372.
  523
Stevens, John 151-2 ■Strong 女 585
Suck/er as good 164.358.543
Suckling 454. ■ Sunao-ism 138
Surimono 628.688 =>*Kyôka Varieties*
Swift 105.400.522.554. ■ Syllabet 26
Takanashi (,) Hiroko 356.563-8
Take-offs 19■Takuan man+pickle 141
Tanabata => Star Lovers
Tanaka, Rokuo 11.12.92.486.538
Tanaka Yûko 91 ■ Tanka 630.670-1
Taoism => Daoism
Tawara Machi > Salad. ■Taxing 618
Tears => Metaphor.
Teetotalers vs Drunks 178-81.490.
  515-6
Teiryû 610 ■ Teitoku's best 282.541
Tenmei Nom de Plume 592-594
The Cremation of Sam McGee 508
Thin man roast 56.87.599.defense 394
Thrush => Uguisu ■ Thomas R.K.
606.630

Time's Arrow 356.543 ■ Toad 281
Tobacco 76.100.299.304-5.316.427.
  547
To be is not to be 208. ■ Tôfu 86.504.
Tongue-twisters 308-9.549-50
Toothpick 416-7 ■ ~ hardening 579
Tortoise=teacher 171
Tourism 414-23.574-8.
Transcribing 436.517.8
Translation 23-5.27.160.173.311.356.
  358-9.362.364-9.378.402! 432.436-7.
  452.454.457-61. 462-3.483.495.498.
  517-8. 529.536.551-2.
Trash 129. ■ Treyvaud, Matt 605
Tsurayuki 34,71.206.219.475.521
Tubbs, Ernest 36
Turco, Lewis 404. Twain 19
U 569. ■ Ugly woman otafuku 458-9
Uguisu ~ name problem 516-7. other
  44.103.165.186-8.192.209.236.
  242.246.316.334.345.372.417.420.
  425.428.440.469.474.546. 552-3.
  556.691.702
Unanswered Prayers 494.
Unsolved poems: *king of hell* 64.477.
  otter 82, 129. & many more!
Unfaithful lover 142.190.502-3.519
Untranslatable 366-9.479.511.538.562
Urashima Tarô's box 238.442.470
Usania 19.671 ■ *Ushin* vs *Yûshin* 608
Visual puns 26-7.434-5.594.672
Wacking women 445
Waka *eg.* 118-19. *def.* 673.~ *& me* 710
  ~ *or kyôka?* 519.532.544.562
  ~ *revival* (Kotomichi) 360-1
  ~ *ushin* vs *mushin* 635-6
Wakashu 51. ■Waley, Arthur 23
Warbler => Uguisu
Ward, Sydney 424. ■ Watermelon 182
Watson, Burton 33.497-8
Wells, HG 541. ■ When I die 177
White powder make-up 41.376-7.482
White snake 438 ■ Wilde 596
Window-side study 351.381.563
Women r blessed 150 ■Wordplay 188
Wrinkles 250.413.424
Wynette, Tammy 192
Yabai 217. Yayû 257
Year End debt 234-5.241.351
Year's end *send-off* 529. *last day* 337.
Yomisute 607 ■ Young greens 374
Yoshioka Ikuo 10,22
Yoshiwara 117.445.536-9
Yûchôrô 95 ■ Yuraku 597-8
Zen kyôshi (Chinese poems) 506-9
Zen mondô 162-3 ■Zhuang-ze 84,
Zhuangzhi 168 & other spellings!)

POE*T* INDEX

You will find the names terribly inconsistent in this book. I will not say there is a method to the madness, but there are reasons for it, so whether inconsistancy bothers or intrigues you, please read the below.

◆ The Problem with Mad Poet Names ◆
A caveat for *all* readers, or the picky ones, anyway.

If we stuck to 16-17c *kyôka* poets who, despite being nobles or high-ranking samurai with long names, mostly used the same two-character pen-names that were the fashion in link-verse *haikai*, there would have been few problems with orthography or design, for the pronunciation was relatively constant and the short names would always fit the small space left before the margin of a line with a whole 31-syllabet poem crammed in it, excepting those poems from parodies of classic poetry, such as the Dog/pseudo *Hundred Poets One Poem* anthology of 1669 (犬百人一首) that used joking pseudonyms resembling those of the ancient poets, or utterly fantastic ones found in mad poem 'contests' such as the Four Families of Life Match (四生の歌合) of 1643 with its *"nama-unagi-nukari-no-bô* = raw-eel-slush-monk" vs. *"namazu-no-hyon-tarô* = cat-fish-droll-boy." But, in this book we chase the mad poem back even before link-verse *haikai* to a time when the noble *waka* poets usually but not always used the lengthy version of their names. For the well-known poets, the last of their names, which is to say their personal name – the order is the reverse of English – alone suffices (eg., Shunzei, Tsurayuki). I follow the practice of many books written in Japanese, using that alone. And I take it further by using it for poets translated enough in this book that economy made sense. Lady Daibu and Shikibu, for example. The former is usually called Kenreimon-in Ukyô no Daibu (the first, the name of the ex-Empress she served) and there are *two* Shikibu, Murasaki, who wrote the *Tale of Genji* and Izumi who wrote the wittier poems. Our Shikibu is the latter. Such confusion is rarer than an English speaker might think. Readers not fluent in Japanese should note that thousands of poets can be told apart by a single name. Unlike English personal names, until recently limited to a small number, Japanese (like Balinese, though confined to adults) believed in giving humans individual names and did not hesitate to coin new ones, so they are abundant. The only problem is that, depending on the time period, some *pronounce* their names in the long Japanese style and others in a short Chinese one and I did not have time or money to check; and even if I had the resources, for many, no one knows which is correct and in some cases, more than one pronunciation was acceptable. When in doubt, I have usually chosen the short name. With the late-17c and early-18c *kyôka* poets, the *nome de plume* was sometimes extended to the last name as well but, even then, the two-character pen-name which pretty much functioned as a personal name usually sufficed. With late-18c or Tenmei *kyôka* poets, long pen-names become standard. Often parodies of the names of ancient *waka* poets or interesting idiom in the guise of heterographic homophones, they lose their *meaning*, which is to say *wit*, when only part is used. This makes me want to use the whole name as many books do in Japan. But, most books still abbreviate them alot, using the full name only once, the first time it appears. The names of poets we see a lot of are generally shortened (~~Yomo no~~ Akara, ~~Akera no~~ Kankô, ~~Yadoya no~~ Meshimori).

In this book, with more poets and space between filled with explanation, a full name needs more than one introduction. But, where poems must fit horizontally rather than vertically, as in Japanese books, space for long names is just not there, unless they are put in a separate line. Were this book to be printed in volume, the names might get their own lines; with print-on-demand, however, the only way to keep a given content cheap is to cram it into as few pages as possible. So said, the designer side of me compensates for the lack of white-space by at least demanding symmetry and smooth outlines. If that means chopping names in half or, to the contrary, using a full name where a short one would do, etc., so be it. *One cannot be consistent in design and spelling both.*

Then there are poems that are not by anonymous authors whose names I cannot yet provide because I am poor and isolated. That sounds ridiculous, perhaps, but it is true. The major *waka* data bank for those of us without the academic affiliations or money to use or buy the *waka taikan* or the *koten bungaku taikei*, Nichibun, only gives the names of the major poets in the anthologies. Others that are named in the original are given only as "un-numbered" 番号外. So, we have many *waka* by ng, which is to say, Not Given. When the poem is particularly interesting it hurts not to be able to credit the poet. Readers with access and time are welcome to supply names for future editions. Also, we have a hundred or so poems from a book printed in the late-19c with what seem to be late-18c and, perhaps, early 19c *kyôka* which gave only two Chinese characters for all poets. Some I recognize, most I do not. It is possible that one of the dictionaries my small budget did not permit me to buy had 18-19c kyôka poets listed by their abbreviated names as well as full ones, but who knows. At present, I only have that for the 19c *surimono* poets in Carpenter: 2008 compiled by Miwako Hayashi. Unfortunately, few 18c poets are in it and the index to the Tokuwa anthology (the only index I have for *kyôka*) only lists the full name. I have neither the memory to recall most names I read nor the time to skim through all the names to find one. Nor do I want to waste the time of my respondent, whom I prefer to bother about matters of more importance. So for this edition, in many cases, all I can do is guess. As Hayashi writes in the preface to her index, that often means "choosing the pronunciation that is the most euphonious or clever-sounding." If *anyone* or institution finds something of particular value in *kyôka,* the names from the dictionary (I think it is pre-copyright) should be put on-line open to all – as the names of *haikai* poets are – so they may be efficiently searched.

Worse yet, I do not even have the authors or dates of some of the reprints in *Broadview* (things which my respondent has slowly but surely been adding to his website), did not do a good job of separating anonymous from author not known from playful pseudonyms for it was all I could do to roughly index as my aging eyes tire me so much my brain kicks back to survival mode (otherwise, I might have thought to separate "moral" and "proverb" poems out from other anon. poems earlier – many are lost in anon.), had no time nor resources on hand to find out, say, which of the poems in the Shokusan-kashû or house/personal collection of Ôta Nanpo belong to his Yomo no Akara period and hence, rather than just having a dozen or so of his poems found in the Tokuwa-shû credited to Akara decided to just index all together under Shokusanjin, and even less inclination to get the long names and titles (including little things like Emperor or Prince) of the waka folk straight – maybe I got some right, you are cautioned not to use this book for proper identification. Still, you will find more information – including correction of previously published material – in respect to the names of some kyôka poets. Anyone to whom this sort of detail work is not sheer torture is welcome to try to sort things out better.

Alphabetization is Absolute – breaks & hyphens do not count – & pardon the guesses!

Abe no nakamaro (701-70) 291
aisô 愛宗 1679 銀葉夷 170
akara 赤良 => Shokusanjin
akazome emon 赤染衛門 295
akera => kankô
akinaga? monoyana 秋長堂物築？436
akinari 秋成 674.675
akitsuna? 藤原章網 124
anjû 庵住 一万 249

ANONYMOUS. Most under Anom. are specifically deemed so in the books.

Where names are given but not to the data base I had to rely upon, I put it under NG (not given). Where it was unclear if an author of a book was the author of a poem I sometimes gave the author the benefit of the doubt & sometimes did not. Where the authorship of an entire book is unclear, poems may be numbered under the book title (Eg. *Ise*, Tales of & its parody *Nise* – I am afraid this index is more useful for checking the respectivecontributions of individual poets than anything else.

General.73. 103.123.124.126. 150. 171? 173.174. 177.177.193.222. 270. 285.285.288. 323.327.328.329.364. 368.377?377? 379.449? 467.493.513. 533.533.540? 560.570.573.573.598

Chikuba kyôginshû (bk) 1499
273.273.273.273. 541.541.619

Folk/ryôjinhisshô 梁塵秘抄 12c imayo etc. 95. 220. 368. 378. 473. 473. 477.

Inu-tsukubashû 1539 犬筑波集
201.272.272.465.543 (=>Sôkan?)

ANONYMOUS ~ continued ~

　Kkrj　古今和歌六帖 c.985 or 976-82 Kokinwakarokujô　63.77. 119.119.142. 142.142.142.143. 143.143.143. 293. 459.

　Kks 905 (Kokinwakashû) 40.59. 70.71.80.155. 188.217.260.309. 309.458.481.481. 483.493.527. 539.555.567.581.603

　Mys (manyôshû) 8c54.54.55. 55.58.59.62.62.63.63.70.80.81. 106.107.136.138.183.309.371. 409.457.474. 599.599

　Skks (shinkokinwakashû) 1205 120.121.121.121.565

　Shinsen inu tsukubashû (bk) 1667 50.105.175.268

　Moral 道歌 172.172.172.550.550 . .

　Proverb 170.170.170.171.515. . . .

　Senryû yanagidaru (y) 18-19c 柳多留 12. 118.137.137.137.140. 148. 159.191.290. 291.293.295.296. 296.297.300.301.301.391.399.471. 480. 515.537.537.545.582.681.

　Squib 落首 109.109.110.111.111. 111.293.492.619. 619.641.641.642. 642.642.642.643

　Zappai mutamagawa 83. 391

End Anonymous

Continue Individual Poets

ANRAKU Sakuden 1554-1642 安楽庵策伝 (from 醒睡笑 1623, some his, some found) 110.402.402. 402. 402. 403.403.403. 403. 404.404.405. 405.405.406. 406. 406 .406 .407.

ASAHI BUNZAEMON/Monzaemon 朝日文左衛門 1674-1718 鸚鵡籠中記 c.1707 I have no idea how many of the poems are his or just collected: 621.621.621.621.621. 621.622. 622. 622.622.623.623.623.623. 623.623.624.624.624.624.625. 625.625.625.625.626. 640?640? 640?640?640?

asahi no sajubô 旭佐易方? c1830? 436
asakusa an c.1800 浅草庵 224.444
asanoya naonari 1820's 麻屋直成 446

ato ichijô? 後一条入道関白 129
baba kinrachi 1750-1807 馬場金埒 74
baikadô nerikata 梅花堂煉方 442
BASHÔ 1644-94 松尾芭蕉 103. 440. 666. 675. 675
bokubokutei kineo 1834 441
bokuryû 1785 卜柳 677
bokutan p1740 栗柯亭木端 231.376
BOKUYÔ 1607-1678 半井卜養 101?101?101?101?178.178.178.178. 179.179.179.180.180.181.181. 319. 356.357.357.358.358.359.359.359. 359. 482.490.490. 515-16. 565.568. 676.676.676. 677.677.677.677
bôshin 1740 迎月楼暮新嵐/百 377
bôun 1785 白鯉館卯雲 224
bunôsha naoki 文桜舎直樹 447
Bunzaemon=>Asahi Bunzaemon
BUSAI? 沸斉 17c 日本酒仙伝出典 178.178.178.179.179.180.180.181.181
CHIE NO NAISHI 1735-1807. 智恵内子 93.238.381.399.444.444.516
CHIKAMASA d.1448 親当 (蜷川新右衛門) 73.162.163.163. 470.511
CHIKUSAI (fictional) 竹斎 1623? 杉楊枝? 176.176.286.380.510
chikushôen? c.1800? 竹壽園 83
CHINKEN 1723-88=内山椿軒=賀邸 Uchiyama Gatei 88.99.480
chôchôtei somabito 1820 427
Chôka p1672 重香 527.576
chôkô 1666 長好 325
chôshô? 1672 重正 576
CHÔSHÔSHI p1643 木下長嘯子 also 木下勝俊 kinoshita katsutoshi 1569-1649 四生の歌合 60.61.104. 514.
chûritsu 中栗 479
DAIBU, lady12-13c 建礼門院右京大夫 208.208.209.209.210.211.213. 213.213.213.213.213. 213.522
daiso sôgyônin 1669 佐心子賀近 296
Daisan? p1740 則本太山? 狂歌餅月夜 528.703
dôgen 道元和尚 612
dôin, monk b.1090 fujiwara no atsu-yori 119
dôshi 童子 591

dôtomo shironushi 1785 堂伴白主 449
edanoya chitoyo 枝屋千豊 443
eiga-monogatari 11c 栄花物語 473
eiri 1672?/8? 永利 420
enma? early-19c 烏亭焉馬 688
enzô? 1264 権僧正公朝 家集 129
Esshi, Princess 1259-1332 448
Fake Ise => Nise
folk 573
fudenari 筆成 c.1800 177
Fujimoto Yûki? fl.ca.1647-1726 藤本由己 春駒狂歌 679.679.679.679.679
fujiwara no okikaze 古今 #745 365
fukukô lr 腹藁 編? 失典 466
fukurochô? 袋町一萬集 p1897 77
fûrai sanjin 風来山人 245
furu no imamichi kks #227 216
fuse yajirô d. 1787 布施弥次郎 383
fusei 1734 永田布声 703
fuseki 1729 桴雪 華紅葉 95
FUSHIMATSU NO KAKA 1785 節松嫁嫁/嫁ゝ 92.265.472.484.486
Fushimi ret.emp.1313 伏見院 496
futoku 不得 1697 大三物 45
Futome? 1670's 太女 51.421.421.421
fûyû? 1678 富由 422
fûzokuko? 1740 同所風俗子都則 703
GAKIN 賀近 犬百人一首 1669 著佐心子賀近 ame no nakagai 飴中買 mimeyoshi no muko 眉見よしの聟 酔狂法師、など作名 119. 543. 544
genan 1666 元安 545
gendô 17c 元藤 211
genin 1679 言因 銀葉夷歌集 164
genkô 1666 玄康 318
genkô 天地玄黄 狂歌一万 536
Gennai => Hiraga Gennai
Genshin 1672?1729? 元信 485. 510
Genzaemon (yamanaka ~ d.1645) 山中源左衛門 392. 572
GETSUDÔKEN 黒田 Kuroda 月洞軒 (my favorite) fl.1688-1703 大団 182.223.252.330.330.330.331.331. 332.332.332.333.333.333.334.334. 334.335.335.335.335.336.336.336. 337.337. 337.337. 338.338.339.339. 339.339.340.340.340.341.341.342. 342.342.343. 343.343.343. 462.486. 551.557.557.558.558.559.560.560.680. 680.680.680

gisai 1666 宜斉 316
goa c.1700 其阿上人 557
Go-kyôgoku sesshô saki no daijô-daijin
    1169-1206 取?政太政大臣
    後京極摂政前太政大臣 44.122

gonsui d. 1719 言水 427

GOSAI, emperor. 1638-85
    後西上皇 69. 616

goshintei san'en 1834 護心亭三猿 441
gôshû hino ryûjôen umeyasu 1832 583
gosokusai kabenuri 1820s 五息斎壁塗
    546
gôto masaharu 後藤昌治 1

GO TOBA 1180-1239 retired.emp.
    後鳥羽院宮内卿 205.300.334.552

Gubutsu 愚佛 犬咬合 狂詩大全 573
Gyôgetsu-bô => kyôgetsu-bô
gyokuho? 1740 八雲軒玉峯? 703
gyôshi? c.1800 業枝 231
Gyôson 1055-1135 abbot / arch bish.
    前大僧正行尊 35. 296
haji no kakiyasu1785 掻安 276

HAKUIN 1685-1768 白隠 306.396
hakurikanbôun 1785 白鯉館卯雲 394
hakusanyô? 白山羊 contemp. 379
hakushi 1689 薄芝 あらの 195
Hakushû 白秋 20c 雀の卵 145
hakusui 1679 伯水 490
hakyûtei sakai?1806 柏乗亭さかえ? 426

HAMABE NO KUROHITO
    1719-90 濱邊黒人 93. 380
hannya-bô 17-18? 般若房宗煕 306
harawara? fukuyo? 腹藁? 489
hyakurintei masugi1822 百林亭真杉 581
Hayashi amari 林あまり 588.588.588
Hayashi Shihei 1738-93 林子平 384
hayatomo 早鞆和布刈盲目の大学
    者,塙保己一? 岩 57 狂歌解説 537

HENJÔ arch-bishop 816-90 僧正
    遍照 or 遍昭 166. 216.216.293.499.
    499.499.500.500.500.501.501

hikamasa d.1448(醒睡笑 1623) 550
hikaru 1785 ひかる 百鬼夜狂 274
hikikata? 引方 同一萬集 74

Hiraga Gennai 1728-1779 源内
    232.232

Hiroshige 広重 maybe poem, too 396
Hiroshige II? maybe poem, too 549

Hisago no Karazake 瓢のから酒
    1785 徳和 166
hisakataya c.1830 久堅屋 寛政 434

HITOMARO 柿本人丸 290. 408
hodô? (一茶全集 2-170) 甫道? 344
hokusai? 1821 581
Hokushi d. 1718 北枝辞世 388
Honami kôetsu 本阿弥光悦 258
Honami Nishita1785 帆南西太 528
Honda-bô 1558-1623 本因坊算砂 384
hônen-jônin 1574-89 法然上人 408
honin? 本院侍従 1312 玉葉 309
hôrai kikyô 蓬莱(山人) 帰橋 88
horaisha nobe? 宝来舎述+ c.1850
    (= kuniyoshi?) 548
hôseki 方碩 1679 銀葉夷歌集 50
hoshiya mitsuji 1785 星屋光次 243
hoyû 1666. f 1645 保友 316
Hôzumi, emp.8c 穂積親王 80.410
hyakuma sensei 亭主 百間先生 183
hyakutei sakai early 19c. 426
hyakutensha baichô 1821-2 百囀舎
    梅鳥 448

icchô 一朝談 林十百韻 222
ichihan? jônin. ochikochi 1574-89
    一反上人 408
ichimu 一夢 1854, 51 歳 388
ichiyô josui? 一陽如酔 狂歌師藤
    根堂 387
ichiyô 一蓉 1811 春山集 250
ichô mitsukado 1785 銀杏満門 89.
    479. 537.
Ichû 1638-1711 惟中 41

IETAKA 1158-1237 家隆
    fujiwara no ~ 123.125.496

IKKU jippensha ~ 十返舎一九 19c
    369.568.682.682

IKKYÛ 1394-1481 一休 36.73.
    73. 73.103.150?151.152.153.161.
    161.162.162.163.163.282?288.
    289.390.470.640.641.641.641

Ise monogatari / tales of ~ => Anon.

ISE, LADY fl.930 伊勢女 374.
    374. 375.375.375.375.487.524.
    570.570.682.702

Ise no ôsuke?or taifu?? 伊勢 大輔
    989-1060 53

ISE, Tales of c.900 伊勢物語 70.98.
    224.261.284.284.352.353.353.354.
    355.355.363. 366. 366.367.367.
    367.545.563.568 (& see Narihira)

ISSA 1763-1827 小林一茶 29.35.39.
    47.47.49.49.52. 66.68.68.84.91.109.
    135.148.149.149.149.154.154.167.
    168.168.168.169.169.169. 169.169.
    169.169.189.196. 201.210. 211.211.
    220.220.221.221.221.221.221.222.
    222.229.257.283.287.465.581. 234.
    235.235. 235.235.241.257.267.267.
    269.286. 286. 314.320.321.338.344.
    344.345.345.345.345.346.346.346.
    346.347.347.347.347.348.348.348.
    348. 349.349.349.349.349.349.349.
    349.350.350.350.350.350.350.351.
    351.438.439.488504.504.511.511.
    512.513.513 518.534.535. 535.535.
    560.560.560.560.560.562.562.562.
    562.563.563.563.580

isseitei muretori c.1800 一声亭群鳥
    433

itadaki? p1897 頂 77
Itteki 18c? 一滴 53
Ittetsu 1515-88 inaba～稲葉一鉄,
    but 1675 談林十百韻? 200

JAKUREN 1139?-1202 寂蓮法師
    121.128.146. 204.205.374.495.
    495.501.501.683

jichin 慈鎮和尚六百番歌合 493.636

JIEN 1155-1225 慈円/ 前大僧正
    慈圓 123.123.126.130.229.469.497

JIHINARI d1833 桜川慈悲成 189.
    307.424.425.429.517.579
jikko 1791 笑い艸十・口 69 歳 388
jikyoku 1666 自曲 701

JINKYÛ 17c (pre. 1707) 甚久法師
    515.683.683-4.684.684.684.684.
    684.684.684.684.684.684.684.684.
    684.684. 684.684

jitei? 治貞 1666 488-9

Jitô (Empress 645-702) 持統天皇 140

Jizori c.1700 自剃 (大団の中で) 337

Jôha 1523-1602 紹巴 191
Jôjin's mother 成尋法師母 126
jôji 1666 浄治 147
jokyô? 1740 如挙 377
joryû 1740 如柳 704
jôseki 1779 丈石 85 歳 388

JUNPO? d. 1548 釈三卜 栖雲寺潤甫
    和尚 1532=玉吟抄 199. 202
同和尚? 山蒼斎称名院三条西殿 202

Juntoku 順徳院 1197-1242 r.emp. 301

KABE NO NAKANURI c1785
加陪仲塗 240. 241. 479. 532

Kabocha no Motonari 加保茶元成 244. 398.

kachû no tsuma? 1666 夏虫妻 318

kaida rotei? 17-18c? 参 45 貝田露程 諸国落首咄 305

kajitsutei tokiwa c.1822 花実亭常盤 445

kameya ichimaru 亀屋一丸 435

kamo no chômei earl-13c 鴨長明 487

kanesada 1666 藤原兼定卿 326

KANKÔ 1740-1800 AKERA ~ 朱楽管江 223.234.240.260.262.563

kansui 1740 (dorokusai kansui) 土碌斎寛水 704

karagoromo => kisshû

kariho 苅穂 ls 147

Kasei d.1859-2-2 歌成 383

kashô 1740 kusodôkashô 鈎帯堂可笑 704

kasukusai yotanbô 糟句斎よたん坊 1786 吾妻 569

katatsumuri hikaru c.1800 蝸光 72

katsuho p1672,1679 且保 331.542

katsura s 桂 p? 244

kawabito??? c.1800 皮人 73

keiin = 1663-1742 契因= 1740 紀海音か? 狂歌活玉集 89

keikôsha narimasu c.1810 桂香舎成益 485

kenshô 顕昭 1310 125. 492

kichiuemon d.1747 寺坂吉右衛門 395

kihô? c1800? 季保 479

kii lady 紀伊 p905 祐子内親王家 103

kiin 希因 古選-1748 45

Kikaku? d.1707 其角 五元集 138? 432

kikô 1740 其考 704

kinjitei sunago c1825 金地亭砂子 450

kinki? p1897 近喜一萬集同 74

ki-no-harunaga 1785 紀春長 467

KI NO SADAMARU 1760-1841 紀定丸 / 紀 定麿 454. 574. 587. 686

Ki no Tsurayuki => tsurayuki

kintsune (fuji.) 公経 1171-1244 299

kiritsubo no kôi 657-8

Kisen Monk 9c 喜撰法師 544

kisen 喜撰 1313 205

kishijo きし女 1785 徳和 487

KISSHÛ 1739-1802 karagoromo ~ 唐衣橘洲 50.100.233.239.470.479. 685.685

kita-in?shukaku hoshinnô? 喜多院入道 p1310 北院御室御集 で守覚法親王(d.1202)? 203

kitamuki sabuki 1785 北向左武喜 165

Kiun 中川喜雲著 Maybe ryôi 了意? =京雀(1612-1691) 1658 京童跡追 (1667 in 地誌所載狂歌抄) 575

Ko ôigimi 10c 小大君 実方集 314

Kôan p1666 / 1672 行安 552. 576

Kobo-daishi 弘法大師 (d.776) 307

kôchô? mitsushige? 光重 1678 422

kôchô? p1672 公朝 223

Kodaijin, palace woman p.1348 花園左大臣小大進 for emp hanazono 129

koe? 1672 行重 414

KÔFÛ fl. 1666-1678 行風 29.414. 414.414?415.415.416. 416.417.418. 418. 419.419.419.420.423.546?553. 576.576.577.577.577.577.577.638

kôhô 1672 行豊? 421

kôjun 1672 行順 417

kôkô 1666 行好 324

Kôkô-in, emp.光孝院 in skks, also, komatsu no mikado 120.120

komendo 米人 p1897 74

konomich kuraki 1799 此道くらき 516

konononomagohiko 1786 子子孫彦 吾妻 570

Koreaki, prin. 1179-1221 惟明親王 44

korenori 坂上是則 sakanoue no ~ 121

koretada or koremasa d.972 伊尹 120

kôshi 1674 幸之桜川 197

kôshô? 1678 光正 422

kotodaka? c.1800 琴高 77

kotohiki? c.1800 琴弾 72

kotoiedaka? p1205 藤原言家隆 494

KOTOMICHI 1798-1868 大隈言道 360. 360.360.361.361.361.572.605. 686. 686.686.686.687

kôyû? 1678 光友 423

kuretake no yotsuya 1785 呉竹世艶 95

Kuroda => getsudôken 黒田月洞軒

kuroki kaoru 黒木香 588.588.588.588

Kûsui d.1763 空翠 一茶全集 31.160

kusune kanemitsu 1126? 久壽根兼満 165

KYÔGETSU-BÔ 1265-1328 暁月坊 又 教月法師 又 居月坊 96. 97.97.136. 370. 687.687.687

kyôhaku 京博 一万 224

kyoriku 許六 -1715 383

LR lost reference – same thing as ↓

L.S. lost sources 出典失名 226.280. 281.291.297.299.425. 425.526.544

madake-no-fukayabu 1785 真竹深 493

madonoya 窓乃屋 437

magane? p1897 真金 一萬集 75

MAGAO 1753-1829. Shikatsube no ~ 鹿都部 真顔 later, Yomo no utagaki magao 四方歌垣 真顔 also 真兒 244.250.303.428.432.440.583

mahagi? c.1800 真萩 259

manei? 1666 満永 317

manryûtei yotomi 万流亭世富 442

masaari 1241-1301 飛鳥井雅有 131

masachika pre-1310 藤原雅親 127

masafusa p1310 前中納言匡房卿 472

matsuo sp? 松雄 245

MESHIMORI 1752-1830 Yadoya no ~ 宿屋飯盛 32.100.134.135.255. 277.279.465.540.689

michikatsu p1672 原通勝卿 328

michinobu 972-94 藤原道信 360

michitake d.1516 道寸 65

michiyori? 道頼 一萬集 p1897 77

Michizane 845-903 菅家 sugawara no 294

MITOKU 1588-1669 未得 (1649 吾吟我集) 35.158.167.257.317.323.487.524. 528.554.554.584.613.613.614.614.614. 614.614.615.615.615.615.615.616.616. 616.616.617.617.617.617.639.639. 639.639. 639.639.39.639.639

mitsune みつね kks 206

mitsutoshi? fuboku 光俊 1310 467

mitsutoshi?? 光俊 1310 125

moji 1642 茂次 鷹つくば 187

môjin 盲人 私可多咄 710

MOMOKO 塘藩山堂 百子 in 1734 & 狂歌餅月夜 1740 著 490. 513. 523. 537. 574. 690.690.690.690.690.690

momonoya nagatane 桃の屋永胤 443

monogusa tarô 16c 643

moritake d.1549 荒木田守武 550

moriya sen'an d. 1838 488

motoie 基家 496
MOTOKATA c.905 ariwara no ~ 在原元方 34. 81. 483
motonari => kabocha no
moto no mokuami 1680 (character/proverb from 元の木阿弥物語) 253
MOTO NO MOKUAMI (1785) もとの木網, 元の～ 238. 306. 470
motosuke 908-990 拾遺集 #1180 清原元輔 185
mototoshi in skks 藤原基俊 494
motoyoshi prince 元良親王 gss #960 prince 890-943 294
mûan 夢庵 /1623 Anraku S.? 404.405
MUNENAGA prince 1311-85 宗良親王 690.690.690.690-1.691. 691.691.691.691.691.691.691. 691.691-2.692.692.692. 692.692. 692. 692.692.692-3.693.693.693. 693.693.693.693.693.693. 694.694.694.694.694.694. 694.694.694.694

munetaka 宗尊親王 469
muneyama pre.905 525
muneyuki p905 源宗于 148.636
munô jônin 無能上人 396
Murakami emp. c.1005 sis 184
musen sp? 無染 245
Musen-hôshi 1636 無銭法師 新撰狂歌集 (雄長老か) 282
musen 無染 一万 224
Musô ? pre-1666 夢窓国師 90.326
nadehiko c1800? 撫彦 72
Nagaiki hisami 不老庵長生久美? 187.443
nagakata? 1310 長方 124
NAGASAKI IKKEN c.1700? 長崎一見 477. 481. 481. 482. 526
Nakamasa p1310 源仲正 248.472
nakamichi c.1800 中道 77
Nakanuri 仲塗 => Kabe no Nakanuri
Nakarai Bokuyô => Bokuyô
nakasane 1310 仲実朝臣 467
nakatsukasa pre-1310 中務爵 みこ御集蛍 207
namakawa norabito 1785. x2 599
namakawa norabito 1785 奈間川野等人 165
namiki? 次木 後撰夷曲集 1672 78
nanshi no harutsugu 1799 南枝春告 444

NARIHIRA 825-880 在原業平 Ariwara no ~ 伊勢 (& maybe more in Tales of Ise not attrib. etc.) 36.190
NEBOKE sensei 1767 寝惚先生 Shokusanjin's kyôshi 153.675
negao 寝顔 狂歌一万 18-19c 532
nenten x2 坪内稔典 553
NG names not given by Nichibun. 番号外作者 'not yet numbered'
  Gyokushû 1312/13 玉葉集 130. 130.130.130.131.131.172. 204. 204.205. 532.551
  Sensaishû 1187 千載集 247.474. & some I missed so noting ...
  Goblin Poetry ng by Hearn 19c kyôka-hyakumono 狂歌百物語 275.277.278.278.281
NG info re author of poems insuffic. in Broadview –
  1636 新撰狂歌集 319.319.321
  遠近岬 (1574-89) 408. 408
  1659 百物語 305.305.305
nijiku 1740 同所似竺 703
Nijô Nyôbô 1320-88or ~ Yoshimoto 二条女房 609
nina 1740 四弘亭忍阿 704
Nintoku c710 古事記 106
NISE c.1640 nisemonogatari 仁勢物語 poet possibly 烏丸光広 (1579-1637) 190. 284.284.352. 353.353. 354. 355.355.363. 366.494.563
Nishi sanjô (醒睡笑にて 1623) 西三条道遥院殿 => Sanetaka 407
nobutsune 1672 宣恒 417
nobuzane 1176-1265 信実朝臣 82
Nôin, monk 988-1050? 能因法師 207.496
Noin c.1126 野因 金葉 165
Nori no suiyû 1779 則水由 186
Norinaga 1730-1801 本居宣長 167.674
Nyochiku fl.1730-40 如竹 66
NYÛAN p1610 入安 202.324. 325.357.357.357.357
OCHIKOCHIgusa 遠近草 1574-89. Must find author's name! Most poems are gathered or written and attrib. to real or fictional characters: eg.和多利石州・柳意軒・桂外記・喜田監物・源空上人・坂井次郎

大夫・ある人・東堂 ・甘数たゝよし・ある好色の人ある曲者・など 64.410.410. 410.410.410.410. 411.411.411.411.411.411.
Ôe Yoshitoki 大江喜言 473
ôhe no matagusa 大屁股臭 560
OKAMOCHI 手柄岡持 1735-1813 Tegara no ~ 33. 398. 471. 479. 523
omokasa uchidaijin p1310 表笠内大臣 82
ône no futoki? c.1800 大根太木 289
ONO NO KOMACHI c.850 小野小町 292. 364. 501. 613
ono no takamura 10c kks 382
osamaru??? 雄左丸 同 一万? 479
Ôta Nanpo/Nampo => Shokusanjin
Ôtsu, Prince (663-86) 392?
ÔYA NO URAZUMI d.1810 大家裏住 277.289.543.562.677.677.678
Ozawa roan 1723-1801 小沢蘆庵 10. 249
Raizan 1716 来山 63 歳 387
rakuda-en pseudonym 154
rakuseian 1830's? 楽聖庵 586
renshô p.1666 蓮生法し 484
Richibô? 1740 東華堂栗芳 376.377
rikkaen? 栗花園 一万 472
rikyô 1730 李郷 705.705
rinken monk 琳賢法師 497
risai 1666 理西 325
rohan c.1800? 露伴 647
rôjin 17c 老人 かさね草紙 515
rokube c. 12-17c folktales 六部 514
rokusekien meshimochi 六石園飯持 585
ryôi 浅井了意著(-1691) 出来斎京土産 1677 in 地誌所載狂歌抄 575.x2
RYÔKAN, monk. 1758-1831 良寛 86.86.87.87.87.258. 258.387.696.696.
ryôsoku? rinsoku? 18c? 綾足 445
ryôta 蓼太 683
ryôzen monk 良暹法師 11c 298
ryûgaen Isshi 柳芽園一枝 582
ryûin p1737/1740 also 長生 chôshô? 亭柳因 112. 703
ryûsui 1730 流水 528
Sagami, lady fl 1035-61 相模 120. 120. 295
sai miya? 斎宮女 p1312 玉葉集 464-5
saibeito? 1740 西園斎米都 704

SAIGYÔ 1118-90 西行上人 42.79.
88.89.112.112.114.114.114.115.115.
115.116.116.117.117.117.118 . 126.
132.132.133.133.134. 144.144.144.
144.192.192.193.194.194.194.217.
232.246.246.246. 246.247.247 482.
493.497.522.532.533.611.686.
696.696.696

sakekasu? 酒粕 1672   421

sakuden=> anraku ~
sakuragawa => jihinari
sanefusa 1147-1225 藤原実房 204
sanekane? 実兼 1312 玉葉集 487
SANEKATA 958?-98 藤原実方
312.312.312.313.313. 314.315.
315.315.315.519.697

saneo? 実雄 1312 gyokuyôshû 483

SANETAKA? 1536 実隆 I am
unsure if all the poems in 再昌
草 are his but, at any rate: 407.412.412.412.
413. 413.413.413.413.413.413

saneyori 1312 実頼 560
Sanjo ret.emp. 976-1017 三条院 297
sankyô? 三敲 445
sanpû 676
sansôsai? 1608 山蒼斎 称名院三条西
殿 玉吟抄 384
sanuki さぬき kks #1055 493
sanwa さんわ 百鬼夜狂 1785 276
sanyôdô 山陽堂 427
sarumaru? pr905 猿丸大夫 226
sasa maro 1785   636
satobito 里人 pseudo in 17c 行風 512
saû-ni suna yu ni? 1672 妙祐尼 414
seian p1672 成安 後撰曲集 384
seiho 1656 正甫 ゆめみ草   197
seishi? 1672 清紙 576
seiyôkan umeyo 19c 青陽館梅世 579
sekitôrô kokemushi 石唐楼苔蒸 450
semimaru 10c? 蝉丸 292
sen ? 1740 洗鬢   377
sen? 1740 全   377
senboku? 1740 泉墨 529
SENGAI 1750-1837 仙厓和尚 又
仙厓義梵 287.371.371.547.587

shigeka? 1672?8? 重香 420
shigekatsu's wife 1679 重勝妻 183
shigesada? chôtei? 1678 重貞 423
shigetomo 重友 1678 420
shigeyori? enoko-shû 重頼? 犬子
#1609 1633 201

shigeyuki? gsis 1086 源 重之 201
shikanari? c.1800 鹿成 393
SHIKI 子規-1902 47.426
SHIKIBU c970-1030 和泉式部
IZUMI ~ 94.128.129.131.175.194.
201.207.254. 255. 405.515.697.697.
shikô 1740 備前岡山司喉   703
shikyô 1832? 史喬 485
shinagatori manyô (1738)   510
shinjin? 前関白信尋公 449
shinjô? 1679 信澄 531
SHINKAI 1634-88 信海 322.322.
338.554
shinratei manzô II 森羅亭萬象 438
shinryûtei harukaze 1834 441
shinshô 1645 信勝 kebukisô 418
shiriyake no sarundo 尻焼猿人 238
Shirohito => Yamate no
shôbô 1672 尚芳 576
shôbô? 1678 正房 422
shôchô p1666 正長 323.316
shôe 1679 正恵 164
Shohaku d.1722 尚白 393

SHÔI   談林俳人 fl. 1670's 松意
196.200.222.416
shôken 松堅 96 歳 1726 ネット 386
SHOKUSANJIN 1749-1823 蜀山人
also YOMO NO AKARA 四方赤良
& Neboke Sensei 寝惚先生& 家
集の中で隠士赤松金鶏著?Outside
of kyôka, Ôta Nanpo 大田南畝
37.37.60.65.75.84?.85.89.90.91.98.
99.102. 104.108.108.109.112.113.
113.118. 139.140.148.149.158.159.
171.176.176.176.176.182.183.190.
214.214.214.215.215.215.225.226.
226.227.228.230.234.235.236.236.
236.237.241.243.243.248.253. 275.
279.290.290.291.291.292.292.293.
294.294.295.295.296.297.298.299.
299.300.301. 302.304.320.369.370.
390.391.391.391.391.391. 399.465.
470.483.510.522.523.523.30.530.
538.538.541-2.542.544.546.547.
561.563.587.587. 587.685.698.
shôroku: 松緑. 1672 421
shôtetsu 1381-1459 正徹 411
shôun 1740 ㄚ馬 虚楼嘯雲 376
shûhaku? 1679 酒粕 銀葉夷歌集 511
shuho? 1678 衆甫 422
Shûishû c1005 192
shûishû song #597   p 1005 59

shûkyôtei tsuchimaru 1822 581-2
shunjô 1679 春澄 銀葉夷歌集 555
shunman? c.1800 尚左堂俊満
              shôsadô ~ 503
shunsa 1672   俊佐 417
SHUNZEI 1114-1204 俊成卿,俊成
皇太后宮大夫俊成 fujiwara no ~ 33.
45.126. 220? 237. 237. 298. 369. 409.
469. 545. 562. 699

shûshin 酒心 557

SÔBÔ 1642/1666 宗朋 197.317.385

SÔCHÔ 1448-1532 宗長 59.196.
227. 260.261.310. 310.464. 467.527.
699.700

sogan 素丸 1712-95 45

SÔGI 1420-1502 宗祇 193.195.
406.407.551.591.699-700.700.700

sôho 永井走帆 201.705
sôhô? 宗鋪 1666 ♪ 317.552

SÔKAN 1458-1546 / 1465-1553 /
d.1540? 山崎宗鑑 196.271-272.
               382.410.701

someone ある人 p1734   704

sonin? (又人)/ochikochi 1574-89
409
sôno / sôshi? p1672 宗之 575 .577
sonohazu no kotonari 1785 其筈琴成
                  531
Sono no Kochô c.1785? 園胡蝶 259
sônosuke 藤原朝臣奏之 万葉集 5

SOSEI d.c909 そせい法し素性法師
188. 195.295.372.372. 372.372.
372.372. 373.373.373.519.601

sosen 楚泉 1785 224
sôtan 1693 宗旦 58 歳 386
sôtei? 宗定 1672 421
sotoku-in 1119-64 崇徳院御歌 212
sotonari 鬼 x 屋外成 431
sôya? 1666 宗也 318
suigan 1824 晴雪楼翠巌 484
Sukenobu 1740 之信   376. 377.

TABITO 大伴旅人 Ôtomo ~ (father
of ed. of mys 8c) 96.97.97.97.97.488

tachibana no suzunari 1785 橘鈴也 155
tadaaki (prince) 惟明親王 204
tadami? 壬生忠見 (in 袋草子) 602
Tadamine 86-920 壬生忠岑 141
tadatsugu 1666 従四位源 忠次 324
Taigi d.1772 太祇 47. 434

taikyoku 1672 太極　417
tajihi no mahito 8c 丹比真人 40
taka no hatsuga1785i 鷹羽番　587
takachika 15-16c (高親) 小原兵庫頭
　　　　　　　　　　(宗長日記) 527
takafusa fujiwara ~ d.1209 隆房 205
takakura? kôsô? 高倉 465
takamaru? 高丸 ichiman? 237
takamitsu??? 1005 藤原高光 90
takanobu??? d.1205 隆信朝臣 203
takara-no-atsumaru 1779 寶の敦丸
　　　　百千鳥狂歌合せ　514
TAKUAN 1573-1645 沢庵和尚
　　　141.141.141.165. 580.701
Tales of Ise => ise
tamago no kakujo1786 玉子香久女
　　　　　　　　　　　　264
TAMEIE 1310 民部爵為家 minobe
　　　83.122.123.125.126.203.556
tamemori p.1666 為盛 638
Tamochi no ôkimi p.8c 手持女王 382
tarubo 樽坊 553
tatsunomi 辰巳 source? 225
TAWARA Machi 670.670.671.671
Tegara-no-okamochi => Okamochi
teidô 1740 貞堂 狂歌活玉集 594
TEIFU? p1672, 1679 貞富 248.
　　　　　　328. 414.415.504
TEIGA 1734,1740 貞峩関法橋契,
海音堂貞峩,愚弟貞峩 381.653.703
TEIN p1672 貞因 576.577.703
teiji 1642 定時 鷹つくば 426
TEIKA 1162-1241 藤原定家 127.
131.230.409.469.525.527. 547.701.
702. 702.702
teikyû 汀躬 191
TEIN pre-1672.1679 藤原貞因
　　　　　　　　164. 414.416
teirin? p1672.p1679 貞林 51.414
TEIRYÛ 1654-1735 鯛屋=由縁斎
貞柳 46.118.198.199.215.231.231.
291.295.296.298.298.301.304.
520.521.526.528.680.702-3.
703.704.704.705.705.
teiryû II d.1735 貞柳二世? 198
teishitsu 1673 貞室 64歳 386

teishun 1740 木原貞椿 704
TEITOKU 1571-1653 松永貞徳
38.38. 44.48.49.160.212.228.229.
261.272.282.287.316.317.318.
322.471.529.612.642.705.
Tenji emp. 626-71 天智天皇 290
tenmarô wakizumi1820 天馬楼
　　　　　　　　　和吉住 441
Tenmu emp. 7c 天武天皇 308
tenpo no kawanari1785 天保川成 165
Tobuchiri no Batei 飛塵馬蹄 249
Tokiwai-nyûdô Minister p1330 常盤
　　井入道太政大臣 百首御歌 42
Tokiyori 平時頼朝臣 701
tôkôen gensen 1830 東光?
　　　　　　　園源撰僊? 430
TOKUGEN 徳元 1559-1647
　　　　　37. 173. 270. 271
tomoda kinpei. c1789 友田金平 394
tomokazu? 1672 友和　576
tomonori kks 437 とものり 218
tomosada? 友定俳諧遠近集 576
tomoyô? 1678 友易 423
tonsui 1715 呑水 俳諧あふむ石 197
TÔSAKU 1726-89 平鉄東作
　　　Hezutsu ~ 76. 240. 362. 537
TÔSHI 1740 冬之 376.377.572
toshimichi ssmys 893 尚左堂俊満 502
TOSHIYUKI 905 藤原としゆき・
　　としゆきの朝臣 188. 489
tôsui d.1683 桃水和尚 158
tsubouchi nenten 20c 321
TSUBURI NO HIKARI 1753-1796
つぶり光 also, tsuMuri 171.279.504
TSURAYUKI 905 紀貫之 Ki no
tsurayuki, Kokinshû's chief-editor
　　　58.71.71.206.219.459.605
tsurenari? c.1800 連成 72
tsuruoka? 鶴岡 author of 15c?
or 1767? 放生会職人歌合? 575.
tsutsui __? 1788-1859 筒井蠻渓 263
Uchiyama Gatei => Chinken
uguisu no surie 1785 鶯 摺江 242
uji, tales of 宇治拾遺物語 3-11 602
Umaya no Mayasuke1785 馬屋厩輔
　　　　　　　　　　　　233
Urazumi => Ôya no ~

yabe toranosuke d.1615 矢部虎之助
　　　　　　　　　　　395
YAKAMOCHI 718?-785 大伴家持
ed. of Manyôshû 56. 56. 70.209.291
yamanaka genzaemon d.1645 山中源
左衛門 392
YAMATE NO SHIROHITO 1726-
87 山手白人 79 .233. 565. 637
YAYÛ 1702-83 横井也有 67.256.
256.256. 256.256. 256-7.257
yôgen hôshi gsis 572
Yomo no akara => Shokusanjin
Yomo no utagaki magao => Magao
yonenari 米成 431
yorimasu ? 頼益 ichiman? 244
Yoshiakira or katsuakira 10c prince
克明親王? or mod. katsumei kokumei
　　　　in 1679 ginyô? 165
yoshimura yasuyo 1785 266
yoshinobu p1310 能宣朝臣 128
yoshinobu 一礼斎芳信? 306
yoshinobu p1310 能宣 128
yoshino-no-kuzuko 1785 吉野葛子
　　　　　　　　　　　516
yoshio 孝雄・p1814 (1790?)豊蔵坊
　　　　　信海狂歌集 98
YOSHITADA p1310 好忠 122.
　　　　　　123.126.495
yoshitaka? 民部少輔喜隆 1672 後撰
　　　　　　　　夷曲集 318
yotsuya (kuretake no) 呉竹世艶 76
yûchi 1666 友知 323
YÛCHÔRÔ 1547-1602 永雄長老
ei ~ 0.41.95.102.220.242.242.259.
267.283.283.283.286.322.324.404.
475.492.540
yûjo hatamaki 1786 遊女はた巻 264
Yûryaku (r.457-89) emp. 雄略天皇
　　　　　　　　　　　598
Yûsai 幽斎公 1534-1610 in 醒睡笑 41
yûwa 1679 友和　銀葉夷歌 535
yûwa 1672 友和 421
zaishiku 1675 談林十百韻 196
Zôga shônin 917-1003 増賀 僧侶 397
zuigen? 1674 隋言 37

POE*M* INDEX

All *Poems* in *Alphabetical Order*, ~~with Symbols~~

I *intended* to give each poem one of the following thirteen marks, partly to help sort them out for the reader who found my presentation, with many examples perepheral to *kyôka* proper, irregular and confusing, and partly to get a precise count on the number of *kyôka* in this book. I am afraid time+money do not permit it at this time. Poems in English, including mine, English or Japanese, are not included in this index.

☆ ~~*Kyôka*, 31-syllabet mad poems from *bonafide* collections or not.~~
☆ ~~*Kyôka*, ditto for the above but with with an irregular 14-17 break.~~
★ ~~*Kyôka* by content and style in *haikai renga* that are proper 17-14.~~
★ ~~*Kyôka* content & style found in *haikai renga*, improper 14-17.~~
○ ~~*Waka*, 31-syllabet traditional poems called *haikai, mushin* or~~
— ~~so full of wordplay that *anyone* might well call them *kyôka*.~~
● ~~*Waka I* unilaterally 勝手ながら think could be called *kyôka*.~~
● ~~*Waka* parodied or otherwise played by a *kyôka*, or referred to.~~
◎ ~~*Ko-uta, imayo*, or other short songs with a mad spirit.~~
◎ ~~*Sundry* poems, 14-17-14 or whatever, that seem mad.~~
△ ~~*Senryû* or *Mutamagawa zappai*.~~
▲ ~~*Kyôku*. Mad haiku (*hokku, hiraku*, etc.) I would like to call that.~~
□ ~~*Kyôshi*. Mad poems in Japanese-style pure Chinese characters.~~
■ ~~Mad-cap verse (epigrams, grooks) from beyond the Sinosphere.~~
■ ~~Ditto but only mad because I helped make them so.~~

Were circumstances to permit doing this right in the future, I might also add a second sign, perhaps a letter to the *kyôka* stars, to indicate whether the poem was early *kyôka* (up to the late-16c), middle (~ to mid-18c), or late (from mid-18c), in other words, pre-Teitoku, Teitoku and his school, Ôta Nanpo (Yomono Akara, Shokusanjin) and his contemporaries and what came after. Anyone with a bilingual computer, much Japanese ability, the spare time, and an inclination for detail work is always welcome to complete what I leave undone. If more content-oriented detail-work would be preferred, please note that the 900+ holothurian haiku in *Rise, Ye Sea Slugs!* (2003) are still waiting for that Venn Diagram described in the Introduction! That book also awaits a pro wine-tester's description of the taste of sea-cucumber guts (*konowata*).

Alphabetization is Absolute – breaks & hyphens do not count – Haiku & Senryû at End

Abinureba yu ni hada o . . . 544
ada hito no tsukuma 615
agake tote sake ya 119
ahahan to waraite fuku 335
aikei wa onore 307
ajikinaya kimi ni 693
akahan o iza yakubaran 102
akanaku ni 70. ~ nashi to omoeru 411
~ zome ga ineburi o shite 295
ake nureba 684. ~ yukeba moyuru 203
~ kure ni 165. ~ te somuru 678
aki kaze ni murasame 126
aki no no ni iro 560
~ no kusa no tamoto 525
~ no kusamura goto ni 123
aki no ta no ho no ue ni mo 77
~ kariho no io no toma 290

~ kariho no io no utagaruta 290
aki no ta o uetsuke mo 621
~ yo no chiyo o   224
~ yo no 331. ~ wa mata 244
akiretari karimono 641
akuhitsu no 642. ~ nin no 165
ama no iwato furisode 622
ama no michi 414. ~ sumu sato 364
amagoze no tsumakuru susu 165.
amagumo ni iwafune 42. ~ o chie 293.
amai tsuyu furuka furuka to 350.
ama-kudaru 639. ~ amamoyoi 562.
amanogawa hagoromo 212. ~ naedai
    165. ~ nagarete 132. ~ soko no 237.
    ~ towataru kari 556
amanohara furisake 291. ~ narite 480.
    ~ onaji iwatô o izuredomo 89.
amanoshita ari to aru mono naku 310.
amanoto mo shibashi 264
    ~ o hiraku ôgi ni 446. ~ o waga 312.
amaochi no ishi no hekomi ni 348
amari 486. amatsukaze kumo 293
ame furite 274. ~ ame ni yori 326
ame no hara ajiwai mireba . . . 543
amida wa 273. ~ ami no me 143
anagachi ni niwa o sae haku 194
ana koishi 479. ~ miniku 97.~ unagi 60
andon 279.   aoyagi o tsuzurago 440
aranu tokoro 201. araoda o ara 458.
arasowanu kaze no yanagi 303
aratama no fumi 445. ~ no haru 425.
    ~ hatsumotoi 467. ~ kotoshi 467.
    ~ toshi mo 341. ~ uguisu 345
areba tote 133.   ari nomi to 701
ariake no tsurenaku ienu 141. ~ mo141.
arimayama takaki wa bakari 420
    ~ yuna no koe 414
arimayama watakushi-ame ni 422
    ~ no furu 422.   ~ no nuremono 421.
arimayama yuna koi shinobu 414
    ~ no wamekeru 414. ~ o oni 577.
aru toki wa 394.   asa na yû 258
asa yû ni chinchin 514. ~ kamado 68.
asagao o nani wa kanashi to 360
ase mizu ni 540. ~ o nagashite 588
ashihiki no yamadori no o no shidario
    290. ~ shitarigao 290
ashihiki no yamaya 291. ~ wa naku 70
ashi nakute 541. ~ no ura no ito 364.
atama naki 275. atarashii obire 703.
atarashiki inabe no takumi 598
ato made mo 380. ~ no yo ni 560.
atsumetsuru 381. atsurae no 249
au koto no 121. ~ made no 365
    ~ toki wa 523. ~ to mite 494
aware chô(to iu) koto koso 481
    ~ nari fude 220. ~ to iu koto ni 694
    ~ to mo mi 625. ~ to ya omoi 213
    awaseba ya sagi o karasu to go o 144

azumaya no nokiba ni ne sase 551
Bakemono no sumu no no 222.
barabara ni 528. benben to 350.
beniguma no hatsuhi medetaku 447.
benzai no megumi 438. ~ ten e 359.
binbôgami izumo e 542. ~ mari 337.
binbon no kami tote sara ni 283
binbô no bô mo kasegeba 170
binbô no kami mo 403. ~ o ireshi 286.
bô hodo na namida 330. bonnô no 103
bushi ni naru 75. butsudô ni 362

Cha o nomeba nerarenu 554
chichi koishi koishi 321. ~ haha 328
    ~ nomi no chichi-no-shima 145
chigirarenu mono to wa ima zo 479
chihayaburi kami 158. ~ satsuki 640
    ~ oba ashi ni maku mono ka 175
chiisakeredomo 273.   chikurin 547
chinmoku no 671. chirinureba 499
chiru to mite 372. chitose no tsuru 248
chiyo o hitoyo yumiya teppô yoi 343
choku naraba 192.   ~ to ka ya 192

Da ga nagasu 693. daikon o 336
daimon no 576. dana-san 573
danjiri ya chanchiki 95. dan-ochi 55
dare nite mo sake 99. doko kara 684
dokudoku to 349.doteuma no 224

Eda kuchishi 691. ehô yori 621
eteshi kana kuchi ni 577

Fuguri no atari yoku zo arawan 272
fuji no ne 443. ~ yama 46
fukamidori 472. fukimakuru 240
fukitojiyo 293. fukufuku to 548
fuku kaze ni nabiku 204. ~ waga 284
fuku kaze no te ni 524. ~ o 441
fuku kaze no togatogashi 350
fukunokami inoru 170. ~ waga mi 284
fuku wa uchi oni wa soto 357
    ~ o-niwa no matsu 435
fumi o mote 245.   ~ shira wa 710
fuminan wa 240.   fumizuki o 345
fundoshi o sarasu to ya min 523
furitsumeba 705. furitsumoru 259.
furu yuki o 143. furusato e kaeru 408
    ~ no arehateni 682. ~ o kika- 575
fusuma sae ito omogenaru oi no 361
futatsu ma 178. ~ moji 448. ~ naki 71
    ~ yoi koto koso nakere 298
futomomo no shiroki ni mukashi 333
fuyugomori haru 59. ~ ni tatsu 639

Ganjitsu wa ushi no tsuno moji 449
gantan 384. geko 295. ge ni sake 100.
geta no 493. goi nareba 141.

gokuraku de 160. ~ mo jigoku 31.160
    ~ no kogane 325. ~ no uchi ni 358
    ~ wa jûmanokudo 163.
    ~ wa suzushiki 158. ~ ya jigoku 162
go-muri to wa kuchi ni iedomo101.490
    ~ iedo ureshisa 179
go nariseba kô 384.   go sekku 179
go toba-dono 300.   goto naraba 309
gozare tote 357. gozen no mae 569
gururi to ie 287

Hachisu-ha 166. ha ga nukete 346
haha no chichi 171. haikai ni waki 690
hai mawaru 638.
hakaze o ba itoinagara 187. 443
hakkei no naka . . . kuidaore 180
    ~ . .mochiya 180. ~ kurai-daore 101
hako-ire no musume no toshi wa 75
hakone yama 414. hako wa shiri 105
hakufun o kao 490. hamaguri ni 134.
hama mireba masago ni kani 616
hana chirasu 195. ~ chira de tsuki 117
    ~ ike ni 577. ~ iro 623. ~ mireba 360
hana no iro ni koke 501. ~ wa 292
hana no ki 519. ~ na wa yoshi ya 336
hanasasenu tarashi 545.
hana sasô . .wa wagami 299. ~ ushi 299
hana to miba 194. ~ mite oran to 217
    ~ mite te tagoto 704
hana yori mo 111. hana yue ni 403
hanazakari geko mo jôgo mo 515-16
hanbun wa 477. hane no ko no 561
hanuki nara 704. harahara to 331
hara made 529. ~ hara tatsuru 576
harai tamai 165. hare yaranu 94
hari no ana 560. harubaru to 692
haru fukaki 128. ~ goma no 432
    ~ kaeru kari 142. ~ kaze ni 584
    ~ kureba 35. ~ kurete 360. ~ mo 532
    ~ no hi 576. ~ o matsu hito 361
    ~ o matsu mochi 332. haruru 501
    ~ same ni nureshi 441. ~ no furu 692
    ~ sugite natsu ki ni haji 640
    ~ sugite natsu kinikerashi 140
    ~ sugite natsu-ki ni hayaru 621
    ~ tateba 372. ~ tatedo onaji 690
    ~ to shi mo nao 696. ~ wa moe 185
ha shigemi 697. hato no tsue 259
hatsu haru 467. hatsu koe 334.
hatsukusa 355. hatsumono 139
hayaki se 603. hayaku shine 560
hayaoki no tane to mo nareba 225
hazukashisa kowasa 72. ~ ya nado 355
he he he he he 398. he nari to mo 587.
he o 143. hieta 182. higa koto 675
HIGURASHI no nakitsuru nae ni 539
hiki yosuru tabako 76. ~ tsurete 700
hikoboshi no hiku 214. ~ kubeki 215
hiku ito no 213.   ~ ushi no hanage 342

hi-no-kuruma 170
hinomoto no aruji 624. ~ na ni au 405
hi-no-nezumi 149. hiraya naru 619
hiru wa naki 459. hisakata no 33
hito kouru koto 555. ~ namida 122
hitomaro no uta no aji no mumasa 543
hito mienu 413. ~ mo kinu 524.702
hito mo minu yado 254. ~ oshi hito 300
hito ni awan 59. hito no hi wa 550
hito no koi ki 67. ~ mi 207. ~ oni 231
 ~ yuku mae wa chôchin 202
hito o ami e ireta 198. ~ mite hito 639
 ~ nomi umi ni 496
hito ôki hito no naka 307. ~ machi 305
 ~ me o mo shinobi tokei no oto 73
hitori kite hitori . . . mo mayoi 163
  ~ kaeru mo 161
hitori-ne no kachô 487. ~ nezame 696
 ~ toko ni tamareru namida 119
hito shirenu 120. ~ tose ni 467
hitotsuma to aze ka so o iwamu 136
hitotsu o mo chidori 402. ~ tori 369
hito wa ge ni 510. ~ mina oki 108
hitoyo akete 427. ~ neshi 540. ~ o 224
hi wa irite tsuki koso sora ni 575
hôki tatete zôri e kyû o suyuru 253.
honobono to akane 406. ~ akashi 677.
hori-kaeshi 337. hôshi nite fugen 560
hoshiai mo mienu 574. ~ amanoto 522
hoshiai no sugishi yahan mo ushi 224
hôshira no hige 55. hosoboso to 552
hotaru koi chichi 521. ~ o ba 201.
hotoke ni wa 325
hototogisu jiyûjizai 504. ~ koe 247.
 ~ kubeki 196. ~ motenasu 349
 ~ nakitsuru 243. ~ naku sora 346
 ~ nare ga hosokubi 334. ~ tani 247
hyaku no uchi 393
hyôtan no uchi 531. ~ to totemo 341

Ichido iite 576. ~ sae yasetaru 87
ichimai o man 616. ichimotsu mo 73
ieba e ni 354. ie ni arishi 80.
igirisu mo furansu 263. ii-yore 77.
ika de ware tokoyo 246. ~ hodo 140.
 ~ ni sen mono- 464. ~ ni shite 404.
ikabakari ebi 580. ~ hana ya 582.
ikani shite kokoro 61. ikebana 411.
ikita zo o 705. ikubaku no nageki 348
iku chiri 129. ~ iku chiyo mo 177
iku haru ga koe- 341. ~ mo kawa- 442
ikuru koto 387. iku yo heshi 396.
ima kon to 372. ~ koso are ware 340
ima made wa heta 383. ~ me 386
imasara ni hana 691. ~ kumo 50.
 ~ nani ga. 234 imasuke 684.
ima wa tote namida 122. ~ uchi 686
ima ya yume mukashi ya yume to
 mayowa[todara]rete ikani omoedo

utsutsu to zo naki daibu 12-13c 209
ima yori wa uta 684. ~ nozomi 405
ime ni dani mieba 209
imo ga kao 410. ~ na wa chiyo 40
imogako ni kagiri. 325
imo to neba 315. ~ waga nuru 331.
inazuma no chira 76. ~ wa terasa 120
inìshie no midare 484. ~ nara 53
 ~ nomori no 204. ~ shizu no 261.
 ~ yoroi ni kawaru 484
inishie wa 10. inkyô shite 90
inochi koso 233. ~ shirazu to 175
inorite mo 72. io no to o 350
ippai ni 574. irete min 359
iriai no kane 329.553. irizuki ni 532
iro fukaku hito 615. ~ gonomi 200.
 ~ ha ni ho to 573. kawaru 120
 ~ mie de (miete) 613. ~ ni shimi 246
 ~ o mede oreru bakari zo 216
iruka naranu imo 479. iru made 420
isamashiki kao 424. ise no umi 694
ishi hakobi nageki koritsutsu 109
ishinago no ochikuru 349.~ no tama 133
ishi nara de 74. ~ no naka ni 647
iso no nami 691. isshô o ayamaru 178
ita hitoe shita 278. itadaku wa 684
itazura ni mi o 207. ~ waga mi 361.
itokenaki kokoro 587
ito susuki 357.~ tsukete 616.~ yori 594
itsu mite mo 260. itsumo tatsu 690.
itsu no ma 255. itsushika mo ura- 693
itsushika to hana 692. ~ namida 126
 ~ waga torinarete ushirote 686
itsuwari no aru 283. ~ hatsune 691
 ~ naki yo narikeri 230. 527
 ~ naki yo nariseba 527
itsu yori ka 562. itto nomu hito 178.
iwa hodo wa 691. iwama yori 367
 ~ maro ni ware 56. ~ iwa no ue 501
iwato akeshi 236. ~ yaburu 382
iya ware wa 680. iyu shishi o 62
iza kodomo 5. ~ saraba ike 691
 ~ saraba maromeshi 675
izukata ni 173. izuku ni 54
izumoji e 528. izure make 239.

Jigata fukite mawarenu 639
jigokudani 577. jôbaku 377. jômô 306.
jônin no ususumi 408. jôyaku wa 111
jûbun no ue ni ato 181. ~ mo sake 181
jûgatsu ni jû . . . ishi 409. ~ iu 409.
jûgoya no tsuki 97
jûnoji ni hae 622. jûson no ari 305

Ka bakari wa nani yue otsuru 131
ka(a)ka nara 376. kado kado e 690
kadomatsu wa meido . . medetaku 36
 ~ uma kago 470
kaeru kari ni chigau 246. kaerusa 406

kagami kumorite wa waga mi 378
 kagami mochi iza 639. ~ kasumi 579
kagaribi ni 493. kagigoshi ni 357.
kagiri 657. kaibito 575. kakegoi 689.
kaki-chirasu fude 510. ~ kawasu 527.
 ~ kurasu 204
kaku bakari hegataku miyuru 90
  ~ medetaku miyuru 90
 ~ somete 333. ~ sekiwazurawaba 124
kakureite 360. kama no futa 583
kamibukuro 684. kami mo omoi 59.
kamigami no rusu 230. ~ wa 285
kamiko-tachi 41. kaminari no 503
kaminazuki amari 231. ~ fumi 527
 ~ sorya koso shigure itsuwari 528
kamisori no ha yori mo usuki 286
kane hirou yume 102. ~ wa ari 241
kanshin wa 547. kara wa shirazu 703
karabito no hige 450. ~ kasa no 279
karakuri no ito 416.~ no karari 73
 ~ no takeda chikae ga ito kirete 621
karasu hodo ahô- 244. ~ zaki no 144
karegi no 679. kareno uzumu 246
kari no toki 636. kari no yo ni 289
karigamo wa ware o misutete 86
karigane no momiji 247. ~ no yo 245
kariokishi 386. karu kaya o hotaru 142
kasasagi ni hashi 214. ~ no wataseru 291
kashimashi ya 196. kashiwadera 684
kasugano no tobihi no . . . idete 581
   yudete 581
kasugano no wakana 374. ~ ya tsuma 431
kasumi ka 702. ~ tatsu amanogawa 474
kata-fuchi ni mi o naken to wa 177
katakana no to 533. katami koso 703
katana mote nagaruru mizu wa 142
katsu miredo 71. katsumata no ike 599
katsura-hito 487. ~ -otoko kumo 482
ka wa fuji no 199. 520. kawaii ki 377
kawa no ya 421. kawa tsura no 614
kawa wa mina 699. kayaribi no 128
kayuzue ni furimuku imo ga mi 444
kaze dani 194. ~ koete 167. ~ mukau 624
 ~ sasou ane 623. ~ yori mo sotto 66
kazu naranu namida 131. ~ shiranu 686
kemari no kawa 298. kemuri tatsu 557
kemuru oki 434. kenkon no soto 383
kesa hitoha 677. ~ to nareba 425
KIBASAMI o 243. kiegataki kô 128
kikabaya na 210. kikeba hon no 51
ki konyoku 340. kiku no ue ni 375
kiku tabi ni 196. ki mamori ni naru 684
kimi ga kao 40. ~ kogi 583.~ ga senu 120
kimigayo no hisashi 640.
kimigayo wa chiyo ni hitotabi 473.
  ~ yachiyo ni sazai ni shi 41
 ~ yachiyo ni sazareishi musu mame 41
kimigayo wa chiyo to mo sasaji 33
 ~ hikari 129. ~ i-wai sushi ni 690

kimi kôru namida no kawa 497
 ~ shi nakuba karagoromo mune 58
kimi nakute 124.~ shitau 116. ~ yue 405
kingin o tsukai-sutetaru uma-zoroe 110
kinô made maru- 50. ~ shinde 554
kintama no sadamari 336. kiru mono 324
kiuri mo ya namako 482
KOBURI yoki 376. kodakara no 436
kodomo o ba sushi ni suru hodo 323
kogarashi no kozue 350. ~ mi wa 666
kôgen wa yamadori no ya no 291
koi no yami 77.   ~ o shite 64
  ~ shiranu 585. ~ shisa-w/ba ika 79
  ~ to iu 270. ~ wabite 127
koke uzumu 42. kokodaku no tsumi
  mo kiyubeshi 91. koko de chigiri 377
kokoro aru to 636.   ~ etsu tada 193
  ~ kara mono 572. ~ hana no 188.567
  ~ kara kokoro ni 493
kokoro-naki mi 134. ~ nashi to 636.
  ~ kokoro ni mo ara de 297.
kokoro ni wa dô ka 625. ~ dare 236
kokoro o ba 117. kokorozashi aru 271
komatsu ni wa 450. komu to iu 309
konata ni wa 615. kono fukuro 701
konoha o ba 422. kono hodo wa 544
kono ie wa 289. kô no ishi o 143
kono koro no waga 63. ~ wa nami 694
ko no ma 205
kono tabi wa . . . yama mada 294
         ~ yama momiji 294
kono uta no kokoro o ika ni gaten 462
         ~ wa shiraji 591
kono yo ni shi 97.   ~ nite jihi 162
  ~ o mo ato 128. ~ oba doriya 369.568
kon to shirite 260. konya kuu 676.
ko-oroshi no nyôbo to miete 277
kore hodo wa 319. kôre-ochishi 496
kore o hito no kokoro to 176
koreya kono yuku . .ebisu-banashi 293
         ~. wakarete 292
kôri toku kaze 426. koro mono 546.
koromo shi mo 183. ~ gae no 317
koro mo ushi 130
kotonoha mo migakisuna 415
  ~ mo mukashinagara 703
  ~ no tanomubeshi 502
koto shi araba 62. kowagowa mo 479
koyoi kon 372. ~ kono 88. ~ koso123
kozue fuku192. kozutaeba onoga 188
KUBI bakari 275. kuchibashi no 576
kuchi-naka no 417. kuchinawa no 616
kudô naru 256.   kueba heru 394
kuge wa yake buke 624. ~ hikeshi 624
kuitaranu uwasa mo kikazu 93
kuji kenka jishin 387. ~ wadan 181
kumo no koromo 50. kumori-naki 692.
kumo to nari 339. kurehatenu 467
kure o matsu 205. kure yuku to 242

kuretake to kikeba 523
kurikaeshi ei/yoi no maw-101.181.490
  ~ onaji koto 261. ~ koyomi no 538
kurogami mo 215. kurogoma no 677
kurozuka no 679. kurukurushiku 272
kurushi to mo 479. kuruyo nite 327
kusamura ni hotaru 204. ~ musato 147
kuse to shite 305.   kuu goto 568
kyôgetsu ni ke no muku-muku 687
kyôka ni wa jiman 322. ~ yomi no 337
kyô mo 349. kyonen no kyô 403. kyô
sake 225. kyôshitsu ni 670 kyôtoku
mo seritatete 637. kyô yori 643

Magarite mo 109. mai hibari 530
maku mame o iwai osamete 335
makura ni mo 44. ~ no ue no 273
  ~ nomi uku 121. ~ yori ato yori 80
manaita no 77. maneku tote 525. 702
mannen ka 420. ~ mo hanare 318
maotoko ga 551. marebito wa 684
marokarazu 612. maru hadaka 296
marukareya 176.
maruku to mo . . . komageta 176
         ~ hitokado 176
marukute marukute 332. masurao 430
matagarishi 112. mata hitotsu 238.470
mata koko 419.~ kujira 625.~ shite 256
mata to yo ni aru 356. 565
matsu mo ushi 694. matsuyama 115
matsu yoi no 406. mayoi zo to 171
medetai to ieba medetai to iu 316
meidô kara . . .yasohachi 391
         ~ kyûjûkyû 391
meigetsu ni kono yo 704
me ni mienu haru 692.   ~ oni 412
me ni wa 284. ~ no mae ni 277
 ~ to kuchi 296. ~ wa kagami 281
meoto naka ni 243. ~ shite hashi 690
meshi wa mina kuitsukushitaru 166
mezurashiki 694. mezurashiku 416
MI hitotsu 403. ~ mo tsuraku 483
 ~ ni sou 256-7. ~ no ru su ni 617
 ~ o kakusu 402. ~ o sutete 177
michi naka ni 546. michinobe 696
michinoku no 563. michinoshiri 106
michi sugara 533. migoto nite 167
mijika yo mo 78. mi-kari ni 614.639
mime no yoki yuna 576.
minabito no moshi 324. ~ wa hana 499
  ~ wa shinuru 687. minakuchi 353
minaregawa 124. minasoko ni 353
minu mo mie 82. miru hodo no 377
miru ni kokoro 481. misogi shite 343
mite suzumu 510.
mitorete wa tsui 236. ~ yodare o 377
mitsuidera no chigo wa hajiro ni 491
miwataseba miyako 624. ~ ya-nami 623
miyakobito 312. ~ yori kuge ga 640

miyoshino no yoshi 348 ~ wa yama 565
mizu chikaku 333. ~ha sasu 397
 ~ ni sumu kaeru 317. ~ mizu no 545
môde suru 359. momijiba wa 240
momo no yumi 443. mômoku to 410
momoshiki no onka 301.
         ~ ya furuki fusuma 546
         ~ ya furuki nokiba 301
         ~ ya furuki utabito 301
momozutau 392.   mono iwanu 320
mono iwazu 641. mono no na 173
mono omoeba kokoro 209. ~ sawa 201
monogoto ni araba 554. ~ taranu 551
mononô no kokoro 466. ~ yatake 472
mono-omou 115. morokoshi no 405
moromoro no 577. morotomo ni aware
   . .otsukisama 297. ~ yamazakura 296
moto yori mo chiri .. ja tote akutare 95
         ~ nareba tsuki 94
moto yori mo kari no yo 288
mukashi yori amidabotoke 602
 ~ kitoku arima 407. ~ koko 576
mumasôna yuki 241. ~ kashi o ba 412
mumoregi no 203. mune no hi 641
munen nagara 271. murasame no 560
musashi/kasuga-no wa kyô 98
musashino ni habakaru 338
musashino no suehirogari ni 339
 ~ wa kyô wa na yaki so asakusa 363
 ~ wa kyô wa na yaki so wakakusa 363
musasô de kireina 612. musekaeru 414
mushi-jigoku e ochite mo mizu 417
muzukashiku nejikaeritaru jôgo 179
         ~ toitari mata wa 164

Nadeshiko no hana no kuchibiru 331
nagaiki no ie 559. ~ o sureba 483
         ~ wa haji ôkeredo 257
na g/ka ki yo wa 617. ~ -no-to- 573
nagarete wa izure 497
nageke tote tsuchi-yawamono 118
         ~ tsuki ya wa mono o 118
nageki de mo 213. nagekitsutsu 464-5
nakamaro wa ikai habushi no 291
nakanaka ni hito to 97. ~ nani ka 58
         ~ tokidoki kumo 88. 482
naki ato 704. ~ haha ga 588
 ~ kaeru kari 126. nakitsumeshi 119
naku koe ni 375. ~ namida 382
 ~ shika no koe kiku tabi ni 226
namadai no sebone 354.~ei no reisha 563
namidagawa ause 493. ~ haru no 127
 ~ ko(h)i yori idete 496. ~ makura 481
 ~ marone 496. ~ mi 121.
 ~ sakamaku 116. ~ segaruru 693
namida ni zo nure 367. ~ no mi uki 120.
 ~ nomi itodo 130. ~ nomi shiru 570
namima yori urashima tarô tsuki 485.
nanakusa no hana 182. ~ kayui 425

nananenki iza 703. ~ ni 683-4. ~ o 704
nanasekawa yasetaru uma 611
nanatsu ume 485. nani o ga . . 73
nanigoto mo kokoro 407. ~ mina 390
　~ mizaru iwazaru 640. mo nashi 701
nanigoto mo otame otame to 625
nani sen ni sode 692-3. ~ ware 125
na ni shi ou ningyô 416. ~ owaba 638.
na ni takaki 623. nani toka ya tsuki 605.
naniwa hito 138. ~ naru ashi 694
~ -e no ashi koshi 421. ~ no itami 414
nani yue ka saigyô hodo no kyôyû 118
na nomi shite 615. ~ noru beki 693
　~ o mede 216. nao saete yama 690
naseba naru nasaneba naranu 550
natsumushi no mi 375. ~ o nani 206
　~ wa urayamashiku ya 207
natsu no yo 557. ~ yase to hito 72
negawakuba ware wa hechima 421
　　~ waga ato no yo wa oni 164
negawashishi iza 411. negi goto 493
neko no goto 418. ~ no ha ni 615
　~ no me no kawaru kokoro 74
　　　　　　　~ ni tsukete 176
neko no tsuma moshi koi- 69. 616
nenbutsu 158. nengô wa 492
nete matedo 159. nezame ni mo 164
nigiyaka ni 178;
nijusanyo no tsuki 357. nikkori to 565
nippori no 532. nishi muki 326.
nishiki kite 504. niwatazumi 344
nodoka naru 441.
noki chikaki tonari 282. ~ ku fufû 186
noki ni kite 334. ~ shiroki tsuki 205
no mo yama 469. ~ nomu kara 702-3
no to naraba 545. nozomu o ba 411
nubatama no 598. nukarumai to 77
nurete hosu 372. nushi shiranu ka 372
nyôin no gozen no hiroku naru 370

Ochikereba inochi bakari wa 619
odosu to mo 408. ô-eda o kirite 336
ôfuguri kura 410. ofuji-sama yuki 623
ôgiku o mezuru 237. ogura yama 219
ôhara ya mushi 224. ohashita no 228
ôhei ni hito 560.
oinuredo mata 237 ~ to mo mata 237
oiraku no kasanaru 344. ~ kon to 260
oiraku o da ga hajimeken 87. 258
　~ wa waga mi 131. oiran ni sô 537
ôkami ni koromo 679
ôkata no yo o 87. ~ wa tsuki o 36
okosode wa 183. okuretaru ichiwa 244
okuyama e kakuren yori wa kame 171
　　~ ni momiji fumiwake 226
　　~ mi no kyaku 226. ~ nagamete 526
　　~ o chirasu 526.　~ ori taki 526
　　~ to mite ya sarumaro ga shiri 226
okuyuki mo 73. omatsuri wa 109

omeiko ni bobo shita bachi ya 335
ominaeshi ike no 217. ~ kazari 684
　~ koke no 501. ~ namameki 227
　~ ushi to mitsutsu zo 216
omoboezu sode 121. omoedomo 126
omôezu hitai ni nami no 494
omoi areba sode 495. omoiidete 614
omoi-izuru ori-takenu 334 ~ taku 334
omoikanuru 123. omoi-kawa 83
omoiki ya kumoi no aki no sora 344
omoitsutsu nureba ya hito no 613
　　　　　　~ wakashu 613
omoiwabinu semete 691 ~ sate 119
omoshiroki kono kotonoha mo 413
o mo shiroshi kashira mo 319
omou kata futatsu 402. ~ no mo 377
　~ to mo karenan 373
omo wasure dani 80
omowazu yo 537. onaji yo to 208.
oni koyoi hana 335. ~ naranu kami 231
　~ wa uchi 259.
onna hodo medetai 150. ~ o ba hô 150
onoga ne ni 345. onozukara 614
on-sudare 238. ori kara no momo 523
oriyoku wa 449. osaete mo 495
osamareru miyo 427. osanago no 587
oshi to omou 372. oshinabete 70.
oshiroi de kakushite 376
osoku izuru tsuki 71. osoroshiki 415
otohime no suitsuke 470.
otoko ichi kawayurashiki 557
　~ onna　mina 527
　~ yama kotoba 680. oto mo 201
oto ni kiku arima 407. ~ takashi 103
　　~ tsutsumi no taki 321
oto ni nomi 373. ototoshi mo 408
otowa kawa sese 203. ôtsuchi 81
ouko yori daku 323. ôyabu no 349
oyaman to 85. oya mo nashi ko mo
　nashi 384. ~ tsuma nashi 384
oya wa oya take 676. ôyodo no 366
ôzo no kuru 705.
ôzora ni na-dakaki 89. ~ tsuma inoru 68

Pisshari to ka 198. p[h]okkuri to 385
purupuru to furue 588

Raizan wa umareta toga de 387
rakugaki 147. rengashi wa onnago 322
ri na ku to mo ri no 413
rô ga mi no 258. ~ no mi wa 351
rokudenaki 179. 　jû wa kawa e 684
　~ roku no iroko no 587
rusu naraba kaeri o matsu to 391

Sabishisa ni shomotsu toridete 298
sabishisa ni yado o . . . tabako 299
　　　　　　~ izuko mo 298
sabishisa no tane to wa shira de 404

~ o aware to 296. ~ yo aki no 299
sage-obi 155. sagijima no goishi 144
saho hime no kasumi no 444
saigyô no omekake 560. ~ tabako 304
sakasama ni koi 202. sakashimi to 488
sakazuki e tobi- 99. ~ no kazu o 485
　~ no sumi 307. ~ no uchi ni 489
sake naranu 685. ~ no ei abunai 377
　~ no na o hijiri 97. ~ nomeba 98
　~ nonde sake 490. ~ wa nomu 285
saku hana no kokage ni yorite 441
　~ o tazunete yukeba itsu yori 686
saku koro 395. sakurabana saki 371
sakura ni wa aranu 475. ~ saku 560
saku toki wa hana no kazu ni 395
samazama ni omoiyari 213. 522
samidare no hi 541. ~ shitagoshirae 562
samuki yo ni ki-atatamenuru 342
　~ wa ikanaru uta mo 318
samuku nashi 684. san suji made 250
sangoku no yama no uchi demo 338
sansan-no-ku 178. ~ sanzan ni geko 178
saohime no koromo 444. ~ suso 48
saotome no kasa 479. ~ omoi kake 677
saranaru sakana 465. saritote wa 96
sasagani no ito ni tsuranuku tsuyu 132
　~ kumo no igaki 313. ~ sora ni 500
sato no ko 223. satô yori amamitsu 419
satsujinki no 588. sawarabi ga 530
sayo fukete ima 184. sayuru yo ni 126
sazare-ishi no iwa hodo nareru 176
　~o to narite 680. ~ to nareru koke 694
　~ to nareru yamakawa 472
seiri-chû no fuakku wa atsushi chi 588
sekken wa byôshi 324. ~ yo fushigi 420
senaka ni mo 684.　sen kin no 89
sennin mo tengu 135. sentaku sen 268
shaka daruma teika 591. ~ sama ni 359
shakkin mo ima 234. ~ mo yamai 282
shakkin no fuchi hodo 323. ~ ni 351
shakkin o outaru 682. ~ wa bake- 276
　~ wa fuji 682. ~ wa kubi dake 241
shamisen no komaka ni 343
SHIBARAKU mo yotoko ni shiri o 262
shichihô mo meshi 180. ~ no sakazuki 180
shigemori to imasara nani o 423
shijûkara ga 514. ~ oi no naka e 515
　~ to kimi ni 514. ~ wa oi no 174
shika no ke 220. shikai nami mede- 178
shikarubeki sono hitogara mo 101.179
shikishima no miichi wa kami yori 653
　~ yamatogokoro no nantoka no 674
　~ yamatogokoro o hito ni towaba 674
shiku namida 123. shimaginu o 677
shimozuki ni shimo no furu koso 409
shina takaki 572. ~ yatte-kuru 376
shinagatori aha ni tsugitaru 510.
shinanogawa nanasei 410. ~ naru 352
shinde ato towan 511

~ kara hotoke ni 163. ~ to iu 162
shindeyuku jigoku no sata 396
shini wakarete yori 704
shinimasu to iishi 641. ~ iute 330
shinobe to ya 701. shinobu beki 697
shiorashi ya 642. shi o tsukuri uta 113
shiozuke 557. shippori 421. shiraga 352
shirakawa no kiyoki ni uo mo 109
shirami hodo 322. ~ kite hirunaka 504
   ~ -ko no mi no yukusue o 368
shira sagi wa 304. shiratama to mie 206
shiratsuyu ni aji 168. ~ o tama ni 218
shirayuki o itadakeba 515. ~ itadaki 515
shirazariki kumoi no yoso ni mishi 522
shiri no hida 342. ~ kage nite na o 201
shiro-aka to 428. ~ shiro kabe o 705
shi ro ka mi wa ma i 617
shirubenaki 123. shiru hito ni 270
shirushi-naki 96. shiru shiranu 381.570
shitabara ni ke no naki go-uchi 680
shita tôru namida ni 125. 492
shita tsuzumi 320. shitazori no ue 73
shiwa wa yoru 256. shizu ya shizu 538
shôben ga ichi mon 642
shôjiki no atama 231. shômotsu-mo 29
shu o mazete 404. sobô sojî hiuba 324
sochi mo shian 577. sode nurete 367
sode wa hiji 126. sôkan wa doko 382
someru yara 264. somuru to wa 692
sono hito no shirushi 570. ~ wa 704
sono mama ni 291. sono mukashi 170
sora ni naru hito 255. sora wa kao 329
sore to miyo 129. soriotoshi 267
sorosoro ni 643. soshite mata 537
sosori tatsu 588. sotôri no uta 292
soyo to harube 53. sue no yo no 117
sugajima ya tôshi 144. sugu naru 380
suisui kaze 619. sui suru ni 412
sukashi-he no 454. sumi-narete 703
sumiyoshi to hito 282. sunao naru 622
su o ba ato ni nokoshi idetaru 242
surikôgi tami no 623. ~ -machi wa 621
susu hokori haka de kono yo o furu 235
~ haki no uchi 51. ~ kuroki 416
sutehatete mi wa . . . mara no tatsu 232
      ~ yuki no furu 232
suterarenu shudô 555. suzumedono 302

T abako nomu uchi yori haru wa 316
tabi goto ni 310. ~ goromo arai 684
~ meku ya 560. ~ yase no ashi 690
tachi wa saya ni osameru miyo 423
tachimagau 194. ~ tachisawagu 693
tada hitoyo ake no karasu 189.517
ta ga tame ni 312. ~ tane o 531
tagui naki 213. taihei no nemuri 110
taikô no moto 141. takaki na no 683
takasago no jii mo mukashi wa 340
take no muma wa fushi kage ni 637

takeuma o hatsu-uma 112. ~ o tsue 112
~ wa fushi-gachi ni shite 602
tako o mite 690. takuri-hokuri 535
tamadare no ko- 489. tama-hôki 129
tamakushige 277. tamamushi no 581
tamashii mo 131. tamawaru wa 516
tamuke ni wa tsuzuri no sode mo 295
tanabata mo susurite wa naki 215
~ ni kokoro 213. ~ no chigiri 213
~ no hito 347. ~ no hiyoku 214
~ no kokochi 313. no matsu 693
~ no morote 314. ~ o omoeba 215
tanigake no 474. ta no hata ni ie 492
tanomezu wa 694. tanomoshina 172
tanomu beki 205. tanoshimi o 694
tanpopo ni te o 705. ~ o to tantan to 319
tan-tan-tan ta'tta 418. taru koto o 311
tasogare ni tamerau 377
tatsu haru wa osanaki 437. ~ tote 639
tayori ni mo aranu omoi no ayashiki 81
te ni irete mite 410. ~ musubi 694
~ toreba hito o sasu to iu igakuri 223
te o nigiri 357. te wa furuu ashi 256
teikin no ôrai 323. teishû tote 614
temukitashi temu 704
tenjin ya hito miorosaba musashi 346
tenka mina haru 38. ~ toru koto 626
tenki yohô 671. ten made wa 687
teppô mo soko 318. ~ no tama 528
teradera no megaki 599. ~ tera-iri 703
~ kodomo hikitaru ushi no 587
teratera to tsuki no katsurao sasu 93
teru tsuki no kage 487. ~ wa uchiwa 703
TO o akete 91. tobimawari 684
tôdô no koromo 411. tôji-naru uri 537
tokaku yo wa 100. tokidoki wa 283
toki o ake yose-kuru ka o ya 199
toki shiranu shiwasu 529. ~ yamai 639
toko chikashi 494. tokonoma ni 278
toko no uchi no 679. ~ no umi ni 123
toko wa umi makura wa yama to 125
tokoyami no 165.599. tokuhô no 413
tokuri no yô 377. ~ tokuri-tokuri 676
tôme ni wa sadaka naranu to 244
tomo mo naku 297. ~ tori mo 245
tomoshibi ni 562. tonikaku ni 83
toreba mata 470. tori-jigoku ni 577
tôrimasu to 238. toru tokoro 59
toshidoshi ni akuma 163. ~ atama 429
toshigoto ni 605. ~ hetaru 472.
~ hisashiki 343. ~ koete hana 316.
~ koshi 470. ~ kureshi 45.
~ kurete hito mono kurenu 701
~ nami no hitai 471. ~ ima ya 37
~ kaeru tebako o urashima mo 442
toshinouchi ni haru tachinu to ya 469
~ haru wa kinikeri 34. ~ kaji wa 625
~ mochi wa tsukikeri 467. 609
toshi no uchi no haru ni mumaruru 35

~ no ya wa 471. ~ toku no kami 248
~ wa tada kureo 413. ~ wakaki 343
~ yoraba* meshi 405. ~ yoreba 575
toshiyori mo mata kuu beki to 253
TSUBO-ori o 436. tsubururu mo 541
tsuchi sakete 249. tsui to tatsu 684
tsuki hi hoshi 332. ~ makuru 588
~ mireba kuni wa 70. ~ nara de 703
~ no uchi ni 487. ~ no yuku 532
~ o mezuru yo 685. ~ o toru 640
~ to hi no nezumi 504. ~ wa min 404
~ yue ni itodo 261. ~ yuki no 570
~ kage no itaranu 410. ~mi hana 513
~ yaki no nakazuri hodo ni 348
tsukunen to arima 422. tsuma sari 280
tsumagi ni mo 691-2. tsumekoto 576
tsumi aru mo 317. tsumu hito 374.683
tsunokuni no tare to fushi ya 315
tsuno moji mo kaku koto nara 449
   ~ no ise ebi o mite futatsu 587
   ~ no ise-ebi ushi to 433
tsuno moji no isoganu haru no hi 448
tsura akami 355. tsure mo naki 79
tsurenaki kimi 677. tsurezure to 697
tsurizao no ito 703
tsuru kame no 248. ~ kyûhyaku 391
~ mo iya kame 390. ~ uchi-ga 423
tsuyu bakari okuramu sode wa 120
~ jimo o tokete 143. ~ shizuku 691

U batama no yobai ni rô no mi 572
uchi-akete 77. uchi-kokete 705
uchi no kaze 172. uchi-taete nageku 114
uchiwa tote amari maruki wa 86
ue kara wa meiji 111. ue yori wa 622
uete miru hito no kokoro ni 519
uguisu ka takeya 420. ~ mo mada 469
~ no hakaze 691. ~ no hô-hôkei 417
~ no namida 44. ~ o tama ni 440
ukauka to nagaki yosugara 92. 486.
uki koto no kagiri 693. ~ o kataru 543
   ~ o oriori goto ni shinobureba 63
uki namida furuki 569. ~ shinobu 479
ukihito ni namida 125. ~ wasuraruru 72
ukihito no kokoro 693
uki o ushi to 131. ukite koso 130
umai-hi o mizu ni 457
ume ga ka ni onara no nioi koki- 52
ume no hana mi ni 188. ~ sake sake 516
umi de mizu aburu 318. unabara ni 688
unjô o toriagerarete 622
uo no na no sore 449. ~ o muza to 528
ura ni taku mo-shio no keburi 121
urameshi ya hito 345.~ waga kakure 371
urami wabi hosanu sode . . . koi ni 295
~ . . . kono shi go nichi wa ame 295
urawaka mi neyoge ni miyuru 355
urayamashi isoji 562. ~ karanu hôshi 558
~ koi ni taetaru 211. ~ kuro kami 575

uruwashi to waga omou imo ga 107
ushi nara de 411. ushi no ko ni 146
uso ja nai itsuka kanarazu kaesu 281
utayomi wa heta koso 32.465.
utsu mono mo utaruru . . . kawarake 65
~ okujochû kawarake naranu 65
utsukushiki fuji 338. ~ hana no 358
utsusemi wa 500. uwanari no yu 422
uzu takaku hidari-nejire no sa-daiben 104

W abinureba ima hata onaji 294
~ koi no kawari ni yoki funa 294
waga an wa nebutai 684. ~ gotoku 379
~ hara no ue ni 337. ~ ie no hitsu 410
~ io wa fuyu zo wa keshiki 575
~ io wa miyako uma/shika 544
~ kado ni mezamashi 406.~ no hairi 691
~ kimi wa chiyo ni yachiyo ni 40
waga koi shi kimi 493. ~ wa hito 552
~ wa michi no ne-nagare 82
waga kokoro akete 74. ~ ushi no 545
waga koto ya kumo no naka ni 375
waga mi koso nani 687. ~ kosu 122
~ nagara mo tôtokarikeri 272
waga mida no yuzuri . . issa 465
wagamono to hoshiki/toboshiki 406
~ hoshisa no mama 700. ~ nao 692
~ waga mune 98. ~ waga namida 115
~ omou hito eda taoru mono 536
waga sode no namida kakaru to 114
~ ni io wa suminu to 142
waga sode wa 693. ~ toshi mo 37
waga tsuma o 136. ~ wa okubi 642
waga ue no tsuyu 337. ~ uta ni 322
waga yado no kaki no moto 307
~ kemomo 409. ~ nokiba no 330
waga yado wa hashira 288.~ michi 500
wagimoko ga koromo 495. ~ kozari 459
wakai shu ya 396. wakaki ko ga 315
waka mizu o 431. waka no ura 411
wakareji no 540.   wakaruredo 314
wakashu koso 558. ~ mo tada 318
~ no kokoro 328. ~ no shiritsuki 328
~ o omohi no tama ka hotarubi 202
waka-tabako nomu kotonoha wa 305
waka-yuna no ha o ba 417
wakiideru yuna 421.wanzakure 392.572
waraigusa 388. warawa domo kusa 54
ware bakari mono arau hito wa 353
~ omou hito ya mata mo aru to 696
~ wa mata mo araji to 353
ware danimo 696. ~ maneku sode 570
~ mo sazo niwa no isago no 112.
~ mo waretari 273. ~ o omou 309.
ware shinaba bizen-irube/shibin 177
~ bizen-irube/tokuri 177
~ sakaya no bin no shita ni 488-9
~ sakaya no kame no shita ni 488
ware to iu 670. ~ wa mo ya 106

~ wa tada yo 161. ~ yori 227.699
waregachi ni 233. warera koto 113
wasurareshi otoko-hideri 74
wasuregusa nani o ka tane to 373
watatsu umi no kame no senaka 473
watatsumi no kazashi . . . kurage 366
~ mo mo 366
wazuka naru kusa no 692

Y akeyakete kaki no moto made 641
yamabito no hirune suredomo 423
yamabuki no hana ga makoto 512
~ iro-goromo nushi ya tare 601
yamadera no 694. ~ guchi 419
~ hime mo 444. ~ kaze ni 499
~ mo kasumi 581-2. ~ mo kaze 576
~ momo no erigui 639. ~ no i 60
~ takami iwane 212
yamazato ni shiri 399. ~ wa haru 690-1
~ wa itsu naku totemo sabishiki 692
~ wa fuyu zo sabishisa . . hitome 148
~ . . yahari shijû ga nigiyaka 148
yamazumi wa he o 399
yaminureba o no 84. yamitsuki de 242
yane to yane 165. yaru fumi no 677
yarumai zo yarumai 317. 552
yasebô no shiwa 413. yasojuya? 391
yasuraka ni fude 586. ~ noki o 617
yasurawa de ne- 295. yasuyasu mo 56
yayo shigure ame 317. ~ mono 229
YODARE tarasu 256. ~ tare hito 683
yoi yoi ni deai 487. yoine asane 257
yokarazaru utsuwa 415. yoki atai 376
yoki hito no 308. yoki hito wa 684
yokuaka o arai 511. ~bukaki hito 172
yominarau uta 516. yomonoharu 579
yomosugara tama 693. yomu iroha 700
yomu uta o 680. yone ni aute 252
yo ni sumaba te o 350. ~ tatsu 685
yononaka ni aru to 171
yononaka ni hito no . . ureshikere 183
~ urusakere 183
yononaka ni ka hodo urasaki 108
~ kaku beki かく(欠く?)べき 550
~ kaku beki 書へき mono 550
~ taete onna/sakura 190. ~ saishi 190
yononaka no chiri 289. ~ hito o 417
~ uki tabigoto 483. ~ wa ima 513
yononaka o hajinu 172. ~ omou 309
~ sukuu kokoro 346
yononaka wa chichi 623. ~ ika ni 483
~ iro to sake to ga kataki nari 698
~ kari no yo . . . kari mo yoshi 704
~ . . . kari-nikushi 704
~ mina shamisen 621. ~ mishi 213
~ sate mo 542. ~ sono tokidoki 625
~ tada hyôtan 386. ~ sumu to 533
yononaka yo michi koso nakere 298

yo o itou mi 266. ~ somuku 501
yoru goto ni shikibu 95. ~ hiru no 408
~ naku wa 224. ~ yonaka 413
yosegire to 563. yoshi hito wa 243
yoshinoyama kozo . . mi chigaete 686
~ . . michi kaete 686
yoshi saraba namida no ike ni 114.126
~ shita ni kuchi 130
yoshi ya mata 265. yoso e yuku 497
yotsu no o no 292. yo ya senu to 89
yôyô to kite mo 465. ~ yôyô to 370
YÛ sareba nobe 369. ~ umaya 349
yûdachi no zatto 679. ~ ya furuki 249
yûdan naku 306. yûgao no sagari 393
yûgure wa izure no kumo no 702
yuki furazu 235. ~ furite secchin 104
~ mi to wa itsu 233. ~ no hada 481
~ no uchi ni haru 469. ~ ore no 339
yukite mimu ima wa. . . 465
yuku aki o 130. ~ hito o shine 276
~ hotaru 205. ~ mizu no 692
yukue shiranu 339. yûmagure 204
yume nara de au 374. ~ no ku ni 38
yunadomo no 414. ~ kouru mi wa 421
~ no na no nabe no heso yori 421
yusen to wa 279. yutakanaru 484
Z atô-no-bô mime 410. zenigane de 316

HAIKU

Link-verse *haikai* that adds up to about 31 syllabets is found above, listed together with the *kyôka* and *waka*. This includes 17-syllabet haiku and that haiku includes *ku* of the mad sort that I call *kyôku*, but not *senryû*.

AJI araba 168. amakaraba sazo 168
ame mizu no 45. ana no aku hodo 210
ara atsushi 535. arakenaya 195
aratama no toshi tachikaeru shirami 267
asagao no yûbe shisu to mo ka 197
BÔFURI mo fure 221. ~ mo okyô 220
~ no hitori 221. ~ no nenbutsu 220
~ ya shôben muyô 221. ~ yo sei 221
chiraba chire 193. dai no ji ni nete 534
dô no hae juzu 267. doko de toshi 154
dote no uma 432. FUKUNOKAMI 169
fukusuke ga 580. fundoshi ni 211
furuzukin binbôgami 286. GE GE 562
gokuraku ni tanjô 388. HAI ni naru 383
hana o kyô tsumite 191. hanaiki ni 47
hane haete zeni ga tobunari 235
haru tatsu ya gu no ue ni mata gu 39
~ nihon medetaki 37. ~ tsurara 45

harugoma wa take 581. hashiiseru 1
hatsuyume ni neko 47. ~ no fuji no 47
hatsuzora ya tabako fuku wa no 427
hi no hajime 45. hi to miyuru 229
hime-uri no yute 576. hitonaka de 272
hitorimushi hito 563. hone hirou 49

HAIKU CONTINUED

hoshimukae io 347. hototogisu nake 196
hyakunen no 379. io no nomi kawai 269
IZA hiroe tsuyu no mage tama 169
 ~ saraba yukimi ni korobu 675
izumo-e-no rosen 287. jiiji chaya 563
KADO no tsuyu 169. kadoguchi ni 37
kaite mitari keshitari 388. kakaru ka 197
kakugo shite kaze hiki ni yuku 676
kane naru ya 189. kanzuki ya kui- 488
kayuzue ni niguru 445. ~ ya yuzu 445
kesa taruru tsurara 44. kite mireba 286
kôri nigaku enso 675. kôrogi fuito 349
kyô no hi 221. MACHITE chire 195
makete tatarenu 257. motainaya 535
muda na mi ni 149. muda-kusa ya 149
mukôzune zabu ni kittaru susuki 222
musashino ya inu 338. nagusami ni 148
naki-haha ya 347. NEKO no kao 426
nemushiro ya shiri 84. nippon ni 154
OGORU na yo 371. oi odoru ahô 518
ominaeshi motto 211. onjaku no 257
oo samushi 287. ôyuki ya deiri 438
rô no mi wa 149. SAKE ya shigure 228
samidare ya tsuzumi 418. sao hime no
tegai naru 426. ~ ya sakura-iro 49
SAO-hime no bari ya koboshite 49
shiratsuyu no teren 167. ~ to shiranu
kodomo ga 512. shôben mo tama 169
 ~ no taki o miseo 349. ~ no tsuyu no
tashi naru 169. SUSU hakite neta 138
takarabune wake no 47. tako oeba kani
mo 434. tama to naru 169. tanpopo ni
doko ga 553. ~ no popo no atari 321.
 ~ no popo no sonogo 553. tatsuda-
bime taya o 228. ~ shito kake 225.
tenpitsu to iu 642. toshidana ya 439
toshinouchi ni haru . . .iranu sewa 35.
 ~ neko no koi 66. tsukuzuku to 135
tsuma o omou 197. tsuyu harari 513
 ~ no tama tsumanda 511. ~ no tama
tsumande mitaru 511. ~ no yo wa 513
UGUISU no hanekaze 187. ~ ya
mochi ni funsuru 103. uke iwai 549
uta o yomu 211. waga io ga tama 169
 ~ no tachi yori 222. ware to hana no
chiraba binbô 193. warutsuchi no 201
YAKENIKERI saredomo hana 388
yami yori yami 563. yaso tose no 250

yoi tsure zo 283. yononaka no 191
 ~ wa kuneri 347. yûbe ni wa 197
yuku toshi wa doko 234. ~ ya kasegu
ni oitsuku 235. yume hitotsu 388

S E N R Y Û

Includes some from Mutama-
gawa sometimes called *zappai*
as well as Yanagidaru classics.

anone moshi 537. chi de hajime 301.
gyôson no 296. hana mono iwazu 296
hana ya chiruran 191. heri wa semai
keredo 137.   HIRU mo ushi 300
hitoana de shusse 480. hyaku no ji 301
jinmoku mo 148. kakochigao 118.
kaze no te de 582. kokoro ni mo 297.
kyûjuku de shinde 391. ~ de shinuru
391. momiji seshi 545. NEN de miru
yume 83. ni san nichi 295. nureta miso
tonari 290. nusumarete 137. ochiba ni
mo korizu 681. odoreme to ieba 537
oku shimo no 291. OSHAKA-sama
umare-ochiru to miso o age 159.
rakuba ni mo korizu 293. sanjûkyû no
kure 515. setchin no 399. tori no fun
kao no hatake 103. yama de hosu 140
yo o sarishi oshi mo mono iu 471

I M A Y O etc. *songs*

Some songs, mostly *Ryôjin-
hisshô,* got mixed up with the
31-syllabet poems somewhere
in the indexing process, and I
have no time to look – the text
may have twice this amount.

binjô uchi mireba 477
hô ni oki-fusu dani mo hotoke 220
kôbe ni asobu wa kashirajirami 368
mangô kame no senaka 473
ryûnyo wa 95
suru nara ôki na koto shiyare 232

K Y Ô S H I

The romanization below is but
a third of the total in the book;
but I am unsure of many of the
pronunciations – not scattered
here and there for comparison

or reference as is the case with
haiku and senryû. If you would
like to index all of them for the
next edition or, better yet, help
me make a whole book of
kyôshi . . . As some blank space
remains, let me put first-lines
below *as is*, without attempting
a pronunciation. In my opinion,
Ikkyû and many others had fun
with that on-yomi pronunciation,
chanting their rhyming fake
Chinese in what we might call
a rap music sort of way. So, I
would have liked to have given
it, but the Japanese books I have
seen ignore the same and I am
afraid that with more than one
pronunciation possible for many
characters, it is beyond my ken.

yô-fu-yoku-sui 155
gan-rai-yû-kô 151
hi-raku-san-shi 154
i-bin-i-ton 153
jaku-shu-ten-zen 153
kaku-kô-ikkyô 156
momo momo mo mata 398
shakka-chin-kû-kai   157
wan wan wan wan 573
yo-getsu-gi-rai 156

元来有口更無言 151
勇巴興尽対妻淫 152
若衆天然好富貴 153
為貧為頓奈世何 153
一 落山師手   154
洋婦浴水海瀬邑 155
夜月凝来夏見霜 156
郭公一叫誤閨情 156
釈迦沈苦界   157
問既一般 506
識得最初句 506
眼流星 507
趙州若在 507
聞名不如見面 507
劍刃上行   508
路逢劍客須呈 508
南泉可謂 509
椀々々々亦椀々 *kyôka*, not *kyôshi* 573

733

Reviews & Supplemental Information about books in English by Robin D. Gill

Rise, Ye Sea Slugs! (1,000 *ku* re. sea cucumbers compiled & transl. from Japanese). paraverse 2003. pp 480 $25.

"I wondered, can one really devote 480 pages to haiku on sea slugs? The answer is emphatically 'yes.' Although difficult to read from beginning to end, this book contains great learning and insight, and deserves a wide reading among specialists and non-specialists alike."

"For many of the haiku, Gill gives multiple translations as a way of showing possible interpretations. I know of no other book of English translations of haiku that goes to such lengths to explain translations, which in Gill's hands are accurate, economical, and often elegant."

"For all the eccentricities one might expect (and does find) in a book devoted entirely to Japanese haiku on the sea slug, the author is an accomplished haiku writer, a very talented and engaging critic, capable of reading with an acute understanding of culture and cultural differences."

–Thomas H. Rohlich, Professor of Japanese Language and Literature at Smith College, from *Metamorphoses: the journal of the five college faculty seminar on literary translation* (Vol. 13.1, Spring 2005).

"This single-topic tome may be our best English-language window yet into the labyrinth of Japanese haikai culture. If you have read Yasuda, Blyth, Henderson, Ueda, and Shirane, then read Gill. He will expand your mind. If you have not read those guys yet, then read Gill first. He's more fun."

– William J. Higginson, author of *Haiku World*, in Modern Haiku (volume 35.1 winter-spring 2004).

♪   *The haiku are from the early-Edo period to the present. The apparently featureless sea cucumber (namako) offered a unique opportunity for poets to treat what amounts to a ding en sich, and the results were poems pushing the limits of natural observation on the one hand and metaphysics on the other. Some of the latter bear resemblence to kyôka in their logic-born dry wit, and are what I call 'kyôku' in this book.*

◎   ◎   ◎   ◎   ◎

Re: **Fly-ku!** (Translations of fly & fly-swatting ku, + an in-depth study of Issa's famous fly-ku,"Don't swat!") 2005

"An American scholar and poet who writes in an extemporaneous style akin to that of Jack Kerouac; thinks like Herman Hesse, Koyabashi Issa, and Lewis Carroll, all rolled into one."

– Robert D. Wilson, founder of the on-line magazine *Simply Haiku* (2005-summer). Also author of *Jack-fruit*.

"Gill strikes us as no less than amazing. Why isn't he teaching at Yale, or the University of California, or Tokyo University? His references include no end of obscure Japanese lore, plus quotes and notes from such artists as Clare, Lovelace, Steinbeck, Dumont, Verdi, Satie, Blyth, Shakespeare, Emily Dickinson."

– Carlos Amantea, author of *The Blob That Ate Oaxaca* R.A.L.P.H. (Review of Art, Literature, Philosophy & History)

♪   *Not as much natural history in this wee bk. as in Rise, Ye Sea Slugs!, but a good discussion of the supposed anthropomorphic fallacy & a comparison of translations of "Don't swat/hit/kill" the fly that gives great detail on what makes "precise" translation between exotic tongues impossible. If you want more on just that problem, with especial attention to* word-order *vs* flow *please read the yet-unreviewed* **Orientalism & Occidentalism** – *Is the mistranslation of culture inevitable? (paraverse press 2004); and see my newest book which shall be published soon after this one,* **A Dolphin In the Woods** – *paraversing, distillation & composite translation. Besides giving examples of poems with two to a score of translations, it gives chapters to books including* Nineteen Ways of Looking at Wang Wei *and* Le Ton beau de Marot.

Re: ***Cherry Blossom Epiphany*** (Three thousand *ku+ka* on blossom-viewing, including many by Sôgi) 2007, pp.740

"It was bad old Ezra Pound, acknowledging his heavy debt to haiku in translation, who affirmed that the first rule of poetry was "Make it new." This is something Gill has done more effectively, as far as remaking haiku in English goes, than anyone else around. . . .

"One of my favorites is on p. 375, where no less than seven translations are proposed, but four of them "sous rature," or _misekechi_ ['erasures shown,' literally]: in old Japanese, words crossed out in a manuscript but left legible enough that the reader can see what was discarded, and imagine why. (Publishers with accountants are not likely to tolerate this kind of haikaiesque mischief. Gill gets away with it only because he is his own publisher.) And (another reason, if needed) in his commentary Gill distances himself from the conventions of pedantry just as effectively as the haikai poets he translates departed from the venerable (and staid and eventually stuffy) traditions of classical linked verse to make something new."

– Lewis Cook, professor of Japanese literature, CUNY (in a blog at one of Gabi Greve's fine haiku *kigo* and Buddhism-related sites, in response to another's questions about my work.

"This book is exceedingly delightful – what word could be more accurate I cannot say! Here is a guide to allow every reader to play with their own translations of these poems – indeed all the important ingredients – are amply included: . . . nothing in this book is cut in stone – it is pure water, ever-flowing – and that is what is so inspiring about it, its generosity and delightful creativity!"   – s.w. at mountainandrivers.org

♪ *Professor Cook has a broader perspective and more discriminating vocabulary to bring to bear upon what I am doing than I have or ever hope to have. Perhaps this book is, in both senses of the word, fresher yet, though I am well aware that Harold Stewart did intelligent and often stylistically pleasing rhymed couplet translations of haiku a half-century ago and some translators of comic tales have rhymed poems of kyôka length (or the thing itself) they correctly recognized were meant to add a witty and comic touch to the narrative   To my mind, the one thing that no reviewer nor anyone that I know of (formally or informally) has attempted to evaluate is the success/failure of the ways in which I chapter, i.e. divide the poems into sub-themes, something different for* Sea Slugs, Flies, Cherry Blossoms *and* the New Year (The Fifth Season, *below*). *I write this partly because the presentation of hyper-short poetry depends on context and because I am afraid the horrible arrangement of Mad In Translation may be noted somewhere.*

◎   ◎   ◎   ◎   ◎

Re: ***The Fifth Season***   (2000 *ku* on 20 New Year themes & first book of ten in the IPOOH series 2007, pp.500)

No reviews interesting enough to quote, so let me explain. Excluding books on *surimono*, beautiful color-prints accompanied by *kyôka*, published by presses or lines of books dedicated to *art* rather than literature, the New Year, once the Original, or First Season, of the *five* seasons of haiku, has been neglected in favor of the other four by Occidental translators. *The Fifth Season* finally gives this supernatural or cosmological season – one that combines aspects of the Solstice, Christmas, New Year's, Easter, July 4th and the Once Upon a Time of Fairy Tales – its due. *This book brings the Moon back into the calendar and humans back into haiku.* On the whole, New Year haiku in Japanese tend to share more with 'mad poems' than those of any other season. That may be why they were short-changed in translation (even by Blyth). And it may also be why readers of *Mad In Translation* may appreciate this book that has sold only a dozen or two copies since being published (*In Praise of Old Hailku* saijiki project has been suspended – not cancelled – until my S.S. Readership comes into sight)!

◆   Other Books by Robin D. Gill 又は、在りし日のロビン・ギルの諸単作は   ◆

See the author's *Biblio* heading for ***Topsy-Turvy 1585*** (Luis Frois re. 611 ways Europeans & Japanese are contrary), a book often cited in this one & my dirty senryû book of two titles. Please the Paraverse Press website for information on *The Cat Who Thought Too Much, A Dolphin In the Woods* and other books to come, health and wealth willing, as well as summaries and reviews of his published books in Japanese.

◎かの『反・日本人論』(工作者)、『誤訳天国』(白水社)のロビン・ギル、いまや◎
robin d. gill 著 paraverse press 出版の本の書評抜粋

Rise, Ye Sea Slugs! （海鼠千句）について。五大学の文芸翻訳誌、Metamorphoses 2005 春号評者＝スミスカレッジ日本語学、日本文学教授トーマス・H・ローリックの書評より

ギルの手によるその翻訳は簡潔で的をえており、しばしば優雅な味わいがある。これほど翻訳を詳細に説明してある俳句の英訳書は、私の知る限り他に類を見ない。すでに熟練した翻訳家であり、俳人でもある（本書中百句以上が敬愚というペンネームをもつ著者の作である）著者は、芸術としての翻訳の強力な擁護者でもある。どの句にも彼の翻訳のあとに続いて、それぞれ微妙に異なる解釈のあいだを日本文学、歴史、現代の文化についての余談、さまざまな色合いの逸話、ときには暴言までが自由に往来する。（中略）文学についても日常生活についても必ず信頼でき、しばしば愉快でもある彼の日本文化観に私は舌を巻くほかなかった。なにしろ徹頭徹尾ナマコが句題の俳句を集めた本と聞けば当然期待される（事実そのとおりの）風変わりな点はともかく、著者はくろうとの俳人であり、文化と文化間の違いを機敏に理解しながらものを読むことのできる優れた才能に恵まれた魅力ある評論家である。興味津々の本書は、広く俳句愛好家、日本文学と海洋生物の研究者、プロ，アマをとわず翻訳家のすべてに喜ばれるにちがいない。

同著について。*Modern Haiku* 現代俳句（2004年冬春35．1号）*Haiku World:* 1996 の著者、ウィリアム J. ヒギンソン の５ページにわたる書評より

一人の翻訳者として、わたしはギルの俳句翻訳に対する姿勢は刺激的で挑戦的であると思う。彼は「翻訳者の原作に対する責任」（「対応する力」＝ ロバート ダンカン）という点で、果たすべき水準をきわめて高いところまで引き上げてきているのだ。（中略）この単一季語の大著は、日本の俳句文化の迷宮への、今までで一番優れた英語の窓口であろう。（中略）もし、ヤスダやブライスや、ヘンダーソンやウエダやシラネ＊［注：過去半世紀の俳句英訳名家］を読んだことがあるなら、ギルもお読みなさい。あなたの意識を深く広く拡大させてくれるから。そして、先の方々の著作を読んだことがないのなら、やっぱり先にギルをお読みなさい。彼のほうがずっとおもしろいから。

科学者の評 ＝「凄い！惚れてしまった。小柄な我が友を何年も研究してきたが、悪態をつかれるか、さもなければ忘れられた存在でしかない、と思っていた。ナマコ文学をめぐる日欧の差！悲しいかな、互いに隔てられた科学と文学には、理論においてはむろんのこと、用語上ですら、とてつもないギャップが隋所にみられる。両者を深いところで見事に融合した本で、科学者も納得させる。恐れ入りました。」Alexander Kerr 博士 ＝ Web of Life プロジェクトの海鼠科担当、独語の海鼠研究（古典）の英訳、環境進化論の研究に従事する気鋭の生物学者。James Cook 大学属。

F/y-ku!（蝿句）について。オンライン句誌 Simply Haiku 創立者かつ編集者ロバート・D・ウイルソンの書評より

書きぶりはジャック・ケルアック流即興を思わせ、ものの考え方はヘルマン・ヘッセ、小林一茶、ルイス・キャロル、このすべてを丸めて一つにしたような本なのだ。。。

桜・花見三千古句の英訳ある 2007 年の新刊 *Cherry Blossom Epiphany:* The Poetry and Philosophy of a Flowering Tree、 又は、今までに、欧米で見逃れてきた新年部句、二千句ほど英訳ある *The Fifth Season: Poetry for the Re-creation of the World* のいずれの内容について、又上記書評の全文などは、http://www.paraverse.org で、ご覧になってください。英訳とはいえども、全句の日本語原文もその索引も全書に入っているから、英語が苦手の方も、一読を、おすすめできます.

御免あれ急用あれは**校正**も　尻をからけてはしりかき哉　信海

◆孝雄狂歌集

〜〜〜
深海は、月洞軒と貞柳の狂歌師。　ようわからんが、そういう感じ、まったく！
資料をたくさん買って腰かけてじっくりと校正できたらいいが、金も暇も無し。
蛇足ながら、「校正」は、敬愚が直した所。正しくは、むろん「御返事」です。

たのむなり此世であはずはあの世でと　おもひすぎはらのかみも仏も　月洞軒

自然っ子流月洞軒ならではの一首。杉原紙の名前すべて利用済み！c.1700
『狂歌大観』本篇　「大団」元禄元年〜同十六年迄　題「寄紙恋」

◎ ~~Writing at the End of the World – or a Mad Rant for Our Time~~ ◎

~~While I may complain about the burden poverty puts on non-fiction writer, there is something worse, something beyond personal handicap, beyond complaint, a cross born by *all* present day writers, rich or poor, whether they know it or not: *How can I write when so much is wrong*?~~ Rereading poems about dry wet-nurses by the kyôka-master Shokusanjin and Issa while searching for the best 100 poems in this book, I learned to my horror that another wetnurse complaint *a thousand years older* – dueling *kyôka* between scholar spouses Ôe no Masahira no Ason and Akazome Emon (*Goshûishû* #1217) – that I thought was in this book was *not*. As there is no longer place for it within the body of the text, and my Godfather, a writer and the first to give an opinion about the reading copy, felt the essay about *writing at the end of the world* did not add anything to the book, I have exiled it to my website to make room for those poems, here.

Native Wit (*Yamato* = big-peace = *gokoro*) Meets Native Tit *a Millennium Ago*

When a woman who came to serve as a wet nurse produced only a thin stream of milk, the husband, Ason raged, in Cranston's translation, *"What a scatterbrain – / To think she could squeeze by /As a wetnurse here /In a learned doctor's house: /Little learning and less milk!"* (Waka vol. 2A pg 552). The mad poem plays on some one *hakanaku*, i.e., frivolously, lacking *milk=chi=learning* coming to a *hakase*, or scholars' house for employment. My mad translation, is not so close to the original (*hakanaku mo omoikeru kana chi mo nakute hakase no ie no menoto sen to wa*) as the professor's, but might amuse you nonetheless:

> *A wet-nurse, with no more brains or milk than a tit-mouse?*
> *How unwise for wizened dugs to shame a Scholars' house!*

The wife's good-tempered reply (*sa mo araba are yamatogokoro shi kashikoku wa hosoji ni tsukete arasu bakari zo*), again, in Cranston's translation, *"Let's be satisfied / If at least her native wit / Deserves respect – / Scant schooling and thin milk, no doubt, / But enough to squeeze her in."* (#1218 ditto) again relies on the same *knowledge/milk* pun, which modified by *hoso=scant/thin* is pronounced *ji* rather than *chi*. I wrote Professor Cranston to express my enthusiasm for his book and, in my rude way, question him, eg.: *"I suspect the yamatogokoro is used as rhetoric for the attitude her hubby should take and may not, as you write, be defending the wetnurse for having native wit/japanese spirit."* In other words, I felt she was saying that *he* ought to be more "big-peace" (how Yamato was often written) in spirit even if that meant reading *arasu* as *arazu*. That is –

> *She is what she is and wisdom born of our Big Peace way*
> *Would not make an issue of two-bit tits: let her stay!*

Cranston thanked me for the additional reading but stuck to his guns and grammar: "I still think *yamatogokoro* applies to the nurse." While taking Yamato literally falls within poetic license, let me use the far better expression used by Cranston, *native wit*:

> *What she is she is – does not our native wit set us free*
> *Not to nit-pick like Chinese, but let the little things be?*

With the rhetorical usage of *yamatogokoro*, I would hope the interpretation of the poem would interest other scholars of both ancient Japanese literature and politics and look forward to hearing from them.

Perhaps I lost not only these poems but a whole chapter, as each chapter in my book is only two-pages. Microsoft's automatic updates sometimes caught me by surprise and I came back from chores (feeding the cows and cat, crossing the rail-track for the mail, etc.) to find an entire day's work destroyed. A term in the professor's first translation *"what a scatterbrain"* applies well to me, for when such a thing happened (maybe thrice in the last year), I could not recall what exactly was lost!

www.ingramcontent.com/pod-product-compliance
Lightning Source LLC
Chambersburg PA
CBHW082017300426
44117CB00015B/2260